Lecture Notes in Artificial Intelligence 13368

Subseries of Lecture Notes in Computer Science

More information about this subseries at https://link.springer.com/bookseries/1244

Gerard Memmi · Baijian Yang · Linghe Kong ·
Tianwei Zhang · Meikang Qiu (Eds.)

Knowledge Science, Engineering and Management

15th International Conference, KSEM 2022
Singapore, August 6–8, 2022
Proceedings, Part I

 Springer

Editors
Gerard Memmi
Télécom Paris
Paris, France

Baijian Yang
Purdue University
West Lafayette, IN, USA

Linghe Kong
Shanghai Jiao Tong University
Shanghai, Shanghai, China

Tianwei Zhang
Nanyang Technological University
Singapore, Singapore

Meikang Qiu ⓘ
Texas A&M University – Commerce
Commerce, TX, USA

ISSN 0302-9743   ISSN 1611-3349 (electronic)
Lecture Notes in Artificial Intelligence
ISBN 978-3-031-10982-9   ISBN 978-3-031-10983-6 (eBook)
https://doi.org/10.1007/978-3-031-10983-6

LNCS Sublibrary: SL7 – Artificial Intelligence

This Springer imprint is published by the registered company Springer Nature Switzerland AG
The registered company address is: Gewerbestrasse 11, 6330 Cham, Switzerland

Preface

This three-volume set contains the papers presented at the 15th International Conference on Knowledge Science, Engineering, and Management (KSEM 2022), held during August 6–8, 2022, in Singapore.

There were 498 submissions. Each submission was reviewed by at least 3, and on average 3.5, Program Committee members. The committee decided to accept 150 regular papers (30% acceptance rate) and 19 special track papers, giving a total of 169 papers. We have separated the proceedings into three volumes: LNCS 13368, 13369, and 13370.

KSEM 2022 was the fifteenth in this series of conferences which started in 2006. The aim of this interdisciplinary conference is to provide a forum for researchers in the broad areas of knowledge science, knowledge engineering, and knowledge management to exchange ideas and to report state-of-the-art research results. KSEM is in the list of CCF (China Computer Federation) recommended conferences (C series, Artificial Intelligence).

KSEM 2022 was held in Singapore, following the traditions of the 14 previous successful KSEM events in Guilin, China (KSEM 2006); Melbourne, Australia (KSEM 2007); Vienna, Austria (KSEM 2009); Belfast, UK (KSEM 2010); Irvine, USA (KSEM 2011); Dalian, China (KSEM 2013); Sibiu, Romania (KSEM 2014); Chongqing, China (KSEM 2015), Passau, Germany (KSEM 2016), Melbourne, Australia (KSEM 2017), Changchun, China (KSEM 2018); Athens, Greece (KSEM 2019), Hangzhou, China (KSEM 2020), and Tokyo, Japan (KSEM 2021).

The objective of KSEM 2022 was to bring together researchers and practitioners from academia, industry, and government to advance the theories and technologies in knowledge science, engineering, and management. KSEM 2022 focused on three broad areas: Knowledge Science with Learning and AI (KSLA), Knowledge Engineering Research and Applications (KERA), and Knowledge Management with Optimization and Security (KMOS).

We would like to thank the conference sponsors: Springer, Nanyang Technological University, Singapore, and Princeton University, USA. Moreover, we would like to express our gratitude to the honorary chairs and the KSEM Steering Committee chairs, Ruqian Lu (Chinese Academy of Sciences, China) and Dimitris Karagiannis (University of Vienna, Austria), and the members of the Steering Committee, who provided insight and guidance during all the stages of this effort. The KSEM 2022 general co-chairs, Ruby B. Lee (Princeton University, USA), Tianwei Zhang (Nanyang Technological University, Singapore), and Yaxin Bi (Ulster University, Jordanstown, UK), were extremely supportive in the conference organizing, call for papers, and paper review processes, and we thank them for the general success of the conference.

August 2022   Gerard Memmi
                                                        Baijian Yang
                                                        Linghe Kong
                                                        Tianwei Zhang
                                                        Meikang Qiu

Organizations

Honorary General Chairs

Ruqian Lu   Chinese Academy of Sciences, China
Dimitris Karagiannis   University of Vienna, Austria

General Co-chairs

Ruby B. Lee   Princeton University, USA
Tianwei Zhang   Nanyang Technological University, Singapore
Yaxin Bi   Ulster University, Jordanstown, UK

Program Chairs

Gerard Memmi   Telecom Paris, France
Baijian Yang   Purdue University, USA
Linghe Kong   Shanghai Jiao Tong University, China

Steering Committee

Ruqian Lu (Honorary Chair)   Chinese Academy of Sciences, China
Dimitris Karagiannis (Chair)   University of Vienna, Austria
Hui Xiong   Rutgers, The State University of New Jersey, USA
Yaxin Bi   Ulster University, Jordanstown, UK
Zhi Jin   Peking University, China
Claudiu Kifor   Sibiu University, Romania
Gang Li   Deakin University, Australia
Yoshiteru Nakamori   Japan Advanced Institute of Science and
                            Technology, Japan
Jorg Siekmann   German Research Centre for Artificial
                            Intelligence, Germany
Martin Wirsing   Ludwig-Maximilians-Universität München,
                            Germany
Bo Yang   Jilin University, China
Chengqi Zhang   University of Technology Sydney, Australia
Zili Zhang   Southwest University, China
Christos Douligeris   University of Piraeus, Greece
Xiaoyang Wang   Zhejiang Gongshang University, China
Meikang Qiu   Texas A&M University–Commerce, USA

Publication Co-chairs

Meikang Qiu   Texas A&M University–Commerce, USA
Cheng Zhang   Waseda University, Japan

Publicity Chair

Shangwei Guo   Chongqing University, China

Technical Committee

Aniello Castiglione   University of Salerno, Italy
Beibei Li   Sichuan University, China
Bo Luo   University of Kansas, USA
Bowen Zhao   Singapore Management University, Singapore
Chaoshun Zuo   Ohio State University, USA
Cheng Huang   Sichuan University, China
Chunxia Zhang   Beijing Institute of Technology, China
Daniel Volovici   ULB Sibiu, Romania
Ding Wang   Peking University, China
Dongxiao Liu   University of Waterloo, Canada
Guangxia Xu   Chongqing University of Posts and
                             Telecommunications, China
Guilin Qi   Southeast University, China
Guowen Xu   Nanyang Technological University, Singapore
Han Qiu   Tsinghua University, China
Hansi Jiang   SAS Institute Inc., USA
Hao Ren   The Hong Kong Polytechnic University, China
Hechang Chen   Jilin University, China
Jiahao Cao   Tsinghua University, China
Jianfei Sun   Nanyang Technological University, Singapore
Jianting Ning   Fujian Normal University, China
Jiaqi Zhu   Chinese Academy of Sciences, China
Jue Wang   SCCAS, China
Jun Zheng   New Mexico Tech, USA
Kewei Sha   University of Houston–Clear Lake, USA
Krzysztof Kluza   AGH University of Science and Technology,
                             Poland
Leilei Sun   Beihang University, China
Man Zhou   Huazhong University of Science and Technology,
                             China
Md Ali   Rider University, USA
Meng Li   Hefei University of Technology, China

Ming Li	Singapore Management University, Singapore
Neetesh Saxena	Bournemouth University, UK
Nhien An Le Khac	University College Dublin, Ireland
Pengfei Wu	National University of Singapore, Singapore
Pietro Ferrara	Università Ca' Foscari di Venezia, Italy
Qiang Gao	Southwestern University of Finance and Economics, China
Richard Hill	University of Huddersfield, UK
Robert Andrei Buchmann	Babeş-Bolyai University of Cluj Napoca, Romania
Salem Benferhat	University d'Artois, France
Serge Autexier	DFKI, Germany
Shangwei Guo	Chongqing University, China
Shaojing Fu	National University of Defense Technology, China
Shengmin Xu	Singapore Management University, Singapore
Shudong Huang	Sichuan University, China
Shuiqiao Yang	University of Technology Sydney, Australia
Songmao Zhang	Chinese Academy of Sciences, China
Ulrich Reimer	University of Applied Sciences St. Gallen, Switzerland
Wei Luo	Deakin University, Australia
Weipeng Cao	Shenzhen University, China
Wenyu Yang	Peking University, China
William de Souza	Royal Holloway, University of London, UK
Xiang Zhao	National University of Defense Technology, China
Xiangyu Wang	Xidian University, China
Xiaokuan Zhang	Georgia Institute of Technology, USA
Ximing Li	Jilin University, China
Xinyi Huang	Fujian Normal University, China
Yangguang Tian	Osaka University, Japan
Yaru Fu	Singapore University of Technology and Design, Singapore
Ye Zhu	Monash University, Australia
Yi Zheng	Virginia Tech, USA
Yiming Li	Tsinghua University, China
Yuan Xu	Nanyang Technological University, Singapore
Yuan Zhang	University of Electronic Science and Technology of China, China
Yueyue Dai	Nanyang Technological University, Singapore
Yunxia Liu	Huazhong University of Science and Technology, China

Contents – Part I

Contents – Part II

Contents – Part III

Knowledge Science with Learning and AI (KSLA)

A Decoupled YOLOv5 with Deformable Convolution and Multi-scale Attention

Gui Yuan, Gang Liu$^{(\boxtimes)}$, and Jian Chen

School of Computer, Hubei University of Technology, Wuhan 430068, China
1g0061408@126.com

Abstract. YOLO series are very classic detection frameworks in the field of object detection, and they have achieved remarkable results on general datasets. Among them, YOLOv5, as a single-stage multi-scale detector, has great advantages in accuracy and speed, but it still has the problem of inaccuracy localization when detecting the objects. In order to solve this problem, we propose three methods to improve YOLOv5. First, due to the conflict between classification and regression tasks, the classification and the localization in the detection head in our method are decoupled. Secondly, because the feature fusion method used by YOLOv5 can cause the problem of feature alignment, we added the deformable convolution to automatically align the features of different scales. Finally, we added the proposed multi-scale attention mechanism to the features of adjacent scales to predict a relative weighting between adjacent scales. Experiments show that our method on the PASCAL VOC dataset can obtain a mAP0.5 of 85.11% and a mAP0.5:0.95 of 63.33%.

Keywords: Object detection · Decoupled head · Deformable convolution · Multi-scale attention · YOLOv5

1 Introduction

The object detection methods based on deep learning [23] have greatly exceeded the traditional object detection methods [5,27] since deep learning was proposed. Currently, object detection methods based on deep learning have been developed rapidly and widely used in transportation [29], medical treatment [10], surveillance [16], and other fields.

The current mainstream object detection methods are divided into two categories: one-stage methods and two-stage methods. Two-stage methods are mainly the RCNN series and their derivative methods [2,9,12,21]. Fast R-CNN [9] shares the feature extractor to avoid repeated convolution operations and speed up detection. Faster R-CNN [21] proposed the region proposal network (RPN) to generate proposal regions, which further accelerates the detection

The work described in this paper was support by National Natural Science Foundation of China Foundation No. 61902116. Any conclusions or recommendations stated here are those of the authors and do not necessarily reflect official positions of NSFC.

speed. Feature pyramid network (FPN) [12] solves the problems of insufficient semantic information of the low-level features and insufficient localization information of the high-level features by establishing top-down and horizontal connections between the features of different scales. The feature fusion method in FPN can improve the ability to detect small objects, thereby improving the accuracy of detection. Cascade R-CNN [2] is based on Faster R-CNN and uses different IOU thresholds to fine-tune and optimize the proposal regions many times.

One-stage methods can directly generate the classification probabilities and the localization coordinate values of the objects in one stage. Compared with two-stage methods, the region proposal stage is not required in one-stage methods and the overall process of the one-stage methods is simpler. The YOLO series [1, 17–20] are the classic one-stage methods. The YOLO series determine the localization and classification of the predicted object based on the grid cell where the object center is located. In the YOLO series, the classification probabilities and the localization coordinates of the objects are directly regressed. Compared with other YOLO methods, YOLOv5 [17] mainly uses 3 improved methods. These methods are: 1) mosaic data enhancement; 2) adaptive anchor box calculation; 3) combination of FPN and PAN [14] for multi-scale feature fusion. Furthermore, YOLOv5 replaces the original bounding box loss with GIOU loss [22]. These improvements have allowed YOLOv5 to obtain the best detection effect in the YOLO series. However, the detection accuracy of YOLOv5 still needs to be improved and the bounding box containing the object in YOLOv5 does not fit well with the object.

In order to solve these problems, this paper proposed a decoupled YOLOv5 with deformable convolution and multi-scale attention. We mainly uses 3 methods to improve YOLOv5. First, in YOLOv5, the focus of the classification task and the localization task in the convolution process of the detection head is different. The coupled detection head will reduce the detection accuracy. Therefore, the coupled detection head of YOLOv5 is decoupled and two different branches are used to predict the classification and localization of the objects. Secondly, the up and down sampling operations are frequently applied in the feature fusion stage. The sampling operations will cause the position of each object in the feature to shift. As the sampling operations continue to act on the feature, the shifts will continue to accumulate, eventually leading to a large deviation in the position of each object. The deformable convolution [4] is added in the feature fusion stage to solve the problem of feature alignment. Finally, YOLOv5 uses the features of different scales to detect objects of different sizes. Because the features of each scale focus on different object sizes, the attention mechanism is needed to highlight the object information of the corresponding scale in each feature and suppress the object information of other scales. Inspired by the hierarchical multi-scale attention mechanism [25], we proposed a novel multi-scale attention mechanism to suit our needs. The novel attention mechanism is used to focus on the object that each feature is responsible for detecting and suppress other objects. We evaluated our method on the PASCAL VOC dataset, and achieved better performance than other state-of-the-art object detection methods with a mAP0.5 of 85.11% and a mAP0.5:0.95 of 63.33%.

The remainder of this paper is organized as follows. The related work are described in Sect. 2. The proposed improved YOLOv5 method is presented in Sect. 3. Experimental dataset and results are reported in Sect. 4. Finally, some conclusions are given in Sect. 5.

2   Related Work

Two-stage methods mainly include the following 2 stages: 1) classifying the foreground and background in the image to filter out the candidate boxes from a large number of the anchor boxes; 2) adjusting the positions of the candidate boxes and classifying the objects in the candidate boxes. Generally, the two-stage detectors have higher accuracy but will consume more inference time. Since the one-stage detectors have no the stage to classify the foreground and the background, the detection speed is faster than the two-stage detectors but the detection accuracy is generally not as good as the two-stage detectors. For the application scenarios that require detection speed, the one-stage detectors are more suitable.

One-stage detectors can be divided into two categories: anchor-based detectors and anchor-free detectors. The representative anchor-based detectors are the YOLO series. Due to the excellent detection performance of the YOLO series, the improvements of the YOLO series have become an important research hotspot. Ge [8] presented some experienced improvements to the YOLO series, named YOLOX. The YOLOX detectors use an anchor-free manner and conduct other advanced detection techniques. These techniques mainly are a decoupled head and the leading label assignment strategy SimOTA. Chen [3] pointed out that the success of FPN is due to its divide-and-conquer solution to the optimization problem in object detection rather than multi-scale feature fusion and presents You Only Look One-level Feature (YOLOF). In YOLOF, dilated encoder and uniform matching are proposed and bring considerable improvements.

Except for the YOLO series, some other one-stage methods have been proposed. Liu [15] presented SSD (single shot multibox detector). SSD generates scores for the presence of each object category in each default box and produces adjustments to the box to better match the object shape. SSD combines predictions from multiple feature maps with different resolutions to handle objects of various sizes. Lin [13] proposed a novel focal loss which solves the class imbalance by reshaping the standard cross entropy loss such that it down-weights the loss assigned to well-classified examples. The focal loss focuses training on a sparse set of hard examples and prevents the vast number of easy negatives from overwhelming the detector during training. In the literature [13], a novel one-stage method, RetinaNet is also proposed except for the focal loss.

Anchor-free detectors mainly rely on the keypoints to locate the objects and do not use anchor boxes. The representative anchor-free detectors mainly are [6,7,11]. The advantages of these methods mainly include avoiding the problem of imbalance between positive and negative samples and reducing the impact of hyperparameters.

3   Our Method

Although YOLOv5 has a great advantage in speed, it needs to be further improved in detection accuracy. In YOLOv5, the coupled detection head, the problem of feature alignment and the problem of object information interference in the divide-and-conquer detection strategy will cause the detection accuracy to decrease. In response to the above problems, this paper proposed three methods to improve YOLOv5 to obtain higher accuracy. For the coupled detection head, we decoupled the coupled detection head of YOLOv5 and use two different branches to predict the classification and localization of the objects. For the problem of feature alignment, the deformable convolution is used to solve this problem. For the problem of object information interference in the divide-and-conquer detection strategy, we proposed a novel multi-scale attention mechanism to highlight the object information of the corresponding scale in each layer of the feature pyramid.

The improved model structure is shown in Fig. 1. On the original structure of YOLOv5, we added three novel modules. The decoupled detection heads replace the original coupled detection heads. The multiple multi-scale attention modules and the multiple deformable convolution modules are added to the feature fusion stage. In Fig. 1, C1 is the feature map obtained by using the feature extraction network, C2 is the FPN feature map, and C3 is the PAN feature map. In the feature fusion stage, the feature maps are fed into the multi-scale attention modules, and then the features processed by the attention modules are sent to the deformable convolution modules for feature alignment. Finally, the features of each layer in C3 are sent to multiple decoupled detection heads to detect the objects.

3.1   Decoupled Head

The literature [24] pointed out that there is a problem of spatial misalignment problems in classification and localization tasks. Moreover, the literature [28] believed that the fully connected layer is more suitable for classification task, and the convolutional layer is more suitable for the localization task. However, both classification and localization tasks are completed by the convolution operations on the same feature in YOLOv5, which will harm the performance of YOLOv5. Our method uses the decoupled detection heads to replace the original coupled detection heads in YOLOv5, and the decoupled detection head is shown in Fig. 2.

In Fig. 2, the feature A is the feature in the feature pyramid, the feature B is responsible for object classification, the feature C is responsible for object localization and the feature D is responsible for classifying foreground and background. The classification branch and localization branch are completely decoupled. But the structure of these two branches is exactly the same and both are composed of two CBL modules and a convolution module. The view operation is to keep the shape of the feature outputted by the new detection head unchanged. The size of the convolution kernels in CBL is 3×3 and the size of the other convolution kernels is 1×1.

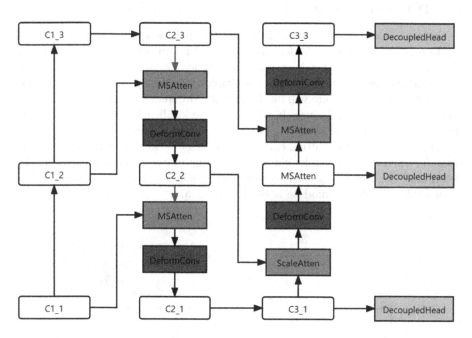

Fig. 1. An overview of our method. The red line is down-sampling and the green line is up-sampling. MSAtten is the multi-scale attention module and deformconv is the deformable convolution module.

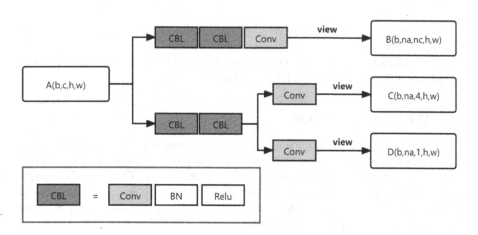

Fig. 2. The decoupled detection head. 'view' represents the resize operation of the feature tensor. The h is the height of the feature, w is the width of the feature and c is the channel of the feature, b is batch size. The na is the number of anchors and nc is the number of classifications. BN means batch normalization.

3.2   Deformable Convolution

In the process of feature fusion, the sampling operation will cause the original position of the objects in the feature to shift. The object position offset is not obvious in the features that have only undergone one sampling operation. However, when the feature has undergone multiple sampling operations, the position of the objects in the feature will be significantly different from the position of the objects in the original feature. It will affect the localization accuracy in object detection and cause the bounding box to not fit the object well.

The deformable convolution can learn the offset of the convolution kernel and resample the original convolution without changing the input data. Hence, the deformable convolution is used to solve the problem of feature alignment. The deformable convolution module is shown in Fig. 3.

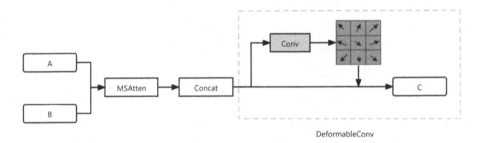

Fig. 3. The deformable convolution module. A and B are the features in the feature pyramid. C is the output feature.

In Fig. 3, the features outputted by the attention mechanism are concatenated and sent to the deformable convolution module. The error caused by the sampling operation will be corrected by the deformable convolution module. The size of the deformable convolution kernel is 3.

3.3   Multi-scale Attention

The hierarchical multi-scale attention mechanism can learn a relative attention mask between adjacent scales. Inspired by it, this paper proposes a similar multi-scale attention mechanism for multi-scale feature fusion. The proposed multi-scale attention mechanism can focus on the object of the corresponding size in the feature of the current scale and suppress the object information of other sizes. The proposed multi-scale attention mechanism is shown in Fig. 4.

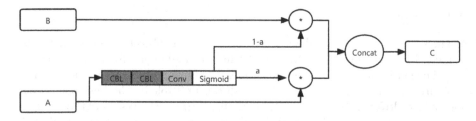

Fig. 4. The proposed multi-scale attention mechanism. A and B are the features in the feature pyramid. C is the output feature. 'concat' is the concatenation operation. '*' is pixel-wise multiplication.

As shown in Fig. 2, the proposed multi-scale attention mechanism contains the CBL modules, the convolution layer and sigmoid activation function. The feature map A is convolved to obtain the feature mask a. Then a is multiplied by the feature map A and the feature map B is multiplied by $1 - a$. Finally, two products are concatenated. The equation of the proposed multi-scale attention mechanism can be formalized as:

$$Output = Concat(a * A + (1 - a) * B) \qquad (1)$$

In this paper, the proposed multi-scale attention modules are added to the feature fusion stage of YOLOv5. Unlike the self-attention mechanism used in the transformer to capture global information, the attention mechanism in our method is used to learn the relative attention mask between the features of adjacent scales and reduce the interference between the objects of different sizes.

4   Experiments

4.1   Data, Parameter Settings and Performance Metrics

The dataset used in the experiments is PASCAL VOC07 and PASCAL VOC12, with a total of $16,551$ training images and $4,952$ verification images. The dataset divides the objects into 20 categories. Since there are many versions of YOLOv5, the version of YOLOv5 used in this paper is YOLOv5s. Compared with other versions of YOLOv5, YOLOv5s has fewer parameters and is faster. Each experiment is trained for 300 epochs. The training batch size for the dataset is set as 16. A back-propagation algorithm with SGD stochastic optimization method is used to train the network through time with the learning rate of 0.01. We use the Pytorch framework to train on an Nvidia GTX 2080ti GPU.

The experiments use mAP (mean average precision) to evaluate the performance of our model. The larger mAP is, the better the model should be. The range of mAP is between $[0, 1]$. Mean average precision (AP) over different IoU thresholds, from 0.5 to 0.95 (written as mAP 0.5: 0.95) and 0.5 (written as mAP 0.5), is used the evaluation metric. They are commonly used performance metrics in object detection.

4.2   Results

We first compare our method with the state-of-the-art object detection methods, namely, FPN, FCOS [26], YOLOv3, RetinaNet, YOLOv5, SSD and CoupleNet [30]. The performance of all methods is measured by mAP0.5 on the test set. The comparison results of these models are shown in Table 1. The best results are shown in **boldface**. As shown in Table 1, our method achieves a mAP of 85.11% and it outperforms all other methods. Compared with YOLOv5 and YOLOv3, our method gives the relative improvements of 0.51% and 1.43%. Compared with the two-stage method FPN, our method gives the relative improvements of 4.17%. Compared with other one-stage methods FCOS, SSD, CoupleNet and RetinaNet, our method gives the relative improvements of 6.01%, 8.31%, 2.41% and 8.21%. These results indicate that our method can effectively improve the detection accuracy of YOLOv5.

Table 1. Comparison of the results of different methods.

Network	mAP 0.5
FPN	80.94%
FCOS	79.10%
SSD	76.8%
CoupleNet	82.7%
RetinaNet	76.9%
YOLOv3	83.68
YOLOv5	84.6%
Ours	**85.11%**

To further investigate the effect of the proposed improvement methods in YOLOv5, a set of experiments are to investigate the effect of these factors. The mAP 0.5 and mAP 0.5: 0.95 are used the evaluation metrics. The results of the ablation experiments are presented in Table 2. YOLOv5_h represents YOLOv5 with the decoupled head, YOLOv5_c represents YOLOv5 with the deformable convolution, YOLOv5_a represents YOLOv5 with the multi-scale attention, YOLOv5_hc represents YOLOv5 with the decoupled head and the deformable convolution, YOLOv5_ca represents YOLOv5 with the deformable convolution and the multi-scale attention, YOLOv5_ha represents YOLOv5 with the decoupled head and the multi-scale attention, YOLOv5_hca represents our method.

Table 2. Effect of each component on the performance of our method.

Method	Decoupled head	Deformable convolution	Multi-scale attention	mAP 0.5	mAP 0.5:0.95	Parameters
YOLOv5				84.6%	59.02%	7.1M
YOLOv5_h	✓			85.26%	61.23%	14.74M
YOLOv5_c		✓		**85.43%**	61.85%	13.2M
YOLOv5_a			✓	84.86%	60.28%	11.2M
YOLOv5_hc	✓	✓		85.33%	63.11%	20.9M
YOLOv5_ca		✓	✓	85.23%	61.92%	17.4M
YOLOv5_ha	✓		✓	84.25%	60.64%	18.9M
YOLOv5_hca	✓	✓	✓	85.11%	**63.33%**	25M

As shown in Table 2, it can be seen that the decoupled head, deformable convolution and multi-scale attention have a significant impact on the performance of our method. Among all models mentioned above, YOLOv5_hca obtains the best result on mAP 0.5:0.95. When only deformable convolution is used, mAP 0.5 of YOLOv5_c can reach the best result of 85.43% and mAP 0.5:0.95 of YOLOv5_c is improved by 2.83% compared with YOLOv5. It can be seen that the deformable convolution has a significant contribution to improving mAP 0.5 and mAP 0.5:0.95. When only the decoupled head is used, mAP 0.5 of YOLOv5_h is improved by 0.66% and mAP 0.5:0.95 of YOLOv5_h is improved by 2.21% compared with YOLOv5. When only multi-scale attention is used, mAP 0.5 of YOLOv5_a is improved by 0.26% and mAP 0.5:0.95 of YOLOv5_a is improved by 1.26% compared with YOLOv5. It shows that the decoupled head has a higher impact on accuracy than multi-scale attention.

Compared with YOLOv5, our approach gives the relative improvements of 0.51% on mAP 0.5 and 4.31% on mAP 0.5:0.95. When the decoupled head and the deform convolution are used, mAP 0.5 of YOLOv5_hc can reach 85.33% and mAP 0.5:0.95 of YOLOv5_hc can reach 63.11%. Compared with YOLOv5, the combination of the decoupled head and the deformable convolution gives the relative improvements of 0.73% on mAP 0.5 and 4.09% on mAP 0.5:0.95. As can be seen from Table 2, other combinations will also improve mAP 0.5 and mAP 0.5:0.95. The experimental results show that all three improvement methods help to further enhance the detection accuracy of YOLOv5. It also shows that the decoupled head and the deformable convolution improve mAP more obviously than the proposed multi-scale attention. Figure 5 shows the detection results of the test set. It can be clearly seen that, compared with YOLOv5, the bounding box is more suitable for the object.

Fig. 5. The detection result of the test set. The number on the bounding boxes is the probability of classification.

5   Conclusions

In this paper, we proposed three methods to improve the detection accuracy of the YOLOv5 model. The three methods are: 1) the decoupled head is used to replace the coupled head in YOLOv5; 2) the deformable convolution is used to solve the problem of feature alignment; 3) the multi-scale attention mechanism is used to solve the problem of object information interference in divide-and-conquer detection strategy. The experimental results show that our method effectively improves the detection accuracy of YOLOv5 and has obvious advantages over other state-of-the-art methods in the general detection task. In the experiments we also analyze the effects of three improved methods on detection accuracy. The ablation experiments show that all three methods can improve the accuracy of detection. In future work, we will further improve YOLOv5 to achieve more accurate detection results.

References

1. Bochkovskiy, A., Wang, C., Liao, H.M.: Yolov4: optimal speed and accuracy of object detection. CoRR abs/2004.10934 (2020)
2. Cai, Z., Vasconcelos, N.: Cascade R-CNN: delving into high quality object detection. In: Proceedings of 2018 IEEE/CVF Conference on Computer Vision and Pattern Recognition, CVPR 2018, Salt Lake City, UT, United states, pp. 6154–6162 (2018)
3. Chen, Q., Wang, Y., Yang, T., Zhang, X., Cheng, J., Sun, J.: You only look one-level feature. CoRR abs/2103.09460 (2021)
4. Dai, J., Qi, H., Xiong, Y., Li, Y., Zhang, G., Hu, H., Wei, Y.: Deformable convolutional networks. CoRR abs/1703.06211 (2017)
5. Dalal, N., Triggs, B.: Histograms of oriented gradients for human detection. In: Proceedings of 2005 IEEE Computer Society Conference on Computer Vision and Pattern Recognition, CVPR 2005, San Diego, CA, USA, pp. 886–893 (2005)
6. Dong, Z., Li, G., Liao, Y., Wang, F., Ren, P., Qian, C.: Centripetalnet: pursuing high-quality keypoint pairs for object detection. In: Proceedings of 2020 IEEE/CVF Conference on Computer Vision and Pattern Recognition, CVPR 2020, Virtual, Online, United States, pp. 10516–10525 (2020)
7. Duan, K., Bai, S., Xie, L., Qi, H., Huang, Q., Tian, Q.: CenterNet: keypoint triplets for object detection. In: Proceedings of 2019 International Conference on Computer Vision, ICCV 2019, Seoul, Republic of Korea, pp. 6568–6577 (2019)
8. Ge, Z., Liu, S., Wang, F., Li, Z., Sun, J.: YOLOX: exceeding YOLO series in 2021. CoRR abs/2107.08430 (2021)
9. Girshick, R.: Fast R-CNN. In: Proceedings of 2015 IEEE International Conference on Computer Vision, ICCV 2015, Santiago, Chile, pp. 1440–1448 (2015)
10. Hardalaç, F., et al.: Fracture detection in wrist x-ray images using deep learning-based object detection models. CoRR **abs/2111.07355** (2021)
11. Law, H., Deng, J.: CornerNet: detecting objects as paired keypoints. Int. J. Comput. Vision **128**(3), 642–656 (2020)
12. Lin, T.Y., Dollr, P., Girshick, R., He, K., Hariharan, B., Belongie, S.: Feature pyramid networks for object detection. In: Proceedings of 30th IEEE Conference on Computer Vision and Pattern Recognition, CVPR 2017, Honolulu, HI, United States, pp. 936–944 (2017)
13. Lin, T.Y., Goyal, P., Girshick, R., He, K., Dollar, P.: Focal loss for dense object detection. IEEE Trans. Pattern Anal. Mach. Intell. **42**(2), 318–327 (2020)
14. Liu, S., Qi, L., Qin, H., Shi, J., Jia, J.: Path aggregation network for instance segmentation. In: Proceedings of 2018 IEEE/CVF Conference on Computer Vision and Pattern Recognition, CVPR 2018, Salt Lake City, UT, United States, pp. 8759–8768 (2018)

15. Liu, W., et al.: SSD: single shot multibox detector. In: Leibe, B., Matas, J., Sebe, N., Welling, M. (eds.) ECCV 2016. LNCS, vol. 9905, pp. 21–37. Springer, Cham (2016). https://doi.org/10.1007/978-3-319-46448-0_2

16. Oh, H., Lee, M., Kim, H., Paik, J.: Improved deeplab v3+ with metadata extraction for small object detection in intelligent visual surveillance systems. IEIE Trans. Smart Process. Comput. **10**(3), 209–218 (2021)

17. Redmon, J.: Yolov5. OL (2021). https://github.com/ultralytics/yolov5

18. Redmon, J., Divvala, S., Girshick, R., Farhadi, A.: You only look once: unified, real-time object detection. In: Proceedings of 29th IEEE Conference on Computer Vision and Pattern Recognition, CVPR 2016, Las Vegas, NV, United States, pp. 779–788 (2016)

19. Redmon, J., Farhadi, A.: Yolo9000: better, faster, stronger. In: Proceedings of 30th IEEE Conference on Computer Vision and Pattern Recognition, CVPR 2017, Honolulu, HI, United States, pp. 6517–6525 (2017)

20. Redmon, J., Farhadi, A.: Yolov3: an incremental improvement. CoRR abs/1804.02767 (2018)

21. Ren, S., He, K., Girshick, R., Sun, J.: Faster R-CNN: towards real-time object detection with region proposal networks. IEEE Trans. Pattern Anal. Mach. Intell. **39**(6), 1137–1149 (2017)

22. Rezatofighi, H., Tsoi, N., Gwak, J., Sadeghian, A., Reid, I., Savarese, S.: Generalized intersection over union: a metric and a loss for bounding box regression. In: Proceedings of 2019 IEEE/CVF Conference on Computer Vision and Pattern Recognition, CVPR 2019, Long Beach, CA, United States, pp. 658–666 (2019)

23. Schmidhuber, J.: Deep learning in neural networks: an overview. Neural Netw. **61**(January 01, 2015), 85–117 (2015)

24. Song, G., Liu, Y., Wang, X.: Revisiting the sibling head in object detector. In: Proceedings of 2020 IEEE/CVF Conference on Computer Vision and Pattern Recognition, CVPR 2020, Virtual, Online, United States, pp. 11560–11569 (2020)

25. Tao, A., Sapra, K., Catanzaro, B.: Hierarchical multi-scale attention for semantic segmentation. CoRR abs/2005.10821 (2020)

26. Tian, Z., Shen, C., Chen, H., He, T.: Fcos: fully convolutional one-stage object detection. In: Proceedings of 2019 International Conference on Computer Vision, ICCV 2019, Seoul, Republic of Korea, pp. 9626–9635(2019)

27. Viola, P., Jones, M.J.: Robust real-time face detection. Int. J. Comput. Vision **57**(2), 137–154 (2004)

28. Wu, Y., et al.: Rethinking classification and localization for object detection. In: Proceedings of 2020 IEEE/CVF Conference on Computer Vision and Pattern Recognition, CVPR 2020, Virtual, Online, United States, pp. 10183–10192 (2020)

29. Zhang, H., Wang, K., Tian, Y., Gou, C., Wang, F.Y.: MFR-CNN: incorporating multi-scale features and global information for traffic object detection. IEEE Trans. Veh. Technol. **67**(9), 8019–8030 (2018)

30. Zhu, Y., Zhao, C., Wang, J., Zhao, X., Wu, Y., Lu, H.: CoupleNet: coupling global structure with local parts for object detection. In: Proceedings of 2017 IEEE International Conference on Computer Vision, ICCV 2017, Venice, Italy, pp. 4146–4154 (2017)

OTE: An Optimized Chinese Short Text Matching Algorithm Based on External Knowledge

Haoyang Ma[1,2], Zhaoyun Ding[2(✉)], Zeyu Li[3], and Hongyu Guo[1]

[1] North China Institute of Computing Technology, Beijing, China
guohongyu@sina.com
[2] Science and Technology on Information Systems Engineering Laboratory, National University of Defense Technology, Changsha, China
{mhy99,zyding}@nudt.edu.cn
[3] Communication University of China, Beijing, China
lizeyu@cuc.edu.cn

Abstract. Short text matching is a key problem in natural language processing (NLP), which can be applied in journalism, military, and other fields. In this paper, we propose an optimized Chinese short text matching algorithm based on external knowledge (OTE). OTE can effectively eliminate semantic ambiguity in Chinese text by integrating the HowNet external knowledge base. We use SoftLexicon to optimize the word lattice graph to provide more comprehensive multi-granularity information and integrate the LaserTagger model and EDA for data augmentation. Experimental results show that OTE has an average accuracy improvement of 1.5% in three datasets compared with existing models.

Keywords: Text matching · Multi-granularity information · Data augmentation · External knowledge · Pre-training · Natural language processing

1 Introduction

Short text matching is a critical technology in NLP. Given a pair of sentences, the text matching is to calculate their text similarity. This technology has extensive research needs in question answer systems [1], recommendation systems [2], and public opinion monitoring [3].

However, there are many challenges in studying similarity in Chinese short texts. (a) The limited length of Chinese short texts leads to the sparsity of text features, resulting in unavailability of adequate information. Moreover, traditional models can neither provide adequate semantic information of Chinese, nor offer enough multi-granularity information. (b) The fusion of deep learning technologies improves the accuracy of model matching degrees. In real scenarios, it takes time and effort to obtain label data.

Supported by the Ministry of Science and Technology of China (No. 2020AAA0105100).

G. Memmi et al. (Eds.): KSEM 2022, LNAI 13368, pp. 15–30, 2022.
https://doi.org/10.1007/978-3-031-10983-6_2

As a result, the data scale is not large enough, and the number of label categories is not balanced.

Word segmentation tools are usually used to construct word lattice graphs [4], but insufficient multi-granularity information may sometimes occur. To address this problem, we can use SoftLexicon model [5] to build a word lattice graph to provide adequate multi-granularity information SoftLexicon is an optimized model based on Lattice-LSTM [6]. Lattice-LSTM has a complex model architecture, limiting its application in many industrial fields. SoftLexicon incorporates word lexicon into character representations, avoiding the need to design a complex sequence modelling architecture while easily being used with pre-trained models such as BERT.

Meanwhile, Chinese words may contain many meanings, leading to ambiguity in judgment [7]. As is shown in Fig. 1, the Chinese word "老古董" may mean an old object (antique) or a rigid person (old fogey). In this paper, we use HowNet [8] as an external knowledge source to provide more relevant senses to solve this problem. HowNet, which was put forward in the middle of this century, has been thoroughly improved after more than ten years of development. In HowNet, "老古董" has two different senses, i.e. "antique" and "old fogey". "Old fogey" contains two sememes: "human" and "stiff", which are also the sememes of "stubborn", so we can draw that these two words are highly similar. Therefore, the model can better disambiguate and match two sentences that might be similar.

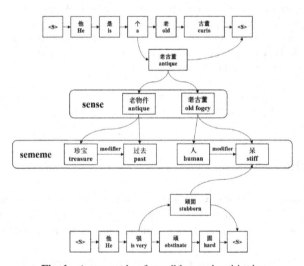

Fig. 1. An example of possible word ambiguity

For the second problem, we use a hybrid data augmentation method based on Easy Data Augmentation (EDA) [9] and text generation model LaserTagger [10]. A random swap strategy augments the original text in the EDA method. Then the EDA improved text and the original text form text pairs into the LaserTagger model to obtain the rephrased text about the input text pairs. The final augmented text received by the hybrid method is mixed with the original text as training data.

In this paper, we mainly complete the following tasks: (a) proposing an optimized short text matching algorithm based on external knowledge by using the SoftLexico model and hybrid data augmentation model; (b) proving that multi-granularity information, semantic information, and data augmentation can improve the accuracy of text matching.

2   Related Work

2.1   Pre-trained Models

Google proposed a pre-trained model named BERT [11] in 2018, which achieved good results in 11 NLP tasks. This model uses the encoder part of Transformer [12] to capture word-level and sentence-level text representations. Therefore, vectors generated by such model are called "dynamic word embeddings". Subsequently, Liu et al. [13] proposed RoBERTa model in 2019 without changing the structure of the BERT model. The BERT pre-training method was optimized by removing the next sentence prediction and introducing dynamic coding tasks to improve the pre-training model's performance. In the same period, many scholars improved the problems in different aspects of BERT and produced a variety of variants. Among them, Lan et al. [14] proposed ALBERT model, a lightweight pre-training model improved based on BERT, to address BERT's shortcomings of high GPU/TPU and longer training times. The two parameter-reduction techniques greatly lowered the memory consumption and increased the training speed of BERT. Zhang et al. [15] proposed ERNIE model, which is an enhanced language representation model trained by large-scale textual corpus and combined knowledge graphs. Yang et al. [16] proposed XLNet model, an extensible autoregressive language model that enables bidirectional prediction by adopting the principle of permutation and combination and overcomes BERT's limitations due to the autoregressive method.

2.2   Data Augmentation

Synonym Replacement (SR) [17] is a simple and intuitive data augmentation method, which generates new text by replacing some words in the original text with their synonyms. The advantage of SR is that it does not destroy the original text information, but the similarity between old and new data is too high. To solve this problem, Wei et al. [9] proposed an easy data augmentation (EDA). In addition to SR, EDA also incorporates random deletion (RD), random swap (RS), and random insertion (RI) for text processing. Still, its excessive reliance on the unexpected way is easy to destroy the context of the text. Sennrich et al. [18] proposed the use of Back Translation for data augmentation in machine translation tasks. The method is used to translate the source language of the corpus into other languages and then back translate it into the source language to obtain new corpus information. Xie et al. [19] used WMT'14 English-French translation models to perform back-translation on sentences. Back-translation can directly call the existing translation software and preserve the original text's context as much as possible. However, its over-reliance on the accuracy of the translation software may introduce a lot of noise to a certain extent. Many scholars have chosen EDA and back-translation due to their high efficiency and simple operation. Among complex data augmentation methods, Kobayashi [20] proposed Contextual Augmentation (CA), which predicts available candidate words by observing contextual information of the target word through a bidirectional language model, and then randomly selects candidate words to replace the current target word. Hu et al. [21] proposed a model for text generation, VAEHD, which combines variational auto-encoders (VAE) and holistic attribute discriminators. It can learn interpretable latent representations and generate sentences with given sentiment and tense. Although the above three methods can improve the quality of data augmentation to a certain extent, they are not conducive to improving the efficiency of data augmentation due to their high algorithm complexity and high training cost.

2.3 Multi-granularity Information

Multi-granularity information is essential in natural language processing. Different models may cause semantic ambiguity, and different tools may provide different granularities. Lattice LSTM [6] model can obtain multi-granularity sentence expression by using word information without word segmentation. Lattice LSTM encodes the input characters and all matched words in a lexicon into the model, selects the most relevant terms from the glossary to reduce the probability of ambiguity, and considers the input of both character and word granularity. The model has achieved significant improvement in multiple NLP tasks. In particular, in the named entity recognition (NER) task, the Lattice LSTM-based model [22] can encode a sequence of input characters and all potential words that match a lexicon to obtain better NER results. Inspired by the success of Lattice in other NLP tasks, as for the text matching task in 2019, LAI used the lattice-based convolutional neural networks [23] to extract sentence-level features from word lattice. LET [24] proposes a Chinese short text matching method based on word lattice and HowNet. This paper improves on this model.

3 Model

In this paper, we follow the steps below to complete the task of Chinese short text matching. First, we use data augmentation model to augment the data of the training set. Define each text pair as $C^a = \{c_1^a, c_2^a, \ldots, c_{T_a}^a\}$ and $C^b = \{c_1^b, c_2^b, \ldots, c_{T_b}^b\}$. We need method $f(C^a, C^b)$ to predict whether the senses of C^a and C^b are equal.

We propose an optimized short text matching algorithm based on external knowledge. For each text, we use SoftLexicon model to generate a word lattice graph $G = (V, E)$. A word w_i is its corresponding node $x_i \in V$ in the word lattice graph. Then we can obtain all senses through the HowNet. If there is an edge connecting nodes x_i and x_j, we define x_i itself and all its reachable nodes in its forward and backward directions as $N_{fw}^{+-}(x_i)$ and $N_{bw}^{+-}(x_i)$. For each text pair, we have two graphs G^a and G^b, which can be used for similarity prediction.

The schematic diagram of the OTE model structure is shown in Fig. 2. OTE model consists of the following five parts: data augmentation model, input model, semantic information transformer, sentence matching layer, relation classifier.

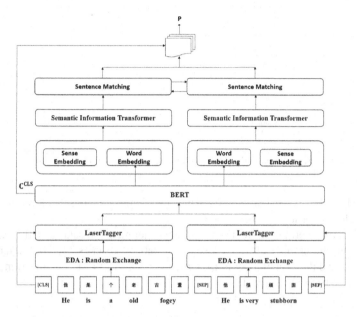

Fig. 2. Schematic diagram of OTE model structure

3.1 Data Augmentation Model

The data augmentation model combines the EDA model and the LaserTagger model. The schematic diagram of the data augmentation model structure is shown in Fig. 3. We adopt the method of random swap, in which two words are randomly selected from a sentence and repeated once, and then their positions are swapped.

The LaserTagger model can complete the text rephrase task and rewrite text A into text B with similar meaning to achieve the effect of data augmentation. The LaserTagger model needs to tag a sequence of characters, and then convert the tag sequences into text. It assigns a tag to each character. A tag is composed of two parts: a base tag and an added phrase. The base tag is either *KEEP* or *DELETE*, and the added phrase is denoted by P. We first align each source text with its target text, that is, use the Longest Common Subsequence (LCS) algorithm [25] to find their longest common substring. Then, all the phrases in the target text that are not part of the LCS are included in the phrase set V, and finally, the most frequent phrases l are selected as the final phrase set V. After the source text with length n_s is converted into tag sequences with the same length, the new text needs to be converted according to the tag of each position. The *KEEP* tag indicates keeping corresponding word, the *DELETE* tag means deleting corresponding word, and the added phrase means adding a phrase before, the corresponding word.

Taking AFQMC [26] dataset as an example, there are 102,477 items in this dataset, including 83,793 items with label 0 and 18,684 items with label 1. The dataset is not pre-divided into training, validation and test sets, so we divide it into these three sets with a ratio of 6:2:2 (a classical ratio for small-scale datasets in machine learning). After division, there are 61,486 training sets, among which 49,352 are labeled 0 and

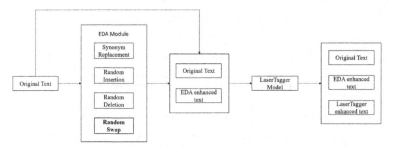

Fig. 3. Schematic diagram of data augmentation model structure

12,134 are labeled 1, with a ratio of 4:1. Thus, problems of small size of training set and unreasonable proportion of labels occur.

To address such problems, we use the model to augment the data labeled 1. After data augmentation, the number of training sets with label 1 reaches 24,270, the label ratio becomes 2:1, and the total number of training sets reaches 73,621. The above-mentioned problems have been well solved.

3.2 Input Model

To generate graph attention network, we use SoftLexicon model to generate a word lattice graph $G = (V, E)$. SoftLexicon divides all matched words of each character into four word sets $seq = \{B, M, E, S\}$, which represents a set of words with characters in different positions. The specific formula is as follows,

$$B(c_i) = \{w_{i,k}, \forall w_{i,k} \in L, i < k \leq n\},$$

$$M(c_i) = \{w_{j,k}, \forall w_{j,k} \in L, 1 \leq j < i < k \leq n\},$$

$$E(c_i) = \{w_{j,i}, \forall w_{j,i} \in L, 1 \leq j < i\},$$

$$S(c_i) = \{c_i, \exists c_i \in L\} \tag{1}$$

Where L stands for lexicon. Then the word set is compressed, mainly to compress each category of word embedding into one embedding, using the word weighting method as follow,

$$v^s(S) = \frac{4}{Z} \sum_{w \in S} z(w) e^w(w), \tag{2}$$

where S represents the word set, and $Z = \sum_{w \in \text{BUMUEUS}} z(w)$. The frequency of occurrence of each word in a static dataset is used as the weight to speed up the training. Meanwhile, if w is overwritten by another subsequence that matches the lexicon, the frequency of w will not increase. This prevents the problem that the frequency of the shorter word is always less than that of the longer word overwriting it.

Then we need generate a graph attention network base on word lattice graph. In 2018, Petar et al. [27] proposed a graph attention network applied to graph structured data. The set of all nodes connected to x_i is denoted by $N^+(x_i)$. We use h_i and h_i' to represent the feature vector and the new feature vector of the node x_i. The weight coefficient of neighboring node x_j to x_i can be set as $\alpha_{ij} = a(Wh_i, Wh_j)$. After calculation, the degree of relevance between x_i and all neighboring nodes can be obtained. After normalization by softmax, the attention weight of x_i and all neighboring nodes can be obtained. The weighted average value of updated node h_i' can be calculated as:

$$h_i^l = \sigma\left(\sum\nolimits_{x_j \in \mathcal{N}^+(x_i)} \alpha_{ij}^l \cdot \left(W^l h_j^{l-1}\right)\right) \tag{3}$$

To avoid the possible limitations in the capacity to model complex dependencies, Shen et al. proposed a multi-dimensional attention mechanism [28]. For each h_j^{l-1}, a feature-wise score vector is first calculated and then normalized using feature-wise multi-dimensional softmax, which is denoted by β,

$$\alpha_{i,j}^l = \beta_j\left(\hat{\alpha}_{i,j}^l + f_m^l\left(h_j^{l-1}\right)\right), \tag{4}$$

where f_m^l is used to estimate the contribution of each feature dimension of h_j^{l-1},

$$f_m^l\left(h_j^{l-1}\right) = W_2^l \sigma\left(W_1^l h_j^{l-1} + b_1^l\right) + b_2^l, \tag{5}$$

then the Eq. (3) can be revised as:

$$h_i^l = \sigma\left(\sum_{x_j \in \mathcal{N}^+(x_i)} \alpha_{ij}^l \odot \left(W^l h_j^{l-1}\right)\right) \tag{6}$$

We need to input text pairs into the BERT model to get a contextual representation of each character as $\{c^{CLS}, c_1^a, c_2^a, \ldots, c_{T_a}^a, c^{SEP}, c_1^b, c_2^b, \ldots, c_{T_b}^b, c^{SEP}\}$. Then we use a feed forward network to obtain a feature-wise score vector for each character, which is denoted by γ. After that, we can normalize it with feature-wise multi-dimensional softmax,

$$u_k = \beta_k(\gamma(c_k)), \tag{7}$$

then we can obtain contextual word embedding:

$$v_i = \sum\nolimits_{k=t_1}^{t_2} u_k \odot c_k \tag{8}$$

To get sense embedding, we need to use HowNet. HowNet has a well-established sense and sememe architecture. As an example of the HowNet structure, the Chinese word " 老古董" has two senses, i.e. "antique" and "old fogey", and the "old fogey" has two sememes: "human" and "stiff". HowNet makes it easier to calculate whether two sentences match.

We generate the set of the senses as $S^{w_i} = \{s_{i,1}, s_{i,2}, \ldots, s_{i,k}\}$ for each word w_i, then generate the set of sememes as $O^{s_{i,k}} = \{o^1_{i,k}, o^2_{i,k}, \ldots, o^n_{i,k}\}$ for each sense. We use sememe attention over target model [29] to calculate each sememe's embedding vector $e^n_{i,k}$, then use multi-dimensional attention function to calculate each sememe's representation $o^n_{i,k}$ as:

$$o^{n'}_{i,k} = \beta(e^n_{i,k}, \{e^{n'}_{i,k} | o^{n'}_{i,k} \in O^{s_{i,k}}\}) \tag{9}$$

For the embedding of each sense, we can obtain it with attentive pooling of all its sememe representations:

$$s_{i,k} = AP(\{o^n_{i,k} | o^n_{i,k} \in O^{s_{i,k}}\}) \tag{10}$$

3.3 Semantic Information Transformer

Contextual information is now separated from semantic information. In order to get more useful information, we propose a word lattice graph transformer. For word w_i, we use v_i and $s_{i,k}$ as the original word representation h^0_i, the sense $s_{i,k}$ as the original sense representation $g^0_{i,k}$. Then update them iteratively.

To update sense representation from $g^{l-1}_{i,k}$ to $g^l_{i,k}$, we need both backward information and forward information of x_i, then update its representation with a gated recurrent unit (GRU) [30],

$$m^{l,bw}_{i,k} = \beta\left(g^{l-1}_{i,k}, \left\{h^{l-1}_j | x_j \in N^+_{bw}(x_i)\right\}\right),$$

$$m^{l,fw}_{i,k} = \beta\left(g^{l-1}_{i,k}, \left\{h^{l-1}_j | x_j \in N^+_{fw}(x_i)\right\}\right),$$

$$g^l_{i,k} = GRU(g^{l-1}_{i,k}, m^l_{i,k}) \tag{11}$$

Where $m^l_{i,k} = \{m^{l,bw}_{i,k}, m^{l,fw}_{i,k}\}$. We use GRU to control the mix of contextual information and semantic information because $m^l_{i,k}$ contains contextual information merely. Then we use $g^l_{i,k}$ to update the word representation from h^{l-1}_i to h^l_i. The transformer uses multi-dimensional attention to obtain the first sense of word w_i from its semantic information, then updates it with GRU.

$$q^l_i = \beta\left(h^{l-1}_i, \left\{g^l_{i,k} | s_{i,k} \in S^{w_i}\right\}\right),$$

$$h^l_i = GRU(h^{l-1}_i, q^l_i) \tag{12}$$

3.4 Sentence Matching Layer

To incorporate word representation into characters, we use characters in C^a as example. We generate a set $W^{c_i^a}$ that contains the words using character c_t^a, then use attentive pooling to get $\hat{c}_t^a$ of each character:

$$\hat{c}_t^a = AP(\{h_i^a | w_i^a \in W^{c_i^a}\}) \tag{13}$$

After obtaining $\hat{c}_t^a$ and c_t^a, we use layer normalization to get semantic information enhanced character representation y_t^a:

$$y_t^a = LN(\hat{c}_t^a + c_t^a) \tag{14}$$

Then for each character c_t^a, we can use multi-dimensional attention to obtain its aggregative information from C^a and C^b, which are denoted by m_t^s and m_t^c. When they are almost equal, we can know that these two sentences are matched. To compare them, we need use multi-perspective cosine distance [31],

$$m_t^s = \beta\left(y_t^a, \left\{y_{t'}^a | c_{t'}^a \in C^a\right\}\right),$$

$$m_t^c = \beta\left(y_t^a, \left\{y_{t'}^a | c_{t'}^b \in C^b\right\}\right),$$

$$d_k = CD\left(w_k^{cos} \odot m_t^s, w_k^{cos} \odot m_t^c\right) \tag{15}$$

where w_k^{cos} represents the different weights of different dimensions of a text. We can get the final character representation $d_t := [d_1, d_2, \ldots, d_k]$ using feed forward networks, then use attentive pooling to obtain the sentence representation vector:

$$\hat{y}_t^a = \gamma\left([m_t^s, d_t]\right),$$

$$r^a = AP(\hat{y}_t^a | \hat{y}_t^a \in \hat{Y}^a) \tag{16}$$

3.5 Relation Classifier Layer

Finally, our model can predict the similarity between two sentences by using r^a, r^b, and c^{CLS}.

$$P = \gamma\left([c^{CLS}, r^a, r^b, \left|r^a - r^b\right|, r^a \odot r^b]\right). \tag{17}$$

For each $\{C_i^a, C_i^b, y_i\}$ raining sample, our ultimate goal is to reduce the BCE loss:

$$\mathcal{L} = -\sum_{i=1}^{N}(y_i log(p_i) + (1 - y_i)\log(1 - p_i)) \tag{18}$$

where $y_i \in \{0, 1\}$ is the label of the i-th training sample we input to the model and $p_i \in [0, 1]$ is the prediction of our model taking sentence pairs as input.

4 Experiment

4.1 Experiment Dataset

In the experimental part, we use three Chinese datasets, i.e. LCQMC [32], AFQMC [26] and BQ [33], to test our model.

The LCQMC dataset is a question semantic matching dataset constructed by Harbin Institute of Technology in COLING2018. Its format consists of sentence pair number, two sentences to be compared and 4 columns of similarity labels. It contains 260,068 pieces of data in total, including 238,766 for training set, 12,500 for test set and 8,802 for validation set. LCQMC is widely used in Chinese short text similarity calculation.

The AFQMC dataset is the dataset of ANT Financial ATEC: NLP Problem Similarity Calculation Competition, and it is a dataset for classification task. All data are from the actual application scenarios of Ant Financial's financial brain, that is, two sentences described by users in a given customer service are determined by algorithms to determine whether they represent the same semantics. Synonymous sentences are represented by 1, non-synonymous sentences are represented by 0, and the format is consistent with LCQMC dataset. Since the AFQMC dataset was not pre-divided into training set, test set and validation set, we divide the dataset by the ratio of 6:2:2 in this experiment. The data volumes of training set, test set and validation set are 61,486, 20,496, and 20,495, respectively, and the total number of all samples is 102,477.

The BQ dataset is a question matching dataset in the field of banking and finance. Comprising question text pairs extracted from one year of online banking system logs, it is the largest question matching dataset in the banking domain. It classifies two paragraphs of bank credit business according to whether they are semantically similar or not. 1 represents the similarity judgment while 0 represents the dissimilarity judgment. The BQ dataset contains 120,000 pieces of data in total, including 100,000 for training set, 10,000 for validation set and 10,000 for test set.

4.2 Experiment Result

Accuracy (ACC.) and F1 score are used as the evaluation metrics. The calculation formula of ACC is as follows,

$$ACC. = \frac{TP + TN}{TP + TN + FP + FN} \tag{19}$$

Where True Positive (TP) indicates the number of cases correctly predicted as positive, False Positive (FP) indicates the number of cases incorrectly predicted as positive, True Negative (TN) indicates the number of cases correctly predicted as negative, False Negative (FN) indicates the number of cases incorrectly predicted as negative. Based on this, precision rate (P), Recall (R) and F1 values can be calculated. Their calculation formulas are shown below:

$$P = \frac{TP}{TP + FP}. \tag{20}$$

$$R = \frac{TP}{TP + FN}. \tag{21}$$

$$F1 = \frac{2 * P * R}{P + R}. \tag{22}$$

We use SoftLexicon model to generate the word lattice graph, use OpenHowNet to acquire external knowledge for semantic information embedding. We use a method that integrates the LaserTagger model and EDA for data augmentation. In order to prevent over-fitting, 50% down-sampling is performed on the original data. The batch size of LCQMC, AFQMC and BQ is 32,32 and 64, respectively. The number of epoch is set to 4. Word representation, sense representation and hidden layer's dimension are all 128.

Data Augmentation Validation. In order to verify the effectiveness of data augmentation, taking AFQMC dataset as an example, we design three groups of comparative experiments, the training sets of which are original text, downsampling and data augmentation, respectively. In the downsampling method, 50% of the training set labeled 0 were randomly selected as the final training samples. Therefore, the training set samples for the final experiment were 24,622 less than the original training set. Data augmentation augments the data labeled as 1 to obtain a dataset with 2:1 of 0 and 1 labels. Compared with the original text method and the downsampling method, the accuracy of the data augmentation method is improved by 3.7% and 3%, respectively. The experimental results are shown in Table 1. We think this is due to the large deviation of the label ratio in the original text. Although the downsampling method solves the problem of ratio, it causes the loss of original data.

Table 1. Comparison of data augmentation results

Method	ACC.	F1
Original	72.98	71.87
Downsampling	73.43	73.95
Data Augmentation	**75.69**	**75.88**

To verify the effectiveness of hybrid data augmentation, we compare the original text, the text generated by back translation, and the text generated by combining LaserTagger and EDA. Back translation means that Chinese text is converted into English text and then back translated into Chinese text through translation tools. In this experiment, Youdao Translation and Google Translation are used separately to achieve this step. Taking AFQMC dataset as an example, the experimental results are shown in Table 2. Compared with original text and back translation, the hybrid method improves the accuracy by 2.9% and 2.3% respectively. Therefore, the hybrid data augmentation method can effectively avoid the introduction of noise to the data-augmented text and improve the accuracy of the Chinese short text semantic similarity calculation model.

Multi-granularity Information Validation. In order to verify the impact of multi-granularity information on the model, we also set up a comparative experiment. The

Table 2. Comparison of hybrid data augmentation results

Method	ACC	F1
Original	73.56	74.22
Back translation	74.01	74.78
Hybird	**75.69**	**75.88**

experiment is divided into three categories: no word segmentation, jieba and word lattice graph. AFQMC is also used as an example in this experiment, and the experimental results are shown in Table 3. As can be seen from the experimental results, the accuracy of lattice is improved by 2.7% and 2.1% respectively compared with that of no word segmentation and jieba. We believe that jieba does not provide enough multi-granularity information, and there may be word segmentation errors, leading to the insignificant improvement of accuracy. This experiment proves that the introduction of multi-granularity information can effectively improve the accuracy of Chinese short text similarity calculation.

Table 3. Multi-granularity information results comparison

Method	ACC.	F1
No	73.72	74.04
Jieba	74.13	74.22
SoftLexicon	**75.69**	**75.88**

Semantic Information Validation. At the same time, in order to test the effectiveness of semantic information, we also set up the experiment without HowNet. Because short texts don't contain enough contextual information, HowNet can provide more semantic information. In this experiment, we remove the updating and embedding of semantic information in the model. Taking AFQMC dataset as an example, through experimental comparison, there is a 1.4% decrease in accuracy and 0.9% decrease in F1 score after removing HowNet. This experiment proves that semantic information provided by integrating external knowledge can increase the accuracy of Chinese short text similarity calculation.

Ablation Experiment. To demonstrate the effectiveness of the joint use of data augmentation and multi-granularity information, we set up an ablation experiment, which is divided into four groups: Neither, Only DA (data augmentation), Only MI (multi-granularity information) and Both When data augmentation is not included, original text is used as the training sample. When multi-granularity information is not included, we cancel the embedding of semantic information and only use BERT as word embedding. The experimental results are shown in Table 4. The bar chart is shown in Fig. 4.

According to the experimental data, compared with Neither group, the Only DA and Only MI can improve the accuracy by 1.5% and 2.4%, respectively. As for the Both group, the accuracy is improved by 5.4%. We believe that because the multi-granularity information model contains more semantic information, the improvement is greater than the data augmentation. Therefore, it can be proved that the combination of data augmentation and multi-granularity information can better improve the accuracy of similarity calculation of Chinese short texts.

Table 4. Ablation experiment

DA	MI	ACC	F1
×	×	71.79	71.86
√	×	72.87	71.95
×	√	73.53	73.72
√	√	**75.69**	**75.88**

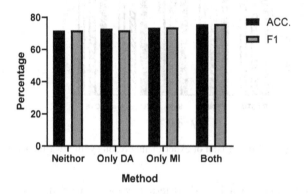

Fig. 4. Ablation experiment

Model Comparison. For the control group, we select BiLSTM [34], ERNIE [15], BERT [11], and BERT-wwm-ext [35] models(BERT(W)). The comparison of experimental results with other models is shown in Table 5. The accuracies of LCQMC, AFQMC and BQ are increased by 1.8%, 2.2% and 0.6%, respectively. The F1 scores of LCQMC, AFQMC and BQ are increased by 1.1%, 0.7% and 1%, respectively.

Table 5. Comparison of experimental results with other models

MODEL	LCQMC		AFQMC		BQ	
	ACC	F1	ACC	F1	ACC	F1
BiLSTM	76.10	78.90	64.68	54.53	73.51	72.68
ERNIE	87.04	88.06	73.83	73.91	84.67	84.20
BERT	85.73	86.86	73.70	74.12	84.50	84.00
BERT(W)	86.68	87.77	74.07	74.35	84.71	83.94
OTE	**88.29**	**88.72**	**75.69**	**75.88**	**85.26**	**84.77**

The bar chart for comparison of experimental results is shown in Fig. 5.

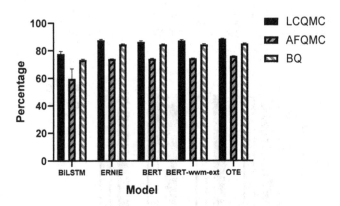

Fig. 5. Comparison of experimental results with other models

BiLSTM is a bidirectional long short-term memory network that can. BERT is essentially a two-stage NLP model. The first stage is called pre-training, which, like word embedding, trains a language model using existing unlabeled corpus. The second stage is called fine-tuning, which uses pre-trained language models to complete specific downstream tasks of NLP. Both Bert-wwm-ext and ERNIE are BERT variants. ERNIE aims to learn the language representation enhanced by knowledge masking strategy. Bert-wwm-ext mainly changes the generation strategy of training samples in the original pre-training stage, and increases the training dataset and the number of training steps. According to the experimental results, compared with BiLSTM, OTE has a great improvement, and also has a certain improvement as compared to BERT-based models. The experimental results show that OTE has an average accuracy improvement of 16.3% as compared to BiLSTM. Compared with BERT-based models, the accuracy has been improved to a certain extent. Among them, the accuracy is improved by 2% on average compared with BERT model and 1.3% on average compared with ERNIE model.

5 Conclusion

In this paper, we propose an optimized short text matching algorithm based on external knowledge, using HowNet as an external data source to generate semantic knowledge. We use SoftLexicon to optimize the word lattice graph to provide more comprehensive multi-granularity information and integrate the LaserTagger model and EDA for data augmentation. We have obtained good experimental results. Compared with other pre-training models, it is proved that multi-granularity information, semantic information and data augmentation can better improve the accuracy of the model.

References

1. Tan, M., Dos Santos, C., Xiang, B., Zhou, B.: Improved representation learning for question answer matching. In: Proceedings of the 54th Annual Meeting of the Association for Computational Linguistics (Volume 1: Long Papers), pp. 464–473 (2016)
2. Chen, H.: Personalized recommendation system of e-commerce based on big data analysis. J. Interdisc. Math. **21**, 1243–1247 (2018)
3. Kilimci, Z., Omurca, S.: Extended feature spaces based classifier ensembles for sentiment analysis of short texts. Inf. Tech. Control. **47**(3), 457–470 (2018)
4. Chen, L., et al.: Neural graph matching networks for Chinese short text matching. In: Proceedings of the 58th Annual Meeting of the Association for Computational Linguistics, pp. 6152–6158 (2020)
5. Ma, R., Peng, M., Zhang, Q., Huang, X.: Simplify the usage of lexicon in Chinese NER. arXiv preprint arXiv:1908.05969 (2019)
6. Zhang, Y., Wang, Y., Yang, J.: Lattice LSTM for Chinese sentence representation. IEEE/ACM Trans. Audio Speech Lang. Process. **28**, 1506–1519 (2020)
7. Xu, J., Liu, J., Zhang, L., Li, Z., Chen, H.: Improve Chinese word embeddings by exploiting internal structure. In: Proceedings of the 2016 Conference of the North American Chapter of the Association for Computational Linguistics: Human Language Technologies, pp. 1041–1050 (2016)
8. Dong, Z., Dong, Q.: HowNet-a hybrid language and knowledge resource. In: International Conference on Natural Language Processing and Knowledge Engineering, 2003, Proceedings. 2003, pp. 820–824. IEEE (2003)
9. Wei, J., Zou, K.: EDA: easy data augmentation techniques for boosting performance on text classification tasks. arXiv preprint: arXiv:1901.11196 (2019)
10. Malmi, E., Krause, S., Rothe, S., Mirylenka, D., Severyn, A.: Encode, tag, realize: high-precision text editing. arXiv preprint arXiv:1909.01187 (2019)
11. Devlin, J., Chang, M.W., Lee, K., Toutanova, K.: BERT: pre-training of deep bidirectional transformers for language understanding (2018)
12. Vaswani, A., et al.: Attention is all you need. In: Advances in Neural Information Processing Systems, pp. 5998–6008 (2017)
13. Liu, Y., et al.: RoBERTa: a robustly optimized bert pretraining approach. arXiv preprint arXiv: 1907.11692 (2019)
14. Lan, Z., Chen, M., Goodman, S., Gimpel, K., Sharma, P., Soricut, R.: ALBERT: a lite BERT for self-supervised learning of language representations. arXiv preprint arXiv:1909.11942 (2019)
15. Zhang, Z., Han, X., Liu, Z., Jiang, X., Sun, M., Liu, Q.: ERNIE: enhanced language representation with informative entities. arXiv preprint arXiv:1905.07129 (2019)

16. Yang, Z., Dai, Z., Yang, Y., Carbonell, J., Salakhutdinov, R.R., Le, Q.V.: XLNet: generalized autoregressive pretraining for language understanding. In: Advances in Neural Information Processing Systems, vol. 32 (2019)
17. Zhang, X., Zhao, J., LeCun, Y.: Character-level convolutional networks for text classification. Adv. Neural Inf. Process. Syst. **28**, 649–657 (2015)
18. Sennrich, R., Haddow, B., Birch, A.: Improving neural machine translation models with monolingual data. arXiv preprint arXiv:1511.06709 (2015)
19. Xie, Q., Dai, Z., Hovy, E., Luong, M.-T., Le, Q.V.: Unsupervised data augmentation for consistency training. arXiv preprint arXiv:1904.12848 (2019)
20. Kobayashi, S.: Contextual augmentation: data augmentation by words with paradigmatic relations. arXiv preprint arXiv:1805.06201 (2018)
21. Hu, Z., Yang, Z., Liang, X., Salakhutdinov, R., Xing, E.P.: Toward controlled generation of text. In: International Conference on Machine Learning, PMLR, pp. 1587–1596 (2017)
22. Zhang, Y., Yang, J.: Chinese NER using lattice LSTM. arXiv preprint arXiv:1805.02023 (2018)
23. Lai, Y., Feng, Y., Yu, X., Wang, Z., Xu, K., Zhao, D.: Lattice CNNs for matching based Chinese question answering. In: Proceedings of the AAAI Conference on Artificial Intelligence, pp. 6634–6641 (2019)
24. Lyu, B., Chen, L., Zhu, S., Yu, K.: LET: linguistic knowledge enhanced graph transformer for Chinese short text matching. arXiv preprint arXiv:2102.12671 (2021)
25. Hirschberg, D.S.: Algorithms for the longest common subsequence problem. J. ACM (JACM). **24**, 664–675 (1977)
26. Xu, L., Zhang, X., Dong, Q.: CLUECorpus2020: a large-scale Chinese corpus for pre-training language model. arXiv preprint arXiv:2003.01355 (2020)
27. Veličković, P., Cucurull, G., Casanova, A., Romero, A., Lio, P., Bengio, Y.: Graph attention networks. arXiv preprint arXiv:1710.10903 (2017)
28. Shen, T., Zhou, T., Long, G., Jiang, J., Pan, S., Zhang, C.: DiSAN: directional self-attention network for RNN/CNN-free language understanding. In: Proceedings of the AAAI Conference on Artificial Intelligence (2018)
29. Niu, Y., Xie, R., Liu, Z., Sun, M.: Improved word representation learning with sememes. In: Proceedings of the 55th Annual Meeting of the Association for Computational Linguistics (Volume 1: Long Papers), pp. 2049–2058 (2017)
30. Caruana, R.: Learning many related tasks at the same time with backpropagation. In: Advances in Neural Information Processing Systems, pp. 657–664 (1995)
31. Wang, Z., Hamza, W., Florian, R.: Bilateral multi-perspective matching for natural language sentences. arXiv preprint arXiv:1702.03814 (2017)
32. Liu, X., Chen, Q., Deng, C., Zeng, H., Chen, J., Li, D., Tang, B.: LCQMC: a large-scale Chinese question matching corpus. In: Proceedings of the 27th International Conference on Computational Linguistics, pp. 1952–1962 (2018)
33. Chen, J., Chen, Q., Liu, X., Yang, H., Lu, D., Tang, B.: The BQ corpus: a large-scale domain-specific Chinese corpus for sentence semantic equivalence identification. In: Proceedings of the 2018 Conference on Empirical Methods in Natural Language Processing, pp. 4946–4951 (2018)
34. Mueller, J., Thyagarajan, A.: Siamese recurrent architectures for learning sentence similarity. In: Proceedings of the AAAI Conference on Artificial Intelligence (2016)
35. Cui, Y., et al.: Pre-training with whole word masking for Chinese BERT. arXiv arxiv:1906.08101 (2019)

KIR: A Knowledge-Enhanced Interpretable Recommendation Method

Yuejia Wu[1,2,3,4,5,6,7], Jiale Li[1,2,3,4,5,6,7], and Jiantao Zhou[1,2,3,4,5,6,7]([envelope])

[1] College of Computer Science, Inner Mongolia University, Hohhot, China
wuyuejia@imudges.com, 1052549239@qq.com, cszjtao@imu.edu.cn
[2] Engineering Research Center of Ecological Big Data, Ministry of Education,
Hohhot, China
[3] National and Local Joint Engineering Research Center of Mongolian Intelligent
Information Processing Technology, Hohhot, China
[4] Inner Mongolia Cloud Computing and Service Software Engineering Laboratory,
Hohhot, China
[5] Inner Mongolia Social Computing and Data Processing Key Laboratory,
Hohhot, China
[6] Inner Mongolia Discipline Inspection and Supervision Big Data Key Laboratory,
Hohhot, China
[7] Inner Mongolia Big Data Analysis Technology Engineering Laboratory,
Hohhot, China

Abstract. Recommendation System (RS) is of great significance for screening adequate information and improving the efficiency of information acquisition. The existing recommendation methods can improve the accuracy of the recommendation results to a certain extent. However, due to the lack of interpretability, the recommendation results are insufficient and burdensome to satisfy the desire of some users to understand the recommendation basis. For this reason, the Knowledge Graph (KG) is introduced as auxiliary information of the RS. It calculates the importance of entities and relations and uses them as the recommendation's basis. First, item categories are introduced to enhance the impact on user preferences. Second, an Attention Mechanism (AM) is proposed to distinguish users' interests in different contextual entity-relation sets in the KG. Finally, multiple feature information is input into the Convolutional Neural Network (CNN) to extract users' preferences. The experimental results prove that the model can improve the accuracy of the recommendation effect, and at the same time, it can better explain the reasons for the recommendation.

Keywords: Recommender system · Knowledge graph · Attention mechanism · Interpretability · Deep learning

1 Introduction

Massive data contains a rich value and huge potential, bringing revolutionary development to human society. However, it also brings serious information overload problems. Recommender Systems (RS), which is an effective way to solve

© The Author(s), under exclusive license to Springer Nature Switzerland AG 2022
G. Memmi et al. (Eds.): KSEM 2022, LNAI 13368, pp. 31–43, 2022.
https://doi.org/10.1007/978-3-031-10983-6_3

the problem of information overload [1], has been successfully used in many fields, including e-commerce, information retrieval, social networks, and news feeds.

Personalized recommendation algorithm is the core of RS [2], which can be divided into three categories: content-based recommendation algorithm [3], collaborative filtering-based recommendation algorithm [4], and hybrid recommendation algorithm [5,6]. Knowledge Graph (KG) is effective auxiliary information in the mixed RS, linking the users and the items to enhance the semantics of the data information and improve recommendations' accuracy. It has become one of the active branches of recommender system research, attracting much attention from researchers [7–11] in recent years.

Existing recommendation methods based on KG can be divided into three categories [12]: feature-based recommendation method, path-based recommendation method, and embedding recommendation method. However, these methods do not detail the effect of item categories on user preferences, which may deviate from actual user preferences, resulting in lower recommendation results than expected. In addition, there is no practical method to explain the recommended items, which will affect the credibility of users to the system.

In order to further characterize user preferences, improve the performance of Recommendation System, and give as valid reasons as possible for recommended items, we propose the Knowledge-enhanced Interpretable Recommendation algorithm (KIR). It combines the item category information with the information in the KG, uses the Attention Mechanism to calculate users' interest in different entity-relation in the KG, and the recommendation reasons for the items to be recommended are given as accurately as possible. The main contributions of this paper are as follows:

- An interpretable recommendation method for knowledge enhancement, KIR, is proposed to enhance user preferences by introducing category information of items and combining entity-relation information in the KG.
- An Attentional Mechanism is designed according to the categories of items and KG information to distinguish users' interest in the KG's entity-relation tuples of different contexts.
- Experimental results show that our KIR method can effectively improve the performance of the recommendation and explain the recommendation results.

2   Related Work

Feature-based recommendation methods mainly input features extracted from KG into traditional models. For example, LibFM [13], which analyzes user preferences by taking the attributes of users and items in the KG as input. Path-based recommendation methods mainly mine multiple connection relationships between users and items in the KG [14–16]. Taking PER [13] as an example, it uses KG from the path-based perspective. The recommended method of embedding-based KG is mainly to represent the entities and relations through graph embedding. This method can be divided into two research directions [17].

One is to use the rich content information in the KG to enhance the recommendation performance. For example, Zhang et al. [8] used the KG method to generate user and item representations for the recommendation. Huang et al. [9] adopted a storage network for recommendation in KG embedding. Wang et al. [10] proposed a multi-hop KG recommendation method based on embedding to solve the problems of feature-based and path-based methods. Another research direction is to use entity and path information in the KG to make interpretable recommendations. The purpose of the explainable recommendation is to give the reasons for recommendation while recommending items to users to improve the reliability of RS [18].

At present, the explainable RS based on the KG designed by researchers mainly makes recommendations according to the path in the KG. For example, Ai et al. [19] incorporated the method of KG embedding learning into interpretable recommendations. Wang et al. [11] proposed a model based on Recurrent Neural Network (RNN) to carry out inference recommendations through KG. Song et al. [20] designed the Attention Mechanism to calculate the weight of the recommendation results obtained from different paths. Several main reasons for the recommendation results can be given through the difference in weight.

However, the above method does not consider the impact of item categories on users, who in general may prefer items of the same category-for example, books, movies, and music in the same genre. In addition, although most of the existing combined with the method of KG is to calculate the weight based on AM for recommendation results explanation, they only consider the entity-relation in KG but do not consider the relationships between entities. In contrast, the relationship between the head and tail entities can be expressed according to the two entities so that more features can be integrated and user preferences can be better expressed.

In order to further improve the performance and the interpretability of the RS, this paper proposes the KIR, an interpretable recommendation algorithm based on knowledge enhancement. KIR algorithm introduces the classification and relationship between the entity, calculates the recommended items and the connection degree of user preferences by the Attention Mechanism, and lists all relationships in descending order. The relationship with the highest weight is considered the recommendation reason.

3   Problem Description

Definition 1. *Recommendation System: In Recommendation System, let $\mathcal{U} = \{u_1, u_2\text{-}, ..., u_M\}$ and $\mathcal{V} = \{v_1, v_2, ..., v_N\}$ respectively represent the set of M users and N items. According to whether the user has clicked on a certain item, defined the user-item interaction matrix is $Z \in \mathcal{R}^{M \times N}$. $Z_{uv} = 1$ indicates that the user u has browsed or clicked on item v, and conversely, $Z_{uv} = 0$.*

Definition 2. *Item Category: For each different item in $\mathcal{V}$, there may be one or more categories, so let $S = \{s_1, s_2, ..., s_{|S|}\}$ is all categories of collection of the item, $|S|$ is the number of all categories.*

Definition 3. *Knowledge Graph: Given a graph* $\mathcal{G} = \{\mathcal{X}, \mathcal{Y}, \mathcal{T}\}$, $\mathcal{X}$, $\mathcal{Y}$, *and* $\mathcal{T}$ *represent the set of triples of entities, relationships, and facts, respectively. For* $\forall$ $\mathbf{h}, \mathbf{t} \in \mathcal{X}, \mathbf{r} \in \mathcal{Y}$, *if* $\mathbf{r}$ *connects* $\mathbf{h}$ *and* $\mathbf{t}$ *directly, and the direction of the relationship is such that* $\mathbf{h} \rightarrow \mathbf{t}$, $\mathbf{h}$, $\mathbf{r}$ *and* $\mathbf{t}$ *form a triple* $(\mathbf{h}, \mathbf{r}, \mathbf{t})$. *The KG notes for* $\mathcal{G} = \{\mathcal{X}, \mathcal{Y}, \mathcal{T}\} = \{(\mathbf{h}, \mathbf{r}, \mathbf{t}) | \mathbf{h}, \mathbf{t} \in \mathcal{X}, \mathbf{r} \in \mathcal{Y}\}$.

Definition 4. *Contextual entity-relation set: Given an entity* $h \in \mathcal{H}_u$, *the q's hop contextual entity-relation set of* $\mathcal{H}$ *is defined as follows:*

$$C_h^q = \{(\mathbf{h}, \mathbf{r}, \mathbf{t}), \mathbf{t} \in \mathcal{X}, \mathbf{r} \in \mathcal{Y} | d(\mathbf{h}, \mathbf{t}) = q\} \tag{1}$$

where the $d(\mathbf{h}, \mathbf{t})$ represents the length of the shortest path between two entities H and T in the KG, and $\mathbf{h}, \mathbf{t} \in \mathcal{X}, \mathbf{r} \in \mathcal{Y}$, $\mathbf{r}$ is the relation directly connected with $\mathbf{t}$. For each user u, there is a click history set $\mathcal{H}_u$, so the q-hop contextual entity-relation set for user U is defined as follows:

$$C_u^q = \cup_{(h \in \mathcal{H}_u)} C_h^q, q = 1, 2, \ldots, Q \tag{2}$$

Definition 5. *Recommended Task: Given the user-item interaction matrix* Z *and KG* $\mathcal{G}$, *the prediction function of probability* $\hat{Z}_{uv}$ *that user u clicks candidate item v in the future is defined as follows:*

$$\hat{Z}_{uv} = F(u, v | \theta, Z, \mathcal{G}, S) \tag{3}$$

where the θ *represents the set of parameters in the method.*

To make the calculation pattern for each batch fixed and more efficient, we sample a fixed size set of context entity-relation for each hop rather than using its complete contextual entity-relation set. The contextual entity-relation set is randomly selected in each hop, and K represents the number of contextual entity-relation tuples in each hop, that is, C_u^q selects K tuples in q-hop.

4   Method

4.1   KIR Framework

Figure 1 shows the framework of our proposed model, KIR. The category attributes and KG information of items are used. The embedding layer maps each category item, KG entities, and relations into a dense, continuous dimensional vector space. The category feature is represented by $\mathbf{P_s}$, and the weight a_k is calculated by Attention Mechanism in combination with the contextual entity-relation set in the KG. At the same time, $\mathbf{P_s}$ and the contextual entity-relation set of the KG are combined into the convolutional neural network to extract the feature $\mathbf{E_k}$ of the KG tuple. All the calculated weights a_k are then multiplied and summed with the corresponding eigenvector $\mathbf{E_k}$ to obtain the user preference $\mathbf{T_u}$. Finally, calculate the hit probability $\hat{Z}_{uv}$ by multiplying $\mathbf{T_u}$ and item v. In this paper, we use bold notation to represent vectors.

4.2   Category Feature

To improve recommendation performance, KIR will incorporate more auxiliary information, namely the category attributes of the item. In KIR, categories are indexed by ID, and the input is a one-hot encoding vector, which only sets the value at the corresponding position of one category to 1 and the value at the other position to 0. At this moment, each input one-hot coding vector is a vector length as $|S|$ category. The embedding layer then maps each category from the ID space to a dense and continuous vector space.

$$\mathbf{P_s} = \mathbf{o_s} W^{stype} \tag{4}$$

where $\mathbf{o_s}$ is one-hot vector of category, fully connects the weight matrix $W^{stype} \in R^{(|S| \times |F_s|)}$ with the input of one-hot vectors, and codes a category S one-hot vector to embedded vector $\mathbf{P_s}$. The $|F_s|$ is the length of the categories of potential space, and it is usually less than the length of the $|S|$. The vector $\mathbf{P_s}$ calculated by the formula (4) is called category eigenvectors. Each item has one or more categories, such as story, romance, and disaster for the Titanic movie. Therefore, an item will contain multiple category feature vectors, which we will describe in the next subsection.

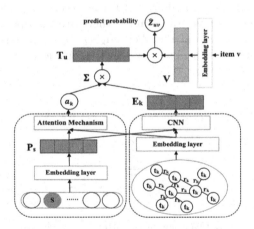

Fig. 1. The overall framework of KIR

4.3   Attention Mechanism

A user might buy or click by item category in the real world. For example, suppose the user has clicked on electronic products frequently, which is the same category of items. In that case, the user can be recommended for this category of items, reducing the range of recommended items and improving the recommendation performance to a certain extent. In addition, an item may contain multiple categories. In order to distinguish users' interest in different contextual entity-relation sets in the KG, different weights can be assigned to them. For each set of the contextual entity-relation tuple $(h_k, r_k, t_k) \in C_u^q$ of a user u, users have different interests, so the Attention Mechanism as shown in Fig. 1 is designed to assign weight a_k to each tuple. The detailed design of the Attention Mechanism is as follows:

$$a_k = \delta(FC(\textbf{concatenate})) \qquad (5)$$

where the δ stand for softmax function and the FC means fully connected layer, the *concatenate* is the result of feature vector splicing, which is expressed as follows:

$$\textbf{concatenate} = concat(\mathbf{h_k}; \mathbf{r_k}; \mathbf{t_k}; \mathbf{P_s}) \qquad (6)$$

where $\mathbf{h_k} \in R^d$ is the vector representation of the head entity $\mathbf{h_k}$, $\mathbf{t_k} \in R^d$ is the vector representation of the tail entity, $\mathbf{r_k} \in R^d$ is the vector representation of the relation $\mathbf{r_k}$, and d represents the dimension of the vector. In the Attention Mechanism we designed, besides the input triples (h_k, r_k, t_k), we also included $\mathbf{h_k} - \mathbf{t_k}$, $\mathbf{P_s}$. $\mathbf{h_k} - \mathbf{t_k}$ can represent the implicit relationship between $\mathbf{h_k}$ and $\mathbf{t_k}$ in the vector graph. At the same time, $\mathbf{r_k}$ is taken as the feature to learn better which relationships users like to explain the recommendation results for users and enhance the credibility. In addition, the class vector $\mathbf{P_s}$ is introduced, which is the corresponding class vector of $\mathbf{h_k}$. If there are multiple categories $\mathbf{h_k}$, so multiple categories vector and the above $\mathbf{h_k}, \mathbf{r_k}, \mathbf{t_k}$ characteristics all stitched and transported into the neural network can be considered in the user's interest in different categories.

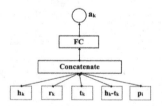

Fig. 2. Overview of the attention mechanism

It can be seen from Fig. 2 and Formula (6) that multiple feature vectors are spliced to retain the features of multiple vectors. If vector splicing is replaced by vector addition, multiple vectors are merged into one, making it difficult to extract the feature information of each vector. Therefore, we choose vector concatenation rather than simple addition. A weight value a_k can now be calculated for each tuple, using the user's preference for entity-relation tuples in different contexts. Then, based on users' preferences for different tuples, the preferences closer to the real are mined from the KG to improve recommendation performance and interpretation.

4.4 Building User Preferences

User preferences are constructed by assigning a weight a_k to each set in this section. The contextual entity-relation tuple (h_k, r_k, t_k). In order to facilitate calculation and extract the key information in the tuple, (h_k, r_k, t_k) needs to be represented by a feature vector $\mathbf{E_k}$. Inspired by the successful application of convolutional neural networks in computer vision, the model based on CNN can be introduced into Recommendation System. For each tuple $(h_k, r_k, t_k) \in C_u^q$, $\mathbf{h_k}$ has one or more category features $\mathbf{P_s}$. Therefore, $\mathbf{h_k}, \mathbf{r_k}, \mathbf{t_k}, \mathbf{P_s}$ feature vectors can be combined and regarded as the vector representation of a picture, and their combined vector representation is as follows:

$$W = [[\mathbf{h_k}], [\mathbf{r_k}], [\mathbf{t_k}], [\mathbf{P_s}]] \in R^{n \times d}, (h_k, r_k, t_k) \in C_u^q \tag{7}$$

where n represents the number of feature vectors, d is the dimension of each feature vector, W matrix is the original input of CNN, then the convolution kernel $\mathbf{g} \in R^{n \times l}$ is applied to W matrix for convolution operation, $l(l < d)$ is the size of the kernel, and the feature vector after the convolution operation is:

$$\mathbf{c} = f(\mathbf{g} * \mathbf{W_{i:i+l-1}} + \mathbf{b}) \tag{8}$$

where f is a non-linear function, $*$ is the convolution operation, $\mathbf{b}$ is error, $\mathbf{W_{i:i+l-1}}$ is the sub-matrix of W and the dimension is the same as the convolutional kernel, and then, the maximum pooling method is used to identify the most critical features on feature vector C:

$$\mathbf{E_k} = max\{\mathbf{c}\} \tag{9}$$

At this stage the user u's preference is:

$$\mathbf{T_u} = \Sigma \ \mathbf{a_k E_k} \tag{10}$$

Each tuple in the contextual entity-relation set of the user u can obtain the corresponding feature vector $\mathbf{E_k}$ through the convolution pooling operation, then the user preference $\mathbf{T_u}$ can be obtained by multiplying its calculated weight.

4.5   Learning Algorithm

Algorithm 1. KIR algorithm

Require: Knowledge Graph G; interaction matrix Z; category information S; index
  k;
Ensure: The predicted probability value $\hat{Z}_{uv}$;
 1: $C_u^q \leftarrow ContextEntityRelation(G, Z)$; /* Calculates the set of contextual entity-
    relation for each user u
 2: **for** (u, v) *in* Z **do**
 3:    $\forall (h_k, r_k, t_k) \in C_u^q$;
 4:    $\mathbf{P_s} \leftarrow \mathbf{o_s} W^{stype}$;
 5:    $a_k \leftarrow \delta(FC(concat(\mathbf{h_k}; \mathbf{r_k}; \mathbf{t_k}; \mathbf{P_s})))$;
 6:    $W \leftarrow [[\mathbf{h_k}], [\mathbf{r_k}], [\mathbf{t_k}], [\mathbf{p_s}]] R^{n \times d}$;
 7:    $\mathbf{E_k} \leftarrow getFeature(W)$;
 8:    $\mathbf{T_u} = \Sigma\, a_k \mathbf{E_k}$;
 9:    $\hat{Z}_{uv} = \sigma(\mathbf{T_u v})$;
10:    The parameters are updated with the learning rate η by gradient descent.
11: **end**
12: **return** $\hat{Z}_{uv}$

In this section, the process of learning algorithms will be introduced. First, the click probability prediction function is as follows:

$$\hat{Z}_{uv} = \sigma(\mathbf{T_u v}) \tag{11}$$

where σ is the *sigmoid* function. In addition, in KIR, entities, and relations in the KG are indexed by ID, and the input is also a one-hot coding vector. As a result, the input of entity composed of vector length is $|X|$ entities, the relationship between the input by the length of $|Y|$ of the relationship between vector, $|X|$ and $|Y|$ respectively the total number of entities and relationships. Then, embedded layer through weight matrix $W^{entity} \in R^{|X| \times |d|}$ and $W^{relation} \in R^{|Y| \times |d| \times |d|}$ respectively each entity and relationships from the ID space mapping to the intensive and continuous dimensional vector space, weight matrix $W^{entity} \in R^{|X| \times |d|}$ and $W^{relation} \in R^{|Y| \times |d| \times |d|}$ respectively with the input of one-hot entities and relationships vector from the fully-connection can embed one-hot vector coding for vector. The complete loss function is as follows:

$$
\begin{aligned}
min\; L = \Sigma_{(u,v) \in Z} &- (Z_{uv} \cdot log\sigma(\hat{Z}_{uv}) + (1 - Z_{uv}) \cdot log(1 - \sigma(\hat{Z}_{uv}))) \\
&+ \lambda(\|W^{entity}\|_2^2 + \|W^{relation}\|_2^2 + \|W^{stype}\|_2^2)
\end{aligned} \tag{12}
$$

In Formula (12), the first term is the cross-entropy loss between the real interaction probability value (1 if clicked, 0 if not clicked) and the predicted probability value, the remaining terms are L2 regularization terms used to prevent overfitting. Then Adam algorithm is used to optimize the loss function iteratively, and it uses the global learning rate η to update all parameters. The formal description of specific steps is given in Algorithm 1. Then, the loss function L gradient is calculated according to the model parameter θ, and all parameters are updated by backpropagation according to the sampled data.

5 Experiments and Results

5.1 Datasets and Experimental Settings

As shown in Table 1, the datasets used in the experiment are MovieLens-20M, Book-Crossing, and Last.FM [10], where K represents the size of context entities per hop, Q represents the hop number, d represents the embedded dimension, and η represents the learning rate of the Adam algorithm. Our task is to make predictions in the CTR scenario, using AUC and F_1 test indicators. Similar to the literature [21], we also use the same comparison model, which is as follows: SVD [22], LibFM [13], PER [14], CKE [8], RippleNet [10], and KGCN [21].

Table 1. Basic Statistics and Hyper-Parameter of The Three Datasets.

	MovieLens-20M	Book-crossing	Last.FM
Users	138159	19676	1872
Items	16954	20003	3846
Entities	102569	25787	9366
Relations	32	18	60
K	6	8	6
Q	2	2	2
d	32	64	16
η	2×10^{-2}	2×10^{-4}	5×10^{-4}
λ	10^{-7}	10^{-5}	2×10^{-4}
Batch size	65536	2048	50

5.2 Results and Analysis

Validity of KIR Algorithm

This experiment verified the effectiveness of introducing categories and the attention mechanism on the model. In addition to the selected six groups of comparison models, there were also four groups of self-comparison experiments, namely removing category features (KIRWS), removing Attention Mechanism (KIRWA), removing both (KIRWSA) and KIR. As shown in Table 2, the experimental results show that KIR has the best performance. In contrast, the experimental indexes of other forms of KIR are lower than that of KIR, indicating that category features and the Attention Mechanism have a specific improvement on the model effect and prove the effectiveness of the two. In addition, due to the sparsity, the experiment performed poorly on the Book-Crossing dataset compared with the other two datasets.

Table 2. AUC and F_1 of different forms of KIR in three datasets

Model	MovieLens-20M		Book-crossing		Last.FM	
	AUC	F_1	AUC	F_1	AUC	F_1
SVD	0.963	0.919	0.672	0.635	0.769	0.696
LibFM	0.959	0.906	0.691	0.618	0.778	0.710
PER	0.832	0.788	0.617	0.562	0.663	0.596
CKE	0.924	0.871	0.677	0.611	0.744	0.673
RippleNet	0.968	0.912	0.715	0.650	0.780	0.702
KGCN	0.978	0.932	0.738	0.684	0.794	0.712
KIRWS	0.982	0.977	0.758	0.679	0.938	0.840
KIRWA	0.974	0.964	0.754	0.675	0.935	0.838
KIRWSA	0.965	0.961	0.75	0.673	0.932	0.832
KIR	**0.987**	**0.983**	**0.762**	**0.688**	**0.945**	**0.848**

The Effect of KIR on Different Sizes of Sets

This experiment studies the effect of KIR selecting a set of contextual entity-relation of different sizes in each hop. Table 3 lists the AUC and F_1 results of these three datasets at different K. It is show that the practical effect is best when 6 or 10 tuples are selected per q-hop. When K is small, the selected KG information is minimal challenging to recommend accurately. When K is large, the selected KG information may contain many interference information, affecting the recommendation results.

Table 3. The effect of KIR in different sizes of contextual entity-relation sets

K	MovieLens-20M		Book-crossing		Last.FM	
	AUC	F_1	AUC	F_1	AUC	F_1
2	0.978	0.974	0.758	0.68	0.938	0.841
6	**0.987**	**0.983**	0.76	0.685	**0.945**	**0.848**
10	0.986	0.98	**0.761**	**0.687**	0.942	0.846
20	0.982	0.979	0.759	0.683	0.940	0.842
30	0.98	0.977	0.758	0.675	0.936	0.84

The Effect of KIR in Different Hop Counts

This experiment verifies the effect of KIR by changing the hop count, that is, the effect of KIR under different Q conditions. The experimental results show that the model achieves the optimal effect when Q is two because the selected KG information is insufficient when Q is one. When Q is three or more significant, it will contain more interference information and cost much time. Table 4 lists the AUC results of these three datasets at different Q's.

Table 4. The effect of KIR in different hops

Q	MovieLens-20M	Book-crossing	Last.FM
	AUC	AUC	AUC
1	0.982	0.756	0.943
2	**0.987**	**0.762**	**0.945**
3	0.984	0.761	0.944

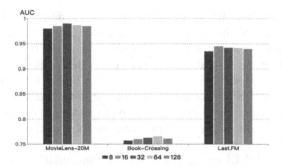

Fig. 3. Overview of the Attention Mechanism

The Effect of KIR Under Different Dimensions

This experiment discusses the effect of the KIR model under different dimensions d. As shown in Fig. 3, different dimensions d will influence the model effect. When d is 32, 64, and 16, KIR achieves the optimal effect in the three datasets, respectively. This may be because when d is small, it is not enough to encode more helpful information, while when d is large, there is a risk of over-fitting.

The Interpretability of KIR Model

Table 5. The explanation of the recommended Titanic

Contextual entity-relation sets	Weight
(Terminator, Director, Titanic)	0.213
(Terminator, Type, Titanic)	0.148
(Terminator, Rate, Titanic)	0.122
(Terminator, Region, Titanic)	0.167
(Avatar, Director, Titanic)	0.205

This experiment discusses the interpretability of the KIR model. Assuming users have already seen Terminator and Avatar, we will recommend Titanic after KIR's calculation. According to the model calculation, we will give the following explanation, as shown in Table 5, which contains the different contextual entity-relation sets for the movie Titanic to be recommended. As can be seen from the table, users have different weights for different tuples, especially for movies with the same director. Therefore, we recommend Titanic because users like drama movies, especially movies with the same director as Terminator.

6 Conclusion

This paper proposes a Knowledge-enhanced Interpretable Recommendation algorithm, KIR. It first introduces the items' category information to explore the user preferences of different categories, then combines the entity-relation in the KG and design an Attention Mechanism to distinguish users' interest in different contextual entity-relation tuples in the KG. Finally, according to the items' categories and KG information, Calculate the items that users are most likely to preference, and calculate the correlation between the recommended item and other related items, using the tuple with the most significant proportion as the possible cause of this recommendation. Verification by selecting different datasets shows that KIR can improve the recommendation performance to a certain extent and give a possible explanation based on different recommendation results.

Future work can rely on a dynamic RS to dynamically optimize our recommendation algorithm to explain the reasons for items recommended by RS as much as possible.

Acknowlegements. This work is supported by the National Natural Science Foundation of China under Grant No. 62162046, the Inner Mongolia Science and Technology Project under Grant No. 2021GG0155, the Natural Science Foundation of Major Research Plan of Inner Mongolia under Grant No. 2019ZD15, and the Inner Mongolia Natural Science Foundation under Grant No. 2019GG372.

References

1. Yu, H., Li, J.H.: A recommendation algorithm to solve the cold start problem of new item. J. Softw. **06**, 135–148 (2015)
2. Adomavicius, G., Tuzhilin, A.: Toward the next generation of recommender systems: a survey of the state-of-the-art and possible extensions. IEEE Trans. Knowl. Data Eng. **17**(6), 734–749 (2005)
3. Pazzani, M.J., Billsus, D.: Content-based recommendation systems. In: Brusilovsky, P., Kobsa, A., Nejdl, W. (eds.) The Adaptive Web. LNCS, vol. 4321, pp. 325–341. Springer, Heidelberg (2007). https://doi.org/10.1007/978-3-540-72079-9_10
4. Su, X., Khoshgoftaar, T.M.: A survey of collaborative filtering techniques. Adv. Artif. Intell. 1–19 (2009)
5. Burke, R.: Hybrid recommender systems: survey and experiments. User Model. User-Adap. Inter. **12**(4), 331–370 (2002)

6. Bellogín, A., Cantador, I., Díez, F., et al.: An empirical COMPAR ISON of social, collaborative filtering, and hybrid recommenders. ACM Trans. Intell. Syst. Technol. (TIST) **4**(1), 1–29 (2013)
7. Wang, H., Zhang, F., Xie, X., et al.: DKN: deep knowledge-aware network for news recommendation. In: Proceedings of the 2018 World Wide Web Conference, pp. 1835–1844 (2018)
8. Zhang, F., Yuan, N.J., Lian, D., et al.: Collaborative knowledge base embedding for recommender systems. In: Proceedings of the 22nd ACM SIGKDD International Conference on Knowledge Discovery and Data Mining, pp. 353–362 (2016)
9. Huang, J., Zhao, W.X., Dou, H., et al.: Improving sequential recommendation with knowledge-enhanced memory networks. In: The 41st International ACM SIGIR Conference on Research and Development in Information Retrieval, pp. 505–514 (2018)
10. Wang, H., Zhang, F., Wang, J., et al.: RippleNet: propagating user preferences on the knowledge graph for recommender systems. In: Proceedings of the 27th ACM International Conference on Information and Knowledge Management, pp. 417–426 (2018)
11. Wang, X., Wang, D., Xu, C., et al.: Explainable reasoning over knowledge graphs for recommendation. In: Proceedings of the AAAI Conference on Artificial Intelligence, vol. 33, no. 01, pp. 5329–5336 (2019)
12. Wang, H., Zhang, F., Wang, J., et al.: Exploring high-order user preference on the knowledge graph for recommender systems. ACM Trans. Inf. Syst. (TOIS) **37**(3), 1–26 (2019)
13. Rendle, S.: Factorization machines with LibFM. ACM Trans. Intell. Syst. Technol. (TIST) **3**(3), 1–22 (2012)
14. Yu, X., Ren, X., Sun, Y., et al.: Personalized entity recommendation: a heterogeneous information network approach. In: Proceedings of the 7th ACM International Conference on Web Search and Data Mining, pp. 283–292 (2014)
15. Sun, Y., Han, J., Yan, X., et al.: PathSIM: meta path-based top-k similarity search in heterogeneous information networks. Proc. VLDB Endow. **4**(11), 992–1003 (2011)
16. Yu, X., Ren, X., Sun, Y., et al.: Recommendation in heterogeneous information networks with implicit user feedback. In: Proceedings of the 7th ACM Conference on Recommender Systems, pp. 347–350 (2013)
17. Xian, Y., Fu, Z., Muthukrishnan, S., et al.: Reinforcement knowledge graph reasoning for explainable recommendation. In: Proceedings of the 42nd International ACM SIGIR Conference on Research and Development in Information Retrieval, pp. 285–294 (2019)
18. Chen, Z., Wang, X., Xie, X., et al.: Co-attentive multi-task learning for explainable recommendation. In: IJCAI, pp. 2137–2143 (2019)
19. Ai, Q., Azizi, V., Chen, X., et al.: Learning heterogeneous knowledge base embeddings for explainable recommendation. Algorithms **11**(9), 137 (2018)
20. Song, W., Duan, Z., Yang, Z., et al.: Explainable knowledge graph-based recommendation via deep reinforcement learning. arXiv preprint arXiv:1906.09506 (2019)
21. Wang, H., Zhao, M., Xie, X., et al.: Knowledge graph convolutional networks for recommender systems. In: The World Wide Web Conference, pp. 3307–3313 (2019)
22. Koren, Y.: Factorization meets the neighborhood: a multifaceted collaborative filtering model. In: Proceedings of the 14th ACM SIGKDD International Conference on Knowledge Discovery and Data Mining, pp. 426–434 (2008)

ICKEM: A Tool for Estimating One's Understanding of Conceptual Knowledge

Gangli Liu[✉]

Tsinghua University, Beijing 100084, China
gl-liu13@mails.tsinghua.edu.cn

Abstract. People learn whenever and wherever possible, and whatever they like or encounter – Mathematics, Drama, Art, Languages, Physics, Philosophy, and so on. With the bursting of knowledge, evaluation of one's understanding of conceptual knowledge becomes increasingly difficult. There are a lot of demands for evaluating one's understanding of a piece of knowledge, e.g., facilitating personalized recommendations; discovering one's expertises and deficiencies in a field; recommending a learning material to practice meaningful learning etc. Assessment of understanding of knowledge is conventionally practiced through tests or interviews, but they have some limitations such as low-efficiency and in-comprehensive. We propose a new method to estimate one's understanding of conceptual knowledge, by keeping track of his/her learning activities. It overcomes some limitations of traditional methods, hence complements traditional methods.

Keywords: Lifelong learning · Knowledge tracking · Meaningful learning

1 Introduction

Our world is bursting with knowledge. Nearly every discipline has been subdivided into numerous sub-disciplines. People learn whenever and wherever possible. People's learning of knowledge is not confined to childhood or the classroom but takes place throughout life and in a range of situations; it can take the form of formal learning or informal learning [20], such as daily interactions with others and with the world around us. Lifelong learning is the "ongoing, voluntary, and self-motivated" pursuit of knowledge for either personal or professional reasons [5]. According to Tough's study, almost 70% of learning projects are self-planned [25].

As people learn eternally, one significant issue is to evaluate how much knowledge an individual is possessing at a particular time. E.g., suppose we have a database that records all the entries of Wikipedia and a person's understanding degree of each entry (e.g., on a scale of 1 to 10). With this information, a lot of new applications are becoming practical. Following are some examples:

© The Author(s), under exclusive license to Springer Nature Switzerland AG 2022
G. Memmi et al. (Eds.): KSEM 2022, LNAI 13368, pp. 44–57, 2022.
https://doi.org/10.1007/978-3-031-10983-6_4

- **Determine a person's knowledge state.** If we set a threshold to the understanding grades, and assume the subject has understood a knowledge entry if its grade is larger than the threshold, then we can estimate a person's knowledge state and knowledge composition at a particular time. Like Fig. 1.
- **Discover a person's expertises and deficiencies.** Expertise finding is critical for an organization or project. Since the participation of experts plays an important role for the success of an organization or project. With the understanding evaluation database, it is convenient to discover a person's domain-level expertise and topic-level expertise. Besides expertise, we can also discover a person's deficiencies in a field, so he can remedy the deficiencies.
- **Make personalized recommendations.** If we know a person's understanding degree to each piece of knowledge, it is convenient to make personalized recommendations to the subject based on the information, e.g., helping the subject to practice meaningful learning.

1.1   Procedural and Conceptual Knowledge

Studies of knowledge indicate that knowledge may be classified into two major categories: procedural and conceptual knowledge [10]. Procedural knowledge is the knowledge exercised in the accomplishment of a task, and thus includes knowledge which cannot be easily articulated by the individual, since it is typically nonconscious (or tacit). It is commonly referred to as "know-how". Such as knowing how to cook delicious food, how to fly an airplane, or how to play basketball etc. Conceptual knowledge is quite different from procedural knowledge. It involves understanding of the principles that govern a domain and of the interrelations between pieces of knowledge in a domain; it concerns understanding and interpreting concepts and the relations between concepts. It is commonly referred to as "know-why", such as knowing why something happens in a particular way. In this article, we only deal with evaluating a person's understanding of conceptual knowledge.

1.2   The Framework

At present, assessment of one's understanding of conceptual knowledge is primarily through tests [12,21] or interviews, which have some limitations such as low-efficiency and in-comprehensive. E.g., it needs other people's cooperation to accomplish the assessment, which is time-consuming; moreover, only a small portion of topics in a domain is evaluated during an assessment, which cannot comprehensively reflect a person's knowledge state of the domain.

We propose a new model called Individual Conceptual Knowledge Evaluation Model (ICKEM) to evaluate one's understanding of a piece of conceptual knowledge quantitatively. It has the advantages of evaluating a person's understanding of conceptual knowledge independently, comprehensively, and automatically. It keeps track of one's daily learning activities (reading, listening, discussing, writing etc.), dividing them into a sequence of learning sessions, then analyzes the text content of each learning session to discover the involved knowledge topics and their shares in the session. It maintains a leaning history for *each* knowledge topic. After a period of time (e.g., several years or decades), the subject's leaning history about a topic is generated. Based on the learning history, the subject's familiarity degree to a knowledge topic is evaluated. Finally, it estimates one's understanding degree to a topic, by comprehensively evaluating one's familiarity degrees to the topic itself and other topics that are essential to understand the topic. Figure 2 is the framework of ICKEM. Each hexagon of the diagram indicates a processing step; the following rectangle indicates the results of the process.

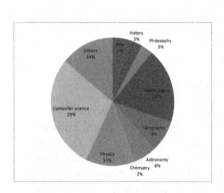

Fig. 1. A person's knowledge composition (imaginary)

Fig. 3. A person's reading learning sessions logged in a database.

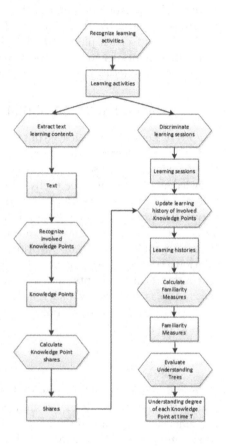

Fig. 2. The framework of ICKEM

The remainder of this paper is organized as follows. Section 2 discusses how to calculate a person's familiarity degree to a knowledge topic. Section 3 introduces a method to estimate a person's understanding degree to a topic, by checking the familiarity degrees of the topic's Understanding Tree. Section 4 discusses related issues about evaluating one's understanding of conceptual knowledge. We cover related work in Sect. 5, before concluding in Sect. 6.

2   Evaluate Familiarity Degree

This section introduces the procedures that are devised to evaluate a person's familiarity degree to a knowledge topic. It starts by presenting a formal definition of knowledge and learning, then discusses how to divide a person's daily learning activities into a series of learning sessions, and analyze the text learning content to obtain a topic's share in a session. After these procedures, a knowledge topic's learning history can be generated. Finally, based on the learning history, the subject's familiarity degree to a topic is calculated.

2.1   Definition of Knowledge and Learning

Knowledge is conventionally defined as beliefs that are true and justified. To be 'true' means that it is in accord with the way in which objects, people, processes and events exist and behave in the real world. However, exactly what evidence is necessary and sufficient to allow a true belief to be 'justified' has been a topic of discussion (largely among philosophers) for more than 2,000 years [12]. In ICKEM, a Knowledge Point is defined as a piece of conceptual knowledge that is explicitly defined and has been widely accepted, such as Bayes' theorem, Euler's formula, mass-energy equivalence, Maxwell's equations, gravitational wave, and the expectation-maximization algorithm etc.

Learning is the process of acquiring, modifying, or reinforcing knowledge, behaviors, skills, values, or preferences in memory. An individual's possessing of knowledge is the product of all the experiences from the beginning of his/her life to the moment at hand [12]. Learning produces changes in the organism and the changes produced are relatively permanent [23].

2.2   Discriminate Learning Sessions

In ICKEM, a person's daily activities are classified into two categories: learning activities and non-learning activities. An activity is recognized as a learning activity if its content involves at least one Knowledge Point of a predefined set. In addition, the learning activities are divided into a sequence of learning sessions, since it is essential to know how many times and how long for each time the individual has learned a Knowledge Point. An individual may employ many methods to learn conceptual knowledge, such as reading, listening, discussing, and writing. Different strategies should be used to discriminate learning sessions for different learning methods. E.g., for leaning by reading electronic documents (e-documents), the learning sessions can be discriminated by monitoring the foreground of the user's personal computer, and detecting opening, closing, and page switching of an e-document.

Figure 3 shows some examples of discriminated learning sessions when reading e-documents. Attribute "*did*" means document ID, which indexes a document uniquely. Attribute "*actiontype*" indicates the type of an action. "*Doc Act*" means a document has been activated. "*Page Act*" is defined similarly.

"Doc DeAct" means a document has been deactivated. That is to say, a learning session has stopped. Attribute *"page"* indicates a page number. Attribute *"duration"* records how long a page has been activated in seconds. If two learning sessions' interval is less than a certain threshold, and their learning material is the same (e.g., the same document), they are merged into one session. Therefore, "Session 2" and "Session 3" are merged into one session.

For other learning methods, it is more complicated to divide learning sessions. However, there are already some attempts for detecting human daily activities [24]. Sung et al. devised an algorithm for recognizing human daily activities from RGB-D Images [24]. They tested their algorithm on detecting and recognizing twelve different activities (brushing teeth, cooking, working on computer, talking on phone, drinking water, talking on a chair etc.) performed by four people and achieved good performance.

2.3 Capture the Text Learning Content

Most learning processes are associated with a piece of learning material. E.g., reading a book, the book is the learning material; attending a course or discussion, the course and discussion contents can be regarded as the learning material. Some learning materials are text or can be converted to text. E.g., discussing a piece of knowledge with others. The discussion contents can be converted to text by exploiting Speech Recognition. Similarly, if one is reading a printed book, the contents of the book can be captured by wearable computers like Google Glass and then converted to text through Optical Character Recognition (OCR). If the book is electronic, no conversion is needed; the text can be extracted directly.

2.4 Calculate a Knowledge Point's Share

A learning session may involve many topics, it is necessary to know how much a learning session involves a topic. To calculate a Knowledge Point's share, maybe the simplest way is to deem the text learning content as a bag of words, and calculate a Knowledge Point's share based on its Term Frequency (TF) or normalized TF, like in Eqs. 1 and 2. N_i is term i's normalized TF. It is calculated with Eq. 1, where T_i is term i's TF, $Max(TF)$ is the maximum TF of the captured text content, α is a constant regulatory factor.

$$N_i = \alpha + (1 - \alpha) * T_i/Max(TF) \tag{1}$$

$$\xi_i = \frac{N_i}{\sum_{j=1}^{m} N_j} \tag{2}$$

Another method of discovering a Knowledge Point's share is to analyze the text learning content with topic model. A topic model is a type of statistical model for discovering the abstract "topics" that occur in a collection of documents. Topic model is a frequently used text-mining tool for discovery of hidden semantic structures in a text body [3,11].

The inputs of a probabilistic topic model are a collection of N documents, a vocabulary set V, and the number of topics k. The outputs of a probabilistic topic model are the following:

- k topics, each is word distribution : $\{\theta_1, ..., \theta_k\}$;
- Coverage of topics in each document d_i: $\{\pi_{i1}, ..., \pi_{ik}\}$;
  π_{ij} is the probability of document d_i covering topic θ_j.

The subject's N learning sessions' text-contents can be deemed as a collection of N documents, then the document collection is analyzed with a topic model like LDA. Based on the outputs of topic model, Eq. 3 can be used to calculate the share of Knowledge Point t_m in learning session d_i. $p(t_m|\theta_j)$ is the probability of Knowledge Point t_m in topic θ_j.

$$p(t_m|d_i) = \sum_{j=1}^{k} \pi_{ij} p(t_m|\theta_j) \tag{3}$$

2.5   The Subject's State and Learning Method

The subject's physical and psychological status may influence the effect of a learning session. Different learning methods like reading or discussing may also affect the learning result. The "physical and psychological status factor" and "learning method factor" are used to discount the effect of each learning session. The status can be detected by some sensors, such as a Smart Bracelet.

2.6   A Knowledge Point's Learning History

With the discriminated learning sessions, a Knowledge Point's share in each session, the subject's physical and psychological status during a session, and the "learning method factor", after a period of time, the subject's learning histories about each Knowledge Point can be generated. Figure 4 shows an exemplary learning history. It records a person's each learning experience about a Knowledge Point. "LCT" stands for "learning cessation time". It is used to calculate the interval between the learning time and the evaluation time, which is then used to estimate how much information has been lost due to memory decay. "Duration" is the length of a learning session. "Proportion" is the Knowledge Point's share during a learning session. "PPS factor" stands for the "physical and psychological status factor". It is a number between 0 and 1 that is calculated based on the subject's average physical and psychological status during a session. "LM factor" stands for the "learning method factor". It is also a number between 0 and 1 that is allocated to a learning method according to its effectiveness level.

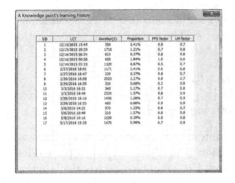

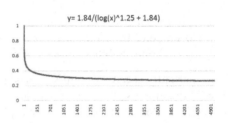

Fig. 4. A person's learning history of a Knowledge Point

Fig. 5. The percentage of memory retention over time calculated by Eq. 4

2.7 Memory Retention of a Learning Experience

People learn all the time; meanwhile, people forget all the time. Human memory declines over time. Interestingly, most researchers report there is no age difference for memory decay [22]. To calculate the familiarity degree, we need to address how the effect of a learning experience decays over time. However, there is no consensus of how human memory decays. Psychologists have suggested many functions to describe the monotonic loss of information with time [22]. But there is no unanimous agreement of which one is the best. The search for a general description of forgetting is one of the oldest unresolved problems in experimental psychology [2].

We propose to use Ebbinghaus' forgetting curve equation [7] to describe the memory retention of a learning experience over time. Since it is the most well-known forgetting curve equation and its soundness has been proved by many studies [19]. Ebbinghaus found Eq. 4 can be used to describe the proportion of memory retention after a period of time[1], where t is the time in minutes counting from one minute before the end of the learning, k and c are two constants that equal 1.84 and 1.25, respectively. Figure 5 shows the percentage of memory retention over time calculated by Eq. 4. The Y axis is the percentage of memory retention; the X axis is the time-since-learning in minutes. It can be seen that memory retention declines drastically during the first 24 h (1,440 min), then the speed tends to be steady.

$$b(t) = k/((\log t)^c + k) \tag{4}$$

2.8 Calculate the Familiarity Degree

Based on the learning history, Eq. 5 is utilized to calculate the subject's Familiarity Measure to a Knowledge Point k_i at time t. A Familiarity Measure is defined

---

[1] It can be found at http://psychclassics.yorku.ca/Ebbinghaus/memory7.htm.

as a score that depicts a person's familiarity degree to a Knowledge Point at a particular time. The input is k_i's learning history – a sequence of m learning sessions (like Fig. 4). d_j is session j's duration; ξ_{ij} is Knowledge Point k_i's share in session j; t_j is session j's "learning cessation time", $b(t - t_j)$ calculates the percent of memory retention of session j at time t with Eq. 4; F_j^{pps} is the "physical and psychological status factor" of session j; F_j^{lm} is the "learning method factor" of session j.

$$f(k_i, t) = \sum_{j=1}^{m} d_j * \xi_{ij} * b(t - t_j) * F_j^{pps} * F_j^{lm} \tag{5}$$

The computation hypothesizes each learning experience about a Knowledge Point contributes some effect to the subject's current understanding of it, and the learning effect declines over time according to Ebbinghaus' forgetting curve. Other attributes (the subject's physical and psychological status, learning method) that may affect the learning effect are counted in as numeric factors.

3   Estimate Understanding Degree

Understanding is quite subtle to measure. We hypothesize that if a person is familiar with a Knowledge Point itself and all the background knowledge that is essential to understand it, he should have a good understanding about it. Because Familiarity Measure depicts the cumulative effects of one's learning experiences about a topic, high levels of Familiarity Measures imply intensive learning activities about the cluster of knowledge topics. Intensive learning activities usually result in a good understanding.

The background Knowledge Points that are essential to understand a Knowledge Point can be extracted by analyzing its definition. Table 1 lists eight reduced documents, each of them is a definition of a Knowledge Point in Probability Theory or Stochastic Process. The texts are quoted from Wikipedia and other websites. The third column of Table 1 lists the involved Knowledge Points in the documents, which are deemed as the background knowledge to understand the host Knowledge Point.

An Understanding Tree is a treelike data structure which compiles the background Knowledge Points that are essential to understand the root Knowledge Point. The nodes of the tree can be further interpreted by other Knowledge Points until they are Basic Knowledge Points (BKP). A BKP is a Knowledge Point that is simple enough so that it is not interpreted by other Knowledge Points. Figure 6 shows an exemplary Understanding Tree which is constructed based on the definitions of Table 1. Each node is tagged with an artificial Familiarity Measure, which can be calculated with Eq. 5 in practice. The leaf nodes of an Understanding Tree are BKPs. Understanding Tree can be used to evaluate a person's topic-level expertise, e.g., evaluating a person's understanding degree to the expectation-maximization (EM) algorithm.

Table 1. A list of documents and their involved knowledge points

Doc	Content	Knowledge points
D1	A Strictly Stationary Process (SSP) is a Stochastic Process (SP) whose Joint Probability Distribution (JPD) does not change when shifted in time	SSP, JPD, Time, SP
D2	A Stochastic Process (SP) is a Probability Model (PM) used to describe phenomena that evolve over time or space. In probability theory, a stochastic process is a Time Sequence (TS) representing the evolution of some system represented by a variable whose change is subject to a Random Variation (RaV)	SP, PM, TS, Time, Space, System, Variable, RaV
D3	In the study of probability, given at least two Random Variables (RV) X, Y, ... that are defined on a Probability Space (PS), the Joint Probability Distribution (JPD) for X, Y, ... is a Probability Distribution (PD) that gives the probability that each of X, Y, ... falls in any particular range or discrete set of values specified for that variable	JPD, RV, PS, PD, Variable, Probability
D4	A Probability model (PM) is a mathematical representation of a random phenomenon. It is defined by its Sample Space (SS), events within the SS, and probabilities associated with each event	PM, SS, Event, Probability
D5	In probability and statistics, a Random variable (RV) is a variable quantity whose possible values depend, in some clearly-defined way, on a set of random events	RV, Variable, Event
D6	A Probability Space (PS) is a Mathematical Construct (MC) that models a real-world process consisting of states that occur randomly. It consists of three parts: a Sample Space (SS), a set of events, and the assignment of probabilities to the events	PS, MC, SS, Probability, Event
D7	A Probability Distribution (PD) is a table or an equation that links each outcome of a statistical experiment with its probability of occurrence	PD, Probability
D8	The Sample Space (SS) is the set of all possible outcomes of the samples	SS, Sample

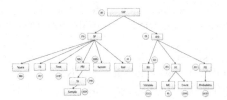 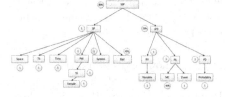

Fig. 6. An understanding tree tagged with familiarity measures

Fig. 7. Familiarity measures transformed into percentages

3.1   Calculation of Understanding Degree

If all the Familiarity Measures of an Understanding Tree exceed a threshold, it is assumed that the person has understood the root Knowledge Point. Then the

Knowledge Point is classified as "Understood"; otherwise, it is classified as "Not Understood". Due to the differences of people's intelligence and talent, different people may have different thresholds.

If a Familiarity Measure is less than the threshold, a percentage is calculated by dividing it by the threshold, indicating the subject's percent of familiarity of the node; if the Familiarity Measure is greater than the threshold, the percentage is set to 1, implying the quantity of familiarity of this node is large enough for understanding the root, extra familiarity is good but not necessary. Equation 6 is used to calculate the percentage of familiarity, $f(k_i, t)$ is the subject's Familiarity Measure to Knowledge Point k_i at time t, f_T is the threshold.

If a Knowledge Point is classified as "Not Understood", a percent of understanding is calculated with Eq. 7. $P_u(k_r, t)$ is the subject's percent of understanding of the root Knowledge Point at time t, $P_f(k_r, t)$ is the percent of familiarity of the root, $\frac{1}{m} \sum_{j=1}^{m} P_f(k_j, t)$ calculates the average percent of familiarities of its descendants (not including the root). E.g., Fig. 7 is the Understanding Tree of Fig. 6 with Familiarity Measures transformed into percentages (assuming f_T equals 100). The $P_f(k_r, t)$ of it equals 85%, and $\frac{1}{m} \sum_{j=1}^{m} P_f(k_j, t)$ equals 89%, so the $P_u(k_r, t)$ equals 76%, indicating the subject's understanding of the root Knowledge Point is 76%.

If $P_u(k_r, t)$ is less than 100%, the Knowledge Point is classified as "Not Understood". Thus it can be seen that we are using a conservative strategy for estimating the subject's understanding. For a Knowledge Point to be classified as "Understood", the subject must be familiar with *every* node of its Understanding Tree.

$$P_f(k_i, t) = \begin{cases} 1 & f(k_i, t) \geq f_T \\ f(k_i, t)/f_T & f(k_i, t) < f_T \end{cases} \tag{6}$$

$$P_u(k_r, t) = P_f(k_r, t) * \frac{1}{m} \sum_{j=1}^{m} P_f(k_j, t) \tag{7}$$

Another choice for calculating $P_f(k_r, t)$ or $P_f(k_i, t)$ is to use a sigmoid function.

$$P_f(k_i, t) = \frac{1}{1 + e^{-a(f(k_i, t) - b)}}$$

where $f(k_i, t)$ is the subject's Familiarity Measure of Knowledge Point k_i at time t, a and b are two constant parameters to be optimized. The time complexity of ICKEM is $\mathcal{O}(nm)$, where n is the total number of learning sessions, m is the size of an Understanding Tree.

4 Discussion

Assessing a person's understanding of conceptual knowledge is not easy; as an experimental model aimed to accomplish this, a great deal of thought and research are required to realize its potential.

4.1 Trade-Offs Between Different Methods

Quantitatively assessing one's understanding of conceptual knowledge seems to be a good thing, but there are risks that it introduces some harmful effects. For example, if the Familiarity Measures and understanding degrees calculated are inaccurate, it may lead to wrong decisions. In addition, it cannot detect a person's talent and potential in a field. On the other hand, traditional exams or interviews have their limitations. E.g., it needs other people's cooperation to accomplish the evaluation; it only assesses one's knowledge in a particular field at a time, and the evaluation is not comprehensive. Since it only assesses questions being asked, not all of the topics in a field are evaluated. ICKEM assesses one's knowledge independently, comprehensively, and automatically. Therefore, the methods of evaluating one's understanding of knowledge should be used cooperatively, complementing one another.

4.2 Privacy Issues

Recording one's learning history will inevitably violates privacy. To protect privacy, the learning histories can be password protected or encrypted and stored in personal storage; they should not be revealed to other people. The only information that can be viewed by the outside world is the individual's knowledge measures of some Knowledge Points. Every output of them should be authorized by the owner.

4.3 Analyzing with Topic Models

Since we can calculate a person's Familiarity Measures to different Knowledge Points. The Familiarity Measures can be considered as term frequencies in a document. Therefore, at a given time, a person is equivalent to a document. Thus we can use probabilistic topic models [3,11] to analyze multiple people's expertise of knowledge, or using Understanding Map Supervised Topic Model (UM-S-TM) [17] to analyze an individual.

5   Related Work

Many research fields focus on the collection of personal information, such as lifelogging, expertise finding, and personal informatics. Bush envisioned the 'memex' system, in which individuals could compress and store personally experienced information, such as books, records, and communications [4]. Inspired by 'memex', Gemmell et al. developed a project called MyLifeBits to store all of a person's digital media, including documents, images, audio, and video [9]. In [18], a person's reading history about an electronic document is used as attributes for re-finding the document. ICKEM is similar to 'memex' and MyLifeBits in that it records an individual's digital history, although for a different purpose. 'Memex' and MyLifeBits are mainly for re-finding or reviewing personal data; ICKEM is for quantitatively evaluating a person's knowledge.

Personal informatics is a class of tools that help people collect personally relevant information for the purpose of self-reflection and gaining self-knowledge [15]. Various tools have been developed to help people collect and analyze different kinds of personal information, such as location [16], finances [14], food [6], weight [13], and physical activity [8]. ICKEM facilitates a new type of personal informatics tool that helps people discover their expertise and deficiencies in a more accurate way, by quantitatively assessing an individual's understanding of knowledge.

Expertise is one's expert skill or knowledge in a particular field. Expertise finding is the use of tools for finding and assessing individual expertise [26]. As an important link of knowledge sharing, expertise finding has been heavily studied in many research communities [1]. Many sources of data have been exploited to assess an individual's expertise, such as one's publications, documents, emails, web search behavior, other people's recommendations, social media etc. ICKEM provides a new source of data to analyze one's expertise – one's learning history about a topic, which is more comprehensive and straightforward than other data sources. Because one's expertise is mainly obtained through learning.

6   Conclusion

People's pursuing of knowledge is never stopping. Most conceptual knowledge is transmitted through language; it is hard to imagine how a person can obtain conceptual knowledge without using language. A piece of written or spoken language can be converted to text. We proposed a new framework for estimating a person's understanding of a piece of conceptual knowledge, by analyzing the text content of one's all learning experiences about a knowledge topic. The computation of familiarity degree took into account the total time the subject had devoted to a knowledge topic, a topic's share in a learning session, the subject's physical and psychological status during a session, the memory decay of each learning experience over time, and the difference among learning methods. To estimate a person's understanding degree to a knowledge topic, it comprehensively evaluated one's familiarity degrees to the topic itself and other topics that are essential to understand the topic. Quantitatively evaluating a person's understanding of knowledge facilitates many applications, such as personalized recommendation, meaningful learning, expertise and deficiency finding etc. With the prevailing of wearable computers like Google Glass and Apple Watch, and maturing of technologies like Speech Recognition and Optical Character Recognition (OCR), it is practicable to analysis people's daily learning activities like talking, listening, and reading. Therefore, ICKEM is technically feasible.

References

1. Ackerman, M.S., Dachtera, J., Pipek, V., Wulf, V.: Sharing knowledge and expertise: the CSCW view of knowledge management. Comput. Support. Coop. Work (CSCW) **22**(4–6), 531–573 (2013)

2. Averell, L., Heathcote, A.: The form of the forgetting curve and the fate of memories. J. Math. Psychol. **55**(1), 25–35 (2011)
3. Blei, D.M., Ng, A.Y., Jordan, M.I.: Latent Dirichlet allocation. J. Mach. Learn. Res. **3**, 993–1022 (2003)
4. Bush, V.: As we may think. ACM SIGPC Notes **1**(4), 36–44 (1979)
5. Cliath, B.Á., Rialtais, O.D.F., Alliance, T.S., Laighean, S.T., Rialtais, F., Posttráchta, A.R.: Learning for life. In: White paper on adult education (2000)
6. Cordeiro, F., et al.: Barriers and negative nudges: exploring challenges in food journaling. In: Proceedings of the 33rd Annual ACM Conference on Human Factors in Computing Systems, pp. 1159–1162. ACM (2015)
7. Ebbinghaus, H.: Memory: A Contribution to Experimental Psychology, no. 3. University Microfilms (1913)
8. Fritz, T., Huang, E.M., Murphy, G.C., Zimmermann, T.: Persuasive technology in the real world: a study of long-term use of activity sensing devices for fitness. In: Proceedings of the SIGCHI Conference on Human Factors in Computing Systems, pp. 487–496. ACM (2014)
9. Gemmell, J., Bell, G., Lueder, R., Drucker, S., Wong, C.: Mylifebits: fulfilling the memex vision. In: Proceedings of the tenth ACM International Conference on Multimedia, pp. 235–238. ACM (2002)
10. Hiebert, J.: Conceptual and Procedural Knowledge: The Case of Mathematics. Routledge, Abingdon (2013)
11. Hofmann, T.: Probabilistic latent semantic indexing. In: Proceedings of the 22nd Annual International ACM SIGIR Conference on Research and Development in Information Retrieval, pp. 50–57. ACM (1999)
12. Hunt, D.P.: The concept of knowledge and how to measure it. J. Intellect. Cap. **4**(1), 100–113 (2003)
13. Kay, M., Morris, D., Kientz, J.A., et al.: There's no such thing as gaining a pound: reconsidering the bathroom scale user interface. In: Proceedings of the 2013 ACM International Joint Conference on Pervasive and Ubiquitous Computing, pp. 401–410. ACM (2013)
14. Kaye, J.J., McCuistion, M., Gulotta, R., Shamma, D.A.: Money talks: tracking personal finances. In: Proceedings of the SIGCHI Conference on Human Factors in Computing Systems, pp. 521–530. ACM (2014)
15. Li, I., Dey, A., Forlizzi, J.: A stage-based model of personal informatics systems. In: Proceedings of the SIGCHI Conference on Human Factors in Computing Systems, pp. 557–566. ACM (2010)
16. Lindqvist, J., Cranshaw, J., Wiese, J., Hong, J., Zimmerman, J.: I'm the mayor of my house: examining why people use foursquare-a social-driven location sharing application. In: Proceedings of the SIGCHI Conference on Human Factors in Computing Systems, pp. 2409–2418. ACM (2011)
17. Liu, G.: Topic model supervised by understanding map. arXiv preprint arXiv:2110.06043 (2021)
18. Liu, G., Jiang, B., Feng, L.: A PDF document re-finding system with a Q&A wizard interface. Knowl.-Based Syst. **131**, 1–9 (2017)
19. Murre, J.M., Dros, J.: Replication and analysis of Ebbinghaus' forgetting curve. PLoS ONE **10**(7), e0120644 (2015)
20. Paradise, R., Rogoff, B.: Side by side: learning by observing and pitching in. Ethos **37**(1), 102–138 (2009)
21. O. PISA. Measuring student knowledge and skills. The PISA Assessment of Reading. Mathematical and Scientific Literacy (2000)

22. Rubin, D.C., Wenzel, A.E.: One hundred years of forgetting: a quantitative description of retention. Psychol. Rev. **103**(4), 734 (1996)
23. Schacter, D.L.: Psychology, 2nd edn. Worth Publishers, New York (2011)
24. Sung, J., Ponce, C., Selman, B., Saxena, A.: Unstructured human activity detection from RGBD images. In: 2012 IEEE International Conference on Robotics and Automation (ICRA), pp. 842–849. IEEE (2012)
25. Tough, A.: The adult's learning projects. A fresh approach to theory and practice in adult learning (1979)
26. Vivacqua, A.S.: Agents for expertise location. : Proceedings of 1999 AAAI Spring Symposium Workshop on Intelligent Agents in Cyberspace, pp. 9–13 (1999)

Cross-perspective Graph Contrastive Learning

Shiyang Lin, Chenhe Dong, and Ying Shen[(✉)]

School of Intelligent of Systems Engineering, Sun Yat-sen University, Shenzhen, China
{linshy56,dongchh}@mail2.sysu.edu.cn, sheny76@mail.sysu.edu.cn

Abstract. Attributed graph representation has attracted increasing attention recently due to its broad applications such as node classification, link prediction and recommendation. Most existing methods adopt Graph Neural Network (GNN) or its variants to propagate the attributes over the structure network. However, the attribute information will be overshadowed by the structure perspective. To address the limitation and build a link between nodes features and network structure, we aim to learn a holistic representation from two perspectives: topology perspective and feature perspective. To be specific, we separately construct the feature graph and topology graph. Inspired by the network homophily, we argue that there is a deep correlation information between the network structure perspective and the node attributes perspective. Attempting to exploit the potential information between them, we extend our approaches by maximizing the consistency between structural perspective and attribute perspective. In addition, an information fusion module is presented to allow flexible information exchange and integration between the two perspectives. Experimental results on four benchmark datasets demonstrate the effectiveness of our proposed method on graph representation learning, compared with several representative baselines.

Keywords: Graph representation · Graph convolution networks · Contrastive learning · Self-attention mechanism · Semi-supervised learning

1 Introduction

Attributed graph representation aims to learn low dimensional node representation by fully exploiting the rich information of topological structure, node features, and correlation between them. As typical methods in graph representation learning, the representation learned by GNNs has been proved to be effective in achieving the state-of-the-art performance in a variety of graph datasets such

This work was supported in part by the 173 program No. 2021-JCJQ-JJ-0029, the Shenzhen General Research Project under Grant JCYJ20190808182805919 and in part by the National Natural Science Foundation of China under Grant 61602013.

G. Memmi et al. (Eds.): KSEM 2022, LNAI 13368, pp. 58–70, 2022.
https://doi.org/10.1007/978-3-031-10983-6_5

as citation networks [1], social networks [2] and recommended systems [4]. The underlying graph structure is utilized by GNNs to operate convolution directly on the graph by passing node features to neighbors, or perform convolution in the spectral domain using the Fourier basis of a given graph.

However, some recent studies disclose these GNNs methods tend to suffer from certain weaknesses of the state-of-the-art GNNs in fusing node features with network structure. For example, GNNs only perform low-pass filtering on feature vectors and node representation will become indistinguishable when we always utilize a low-pass filter, causing the over-smoothing problem [25]. GNNs also mainly retain the commonality of node features, which ignores the difference, so that the learned representations of connected nodes become similar [3]. Therefore, separately generating a feature graph and a topology graph for GNNs is a fundamental problem.

GNNs models are built with a supervised pattern, which require lots of labeled nodes for training. Recently, graph contrastive representation learning [13,15] arouses a growing interest, which seeks to maximize the mutual information between input and its representation by contrasting positive pairs with negative-sampled counterparts. For example, [15] learns node representation with graph-structured data in an unsupervised manner. And a contrastive objective is proposed to maximize the mutual information between local node embedding and a summary global embedding. [16] considers mutual information in terms of graphical structure and proposes mutual information between input graphs and high-level embeddings in a straightforward pattern. [14] performs augmentation on the input graph to obtain two graph views, and maximize the mutual information between two graph views. However, these contrastive representation learning methods propagate feature information over topology graphs and contrast node-level embeddings to global ones.

In this paper, we propose a **Cross-perspective Graph Contrastive Learning** (CpGCL) for attributed network embedding. We construct a feature graph via the k-nearest neighbor algorithm and then perform graph convolution operation over both topology graph and feature graph. Then, with the feature representation and topology representation, to the best of our knowledge, we are the first to explore the consistency between feature perspective and topology perspective with contrastive learning. Finally, the information fusion module is designed to propagate the potential information and fuse the different perspective vectors. The major contributions of this paper are summarized as follows.

- Different from existing works on graph contrastive representation learning, we propose a novel training strategy to exploit the correlation between topology structure perspective and node features perspective.
- We develop a cross-perspective propagation-based architecture, which constructs feature graph and topology graph separately and performs graph convolution operation on both feature perspective and topology perspective. Combined with contrastive learning, heterogeneous information can be adequately fused.

- We conduct extensive experiments to demonstrate the effectiveness of the proposed method on four benchmark datasets.

We organize the rest of this paper as follows: Sect. 2 introduces related background on graph neural network and contrastive learning. Section 3 describes our proposed framework and provides motivation of our method. Section 4 reports our experimental results, followed by the conclusion in Sect. 5.

2   Related Work

Graph Neural Network. GNNs have been a mainstream strategy to learn low dimensional node representation and have developed for a wide range of tasks, which propagate features information over network topology to node embedding. GraphSAGE [17] utilizes several aggregators and recursively aggregate features with sampled neighbors. Graph attention networks (GAT) [7] improves GNN with the attention mechanism on sampled neighbor nodes. GraphRNA [18] considers node attribute as a bipartite graph and advance graph convolutional networks to a more effective neural architecture. MixHop [12] proposes a graph convolutional layer that utilizes multiple powers of the adjacency matrix to learn both first-order and higher-order neighbors.

Contrastive Learning. The main idea of contrastive learning is to learn representations by contrasting positive and negative samples. Contrastive learning can be applied to both supervised and unsupervised data and has been shown to achieve good performance on a variety of vision and language tasks [19]. Contrastive learning aims to learn representation by maximizing representation in different views. DGI [15] and MVGRL [26] propose to learn a global graph-level embedding and a local node-level embedding, and maximize the global embedding and local embedding. GCA [13] and GRACE [14] design two graph views by novel data augmentation schemes and maximize the agreement between node embeddings in these two views. SCRL [20] finds a "target" for the projection of prototype vectors and utilizes pseudo label using iteratively Sinkhorn algorithm, then sets up "exchanged problem" to predict.

3   Methodology

An attributed network is denoted as $G = (\mathbf{A}, \mathbf{X})$, where $\mathbf{A} \in \mathbb{R}^{n \times n}$ is the adjacency matrix of the input network with n nodes and $\mathbf{X} \in \mathbb{R}^{n \times d}$ if the matrix of node attributes where d is the dimension of the node features. Specifically, $A_{ij} = 1$ represents there is an edge between nodes i and j, otherwise, $A_{ij} = 0$.

Given an attributed network $G = (\mathbf{A}, \mathbf{X})$, attributed network embedding aims to learn a function $f : v_i \rightarrow y_i$ that maps each node v_i to a low dimensional representation vector y_i. Specifically, we use feature graph and topology graph to capture the underlying information in feature space and topology space, and adopt graph convolution over feature graph and topology graph specifically to aggregate the information (Sect. 3.1). Then a cross-perspective contrastive learning module is designed to exploit the consistency of feature information and topology information (Sect. 3.2). Afterwards, we introduce an information fusion module to propagate important information over both two graphs and integrate a common embedding from two perspectives (Sect. 3.3). Finally, we employ a contrastive objective (i.e., a discriminator) that enforces the encoded embeddings of each node in the two different perspectives agree with each other (Sect. 3.4).

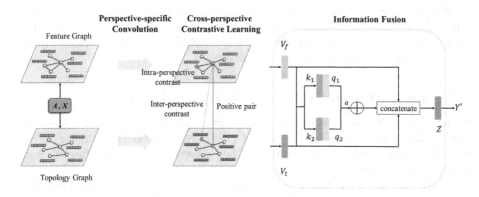

Fig. 1. The framework of CpGCL model. Given an attributed graph $G = (\mathbf{A}, \mathbf{X})$, feature graph and topology graph are constructed. CpGCL consists of three parts: Perspective-specific Convolution Module, Cross-perspective Contrastive Learning Module and Information Fusion Module.

3.1   Perspective-specific Convolution Module

Merely propagating the feature information over the topology graph may only perform low-pass filtering on feature vectors and will smooth the difference between node features. A nature idea is to separately construct a feature graph and a topology graph, then adopt graph convolution operation over them.

To represent the node with feature perspective, we construct the feature graph $G_f = (\mathbf{A}_f, \mathbf{X})$ via k-nearest neighbour algorithm, where $\mathbf{A}_f$ is the adjacency matrix of feature graph and $\mathbf{X}$ is the feature matrix of graph. Concretely, we calculate the similarity matrix $\mathbf{S} \in \mathbb{R}^{n \times n}$ with cosine similarity formula:

$$S_{ij} = \frac{x_i \cdot x_j}{|x_i| \cdot |x_j|}, \tag{1}$$

where S_{ij} is the similarity between node feature x_i and node feature x_j. Then we choose top k similar node pairs for each node and establish edges. Finally, we obtain the adjacency matrix of feature graph $\mathbf{A}_f$.

To extract meaningful information from the feature graph, we adopt graph convolution over the feature graph. With the input graph $(\mathbf{A}_f, \mathbf{X})$ in feature space, the l-th output layer can be represented as:

$$f^{(l)} = ReLU(\hat{D}_f^{-\frac{1}{2}} \hat{A}_f \hat{D}_f^{-\frac{1}{2}} f^{(l-1)} W_f^{(l)}), \tag{2}$$

where $ReLU$ is the activation function, $\hat{A}_f = A_f + I_f$, $\hat{D}_f$ is the diagonal matrix of $\hat{A}_f$, $W_f^{(l)}$ is the weight matrix of the l-th layer in GCN, $f^{(l)}$ is the last layer output of GCN in feature perspective.

As for the topology perspective, we have the topology graph $G_t = (\mathbf{A}_t, \mathbf{X})$, where $\mathbf{A}_t$ is the adjacency matrix of topology graph and $\mathbf{X}$ is the feature matrix. So we can obtain the last layer output $t^{(l)}$ of GCN in topology perspective in the same way as in the perspective of feature.

3.2 Cross-perspective Contrastive Learning Module

Contrary to previous works [15,16] that learn representations by the node-level to the graph-level contrastive scheme, in CpGCL, we define the contrastive objective at the node-level and exploit the correlation between feature perspective and topology perspective.

To be specific, with feature embeddings $\mathbf{V}_f$ and topology embeddings $\mathbf{V}_t$, we employ a contrastive objective that distinguishes the embeddings of the same node in these two different perspectives from other node embeddings. For any node v_i, its embedding generated in feature perspective, V_f, is treated as the anchor, the embedding of it generated in topology perspective, t, is treated as the positive sample, and embeddings of nodes other than V_t in the two perspectives are naturally regarded as negative samples. Formally, we define the critic $\theta(f,t) = s(g(f), g(t))$, where s is the cosine similarity and g is the nonlinear projection to enhance the expression power of the critic. The projection g is implemented with a two-layer multilayer perceptron (MLP). We define the pairwise objective for each positive pair (f, t) as

$$l(V_f, V_t) = \log \frac{e^{\theta(f_i, t_i)/\tau}}{e^{\theta(f_i, t_i)/\tau} + \sum_{k \neq i} e^{\theta(f_i, t_i)/\tau} + \sum_{k \neq i} e^{\theta(f_i, t_k)/\tau}}, \tag{3}$$

where τ is a temperature parameter, $e^{\theta(f_i, t_i)/\tau}$ is the positive pair, $e^{\theta(f_i, t_i)/\tau}$ is the inter-perspective negative pairs and $e^{\theta(f_i, t_k)/\tau}$ is the intra-perspective negative pairs. Therefore, negative pairs come from two sources. Since two perspectives are symmetric, the loss for another perspective can be defined similarly for $l(t_i, f_i)$. The overall contrastive objective is defined as the average of two different forms:

$$L_c = \frac{1}{2N} \sum_{i=1}^{N} [l(f_i, t_i) + l(t_i, f_i)]. \tag{4}$$

To sum up, CpGCL first constructs feature graph G_f and topology graph G_t separately. Obtaining feature representation v of G_f and topology representation

t of G_t, we respectively use GNNs encoder to propagate the feature information and topology information. Finally, we learn embeddings by maximizing the agreement between feature representation v and topology representation t.

3.3   Information Fusion Module

In order to exchange the information between feature perspective and topology perspective, another design goal of CpGCL framework is to propagate critical information along the network structure and maintain the discriminative features in node attributes. Previous work [8] designs a Common-GCN with parameter sharing strategy to get the embeddings shared in two spaces. Instead, we utilize the self-attention mechanism [22] to exchange features between perspectives. The intuition includes two aspects. First, the self-attention mechanism is designed to learn the importance of two perspectives, without having one perspective separated from another. Second, the self-attention mechanism can adaptively obtain one vector for each perspective, so that the information fusion module can be naturally stacked.

Specifically, given the feature representation V_f and topology representation V_t, following standard self-attention, we calculate the query vector q and key vector k for each node,

$$\begin{aligned} q_1 &= V_f W^Q, & q_2 &= V_t W^Q, \\ k_1 &= V_f W^K, & k_2 &= V_t W^K, \end{aligned} \tag{5}$$

where d is the embedding dimension, $W_Q, W_K \in \mathbb{R}^{d \times d}$ denotes the transformation matrices for query vector and key vectors, respectively. Then we fuse the new node representation V_1 and V_2 with the following computation,

$$\begin{aligned} \alpha_{i,j} &= \frac{\exp(q_i k_j^\top)}{\sum_{k \in \{k_1,k_2\}} \exp(q_i k^\top)}, \\ V_1 &= \mu(\alpha_{1,1} V_f + \alpha_{1,2} V_t), \\ V_2 &= \mu(\alpha_{2,1} V_f + \alpha_{2,2} V_t). \end{aligned} \tag{6}$$

where $\alpha_{.,.}$ denotes the relative weights of the intermediate features V_f and V_t for the node representations, and μ is the activation function.

Then we combine these two node representation V_1 and V_2 to obtain the common embedding V of two perspectives.

$$V = (V_1 + V_2)/2, \tag{7}$$

3.4   Optimization Objective

To preserve the information from feature perspective and topology perspective, V_f, V_t and V are concatenated as the final embedding Z. Then we use Z for semi-supervised classification with a linear transformation and softmax function. Y' is the prediction result and Y'_{ij} is the probability of node i belonging to class j. W and a is the weight and bias of the linear layer, respectively.

$$Y' = (W \cdot Z + b). \tag{8}$$

Suppose there are T nodes in training set, we adopt cross-entropy loss to measure the difference between predicted label Y'_{ij} and truth label Y_{ij}.

$$L_t = \sum_{i=1}^{T} \sum_{j=1}^{C} Y_{ij} \ln Y'_{ij}. \tag{9}$$

Combining the node classification task and contrastive learning, we have the following overall objective function:

$$L = L_t + \beta L_c, \tag{10}$$

where β is the consistency balancing hyper-parameter.

4   Experimental Analysis

In this section, we conduct extensive experiments to evaluate the effectiveness of the cross-perspective graph contrastive learning framework for node classification on attributed graph representation.

4.1   Datasets

For a comprehensive comparison, we use four widely-used datasets, including ACM [27], Citeseer [21], UAI2010 [23] and Cora to study the performance of node classification; their detailed statistics is summarized in Table 1. Moreover, we provide all the data websites in the supplement for reproducibility.

ACM[1] contains papers published in KDD, SIGMOD, SIGCOMM, Mobi-COMM, and VLDB and are divided into three classes (Database, Wireless Communication, Data Mining). The constructed graph comprises 3,025 papers, 5,835 authors, and 56 subjects. Paper features correspond to elements of a bag-of-words represented of keywords. **Citeseer**[2] consists of 3,312 scientific publications classified into one of six classes and 4,732 links. Each publication in the dataset is described by a 0/1-valued word vector indicating the absence/presence of the corresponding word from the dictionary. **UAI2010**[3] contains 3,067 nodes in 19 classes and it has been tested in GCN for community detection. The attribute dimension of each node is 4,973. **Cora**[4] is a paper citation network, which contains 2,708 papers as nodes and 5,249 citation links as edges. These papers are divided into seven categories. The attribute of each node is a binary vector of 1,433 dimensions.

---

[1] https://github.com/Jhy1993/HAN.
[2] https://github.com/tkipf/pygcn.
[3] http://linqs.umiacs.umd.edu/projects//projects/lbc/index.html.
[4] Cora dataset is available at https://linqs.soe.ucsc.edu/data.

Table 1. The statistic of the datasets

Dataset	Nodes	Edges	Classes	Features
ACM	3,025	13,128	3	1,870
Citeseer	3,327	4,732	6	3,702
UAI2010	3,067	28,311	19	4,973
Cora	2,708	5,429	7	1,433

4.2 Baselines

We compare the CpGCL framework with graph representative baselines to verify the performance.

- **DeepWalk** [6] is a classical graph embedding method which uses random walk and skipgram to learn network representations.
- **Line** [9] preserves the first-order or second-order proximity in the network by optimizing the carefully designed objective function.
- **ChebNet** [10] is a spectral-based GCN that uses Chebyshev filters to reduce computation complexity.
- **GCN** [5] is a semi-supervised network embedding method that applies average aggregation in the local neighborhood.
- **kNN-GCN** [8] uses the sparse k-nearest neighbour graph calculated from feature matrix as input graph of GCN and represent it as kNN-GCN.
- **GAT** [7] is a semi-supervised neural network which learn the importance between nodes and its neighbors and fuse the neighbors to perform node classification.
- **DNet** [11] is a degree-specific graph neural network using multi-task graph convolution for node classification.
- **MixHop** [12] is a propagation-based method that mixes the node representation of highter-order neighbours in one graph convolutional layer.
- **GRACE** [13] is a proposed graph contrastive learning framework. It generates two graph view and maximize the agreement of node representations of two views.
- **AMGCN** [8] exploits the information from both feature space and topology space. Then it uses the attention mechanism to learn adaptive importance weights of the embeddings.
- **SCRL** [20] presents a self-supervised framework to learn a consensus representation for attributed graph. It fuses the topology information and node feature information of the graph.

Table 2. Node classification results(%). (Bold: best; underline: runner-up)

Dataset	ACM						Citeseer					
L/C	20		40		60		20		40		60	
Metrics	ACC	F1	ACC	F1	ACC	F1	ACC	F1	ACC	F1	ACC	F1
DeepWalk [6]	62.69	62.11	63.00	61.88	67.03	66.99	43.47	38.08	45.15	43.18	48.86	48.01
LINE [9]	41.28	40.12	45.83	45.79	50.41	49.92	32.71	31.75	33.32	32.42	35.39	34.37
ChebNet [10]	75.37	74.93	81.68	81.33	85.78	85.32	69.64	65.91	71.52	68.23	73.21	70.24
GCN [5]	87.64	87.80	88.96	89.02	90.37	90.43	70.30	67.42	72.98	69.66	74.43	71.29
kNN-GCN	78.54	78.14	81.61	81.55	81.94	81.89	61.37	58.83	61.59	59.42	62.46	60.13
GAT [7]	87.47	87.59	88.51	88.47	90.26	90.33	72.53	68.17	73.02	69.59	74.71	70.37
DNet [11]	84.48	84.17	85.64	84.78	86.65	84.09	69.52	67.81	70.39	66.92	71.88	68.24
MixHop [12]	81.08	81.42	82.37	81.09	83.03	82.36	71.40	66.96	71.56	67.47	72.31	69.37
GRACE [13]	89.04	89.00	89.46	89.36	91.08	91.03	71.70	68.14	72.38	68.74	74.20	70.73
AMGCN [8]	<u>90.40</u>	<u>90.43</u>	<u>90.76</u>	90.66	91.40	90.69	<u>73.12</u>	68.44	<u>74.62</u>	69.84	<u>75.56</u>	70.94
SCRL [20]	88.70	88.46	90.70	<u>90.71</u>	<u>91.80</u>	<u>91.83</u>	73.00	<u>68.81</u>	73.80	<u>70.17</u>	75.50	<u>71.86</u>
CpGCL	**91.82**	**91.68**	**91.92**	**91.84**	**92.20**	**92.15**	**73.40**	**70.30**	**75.90**	**71.42**	**76.60**	**72.80**

Dataset	UAI2010						Cora					
L/C	20		40		60		20		40		60	
Metrics	ACC	F1	ACC	F1	ACC	F1	ACC	F1	ACC	F1	ACC	F1
DeepWalk [6]	42.15	33.04	50.71	46.24	54.71	46.59	73.22	71.90	75.12	73.88	76.10	74.56
LINE [9]	43.43	37.16	45.83	39.81	50.41	43.71	73.56	72.04	74.84	73.36	75.42	74.28
ChebNet [10]	50.12	33.75	58.18	38.82	59.74	40.77	76.68	75.82	77.56	76.34	78.21	77.24
GCN [5]	49.98	32.96	51.87	33.90	54.53	32.31	77.30	76.53	78.98	77.79	79.83	78.84
kNN-GCN	66.06	52.43	68.74	54.45	71.68	54.82	61.57	58.83	64.59	61.24	67.48	63.28
GAT [7]	56.87	39.59	63.71	45.11	68.47	48.92	78.53	77.38	79.82	78.56	80.71	79.57
DNet [11]	23.71	16.90	30.57	26.64	34.53	29.31	76.40	75.43	77.33	76.82	77.89	76.46
MixHop [12]	61.56	49.23	65.11	53.93	67.71	56.42	72.40	70.88	73.56	72.47	75.31	73.82
GRACE [13]	65.59	48.43	66.71	49.57	68.71	51.49	76.84	75.72	78.26	77.20	79.18	78.22
AMGCN [8]	70.14	55.67	73.17	<u>64.91</u>	74.42	66.08	<u>80.80</u>	<u>79.98</u>	83.57	82.39	<u>84.21</u>	83.17
SCRL [20]	<u>71.90</u>	<u>58.40</u>	<u>73.52</u>	64.70	<u>74.90</u>	<u>66.54</u>	80.60	79.72	<u>84.17</u>	<u>83.28</u>	84.06	<u>83.72</u>
CpGCL	**73.70**	**62.06**	**74.50**	**66.42**	**75.84**	**68.62**	**82.50**	**82.02**	**85.10**	**84.42**	**85.36**	**84.60**

4.3 Parameters Setting

For all the baseline methods, we use the implementations provided by either their authors or open-source libraries. By default, we build a 2-layer GCN with the same hidden layer dimension $n \in \{512, 768\}$ and train our model utilizing Adam [24] optimizer with learning rate range from 0.0001 to 0.0005. In order to prevent the over-fitting problem, we set the dropout rate to 0.5. In addition, we set weight decay $\in \{5e-4, 5e-3\}$, temperature parameter $\tau \in \{0.8, 0.9, 1.0, 1.1\}$ for contrastive objective and $k \in \{2, ..., 9\}$ for the kNN graphs. The balancing hyper-parameter is set from 0.7 to 1.0. For fairness, we follow [8] and select three label rates for the training set (i.e., 20, 40, 60 labeled nodes per class) and choose 1000 nodes as the test set. The selection of labeled nodes on each dataset is identical for all compared baselines. We repeatedly train and test our model for 5 times with the same partition and evaluate the performance of our model by Accuracy (ACC) and Macro-F1 (F1).

4.4 Node Classification Results

The node classification results are reported in Table 2, where L/C means the number of labeled nodes per class for training. We have the following observations.

- Compared with all baselines, the proposed CpGCL generally achieves the best performance on all datasets with all label rates. Compared with the best competitor (SCRL), CpGCL improves it by 1.35% and 1.68%for ACC and F1 respectively across all datasets. The results implicate the effectiveness of the cross-perspective contrastive learning and information fusion modules. CpGCL can better capture the difference between nodes and their neighbor nodes pairs.
- In some situations, the feature graph shows better performance than on topology graph, such as UAI2010. Comparing with GCN, kNN-GCN and GAT, CpGCL achieves substantial improvement on all datasets, which further confirms the necessity of the feature graph.
- CpGCL consistently outperforms GRACE on all the datasets, indicating the effectiveness of cross-perspective contrastive learning in CpGCL, because CpGCL effectively learns the correlation between feature perspective and topology perspective.

4.5 Ablation Study

Here, we conduct an ablation study by discarding some of the design choices shown in Fig. 1. The node classification results on ACM, Citeseer, UAI2010, and Cora are shown in Table 3. In the table, **CpGCL - IF** means discarding the information fusion module, **CpGCL - CL** means CpGCL without the cross-perspective contrastive learning module and removing the contrastive objective loss. As we can see from the Table 3, the results of CpGCL are obviously better than all its variants on all datasets with all labeled rates, verifying that information fusion module and cross-perspective contrastive learning module are effective in terms of improving the node representation results for classification.

Table 3. The results of CpGCL and its variants on four datasets.

Dataset	Metrices	L/C	CpGCL	CpGCL-IF	CpGCL-CL
ACM	ACC	20	91.82	89.95	89.70
		40	91.92	89.70	89.50
		60	92.20	90.20	90.20
	F1	20	91.68	90.10	89.22
		40	91.84	90.20	89.47
		60	92.15	90.49	90.22
Citeseer	ACC	20	73.40	72.20	72.40
		40	75.90	72.70	73.30
		60	76.60	74.90	74.70
	F1	20	70.30	67.93	68.58
		40	71.42	69.46	69.95
		60	72.80	71.96	71.43
UAI2010	ACC	20	73.70	69.90	69.30
		40	74.50	73.50	73.40
		60	75.84	74.40	75.20
	F1	20	62.06	59.42	59.31
		40	66.42	64.89	64.49
		60	68.42	66.56	67.55
Cora	ACC	20	82.50	82.26	80.79
		40	85.10	82.42	82.33
		60	85.36	82.66	82.88
	F1	20	82.02	81.36	81.20
		40	84.42	83.20	83.10
		60	84.60	83.80	83.70

4.6   Parameter Sensitivity

We also study the sensitivity of the one major hyper-parameter k-nearest neighbor graph k on ACM and UAI2010 datasets.

Parameter k: We study the impact of the top k neighborhoods in the kNN graph with k range from 2 to 9. We conduct experiments on ACM and UAI2010 datasets, their accuracies have similar trends. The results are shown in Fig. 2. The accuracy witness a climb first, which is followed by a decrease. The reason is that larger k can provide more useful feature information but too many neighbors will also introduce noisy edges.

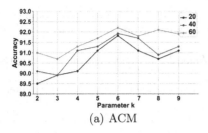
(a) ACM

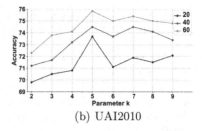
(b) UAI2010

Fig. 2. Analysis of parameter k

5   Conclusion

In this paper, we propose a cross-perspective graph contrastive learning framework on the attributed graph, which is able to explore the attribute information and topology information adaptively. Requiring the embeddings of feature graph and topology graph, the cross-perspective contrastive learning module is proved to be effective to learn the consistent information between feature perspective and topology perspective. To further fuse the information, we introduce the information fusion module to flexibly exchange and integrate information between the two perspectives. Experimental results on real-world datasets demonstrate the superiority of our proposed method on attributed graph representation.

References

1. Song, Q., Wang, X., Wang, R.: Knowledge network and visual analysis of knowledge graph research. In: ICVRS, pp. 61–66 (2021)
2. Qiu, J., Tang, J., Ma, H., et al.: DeepINF: social influence prediction with deep learning. In: SIGKDD, pp. 2110–2119 (2018)
3. Bo, D., Wang, X., Shi, C., et al.: Beyond low-frequency information in graph convolutional networks. In: AAAI (2021)
4. Ying, R., He, R., Chen, K., et al.: Graph convolutional neural networks for web-scale recommender systems. In: SIGKDD, pp. 974–983 (2018)
5. Kipf, T.N., Welling, M.: Semi-supervised classification with graph convolutional networks. In: ICLR (2016)
6. Perozzi, B., Al-Rfou, R., Skiena, S.: Deepwalk: online learning of social representations. In: SIGKDD, pp. 701–710 (2014)
7. Velickovic, P., Cucurull, G., Casanova, A., Romero, A., Lio, P., Bengio, Y.: Graph attention networks. In: ICLR (2017)
8. Wang, X., Zhu, M., Bo, D., Cui, P., Shi, C., Pei, J.: AM-GCN: adaptive multi-channel graph convolutional networks. In: SIGKDD, pp. 1243–1253 (2020)
9. Tang, J., Qu, M., Wang, M., et al.: Line: large-scale information network embedding. In: WWW, pp. 1067–1077 (2015)
10. Defferrard, M., Bresson, X., Vandergheynst, P.: Convolutional neural networks on graphs with fast localized spectral filtering. In: NeruIPS, p. 29 (2016)
11. Wu, J., He, J., Xu, J.: Net: degree-specific graph neural networks for node and graph classification. In: SIGKDD, pp. 406–415 (2019)

12. Abu-El-Haija, S., Perozzi, B., Kapoor, A., et al.: Mixhop: higher-order graph convolutional architectures via sparsified neighborhood mixing. In: PLMR, pp. 21–29 (2019)
13. Zhu, Y., Xu, Y., Yu, F., Liu, Q., Wu, S., Wang, L.: Deep graph contrastive representation learning. In: ICML (2020)
14. Zhu, Y., Xu, Y., Yu, F., et al.: Graph contrastive learning with adaptive augmentation. In: WWW, pp. 2069–2080 (2021)
15. Velickovic, P., Fedus, W., Hamilton, W.L., et al.: Deep graph infomax. In: ICLR (2019)
16. Peng, Z., Huang, W., Luo, M., et al.: Graph representation learning via graphical mutual information maximization. In: WWW, pp. 259–270 (2020)
17. Hamilton, W., Ying, Z., Leskovec, J.: Inductive representation learning on large graphs. In: NeruIPS, pp. 1024–1034 (2017)
18. Huang, X., Song, Q., Li, Y., et al.: Graph recurrent networks with attributed random walks. In: SIGKDD, pp. 732–740 (2019)
19. He, K., Fan, H., Wu, Y., Xie, S., Girshick, R.: Momentum contrast for unsupervised visual representation learning. In: CVPR, pp. 9726–9735 (2020)
20. Liu, C., Wen, L., Kang, Z., et al.: Self-supervised consensus representation learning for attributed graph. In: MM, pp. 2654–2662 (2021)
21. Kipf, T.N., Welling, M.: Semi-supervised classification with graph convolutional networks. In: ICLR (2017)
22. Vaswani, A., et al.: Attention is all you need. In: NeurIPS, pp. 5998–6008 (2017)
23. Wang, W., Liu, X., Jiao, P., et al.: A unified weakly supervised framework for community detection and semantic matching. In: PAKDD, pp. 218–230 (2018)
24. Kingma, D.P., Ba, J.: Adam: a method for stochastic optimization. In: ICLR (2015)
25. Zhu, R., Tao, Z., Li, Y., et al.: Automated graph learning via population based self-tuning GCN. In: SIGKDD, pp. 2096–2100 (2021)
26. Hassani,K., Khasahmadi,A.H.: Contrastive multi-view representation learning on graphs. In: PMLR (2020)
27. Wang, X., Ji, H., Shi,C., et al.: Heterogeneous graph attention network. In: WWW, pp. 2022–2032 (2019)

A Multi-scale Convolution and Gated Recurrent Unit Based Network for Limit Order Book Prediction

Borui Xu, Tong Zhang, and Weiguo Liu[✉]

School of Software, Shandong University, Jinan, Shandong, China
{boruixu,202035309}@mail.sdu.edu.cn, weiguo.liu@sdu.edu.cn

Abstract. Nowadays, with the development of high-frequency trading (HFT), many people have started to pay attention to limit order book (LOB) data which records the orders in market trading. There have been many works using LOB data to make predictions, but these works do not distinguish between the orders of buyers and sellers. Intuitively, the transaction in the financial market is a process of the game between buyers and sellers, and it is important to represent the features of both sides. Inspired by this thought, in this paper, we propose a novel multi-scale deep learning model to represent the features of buyer and seller, respectively, and make predictions of the future trend of LOB data based on the changes in the features of both sides. Our model uses convolutional networks to extract the independent features of buyers and sellers and gated recurrent unit (GRU) networks to capture the market state. And it combines the features of both sides with the market state using the gating mechanism to represent features better. Experiments on the FI-2010 benchmark dataset and a bitcoin cryptocurrency dataset (BTC-2021) all show that our model can achieve state-of-the-art performance.

Keywords: Financial time series · Limit order book · Price prediction · Deep learning · Gating mechanism

1 Introduction

Due to a large amount of noise and stochastic events in the financial market, it is a complex problem to predict the trend of financial time series effectively for a long time [5]. Many researchers and investors have devoted a lot of time to this domain. At first, many mathematical methods have been tried to capture changes in share prices, such as the vector autoregressive model (VAR) [22], the autoregressive integrated moving average model (ARIMA) [1] and so on. But in practice, these models can not produce satisfactory performance because of too many assumptions about data distribution. After that, machine learning attracts people's attention, many related models like support vector machines [6] and random forest [13] have been used and proved to outperform statistical

© The Author(s), under exclusive license to Springer Nature Switzerland AG 2022
G. Memmi et al. (Eds.): KSEM 2022, LNAI 13368, pp. 71–84, 2022.
https://doi.org/10.1007/978-3-031-10983-6_6

models. In recent years, with the development of deep learning, time series prediction has made great progress in many domains [2,21]. So people also expect to explore some deep learning models to improve the performance of financial time series prediction [16,17]. How to combine financial time series and deep learning technology to improve the accuracy and efficiency of prediction has become an interesting problem.

Limit Order Books (LOBs), as a kind of financial time series, are often used in high-frequency trading (HFT). This data records all the submitted orders waiting to be executed. Orders are sorted by price, which constitutes different levels. At a specific level, orders will be executed by the arrival time. LOB data contains quite a number of the trading information in the financial market. This data can be divided into two parts: ask orders part and bid orders part. If a trader wants to buy an asset at or below a specified price, he will submit a bid order; on the contrary, if he wants to sell, he will submit an ask order. Both ask order and bid order include price $(P_a(t), P_b(t))$ and volume $(V_a(t), V_b(t))$. Figure 1 illustrates the structure of the LOB data in detail.

Bid Volume	Price	Ask Volume
	10.2	5
	10.1	6
	10.0	2
3	9.9	
5	9.8	
17	9.7	

Fig. 1. An example of LOB data, left part is the volume of bid orders, right part is the volume of ask orders. 10.0 (9.9) is the first level of ask (bid) orders, 10.1 (9.8) is the second level of ask (bid) orders and so on.

Deep learning technology has been used in this domain for many years [9,15, 16,18,20]. And these works demonstrate that forecasting the trend of LOB data in a short time is feasible. However, since this data is noisy and nonstationary, the prediction results are still unsatisfactory. And there are also some problems with the existing works. Firstly although the transaction is between the buyer and the seller, few of them consider representing ask and bid features separately. Most works combine ask features and bid features at the beginning expecting to get global features from them. This operation may lead to the destruction of single side features. Besides that, most works ignore the use of feature engineering in deep learning and only use basic features to make the models learn features by themselves. Moreover, when it comes to how to use handcrafted features, existing models always process them as well as basic features in the same way, which does not show the advantages of basic features and handcrafted features.

In order to represent features of LOB data better and make more accurate predictions, in this paper, we propose a new multi-scale deep learning model which can represent independent ask and bid features and utilize different network structures to deal with various input types. First, it uses basic data in convolutional networks to learn and extract independent ask and bid features. After that, it uses handcrafted data in a GRU-based module so-called RGRU [9] to represent the market state. Then it integrates these independent ask and bid features with the market state through a gating mechanism to consider the impact of the market state on trading. Finally, it uses a temporal attention mechanism to get the current features and make predictions. We test our model on a public LOB benchmark dataset called FI-2010 [11] and a bitcoin cryptocurrency dataset (BTC-2021) [12]. Experiments show that our model exceeds the state-of-the-art models.

The major contributions of this paper are summarized as follows:

1. We propose a novel model that can represent independent ask and bid features using a gating mechanism. As far as we know, it is the first model which can represent independent ask and bid features.
2. Compared with the existing works, we pay more attention to the feature engineering, we use handcrafted features to express the market state and select different networks according to different input data types, which is more reasonable for feature representation.
3. Experiments show our model can achieve state-of-the-art performance on both FI-2010 dataset and BTC-2021 dataset.

The rest of this paper is organized as follows. In Sect. 2, we give an overview of the related work. Section 3 formulates this problem and illustrates the structure of our model. Section 4 starts with introducing the dataset and experimental settings, then provides and analyzes the results. In Sect. 5, we summarize this paper and discuss possible future work.

2   Related Work

Millions of LOB data generated every day provide deep learning models with a large amount of data for training and testing. Since the Convolutional Neural Network (CNN) [7] was used by Tsantekidis et al. [16], deep learning models have been greatly developed to predict the future trend of LOB data. To sum up, all deep learning models can be simply divided into two categories: using only basic features and using both basic features and handcrafted features.

Basic features usually refer to the price and volume of LOB data. Tsantekidis et al. [16] first uses the CNN module to extract the potential features in the basic features. This model only uses 10 level basic features to predict the trend. They [17] also tried the Long Short-Term Memory Units (LSTM) [4] on

LOB data and got a better result. After that, Tran et al. [15] design a Temporal Attention-Augmented Bilinear Layer (TABL) module to learn the features in the historical time series. Zhang et al. [20] propose a deep convolutional neural network (DeepLOB) to address the prediction problem. They analyze the characteristic of LOB data and used carefully designed CNN module to extract features, also use an inception module [14] to capture the feature in time horizon and got an impressive result. Wallbridge [19] tries Transformers structure in his model. Liu et al. [8] propose a Multi-scale Two-way Deep Neural Network (MTDNN) for stock trend prediction. They combine traditional discrete wavelet transform and XGBoost with CNN and LSTM to get the result.

Only a few deep learning models pay attention to the feature engineering and design handcrafted features to predict the LOB data. Tsantekidis et al. [18] consider the drawback of the basic features normalized by z-score and design a set of stationary features to overcome that. He propose a CNN-LSTM model. The input of this model includes both basic features and handcrafted features. Lv and Zhang [9] also use both features in their stacked residual gated recurrent unit (SRGRU) network. However, the existing works do not consider the differences between the two features, which may lead to terrible performance. In our work, we utilize different modules to deal with them and get better results.

Table 1. Input sets

Input data	Description
Basic	$v_1 = \{P_i^{ask}, V_i^{ask}, P_i^{bid}, V_i^{ask}\}_{i=1}^n$
Handcrafted	$v_2 = \{(P_i^{ask} - P_i^{bid}), (P_i^{ask} + P_i^{bid})/2\}_{i=1}^n$
	$v_3 = \{|P_n^{ask} - P_1^{ask}|, |P_n^{bid} - P_1^{bid}|, |P_{i+1}^{ask} - P_i^{ask}|, |P_{i+1}^{bid} - P_i^{bid}|\}_{i=1}^n$
	$v_4 = \{\frac{1}{n}\sum_{i=1}^n P_i^{ask}, \frac{1}{n}\sum_{i=1}^n P_i^{bid}, \frac{1}{n}\sum_{i=1}^n V_i^{ask}, \frac{1}{n}\sum_{i=1}^n V_i^{bid}\}$
	$v_5 = \{\sum_{i=1}^n (P_i^{ask} - P_i^{bid}), \sum_{i=1}^n (V_i^{ask} - V_i^{bid})\}$
	$v_6 = \{dP_i^{ask}/dt, dP_i^{bid}/dt, dV_i^{ask}/dt, dV_i^{bid}/dt\}_{i=1}^n$

3 Proposed Method

3.1 Problem Formulation

To predict the LOB data, we use the historical LOB time series data as input. Referring to [9,11], the input data we used are shown in Table 1. Here we denote the input as $\mathbf{X} = \{x_1, x_2, \ldots, x_T\}$, where T is the length of time steps. As for a specific time step, we denote the features as $x \in \mathbb{R}^{12n+6}$, where n is the levels used in LOB data. In this paper, $n = 10$. And we describe the prediction problem as three classification problems: down, stationary, and up. We use the percentage change of the mid-price on the next few days to label the data as our prediction target. Mid-price and rising percent are calculated as follows:

$$p_t = \frac{p_a^{(1)}(t) + p_b^{(1)}(t)}{2} \qquad (1)$$

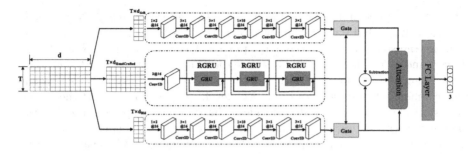

Fig. 2. The structure of the proposed model. It combines the independent features of both sides and the market state to better perform feature representation and prediction.

$$\alpha_t = \frac{s_+(t) - p_t}{p_t} \tag{2}$$

$$\alpha_t = \frac{s_+(t) - s_-(t)}{s_-(t)} \tag{3}$$

where p_t is the mid price at time t, $p_a^{(1)}(t)$ and $p_b^{(1)}(t)$ are the first level price of ask and bid orders at time t, α_t is the rising percent, $s_+(t)$ is the mean of the next k mid prices (not including p_t), $s_-(t)$ is the mean of the previous k mid prices (including p_t). Equation (2) is used in FI-2010 dataset to get rising percent. In order to compare with other models, we also use this calculation method on FI-2010 dataset. However, [20] has pointed out this calculation method only smooths the future prices, not the previous prices, which is not suitable for the design of trading algorithms. Therefore, they suggest using Eq. (3) to calculate the rising percent. And we use Eq. (3) in BTC-2021 dataset. For a fixed threshold α, if $\alpha_t < -\alpha$, α_t is defined as 0 (down), if $\alpha_t > \alpha$, α_t is defined as 2 (up). In other cases, α_t is defined as 1 (stationary).

In this paper, we aim to propose a model to map the input features X to three classes. Firstly it mainly uses basic input data to extract the latent independent ask and bid features and handcrafted data to extract the market state. Then in order to reflect the impact of the market state, it combines market state and independent features using the gating mechanism to get the final features representation. In the end, it uses a temporal attention mechanism and linear layers to obtain the prediction results. The general structure of our model is described in Fig. 2.

3.2 Independent Feature Representation

Convolutional layers are often used to extract local features, and there have been lots of works using convolutional modules to get features from financial time series [16,18,20]. Zhang et al. [20] are the first to consider the structure features of LOB data when using CNN. It extracts data features hierarchically. However, it also ignores the parameter sharing mechanism of CNN. In the process of combining price and volume at every level, they use the same CNN module to process ask and bid data, assuming that both sides have the exact nature and can use the same weights to combine price and volume features. Nevertheless, buyers and sellers do not necessarily have the same characteristics. Besides that, all existing works ignore the nature of the game between buyers and sellers and just combine ask and bid features at each level, which can not reflect the change in historical characteristics of both sides. Therefore, we propose to use different modules of the same convolutional structure to extract independent features. It can not only solve the influence of sharing parameter mechanism on feature representation, but also reflect the independent feature changes of both sides. The ask input and bid input are as follows:

$$X_{ask} = \{\{p_a^{(i)}(t), v_a^{(i)}(t)\}_{i=1}^{n=10}\}_{t=1}^{T} \tag{4}$$

$$X_{bid} = \{\{p_b^{(i)}(t), v_b^{(i)}(t)\}_{i=1}^{n=10}\}_{t=1}^{T} \tag{5}$$

Here, we take the extraction of independent ask features as an example. As shown in Fig. 2, we use convolutional kernels to combine the price and volume at each level first. In order to ensure the combination of price and volume at the same level, the size of the first kernel is (1×2) with the stride of (1×2). After that, we use convolutional kernels of (3×1) to interact with the features in the local horizon. Moreover, we pad zero to the input to keep the time series length unchanged. Then we use kernels with the size of (1×10) to combine all level features into one dimension. Convolutional kernels of (3×1) follow as well. All activation functions used in this module are Leaky Rectifying Linear Units (Leaky-ReLU) [10].

3.3   Market State Representation

We believe that the current market state also has a specific impact on the future price trend. And we use handcrafted input data shown in Table 1 to extract corresponding market state features. Handcrafted features include the information on ask and bid sides. Therefore, we use them to represent the change in the market state. Unlike basic features, handcrafted features have already represented potential features on a single time step. Hence we pay more attention to the interaction during the time step. Gated Recurrent Unit (GRU) [3] is a variant of Recurrent Neural Network (RNN). While ensuring the transmission of information, GRU solves the problem of gradient vanishing in RNN. Lv and Zhang [9] propose a structure called RGRU, which bases on GRU and residual thought. We use the RGRU module to process the handcrafted features and get the latent market state.

We will illustrate the details of an RGRU cell first. At time step t, the inputs of an RGRU cell are the previous state h_{t-1} and the information i_t on the current time step t. The reset gate r_t controls how much previous information can be used to get the current updated state $\tilde{h}_t$, and the update gate z_t controls the proportion of h_{t-1} and $\tilde{h}_t$ to get the new state h_t. To enhance the expression of original features, the output m_t of the RGRU module is the element-wise addition between the input of the GRU block and the output of the GRU block. The following formula describes this process:

$$r_t = \sigma(W_r \cdot [h_{t-1}, i_t]) \tag{6}$$

$$z_t = \sigma(W_z \cdot [h_{t-1}, i_t]) \tag{7}$$

$$\tilde{h}_t = tanh(W_{\tilde{h}} \cdot [r_t * h_{t-1}, i_t]) \tag{8}$$

$$h_t = z_t * \tilde{h}_t + (1 - z_t) * h_{t-1} \tag{9}$$

$$m_t = h_t + i_t \tag{10}$$

where σ is the sigmoid function, $W_r, W_z, W_{\tilde{h}}$ are the trainable parameter matrices. In addition, to get better performance and perform dimension conversion, we add a one-dimension convolutional layer to process the input of the RGRU modules.

3.4   Feature Fusion

After obtaining the independent features and market state features, in this part, we add the influence of the market state on both sides to the independent ask and bid features. This is because the market state has an impact on transactions. So in order to measure the degree of influence of market state on both sides, we use the gating mechanism to combine independent features with the market state features. Since the effects on buyers and sellers may not be the same, we use two independent gating functions. The formula is as follows:

$$C_a = \sigma(W_a \cdot [A, M]) \tag{11}$$

$$A_{new} = C_a * A + (1 - C_a) * M \tag{12}$$

$$C_b = \sigma(W_b \cdot [B, M]) \tag{13}$$

$$B_{new} = C_b * B + (1 - C_b) * M \tag{14}$$

where W_a, W_b are the trainable parameter matrices. A, B mean the independent ask and bid feature matrices. M means the market feature matrix. C_a and C_b mean combination ratio matrices. A_{new}, B_{new} are the final ask and bid feature matrices. In addition, we use the difference of final feature matrices to indicate the difference between these two features, which can be described as $D_{AB} = A_{new} - B_{new}$.

3.5 Temporal Attention Module

In this part, we concatenate final ask features, final bid features, and difference features in the last dimension forming a feature matrix F_{total}. Considering that the features of different time steps have different effects on the future prediction results and the attention mechanism can help us pay more attention to the important parts, we take a temporal attention module to enhance the effect of important time steps. We get the corresponding attention value in different time steps through a linear layer. Moreover, a softmax function is used to normalize the attention value. Finally, we calculate the final mixed feature vector with a weighted sum of each time step. The formula is as follows:

$$o_t = \sigma(W_m f_t + b_m) \tag{15}$$

$$atten_t = \frac{exp(o_t)}{\sum_j exp(o_t)} \tag{16}$$

$$v = \sum_{t=0}^{T} atten_t * f_t \tag{17}$$

where f_t is the feature vector at time t in F_{total}, W_m is the trainable parameter matrix, b_m is the bias vector, o_t is the attention score, $atten_t$ is the weight at time t, v is the weighted sum result vector. Through this part, we incorporate all time steps feature vectors together. In the end, we use the vector v to do the classification task. A simple linear network is used to generate the category prediction results.

4 Experiments

4.1 Experiments Settings

In this section, we name our model CNN-GRU. We implement it with Pytorch and train it using a single Nvidia RTX 3090 GPU. Categorical cross-entropy loss is adapted as the loss function. And we use the ADAM algorithm to optimize our model parameters. The initial learning rate is 0.001 and will decrease with the factor of 0.5 when the loss value stops decreasing in four epochs. Other optimization parameters are the default value set by Pytorch.

In all experiments, the mini-batch is 64, and the unit number of a GRU cell is 16. The length of the input time series T is 10. On FI-2010 dataset, it needs approximately 100 epochs to get the best effect. On BTC-2021 dataset, it requires about 10 epochs to get the best result. To ensure performance, we train all models for 200 epochs.

4.2   Dataset

FI-2010 dataset is the first public benchmark dataset to test the model's ability to predict LOB data. Most existing works test performance on this dataset. It provides about 4.5 million events of the LOB data of 5 stocks in the Nasdaq Helsinki Stock Exchange for 10 consecutive trading days from June 1 to June 14, 2010. The dataset offers three kinds of normalized data: z-score, min-max, and decimal precision normalization. We choose data normalized by z-score as the input, which is chosen by most existing works. For the convenience of testing, the data set is divided into 10 folds. And there are 5 prediction horizons (10, 20, 30, 50, 100) labeled by the threshold $\alpha = 0.002$.

BTC-2021 contains approximately one million LOB data of bitcoin to US dollar from March 1 to March 14, 2021. It also has 10 levels of the ask (bid) depth. Each data is separated by 100 ms. z-score is used to normalize each dimension. More specifically, we use the last 12 of seconds data to normalize the current data. Handcrafted features are calculated based on basic price and volume. We divide the dataset into three classes with equal proportions and get 3 prediction horizons (10, 20, 50).

4.3   Results

In this section, many experiments are conducted to evaluate the performance of our model. We compare our model with traditional machine learning methods and new deep learning methods. We use accuracy, precision, recall, and F1 score as our metrics. Since the FI-2010 dataset is unbalanced, we follow the suggestion by Ntakaris et al. [11] to use the F1 score as the primary metrics on the FI-2010 datset. We also provide an ablation study to prove and understand the effectiveness of every part of our model.

Results on FI-2010. We use a common division method used in [16–18,20] to evaluate our model. We use first 7 days to train and validate our model, and select the best model on validation dataset to test on the last 3 days. For the training process, we use the first 80% data for training, the rest 20% data for validation. We compare our model with SVM [17], MLP [17], CII-I [16], LSTM [17], C(TABL) [15], DeepLOB [20], MTDNN [8] and SRGRU [9]. Table 2 shows the results on FI-2010.

In Table 2, we can see our model CNN-GRU can achieve the best performance in all prediction horizons. It suggests that CNN-GRU can capture and express the latent features better. Unlike CNN-I, CNN-II, and DeepLOB, we combine ask features and bid features later in the model, which shows a better effect. Compared with SRGRU on the F1 score, our results have a maximum improvement of about 5%, which is difficult in the financial domain.

Table 2. Results on FI-2010

Model	Accuracy (%)	Precision (%)	Recall (%)	F1-score (%)
Prediction horizon k = 10				
SVM	-	39.62	44.92	35.88
MLP	-	47.81	60.78	48.27
CNN-I	-	50.98	65.54	55.21
LSTM	-	60.77	75.92	66.33
C(TABL)	84.70	76.95	78.44	77.63
DeepLOB	84.47	84.00	84.47	83.40
SRGRU	86.76	86.24	86.76	86.83
CNN-GRU	87.80	87.35	87.80	**87.35**
Prediction horizon k = 20				
SVM	-	45.08	47.77	43.20
MLP	-	51.33	65.20	51.12
CNN-I	-	54.79	67.38	59.17
LSTM	-	59.60	70.52	62.37
C(TABL)	73.74	67.18	66.94	66.93
DeepLOB	74.85	74.06	74.85	72.82
SRGRU	84.25	83.81	84.25	83.48
CNN-GRU	88.55	88.52	88.55	**88.53**
Prediction horizon k = 30				
CNN-I	67.98	66.52	67.98	65.72
DeepLOB	76.36	76.00	76.36	75.33
SRGRU	85.83	85.56	85.83	85.58
CNN-GRU	89.09	89.06	89.09	**89.07**
Prediction horizon k = 50				
SVM	-	46.05	60.30	49.42
MLP	-	55.21	67.14	55.95
CNN-I	-	55.58	67.12	59.44
LSTM	-	60.03	68.58	61.43
C(TABL)	79.87	79.05	77.04	78.44
DeepLOB	80.51	80.38	80.51	80.35
MTDNN	81.12	-	-	81.05
SRGRU	86.43	86.34	86.43	86.36
CNN-GRU	89.37	89.40	89.37	**89.38**
Prediction Horizon k = 100				
CNN-I	64.87	65.51	64.87	65.05
DeepLOB	76.72	76.85	76.72	76.76
SRGRU	83.25	83.41	83.25	83.30
CNN-GRU	88.45	88.47	88.45	**88.46**

Results on BTC-2021. We use the first 80% data to train and validate models and the last 20% data to test models. We select DeepLOB and SRGRu as comparison objects because they can achieve a bit better results on FI-2010 than other models. We use the source codes provided by the authors to train all models.

Results are presented in Table 3. Our model CNN-GRU achieves the best performance when the prediction horizon is 10 and 20. When the prediction horizon is 10, CNN-GRU achieves the highest accuracy, 61.19%, and F1 score, 61.33%, and is the only model whose metrics exceed 60%. Although DeepLOB gets the best results when the prediction horizon is 50, it performs terribly on other prediction horizons. It also suggests that CNN-GRU can express features and make predictions better in most cases.

Table 3. Results on BTC-2021

Model	Accuracy (%)	Precision (%)	Recall (%)	F1-score (%)
Prediction horizon k = 10				
DeepLOB	48.17	47.65	48.17	46.90
SRGRU	59.29	59.09	59.29	58.73
CNN-GRU	61.19	61.67	61.19	**61.33**
Prediction horizon k = 20				
DeepLOB	41.45	42.28	41.45	33.81
SRGRU	52.44	52.05	52.44	51.68
CNN-GRU	53.15	53.37	53.15	**53.23**
Prediction horizon k = 50				
DeepLOB	49.28	49.26	49.28	**49.24**
SRGRU	46.61	46.37	46.61	45.96
CNN-GRU	46.21	46.43	46.21	44.29

Ablation Study. In order to explore and understand which part of the model plays a role, we conduct detailed experiments by simplifying some parts of the CNN-GRU model. We use three variants of CNN-GRU to test the effect of every part. First of all, in order to prove the superiority of representing ask and bid features separately, we use the CNN module used by [20] to replace our two independent CNN modules. The CNN module used by [20] can process basic ask and bid input together. Moreover, due to changes in model structure, we only use a gating function in this variant model and cancel the subtraction between features. We name it Variant-1. We also design a variant model to test the performance of the gating mechanism. Instead of gating functions, we use addition to integrate independent features and market state features. We call it Variant-2. We also test the effect of the temporal attention module. In Variant-3, we use the average features of all time steps instead of the results of the temporal attention mechanism. We train all models on the first 7 days of the FI-2010 dataset and test on the last 3 days of the FI-2010 dataset. The prediction horizon is 20 and 100 in this part. Table 4 shows the comparison results.

Table 4. Results of ablation study

Model	Accuracy (%)	Precision (%)	Recall (%)	F1-score (%)
Prediction horizon k = 20				
Variant-1	84.23	85.20	84.23	84.51
Variant-2	85.23	85.62	85.23	85.31
Variant-3	86.02	85.77	86.02	85.84
CNN-GRU	88.55	88.52	88.55	**88.53**
Prediction horizon k = 100				
Variant-1	86.07	86.08	86.07	86.08
Variant-2	86.62	86.70	86.62	86.65
Variant-3	86.66	86.78	86.66	86.49
CNN-GRU	88.45	88.47	88.45	**88.46**

From the results of Variant-1, we can see that representing the independent ask and bid features does make models work better. This suggests that we can not simply process ask and bid data together, which may destroy the representation of the features of both sides. And fine-grained representation of LOB data helps us improve models' expression and prediction ability.

The results of Variant-2 demonstrate the ability of the gating mechanism. Using simple addition to integrate independent features and market state can not reflect the exact impact of the market state on both buyers and sellers. And the gating mechanism can determine the degree of market influence according to the changes in independent ask and bid features. This is a critical thought in our model.

And Variant-3 shows the importance of the temporal attention mechanism. Average addition leads to the loss of information in important time steps. Thus, we consider using the temporal attention mechanism to solve the problem, and it does work.

5   Conclusion

In this paper, we propose a novel multi-scale convolution and GRU based deep learning model to predict the future trend of LOB data. It can represent ask and bid features, respectively and add the impact of the market state on both sides. And we carefully design different network structures according to the characteristics of input data types. Experiments on the FI-2010 dataset and BTC-2021 dataset show that our model can achieve state-of-the-art performance, suggesting that our model can better extract and represent features.

References

1. Ariyo, A.A., Adewumi, A.O., Ayo, C.K.: Stock price prediction using the Arima model. In: 2014 UKSim-AMSS 16th International Conference on Computer Modelling and Simulation, pp. 106–112. IEEE (2014)
2. Bai, S., Kolter, J.Z., Koltun, V.: An empirical evaluation of generic convolutional and recurrent networks for sequence modeling. arXiv preprint arXiv:1803.01271 (2018)
3. Cho, K., et al.: Learning phrase representations using RNN encoder-decoder for statistical machine translation. arXiv preprint arXiv:1406.1078 (2014)
4. Hochreiter, S., Schmidhuber, J.: Long short-term memory. Neural Comput. **9**(8), 1735–1780 (1997)
5. Hu, Z., Liu, W., Bian, J., Liu, X., Liu, T.Y.: Listening to chaotic whispers: a deep learning framework for news-oriented stock trend prediction. In: Proceedings of the Eleventh ACM International Conference on Web Search and Data Mining, pp. 261–269 (2018)
6. Kercheval, A.N., Zhang, Y.: Modelling high-frequency limit order book dynamics with support vector machines. Quant. Financ. **15**(8), 1315–1329 (2015)
7. LeCun, Y., Bengio, Y., et al.: Convolutional networks for images, speech, and time series. Handb. Brain Theory Neural Netw. **3361**(10), 1995 (1995)
8. Liu, G., et al.: Multi-scale two-way deep neural network for stock trend prediction. In: IJCAI, pp. 4555–4561 (2020)
9. Lv, X., Zhang, L.: Residual gated recurrent unit-based stacked network for stock trend prediction from limit order book. In: Qiu, H., Zhang, C., Fei, Z., Qiu, M., Kung, S.-Y. (eds.) KSEM 2021. LNCS (LNAI), vol. 12816, pp. 351–363. Springer, Cham (2021). https://doi.org/10.1007/978-3-030-82147-0_29
10. Maas, A.L., Hannun, A.Y., Ng, A.Y., et al.: Rectifier nonlinearities improve neural network acoustic models. In: Proceedings of ICML, vol. 30, p. 3. Citeseer (2013)
11. Ntakaris, A., Magris, M., Kanniainen, J., Gabbouj, M., Iosifidis, A.: Benchmark dataset for mid-price forecasting of limit order book data with machine learning methods. J. Forecast. **37**(8), 852–866 (2018)
12. Özyar, M.I.: Learning the Limit Order Book: a comprehensive mix between stochastic and machine learning models for generation and prediction. Master's thesis, Delft University of Technology (2021)
13. Patel, J., Shah, S., Thakkar, P., Kotecha, K.: Predicting stock and stock price index movement using trend deterministic data preparation and machine learning techniques. Expert Syst. Appl. **42**(1), 259–268 (2015)
14. Szegedy, C., et al.: Going deeper with convolutions. In: Proceedings of the IEEE Conference on Computer Vision and Pattern Recognition, pp. 1–9 (2015)
15. Tran, D.T., Iosifidis, A., Kanniainen, J., Gabbouj, M.: Temporal attention-augmented bilinear network for financial time-series data analysis. IEEE Trans. Neural Netw. Learn. Syst. **30**(5), 1407–1418 (2018)
16. Tsantekidis, A., Passalis, N., Tefas, A., Kanniainen, J., Gabbouj, M., Iosifidis, A.: Forecasting stock prices from the limit order book using convolutional neural networks. In: 2017 IEEE 19th Conference on Business Informatics (CBI), vol. 1, pp. 7–12. IEEE (2017)
17. Tsantekidis, A., Passalis, N., Tefas, A., Kanniainen, J., Gabbouj, M., Iosifidis, A.: Using deep learning to detect price change indications in financial markets. In: 2017 25th European Signal Processing Conference (EUSIPCO), pp. 2511–2515. IEEE (2017)

18. Tsantekidis, A., Passalis, N., Tefas, A., Kanniainen, J., Gabbouj, M., Iosifidis, A.: Using deep learning for price prediction by exploiting stationary limit order book features. Appl. Soft Comput. **93**, 106401 (2020)
19. Wallbridge, J.: Transformers for limit order books. arXiv preprint arXiv:2003.00130 (2020)
20. Zhang, Z., Zohren, S., Roberts, S.: DeepLOB: deep convolutional neural networks for limit order books. IEEE Trans. Sig. Process. **67**(11), 3001–3012 (2019)
21. Zhou, H., et al.: Informer: beyond efficient transformer for long sequence time-series forecasting. In: Proceedings of AAAI (2021)
22. Zivot, E., Wang, J.: Vector autoregressive models for multivariate time series. In: Modeling Financial Time Series with S-Plus®, pp. 385–429 (2006)

Pre-train Unified Knowledge Graph Embedding with Ontology

Tengwei Song⬤, Jie Luo$^{(\boxtimes)}$⬤, and Xiangyu Chen

State Key Laboratory of Software Development Environment,
School of Computer Science and Engineering, Beihang University,
Beijing, China
{songtengwei,luojie,xiangyu_chen}@buaa.edu.cn

Abstract. Existing knowledge graph embedding models mainly focus on a single task, such as link prediction or entity typing, which actually cannot ensure the generalization capability of the model. Recent research shows that introducing additional ontology information can naturally convert the entity typing task to a specific case of link prediction between the instance and ontology layers. However, the unbalanced scale of the two layers brings difficulty for learning. To this end, we pre-train the knowledge graph embedding on the instance and schema layers of KG respectively on the basis of Rot-Pro, a model that is capable to express the transitivity relation pattern occurred in class hierarchy of the ontology. Furthermore, we construct a dataset by integrating entity type and class hierarchy information based on YAGO3 for evaluating the model efficiency on both link prediction and entity typing tasks. Experimental result shows that our model provided a unified and effective approach for both tasks.

Keywords: Knowledge graph · Representation learning · Embedding

1 Introduction

Knowledge graph (KG) depicts various instances and concepts that exist in the real world, as well as the relations between them. In order to enable the structured data in KGs to be modeled and learned by machine, most existing knowledge graph embedding (KGE) methods [1,10,12] dedicate to propose various machine learning strategies to convert the instances information into continuous vectors for link prediction tasks, which intends to predicting the missing/new facts in KGs.

Meanwhile, many KGs also suffer from incomplete entity types [2]. Entity type information is one of the inherent attributes of the entity and represents the semantic category to which the entity belongs. In order to further predicting the missing entity type information in KGs, previous work [15] developed model that map the entities to entity type space and performed well on certain entity

© The Author(s), under exclusive license to Springer Nature Switzerland AG 2022
G. Memmi et al. (Eds.): KSEM 2022, LNAI 13368, pp. 85–92, 2022.
https://doi.org/10.1007/978-3-031-10983-6_7

typing benchmarks. However, they pay less attention to finding a unified embedding that is capable of handling both tasks hence causing poor generalization performance on other tasks.

To solve this issue, we concentrate on the schema layer of KGs, which is also commonly referred to as ontology. The schema layer of a KG contains the definitions and relationships of concepts based on description logic, including the semantic hierarchy between classes or the type information between entities and classes. Similar to the idea of ETE [2], we simply convert the entity typing task to the link prediction task between the instance layer and schema layer by uniformly considering the link between two layers as a single relation *rdfs:type*, because the ontology naturally contains the class information of entities. However, there exists a problem of embedding the two layers uniformly because the scale of schema is far smaller than that of instance. One feasible solution is to train the embedding of instance and ontology separately for preparation of entity typing task [5]. Therefore, a new KGE model can be proposed by pre-training a base KGE model on two layers simultaneously to learn an initial representations and then fine-tune the model with intra layer data. The pre-train process has two benefits: (1) Learning representations independently alleviate the unbalanced scale of two layers. (2) Speed up the convergence for the whole model.

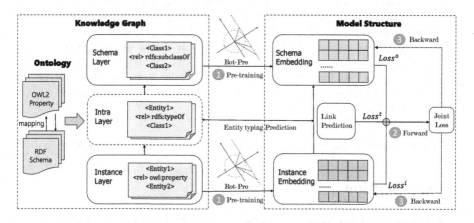

Fig. 1. The structure of PEMO. A complete KG can be regarded as a three layer graph after incorporating the OWL property and RDF schema. PEMO first uses the Rot-Pro model for pre-training the embedding of schema layer and instance layer separately. Then the entity typing task can be uniformly treated as link prediction by regarding the relation between the two layers as rdfs:type.

Furthermore, to capture more relation patterns of schema layer, we choose Rot-Pro [10] as our base model, which is a recent KGE model that is capable of modeling five common relation patterns especially transitivity. We illustrate that the Rot-Pro model is suitable for modeling class hierarchy and demonstrate that it could be extended to embed the two layers of KGs as well as conducting link prediction and entity typing tasks within or between layers.

Hence we present PEMO, a **Pre-Train KG Embedding Model with O**ntology. To evaluate the effectiveness of PEMO, we conduct link prediction and entity typing tasks on a large-scale knowledge graph dataset to empirically study the generalization capability of the model.

2   Related Work on Entity Typing Task

KGE Models for Link Prediction Task. Most work focus on instance layer alone for regarding relations as a specific transformation according to its property. Translation-based models as TransE [1], TransH [13], TransR [14], and TransD [4] assumes the added embedding of subject entity and relation should be close to the embedding of object entity in the same space or transformed spaces. RotatE [12] consider a relation as a rotation from head entity to tail while Rot-Pro [10] considers it as projection on entities and a additional rotation from head entity to tail for capturing transitive relation patterns.

KGE Models for Entity Typing Task. Previous models such as LM and PEM [8]. Introduced entity classification task into KGE by constructing a large-scale dataset and designing an evaluation methodology. The problem of this work is ignoring the global triples which plays an important role in KGs. To address this problem, ETE [2] embeds entity types close to their entities and achieved higher accuracy for inferring missing entity types. Recently, ConnectE [15] thought that the method of embedding entities and entity categories into the same space was irrational, and build two distinct knowledge-driven type inference mechanisms. For universal representations of KGs, JOIE [5] designed a mechanism to categorize KGs as an instance view and ontology view, and designed a specified mapping method by assuming that any instances are close to their corresponding concept in the same space, or in the transformed space.

3   Background and Methodology

A complete KG consists of a schema (or ontology) as well as a set of instances, which can be denoted as $\mathcal{G} = (\mathcal{O}, \mathcal{I})$. The schema of KG is an ontology specified in description languages such as RDF schema (RDFS) or OWL2 RL [3].

However, in general KGs, the scale of ontologies is far smaller than that of instances, i.e., $|\mathcal{O}| \ll |\mathcal{I}|$. Furthermore, the schema layer in KGs is generally sparse, i.e., there are only a few relations in the ontology. The instance layer in KGs tends to be denser and contains more relations. This results in unbalanced information between the two layers, which also limits the ability to discover new relation instances between layers.

3.1   Rot-Pro Model

Rot-Pro is a recent KGE model build on instance layer [10]. Rot-Pro models transitivity relation pattern as projection translation simultaneously on both head and tail entity in complex space to ensure that the entities in the transitive chain transfer after n times is equivalent to transfer once. Rot-Pro further conducts a rotation operation after the projection to make the model support other common relation patterns, which are symmetry, asymmetry, inversion, composition. The scoring function of Rot-Pro is defined as:

$$f_r(\mathbf{e}_h, \mathbf{e}_t) = -\|rot(p_r(\mathbf{e}_h), \theta_r) - p_r(\mathbf{e}_t)\|, \tag{1}$$

where p_r is the projection operation on an entity with additional learnable parameter to decide whether non-trivial projection should be performed before rotation and rot is the rotation operation with the relational rotation phase θ_r.

4 Method

To resolve the problem of unbalanced scale between layers that mentioned above, we train the Rot-Pro model simultaneously on both the schema and instance layers to obtain the pre-trained embedding of entities, classes and relations. The pre-train process is illustrated as step 1 in Fig. 1.

Generally, an arbitrary KGE model which could handle the triplet instance is feasible to learn the representation within each layer. However, considering the class hierarchy exists in schema layer as well as the intra layer type relation, we try to find a proper KGE model that is capable of modeling the main relation patterns occurred in class hierarchy. We discovered that there exist two specific relation patterns in the schema layer and the intra layer, which are illustrated in Table 1. Therefore, to better fit the relational properties in KG, we choose the Rot-Pro model having considered the different relation patterns *within* and *between* layers.

Table 1. Main relation patterns occurred in schema and intra layers.

Layer	Pattern	Rule form
Schema	Transitivity	$r(c_1, c_2) \wedge r(c_2, c_3) \Rightarrow r(c_1, c_3)$
Intra	Composition	$r_1(e_1, c_1) \wedge r_2(c_1, c_2) \Rightarrow r_1(e_1, c_2)$

4.1 Relation Patterns Within Each Layer

The main relational property in schema layer is the class hierarchy, which in fact, essentially exhibits transitivity relation pattern. For example, given two instances on a class hierarchy chain *(Singer, subClassOf, Artist)* and *(Artist, subClassOf, Person)*, it can be inferred that *(Singer, subClassOf, Person)*. Other geometric based KGE models could not model such transitivity pattern, since its special topological property.

It is proved by Rot-Pro that it could model all five common relation patterns in instance layer [10], we focus on analyzing the expressiveness of Rot-Pro on schema layer.

4.2   Relation Patterns Between Layers

The relation between the schema and instance layers is essentially a special case of composition relation pattern, in which the result of composition is also one of the relations being composited. For example, given *(Honolulu, type, City)* and *(City, subClassOf, Place)*, there should exist a fact *(Honolulu, type, Place)*.

According to the analysis of the relational property within schema layer, we proved that Rot-Pro can also model the special case of composition relation pattern, by substituting the conditions in composition rule form in Table 1 into Eq. (1):

$$\begin{cases} p_r(c_1) = rot(p_r(e_1), \theta_{r_1}), \\ p_r(c_2) = rot(p_r(c_1), \theta_{r_2}). \end{cases}$$

That is: $p_r(c_2) = rot(rot(p_r(e_1), \theta_{r_1}), \theta_{r_2})$. When θ_{r_2} equals to 2π, we further got $p_r(c_2) = rot(p_r(e_1), \theta_{r_1})$, which satisfies the scoring function of Equation (1). Thus, (e_1, r_1, c_2) holds.

Therefore, it is proved that it is also capable to model relation patterns between layers by Rot-Pro.

4.3   Optimization Objective

To ensure the generalization capability of PEMO across two tasks, we conduct negative sampling on three layers respectively and integrate a weighted joint loss for fine-tuning the model. The optimization process is illustrated in step 2 and 3 in Fig. 1.

Let us denote the loss of schema layer as $\mathcal{L}_o$; the loss of instance layer as $\mathcal{L}_i$ and loss of the intra layer as $\mathcal{L}_t$. By combining all the three part of losses, the unified joint loss $\mathcal{L}_j$ is defined as follows:

$$\mathcal{L}_J = \mathcal{L}_o + \alpha_1 \cdot \mathcal{L}_i + \alpha_2 \cdot \mathcal{L}_t \qquad (2)$$

where α_1 and α_2 are hyper-parameters for tuning the weights between three losses. $\mathcal{L}_{o,i,t}$ is the negative sampling loss with self-adversarial training defined in [10, 12].

5   Experiment

5.1   Datasets

To integrate the instance layer with ontology, JOIE [5] proposed two datasets: YAGO26K-906 and DB111K-174, which are extracted from YAGO [11] and DBpedia [9] respectively. However, we find there are several problems on the datasets. First, there is duplicated data in testing set from training set. Second, there exist incorrect ontology information, such as: *wordnet_city_108524735 isa wordnet_book_106410904*.

For better evaluating the KGE methods, we constructed a new dataset, YAGO3-1668K which integrated both entity types (classes) and class hierarchy information based on the following three parts of YAGO3 [6]:

- YAGO3-10 instances, which is a commonly used benchmark in the field of KGE on instance layer.
- *YAGOTypes*, which contains the types of entities in YAGO3. Each entity may belong to multiple types, which are connected by relation *rdfs:type*. Entity types in WordNet [7] format are more abstract, and the ones in Wikipedia format contain a large number of restrictive attributes, which is more specific in semantics.
- *YAGOTaxonomy*, which mainly describes the relationship between type data of YAGO3, which is connected by relation *rdfs:subClassOf*.

Concretely, for the entity set of YAGO3-10, we extract the corresponding entity types from the *YAGOTypes*, and for each entity type, we further find its parent class in *YAGOTaxonomy*. We construct the schema layer manually by adding each parent class on the searching path which is connected by relation *rdfs:subClassOf*. The statistics of the datasets are showed in Table 2.

Table 2. Statistics of YAGO3-1668K.

	#Ent	#Type	#Rel	#Train	#Valid	#Test
Instance layer	123,182	0	37	1,079,040	5,000	5,000
Schema layer	0	1,492	1	4,574	538	550
Intra-layer	112,260	1,086	1	458,925	57,355	57,357

5.2   Experimental Settings

Implementation Details. Most of the hyper-parameters in training are consistent with those given by RotatE and Rot-Pro for YAGO3-10. In addition, in order to adapt to the new task, we also try the following hyper-parameters settings, including: the embedding dimension $d \in \{200, 500, 1000\}$, learning rate $l \in \{0.00001, 0.000005, 0.000001\}$, margin $\gamma \in \{12.0, 16.0, 24.0\}$, adversarial temperature $a \in \{1.0, 1.5\}$; the proportion of $\alpha_1{:}\alpha_2 \in \{1{:}1, 1{:}2, 1{:}3, 1{:}5, 1{:}6, 1{:}8\}$.

Baseline Models. We conduct a similar pre-train process on another two KGE models focused on instance layer, which are TransE [1] and RotatE [12]. The unified embedding methods on the basis of TransE and RotatE are denoted as **TransE-pe** and **RotatE-pe** respectively.

Furthermore, to validate the effectiveness of the pre-train process, we built a baseline model as **PEMO-base**, which learns the representation on the whole YAGO3-1668K dataset without pre-train, i.e., using the whole triples among three layers as training data and let the model learn the final representations.

Evaluation Protocol. By treating entity typing uniformly as link prediction, we follow the evaluation protocol of link prediction of previous work [1,10]. All the models are evaluated in a *filtered* setting, i.e., corrupted triples that appear in training, validation, or test sets are removed during ranking. The valid triple and filtered corrupted triples are ranked in ascending order based on their prediction scores. We evaluate the PEMO and baseline models on three common evaluation metrics: mean reciprocal rank (MRR), and top-k Hit Ratio (Hit@k). Higher MRR or Hit@k and lower MR indicate better performance.

5.3 Experimental Results

Table 3 show the results on three KG layers respectively. The best results are bold-faced. We can see from the results that the performance of PEMO is generally better than baseline models among three tasks, which demonstrates the generalization capability of PEMO. Furthermore, according to the ablation study between PEMO-base and PEMO, it empirically illustrates that the pre-train process indeed benefits the unified embedding. Similarly, the outperformance of PEMO over other pre-train models also coincides with our conjecture that Rot-Pro is effective on expressing class hierarchy.

Table 3. Link prediction results of PEMO as well as baseline models on schema layer and entity typing results on intra layer.

		MRR	MR	Hit@1	Hit@3	Hit@10
Instance layer	TransE-pe	0.471	**928**	36.9	53.6	65.2
	RotatE-pe	0.467	935	37.4	51.8	64.4
	PEMO-base	0.540	1417	**46.3**	59.5	68.5
	PEMO	**0.541**	1206	45.5	**59.9**	**69.9**
Schema layer	TransE-pe	0.471	**928**	36.9	53.6	65.2
	RotatE-pe	0.467	935	37.4	51.8	64.4
	PEMO-base	0.540	1417	**46.3**	59.5	68.5
	PEMO	**0.541**	1206	45.5	**59.9**	**69.9**
Intra layer	TransE-pe	0.587	7.6	42.5	70.4	88.0
	RotatE-pe	0.589	6.8	42.6	70.8	**88.6**
	PEMO-base	0.598	7.3	44.0	71.1	88.0
	PEMO	**0.612**	**6.5**	**46.3**	**71.8**	88.2

6   Conclusion

We proposed PEMO, a pre-train unified knowledge graph embedding model with ontology. PEMO dedicated to extending the model generalization across link prediction and entity typing tasks by introducing joint loss from three layers of KG on the basis of Rot-Pro, a KGE method which was capable of modeling the relation patterns occurred in class hierarchy and entity typing. Experimental result showed that PEMO had empirical generalization capability on both link prediction and entity typing tasks.

Acknowledgement. This work was supported by the National Key R&D Program of China (Grant No. 2021ZD0112901).

References

1. Bordes, A., Usunier, N., Garcia-Duran, A., Weston, J., Yakhnenko, O.: Translating embeddings for modeling multi-relational data. In: Advances in Neural Information Processing Systems, vol. 26, pp. 2787–2795 (2013)
2. Chang Moon, P.J., Samatova, N.F.: Learning entity type embeddings for knowledge graph completion. In: Proceedings of CIKM, p. 2215–2218 (2017)
3. Group, W.O.W.: Owl 2 Web Ontology Language Document Overview, 2nd edn. W3C Recommendation 11 December 2012 (2012)
4. Ji, G., He, S., Xu, L., Liu, K., Zhao, J.: Knowledge graph embedding via dynamic mapping matrix. In: Proceedings of the 53rd Annual Meeting of the Association for Computational Linguistics and the 7th International Joint Conference on Natural Language Processing, pp. 687–696 (2015)
5. Hao, J., Chen, M., Yu, W., Sun, Y., Wang, W.: Universal representation learning of knowledge bases by jointly embedding instances and ontological concepts. In: Proceedings of the 25th ACM SIGKDD International Conference on Knowledge Discovery and Data Mining. KDD 2019, pp. 1709–1719 (2019)
6. Mahdisoltani, F., Biega, J., Suchanek, F.M.: Yago3: a knowledge base from multilingual Wikipedias. In: Proceedings of CIDR 2015 (2015)
7. Miller, G.A.: WordNet: a lexical database for English. Commun. ACM **38**(11), 39–41 (1995)
8. Neelakantan, A., Chang, M.W.: Inferring missing entity type instances for knowledge base completion: new dataset and methods (2015)
9. Auer, S., Bizer, C., Kobilarov, G., Lehmann, J., Cyganiak, R., Ives, Z.: DBpedia: a nucleus for a web of open data. In: The Semantic Web, pp. 722–735 (2007)
10. Song, T., Luo, J., Huang, L.: Rot-Pro: modeling transitivity by projection in knowledge graph embedding. In: Proceedings of the Thirty-Fifth Annual Conference on Advances in Neural Information Processing Systems (NeurIPS) (2021)
11. Suchanek, F.M., Kasneci, G., Weikum, G.: Yago: a core of semantic knowledge. In: Proceedings of the 16th International Conference on World Wide Web, pp. 697–706 (2007)
12. Sun, Z., Deng, Z.H., Nie, J.Y., Tang, J.: Rotate: knowledge graph embedding by relational rotation in complex space. In: International Conference on Learning Representations (2019)
13. Wang, Z., Zhang, J., Feng, J., Chen, Z.: Knowledge graph embedding by translating on hyperplanes. In: AAAI Conference on Artificial Intelligence (2014)
14. Lin, Y., Liu, Z., Sun, M., Liu, Y., Zhu, X.: Learning entity and relation embeddings for knowledge graph completion. In: Proceedings of the 29th AAAI Conference on Artificial Intelligence, pp. 2181–2187 (2015)
15. Zhao, Y., Zhang, A., Xie, R., Liu, K., Wang, X.: Connecting embeddings for knowledge graph entity typing. In: Proceedings of the 58th Annual Meeting of the Association for Computational Linguistics, pp. 6419–6428. Association for Computational Linguistics, Online, July 2020. https://www.aclweb.org/anthology/2020.acl-main.572

Improving Dialogue Generation with Commonsense Knowledge Fusion and Selection

Dongjun Fu[1], Chunhong Zhang[2(✉)], Jibin Yu[1], Qi Sun[2], and Zhiqiang Zhan[1]

[1] State Key Laboratory of Networking and Switching Technology,
Beijing University of Posts and Telecommunications, Beijing 100876, China
{fudongjun,yujibin,zqzhan}@bupt.edu.cn
[2] Key Laboratory of Universal Wireless Communications, Ministry of Education,
Beijing University of Posts and Telecommunications, Beijing 100876, China
{zhangch,qisun}@bupt.edu.cn

Abstract. Knowledge-aware dialogue generation aims to generate informative and meaningful responses with external knowledge. Existing works are still insufficient to encode retrieved knowledge regardless of the dialogue context, which probably leads to the introduction of irrelevant information. In this paper, we propose a dialogue generation model named CKFS-DG, which filters out context-irrelevant and off-topic knowledge to reduce the influence of redundant knowledge. Specifically, we design a knowledge-enriched encoder and a topic fact predictor to improve the quality of fusion knowledge. For achieve the knowledge-enriched encoder, we put forward a context-knowledge attention mechanism to dynamically filter out irrelevant knowledge conditioned on context. For the topic fact predictor, we utilize the probability distribution on retrieved facts to retain on-topic knowledge. The experimental results on English Reddit and Chinese Weibo dataset demonstrate that CKFS-DG outperforms the state-of-the-art neural generative methods in knowledge utilization, and CKFS-DG could reduce the influence of irrelevant knowledge to generate reasonable responses.

Keywords: Dialogue generation · Knowledge aware · Knowledge selection · Attention mechanism · Topic prediction

1 Introduction

The open-domain dialogue generation task is designed to generate a reasonable response for a given post. However, different from a human, a machine can merely extract limited information from the post and cannot associate the dialogue with background knowledge [1]. Consequently, it is difficult for a machine to completely comprehend the post and thus generate diverse and informative response. To address this problem, some prior studies begin to enhance the performance of dialogue generation by external knowledge [2]. In recent years,

G. Memmi et al. (Eds.): KSEM 2022, LNAI 13368, pp. 93–108, 2022.
https://doi.org/10.1007/978-3-031-10983-6_8

many researches integrate commonsense knowledge graphs as additional representations, and generate responses conditioned on both the post and the extra knowledge.

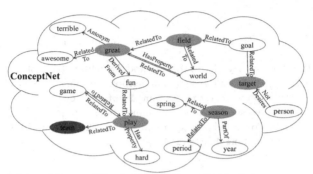

Post: that would be great if they had to play at target field the first season .
Ground-truth Response: its about time a mn team won there .
Generated Response 1 : well that would be a great idea . and that 's pretty awesome
Generated Response 2 : well , if the hawks had to play at target , they 'd be a great team .

Fig. 1. An example of dialogue generation, including a post-response pair and retrieved facts from knowledge graph based on the entity words (orange words) in the post. The fact whose tail entity (blue words) appears in the truth response is the golden fact. The two generated responses are given without/with considering the topic of the dialogue. (Color figure online)

To fully leverage the retrieved facts, Seq2Seq [3] framework with knowledge-aware mechanism is proposed to integrate the retrieved facts in encoder and generator module [1,2]. In encoder module, retrieved knowledge facts are encoded into additional semantic representation, which facilitates the understanding of the post. In generator module, retrieved facts are read as one of the word sources for response generation. However, most frameworks to retrieve knowledge facts do not consider specific dialogue context, which probably results in introducing noise in knowledge integration. On the one hand, some candidate facts retrieved by off-topic entity words in the post may be redundant. As illustrated in Fig. 1, generated response 1 is generic because the model focuses on the entity "great", and generated response 2 is relatively reasonable because of noting "play" that is the topic of this dialogue. Obviously, topic entities are essential and retrieved facts through them may be more meaningful for developing conversation [4]. On the other hand, an entity may have multiple meanings, but only one specific meaning is involved in a particular context. Some retrieved knowledge facts based on the multi-meaning entity can be irrelevant to the current dialogue [5]. If irrelevant facts are encoded in knowledge integration, it might introduce redundant information for response generation. Therefore, we argue that it will be necessary to fuse relevant knowledge facts in post representation and select appropriate topic facts in response generation.

To address the aforementioned challenges, in this paper, we propose CKFS-DG (a model for dialogue generation with **C**ommonsense **K**nowledge **F**usion and **S**election) based on the Seq2Seq framework with two major knowledge-aware components, (1) a *knowledge-enriched encoder* that fuses filtered knowledge as additional semantic representation of the post, and (2) a *topic fact predictor* that predicts topic entities and facts, which facilitates the selection of appropriate knowledge facts for response generation. The motivation to design the knowledge-enriched encoder is to enhance the semantic of the post by combining relevant knowledge representations. Contextual knowledge attention mechanism is designed as a filter to dynamically filter out irrelevant knowledge based on the contextual vector of the post. For selecting appropriate topic facts, topic fact predictor is introduced to generate topic fact probability distribution over the retrieved facts, whose probability is adopted to guide word selection in response generation. We evaluate CKFS-DG on English Reddit and Chinese Weibo dataset [5] to demonstrate its effectiveness over the state-of-the-art dialogue generation methods. Our contributions are summarized as follows:

- We propose a knowledge-enriched encoder with context-knowledge attention mechanism to dynamically filter out irrelevant knowledge and enhance the semantic of the post by combining external knowledge representations;
- We design a topic fact predictor to generate topic fact distributions over the retrieved facts, which facilitates accurate knowledge selection;
- Experiments on Reddit and Weibo demonstrate the effectiveness of the proposed method on benchmarks of knowledge-aware dialogue generation.

2   Related Works

Knowledge-aware dialogue generation aims to generate informative and meaningful responses with external knowledge, such as additional texts [6] or knowledge graphs [4,7]. CCM [2] first applies a large-scale commonsense knowledge graph to facilitate the generation of a response with one-hop graph attention mechanisms. Some studies consider that the multi-hop graph is likely to contain more informative knowledge [1,4]. However, these models encode all retrieved knowledge to a representation, ignoring that the retrieved knowledge may contain irrelevant information that are useless for dialogue generation.

Hence, knowledge selection module that could select the appropriate knowledge gains much attention in knowledge-aware dialogue generation [8]. Generally, existing methods for combining knowledge selection and response generation can be grouped into two categories: a joint way and a pipeline way [9]. The joint approaches integrate knowledge selection into the generation process, that consistently select knowledge related to the current decoding step [9,10]. The joint ways result in the decoder being designed more complexly. The pipeline approaches separate knowledge selection from generation [11,12]. Some studies adopt attention mechanism [13,14] to filler out irrelevant knowledge, but could not utilize the actual knowledge as supervised training. ConKADI [5] utilizes the posterior knowledge distribution over the retrieved facts to select felicitous facts for generation. However, these works hardly consider the role of topic entities for generating on-topic responses. Different from some works attempting to capture the topic in the dialogue [4,15], we predict topic words and facts based on posterior information in responses, that is proven useful for knowledge selection.

In this work, we adopt a pipeline approach to focus on the knowledge selection easily. Different from previous works, we design context-knowledge attention mechanism to filter out irrelevant knowledge based on context, and a topic fact predictor as posterior knowledge selection module for reducing the influence of irrelevant knowledge in dialogue generation.

3   Methodology

3.1   Task Formulation and Model Overview

Knowledge-aware dialogue generation is defined as given a post $X = (x_1, ..., x_n)$ and a set of candidate knowledge facts $F = \{f_1, f_2, .., f_N\}$ to generate a response $Y = (y_1, ..., y_m)$. The words in the post X can be divided into entity words and common words. Candidate facts are retrieved from knowledge graph based on the entity words in the post [2]. A candidate fact f_i is formally a triple $< h_i, r_i, t_i >$, including head entity, relation and tail entity. In particular, knowledge aware dialogue generation targets to generate a response which can not only express consistent semantics as the post, but also embody the entity words contained in the candidate knowledge facts explicitly. The goal of training is to maximize the posterior probability of generating the truth response $\sum_{(X,Y,F) \in \mathcal{D}} \frac{1}{|\mathcal{D}|} p(Y|X,F)$.

The overview of the proposed model is shown in Fig. 2, which is consists of four components. First, *Context Encoder* encodes an utterance into contextual representation. Second, *Knowledge-enriched Encoder* encodes the post by fusing the filtered knowledge. Context-knowledge attention mechanism is proposed to dynamically filter out irrelevant facts in word-level based on the context. Third, *Topic Fact Predictor* calculates the topic fact probability distributions over retrieved facts to guide the generation. Finally, *Response Generator* generates a response by selecting from vocabulary, entity words, and copied words.

3.2   Context Encoder

The context encoder extracts information from the utterance by encoding the sequence into contextual representations, with bi-directional GRU network [16]:

$$\begin{aligned}
\mathbf{h}_t^f &= GRU^f\left(\mathbf{h}_{t-1}^f, \mathbf{x}_t, \mathbf{e}_{\mathbf{x}_t}\right) \\
\mathbf{h}_t^b &= GRU^b\left(\mathbf{h}_{t+1}^b, \mathbf{x}_t, \mathbf{e}_{\mathbf{x}_t}\right)
\end{aligned} \tag{1}$$

where $\mathbf{x}_t \in \mathbb{R}^K$ is the word embedding corresponding to x_t. To enhance semantics, we add the matched entity embedding vector $\mathbf{e}_{\mathbf{x}_t} \in \mathbb{R}^{d_e}$ of x_t, which will be a d_e-dimensional zero vector if x_t is a common word. The contextual state of the post is denoted as $H^x = (\mathbf{h}_1^x, ..., \mathbf{h}_n^x)$, and $\mathbf{h}_t^x = \left[\mathbf{h}_t^f; \mathbf{h}_t^b\right]$.

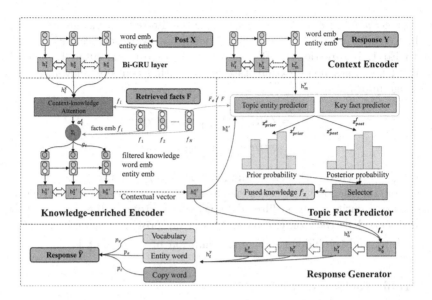

Fig. 2. Overall architecture of the proposed CKFS-DG. It contains four parts: Context Encoder, Knowledge-enriched Encoder, Topic Fact Predictor and Response Generator.

3.3   Knowledge-Enriched Encoder

The knowledge-enriched encoder is designed to encode the post by combining retrieved knowledge as additional semantic representations, which facilitates the understanding of a post. Apparently, as shown in Fig. 1, some preliminary retrieved knowledge facts may be irrelevant to the dialogue. Therefore, when using external knowledge to enhance context representation, it is necessary to filter out irrelevant knowledge based on the dialogue context.

Context-knowledge Attention Mechanism. We design the context-knowledge attention mechanism to dynamically filter out irrelevant knowledge in the word-level, inspired by previous works [14]. The major difference lies in that the context-knowledge attention mechanism generates filtered fact vector g_t^x for t-th word x_t in post, because each word may focus on different parts of the candidate facts. Formally, filtered fact vector is calculated:

$$g_t^x = \sum_{i=1}^{N} \alpha_i^t f_i, \alpha_i^t = softmax(\beta_i^t) \tag{2}$$

$$\beta_i^t = (\mathbf{W_h h_t^x})^\top \tanh(\mathbf{W_f f_i}) \tag{3}$$

where $f_i = [h_i; r_i; t_i] \in \mathbb{R}^{d_e+d_r+d_e}$ is the embedding vector of i-th fact. $\mathbf{W_h}$ and $\mathbf{W_k}$ are trainable. α_i^t is the attention weight that measures the relevance of the contextual state $\mathbf{h_t^x}$ and the fact f_i. Given contextual state $\mathbf{h_t^x}$, context-knowledge attention mechanism tries to discard the redundant parts of candidate facts, and remain relevant parts to form the filtered knowledge vector g_t^x.

Knowledge-Enriched Encoder. To better fuse the filtered knowledge, knowledge-enriched encoder encodes the post into knowledge-aware representation. Referring to Eq. 1, bi-directional GRU network reads post and filtered knowledge vector, then outputs a contextual state sequence that contains relevant external knowledge information:

$$
\begin{aligned}
\mathbf{h}_t^{f'} &= GRU^{f'}\left(\mathbf{h}_{t-1}^{f'}, \mathbf{x}_t, \mathbf{e}_{\mathbf{x}_t}, \boldsymbol{g}_t^x\right) \\
\mathbf{h}_t^{b'} &= GRU^{b'}\left(\mathbf{h}_{t+1}^{b'}, \mathbf{x}_t, \mathbf{e}_{\mathbf{x}_t}, \boldsymbol{g}_t^x\right)
\end{aligned}
\tag{4}
$$

where $\mathbf{e}_{\mathbf{x}_t}$ is matched entity embedding vector and $\boldsymbol{g}_t^x$ is filtered knowledge vector. In context encoding, the encoder encodes information from three aspects: word vectors, entity vectors, filtered knowledge vectors. After the knowledge-enriched encoder, the contextual state of the post is denoted as $H^{x'} = (\mathbf{h}_1^{x'}, ..., \mathbf{h}_n^{x'})$, and the hidden state representation $\mathbf{h}_t^{x'} = \left[\mathbf{h}_t^{f'}; \mathbf{h}_t^{b'}\right]$.

3.4 Topic Fact Predictor

Considering that some retrieved facts may be redundant for current dialogue, we select appropriate facts for generating responses via the topic fact predictor. The topic fact predictor mainly consists of topic entity predictor and key fact predictor. The topic entity predictor predicts distribution over entity words in the post, denoting the probability of an entity word becoming discussion topic. The key fact predictor is designed to predict distribution over candidate facts, meaning that the probability of a fact selected in response generation.

Topic Entity Predictor. The topic entity predictor infers the topic probability over entity words in the post. As seen in Fig. 1, candidate facts are retrieved by entity words such as "great" and "play". But "play" looks more like a discussion topic. The candidate facts retrieved through topic entity may be more useful for response generation. Inspired by teacher-student network [14], posterior knowledge selection takes the context and response as input and generates the posterior distribution $\mathbf{z}_{post}^e$ over entities as soft label. The prior distribution $\mathbf{z}_{prior}^e$ is trained to be close to the posterior, and generates without response as input:

$$
\begin{aligned}
\mathbf{z}_{post}^e &= softmax\left(tanh\left(\mathbf{F}_e \mathbf{W}_{post}^e\right) \cdot tanh\left(\left[\mathbf{h}_n^{x'}; \mathbf{h}_m^y\right] \mathbf{W}_{post}^{h,e}\right)^{\top}\right) \\
\mathbf{z}_{prior}^e &= softmax\left(tanh\left(\mathbf{F}_e \mathbf{W}_{prior}^e\right) \cdot tanh\left(\mathbf{h}_n^{x'} \mathbf{W}_{prior}^{h,e}\right)^{\top}\right)
\end{aligned}
\tag{5}
$$

where $\mathbf{F}_e \in \mathbb{R}^{|\mathcal{T}| \times d_e}$ is the embedding matrix of entity words in the post, and $\mathcal{T}$ is the set of entities. $\mathbf{W}_{post}^e, \mathbf{W}_{prior}^e, \mathbf{W}_{post}^{h,e}$ and $\mathbf{W}_{prior}^{h,e}$ are trainable parameters. *softmax* and *tanh* are activation functions. $\mathbf{h}_n^{x'}$ is the contextual representation of the post X obtained by the knowledge-enriched encoder and $\mathbf{h}_m^y$ is the contextual representation of the response Y obtained by the context encoder.

Key Fact Predictor. The key fact predictor selects the facts that highly coincide with the dialogue. Given the context and fact representation, the predictor outputs a probability distribution $\mathbf{z}^f$ over the F by feedforward neural networks:

$$
\begin{aligned}
\mathbf{z}_{\text{post}}^f &= softmax\left(tanh\left(\mathbf{F}\mathbf{W}_{\text{post}}^{\text{f}}\right) \cdot tanh\left(\left[\mathbf{h}_n^{x'}; \mathbf{h}_m^y\right]\mathbf{W}_{\text{post}}^{\text{h,f}}\right)^{\top}\right) \\
\mathbf{z}_{\text{prior}}^f &= softmax\left(tanh\left(\mathbf{F}\mathbf{W}_{\text{prior}}^{\text{f}}\right) \cdot tanh\left(\mathbf{h}_n^{x'}\mathbf{W}_{\text{prior}}^{\text{h,f}}\right)^{\top}\right)
\end{aligned}
\tag{6}
$$

where $\mathbf{F} \in \mathbb{R}^{N \times (d_e + d_r + d_e)}$ is the embedding matrix of candidate facts F. We calculate the probability distribution $\mathbf{z}^p$ of candidate facts:

$$
\mathbf{z}^p = \begin{cases} \lambda\mathbf{z}_{\text{post}}^e + (1-\lambda)\mathbf{z}_{\text{post}}^f & \text{if train} \\ \lambda\mathbf{z}_{\text{prior}}^e + (1-\lambda)\mathbf{z}_{\text{prior}}^f & \text{else} \end{cases}
\tag{7}
$$

where λ is a hyperparameter to control the contribution of distribution. $\mathbf{z}^p$ is used to calculate the topic fact representation: $\mathbf{f_z} = \mathbf{z}^p \cdot \mathbf{F}$.

The loss function of topic fact predictor consists of three parts: the Bag-of-Words (BoW) [17], Cross Entropy (CE) and Kullback-Leibler divergence (KLD) loss [18]. The purpose of the BoW loss is to measure the accuracy of contextual and topic fact vector to response generation. Meanwhile, the label $\mathbf{I}^e, \mathbf{I}^f$ are 0–1 indicator vectors to supervise the training of $\mathbf{z}_{\text{post}}^e$ and $\mathbf{z}_{\text{post}}^f$. $\mathbf{I}_i^e$ is either 1 or 0, denoting whether the i-th entity word in post is one of topic entities or not. $\mathbf{I}_i^f$ indicates whether the target entity in i-th facts is in the truth response or not. The labels are applied in CE loss. KLD loss is used to force prior distribution and posterior distribution to become as close as possible. Thus, the training objective of the key fact predictor module is to minimize a loss:

$$
\begin{aligned}
\mathcal{L}_p &= \mathcal{L}_{BoW} + \mathcal{L}_{CE}(\mathbf{z}_{\text{post}}^e, \mathbf{I_e}) + \mathcal{L}_{CE}(\mathbf{z}_{\text{post}}^f, \mathbf{I_f}) \\
&+ \mathcal{L}_{KLD}(\mathbf{z}_{\text{post}}^e, \mathbf{z}_{\text{prior}}^e) + \mathcal{L}_{KLD}(\mathbf{z}_{\text{post}}^f, \mathbf{z}_{\text{prior}}^f)
\end{aligned}
\tag{8}
$$

3.5 Response Generator

The response generator is used to generate the sentence conditioned on context and topic fact vector. Formally, the hidden states of decoder are computed:

$$
\mathbf{h}_t^y = GRU\left(\mathbf{h}_{t-1}^y, [\mathbf{u}_{t-1}; \mathbf{c}_{t-1}]\right)
\tag{9}
$$

where $\mathbf{u}_{t-1} = [\mathbf{y}_{t-1}; \mathbf{e}_{y_{t-1}}]$ connects word embedding and entity embedding of the last predicted token y_{t-1}; $\mathbf{c}_{t-1}$ is attentive context vector [19]; the initialization state of the decoder is $\mathbf{h}_0^y = \tanh([\mathbf{h}_n^{x'}; \mathbf{f_z}]\mathbf{W}_{\text{init}})$.

The current word y_t is generated by choosing from the vocabulary, entity words or copy words. Therefore, P_v, P_e, P_c are the probability distributions over vocabulary, entity words and copy words, respectively, calculated as follows:

$$P_v(y_t) = softmax(elu([\mathbf{h}_t^y; \mathbf{u}_{t-1}; \mathbf{c}_t]\mathbf{W}_{v_1})\mathbf{W}_{v_2})$$

$$P_e(y_t) = \gamma_t \mathbf{z}^p + (1 - \gamma_t)softmax(elu(\mathbf{FW}_{ef}) \cdot elu([\mathbf{h}_t^y; \mathbf{u}_{t-1}]\mathbf{W}_{et})^\top) \quad (10)$$

$$P_c(y_t) = softmax(elu(H^{x'}\mathbf{W}_{cx}) \cdot elu([\mathbf{h}_t^y; \mathbf{u}_{t-1}; \mathbf{c}_t]\mathbf{W}_{ct})^\top)$$

where $\mathbf{z}^p$ is topic fact distribution, calculated in topic fact predictor. $\gamma_t = $ sigmoid$([\mathbf{h}_t^y; \mathbf{u}_t; \mathbf{c}_t]\mathbf{W}_\gamma)$ is a gate to control the contribution of topic fact distribution. Next, we employ three selection gates to dynamically generate different kinds of words:

$$p(y_t) = \nu_t^v p_v(y_t) + \nu_t^e p_e(y_t) + \nu_t^c p_c(y_t) \quad (11)$$

$$\nu_t = [\nu_t^v, \nu_t^e, \nu_t^c] = softmax([\mathbf{h}_t^y; \mathbf{u}_{t-1}; \mathbf{c}_t]\mathbf{W}_p) \in \mathbb{R}^3 \quad (12)$$

where ν is the gate to control the contribution of three types of words. The loss function $\mathcal{L}_n$ of the generator module consists of two parts: the first part is the log-likelihood of the generated response; the second part is cross-entropy loss, which aims to supervise the gated prediction distribution:

$$\mathcal{L}_n = -\sum \log P(y_t \mid y_{t-1:1}, X, F) - \sum \mathbf{I}_t \cdot \log(\nu_t) \quad (13)$$

where $\mathbf{I}_t \in \mathbb{R}^3$ is a 0–1 indicator vector. For example, if t-th word in truth response is an entity word, $\mathbf{I}_t = [0, 1, 0]$. Finally, the overall loss to train CKFS-DG is computed: $\mathcal{L} = \mathcal{L}_n + \mathcal{L}_p$.

4   Experiments

4.1   Datasets

We conduct experiments on two large-scale dialogue datasets: English Reddit [2] and Chinese Weibo [5], which are open-domain single-round dialogue datasets. Both datasets are aligned with the commonsense knowledge graph ConcetNet[1]. The statistics of Reddit and Weibo dataset are provided in Table 1. The statistics table includes the number of dialogue pairs in training and test sets. Additionally, the number of candidate facts and the average number of facts per dialogue pair are included. Golden facts are the facts whose target entity appears in the response Y. According to statistics, each dialogue pair involves a large number of candidate facts and few golden facts, that makes it difficult to select appropriate facts for response generation.

---

[1] Available at: https://conceptnet.io.

Table 1. The statistics of knowledge-aware dialogue dataset Reddit and Weibo.

Datasets	Train	Test (valid)	Facts	Avg facts	Avg golden facts
Reddit [2]	1,352,961	40,000	149,803	85.01	1.009
Weibo [5]	1,019,908	56,661	696,466	77.66	1.293

4.2 Baselines

We compare the performance of CKFS-DG with seven neural generative methods. These models are divided into three categories: without knowledge as input, with one-hop knowledge graph and with two-hop knowledge graph. Firstly, **Seq2Seq** [3] takes the post as input. **Copy** [20] can reproduce words from posts. And then, **GenDS** [7] utilizes entity words in one-hop knowledge graph. **CCM** [2] exploits knowledge graph with graph attention mechanisms to capture the semantics of the knowledge facts. **ConKADI** [5] designs felicitous fact recognizer to detect the facts that highly coincide with the dialogue context. Finally, **ConceptFlow** [1] simulates the dialogue flow in the two-hop knowledge graph space. **TSGADG** [4] employs two-hop based static graph attention to deepen the understanding of context. Considering that our model only utilizes one-hop knowledge graph, we mainly compare with the first two categories.

4.3 Experimental Setup

In the experiment, our model is implemented with Tensorflow[2]. Most hyperparameters are consistent with ConKADI [5]. In detail, we use a fixed English vocabulary of 30,000 words, and a Chinese vocabulary of 50,000 words. The word embeddings adopt the Glove word embeddings with the dimension of 300. TransE embedding [21] is used for the entity and relations representations in the facts, whose dimension is 100. The state size of GRU network, used in encoder and decoder, is 512. The adam optimizer is used for training, and the initial learning rate is 0.0001. We halve the learning rate when perplexity [22] increases on validation data, and stop training if the perplexity improves for two successive iterations. The batch size is 100. The maximum number of epochs is 25.

4.4 Evaluation Metrics

To measure the quality of the generated responses, we introduce the common evaluation metrics [5,10] from five aspects:

Knowledge Utilization: E_{match} [2] is the average number of overlapping entities in the generated responses and candidate facts, that measures the model's ability to use the tail entities in the candidate facts. E_{use} [5] further considers the number of head entities to evaluate the utilization of entities. E_{recall} [5] is the ratio of overlapping entities between the generated responses and the ground-truth responses, which evaluates the accuracy of knowledge selection.

---

[2] https://github.com/tensorflow/tensorflow.

Embedding-Based Relevance: Emb_{avg} [23] evaluates the similarity between the generated responses and the ground-truth responses by using the averaged word embedding. Emb_{ex} [23] uses each dimension's extreme value of word embedding.

Overlapping-Based Relevance: BLEU-2 [24] measures n-gram overlap rate between the generated response and the ground-truth response.

Diversity: Distinct-2 [25] is a ratio of distinct bigrams in the generated responses, assessing the diversity of generated responses.

Informativeness: Entropy [26] is computed by averaging word-level entropy in the generated responses, measuring informativeness of generated responses.

4.5   Results and Analysis

Experimental Results. We compare CKFS-DG with the baselines on Reddit and Weibo dataset. Experiment results are shown in Tables 2 and 3.

In knowledge utilization evaluation, CKFS-DG outperforms the baseline methods in selecting appropriate knowledge, which can be proved by E_{recall} on Reddit dateset. The E_{recall} of our model is improved by 21.4% compared to ConKADI. The proposed topic fact predictor has the potential to select the accurate facts from candidate knowledge facts. Although E_{match} drops by 3.2%, the overall E_{use} increases by 12.6%. The advantages of our model lie in utilizing the copy mechanism, that exploits entity words in posts. The experiments on the Weibo dataset also basically achieve the effectiveness of ConKADI. The results demonstrate that our model selects entity words in candidate facts and has high utilization of the knowledge for response generation.

In embedding-based relevance evaluation, Emb_{ex} of our model improves by 15% compared to ConKADI on Reddit, indicating that the semantics between the responses generated by our model and the ground-truth responses are more similar. In overlapping-based relevance and diversity evaluation, BLUE-2 and dist-2 value are moderate compared to other models. Analysis of these two

Table 2. Experimental Results on Reddit. [†] means that the result is borrowed from ConKADI [5] and [§] means that the result is borrowed from TSGADG [4].

Metrics	Entity Score			Embedding		Overlap (%) BLEU-2	Diversity (%) dist-2	Informativeness Entropy
	E_{match}	E_{use}	E_{recall}	Emb_{avg}	Emb_{ex}			
Seq2Seq[†] [3]	0.41	0.52	0.04	0.868	0.837	4.81	1.77	7.59
Copy[†] [20]	0.14	0.67	0.09	0.868	0.841	**5.43**	8.33	7.87
GenDS[†] [7]	1.13	1.26	0.13	0.876	0.851	4.68	3.97	7.73
CCM[†] [2]	1.08	1.33	0.11	0.871	0.841	5.18	5.29	7.73
ConKADI[†] [5]	1.24	1.98	0.14	0.867	0.852	3.53	18.78	8.50
ConceptFlow[§] [1]	1.26	-	-	0.82	0.81	5.14	12.28	8.14
TSGADG[§] [4]	**1.57**	-	-	0.88	0.63	5.15	**27.25**	**8.53**
CKFS-DG(Ours)	1.20	**2.23**	**0.17**	**0.88**	**0.865**	4.93	14.39	8.42

Table 3. Experimental Results on Weibo. [†] means that the result is borrowed from ConKADI [5].

Metrics	Entity Score			Embedding		Overlap (%) BLEU-2	Diversity (%) dist-2	Informativeness Entropy
	E_{match}	E_{use}	E_{recall}	Emb_{avg}	Emb_{ex}			
Seq2Seq[†] [3]	0.33	0.58	0.13	0.770	0.500	2.24	1.04	6.09
Copy[†] [20]	0.33	0.68	0.13	0.786	0.501	2.28	2.18	6.13
GenDS[†] [7]	0.75	0.84	0.26	0.789	0.524	2.09	1.66	5.89
CCM[†] [2]	0.99	1.09	0.28	0.786	0.544	3.26	2.59	6.16
ConKADI[†] [5]	**1.48**	**2.08**	**0.38**	**0.846**	0.577	**5.06**	23.93	9.04
CKFS-DG(Ours)	1.44	2.00	**0.38**	0.816	**0.592**	4.32	**24.88**	**9.57**

indicators by CCM and ConKADI, the high BLUE-2 based on word character similarity losts the diversity of generated responses to a certain extent [5]. In informativeness evaluation, entropy of our model improves by 5.8% compared to ConKADI on Weibo, that further confirms the advantages of our model in integrating knowledge and generating informative responses. We also found that the entropy is slightly lower than ConKADI on Reddit. The reason may be that the collected sources of the two datasets are different, and there are inherent differences of datasets, as mentioned in [5]. The experimental results prove that our method has the ability to selecting appropriate knowledge facts to generate informative responses.

Ablation Study. We conduct further ablation experiments to dissect our model. The experimental results are shown in Table 4. We analyze the influence and role of each module by comparing the experimental results of the model with and without this module. Specifically, (1) **w/o TEP** is the model without topic entity predictor, whose role is to predicte dialogue topic entity in the post. (2) **w/o KE** is the model removing knowledge-enriched encoder, which is based on the context-knowledge attention mechanism and generates knowledge-enriched contextual representation of post. (3) **w/o TFP** is the model without topic fact predictor, including topic entity and fact prediction of the current dialogue.

Table 4. Results of ablation study on Reddit and Weibo. Comparative experiments include: (1) "-w/o TEP" without Topic Entity Predictor, (2) "-w/o KE" without Knowledge-enriched Encoder and (3) "-w/o TFP" without Topic Fact Predictor.

Metrics	Reddit					Weibo				
	E_{recall}	Emb_{ex}	BLEU-2	dist-2	Entropy	E_{recall}	Emb_{ex}	BLEU-2	dist-2	Entropy
CAFS-DG	**16.4**	**0.865**	4.938	14.392	8.426	**37.45**	**0.592**	4.321	24.877	**9.566**
- w/o TEP	15.93	0.571	5.154	**24.059**	**8.971**	36.12	0.588	4.085	**27.587**	9.541
- w/o KE	13.59	0.849	3.966	15.764	8.263	36.46	0.567	4.127	26.611	9.462
- w/o TFP	12.6	0.855	**5.614**	7.374	7.857	32.34	0.542	3.671	4.590	6.579

The results show that (1) when our model removes the topic entity predictor, E_{recall} drops by 2.8% and Emb_{ex} drops by 33.9% on Reddit. It shows that predicting the topic entities helps the model generate responses related to the topic, and there is a high semantic similarity between the generated responses and the target responses. Intuitively, the topic entity predictor will make the model pay more attention to candidate facts related to topic entities in response generation. Without topic entity predictor, dict-2 decreases by 10.9% on Weibo, indicating that focusing on the topic of the dialogue may lose the diversity of generated responses. (2) Without knowledge-enriched encoder, E_{recall} and BLEU-2 decrease by 17.1% and 19.7% on Reddit respectively. The module uses the context-knowledge attention mechanism to construct filtered knowledge representation, and generates knowledge-enriched contextual vector of post. The performance of the model is improved with this module, showing that the knowledge-enriched encoder module is helpful to strengthen the semantic representation of the post. (3) Removing the topic fact predictor, E_{recall} drops by 13.6% and entropy drops by 31.3% on Weibo. It demonstrates the importance of topic fact predictor to generate informative and diverse responses with appropriate entities in retrieved facts.

Case Study. As shown in Table 5, we discuss two typical cases, including generated responses by our model and baselines CopyNet, CCM and ConKADI.

In case 1, candidate facts were retrieved based on the entity words in the post such as "great" and "play". The retrieved facts whose head entity is "play" should receive more attention. Comparing with "great", "play" is more likely to be the topic point of the current conversation. CCM and ConKADI do not select golden facts and generate generic responses. Our model focuses on the topic entity "play" and selects facts to generate a reasonable response. From the perspective of response quality, our model generates a natural response according to dialogue topic.

In case 2, it is obvious that "paper" and "work" in the post are important topic entities, but "zombies" are not. ConKADI paid attention to the "paper" while also paying attention to the "zombies" when generating responses. Our model utilizes candidate facts to infer "graduation" from "work" and generates relatively fluent responses.

We further visualize the probability distribution over candidate facts for the above cases in Fig. 3. The distribution plots on the left are generated by ConKADI, and the plots on the right are generated by CKFS-DG. In each plot, the words on the left are the entity words in the post, and no more than 25 knowledge facts are retrieved based on each entity word. The probability distribution value for each fact is distinguished by the color of the plots.

Obviously, in case 1, the focus of ConKADI is the candidate facts whose head entity word is "great". Different from ConKADI, our model pays attention to the facts "⟨play, RelatedTo, team⟩" which is used for generate responses. In case 2 our model focuses on knowledge facts related to "work". Our model further utilizes candidate facts to infer the word "graduation" based on the dialogue

Table 5. Two cases of knowledge-aware dialogue generation. The comparison models include CopyNet, CCM, ConKADI, and our model CKFS-DG. The orange words are the entity words in the post, the blue words are the entity words in the true response, and the green words are entity words in the candidate facts.

case 1 (Reddit)	Post	that would be great if they had to play at target field the first season
	Knowledge	⟨play, RelatedTo, team⟩ ⟨great, RelatedTo, awesome⟩ ⟨great, RelatedTo, money⟩ ⟨great, HasContext, music⟩ ...
	Golden Fact	⟨play, RelatedTo, team⟩
	True Response	its about time a mn team won there.
	GenDS [7]	i would n't be surprised if they did n't have to play at target field field
	CCM [2]	i 'd be happy with that .
	ConKADI [5]	well that would be a great idea. and that 's pretty awesome.
	CKFS-DG(Ours)	well, if the hawks had to play at target, they 'd be a great team.
case 2 (Weibo)	Post	被论文和工作弄疯了，现在暂时缓了一下下，但是一大波僵尸还在前方啊 Be crazy for the papers and work, now it is temporarily slowing down, but a large wave of zombies is still ahead.
	Knowledge	⟨毕业,Causes,工作⟩ ⟨加油,MotivatedByGoal,工作⟩ ⟨graduation,Causes,work⟩ ⟨Come on,MotivatedByGoal,work⟩ ⟨工作,HasProperty,苦⟩ ⟨麻烦,NotDesires,工作⟩ ... ⟨Work,HasProperty,bitter⟩ ⟨Trouble, NotDesires, work⟩ ...
	Golden Fact	⟨毕业,Causes,工作⟩ ⟨graduation,Causes,work⟩
	True Response	劳逸结合，熬过毕业季 Combine work and rest to survive the graduation season
	ConKADI [5]	是啊，加油，我把论文写完了，前方的僵尸 Yes, come on, I have finished writing the thesis, the zombie in front
	CKFS-DG(Ours)	弄的挺麻烦，你说，毕业的时候，加油 It was very troublesome , say that I will work hard when I graduate

context. Compared to ConKADI, our model introduces topic entity predictor to focus on the relevant topic entities, which helps to select appropriate knowledge.

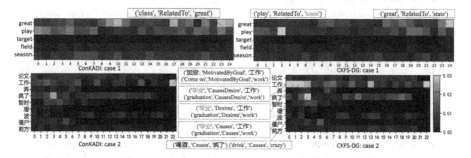

Fig. 3. Visualization of probability distributions over candidate facts for the two cases. We only show the 25 candidate facts retrieved for each entity word in posts.

5   Conclusion and Future Work

We propose a knowledge-aware dialogue generation model CKFS-DG to integrate external knowledge into response generation. In particular, we design context-knowledge attention mechanism to filter out redundant knowledge for knowledge enhanced context representation, and topic fact prediction mechanism to select appropriate knowledge facts for response generation. Experimental results on Reddit and Weibo datasets demonstrate the effectiveness of CKFS-DG in selecting appropriate knowledge and generating informative responses. In the future, we intend to introduce different forms of knowledge into the generation model effectively and naturally.

Acknowledgements. This work was supported by the National Key R&D Program of China under Grant No. 2019YFF0302601.

References

1. Zhang, H., Liu, Z., Xiong, C., Liu, Z.: Grounded conversation generation as guided traverses in commonsense knowledge graphs. In: Proceedings of the 58th Annual Meeting of the Association for Computational Linguistics, pp. 2031–2043 (2020)
2. Zhou, H., Young, T., Huang, M., Zhao, H., Xu, J., Zhu, X.: Commonsense knowledge aware conversation generation with graph attention. In: Proceedings of the 27th International Joint Conference on Artificial Intelligence, pp. 4623–4629 (2018)
3. Sutskever, I., Vinyals, O., Le, Q. V.: Sequence to Sequence Learning with Neural Networks. In: Advances in Neural Information Processing Systems, pp. 3104–3112 (2014)
4. Zhou, S., Rong, W., Zhang, J., Wang, Y., Shi, L., Xiong, Z.: Topic-aware dialogue generation with two-hop based graph attention. In: IEEE International Conference on Acoustics, Speech and Signal Processing, pp. 7428–7432 (2021)
5. Wu, S., Li, Y., Zhang, D., Zhou, Y., Wu, Z.: Diverse and informative dialogue generation with context-specific commonsense knowledge awareness. In: Proceedings of the 58th Annual Meeting of the Association for Computational Linguistics, pp. 5811–5820 (2020)
6. Ghazvininejad, M., et al.: A knowledge-grounded neura conversation model. In: Proceedings of the AAAI Conference on Artificial Intelligence, pp. 5110–5117 (2018)
7. Zhu, W., Mo, K., Zhang, Y., Zhu, Z., Peng, X., Yang, Q.: Flexible end-to-end dialogue system for knowledge grounded conversation. CoRR, abs/1709.04264 (2017)
8. Moon, S., Shah, P., Kumar, A., Subba, R.: Opendialkg: Explainable conversational reasoning with attention-based walks over knowledge graphs. In: Proceedings of the 57th Annual Meeting of the Association for Computational Linguistics, pp. 845–854 (2019)
9. Lin, X., Jian, W., He, J., Wang, T., Chu, W.: Generating informative conversational response using recurrent knowledge-interaction and knowledge-copy. In: Proceedings of the 58th Annual Meeting of the Association for Computational Linguistics, pp. 41–52 (2020)

10. Wang, W., Gao, W., Feng, S., Chen, L., Wang, D.: Adaptive posterior knowledge selection for improving knowledge-grounded dialogue generation. In: Proceedings of the 30th ACM International Conference on Information and Knowledge Management, pp. 1989–1998 (2021)

11. Liu, Z., Niu, Z. Y., Wu, H., Wang, H.: Knowledge aware conversation generation with explainable reasoning over augmented graphs. In: Proceedings of the 2019 Conference on Empirical Methods in Natural Language Processing and the 9th International Joint Conference on Natural Language Processing, pp. 1782–1792 (2019)

12. Wang, J., Liu, J., Bi, W., Liu, X., He, K., Xu, R., Yang, M.: Improving Knowledge-Aware Dialogue Generation via Knowledge Base Question Answering. In: Proceedings of the 34th AAAI Conference on Artificial Intelligence, pp. 9169–9176 (2020)

13. Dinan, E., Roller, S., Shuster, K., Fan, A., Auli, M., Weston, J.: Wizard of Wikipedia: Knowledge-Powered Conversational Agents. In: Proceedings of the 7th International Conference on Learning Representations, (2019)

14. Wang, Y., Wang, Y., Lou, X., Rong, W., Hao, Z., Wang, S.: Improving Dialogue Response Generation Via Knowledge Graph Filter. In: 2021 IEEE International Conference on Acoustics, Speech and Signal Processing(ICASSP), pp. 7423–7427 (2021)

15. Zhong, P., Liu, Y., Wang, H., Miao, C.: Keyword-guided neural conversational Model. In: Proceedings of the AAAI Conference on Artificial Intelligence, pp. 14568–14576 (2021)

16. Cho, K., et al.: Learning phrase representations using RNN encoder-decoder for statistical machine translation. In: Proceedings of the 2014 Conference on Empirical Methods in Natural Language Processing, pp. 1724–1734 (2014)

17. Zhao, T., Zhao, R., Eskenazi, M.: Learning discourse-level diversity for neural dialog models using conditional variational autoencoders. In: Proceedings of the 55th Annual Meeting of the Association for Computational Linguistics, pp. 654–664 (2017)

18. Kullback, S., Leibler, R.A.: On information and sufficiency. The annals of mathematical statistics, pp. 79–86 (1951)

19. Luong, M.T., Pham, H., Manning, C.D.: Effective approaches to attention-based neural machine translation. CoRR, abs/1508.04025 (2015)

20. Gu, J., Lu, Z., Li, H., Li, V.O.: Incorporating copying mechanism in sequence-to-sequence learning. In: Proceedings of the 54th Annual Meeting of the Association for Computational Linguistics, pp. 199–208 (2016)

21. Bordes, A., Usunier, N., Garcia-Duran, A., Weston, J., Yakhnenko, O.: Translating embeddings for modeling multi-relational data. In: Advances in Neural Information Processing Systems, pp. 2787–2795 (2013)

22. Serban, I. V., Sordoni, A., Bengio, Y., Courville, A., Pineau, J.: Hierarchical neural network generative models for movie dialogues. CoRR, abs/1507.04808, pp. 434–441 (2015)

23. Liu, C. W., Lowe, R., Serban, I. V., Noseworthy, M., Charlin, L., Pineau, J.: How not to evaluate your dialogue system: an empirical study of unsupervised evaluation metrics for dialogue response generation. In: Proceedings of the 2016 Conference on Empirical Methods in Natural Language Processing, pp. 2122–2132 (2016)

24. Tian, Z., Yan, R., Mou, L., Song, Y., Feng, Y., Zhao, D.: How to make context more useful an empirical study on context-aware neural conversational models. In: Proceedings of the 55th Annual Meeting of the Association for Computational Linguistics, pp. 231–236 (2017)

25. Li, J., Galley, M., Brockett, C., Gao, J., Dolan, B.: A diversity-promoting objective function for neural conversation models. In: Proceedings of the 2016 Conference of the North American Chapter of the Association for Computational Linguistics: Human Language Technologies, pp. 110–119 (2015)
26. Mou, L., Song, Y., Yan, R., Li, G., Zhang, L., Jin, Z.: Sequence to backward and forward sequences: a content-introducing approach to generative short-text conversation. In: Proceedings of COLING 2016, the 26th International Conference on Computational Linguistics: Technical Papers, pp. 3349–3358 (2016)

A Study of Event Multi-triple Extraction Methods Based on Edge-Enhanced Graph Convolution Networks

Yu Zhang, Yimeng Li, Chaomurilige[✉], and Yu Weng[✉]

School of Information Engineering, Minzu University of China, Beijing 100081, China
leia_wang@163.com, dr_wengyu@126.com

Abstract. The event multi-triple extraction task consists of identifying event trigger words and extracting relevant event arguments, and is the basis for some natural language processing downstream tasks. Joint approaches are often considered in existing work, but the coupling and constraints of trigger word recognition and argument recognition pose difficulties for concrete implementation. In this paper, we propose a pipelined approach to event multi-triple extraction, use the event trigger words and event categories generated by EE-GCN as an indication of event extraction, NER as a technical tool to extract event indicator. Based on syntactic dependencies we propose syntactic rules for the selection of arguments, According to this rule, event category, event trigger words and their corresponding arguments are formed into event Multi-triple. The experimental results show that the method is effective in extracting event multi-triple from the text in the ACE2005 dataset.

Keywords: Event multi-triple · EE-GCN · NER · Syntactic rules · Extraction

1 Introduction

Event extraction is a specific operation of information extraction for a particular piece of information. It is the basis for natural language processing downstream tasks. It has also been successfully used in many important areas such as network monitoring, emergency alerting, intelligence gathering, business and economics, automated response, human-computer interaction, and biomedicine [3–10].

Event extraction consists of two primary tasks: event detection and argument recognition [2, 3]. In recent years, deep learning (especially deep and graphical convolutional neural networks) is emerging with its powerful characterization and learning capabilities Event extraction based on deep learning can be divided into pipeline methods and joint methods. Theoretically, the joint learning approach is superior to the pipeline approach [2]. However, because trigger word recognition and argument recognition are coupled and mutually constrained, both the learning algorithm and the training model are complex and pose certain difficulties for concrete implementation.

One effective way to solve the above problem is to use the pipeline method. Based on study [11], a new event detection model EE-GCN was proposed by Cui et al. [12]. Event trigger words and event categories are identified using Edge-Enhanced GCN and

G. Memmi et al. (Eds.): KSEM 2022, LNAI 13368, pp. 109–119, 2022.
https://doi.org/10.1007/978-3-031-10983-6_9

SoftMax, and validated on the ACE2005 dataset. Both theory and experiments have proven this method to be one of the most effective methods of event detection.

However, EE-GCN has only completed the first subtask of event extraction, i.e. event detection. Inspired by this article on the EE-GCN, using the event triggers and event categories generated by EE-GCN as indicators for event extraction, a pipelined approach was used to extract event multi-triple, using arguments roles defined by ACE2005 evaluation meeting as the baseline and NER as the technical tool. Finally, general event multi-triple according to grammatical rules.

2   Related Works

In earlier studies, researchers focused on pattern matching methods. Methods for machine learning such as HMM [15], SVM [16], CRF [17], and plain Bayesian [18] have been proposed one after another.

With the development of information technology, deep learning and graph convolutional neural networks are increasingly being used in event extraction tasks. With the rise of GCNs (Kipf and Welling [19]), Orr et al. [14] proposed a directed acyclic graph GRU model that introduces syntactic structure into sequence structure. Nguyen and Grishman et al. [20] proposed to transform syntactic dependency trees into graphs and use GCN for event detection through information propagation on graphs. Few of them consider dependency label information. Cui et al. [12] proposed the EE-GCN model, which combines both syntactic dependency structures and typed dependency labels for event detection.

However, less research has been done on the theoretical element recognition task, making the event extraction task imperfect. Ahn [21] explicitly divided event extraction into four steps. It divides event detection and argument extraction into two independent models, making the model more flexible. So our paper adopts the pipelined approach, using the results of EE-GCN as an indication, and then extracting relevant arguments according to the argument roles corresponding to the events to form event multi-triple.

3   Proposed Approach

The event triggers and event categories generated by EE-GCN are used as indicator for event extraction, and the NER is used as a technical tool to extract the arguments corresponding to event trigger words and event categories, using the arguments roles defined at the ACE2005 as a benchmark. The event trigger words and event categories, together with their corresponding arguments, are formed into event multi-triple according to grammatical rules. The overall structure is shown in Fig. 1.

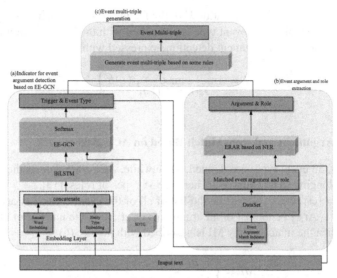

Fig. 1. The overall architecture of Event Multi-triple Extraction Methods Based on Edge-Enhanced Graph Convolution Networks. SDTG: syntactic dependency tensor generation.

3.1   Indicator for Event Argument Detection Based on EE-GCN

Given that the input text consist of M words, i.e. $= \{w_1, w_2, \ldots, w_M\}$, let $w_i (i \in [1, M])$ be encoded into sematic word embedding $\overline{w}_i$ with skip-gram [12]. At the same time, let w_i be encoded into entity type embedding $\widehat{w}_i$ [10]. Then $x_i = [\overline{w}_i, \widehat{w}_i]$ which is fed into the BiLSTM. The BiLSTM output $N^0 = [h_1^0, h_2^0, \ldots, h_M^0]$ $N^0 \in R^{M \times d}$ (d is dimension of h) is taken as the initial node input of EE-GCN [12].

Dependency analysis [26] is performed on the input text P. The result is a tensor $E^o = \{E_{:,:,:}^0\} \in R^{M \times M \times K}$ and taken as the initial edge input of EE-GCN [12], Thus, the update of the nodes and the edges of the EE-GCN is calculated with Eq. (1)–(3) [12]:

$$N^l = relu\Big(Average\_pooling\Big(N_1^l, N_2^l, \ldots, N_K^l\Big)\Big) \tag{1}$$

$$N_i^l = E_{:,:,i}^{l-1} N^{l-1} W_N \tag{2}$$

$$E_{i,j,:}^l = W_E\Big[E_{i,j,:}^{l-1} \oplus h_i^l \oplus h_j^l\Big], i, j \in [1, M] \tag{3}$$

where $E_{:,:,i}^{l-1}$ is the ith channel of E^{l-1}, and $E_{i,j,:}^{l-1} \in R^K$ represents the (i, j) element of $E^{l-1} \in R^{M \times M \times K}$ with K-Dimension syntactic dependency embedding vector, $W_N \in R^{d \times d}$ is a learnable weight matrix, $W_E \in R^{(2 \times d + K) \times K}$ is a learnable weight matrix.

Let $T = [t_1, t_2, \ldots, t_q]$ stands for the set of all event types, where t_i represents the ith event type, q is the number of all the event types. At the last layer, each node h_i^l is fed into a fully connected network (FCN$_i$), followed by a Softmax (softmax$_i$(.)) used to calculate the probabilities of h_i^l for all event types, expressed as Eq. (4) [12].

$$p\big(t_j|h_i^l\big) = softmax_j\big(w_j h_i^l + b_j\big), i \in [1, M], j \in \big[1, q\big] \tag{4}$$

where w_j maps the node representation h_i^l to the feature score for each event type and b_j is a bias term. Then the final event type is calculated with the Eq. (5), and it is taken as the indicator of the event argument detection, expressed with I.

$$I = Arc \max_{i\in[1,M],j\in[1,q]} p\left(t_j|h_i^l\right) \tag{5}$$

3.2 Event Argument and Role Match Based on ACE2005

In ACE2005, 33 event types are defined. Meanwhile, ACE2005 defines the role of the argument belonging to that subtype. There are 35 types of roles. [13].

Let $ET = [et_1, et_2, \ldots, et_{33}]$ be the list of all of the event types. Let $argument_i = [Ar_1, Ar_2, \ldots, Ar_{ai}]$ be the list of all arguments of et_i, ai is the number of elements in $argument_i$, then the match policy MI is described with the Eq. (6)

$$MI = \begin{cases} 1, ifI = et_i, i \in [1, 33] \\ \quad 0, others \end{cases} \tag{6}$$

According to the calculating result of Eq. (6), the matched event sub-type is obtained with Eq. (7).

$$et_j = arcMI, I = et_j \tag{7}$$

Then the corresponding argument is $argument_j = \left[Ar_1, Ar_2, \ldots, Ar_{aj}\right]$.

3.3 Event Argument and Role Extraction Based on NER

Based on the results of Eq. (6) and Eq. (7), the event argument to be determined is $Ar_1, Ar_2, \ldots, Ar_{aj}$. In addition, seen from Sect. 3.2, each event argument also corresponds to a different entity type. We obtain the entity type Entity Word (EW) for each word in the text by named entity recognition, described as $EW_i, i \in [1, M]$. The entity matching $Ar_1, Ar_2, \ldots, Ar_{aj}$ from $EW_i, i \in [1, M]$ is selected as the argument element of the event and is described by Eq. (8). The process is shown in Fig. 2 and Algorithm 1.

$$Ar_k = \begin{cases} EW_i, & if Ar_k \text{ matched } EW_i, i \in [1, M], k \in \left[1, aj\right] \\ NULL, others \end{cases} \tag{8}$$

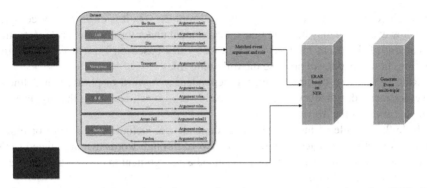

Fig. 2. The overview of the method of event role and argument extraction based on NER. The dataset event arguments defined by ACE2005. ERAR: event role and argument recognition.

Algorithm 1 ERAR based on NER

Input: Event type E, Event Argument Dataset S, the initial empty argument dictionary D, Input text T.
Output: the final argument dictionary D.

```
roles ← S.get(E)
ner_results ← NER(T)
for e ← roles do
    role_name ← e[0]
    role_entity_type ← e[1...len(e)]
    temp_words ← [ ]
    for v ← ner_results.values do
        if v in role_entity_type then
            add the key corresponding to the value to
the temp_words
        end if
    end for
    D.put(role_name,temp_words)
end for

return D
```

3.4 Event Multi-triple Generation

Based on the results of Eq. (6), Eq. (7) and Eq. (8) matching, the basic form of our extracted event multigroup can be described as:

$$\text{Event multi} - \text{triple} = \{\text{event type, trigger word}, Ar_1, Ar_2, \ldots, Ar_{aj}\} \qquad (9)$$

where trigger word is the event trigger word. From Eq. (9), it is clear that for complex texts, however, there may be more than one argument under the argument role. A further refinement of the event multi-triple by certain rules based on Eq. (9) is an effective solution. In this paper, we propose the following rules:

Rule 1: The rule of direct syntactic dependence. A word or phrase that defines a direct syntactic dependency (e.g. subject-verb, verb-object, etc.) with the trigger word is an argument in the event.

Rule 2: The rule of indirect syntactic dependence. Definition If a word or phrase can be indirectly associated with the trigger word through words that are related to the trigger word. Then the word or phrase can also be an argument in the event. The process pseudocode is as follows.

Algorithm 2 Event multi-triple generation

Input: trigger G, argument dictionary D, dependency relation matrix R.
Output: the final argument dictionary D.

```
direct_list ← Find words in R that are connected to G
indirect_list ← [ ]
for d ← direct_list do
    w ← Find words in R that are connected to d
    indirect_list.add(w)
end for
for Ar ← D.values do
    if Ar in direct_list or Ar in indirect_list then
        contiune
    else
        Delete Ar from D
    end if
end for

return D
```

---

4 Experimental Evaluation

4.1 Experimental Setup

The experiments were conducted on a machine with 12GB of RAM, an Intel i7-7500U CPU and an NVIDIA 940mx GPU. The operating system is Window 10 Professional, the programming language is python 3.7, the deep learning platform is PYTORCH. Using ACE2005 as a dataset [13].

4.2   Experimental Design

The design of this experiment required experiments to verify the following. (1) The ability to correctly generate an Indicator for event extraction as the basis for subsequent experiments. (2) Validating the usability of our proposed theoretical element extraction method for named entity recognition in real texts. (3) Verify the validity of the proposed event multivariate group extraction rule. Corresponds to Sects. 4.3, 4.4 and 4.5

4.3   Generate Indicator for Event Argument Detection

Table 1. Indicator generates results.

Sentence id	Sentence	Indicator
1	Jordan met with the Sixers on Sunday, according to a person close to the situation	Trigger:met EventType:Meet
2	Hunter,34,filed for divorce in Los Angeles Superior Court	Trigger:divorce EventType:Divorce
3	katie was born on christmas day in America	Trigger:born EventType:Be-Born
4	Ranjha Masih guilty of defiling Koranic verses during a protest rally by the minority Christian community in 1998	Trigger:rally EventType:Demonstrate
5	Hu , who was appointed to the top job in March , will meet his Russian counterpart Vladimir Putin during his three-day state visit from May 26 to 28	Trigger:meet EventType:Meet
6	Thousands of Iraq's majority Shiite Muslims marched to their main mosque in Baghdad to mark the birthday of Islam 's founder Prophet Mohammed	Trigger:marched EventType:Demonstrate

We use the EE-GCN model for the task of detecting trigger words and classifying events, and combine the two into an Indicator for event extraction. The first column in the table is the id value of each sentence of text, the second column is the text information of the sentence, and the third column is the experimentally obtained INDICATOR.

4.4   Argument Extraction

In this section, the experiments performed are designed to validate the usability of our proposed named entity recognition-based argument extraction method in real texts. The input data consisted of two parts, one being the same sentences as in the experiments in Sect. 4.3, and the other being the trigger words and event types output in the experiments in Sect. 4.3. Outputs the results of argument extraction under each argument role.

The results of the experiment to test the ability to extract multi-triple of events are shown below. The second column is the indicator of the event extraction obtained in Sect. 4.3, and the third column is the result of the argument extraction.

Table 2. Arguments generates results.

Sentence id	Indicator	Result
1	Trigger:met EventType:Meet	EventType:Meet trigger:met Entity:['Jordan','Sixers'] Time:['Sunday'] Place:[]
2	Trigger:divorce EventType:Divorce	EventType:Divorce trigger:divorce Person:['Hunter'] Time:[] Place:['Los Angeles']
3	Trigger:born EventType:Be-Born	EventType:Be-Born trigger:born Person:'katie'] Time:['christmas day'] Place:[America]
4	Trigger:rally EventType:Demonstrate	EventType:Demonstrate trigger:rally Entity:['Ranjha Masih'] Time:[1998] Place:[Pakistan]
5	Trigger:meet EventType:Meet	Trigger:meet EventType:Meet Entity: ['Hu','Vladimir Putin'] Time: ['three-day','May 26 to 28','March'] Place: ['Russian']
6	Trigger:marched EventType:Demonstrate	Trigger:marched EventType:Demonstrate Entity: ['Shiite Muslims', 'Islam','Prophet Mohammed'] Time: [''] Place: ['Iraq', 'Baghdad']

In this experiment, the theoretical elements of both sentence 3 and sentence 4 were extracted completely and uniquely. At the same time, there are missing arguments in extracting the event multi-triple of sentence 1 and sentence 2.

What we can notice is that the arguments extracted under the theoretical role are not unique when the targuments are extracted for sentences 5 and 6.

4.5 Generate Event Multi-triple

In Sect. 3.4, we propose Event multi-triple generation rules to deal with the case where there are multiple arguments under a single argument role after extraction by the proposed argument extraction method under complex texts. For the results in Sect. 4.4 the application rules are further processed and the results are shown in Table 3. The second column is the result of the output in Sect. 4.4, and the third column is the final output of the event multi-triple.

Table 3. Event multi-triple result

Sentence id	Argument extraction	Event multi-triple
5	Trigger:meet EventType:Meet Entity: ['Hu','Vladimir Putin'] Time: ['three-day','May 26 to 28','March'] Place: ['Russian']	Trigger:meet EventType:Meet Entity: ['Hu','Vladimir Putin'] Time: [May 26 to 28] Place: ['Russian']
6	Trigger:marched EventType:Demonstrate Entity: ['Shiite Muslims', 'Islam','Prophet Mohammed'] Time: [''] Place: ['Iraq', 'Baghdad']	Trigger:marched EventType:Demonstrate Entity: ['Shiite Muslims'] Time: [''] Place: ['Baghdad']

After the rules have been applied to the text, the final event multi-triple can be extracted.

In sentence 5, after the extraction of arguments, there are two arguments under the role of Entity, and three arguments under Time. There is a direct syntactic dependency between 'Hu' and the trigger word 'meet', a subject-predicate relationship between 'Hu' and 'meet', and no direct syntactic dependency between 'Vladimir Putin' and the trigger word, but there is an indirect syntactic dependency between the two through the 'counterpart' as a transit. Thus, 'Hu', 'Vladimir Putin' can all be used as arguments under the argument role Entity.

5 Conclusion and Future Works

In this paper, we propose a method of event multi-triple extraction based on EE-GCN. Our experiments demonstrate the effectiveness of the method. In the future, we also try to transfer the algorithm model to other datasets. For example, this can be applied to news datasets, where knowledge graphs can be built to sort out news events.

Acknowledgements. This work was supported in part by the National Key Research and Development Program of China under Grant 2020YFB1406702-3, in part by the National Science Foundation of China under Grant 61772575.

References

1. Hogenboom, F., Frasincar, F., Kaymak, U., de Jongm, F., Caron, E.: A survey of event extraction methods from text for decision support systems. Decis. Support Syst. **85**(C), 12–22 (2016)

2. Gao, L., Zhou, G., Luo, J., Lan, M.: Survey on meta-event extraction. Comput. Sci. **46**(8), 9–15 (2019)
3. Zhan, L., Jiang, X.: Survey on event extraction technology in information extraction research area. In: IEEE 3rd Information Technology, Networking, Electronic and Automation Control Conference (ITNEC), pp. 2121–2126 (2019)
4. Xiang, W., Wang, B.: A survey of event extraction from text. IEEE Access **7**, 173111–173137 (2019)
5. Conlon, S.J., Abrahams, A.S., Simmons, L.L.: Terrorism information extraction from online reports. J. Comput. Inf. Syst. **55**(3), 20–28 (2015)
6. Tanev, H., Piskorski, J., Atkinson, M.: Real-time news event extraction for global crisis monitoring. In: Kapetanios, E., Sugumaran, V., Spiliopoulou, M. (eds.) NLDB 2008. LNCS, vol. 5039, pp. 207–218. Springer, Heidelberg (2008). https://doi.org/10.1007/978-3-540-69858-6_21
7. Atkinson, M., Du, M., Piskorski, J., Tanev, H., Yangarber, R., Zavarella, V.: Techniques for multilingual security-related event extraction from online news. In: Przepiórkowski, A., Piasecki, M., Jassem, K., Fuglewicz, P. (eds.) Computational Linguistics, pp. 163–186. Springer, Heidelberg (2013). https://doi.org/10.1007/978-3-642-34399-5_9
8. Nuij, W., Milea, V., Hogenboom, F., Frasincar, F., Kaymak, U.: An automated framework for incorporating news into stock trading strategies. IEEE Trans. Knowl. Data Eng. **26**(4), 823–835 (2014)
9. Capet, P., Delavallade, T., Nakamura, T., Sandor, A., Tarsitano, C., Voyatzi, S.: A risk assessment system with automatic extraction of event types. In: Zhongzhi Shi, E., Mercier-Laurent, D.L. (eds.) Intelligent Information Processing IV, pp. 220–229. Springer US, Boston, MA (2008). https://doi.org/10.1007/978-0-387-87685-6_27
10. Vanegas, J.A., Matos, S., González, F., Oliveira, J.L.: An overview of biomolecular event extraction from scientific documents. Comput. Math. Methods Med. **2015**, 1–19 (2015)
11. Nguyen, T.H., Grishman, R.: Graph convolutional networks with argument-aware pooling for event detection. In: Thirty-Second AAAI Conference on Artificial Intelligence, vol. 32, p. 1 (2018)
12. Cui, S., Yu, B., Liu, T., et al.: Edge-enhanced graph convolution networks for event detection with syntactic relation. In: EMNLP, Punta, Cana, pp. 2329–2339 (2020)
13. Walker, Christopher, et al.(2006) ACE 2005 Multilingual Training Corpus LDC2006T06. Web Download. Philadelphia: Linguistic Data Consortium
14. Walker Orr,Prasad Tadepalli,and Xiaoli Fern.(2018)Event detection with neural networks:A rigorous empirical evaluation.In:Proceedings of the 2018 Conference on Empirical Methods in Natural Language Processing,Brussels,Belgium.Association for Computational Linguistics.pp. 999–1004
15. Eddy, S.R.: Hidden markov models. Curr. Opin. Struct. Biol. **6**(3), 361–365 (1996)
16. Suykens, J.A., Vandewalle, J.: Least squares support vector machine classifiers. Neural Process. Lett. **9**(3), 293–300 (1999)
17. Laffaty,J.,Mccallum,A.,Pereira,F.,et al.: Conditional random fields: probabilistic models for segmenting and labeling sequence data. In: International Conference on Machine Learning, pp. 282–289 (2001)
18. Mccallum, A., Nigam, K.: A comparison of event models for naive bayes text cassification. In: The 15th AAAI Conference on Artificial Intelligence, pp. 41–48 (1998)
19. Kipf, T.N., Welling, M.: Semi-supervised classification with graph convolutional networks. In: 5th International Conference on Learning Representations. arXiv preprint arXiv:1609.02907 (2016)
20. Nguyen, T.H., Grishman, R.: Graph convolutional networks with argumant-aware pooling for event detection. In: The 32nd AAAI Conference on Artificial Intelligence, pp. 5900–5907 (2018)

21. Ahn, D.: The stages of event extraction. In: Proceedings of the Workshop on Annotating and Reasoning about Time and Events, pp. 1–8 (2006)
22. Graves, A.: Supervised Sequence Labelling with Recurrent Neural Networks. Springer, Heidelberg (2012). https://doi.org/10.1007/978-3-642-24797-2
23. Marcheggiani, D., Titov, I.: Encoding sentences with graph convolutional networks for semantic role labeling. arXiv preprint arXiv:1703.04826 (2017)
24. Chen, Y., Yang, H., Liu, K., Zhao, J., Jia, Y.: Collective event detection via a hierarchical and bias tagging networks with gated multi-level attention mechanisms. In: Proceedings of the 2018 Conference on Empirical Methods in Natural Language Processing, Brussels, Belgium. Association for Computational Linguistics, pp. 1267–1276 (2018)
25. Guo, Z., Zhang, Y., Lu, W.: Attention guided graph convolutional networks for relation extraction. In: Proceedings of the 57th Annual Meeting of the Association for Computational Linguistics, Florence, Italy. Association for Computational Linguistics, pp. 241–251 (2019)
26. Qi, P., Zhang, Y., Zhang, Y., Bolton, J., Manning, C.D.: Stanza: a Python natural language processing toolkit for many human languages. In: Association for Computational Linguistics (ACL) System Demonstrations (2020)
27. Qiu, H., Zheng, Q., Msahli, M., Memmi, G., Qiu, M., Lu, J.: Topological graph convolutional network-based urban traffic flow and density prediction. IEEE Trans. Intell. Transp. Syst. **22**(7), 4560–4569 (2021). https://doi.org/10.1109/TITS.2020.3032882

Construction Research and Applications of Industry Chain Knowledge Graphs

Boyao Zhang[1,2] , Zijian Wang[1], Haikuo Zhang[3(✉)] , Yonghua Zhao[1], Jingqi Sun[1], and Jing Wang[1]

[1] Computer Network Information Center, Chinese Academy of Sciences, Beijing, China
{zhangby,yhzhao}@sccas.cn, {wangzj,jqsun,wangjing}@cnic.cn
[2] University of Chinese Academy of Sciences, Beijing, China
[3] China Internet Network Information Center, Beijing, China
zhanghaikuo@cnnic.cn

Abstract. Research on listed companies is an important part of stock analysis. This study proposes an automatic construction method of the knowledge graph for the financial industry chain, which can better track and study the relationship between the production and operation of listed companies from the perspective of the graph. To solve the problems of high expert labor costs, late update and maintenance, and unstandardized and label-lacking datasets during the construction of vertical domain knowledge graphs, this study conducts knowledge extraction of unstructured text by integrating two dependency parsing methods, phrase structure trees, and dependency parse trees. Furthermore, this study uses automatically labeled datasets to train a deep learning-based named entity recognition model. This method, which integrates the two abovementioned methods, improves normalization ability and allows for the automatic construction of a financial industry chain knowledge graph.

Keywords: Knowledge graph · Dependency parsing · Named entity recognition · Construction · Phrase structure tree · Dependency parse tree

1 Introduction

The stock market is an important channel for corporate financing and resource allocation because it is a significant part of the capital market. The stock price reflects the value of the listed company, making stock price analysis inseparable from listed company research [1]. The evaluation of a listed company's value is often based on its fundamental dimensions, including its production and operation, the future development prospects of its industry, and the impact of macroeconomic policies. However, listed companies are often related to and influenced by each other. Particularly in the production and operation processes of listed companies, there are often complex relationships between upstream and downstream suppliers, partners, or competitors.

The financial industry has accumulated a large amount of structured and unstructured data, and many high-performance big data processing technologies [2] have made significant contributions to financial security and data analysis [3, 4]. A knowledge graph is

G. Memmi et al. (Eds.): KSEM 2022, LNAI 13368, pp. 120–132, 2022.
https://doi.org/10.1007/978-3-031-10983-6_10

a semantic web that describes the relationship between real objective entities and records attributes of entities and their interrelationships in a "entity-relation-entity" triple set. Knowledge graphs have become increasingly popular in the financial industry in recent years for financial investment [5], fraud detection [6], and *Knowledge Graph-based Question and Answer* (KBQA) [7].

Previous research on the correlation and influence between listed companies has demonstrated that a knowledge graph can not only link the entity knowledge buried in the text in a network, but also perform vectorized mapping of the embedding space for the graph using matrix decomposition [8], random-walk based embedding [9, 10], graph neural networks [11], and other powerful graph embedding technologies. Finally, during the downstream task, the mapped knowledge graph can be used to extract entity attributes and additional information hidden in the graph structure, or it can be integrated with other knowledge graphs.

The present study proposes a method which automatically extract entities such as raw materials and products from the texts describing production and operation activities of listed companies, and then construct a knowledge graph of the company's industry chain. Listed companies usually provide detailed information on their main products and raw materials used for production in their *Initial Public Offering* (IPO) prospectus and annual financial reports. Natural language texts describing production and operation can differ significantly across industries and even between companies within the same industry. Furthermore, many entity names are long and contain complex relationships. Therefore, recognizing financial industry chain entities is more difficult than recognizing named entities in the common field.

The construction of a financial knowledge graph has its own challenges because the required dataset is extracted from descriptive unstructured text in prospectuses and annual financial reports of listed companies, and there is no labeled dataset of enterprise upstream and downstream industry chains. Manual data labeling is almost equivalent to manually constructing a knowledge graph, and the text materials of listed companies are continuously updated. Thus, building and maintaining a knowledge graph of the industry chain is time consuming. Therefore, an automated extraction and labeling method is urgently required. The *Named Entity Recognition* (NER) is the most important technique for building a knowledge graph [12]. Currently, extracting accurate company information from prospectuses and annual financial statements of listed companies using the general domain NER model is difficult. Downstream industry chain entity information urgently requires an automated construction method.

The main objectives of this study are as follows. First, this study proposes combining phrase structure tree [13] and dependency parse tree [14] to analyze the subject-predicate-object structure, sentence components, corresponding parts of speech, and other information from relatively regular sentences to address the lack of labeled data in the financial industry chain. Second, this study combines a set of manual rules to complete the task of extracting financial entities. Third, automatic data labeling is achieved by reverse-mapping the dictionary generated from the financial entities extracted from the entity extraction task into the original text. Manual labeling cost can thus be significantly reduced. Finally, based on the financial text annotation dataset, the present study constructs a NER model for the financial industry chain based on the pre-training model and Bi-LSTM+CRF [15]. The accuracy and recall rate of entity extraction in the financial industry chain have been effectively improved through the integration and optimization of phrase structure tree, dependency parse tree, and the NER model.

This article contains the following sections: in Sect. 2, we introduce related work on construction of knowledge graphs in vertical domains; in Sect. 3, we introduce the method for constructing industry chain knowledge graph, including ontology modeling and knowledge extraction methods; in Sect. 4, experiments are conducted on the knowledge extraction, which proposes the effectiveness of knowledge extraction methods in this paper for construction of industry chain knowledge graph; Sect. 5 is conclusion.

2   Related Work

This section discusses related work on knowledge graph construction, vertical domain knowledge extraction, and dependency parsing. With the rapid advances in computer capabilities [16, 17], network facilities [18, 19], and the new algorithms [20, 21], large amounts of data [22, 23] can be collected and processed quickly, safely [24, 25] and accurately to generate the useful information or knowledge with the aid of machine learning [26, 27] and artificial intelligence [28, 29] techniques.

A *knowledge graph* is a technology that uses a graph model to describe knowledge and model the relationships between everything in the world. Recently, the accumulation of crowdsourced data on the World Wide Web has led to the creation of various knowledge graphs in the general domain, including Freebase [30], DBpedia [31], Yago [32], and Baidu Graph [33]. Unlike general domain knowledge graphs, vertical domain knowledge graphs are usually developed to solve a specific problem in a specific profession, and they have a higher practicability. Typical examples of such knowledge graphs include the e-commerce domain knowledge graph from Alibaba [34], Linked Life Data medical domain knowledge graph [35], and Chinese medicine knowledge graphs [36].

When constructing a vertical domain knowledge graph, domain ontology modeling, knowledge extraction, knowledge fusion, and knowledge storage are all required technologies. Knowledge extraction methods for unstructured text are mainly classified into four categories: extracting knowledge based on expert-created rules, extracting knowledge based on statistical models such as *Hidden Markov Model* (HMM) and *Conditional Random Field* (CRF) [37, 38], extracting knowledge based on dependency parsing combined with domain knowledge [39, 40], and extracting knowledge based on deep learning methods such as pre-trained models and recurrent neural networks [41]. The development of a knowledge extraction method based on manually created rules often requires high labor costs owing to the need to involve a large group of experts and the need for professionals to maintain time and update. However, knowledge extraction methods based on statistical models and deep learning models usually require a large number of labeled datasets in vertical domains to be input.

To solve the problems of high labor costs, late updates, and lack of labeled datasets that occur when developing knowledge graphs in the financial industry chain, this study proposes a knowledge extraction model based on dependency parsing technology. This study uses this foundation to label unstructured texts and use the labeled data as inputs to train a depth-based NER model Finally, the problem of the insufficient generalization ability of a single method is solved by integrating the two models, and the automatic construction of the knowledge graph for the financial industry chain can be achieved.

3   Construction Method of Industry Chain Knowledge Graph

First, the ontology of the knowledge graph in the financial field is constructed in this section using the analytical logic used when researching listed companies. Subsequently, a knowledge extraction method for industry chains based on dependency parsing is proposed. According to the extraction results, this study performed an automatic labeling task and used deep learning to train the NER model. Finally, the generalization ability of knowledge extraction is improved using model fusion, and the method proposed in this study can automatically develop an industry chain knowledge graph in the financial field.

3.1   Ontology Modeling of Knowledge Graphs in Financial Field

Ontology is the foundation and framework of a knowledge graph. An ontology is a semantic model that defines entity types, entity attributes, and associations between entities in a knowledge graph [42]. A knowledge graph in the financial field developed in this study must support the fundamental analysis of listed companies; therefore, the logical structure of the ontology must be consistent with stock research methods. The ontology must include not only listed companies and entities related to them, but also the relationships between entities and the unique attribute information of each entity.

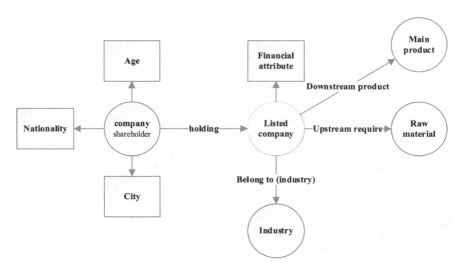

Fig. 1. The ontology of knowledge graphs in the financial field. Circles represent entities, squares represent attributes, and lines with text represent edges. The listed company entity is the core of the knowledge graph, and other industry entities, shareholder entities, etc. are connected to the listed company entities through edges.

The ontology of the financial knowledge graph developed in this study, as shown in Fig. 1, includes the following:

1. Entity types are defined as listed companies, raw materials, main products, industry, and company shareholders.
2. Following the definition of entity types, the relationship types between them are also defined. The relationship type between the listed company entity and the industry entity; for example, is "belong to (industry)," and between the listed company entity and the main product entity is a "downstream product."
3. The attribute information of each entity is also defined; for example, the entity attributes of the company shareholder entity include age, nationality, and city.

A graph definition includes a series of triplets. In this study, we are mainly concerned with extracting < listed company-downstream product-main product > and < listed company-upstream needs-raw materials > knowledge in the form of triples.

As shown in Table 1, the data used in this study to develop an industry chain knowledge graph mainly comes from the IPO prospectus and annual financial statements of listed companies. The specific data used included statements, shareholder data, and tabular and text data describing the main product and raw materials.

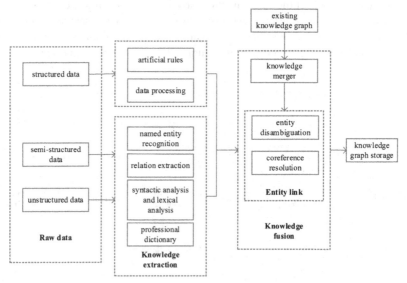

Fig. 2. The framework shows the general steps to construct a knowledge graph. From left to right, it shows a typical process from raw data, knowledge extraction, knowledge fusion to finally constructing a graph and storing it.

Figure 2 depicts the financial knowledge graph construction process. Raw data were divided into three types: structured, semi-structured, and unstructured. Structured data are directly extracted from listed company entities using manual rules and used to supplement the attribute information. Semi-structured data are used to produce share-holder and main product information of listed companies. Unstructured data is used to extract upstream raw material information from the text of the listed company, which describes its production and operation processes. The extracted knowledge is fused with the existing knowledge graph to produce a final knowledge graph.

Table 1. Data sources for building knowledge graph.

Data type	Data content	Knowledge graph
Structured data	Statement data in Annual Financial Statements	Financial attribute of listed company
Semi-structured data	Shareholder data in Annual Financial Statements	Information about shareholders
Semi-structured data	Tabular data describing the downstream main product of listed company in Annual Financial Statements	Main product entity
Unstructured data	Text data describing upstream raw materials of listed company in Annual Financial Statements and prospectus	Raw material entity

3.2   Knowledge Extraction Based on Dependency Parsing

Dependency parsing is one of the most important tasks in natural language processing. It is a prerequisite for an in-depth understanding of natural language. It performs a

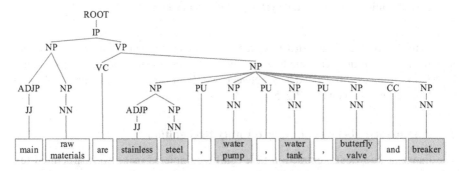

Fig. 3. The example of extracting entities from sentences and building knowledge graphs based on the phrase structure tree method. The sample is a sentence of a listed company describing the raw materials needed for its production. In the typical example of the phrase structure tree, the NP words appearing after VC (marked in bright yellow) are raw material entities. (Color figure online)

structural analysis of natural language, splitting different sentence structures and their dependencies into a tree-like structure logic, which is easy to understand and analyze. Dependency parsing techniques can be divided into two language structure disassembly methods: phrase structure trees and dependency parse trees. This study proposes a raw material entity extraction method based on these two language structure disassembly methods.

The phrase structure tree divides sentence from top to bottom based on *Probabilistic Context-Free Grammar* (PCFG) and recursively decomposes them into *Inflection Phrase* (IP), *Verb Phrase* (VP), *Noun Phrase* (NP), and other structures according to the phrase structure tree, as shown in Fig. 3. In this study, the knowledge extraction task was implemented according to the NP structure division.

The theory of dependency parsing is used to create a dependency parse tree. It generates a dependency syntax tree for a sentence and focuses on the dependencies between words in the sentence, such as the definite relationship, subject-predicate relationship, and nouns juxtaposition, as shown in Fig. 4. In this study, the knowledge extraction task is mainly accomplished by extracting the object and the *coordinate word* (COO) based on dependencies such as the *verb-object* (VOB).

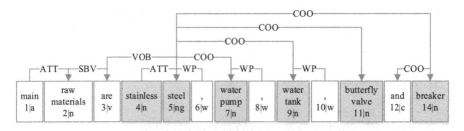

Fig. 4. The example of extracting entities from sentences and building knowledge graph based on the dependency parse tree method. The sample is a sentence of a listed company describing the raw materials needed for its production. In the typical example of the dependency parse tree, the words pointed to by the VOB relation and the words associated with it (by COO relation) are raw material entities (marked in bright yellow). (Color figure online)

In this study, the phrase structure tree and dependency parse tree were combined to extract joint entities. This method not only considers the sentence phrase structure, but also introduces the dependency between words to obtain a better financial entity extraction effect, as shown in Fig. 5.

3.3 Automatic Labeling and Named Entity Recognition

The financial knowledge extraction task can be completed using well-structured text using a dependency parsing-based method. Owing to the diversity of the semantic structure of financial texts, a dependency parsing-based method cannot completely cover all scenarios. Therefore, this method has certain limitations. In this study, the NER model is used to cover other less regular sentences and is combined with dependency parsing to improve generalization ability.

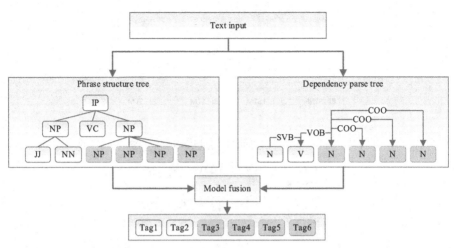

Fig. 5. The framework shows the model fusion process of phase structure trees and the dependency parse trees. The input text describes the raw materials required for production. The output is the union of the results of the knowledge extraction of the two models. The fusion model takes into account both sentence phrase structure and dependency between words.

In this study, the dependency parsing module was used to complete part of the entity extraction tasks. The extracted entity information can be customized into dictionaries for various industries, and then mapped back to the text using manual rule-matching to complete the automatic labeling task. The BIO labeling mode is used for data set labeling, which means that non-entity data are marked with "O," and the first character of the upstream raw material entity is marked as B_PM, and the internal character is marked as I_PM. After the automatic data labeling was completed, to scientifically and reasonably evaluate the performance of the model trained in this study, the labeled data were divided according to a certain proportion, of which 28,000 pieces were divided into training data sets, and the remaining 1000 pieces of data were manually annotated by experts to form the test dataset.

The NER method developed in this study uses the encoder of the pretraining model as a feature extractor. The embedding sequence of the sentence was used as input into the Bi-LSTM model for re-encoding, yielding a better representation of the input features. Bi-LSTM is adopted instead of the other versions of LSTM to achieve the retention of information transfer between the context and the context. Finally, SoftMax function is combined with the CRF to produce the optimal label sequence. The pre-training model and the downstream task model are combined to generate a deep bidirectional language representation using ALBERT as a pre-training model [43]. Bi-LSTM can effectively use the bidirectional data features of the sequences. Owing to the existence of the CRF layer, the model can also use the constraint information between sentence-level tags, as shown in Fig. 6.

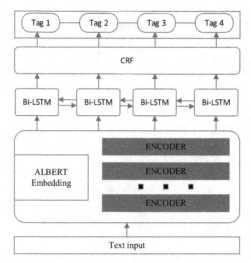

Fig. 6. Named Entity Recognition model. The samples used for training are annotated by the method based on dependency parsing in Sect. 3.2.

4   Experiment

In this section, experiments are conducted on the knowledge extraction model based on the dependency parsing method and the NER model based on an automatic labeling task. Unstructured texts from the IPO prospectuses and annual financial statements of listed companies that describe their production and operations were used as data. Among them, 28,000 samples were classified as training datasets, while the remaining 1,000 samples were manually annotated by stock analysis experts to create test datasets. The experimental results were used to compare model performance, including *Precision*, *Recall* and $F1 - Score$, which are commonly used evaluation metrics in knowledge extraction tasks.

Precision was used for the prediction results, and it indicates how many of the predicted positive samples were true positive. *Precision* is determined as follows:

$$Precision = \frac{TP}{TP + FP} \tag{1}$$

where *TP* (true positives) is the number of samples that the model predicts positive classes as positive, and *FP* (false positives) is the number of samples that the model predicts negative classes as positive.

Recall is for the original sample, which indicates how many positive examples in the sample were predicted correctly. *Recall* is determined as follows:

$$Recall = \frac{TP}{TP + FN} \tag{2}$$

where *FN* (false negatives) is the number of samples that the model predicts a positive class as negative. Because the p *recision* and *recall* indicators sometimes contradict each other, they must be considered comprehensively. The most used method is $F1 - Score$, which is calculated as follows:

$$F1 - Score = \frac{2 \times Precision \times Recall}{Precision + Recall} \quad (3)$$

This study uses the Stanford CoreNLP + NLTK technologies [44] and the Baidu artificial intelligence platform [33] to achieve knowledge extraction based on a phrase structure tree and dependency parse tree. This study also proposes a joint extraction method that combines the two models, allowing for simultaneous consideration of the phrase structure of the sentence and dependencies between words. Table 2 shows the specific experimental results, the F1 score of the fusion model is higher than the individual models, which shows that after integrating the phrase structure and dependency parse, the ability to extract knowledge has further improved.

Table 2. Knowledge extraction based on dependency parsing.

	Precision	Recall	F1-socre
Phrase structure tree	0.6335	0.5605	0.5948
Dependency parse tree	0.7844	0.6559	0.7144
Phrase structure tree + Dependency parse tree	0.7917	0.7110	0.7492

The dataset obtained after completing the labeling task based on the dependency parsing module is used to train the NER model of ALBERT + Bi-LSTM + CRF. The parameters for training the entity recognition model: GELU was used as the loss function, the hidden layer size was 768, a 12-head attention mechanism was used, a 12-layer transformer encoding structure was used, which supported a maximum encoding length of 512 bytes, and the hidden layer of Bi-LSTM was 128 neurons. During the training process, the epoch was set to five, and the batch size was set to 128, the initial learning rate was set to 0.001, and the number of training rounds was automatically corrected.

The proposed dependency parsing-based knowledge extraction method can directly extract industrial chain entities from well-structured sentences. The entity extraction task for other less-regular sentences can be better accomplished by developing a NER model. Finally, this study used two models to jointly complete the entity extraction task.

Compared with English NER, Chinese NER is different since it usually involves word segmentation. Two Chinese NER mothods, FLAT [45] and UIE [46], are used for performance comparison. FLAT is Flat-LAttice Transformer, which leverages the span position encoding. UIE is Universal Information Extraction, which uses a unified text-to-structure generation framework. As shown in Table 3, in the entity extraction task of the financial industry chain, FLAT uses more word segmentation information, so it has a high recall score, while the precision descends heavily. Instead, UIE has a more smooth Precision and Recall. Compared with a single model, the fused model in this paper gets a higher F1-Score and significantly improved Recall, and improves generalization and knowledge extraction abilities.

Table 3. Named entity recognition based on deep learning.

	Precision	Recall	F1-socre
Phrase structure tree + Dependency parse tree	0.7917	0.7110	0.7492
NER (ALBERT + Bi-LSTM + CRF)	0.7565	0.6616	0.7059
FLAT	0.5937	0.8311	0.6826
UIE	0.6970	0.7252	0.7110
Phrase structure tree + Dependency parse tree + NER	0.7097	0.8076	0.7555

5   Conclusion

This study proposed a knowledge extraction method based on a dependency parsing that combined phrase structure trees and dependency parse trees to extract industry chain knowledge and perform automated labeling tasks. This study used the obtained dataset to train the NER model based on ALBERT + Bi-LSTM + CRF and fused it with the dependency parsing knowledge extraction model, which improved generalization ability and allowed for the automatic construction of an industry chain knowledge graph. This automated knowledge graph construction technology can assist in automatically tracking and studying associations between listed companies.

Acknowledgements. The authors would like to acknowledge the support of this research by National Key R&D Program of China (no. 2019YFF0301300).

References

1. Fama, E.F., French, K.R.: The cross-section of expected stock returns. J. Finance **47**(2), 427–465 (1992)
2. Lu, R., Jin, X., Zhang, S., Qiu, M., Wu, X.: A study on big knowledge and its engineering issues. IEEE Trans. Knowl. Data Eng. **31**(9), 1630–1644 (2018)
3. Qiu, M., Zhang, L., et al.: Security-aware optimization for ubiquitous computing systems with SEAT graph approach. J. Comp. Sys. Sci. **79**(5), 518–529 (2013)
4. Gai, K., Qiu, M., Thuraisingham, B., Tao, L.: Proactive attribute-based secure data schema for mobile cloud in financial industry. In: EEE 17th HPCC, pp. 1332–1337 (2015)
5. Liu, Y., Zeng, Q., Ordieres Meré, J., Yang, H.: Anticipating stock market of the renowned companies: a knowledge graph approach. In: Complexity 2019 (2019)
6. Wang, J., Guo, Y., Wen, X., Wang, Z., Li, Z., Tang, M.: Improving graph-based label propagation algorithm with group partition for fraud detection. Appl. Intell. **50**(10), 3291–3300 (2020)
7. Cao, Z., Ni, L., Dai, L.: A review of knowledge graph-based question and answer system research and its application in chronic disease diagnosis. Acad. J. Comput. Inf. Sci. **4**(4), 1–11 (2021)
8. Bordes, A., Usunier, N., Garcia-Duran, A., Weston, J., Yakhnenko, O.: Translating embeddings for modeling multi-relational data. In: Advances in Neural Information Processing Systems, vol. 26 (2013)

9. Perozzi, B., Al-Rfou, R., Skiena, S.: Deepwalk: online learning of social representations. In: 20th ACM SIGKDD Conference on Knowledge Discovery and Data Mining, pp. 701–710 (2014)

10. Grover, A., Leskovec, J.: node2vec: scalable feature learning for networks. In: 22nd ACM SIGKDD Conference on Knowledge Discovery and Data Mining, pp. 855–864 (2016)

11. Scarselli, F., Gori, M., Tsoi, A.C., Hagenbuchner, M., Monfardini, G.: The graph neural network model. IEEE Trans. Neural Netw. **20**(1), 61–80 (2008)

12. Nadeau, D., Sekine, S.: A survey of named entity recognition and classification. Lingvisticae Investigations **30**(1), 3–26 (2007)

13. De Marneffe, M.C., MacCartney, B., Manning, C.D.: Generating typed dependency parses from phrase structure parses. Lrec **6**, 449–454 (2006)

14. Nivre, J.: Dependency grammar and dependency parsing. MSI Report **5133**(1959), 1–32 (2005)

15. Huang, Z., Xu, W., Yu, K.: Bidirectional LSTM-CRF models for sequence tagging. arXiv preprint arXiv:1508.01991 (2015)

16. Qiu, M., Xue, C., Shao, Z., Sha, E.: Energy minimization with soft real-time and DVS for uniprocessor and multiprocessor embedded systems. In: IEEE DATE Conference, pp. 1–6 (2007)

17. Qiu, M., Khisamutdinov, E., et al.: RNA nanotechnology for computer design and in vivo computation. Philos. Trans. R. Soc. A **371**(2000), 20120310 (2013)

18. Lu, Z., Wang, N., et al.: IoTDeM: an IoT big data-oriented MapReduce performance prediction extended model in multiple edge clouds. JPDC **118**, 316–327 (2018)

19. Liu, M., Zhang, S., et al.: H infinite state estimation for discrete-time chaotic systems based on a unified model. IEEE Trans. Syst. Man Cybern. (B) **42**(4), 1053–1063 (2012)

20. Qiu, L., Gai, K., Qiu, M.: Optimal big data sharing approach for tele-health in cloud computing. In: IEEE SmartCloud, pp. 184–189 (2016)

21. Qiu, M., Chen, Z., Niu, J., Zong, Z., Quan, G., Qin, X., Yang, L.T.: Data allocation for hybrid memory with genetic algorithm. IEEE Trans. Emerg. Top. Comput. **3**(4), 544–555 (2015)

22. Wu, G., Zhang, H., Qiu, M., et al.: A decentralized approach for mining event correlations in distributed system monitoring. JPDC **73**(3), 330–340 (2013)

23. Qiu, M., Cao, D., et al.: Data transfer minimization for financial derivative pricing using Monte Carlo simulation with GPU in 5G. Int. J. Comm. Sys. **29**(16), 2364–2374 (2016)

24. Qiu, M., Gai, K., Xiong, Z.: Privacy-preserving wireless communications using bipartite matching in social big data. FGCS **87**, 772–781 (2018)

25. Shao, Z., Xue, C., et al.: Security protection and checking for embedded system integration against buffer overflow attacks via hardware/software. IEEE TC **55**(4), 443–453 (2006)

26. Qiu, H., Qiu, M., Lu, Z.: Selective encryption on ECG data in body sensor network based on supervised machine learning. Inf. Fusion **55**, 59–67 (2020)

27. Li, C., Qiu, M.: Reinforcement Learning for Cyber-Physical Systems: with Cybersecurity Case Studies. Chapman and Hall/CRC (2019)

28. Li, Y., Song, Y., et al.: Intelligent fault diagnosis by fusing domain adversarial training and maximum mean discrepancy via ensemble learning. IEEE TII **17**(4), 2833–2841 (2020)

29. Qiu, H., Zheng, Q., et al.: Topological graph convolutional network-based urban traffic flow and density prediction. In: IEEE Trans on ITS (2020)

30. Bollacker, K., Cook, R., Tufts, P.: Freebase: a shared database of structured general human knowledge. In: AAAI, vol. 7, pp. 1962–1963 (2007)

31. Lehmann, J., Isele, R., Jakob, M., Jentzsch, A., et al.: Dbpedia–a large-scale, multilingual knowledge base extracted from wikipedia. Semantic Web **6**(2), 167–195 (2015)

32. Mahdisoltani, F., Biega, J., Suchanek, F.: Yago3: a knowledge base from multilingual wikipedias. In: 7th Biennial Conference on Innovative Data Systems Research. CIDR Conference (2014)

33. Baidu Artificial Intelligence Platform. https://ai.baidu.com/. Accessed 12 Mar 2022
34. Luo, X., Liu, L., Yang, Y., Bo, L., et al.: AliCoCo: Alibaba e-commerce cognitive concept net. In: ACM SIGMOD Conference on Management of Data, pp. 313–327 (2020)
35. Linked Life Data homepage. http://linkedlifedata.com/. Accessed 12 Mar 2022
36. Yu, T., Li, J., Yu, Q., Tian, Y., et al.: Knowledge graph for TCM health preservation: design, construction, and applications. Artif. Intell. Med. **77**, 48–52 (2017)
37. Finkel, J.R., Grenager, T., Manning, C.D.: Incorporating non-local information into information extraction systems by Gibbs sampling. In: 43rd ACL, pp. 363–370 (2005)
38. Liu, F., Zhao, J., Lv, B., Xu, B., Yu, H.: Product named entity recognition based on hierarchical hidden Markov model. In: 4th SIGHAN Workshop on Chinese Language Processing (2005)
39. McClosky, D., Surdeanu, M., Manning, C.D.: Event extraction as dependency parsing. In: 49th Meeting of the Association for Computational Linguistics: Human Language Technologies, pp. 1626–1635 (2011)
40. Zamiralov, A., Sohin, T., Butakov, N.: Knowledge graph mining for realty domain using dependency parsing and QAT models. Procedia Comp. Sci. **193**, 32–41 (2021)
41. Lample, G., Ballesteros, M., Subramanian, S., Kawakami, K., Dyer, C.: Neural architectures for named entity recognition. In: Proceedings of NAACL-HLT, pp. 260–270 (2016)
42. Brachman, R.J., Schmolze, J. G.: An overview of the KL-ONE knowledge representation system. In: Readings in Artificial Intelligence and Databases, pp. 207–230 (1989)
43. Lan, Z., Chen, M., Goodman, S., et al.: Albert: a lite bert for self-supervised learning of language representations. arXiv preprint arXiv:1909.11942 (2019)
44. Stanford-CoreNLP-API-in-NLTK.   https://github.com/nltk/nltk/wiki/Stanford-CoreNLP-API-in-NLTK. Accessed 12 Mar 2022
45. Li, X., Yan, H., Qiu, X., Huang, X.: FLAT: Chinese NER using flat-lattice transformer. In: 58th Annual Meeting of the Association for Computational Linguistics, pp. 6836–6842 (2020)
46. Lu, Y., Liu, Q., Dai, D., Xiao, X., et al.: Unified structure generation for universal information extraction. In: 60th Meeting of the Association for Computational Linguistics, pp. 5755–5772 (2022)

Query and Neighbor-Aware Reasoning Based Multi-hop Question Answering over Knowledge Graph

Biao Ma[1], Xiaoying Chen[1,2(✉)], and Shengwu Xiong[1,3]

[1] School of Computer Science and Artificial Intelligence,
Wuhan University of Technology, Wuhan, China
{lilma,xiaoying.chen,xiongsw}@whut.edu.cn
[2] Hubei Credit Information Center, Wuhan, China
[3] Sanya Science and Education Innovation Park of Wuhan University of Technology,
Sanya, China

Abstract. Multi-hop Question Answering over Knowledge Graph (multi-hop KGQA) is a challenging task since it requires reasoning with multiple triplets over knowledge graph to find the correct answer entities. Benefiting from expeditious development of attention mechanism and graph neural network, recent works in multi-hop KGQA based on information retrieval have made great progress. However, most existing works focus on encoding questions and knowledge graph in isolation so that the reasoning module lacks interaction of encoding information. Additionally, they only consider matching relation embeddings with the encoded queries at each hop, hence the complex questions, such as those containing one-to-many relation, are hard to answer. In this paper, we propose a query and neighbor-aware reasoning based multi-hop KGQA model to solve the above problems by introducing the CoAttention module and the neighbor-aware reasoning module. Experiments show that our model can not only keep competitive performance on MetaQA datasets but also improve performance than the state-of-the-art baselines on the wide-used benchmarks WebQSP and CWQ.

Keywords: Knowledge graph · Multi-hop question answering · Information retrieval · Graph neural network · Deep learning

1 Introduction

Recent years have seen great popularization of knowledge graph (KG), which is a directed graph with nodes and edges representing entities and relations between entities, respectively. Question Answering over Knowledge Graph (KGQA) aims to automatically answer natural language questions by utilizing the abundant and structured information stored in KG [1–3]. KGQA requires models to understand the factoid questions and predict the answers with KG.

Multi-hop KGQA aims to reason with the entities and relations at multiple steps over KG [4–6]. This task is challenging since it lacks a specific relation

© The Author(s), under exclusive license to Springer Nature Switzerland AG 2022
G. Memmi et al. (Eds.): KSEM 2022, LNAI 13368, pp. 133–145, 2022.
https://doi.org/10.1007/978-3-031-10983-6_11

path as input of models. Additionally, the KGs, also as search space, are usually remarkably large for searching the answer entities. Existing methods in multi-hop KGQA can be divided into two mainstream categories: semantic parsing and information retrieval. We develop our work with the idea of information retrieval.

However, existing works [7–10] mainly focus on encoding question and KG in isolation, which is also known as sequence-to-sequence task and KG embedding task. Therefore, the natural language questions and entities in KG lack interaction of encoding information, and the reasoning module is unable to select candidate entities that are the most relevant to the question, either. Moreover, most existing works only consider matching relation embeddings with the encoded queries at each hop. Those works fail to handle the complex relation types in KG, such as one-to-many relation. Consequently, the reasoning ability is constrained in relation encoding. For example, given a question *Who played obi wan in episode 2?*, the model needs to recognize the semantic information from it and find the answer about the entity *Star War Episode 2*, otherwise the wrong answers of the other episodes such as *Star War Episode 1* would be predicted. However, whether *Star War Episode 1* or *Star War Episo— de 2*, the reasoning relation path is always same as *Obi Wan* $\xrightarrow{portrayed\_in\_films}$ *movie* $\xrightarrow{actor}$ *answer entity*, hence it is necessary for the model to discriminate which movie matches the query better.

To solve the problems mentioned above, we propose a method called Query and Neighbor-aware Reasoning based KGQA (QNRKGQA) as illustrated in Fig. 1. A CoAttention module is added to generate query-aware entity embeddings as input of the neighbor-aware reasoning module. Besides, to take full advantage of the learned query-aware entity embeddings, we build our neighbor-aware reasoning module in a way of Graph Neural Network (GNN). Our model can generate entity embeddings integrated with the question information, and handle complex relation types in KG to answer the more complex questions.

In general, we summarize our contribution as follows:

- The CoAttention module is introduced into our QNRKGQA model to solve the independent encoding problem, and it generates entity embeddings integrated with encoded question information as the input of the reasoning module.
- We focus on the complex relation types such as one-to-many relation in KG and a neighbor-aware reasoning module is proposed to lead triplets matching the query at each reasoning step. With the query-aware entity embeddings as input, our proposed QNRKGQA model manages to deal with the more complex questions.
- Experiments show that our model can not only keep competitive performance on structured benchmark MetaQA (MetaQA-1hop, MetaQA-2hop, and MetaQA-3hop) but also improve performance than the state-of-the-art baselines on Hits@1 metric of more complex benchmarks WebQSP and CWQ.

The rest of this paper is organized as follows: Sect. 2 summarizes the recent KGQA works related to our work. Section 3 presents our approach with particular attention to the CoAttention and neighbor-aware reasoning module. In Sect. 4, we show our experiments on different benchmarks, providing a detailed exploration of analysis of performances, ablation study, and case study. Finally, Sect. 5 concludes our work.

2   Related Work

2.1   Multi-hop KGQA

As mentioned above, existing works in multi-hop KGQA can be divided into two mainstream categories: semantic parsing and information retrieval. Methods based on semantic parsing commonly convert natural language questions into formal queries, like query graph [14–16], and then execute the queries to find the answers. Methods based on information retrieval need to extract subgraphs centered by labeled topic entities firstly. These methods regard all the entities except topic entities in the subgraph as candidate answers, then find answers with max probability based on semantic similarity between natural language questions and candidate entities, like score function [18] and other customized methods [7–9]. With the convenience and impressive performance achieved by information retrieval, plenty of works have developed recently. The memory network utilized an external memory to perform reasoning module [19], which can be updated during multi-hop reasoning. Some works treated multi-hop KGQA as a reinforcement learning task [9]. Besides, several works incorporated external knowledge for this task, like corpus [7,8] and SPARQL [15].

2.2   Attention in KGQA

Relying on huge success by attention mechanism, a large number of works on KGQA utilized attention mechanism to improve their performance. MTQA-net [25] proposed multi-view attention to learn more comprehensive sentence representations. BAMnet [20] added bidirectional attention to memory network. CFC [11] proposed a coarse-grain module and a fine-grain module to combine information from evidence across multiple documents. However, these works either lacked excellent reasoning capacity or neglected the independent encoding problem.

2.3   GNN in KGQA

GNN has been widely used in many domains, including node classification [12] and graph embedding [13,17]. Also, some works apply GNN to multi-hop KGQA task. GraftNet [7] encoded subgraphs extracted by GNN to find the answers. PullNet [8] proposed a retrieve-and-reason process to solve the low recall problem. NSM [10] proposed a special GNN reasoning module, which achieved remarkable competitive performance. However, these models only considered matching the relation embeddings with the encoded queries at each hop and neglected the complex relation type in KGs like one-to-many relation, thus failing to deal with the more complex questions.

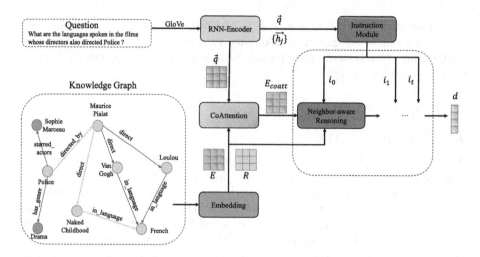

Fig. 1. The framework of our proposed QNRKGQA model.

3   Methodology

3.1   Preliminary

A KG can be denoted as $G = \{V, E\}$, where V represents the set of entities, also known as nodes, and E represents the set of relations, known as edges. $E \in \mathbb{R}^{n_e \times d}$ and $R \in \mathbb{R}^{n_r \times d}$ denote entity embedding matrix and relation embedding matrix in KG respectively. n_e and n_r denote the number of entities and relations, respectively, and d represents the embedding dimension. A KG consists of multiple triplets (h, r, t), where $h \in \mathbb{R}^d$ denotes head entity, $t \in \mathbb{R}^d$ denotes tail entity and $r \in \mathbb{R}^d$ denotes the relation between h and t. For instance, *(Lone Star, written_by, John Sayles)*. Especially, N_e denotes the set of neighbor entities that have edges connected to the entity e.

The given natural language question is labeled with entities, which are called topic entities. As shown in Fig. 1, given a question *What are the languages spoken in the films whose directors also directed Police?*, the labeled topic entity is *Police*. Multi-hop KGQA task aims to reason from topic entities to answer entities with the context of the given question.

3.2   Instruction Module and KG Initialization

Given a natural language question Q with $|Q|$ words, i.e. $Q = \{w_0, w_1, \ldots, w_{|Q|}\}$, we treat it as a sequence-to-sequence task by using pretrained word vector (i.e. GloVe [21]) to transfer the raw query words into query embeddings firstly. Then a bidirectional LSTM [22] is used to encode the question as $H = \{h_0, h_1, \ldots, h_{|Q|}\}$, which is the sequence of hidden states. The output of bidirectional LSTM q is regarded as the representation of the given question.

Following Neural State Machine [23] and NSM [10], we obtain instruction vector as input query information at each steps. The attention mechanism is utilized to generate instruction vector i^k, which represents encoded query dynamically at the k-th reasoning step:

$$i^k = \sum_j^{|Q|} \alpha_j^k h_j, \tag{1}$$

$$\alpha_j^k = softmax_j(W_\alpha^k(q^k \odot h_j) + b_\alpha^k), \tag{2}$$

$$q^k = W_q^k(i^{k-1} \parallel q) + b_q^k, \tag{3}$$

where $W_\alpha^k \in \mathbb{R}^{d \times d}$, $W_q^k \in \mathbb{R}^{2d \times d}$ denote the linear transformation matrices, $b_\alpha^k, b_q^k \in \mathbb{R}^d$ are corresponding biases, and $\odot$ represents element-wise product. Instruction module can offer different focuses at different steps, making the reasoning process more robust.

As for KG initialization, since the search space is remarkably large, relation embeddings are utilized to initialize entity embeddings, which can be formulated as:

$$e_{init} = relu(\sum_{(h,\ r,\ t) \in N_e} W_{init}r + b_{init}), \tag{4}$$

where $W_{init} \in \mathbb{R}^{d \times d}$, $b_{init} \in \mathbb{R}^d$ are linear transformation parameters, $e_{init} \in \mathbb{R}^d$. $E_{init} \in \mathbb{R}^{n_e \times d}$ denotes the initialization entity embedding matrix, which consists of all the entities e_{init} of each subgraph.

3.3 CoAttention Module

To build interaction of encoding information, the CoAttention module is used to generate the codependent representation of encoded query and entity embeddings in KG. We take the query representation q and initialization entity embedding matrix E_{init} as input. Inspired by CFC [11], firstly we can get the affinity matrix between them:

$$F_{eq} = E_{init}(q^T). \tag{5}$$

Then the entity summary vector and the query summary vector are calculated as follow:

$$s_e = softmax\,(F_{eq})\,q, \tag{6}$$

$$s_q = softmax\,(F_{eq}^T)\,E_{init}, \tag{7}$$

where $softmax(\cdot)$ represents column-wise normalization. To make sure that the encoding information becomes more similar, bidirectional LSTM is used to generate the query-aware entity embeddings:

$$D_e = BiLSTM(softmax\,(F_{eq})\,s_q), \tag{8}$$

$$E_{coatt} = W_{sd}(s_e \| D_e) + b_{sd}, \tag{9}$$

where $E_{coatt} \in \mathbb{R}^{n_e \times d}$, $||$ denotes concatenation, $W_{sd} \in \mathbb{R}^{d \times 2d}$, $b_{sd} \in \mathbb{R}^d$ are linear transformation parameters. Note that our CoAttention module is designed to build interaction between encoded questions and KGs. The generated query-aware entity embeddings contain more information than the counterpart in knowledge graph embedding, which helps the reasoning module assign a larger probability to those entities matching the query.

3.4   Neighbor-Aware Reasoning

According to our observation, the reasoning process in multi-hop KGQA requires an excellent capacity to filter which triplet is more reasonable at the next hop. In consideration of query-aware entity embeddings, we develop our reasoning module in a way of GNN. The correlation between triplets and the instruction at k-th step can be formulated by:

$$c_{hrt}^k = i^k \bigodot W_{tr}[h \mid\mid r \mid\mid t], \tag{10}$$

where $W_{tr} \in \mathbb{R}^{3d \times d}$, h and t are obtained from entity embeddings at k-th step. To learn the importance of each triplet matching the query, we perform a linear transformation parameterized by a weight matrix $W_c \in \mathbb{R}^{d \times d}$ and bias $b_c \in \mathbb{R}^d$:

$$\beta_{hrt}^k = LeakyReLU(W_c c_{hrt}^k + b_c). \tag{11}$$

The importance message can be aggregated by the entity distribution at the previous step:

$$e^k = ||_{m=1}^M \sum_{<h,r,t> \in N_e} \beta_{hrt}^k d^{k-1}, \tag{12}$$

where $||$ denotes concatenation and M is a hyperparameter. To update the entity embeddings, multi-head attention is used to permit the reasoning module to make multiple choices, which enables our model to lessen the effect of noise and deviation, and we name it multi-choices below. Theoretically, the whole model can converge faster due to the efficiency of multi-choices.

Finally, the entity distribution at current reasoning step is calculated by softmax:

$$d^k = softmax(W_e([e^{k-1} \mid\mid e^k]) + b_e), \tag{13}$$

where $W_e \in \mathbb{R}^{(M+1)d \times d}$, $b_c \in \mathbb{R}^d$ are parameters to be learned. We execute this module step-by-step, and the whole reasoning process is explicit and explainable.

To train our model, KL-divergence is used between prediction results and labeled answer entities as objection function to compute loss during training:

$$L = KL(d^T, \ a), \tag{14}$$

where d^T is the predicted entity distribution at the last reasoning step T, and a is the distribution of labeled answer entities.

Inspired by the knowledge distillation method in NSM$_{+h}$ [10], hybrid reasoning is used to rich the supervision signal of our QNRKGQA model. The backward reasoning process from predicted answer entities generated by aforementioned forward reasoning to topic entities is the teacher network. The intermediate entity distribution can be regarded as intermediate supervision signal. We name it QNRKGQA$_{+h}$, and the corresponding objection function is formulated as:

$$L_h = KL(d^T, a) + \lambda KL(d^k, d_t^k), \tag{15}$$

where d^k denotes the intermediate entity distribution at k-th reasoning step, λ is a hyperparameter and d_t^k denotes the counterpart generated by the teacher network of backward reasoning:

$$d_t^k = (d^k + d_b^{T-k})/2, \tag{16}$$

where d_b^k denotes the intermediate entity distribution at $(T - k)$-th backward reasoning step.

4   Experiment

4.1   Dataset

We verify the effectiveness of our proposed method and compare ours with other state-of-the-art baselines on three widely used datasets: (1) MetaQA [24] is based on WikiMovies [19], and it consists of more than 400k questions from single-hop questions to 3-hop questions, which is generated by the templates. (2) WebQSP [26] is based on Freebase, and its knowledge graph contains more than 50 domains. It consists of 4.7k questions and these questions require single-hop or 2-hop reasoning. (3) ComplexWebQuestion (CWQ) [27] is generated by extending the WebQSP questions to make them more complex and consists of 34k questions. There are four types of questions in CWQ: composition, conjunction, comparative, and superlative.

Following NSM [10], the PageRank-Nibble algorithm is adopted to extract the subgraphs of each question with labeled topic entities in original datasets. The details of these datasets are listed in Table 1.

4.2   Implementation Details

As for the general experiment setting, we adopt dropout for bidirectional LSTM to make the training process more stable and the dropout probability is set to 0.3. For model training, we set the batch size to 80 for MetaQA and CWQ datasets and 20 for WebQSP dataset. The models on these datasets are all optimized by using Adam [28] with the learning rate 0.0005.

On MetaQA datasets, the reasoning step number is set to $T = 1$, $T = 2$ and $T = 3$ on MetaQA-1hop, MetaQA-2hop and MetaQA-3hop datasets respectively. Therefore, we have evaluation results of QNRKGQA$_{+h}$ on MetaQA-2hop and MetaQA-3hop datasets, which is more reasonable and explainable than NSM$_{+h}$. We set the embedding dimension to 80 on three datasets. For the neighbor-aware reasoning module, the parameter M is set to 2. We add inverse relation

Table 1. The statistics of MetaQA(MetaQA-1hop, MetaQA-2hop, MetaQA-3hop), WebQSP and CWQ datasets. #*Total entities* denotes the total entity number of all subgraphs in a dataset, and #*Total relations* denotes the total relation number of all subgraphs in a dataset.

Dataset	Train	Dev	Test	#Total entities	#Total relations
MetaQA-1hop	96,106	9,992	9,947	43,234	9
MetaQA-2hop	118,980	14,872	14,872	43,234	9
MetaQA-3hop	114,196	14,274	14,274	43,234	9
WebQSP	2,848	250	1,639	1,441,420	6,102
CWQ	27,639	3,519	3,531	2,429,346	6,649

into MetaQA datasets, contributing to representing relations in natural language questions, such as *direct* and *directed_by*.

In terms of WebQSP and CWQ datasets, we set the reasoning step number T = 3 and T = 4 respectively, and the embedding dimension is set to 100 and 80 respectively. M in the multi-choices module is set to 3 on both two datasets. To deal with the questions with uncertain hops, we add self-loop relation into both two datasets.

Table 2. Comparison of our method and other baselines on WebQSP, CWQ, and MetaQA datasets with Hits@1. Note that the results of baselines are taken from NSM [10] and reported in percentage. Bold and underlined fonts denote the best and the second best performance.

Models	Webqsp	CWQ	MetaQA-1hop	MetaQA-2hop	MetaQA-3hop
KV-Mem	47.6	21.1	96.2	82.7	48.9
GraftNet	66.4	32.8	97.0	94.8	77.7
PullNet	68.1	45.9	97.0	99.9	91.4
SRN	-	-	97.0	95.1	75.2
EmbedKGQA	66.6	-	**97.5**	98.8	94.8
NSM	68.7	47.6	97.1	**99.9**	**98.9**
NSM$_{+p}$	73.9	48.3	<u>97.3</u>	**99.9**	**98.9**
NSM$_{+h}$	74.3	48.8	97.2	**99.9**	**98.9**
QNRKGQA	<u>74.9</u>	<u>50.5</u>	<u>97.3</u>	**99.9**	**98.9**
QNRKGQA$_{+h}$	**75.7**	**51.5**	-	**99.9**	**98.9**

4.3   Results and Analysis

To assess the effectiveness of our proposed method, we compare our method with several state-of-the-art baselines, including KV-Mem [19], GraftNet [7],

PullNet [8], SRN [9], NSM [10], NSM_{+p} [10] and NSM_{+h} [10]. Table 2 shows our evaluation results on these datasets compared with other baselines.

Specifically, we show that our QNRKGQA and $QNRKGQA_{+h}$ can not only keep competitive performance on MetaQA-1hop, MetaQA-2hop, and MetaQA-3hop datasets with a more reasonable and explainable reasoning step number but also improve performance than the state-of-the-art baselines on Hits@1 metric of WebQSP and CWQ datasets. Moreover, the improvement of QNRKGQA and $QNRKGQA_{+h}$ on WebQSP and CWQ datasets is incremental, which also demonstrates our model can earn a better performance when handling the more complex questions.

4.4 Ablation Study

To estimate the effectiveness of the different factors, the ablation experiments are implemented in the following aspects: We utilize the proposed method without the CoAttention module (i.e. QNRKGQA-coatt and $QNRKGQA_{+h} - coatt$) or the neighbor-aware reasoning module (i.e. QNRKGQA-na and $\{QNRKGQA_{+h} - na\}$). Table 3 shows the results of the ablation study on WebQSP and CWQ datasets. In implementation, we remove the neighbor-ware module by removing the multi-choices and the neighbor entity embeddings (head entity and tail entity) to make the encoded query match the relation embeddings directly.

We also show F1 matric in ablation study to compare QNRKGQA and $QNRKGQA_{+h}$ with NSM and NSM+h since few baselines report F1 in their original papers. And QNRKGQA and $QNRKGQA_{+h}$ also achieve significant improvement on the F1 metric.

Table 3. Performance of ablation study on WebQSP and CWQ datatsets.

Models	Webqsp		CWQ	
	Hits@1	F1	Hits@1	F1
NSM_{+h}	74.3	67.4	48.8	44.0
$QNRKGQA_{+h}$	**75.7**	**70.8**	**51.5**	**48.1**
$QNRKGQA_{+h} - coatt$	74.9	69.0	49.7	46.6
$QNRKGQA_{+h} - na$	74.6	69.4	49.2	44.2
NSM	68.7	62.8	47.6	42.4
QNRKGQA	<u>74.9</u>	<u>68.9</u>	<u>50.8</u>	<u>46.9</u>
QNRKGQA − coatt	73.5	67.8	48.1	45.5
QNRKGQA − na	73.4	66.4	48.2	43.3

4.5 Influence of Parameters

Note that the CoAttention module is parameter-free, hence we do not study the parameter sensitivity analysis on this module but on the neighbor-aware module. Here we conduct the parameter sensitivity analysis to determine the value of M in multi-choices, and we set the value among $\{1, 2, 3, 4, 5\}$. Figure 2(a) shows the results of F1 under these values of M. QNRKGQA achieves the best performance when $M = 3$.

Furthermore, we conduct the model efficiency on dev datasets of WebQSP as shown in Fig. 2(b). We show that QNRKGQA converges faster than NSM, which confirms our theoretical conjecture. Evidently, QNRKGQA starts converging after 50 epochs while NSM starts converging after 150 epochs.

As for the other parameters, we tuned the value of λ among 0.01, 0.05, 0.1, 0.5, 1.0, 5.0 and $QNRKGQA_{+h}$ achieves best performance when $\lambda = 0.05$. In the same way, the learning rate and embedding dimension are tuned amongst $\{0.00005, 0.0003, 0.0005, 0.0007, 0.005\}$ and $\{50, 80, 100, 120, 150\}$. We do not state the details of tuning these parameters.

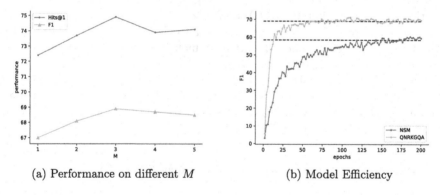

(a) Performance on different M (b) Model Efficiency

Fig. 2. Parameter sensitivity analysis of M in multi-choices, performance on the left and efficiency on the right.

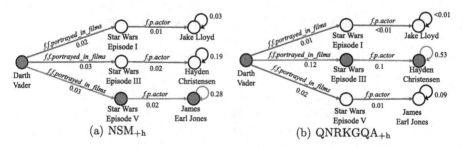

(a) NSM_{+h} (b) $QNRKGQA_{+h}$

Fig. 3. Case from WebQSP: *Who did the voice of darth vader in episode 3?* Correct answer is *Hayden Christensen*. We simplify the relation name *film. film_character.portrayed_in_films* as *f.f.portrayed_in_films*, *film.p− erformance. actor* as *f.p.actor*. The numbers beside the edges are entity probabilities at every hop.

4.6 Case Study

To illustrate how QNRKGQA performs on complex questions, we conduct a case study on WebQSP questions to show how our model works on complex questions. Note that we use the reasoning step number T = 3 on WebQSP dataset, hence the last step commonly lies on self-loop relation to increase answer entities' probability.

As shown in Fig. 3, given a question *Who did the voice of darth vader in episode* 3? with labeled topic entity *darth vader*, the reasoning module needs to discriminate the intermedia entities, also known as CVT nodes, from different episodes of Star Wars based on the query. Whether the forward reasoning or the backward reasoning process, the difference of episodes cannot be differentiated in NSM_{+h} since the relation of each hop is fixed. Thanks to the CoAttention module and neighbor-aware reasoning module, $QNRKGQA_{+h}$ obtains the query-aware entity embeddings and predicts the more reasonable relation path with a greater probability about the entity Star War Episode 3.

5   Conclusion

In this paper, we proposed a query and neighbor-aware reasoning based model for multi-hop KGQA. It leveraged the independent encoding problem and complex relation type problem by introducing the CoAttention module and the neighbor-aware reasoning module. The evaluation experiments show that our model can not only keep competitive performance on MetaQA datasets but also improve performance than the state-of-the-art baselines on the wide-used benchmarks WebQSP and CWQ. Extra analysis and study show that our model also possesses high efficiency and explainability.

Acknowledgements. This work was in part supported by NSFC (Grant No. 62176194, Grant No.62101 393), the Major project of IoV (Grant No. 2020AAA001), Sanya Science and Education Innovation Park of Wuhan University of Technology (Grant No. 2021KF0 031), CSTC (Grant No. cstc2021jcyj-msxmX1148) and the Open Project of Wuhan University of Technology Chongqing Research Institute (ZL2021-6). We thank MindSpore for the partial support of this work, which is a new deep learning computing framework (https://www.mindspore.cn/).

References

1. Berant, J., Chou, A., Frostig, R., Liang, P.: Semantic parsing on freebase from question-answer pairs. In: EMNLP, pp. 1533–1544, October 2013
2. Bast, H., Haussmann, E. More accurate question answering on freebase. In: ICKM, pp. 1431–1440 (2015)
3. Abujabal, A., Yahya, M., Riedewald, M., Weikum, G.: Automated template generation for question answering over knowledge graphs. In: WWW, pp. 1191–1200 (2017)
4. Zhang, Y., Dai, H., Kozareva, Z., Smola, A. J., Song, L.: Variational reasoning for question answering with knowledge graph. In: AAAI, pp. 6069–6076 (2018)

5. Zhou, M., Huang, M., Zhu, X.: An interpretable reasoning network for multi-relation question answering. In: COLING, pp. 2010–2022 (2018)
6. Lan, Y., Wang, S., Jiang, J.: Multi-hop knowledge base question answering with an iterative sequence matching model. In: ICDM, pp. 359–368 (2019)
7. Sun, H., Dhingra, B., Zaheer, M., Mazaitis, K., Salakhutdinov, R., Cohen, W.W.: Open domain question answering using early fusion of knowledge bases and text. In: EMNLP, pp. 4231–4242 (2018)
8. Sun, H., Bedrax-Weiss, T., Cohen, W.W.: Pullnet: pen domain question answering with iterative retrieval on knowledge bases and text. In: EMNLP/IJCNLP, pp. 2380–2390 (2019)
9. Qiu, Y., Wang, Y., Jin, X., Zhang, K.: Stepwise reasoning for multi-relation question answering over knowledge graph with weak supervision. In: WSDM, pp. 474–482 (2020)
10. He, G., Lan, Y., Jiang, J., Zhao, W.X., Wen, J.R.: Improving multi-hop knowledge base question answering by learning intermediate supervision signals. In: WSDM, pp. 553–561 (2021)
11. Zhong, V., Xiong, C., Keskar, N.S., Socher, R.: Coarse-grain fine-grain coattention network for multi-evidence question answering. In: ICLR (2019)
12. Kipf, T.N., Welling, M.: Semi-supervised classification with graph convolutional networks. In: ICLR (2017)
13. Nathani, D., Chauhan, J., Sharma, C., Kaul, M.: Learning attention-based embeddings for relation prediction in knowledge graphs. In: ACL, pp. 4710–4723 (2019)
14. Luo, K., Lin, F., Luo, X., Zhu, K.: Knowledge base question answering via encoding of complex query graphs. In: EMNLP, pp. 2185–2194 (2018)
15. Bhutani, N., Zheng, X., Jagadish, H.V.: Learning to answer complex questions over knowledge bases with query composition. In: CIKM, pp. 739–748 (2019)
16. Lan, Y., Jiang, J.: Query graph generation for answering multi-hop complex questions from knowledge bases. In: ACL, pp. 969–974 (2020)
17. Schlichtkrull, M., Kipf, T.N., Bloem, P., Van Den Berg, R., Titov, I., Welling, M.: Modeling relational data with graph convolutional networks. In: ESWC, pp. 593–607 (2018)
18. Saxena, A., Tripathi, A., Talukdar, P.: Improving multi-hop question answering over knowledge graphs using knowledge base embeddings. In: ACL, pp. 4498–4507 (2020)
19. Miller, A., Fisch, A., Dodge, J., Karimi, A.H., Bordes, A., Weston, J.: Key-value memory networks for directly reading documents. In: EMNLP, pp. 1400–1409 (2016)
20. Chen, Y., Wu, L., Zaki, M.J.: Bidirectional attentive memory networks for question answering over knowledge bases. In: NAACL, pp. 2913–2923 (2019)
21. Pennington, J., Socher, R., Manning, C.D.: Glove: global vectors for word representation. In: EMNLP, pp. 1532–1543 (2014)
22. Hochreiter, S., Schmidhuber, J.: Long short-term memory. Neural Comput. **9**(8), 1735–1780 (1997)
23. Hudson, D.A., Manning, C.D.: Learning by abstraction: the neural state machine. In: NeurIPS, pp. 5901–5914 (2019)
24. Zhang, Y., Dai, H., Kozareva, Z., Smola, A.J., Song, L.: Variational reasoning for question answering with knowledge graph. In: AAAI, pp. 6069–6076 (2018)
25. Deng, Y., Xie, Y., Li, Y., Yang, M., Du, N., Fan, W., Shen, Y.: Multi-task learning with multi-view attention for answer selection and knowledge base question answering. In: AAAI, pp. 6318–6325 (2019)

26. Yih, S.W.T., Chang, M.W., He, X., Gao, J.: Semantic parsing via staged query graph generation: Question answering with knowledge base. In: ACL, pp. 1321–1331 (2015)
27. Talmor, A., Berant, J.: The web as a knowledge-base for answering complex questions. In: NAACL, pp. 641–651 (2018)
28. Kingma, D. P., Ba, J.: Adam: a method for stochastic optimization. In: ICLR (2015)

Question Answering over Knowledge Graphs with Query Path Generation

Linqing Yang, Kecen Guo, Bo Liu[✉], Jiazheng Gong, Zhujian Zhang, and Peiyu Zhao

College of Information Science and Technology, Jinan University, Guangzhou, China
joesphy_yang@163.com, {gkc0421,gongjiazheng}@stu2020.jnu.edu.cn,
ddxllb@163.com, {zzj2021,jnuzpy}@stu2021.jnu.edu.cn

Abstract. Knowledge graphs have been applied in question answering. Many researchers have proposed methods based on query graph generation, but there are some defects such as high cost of query graph generation and large search scope of knowledge graphs. Especially for the complex questions, which refer to those with multi-hop relations and constraints, there are problems such as incomplete search and inaccurate selection of answers. In order to solve the problems mentioned above, this paper proposes a staged query path generation method. The approach firstly takes the predicate sequence of the question in knowledge graphs as the breakthrough and constructs the core path. Then, the constraints are obtained by analyzing the question. And on this basis, the core path is extended to generate the query path. Finally, the final answer to the question is determined through the query path. Experimental results show that the Hit score of proposed approach is higher than that of many competitive state-of-the-art baselines.

Keywords: Question answering · Knowledge graphs · Query path generation · Predicate sequence · Complex questions

1 Introduction

Question answering (QA) is the advanced form of information retrieval, which aims at answering the questions in natural language. Moreover, question answering over knowledge graph (KGQA) has the following data advantages. Firstly, in the knowledge graph (KG), an entity is associated with other entities or its attribute values through edges with semantic information. Secondly, constructing the KG usually requires the participation of experts, so it has higher accuracy. Thirdly, the structured form of KG not only improves the retrieval efficiency of computer, but also makes it possible to locate answers accurately.

Supported by the National Key Research and Development Project of China (2018YFC2002500).

G. Memmi et al. (Eds.): KSEM 2022, LNAI 13368, pp. 146–158, 2022.
https://doi.org/10.1007/978-3-031-10983-6_12

Nowadays, methods of KGQA can be divided into 5 categories: template-based [2,3], query graph-based [7,10,14,16], network-based [8,11–13,15], question graph alignment-based [1] and embedding-based [4–6,9] methods. However, the above approaches have several shortcomings. More specifically, in the template-based approach, it's not possible to cover all situations with manually defined templates. In the query graph-based approach, establishing the relationship between the question and each candidate query graph has some defects such as high cost of query graph generation, large search scope of knowledge graphs and low search efficiency. In embedding-based approach, the black box has poor interpretability. In addition, for complex questions, which refer to those with multi-hop relations and constraints, there are problems such as incomplete search and inaccurate selection of answers.

The research goal of our paper is how to answer the natural language questions, especially for the complex questions with multi-hop relations and constraints. The proposed method can save the cost of query graph generation, improve the interpretability of model, reduce the search scope of KG, and improve the accuracy of QA.

The main contributions of this paper can be summarized as follows:

- This paper takes the predicate sequence of the question in KG as the breakthrough and proposes a staged query path generation method, including predicate sequence detector training model and query path generation and answer selection model.
- The predicate sequence detector can transform the question answering model from query graph level to predicate level. The QA model firstly learns not the features of the query graph, but the predicates corresponding to the question in the KG. Furthermore, associate questions with predicate sequences and extended triples in KG, rather than directly with query graphs.
- Our model can not only enhance the interpretability of QA and solve the problem of high cost of query graph generation, but also accurately understand the intention of the question, greatly narrow the range of answer choices and save the consumption of computing resources.

The paper is organized as follows: in Sect. 2, we introduce the related work of KGQA. We describe the proposed approach in Sect. 3. In Sect. 4, the results and analysis of experiment are described. After that, conclusions are given in Sect. 5.

2 Related Work

The section introduces the work of KGQA, including template-based, query graph-based, network-based, question graph alignment-based and embedding-based methods.

Template-based question answering rely on templates to translate natural language sentences into pre-defined logical forms [2,3]. Additionally, a staged query path generation method was proposed in work [7,14]. The work [10] proposed a question answering system with predicate constraints, including dictionary construction module and dictionary-based QA module. And the work [16] proposed a framework to answer natural language questions in a user-interactive manner while keeping the cost as low as possible.

Furthermore, the key-value memory network retrieves answers with data table and the table stores facts and text encoded as key-value pairs in work [8]. In order to solve the noise problem of natural language and multi-hop inference based on knowledge graphs, the work [15] introduced an end-to-end variational inference network, which could simultaneously locate the topic entity of the question and find the unknown inference steps leading to the answer based on the question-answer pairs. The work [12] proposed a GRAFT-Net model, which creates problem-specific subgraphs containing facts, entities, and textual sentences with heuristic method and performs reasoning with variant Convolutional Neural Network (CNN). PullNet was proposed in work [11] and the model could extract facts and sentences from data to create more relevant subgraphs and perform reasoning with graph CNN. The work [13] introduced a semantic fusion model, which uses Recurrent Neural Network (RNN) to build sequence annotation module and design dynamic candidate path generation algorithm to achieve multi-hop reasoning.

A novel framework for resource description framework (RDF) question answering based on data-driven graph similarity was proposed in [1]. And a method based on knowledge embedding for KGQA was introduced in [5]. In addition, the work [9] proposed EmbedKGQA model to solve multi-hop QA mission based on knowledge graph. The work [6] proposed the RceKGQA model, which introduced relational chain reasoning to improve the multi-hop reasoning.

3   Approach

3.1   Related Definition

Definition 1. *Knowledge graph (KG) is represented as a quadruple, namely $KG = (E, R, P, PV)$. Where E is the set of entities, R is the set of relations, P is the set of attributes and PV is the set of attribute values.*

Definition 2. *Triplet is the basic unit of KG, which consists of subject s, predicate p and object o, namely $t = (s, p, o), s \in E, p \in R \cup P, o \in E \cup PV$. In the KG, the subject and object of triplet correspond to nodes, and edges correspond to predicates.*

Definition 3. *Focus word is the entity linked to the topic entity mention in the question and is the starting point for finding answers in the KG.*

Definition 4. *Predicate sequence is the sequence of predicates on the path from the focus word to the answer in KG.*

Definition 5. *Core path is the subgraph of knowledge graph, including focus word, predicate sequence and the nodes linked by the predicate sequence.*

Definition 6. *Query path is a subgraph of knowledge graph, which is formed by linking one or more triples with the core path according to the constraints of the question. If the question has no constraints, the query path is equivalent to the core path.*

For example, Fig. 1 is an example of a subgraph of KG, where nodes represent entities and edges represent predicates of links between entities.

For the question "What is the name of Justin Bieber brother?", our method can obtain the following key information step by step. Suppose that the predicate "*/people/person/sibling_s*" is represented by "$Predicate_1$", the predicate "*people/sibling_relationship/sibling*" is represented by "$Predicate_2$" and the predicate "*/people/person/gender*" is represented by "$Predicate_3$". Similarly, the node "*Justin Bieber*" is represented by "$Node_1$", the node "*Jaxon Bieber*" is represented by "$Node_2$" and the node "*Jazmyn Bieber*" is represented by "$Node_3$".

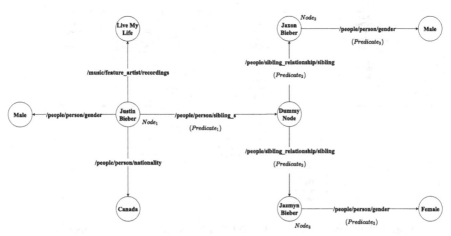

Fig. 1. Example of a subgraph of KG

Focus Word: "$Node_1$";

Predicate Sequence: "$[Predicate_1, Predicate_2]$";

Core Paths: "$Node_1 - Predicate_1 - Dummy\,Node - Predicate_2 - Node_2$" and "$Node_1 - Predicate_1 - Dummy\,Node - Predicate_2 - Node_3$";

Constraints on the Question: "*brother*";

In order to acquire the query path, the triplets $(Node_2, Predicate_3, Male)$ and $(Node_3, Predicate_3, Female)$ need to be linked into the two core paths.

Query Paths: "$Node_1 - Predicate_1 - Dummy\,Node - Predicate_2 - Node_2 - Predicate_3 - Male$" and "$Node_1 - Predicate_1 - Dummy\,Node - Predicate_2 - Node_3 - Predicate_3 - Female$";

Answer: "$Node_2$".

3.2   The Framework of KGQA Based on Query Path Generation

The process of KGQA in our paper is shown in Fig. 2 and the model framework is shown in Fig. 3. In this paper, the whole question answering over knowledge graph model mainly includes predicate sequence detector training model and query path generation and answer selection model.

Fig. 2. Process of KGQA

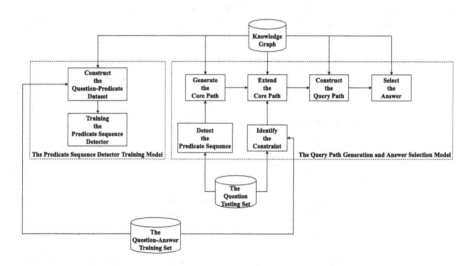

Fig. 3. The model framework of KGQA based on query path generation

Predicate Sequence Detector Training Model. The predicate sequence detector training model is mainly composed of constructing question-predicate sequence dataset module and training predicate sequence detector module. More specifically, the constructing question-predicate sequence dataset module takes the focus word, the answer and KG dataset as input, and outputs the predicate sequence. In addition, the training predicate sequence detector module takes question-predicate dataset as input, and outputs the predicate sequence detector.

In the predicate sequence detector training model, firstly the focus word and an answer of the question are extracted by question-answer training dataset, and a predicate sequence of this question is obtained after searching and filtering the

KG. By this way, the question-predicate sequence dataset is constructed. Then, the predicate sequence detector is trained with the above question-predicate sequence dataset based on RoBERTa model and Multi-Layer Perceptron (MLP).

Suppose that the predicate sequence detector is denoted as P-Detector. And the structure of P-Detector is shown in Fig. 4. In the training model, the input question goes through the Embedding module, the Encoding module and the Classifying module to get one or more predicates. For the design of P-Detector, both single-hop and multi-hop questions are considered. The question and the obtained previous predicate are inputted into P-Detector to predict the next hop predicate. Once the obtained predicate is empty, the prediction is terminated. It should be noted that in Fig. 4, the P-Detector outputs each predicate of the question in order. That is, if the first predicate is output, the corresponding input has only the question. If the subsequent predicate is output, it is used as input to P-Detector along with the question.

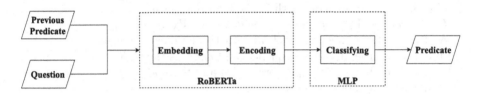

Fig. 4. The structure of P-Detector

Query Path Generation and Answer Selection Model. In the query path generation and answer selection model, firstly, the predicate sequence of question is identified by the trained P-Detector. Secondly, the core path is constructed through the focus word, the predicate sequence of the question and the nodes linked by the predicate sequence. Thirdly, the constraints are obtained by analyzing the question and the core path is extended to generate the query path based on the constraints. Finally, the candidate answers based on the query path are selected to determine the final answer to the question. Table 1 describes the algorithm of the query path generation and answer selection model, referred to as QPath-Answer.

Besides, the time complexity of QPath-Answer is $O(max(n^2, m^2, p * q^2))$. Where, n represents the length of the word sequence input by the P-Detector, m represents the sum of the word sequence length of the original problem and the problem with the focus word removed, p represents the number of query paths, which is equal to the number of candidate answers, and q represents the length of the word sequence input when the similarity calculation is completed using the RoBERTa classification task.

QPath-Answer Algorithm is explained as follows:

Line 1: Obtain the focus word of the question in KG. Since the focus words of the question have been provided in the experimental dataset, this paper does not study how to find the focus words.

Table 1. QPath-answer algorithm

Algorithm name: QPath-Answer
Input: The question of testing set (*question*) and dataset of knowledge graph (*KG*)
Output: The answer of question (*answer*)
1: $focus\_word$ = EXTRACT_FOCUS_WORD(*question*)
2: $predicate\_sequence$ = P-Detector(*question*)
3: $core\_path\_set$ = GENERATE($KG, focus\_word, predicate\_sequence$)
4: $constraints$ = IDENTIFY(*question*)
5: $query\_path\_set$ = CONSTRUCT($KG, core\_path\_set, constraints$)
6: for qp in $query\_path\_set$:
7:    answer.append(SELECT(qp))
8: end for

Line 2: Detect the predicate sequence of the question with P-Detector.

Line 3: Generate the core path in the following form:

$$Focus\,word - W_1 - node_1 - ... - node_{N-1} - W_N - node_N;$$

And N is the number of predicates in the predicate sequences, W_i is the i-th predicate in the predicate sequence, and $node_i$ is the node in the core path. Note that there may be multiple core paths, and the $node_N$ in each core path is selected as the candidate answer.

Line 4: Identify the constraints on the question. The constraints considered in our paper include label value constraint, entity constraint, time constraint and ordinal constraint. The examples of constraints for questions are shown in Table 2. The constraint discrimination rules are as follows:

(1) If the question has a noun and the noun is closest to the interrogative word, as the same time, the noun indicates the entity label value in KG, then the entity label value indicated by the noun is the label value constraint of the question.

(2) If the question has a noun and the noun has obviously indication function in KG, then the noun is the entity constraint of the question.

(3) If there is a cardinal word in the question, the cardinal word is an explicit time constraint of the question. If there is a time indicator, the adverbial containing the time indicator is the adverbial time constraint. In addition, if the constraints are implicit in the tense of the question, then the tense of the question is the implicit time constraint.

(4) If the question has an ordinal word, then the ordinal word is the ordinal constraint.

Line 5: Construct the query path. The key is to decide whether to extend the core path based on the constraints of the question. If the constraint is empty or the constraint is label value data, then the core path is directly used as the query path without extension. However, if the constraint is entity data, time data or ordinal data, then the core path needs to be extended. In other words, the corresponding constraint in KG is identified and linked to the core path.

Table 2. Examples of constraints for questions

Type	Question	Constraint
Label Value	What country is the Grand Bahama in?	Country
Entity	What is the name of Justin Bieber brother?	Brother
Explicit Time	Who is the current president of the Dominican Republic in 2010?	2010
Adverbial Time	What did Abraham Lincoln do before he was president?	Before he was president
Implicit Time	Who does Joakim Noah play for?	"Does" implies the present
Ordinal	What is the name of the first Harry Potter literary series novel?	First

The linked triplet is called extended triplet, and the query path is obtained by linking extended triplets with the core path.

Line 6–8: Select the answer. The rules are as follows:

(1) For the unconstrained question, the candidate answers obtained in the core paths are determined as the final answers.

(2) For the question with the label value constraint, if the label value of a candidate answer is consistent with the constraint in its query path, the candidate answer is selected as a final answer.

(3) For the question with the entity constraint, the candidate answer of the query path where the determinative object is located is selected as a final answer. More specifically, the way to determine the determinative object is as follows: obtain each extended triplet in the query path, calculate the semantic similarity score between the object of each extended triplet and the question with the focus word removed, in this way, the object with the highest score is determinative object.

(4) For the question with the time constraint, the candidate answer of the query path where the determinative object resides is selected as a final answer. Specifically, the ways to determine the determinative object are as follows:

For the question with the explicit time constraint, the object of extended triplet is the determinative object if its time range contains the explicit time of the question.

For the question with the adverbial time constraint, firstly, the candidate answer with the highest semantic similarity with the adverbial clause of time is determined, then the time range of the object of the extended triplet corresponding to the above candidate answer is determined, and finally, the time range corresponding to the time indicator is inferred. The object of the extended triplet of the query path is the determinative object if the time range of the object contains the time range of the inference.

For the question with the implicit time constraint, the time range is inferred through the question tense. The object of the extended triplet of the query path is the determinative object if the time range of the object contains the time range of the inference.

(5) For the question with the ordinal constraint, the candidate answer of the query path where the determinative object resides is selected as the final answer. And the determinative object is determined by the ordering of the object of extended triplet in the query path.

4 Experimental Results and Analysis

4.1 Experimental Datasets

In the experiment, our datasets are divided into two types: KG dataset and QA dataset. Specifically, the KG dataset includes MetaKG and Freebase, and the QA dataset includes MetaQA (MQA) and WebQuestions Semantic Parses (WSP). In addition, the MQA dataset corresponds to MetaKG and the WSP dataset corresponds to Freebase.

The number of triplets of MetaKG is 134,741 with 43,234 entities and 9 relations. And the triple number of complete Freebase is 1.9 billion, while the number of triplets in Freebase ExQ selected in our experiment is 306,733,220 with 72,407,365 entities and 4,335 relations. In order to improve the efficiency of QA, the MetaKG and Freebase ExQ are imported into Neo4j database in our research. Moreover, the Meta KG is imported into Neo4j with the designed Cypher statement and Freebase ExQ is imported with the Freebase Neo4j Importer tool (https://github.com/kuzeko/neo4j-freebase).

In MQA, there are 329,282 training questions, 39,138 validation questions and 39,093 testing questions, including 1-hop, 2-hop and 3-hop relations. In WSP, there are 3,098 training questions and 1,639 testing questions, including 1-hop and multi-hop relations and the questions with constraints.

4.2 Baseline and Evaluation Metrics

Our model is compared with Bordes, Chopra, and Weston's QA system [4], KV-MemNN [8], VRN [15], GRAFT-Net [12], PullNet [11] and EmbedKGQA [9].

Hit evaluation metrics is used to evaluate the accuracy of QA. If the predicted answer is exactly the same as the ground truth answer, the result is a correct. Otherwise, the result is a incorrect. The calculation formula is shown in Eq. 1, where the *pos* refers to the number of questions answered correctly and *neg* refers to the number of questions answered incorrectly.

$$Hit = \frac{pos}{pos + neg} \tag{1}$$

4.3   Experimental Results and Analysis

The QA performance for MQA and WSP dataset is obtained with Hit evaluation metrics, as shown in Table 3 and Table 4.

According to the results in Table 3, the 1-hop questions get the Hit score of 93.9%. Compared with previous studies, although our method is not the best for 1-hop questions in MQA, it is the best for 2-hop and 3-hop questions.

According to the results in Table 4, the Hit score of our model is 71.1% on the WSP dataset, which is 4.4% higher than the second best model, PullNet.

Table 3. QA performance of MQA dataset

Model	1-hop Hit	2-hop Hit	3-hop Hit
Bordes, Chopra, and Weston's QA system	95.7%	81.8%	28.4%
KV-MemNN	96.2%	82.7%	48.9%
VRN	**97.5%**	89.9%	62.5%
GRAFT-Net	97.0%	94.8%	77.7%
PullNet	97.0%	**99.9%**	91.4%
EmbedKGQA	**97.5%**	98.8%	94.8%
Ours	93.9%	**99.9%**	**98.5%**

Table 4. QA performance of WSP dataset

Model	Hit
KV-MemNN	46.7%
GRAFT-Net	66.4%
PullNet	68.1%
EmbedKGQA	66.6%
Ours	**71.1**

4.4 Case Study

This section will describe three examples as follows:

(1) Question 1: "Who was vp for Richard Nixon?"

This is a question with multi-hop relations.

And the predicate sequence detector model can correctly identify its predicate sequence "[*government/us_president/vice_president*]" in KG. And the core path is generated correctly. Because no constraint is identified, the two core paths are the query paths. Therefore, the two candidate answers (Gerald Ford, Spiro) on the core paths are selected as the final answer, and the result is correct.

(2) Question 2: "Who did Samir Nasri play for before arsenal?"

This is a question with multi-hop relations and the adverbial time constraints. And the predicate sequence detector model can identify its predicate sequence "[*/sports/pro_athlete/teams, /sports/sports_team_roster/team*]". In addition to that four core paths are generated, whose candidate answers are "Arsenal F.C.", "France national football team", "Manchester City F.C." and "Olympique de Marseille". And moreover, it is identified that the question has the adverbial time constraint, and the constraint corresponding to the core paths: "[*/sports/sports_team_roster/from, /sports/sports_team_roster/to*]".

And the time "from 2008" and "to 2011" are determined by extending the core paths with time constraints. Then through the time indicator "before", the time range is inferred to be before 2008, and the answer is "Olympique de Marseille".

(3) Question 3: "What jobs did John Adams have before he was president?"

For this question, in the work [7], the author holds that their method can not find the query graph. In contrast, our model can find the core paths corresponding to this question. Although the constraint is misidentified in KG, four correct answers and one wrong answer are obtained.

5   Conclusion

This paper proposed a staged query path generation method for KGQA, especially for the complex questions with multi-hop relations and constraints. More specifically, our method mainly includes the predicate sequence detector training model and query path generation and answer selection model. Taking the predicate sequence of the question in KG as the breakthrough point, the question is associated with the predicate sequence and extended triplets in KG, rather than directly with the query graph. The process of QA is highly interpretable and it can accurately understand the intent of the question, greatly reduce the range of choices, and improve the efficiency of QA.

In this work, only 4 types of question constraints were studied. The next step will be to study the answers to the questions with comparative, superlative and aggregate constraints. And further explore how to accurately identify various constraints in natural language questions.

References

1. Bakhshi, M., Nematbakhsh, M., Mohsenzadeh, M., Rahmani, A.M.: Data-driven construction of SPARQL queries by approximate question graph alignment in question answering over knowledge graphs. Expert Syst. Appl. **146**, 113205 (2020)
2. Bast, H., Haussmann, E.: More accurate question answering on freebase. In: Proceedings of the 24th ACM International Conference on Information and Knowledge Management, CIKM 2015, Melbourne, VIC, Australia, 19–23 October, 2015, pp. 1431–1440. ACM (2015)
3. Berant, J., Liang, P.: Semantic parsing via paraphrasing. In: Proceedings of the 52nd Annual Meeting of the Association for Computational Linguistics, ACL 2014, June 22–27, 2014, Baltimore, MD, USA, Volume 1: Long Papers, pp. 1415–1425. The Association for Computer Linguistics (2014)
4. Bordes, A., Chopra, S., Weston, J.: Question answering with subgraph embeddings. In: Proceedings of the 2014 Conference on Empirical Methods in Natural Language Processing, EMNLP 2014, October 25–29, 2014, Doha, Qatar, A meeting of SIGDAT, a Special Interest Group of the ACL, pp. 615–620. ACL (2014)
5. Huang, X., Zhang, J., Li, D., Li, P.: Knowledge graph embedding based question answering. In: Proceedings of the Twelfth ACM International Conference on Web Search and Data Mining, WSDM 2019, Melbourne, VIC, Australia, February 11–15, 2019, pp. 105–113. ACM (2019)
6. Jin, W., Yu, H., Tao, X., Yin, R.: Improving embedded knowledge graph multi-hop question answering by introducing relational chain reasoning. CoRR abs/2110.12679 (2021)
7. Lan, Y., Jiang, J.: Query graph generation for answering multi-hop complex questions from knowledge bases. In: Proceedings of the 58th Annual Meeting of the Association for Computational Linguistics, ACL 2020, Online, 5–10 July, 2020, pp. 969–974. Association for Computational Linguistics (2020)
8. Miller, A.H., Fisch, A., Dodge, J., Karimi, A., Bordes, A., Weston, J.: Key-value memory networks for directly reading documents. In: Proceedings of the 2016 Conference on Empirical Methods in Natural Language Processing, EMNLP 2016, Austin, Texas, USA, 1–4 November, 2016, pp. 1400–1409. The Association for Computational Linguistics (2016)
9. Saxena, A., Tripathi, A., Talukdar, P.P.: Improving multi-hop question answering over knowledge graphs using knowledge base embeddings. In: Proceedings of the 58th Annual Meeting of the Association for Computational Linguistics, ACL 2020, Online, 5–10, July 2020, pp. 4498–4507. Association for Computational Linguistics (2020)
10. Shin, S., Jin, X., Jung, J., Lee, K.: Predicate constraints based question answering over knowledge graph. Inf. Process. Manag. **56**(3), 445–462 (2019)
11. Sun, H., Bedrax-Weiss, T., Cohen, W.W.: Pullnet: open domain question answering with iterative retrieval on knowledge bases and text. In: Proceedings of the 2019 Conference on Empirical Methods in Natural Language Processing and the 9th International Joint Conference on Natural Language Processing, EMNLP-IJCNLP 2019, Hong Kong, China, 3–7 November 2019, pp. 2380–2390. Association for Computational Linguistics (2019)
12. Sun, H., Dhingra, B., Zaheer, M., Mazaitis, K., Salakhutdinov, R., Cohen, W.W.: Open domain question answering using early fusion of knowledge bases and text. In: Proceedings of the 2018 Conference on Empirical Methods in Natural Language Processing, Brussels, Belgium, October 31–4 November, 2018, pp. 4231–4242. Association for Computational Linguistics (2018)

13. Xiong, H., Wang, S., Tang, M., Wang, L., Lin, X.: Knowledge graph question answering with semantic oriented fusion model. Knowl. Based Syst. **221**, 106954 (2021)
14. Yih, W., Chang, M., He, X., Gao, J.: Semantic parsing via staged query graph generation: Question answering with knowledge base. In: Proceedings of the 53rd Annual Meeting of the Association for Computational Linguistics and the 7th International Joint Conference on Natural Language Processing of the Asian Federation of Natural Language Processing, ACL 2015, 26–31 July, 2015, Beijing, China, Volume 1: Long Papers. pp. 1321–1331. The Association for Computer Linguistics (2015)
15. Zhang, Y., Dai, H., Kozareva, Z., Smola, A.J., Song, L.: Variational reasoning for question answering with knowledge graph. In: Proceedings of the Thirty-Second AAAI Conference on Artificial Intelligence, (AAAI-18), the 30th innovative Applications of Artificial Intelligence (IAAI-18), and the 8th AAAI Symposium on Educational Advances in Artificial Intelligence (EAAI-18), New Orleans, Louisiana, USA, February 2–7, 2018, pp. 6069–6076. AAAI Press (2018)
16. Zheng, W., Cheng, H., Yu, J.X., Zou, L., Zhao, K.: Interactive natural language question answering over knowledge graphs. Inf. Sci. **481**, 141–159 (2019)

Improving Parking Occupancy Prediction in Poor Data Conditions Through Customization and Learning to Learn

Haohao Qu, Sheng Liu, Zihan Guo, Linlin You, and Jun Li[✉]

School of Intelligent Systems Engineering, Sun Yat-Sen University, Guangzhou, China
{quhaoh,liush235,guozh29}@mail2.sysu.edu.cn
{youlllin,stslijun}@mail.sysu.edu.cn

Abstract. Parking occupancy prediction (POP) can be used for many real-time parking-related services to significantly reduce the unnecessary cruising for parking and additional congestion. However, accurate and fast forecasting in data-poor car parks remains a challenge. To tackle the bottleneck, this paper proposes a knowledge transfer framework that can customize a lightweight but effective pre-trained network to those data-deficient parking lots for POP. The proposed approach integrates two novel ideas, namely Customization: select source domain utilizing reinforcement learning based on parking-related feature matching; and Learning to Learn: extract insightful prior knowledge from the selected sources using Federated Meta-learning. Results of a real-world case study with 34 parking lots in Guangzhou City, China, from June 1 to 30, 2018, show that compared to the baseline, the proposed approach can 1) bring approximately 21% extra performance improvement; 2) improve the model adaptation and convergence speed dramatically; 3) stabilize predictions with error minor variance.

Keywords: Knowledge-based application · Knowledge transfer · Parking occupancy prediction · Federated meta-learning · Reinforcement learning

1 Introduction

Growing applications of parking occupancy prediction (POP) have been witnessed in various parking-related smart services, such as parking guidance [1], dynamic parking charging [2] and parking spaces sharing [3], they alleviate the shortage of parking space, and the associated impact of traffic congestion [4]. However, an emerging bottleneck hinders the mass acceptance of POP services: under-performing in poor data cases. To tackle the bottleneck, this paper proposed an integrated approach, Customization and Learning to Learn (CLL), which can provide a lightweight but effective customized model for the parking lots that lack reliable historical data.

The research is supported by National Natural Science Foundation of China (62002398).

G. Memmi et al. (Eds.): KSEM 2022, LNAI 13368, pp. 159–172, 2022.
https://doi.org/10.1007/978-3-031-10983-6_13

In the literature, data augmentation and structure optimization are two common ways to handle the small-sample prediction task in POP. They improve the performance by incorporating heterogeneous data, but the heavy data dependence on a specific area and the capacity to predict under null-data conditions remain challenges in these studies [5–7]. By contrast, knowledge transfer is a new and effective way to address these problems, using the prior knowledge extracted from the POP tasks in other parking lots (e.g., parking patterns shared between target and source domains) to pre-train a predictive model for car parks with insufficient data [8,9]. However, while transferring extra information for model training to alleviate data shortage, the extra distraction would also accumulate during learning iterations which can deteriorate the performance [10]. Therefore, what and how to transfer becomes the major topic for researchers and a knowledge learning method that can counteract misinformation is required to improve the accuracy of small-sample POP.

To fill the gap, we improve knowledge transfer by adopting two novel ideas, Customization and Learning to Learn, namely 1) Customization: select appropriate source domains (i.e., "guiders") by utilizing reinforcement learning based on feature matching to facilitate the knowledge learning; 2) Learning to Learn: find the update direction by leveraging Federated Meta-learning [11] to pre-train an effective model.

In particular, the main contributions of this paper are as follows:

- Through the integration of Customization and Learning to Learn, the proposed approach provides a new and effective way to solve the small-sample issues in parking occupancy prediction.
- Unlike existing approaches, CLL can learn more insightful knowledge and reduce negative transfer by enabling the pre-training process using federated meta-learning and the client selection using reinforcement learning.
- Experiment on a real-world dataset with 34 parking lots in Guangzhou empirically show that CLL brings nearly 21% extra performance improvement compared with several representative methods.

The remainder of this paper is structured as follows. In Sect. 2 a literature review is presented to summarize the current challenges and solutions in small-sample POP. Then, Sect. 3 introduces the proposed approach for small-sample POP, which is evaluated in Sect. 4. Finally, Sect. 5 concludes the work and discusses future research directions.

2 Related Work

While applying prediction model for the small-sample predictions of parking occupancy and other traffic conditions, several challenges are emerging and quite a few solutions are proposed.

Summary of Challenges. 1) Data shortage: The incompleteness of local parking records puts the personalized models' training in a difficult circumstance that is likely to be trapped in local optimum or over-fitting [12]. 2) Knowledge learning: Disinformation accumulates as additional data is introduced, so avoiding negative learning is vital to model training [13]. 3) Guider selection: The optimization of customization depends crucially on how the clients are selected, as they are the sources of prior knowledge [14]. 4) Generalizability: A flexible data fusion mechanism is required to be capable of handling various degrees of missing data from different car parks.

Related Solutions. Deep learning methods has achieved great success in traffic condition prediction, they emphasize the advantages of data augmentation and heterogeneous data fusion, e.g., R-GANs [15], which provide data recovery by generating samples that look closer to the original data; WoT-NNs [16], which leverages the techniques of Web of Things (WoT) to collect additional information and incorporate them into neural networks; and ToGCN [7], which uses a Topological GCN followed with a Sequence-to-sequence framework to predict future traffic flow and density with temporal correlations. However, they have heavy dependence on availability of other data sources in a specific area and their burdensome structures may cause the lagging in model updates. Differently, knowledge transfer methods provide target domains prior knowledge extracted from source domains through a pre-training process, so that the models can be trained without much historical data. An illustration is a traffic prediction method bringing about 4–13% extra performance improvements by adopting transfer learning framework [8]. However, traditional transfer methods may suffer the negative learning issue to train a biased model because of its direct "reproduction", which fosters the study of improving knowledge transfer. A representative approach is FADACS [9], a GAN-based ConvLSTM transfer learning framework that generates a parking occupancy prediction model utilizing mutual attack of target and source with graph-based patterns. But, as a foundation to optimize the knowledge adaptation for transfer methods, source selection is overlooked yet.

Table 1. Emerging challenges and representative solutions (●: Solved; ◑: Partially; ○: Not-solved)

Challenges	WoT-NNs (2020)	ToGCN (2021)	FADACS (2021)	CLL*(proposed)
Data shortage	●	●	●	●
Knowledge learning	○	◑	●	●
Client selection	○	○	◑	●
Generaliz-ability	◑	◑	◑	●

In summary, Table 1 shows the evaluation of the reviewed methods by their abilities in addressing the four challenges. The knowledge transfer methods (i.e.

FADACS) can outperform the typical deep learning models (i.e., ToGCN) in knowledge learning. However, the source selection is still inadequate, which may make them easier to be misled by the negative transfer. To fill the gap, this paper proposes a novel approach, i.e. CLL, which integrates federated meta-learning and reinforcement learning to pre-train a simple but efficient POP model for data-deficient parking lots.

3   Approach

As illustrated in Fig. 1, the proposed approach consists of A) a model training module, which employs a neural network with LSTM as the backbone; B) a model pretraining Module, which utilizes FedFOMAML (i.e., the Learner) to learn, integrate and transfer prior knowledge from "guiders", then provides the targets a customized and well-trained prediction model; and C) a client selection module, which produces an appropriate client-selecting strategy (i.e., build a Selector). Each part of the proposed approach will be described in the following subsections.

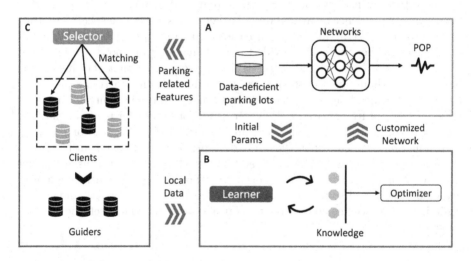

Fig. 1. Overall structure of the proposed approach: A) model training module using LSTM, B) model pretraining module applying FML, C) client selection module based on feature matching.

3.1   The Model Training Module

We utilize Recurrent Neural Network (RNN) which is a widely recognized deep learning approach to process temporal signals, and we pick LongShort-Term-Memory (LSTM) as the building block in RNN due to its success in numerous real-world applications [17]. Briefly, the state transition equation of LSTM is presented in Eq. (1).

$$i_t = \sigma(W_{ii}x_t + b_{ii} + W_{hi}h_{t-1} + b_{hi})$$
$$f_t = \sigma(W_{if}x_t + b_{if} + W_{hf}h_{t-1} + b_{hf})$$
$$g_t = \tanh(W_{ig}x_t + b_{ig} + W_{hg}h_{t-1} + b_{hg}) \tag{1}$$
$$o_t = \sigma(W_{io}x_t + b_{io} + W_{ho}h_{t-1} + b_{ho})$$
$$c_t = f_t \odot c_{t-1} + i_t \odot g_t$$
$$h_t = o_t \odot \tanh(c_t)$$

where h_t is the hidden state at time t, c_t is the cell state at time t, x_t is the input at time t, h_{t-1} is the hidden state of the layer at time $t-1$ or the initial hidden state at time 0, and i_t, f_t, g_t, o_t are the input, forget, cell, and output gates, respectively. σ is the sigmoid function, and $\odot$ is the Hadamard product.

3.2   The Model Pretraining Module

Unlike traditional transfer learning, meta-learning takes a longer-term and comprehensive horizon, i.e., it integrates gradients from multi-domains and updates a global network instead of employing network parameters obtained from source domains, which enables the learner learn more insightful knowledge and reduce the adverse impact of negative transfer. The following subsections will describe the meta-learning mechanism and its integration with federated learning for small-sample parking occupancy prediction.

Meta-learning. We adopt a simple but effective meta-learning method, First-order Model-agnostic Meta-learning (FOMAML) [18], which is simplified based on the Model-agnostic Meta-learning (MAML) by ignoring the second derivative terms to reduce the number of gradient steps in finding the best match. Given that M defines the number of pre-training tasks, the objective function of MAML can be defined by (2), which is to find a set of initial parameters minimizing the learner loss. Thereinto, θ represents the intermediate parameter related to the initial parameter ϕ; θ^m denotes the current parameter in task m; $l^m(\theta^m)$ indicates the error with θ^m in task m; and $L(\phi)$ is the total after-training loss of initial parameter ϕ.

$$\min L(\phi) = \sum_{m=1}^{M} l^m(\theta^m) \tag{2}$$

The derivative of (2) is the gradient function. To reduce computational complexity, the second derivative terms can be ignored [18]. It means $\nabla_\phi l^m(\theta^m)$ can be replaced to $\nabla_\theta l^m(\theta^m)$, and the gradient function can be written as (3).

$$\nabla_\phi L(\phi) = \sum_{m=1}^{M} \nabla_\phi l^m(\theta^m) \approx \sum_{m=1}^{M} \nabla_\theta l^m(\theta^m) \tag{3}$$

where $\nabla_\phi L(\phi)$ is the gradient of $L(\phi)$ with respect to ϕ; $\nabla_\phi l^m(\theta^m)$ is the gradient of $l^m(\hat{\theta}^m)$ with respect to ϕ; and $\nabla_\theta l^m(\theta^m)$ is the gradient of $l^m(\theta^m)$ with respect to θ.

FedFOMAML for POP. The integration is implemented through a pre-training process as illustrated in Algorithm 1, where the clients and targets are Train set and Test set. Furthermore, these two sets are divided into four separate parts, namely 1) Train-Support R_1, for obtaining local iterative parameters; 2) Train-Query R_2, for getting local gradients; 3) Test-Support R_3, which represents the "few-sample" that target parking lots have for fine-tuning the personalized network; and 4) Test-Query R_4, for evaluating performance. Expressly, assume there are N parking lots in the federation, and M clients are selected as guiders. In a particular epoch p, local gradients are obtained from each guider via a local pre-training based on local data, then the global network parameter ϕ_p can be updated to ϕ_{p+1} the global parameter of the next epoch with the aggregation of local gradients by FedFOMAML mechanism [11]. Given that R_1^m and R_2^m represent local Train-Support set and Train-Query set, respectively, lr denotes learning rate, and θ^m is the iterative parameter in pre-training task m, the process can be written as (4).

$$\phi_{p+1} = \phi_p - \frac{lr}{M} \sum_{m=1}^{M} \nabla_\theta l^m(\theta^m, \ R_2^m)$$

$$s.t. \ \theta^m = \phi_p - lr \nabla_\phi l^m(\phi_p, \ R_1^m) \tag{4}$$

Algorithm 1. Learner: FedFOMAML - pseudocode

Require: Batch of pre-training tasks $m = 1, ..., M$ selected from federation
1: initialize ϕ, learning rate lr, pre-training and fine-tuning max-epochs p, p_f
2: divide data set into R_1, R_2, R_3, R_4
3: **while** not done **do**
4:     **for** $i = 1, ..., p$ **do**
5:         **for** each pre-training task m **do**
6:             compute $g_1^m = \nabla_\phi l^m(\phi, \ R_1^m)$
7:             update ϕ to θ^m with g_1^m
8:             obtain $g_2^m = \nabla_\theta l^m(\theta^m, R_2^m)$
9:         **end for**
10:       update $\phi = \phi - lr \sum_{m=1}^{M} g_2^m$
11:     **end for**
12:     initiate personalized net $\phi' = \phi$
13:     **for** $j = 1, ..., p_f$ **do**
14:         update ϕ' with R_3
15:     **end for**
16: **end while**
17: evaluate predicting performance in R_4

3.3 The Client Selection Module

Feature matching is a common way to select clients, but the weight setting of features remains challenge. Therefore, we employ asynchronous advantage actor-critic (A3C) [19] to train a Selector network to provide a selection strategy according to the predicting performance (reward) and feature matching (state). A3C is a conceptually simple and lightweight framework of deep reinforcement learning (RL) that uses asynchronous gradient descent to optimize deep neural network controllers, and it can significantly shorten the RL training time and make the learning process stable.

Selector Training. The Selector Module consists of a Selector (3-layer MLP) and a Critic (2-layer MLP). The Selector outputs actions (i.e., "guiders" selection) according to the present state modeled with parking-related features, and the Critic is used to evaluate the selection strategies. The process of Selector training using the A3C framework is presented in Algorithm 2. Firstly, we adopt an off-policy strategy for sampling and obtain the rewards through a reward function presented in (5).

$$r(a,\ S_i)\ =\ \lambda \div F(a,\ S_i) \tag{5}$$

The reward r is straightforwardly measured by the testing loss of the Learner module given the specific state S_i and actions a. We set a positive constant λ empirically as a threshold value.

After sampling, the coordinator collects all states, actions, and rewards into a buffer. In the case of parking occupancy prediction (POP), the number of training states is equal to the number of clients in the federation, and there will be C_N^M actions given N states and M parking lots to select. Each client utilizes Advantage Actor-Critic (A2C) to calculate local gradients of Selector and Critic, respectively, then update the global network's parameters with the aggregation of batch local gradients.

In term of Critic updating, a value-based method is employed for the Critic updating. The estimated Value V_π^s indicates the approximate expectation of rewards in a particular state s, which is defined by (6).

$$V_\pi^s = E_\pi\left(r\left(\widetilde{a}, s\right)\right) = \frac{1}{T} \sum_{t=1}^{T} r\left(a_t, s\right) \frac{\rho_\pi\left(a_t | s\right)}{\rho_{\pi'}\left(a_t | s\right)} \tag{6}$$

where $E_\pi\left(r\left(\widetilde{a}, \hat{s}\right)\right)$ represents the expected value of the reward r for all actions $\widetilde{a}$ in a specific state $\hat{s}$ using Selector π; V_π^s indicates how good the Selector could do; T is the number of actions in one state; $r(a_t, \hat{s})$ denotes the reward of action a_t in the state $\hat{s}$; $\rho_\pi(a_t | \hat{s})$ represents the probability of that the Selector takes action a_t using parameter π; and $\rho_{\pi'}(a_t | \hat{s})$ indicates the global sampling distribution that could be omitted if it were a uniform distribution.

Then, Critic gradients of state s_m can be calculated through the square error (SE) regression between the Critic's output $V_{critic}^{s_m}$ and the observed value $V_\pi^{s_m}$. Under the federation framework, we update the global Critic net π_c using the aggregated gradients as Eq. (7).

$$\pi_c' = \pi_c - \beta \sum_{m=1}^{M} \nabla_{\pi_c}(V_\pi^{s_m} - V_{critic}^{s_m})^2 \tag{7}$$

In term of Selector updating, according to the idea of policy-based advantage function [19], when the reward of an action is greater than the valuation of Critic V_critic, its probability goes up, otherwise, goes down. Then, the gradient of Actor (i.e., Selector) $\nabla \bar{R}_\pi^s$, can be written as (8).

$$\nabla \bar{R}_\pi^{\hat{s}} = \frac{1}{T} \sum_{t=1}^{T} (r(a_t, \hat{s}) - V_{critc}) \nabla_{\pi_a} \log \rho_\pi(a_t | \hat{s}) \tag{8}$$

Similar to the updating process of Critic net, that of Selector net π_a also can leverage the aggregated local gradients as illustrated in Eq. (9).

$$\pi_a' = \pi_a - \beta \sum_{m=1}^{M} \nabla \bar{R}_\pi^{s_m} \tag{9}$$

Finally, after iterative updating, the Selector would be able to find a "best" policy that selecting a certain number of good "guiders" for the Learner module.

Algorithm 2. Selector Training: A3C - pseudocode

Require: the Learner module, parking-related features
1: assume that the numbers of clients and selected guiders are N and M, then the amount of states and actions are N and $T = C_N^M$ respectively
2: initialize global Selector and Critic net π_a and π_c; model state s with features
3: **for** episode **do**
4:     sample distribution $\pi' = \pi$
5:     sample local states and actions to global buffer
6:     compute rewards with Learner and reward function
7:     distribute samples (s, a, r) to corresponding member
8:     **for** each member m **do**
9:         freeze π_a
10:         $d\pi_c \leftarrow 0$
11:         compute $V_\pi^{s_m}$
12:         obtain $d\pi_c^m$ by regression
13:     **end for**
14:     update π_c, release π_a
15:     **for** each member m **do**
16:         freeze π_c
17:         $d\pi_a \leftarrow 0$
18:         obtain $d\pi_a^m$ by advantage function
19:     **end for**
20:     update π_a, release π_c
21: **end for**

---

4 Experiments and Results

In this section, we deploy the proposed method on a real-world parking occupancy prediction case, and the predicting performance will be evaluated together with other representative forecasting methods based on the same evaluation metrics. Moreover, the results will be analyzed to demonstrate the improvements achieved.

4.1 Evaluation Preparation

Data Declaration. A shared dataset with a minimum resolution of 5 min was created based on the parking occupancy data of 34 parking lots in Guangzhou City, China, from June 1 to 30, 2018. There are four parking lots (Target 1–4) for testing and 30 (Client 1–30) for training. The parking-related features include: 1) parking-related points of interest (POI), which are collected from Gaode API, and the kernel density are clustered into 20 classes; 2) parking lot types, which are divided into six categories according to the land use, namely Commercial, Office, Residential, Hospital, Recreational, Tourism.

Dataset division: the Train-Support set and Train-Query set are (Day 1–18) and (Day 19–24) for FOMAML pre-training; the Test-Query set is (Day 25–30) for model performance evaluation. Expressly, we consider five data conditions of the Test-Support set, namely complete data (Day 1–24, 24d), partial data (Day 18–24, 6d), small data (Day 21–24, 3d), few data (Day 24, 1d), empty data (null).

Baselines and Competitive Approaches. Several representative methods for time-series prediction are compared. Including, 1) Fully Connected Neural Network (FCNN): which is widely used in function approximation and general regression problems, but it relies on feature extraction and cannot distinguish between temporal features and spatial features; 2) Long Short-Term Memory (LSTM) [17]: a recurrent-based method that is widely used in many time-series prediction tasks, which is set as the baseline; 3) Gated Recurrent Unit (GRU) [20]: a simplified LSTM structure which has advantages of rapidly computing; and 4) Bi-directional Long Short-Term Memory (BiLSTM) [21]: a combination of forward LSTM and backward LSTM, which is often used to model context information in natural language processing tasks. 5) Auto-regressive Integrated Moving Average (ARIMA) [22]: A statistical model which can be used to model time series as long as the data or the difference of the data is stationary. 6) Support Vector Regression (SVR) [23]: A typical machine learning model. 7) a traditional transfer learning method named Transfer-LSTM [24] deploys LSTM as backbone network for time-series prediction. In addition, to validate the Selector, we also evaluate the performance of FML (i.e., the Learner) which selects "guiders" randomly. The running configuration is illustrated in Table 2.

Table 2. Running configurations

Model	Param	Value	Comment
*	(N, M, T)	(30, 3, 4060)	The number of (states, guiders, and actions)
	Channel	(1, 6, 1)	(Input channel, sequence length, output channel)
	Learning rate	(0.03, 0.02, 0.05)	(Pretraining, Fine-tuning, Selector training)
	Max epochs	(200, 400, 5000)	(Pretraining, Fine-tuning, Selector training)
	Optimizer	BGD | Adam	Pretraining | Fine-tuning & Selector training
	Loss function	MSE | CE	Pretraining & Fine-tuning | Selector training
ARIMA	(p, d, q)	(2, 1, 1)	Implemented on Statsmodels
SVR	Kernel, epsilon	RBF, 0.001	Implemented on Scikit-learn (sklearn)

* CLL, FML, transfer-LSTM and NNs.

Experiment Setting. The objective is to predict the parking occupancy rate for the next 30 min (6 timesteps as accurately as possible in the last six days (25–30) of June 2018. The evaluation metrics are Mean Absolute Percentage Error (MAPE), Root Mean Squared Error (RMSE), Relative Absolute Error (RAE), and Coefficient of Determination (R-square). Finally, All the experiments are conducted on a Windows workstation with four NVIDIA GeForce RTX 3090 GPU, an Intel Gold 5218R Two-Core Processor CPU, and 512 G RAM. The pretraining process takes about 20 min, but the Selector training process costs around two weeks for the experiment. It is worth noting that for reproductivity, the dataset and code used by this paper are shared on Github and downloadable from the link[1].

4.2   Result and Discussions

Forecasting Error. As shown in Table 3, the average metrics of compared models in the five different data volumes (empty, few, small, partial, and complete data) are summarized. We can see the methods with a knowledge transfer learning framework are much superior to those without, and the proposed approach reduces the prediction errors significantly with the highest scores in all the four evaluation metrics, namely MAPE 4.77%, RMSE 0.0312, RAE 15.66%, and R2 96.36%. Compared to its backbone network LSTM, CLL brings nearly 21% extra performance improvements. Furthermore, the LSTM model using CLL outperforms that using FML, demonstrating the effectiveness of our auto-selector. As shown in Table 4, the selection result indicates that our selector views clients with a closer density of POI to the target as a good "guider". Moreover, it is better if the client is in the same type of parking as the target.

Convergence Profile. We compare the convergence profiles of CLL and its backbone network LSTM (i.e., the baseline), and the first-100-epochs MSE-loss curves are given in Fig. 2. We can see that the errors at the beginning of the curves for ALL-LSTM are smaller than that at the 100th iteration of LSTM, indicating the advantage of ALL for knowledge extraction and propagation.

---

[1] https://github.com/Quhaoh233/CLL.

Table 3. List of average metrics of the compared models

Model	RMSE (10^{-2})	MAPE (%)	R2 (%)	RAE (10^{-2})
CLL-LSTM	3.12	4.77	96.36	15.66
FML-LSTM	3.36	5.05	95.94	16.41
Transfer-LSTM	3.76	5.79	95.33	17.72
SVR	3.90	5.83	94.31	19.01
LSTM	3.97	5.40	94.96	17.23
BiLSTM	4.10	6.24	93.71	20.23
GRU	5.27	8.19	88.10	26.24
FCNN	5.85	8.87	84.86	30.11
ARIMA	6.03	9.40	80.45	33.54

The metrics are averaged based on the result of 20 tasks (4 parking lots × 5 data volumes).

Table 4. Parking-related features of the targets and selected clients

Feature	Target1	Client1	Client5	Client11	Target2	Client5	Client8	Client10
Density of POI	12	8	14	10	18	14	17	18
Type of car parks	A	A	A	B	A	A	A	A
Feature	Target3	Client3	Client14	Client25	Target4	Client12	Client17	Client27
Density of POI	4	3	2	2	11	9	12	11
Type of car parks	C	A	C	E	D	B	C	F

A: Commercial; B: Hospital; C: Office; D: Residential; E: Recreational; F: Tourism.

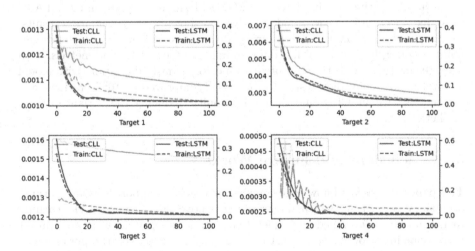

Fig. 2. Comparison of convergence profile between CLL-LSTM and LSTM

Error Variance. To emphasize the stability brought by the meta-learning pre-training and client selection, we give an illustration in Fig. 3, which reveals that using knowledge transfer (i.e., Transfer-LSTM) can lower the error variance of the learning model (i.e., LSTM). Further, using the CLL pre-training framework gives the prediction model a smaller error box than using the traditional transfer learning. The above results demonstrate that the proposed framework can stabilize prediction, improving its application significance in real-world scenarios.

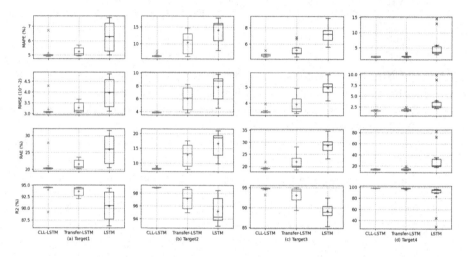

Fig. 3. Boxplot of the metrics in four target prediction tasks respectively, the baseline is LSTM

In summary, the combination of FedFOMAML in model pretraining and A3C in source selection is efficient and effective. As shown by the evaluation results, the proposed approach has the following advantages, 1) high accuracy and scalability, scoring highest in all five data groups and four evaluation metrics, with a significant reduction of 21% in prediction error; 2) fast adaptation, with model adaptation and convergence speed substantially improved by 10^2 iterations over the model without CLL; and 3) good stability, reducing the variance of the predictions.

5   Conclusions and Future Works

This paper proposed a knowledge transfer approach to support few-data parking occupancy prediction, which integrated two novel ideas, namely 1) Learning to Learn: which leveraged the Federated Meta-learning framework to transfer multi-domains knowledge; 2) Customization: which improved the performance via training a Selector for client selection. The evaluation results showed that the proposed approach CLL outperformed the compared methods in three aspects:

significant performance, fast adaptation, and more minor variances. It provided a simple but effective way to solve small-sample parking occupancy prediction. In the future, the work will be further enhanced:

1) To extend its application: The ideas of Customization and Learning to Learn will be extended to more scenarios, e.g., traffic flow, density and speed prediction in limited-sensing roads.
2) To consider data security: The proposed approach will be improved by integrating advanced federated learning method to avoid data leakage and bridge data islands among parking facilities.

Acknowledgements. The research is supported by National Natural Science Foundation of China (62002398).

References

1. Xiao, J., Lou, Y.: An online reinforcement learning approach for user-optimal parking searching strategy exploiting unique problem property and network topology. IEEE Trans. Intell. Transp. Syst. 1–13 (2021)
2. Ding, H., Qian, Y., Zheng, X., Bai, H., Wang, S., Zhou, J.: Dynamic parking charge-perimeter control coupled method for a congested road network based on the aggregation degree characteristics of parking generation distribution. Physica A-Stat. Mech. Appl. **587**, 126481 (2022)
3. Zhang, F., Liu, W., Wang, X., Yang, H.: Parking sharing problem with spatially distributed parking supplies. Transp. Res. Part C-Emerg. Technol. **117**, 102676 (2020)
4. Bock, F., Di Martino, S., Origlia, A.: Smart parking: using a crowd of taxis to sense on-street parking space availability. IEEE Trans. Intell. Transp. Syst. **21**(2), 496–508 (2020)
5. Wang, Y., Zhang, H.: Introducing graph neural networks for few-shot relation prediction in knowledge graph completion task. In: The 14th International Conference on Knowledge Science, Engineering and Management, pp. 294–306 (2021)
6. Yang, S., Ma, W., Pi, X., Qian, S.: A deep learning approach to real-time parking occupancy prediction in transportation networks incorporating multiple spatio-temporal data sources. Transp. Res. Part C Emerg. Technol. **107**, 248–265 (2019)
7. Qiu, H., Zheng, Q., Msahli, M., Memmi, G., Qiu, M., Lu, J.: Topological graph convolutional network-based urban traffic flow and density prediction. IEEE Trans. Intell. Transp. Syst. **22**(7), 4560–4569 (2021)
8. Zhang, C., Zhang, H., Qiao, J., Yuan, D., Zhang, M.: Deep transfer learning for intelligent cellular traffic prediction based on cross-domain big data. IEEE J. Sel. Areas Commun. **37**(6), 1389–1401 (2019)
9. Shao, W., et al.: FADACS: a few-shot adversarial domain adaptation architecture for context-aware parking availability sensing. In: 2021 IEEE International Conference on Pervasive Computing and Communications (PerCom), pp. 1–10 (2021)
10. Gui, L., Xu, R., Lu, Q., Du, J., Zhou, Yu.: Negative transfer detection in transductive transfer learning. Int. J. Mach. Learn. Cybern. **9**(2), 185–197 (2017). https://doi.org/10.1007/s13042-016-0634-8

11. Lin, S., Yang, G., Zhang, J.: A collaborative learning framework via federated meta-learning. In: 2020 IEEE 40th International Conference on Distributed Computing Systems (ICDCS), pp. 289–299 (2020)

12. Yang, M.: A survey on few-shot learning in natural language processing. In: 2021 International Conference on Artificial Intelligence and Electromechanical Automation (AIEA), pp. 294–297 (2021)

13. Khan, A., Kim, J.-S., Kim, H.S.: Damage detection and isolation from limited experimental data using simple simulations and knowledge transfer. Mathematics **10**(1) (2022)

14. Jie, X., Wang, H.: Client selection and bandwidth allocation in wireless federated learning networks: a long-term perspective. IEEE Trans. Wireless Commun. **20**(2), 1188–1200 (2021)

15. Sun, Y., Peng, L., Li, H., Sun, M.: Exploration on spatiotemporal data repairing of parking lots based on recurrent GANs. In: 2018 21st International Conference on Intelligent Transportation Systems (ITSC), pp. 467–472 (2018)

16. Provoost, J.C., Kamilaris, A., Wismans, L.J.J., Van der Drift, S.J., Keulen, M.V.: Predicting parking occupancy via machine learning in the web of things. Internet Things **12**, 100301 (2020)

17. Zhao, Z., Chen, W., Wu, X., Chen, P.C.Y., Liu, J.: LSTM network: a deep learning approach for short-term traffic forecast. IET Intell. Transp. Syst. **11**(2), 68–75 (2017)

18. Finn, C., Abbeel, P., Levine, S.: Model-agnostic meta-learning for fast adaptation of deep networks. In: The 34th International Conference on Machine Learning (ICML), vol. 70, pp. 1126–1135 (2017)

19. Mnih, V., et al.: Asynchronous methods for deep reinforcement learning. In: International Conference on Machine Learning (ICML) (2016)

20. Cho, K., van Merrienboer, B., Bahdanau, D., Bougares, F., Schwenk, H., Bengio, Y.: Learning phrase representations using RNN encode-decoder for statistical machine translation. In: Conference on Empirical Methods in Natural Language Processing (EMNLP) (2014)

21. Schuster, M., Paliwal, K.K.: Bidirectional recurrent neural networks. IEEE Trans. Signal Process. **45**(11), 2673–2681 (1997)

22. Jaynes, E.T.: On the rationale of maximum-entropy methods. Proc. IEEE **70**(9), 939–952 (1982)

23. Wu, C.H., Ho, J.M., Lee, D.T.: Travel-time prediction with support vector regression. IEEE Trans. Intell. Transp. Syst. **5**(4), 276–281 (2004)

24. Li, J., Guo, F., Wang, Y., Zhang, L., Na, X., Hu, S.: Short-term traffic prediction with deep neural networks and adaptive transfer learning. In: IEEE 23rd International Conference on Intelligent Transportation Systems (ITSC) (2020)

Knowledge Concept Recommender Based on Structure Enhanced Interaction Graph Neural Network

Yu Ling[1] and Zhilong Shan[1,2(✉)]

[1] School of Computer Science, South China Normal University, Guangzhou, China
kakawater@icloud.com, ZLshan@m.scnu.edu.cn
[2] School of Distance Education, South China Normal University, Guangzhou, China

Abstract. Online education is becoming more and more popular. Although there are many online courses, this brings users trouble: (1) courses with the same name have different emphases; (2) there is dependence between courses in learning order. These phenomena make learners spend a certain amount of energy to find suitable courses, reducing their interest in online education. To help learners better conduct online learning, we study the problem of knowledge concept recommendation. This paper proposes a knowledge concept recommendation model based on a structure-enhanced interactive graph neural network (KCRec-SEIGNN). As for user representation, multiple entities in the knowledge concept recommendation scenario are organized into a heterogeneous graph and then graph convolution based on meta-path guidance to learn user entity representation on the heterogeneous graph. As for knowledge concept representation learning, we capture the co-occurrence information of knowledge points in the interaction sequence by using the knowledge concept interaction sub-sequence as a wizard and then build a knowledge concept interaction graph using the co-occurrence information. When aggregating the neighbor node information, we retain the structure information between the neighbor node and the target node and use an attention mechanism to distinguish the contributions of different neighbor nodes. Lastly, input the representation of user entities and knowledge concepts into a rating layer based on extended matrix decomposition to recommend knowledge concepts by rating. We conduct a series of Experiments on public real-world datasets, XuetangX, showing that the model is more effective for knowledge concept recommendation than some of the latest methods.

Keywords: Recommender system · Heterogeneous graph neural networks · Interaction graph · Graph embedding · MOOC

1 Introduction

With the prevalence of the Internet, online education has become an innovative way to learn knowledge, and an increasing number of people have begun to learn online [1, 2]. But there are some problems with online education. (1) Many courses often rely on certain knowledge concepts from specific pre-requisite courses [3]. (2) There are

G. Memmi et al. (Eds.): KSEM 2022, LNAI 13368, pp. 173–186, 2022.
https://doi.org/10.1007/978-3-031-10983-6_14

many courses with the same name or similar names, but they have different emphases and require different concepts of advanced knowledge [4]. These problems increase the burden for students to choose the appropriate course. Therefore, the knowledge concept recommendation system arises at the historic moment.

Scholars have done some research on knowledge concept recommendation systems [4, 5]. ACKRec [4] first organizes various entities in the knowledge recommendation system into a heterogeneous graph [6], then gets embedding representations of users and knowledge concepts on several meta-paths. Finally, an attention mechanism is used to aggregate the embedding representation of user and knowledge concept on different meta-paths to obtain the final representation of user and knowledge concept. Based on ACKRec, CEREC-ME [5] defines the entity community and measures the similarity of nodes in the entity community. Finally, the structural information of the community and the neighborhood information of nodes are added to the loss function to improve the recommendation performance of the model.

However, existing knowledge concept recommendation models fail to fully mine the rich context information contained in user interaction records. Considering the challenge, we propose a knowledge concept recommendation system based on the knowledge concept Interaction Graph.

The main contributions of this paper are as follows:

- In the embedding representation learning of knowledge concepts, we first find the co-occurrence information between knowledge concepts according to the sub-sequence of knowledge concept interaction sequences. Then we build a knowledge concept interaction graph by using the co-occurrence information.
- To retain the structure information between the neighbor node and the target node for a better representation, we correlate each neighbor node with a learnable directed edge's weight embedding when aggregating the neighbor node information.
- An attention mechanism based on structural information is proposed to distinguish the contributions of different neighbor nodes and generate the final representation of knowledge concepts.
- We verify the validity of our proposed model on an open dataset. Comprehensive experiments and analysis show that the proposed model is superior to some of the latest methods.

The rest of the paper is organized as follows. Section 2 summarizes the related work on knowledge concept recommender systems. Section 3 introduces the preliminary concepts of our model. Section 4 gives an overview of our framework and explains the implementation details. The experiment results are discussed in Sect. 5, followed by the conclusion and future work of this paper in Sect. 6.

2 Related Work

Data sparsity is one of the common problems faced by recommendation systems. A popular method is to build a recommendation system based on the heterogeneous graph [6] to solve this problem [6, 8–11]. The basic idea is to alleviate the problem of data sparsity by introducing additional side information or auxiliary information. In building recommendation systems based on heterogeneous graphs, how to embed nodes in heterogeneous graphs has become a hot research field. The primary way of learning node representation based on heterogeneous graphs is using meta-paths [7]. Meta-path2vec [12] uses meta-path to carry out random walks and generates an embedding representation of nodes with the help of a skip-Gram model. HAN [13] transforms the heterogeneous graph into an isomorphic graph connected by multiple meta paths, then aggregates the information of the neighbor based on the meta path by using the attention mechanism on each meta path, and finally aggregates the node representations obtained on various meta paths by using the attention mechanism. MAGNN [14] also considers the embedding of intermediate nodes in the meta-path when learning the node representation based on the meta-path. Unlike these efforts [4, 5], this paper proposes a structure-enhanced interaction graph neural network, which learns co-occurrence relations between items based on subsequences in interaction sequences to obtain better item representation.

3 Preliminary

In this section, we formulate the problem of knowledge concept recommendation and introduce some key concepts about the knowledge concept interaction graph proposed in the paper.

3.1 Problem Statement

The goal of the knowledge concept recommendation system is to rate each knowledge concept according to the user's interaction record to obtain the recommendation list composed of the top N knowledge concepts with the highest score. More formally, given a set of interaction records for user u, learn a predictive function $f : u \rightarrow \{k_i \mid k_i \in K, i < N\}$ to generate a recommended list of knowledge concepts. Where K represents the set of knowledge concepts, k_i represents the i-th knowledge concept in the recommended knowledge concept list, and N means the length of the recommended knowledge concept list.

3.2 Key Concept

User interaction records contain rich context information. This paper proposes a way to organize knowledge concepts into a knowledge concept interaction graph according to users' knowledge concepts interaction records and then learn representations of user entities by the graph for knowledge concept recommendation.

Let $U = \{u_1, u_2, \cdots, u_m\}$ and $K = \{k_1, k_2, \cdots, k_n\}$ represent a user set and a knowledge concept set, respectively. $S^u = [h_1, h_2, \cdots, h_{|S^u|}]$ is the knowledge concept interaction sequence of user $u \in U$, where $h_i \in K$ represents the i-th element in S^u, and $|S^u|$ means the length of S^u.

Definition 1. Knowledge Concept Learning Path.

Given a knowledge concept interaction sequence S^u, $S^{u'}$ is obtained after dedupli-cation of elements in the S^u, and a sliding window with length l is used to slide from front to back on $S^{u'}$. The sequence in the sliding window is treated as a knowledge con-cept learning path $Path_i^u = \left[S^{u'}_{m-l+1}, \cdots, S^{u'}_{m-1}, S^{u'}_m \right]$ every time the sliding window moves a position. $Path_i^u$ represents the i-th learning path obtained by $S^{u'}$. If $l > \left| S^{u'} \right|$, $Path_0^u = S^{u'}$. Obviously, if $l \leq \left| S^{u'} \right|$, $\left| S^{u'} \right| - l + 1$ learning paths can be obtained accord-ing to $S^{u'}$. As shown in Fig. 1, $l = 3$, given the knowledge concept interaction sequence $S^{u_3} = [k_1, k_2, k_3, k_1, k_4, k_5, k_2, k_1, k_6]$ of user u_3, $S^{u_3'} = [k_1, k_2, k_3, k_4, k_5, k_6]$. And then we can get $Path_0^{u_3} = [k_1, k_2, k_3]$, $Path_1^{u_3} = [k_2, k_3, k_4]$, $Path_2^{u_3} = [k_3, k_4, k_5]$ and $Path_3^{u_3} = [k_4, k_5, k_6]$.

Definition 2. Knowledge Concept Interaction Graph.

Given a knowledge concept learning paths set $Path = \left[Path_1, Path_2, \cdots, Path_{|Path|} \right]$, a knowledge concept interaction graph can be gen-erated, where $|Path|$ represents the number of elements in $Path$. The knowledge con-cept interaction diagram can be expressed as Graph $G_I = (K, E_I)$, where E_I is the edge set. Each edge $k_i \xrightarrow{distance} k_j$ in E_I indicates a learning path $Path_q$ that makes k_i and k_j the elements of $Path_q$, and the subscripts $Index_{k_i}{}^q$ and $Index_{k_j}{}^q$ correspond-ing to k_i and k_j in $Path_q$ satisfy the equation: $Index_{k_j}{}^q - Index_{k_i}{}^q = distance$ or $Index_{k_j}{}^q - Index_{k_i}{}^q = -distance$. where $distance$ is the weight of edge $k_i \xrightarrow{distance} k_j$ and represents the distance from k_i to k_j in $Path_q$. Obviously, the knowledge concept interaction graph will be constructed as a directed multiple graph. Taking Fig. 1 as an example, for learning path $Path_0^{u_3}$, there will be these directed edges between k_1, k_2, and k_3 in the knowledge concept interaction diagram: $k_1 \xrightarrow{1} k_2, k_1 \xrightarrow{2} k_3, k_2 \xrightarrow{-1} k_1, k_2 \xrightarrow{1} k_3$, $k_3 \xrightarrow{-2} k_1$, and $k_3 \xrightarrow{-1} k_2$.

Definition 3. Knowledge Concept Learning Path based Neighbor.

Given a knowledge concept learning path set $Path$ and its corresponding knowledge concept interaction graph G_I, let $Path_i = [k_i, k_m, \cdots, k_n] \in Path$, then each knowledge concept in $Path_i$ is the neighbor of each other based on learning path $Path_i$. We use $N_j^{Path_i}$ to represent the neighbor set of knowledge concept node k_j based on learning path $Path_i$. We use N_j^{Path} to represent the set of neighbors of the knowledge concept node k_j based on all learning paths. As shown in Fig. 1, given a node k_3 in the knowledge concept interaction graph, we obtain its neighbor node set $N_3^{Path} = \{k_1, k_2, k_3, k_4, k_5, k_7\}$.

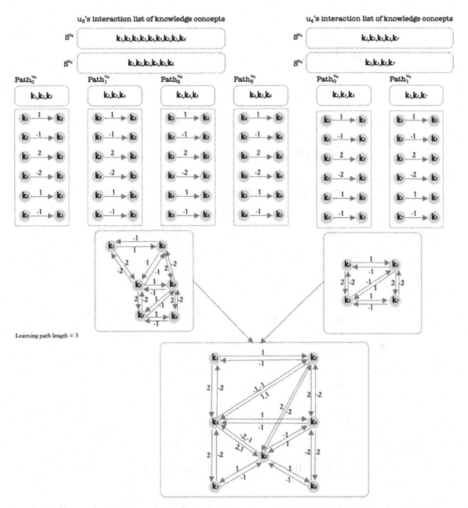

Fig. 1. An illustration of the terms defined in Sect. 3.2

4 Proposed Method

The framework of the knowledge concept recommendation system proposed in this paper is shown in Fig. 2. It consists of the following components:

– Entity Feature Extraction and Entity Relation Extraction. Before entity representation learning, feature extraction of user entity and knowledge concept entity is helpful to obtain better entity representation. In addition, obtaining the relationship between user entities and knowledge conceptual entities can be beneficial for learning entity representation based on graph convolution in heterogeneous graphs.

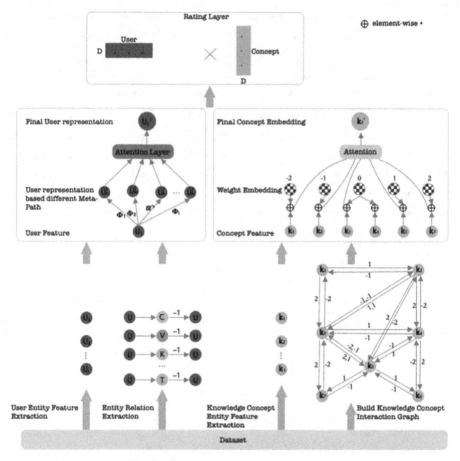

Fig. 2. Illustration of our proposed model.

- Knowledge Concept Representation Learning Based on Structure-Enhanced Interaction Graph Neural Network. This component will learn the representation of knowledge concepts entity using all users' interaction sequence of knowledge concepts and the knowledge concepts entity feature extracted in the previous step. Specifically, we first construct a knowledge interaction graph described in Sect. 3.2 according to all users' interaction sequences of knowledge concepts. Then when learning target node representation based on neighbor node information aggregation, the Structure-enhanced Fusion proposed in the paper is used to fuse the structure information with neighbor node information and an attention mechanism within Attention-based Structure-enhanced Aggregator is used to distinguish the contributions of different neighbor nodes.
- User Representation Learning Based on Heterogeneous Graph Neural Network. After extracting user entity features and user entity relationships, we use the method proposed in ACKRec [4] to learn the representation of user entities.

– Rating Prediction. After obtaining the entity representation of users and knowledge concepts, they are input into a rating layer based on extended matrix decomposition to recommend knowledge concepts by rating.

4.1 Entity Feature Extraction and Entity Relation Extraction

Entity Feature Extraction

Feature Extraction of Knowledge Concept Entity
Generally, the name of knowledge concept is a generalization of the content covered by knowledge concepts, such as Indefinite Integration, attributive clause, and binary tree, which contain rich semantic information. Therefore, we can use the word embedding of name to generate the features of knowledge concept entities. Specifically, we use Word2vector [15] to generate word embeddings.

Feature Extraction of User Entities
For the features of user entities, we can use one-hot encoding to generate the user's knowledge concept state as its features.

Entity Relation Extraction. Entity relation extraction aims at generating an adjacency matrix of nodes according to a given meta path [7]. Take the meta-path User $\xrightarrow{click}$ Concept $\xrightarrow{click^{-1}}$ User as an example, we generate a user- knowledge concepts adjacency matrix A_1^u. Where its row number indicates the user ID, and its column number indicates the knowledge concept ID. element $a_{i,j}^1 \in \{0, 1\}$ in A_1^u indicates whether user u_i clicked on knowledge concept e_j.

4.2 Knowledge Concept Representation Learning Based on Structure-Enhanced Interaction Graph Neural Network

Structure-Enhanced Fusion. As shown in the Fig. 2, given a node k_3 in the knowledge concept interaction graph, we obtain its neighbor node set $N_3^{Path} = \{k_1, k_2, k_3, k_4, k_5, k_7\}$ and the directed edge set from node k_3 to its neighbor node:

$$\{k_3 \xrightarrow{-2} k_1, k_3 \xrightarrow{-1} k_2, k_3 \xrightarrow{-1} k_2 k_3 \xrightarrow{0} k_3, k_3 \xrightarrow{1} k_4, k_3 \xrightarrow{1} k_5, k_3 \xrightarrow{2} k_5, k_3 \xrightarrow{2} k_7\}$$

Inspired by transformer's related work [16, 17], to capture the structural information in the knowledge concept interaction graph, we correlate each neighbor node with a learnable directed edge's weight embedding $D \in R^{|D| \times d}$ to capture the structural information of the neighbor node relative to the current node k_3.

$$\widehat{E_i} = E_i + D_j \tag{1}$$

where E_i is the embedding representation corresponding to k_i, the neighbor node of node k_3, and D_j is the embedding representation corresponding to the weight on the directed edge $k_3 \overset{weight}{\to} k_i$. Knowledge concept interaction graph is a directed multigraph; there may be multiple directed edges in the same direction between two nodes. We can choose one of the directed edges as the directed edge between the two nodes for node representation learning. Take the set of directed edges from k_3 to k_5 as an example, $\{k_3 \overset{1}{\to} k_5, k_3 \overset{2}{\to} k_5\}$. This paper selects one of the directed edges corresponding to the weights that appear most frequently. If multiple weights occur most frequently, choose the least of them. Here we choose $k_3 \overset{1}{\to} k_5$ as the directed edge between k_3 and k_5. We can also use the attentional mechanism to take advantage of multiple co-directed edges between two nodes, which we leave for future work.

Attention-Based Structure-Enhanced Aggregator. Using the Structure-enhanced Fusion, we get the embedding representation of the neighbor node relative to the current node after fusing its structure information relative to the current node. however, different neighbor nodes should not be considered equally to solve this problem, this paper proposes an attention-based structure-enhanced aggregator.

As shown in the Fig. 2, take node k_3 as an example. For node k_3, since different neighbor nodes make different contributions to the current node k_3, we calculate the cosine similarity of the embedding representation $\widehat{E}_3$ of the current node k_3 and the embedding representation $\widehat{E}_i$ of each neighbor node k_i as the neighbor node's attention value to the current node k_i.

$$attn(e_3, e_i) = Cosine\left(\widehat{E}_3, \widehat{E}_i\right) = \frac{\widehat{E}_3 \cdot \widehat{E}_i}{\|\widehat{E}_3\| \cdot \|\widehat{E}_i\|}, \; e_i \in N_3^{Path} \tag{2}$$

Here, $attn(e_3, e_i)$ represents the attention value of compute node e_i to e_3. Other measuring attention can also be applied, and we leave it for future work.

We use the softmax function to normalize the attention value $attn(e_3, e_i)$ of all neighbor nodes of the current node k_3. Then we can obtain the aggregation weight α_{3j} from each neighbor node of k_3 to k_3.

$$\alpha_{3j} = \frac{exp(attn(e_3, e_i))}{\sum_{e_j \in N_3^{Path}} exp\left(attn(e_3, e_j)\right)} \tag{3}$$

We use the weights of aggregation to aggregate the information $\widehat{E}_i$ of k_3's neighbor node to k_3.

$$E_3' = \sum_{e_i \in N_3^{Path}} \alpha_{3i} \cdot \widehat{E}_i \tag{4}$$

where E_3' represents the final representation of node k_3 obtained by structure-enhanced interaction graph neural network.

4.3 User Representation Learning Based on Heterogeneous Graph Neural Network

This section adopts the method proposed in ACKRec [4] for user representation learning based on heterogeneous graphs [6]. After obtaining the features and relations of the user entity, they are input into a graph convolutional network to learn the representation of the user entity. The graph convolutional network layer adopted by us is as follows:

$$U^{l+1} = \sigma\left((PU^l)W^l\right) \tag{5}$$

where U^{l+1} represents the user entity representation obtained through the convolution layer of the l-th graph. In particular, U^0 is the input we provide at the beginning, the user entity feature obtained in Sect. 4.1. $P = \tilde{D}^{-\frac{1}{2}}\tilde{A}\tilde{D}^{-\frac{1}{2}}$, $\tilde{A} = A + I$, which represents the adjacency matrix A plus its identity matrix I. A is the adjacency matrix corresponding to a particular meta-path. $\tilde{D} = diag\left(\tilde{A}1\right)$, 1 represents a vector of all-ones. $\sigma(\cdot)$ is defined as $ReLU(\cdot)$, where $ReLU(a) = max\{0, a\}$ is a linear rectifier activation function. l represents the l-th layer of graph convolution, and W^l means the trainable shared weight matrix of the l-th layer of graph convolution. This article set the number of graph convolution layers to 3. Finally, the user entity representation obtained after three graphs convolution layer is expressed as:

$$U' = U^3 = ReLU\left((PU^2)W^2\right) \tag{6}$$

Then, as shown in Fig. 2, we use the attention mechanism to aggregate the entity representation of user u_i on different meta-paths, to obtain the final user entity representation U_i'.

$$U_i' = \sum_{i=1}^{|MP|} \alpha_{\Phi_i} \hat{U}_{\Phi_k}^i \tag{7}$$

where $|MP|$ represents the number of meta-paths, and α_{Φ_i} means the attention weight of meta-path Φ_i.

4.4 Extended Matrix Factorization for Knowledge Concept Recommendation

We use a method based on extended matrix decomposition to recommend knowledge concepts to users. We treat the number of times users click on knowledge concepts as the rating matrix. According to matrix decomposition, users' ratings of knowledge concepts are defined as follows:

$$\hat{r}_{u,k} = x_u^T y_k \tag{8}$$

where $x_u \in R^{D \times |U|}$ and $y_k \in R^{D \times |K|}$ represent the latent factor vector of users and knowledge concepts, respectively. D is the number of latent factors. $|U|$ and $|K|$ are the numbers of user entities and knowledge concept entities, respectively. As shown below, to use the obtained user entity representations U' and knowledge concept entity representations E' to recommend knowledge concepts, we input them into the rating prediction layer for rating prediction.

$$\hat{r}_{u,k} = x_u^T y_k + \beta_u \cdot U'^T t^k + \beta_k \cdot t^{u^T} E' \tag{9}$$

Here we introduce trainable parameters t^k and t^u to ensure that U' and E' are in the same space. In addition, β_u and β_k are tuning parameters. To obtain appropriate rating prediction, the objective function of MF is defined as follows:

$$\min_{U,K} \frac{1}{|U| \times |K|} \sum_{u=1}^{|U|} \sum_{k=1}^{|K|} \left(r_{u,k} - \hat{r}_{u,k} \right)^2 \tag{10}$$

We further add regularization terms to the function. Therefore, the final objective function is formulated as follows:

$$\min_{U,K} \frac{1}{|U| \times |K|} \sum_{u=1}^{|U|} \sum_{k=1}^{|K|} \left(r_{u,k} - \hat{r}_{u,k} \right)^2 + \lambda \left(\|x_u\| + \|y_k\| + \|t^u\| + \|t^k\| \right) \tag{11}$$

where λ is a regularization parameter. Then the stochastic gradient descent algorithm is used to optimize the local minimum of the final objective function.

5 Experiments

5.1 Dataset Description

To verify the effectiveness of the proposed model, we validated the model on a real open dataset[1], which is provided by the XuetangX[2] MOOC platform. The dataset treats students' course enrollment behaviors from October 1st, 2016, to December 30th, 2017, as the training set and those from January 1st, 2018, to March 1st, 2018, as the test set. Each instance of the training set and test set is a sequence that represents the user's history of click behaviors. In the training process, we generate a corresponding negative instance for each positive instance by replacing the target knowledge concept with a randomly sampled knowledge concept from the knowledge concept set. In the testing process, each item in sequences in the test set is treated as the target knowledge concept; The corresponding positive instances in the training set are taken as the past behaviors to obtain several positive instances. To evaluate the proposed model's recommendation performance, each positive instance in the test set is paired with 99 randomly sampled negative instances generated in the same way as previously described, and the prediction scores for the 100 instances are output [18].

5.2 Evaluation Metrics

We use common evaluation metrics to evaluate all models, including the area under the ROC curve (AUC), Hit Ratio of top-K items (HR@K), Normalized Discounted Cumulative Gain of top-K items (NDCG@K) [19], and mean reciprocal rank (MRR). We set K to 5 and 10, and report the average metrics for all users in the test set.

---

[1] The dataset is available at https://github.com/JockWang/ACKRec.
[2] https://www.xuetangx.com.

5.3 Evaluation of Model Parameters

The length of the Learning Path is a critical parameter when learning knowledge concept representation. Therefore, we compare the model's performance under different lengths of the Learning Path. As shown in Table 1, we tune the length of the Learning Path from 10 to 60 in increments of 10. Then we can see that the performance growth flattens out as the length of the Learning Path increases. When the length of Learning Path is 40, the model can produce the best performance.

Table 1. Different results from different length of Learning Path.

Length	HR@5	HR@10	NDCG@5	NDCG@10	MRR	AUC
10	0.7790	0.8844	0.6779	0.7120	0.6644	0.9466
20	0.7818	0.8937	0.6628	0.6990	0.6440	0.9537
30	0.7837	0.8909	0.6808	0.7158	0.6670	0.9504
40	0.8001	0.8951	0.6946	0.7255	0.6781	0.9499
50	0.7870	0.8890	0.6790	0.7122	0.6624	0.9494
60	0.7945	0.8913	0.6909	0.7249	0.6758	0.9485

5.4 Baseline Methods

To evaluate the proposed KCRec-SEIGNN, we selected the following comparative model in the experiment. CERec-ME [5] is a knowledge concept recommendation method based on heterogeneous graph neural networks and enhanced by utilizing community structure information between entities. ACKRec [4] is a knowledge concept recommendation method based on heterogeneous graph neural networks. NAIS [18] is an item-to-item collaborative filtering algorithm but uses an attentional mechanism approach to distinguish the weights of different online learning behaviors. FISM [20] is an item-to-item collaborative filtering algorithm that conducts recommendations based on the average embeddings of all behavior histories and the embeddings of the target knowledge concept. KCRec-SEIGNN$_{no-attn}$ is a variant of KCRec-SEIGNN. KCRec-SEIGNN$_{no-attn}$ ignores the attention mechanism into account when generating knowledge concept representations. KCRec-SEIGNN$_{no-attn-structure}$ is also a variant of KCRec-SEIGNN. KCRec-SEIGNN$_{no-attn-structure}$ ignores the structure information between the neighbor node and the target node and the attention mechanism when generating knowledge concept representations.

5.5 Experiment Setup

To fairly compare with previous meta-path-based models, in the user entities representation learning, we use the same meta-paths proposed in ACKRec [4] to learn user entity representation and set the number of GCN layers and the dimension of the user entities representation as 3 and 100, respectively. The meta-paths are shown in Table 2. For the same purpose, in the extended matrix factorization (MF) based Rating Layer, we set the number of latent factors as 30. We set the length of Learning Path as 40.

Table 2. Meta-Paths used in user entities representation learning.

Meta-Path	Explanation
User $\overset{click}{\rightarrow}$ Concept $\overset{click^{-1}}{\rightarrow}$ User	Two users click on the same knowledge concept
User $\overset{enrolled}{\rightarrow}$ Course $\overset{enrolled^{-1}}{\rightarrow}$ User	Two users take the same course
User $\overset{watched}{\rightarrow}$ Video $\overset{watched^{-1}}{\rightarrow}$ User	Two users watched the same video
User $\overset{enrolled}{\rightarrow}$ Course $\overset{take}{\rightarrow}$ Teacher $\overset{take^{-1}}{\rightarrow}$ Course $\overset{enrolled^{-1}}{\rightarrow}$ Teacher	Both users have taken classes with the same teacher

5.6 Results

As shown in Table 3, we compare KCRec-SEIGNN with the other comparison methods on the knowledge concept recommendation task. Note that for a fair comparison, we use the same meta-path in CERec-ME [5] and ACKRec [4], and in the components for user entity representation learning in KCRec-SEIGNN$_{no-attn-structure}$, KCRec-SEIGNN$_{no-attn}$, KCRec-SEIGNN, we use the same meta-path proposed in ACKRec to learn user entity representation. We can observe that:

- The methods based on heterogeneous graph neural networks, including CERec-ME, ACKRec, KCRec-SEIGNN, and KCRec-SEIGNN's variants, have better performance than other methods. It indicates that the additional side information introduced by the heterogeneous graph makes better performance on knowledge concept recommendation.
- Compared with CERec-ME and ACKRec, KCRec-SEIGNN and its variants use structure-enhanced interactive graph neural network instead of heterogeneous graph neural network for knowledge concept representation learning, has better performance. It indicates that the co-occurrence information between knowledge concepts introduced by Learning Path-based interactive graph neural network contributes to better performance on knowledge concept recommendation.
- By comparing KCRec-SEIGNN and its variants, it shows that taking the structure information between neighbor nodes and target nodes into account when aggregating neighbor node information to generate target node information is helpful to generate better node representation.
- By comparing KCRec-SEIGNN$_{no-attn}$ and KCRec-SEIGNN, it shows that introducing an attention mechanism when aggregating the neighbor node information to generate target node information helps obtain better node representation.

Table 3. Comparison of different models.

	HR@5	HR@10	NDCG@5	NDCG@10	MRR	AUC
NAIS	0.4112	0.6624	0.2392	0.3201	0.2392	0.8863
FISM	0.5849	0.7489	0.3760	0.4203	0.3293	0.8532
ACKRec	0.6470	0.8122	0.4635	0.5170	0.4352	0.9232
CERec-ME	0.6532	0.8221	0.4712	0.5284	0.4453	0.9412
KCRec-SEIGNN$_{\text{no-attn-structure}}$	0.6760	0.8446	0.4826	0.5372	0.4491	0.9171
KCRec-SEIGNN$_{\text{no-attn}}$	0.7527	0.8644	0.6464	0.6951	0.5807	0.9430
KCRec-SEIGNN	0.8001	0.8951	0.6946	0.7255	0.6781	0.9499

6 Conclusion

In this paper, we propose a knowledge concept recommendation model based on a structure-enhanced interactive graph neural network, an end-to-end graph neural network. To make more effective use of rich context information contained in the user's historical interaction sequence of knowledge concept, we construct all user's historical interaction sequence of knowledge concept into a knowledge concept interaction graph according to the Learning Path, which helps to discover co-occurrence information between knowledge concepts. Then, to obtain a better knowledge concepts representation, we retain the structure information between the neighbor node and the target node when aggregating the neighbor node information. Finally, an attention mechanism is used to improve the representation of knowledge concepts further. To verify the effectiveness of the proposed method, experiments are conducted on an open dataset. The results show that the performance of this method is better than the most advanced methods.

Acknowledgments. This work is supported by the National Science Foundation of China (No. 62192711) and the Guangzhou Science and Technology Project (No. 201904010195).

References

1. King, C., Robinson, A., Vickers, J.: Targeted MOOC captivates students. Nature **505**(7481), 26 (2014)
2. Zhang, J.: Can MOOCs be interesting to students? An experimental investigation from regulatory focus perspective. Comput. Educ. **95**, 340–351 (2016)
3. Pan, L., Li, C., Li, J., Tang, J.: Prerequisite relation learning for concepts in MOOCs. In: Annual Meeting of the Association for Computational Linguistics, pp. 1447–1456 (2017)
4. Gong, J., et al.: Attentional graph convolutional networks for knowledge concept recommendation in MOOCs in a heterogeneous view. In: ACM SIGIR, pp. 79–88 (2020)

5. Ye, B., Mao, S., Hao, P., Chen, W., Bai, C.: Community enhanced course concept recommendation in MOOCs with multiple entities. In: Qiu, H., Zhang, C., Fei, Z., Qiu, M., Kung, S.-Y. (eds.) Knowledge Science, Engineering and Management. Lecture Notes in Computer Science (Lecture Notes in Artificial Intelligence), vol. 12816, pp. 279–293. Springer, Cham (2021). https://doi.org/10.1007/978-3-030-82147-0_23

6. Shi, C., Hu, B., Zhao, W.X., Philip, S.Y.: Heterogeneous information network embedding for recommendation. IEEE Trans. Knowl. Data Eng. **31**(2), 357–370 (2018)

7. Gori, M., Monfardini, G., Scarselli, F.: A new model for learning in graph domains. In: IEEE International Joint Conference of Neural Network, vol. 2, pp. 729–734 (2005)

8. Pham, T.A.N., Li, X., Cong, G., Zhang, Z.: A general recommendation model for heterogeneous networks. IEEE Trans. Knowl. Data Eng. **28**(12), 3140–3153 (2016)

9. Yu, X., et al.: Personalized entity recommendation: a heterogeneous information network approach. In: Proceedings of the 7th ACM International Conference on Web Search and Data Mining, pp. 283–292 (2014)

10. Hu, B., Shi, C., Zhao, W. X., Yu, P.S.: Leveraging meta-path based context for top-N recommendation with a neural co-attention model. In: Proceedings of the 24th ACM SIGKDD International Conference on Knowledge Discovery & Data Mining, pp. 1531–1540. (2018)

11. Shi, C., Zhang, Z., Luo, P., Yu, P.S., Yue, Y., Wu, B.: Semantic path based personalized recommendation on weighted heterogeneous information networks. In: Proceedings of the 24th ACM International on Conference on Information and Knowledge Management, pp. 453–462 (2015)

12. Dong, Y., Chawla, N.V., Swami, A.: metapath2vec: scalable representation learning for heterogeneous networks. In: Proceedings of the 23rd ACM SIGKDD International Conference on Knowledge Discovery and Data Mining, pp. 135–144 (2017)

13. Wang, X., et al.: Heterogeneous graph attention network. In: The World Wide Web Conference, pp. 2022–2032 (2019)

14. Fu, X., Zhang, J., Meng, Z., King, I.: MAGNN: metapath aggregated graph neural network for heterogeneous graph embedding. In: Proceedings of the Web Conference 2020, pp. 2331–2341 (2020)

15. Mikolov, T., Chen, K., Corrado, G., Dean, J.: Efficient estimation of word representations in vector space. In: International Conference on Learning Representations (2013)

16. Devlin, J., et al.: BERT: pre-training of deep bidirectional transformers for language understanding. arXiv preprint arXiv:1810.04805 (2018)

17. Vaswani, A., et al.: Attention is all you need. In: Neural Information Processing Systems, pp. 5998–6008 (2017)

18. He, X., He, Z., Song, J., Liu, Z., et al.: NAIS: neural attentive item similarity model for recommendation. IEEE Trans. Knowl. Data Eng. **30**(12), 2354–2366 (2018)

19. Järvelin, K., Kekäläinen, J.: IR evaluation methods for retrieving highly relevant documents, pp. 41–48. ACM SIGIR (2000)

20. Kabbur, S., Ning, X., Karypis, G.: Fism: factored item similarity models for top-N recommender systems. In: ACM SIGKDD, pp. 659–667 (2013)

Answering Complex Questions
on Knowledge Graphs

Xin Wang[1,2]⬤, Min Luo[2], Chengliang Si[2(✉)], and Huayi Zhan[2]

[1] Southwest Petroleum University, Chengdu, China
[2] Sichuan Changhong Electronic Ltd. Co, Mianyang, China
{chengliang.si,Huayi.zhan}@changhong.com

Abstract. The topic of knowledge-based question answering (KBQA) has attracted wide attention for a long period. A series of techniques have been developed, especially for *simple questions*. To answer *complex questions*, most existing approaches apply a semantic parsing-based strategy that parses a question into a query graph for result identification. However, due to poor quality, query graphs often lead to incorrect answers. To tackle the issue, we propose a comprehensive approach for query graph generation, based on two novel models. One leverages attention mechanism with richer information from knowledge base, for core path generation and the other one employs a memory-based network for constraints selection. The experimental results show that our approach outperforms existing methods on typical benchmark datasets.

Keywords: Complex questions · Knowledge base · Question answering · Attention · Memory network

1 Introduction

Question answering on knowledge bases is an active area since proposed. Its main task is to answer natural language questions from a structured knowledge base. The KBQA system has been used as QA machine in many fields. At its early stage, investigators have proposed techniques for answering *simple questions*.

Driven by practical requirements, techniques for answering *complex questions*, which contain multiple constraints are in urgent demand. However, prior techniques for answering *simple questions* can not be easily adapted for answering *complex questions*. Taking the question **"who plays claire in lost?"** from WebQuestion [4] as an example, if one simply parses it into a triple query ⟨**claire, is_played_by, ?**⟩, the answer will be anyone who played claire in any series. However, the correct answer should be the actor in "lost". Therefore, answering *complex questions* is far more complicated than that of *simple questions*.

To answer *complex questions*, most semantic-parsing-based approaches parse a question into a *query graph* and use that *query graph* to find answers from a KB. Typically, a query graph is defined as a formal graph, whose nodes correspond to the topic entity, answer node, variables and constraints, and edges correspond

G. Memmi et al. (Eds.): KSEM 2022, LNAI 13368, pp. 187–200, 2022.
https://doi.org/10.1007/978-3-031-10983-6_15

to relations [27]. Figure 1 shows two questions along with their query graphs. In each figure, the rectangle with bold font denotes the topic entity, rectangles with normal font denote constraints and rounded rectangle with dotted line includes a core path. The construction of query graphs can be split into three main tasks, *i.e.*, entity linking, core paths generation and constraints selection [3, 8, 10, 15, 17, 27, 28, 30]. Due to semantic diversity, query graphs are often unable to precisely express the meaning of a given question.

The low quality of query graphs mainly lies in two issues. The first issue is the core path generation. For example, question Q_1 in Fig. 1 has two candidate core paths, *i.e.*, $\langle$fiction_character$\rangle$[1] and $\langle$TV_character$\rangle$[2]. It is uneasy to determine which one is the correct one. While, if the *type* information, *e.g.*, "TV Character", of the topic entity can be used, then the candidate selection becomes much easier. Another issue lies in the constraints selection. Most existing works [3, 17, 27, 30] simply add all identified constraints to a query graph without careful justification. Hence, a query graph may carry inappropriate constraints.

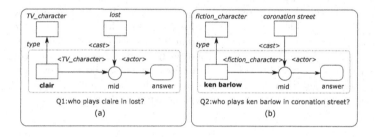

Fig. 1. Questions and their query graphs

Contributions. The contributions of this paper are summarized as follows.

1. We devise a novel metric that is based on *local similarity* and *global similarity* for measuring semantic similarity between a mention and a candidate entity. This new metric shows superiority than its counterparts.
2. We introduce an attention-based model for core path generation. In contrast to prior works, this model incorporates richer implicit information for path identification and shows excellent performance.
3. We propose a memory-based model for constraints selection. The model enables us to choose suitable constraints adaptively.
4. We compared our approach with the state-of-art methods on typical benchmark datasets and show promising results.

The reminder of the paper is organized as follows. We introduce related works in Sect. 2. We illustrate our method in Sect. 3. We conduct experiments to show the performance of our approach in Sect. 4, followed by conclusion in Sect. 5.

---

[1] $\langle$tv.tv_character.appeared_in_tv_program,tv.regular_tv_appearance.actor$\rangle$.

[2] $\langle$fictional_universe.fictional_character.character_created_by$\rangle$.

2   Related Work

The problem of answering complex questions on KBs has been investigated for a period. Investigators have developed several techniques, that can be categorized into *information retrieval* (abbr. IR) and *semantic parsing* (abbr. SP).

Information Retrieval. Methods in this line mainly work as follows: (a) identify the topic entity from the underlying KB for the given question; (b) gain a subgraph around the topic entity over KB; (c) extract features of candidate answers from the subgraph; and (d) match the feature of the query to choose answers.

One bottleneck of IR-based methods is feature extraction. Hence, existing approaches adopt different feature extraction methods to catch important information from the question and the answer, respectively. Early approaches perform as follows. [7,26] first gain candidate answers over KB according to dependency tree, then use feature map to process feature extraction on the question and candidate answers respectively. With the development of neural networks, [11,14] introduce techniques by incorporating CNN and attention mechanism in feature extraction. Moreover, some approaches [9,16] adopted memory networks for the task.

Since IR-based approaches retrieve answers from a KB, the completeness of the KB is imperative. [13,20] make efforts on reasoning under incomplete KB. While [22,29] proposed techniques to dynamically update reasoning instructions.

Semantic Parsing. Most semantic parsing approaches show better performance on complex KBQA [8,9,15]. Methods in this line mainly work as follows: (a) question understanding: understand a given question via semantic and syntactic analysis; (b) logical parsing: translate the question into logical forms; (c) KB grounding: instantiate logical forms by conducting semantic alignment on underlying KB; (d) KB execution: execute the logical forms to obtain answers.

In the early stage, traditional semantic parsing methods [4,12] used templates to conduct logical parsing. Recently, for question understanding, syntax dependencies [1,2,17] were introduced to accomplish the task, while [21] treats a complex question as the combination of several simple questions.

The logical form generation is crucial for SP-based methods, approaches, *e.g.,* [8,27] focus on the task. A staged query graph generation mechanism was introduced by [27], where each stage added some semantic components with rules. Followed by [27], [3] further investigated the staged query graph generation, and summarized the types of constraints. A hierarchical representation that based on words, questions and relation levels was proposed by [28]. [15] developed a state-transition model to generate query graphs. While [17] and [18] improved techniques for ranking query graphs. [10] analyzed historical datasets and put forward a set of structured templates for generating complex query graphs. Followed by [10], [8] proposed a generative model to generate abstract structures adaptively, and match the abstract structures against a KB to gain formal query graphs.

3   Approach

Problem Formulation. The task of complex question answering on KBs can be formulated as follows. Given a natural language question **Q** represented as a sequence of words $\mathcal{L}_Q = \{w_1, ..., w_T\}$ and a background knowledge base KB as input, it is to find a set of entities in KB as answers for the question **Q**.

Typically, SP-based techniques, which gain better performances, involves *question patterns* and *query graphs* (*a.k.a.* semantic graphs). We next formally introduce the notions (rephrased) as follows.

Question Pattern. Given a question **Q**, one can generate a new question by replacing an entity mention in **Q** with a generic symbol ⟨e⟩. Then this new question is referred to as a *question pattern* (denoted by **P**) of **Q**. For example, a *question pattern* of **"who plays claire in lost?"** is **"who plays ⟨e⟩ in lost?'**, where the entity mention "claire" in **Q** is replaced by ⟨e⟩.

Query Graph. Typically, a query graph Q_g is defined as a logical form in λ-calculus [27] and consists of a core path and various constraints. Specifically, a core path includes a topic entity, a middle node (not essential), an answer node and some predicates among these nodes. Constraints are categorized into four types according to their semantics, *e.g.*, entity constraints, type constraints, time constraints, and ordinary constraints. Two query graphs are shown in Fig. 1.

Overview. Our approach consists of three modules *i.e., Topic Entity Recognition*, *Core Path Generation* and *Constraints Selection*. In a nutshell, given a question **Q** issued on a KB, the *Topic Entity Recognition* module first retrieves mentions from it and identifies a set of topic entities as candidates from the underlying KB. On the set of candidate entities, the *Core Path Generation* module identifies the core path with an attention-based model. Finally, the *Constraints Selection* module employs a memory-based model to select the most suitable constraints, which are then used to produce the query graph. Below, we illustrate the details of these modules in Sects. 3.1, 3.2 and 3.3, respectively.

3.1   Topic Entity Recognition

The *Topic Entity Recognition* module works as follows. (1) It employs, *e.g.*, BiLSTM + CRF to recognize entity mentions from a given question **Q**. (2) It performs the entity linking task with the state-of-the-art entity linking tool, *i.e.*, S-MART [24] to link a mention to entities in a KB. Note that, a mention may be linked to multiple entities in a KB. Hence, after above process, a collection of triples $\langle m, e, s_e \rangle$ are returned, where m, e and s_e represent a mention, an entity that is linked from m and a score measuring semantic similarity between m and e, respectively. (3) It determines the best topic entity according to a novel metric for measuring semantic similarity between a mention and an entity in a KB.

Similarity Metric. Given a question **Q**, a list of n mentions $[m_1, m_2, ..., m_n]$ can be extracted from it. For a mention m_i ($i \in [1, n]$), it is linked to k different entities $[e_i^1, e_i^2, \cdots, e_i^k]$ in a KB and each entity e_i^j is assigned with a value s_i^j

indicating the matching degree between m_i and e_i^j ($j \in [1, k]$). We define the largest matching degree $\hat{s}_i$ of m_i as $\hat{s}_i = \max\{s_i^1, s_i^2, \cdots, s_i^k\}$, then the entity with $\hat{s}_i$ is considered the best entity of m_i. The *local similarity* l_i^j and *global similarity* g_i^j between a mention m_i and its j-th entity e_i^j are hence defined as $l_i^j = s_i^j / \hat{s}_i$ and $g_i^j = \frac{s_i^j}{\max\{\hat{s}_1, \hat{s}_2, \cdots, \hat{s}_n\}}$, respectively. The final semantic similarity τ is defined as below.

$$\tau = \beta \cdot l_i^j + (1 - \beta) \cdot g_i^j, \tag{1}$$

where β is an adjustment coefficient tuned by users.

Based on the metric τ, the best topic entity e is determined and returned to the core path generation module for further processing.

3.2 Core Path Generation

Given the topic entity e of a question $\mathbf{Q}$, one can generate a set $\mathbf{R} = \{R_1, \cdots, R_T\}$ of *core paths* as candidates, where each R_i takes e as the initial node and consists of h hop nodes and edges of e in a KG. Then one only needs to determine the best one from multiple candidates. Here, the quality of a core path R_i *w.r.t.* $\mathbf{Q}$ indicates the semantic distance between R_i and the question pattern of $\mathbf{Q}$.

To tackle the issue, a host of techniques *e.g.*, [3,17,27] have been developed. These techniques mostly learn correlation between a question pattern and corresponding candidate core paths for the best core path determination. While, the correlation from explicit information alone is insufficient. For example, given

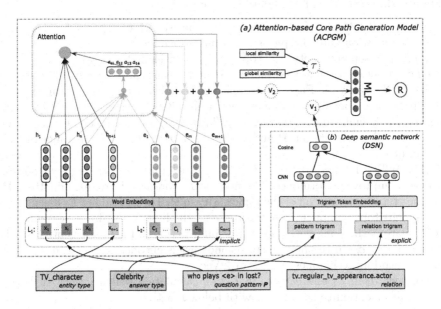

Fig. 2. Attention-based core path generation model & Deep semantic network

the question **"who plays ken barlow in coronation street?"**, it is easy to obtain a topic entity as well as a question pattern **"who plays ⟨e⟩ in coronation street?"**. Note that the pattern corresponds to multiple candidate paths (*a.k.a.* relations) in a KG, *e.g.,* ⟨fiction_character⟩ and ⟨TV_character⟩, while only one "golden" path exists. If the "type" information of the topic entity, *i.e.,* 'TV Character', can be incorporated, one can easily determine the *golden* path: ⟨TV_character⟩. This example shows that *implicit information, e.g., type* of the topic entity, plays a crucial role in determining the *golden* path.

Motivated by this, we develop an **A**ttention-based **C**ore **P**ath **G**eneration **M**odel, denoted as ACPGM, to generate a core path for a given question.

Model Details. As shown in Fig. 2(a), ACPGM learns correlation between a question and a core path by using *explicit correlation* v_1 and *implicit correlation* v_2 and semantic similarity τ of the topic entity. In particular, the degree of *explicit correlation* is calculated with a deep semantic network, which is shown in Fig. 2(b). We next illustrate with more details.

Explicit & Implicit Correlation. Intuitively, the semantic correlation between a question pattern **P** and a core path R_i is referred to as the *explicit correlation*. On the contrary, the correlation that is inferred from certain *implicit information*, is referred to as *implicit correlation*. Taking the question pattern **"who plays ⟨e⟩ in lost?"** of $\mathbf{Q}_1$ as example, it corresponds to multiple candidate paths, among which ⟨fictional_character⟩ and ⟨TV_character⟩ are typical ones. Observe that the "type" (as one kind of implicit information) of the topic entity is "TV Character", which already appeared in the second candidate. If the "type" information can be used to guide the selection, then the correct answer can be obtained since the second candidate is more preferred.

Structure of the Model. The entire model consists of two parts for learning *explicit* correlation and core paths selection, respectively.

(I) A deep semantic network (abbr. DSN) is developed to capture the *explicit* correlation between a question pattern **P** and a candidate path R_i. The structure of DSN is shown in Fig. 2 (b). It encodes **P** and R_i as letter-trigram vectors, and applies two convolutional neural networks with the same structure to learn their semantic embeddings, respectively. Then DSN computes semantic similarity (denoted by v_1) between **P** and R_i by calculating the cosine distance of two embeddings.

(II) ACPGM takes two lists L_1 and L_2 as input and leverages attention scheme to improve performance. The first list L_1 consists of a question pattern **P** and the "type" information of the topic entity in **P**. The second list L_2 essentially corresponds to the implicit information, *e.g.,* the first two and the last entry of a candidate path, along with the "type" information of the answer entity. Each word x_i (resp. c_i) in the first (resp. second) list is encoded as h_i (resp. e_j), via certain encoding techniques, *e.g.,* Word2Vec.

For each h_i in L_1 and each e_j in L_2, we calculate a weight w_{ij} of each pair $\langle h_i, e_j \rangle$, as attention to the answer with below function.

$$w_{ij} = W^T(h_i \cdot e_j) + b, \tag{2}$$

where · operates as the dot product, $W^T \in \mathbb{R}$ and b are an intermediate matrix and an offset value, respectively; they can be randomly initialized and updated during training. Note that there are in total $l = |L_1| * |L_2|$ pairs of weights for each input. Accordingly, the attention weight a_{ij} of the pair $\langle h_i, e_j \rangle$, in terms of the implicit information can be computed via below function.

$$a_{ij} = \frac{exp(w_{ij})}{\sum_{k=1}^{l} exp(w_{ik})} \qquad (3)$$

The attention weights are then employed to compute a weighted sum for each word, leading to a semantic vector that represents the question pattern. The similarity score v_2 between a question $\mathbf{Q}$ and a core path R_i is defined as below.

$$q_i = \sum_{j=1}^{n+1} a_{ij} h_j \qquad (4)$$

$$v_2 = \sum_{i=1}^{m+1} q_i e_i \qquad (5)$$

By now, the *explicit* and *implicit* correlation between a question and a candidate core path, i.e., v_1 and v_2 are obtained. Together with score τ for measuring topic entity, a simple multi-layer perceptron, denoted by $f(\cdot)$ is incorporated to calculate the final score that is used for core paths ranking.

$$v = f(v_1, v_2, \tau) \qquad (6)$$

Here, the loss function of ACPGM is defined as follows.

$$Loss(\mathbf{Q}, R) = max(\gamma + v(\mathbf{Q}, a_0) - v(\mathbf{Q}, a), 0), \qquad (7)$$

where γ is the margin parameter, a and a_0 refer to the positive and negative samples, respectively. The intuition of the training strategy is to ensure the score of positive question-answer pairs to be higher than negative ones with a margin.

3.3 Constraints Selection

Given a core path, it is still necessary to enrich it with constraints imposed by the given question and produce a query graph for seeking the final answer. To this end, we first categorize constraints into four types, i.e., *entity constraint, type constraint, time constraint* and *ordinary constraint*, along the same line as [17], and then apply an approach, that works in two stages, for constraints selection.

Candidates Identification. As the first stage, this task targets at collecting valid constraints as candidates. Given a question $\mathbf{Q}$ and its corresponding core path p_c (identified by ACPGM), we first identify 1-hop entities e_c connected to nodes (excluding the topic entity and answer node) of p_c from the underlying KB. For each identified entity e_c, if part of its name appears in the original question $\mathbf{Q}$, e_c

is considered as a possible *entity constraint*. Moreover, we treat type information associated to the answer node as *type constraint*. The *time constraint* is recognized via certain regular expression, and *ordinary constraint* is distinguished via some typical hand-weaved rules. All the identified constraints are then included in a set of size n for further process.

Constraints Selection. Given the set of candidate constraints, a **Memory-based Constratint Selection Model**, denoted as MCSM, is developed to choose constraints. The idea of MCSM is to measure the relevance between a question and its constraints and then select the most suitable ones to update the core path.

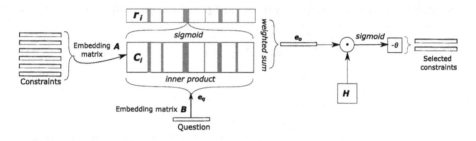

Fig. 3. Constraint selection model

It works as follows. For each candidate constraint, it is converted into a vector c_i ($i \in [1, n]$) of dimension d with an embedding matrix $A \in \mathbb{R}^{d \times n}$, which is initialized randomly and learned during training. The set of embedding $\mathbf{C} = \{c_1, c_2, \cdots, c_n\}$ will be stored in memory for querying. The input question is also encoded as a matrix e_q of dimension d with another matrix $B \in \mathbb{R}^{d \times n}$. Via encoding, the relevance r_i between a candidate constraint and the question can be measured with Eq. 8.

$$r_i = \sigma(\mathbf{e}_q \cdot c_i) \tag{8}$$

Here σ indicates a nonlinear transformation with sigmoid function. In this way, r_i can be deemed as the relevance degree between the i-th constraint and the question. Based on the relevance set, a new embedding $\mathbf{e}_o$ as the representation of the output memory can be generated as follows:

$$\mathbf{e}_o = \sum_{i=1}^{n} c_i \times r_i \tag{9}$$

Intuitively, $\mathbf{e}_o$ captures the total relevance between a question and all its constraints. Finally, the output embedding $\mathbf{e}_o$ is transformed via Eq. 10 to be a numerical number *val* for judgement.

$$val = \sigma(H^T \cdot \mathbf{e}_o) - \theta \tag{10}$$

Here, matrix $H \in \mathbb{R}^{n \times d}$ is randomly initialized and optimized via training, and θ is a predefined threshold for constraint selection, *i.e.*, a constraint with *val* above zero can be accepted.

After constraints are determined, the core path p_c is updated as follows. For an *entity constraint*, it is associated with a node (excluding the topic entity and answer node) in p_c. For a *type constraint*, it is connected to the answer node directly. If the constraint is a *time constraint* or *ordinary constraint*, p_c is extended by connecting the constraint to the middle node or answer node. After above steps, the query graph is generated. Then the final answer can be easily obtained.

4 Experimental Studies

4.1 Settings

We introduce details of model implementation, dataset and baseline methods.

Model Implementation. Our models were implemented in Keras v2.2.5 with CUDA 9.0 running on an NVIDIA Tesla P100 GPU.

Knowledge Base. In this work, we use Freebase [6], which contains 5,323 predicates, 46 million entities and 2.6 billion facts, as our knowledge base. We host Freebase with the Virtuoso engine to search for entities and relations.

Questions. We adopted following question sets for performance evaluation.

- CompQuestion [3] contains 2,100 questions collected from Bing search query log. It is split into 1,300 and 800 for training and testing, respectively.
- WebQuestion [4] contains 5,810 questions collected from Google Suggest API and is split into 3,778 training and 2,032 testing QA pairs.

Baseline Methods. We compared our approach with following baseline methods: (1) Yih *et al.* 2015 [27], a technique for staged query graph generation; (2) Bao *et al.* 2016 [3], extended from Yih's work with techniques for constraint detection and binding; (3) Luo *et al.*, 2018 [17], that treats a query graph as semantic components and introduces a method to improve the ranking model; (4) Hu *et al.* 2018 [15] which gains the best performance on WebQuestion with a state-transition mechanism; and (5) Chen *et al.* 2020 [8], that achieves the best performance on CompQuestion.

4.2 Model Training

We next introduce training strategies used by our models.

Training for DSM. The DSM is fed with a collection of question pattern and core path pairs for training. To improve performance, a subtle strategy is applied to ensure the correctness of positive samples as much as possible. Specifically, for each question **Q** in the original training set, a core path that takes topic entity

e in $\mathbf{Q}$ as starting node, with length no more than two in the underlying KB and $F1$ score no less than 0.5 is chosen as training data. Here $F1$ is defined as $\frac{2*precision*recall}{precision+recall}$, where $precision = \frac{\#true\_paths\_predicted}{\#predicted\_paths}$ and $recall = \frac{\#true\_paths\_predicted}{\#true\_paths}$.

Training for ACPGM. To train ACPGM, a collection of question pattern and core path pairs $\langle \mathbf{P}, R \rangle$ needs to be prepared. Besides the set of paths identified for training DSM, n incorrect paths were chosen randomly as negative samples, for each question pattern $\mathbf{P}$; In this work, margin γ is set as 0.1, n is set as 5 and h, indicating number of hops, is set as 3.

Training for MCSM. The constraint with the largest $F1$ score is deemed as the *golden* constraint. As a multi-classification model, MCSM calculates the binary cross entropy loss for each class label, and sum all the label loss as the final loss. The probability threshold θ is set to 0.8.

During the training, we use a minibatch stochastic gradient descent to minimize the pairwise training loss. The minibatch size is set to 256. The initial learning rate is set to 0.01 and gradually decays. We use wiki answer vectors as the initial word-level embedding.

4.3   Results and Analysis

We use the $F1$ score over all questions as evaluation metric. Here, $F1$ score for final answer is defined similarly as before, with the exception that the precision and recall are defined on answer entities rather than core paths.

Overall Performance. Table 1 shows the results on two benchmark datasets. As can be seen, our method achieves 53.2% and 42.6% $F1$ values on WebQuestion and CompQuestion, respectively, indicating that our method excels most of the state-of-the-art works, *w.r.t.* $F1$ score.

Table 1. Performance evaluation ($F1$)

Methods	CompQuestion (%)	WebQuestion (%)
[Dong *et al.*, 2015] [11]	–	40.8
[Yao *et al.*, 2015] [25]	–	44.3
[Berant *et al.*, 2015] [5]	–	49.7
[Yih *et al.*, 2015] [27]	36.9	52.5
[Bao *et al.*, 2016] [3]	40.9	52.4
[Xu *et al.*, 2016] [23]	36.9	52.5
[Abujabal *et al.*, 2017] [2]	–	51.0
[Luo *et al.*, 2018] [17]	42.8	52.7
[Hu *et al.*, 2018] [15]	–	53.6
[Zhu *et al.*, 2020] [30]	–	52.1
Ours	42.6	53.2

We noticed that Chen *et al.*, 2020[8] claimed higher performance on both dataset. However, this work introduced additional information, proposed in [17] as ground truth during training, while we just use the original WebQuestion. Moreover, Hu *et al.*, 2020[15] introduced external knowledge to solve implicit relation to achieve higher performance on WebQuestion.

Performance of Sub-modules. As our approach works in a pipelined manner, the overall performance is influenced by the sub-modules. It is hence necessary to show the performance of each sub-module. To this end, we introduce a metric, which is defined as $Acc_u = \frac{|TP|}{|test|}$, where TP is a set consisting of intermediate results returned by a sub-module, such that each of them can imply a correct answer, and test refers to the test set. Intuitively, the metric Acc_u is used to show the upper bound of the prediction capability of each sub-module. Besides Acc_u, the metric $F1$ is also applied for performance evaluation. Table 2 shows Acc_u and $F1$ scores of sub-modules on WebQuestion and CompQuestion, respectively.

Table 2. Performance evaluation *w.r.t.* sub-modules

Sub-modules	WebQuestion		CompQuestion	
	Acc_u (%)	$F1$ (%)	Acc_u (%)	$F1$ (%)
Topic entity recognition	93.5	77.4	93.4	64.4
Core path generation	65.0	54.7	60.3	44.3
Constraints selection	56.8	53.2	52.1	42.6

Topic Entity Recognition. For an identified entity, if it can lead to the "golden" answer, it is treated as a correct entity, otherwise, it will be regarded as an incorrect prediction. Based on this assertion, the Acc_u and $F1$ score *w.r.t.* topic entity recognition can be defined. As is shown, the Acc_u of the sub-module reaches 93.5% on WebQuestion and 93.4% on CompQuestion. This shows that our sub-module for topic entity recognition performs pretty well. However, the $F1$ scores of the sub-module reaches 77.4% and 64.4% on WebQuestion and CompQuestion, respectively. The gap between the Acc_u and $F1$ scores partly lies in the incompleteness of the answer set of a question in the test set. Taking WebQuestion as an example, it was constructed by Amazon Mechanical Turk (AMT) manually, for each question, it only corresponds to no more than ten answers.

Core Path Generation. As shown in Table 2, the Acc_u of our core path generation sub-module is 65% on WebQuestion and 60.3% on CompQuestion, respectively; while the $F1$ scores on WebQuestion and CompQuestion are 54.7% and 44.3%, respectively. The figures tell us following. (1) It is more difficult to determine a correct core path on CompQuestion than that on WebQuestion, as both Acc_u and $F1$ score on CompQuestion are lower than that on WebQuestion, which is also consistent with the observation on both dataset. (2) Both metrics of the sub-module are significantly lower than that of Compared with the sub-module for topic entity recognition,

There still exists a big gap between Acc_u and F_1 scores on two dataset. We will make further analysis in Error analysis part.

Constraints Selection. After constraints selection, the final answers are obtained. Thus the $F1$ score of the sub-module is the same as that of the entire system.

We also compared the MCSM with a variant (denoted as MemN2N) of the model introduced by [19] to show its advantages *w.r.t.* training costs. Compared with MCSM, MemN2N leverages two matrices to produce different embedding of constraints, which brings trouble for model training. As shown in Table 3, MCSM consumes less time for model training, while achieves almost the same $F1$ score, no matter how training set and validation set are split. This sufficiently shows that the MCSM is able to achieve high performance with reduced training cost.

Table 3. MCSM v.s MemN2N

Train/Validation	MemN2N		MCSM	
	Training time (s)	$F1$ (%)	Training time (s)	$F1$ (%)
4:1	2549	52.8	2031	52.8
9:1	1610	52.8	1211	52.7
All Train	2340	52.7	1657	52.8

5   Conclusion

In this paper, we proposed a comprehensive approach to answering complex questions on knowledge bases. A novel metric for measuring entity similarity was introduced and incorporated in our topic entity recognition. As another component, our attention-based core path generation model leveraged attention scheme to determine the best core paths, based on both explicit and information. A memory network with compact structure was developed for constraints selection. Extensive experiments on typical benchmark datasets show that (1) our approach outperformed most of existing methods, *w.r.t.* $F1$ score; (2) our sub-modules performed well, *i.e.*, with high $F1$ values; (3) our sub-module *e.g.*, the constraints selection model was easy to train and consumes less training time; and (4) implicit information was verified effective for determining core paths.

Acknowledgement. This work is supported by Sichuan Scientific Innovation Fund (No. 2022JDRC0009) and the National Key Research and Development Program of China (No. 2017YFA0700800).

References

1. Abujabal, A., Saha Roy, R., Yahya, M., Weikum, G.: Never-ending learning for open-domain question answering over knowledge bases. In: Proceedings of the 2018 World Wide Web Conference, pp. 1053–1062 (2018)
2. Abujabal, A., Yahya, M., Riedewald, M., Weikum, G.: Automated template generation for question answering over knowledge graphs. In: Proceedings of the 26th International Conference on World Wide Web, pp. 1191–1200 (2017)
3. Bao, J., Duan, N., Yan, Z., Zhou, M., Zhao, T.: Constraint-based question answering with knowledge graph. In: Proceedings of COLING 2016, the 26th International Conference on Computational Linguistics: Technical Papers, pp. 2503–2514 (2016)
4. Berant, J., Liang, P.: Semantic parsing via paraphrasing. In: Proceedings of the 52nd Annual Meeting of the Association for Computational Linguistics, pp. 1415–1425 (2014)
5. Berant, J., Liang, P.: Imitation learning of agenda-based semantic parsers. Trans. Assoc. Comput. Linguistics 3, 545–558 (2015)
6. Bollacker, K.D., Evans, C., Paritosh, P.K., Sturge, T., Taylor, J.: Freebase: a collaboratively created graph database for structuring human knowledge. In: Proceedings of the International Conference on Management of Data, pp. 1247–1250 (2008)
7. Bordes, A., Chopra, S., Weston, J.: Question answering with subgraph embeddings. In: 2014 Conference on Empirical Methods in Natural Language Processing, EMNLP 2014, pp. 615–620 (2014)
8. Chen, Y., Li, H., Hua, Y., Qi, G.: Formal query building with query structure prediction for complex question answering over knowledge base. In: International Joint Conference on Artificial Intelligence (IJCAI) (2020)
9. Chen, Y., Wu, L., Zaki, M.J.: Bidirectional attentive memory networks for question answering over knowledge bases. In: Proceedings of NAACL-HLT, pp. 2913–2923 (2019)
10. Ding, J., Hu, W., Xu, Q., Qu, Y.: Leveraging frequent query substructures to generate formal queries for complex question answering. In: Proceedings of the Conference on Empirical Methods in Natural Language Processing and the International Joint Conference on Natural Language Processing, pp. 2614–2622 (2019)
11. Dong, L., Wei, F., Zhou, M., Xu, K.: Question answering over freebase with multi-column convolutional neural networks. In: Proceedings of the 53rd Annual Meeting of the Association for Computational Linguistics and the 7th International Joint Conference on Natural Language Processing, pp. 260–269 (2015)
12. Fader, A., Zettlemoyer, L., Etzioni, O.: Open question answering over curated and extracted knowledge bases. In: Proceedings of the 20th ACM SIGKDD International Conference on Knowledge Discovery and Data Mining, pp. 1156–1165 (2014)
13. Han, J., Cheng, B., Wang, X.: Open domain question answering based on text enhanced knowledge graph with hyperedge infusion. In: Proceedings of the Conference on Empirical Methods in Natural Language Processing, pp. 1475–1481 (2020)
14. Hao, Y., Zhang, Y., Liu, K., He, S., Liu, Z., Wu, H., Zhao, J.: An end-to-end model for question answering over knowledge base with cross-attention combining global knowledge. In: Proceedings of the 55th Annual Meeting of the Association for Computational Linguistics, pp. 221–231 (2017)
15. Hu, S., Zou, L., Zhang, X.: A state-transition framework to answer complex questions over knowledge base. In: Proceedings of the 2018 Conference on Empirical Methods in Natural Language Processing, pp. 2098–2108 (2018)

16. Jain, S.: Question answering over knowledge base using factual memory networks. In: Proceedings of the NAACL Student Research Workshop, pp. 109–115 (2016)
17. Luo, K., Lin, F., Luo, X., Zhu, K.: Knowledge base question answering via encoding of complex query graphs. In: Proceedings of the 2018 Conference on Empirical Methods in Natural Language Processing, pp. 2185–2194 (2018)
18. Suchanek, F.M., Kasneci, G., Weikum, G.: Yago: a core of semantic knowledge. In: Proceedings of the International Conference on WWW, pp. 697–706 (2007)
19. Sukhbaatar, S., Weston, J., Fergus, R., et al.: End-to-end memory networks. Advances in neural information processing systems 28 (2015)
20. Sun, H., Bedrax-Weiss, T., Cohen, W.: Pullnet: open domain question answering with iterative retrieval on knowledge bases and text. In: Proceedings of the Conference on Empirical Methods in Natural Language Processing and the International Joint Conference on Natural Language Processing, pp. 2380–2390 (2019)
21. Sun, Y., Zhang, L., Cheng, G., Qu, Y.: Sparqa: skeleton-based semantic parsing for complex questions over knowledge bases. In: Proceedings of the AAAI Conference on Artificial Intelligence, vol. 34, pp. 8952–8959 (2020)
22. Xu, K., Lai, Y., Feng, Y., Wang, Z.: Enhancing key-value memory neural networks for knowledge based question answering. In: Proceedings of the 2019 Conference of the North American Chapter of the Association for Computational Linguistics: Human Language Technologies, pp. 2937–2947 (2019)
23. Xu, K., Reddy, S., Feng, Y., Huang, S., Zhao, D.: Question answering on freebase via relation extraction and textual evidence. In: Proceedings of the 54th Annual Meeting of the Association for Computational Linguistics, pp. 2326–2336 (2016)
24. Yang, Y., Chang, M.W.: S-mart: Novel tree-based structured learning algorithms applied to tweet entity linking. In: Proceedings of the 53rd Annual Meeting of the Association for Computational Linguistics and the 7th International Joint Conference on Natural Language Processing, pp. 504–513 (2015)
25. Yao, X.: Lean question answering over freebase from scratch. In: Proceedings of the 2015 Conference of the North American Chapter of the Association for Computational Linguistics: Demonstrations, pp. 66–70 (2015)
26. Yao, X., Van Durme, B.: Information extraction over structured data: question answering with freebase. In: Proceedings of the 52nd Annual Meeting of the Association for Computational Linguistics, pp. 956–966 (2014)
27. Yih, S.W.t., Chang, M.W., He, X., Gao, J.: Semantic parsing via staged query graph generation: question answering with knowledge base (2015)
28. Yu, M., Yin, W., Hasan, K.S., dos Santos, C., Xiang, B., Zhou, B.: Improved neural relation detection for knowledge base question answering. In: Proceedings of the ACL, pp. 571–581 (2017)
29. Zhou, M., Huang, M., Zhu, X.: An interpretable reasoning network for multi-relation question answering. In: Proceedings of the 27th International Conference on Computational Linguistics, pp. 2010–2022 (2018)
30. Zhu, S., Cheng, X., Su, S.: Knowledge-based question answering by tree-to-sequence learning. Neurocomputing **372**, 64–72 (2020)

Multi-attention User Information Based Graph Convolutional Networks for Explainable Recommendation

Ruixin Ma[1,2], Guangyue Lv[1,2], Liang Zhao[1,2(✉)], Yunlong Ma[1,2], Hongyan Zhang[1,2], and Xiaobin Liu[3]

[1] School of Software Technology, Dalian University of Technology, Dalian, China
maruixin@dlut.edu.cn,
{1069098299,m1804069847,zhanghhongyan}@mail.dlut.edu.cn
[2] The Key Laboratory for Ubiquitous Network and Service Software of Liaoning Province, Dalian University of Technology, Dalian, China
liangzhao@dlut.edu.cn
[3] 32127 Division of PLA, Dalian, Liaoning, China
522196928@qq.com

Abstract. Dealing with sparsity and cold-start problems in recommendation systems has always been a challenge. We propose a Multi-Attention User Information based graph convolutional networks for explainable Recommendation model (MAUIR), which can aggregate user and item simultaneously through higher-order information. Our model contains two kinds of attention mechanisms-hierarchical attention and inter-level attention. The first is to explore the different contributions of neighboring entities to the central entity, and the second is to capture the influence of the higher-order structure on the central entity. Therefore, these measures are used to better obtain the final representation of the entity, and the model predicts more accurately. In addition, we also add auxiliary information to the dataset to enrich the user representation to make the model more explanatory. Experiments on three data sets show that our model exceeds the baselines.

Keywords: Recommender system · Attention mechanism · Knowledge graph · Graph convolutional networks · Information aggregation

1 Introduction

The proliferation of online content and services has made Recommendation Systems(RS) [3,4] a must, and much research has been devoted to collaborative filtering (CF) [1,2], which has excellent performance but does not address cold-start and sparsity issues. Knowledge Graph(KG) contains rich information and can provide the accuracy of recommendation, which is a multi-relation directed graph composed of a large number of entities and relationships. For example, as shown in Fig. 1, Triple (Hamlet, author, Shakespeare) represents Shakespeare

G. Memmi et al. (Eds.): KSEM 2022, LNAI 13368, pp. 201–213, 2022.
https://doi.org/10.1007/978-3-031-10983-6_16

is the author of the book Hamlet. In recent years, knowledge graphs have been successfully applied to various applications. This motivates researchers to use knowledge graphs to improve the performance of Recommendation Systems.

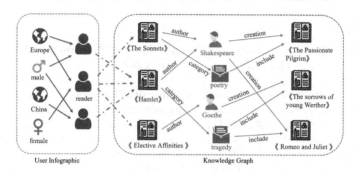

Fig. 1. Knowledge graph example.

Recommendations based on knowledge graph are divided into three categories: The first category is based on the knowledge embedding method [6], including TransE [15], TransR [7], etc. However, most of them are more suitable for classification [10], entity link prediction [11], and relation fact extraction [12,13] tasks, The high-level connectivity between users and items cannot be fully exploited to improve the accuracy of recommendations. The second category is path-based method [14,19], which can effectively obtain representations between users and items, but are highly dependent on whether the designed path satisfies a specific scenario. It is difficult to achieve the best results in practice. The third method is the method of combining the first two categories. The representative methods with excellent performance at present are KGCN [8] and RippleNet [9]. However, they still contain some disadvantages: (1) Neither KGCN nor RippleNet consider the importance of user attribute information to users. (2) The semantic information of the relationship between entities is not fully explored, resulting in the loss of information in the message transmission process. For example, As shown in Fig. 1, Men may prefer to watch the hamlet, while women may prefer the sonnets, gender is an attribute of the user. Most of the existing work does not take this into account.

In order to solve the above-mentioned challenges, we proposed Multi-Attention User Information Based Graph Convolutional Networks Explainable Recommendation model (MAUIR). MAUIR aims to explore the importance of different entities by fully utilizing KG to propose an intra-level attention mechanism, which can better obtain the user's potential preferences from the high-level connection structure. MAUIR contains inter-level attention mechanism to automatically mine and obtain the importance of information aggregation of different items in the high-level knowledge structure. Furthermore, user attribute information is added to the dataset, addressing the inadequacy of previous models. Experiments on the CTR prediction task and the top-K recommendation task were carried out on three data sets, which proved the best performance and robustness of MAUIR.

The rest of the paper is organized as follows. Section 2 reviews the commonly used related terms in knowledge graphs, and Sect. 3 presents our approach after an in-depth study, followed by experiments on existing benchmark datasets and a comparative discussion of various models with excellent performance in Sect. 4. Finally, Sect. 5 concludes and discusses future work.

2   Preliminaries

In this section, we clarify some of the terms used in this thesis, including foggy feedback and knowledge graph integration.

2.1   Foggy Feedback

Compared with evident feedback, the recommendation tasks considered in this paper are richer fuzzy feedback, e.g., click history, book reading memory and music listening record. In a typical recommender system, user set and item set are denoted by $U = \{u_1, u_2, u_3...u_U\}$ and $V = \{v_1, v_2, v_3...v_V\}$ respectively. The user-item interaction matrix is denoted as $Y = \{y_{uv}|u \in U, v \in V\}$, where

$$y_{uv} = \begin{cases} 1 \;\; if \; u \; and \; v \; interaction \; is \; real \\ 0 \;\; other \; cases \end{cases} \tag{1}$$

$y_{uv} = 1$ means that user u clicked on item v, which is usually considered to be positive feedback. However, the case of $y_{uv} = 0$ is considered negative feedback.

2.2   Knowledge Graph Integration

Knowledge graph integration connects multiple graphs by sharing user behavior and the same entity, the user attribute information graph connects the user history interaction graph with the user as a bridge, and then the user clicks on the history graph to align the entities with the knowledge graph through the clicked records, and finally form a joint graph.

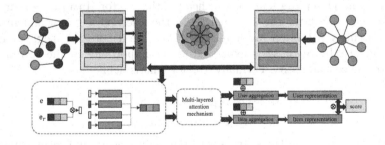

Fig. 2. The overall structure of MAUIR

3   Methodology

The overall structure of the proposed MAUIR model is shown in Fig. 2. It is mainly composed of four parts: (1). KG embedding layer: Interaction graphs, user information graphs, and knowledge graphs are embedded in low-dimensional vectors. This layer is used to obtain the self-representations of entities and relationships. (2). Perceptual bias layer: This layer explores the importance of the relationship between user u and the item v to be tested. (3). Attention characteristic aggregation layer: It can aggregate higher-order information by expanding from the inside to the outside to capture the importance of each layer. (4). Prediction layer: This layer aggregates the information representations of user and item themselves and all perceptual layers, and output the predicted click probability score.

The task of MAUIR is to input a user and an item, and output the predicted probability of the user clicking on the item, we use vector u to represent the input user vector, and use vector v to represent the input item vector. Since the prediction model is a binary classification task, we use the sigmoid function $\sigma(\cdot)$ as the activation function. Finally, The CTR prediction task can be achieved. In the subsection, we will introduce the model in detail.

$$\hat{y} = \sigma(u^T v) \tag{2}$$

3.1   KG Embedding Layer

In the KG, an entity may have more than one entity connected to multiple entities, and there are also a variety of corresponding relationships. Knowledge graph embedding is a method that can not only maintain the graph structure, but also effectively represent the entity as a low-dimensional vector. In this paper, each entity is represented by applying TransR [7]. A triple (h, r, t) exists in the knowledge graph. We can translate into three vectors e_h, e_r and e_t.

$$e_h + e_r \approx e_t \tag{3}$$

Therefore, the energy score for a given triplet (h, r, t) can be expressed as:

$$g(h, r, t) = \|W_r e_h + e_r - W_r e_t\|_2^2 \tag{4}$$

where W_r represents the transformation matrix of the relation r. The lower the $g()$ score, the closer the sum of the head entity vector. In order to enhance the efficiency. We filter the information in the knowledge graph and propose the Hierarchical Attention Mechanism (HAM). We denote the neighbor nodes around node v by $S(v)$. M is expressed as the importance of the surrounding nodes to the central entity. Formally, the formula is defined as

$$M = \{v \cdot v_1 | v \in G, v_1 \in S(V)\} \tag{5}$$

$$\tilde{M} = \{m_1, m_2, m_k...m_k | m_1, m_2...m_k \in M\} \tag{6}$$

Herein, $m_1, m_2...m_k$ are the k items with the highest score, indicating that they are most relevant to the central entity.

3.2 Perceptual Bias Layer

Knowledge graph carries the complex relationship between various entities and entities. For the same user, not all entities have the same importance in identifying user interests. Many entities have nothing to do with specific users. In order to reduce the impact of noise, We integrate entities propagated in user click history along the knowledge graph according to different attention levels, in order to better filter out the items that users may be interested in. Specifically, given a specific user u, we record the user's click history or browsing history as $Z_u = \{v_{u,i}|i = 1, 2, 3...N\}$, Among them, $v_{u,1}$ represents the item that the user clicked for the first time. Then we try to pay attention to the first-order higher-order neighbors of $v_{u,1}$. However, different neighbors have different importance to user u. We use $N_{v_{u,i}}$ to represent the neighbors directly connected to $v_{u,i}$. In order to give different degrees of attention, we use points to calculate the importance of statistics. $r_{v_{u,i}v}$ represents the relationship between $v_{u,i}$ and v directly, where v is an instance in the $N_{v_{u,i}}$ set. Use dot product to calculate user and relationship score. Formally, define the following formula:

$$S_r^u = g(u, r_{v_{u,i}v}) \tag{7}$$

where u and $r_{v_{u,i}v}$ respectively represent the user u and the relationship $r_{v_{u,i}v}$. Generally, S_r^u describes the importance of the user u and the relationship $r_{v_{u,i}v}$. Finally, we get all the relationship scores with user u in $N_{v_{u,1}}$, and then normalize them to get the normalized user relationship score. Formally defined as:

$$S_{r_{v_{\iota},v}}^{\ddot{u}} = \frac{exp(S_{r_{v_i},v}^u)}{\sum_{v \in N_{v_{u,i}}} exp(S_{r_{v_i},v}^u)} \tag{8}$$

In order to better represent the topological structure of the node $v_{u,i}$, we calculated the linear combination of $v_{u,i}$ neighbors. Formally defined as:

$$V_{N_{v_{u,v}}}^u = \sum_{e \in N_{v_{u,i}}} S_{r_{v_{\iota},v}}^{\ddot{u}} e \tag{9}$$

3.3 Attention Characteristic Aggregation Layer

Generally, for a model input item (u, v), the representation of the user u and the item v cannot only calculate the first-level high-order neighbors. Other high-level neighbors also contribute to the central entity. For example, it is like a stone being thrown into the sea. The process of the stone touching the surface of the water is when the user evaluates a book he has read, or the user has clicked on a web page on the Internet. The ripples gradually weaken from the center to the outside. In order to describe this reality, certain strategies must be adopted to perfectly describe this fact. Therefore, we propose a inter-level attention mechanism (ILAM), which can better adapt to the local structure, and simulates that higher-order entities should be assigned different weights to increase the accuracy and interpretability of the recommendation system. This strategy can obtain both user and item representations. Specifically, given an input pair (u, v), The final representation of users and items is as follows:

$$V_{rep} = aggregate(N_v + v) \tag{10}$$

$$U_{rep} = aggregate(N_u + u) \tag{11}$$

Among them, the subscripts v and u of N_v and N_v represent the higher-order aggregate representation of item v and user u, respectively. v and u respectively represent its embedding vector. V_{rep} and U_{rep} represent the final representation of v and u, aggregate is a designed aggregator. The details are as follows:

$$V_{rep} = aggregate(N_v + v) = \sigma((W_v(g(N_v) + v) + b_v) \tag{12}$$

where W_v and b_v are the weight and bias parameters learned during the model training process, σ is a non-linear transformation, such as tanh or Softsign, where $g(N_v)$ is the aggregation of multi-layer high-order neighbors of the entity v. Expressed as follows:

$$g(N_v) = F(v, R_v, N_v, H) \tag{13}$$

The $F()$ function is designed as an entity information aggregation module. For the central entity v, its neighboring entities and mutual relations are the key factors to maintain the network structure. Its neighbor set is represented by N_v, R_v is the set of high-level relations, and H is the aggregation Number of layers, expressed as $H = \{0, 1 \ldots h \ldots H\}$. The h-th layer is expressed as the aggregation of the h-1 layer and itself, expressed as:

$$g(N_e^h) = F(e, R_e, N_e, h) \tag{14}$$

$$E_{h-1}^u = \sum_{v \in N_e} S_{r_{e,v}}^{\ddot{u}} e_{h-1}^u \tag{15}$$

$$E'^u_{h-1} = kE_{h-1}^u \tag{16}$$

$$g(N_e^h) = e_h^u = agg(E'^u_{h-1}, e_{h-1}^u) \tag{17}$$

where N_e^h represents the neighbor of e when the h-th layer is represented, and R_e represents the relationship set of item e. N_e represents the set of neighbors of item e. attention coefficient is the k, which can take the value $k = e^{-1/(h+b)}$. E'^u_{h-1} is the final representation of information aggregation after increasing hierarchical attention. e_h^u The final representation of the h-th layer. Finally, the final representation of item v is as follows:

$$V_{rep} = g(N_v) = g(N_v^1) + g(N_v^2) + \ldots + g(N_v^H) \tag{18}$$

Similar to the item aggregation information, the input user u also has its attribute information and click record information around it. The layer h is represented by the aggregation of the h-1 layer and itself, which is represented as:

$$E_{h-1}^v = \sum_{e' \in N_e} S_{r_{e,e'}}^{\ddot{v}} e_{h-1}^v \tag{19}$$

$$g(N_e^h) = e_h^v = agg(E'_{h-1}^{v}, e_{h-1}^v) \tag{20}$$

Finally, aggregate the information of each layer to get the final representation of user U_{rep}.

The time complexity of the MAUIR algorithm is $O(n_1 * n_2 * n_3)$, where n_1 represents the number of pairs of all users and entities to be tested. Taking item information aggregation as an example, n_2 represents the high-level number of attention mechanisms between levels, and n_3 represents item information aggregation in hierarchical attention.

3.4 Prediction Layer

Just as the multiple attention aggregation mechanisms mentioned above-hierarchical attention mechanism and inter-level attention mechanism, MAUIR can finally get the representation u and v of users and items. In the end, the probability that u may be interested in v is as follows:

$$\hat{y}_{uv} = f(u, v) = \sigma(u^T v) \tag{21}$$

where prediction function $f()$ implements an inner product operation. We adopted a negative sampling strategy in the training process. The complete loss function is as follows:

$$\mathcal{L} = u \sum_{u \in U} (\sum_{v:y_{uv}} \mathcal{J}(y_{uv}, \hat{y}_{uv}) - \sum_{i=1}^{T^u} E_{v_i \sim P(v_i)} \mathcal{J}(y_{uv}, \hat{y}_{uv})) + \|\mathcal{F}\|_2^2 \tag{22}$$

where $\mathcal{J}$ is cross-entropy loss and the last term is the L2-regularizer. P is a negative sampling distribution, and T^u is the number of negative samples for user u. In this paper, $T^u = |\{v : y_{uv} = 1\}|$ and P follows a uniform distribution.

4 Experiments

In this section, we will evaluate the performance of the MAUIR model on three public datasets: Book-Crossing, Last.FM, and Movielens-20M. First of all, we introduce the dataset, comparative baselines, and evaluation metrics. Then, the experimental settings are stated, and finally, we compare MAUIR with the state-of-the-art baselines in detail to demonstrate the excellent performance of MAUIR.

4.1   Datasets

To verify the effectiveness of MAUIR in different application scenarios, we use three benchmark datasets from different fields (books, music, and movies). Corresponding to Book-Crossing[1], Last.FM[2], and Movielens-20M[3], respectively.

Considering that the design of MAUIR model is based on exploring user interest in implicit feedback to make recommendations, in order to be consistent with implicit feedback, we need to convert the above realistic feedback data sets (Book-Crossing, Last.FM and Movielens-20M) into implicit feedback data. For Book-Crossing data sets, all interaction records are set to positive feedback. For the other two datasets (Last.fm and Movielens-20M), implicit feedback is obtained by setting thresholds. Only those with a score of 4 or 5 are considered to be positive implicit feedback. the detailed basic statistics of three datasets are shown in Table 1. Since this paper also explores the importance of user information to the recommendation system, in addition to integrating knowledge graphs and user click records, we also add user information to three public datasets to simulate the impact of user information on the recommendation system. In Table 1, u-items, u-rela and t-Triples represent the number of entities, the number of relations and the number of triples in the user knowledge graph, respectively.

Table 1. Statistics for the three datasets.

	Users	Items	Interactions	Relations	KG Triples	u-items	u-rela	u-Triples
Book-Crossing	17860	14910	139746	25	19876	64	2	23218
Last.fm	1872	3846	42346	60	15518	23	2	3744
Movielens-20M	138159	16954	13501622	32	499474	28	2	184215

4.2   Baselines

In order to verify the superiority of our model, we choose five advanced models as benchmarks and compare them with our MAUIR. As shown in Table 2, they are LibFM [5], CKE [16], Wide&Deep [18], PER [17] and KGCN [8], respectively.

---

[1] http://www2.informatik.uni-freiburg.de/~cziegler/BX/

[2] https://grouplens.org/datasets/hetrec-2011/

[3] https://grouplens.org/datasets/movielens/

Table 2. Comprehensive performance on the CTR prediction task.

	Book-Crossing		Last.fm		Movielens-20M	
	AUC	F1	AUC	F1	AUC	F1
LibFM	0.693	0.618	0.778	0.71	0.959	0.906
CKE	0.677	0.611	0.744	0.673	0.924	0.871
Wide&Deep	0.709	0.62	0.756	0.688	0.953	0.905
PER	0.623	0.588	0.633	0.596	0.832	0.871
KGCN	0.684	0.623	0.794	0.695	0.976	0.929
MAUIR(ATT)	0.695	0.634	0.798	0.708	**0.979**	0.928
MAUIR(ATT-UI)	**0.744**	**0.669**	**0.808**	**0.746**	**0.979**	**0.936**

4.3 Experiments Setup

We use TensorFlow to implement our model. In the MAUIR model, we first randomly divide the data set we use into blocks, and the proportion of training set, evaluation set and test set is 6:2:2. In order to improve the best effect of the model, we use the verification set to find the optimal hyperparameters. Repeat each experiment 10 times, and then report the average performance. In addition, all trainable parameters are optimized by Adam algorithm. We evaluated our approach in two lab tasks: the click-through rate (CTR) task and the top-K recommendation task. In the previous task, we applied the trained model to predict each interaction in the test set, using metrics AUC and F1. In the second task, we chose Recall@k as the evaluation indicator for this task. Use the trained model to select the item with the highest click probability for each user in the test set. More settings will be discussed in Sect. 4.5.

4.4 Performance Comparison

In this section, we compare our designed MAUIR with five state-of-the-art models that perform in CTR prediction tasks and top-K recommendation tasks. The MAUIR (ATT) model only adds hierarchical attention and inter-level attention mechanisms. The MAUIR (ATT-UI) model adds the attribute information of the simulated user on the basis of MAUIR (ATT). The baseline and MAUIR results for the two tasks are shown in Table 2 and Fig. 3, respectively. We have the following observations.

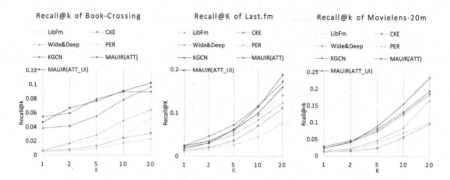

Fig. 3. The results in top-K recommendation.

- Compared with the results of KGCN in the two tasks, MAUIR scored higher and performed better on all data sets, which indicates that the MAUIR model can alleviate the limitations of KGCN by learning the aggregate representation of users and item and making use of hierarchical attention mechanism and inter-level attention mechanism.

- MAUIR performs best on the three datasets in the CTR prediction scenario and the top-K recommendation scenario. The results show that MAUIR has the ability to mine users' potential preferences from the knowledge graph of high-order connectivity, and that MAUIR can make full use of KG information to improve the performance of recommendation.

- The experimental results also prove the importance of biased selection of neighbor nodes and the effectiveness of knowledge graph high-order neighbor information aggregation. In addition, the results also show that because the information dissemination mechanism is more effective, and the attention entity attention information dissemination strategy is more effective, MAUIR can explore deeper semantic information.

- LibFM and Wide&Deep have achieved good results on three data sets. In our experiment, in addition to knowledge graph and user interaction records, we also simulated the addition of user auxiliary information. This means that additional KG data can also be learned to promote recommended performance because of the lack of KG in their original paper.

- The PER performance is not very good because it is difficult for us to design meta-paths that require a lot of expertise. CKE performs poorly because it requires textual content and visual images to represent an item, which are not present in the experiments.

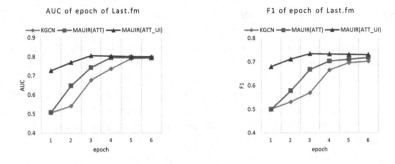

Fig. 4. The results of AUC and F1 are in different epochs

4.5 Specific Comparison

In this section, Since the advantage of the MAUIR (ATT) model in the Last.fm data set is not very obvious, we first conducted a complete training after each epoch AUC test and F1 test, as well as the average after 10 times of training. KGCN is a model with excellent performance, we only compare it with KGCN. We randomly sampled an experiment to explore the stability of our model, through six iterations to compare with the most advanced model, because the effect of KGCN is the best, so we only do the comparative experiment with KGCN. It is worth noting that our model can achieve the optimal effect faster and better than the KGCN model in each training. As shown in Fig. 4.

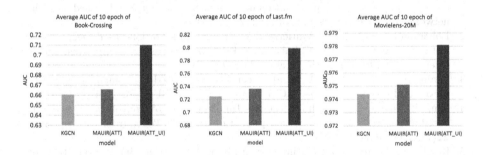

Fig. 5. The average results of AUC

After that, the average AUC value of the three data sets was tested after a complete training of the model. As shown in Fig. 5, we found that adding attention mechanism and user information can effectively improve AUC.

5   Conclusion and Future Work

In this paper, we proposed a new model called MAUIR, which aims to infer the potential interest of users by combining a variety of knowledge graphs to infer the potential interest of users, so as to solve the problems of sparsity and cold start in traditional recommendation systems. By effectively combining GCN and aggregating high-order neighbor information through a variety of attention mechanisms and biased information, we can learn the representation of central entities by learning adjacent topologies. In addition, in order to be closer to the real-world scene, we actively increase the knowledge graph of user information, which makes the recommendation effect grow by leaps and bounds, and enhances the knowledge connectivity of the knowledge graph. Finally, our model is tested on three common data sets, and satisfactory results are achieved in the CTR prediction task and the top-K recommendation scenario.

In the future, we will continue to expand our work, because most of the existing work only uses text modalities, which is incomplete for item and user representation, we can add multi-modal content such as visual images, and add elements of knowledge graphs information, and make better use of it for accurate recommendations.

Acknowledgements. This work is supported by the National Natural Science Foundation of China (61906030), the Science and Technology Project of Liaoning Province (2021JH2/10300064), the Natural Science Foundation of Liaoning Province (2020-BS-063) and the Youth Science and Technology Star Support Program of Dalian City (2021RQ057)

References

1. Chen, R., Hua, Q., Chang, Y.S., et al.: A survey of collaborative filtering-based recommender systems: from traditional methods to hybrid methods based on social networks[J]. IEEE Access **6**, 64301–64320 (2018)
2. Bobadilla, J., Ortega, F., Gutiérrez, A., et al.: Classification-based Deep Neural Network Architecture for Collaborative Filtering Recommender Systems. Int. J. Interactive Multimed. Artif. Intell. **6**(1) 2020
3. Zhang, S., Yao, L., Sun, A., et al.: Deep learning based recommender system: a survey and new perspectives. ACM Comput. Surv. (CSUR) **52**(1), 1–38 (2019)
4. Qiu, H., Zheng, Q., Msahli, M., et al.: Topological graph convolutional network-based urban traffic flow and density prediction[J]. IEEE Trans. Intell. Transp. Syst. **22**(7), 4560–4569 (2020)
5. Rendle, S.: Factorization machines with libfm. ACM Trans. Intell. Syst. Technol. (TIST) **3**(3), 1–22 (2012)
6. Piao, G., Breslin, J.G.: Transfer learning for item recommendations and knowledge graph completion in item related domains via a co-factorization model. In: Gangemi, A., Navigli, R., Vidal, M.-E., Hitzler, P., Troncy, R., Hollink, L., Tordai, A., Alam, M. (eds.) ESWC 2018. LNCS, vol. 10843, pp. 496–511. Springer, Cham (2018). https://doi.org/10.1007/978-3-319-93417-4_32
7. Lin, Y., Liu, Z., Sun, M., et al.: Learning entity and relation embeddings for knowledge graph completion. In: Twenty-Ninth AAAI Conference on Artificial Intelligence (2015)
8. Wang, H., Zhao, M., Xie, X., Li, W., Guo, M.: Knowledge graph convolutional networks for recommender systems. In: The World Wide Web Conference, pp. 3307–3313 (2019)

9. Wang, H., Zhang, F., Wang, J., et al.: Ripplenet: propagating user preferences on the knowledge graph for recommender systems. In: Proceedings of the 27th ACM International Conference on Information and Knowledge Management, pp. 417–426 (2018)

10. Wang, J., Wang, Z., Zhang, D., et al.: Combining Knowledge with Deep Convolutional Neural Networks for Short Text Classification. IJCAI. 350 (2017)

11. Zhang, Z., Cai, J., Zhang, Y., et al.: Learning hierarchy-aware knowledge graph embeddings for link prediction. In: Proceedings of the AAAI Conference on Artificial Intelligence, vol. 34(03), pp. 3065–3072 (2020)

12. Zhang, N., Deng, S., Sun, Z., et al.: Long-tail relation extraction via knowledge graph embeddings and graph convolution networks. arXiv preprint arXiv:1903.01306 (2019)

13. Li, Y., Shen, T., Long, G., et al.: Improving long-tail relation extraction with collaborating relation-augmented attention. arXiv preprint arXiv:2010.03773 (2020)

14. Dai, F., Gu, X., Li, B., Zhang, J., Qian, M., Wang, W.: Meta-graph based attention-aware recommendation over heterogeneous information networks. In: Rodrigues, J.M.F., Cardoso, P.J.S., Monteiro, J., Lam, R., Krzhizhanovskaya, V.V., Lees, M.H., Dongarra, J.J., Sloot, P.M.A. (eds.) ICCS 2019. LNCS, vol. 11537, pp. 580–594. Springer, Cham (2019). https://doi.org/10.1007/978-3-030-22741-8_41

15. Qian, W., Fu, C., Zhu, Y., et al.: Translating embeddings for knowledge graph completion with relation attention mechanism. IJCAI, pp. 4286–4292 (2018)

16. Zhang, F., Yuan, N.J., Lian, D., et al.: Collaborative knowledge base embedding for recommender systems. In: Proceedings of the 22nd ACM SIGKDD International Conference on Knowledge Discovery and Data Mining, pp. 353–362 (2016)

17. Yu, X., Ren, X., Sun, Y., et al.: Personalized entity recommendation: a heterogeneous information network approach. In: Proceedings of the 7th ACM International Conference on Web Search and Data Mining, pp. 283–292 (2014)

18. Cheng, H.T., Koc, L., Harmsen, J., et al.: Wide & deep learning for recommender systems. In: Proceedings of the 1st Workshop on Deep Learning for Recommender Systems, pp. 7–10 (2016)

19. Chen, H., Yin, C., Fan, X., Qiao, L., Rong, W., Zhang, X.: Learning path recommendation for MOOC platforms based on a knowledge graph. In: Qiu, H., Zhang, C., Fei, Z., Qiu, M., Kung, S.-Y. (eds.) KSEM 2021. LNCS (LNAI), vol. 12816, pp. 600–611. Springer, Cham (2021). https://doi.org/10.1007/978-3-030-82147-0_49

Edge-Shared GraphSAGE: A New Method of Buffer Calculation for Parallel Management of Big Data Project Schedule

Yawei Zhao[1](✉), Yangyuanxiang Xu[1], and Zhiwei Wang[1,2]

[1] University of Chinese Academy of Sciences, Beijing, China
zhaoyw@ucas.ac.cn, xuyangyuanxiang20@mails.ucas.ac.cn
[2] Institute of Computing Technology, Chinese Academy of Sciences, Beijing, China
wangzhiwei20s@ict.ac.cn

Abstract. Schedule network is essential for project schedule management. Critical Chain Method (CCM) is the most commonly used method on a schedule network to avoid project extension. The key to CCM lies in setting the proper buffer size. However, little work has considered the interdependence of nodes into buffer size calculating. In this paper, we present Edge-shared GraphSAGE, a model based on Graph Neural Network (GNN) for improving the result of buffer size prediction. Edge-shared GraphSAGE constructs undirected edges between schedule networks of projects sharing resources with each other. Fed by historical data of previous projects, the model predicts Safe-time Utilization Rate of each node of current project, so as to calculate the predicted size of the buffer. To the best of our knowledge, this is the first time that GNN is used in calculating buffer size. In several real projects, the proposed method outperforms Rule-based method and Machine Learning method.

Keywords: Schedule management · Project network · Edge-shared GraphSAGE · Buffer calculation · Parallel big data project

1 Introduction

Research shows that 65–100% of big data projects end in failure. Gartner [1] believes that 60% of BDA projects fail for being out of the budget or the plan. Therefore, in the actual implementation of big data projects, not only advanced technology is needed to complete some challenging tasks, but also the management of project process should be paid attention to. Generally, the project is broken down into some processes. Each process can be seen as nodes, and the sequence relationship between the processes can be abstracted into edges. Thus, a huge schedule network is formed, on which the process management of the project is carried out.

As shown in Fig. 1, the network shows a complete big data project, including the logical relationship order for all processes, in which a node represents a

© The Author(s), under exclusive license to Springer Nature Switzerland AG 2022
G. Memmi et al. (Eds.): KSEM 2022, LNAI 13368, pp. 214–226, 2022.
https://doi.org/10.1007/978-3-031-10983-6_17

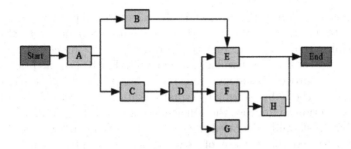

Fig. 1. Schematic diagram of network progress

process. Such network is called an Activity-on-node (AON) network. AON networks are particularly critical to the management of big data projects, especially the optimization of project progress. There is a problem in big data projects, that some operations often have a higher risk of delay due to their high level of uncertainty, which requires more buffer time to prevent such processes from affecting the completion of the entire project.

For the management of big data projects, the Critical Chain Method (CCM) in the management method can usually be used for analysis and optimization. The key of CCM is to find a suitable critical chain and set a reasonable buffer size. Traditional buffer size prediction methods are usually based on rules, which are too subjective and lack the learning of historical data. Besides, most rule-based methods consider the processes to be independent of each other, ignoring the successive logical relationship among processes.

We propose a new method based on graph neural network (GNN) to predict the buffer size in the process, which achieves better results. We also compared our method with the rule-based method and the regression methods of machine learning to verify its effectiveness.

The contributions of our paper are as follows:

(1) We construct feature indicators of different nodes through expert experience using the historical network data, and define Safe-time Utilization Rate θ_i as the dependent variable.
(2) According to the resource sharing of nodes, we merge the network of these projects to construct a parallel project schedule heterogeneous network.
(3) We propose Edge-shared GraphSAGE method based on graph neural network (GNN) to predict the Safe-time Utilization Rate of each node in the network, so as to indirectly calculate the buffer size of each process. Compared with other methods(include Rule-Based method and Machine Learning method), this method shows the superiority.

2   Related Work

In the field of schedule management, the Critical Chain Method has been widely used in recent years. For the setting of the buffer size, there are some methods that many scholars have proposed.

For the calculation of the Project Buffer, the most typical methods are the cut and paste method (C&PM) and the root square error method (RSEM) [2]. The shortcomings of C&PM include that if there are more processes in a project, the buffer that needs to be set will also be enlarged. For RSEM, its priori assumption is that each process is independent, but in fact it is difficult to strictly hold, which will make the buffer setting too small. Ashtiani B (2008) [3] used the Lognormal distribution to improve the deficiencies of the RSEM method, integrated the risk of the task, and calculated the parameters of the distribution. Gong Jun (2019) [4] proposed the concept of using information entropy and introduced an interval intuitionistic trapezoidal fuzzy number algorithm to quantify the impact of uncertain factors on the process, thereby modifying the root variance method. Zhou Yaoyao (2020) [5] proposed a calculation method for the critical chain buffer based on comprehensive constraints, using a piecewise fuzzy function to determine specific resource constraint coefficients. Xu Ye (2014) [6] used the linear regression equation method to predict the time schedule of different processes in the project, and optimized the schedule and construction period of the project by importing buffers, thereby shortening the construction period. Yadav S (2020) [7] used the principal component analysis (PCA) method to improve the root variance method, reduced the dimension of some indicators, merged them into the buffer, and gave actual cases to shorten the construction period.

However, for the setting of buffer size, most methods consider that each node in the network is independent, and a few researchers have only conducted the study of the previous and the latter projects. Especially for the schedule management of parallel big data projects, there are huge differences in their uncertainties, which is usually closely related to the position of the node in the entire graph. For example, there are some process nodes with large uncertainties, which are at the beginning and end of the network, also have significantly different buffer sizes.

In recent years, researches on graph analysis method are emerging in the computer field. The mainstream methods are a series of derivative and extended methods including GCN [8,12], such as GraphSAGE [9], GAT [10], etc. Some authors applied the GNN model to the prediction of traffic flow [11,13,14], which has a very good prediction effect. Aiming at the optimization of the schedule network, we try to apply GNN to the field of progress management for the first time. For buffer calculation, we consider the impact of the overall network on the buffer size of each process, and propose a new method of buffer size calculation based on Edge-shared GraphSAGE. In addition, we compare this method with the Rule-based method and the regression methods of Machine Learning, and the result demonstrates that Edge-shared GraphSAGE performs well to some degree.

3   Background

This section introduces theories of schedule network which is used in the modeling process.

3.1   Schedule Network

In a complete project process, it is necessary to describe the logical sequence of each activity. We define each activity of the project as a process, and define the logical sequence structure of a project as edges in the network. For two adjacent nodes, each node represents the operation of a process, and each edge represents the completion of the previous process and the beginning of the next process.

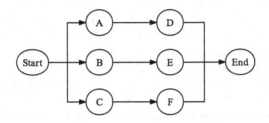

Fig. 2. Network diagram of a project

As shown in Fig. 2, each node represents each processing procedure in the big data project. For this network, the former procedure must be completed before the latter procedure can be executed, and there is a strong logical dependence in it.

3.2   Critical Chain Method

At the beginning of the project, the schedule network needs to be drawn based on the duration estimation, the given dependencies and constraints. Then the critical path is calculated. After the critical path is determined, the availability of resources is considered, so as to develop a resource-constrained schedule, in which the critical path is usually different from the previous ones. And the resource-constrained critical path in the schedule is called the critical chain [11].

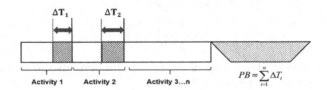

Fig. 3. Schematic diagram of the Project Buffer

The method above is called Critical Chain Method (CCM), which is based on Parkinson's law. CCM is a resource-constrained schedule network analysis tool. By setting a buffer to ensure network progress, it can effectively solve the situation of work delays. As shown in Fig. 3, through CCM, the accumulated buffer time will be eventually placed at the end of the project to form a Project Buffer. Import Buffer ensures that the critical chain will be successfully imported without affecting the process.

3.3 Buffer Size

In a large number of previous studies, there is a lack of constructing comprehensive quantitative indicators to analyze the size of the buffer, and also short of some indicators to measure the specific impact of process delaying. So it is necessary to set relevant feature indicators for the buffer of each process. The 90% of probability estimate of the i-th process duration is noted as S_{i1}, and the 50% of probability estimate is noted as S_{i2}. For the i-th process, the safe time of the process is noted as $\Delta S = S_{i1} - S_{i2}$. In a big data project, different processes have different actual buffer size, which is noted as ΔT.

Define θ_i as the Safe-time Utilization Rate of the i-th process:

$$\theta_i = \frac{\Delta T_i}{\Delta S_i} \tag{1}$$

where ΔT_i is the buffer time applicable to the i-th process in a big data project, and ΔS_i is the safe time of the i-th process. Because the uncertainty is different in different processes of real implementation of the project, θ_i is also different [12]. If the uncertainty of the sub-process is higher, the corresponding θ_i is larger and the greater ΔT_i is needed to ensure the completion of the process, otherwise, the θ_i is smaller.

Set $X = [x_1, x_2, x_3, \cdots, x_n]$ as the impact factor of the buffer size, which is defined as an independent variable. θ is the Safe-time Utilization Rate, which is defined as a dependent variable. Therefore, a nonlinear regression relationship between X and θ can be established, namely $\theta_i = f(x_1, x_2, x_3, \cdots, x_n)$.

3.4 Evaluation Index

The predicted value of the buffer size of each node in the process network is a continuous value. Therefore, we use R^2 to calculate the effectiveness of fitting results between the predicted value and the true value:

$$R^2 = \frac{\sum(\widehat{y}_i - \overline{y})^2}{\sum(y_i - \overline{y})^2} \tag{2}$$

where y_i represents the true value of the model, $\overline{y}$ represents the average of true values, and $\widehat{y}_i$ represents the predicted value.

4   Edge-Shared GraphSAGE

4.1   Global Network Without Resource Sharing

Define the network topology graph set $G = \{G_1, G_2, G_3, \cdots, G_n, G_s\}$, which means a collection of $(n+1)$ schedule network of projects. As shown in Fig. 4a, this set contains n schedule networks G_j, $j \in [1, 2, 3, \cdots, n]$ of projects already done before, whose nodes contain numerical labels, and a network G_s whose nodes need to be predicted.

The projects are not connected to each other, i.e. they are independent of each other. We call the individual elements G_j, $j \in [1, 2, 3, \cdots, n]$ a sub-network of G. Each process node in G has its specific attribute value X as an independent variable. Besides, all nodes on G have a corresponding Safe-time Utilization Rate θ as a dependent variable. The labels of all nodes in sub-network G_s are unknown and need to be predicted.

For G_i and G_j, there will be resource sharing in some processes. If there are nodes sharing the same resources in G_i and G_j, define these nodes as shared nodes, and their connecting edges as shared edges e_{ij}.

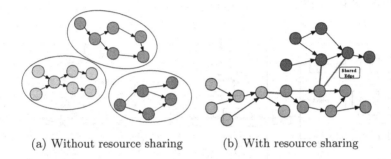

(a) Without resource sharing   (b) With resource sharing

Fig. 4. Global network with/without resource sharing

4.2   Global Network with Resource Sharing

For the whole network, the edge whose ends belonging to the same project schedule sub-network, is called a directed edge, otherwise, an undirected edge which connects two different sub-networks. As shown in Fig. 4b, edges in brown are shared edges.

$$e_{ij} = \begin{cases} G_i \rightarrow G_j, & \text{if } (i \in G_i) \cap (j \in G_j) \cap (i = j) \\ G_i \leftrightarrow G_j, & \text{if } (i \in G_i) \cap (j \in G_j) \cap (i \neq j) \end{cases} \qquad (3)$$

4.3   Features of the Node

The attributes of each node in G are noted as $X = \{x_1, x_2, x_3, x_4, x_5\}$, where x_1 represents resource tensity of data, x_2 represents implementation difficulty of the process, x_3 represents connection level of data, x_4 represents changing probability of the process result, and x_5 represents importance of the process. These 5 features above are core factors affecting the prediction of buffer size.

Let experts score each process according to the indicators mentioned above, and the score ranges from *1* to *5*. *5* means the risk level of the indicator is *extremely high*, *4* means *high*, *3* means *fair*, *2* means *low*, and *1* means *extremely low*.

We conduct a number of project managers with rich experience to perform quantitative evaluations on the historical projects of the company to obtain features of historical data. We use the historical buffer time, the expected probability of 50% and of 90% to calculate the utilization rate of safe time θ.

4.4   Edge-Shared GraphSAGE

For most tasks, GNN is used to solve classification problems requiring some labels of nodes which are generally discrete values. We use GraphSAGE [12] as backbone to build a regression model that outputs continuous values for prediction, and we only consider the use of *Mean aggregation* to reduce the complexity of our model.

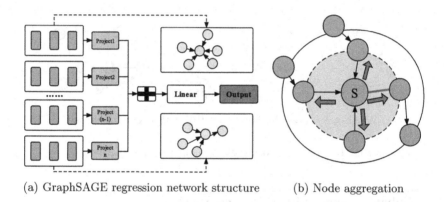

(a) GraphSAGE regression network structure   (b) Node aggregation

Fig. 5. Analytical diagram of the algorithm architecture (Color figure online)

As shown in Fig. 5a, different schedule sub-networks are input as nodes, and they are connected and aggregated through sharing edges when they share the same resources in the schedule, thereby forming a big network with historical data and current data. The schedule network is input to GraphSAGE for prediction. In order to fit continuous values, on the top layer, we replaced the Softmax layer with the Linear layer, which played an important role in predicting continuous data.

For the entire network, there will be a clear distinction between the internal connections of the sub-network and the connections between the sub-networks. This is because the networks of different schedules are heterogeneous networks, there is a distinct difference between their characteristics, and it cannot be treated the same during aggregation. We add parameters λ and fine-tuned the weights of these two parts above for trade-off to better adapt to the current regression prediction. The improved model is named Edge-shared GraphSAGE. The aggregation of the model is shown as Fig. 5b. The center node is the target aggregation node, noted as S. This figure contains two types of schedule networks, which are in blue and in yellow respectively. Similar to GraphSAGE, the neighbors of S are aggregated.

The aggregation function in GraphSAGE is expressed as:

$$h^l_{N(v)} \leftarrow Aggregate_l(\{h^{l-1}_u, \forall u \in N(v)\}) \tag{4}$$

We use the Mean aggregation function here, namely:

$$h^l_{N(v)} \leftarrow \sigma(W \cdot mean(\{h^{l-1}_u\} \cup \{h^{l-1}_u, \forall u \in N(v)\})) \tag{5}$$

Notes: $N(v)$ represents nodes connected to v

During aggregation, different projects connect to each other with shared edges, so as to form a big network. A project contributes differently to aggregation than its neighbor project, so we set weight λ for trade-off.

Define $u \in N(v)$. If u, v belong to the same project progress subgraph, mark u as $N^+(v)$. If u, v don't belong to the same subgraph, mark u as $N^-(v)$. The resulting aggregation function of Edge-shared GraphSAGE is denoted as:

$$h^l_{N(v)} \leftarrow \sigma(W \cdot mean(h^{l-1}_v \cup \{h^{l-1}_{u_1}, \forall u_1 \in N^+(v)\} \cup \{h^{l-1}_{u_2}, \forall u_2 \in N^-(v)\})) \tag{6}$$

λ is a hyper-parameter, which controls the degree of connectivity between different sub-networks and can be optimized through experimental tuning. When $\lambda = 1$, the weight between sub-networks is considered to be the same as the weight into the sub-network, which is to say, this structure is the Mean aggregation form of GraphSAGE. The pseudo code of the method is as Algorithm 1.

Algorithm 1: Edge-shared GraphSAGE: node value prediction (forward propagation) algorithm

---

Input: Graph $G(V, E) = \{G_1, G_2, \cdots, G_n\}$; input features $x_v, \forall v \in V$; depth K; weight matrices $W^k, \forall k \in \{1, \cdots, K\}$; non-linearity function σ; linear function $Linear$; mean aggregator function $MEAN$; positive neighborhood function $N^+ : v \rightarrow 2^v$; negative neighborhood function $N^- : v \rightarrow 2^v$; hyperparameter λ

Output: Predicted value z_v for all $v \in V$

1 $h^0_v \leftarrow x_v, \forall v \in V$;

2 **for** $k = 1, \cdots, K$ **do**

3   **for** $v \in V$ **do**

4        $h^k_{N^+(v)\cup N^-(v)} \leftarrow MEAN(\{h^{k-1}_{u_1}, \forall u_1 \in N^+(v)\} \cup \{\lambda \cdot h^{k-1}_{u_2}, \forall u_2 \in N^-(v)\})$;

5        $h^k_v \leftarrow \sigma(W^k \cdot CONCAT(h^{k-1}_v, h^k_{N^+(v)\cup N^-(v)}))$;

6   **end**

7     $h^k_v \leftarrow h^k_v / \|h^k_v\|_2, \forall v \in V$;

8 **end**

9 $z_v \leftarrow Linear(h^K_v), \forall v \in V$;

10 **return** z_v;

4.5   Calculate the Project Buffer and Import Buffer

The Safe-time Utilization Rate is used to calculate the real buffer time of each process. The Project Buffer(PB) is the sum of all buffer times in the critical chain, namely:

$$\Delta T_i = \Delta S_i \cdot \theta_i; PB = \sum_{i=1}^{n} \Delta T_{i \in CriticalChain} \tag{7}$$

When the increasing of the Import Buffer does not affect the critical chain, let the Import Buffer be the sum of all buffers on the non-critical chain.

5   Experiment

5.1   Data

We investigate a company's implementation of big data projects in the past 4 years, and conduct two experiments on its relative schedule networks. One uses the existing data (5 schedule networks with known node labels, and a schedule network with unknown node labels) for comparative analysis, and let the invited experts to score the attributes of nodes in the network. The other uses similar pattens to increase random items of data, and automatically generates 50 similar projects for analysis and comparison.

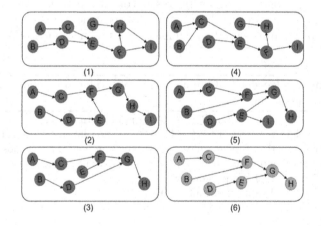

Fig. 6. A set of project network diagrams (Color figure online)

Figure 6 shows the topological structure of the project schedule network. Networks in blue are historical projects. This data set has a total of 44 nodes and 40 directed edges. The network in yellow is current project which is marked as true dataset. In addition, an analog dataset of 50 similar projects is generated, who has a total of 498 nodes and 477 edges. The historical data set is divided into 60% and 40% as training set and testing set, respectively. Compare the results of different methods in the testing set.

5.2   Method

Rule-Based Method. When setting up the critical chain for schedule management, the 50% shearing method is usually used to directly determine the size of each buffer. For these historical projects, each node has a corresponding buffer size. The essence of the Rule-Based method (Shearing method) is to directly take 50% of the process as the size of the safety time, which θ is always equal to 0.5. The R^2 of this method in the testing set is only 0.319, that is to say, the prediction accuracy of the buffer size for each node is low.

However, the advantage of this method is that it is relatively simple and intuitive. Because there is no reference to relevant historical data, the safety time prediction of each node cannot reflect the characteristics of the project itself, and the prediction is poor.

Machine Learning Method. For the nodes of each schedule network, suppose the nodes are independent of each other, we use three machine learning models for training, including: (1) Decision Tree Regression (2) Random Forest Regression (3) GBDT Regression. They are verified in the testing set, and measured by R^2. Although the original data form is graph, there is no node relationship information used in the calculation, which only uses the own information of each node. The results are shown in Table 1.

Table 1. Comparison of experimental results of different methods

Method	Dataset 1			Dataset 2		
Results	Test 1	Test 2	Test 3	Test 1	Test 2	Test 3
Decision Tree	0.613	0.628	**0.632**	0.593	0.608	**0.637**
Random Forest	0.707	0.695	**0.713**	0.683	**0.693**	0.686
GBDT	**0.643**	0.623	0.637	**0.607**	0.585	0.586

We conduct 10 tests on each dataset of each model and take down the best three results after adjusting parameters. Table 1 (Dataset 1) gives the prediction of three models using the historical data of the company. It can be seen that the best result is from *Random Forest*, whose R^2 reaches 0.713, which is much better than the Rule-based method. The results of both *Decision Tree* and *GBDT* are not as good as that of *Random Forest*. Table 1 (Dataset 2) shows the result on an expended data set of generated 50 similar projects. The overall R^2 is slightly lower than that in Dataset 1(historical data). The results indicate that when data expands, the data is less accidental, the result of prediction is worse.

Edge-Shared GraphSAGE. In previous sections, the topological structure of the network is not considered in experiments. In this section, we consider the topological information, so the prediction θ learns the relationship between nodes. In addition, the resources between projects are usually shared (e.g. people involved in one project are involved in other projects at the same time). As a result, we add edges between nodes where resources are shared and established strong correlation between projects.

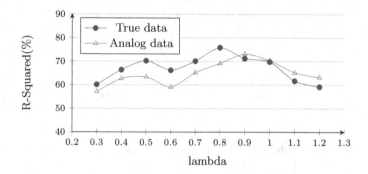

Fig. 7. The test results of Weight-GraphSAGE (Color figure online)

As show in Fig. 4b, node A in both two sub-networks is the process in which the same project manager participates. Two schedule networks share the same resource, so they are defined as shared edges. For some projects that don't have any shared resource, they are excluded from the calculation. Thus, a connected graph G can be obtained. We use Edge-shared GraphSAGE to make predictions on G. When $\lambda = 1$, the model degrades to GraphSAGE. We conduct experiments on the true dataset and simulated dataset separately, and select 9 groups of parameters where $\lambda \in \{0.3, 0.4, 0.5, 0.6, 0.7, 0.8, 0.9, 1.0, 1.1, 1.2\}$, for analysis and comparison. We use R^2 as the evaluation metrics to measure the fit of the model. The results of Edge-shared GraphSAGE are shown in Fig. 7. Points in blue are the results of the real data, and points in red are the results of the expanded analog data. Relatively speaking, the real data is sparse, the quantity is small, so the stability is poor. We test the model using different value of λ, When $\lambda = 0.8$, R^2 is 0.758, the result is better than which of Machine Learning methods and GraphSAGE ($\lambda = 1$). When λ diminishes, the accuracy decreases, which may be caused by the reduced features that learned from adjacent sub-network. For what kind of parameters to choose is highly depend on the characteristics of the pattern and the distribution of degrees of schedule networks.

Therefore, we could not give the optimal parameters for all network to predict buffer size accurately. However, what is certain is that when the topology information and associated network information are added, the prediction results of each sub-network is improved. (e.g. R^2 of the true dataset is increased from 0.713 to 0.758, and which of the simulation dataset is increased from 0.693 to 0.731.) It shows that the model can learn information from the adjacent nodes, and leads to the best prediction of Safe-time Utilization Rate for each node.

5.3   Comparision

For real projects, the rule-based method (shearing method) is usually very convenient and has certain practical effects. But it doesn't take the mutual influence between nodes into account, and it also ignores the historical information of nodes. Therefore, we introduce historical data and use Machine Learning method to capture the characteristics of buffer settings in different nodes.

Table 2. Comparison of experimental results of different methods

Method	Best R^2 of true data	Best R^2 of analog data
Rule-Based Method	0.319	0.407
Machine Learning Method (RF)	0.713	0.693
GraphSAGE ($\lambda = 1$)	0.698	0.703
Edge-shared GraphSAGE ($\lambda = 0.8$)	**0.758**	**0.731**

As shown in Table 2, Machine Learning methods have improved the prediction greatly compared with the Rule-based method, and make more targeted predictions for different types of schedules. However, the information of the adjacent nodes is not used, so the prediction is not complete in theory. So we propose Edge-shared GraphSAGE method to capture the information of adjacent nodes, and the effect has been greatly improved.

Through networks, Edge-shared GraphSAGE learns the internal connection of nodes sharing the same resources, which will make the regression fit better. However, if the parameters are not selected properly, each project would take a negative impact on its adjacent projects. Therefore, it is necessary to constantly optimize the parameters to ensure the best results of the model.

6   Conclusion

We discussed how to optimize the buffer size in schedule management of parallel big data projects, so as to improve the ability to resist uncertainty of the project. The traditional method had the problem of excessive subjectivity and poor fit with real data. Therefore, we proposed Edge-shared GraphSAGE, a GNN-based model for regression analysis, which models the correlation between nodes, further improved the result of buffer size prediction, and provided a reference for the node regression problem of heterogeneous graphs.

For big data parallel projects, due to the large number of resources and the serious problem of resource conflication, if buffer settings were unreasonable, the process would be seriously affected. Introducing the Graph Neural Network prediction technology into the Critical Chain method, we could reduce the error of the schedule forecast of real project to a certain extent, avoided the delay of the big data project, and reduced the cost of the project. Therefore, the model was worthy of application and recommendation in the engineering field.

Acknowledgement. This work was supported in part by the National Key Research and Development Program of China under Grants 2020YFC1807104.

References

1. Toku, A.A., Uran, Z.E., Tekin, A.T.: Management of Big Data Projects: PMI Approach for Success, pp. 279–93. IGI Global (2019)
2. Jiang, h.: Summary and prospect of research on critical chain project management method. Build. Constr. **41**(09), 1764–1769 (2019)
3. Fallah, M., Ashtiani, B., Aryanezhad, M.B.: Critical chain project scheduling: utilizing uncertainty for buffer sizing. Int. J. Res. Rev. Appl. Sci. **3**(3), 280–289 (2010)
4. Gong, J., Hu, T., Yao, L.: Buffer setting method of critical chain based on information entropy. Acta Automatica Sinica **45**(x), 1–10 (2019)
5. Xiaoxiao, Z., Mengrui, L., Xunguo, Z., et al.: Critical chain size calculation method based on comprehensive resource constraints. J. Civ. Eng. Manag. **37**(06), 145–51 (2020)
6. Xu, Y.: Research on the application of critical chain multi-project schedule management in mobile phone projects. Shanghai Jiaotong University (2014)
7. Yadav, S., Singh, S.P.: Blockchain critical success factors for sustainable supply chain. Resour. Conserv. Recycl. **152**, 104505 (2020)
8. Abu-El-Haija, S., Kapoor, A., Perozzi, B., et al.: N-GCN: multi-scale graph convolution for semi-supervised node classification. In: Uncertainty in Artificial Intelligence, pp. 841–851. PMLR (2020)
9. Xiao, L., Wu, X., Wang, G.: Social network analysis based on graph SAGE. In: 2019 12th International Symposium on Computational Intelligence and Design (ISCID), vol. 2, pp. 196–199. IEEE (2019)
10. Veličković, P., Cucurull, G., Casanova, A., et al.: Graph attention networks. arXiv preprint arXiv:1710.10903 (2017)
11. Msahli, M., Qiu, H., Zheng, Q., et al.: Topological graph convolutional network-based urban traffic flow and density prediction. IEEE Trans. Intell. Transp. Syst. **22**, 4560–4569 (2020)
12. Hamilton, W., Ying, Z., Leskovec, J.: Inductive representation learning on large graphs. In: Advances in Neural Information Processing Systems, pp. 1024–1034 (2017)
13. Yu, B., Yin, H., Zhu, Z.: Spatio-temporal graph convolutional networks: a deep learning framework for traffic forecasting. arXiv preprint arXiv:1709.04875 (2017)
14. Wu, Z., Pan, S., Long, G., et al.: Graph WaveNet for deep spatial-temporal graph modeling. arXiv preprint arXiv:1906.00121 (2019)

Tackling Solitary Entities for Few-Shot Knowledge Graph Completion

Yi Liang[1], Shuai Zhao[1(✉)], Bo Cheng[1], Yuwei Yin[2], and Hao Yang[2]

[1] Beijing University of Posts and Telecommunications, No. 10. Xitucheng Road, Haidian, Beijing, China
{liangyi,zhaoshuaiby,chengbo}@bupt.edu.cn
[2] 2012 Labs, Huawei Technologies, CO., LTD., Shenzhen, China
{yinyuwei,yanghao30}@huawei.com

Abstract. Few-Shot Knowledge Graph Completion (FSKGC) aims to predict new facts for relations with only a few observed instances in Knowledge Graph. Existing FSKGC models mostly tackle this problem by devising an effective graph encoder to enhance entity representations with features from their directed neighbors. However, due to the sparsity and entity diversity of large-scale KG, these approaches fail to generate reliable embeddings for solitary entities, which only have an extremely limited number of neighbors in KG. In this paper, we attempt to mitigate this issue by modeling semantic correlations between entities within an FSKGC task and propose our model YANA (**Y**ou **A**re **N**ot **A**lone). Specifically, YANA introduces four novel abstract relations to represent inner- and cross- pair entity correlations and construct a Local Pattern Graph (LPG) from the entities. Based on LPG, YANA devises a Highway R-GCN to capture hidden dependencies of entities. Moreover, a query-aware gating mechanism is proposed to combine topology signals from LPG and semantic information learned from entity's directed neighbors with a heterogeneous graph attention network. Experiments show that YANA outperforms the prevailing FSKGC models on two datasets, and the ablation studies prove the effectiveness of Local Pattern Graph design.

Keywords: Knowledge graph completion · Few-shot learning · Link prediction · Graph learning · Representation learning

1 Introduction

Knowledge Graph is a vital resource for many downstream applications such as recommendation system [21], question answering [12], urban computing [10], fault detection [7] and medical data processing [5]. A knowledge graph (KG) represents facts in the form of triple (h, r, t), describing relation r between head entity h and tail entity t. Despite their large scale, KGs are usually incomplete. Thus, knowledge graph completion (KGC), which is to infer new facts from existing triples [17], has attracted widely attention in recent years.

© The Author(s), under exclusive license to Springer Nature Switzerland AG 2022
G. Memmi et al. (Eds.): KSEM 2022, LNAI 13368, pp. 227–239, 2022.
https://doi.org/10.1007/978-3-031-10983-6_18

Current KGC approaches roughly follow encoder-decoder framework [13], while encoder focuses on learning entity and relation embeddings and the decoder aims to compute scores for new queries. These models mainly rely on sufficient triples for each relation and entity to learn a good representation. Unfortunately, due to the long-tail phenomenon in real-world KGs, a large proportion of relations have only a *few* triples [23]. Predicting new facts for these relations is called few-shot knowledge graph completion (FSKGC) [2,24]. Generally, a K-shot knowledge graph completion task aims to predict tail entities for query $(h_q, rel, ?)$ with only K associated entity pairs of relation rel as the support set. Figure 1(a) gives an example of FSKGC task.

Previous researches on FSKGC can be roughly grouped into sub-graph based models and full graph models according to different network architecture. Sub-graph models [9,14,23,24] capture signals from entity's one-hop neighbors. Unlike sub-graph models, full graph models [6,11,13,22] mainly encode entities with multi-layer message passing neutral network [13] to capture features from multi-hop neighbors.

Despite their variant designs, all these methods only consider **intrinsic** topology signals from existing KG, and thus have two major limitations. **1) Graph sparsity**: A large amount of entities has a minimal number of neighbors in KG. For example, 99.2% entities of Wikidata [20] have fewer than five neighbors. **2) Neighbor diversity**: In a real-world KG, neighbors of entities are mostly irrelevant to new few-shot relations [9]. It is difficult for current models to generate reliable embeddings for these **solitary entities** with unrelated neighbors.

Intuitively, the correlations between entities in the same FSKGC task could provide semantic meanings towards current relation. For instance, the embedding of "Zuckerburg" may influence the representation of "Cook" in the context of relation "ceo_of" since they both act as the head entity of associated triples.

In light of this observation, in this paper, we propose a novel sub-graph based model YANA (**Y**ou **A**re **N**ot **A**lone) to tackle solitary entity issue by modeling hidden semantic correlations between entities in the same task. Specifically, as shown in Fig. 1(b), YANA collects entities involved in the FSKGC task in Fig. 1(a) to construct an entity set named *relation-query association*. Then we introduce four novel abstract relations in two categories to describe entity correlations in *relation-query association* and construct a multi-relation graph called *local pattern graph (LPG)*. With LPG, YANA devises a Highway R-GCN [13] to learn entity embeddings. A query-aware gating mechanism is proposed to integrate semantic meanings from LPG with intrinsic topology information from one-hop neighbors in KG to refine entity representations. Moreover, a transformer relation learner followed with an attentive prototypical network is applied to encode entity pairs and make predictions.

Our contributions could be summarized as follows: 1) This paper concerns the limitation of current FSKGC models on representing solitary entities and proposes a novel model YANA to address this problem by modeling correlations between entities shared the same few-shot relation task. 2) Experiments demonstrate that YANA achieves state-of-the-art performances on large-scale

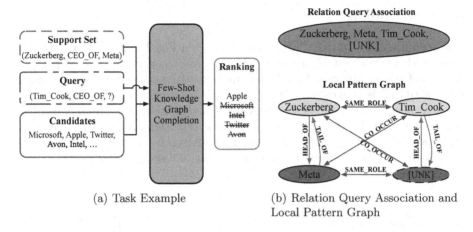

(a) Task Example

(b) Relation Query Association and
Local Pattern Graph

Fig. 1. 1(a) gives an example of 1-shot knowledge graph completion task. 1(b) illustrates the corresponding *relation-query association* and the corresponding *local pattern graph* of 1(a). We devise four abstract relations to describe the correlations between entities and introduce a unified node [UNK] to represent the unknown tail entity of queries.

and sparse dataset Wiki and encouraging performances on the NELL. Extensive experiments also show the effectiveness of each module.

The rest of the paper is organized as follows. Section 2 introduces basic preliminaries. Section 3 gives the details of our proposed model. Section 4 presents the details of experiments. Finally, Sect. 5 concludes our work.

2   Preliminaries

Knowledge Graph. A knowledge graph $\mathcal{G}$ is formulated as $\mathcal{G} := \{\mathcal{E}, \mathcal{R}, \mathcal{T}\}$, in which $\mathcal{E}$ is entity set, $\mathcal{R}$ is relation set and $\mathcal{T} := \{(h, r, t) | h, t \in \mathcal{E}, r \in \mathcal{R}\}$ is triple set. Background graph $\mathcal{BG}$ of $\mathcal{G}$ denotes a set of known triples available in training. Here we have $\mathcal{BG} \subset \mathcal{G}$.

K-Shot Knowledge Graph Completion. Every few-shot relation $r \notin \mathcal{BG}$ is formulated as $\mathcal{D}_r = \{r, \mathcal{P}_r, \mathcal{C}_r\}$, in which $\mathcal{P}_r := \{(h, t) | (h, r, t) \in \mathcal{G}\}$ and $\mathcal{C}_r$ denote entity pairs and candidate entities of r respectively. A K-Shot Knowledge Graph Completion task refers to given a few-shot relation r with K entity pairs as support set $\mathcal{S}_r$ and a query entity pair $(h_q, ?)$, ranking golden tail entity t_q higher than other entities in $\mathcal{C}_r$.

Relation-Query Association. We formally define the *relation-query association* of a few-shot relation r with support set $\mathcal{S}_r$ and query $(h_q, ?)$ as an entity set $\mathcal{A}_r^q := \{h_1, h_2, \ldots, h_K, h_q\} \cup \{t_1, t_2, \ldots, t_K, t_{[UNK]}\}$. Here, we introduce a unified virtual node $t_{[UNK]}$ to denote the unknown tail entity in queries to ensure each query has a unique $\mathcal{A}_r^q$. For a K-shot task, we have $|\mathcal{A}_r^q| = 2K + 2$.

3   Methodology

The overall architecture of YANA is illustrated in Fig. 2. Given a query $(h_q, ?)$ along with support set $\mathcal{S}_r$ and candidates, YANA constructs a local pattern graph and applies Highway R-GCN to capture entities correlations. At the same time, a HGAT is proposed to learn from one-hop neighbors of each entity. A query-aware gating mechanism is proposed to merge information from two graph neutral networks. Latter, YANA learns relation representation and make predictions by a Transformer Relation Learner and Attentive Prototypical Network. Details of these modules will be presented in the following subsections.

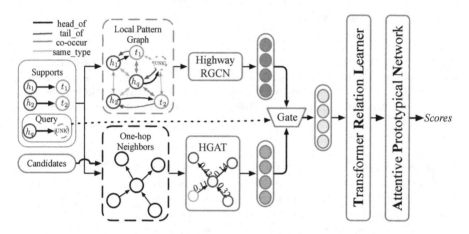

Fig. 2. Overall architecture of our model YANA.

3.1   Local Pattern Graph Construction

To model the relatedness between entities in $\mathcal{A}_r^q$, we consider two aspects of correlations and introduce four different abstract relations to convert $\mathcal{A}_r^q$ to a local pattern graph $\mathcal{G}_L$:

Inner-Pair Correlations: Two abstract relations HEAD_OF and TAIL_OF are introduced to describe the correlations of two entities within entity pair, e.g., for (Zuckerburg, ceo_of, Meta), we have (Zuckerburg, HEAD_OF, Meta) and (Meta, TAIL_OF, Zuckerburg).

Across-Pair Correlations: We introduce two abstract relations SAME_ROLE and CO_OCCUR to reflect the relatedness of two entities from different triples. SAME_ROLE allows an entity to connect with the other K entities shared the same role (head-to-head and tail-to-tail). Meanwhile, with CO_OCCUR, an entity can aggregate message from the other K entities in different role (head-to-tail and tail-to-head). For entity pair (Zuckerburg, ceo_of, Meta) and (Hans, ceo_of, Version), we can have (Zuckerburg, SAME_ROLE, Hans) and (Hans, CO_OCCUR, Meta) in $\mathcal{G}_L{}^1$.

3.2   Message Passing over Local Pattern Graph

Relational Graph Convolution Network (R-GCN) [13] is a powerful architecture for producing latent representations of entities in multi-relational data. Thus, based on $\mathcal{G}_L$, we propose an L_R-layers Highway R-GCN network to update entity embeddings. Specifically, the $l + 1$-th R-GCN layer computes the entity representation follows:

$$\mathbf{h}_i^{'l+1} = \sigma(\sum_{r=1}^{4} \sum_{j \in \mathcal{N}} (\mathbf{h}_i^l \mathbf{W}_r^l)), l = 0, 1, \ldots, L_R \tag{1}$$

$\mathbf{W}_r^l$ is relation specific matrix for the r-th relation. $\mathbf{h}_i^l$ is the l-th layer output of node i. σ indicates non-linear activation function and we use ReLU [8]. To overcome **over-smoothing problem** in multi-layer GNNs [22], we introduce highway mechanism [3, 15] to enable cross layer interactions and obtain the $l+1$-layer output $\mathbf{h}_i^{l+1}$:

$$\begin{aligned} g^{l+1} &= \text{Sigmoid}(\mathbf{W}_h^{l+1}\mathbf{h}_i^{'l+1} + b_h^{l+1}) \\ \mathbf{h}_i^{l+1} &= g^{l+1} \odot \mathbf{h}_i^{'l+1} + (1 - g^{l+1}) \odot \mathbf{h}_i^l \end{aligned} \tag{2}$$

wherein $\mathbf{W}_h^{l+1} \in \mathbb{R}^{d_e}$ and $b_h^{l+1} \in \mathbb{R}$ are layer-specific learnable parameters. $\odot$ is element wise dot product. We take the L-th layer output $\mathbf{h}_i^{L_R}$ as the task-specific embedding $\hat{\mathbf{e}}_i$ of the i-th entity e_i.

Note that, we assign entity i except $t_{[\text{UNK}]}$ in LPG with a d_e dimensional vector $\mathbf{x}_i \in \mathcal{R}^{d_e}$ obtained with embedding model ComplEx [17] and regard $\mathbf{x}_i$ as the input of Highway R-GCN, i.e., $\mathbf{h}_i^0 = \mathbf{x}_i$. Besides, we represent $t_{[\text{UNK}]}$ with learnable vector $\mathbf{x}_{[\text{UNK}]} \in \mathcal{R}^{d_e}$ which initial values drawn from the normal distribution $\mathcal{N}(0, 0.5)$. To prevent noise from $\mathbf{x}_{[\text{UNK}]}$ to other entities, we introduce a punishment factor $\mathcal{L}_{\text{reg}} = \|\mathbf{x}_{[\text{UNK}]}\|_2$, in which $\| \cdot \|_2$ is the Euclidean norm.

3.3   HGAT for Encoding One-Hop Neighbors

Apart from entity correlations, direct neighbors in background graph are still a vital source to encode entities [9, 14, 23, 24]. Hence, we devise a heterogeneous graph attention (HGAT) encoder generate the intrinsic embedding of entities in $\mathcal{A}_r^q \backslash \{t_{[\text{UNK}]}\}$ and $\mathcal{C}_r$ from its one-hop neighbors.

First we extract one-hop neighbors $\mathcal{N}_e = \{(r_i, t_i)\}$ starting with e from $\mathcal{BG}$. We calculate the impacts of (r_i, t_i) following:

---

[1] There will be eight edges for two pairs. We omit the other six samples for brevity.

$$\mathbf{n}_i = \tanh(\mathbf{W}_1(\mathbf{v}_{r_i} \| \mathbf{v}_{t_i}))$$
$$d_i = \text{LeaklyReLU}(\mathbf{u}^T \mathbf{n}_i + b_1)$$
$$\alpha_i = \frac{\exp(d_i)}{\sum_{(r_j, e_j) \in \mathcal{N}_e} \exp(d_j)} \tag{3}$$

in which $\mathbf{n}_i$ is the representation of (r_i, t_i), d_i and α_i are absolute and normalized attention value respectively. $\mathbf{v}_{r_i}$ and $\mathbf{v}_{t_i}$ are the initial embedding with dimension d_e of r_i and t_i. $\mathbf{W}_1 \in \mathbb{R}^{d_e \times 2d_e}$, $\mathbf{u} \in \mathbb{R}^{d_e}$ and $b_1 \in \mathbb{R}$ are learnable parameters. Finally, we have the intrinsic embedding $\bar{\mathbf{e}} = \sum_{i=1}^{|\mathcal{N}_e|} \alpha_i \mathbf{n}_i$.

3.4 Query-Aware Gating Mechanism

In order to automatically select relevant features and filter unrelated noises, we propose a query-aware gating mechanism to incorporate task-specific embedding $\hat{\mathbf{e}}$ with intrinsic embedding $\bar{\mathbf{e}}$ and generate reliable entity embedding:

$$g_q = \text{Sigmoid}(\mathbf{u}_{g_q}^T[\hat{\mathbf{h}}_q \odot \bar{\mathbf{h}}_q; \hat{\mathbf{t}}_q] + b_{g_q})$$
$$\mathbf{h}_e = \text{ReLU}(g_q \hat{\mathbf{e}} + (1 - g_q)\bar{\mathbf{e}}) \tag{4}$$

wherein, $\mathbf{u}_{g_q} \in \mathbb{R}^{2d_e}$ and $b_{g_q} \in \mathbb{R}$ learnable parameters.

3.5 Transformer Relation Learner

With entity representations, we are going to encode entity pairs. A major challenge is to preserve relation patterns when extracting hidden semantic features. Inspired by the great success of transformer [14,18], we devise a transformer relation learner (TRL) to represent entity pairs. Taking an entity pair (h, r, t) of few-shot relation r as an example. We regard the pair as a sequence $X = \{h, r, t\}$. The input representation of each element follows:

$$\mathbf{z}_i^0 = \mathbf{x}_i^{\text{org}} + \mathbf{x}_i^{\text{pos}}, i = 1, 2, 3 \tag{5}$$

wherein, $\mathbf{x}_i^{\text{org}} \in \mathbb{R}^{d_e}$ is the origin embedding and $\mathbf{x}_i^{\text{pos}} \in \mathbb{R}^{d_e}$ is the learnable positional signals. With such positional signals, the multi-head self-attention module in transformer can distinguish the roles of input elements (i.e. head, tail entity and relation). Embeddings of h and t are from Eq. 4. As for $\mathbf{x}_r$, we use a unified random d_e dimensional vector as the initial embedding. Later, we pack the embeddings into matrix $\mathbf{Z}^0$ and feed into an L_T successive Transformer layers[2]:

$$\mathbf{Z}^l = \text{Transformer}(\mathbf{Z}^{l-1}), l = 1, 2, \ldots, L_T \tag{6}$$

---

[2] Due to paper length restrictions, we omit the details of transformer and refer readers to the origin paper [18].

Finally, we apply a Mean Pooling layer over the L_T-layer output $\mathbf{Z}^{L_T}$ to obtain pair representation:

$$\mathbf{z}_p = \text{MeanPooling}(\mathbf{z}_h^{L_T}, \mathbf{z}_r^{L_T}, \mathbf{z}_t^{L_T}) \tag{7}$$

3.6   Attentive Prototypical Network

Support instances may have various contributions when matching with different queries [4,14]. To allow YANA to focus more on relevant instances and filter noises during the prediction stage, we introduce an instance-level Attentive Prototypical Network (APN) to generate query-aware relation representation $\mathbf{r}_q$ and compute the matching score by automatically determine the importance of each instances towards the current query follows:

$$d(\mathbf{q}, \mathbf{s}_i) = \|\mathbf{q} - \mathbf{s}_i\|_2$$
$$\beta_i = \frac{\exp(-d(\mathbf{q}, \mathbf{s}_i))}{\sum_{j=1}^{K} \exp(-d(\mathbf{q}, \mathbf{s}_i))}$$
$$\mathbf{r}_q = \sum_{i=1}^{K} \beta_i \mathbf{s}_i \tag{8}$$
$$\text{score}(q, r) = -d(\mathbf{q}, \mathbf{r}_q)$$

wherein, $\|\cdot\|_2$ is the Euclidean norm. $\mathbf{q}$ and $\mathbf{s}_i$ are the representations of query and the i-th instance learned from TRL. β_i denotes the normalized semantic similarity between q and s_i.

3.7   Model Training

We follow previous FSKGC models' training regime [14,23,24] and conduct meta-training to optimize our model. In each training step, we randomly sample a relation r from $\mathcal{D}_{train}$ along with K instances from $\mathcal{P}_r$ as the support set $\mathcal{S}_r$. Positive queries $\mathcal{Q}_r^+$ are from $\mathcal{P}_r \backslash \mathcal{S}_r$. Then we obtain negative samples $\mathcal{Q}_r^-$ by polluting tail entity of each pair (h_l, t_l) in $\mathcal{Q}_r^+$ s.t. $t_n \in \mathcal{C}_r$ and $(h_l, t_n) \notin \mathcal{KG}$.

Finally, we apply margin-ranking loss along with $\mathcal{L}_{reg}$ to optimize our model:

$$\mathcal{L} = \mathcal{L}_{\text{rank}} + \xi \mathcal{L}_{\text{reg}}$$
$$\mathcal{L}_{\text{rank}} = \frac{1}{N} \sum_r \sum_{(h_l, t_l) \in \mathcal{Q}_r^+} \sum_{(h_l, t_n) \in \mathcal{Q}_r^-} \max(\gamma + \text{score}_{(h_l, t_n)} - \text{score}_{(h_l, t_l)}, 0) \tag{9}$$

wherein hyper-parameter ξ is the trade-off factor between $\mathcal{L}_{\text{rank}}$ and $\mathcal{L}_{\text{reg}}$. γ is the margin distance.

Table 1. Statistics of datasets.

Dataset	Entities	Relations	Tuples	Avg-Deg	Solitary	#Train	#Valid	#Test
NELL	68545	291	181,109	5.284	85.18%	51	5	11
Wiki	4,838,244	539	5,859,240	2.422	99.20%	133	16	34

4 Experiments

4.1 Datasets and Baselines

Dataset: We conduct experiments on two FSKGC datasets, NELL and Wiki proposed by [23]. Relations with more than 50 but less than 500 instances are selected to construct train/valid/test set. Also, each relation has its own candidate set $\mathcal{C}_r$ constructed based on the entity type constraint. Table 1 lists statistics of these two datasets. Avg-Deg means the average degree of entities (including inverse relations). Solitary means the percentage of entities with less than five directed neighbors. #Train, #Valid and #Test indicate the number of tasks in train, valid and test set, respectively.

Baselines: We compare YANA with following baselines to measure the effectiveness of our model. *1) Sub-Graph Models*: **GMatching** [23]: The first model for one-shot relation learning. We extend GMatching to few-shot scenario by applying a max pooling (MaxP) or a mean pooling (MeanP) layer over K support instances to obtain 5-shot results. **FSRL** [24]: A metric-learning model with heterogeneous graph encoder and an LSTM auto-encoder for modeling instances interaction. **FAAN** [14]: A model with dynamic graph encoder discerning entity properties in different relations. **GANA** [9]: A model incorporating pre-train embeddings with sub-graph GNN to improve low-degree entity representations. *2) Full Graph models* We compare YANA with five full graph relation prediction models including **R-GCN** [13], **GNN** [11], **RA-GCN** [16], **I-GCN** [6] and **GNN-FSRP** [22]. Results of these models are taken from [22]. *3) Meta-Embedding Model*: **MetaR** [2]: A meta-learning model over TransE [1] for FSKGC. We directly report 5-shot results of MetaR from the origin paper.

4.2 Implementation Details

We initialize entities and relations in the background graph with ComplEx [17] embeddings which dimensionality is 100 for NELL and 50 for Wiki. We set the number of transformer layers to 3 and 4, and the number of heads to 4 and 8 for NELL and Wiki, respectively. The number of R-GCN layers is set to 2. Dropout with rate tuned in $\{0.1, 0.3, 0.5\}$ is applied to avoid over-fitting. Adam is used to optimize our model. We linearly increase the learning rate to $5e^{-5}$ for NELL and $6e^{-5}$ for Wiki at the very first 10k steps and decrease to 0 until the last epoch. We evaluate every 10k steps on the validation set and select models achieving the highest HITS@10 within 300k steps to make predictions on the test set. The margin γ is set to 5.0, and the trade-off ξ is 0.1. The sizes of $\mathcal{Q}_r^+$ and $\mathcal{Q}_r^-$ are both set to 128. We fix the maximum number of neighbors M to 30 for all sub-graph models to obtain results in our environment for a fair comparison.

Metrics: We use MRR and HITS@N to measure the performance of all methods. MRR is the mean reciprocal rank, and HITS@N is the proportion of correct entities ranked in the top N, with $N = 1, 5, 10$. For both HITS@N and MRR, a higher score means better performance. We perform a 5-shot KGC task for all models, *i.e.*, $K = 5$.

4.3 Main Results

Table 2. Experiment results. Best results are in boldface. <u>Underline</u> indicates the second-best results.

Model	NELL				Wiki			
	HITS@1	HITS@5	HITS@10	MRR	HITS@1	HITS@5	HITS@10	MRR
GMatching (MaxP)	.113	.223	.286	.174	.197	.331	.427	.273
GMatching (MeanP)	.119	.255	.348	.188	.213	.335	.391	.284
FSRL	.169	.284	.352	.230	.167	.295	.354	.253
FAAN	.188	.361	.437	.271	.270	.391	<u>.448</u>	.339
GANA	.194	<u>.395</u>	<u>.482</u>	.291	<u>.289</u>	<u>.392</u>	.436	<u>.347</u>
MetaR (BG:In-Train)	.168	.350	.437	.261	.178	.264	.302	.221
MetaR (BG:Pre-Train)	.141	.280	.355	.209	.270	.385	.418	.323
R-GCN	.139	.346	.427	.270	.141	.310	.351	.233
GNN	.140	.351	.451	.273	.143	.316	.365	.235
RA-GCN	.144	.358	.442	.280	.146	.321	.364	.241
I-GCN	.142	.353	.436	.275	.144	.317	.358	.238
GNN-FSRP	<u>.218</u>	**.442**	**.518**	**.336**	.161	.338	.420	.252
YANA (Ours)	**.230**	.364	.421	<u>.294</u>	**.327**	**.442**	**.523**	**.380**

Table 2 demonstrates that YANA achieves consistent improvements compared with baseline models. To be concrete, 1) YANA achieves the state-of-the-art performance on the Wiki dataset. Note that Wiki is a large-scale and sparse dataset, where nearly 99% of entities only have less than 5 neighbors, leading to sub-optimal performance for existing models. Nevertheless, our proposed model YANA gains 3.1%, 5.0%, 7.5% and 3.3% performance improvements in HITS@1, HITS@5, HIST@10 and MRR, respectively. 2) Unlike Wiki, NELL can provide sufficient and related neighborhood information for FSKGC. The results show that full-graph models leveraging signals from multi-hop neighbors are generally more expressive than sub-graph models. Even so, YANA achieves the best HITS@1 performance, which means that our model can make more precise predictions than others.

4.4 Ablation Study

LPG Variants. The major contribution of our work is that we construct local pattern graphs by proposing two categories of abstract relations for few-shot

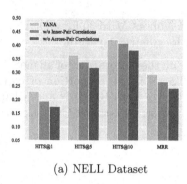
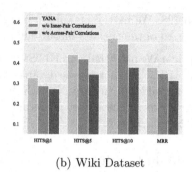

(a) NELL Dataset   (b) Wiki Dataset

Fig. 3. Ablation study results of abstract relations. *w/o Inner-Pair Correlations* denotes LPG without abstract relations HEAD_OF and TAIL_OF. *w/o Across-Pair Correlations* means removing CO_OCCUR and SAME_ROLE in LPG.

relation tasks. To examine the legitimacy of these abstract relations, we conduct experiments on NELL and Wiki with two different LPG constructed by removing two categories of relations, respectively. Overall results are shown in Fig. 3. From these results, we observe that on both datasets, the removal of *Inner-Pair Correlations* or *Across-Pair Correlations* leads to the performance decrement, which means that modeling the correlations between entities is beneficial to final predictions. In terms of different datasets, these entity correlations have more significant impacts on Wiki than that on NELL. It is reasonable because Wiki is far more sparse than NELL and therefore more dependent on dynamic neighbors from LPG to encode entities.

Module Variants. We further conduct ablation studies on NELL to investigate the effectiveness of each module of YANA. *w/o LPG* generates entity representation only by aggregating its one-hop neighbor embeddings with our devised HGAT module. *w/o HGAT* omits the HGAT module and allows the query-aware gating mechanism to combine the outputs of Highway R-GCN and pre-trained embeddings to represent entities. *w/o GNNs* removes the LPG and HGAT at the same time and represents entities with pre-trained embeddings learned with ComplEx [17] to examine the effectiveness of graph encoders. *w/o TRL* removes the transformer relation learner (TRL) and follows previous works [9,23,24] to represent (h, t) with the concatenation of head and tail embeddings, i.e., $\mathbf{z}_p = [\mathbf{h}; \mathbf{t}]$. *w/o APN* replaces the attentive prototypical network (APN) with an LSTM matching network [19] to compute scores of queries.

Overall results are listed in Table 3. We can observe that: 1) **Impacts of Entity Encoder**: The results of *w/o HGAT* prove the ability of our Highway R-GCN to capture semantic meanings from LPG for FSKGC problem. Furthermore, the results of *w/o LPG* reveal the effectiveness of our sub-graph encoding module. Besides, model performances drop sharply without graph encoders. 2) **Impacts of TRL and APN**: We devise a transformer relation learner (TRL) to encode entity pairs and apply an attentive prototypical network (APN) to

Table 3. Results of model variants on NELL dataset with 5-shot. Best results are in boldface.

Models	HITS@1	HITS@5	HITS@10	MRR
YANA	**.230**	**.364**	**.421**	**.294**
w/o HGAT	.162	.315	.398	.235
w/o LPG	.181	.332	.400	.252
w/o GNNs	.097	.217	.268	.156
w/o TRL	.156	.272	.334	.221
w/o APN	.143	.309	.402	.229

compute scores for queries. Results of *w/o TRL* and *w/o APN* prove the validness of these modules.

5 Conclusion

This paper concentrated on the solitary entity issue in the few-shot knowledge graph completion problem and proposed our model YANA. Different from previous approaches relying on learning knowledge graph structure to represent entities, YANA introduces four novel abstract relations to exploit hidden correlations between entities within a few-shot relation task. With a gating mechanism, YANA can effectively combine neighbor signals from knowledge graph and task-specific features to learn more reliable embeddings for solitary entities. Experiments on two benchmark datasets NELL and Wiki demonstrated the effectiveness of YANA. Extensive ablation studies validated the effects of each module in YANA and proved the importance of the four abstract relations. Our future work may consider learning the contribution of different entities within a task and explore the interaction of task structure and the background graph.

Acknowledgements. This work is supported by Beijing Nova Program of Science and Technology (Grant No. Z191100001119031), National Natural Science Foundation of China (Grant No. U21A20468), Guangxi Key Laboratory of Cryptography and Information Security (Grant No. GCIS202111), The Open Program of Zhejiang Lab (Grant No. 2019KE0AB03), and Zhejiang Lab (Grant No. 2021PD0AB02). Yi Liang is supported by BUPT Excellent Ph.D. Students Foundation under grant CX2019136. Shuai Zhao is the corresponding author.

References

1. Bordes, A., Usunier, N., García-Durán, A., Weston, J., Yakhnenko, O.: Translating embeddings for modeling multi-relational data. In: NIPS, pp. 2787–2795 (2013)
2. Chen, M., Zhang, W., Zhang, W., Chen, Q., Chen, H.: Meta relational learning for few-shot link prediction in knowledge graphs. In: EMNLP, pp. 4216–4225. Association for Computational Linguistics (2019)

3. Dai, D., Zheng, H., Sui, Z., Chang, B.: Incorporating connections beyond knowledge embeddings: a plug-and-play module to enhance commonsense reasoning in machine reading comprehension. arXiv:2103.14443 (2021)
4. Gao, T., Han, X., Liu, Z., Sun, M.: Hybrid attention-based prototypical networks for noisy few-shot relation classification. In: AAAI (2019)
5. Hu, F., Lakdawala, S., Hao, Q., Qiu, M.: Low-power, intelligent sensor hardware interface for medical data preprocessing. IEEE Trans. Inf. Technol. Biomed. **13**, 656–663 (2009)
6. Ioannidis, V.N., Zheng, D., Karypis, G.: Few-shot link prediction via graph neural networks for Covid-19 drug-repurposing. arXiv:2007.10261 (2020)
7. Li, Y., Song, Y., Jia, L., Gao, S., Li, Q., Qiu, M.: Intelligent fault diagnosis by fusing domain adversarial training and maximum mean discrepancy via ensemble learning. IEEE Trans. Industr. Inf. **17**, 2833–2841 (2021)
8. Nair, V., Hinton, G.E.: Rectified linear units improve restricted Boltzmann machines. In: ICML, pp. 807–814. Omnipress (2010)
9. Niu, G., et al.: Relational learning with gated and attentive neighbor aggregator for few-shot knowledge graph completion. In: Proceedings of the 44th International ACM SIGIR Conference on Research and Development in Information Retrieval (2021)
10. Qiu, H., Zheng, Q., Msahli, M., Memmi, G., Qiu, M., Lu, J.: Topological graph convolutional network-based urban traffic flow and density prediction. IEEE Trans. Intell. Transp. Syst. **22**, 4560–4569 (2021)
11. Satorras, V.G., Bruna, J.: Few-shot learning with graph neural networks. arXiv:1711.04043 (2018)
12. Saxena, A., Tripathi, A., Talukdar, P.P.: Improving multi-hop question answering over knowledge graphs using knowledge base embeddings. In: ACL (2020)
13. Schlichtkrull, M., Kipf, T.N., Bloem, P., van den Berg, R., Titov, I., Welling, M.: Modeling relational data with graph convolutional networks. In: Gangemi, A., et al. (eds.) ESWC 2018. LNCS, vol. 10843, pp. 593–607. Springer, Cham (2018). https://doi.org/10.1007/978-3-319-93417-4_38
14. Sheng, J., et al.: Adaptive attentional network for few-shot knowledge graph completion. In: EMNLP, pp. 1681–1691. Association for Computational Linguistics (2020)
15. Srivastava, R.K., Greff, K., Schmidhuber, J.: Highway networks. arXiv:1505.00387 (2015)
16. Tian, A., Zhang, C., Rang, M., Yang, X., Zhan, Z.: RA-GCN: relational aggregation graph convolutional network for knowledge graph completion. In: Proceedings of the 2020 12th International Conference on Machine Learning and Computing (2020)
17. Trouillon, T., Welbl, J., Riedel, S., Gaussier, É., Bouchard, G.: Complex embeddings for simple link prediction. In: ICML, vol. 48, pp. 2071–2080. JMLR.org (2016)
18. Vaswani, A., et al.: Attention is all you need. In: NIPS, pp. 5998–6008 (2017)
19. Vinyals, O., Blundell, C., Lillicrap, T., Kavukcuoglu, K., Wierstra, D.: Matching networks for one shot learning. In: NIPS, pp. 3630–3638 (2016)
20. Vrandečić, D., Krötzsch, M.: Wikidata: a free collaborative knowledgebase. Commun. ACM **57**(10), 78–85 (2014)
21. Wang, X., He, X., Cao, Y., Liu, M., Chua, T.S.: KGAT: knowledge graph attention network for recommendation. In: Proceedings of the 25th ACM SIGKDD International Conference on Knowledge Discovery & Data Mining (2019)
22. Wang, Y., Zhang, H.: Introducing graph neural networks for few-shot relation prediction in knowledge graph completion task. In: KSEM (2021)

23. Xiong, W., Yu, M., Chang, S., Guo, X., Wang, W.Y.: One-shot relational learning for knowledge graphs. In: EMNLP, pp. 1980–1990. Association for Computational Linguistics, Brussels, Belgium, October–November 2018
24. Zhang, C., Yao, H., Huang, C., Jiang, M., Li, Z., Chawla, N.: Few-shot knowledge graph completion. In: AAAI, vol. 34, pp. 3041–3048, April 2020

CP Tensor Factorization for Knowledge Graph Completion

Yue Luo[1], Chunming Yang[1,3(✉)], Bo Li[1], Xujian Zhao[1], and Hui Zhang[2]

[1] School of Computer Science and Technology, Southwest University of Science and Technology, Mianyang 621010, Sichuan, China
yangchunming@swust.edu.com
[2] School of Science, Southwest University of Science and Technology, Mianyang 621010, Sichuan, China
zhanghui@swust.edu.com
[3] Sichuan Big Data and Intelligent System Engineering Technology Research Center, Mianyang 621010, Sichuan, China

Abstract. The problem of incomplete knowledge caused by the lack of relations in large-scale knowledge graphs increases the difficulty of downstream application tasks. Predicting the missing relations between entities according to the existing facts is the main means of knowledge graph completion. The triple of knowledge graph can be seen as a third-order binary tensor element that linearly transforms entities and relations into low-dimensional vectors through tensor decomposition to determine the probability that the triple of missing relations is true. However, the non-deterministic polynomiality in determining the tensor rank can lead to overfitting and unfavorable to the generation of low-rank models. Aiming at this problem, we propose to use CP decomposition to decompose the third-order tensor into the sum of multiple rank-one tensors, which is the sum of the outer products of the head entity embedding, relation embedding, and tail entity embedding for each triple, and convert it into a super-diagonal tensor product the factor matrix of each mode, and use scoring function calculate the probability that the triple of missing relation is true. Link prediction experimental results from four different domains of benchmarks knowledge graph datasets show that the proposed methods are better than other comparison methods, it also can express the complex relations of knowledge graph, and the decomposition has uniqueness, reduces the total amount of calculations and parameters, avoids overfitting.

Keywords: Knowledge graph completion · Tensor decomposition · CP decomposition

1 Introduction

Knowledge Graphs (KGs) are large-scale semantic networks that store human knowledge in the form of graphs, where nodes represent entities and edges represent specific factual relations that connect two entities, usually represented as triples, namely (head entity, relation, tail entity). KGs, which allow computers to model complex data in the form

G. Memmi et al. (Eds.): KSEM 2022, LNAI 13368, pp. 240–254, 2022.
https://doi.org/10.1007/978-3-031-10983-6_19

of structured storage of knowledge and have been widely used in automated question-answering, information retrieval, and recommendation systems [1–3]. At present, a large number of large-scale KGs have been constructed by manual and semi-automatic methods, such as Freebase [4], YAGO [5], NELL [6], etc., but there are problems such as the lack of entity attributes and relations between entities. For example, about 70% of people lack birthplace information, WordNet [7] and NELL also have different degrees of lack of relations such as race and part of speech [8]. The lack of data in KGs leads to data sparseness and knowledge incomplete, which increases the computational difficulty of downstream tasks [1–3]. Knowledge representation learning [8, 9, 11] maps entities and relations in KGs into a low-dimensional continuous space through representation learning, and uses a scoring model with low latitude embedding as input to score the triple, so as to determine the probability that the triple is true, and achieve the purpose of completing KGs quickly, which can effectively solve the data sparseness problem and improve the calculation efficiency of downstream tasks.

Knowledge representation learning can be divided into non-linear [9, 11] and linear models [8]. Nonlinear models mainly include translation models and neural network models. The translation model [9] assumes that the relation is the translation from head entity to tail entity, and projects the head and tail entities into a vector space of the same dimension by the relations vector/matrix, and calculate the distance between the projection vectors to determine the confidence level that exists relations between entities. The translation model uses the distance between two entities to measure the rationality of a fact, and cannot accurately describe the semantic connection between two entities. Therefore, the synergy between entities is poor, cannot effectively solve the complex relation problem of triple, such as Trans E [10]. The neural network model [11] adopts the nonlinear model of a single-layer neural network to further describe the semantic correlation of entities under relations, but it is opaque, understandable and interpretable, and has high computational complexity. Linear models regard knowledge graph (KG) as a third-order binary tensor, where each element corresponds to a triple, 1 indicating a true fact and 0 indicating the unknown (either a false or a missing fact). The goal of KG completion is to linearly transform entities and relations into low-dimensional vectors through tensor decomposition [12], and then embed entities and relations to calculate the probability that triplets are true by product.

Tensor decomposition is the recovery of low rank components by approximating low-rank structure of data tensors, making full use of the information from all dimensions of data to effectively recover or predict the lost data. However, the non-deterministic polynomials that determining the rank of the tensor [13], such as TuckER [14], can lead to overfitting that unfavorable to the generation of low-rank models, which affects the accuracy of KG completion. To solve the above problems, we propose a method of using CP decomposition [15] for KG completion, which uses CP decomposition to decompose the third-order tensor into a sum of component rank-one tensors, which is the sum of the outer products of the head entity embedding, relation embedding, and tail entity embedding for each triple, and we convert it into a super-diagonal tensor product the factor matrix of each mode, and use the scoring function to calculate the score of each triple to infer the probability that each triple is true. CP decomposition ensures the uniqueness of tensor rank, reduces the amount of calculation and the total number of parameters. We conduct a completion experiment on four different domains of standard datasets, the results show that this method has better prediction accuracy.

The rest of the paper is organized as follows: Section "Related Work" introduces the basic concepts of knowledge representation learning and existing embedding methods and their advantages and disadvantages. Section "Knowledge graph completion based on CP decomposition" describes the proposed CP model in detail. Section "Experiments and Results" compares CP with the most typical and state-of-the-art embedding models followed by a conclusion in the "Conclusions".

2   Related Work

Knowledge representation learning maps entities and relations in KGs into dense low-latitude real-valued vectors respectively while keeping the semantic relations unchanged, and then calculates complex semantic associations between entities and relations in low-dimensional space to improve the computational efficiency of downstream tasks. The mapping method mainly includes non-linear and linear models. Nonlinear models consist of translation models and neural network models.

Translation-based models regarding the relation as a mapping from head entity to tail entity, and measure the plausibility of a fact as the distance between two entities. The representative model is Trans E [10], Trans E models a real triple (h, r, t) as $h + r \approx t$, where $h, r, t \in \mathbb{R}^k$ represents the head entity, relations, and tail entity respectively. k denotes vector dimensions, it can perform well on link prediction, but cannot handling 1-N, N-1, N-N relations. Trans R [16] embeds entities and relations into separate vector spaces, which is better in handling N-N relations, but has high time and space complexity. In addition, there are also translation models such as Trans M [17], Manifold E [18], and Tran Spare [19] that have made relevant improvements for complex relational problems, all of which have achieved better results. However, the translation model uses two different matrices to project the head and tail entities, so that the semantic connections between the entities cannot be accurately characterized, such as Trans H [20], so the synergy between entities is not good and it is still difficult to deal with the complex relations of KGs.

Neural network model uses neural networks to replace the bilinear transformation of linear models to calculate the scoring function of triple, NTN [21] portrays the semantic connections between entities and relations through nonlinear operations of single-layer neural networks, whose scoring functions is defined as a neural network-like output, it can portray complex semantic relations between entities more accurately, but too many parameters also bring an increase in complexity. Dong [22] et al. proposed an ER-MLP model that can be considered a simplified version of NTN to reduce the number of parameters. Models such as R-GCN [23], Conv E [24] and Conv KB [25] use convolutional neural networks to learn vector representations of entities and relations in KGs, R-GCN uses relational graph convolutional neural networks to model relational paths in KGs. Conv E combines entities and relations embedding into a two-dimensional matrix, and then performs a 2D convolution operation on this matrix, Conv KB uses only one-dimensional convolution. Although the prediction accuracy of the neural network model is considerable, the model is not transparent and understandable and high computational complexity.

Linear model treats each triple of KG as an element in a tensor (matrix) and uses tensor decomposition to decompose high-dimensional arrays into multiple low-dimensional ones for representation learning. Typical models include RESCAL [26], DisMult [27], ComplEx [28], SimplE [29], and TuckER [14], all of which apply different decomposition methods for this third-order binary tensor to solve the KG completion problem. RESCAL uses vectors to represent the potential semantics of entities, matrices to represent the relations between entities, and uses relation matrices to model potential factors with interactions, which makes the algorithm complex, parameter-rich and more prone to the risk of overfitting since each relation corresponds to a relation matrix. DisMult compensates for this risk by restricting the relation matrix to a diagonal matrix, which reduces complexity of the model but failing to establish triples of asymmetric relations. ComplEx represents entities and relations as complex vectors to capture triples of anti-symmetric relations. SimplE learns each relation as two independent embedding, one for normal relations and the other for reverse ones. TuckER decomposes the tensor into a core tensor multiplied by the product of three factor matrices in three modes, each row of which represents subject entity, relation, and object entity respectively, and the core tensor characterizes the level of interaction between them and is a fully expressive model. However, TuckER decomposition is an approximation of n-rank and low rank, for fixed n-rank, the uniqueness of TuckER decomposition cannot be guaranteed, the core tensor is not constrained, and the correlation between entities and relations are not better handled, so it is prone to the risk of overfitting.

When we regard KGs as third-order binary tensors, the third-order KG tensor is decomposed into the sum of the outer product of embedding of each triple head entity, relation, and tail entity by CP decomposition, at which point we are able to build each triple that can express any relations of KGs (including complex relations such as many-to-many, multi-level, asymmetric, etc.). Meanwhile CP decomposition is an approximation of rank and low rank, decomposition has uniqueness, which can decompose high-dimensional tensors into the sum of component rank-one tensors, with each nucleus consisting of the outer product of vectors, reducing the rank of the weight, the amount of computation and the total amount of parameters, avoiding overfitting.

3   Knowledge Graph Completion Based on CP Decomposition

3.1   Problem Definition

For a given knowledge graph $KG = (\varepsilon, \mathcal{R})$, ε denotes the set of all entities, $\mathcal{R}$ the set of all relations, and Δ denotes the set of ground truth triples in KG. The triple (h, r, t) represents a fact, $h, t \in \epsilon$ denotes head entity and tail entity, $r \in \mathcal{R}$ the relations between head and tail entities. KG can be represented as a third-order binary tensor $\chi \in \mathbb{R}^{I \times J \times K}$, $h_i \in \mathbb{R}^I, r_i \in \mathbb{R}^J, t_i \in \mathbb{R}^K$ represents head entity, relation, and tail entity of a triple, KG of the third-order binary tensor can be decomposed into (Fig. 1):

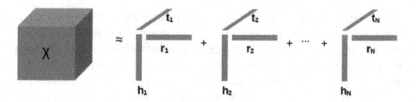

Fig. 1. CP decomposition of KG

Expanding the above CP decomposition:

$$\chi = h_1 \circ r_1 \circ t_1 + h_2 \circ r_2 \circ t_2 + \cdots + h_N \circ r_N \circ t_N \approx \sum_{i=1}^{N} h_i \circ r_i \circ t_i \quad (1)$$

where $\circ$ denotes the outer product of vector, N is a positive integer, and CP decomposition can also be expressed in terms of mod-i multiplication:

$$\chi = \mathcal{J} \times_1 H \times_2 R \times_3 T \quad (2)$$

where $\mathcal{J} \in \mathbb{R}^{N \times N \times N}$ is the unit tensor, indicating the degree of reciprocity between different components, with all its super-diagonal elements being 1 and others being 0, $H = \{h_1, h_2, ..., h_N\} \in \mathbb{R}^{I \times N}$, $R = \{r_1, r_2, ..., r_N\} \in \mathbb{R}^{J \times N}$, $T = \{t_1, t_2, ..., t_R\} \in \mathbb{R}^{K \times N}$ are embedding matrix of head entity, relation and tail entity, and $\times_n$ denotes the tensor product along pattern n. When left equals right, the rank of χ is N. When H, R, T is orthogonal, it can be considered as the main constituent factor in each mode.

3.2 Model Definition

KG completion based on CP decomposition decomposes KG of a third-order binary tensor into a super-diagonal tensor product the factor matrix of each mode. Entity embedding matrix E that is equivalent for head and tail entities, i.e., $E = H = T \in \mathbb{R}^{n_e \times d_e}$, and relation embedding matrix R $\in \mathbb{R}^{n_r \times d_r}$, where n_e and n_r present the number of entities and d_e and d_r the dimensionality of entity and relation embedding vectors respectively (Fig. 2).

The scoring function for CP as:

$$f(h, r, t) = \mathcal{J} \times_1 u_h \times_2 v_r^T \times_3 w_t \quad (3)$$

where $d_e = d_r$, $\mathcal{J} \in \mathbb{R}^{d_e \times d_r \times d_e}$ is the super-diagonal tensor of CP decomposition and $\times_n$ is the tensor product along the n-th mode. $u_h, w_t \in \mathbb{R}^{d_e}$ are the rows of E representing the head and tail entity embedding vectors, v_r the rows of R representing the relation embedding vector. We first multiply $\mathcal{J}$-recombinant a matrix with u_h, and the result forms a third-order tensor with the transpose matrix of relation vector for product, and finally multiply with w_t to get a score of the triple. We use the Sigmoid activation function for each triple score $f(h, r, t)$ to get the prediction probability $p = \sigma(f(h, r, t))$ that each triple is true, and the space complexity of cp is $O(n_e d_e + n_r d_r)$.

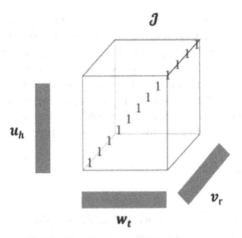

Fig. 2. Visualization of CP architecture

3.3   Model Learning

For learning CP, we assign the diagonal of decomposed third-order tensor to 1 and others to 0 (either a false or a missing fact). For each head entity $u_h^{(i)}$, relation $v_r^{(j)}$, tail entity $w_t^{(k)}$ correspond to the i-th, j-th, and k-th elements of the three factor matrices respectively, and train this three matrices so that the positions (i, j, k) corresponding vectors u_h, v_r, w_t of true triple fall as far as possible on the super-diagonal of decomposed third-order tensor, as shown in Fig. 3:

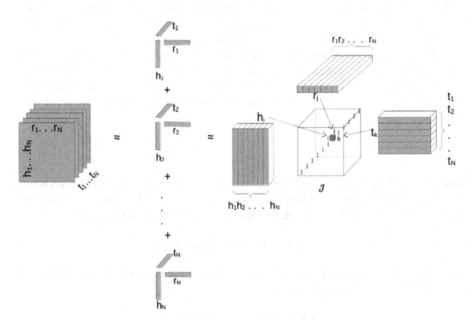

Fig. 3. Flow chart of CP learning

We take only the non-existent triples $(u_h, v_r, \cdot)$ and $(\cdot, v_r, w_t)$ of the observed pairs u_h, v_r and v_r, w_t respectively as negative samples and all observed triples as positive samples. To improve the training speed and accuracy of the algorithm, we refer to the training method of Dettmers et al. [24] and use numerical method to train CP. Using the *1-N* scoring, that is, we simultaneously score a pair u_h, v_r with all entities $w_t \in \epsilon$, in contrast to *1-1* scoring, where individual triples (u_h, v_r, w_t) are trained one at a time. This way improves the training speed of algorithm significantly. We train our model to minimize the Bernoulli negative log-likelihood loss function:

$$\mathcal{L} = \sum_{(h,r,t)\in\mathcal{B}(h,r,t)} l(h, r, t)logp(h, r, t) + (1 - l(h, r, t))\log(1 - p(h, r, t)) \quad (4)$$

where $\mathcal{B}(h, r, t) = \Delta \cup \Delta'$, Δ denotes the set of fact triples, $\Delta' = \left\{\left(u_h, v_r, w_t'\right)|w_t' \in E\right\} \cup \left\{\left(u_h', v_r, w_t\right)|u_h' \in E\right\}$ gets the set of negatively sample triples from positive triples, i.e., we replace head and tail entity of a fact triple randomly, then they may contain other fact triple, which not participate in computation. $\mathcal{B}(h, r, t)$ is the set consisting of fact triples and negatively sampled triples. The value of $l(h, r, t)$ depends on whether the triple is true or not.

$$\mathcal{L} = l(h, r, t) = \begin{cases} -1, if \ (u_h, v_r, w_t) \in \Delta' \\ 1, if \ (u_h, v_r, w_t) \in \Delta \end{cases} \quad (5)$$

3.4 Model Analysis

From Eq. (1) we can see that CP decomposition can completely and directly express every triple and relations between entities (many-to-many, multi-level, asymmetric, and other complex relations), so CP can model complex relations of KG.

Unconstrained decomposition in tensor decomposition leads to uniqueness of the results, which leads to unstable model training and reduces the robustness of the model and affects the prediction effect. the method of first determining the number of rank-one tensors before iterating ensures its uniqueness in CP decomposition. The proof is as follows:

$$\chi = \sum_{r=1}^{N} a_r \circ b_r \circ c_r = \{A, B, C\} \quad (6)$$

where $a_r \in \mathbb{R}^I, b_r \in \mathbb{R}^J, c_r \in \mathbb{R}^K$, and uniqueness means that the above decomposition may be a combination of single-rank matrices (A, B, C), and here the columns of the decomposed single-rank matrix are rearranged using the permutation matrix:

$$\chi = \{A, B, C\} = \{A\Pi, B\Pi, C\Pi\} \quad (7)$$

where Π is the permutation matrix of $N \times N$, and scaling vectors in CP decomposition does not affect the outcome, for example:

$$\chi = \sum_{r=1}^{N} (\alpha_r a_r) \circ (\beta_r b_r) \circ (\gamma_r c_r) \quad (8)$$

where $\alpha_r, \beta_r, \gamma_r = 1, r = 1, ..., R$, so cp decomposition is unique, and the stability of training is ensured by orthogonal constraints on the three factor matrices.

CP decomposition is the sum of all rank-one tensors decomposed by high-dimensional tensors, reduces the rank of weights, which in turn reduce the total amount of calculations and parameters. We convert CP decomposition to obtain a super-diagonal tensor and three factor matrices, where most of elements in super-diagonal tensor are 0, eliminating the interaction between components in every dimension and reducing the overfitting problem of model training to a certain extent.

4 Experiments and Results

4.1 Datasets

To validate our model, we use four benchmark datasets from different domains for link prediction. Since the correlation prediction tasks in WN18 [24] and FB15K [10] are not affected by the inverse relation problems [30], we use FB15k-237 and WN18RR that have filtered out the inverted relations to better train our model. all datasets counted as in Table 1.

WN18RR [24] is an English vocabulary database that filtered out all inverse relations from WN18.

FB15k-237 [31] is a structured KG contributed by community members that filtered out all inverse relations from FB15K.

Table 1. Number of entities, relations, and the dataset partition

Dataset	Rel	Ent	Train	Test	Valid
FB15K237	237	14,541	272,115	20,466	17,535
WN18RR	11	40,934	86,835	3,134	3,034
Nell-995	200	75,492	149678	543	3992
Kinship	25	104	8544	1074	1068

Nell-995 [32] Contains information on coaches, universities, government agencies, etc.

Kinship [33] is a dataset about kinship.

4.2 Implementation and Evaluation

KG completion is to predict missing triples in KG, i.e., find the missing entities or relations in triples. we get the set of all true triples in KG, with the goal of training the scoring function $f(h, r, t)$ corresponding to each triple to guide whether the triples are true or not, and finally be able to accurately score all the missing triples. A positive score for a triple indicates that it is a fact triple and negative overwise. Scoring function is a specific form of tensor factorization.

We evaluate each triple from the test set. For a given triple. We create candidate triples by replacing the head or tail entities with all entities in the dataset, we then rank the scores obtained. We use the filtered setting, i.e., we remove all other true triples apart from the currently observed test triple.

For evaluation, we use two evaluation metrics used across the link prediction literature: mean reciprocal rank (MRR) and $hits@N$, $N \varepsilon \{1, 3, 10\}$, MRR is the average of the inverse of a mean rank assigned to the true triple over all n_e generated triples. $hits@N$ indicates the proportion of correct answers in the top N of all candidate sets. The aim is for our model to achieve high MRR and $hits@N$.

4.3 Experiment Setting

We select hyperparameters by random search algorithm, and choose learning rate $\gamma \in \{0.0005, 0.001, 0.003, 0.005, 0.01\}$, learning rate decay $\gamma' \in \{1, 0.99, 0.95, 0.995\}$. We select the best parameters on each dataset by tuning parameters, as follows:

Table 2. Parameters setting

	Train Times	Learning rate	Number of batches	dimensions
FB15K237	500	0.005	128	200
WN18RR	500	0.01	128	100
Nell-995	500	0.005	128	100
Kinship	500	0.0005	128	100

4.4 Link Prediction Result

We compared several typical linear and nonlinear KG completion models in experiments, link prediction results on all four datasets are shown in Table 3 and 4. In Sect. 3.4, we analyze that CP can better solve the complex relations problem of KG, to test this, we experiment with extracting n-n relations as test-sets on KinShip. Table 5 shows the link predictions results for each model on test set with only complex relations on KinShip.

Table 3. Link prediction results on FB15K237 and WN18RR

	FB15K237				WN18RR			
	MRR	Hit@10	Hit@3	Hit@1	MRR	Hit@10	Hit@3	Hit@1
TransE	.279	.441	.376	.198	.243	.532	.441	.427
RotatE [34]	.338	.533	.375	.241	.476	.571	**.492**	.428

(continued)

Table 3. (*continued*)

	FB15K237				WN18RR			
	MRR	Hit@10	Hit@3	Hit@1	MRR	Hit@10	Hit@3	Hit@1
PairRE [35]	.351	.544	.387	.256	.452	.546	.467	.410
R-GCN	.248	.417	.264	.151	–	–	–	–
Conv E	.325	.501	.356	.237	.430	.520	.440	.400
InteractE [36]	.354	.535	-	.263	.463	.528	–	.430
DisMult	.281	.419	.263	.155	.430	.490	.440	.390
ComplEx	.278	.428	.275	.158	.440	.510	.460	.410
TuckER	.358	.544	.394	.266	.470	.526	.482	.443
CP	**.371**	**.552**	**.399**	**.272**	**.482**	**.547**	.484	**.455**

Table 4. Link prediction results on NELL-995和 and Kinship

	NELL-995				Kinship			
	MRR	Hit@10	Hit@3	Hit@1	MRR	Hit@10	Hit@3	Hit@1
TransE	.401	.501	.472	.344	.271	.623	.345	.090
RotatE	.460	.553	.493	.403	.811	.971	.891	.717
R-GCN	–	–	–	–	–	–	.880	.300
Conv E	**.491**	.613	.531	.403	.833	.981	.917	.738
InteractE	–	–	–	–	.777	.959	.870	.664
DisMult	.485	.610	.524	.401	.516	.867	.581	.367
ComplEx	.482	.606	.528	.399	.677	.963	.795	.526
TuckER	.411	.514	.459	.362	.843	.985	.915	.760
CP	.481	**.614**	**.541**	**.424**	**.880**	**.986**	**.941**	**.812**

From Table 3 and 4, we can see that CP outperforms all previous state-of-the-art models (except Conv E has a higher MRR on NELL-995 and RotatE has a higher Hit@3 on WN18RR), which indicates that CP has a very good performance, not only over other linear models, such as DisMult, ComplEx, and TuckER, but also over complex deep neural networks and reinforcement learning architectures, such as R-GCN, Conv E, and InteractE, reflecting the strong performance of CP.

From the structural analysis of these four datasets, we find that when the number of entities increases sequentially (Kinship, FB15K237, WN18RR, NELL-995), the linear model has progressively superior expressiveness compared with translation models and neural network models. This is because the larger the number of entities, linear models with the parameterization of the relation have more expressive, the better it can handle the richness of the entity. Comparing Kinship, FB15K237 and WN18RR, the model is trained better when the factorization of the higher dimensional tensor is used, such as TuckER, CP. TuckER performed better on FB15K237, WN18RR and Kinship just behind CP, but TuckER did not perform well on NELL-995 and CP still performs the best, which shows that CP is not only more expressive than TuckER but also more stable.

Table 5 shows that for the test set containing only complex relations, CP remains the best and TuckER the second, which indicates that CP is able to handle triples with complex relations in KG excellently, while RESCAL cannot.

Table 5. Link prediction results with n-n relations on KinShip

	Kinship(only n-n relations)			
	MRR	Hit@10	Hit@3	Hit@1
TransR	.266	.769	.436	0
RotatE	.816	.972	.888	.722
Rescal	.011	.001	0	0
DisMult	.539	.873	.598	.391
ComplEx	.677	.963	.795	.526
TuckER	.843	.985	.912	.760
CP	**.874**	**.986**	**.945**	**.803**

To verify that CP can reduce the total number of parameters, that is, a lower embedding dimensionality (i.e., lower rank of the decomposition) compared to other models can also have better results. We trained ComplEx, TuckER, and CP for embedding sizes $d_e = d_r \in \{20, 50, 100, 200\}$ on KinShip, Table 4 shows the obtained MRR on the test set for each of the models.

We can see from Fig. 4 that CP outperforms Tucker and ComplEx in any embedding dimension, and the difference between the MRRs of ComplEx, TuckER and CP is approximately constant and performs best at embedding sizes 100 and 200. However, for lower embedding sizes, the difference between MRRs is larger. At the embedding size is 20, the performance of CP is the least different from that at the optimal embedding dimension compared to ComplEx and TuckER, which supports the hypothesis that CP can reduce the total number of parameters.

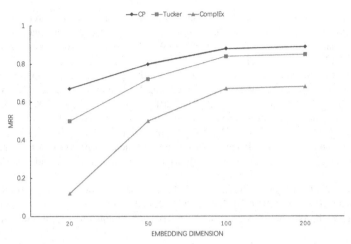

Fig. 4. MRR for ComplEx, TuckER and CP for embedding sizes $d_e = d_r \in \{20, 50, 100, 200\}$ on KinShip

5 Conclusion

In this work, we have introduced CP, a simple but excellent linear model for link prediction in KGs based on CP decomposition, which decomposes KG represented by third-order tensor into a sum of multiple rank-one tensors, with the rank-one tensor consisting of the outer product of embedding of head entity, relation and tail entity of each triple for KG completion. CP is a higher-order expression of factorization models such as RESCAL, DisMult, and SimplE. We analyze that CP can model complex relations of KG, which solve the problem that most of the current KG completion models are difficult to deal with. And we prove that CP decomposition is unique, stable, reduces the total number of computations and parameters, and reduce overfitting. The experiments worked best on four different domains standard datasets and fill KG effectively. It is possible that it is of great practical significance to make link predictions of the knowledge graph of phenotypes (diseases, symptoms), drugs, genes and their relations to explore potential drug treatment mechanisms in the field of medicine.

Future work might include taking into account the semantic hierarchy and relational attributes between entities in triples, and combining the characteristics of the knowledge graph constructed by phenotype (disease, symptom), drug, and gene, to achieve a more intelligent and high-precision knowledge graph completion, explore targeted drugs and disease-treating genes.

References

1. Jiao, J., Wang, S., Zhang, Xiaowang, W.L., Feng, Z., Wang, J.: gMatch: knowledge base question answering via semantic matching. Knowl. Based Syst. 228 (2021). Author, F., Author, S.: Title of a proceedings paper. In: Editor, F., Editor, S. (eds.) CONFERENCE 2016, LNCS, vol. 9999, pp. 1–13. Springer, Heidelberg (2016)

2. Xiong, C., Power, R., Callan, J.: Explicit semantic ranking for academic search via knowledge. graph embedding. In: Barrett, R., Cummings, R., Agichtein, E., et al. Proceedings of the 26th International Conference on World Wide Web, WWW 2017, Perth, Australia, 3–7 April 2017, pp. 1271–1279. ACM (2017)

3. Zhou, Z., Liu, S., Xu, G., Xie, X., Yin, J., Li, Y., Zhang, W.: Knowledge-based recommendation with hierarchical collaborative embedding. In: Phung, D., Tseng, V.S., Webb, G.I., Ho, B., Ganji, M., Rashidi, L. (eds.) PAKDD 2018. LNCS (LNAI), vol. 10938, pp. 222–234. Springer, Cham (2018). https://doi.org/10.1007/978-3-319-93037-4_18

4. Bollacker, K., Evans, C., Paritosh, P., et al.: Freebase: a collaboratively created graph database for. structuring human knowledge. In: Proceedings of the 2008 ACM SIGMOD International Conference on Management of Data - SIGMOD 2008, Vancouver, Canada, p. 1247. ACM Press (2008)

5. Mahdisoltani, F., Biega, J., Suchanek, F.M.: YAGO3: a knowledge base from multilingual. Wikipedias. In: CIDR 2015, Seventh Biennial Conference on Innovative Data Systems Research, Asilomar, CA, USA, 4–7 January 2015, Online Proceedings. www.cidrdb.org (2015)

6. Nathani, D., Chauhan, J., Sharma, C., Manohar, K.: Learning attention-based. embeddings for relation prediction in knowledge graphs. CoRR,2019.abs /1906.01195

7. Miller, G.A.: WordNet: a lexical database for English. Commun. ACM **38**(11), 39–41 (1995)

8. Ji, S., Pan, S., Cambria, E., Marttinen, P., Yu, P.S.: A survey on knowledge graphs: representation, acquisition, and applications. IEEE Trans. Neural Netw. Learn. Syst. **33**(2), 494–514 (2022)

9. Han, X., Minlie, H., Yu, H., Xiaoyan, Z.: TransA: an adaptive approach for. knowledge graph embedding. CoRR,2015, abs/1509.05490

10. Bordes, A., Usunier, N., Garcia-Duran, A., et al.: Translating Embeddings for Modeling Multi-relational Data. Curran Associates Inc. (2013)

11. Msahli, M., Qiu, H., Zheng, Q., et al.; Topological graph convolutional network-based urban traffic flow and density prediction. IEEE Trans. Intell. Transp. Syst. PP(99) (2020)

12. Sedghi, H., Sabharwal, A.: Knowledge completion for generics using guided tensor. factorization. CoRR, abs /1612.03871 (2016)

13. Patents: Polynomial Method of Constructing a Non-Deterministic (NP) Turing Machine. In: Patent Application Approval Process (USPTO 20160012339). Politics & Government Week (2016)

14. Balazevic, I., Allen, C., Hospedales, T.M.: TuckER: tensor factorization for. knowledge graph completion. CoRR,abs/1901.09590 (2019)

15. Kolda, T.G., Bader, B.W.: Tensor Decompositions and applications. SIAM Rev. **51**(3), 455–500 (2009)

16. Lin, Y., Liu, Z., Sun, M., et al.: Learning entity and relation embeddings for knowledge graph. Completion. In: Bonet, B., Koenig, S. (eds.) Proceedings of the Twenty-Ninth AAAI Conference on Artificial Intelligence, 25–30 January 2015, Austin, Texas, USA, pp. 2181–2187. AAAI Press (2015)

17. Fan, M., Zhou, Q., Chang, E., et al.: Transition-based Knowledge Graph Embedding with Relational Mapping Properties (2014)

18. Xiao, H., Huang, M., Zhu X.: From one point to a manifold: knowledge graph embedding for. Precise Link Prediction. In: KAMBHAMPATI S. Proceedings of the Twenty-Fifth International Joint Conference on Artificial Intelligence, IJCAI 2016, New York, NY, USA, 9–15 July 2016, pp. 1315–1321. IJCAI/AAAI Press (2016)

19. Ji, G., Liu, K., He, S., et al.: Knowledge graph completion with adaptive sparse transfer. Matrix. In: Schuurmans, D., Wellman, M.P. (eds.) Proceedings of the Thirtieth AAAI Conference on Artificial Intelligence, 12–17 February 2016, Phoenix, Arizona, USA, pp. 985–991. AAAI Press (2016)

20. Wang, Z., Zhang, J., Feng, J., et al.: Knowledge graph embedding by translating on. Hyperplanes. In: Brodley, C.E., Stone, P. (eds.) Proceedings of the Twenty-Eighth AAAI Conference on Artificial Intelligence, 27–31 July 2014, Québec City, Québec, Canada, pp. 1112–1119. AAAI Press (2014)
21. Socker, R., Chen, D., Manning, C.D., et al.: Reasoning with neural tensor networks for knowledge. Base completion. In: Advances in Neural Information Processing Systems, pp. 926–934 (2013)
22. Nickel, M., Murphy, K., Tresp, V., Gabrilovich, E.: A review of relational machine learning for knowledge graphs. Proc. IEEE **104**(1), 11–33 (2016)
23. Schlichtkrull, M., Kipf, T.N., Bloem, P., van den Berg, R., Titov, I., Welling, M.: Modeling relational data with graph convolutional networks. In: Gangemi, A., Navigli, R., Vidal, M.-E., Hitzler, P., Troncy, R., Hollink, L., Tordai, A., Alam, M. (eds.) ESWC 2018. LNCS, vol. 10843, pp. 593–607. Springer, Cham (2018). https://doi.org/10.1007/978-3-319-93417-4_38
24. Dettmers, T., Minervini, P., Stenetorp, P., et al.: Convolutional 2D knowledge graph. Embeddings. In: Mcilraith, S.A., Weinberger, K.Q. (eds.) Proceedings of the Thirty-Second AAAI Conference on Artificial Intelligence, (AAAI-18), the 30th innovative Applications of Artificial Intelligence (IAAI-18), and the 8th AAAI Symposium on Educational Advances in Artificial Intelligence (EAAI-18), New Orleans, Louisiana, USA, 2–7 February 2018, pp. 1811–1818. AAAI Press (2018)
25. Nguyen, D.Q., Nguyen, T.D., Nguyen, D.Q., et al.: A novel embedding model for knowledge. Base completion based on convolutional neural network. In: Walker, M.A., Ji, H., Stent, A. (eds.) Proceedings of the 2018 Conference of the North American Chapter of the Association for Computational Linguistics: Human Language Technologies, NAACL-HLT, New Orleans, Louisiana, USA, 1–6 June 2018, Volume 2 (Short Papers), pp. 327–333. Association for Computational Linguistics (2018)
26. Nickel, M., Tresp, V., Kriegel, H.-P.: A three-way model for collective learning on multi-relational data. In: Getoor, L., Scheffer, T. (eds.) Proceedings of the 28th International Conference on Machine Learning, ICML 2011, Bellevue, Washington, USA, 28 June–2 July 2011, pp. 809–816. Omnipress (2011)
27. Yang, B., Yih, W., He, X., et al.: Embedding entities and relations for learning and inference in. knowledge bases. In: Bengio, Y., Lecun, Y. (eds.) 3rd International Conference on Learning Representations, ICLR 2015, San Diego, CA, USA, 7–9 May 2015, Conference Track Proceedings (2015)
28. Trouillon, T., Welbl, J., Riedel, S., et al.: Complex embeddings for simple link. Prediction. In: Balcan, M.-F., Weinberger, K.Q. (eds.) Proceedings of the 33nd International Conference on Machine Learning, ICML 2016, New York City, NY, USA, 19–24 June 2016. JMLR.org, vol. 48, pp. 2071–2080 (2016)
29. Kazemi, S.M., Poole, D.: SimplE embedding for link prediction in knowledge. Graphs. In: Bengio, S., Wallach, H.M., Larochelle, H., et al. Advances in Neural Information Processing Systems 31: Annual Conference on Neural Information Processing Systems 2018, NeurIPS 2018, 3–8 December 2018, Montréal, Canada. 2018, pp. 4289–4300 (2018)
30. Akrami, F., Saeef, M.S., Zhang, Q., Hu, W., Li, C.: Realistic Re-evaluation of Knowledge Graph Completion Methods: An Experimental Study. Management of Data (2020)
31. Toutanova, K., Chen, D., Pantel, P., Poon, H., Choudhury, P., Gamon, M.: Representing text for joint embedding of text and knowledge bases. In: Proceedings of the 2015Conference on Empirical Methods in Natural Language Processing (2015)
32. Xiong, W., Hoang, T., Wang, W.Y.: De eppath: a reinforcement learning method for knowledge graph reasoning. arXivpreprint arXiv:1707.06690,201
33. Lin, X.V., Socher, R., Xiong, C.: Multi-hop knowledge graph reasoning with reward shaping. In: Proceedings of the 2018 Conference on Empirical Methods in Natural Language Processing (EMNLP) (2018)

34. Sun, Z., Deng, Z.H., Nie, J.Y., et al.: RotatE: knowledge graph embedding by relational rotation in complex space (2019)
35. Chao, L., He, J., Wang, T., et al.: PairRE: knowledge graph embeddings via paired relation vectors (2020)
36. Vashishth, S., Sanyal, S., Nitin, V., et al.: InteractE: improving convolution-based knowledge graph embeddings by increasing feature interactions. In: Proceedings of the AAAI Conference on Artificial Intelligence, vol. 34, no. 3, pp. 3009–3016 (2020)

Signal Embeddings for Complex Logical Reasoning in Knowledge Graphs

Kai Wang[1], Chunhong Zhang[2(✉)], Jibin Yu[1], and Qi Sun[2]

[1] State Key Laboratory of Networking and Switching Technology, Beijing University of Posts and Telecommunications, Beijing 100876, China
{wk_2016,yujibin}@bupt.edu.cn

[2] Key Laboratory of Universal Wireless Communications, Ministry of Education, Beijing University of Posts and Telecommunications, Beijing 100876, China
{zhangch,qisun}@bupt.edu.cn

Abstract. Complex logical reasoning over Knowledge Graph is one of the fundamental tasks of Artificial Intelligence. Traditional approaches suffer from the incompleteness and noise of knowledge graph, making complex logical reasoning a challenging task. Recent methods propose to embed entities and first-order logic (FOL) queries in low-dimensional vector spaces. However, most of the current models cannot deal with logical negation. In addition, many methods utilize neural networks to model relation projections, which require a large number of parameters and computational expense. In this work, we proposes SignalE that simplifies relation projection operations while being able to handle logical negation. We represent entities and queries by signal embeddings, which can be represented in both time domain and frequency domain interchangeably. The logical negation operation is handled by inverting the amplitude in each dimension of the frequency-domain form of the signal embedding. Furthermore, relational projection operations are simplified into translation between entities. Experiments demonstrate that SignalE significantly outperforms existing state-of-the-art methods on benchmark datasets.

Keywords: Complex logical reasoning · Query embedding · Knowledge graph embedding

1 Introduction

Complex logical reasoning is the task of answering complex queries using logical operations based on known facts [1]. This approach parses complex queries into first-order logic form (FOL) [16], which consists of variable V, predicates (relation) and logical operators *existential quantification* ($\exists$), *conjunction* ($\wedge$), *disjunction* ($\vee$), *negation* ($\neg$). For example, "The capital of a country whose capital has held the Olympic Games and is not located in Europe?" is transformed into $\exists V_? : held(V, Olympic\ Games) \wedge \neg located\_in(V, Europe) \wedge captial\_of(V_?, V)$, where $V_?$ represents target answer, in Fig. 1 (a), which is used to reason out the answer.

© The Author(s), under exclusive license to Springer Nature Switzerland AG 2022
G. Memmi et al. (Eds.): KSEM 2022, LNAI 13368, pp. 255–267, 2022.
https://doi.org/10.1007/978-3-031-10983-6_20

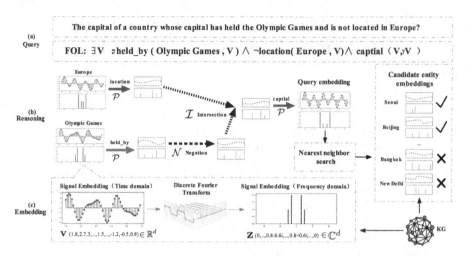

Fig. 1. Reasoning framework of SignalE: (a) A query and its FOL expression. (c) Time domain form and frequency domain form of signal embedding. (b) Reasoning process, which follows steps of query graph transformed from (a) and obtains entities embeddings from (c) for inferring answer entities.

Traditional approaches perform subgraph matching [6–8] suffer from the incompleteness and noise of knowledge graph. To alleviate this issue, some works [2–4] propose query embedding method (QE) which conducts complex logical reasoning in the embedding space and possess the ability of implicit induction of missing information. Particularly, GQE [2] transforms entities into vector embeddings and employs neural networks for relation projection and logical intersection. Q2B [3] maps entities into hypergeometric box embeddings, uses movement and scaling to model relational projection, and apply attention for logical intersection. Both Q2B and GQE model set logic with closed regions, so neither of them can deal with the logical negation problem. BetaE [4] maps entities into beta distribution embeddings, proposes to model set logic with FOL and tackles the negation problem by probability density. However, beta embedding increases the burden of model training and reasoning. Furthermore, beta embedding relies on neural networks for modeling projection operations.

To address the issues raised above, we propose SignalE, a novel complex logical reasoning method on knowledge graph. Entities and relations are modeled by signal embeddings, which have two forms of time domain and frequency domain, as shown in Fig. 1(c). These two forms of signal embedding can be converted into each other, with the same dimension. We represent relations with embeddings rather than neural networks and model relational projection as translation between entities embeddings in frequency domain. Then, neural logical operators that operate on signal embeddings are designed, including negation. Both the time-domain form and the frequency-domain form of the signal embedding are used to calculate the loss for optimization. The advantages of our model include: (1) Signal embedding is less expensive than beta probability distribution and has the ability to model logical negation operation. (2) Translation for relational projection reduces the parameter complexity of the model and the difficulty of training the model on large-scale datasets. (3) Our method is capable of handling logical negation. The intuition behind negation is that the negation operation in FOL is migrated to the embedding space by adjusting the amplitude of the signal embedding in frequency domain. In summary, our contributions are as follows:

- We propose signal embedding for entities and queries and have the ability to handle logical negation operation.
- We propose to use embeddings instead of neural networks to represent relations, and explicitly model relation projection as translation between entity embeddings.
- We propose a novel complex logical reasoning method on knowledge graph named SignalE, which achieves state-of-the-art performance on benchmark datasets.

2   Related Work

Knowledge Graph Embedding. Knowledge Graph Embedding (KGE) puts entities and relations into low-dimensional vector space. There are three basic categories of approaches. Translation-based models are represented by TransE [9], semantic matching-based models are represented by Dismult [18], and neural-based models are represented by ConvE [10]. There are a variety of embedding forms in KGE, including vector [9], probability distribution [12], complex number [5,11] and et al. These embeddings provide the foundation for later applications on KG, such as reasoning.

Complex Logical Reasoning. Traditional methods convert the query into a query graph and conduct subgraph matching [6–8], suffering from the incompleteness and noise of KG. To alleviate this problem, researchers utilize the inductive ability of embedding to represent logical query in the embedding space, inspired by KGE [9,10,12]. According to the different ways of obtaining query embedding, we group these methods into logic-basic methods and nerual-based methods.

The neural-based method leverages different neural networks [14,15,17,21] for reasoning instead of designing specific logical operations. For example, GCN [17], transformer [14], neural link predictors [15] and nerual logical regularizers [21] are applied to process the query graph to get the query embedding. Restricted by the black-box characteristics of neural networks, the interpretability and controllability of such methods are difficult to meet the requirements of complex logical reasoning.

The logic-basic approach transfer the set logic into the vector space and defines explicit logical operators to perform step-by-step operations on known entities. Particularly, geometric embeddings [2,3,19] like vector and box embedding are popular for providing a natural and easily interpretable way to represent entity sets. However, they don't support negation operation. To address this issue, some works [4,13,20] make different efforts. BetaE [4] applies expensive beta embedding to solve negation. LogicE [20] converting set logic into direct real-valued logic. EMQL [13] introduces extra symbolic structures SKTECH structure. Different from these methods, our work aims to find another less expensive embedding that can solve negation under the framework of first-order logic, without introducing additional information.

3   Preliminaries

Knowledge graph is a kind of heterogeneous graph $\mathcal{G} = (\mathcal{E}, \mathcal{R}, \mathcal{T})$, which is composed of fact triples $\mathcal{T}$ that is constructed by entity $e \in \mathcal{E}$ and relations $r \in \mathcal{R}$. Arbitrary natural language queries can be expressed in logical form using first-order logic [16], which contains logical operation symbols such as *existential quantification* ($\exists$), *conjunction* ($\wedge$), *disjunction* ($\vee$), *negation* ($\neg$) and atomic formulas that is composed of anchor entities, intermediate variables V, target variables $V_?$ and predicates (relations).

Query embedding methods implement relational projection for the predicate/relation, intersection operation for the logical conjunction, union operation for the logical disjunction, and negation operation for the logical negation, as shown in Fig. 1 (b). Then, answers $[\![q]\!]$ of query q are derived in embedding space. Relational projection and logical operators are defined as follows:

Relation Projection $\mathcal{P}$: Given a set of entities $S \subseteq \mathcal{E}$ and relation type $r \in \mathcal{R}$, relation projection compute adjacent entities $\cup_{v \in S} A_r(v)$ related to S via r : $A_r(v) \equiv \{v' \in \mathcal{E} : r(v, v') = \text{True}\}$.

Intersection $\mathcal{I}$: Given sets of entities $\{S_1, S_2, \ldots, S_n\}$, $\mathcal{I}$ compute their intersection $\cap_{i=1}^{n} S_i$.

Negation $\mathcal{N}$: Given a set of entities $S \subseteq \mathcal{E}$, $\mathcal{N}$ compute its complement $\bar{S} \equiv \mathcal{E} \backslash S$.

Union $\mathcal{U}$: Given sets of entities $\{S_1, S_2, \ldots, S_n\}$, $\mathcal{U}$ compute their union $\cup_{i=1}^{n} S_i$.

A discrete signal: $x = \{x[n], n = 1, 2, \ldots, N\}$, which is the time domain form and N is the length of discrete signal. A time domain signal x can be transformed into frequency domain X form by discrete fourier transform (DFT):

$$X = \{\sum_{n=0}^{N-1} x[n] e^{-i(2\pi/N)nk}, k = 0, 1, \ldots, N-1\} \tag{1}$$

which is a sequence of complex numbers that corresponds to fundamental signal of different frequency k. Similarly, we can also transform X into x through inverse discrete fourier transform (IDFT). The real part and imaginary part of X are denoted as X^{re} and X^{im}. The amplitude and phase of X and denoted as X^a and X^p.

4   Signal Embedding for Logical Reasoning

4.1   Signal Embedding

We discussed the mathematical definition of a discrete signal and its two forms in Sect. 3. By taking the length N of signal as the embedding dimension d, the signal embedding of ith entity $e_i \in \mathcal{E}$ is defined in time domain form $\mathbf{v}_i \in \mathbb{R}^d$ and frequency domain form $\mathbf{z}_i \in \mathbb{C}^d$, corresponding to the x and X of the signal as defined above, respectively. Specifically, we use $\mathbf{z}^{re}$ to denote the real part of $\mathbf{z}$, $\mathbf{z}^{im}$ to denote the imaginary part of $\mathbf{z}$. $\mathbf{z}^a$ and $\mathbf{z}^p$ is used to denote the amplitude and phase of $\mathbf{z}$. In fact, both the time domain and the frequency domain represent the semantic information of the entity e_i, we only generate the time domain form embedding. We can get the frequency domain embedding directly by DFT: $\mathbf{v}_i \xrightarrow{DFT} \mathbf{z}_i$ and vice versa: $\mathbf{z}_i \xrightarrow{IDFT} \mathbf{v}_i$.

4.2   Signal Logical Operators

Given the embedding form, we design relational projection operator, logical intersection operator, logical negation operator and logical union operator on signal embedding. The input of these operations are one or multiple signal embeddings, and output a new signal embedding.

Relational Projection Operator $\mathcal{P}$: In order to model the relations between entities, we design the signal projection operation to obtain entities that has the relation r_j with the entity e_i. We model j^{th} relation type $r_j \in \mathcal{R}$ as signal embedding whose time domain embedding is denoted as $\mathbf{v}_j$ and frequency domain embedding is denoted as $\mathbf{z}_j$. Inspired by RotatE [5], relational projection performs translation between entity embeddings in frequency domain. Specifically, given entity frequency embedding $\mathbf{z}_i$ and relation frequency embedding $\mathbf{z}_j$, we directly multiply them element-wise to obtain output frequency embedding $\mathbf{z}_{out}$:

$$\mathbf{z}_{out} = \mathbf{z}_i \circ \mathbf{z}_j + \delta_j \tag{2}$$

where $\circ$ represents the Hadamard product, $\mathbf{z}_{out}$ stand for the frequency embedding of a set of entities which has the relation r_j with the entity e_i and δ_j is a bias of $\mathbf{z}_j$.

Intersection Operator $\mathcal{I}$: Intersection operation aims to calculate the intersection of the input, retaining alike features of these embeddings. We employ the attention mechanism in designing logical intersection operation. Given n input frequency embeddings $\mathbf{z}_1, \mathbf{z}_2, ..., \mathbf{z}_n$, we concatenate the real part and imaginary part and put it into the attention network which construct by two linear layer and activation layer to get attentions α about inputs. Finally, we get the output: $\mathbf{z}_{inter}$, based on the input $\mathbf{z}_1, \mathbf{z}_2, ..., \mathbf{z}_n$ and attention coefficients α:

$$\alpha_i = \frac{\exp(MLP_{att}([\mathbf{z}_i^{re}, \mathbf{z}_i^{im}]))}{\sum_j^n \exp(MLP_{att}([\mathbf{z}_j^{re}, \mathbf{z}_j^{im}]))} \tag{3}$$

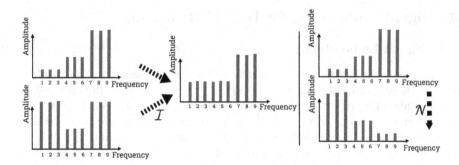

Fig. 2. An explanation of logical intersection (left) and logical negation (right): $\mathcal{I}$ selectively retain the frequency features of input frequency domain embeddings, while $\mathcal{N}$ tends to turn frequency features of input the opposite.

$$\mathbf{z}_{inter} = \sum_{i}^{n} \alpha_i \mathbf{z}_i \tag{4}$$

where [] represents concatenation operation. Notably, this operation satisfies the logical proposition: Given signal embedding $\mathbf{z}$, about intersection I, we have $I(\mathbf{z}, \mathbf{z}, ..., \mathbf{z}) = \mathbf{z}$.

Signal Negation Operator $\mathcal{N}$: Logical negation operation aims to obtain semantically opposite entity embeddings according to the input entity embedding. We accomplish the negation operation by inverting the amplitude of the frequency domain embedding. Specifically, given a signal embedding, we set the amplitude of frequency domain form $\mathbf{z}^m$ to $1 - \mathbf{z}^m$ and keep the phase unchanged:

$$\mathbf{z}_{neg}^a = 1 - \mathbf{z}^a, \mathbf{z}_{neg}^p = \mathbf{z}^p \tag{5}$$

Figure 2 (right) visualizes this operation, which clearly satisfies the logical proposition: $\mathcal{N}(\mathcal{N}(\mathbf{z})) = \mathbf{z}$.

Signal Union Operator $\mathcal{U}$: According to H. Ren, W. Hu, and J [3], arbitrary first-order logical questions can be formulated in Disjunctive Normal Form (DNF), which is the union of several conjunction queries. If the union operation appears anywhere in the computing graph, we move the union operation to the last step. Finally, simply take the union of each conjunction query's results as answer. When dealing with complex queries that require $\mathcal{U}$ operations, we employ this strategy.

For an arbitrary logical query q, we start from the anchor entities' embedding. Then, we follow the steps of the query graph and utilize corresponding operators $\mathcal{P}, \mathcal{I}, \mathcal{N}, \mathcal{U}$ to obtain the query's embedding $\mathbf{z}_q$ in frequency domain. Finally, we perform a nearest neighbor search in the candidate entity set $[\![q]\!]_{candidate}$ to obtain answer entity set $[\![q]\!]_{answer}$.

Table 1. Statistics of entities, relations and query structures. In evaluation and validation, "others" represents $2p/3p/2i/3i/2in/3in/inp/pin/pni/ip/pi/2u/up$ query structures. $\mathcal{N}-$ and $\mathcal{N}+$ represent $1p/2p/3p/2i/3i$ and $2in/3in/inp/pin/pni$, respectively.

Queries			Training		Validation		Evaluation	
Dataset	Entity	Relation	$\mathcal{N}-$	$\mathcal{N}+$	$1p$	Others	$1p$	Others
FB15k	14,951	2,690	273,710	27,371	59,097	8,000	67,016	8,000
FB15k-237	14,505	474	149,689	14,968	20,101	5,000	22,812	5,000
NELL995	63,361	400	107,982	10,798	16,927	4,000	17,034	4,000

4.3   Training

Distance Function: During training, the dissimilarity between them is deform a given query q, we utilize relational projections $\mathcal{P}$ and logical operations $\mathcal{I}, \mathcal{N}, \mathcal{U}$ to obtain the frequency domain embedding $\mathbf{z}_q$, which can generate the time domain embedding $\mathbf{v}_q$. For candidate entities $e \in [\![q]\!]_{candidate}$, the dissimilarity between them is defined as follows:

$$d(q, e) = \beta \|\mathbf{v}_q - \mathbf{v}_e\|_2 + \|\mathbf{z}_q - \mathbf{z}_e\|_2 \tag{6}$$

where $\|\|_2$ denotes L_2 norm, $d_1 = \|\mathbf{v}_q - \mathbf{v}_e\|_2$ is the distance in time domain and $d_2 = \|\mathbf{z}_q - \mathbf{z}_e\|_2$ is the distance in the frequency domain. β is a hyperparameter for balancing d_1 and d_2.

Training Objective: Given a training query q, we optimize a negative sampling loss which is described below:

$$L = -log(\gamma - d(q, e)) - \sum_{j=1}^{m} \frac{1}{m} log(d(q, e'_j) - \gamma) \tag{7}$$

where γ denotes a fixed margin, $e \in [\![q]\!]_{answer}$ represents positive entities of q, e'_j denotes the jth entity in m negative samples.

5   Experiments

5.1   Experiment Setup

Dataset: We conduct experiments on three benchmark datasets [4]: FB15k, FB15k-237, and NELL995. As shown in Fig. 3, the training query structures of datasets include five conjunctive structures $1p/2p/3p/2i/3i$ and five structures $2in/3in/inp/pin/pni$ involving $\mathcal{N}$ operation. In addition, evaluation query structures increase $ip/pi/2u/up$ which are unseen in training for evaluating generalizability of the model. Table 1 shows statistics of entities, relations, and query structures on three datasets.

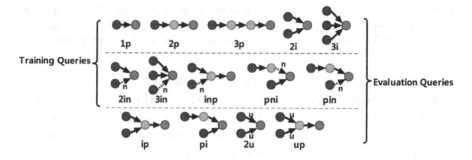

Fig. 3. Query structures used in experiments, where p, i and n stand for projection, intersection and negation, following [4].

Evaluation Protocol: We follow the evaluation protocol in BetaE [4]. Given a logical query q and its corresponding answer entities, we rank answer entities against negative entities and denote the rank as r. Then, we calculate the Mean Reciprocal Rank (MRR): $\frac{1}{r}$, and Hits at $K(H@K) : 1[r \leq K]$ as evaluation metrics.

Baselines: Three state-of-the-art methods GQE [2], Q2B [3], BetaE [4] for answering complex logical queries are considered as baselines. GQE and Q2B can not handle the negation operation. Therefore, We compare SignalE with GQE, Q2B and BetaE on query structures without negation, and compare SignalE with BetaE on query structures with negation operation.

Environment and Hyperparameters: In the experiments, we select embedding dimensionality d in {100-800} in the case of an interval of 100, and hyperparameter β (Eq. (6)) in {0.25, 0.5, 0.75}. The MLP_{att} (Eq. (3)) used in the logical intersection operation is a two-layer fully connected network whose first layer is activated by the relu function and the second layer is normalized by softmax. We choose the minibatch in {256, 512, 1024} queries, and the negative sampling number m in {64, 128, 256}, the learning rate l_r in {0.0001.0.0005, 0.001}. We optimize the loss in Eq. (7) using Adam Optimizer. All types of training structures are simultaneously trained on a single GPU (NVIDIA TITAN RTX). We determine the optimal parameter combination (d = 400, β = 0.25, l_r = 0.001, minibatch = 512 and m = 128) of SignalE by grid search and follow the optimal parameter combination of GQE, Q2B and BetaE in [4].

5.2   Results

Queries Without Negation $\mathcal{N}$: The experimental of answer queries without *negation* $\mathcal{N}$ are shown in Table 2. Overall, on FB15k, FB15k-237 and NELL995, SignalE achieves on average 23.1%, 9.6% and 17.5% improvement over previous state-of-the-art method on MRR, and also significantly outperforms BetaE, Q2B and GQE on Hit@1. The overall performance of SignalE reflects the strong adaptability of signal embedding for logical reasoning tasks. SignalE makes an

Table 2. MRR and Hit@1 results (%) of SignalE, BetaE, Q2B and GQE on answering queries without negation.

Dataset	Method	1p	2p	3p	2i	3i	pi	ip	2u	up	avg
MRR											
FB15k	GQE	54.6	15.3	10.8	39.7	51.4	27.6	19.1	22.1	11.6	28.0
	Q2B	68.0	21.0	14.2	55.1	66.5	39.4	26.1	35.1	16.7	38.0
	BetaE	65.1	25.7	**24.7**	55.8	66.5	43.9	28.1	40.1	25.2	41.6
	SignalE	**76.9**	**28.9**	24.4	**59.5**	**69.4**	**47.3**	**31.3**	**45.8**	**26.1**	**51.2**
FB15k-237	GQE	35.0	7.2	5.3	23.3	34.6	16.5	10.7	8.2	5.7	16.9
	Q2B	40.6	9.4	6.8	29.5	42.3	21.2	12.6	11.3	7.6	20.1
	BetaE	39.0	10.9	**10.0**	28.8	42.5	22.4	12.6	12.4	9.7	20.9
	SignalE	**42.8**	**11.6**	9.8	**32.6**	**46.5**	**24.9**	**14.4**	**13.3**	**10.2**	**22.9**
NELL 995	GQE	32.8	11.9	9.6	27.5	35.2	18.4	14.4	8.5	8.8	18.6
	Q2B	42.2	14.0	11.2	33.3	44.5	22.4	16.8	11.3	10.3	22.9
	BetaE	53.0	13.0	**11.4**	37.6	47.5	24.1	14.3	12.6	8.5	24.6
	SignalE	**54.1**	**13.9**	11.1	**38.2**	**50.0**	**24.3**	**16.3**	**13.7**	**9.6**	**28.9**
Hit@1											
FB15k	GQE	34.2	8.3	5.0	23.8	34.9	15.5	11.2	11.5	5.6	16.6
	Q2B	52.0	12.7	7.8	40.5	53.4	26.7	16.7	22.0	9.4	26.8
	BetaE	52.0	17.0	**16.9**	43.5	53.5	32.3	19.3	18.1	16.9	31.2
	SignalE	**66.3**	**28.9**	16.2	**47.2**	**58.4**	**35.5**	**21.7**	**32.4**	**17.1**	**36.0**
FB15k-237	GQE	22.4	2.8	2.1	11.7	20.9	8.4	5.7	3.3	2.1	8.8
	Q2B	28.3	4.1	3.0	17.5	29.5	12.3	7.1	5.2	3.3	12.3
	BetaE	28.9	5.5	**4.9**	18.3	31.7	14.0	6.7	6.3	4.6	13.4
	SignalE	**32.4**	**6.1**	4.8	**21.7**	**35.8**	**16.4**	**8.5**	**7.2**	**4.9**	**15.3**
NELL 995	GQE	15.4	6.7	5.0	14.3	20.4	10.6	9.0	2.9	5.0	9.9
	Q2B	23.8	8.7	6.9	20.3	31.5	14.3	10.7	5.0	6.0	14.1
	BetaE	43.5	8.1	**7.0**	27.2	36.5	17.4	9.3	6.9	4.7	17.8
	SignalE	**44.7**	**8.7**	6.8	**27.3**	**39.2**	**17.5**	**11.3**	**7.9**	**5.3**	**18.7**

impressive improvement on $ip/pi/2u/up$ queries that are unseen in training. This illustrates the superior generality ability of SignalE. Furthermore, SiganlE significantly improves on $1p/2p$ queries, which indicates that translation is powerful for relational projection. We notice that SignalE has a gap ($\leq 0.3\%$) with BetaE on the $3p$ task on MRR. Empirically, cascading errors [19] may occur during multi-hop reasoning. Increasing the complexity of relation projection may alleviate this issue, but it requires a trade-off between parameter complexity and accuracy. Accordingly, SignalE adopt on average 54% and 40% less parameters (Table 4) than BetaE and GQE on three dataset, and obtains competitive performance.

Queries with Negation $\mathcal{N}$: For query structures $2in/3in/pni/pin/inp$ involving *negation* $\mathcal{N}$, as shown in Table 3. SignalE achieves on average 6.8% improvement compared with BetaE on FB15k dataset. SignalE obtains similar performance to BetaE on FB15k-237 dataset and achieves competitive performance on NELL995 dataset. Obviously, SignalE perform better on FB15k than NELL995. Combining the dataset statistics in Table 1, there are 2690 relations in FB15k and 400 relations in NELL995. This suggests that SignalE has better ability to model knowledge graphs with more relations like FB15k. Admittedly, SignalE is able to handle logical negation and achieve a competitive overall performance on $2in/3in/pni/pin/inp$.

Convergence Speed: As shown in Fig. 4, SignalE achieves a much faster training speed than baselines, with the same compute resources, Adam optimizer and embedding dimension 400. The training loss curve of SignalE appears more smooth, compared to baselines. Furthermore, as shown in Fig. 5, we present the time of models to complete training with optimal parameter combination. Clearly, SignalE trains 2x faster than Q2B and 3x faster than BetaE. This highlights the applicability of SignalE to large-scale knowledge graphs in reality.

Case Study: We choose four query structures $1p/2p/2i/3i$ for presentation. $1p/2i$ stands for simple query structure, $2p/3i$ represents complex query structure. Given a query, we present the top five highest scoring entities with their ranking in Table 5. The query of case #$1p$ is ($IndianaPacers, position, V_?$). Top five predicted entities of BetaE for this query, in order, are $powerforward$, $shootingguard$, $pointguard$, $forward - center$ and $smallforward$. Top five predicted entities of signalE for this query, in order, are $shootingguard$, $smallforward, powerforward, pointguard$ and $center$. The fourth highest scoring entity "forward-center" of BetaE is a negative entity. Likewise, "North Carolina State University" is a negative entity in case #$2i$, and BetaE even ranks it

Table 3. MRR and Hit@10 results (%) of SignalE and BetaE on answering logical queries with negation.

Dataset	FB15k							FB15k-237	NELL995
Metric	Method	2in	3in	inp	pin	pni	avg	avg	avg
MRR	BetaE	14.3	14.7	11.5	**6.5**	12.4	11.8	**5.4**	**5.9**
	SignalE	**14.9**	**15.7**	**12.5**	6.5	**13.2**	**12.6**	5.4	5.5
Hit@10	BetaE	30.8	31.9	23.4	14.3	26.3	25.3	**11.9**	**12.9**
	SignalE	**31.9**	**33.7**	**25.3**	**15.0**	**27.6**	**26.7**	11.2	12.1

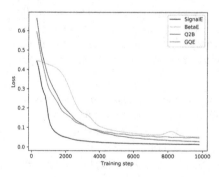

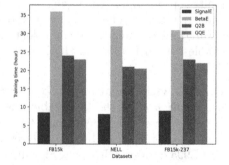

Fig. 4. Convergence curve of SignalE, BetaE, Q2B and GQE on FB15k.

Fig. 5. Training time of SignalE, BetaE, Q2B and GQE on three datasets.

Table 4. Parameters (M) of models in dimension 400.

Model	SignalE	BetaE	Q2B	GQE
FB15k	8.8	19.8	8.7	15.4
FB15k-237	7.4	18.5	6.8	13.2
NELL955	27.3	57.6	26.3	52.3

Table 5. Examples on $1p/2p/2i/3i$ of SignalE and BetaE. V and $V_?$ represents intermediate variables and the target answer of query. $\textbf{Top@5}_{BetaE}$ and $\textbf{Top@5}_{SignalE}$ stand for top 5 entities obtained by BetaE and SignalE. Entities marked by ✗ are negative entities of query.

Rank	$\textbf{Top@5}_{BetaE}$	$\textbf{Top@5}_{SignalE}$
	#1p : $(IndianaPacers, position, V_?)$	
1	power forward	shooting guard
2	shooting guard	small forward
3	point guard	power forward
4	forward-center ✗	point guard
5	small forward	center
	#2p : $(DamianMarley, liveIn, V, birthOf, V_?)$	
1	Eva Mendes	Damian Marley
2	Thomas Ian Nicholas ✗	Pitbull
3	Pitbull	Enrique Iglesias
4	Faith Hill ✗	Debbie Harry
5	Damian Marley	Jennifer Lopez ✗
	#2i: $(chancellor, leader, V_?) \wedge (administration, majorFieldOfStudy, V_?)$	
1	University of Arkansas	University of the West Indies
2	North Carolina State University ✗	Appalachian State University
3	University of Massachusetts Amherst	University of Pittsburgh
4	University of California, Irvine ✗	East Carolina University
5	Washington University in St. Louis	University of Kansas
	#3i : $(publicuniversity, schoolType, V_?) \wedge$ $(MasterofScience, educationDegree, V_?) \wedge (ChicagoCubs, teamOf, V_?)$	
1	Arizona State University ✗	Mississippi State University
2	Mississippi State University	California State University
3	University of South Carolina	University of Oklahoma ✗
4	Louisiana State University ✗	Wichita State University
5	Rice University ✗	University of South Carolina

second. Conversely, there is no negative entity in the top five predicted entities of SiganlE in both case #$1p$ and #$2i$. This shows that in sample query structures ($1p/2i$), SignalE is more accurate and dependable than BetaE. In complex query structures, large deviations appear in top five entities of BetaE. In case $2p$, the second and fourth-ranked entities are negative entities. In case $3i$, the first-ranked entity "Arizona State University" is even a negative entity. Contrastingly, SignalE has only one negative entity in both case #$2p$ and #$3i$. This illustrates that SignalE has higher confidence in selecting the high-ranked entity as the answer of query.

6   Conclusion

In this paper, we proposed a novel reasoning method named SignalE for answer FOL queries over knowledge graphs. We represent entities, relations and queries as signal embedding. SignalE greatly simplifies projection operation by modeling projection as a translation between entities in the frequency domain. Meanwhile, SiganlE has the ability of modeling negation by inverting the amplitude in the frequency domain form of the signal embedding. In the future, we are interested in making significant improvements on negation and investigating how to further improve relational projection operations.

Acknowledgments. This work was supported by the National Key R&D Program of China under Grant 2019YFF0302601.

References

1. Chen, X., Jia, S., Xiang, Y.: A review: knowledge reasoning over knowledge graph. Expert Syst. Appl. **141**, 112948 (2020)
2. Hamilton, W., Bajaj, P., Zitnik, M., Jurafsky, D., Leskovec, J.: Embedding logical queries on knowledge graphs. In: Advances in Neural Information Processing Systems 31 (2018)
3. Ren, H., Hu, W., Leskovec, J.: Query2box: reasoning over knowledge graphs in vector space using box embeddings. arXiv preprint arXiv:2002.05969 (2020)
4. Ren, H., Leskovec, J.: Beta embeddings for multi-hop logical reasoning in knowledge graphs. Adv. Neural. Inf. Process. Syst. **33**, 19716–19726 (2020)
5. Sun, Z., Deng, Z.H., Nie, J.Y., Tang, J.: Rotate: knowledge graph embedding by relational rotation in complex space. arXiv preprint arXiv:1902.10197 (2019)
6. Du, B., Zhang, S., Cao, N., Tong, H.: First: fast interactive attributed subgraph matching. In: Proceedings of the 23rd ACM SIGKDD International Conference on Knowledge Discovery and Data Mining, pp. 1447–1456 (2017)
7. Liu, L., Du, B., Tong, H., et al.: G-Finder: approximate attributed subgraph matching. In: 2019 IEEE International Conference on Big Data (Big Data), pp. 513–522. IEEE (2019)
8. Pienta, R., Tamersoy, A., Tong, H., Chau, D.H.: MAGE: matching approximate patterns in richly-attributed graphs. In: 2014 IEEE International Conference on Big Data (Big Data), pp. 585–590. IEEE (2014)

9. Bordes, A., Usunier, N., Garcia-Duran, A., Weston, J., Yakhnenko, O.: Translating embeddings for modeling multi-relational data. In: Advances in Neural Information Processing Systems 26 (2013)

10. Dettmers, T., Minervini, P., Stenetorp, P., Riedel, S.: Convolutional 2D knowledge graph embeddings. In: Proceedings of the AAAI Conference on Artificial Intelligence, vol. 32 (2018)

11. Trouillon, T., Welbl, J., Riedel, S., Gaussier, É., Bouchard, G.: Complex embeddings for simple link prediction. In: International conference on Machine Learning, pp. 2071–2080. PMLR (2016)

12. He, S., Liu, K., Ji, G., Zhao, J.: Learning to represent knowledge graphs with Gaussian embedding. In: Proceedings of the 24th ACM International on Conference on Information and Knowledge Management, pp. 623–632 (2015)

13. Sun, H., Arnold, A., Bedrax Weiss, T., Pereira, F., Cohen, W.W.: Faithful embeddings for knowledge base queries. Adv. Neural. Inf. Process. Syst. **33**, 22505–22516 (2020)

14. Kotnis, B., Lawrence, C., Niepert, M.: Answering complex queries in knowledge graphs with bidirectional sequence encoders. CoRR, abs/2004.02596 (2020)

15. Arakelyan, E., Daza, D., Minervini, P., Cochez, M.: Complex query answering with neural link predictors. arXiv preprint arXiv:2011.03459 (2020)

16. Barwise, J.: An introduction to first-order logic. In: Studies in Logic and the Foundations of Mathematics, vol. 90, pp. 5–46. Elsevier (1977)

17. Daza, D., Cochez, M.: Message passing query embedding. arXiv preprint arXiv:2002.02406 (2020)

18. Yang, B., Yih, W.t., He, X., Gao, J., Deng, L.: Embedding entities and relations for learning and inference in knowledge bases. arXiv preprint arXiv:1412.6575 (2014)

19. Liu, L., Du, B., Ji, H., Zhai, C., Tong, H.: Neural-answering logical queries on knowledge graphs. In: Proceedings of the 27th ACM SIGKDD Conference on Knowledge Discovery & Data Mining, pp. 1087–1097 (2021)

20. Luus, F., et al.: Logic embeddings for complex query answering. arXiv preprint arXiv:2103.00418 (2021)

21. Shi, S., Chen, H., Ma, W., Mao, J., Zhang, M., Zhang, Y.: Neural logic reasoning. In: Proceedings of the 29th ACM International Conference on Information & Knowledge Management, pp. 1365–1374 (2020)

Data Association with Graph Network for Multi-Object Tracking

Yubin Wu[1,2(✉)] , Hao Sheng[1,2,3] , Shuai Wang[1,2] , Yang Liu[1,2] , Wei Ke[3],
and Zhang Xiong[1,2,3]

[1] State Key Laboratory of Software Development Environment, School of Computer
Science and Engineering, Beihang University, Beijing, China
{shenghao,shuaiwang,liu.yang,xiongz}@buaa.edu.cn
[2] Beihang Hangzhou Innovation Institute Yuhang, Yuhang District,
Xixi Octagon City, Hangzhou, China
yubin.wu@buaa.edu.cn
[3] Faculty of Applied Sciences, Macao Ploytechnic University, Macao SAR, China
wke@mpu.edu.mo

Abstract. Multi-Object Tracking (MOT) methods within Tracking-by-
Detection paradigm are usually modeled as graph problem. It is challenging to associate objects in dense scenes with frequent occlusion. To further model object interactions and repair detection errors, we use graph
network to extract embeddings for data association. Graph neural network makes it possible for embeddings aggregate and update between
vertices (detections and trajectories). We both introduce priori confidence to detection attention and trajectory attention, which consider
the interaction between occluded objects in the same frame. Based on
MHT framework, we train two graph networks for clustering in adjacent
frame and association between long spaced tracklets. Experiments on
MOT17/20 benchmarks demonstrate the significant improving in tracking accuracy of proposed method and show state-of-the-art performance
for MOT with public detections.

Keywords: Data association · Graph neural network · Multiple object
tracking

1 Introduction

Multiple Object Tracking (MOT) is an important component of knowledge
extraction and understanding from images and videos. MOT is usually solved
by Tracking-by-Detection paradigm, which obtain the bounding boxes of objects
by pre-trained detector and transform the problem into data association. These
methods are naturally suitable for graph model. Detections are formulated as
vertices in graphs where edges represent associations between vertices. The task
is to obtain the optimal trajectories of multiple objects by evaluate the association relationship in the graph. With the development of graph neural network,

G. Memmi et al. (Eds.): KSEM 2022, LNAI 13368, pp. 268–280, 2022.
https://doi.org/10.1007/978-3-031-10983-6_21

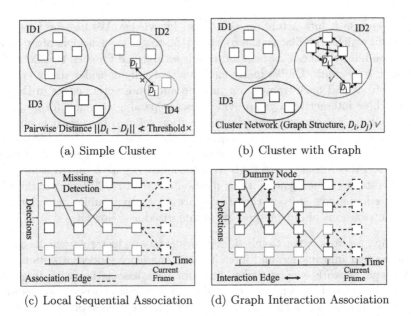

(a) Simple Cluster

(b) Cluster with Graph

(c) Local Sequential Association

(d) Graph Interaction Association

Fig. 1. The squares represent object detections with different color marked for identities. (a): Simple heuristic clustering only considers the distance between two vertices. (b): The proposed graph network exploits the context information between vertices. (c): Sequential association is difficult to model the interactions and recover missing detections. (d): The proposed data association model interactions between objects by graph network.

many effective graph processing methods have been proposed. By aggregating the features of vertices according to the graph structure, vertices can be clustered and classified for downstream tasks[15].

Data association methods are usually divided into two categories: one is to cluster detections within a time window, as shown in Fig. 1(a), and the other is to establish sequential association branches, as shown in Fig. 1(c). However, directly calculating the embedding distance between two detections for decision ignores the context information of adjacent objects. Furthermore, sequential association methods do not fully consider the interactions between objects. Therefore, we combine the two methods to achieve more accurate association in dense scenes with different time intervals. In detail, to solve the occlusion and detection errors caused by complex interaction, we design graph network which utilize context information and cross attention for data association.

In this paper, we first use graph network for detection clustering. Considering the specific MOT problem, we establish the clustering graph for detections, where overlapping detections are regarded as neighboring vertices. Based on graph attention network [21], proposed network model the influence between detections by attention. Graph embeddings are updated to measure the occlusion changes. Here, we consider the confidence information provided by the detector and encode it into attention as a priori knowledge. We use the best clique algorithm, which is similar to the baseline [18], to get the tracklets after clustering. Second, a hypothesis association tree is established for each tracklet following MHT framework. Unlike many methods that only consider the interactions between front and back frames, our method adds interaction edges in the same frame. These interactive edges provide message passing channels for graph networks, but are not considered in the association solving, because it is obviously impossible to associate different objects in the same frame. In addition, considering the interaction in the case of occlusion and using dummy vertices, our method recovers missing detections to reduce false negatives in trajectories. We demonstrate the effectiveness of our method on MOT17/20 benchmarks which achieves competitive state-of-the-art performance using public detections. The main contributions of our method are summarized as follows:

- A graph network extract embeddings for detection clustering which considers the context information and introduces a confidence guided attention.
- A graph network extract embeddings for data association with interaction attention edges between tracklets and dummy vertices for occlusion handling.
- A MOT framework of two-stage association strategy based on graph networks which has good anti occlusion performance in complex scenes.

The paper is organized as follows. Related work is discussed in Sect. 2. Data Association with Graph Network for MOT is presented in Sect. 3. Experimental results are shown and analyzed in Sect. 4 followed by the conclusion in Sect. 5.

2   Related Work

According to whether use subsequent frame information, data association methods are divided into online and offline. Traditional association algorithms usually adopt offline mode to obtain more accurate results, such as min-cost flow [3], Multiple Hypothesis Tracking (MHT) [18], etc. Recently, lifted disjoint path based methods [7,8] associate long-distance trajectories by improving the traditional network flow model and achieve higher trajectory integrity.With the development of deep learning, many online methods [1,23,27] have been proposed based on deep appearance embeddings. Benefiting from the achievements of object detectors, end-to-end methods, such as FairMOT [25] and ByteTrack [24] are proposed to demonstrate detection progress for MOT. These methods rely on the performance of the detector and use lightweight Hungarian algorithm for Bipartite graph matching. Our research focuses on using graph network to explore the relationship between vertices and extract embedding for more accurate global data association. Therefore, we use offline graph association with public detector rather than private detector for more objective evaluation.

For knowledge graph embedding extraction, GCN [10] provides a paradigm for processing non-Euclidean spatial data. In inductive learning task, GAT [21] is proposed based on GCN considering the different importance between vertices. Taking advantage of these achievements, many methods [3,4,12,16,22] use graph

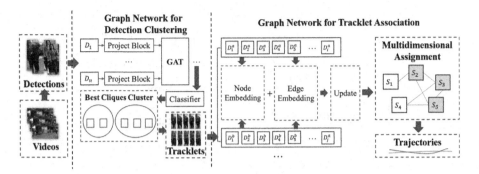

Fig. 2. Proposed MOT framework with graph network. After getting the detection results in each frame of video, our method is divided into two stages. (1) Detections are clustered into tracklets by measuring embeddings extracted with graph network, which encode detection confidence as a priori knowledge and utilize the context information between vertices. (2) Embeddings of tracklets are passing and updating in tracking graph by network with tracklet attention. Then, trajectories are obtained by solving the multidimensional assignment problem according to scores (S_i) of Embeddings.

neural network to deal with MOT problem. Methods proposed in [4,12,16] use graph convolution network to aggregate the feature of objects for data association. Braso et al. [3] propose a neural solver for MOT. Wang et al. However, simple graph network may lead to averaging embeddings and reduce the discrimination in aggregation. On the other hand, these methods do not solve the association with different granularity and make deep use of graph networks. Therefore, without relying on private detection, we propose a two-stage data association strategy with attention mechanism. Based on the previous researches, our method improves both embeddings extraction and data association.

3   Data Association with Graph Network for MOT

In this section, we introduce our MOT framework and graph network design, as shown in Fig. 2. The detailed modules are described in the following sections.

3.1   Framework

In order to model MOT problems using graph networks, we first give definitions. Given a set of detections $\mathcal{D} = \{D_1, D_2, \cdots, D_n\}$, where n is the total number of detections, and trajectory $t = \{D_o, D_p, \cdots, D_q\}$ is the set of detection with the same ID. The goal of MOT is to find an optimal trajectory group $\mathcal{T} = \{t_1, t_2, \cdots, t_m\}$ to maximize the integrity and accuracy of the overall objects.

This problem can be regarded as extracting the ID information of multiple objects from the graph as knowledge. In the process, the embedding of vertices or subgraphs are extracted through the graph network and provide the basis for data association. In graph network, given a graph $\mathcal{G} = \{\mathcal{V}, \mathcal{E}\}$, where $\mathcal{V}$ is

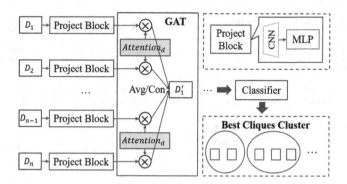

Fig. 3. Structure of graph network for detection clustering. Each detection (D_n) appearance embedding is encoded by the project block and input into GAT. We add detection confidence as priori knowledge into attention ($Attention_d$) to complete embedding aggregation. According to the classification, all tracklets are obtained by solving the best cliques of graph.

vertex set and each vertex represent a detection. Edge $\mathcal{E}$ indicates that there is a potential association between vertices.

Considering that the position and appearance of an object will not change significantly in adjacent frame, clustering the detections as tracklets is an effective method. This strategy can reduce the errors in detection, provide more accurate input for subsequent calculation, and reduce the computational complexity. Therefore, we adopt two-stage association strategy, where the detections are clustered firstly to obtain the tracklets, and the tracklets are further associated as trajectories.

In addition, occlusion and missing detection make the it difficult for long spaced trajectory association. The appearance of objects may change, and the position is difficult to predict with the movement of objects or camera. Therefore, we introduce graph network to build interaction edges, so that the embeddings between occluded objects can be aggregated and updated.

3.2   Graph Network for Detection Clustering

The structure of graph network for detection clustering is shown in Fig. 3. First, the Project Block is used to extract and encoding the appearance embedding of detection D_i from h_{D_i} to h'_{D_i}. The details of Convolutional Neural Network (CNN) in Project Block are described in Sect. 4.1 and the Multilayer Perceptron (MLP) consists of two Full Connection layers (FC) and Rectified Linear Unit (ReLU) with Batchnorm (BN) and dropout.

With appearance embedding of detections, we use self-attention to discover the importance of neighbor vertices. Given vertices pair (v_i, v_j). The importance e_{ij} of vertex j to vertex i is formulated as follows:

$$e_{ij} = Att_d(h'_{D_i}, h'_{D_j}) \cdot C'_{D_j}, \tag{1}$$

where C'_{D_j} is the detection confidence of D_j. The higher the detection confidence, the more reliable the information it provides. Therefore, using the confidence as a priori information can guide the better operation of the attention mechanism. Here we calculate the attention of first-order neighbor vertices Nb_i of v_i (including v_i), that is all the vertices with overlapping areas with v_i in image. Each object and its overlapped objects form a basic subgraph as the calculation set $\{D_1, D_2, D_{n-1}, D_n\}$. We normalize the importance e_{ij} cross all different vertices by Softmax function:

$$\alpha_{ij} = softmax_j(e_{ij}) \tag{2}$$

$$= \frac{exp(\sigma(Att_d(h'_{D_i}, h'_{D_j}) \cdot C'_{D_j}))}{\sum_{x \in Nb_i} exp(\sigma(Att_d(h'_{D_i}, h'_{D_x}) \cdot C'_{D_j}))}, \tag{3}$$

where σ is nonlinear activation function LeakyReLU (with negative input slope $An = 0.2$). Then the embedding of vertex v_i can be aggregated by averaging or concat as follows:

$$h'_{D_i} = \sigma\left(\sum_{j \in Nb_i} \alpha_{ij} h'_{D_j}\right). \tag{4}$$

In order to reduce the time and space cost of algorithm, we use a simple average aggregation function. And to make training process more stable, we extend node level attention to multi-head attention:

$$h'_{D_i} = \Big\|_{k=1}^{K} \sigma\left(\sum_{j \in Nb_i} \alpha_{ij} h'_{D_j}\right), \tag{5}$$

where K is number of multihead attention, which establishes pairwise attention between vertex pairs. In tracking scenes, the association graph between each object is not fixed. The combination of multi-head attention and nonlinear activation makes it possible for the flexible change of graph structure.

As shown in Fig. 3, the appearance embedding of the objects are extracted by multi-layer GAT and transmitted to Classifier, which is composed of FC and sigmoid layer. The classification score are used as the input of the best cliques cluster in the baseline [18] to obtain candidate tracklets. In training, we minimize the cross-entropy loss over all labeled vertices between the ground-truth and the tracklets.

3.3 Graph Network for Tracklet Association

The structure of graph network for tracklet association is shown in Fig. 3. Given a pair tracklets $t^a = \{D_1^a, D_2^a, \cdots, D_i^a\}$ and $t^b = \{D_1^b, D_2^b, \cdots, D_j^b\}$. M denotes average coordinates and size of tracklet. We formulate the spatio-temporal embedding E_{s-t} as:

$$E_{s-t} = \{\frac{|\bar{x}_j - \bar{x}_i|}{W_{img}}, \frac{|\bar{y}_j - \bar{y}_i|}{H_{img}}, \frac{|\bar{w}_j - \bar{w}_i|}{Max(\bar{w}_j, \bar{w}_i)} \tag{6}$$

$$, \frac{|\bar{h}_j - \bar{h}_i|}{Max(\bar{h}_j, \bar{h}_i)}, |\overline{Time_j} - \overline{Time_i}|\}, \tag{7}$$

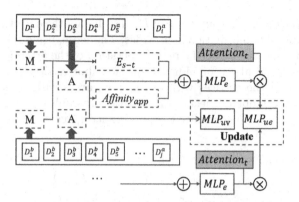

Fig. 4. Structure of graph network for tracklet association. The image coordinates of each detection in tracklets are used to formulate spatio-temporal feature (E_{s-t}). Considering both E_{s-t} and appearance affinity and combining tracklets attention ($Attention_t$), the embedding of edges and vertices are updated by MLP_{ue} and MLP_{uv}.

where $\bar{x}_i, \bar{y}_i, \bar{w}_i, \bar{h}_i, \overline{Time_i}$ are average image coordinates x, y, average width and height w, h, average time or frame of detections in tracklets i. This design is similar to normalization operation, and encodes the motion information of tracklets.

For tracklets association, longer time interval and unpredictable camera motion make the motion information unreliable, so we measure the appearance A at the same time. The cosine distance $Affinity_{app}$ of average appearance feature between tracklets t^a, t^b is concatenate with E_{s-t} through MLP_e. Combining with interaction attention $Attention_t$, all embeddings of associated edges are input to MLP_{ue} to update the edge e_{t^a}. For vertices updates, only the average appearance feature is used as input to MLP_{uv}.

To measure the interaction importance of t^b to t^a,, the weight is formulated as follows:

$$w_{a-b} = \frac{1}{|\mathcal{T}|} \sum_{l \in \mathcal{T}} \mathbf{W} e_{t^l}, \tag{8}$$

where $\mathbf{W}$ is weight matrix for embedding e_{t^l} of tracklet t^l in all connect tracklet set $\mathcal{T}$. The updated e_{t^a} is obtained by MLP_{ue} following with softmax and LeakyReLU layer, which similar as Eq. 3 and Eq. 4.

MLP_e, MLP_{uv} and MLP_{ue}, which size are adapted to the input embeddings, are both consists of two FC and ReLU layer with BN and dropout. The graph network passes the embedding messages for several iteration. Afterwards, we remove the associated edges between vertices in the same frame, and use the maximum weighted independent set algorithm in baseline [18] to solve the multidimensional assignment problem. In training, we minimize the cross-entropy loss over all labeled vertices between the ground-truth and the trajectories.

4   Experiments

Datasets and Metrics: We evaluate our method on MOT17 [14] and MOT20 [5] data sets from MOTChallenge, which is most widely used benchmark. MOT17 includes videos with different lighting conditions and pedestrian density, collected from indoor, outdoor, mobile cameras and static cameras. The dataset provides the three kind of detection results for each video to verify the robustness of MOT method. MOT20 dataset is designed to evaluate tracker in very dense scenes, where a large number of targets in video interact and occlude frequently, which poses a high challenge to the performance of tracker. We use the common CLEAR MOT metrics [2] to evaluate the method. In addition, IDF1 [17] and HOTA [13] two new metrics are introduced, which respectively reflect the ID accuracy and higher order tracking accuracy. These two metrics pay more attention to evaluate the data association algorithm rather than the quality of the detection.

4.1   Implementation Details

Training and Data Augmentation: Two graph networks are trained using MOT17 train set respectively. We train for 10000 iterations with a learning rate $5 \cdot 10^{-4}$, weight decay term 10^{-4} and an Adam Optimizer with β_1 and β_2 set to 0.9 and 0.999, respectively. For the training data from ground truth, we randomly shifting bounding boxes, randomly delete vertices and interpolate between tracklets to simulate the deviation and missing of the detector.

Parameters: By searching the parameters in the train set, we obtained the optimal parameters. In graph network for detection clustering, we set number of attention head K to 6 and set the number of GAT network layers to 4. In graph network for tracklet association, we set the iteration of message passing to 8. All other parameters remain the same as the baseline [18].

Network Model: In order to extract the appearance feature, we use ReID network PCB [20], which provide embeddings of 1536 dimension with ResNet50 [6] as backbone. Two new fully connected layers are added after the convolution layer, to reduce the embedding size to 384. ReID network is pre-trained on Market1501 [26] and all parameters are frozen after pre-training.

Baseline Method: We use TLMHT [18] as the baseline, which provides a simple two-stage multi-target tracking paradigm based on the MHT framework.

Runtime: Our method is tested on computer with CPU i7-9700K and GPU 2080ti and implemented by Python. The runtime of our method is divided into two parts. The first is 10.7FPS of graph network for detection clustering. In the second part, the time complexity of association and solving the optimal trajectory in a single window is $O(n^2 + ne)$, where n and e indicating the number of vertices and edges in the graph. As shown in Table 3 and Table 4, the total calculation efficiency is 8.4FPS and 3.6FPS on MOT17 and MOT20 test sets, which are comparable to previous state-of-the-art offline methods.

Table 1. Ablation study of graph networks and attention mechanism

Settings	MOTA ↑	IDF1 ↑	FP ↓	FN ↓	IDS ↓
base	52.55	61.21	7,834	150,529	1491
base+$\mathcal{N}_d^A$	53.01	61.74	6,195	151,232	894
base+$\mathcal{N}_d^{A_c}$	53.32	62.10	**6,038**	150,632	606
base+$\mathcal{N}_d^{A_c}$+$\mathcal{N}_a$	61.32	71.43	12,882	116,736	682
base+$\mathcal{N}_d^{A_c}$+$\mathcal{N}_a^{A_t}$	**63.94**	**74.48**	11,895	**109,003**	**576**

Table 2. Ablation study of dummy vertex and tracklet appearance representation

Settings	MOTA ↑	IDF1 ↑	FP ↓	FN ↓	IDS ↓
None_Dum	59.15	68.90	9,259	127,875	**477**
App_Avg	61.20	71.28	11,632	118,420	677
Best Setting	**63.94**	**74.48**	**11,895**	**109,003**	576

4.2 Ablation Study

Verification of each component in our method on MOT17 train set is shown in Table 1. We add basic graph network for detection clustering ($\mathcal{N}_d^A$) to the baseline. $\mathcal{N}_d^A$ improve the accuracy of detection clustering by reducing FP and IDS while maintaining a small increase of FN. Making the confidence provided by the detector as prior knowledge of attention, graph network for detection clustering $\mathcal{N}_d^{A_c}$ further reduces FP, IDS and improves the accuracy of detection clustering. The slight improvement of MOTA and IDF1 is due to the detection clustering accuracy of baseline has already reached more than 95% [18]. We add basic graph network for tracklet association ($\mathcal{N}_a$) to the baseline. As shown in Table 1, $\mathcal{N}_a$ deeply explores the interaction between tracklets, and conduct the association over a longer distance. FN decreased by 22.5%, indicating that our method can recover the missing detection under occlusion. The algorithm seeks a balance between the increase of FP and the decrease of FN, so that MOTA and IDF1 are significantly improved by 8 and 9.33. Further, we applied attention to the trajectory in graph network for tracklet association ($\mathcal{N}_a^{A_t}$) and achieved the best results.

On basis of the best results, different optimization strategies are compared in Table 2. Based on the best result in Table 1, we first remove the dummy vertex in association (None_Dum). Because the error information introduced by the dummy vertex is eliminated, FP and IDS are both reduced. However, the effect of missing detection recovery becomes worse without dummy vertex, so FN is increased by 17.3%. So as to tracklet appearance representation, when there is an interval between tracklet pairs, the detection pairs in each tracklet with the highest affinity is selected as the representative embedding of tracklets rather than mean value of all detections. As shown in Table 1, if only the mean value is used for tracklet (App_Avg), all metrics become worse without considering the objects occlusion and the appearance change.

Table 3. Comparison with state-of-the-art methods on MOT17 benchmark

Method	MOTA ↑	IDF1 ↑	HOTA ↑	FP ↓	FN ↓	IDS ↓	FPS ↑
mfi_tst [23]	60.1	58.8	47.2	13,503	209,475	2,065	2.2
ApLift [8]	60.5	65.6	51.1	30,609	190,670	1,709	1.8
Lif_T [7]	60.5	65.6	51.3	14,966	206,619	1,189	0.5
CTTrack [27]	61.5	59.6	48.2	14,076	200,672	2,583	**17.0**
TMOH [19]	62.1	62.8	50.4	10,951	201,195	1,897	0.7
Wang [22]	56.4	42.0	–	17,421	223,974	4,572	–
GNM [16]	57.3	56.3	45.4	14,100	225,042	1,911	1.3
Liang [12]	58.4	62.9	–	**6,526**	225,507	2425	–
MPN [3]	58.8	61.7	49.0	17,413	213,594	1,185	6.5
LPC [4]	59.0	66.8	51.5	23,102	206,948	**1,122**	4.8
Our	**62.3**	**66.7**	**51.8**	16,637	**193,216**	2,672	8.4

Table 4. Comparison with state-of-the-art methods on MOT20 benchmark

Method	MOTA ↑	IDF1 ↑	HOTA ↑	FP ↓	FN ↓	IDS ↓	FPS ↑
Tracktor [1]	52.6	52.7	42.1	6,930	236,680	1,648	1.2
ApLift [8]	58.9	56.5	46.6	17,739	192,736	2,241	0.4
mfi_tst [23]	59.3	59.1	47.1	36,150	172,782	1,919	0.5
TMOH [19]	60.1	61.2	48.9	38,043	165,899	2,342	0.6
GNM [16]	54.5	49.0	40.2	9,522	223,611	2,038	0.1
LPC [4]	56.3	62.5	49.0	**11,726**	213,056	1,562	0.7
MPN [3]	57.6	59.1	46.8	16,953	201,384	**1,210**	**6.5**
Our	**63.1**	**65.2**	**52.5**	71,152	**115,701**	4,041	3.6

4.3 Benchmark Evaluation

We compare our method with state-of-the-art methods on MOT17 and MOT20 benchmark. As shown in Table.3 and Table.4, the best methods with published paper are listed. In order to make a fair comparison and better evaluate the effect of tracker on data association, all methods use the **public detections** provided by the benchmark. By exploring the context information and potential interaction between objects, FN decreased significantly, especially in MOT20.

The tracker [3, 4, 12, 16, 22] listed in the lower part of the Table 3 and Table4 are all based on graph network. Comparing with methods using similar technologies, our proposed method achieves the best results. Overall, our method achieves highest in MOTA, IDF1 and HOTA and the results named GNMOT_IA are published on the official website of the MOTChallenge benchmark[1].

5   Conclusion

This paper aims to solve the difficulties in MOT in complex scenes with graph network. We proposed two graph networks for detection clustering and tracklet association. The proposed networks adopt the attention mechanism and use embeddings aggregation to transfer the context and interactive information between associated vertices. Experiments verify the effectiveness of different components of the method. On the premise of fully respecting of previous state-of-the-art works, our method achieves higher MOT effect in benchmarks over other methods. The proposed method has applications in the fields of video monitoring [11], autopilot, UAV technology and medical image processing [9].

Acknowledgements. This study is partially supported by the National Key R&D Program of China (No. 2018YFB2101100), the National Natural Science Foundation of China (No. 61872025), and the Science and Technology Development Fund, Macau SAR (File no.0001/2018/AFJ) and the Open Fund of the State Key Laboratory of Software Development Environment (No. SKLSDE-2021ZX-03). Thank you for the support from HAWKEYE Group.

References

1. Bergmann, P., Meinhardt, T., Leal-Taixe, L.: Tracking without bells and whistles. In: Proceedings of the IEEE ICCV, pp. 941–951 (2019)
2. Bernardin, K., Stiefelhagen, R.: Evaluating multiple object tracking performance: the clear mot metrics. EURASIP J. Image Video Process. **2008**, 1–10 (2008)
3. Brasó, G., Leal-Taixé, L.: Learning a neural solver for multiple object tracking. In: Proceedings of the IEEE CVPR, pp. 6247–6257 (2020)
4. Dai, P., Weng, R., Choi, W., Zhang, C., He, Z., Ding, W.: Learning a proposal classifier for multiple object tracking. In: Proceedings of the IEEE CVPR, pp. 2443–2452 (2021)
5. Dendorfer, P., et al.: Mot20: a benchmark for multi object tracking in crowded scenes. arXiv preprint arXiv:2003.09003 (2020)
6. He, K., Zhang, X., Ren, S., Sun, J.: Deep residual learning for image recognition. In: Proceedings of the IEEE CVPR, pp. 770–778 (2016)
7. Hornakova, A., Henschel, R., Rosenhahn, B., Swoboda, P.: Lifted disjoint paths with application in multiple object tracking. In: Proceedings of the International Conference on Machine Learning, pp. 4364–4375. PMLR (2020)
8. Hornakova, A., Kaiser, T., Swoboda, P., Rolinek, M., Rosenhahn, B., Henschel, R.: Making higher order mot scalable: an efficient approximate solver for lifted disjoint paths. In: Proceedings of the IEEE ICCV, pp. 6330–6340 (2021)

---

[1] https://motchallenge.net/

9. Hu, F., Lakdawala, S., Hao, Q., Qiu, M.: Low-power, intelligent sensor hardware interface for medical data preprocessing. IEEE Trans. Inf Technol. Biomed. **13**(4), 656–663 (2009)
10. Kipf, T.N., Welling, M.: Semi-supervised classification with graph convolutional networks. arXiv preprint arXiv:1609.02907 (2016)
11. Li, Y., Song, Y., Jia, L., Gao, S., Li, Q., Qiu, M.: Intelligent fault diagnosis by fusing domain adversarial training and maximum mean discrepancy via ensemble learning. IEEE Trans. Industr. Inf. **17**(4), 2833–2841 (2020)
12. Liang, T., Lan, L., Zhang, X., Peng, X., Luo, Z.: Enhancing the association in multi-object tracking via neighbor graph. Int. J. Intell. Syst. **36**(11), 6713–6730 (2021)
13. Luiten, J., Osep, A., Dendorfer, P., Torr, P., Geiger, A., Leal-Taixé, L., Leibe, B.: Hota: a higher order metric for evaluating multi-object tracking. Int. J. Comput. Vision **129**(2), 548–578 (2021)
14. Milan, A., Leal-Taixé, L., Reid, I., Roth, S., Schindler, K.: Mot16: a benchmark for multi-object tracking. arXiv preprint arXiv:1603.00831 (2016)
15. Msahli, M., Qiu, H., Zheng, Q., Memmi, G., Lu, J.: Topological graph convolutional network-based urban traffic flow and density prediction. IEEE Transa. Intell. Transp. Syst. **PP**(99) (2020)
16. Papakis, I., Sarkar, A., Karpatne, A.: Gcnnmatch: Graph convolutional neural networks for multi-object tracking via sinkhorn normalization. arXiv preprint arXiv:2010.00067 (2020)
17. Ristani, E., Solera, F., Zou, R., Cucchiara, R., Tomasi, C.: Performance measures and a data set for multi-target, multi-camera tracking. In: Hua, G., Jégou, H. (eds.) ECCV 2016. LNCS, vol. 9914, pp. 17–35. Springer, Cham (2016). https://doi.org/10.1007/978-3-319-48881-3_2
18. Sheng, H., Chen, J., Zhang, Y., Ke, W., Xiong, Z., Yu, J.: Iterative multiple hypothesis tracking with tracklet-level association. IEEE Trans. Circuits Syst. Video Technol. **29**(12), 3660–3672 (2018)
19. Stadler, D., Beyerer, J.: Improving multiple pedestrian tracking by track management and occlusion handling. In: Proceedings of the IEEE CVPR, pp. 10958–10967 (2021)
20. Sun, Y., Zheng, L., Yang, Y., Tian, Q., Wang, S.: Beyond part models: person retrieval with refined part pooling (and a strong convolutional baseline). In: Ferrari, V., Hebert, M., Sminchisescu, C., Weiss, Y. (eds.) ECCV 2018. LNCS, vol. 11208, pp. 501–518. Springer, Cham (2018). https://doi.org/10.1007/978-3-030-01225-0_30
21. Veličković, P., Cucurull, G., Casanova, A., Romero, A., Lio, P., Bengio, Y.: Graph attention networks. arXiv preprint arXiv:1710.10903 (2017)
22. Wang, Y., Kitani, K., Weng, X.: Joint object detection and multi-object tracking with graph neural networks. In: Proceedings of the IEEE International Conference on Robotics and Automation, pp. 13708–13715 (2021). https://doi.org/10.1109/ICRA48506.2021.9561110
23. Yang, J., Ge, H., Yang, J., Tong, Y., Su, S.: Online multi-object tracking using multi-function integration and tracking simulation training. Appl. Intell. **52**(2), 1268–1288 (2021). https://doi.org/10.1007/s10489-021-02457-5
24. Zhang, Y., et al.: Bytetrack: Multi-object tracking by associating every detection box. arXiv preprint arXiv:2110.06864 (2021)
25. Zhang, Y., Wang, C., Wang, X., Zeng, W., Liu, W.: FairMOT: on the fairness of detection and re-identification in multiple object tracking. Int. J. Comput. Vision **129**(11), 3069–3087 (2021). https://doi.org/10.1007/s11263-021-01513-4

26. Zheng, L., Shen, L., Tian, L., Wang, S., Wang, J., Tian, Q.: Scalable person re-identification: a benchmark. In: Proceedings of the IEEE ICCV, pp. 1116–1124 (2015)

27. Zhou, X., Koltun, V., Krähenbühl, P.: Tracking objects as points. In: Vedaldi, A., Bischof, H., Brox, T., Frahm, J.-M. (eds.) ECCV 2020. LNCS, vol. 12349, pp. 474–490. Springer, Cham (2020). https://doi.org/10.1007/978-3-030-58548-8_28

Knowledge Graph Embedding with Direct and Disentangled Neighborhood Representation Attention Network

Ruiguo Yu[1,2,3], Siyao Gao[1,2,3], Jian Yu[1,2,3], Mankun Zhao[1,2,3], Tianyi Xu[1,2,3], Jie Gao[1,2,3(✉)], Hongwei Liu[4], and Xuewei Li[1,2,3]

[1] College of Intelligence and Computing, Tianjin University, Tainjin, China
{rgyu,siyaogao,yujian,zmk,tianyi.xu,gaojie,lixuewei}@tju.edu.cn
[2] Tianjin Key Laboratory of Advanced Networking (TANKLab), Tianjin University, Tainjin, China
[3] Tianjin Key Laboratory of Cognitive Computing and Application, Tianjin University, Tainjin, China
[4] Foreign Language, Literature and Culture Studies Center, Tianjin Foreign Studies University, Tainjin, China
liuhongwei@tjfsu.edu.cn

Abstract. Knowledge Graph Completion (KGC) has become a focus of attention across the deep learning community owing to its excellent contribution to numerous downstream tasks. Despite the recent surge in KGC work, most existing KGC models deal with triples in Knowledge Graphs (KGs) independently, ignoring the inherent and valuable information from the neighborhoods around entities and the dynamic properties of entities in different link prediction tasks. We propose a novel Direct and Disentangled Neighborhood Representation Attention Network (DDNAN) for KGC, with an adaptive selector to decide what kind of neighborhood information should be aggregated to the current entity. With the assistance of the relation-aware attention aggregator, our model can exploit Knowledge Graphs (KGs) to generate dynamic representations of the given different scenarios and prediction tasks. Extensive experiments on public benchmark datasets have been conducted to validate the superiority of DDNAN over existing methods in terms of both accuracy and interpretability. The code is available at https://github.com/Ariel-Gao/DDNAN.

Keywords: Knowledge graph · Neighborhood information · Disentangled representation · Relation-aware attention

1 Introduction

Knowledge Graphs (KGs) like Freebase [4], DBpedia [1] and NELL [6] are valuable resources for NLP tasks, such as information retrieval [16], machine reading [29], and relation extraction [18]. A typical KG is a multi-relational graph,

G. Memmi et al. (Eds.): KSEM 2022, LNAI 13368, pp. 281–294, 2022.
https://doi.org/10.1007/978-3-031-10983-6_22

represented as triples (h, r, t), indicating that two entities are connected by relation r. Although a KG could contain many triples, it is also known to suffer from incompleteness problems.

Typically, as shown in Fig. 1(a), take "Steve Jobs" and "Robert Downey Jr." for example, the task of querying "nationality" can get the same tail entity "United States", but in relation "profession" the two people indeed exhibit quite a difference. "Nationality" is a n-to-1 relation. Each person has a unique nationality, and countless people have the same nationality. Owing to the common nationalities "America" of "Steve Jobs" and "Robert Downey Jr.", existing methods will naturally pull the representations of the two closer to capture such identity. This static representation ignores that entities may exhibit different roles in different query relations, affecting link prediction performance. Existing methods fail to generate different representations when the prediction tasks change dynamically.

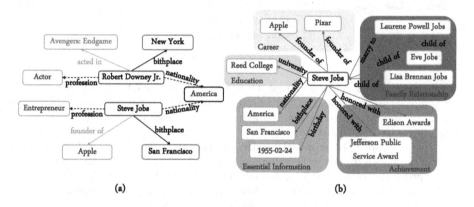

Fig. 1. An example of the "Steve Jobs" neighboring distribution

According to the above mentioned issue, we summarize that (i) simply aggregating neighborhood entities fails to model the critical relations in the specific scenarios effectively. When engaged in different graph contexts, entities and relations might exhibit extremely distinct meanings; (ii) Entities with few associated triples have already represented an independent "theme", directly aggregating neighborhood information would be more suitable; (iii) Entities with more associated triples have formed a relatively complete subgraph, while entities may have multiple aspects, and various relations focus on different aspects of the entity. In Fig. 1(b), the neighborhood of entity "Steve Jobs" contains different "themes" such as "Family Relations", "Career" and "Education". We need to focus on a "theme" that is more relevant to the task. Assume that in the prediction task of (Steve Jobs, profession, ?), it's supposed to pay more attention to the component "Career" such as "founder of Apple" rather than "Family Relations".

The contributions of this paper are summarized as follows:

– We propose a novel Direct and Disentangled Neighborhood Representation Attention Network (DDNAN) that can adaptively learn the direct neighbor feature or the disentangled neighbor feature for the link prediction task.
– For neighborhood information aggregation in different scenarios, We propose Adaptive Selectors(AS) to select appropriate neighbor information.
– We propose Disentangled Neighborhood Information Embedding module(disE) to reinforce entity representation for entities with dense neighborhoods. disE utilizes a dynamic assignment mechanism to collect representations of neighboring entities with a similar "theme" to the current prediction task to enhance the semantic representation of entities.
– For entities with sparse neighborhoods, each adjacent entity already represents an independent "theme", so we propose Direct Neighborhood Information Embedding module(dirE) to reinforce entity representation with direct neighborhood features.
– The experimental results of our approach outperform the state-of-the-art, suggesting that our method is effective and can provide accurate solutions for Knowledge Graph Completion.

2 Related Work

The mainstream models proposed for KGC could be roughly divided into translation based [5,9,10], semantic matching [2,17,24], and neural network based [7,14] models. Despite the success of these approaches, there is still a lack of consideration for the internal structure information in the knowledge graph. CompGCN [21] utilizes a graph neural network to perform a combined operation of entities and relations on each edge connected by a central node. FAAN [20] proposes an adaptive attention network and a transformer encoder to help match references with queries adaptively. KBCPA [8] adds cardinality information to the attention mechanism for different entities. Although these KGC methods exploit the internal structure information of knowledge graphs, they have high computational complexity.

In recent years disentanglement representation has been very effective for dealing with the complex structure of the real-world graph, which has made significant progress in numerous fields, such as image, text, and recommendation. Disentanglement representation aims to learn to embed various disentangled components. IPGDN [15] and ADGCN [22] develop the disentanglement idea of homogeneous networks, while DisenHAN [26] focuses on Heterogeneous networks. Although these methods show, promising results in handling graph structure, applying them to complex knowledge graphs is still challenging. Our work focuses on learning direct and disentangled neighbor features in KGs according to the different sparsity of entities' neighborhoods and generating dynamic entity representations according to the link prediction tasks.

3   Methodology

The Direct and Disentangled Neighborhood Representation Attention Network aims to make full use of each entity's neighborhood to enhance entity representation for improving the performance of knowledge graph completion tasks. Inspired by the huge difference in the roles of entities in triples linked by different relations, DDNAN first selects the appropriate neighborhood information embedding method for different neighborhood sparsity through Adaptive Selector (AS). We use direct neighborhood information for entities with sparse neighborhood and disentangled neighborhood information for entities with dense neighborhood. A final entity representation that aggregates neighborhood information through relation-aware attention. The overall framework is shown in Fig. 2.

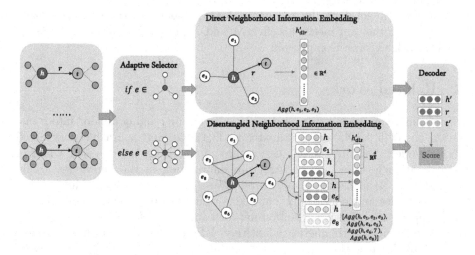

Fig. 2. The overall framework of the model

3.1   Entity Representation with Direct Neighborhood Information

This section refers to the Direct Neighborhood Information Embedding module in Fig. 2 as dirE. To explore more profound connections with other entities, we use the relation-aware neighborhood information attention representation to assign different importance of each neighbor. Link prediction can divide the triple into source entity, query relation and target entity. To focus on the dynamic properties of entities, we design a relation-aware attention neighborhood aggregation method for entities discerning their roles associated with query relations. The neighborhood set of the entity is represented as $N_e = \{(r_i, e_i)|(e, r_i, e_i) \cup (e_i, r_i, e) \in G\}$. We can discern the roles of source entity e according to the relevance between the query relation r and the neighboring relation r_i. Hence, we first define a metric function φ to calculate their relevance score by a bilinear dot product.

$$\varphi(r, r_i) = r^T W_r r_i + b_r \tag{1}$$

where W_r and b_r are learnable parameters. In order to obtain the attention value corresponding to each neighbor, we use a *softmax* function to make it comparable across the neighbors, which is denoted as

$$\alpha_{r_i - r} = softmax(\varphi(r, r_i)) = \frac{exp(\varphi(r, r_i))}{\sum_{(r_i : e_i) \in N_e} exp(\varphi(r, r_i))} \tag{2}$$

In a link prediction task, when neighboring relations are more related to the query relation, $\varphi(\cdot, \cdot)$ will be higher and neighboring entities would play a more critical role in neighbor embeddings. The module aggregate the neighborhood information representation weighted by the attention value $\alpha_{r_i - r}$ to obtain a relation-aware neighbor embedding as

$$e_{dirE} = \sum_{(r_i : e_i) \in N_e} \alpha_{r_i - r} e_i \tag{3}$$

Finally, to generate the embedding of the central entity node with direct neighborhood information e'_{dirE}, we simultaneously couple the source entity embedding e and its direct relation-aware neighbor embedding e_{dirE}.

$$e'_{dirE} = Relu(W_1 e + W_2 e_{dirE}) \tag{4}$$

where $W_1, W_2 \in \mathbb{R}^{d \times d}$ are learnable parameters.

3.2 Entity Representation with Disentangled Neighborhood Information

This section refers to the Disentangled Neighborhood Information Embedding module in Fig. 2 as disE. In order to learn the disentangled representations of entities' neighborhood, we first project the feature vector into different latent spaces, so that each component can extract different semantics from the initial entity node feature. Specifically, for each entity e, we want its embedding to be represented by a K independent component, i.e., $e = [e_1, e_2, ..., e_K]$, where $e_k \in \mathbb{R}^{\frac{d}{K}}$ depicts the k-th aspect of the entity e.

$$e_k^0 = LeakyRelu(W_k e) \tag{5}$$

where the initial embeddings $\{e_k^0\}_{k=1}^K$ are obtained from e through K distinct projection matrix $W = W_1, W_2, ..., W_k$.

However, in this module, we should not use all the neighbors when reconstructing node component e_k as only a subset of neighbors carry the valuable information for the aspect k. For each entity e and each component k, we conduct the following interactions for a specific neighbor e_i with relation r_i:

$$\phi(e, e_i, k) = (e_{r_i}^k)^T \, e_{ir_i}^k \tag{6}$$

where $e_r^k = e_k \circ \theta_r$ represents the k-th relation-aware component representation of entity e in a specific relation-aware subspace. $\theta_r = diag(w_r), \theta_r \in \mathbb{R}^d$ denotes the relation-specific projection matrix. Here θ_r is restricted to be a diagonal matrix for efficiency while ensuring semantic subspace consistency.

We use a softmax function to make it comparable across the neighbors in the k-th component, which is defined as

$$\alpha_{e_{r_i} - e_{ir_i}}^k = softmax(\phi(e, e_i, k))$$
$$= \frac{exp(\phi(e, e_i, k))}{\sum_{(e_i, r_i) \in N(e)} exp(\phi(e, e_i, k))} \tag{7}$$

Based on the hypothesis that the more similar the entity e and the neighbor e_i are in the k-th component in terms of their relation r, the more likely the factor k is to be the reason for the connection. Obtained the attention value $\alpha_{e_{r_i} - e_{ir_i}}^k$, we could aggregate the disentangled representation of each component respectively, which is defined as:

$$e^k = \sum_{(e_i, r_i) \in N(e)} \alpha_{e_{r_i} - e_{ir_i}}^k e_i \tag{8}$$

where e^k denotes the k-th component representation of the entity e.

Hence, sharing the mapping matrix θ_r with the relation-aware aggregator can facilitate a thorough disentanglement of components and distinguish triples that are helpful for prediction. When the query relation of entity e is r, the attention value $\beta_{e,r}^k$ of each component e^k is defined as:

$$\psi(e, r, k) = (e^k \circ \theta_r)^T \cdot r \tag{9}$$

$$\beta_{e,r}^k = softmax(\psi(e, r, k))$$
$$= \frac{exp(\psi(e, r, k))}{\sum_k exp(\psi(e, r, k))} \tag{10}$$

$$e_{disE} = \sum_k \beta_{e,r}^k e^k \tag{11}$$

We generate the embedding of the central entity node with disentangled neighborhood information e'_{disE} using a gate unit to automatically determine the degree of activation of the source entity embedding e and its disentangled neighborhood embedding e_{disE}.

$$e'_{disE} = gate(e_{disE}) + (1 - gate)e + b, g \in [0, 1] \tag{12}$$

3.3   Adaptive Selector for Information Aggregation

As for which kind of information should be aggregated for the current entity, we rationally set the way Adaptive Selector (AS) for different scenarios. Each entity's neighbor already represents an independent "theme" for entities with few associated triples. So, directly aggregating neighborhood information to complement a simple subgraph that is more suitable. However, entities with affluent associated triples have formed a relatively complete neighborhood subgraph. We implement disentanglement and aggregate neighborhood information at the semantic level for such entities.

Inspired by the TranSparse [11], we use the sparsity of entity association triples to determine the number of adjacent nodes to be sampled. The sparsity of entities is defined as:

$$\vartheta_e = 1 - (1 - \vartheta_{min})\frac{degree(e)}{degree(e)_{max}} \tag{13}$$

where $\vartheta_{min}(0 \le \vartheta_{min} \le 1)$ is the lowest entity sparsity. To balance the selection of the number of adjacent nodes, we define the number of sampled neighbor nodes n_e as

$$n_e = \begin{cases} degree(e), & m \le degree(e), \\ \vartheta_e \times degree(e), & otherwise. \end{cases} \tag{14}$$

where m is a hyperparameter. Entities with $n_e = degeree(e)$ will be supplemented with disE module. The remaining entities will be supplemented with dirE module according to the sparsity of the entity e.

Then we use a random selection method to obtain neighbor nodes. This method is suitable for large-scale knowledge graphs, which can improve the training speed of the model and reduce the computational overhead.

3.4   Full Objective

The Convolutional decoder is effective in scoring triplets in KGs with high parameter efficiency. We use ConvE [7] as the decoder in this paper. The score function of ConvE is

$$f(h,r,t) = Relu(vec(Relu[\bar{h};\bar{r}] * \omega)W)t \tag{15}$$

In the training procedure, we define a same listwise loss function as used in ConvE.

$$L = -\frac{1}{N} \sum_{i=1}^{N} [t_i \log p(t_i|h,r) + (1 - t_i) log(1 - p(t_i|h,r))] \tag{16}$$

where t is a label vector whose elements are relations that exist and zero otherwise, and N is the number of entities in a KG. This loss function takes one $< h, r >$ pair and simultaneously scores it against all entities. We tune model parameters from all candidates using the valid set for link prediction and use the standard $L2$ norm of weights as a constraint function.

4   Experiments

4.1   Experimental Setup

Datasets. To verify the performance of DDNAN, we select the two most commonly used public datasets: FB15k-237 [24] and WN18RR [7]. The statistics of datasets are listed in Table 1.

Table 1. Summary statistics for the datasets.

Datasets	Entities	Relations	Triplet		
			Train	Valid	Test
FB15k-237	14,541	237	272,115	17,535	20,466
WN18RR	40,943	11	86,835	3,034	3,134

FB15k-237 is a subset of Freebase related to movies, actors, awards and sports. WN18RR is a subset of WordNet, in which relationships define lexical relations between various words (such as hypernym, hyponym, synonym).

Evaluation Task and Metrics. We evaluate the performance of our method on the task of link prediction. We adopt MRR (the mean reciprocal rank of all correct entities) and Hits@k (the proportion of valid test triples ranking at the top k prediction) metrics. Higher MRR or higher Hits@k indicates better performance.

Hyperparameters. We adopt Adam [13] as the optimizer and Xavier initialization for initializing parameters. Hyperparameter ranges of the grid search were as follows: embedding dropout $\{0.0, 0.1, 0.2, 0.3\}$, embedding size $\{100, 200, 500\}$, batch size $\{64, 128, 256, 512\}$, learning rate $\{0.003, 0.001, 0.0001\}$, and label smoothing $\{0.0, 0.1, 0.2, 0.3\}$.

4.2   Comparisons to State-of-the-Art

In this subsection, we compare our DDNAN with other SOTA methods. Quantitative results of MRR and Hits@n are listed in Table 2 for comparisons in FB15k-237 and WN18RR. Our DDNAN surpasses previous SOTA methods. The promising performance within both dirE and disE modules demonstrates the advancement of our architecture for KGC.

Table 2. Link prediction results of DDNAN compared with the SOTA methods. Best result are shown in bold.

	FB15k-237				WN18RR			
	MRR	Hits@1	Hits@3	Hits@10	MRR	Hits@1	Hits@3	Hits@10
ConvE [7]	.316	23.9	35.0	49.1	.460	39.0	43.0	48.0
RotatE [23]	.338	24.1	37.5	53.3	.476	42.8	49.2	57.1
TuckER [2]	.358	26.6	39.4	54.4	.470	44.3	48.2	52.6
A2N [3]	.317	23.2	34.8	48.6	.483	42.0	46.0	51.0
InteractE [25]	.354	26.3	–	53.5	.463	43.0	–	52.8
HAKE [30]	.346	25.0	38.1	54.2	.497	45.2	51.6	58.2
CompGCN [21]	.355	26.4	39.0	53.5	.479	44.3	49.4	54.6
ReInceptionE [28]	.349	–	–	52.8	.483	–	–	58.2
HittER [19]	.373	**27.9**	40.9	55.8	.503	46.2	51.6	58.4
BiQUE [12]	.365	27.0	40.1	55.5	**.504**	45.9	**51.9**	**58.8**
DDNAN(ours)	**.377**	27.1	**41.2**	**56.9**	**.504**	**46.5**	50.9	58.7

4.3 Performance of Complex Relation Types

As shown in Table 3, we focus on the complex multi-relations task. Following [27], we classify the relations into four groups: 1-to-1, 1-to-n, n-to-1 and n-to-n, based on the average number of tails per head and heads per tail. We choose the FB15k-237 as dataset due to its multi-relations and denser graph structure.

Table 3. Predictions by Categories on FB15k-237.

	Prediction Head (Hits@10)				Prediction Tail (Hits@10)			
	1-to-1	1-to-n	n-to-1	n-to-n	1-to-1	1-to-n	n-to-1	n-to-n
ConvE [7]	50.5	17.0	64.4	45.9	51.0	87.8	15.0	60.3
RotatE [23]	59.3	17.4	**67.4**	47.6	57.8	67.4	13.8	60.8
InteractE [25]	54.7	19.2	64.7	47.6	54.7	88.1	14.1	61.7
CompGCN [21]	60.4	19.0	65.6	47.4	58.9	88.5	15.1	61.6
DDNAN(ours)	**61.4**	**22.4**	65.9	**48.9**	**60.1**	**88.9**	**16.2**	**62.9**

Our model directly aggregates neighbor node information for entities with sparse subgraphs, while entities with dense subgraphs will aggregate those neighbors with similar "theme". The model performs adaptive embedding according to the different sparsity of entity neighborhood subgraphs. Therefore, it outperforms other models in both complex and straightforward relation types.

4.4 Ablation Study

Effects of Different Modules. We gradually add dirE module and disE module to the baseline to investigate the effectiveness of our proposed DDNAN.

"w/o dirE & disE" degenerates into ConvE. As "w/o disE" shows in Fig. 3(b), the direct neighborhood information leads to a gain of 7.2% Hits@10 on WN18RR and 5.4% Hits@10 on FB15k-237. "w/o dirE" showing that disentangled neighborhood information boosts the performance of Hits@10 from 48.0% to 56.4% on WN18RR and from 49.1% to 55.7% on FB15k-237. As shown in Fig. 3(a), the implementation of both dirE and disE modulus combined with Adaptive Selector can further improve the MRR from 0.460 to 0.504 WN18RR, meanwhile, improve the MRR from 0.316 to 0.377 on FB15k-237. This dramatic improvement demonstrates the effectiveness of our proposed DDNAN.

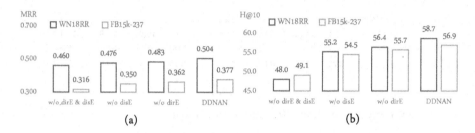

Fig. 3. Ablation experiments of Different Modules on WN18RR and FB15k-237.

Effects of Adaptive Selectors. In this section, we consider the impact of the Adaptive Selector(AS) by replacing it with a binomial distribution or removing it. From the result in Fig. 4, it is evident that the selector has a remarkable influence on WN18RR and FB15k-237. This result is reasonable because the AS is employed to figure out which kind of information should be aggregated for the current entity.

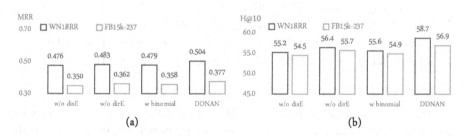

Fig. 4. Ablation experiments of Adaptive Selectors on WN18RR and FB15k-237.

4.5   Visualization

As shown in Fig. 5. Power Morpher is an example of direct neighborhood aggregation due to its few neighbors. When predicting (Power Morpher, genre, ?),

DDNAN assigns the highest attention weights for neighbor (Fox Kids Network, tv_network/programs). Jack London, with many neighbors, is an example of disentangled neighborhood aggregation. DDNAN assigns the highest attention weights for neighbor component "place" when predicting (Jack London, nationality, ?).The entities tend to focus more on the neighbors related to the relation of the prediction task.

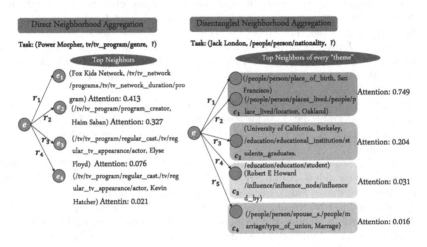

Fig. 5. Explanations of direct or disentangled neighborhood.

5   Conclusion and Future Work

DDNAN utilizes an adaptive selector (AS) to select direct and separated neighborhood features to enhance entity representation. This paper proposes a novel neighborhood-aware model DDNAN for KGC task. For entities with different neighborhood sparsity, DDNAN utilizes an adaptive selector (AS) to select direct and disentangled neighborhood features to reinforce entity representation. Moreover, with relation-aware attention aggregator, our model can exploit KGs to generate dynamic representations of entities in the given scenario and more accurate results on multiple datasets for prediction tasks. In future work, we will consider the influence of other probability distributions in Adaptive Selector and more external knowledge to enhance the representation.

Acknowledgements. This work is jointly supported by National Natural Science Foundation of China (61877043) and National Natural Science of China (61877044).

References

1. Auer, S., Bizer, C., Kobilarov, G., Lehmann, J., Cyganiak, R., Ives, Z.: DBpedia: a nucleus for a web of open data. In: The Semantic Web, 6th International Semantic Web Conference, 2nd Asian Semantic Web Conference, vol. 4825 LNISA, pp. 722 – 735, Busan, Korea (2007)
2. Balaevi, I., Allen, C., Hospedales, T.M.: Tucker: tensor factorization for knowledge graph completion. In: Proceedings of the Conference on Empirical Methods in Natural Language Processing and 9th International Joint Conference on Natural Language Processing, pp. 5185–5194, Hong Kong, China (2019)
3. Bansal, T., Juan, D.C., Ravi, S., McCallum, A.: A2n: attending to neighbors for knowledge graph inference. In: Proceedings of the 57th Annual Meeting of the Association for Computational Linguistics, Conference, pp. 4387–4392. Florence, Italy (2020)
4. Bollacker, K., Evans, C., Paritosh, P., Sturge, T., Taylor, J.: Freebase: a collaboratively created graph database for structuring human knowledge. In: Proceedings of the ACM SIGMOD International Conference on Management of Data, pp. 1247–1249 (2008)
5. Bordes, A., Usunier, N., Garcia-Duran, A., Weston, J., Yakhnenko, O.: Translating embeddings for modeling multi-relational data. In: Advances in Neural Information Processing Systems, Lake Tahoe, NV, United states (2013)
6. Carlson, A., Betteridge, J., Kisiel, B., Settles, B., Hruschka Jr, E.R., Mitchell, T.M.: Toward an architecture for never-ending language learning. In: Proceedings of the National Conference on Artificial Intelligence, vol. 3, pp. 1306–1313 (2010)
7. Dettmers, T., Minervini, P., Stenetorp, P., Riedel, S.: Convolutional 2d knowledge graph embeddings. In: Proceedings of the 32nd AAAI Conference on Artificial Intelligence, pp. 1811–1818. New Orleans, LA, United States (2018)
8. Ding, C., Wei, X., Chen, Y., Zhao, R.: Graph attention mechanism with cardinality preservation for knowledge graph completion. In: Proceedings of the International Conference on Knowledge Science, Engineering and Management, vol. 12815 LNAI, pp. 479 – 490, Tokyo, Japan (2021)
9. Dong, Y., Guo, X., Xiang, J., Liu, K., Tang, Z.: Hypersphere: An embedding method for knowledge graph completion based on hypersphere. In: Proceedings of the International Conference on Knowledge Science, Engineering and Management, vol. 12815 LNAI, pp. 517 – 528, Tokyo, Japan (2021)
10. Guo, X., Gao, N., Wang, L., Wang, X.: TransI: translating infinite dimensional embeddings based on trend smooth distance. In: Proceedings of the International Conference on Knowledge Science, Engineering and Management, vol. 11775 LNAI, pp. 511 – 523, Athens, Greece (2019)
11. Ji, G., Liu, K., He, S., Zhao, J.: Knowledge graph completion with adaptive sparse transfer matrix. In: Proceedings of the 30th AAAI Conference on Artificial Intelligence, pp. 985–991. Phoenix, AZ, United states (2016)
12. Jia Guo, S.K.: BiQUE: biquaternionic embeddings of knowledge graphs. In: Proceedings of the Conference on Empirical Methods in Natural Language Processing (2021)
13. Kingma, D.P., Ba, J.L.: Adam: a method for stochastic optimization. In: Conference Track Proceedings of 3rd International Conference on Learning Representations. San Diego, CA, United states (2015)

14. Li, J., Li, A., Liu, T.: Feature interaction convolutional network for knowledge graph embedding. In: Proceedings of the International Conference on Knowledge Science, Engineering and Management, vol. 12815 LNAI, pp. 369 – 380, Tokyo, Japan (2021)
15. Liu, Y., Wang, X., Wu, S., Xiao, Z.: Independence promoted graph disentangled networks. In: Proceedings of the 34th AAAI Conference on Artificial Intelligence, pp. 4916–4923 (2020)
16. Liu, Z., Xiong, C., Sun, M., Liu, Z.: Entity-duet neural ranking: understanding the role of knowledge graph semantics in neural information retrieval. In: Proceedings of the 56th Annual Meeting of the Association for Computational Linguistics, vol. 1, pp. 2395–2405, Melbourne, VIC, Australia (2018)
17. Nickel, M., Rosasco, L., Poggio, T.: Holographic embeddings of knowledge graphs. In: Proceedings of the 30th AAAI Conference on Artificial Intelligence, pp. 1955–1961, Phoenix, AZ, United states (2016)
18. Ren, X., et al.: CoType: Joint extraction of typed entities and relations with knowledge bases. In: Proceedings of the 26th International World Wide Web Conference, pp. 1015–1024, Perth, WA, Australia (2017)
19. Chen, S., Liu, X., Gao, J., Jiao, J., Zhang, R., Ji, Y.: Hitter: Hierarchical transformers for knowledge graph embeddings. In: Proceedings of the Conference on Empirical Methods in Natural Language Processing (2021)
20. Sheng, J., et al.: Adaptive attentional network for few-shot knowledge graph completion. In: Proceedings of the Conference on Empirical Methods in Natural Language Processing, pp. 1681–1691, Virtual, Online (2020)
21. Vashishth, S., Sanyal, V.N.S., Talukdar, P.: Composition-based multi-relational graph convolutional networks. In: Proceedings of the International Conference on Learning Representations (2020)
22. Zheng, S., et al.: Adversarial graph disentanglement. arXiv preprint arXiv:2103.07295 (2021)
23. Sun, Z., Deng, Z.H., Nie, J.Y., Tang, J.: Rotate: Knowledge graph embedding by relational rotation in complex space. In: Proceedings of the 7th International Conference on Learning Representations, New Orleans, LA, United states (2019)
24. Trouillon, T., Welbl, J., Riedel, S., Ciaussier, E., Bouchard, G.: Complex embeddings for simple link prediction. In: Proceedings of the 33rd International Conference on Machine Learning, vol. 5, pp. 3021–3032, New York City, NY, United states (2016)
25. Vashishth, S., Sanyal, S., Nitin, V., Agrawal, N., Talukdar, P.: InteractE: improving convolution-based knowledge graph embeddings by increasing feature interactions. In: Proceedings of the 34th AAAI Conference on Artificial Intelligence, pp. 3009–3016, New York, NY, United states (2020)
26. Wang, Y., Tang, S., Lei, Y., Song, W., Wang, S., Zhang, M.: DisenHAN: disentangled heterogeneous graph attention network for recommendation. In: Proceedings of the International Conference on Information and Knowledge Management, pp. 1605–1614, Virtual, Online, Ireland (2020)
27. Wang, Z., Zhang, J., Feng, J., Chen, Z.: Knowledge graph embedding by translating on hyperplanes. In: Proceedings of the National Conference on Artificial Intelligence, vol. 2, pp. 1112–1119, Quebec City, QC, Canada (2014)
28. Xie, Z., Zhou, G., Liu, J., Huang, J.X.: ReInceptionE: relation-aware inception network with joint local-global structural information for knowledge graph embedding. In: Proceedings of the Annual Meeting of the Association for Computational Linguistics, pp. 5929–5939, Virtual, Online, United states (2020)

29. Yang, B., Mitchell, T.: Leveraging knowledge bases in LSTMs for improving machine reading. In: Proceedings of the 55th Annual Meeting of the Association for Computational Linguistics, vol. 1, pp. 1436–1446, Vancouver, BC, Canada (2017)
30. Zhang, Z., Cai, J., Zhang, Y., Wang, J.: Learning hierarchy-aware knowledge graph embeddings for link prediction. In: Proceedings of the 34th AAAI Conference on Artificial Intelligence, pp. 3065–3072, New York, NY, United states (2020)

KGESS - A Knowledge Graph Embedding Method Based on Semantics and Structure

Xunhan Chen, Zhiyong Ma, Zhenghong Xiao, Qi Xia, and Shaopeng Liu[✉]

School of Computer Science, Guangdong Polytechnic Normal University,
Guangzhou, Guangdong, China
149265005@qq.com

Abstract. To achieve a better performance in the downstream task of knowledge graph (KG), a good representation of KG is necessary. Sensing from the topological structure of the graph, most conventional methods tend to ignore the semantic features of nodes, which is significant for describing the entity in KG. In this paper, we propose a novel Knowledge Graph Embedding method based on Semantics and Structure (KGESS), which learned the representation of KG from both topological facts and semantic information. It leverages Chinese BERT to obtain semantic features of the entity first. Then it further enhances these features via a neural module, namely Semantic Feature Extractor. To evaluate the performance of KGESS, we utilize an additional linear module to execute the link prediction task. Experimental results demonstrate that KGESS achieves a superior Hit@k score than conventional methods, indicating the effectiveness of the idea of enhancing structure with semantics in the representation task of KG.

Keywords: Knowledge graph embedding · Semantic information · Graph · Pre-training task · Link prediction

1 Introduction

In knowledge representation, Knowledge Graph (KG) is a kind of knowledge base, where the data is integrated through a graph-structured data model or topology. KG commonly used for storing entities that are interconnected with each other, it plays an important role in various kinds of AI tasks, such as link prediction and relation extraction. Proofed by the researches in the last decade, a high-quality representation method can efficiently represent KG and support its downstream task [1,3,9,21]. In this case, Knowledge Graph Embedding (KGE) is generally set as this role. For capturing the hidden information within KG, KGE aims to use low-dimensional and continuous embeddings to represent entities while preserving their semantic meanings.

X. Chen and Z. Ma—Co-author

G. Memmi et al. (Eds.): KSEM 2022, LNAI 13368, pp. 295–308, 2022.
https://doi.org/10.1007/978-3-031-10983-6_23

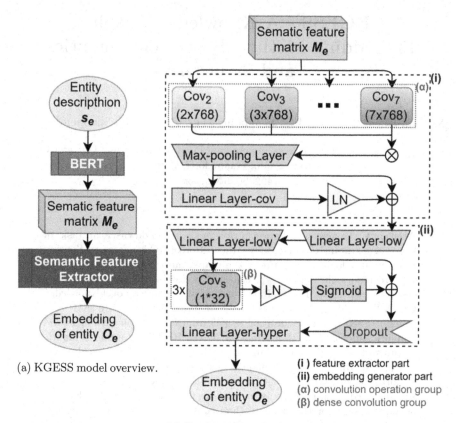

(a) KGESS model overview.

(i) feature extractor part
(ii) embedding generator part
(α) convolution operation group
(β) dense convolution group

(b) Semantic Feature Extractor module architecture.

Fig. 1. (Left) KGESS model overview. (Right) Semantic Feature Extractor module architecture.

Recently, there are lots of great KGE methods being proposed, such as TransE [1], TransH [21], TransR [9], and TransD [7]. These methods are generally implemented by considering the similarity of entities as well as the structure of KG. Although these methods have achieved good performance on several tasks, we found that these methods deeply rely on the structure of graph while ignoring the semantics of entity, which is a significant feature of KG. Therefore, we assume that the semantics of entity, such as the textual description of entity in KG, is a powerful assistance to the representation task.

With the foundation of this assumption, we propose a novel knowledge graph embedding method based on structure and semantics (KGESS) for better KG representation learning. Specifically, KGESS applies a pre-training language model - BERT and a neural module - Semantic Feature Extractor to capture the semantic information within each entity, shown in Fig. 1(a). The key points of KGESS are as follows:

1) We transform task from graph-level to node-level to obtain the entity semantics, which greatly utilizes the semantic information of KG.
2) We discover the interaction of words and extract the local n-gram feature of
entity semantics, which greatly enhance the semantic representation of KG.

Combine with the downstream task - link prediction, we train KGESS and
conduct a comparison of Hit@k on a real dataset about medicine order. Compared to methods only built upon the structure of KG, KGESS achieve a better
performance in the score of Hit@k, which demonstrates the effectiveness of our
idea and the assumption that semantic information is also quite important as
the structure to represent KG. To sum up, the contributions of this work can be
described as follows:

1) Proposing a novel method for knowledge graph embedding based on both
semantics and structure
2) Proposing a neural module for link prediction based on knowledge graph
embedding
3) Our method obtains an ideal performance in terms of Hit@k, compared with
Trans method

The rest of this document is structured as below. In Sect. 2 we review related
work and Sect. 3 introduces KGESS in detail. Section 4 presents empirical experiments, the evaluation results, and analyses. Finally, we conclude the article and
outline future work in Sect. 5. The dataset, along with associated codes, are
accessible at https://gitee.com/xiaqixiaqi/kgess

2 Related Work

2.1 Knowledge Graph Embedding

In KGE field, existing translation-based learning methods attempt to learn entity
embedding from the graph structure between entities directly. TransE [1] considers the relation as a transformation of the head entity towards tail entity. It
is appropriate for 1-to-1 relations, however, there are issues with 1-to-N, N-to-
1, and N-to-N relations. By generating the relation-specific entity embeddings
with mathematical operations, TransH [21] and TransR [9] make it possible for
an entity to have various representations for various relations which the entity it
interacts with, where the former uses hyperplane projection and the latter uses
space projection. TransD [7] enables compute a dynamic mapping and reduce the
dimensional complexity, using two vectors for each entity-relation pair without
projection matrix. Although these methods which learn embeddings from the
graph structure perform well, Wang and Li [22] observe that by directed learning the embeddings from the graph structure, the performance is constrained
due to the sparsity of KG, which is frequent in domain-specific and non-English
cases.

Since the textual information is also a useful part of KG, some researchers
attempt to combine it to improve the representation learning of KG. Gao et al.

[5] propose TransV which simplify relations in a semantic aspect. Lv et al. [10] propose TransC that encodes concepts as spheres and instances as vectors. By using additional unsupervised text corpora, Socher et al. [3] Propose a neural tensor network method, considering the sharing of similar names of entities, to represent entities as word vectors average. Ouyang et al. [12] propose ETRL that can improve triple representations via topic model. Wang et al. [20] propose a method that can embed entities and words jointly into a continuous vector space, utilizing entity names or Wikipedia anchors information. Considering that entity names are usually short and ambiguous, several methods have been proposed to use entity descriptions to further improve performance. Xie et al. [23] propose a knowledge representation learning method embodied by description, which enable to represent entity embedding by modeling both the corresponding fact triples and descriptions. Wang and Li [22] propose a text-enhanced knowledge embedding method TEKE, which can learn different embeddings of relations based on different triples, by combining information such as co-occurrences of entities in corresponding corpus. These methods above can solve the semantic diversity and ambiguous problems of different triples containing entities and relations, however, they are not good at exploiting more rich information in free text data such as syntactics. **Contrary to these methods, we attempt to obtain the semantic information of each entity through a strong pre-trained language model.**

2.2 Pre-trained Language Model

Over the last decade, pre-trained language representation methods have become increasingly popular, with two classes: feature-based methods and fine-tuning methods. As classic word embedding methods, Word2Vec [11] and Glove [13] apply feature-based methods for learning word embeddings, considering words contexts independently, therefore they cannot handle word ambiguity problems. To solve the word ambiguity issues, ELMo [14] learns words representations from context, via a deep bidirectional language model. On the other hand, fine-tuning methods like GPT [16] and BERT [4] utilize pre-trained model and parameters, i.e., data experiences, in the initial phase for various tasks where the pre-trained model can extract rich semantics from free text. In KGE field, the researches of pre-trained language models have also been conducting currently. Regarding KG as the collection of paths between entities, where the paths are represented as random walks of KG, Wang, Kulkarni, and Wang [19] learn context embeddings based on Bi-Directional LSTMs and use these embeddings as the initializations of various KGE models. Zhang et al. [26] enhanc language representation by replenishing informative entities into KG. Bosselut et al. [2] adopt large-scale transformer language models to generate tail phrase tokens by existing seed phrases and relations, in a common senses knowledge base which has constraints on a schema in contrast to normal triples in KG. **In our work, we take the original Chinese BERT as one part of our proposed model KGESS, used for firstly capturing the semantics of entity from entity descriptions in a free text corpus.**

3   Method

A knowledge graph KG is a directed graph where each node is entity and each edge is relation between two objects the edge connected with. Each edge of the triple form (head entity, relation, tail entity) indicates that there exists a relation between head entity and tail entity, and can be formally represented as (h, r, t), where $h, t \in E$ are entities and $r \in R$ is relation. E and R denote the sets of entities and relations respectively. The description of each entity is a continuous and free text sequence, denoted as s_e (for entity $e \in E$).

For conducting KGE, we construct KGESS Model which is shown in Fig. 1. The model construction refers ideas of processing medical data [6] and the structure of other available models [8,15]. KGESS is able to obtain the embedding of entity, i.e., O_e of entity $e \in E$, by text description s_e.

Due to the fact that the semantic feature of entity contributes to the downstream task such as link prediction, we adopt BERT and design a Semantic Feature Extractor, as two main parts of KGESS, to extract semantic feature and obtains embedding of entity. As shown in Fig. 1(a), the BERT first transforms the text description sequence of entity denoted as s_e, to semantic feature matrix denoted as M_e and sends it to the following Semantic Feature Extractor. Secondly, the Semantic Feature Extractor obtain the embedding of entity O_e by a series of operations, such as convolution, residual connection, and normalization. The set of embeddings of all entities, as the embedding of the KG, can be used to further conduct a variety of downstream tasks in KGE fields.

As a bidirectional encoder representation Transformer, the BERT in KGESS - Chinese BERT is based on the initial implementation described by Devlin et al.. Due to the popularity of BERT and our implementation is virtually identical to the original, we refer readers to the source [4] for the detailed background description of the model architecture.

To extract the semantic feature and generate the embedding of entity, the designed Semantic Feature Extractor is composed of 2 main parts: **(i)** and **(ii) embedding generator part**. The details of the Semantic Feature Extractor are shown in Fig. 1(b).

(i) feature extractor part: Inspired by the idea of mining the local semantics within different phrases by convolution [4,18], we build a convolution operation group (α) which is composed of 6 convolutional operators with different kernel sizes $(q, 768)$, where $q \in \{2, 3, 4, 5, 6, 7\}$. It aims to discover the interaction of several words and extract the local n-gram features of entity description. For example, the kernel with different sizes can extract the feature within both the Chinese bigram phrases and trigram phrases, where bigram phrases and trigram phrases occur commonly in Chinese free corpus. This convolution operation group (α) extracts the feature of entity, denoted as C_q, by performing operations on the corresponding semantic feature matrix M_e, as shown in Eq. (1).

$$C_q = Cov_q(M_e), \quad q \in \{2, 3, 4, 5, 6, 7\} \tag{1}$$

For the convenience of subsequent operations, the results of the convolution operation group (α) are concatenated together to one and sent to the following max-pooling layer which produces an output, denoted as O_{cov}, as shown in Eq. (2).

$$O_{cov} = MaxPool([C_2; C_3; \cdots; C_7])$$ (2)

In order to prevent the problems of gradient vanishing and over-fitting, we designed a residual connection to update O_{cov}, where the residual connection includes a linear layer and a layer normalization, followed by an addition, as shown in Eq. (3).

$$O_{cov} := O_{cov} + LN(w_{cov} * O_{cov} + b_{cov})$$ (3)

(ii) embedding generator part: To obtain the embedding O_e of entity and reduce complexity, we utilize two separated linear layers to compress the feature to one with a lower dimension, denoted as O_{low}, as shown in Eq. (4).

$$O_{low} = w'_{low} * (w_{low} * O_{cov} + b_{low}) + b'_{low}$$ (4)

Here, we use residual connection once again, which contains dense convolution group (β) - a stack of 3 different convolution operators with identical kernel sizes, layer normalization, sigmoid function, and follows by an addition. The dense convolution group (β) inside aims to better dig out the internal hidden semantics of description, while the sigmoid function is designed to strengthen the model ability of nonlinear representation. The updated O_{low} is shown in Eq. (5).

$$O_{low} := O_{low} + \sigma(LN(Cov_{s3}(Cov_{s2}(Cov_{s1}(O_{low})))))$$ (5)

For the reason of avoiding over-fitting, we use dropout. In the last step, the linear layer further mines the semantics, by mapping the representation O_{low} to an entity embedding O_e in a hyperplane space, as shown in Eq. (6).

$$O_e = w_{hp} * O_{low} + b_{hp}$$ (6)

For different downstream tasks, the set of embeddings O_es of all entities $e \in E$ in KG, i.e., the embedding of KG, needs to be operated by different modules.

To demonstrate the effectiveness of the convolution operation group (α) and the dense convolution group (β), we conduct an ablation experiment as well, ablating two convolution groups respectively in KGESS. Specifically, the convolution operation group (α) with the concatenation and the max-polling layer are replaced by two simple linear layers, i.e., the Eq. (1) and Eq. (2) are replaced by Eq. (7).

$$O_{cov} = w_{c2} * (w_{c1} * M_e + b_{c1}) + b_{c2}$$ (7)

Additionally, the dense convolution group (β) with the layer normalization and sigmoid function are substituted by a simple linear layer, i.e., the Eq. (5) is substituted by Eq. (8).

$$O_{low} := O_{low} + w_{den} * O_{low} + b_{den}$$ (8)

Both modified KGESS namely $KGESS^{\alpha}_{w/o}$ and $KGESS^{\beta}_{w/o}$ respectively, are trained with the whole training set and tested with 20% amount of the test set.

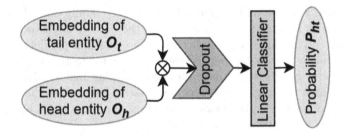

Fig. 2. Link prediction module architecture.

We test the original complete KGESS with the test set(20%) as well. To control variables, the three test sets(20%) are totally the same for these three KGESS.

(iii) **Link Prediction Module** We use the link prediction task to conduct experiments and get evaluations, so we designed the corresponding module, shown in Fig. 2. In this module, the embeddings of head entity h and tail entity t, denoted as O_h and O_t, will be activated by the sigmoid function and concatenated to one feature vector. This feature concatenation enables the KGESS to observe the semantic cross feature of entity. For avoiding over-fitting, we utilize dropout. Then the linear classifier estimates the probability P_{ht} of the missing relation between entities by this feature vector, as shown in Eq. (9).

$$P_{ht} = w_{lc} * ([\sigma(O_h); \sigma(O_t)]) + b_{lc} \tag{9}$$

The trainable parameters in all linear layers are trained with the binary cross entropy (BCE) criterion, shown in Eq. (10), where $|T|$ denotes the number of tail entities t (products), the $\hat{p}_i$ denotes if there is a shopping relation between the user and the i-th product, and the p_i denotes the probability of recommending the i-th product to the user. What should be noticed that this criterion is used for training KGESS as well as Trans models in the experiment.

$$loss = -\frac{1}{|T|} \sum_{i=1}^{|T|} p_i * \log \hat{p}_i + (1 - p_i) * \log(1 - \hat{p}_i) \tag{10}$$

4 Experiment and Analysis

4.1 Dataset Description and Link Prediction Task

Our dataset comes from a real medicine order database. After data preprocessing, we convert the dataset into a KG where entities E correspond to users and goods denoted as h and t, entity textual descriptions correspond to the details of users and goods denoted as s_h and s_t, edges correspond to relations between users and goods denoted as R. In the dataset, the entity descriptions are Chinese free text and the user descriptions are the descriptions of goods that the user had purchased. What should be noticed is that there is only one relation - shopping relations in R. The detailed statistics of the dataset are shown in Table 1. The task we conducted is link prediction, where the link prediction task is to predict the tail entity t given $(h, r, ?)$ where ? refers to the missing element, i.e., to recommend a good given a user who has shopping history. The results are evaluated using a ranking - goods recommendation list, rather than just giving the best answer. Following the work of Bordes et al., Wang et al., and Lin et al., we conduct our experiments using the dataset.

Table 1. Statistics of the dataset.

R	E	h or s_h	t or s_t	(h, r, t) (Train/Valid/Test)		
1	4676	1441	3235	2206	282	264

4.2   Evaluation Protocol

Evaluations of our model and traditional models (transE, transH, transR, and transD) [1,7,9,21] are presented, aiming to show the performance difference between our model - based on semantics and structure both and traditional ones - based on structure only. Following previous works like Yang et al. and Trouillon et al. [17,24], we report 3 indicators: Hits@1, Hits@3, and Hits@10 for evaluations, which are used to evaluate the performance of recommendation systems frequently, where Hits@K denotes the ratio of the test triples that have been ranked among the top k triples. For our model evaluation, the results are evaluated using a ranking produced by the scoring function $f(s_h, s_t)$, i.e., P_{ht} in our method shown in Eq. (9). In each ranking we sort the triples (h, r, t) predicted by corresponding given $(s_h, ?)$ in descending probability P_{ht} order.

To clarify it we present the predicted triples ranking (products recommendation list) of a head entity h (user) as a instance, where the user ID is 3238 and description s_h is "[999]感冒灵颗粒（10g*9袋）—999—风热感冒清热解毒—精选产品+[白云山]小柴胡颗粒（10克×10袋）—白云山—解表散热，疏肝和胃。用于寒热往来，胸胁苦满，心烦喜吐，口苦咽干。—精选产品", shown in Table 2. After getting all user predicted triples rankings, we calculate Hits@1, Hits@3, and Hits@10. The formula of Hit@k is shown in Eq. (8) and a higher Hits@k is better, where $\mathbb{I}[e \leq k]$ denotes the number of correct entities (user purchased products) that are in the predicted top-k entities (recommended top-k products) in the ranking.

$$Hit@k = \frac{1}{|E|} \sum_{e \in E} \mathbb{I}[e \leq k] \tag{11}$$

Table 2. Instance of one predicted triples ranking.

(h, r, t)	h description (s_h)	t description (s_t)	P_{ht}
(3238,0,38)	[999]感冒灵颗粒 (10g*9...	[999]感冒灵颗粒 (10g*9...	0.981
(3238,0,663)	[999]感冒灵颗粒 (10g*9...	[白云山]小柴胡颗粒—白云...	0.972
(3238,0,366)	[999]感冒灵颗粒 (10g*9...	[星群]夏桑菊颗粒无糖(10袋...	0.873
...			
(3238,0,3006)	[999]感冒灵颗粒 (10g*9...	[好邦手]万痛筋骨贴(8cm*...	0.005

This is the predicted triples ranking produced by the scoring function $f(s_h, s_t)$ by given $(s_h, ?)$ in descending probability P_{ht} order. The three integers in (h, r, t) are number IDs of entities and relation, where $r = 0$ is ID of shopping relation.

In the sample shown in Table 2. The description s_h shows that the user h with ID 3238 purchased two goods, "[999]感冒灵颗粒" and "[白云山]小柴胡颗粒", which are two kinds of best-selling cold medicine in China. At the same time, we can see the corresponding goods of descriptions in predicted rankings (products recommendation list), shown in the third column of the Table 2, the top two of them are ones that the user had purchased, and the third one "[星群]夏桑菊颗粒" is also a best-selling cold medicine, while the last one "[好邦手]万痛筋骨贴" is a kind of drug sticker for bone damage, which demonstrated intuitively that the correctness of the prediction.

4.3 Implementation Details

The length of sequence s_e shown in Eq. (1) is not limited. Following the work in [4], the shape of the BERT output matrix M_e shown in Eq. (2) is set as default (512×768). The kernel sizes of 6 convolution operators shown in Eq. (3) are set as $(q, 768)$ separately, where $q \in \{2, 3, 4, 5, 6, 7\}$. The dimension of O_{cov}, as shown in Eq. (3), output by max-pooling layer, is set as 192. As shown in Eq. (6), the output dimension of the first linear layer is set to 64, while that of the second linear layer is set to 32. In the residual connection shown in Eq. (7), the kernel sizes of the 3 convolution operators are all set as (1×32). Other components are not detailed since their dimensions of input and output are the same. The detailed settings of necessary components parameter are shown in Table 3. In addition, in the experiment, to control variables, the dimensions in Trans models are all set to 32, which are the same ones as KGESS'. We separately train several KGESS on three different sizes (10%, 50%, 100%) of the training set, to observe the correlation between dataset amount and model's performance.

Table 3. The hyper-parameters of components in KGESS.

Name	Eq.	Input dim	Output dim
BERT			(512×768)
6 convolution operators & max-pooling layer	(1) (2)	(512×768)	(1×192)
First linear layer	(4)	(1×192)	(1×64)
Second linear layer	(4)	(1×64)	(1×32)
First linear layer	(7)	(512×768)	(512×1)
Second linear layer	(7)	(512×1)	(32×1)

4.4 Result Analysis

The results are presented in Table 4. We observe that **1) KGESS model far outperforms Trans models in terms of Hit@k metrics.** One reason may be that KGESS is essentially a neural embedding, combined with pre-trained BERT, utilizing all KG edges during training, i.e., it captures not only the semantic features of entities but also the geometric features of relations. However, the graph embeddings in Trans models use only structural features - id features. Hence, in comparison to Trans models, the ability of KGESS to capture multifaceted features makes KGESS itself have better performance.

Analyzing the evaluation results of the Trans methods, we discover an interesting point: in terms of Hit@1, TransE, TransD, and TransH scores are almost the same, while TransR performs badly with a score of 0. One reason is that TransR specifically considers multi-faceted entities, but there is only one entity relationship in the experimental dataset. Another reason is that Hit@1 itself is a conceptually difficult indicator to obtain high scores.

Table 4. Performance of models on the dataset.

Method	Hit@1	Hit@3	Hit@10
TransE [1]	0.003788	0.015152	0.181818
TransH [21]	0.003788	0.030303	0.121212
TransD [7]	0.003788	0.049242	0.159091
TransR [9]	0.000000	0.022727	0.123106
KGESS (10% training set)	0.140845	0.151929	0.154930
KGESS (50% training set)	0.053805	0.195737	0.284637
KGESS	**0.063380**	**0.225352**	**0.323944**

The Trans models are trained with the full training set (100%) while the KGESS are trained with three different amounts (10%, 50%, 100%) of the training set. The KGESS performance is highlighted in bold.

The results of the evaluation of KGESS trained on training sets of different sizes(10%, 50%, 100%) are presented in the third block of the Table. We find that the scores of KGESS have nearly reached 0.15 in terms of Hit@k when the amount of training data is relatively scarce (10%). Among them, Hit@1 and Hit@3 of KGESS are even far higher than ones of Trans models trained on the complete training data, and Hit@10 is also similar to Trans models', which demonstrates that **2) KGESS also has good competitiveness in the case of a small amount of data, i.e., KGESS has little dependence on data and high robustness.** Generally speaking, the abilities of general deep learning models are strongly affected by the amount of training data. Compared with general deep learning models, such as Trans models, KGESS has the higher generalization ability and can be applied to a wider range of occasions, the real-world application scenarios where it is difficult to collect ordinary data, such as Pharmaceutical e-commerce platform recommendation systems. Furthermore, we observe that the Hit@3 and Hit@10 gradually increase with the increasing amount of data, which suggests that **3) the performance of KGESS has the potential to improve under normal circumstances.** Finally, we find that with the increase of data volume, KGESS' Hit@1 evaluation has declined. This may be due to the fact that Hit@1 is conceptually difficult to score high, and the requirement for accurate and single prediction is becoming more and more difficult in the case of more and more data.

Table 5. Results of the ablation experiment.

Model	Hit@1	Hit@3	Hit@10	Sum
KGESS	0.066667	0.177778	0.333333	0.577778
KGESS$^{\alpha}_{w/o}$	0.066667	0.177778	0.311111	0.555556
KGESS$^{\beta}_{w/o}$	0.088889	0.133333	0.333333	0.555556

KGESS and ablated KGESS (KGESS$^{\alpha}_{w/o}$ and KGESS$^{\beta}_{w/o}$) are tested with totally the same 20% amount of test sets. The Sum in the table is the sum of the Hit@1, Hit@3, and Hit@10.

In the ablation experiment, we observe that testing with the totally same test set that the complete KGESS also test with, the KGESS score highest in terms of the sum of Hit@k, which demonstrates the effectiveness of both convolution groups. Specifically, we observe that KGESS$^{\alpha}_{w/o}$ without the convolution operation group score lower in terms of Hit@10 and KGESS$^{\beta}_{w/o}$ without the dense convolution group score lower in terms of Hit@3. Additionally, we also observe that KGESS$^{\beta}_{w/o}$ score higher a bit in terms of Hit@1, which demonstrates that although the precision is improved, the recall is reduced, i.e., the dense convolution group enables to improve the model recall performance but the precision.

5   Conclusion and Future Work

In this paper, we propose a novel knowledge graph embedding method named KGESS. KGESS methods can better enhance representation by utilizing the semantics and structure of graph. In contrast with translation-based learning methods, it achieves good results in link prediction on dataset about medicine, which demonstrated that the semantics of knowledge graphs are strongly useful and greatly helpful for representation.

In our future work, we will apply KGESS to more downstream tasks, not only link prediction task within a given KG, but also those within graphs in broader domains. The problems of interaction between model performance and data amount are meaningful for us as well to explore.

Acknowledgements. This work was supported in part by the projects of the National Natural Science Foundation of China (61702119, 62006049), the Natural Science Foundation of Guangdong Province (2016A010101029, 2018A0303130055, 2019A1515012048), Science and Technology Program of Guangzhou (201802010029), and the Science and Technology Program of Guangzhou, China under Grant (201804010236).

References

1. Bordes, A., Usunier, N., Garcia-Duran, A., Weston, J., Yakhnenko, O.: Translating embeddings for modeling multi-relational data. Adv. Neural Inf. Process. Syst. **26** (2013)

2. Bosselut, A., Rashkin, H., Sap, M., Malaviya, C., Celikyilmaz, A., Choi, Y.: COMET: commonsense transformers for automatic knowledge graph construction. In: Proceedings of the 57th Annual Meeting of the Association for Computational Linguistics, pp. 4762–4779. Association for Computational Linguistics, Florence, Italy, July 2019. https://doi.org/10.18653/v1/P19-1470, https://aclanthology.org/P19-1470

3. Danqi, C., Richard, S., et al.: Learning new facts from knowledge bases with neural tensor networks and semantic word vectors. Comput. Sci. **1**, 392–399 (2013)

4. Devlin, J., Chang, M.W., Lee, K., Toutanova, K.: BERT: pre-training of deep bidirectional transformers for language understanding. In: Proceedings of the 2019 Conference of the North American Chapter of the Association for Computational Linguistics: Human Language Technologies, vol. 1 (Long and Short Papers), pp. 4171–4186. Association for Computational Linguistics, Minneapolis, Minnesota, June 2019. https://doi.org/10.18653/v1/N19-1423, https://aclanthology.org/N19-1423

5. Gao, Tianyu, Zhang, Yuanming, Li, Mengni, Lu, Jiawei, Cheng, Zhenbo, Xiao, Gang: Representation learning of knowledge graph with semantic vectors. In: Qiu, Han, Zhang, Cheng, Fei, Zongming, Qiu, Meikang, Kung, Sun-Yuan. (eds.) KSEM 2021. LNCS (LNAI), vol. 12816, pp. 16–29. Springer, Cham (2021). https://doi.org/10.1007/978-3-030-82147-0_2

6. Hu, F., Lakdawala, S., Hao, Q., Qiu, M.: Low-power, intelligent sensor hardware interface for medical data preprocessing. IEEE Trans. Inf Technol. Biomed. **13**(4), 656–663 (2009)

7. Ji, G., He, S., Xu, L., Liu, K., Zhao, J.: Knowledge graph embedding via dynamic mapping matrix. In: Proceedings of the 53rd Annual Meeting of the Association for Computational Linguistics and the 7th International Joint Conference on Natural Language Processing (vol. 1: Long Papers), pp. 687–696 (2015)
8. Li, Y., Song, Y., Jia, L., Gao, S., Li, Q., Qiu, M.: Intelligent fault diagnosis by fusing domain adversarial training and maximum mean discrepancy via ensemble learning. IEEE Trans. Industr. Inf. **17**(4), 2833–2841 (2020)
9. Lin, Y., Liu, Z., Sun, M., Liu, Y., Zhu, X.: Learning entity and relation embeddings for knowledge graph completion. In: Twenty-Ninth AAAI Conference on Artificial Intelligence (2015)
10. Lv, X., Hou, L., Li, J., Liu, Z.: Differentiating concepts and instances for knowledge graph embedding. In: Proceedings of the 2018 Conference on Empirical Methods in Natural Language Processing, pp. 1971–1979. Association for Computational Linguistics, Brussels, Belgium (October–November 2018). https://doi.org/10.18653/v1/D18-1222, https://aclanthology.org/D18-1222
11. Mikolov, T., Chen, K., Corrado, G., Dean, J.: Efficient estimation of word representations in vector space. arXiv preprint arXiv:1301.3781 (2013)
12. Ouyang, X., Yang, Y., He, L., Chen, Q., Zhang, J.: Representation learning with entity topics for knowledge graphs. In: International Conference on Knowledge Science, Engineering and Management, pp. 534–542. Springer (2017). https://doi.org/10.1007/978-3-319-63558-3_45
13. Pennington, J., Socher, R., Manning, C.D.: GloVe: global vectors for word representation. In: Proceedings of the 2014 Conference on Empirical Methods in Natural Language Processing (EMNLP), pp. 1532–1543 (2014)
14. Peters, M.E., et al.: Deep contextualized word representations. In: Proceedings of the 2018 Conference of the North American Chapter of the Association for Computational Linguistics: Human Language Technologies, vol. 1 (Long Papers), pp. 2227–2237. Association for Computational Linguistics, New Orleans, Louisiana, June 2018. https://doi.org/10.18653/v1/N18-1202, https://aclanthology.org/N18-1202
15. Qiu, H., Zheng, Q., Msahli, M., Memmi, G., Qiu, M., Lu, J.: Topological graph convolutional network-based urban traffic flow and density prediction. IEEE Trans. Intell. Transp. Syst. **22**(7), 4560–4569 (2020)
16. Radford, A., Narasimhan, K., Salimans, T., Sutskever, I.: Improving language understanding by generative pre-training (2018)
17. Trouillon, T., Welbl, J., Riedel, S., Gaussier, É., Bouchard, G.: Complex embeddings for simple link prediction. In: International Conference on Machine Learning, pp. 2071–2080. PMLR (2016)
18. Wang, D., Liu, P., Zheng, Y., Qiu, X., Huang, X.: Heterogeneous graph neural networks for extractive document summarization. arXiv preprint arXiv:2004.12393 (2020)
19. Wang, H., Kulkarni, V., Wang, W.Y.: DOLORES: deep contextualized knowledge graph embeddings. CoRR abs/1811.00147 (2018). http://arxiv.org/abs/1811.00147
20. Wang, Z., Zhang, J., Feng, J., Chen, Z.: Knowledge graph and text jointly embedding. In: Proceedings of the 2014 Conference on Empirical Methods in Natural Language Processing (EMNLP), pp. 1591–1601 (2014)
21. Wang, Z., Zhang, J., Feng, J., Chen, Z.: Knowledge graph embedding by translating on hyperplanes. In: Proceedings of the AAAI Conference on Artificial Intelligence, vol. 28 (2014)

22. Wang, Z., Li, J., Liu, Z., Tang, J.: Text-enhanced representation learning for knowledge graph. In: Proceedings of International Joint Conference on Artificial Intelligent (IJCAI), pp. 4–17 (2016)
23. Xie, R., Liu, Z., Luan, H., Sun, M.: Image-embodied knowledge representation learning. arXiv preprint arXiv:1609.07028 (2016)
24. Yang, B., Yih, W.T., He, X., Gao, J., Deng, L.: Embedding entities and relations for learning and inference in knowledge bases. arXiv preprint arXiv:1412.6575 (2014)
25. Yao, L., Mao, C., Luo, Y.: KG-BERT: BERT for knowledge graph completion. CoRR abs/1909.03193 (2019). http://arxiv.org/abs/1909.03193
26. Zhang, Z., Han, X., Liu, Z., Jiang, X., Sun, M., Liu, Q.: ERNIE: enhanced language representation with informative entities. arXiv preprint arXiv:1905.07129 (2019)

Knowledge Structure-Aware Graph-Attention Networks for Knowledge Tracing

Shun Mao[1], Jieyu Zhan[1], Jiawei Li[1], and Yuncheng Jiang[1,2(✉)]

[1] School of Computer Science, South China Normal University,
Guangzhou 510631, People's Republic of China
{shunm,lijiawei}@m.scnu.edu.cn, zhanjieyu@scnu.edu.cn
[2] School of Artificial Intelligence, South China Normal University, Foshan 528225,
People's Republic of China
ycjiang@scnu.edu.cn

Abstract. Knowledge Tracing (KT) aims to assess learners' learning states and predict their performance based on prior interactions. However, most existing KT models depend on knowledge concepts instead of specific exercises, leading to the fine-grained information at the exercise level has been ignored, which may weaken the prediction performance of the models. We herein present Knowledge Structure-aware Graph-Attention Networks (KSGAN) for predicting learners' performance, which uses improved Graph Attention Networks (GATs) to acquire effective exercise representations by taking full advantage of the knowledge structure between knowledge concepts and exercises. Additionally, a representation optimization is devised and integrated into the loss function to alleviate the sparsity of educational data and further improve the prediction performance. Finally, empirical validations on three open benchmark datasets show that our model well outperforms some state-of-the-art models in recent years. Remarkably, our model demonstrates superior prediction performance at exercise level compared to these previous models, without the additional information (e.g., exercise content, temporal information).

Keywords: Knowledge tracing · Exercise recommendation · Intelligent tutoring systems · Graph attention networks

1 Introduction

With the ongoing development of learning technologies in recent years, learners anticipate that intelligent tutoring systems can recommend beneficial learning paths and resources, where Knowledge Tracing (KT) is a core segment in this process. Specifically, the primary goal of KT is to predict learners' performance in the future by using historical learning interactions. To improve the performance in prediction, many KT models have been proposed, including Bayesian

© The Author(s), under exclusive license to Springer Nature Switzerland AG 2022
G. Memmi et al. (Eds.): KSEM 2022, LNAI 13368, pp. 309–321, 2022.
https://doi.org/10.1007/978-3-031-10983-6_24

Knowledge Tracing (BKT) [1] and Deep Knowledge Tracing [2], which are representative models based on traditional methods and deep learning methods, respectively. This paper mainly focuses on KT models based on deep learning methods, which have significantly advanced in the KT field compared with traditional methods in recent years.

Although most existing KT models can well predict learners' performance, these existing models have a notable drawback, that is, none of them consider the information at the fine-grained level. Specifically, these models only take related knowledge concepts into consideration, but the information on exercise level is ignored. The primary reason for this choice is that exercise is terribly sparse compared with knowledge concept in education data, which leads to exercise representations not being effectively trained in the model (see Sect. 4.4 for detailed analysis). Therefore, several methods were proposed to further explore the relation among exercises to tackle this issue. For example, the exercise content is used as a supplement to compute semantic similarity between exercises [3–5]. However, the extra computing resources are used for text processing, which is expensive for KT. To this end, we have to figure out an exercise-level KT model that is both effective and inexpensive.

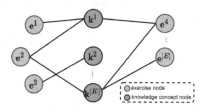

Fig. 1. The knowledge structure composed of exercises and knowledge concepts.

As discussed above, there is a sparsity issue for exercise data, so purely using exercise data leads to overfitting in the KT field. From the viewpoint of data structure, there is a potential knowledge structure between exercises and knowledge concepts, which can also be regarded as the graph structure, shown in Fig. 1. There are two types of nodes in the figure, namely exercise nodes and knowledge concept nodes, wherein an exercise node may cover multiple knowledge concepts, and a knowledge concept is covered by several exercises. It is known that an exercise feature should be closely related to the corresponding knowledge concept feature. Accordingly, we deem it advantageous to fully utilize this knowledge structure to tackle data sparsity issues.

To this end, we propose innovative Knowledge Structure-aware Graph-Attention Networks (KSGAN) for predicting learners' performance. Specifically, inspired by the significant development of Graph neural networks [6], we first present a graph attention layer that aims at acquiring the effective exercise representations from the knowledge structure. Remarkably, our graph attention layer differs from Graph Attention Networks (GATs) [7] because vanilla GATs only aggregates one type of node, while exercise nodes and knowledge concept nodes are both processed in our layer. Moreover, we also develop an integration function within this layer to obtain suitable representations for exercises. Then, we argue that optimizing the exercise representations is also beneficial to further alleviate the sparsity issue. Thus, according to the knowledge structure, we modify the general loss function in the KT task to contain the optimization based on exercise representations and prediction. Finally, we evaluate the proposed KSGAN on several open benchmark datasets, and the experiment results demonstrate that our model outperforms several latest works in prediction performance.

2   Related Work

With the rapid development of deep learning in recent years, several researchers proposed applying deep learning methods to tackle KT issue. A pioneer research work is Deep Knowledge Tracing (DKT) [2] by utilizing a Recurrent Neural Network (RNN) to predict learners' performance. In addition, some basic KT models have been proposed [8–11]. Subsequently, several researchers took temporal information [12,13], prerequisite relation [14] and other additional information into the above models to further improve KT models. However, these works face the same issue that it is hard to greatly improve the prediction performance because ignoring the exercise information lacks certain flexibility and expressiveness.

In addition to these KT models at knowledge concept level, some researchers proposed to use exercise information to improve prediction. For example, several works took exercise content into consideration [3,4]. Nevertheless, there are two limitations in these KT models: high consumption of computing resources and the difficulty of acquiring exercise content. Moreover, the Attentive Knowledge Tracing (AKT) [10], HawkesKT [15] and Knowledge Tracing Machines (KTM) [16] not only used exercises to predict learners' performance but also introduced temporal information to improve prediction performance.

Although these KT models at the exercise level outperform the models at the knowledge concept level, the gap is still slight. Furthermore, we deem that part of the reason for this advantage is that these models introduce some additional information. Considering the above issues in the exercise-level KT model, our model only utilizes the knowledge structure to explore the exercise representations deeply, enabling further improving exercise-level prediction performance.

3   Methodology

3.1   Problem Definition

In KT task, all learning interactions of each learner can be formalized as $S = (s_1, s_2, ..., s_n)$, here the learning interaction denotes the learner's response to a particular exercise. Each learning interaction is defined as a tuple $s_t = (e^i_{t,l}, p_{t,l})$, where $e^i_{t,l}$ represents the exercise e^i was attempted by learner l at time step t, and $p_t \in \{1, 0\}$ (1 means correct and 0 stands for wrong) represents the correctness of the exercise e_t^i which learner attempted. To avoid over-parameterization, the learner index l is neglected in the following discussions. It is worth mentioning that the learner index l is added in Sect. 3.6 because the model calculates the loss for each batch of learners.

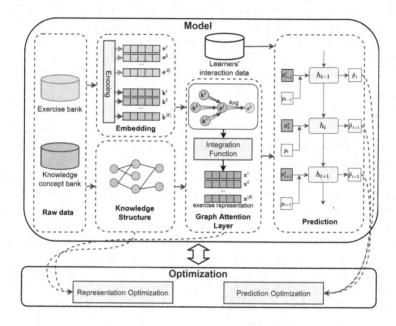

Fig. 2. The architecture of KSGAN.

3.2   Model Overview

As shown in Fig. 2, the KSGAN is divided into the Model and Optimization. In the Model part, we first take exercises and knowledge concepts to acquire embedding vectors. Then, the knowledge structure and embedding vectors are fed into the graph attention layer. Finally, the exercise representations are obtained from graph attention layer and used for predicting learners' performance. In the Optimization part, there are two optimization tasks, namely representation optimization and prediction optimization, which train our model to improve performance.

3.3   Embedding and Knowledge Structure

We first define the set of exercises and knowledge concepts as $\mathcal{E} = (e^1, e^2, ..., e^{|E|})$ and $\mathcal{K} = (k^1, k^2, ..., k^{|K|})$, where $|E|$ and $|K|$ respectively denote the number of exercises and knowledge concepts. Then, we deem that each exercise covers one or multiple knowledge concepts, and each knowledge concept was covered by one or multiple exercises. Accordingly, there is a knowledge structure between exercises and knowledge concepts, which can be summarized as an exercise-knowledge concept relation bipartite graph $\mathcal{G} = ((e^i, r_{(e^i, k^j)}, k^j) | e^i \in \mathcal{E}, k^j \in \mathcal{K})$, where $r_{(e^i,k^j)}$ denotes whether an exercise ^{i} is related to knowledge concept k^j. If exercise e^i covers knowledge concept k^j, $r_{e^i,k^j} = 1$; otherwise, $r_{e^i,k^j} = 0$.

With the above definitions, all knowledge concepts and exercises can be automatically trained as two embedding matrices $\mathbf{E}_{\mathcal{E}} \in \mathbb{R}^{|E| \times d}$ and $\mathbf{E}_{\mathcal{K}} \in \mathbb{R}^{|K| \times d}$ respectively, where d is the number of dimensions. Each row of $\mathbf{E}_{\mathcal{E}}$ or $\mathbf{E}_{\mathcal{K}}$ represents the embedding of a particular exercise or knowledge concept. It means that the i-th row vectors in $\mathbf{E}_{\mathcal{E}}$ and $\mathbf{E}_{\mathcal{K}}$ denote the embedding of e^i and k^i, respectively. Actually, an exercise embedding should contain the information of knowledge concepts covered by this exercise, but it is hard to contain the knowledge concepts in exercise embedding through training directly. Thereby, the exercise-knowledge concept relation bipartite graph $\mathcal{G}$, exercise embeddings $\mathbf{E}_{\mathcal{E}}$ and knowledge concept embeddings $\mathbf{E}_{\mathcal{K}}$ are utilized to tackle this problem in the following process.

3.4 Graph Attention Layer

Inspired by GATs, we present a graph attention layer to obtain the exercise representations. There are two types of data in our task, $\mathbf{E}_{\mathcal{E}} = (\mathbf{e}^1, \mathbf{e}^2, ..., \mathbf{e}^{|E|})$ and $\mathbf{E}_{\mathcal{K}} = (\mathbf{k}^1, \mathbf{k}^2, ..., \mathbf{k}^{|K|})$. Hence, we modify the vanilla GATs model so that these two sets of node features will be aggregated into a new set of node features $\mathbf{X} = (\mathbf{x}^1, \mathbf{x}^2, ..., \mathbf{x}^{|E|})$ through this layer, where each row in $\mathbf{X}$ denotes a particular exercise representation.

In the exercise-knowledge concept relation bipartite graph $\mathcal{G}$, the first-order neighbors of exercise e^i are knowledge concepts that are covered by exercise e^i, such as k^j. Therefore, the model only aggregates the related knowledge concept features for the particular exercise through this graph structure information.

First, our model leverages each exercise embedding to attend on the embedding of all knowledge concepts $\mathbf{E}_{\mathcal{K}}$. As an initial step, the exercise embedding and knowledge concept embedding are concatenated after shared linear transformation, then perform attention computing on the concatenated vector:

$$\beta_{ij} = a\left[\mathbf{W}_1\mathbf{e}^i, \mathbf{W}_1\mathbf{k}^j\right], \tag{1}$$

where $[,]$ indicates the operation that concatenates two vectors, β_{ij} denotes the relevance weights between exercise embedding and knowledge concept embeddings, $\mathbf{W}_1 \in \mathbb{R}^{d \times d}$ and $a \in \mathbb{R}^{1 \times 2d}$ denote a weight matrix of linear transformation and attention computing, respectively.

Secondly, we apply an approach similar to GATs to obtain weight coefficients of knowledge concepts that are covered by a particular exercise. This process only computes weight coefficients α_{ij} for knowledge concept $k^j \in N_i$, where N_i is neighbor nodes (knowledge concept nodes) of exercise node e^i in the relation bipartite graph $\mathcal{G}$. The process of computing weight coefficients can be expressed as:

$$\alpha_{ij} = \frac{\exp(\text{LeakyReLU}(\beta_{ij}))}{\sum_{k^\kappa \in N_i} \exp(\text{LeakyReLU}(\beta_{i\kappa}))}, \tag{2}$$

where the negative input slope of LeakyReLU is set as 0.2 in our experiments.

And then, the weight coefficients are applied to compute a linear combination of related knowledge concept embeddings to serve as the summary vector of knowledge concepts for exercise node e^i. Similarly, as with the above conditions, only the neighbor nodes (knowledge concept nodes) of the exercise node e^i are aggregated in this process. Thus we introduce the summary vector $\mathbf{s}^i \in \mathbb{R}^d$ as follows:

$$\mathbf{s}^i = \sigma\left(\sum_{k^j \in N_i} \alpha_{ij} \mathbf{W}_2 \mathbf{k}^j\right), \tag{3}$$

where $\mathbf{W}_2 \in \mathbb{R}^{d \times d}$, and $\sigma(x)$ denotes Sigmoid activation function that can be formulated as: $\text{Sigmoid}(x) = \frac{1}{1+\exp(x)}$.

Finally, to obtain the suitable exercise representations, we introduce the Integration Function, which incorporates the exercise embedding and related summary vector of knowledge concepts to obtain effective exercise representation:

$$\mathbf{x}^i = \phi(\mathbf{s}^i, \mathbf{e}^i), \tag{4}$$

where $\mathbf{x}^i$ indicates the result of the integration function, the dimension is assumed as D because leveraging different Integration Function results in different dimensions, the details of the integration function are described in the next section. Here, we construct an exercise representation matrix $\mathbf{X} = (\mathbf{x}^1, \mathbf{x}^2, ..., \mathbf{x}^{|E|})$ through the above process for exercise nodes, where each row of $\mathbf{X}$ is a specific exercise representation.

Furthermore, to further focus valuable information from multiple vector subspaces, we adopt multi-head attention to obtain $\mathbf{X}$ for h times, respectively, followed by employing averaging of $\mathbf{X}$ from each head and proceeding to the next step.

To express the correctness of learners' performance on exercise e^i at time step t, we extend the $\mathbf{x}_t^i$ by incorporating a full zero vector $\mathbf{p}_t \in \{0\}^D$ with the exact dimensions as $\mathbf{x}_t^i$. Thus we introduce $\mathbf{y}_t^i \in \mathbb{R}^{2D}$ as follows:

$$\mathbf{y}_t^i = \begin{cases} \left[\mathbf{x}_t^i, \mathbf{p}_t\right], & \text{if } p_t = 1 \\[2mm] \left[\mathbf{p}_t, \mathbf{x}_t^i\right], & \text{if } p_t = 0. \end{cases} \tag{5}$$

Integration Function. Hence, the Integration Functions are introduced to explore the suitable exercise representations. We have tried the following four Integration Functions:

- *Concatenation:* $\phi(\mathbf{s}^i, \mathbf{e}^i) = [\mathbf{s}^i, \mathbf{e}^i]$
- *Multiplication:* $\phi(\mathbf{s}^i, \mathbf{e}^i) = \mathbf{s}^i \odot \mathbf{I} \cdot \mathbf{e}^i$
- *Concatenation and Multiplication:* $\phi(\mathbf{s}^i, \mathbf{e}^i) = [\mathbf{s}^i, (\mathbf{s}^i \odot \mathbf{I} \cdot \mathbf{e}^i)]$
- *Rasch model:* $\phi(\mathbf{s}^i, \mathbf{e}^i) = \mathbf{s}^i + \mu \mathbf{e}^i$,

where $\mathbf{I} \in \mathbb{R}^{d \times d}$ is a trainable transformation matrix, $\odot$ denotes the operation of element-wise multiplication. *Concatenation, Multiplication, concatenation and multiplication* are commons operation to integrate vectors [12]. The *Rasch model* was proposed in AKT [10], where $\mu \in \mathbb{R}^1$ denotes a scalar *difficulty* parameter.

3.5   Prediction

Generally, the learner's learning interactions are modeled as a sequential task, so we use learner's performance as the input of Long Short-Term Memory (LSTM) to obtain learner knowledge state sequentially:

$$\mathbf{h}_t = LSTM(\mathbf{y}_t^i, \mathbf{h}_{t-1}), \tag{6}$$

where $\mathbf{h}_t \in \mathbb{R}^{2d}$. Then, we apply the concatenation of the learner's current knowledge state $\mathbf{h}_t$ and assessment exercise representation $\mathbf{x}_{t+1}^i$ to predict the performance at next time step. The specific process can be formulated as:

$$\mathbf{f}_{t+1} = \text{ReLU}(\mathbf{W_f} \left[\mathbf{h}_t, \mathbf{x}_{t+1}^i\right] + \mathbf{b_f}), \tag{7}$$

$$\widetilde{p}_{t+1} = \sigma(\mathbf{W_p}\, \mathbf{f}_{t+1} + \mathbf{b_p}), \tag{8}$$

where $\mathbf{W_f} \in \mathbb{R}^{d \times (2d+D)}$, $\mathbf{W_p} \in \mathbb{R}^d$, $\mathbf{b_f} \in \mathbb{R}^d$ and $\mathbf{b_p} \in \mathbb{R}^1$ are parameters that are learned during training process.

3.6   Model Optimization

Generally, the standard cross-entropy is used to obtain the loss between $\widetilde{p}_t$ and p_t. Please note that there is another training mission in our model, which is to avoid overfitting. Hence, there are two parts in our loss function: One is the prediction optimization, and the other is representation optimization.

In the first part, we leverage the cross-entropy loss function to compute the loss of prediction performance:

$$\mathcal{L}_1(\widetilde{p}_t, p_t) = -(p_t \log \widetilde{p}_t + (1 - r_p) \log(1 - \widetilde{p}_t)). \tag{9}$$

In the second part, we compute the loss of exercise representations by the following equation:

$$\mathcal{L}_2(i,j) = \begin{cases} 1 - \sigma\left(\mathbf{x}^i \cdot \left(\mathbf{k}^j\right)^{\mathbf{T}}\right), & \text{if } r_{e^i, k^j} = 1 \\ \sigma\left(\mathbf{x}^i \cdot \left(\mathbf{k}^j\right)^{\mathbf{T}}\right), & \text{if } r_{e^i, k^j} = 0 \end{cases}. \tag{10}$$

Finally, to train the trainable parameters in the whole model, we leverage the following loss function to minimize the loss of our model:

$$\mathcal{L} = \frac{1}{L} \sum_{l=1}^{L} \frac{1}{T} \sum_{t=1}^{T} \mathcal{L}_1(\widetilde{p}_{t,l}, p_{t,l}) + \lambda \cdot \frac{1}{|E||K|} \sum_{i=1}^{|E|} \sum_{j=1}^{|K|} \mathcal{L}_2(i,j), \tag{11}$$

where L denotes the number of learners for every batch in the training process, T represents the number of exercises that learner l attempts, and λ is a hyperparameter to tune weight. It is worth mentioning that the learner index is added to Eq. (11) because the model calculates the loss for a batch of learners during every training process.

4   Experimental Results

This section first details the baselines and related experiments[1]. Then, the result of related experiments is reported to justify our superiority. Finally, we discuss our observations from the results.

4.1   Datasets

To evaluate our model, we leverage three following real-world datasets. These datasets are widely used in KT research, and detailed statistics are summed up in Table 1.

Table 1. Dataset Statistics. The last column represents the average number of attempts per exercise.

Dataset	Interactions	Exercises	Concepts	Learners	Attempt
ASSIST09	110.2k	16.9k	111	3.7k	7
ASSIST12	879.5k	50.9k	245	25.3k	17
slepemapy.cz	2877.5k	2.9k	1473	81.7k	992

- **ASSISTments2009 (ASSIST09)**[2]: This dataset comes from ASSISTments online education platform during the school year 2009–2010.
- **ASSISTments2012 (ASSIST12)**[3]: This dataset is similar to ASSIST09. It is collected during the school year 2012–2013.
- **slepemapy.cz.**[4]: This dataset is from the slepemapy.cz. system, an online adaptive system providing adaptive exercise of geography facts.

4.2   Baselines and Experimental Settings

To demonstrate the superiority of the KSGAN, several existing KT models are compared with our model. The details of these models are:

- **DKT** [2] employs RNN to model learning process. We develop DKT with LSTM network in our experiments.
- **DKVMN** [8] is a classic KT model based on deep learning method. It uses modified Memory-Augmented Neural Networks to predict learners' future performance.

---

[1] Source code and datasets will be available at https://github.com/syunnmo/KSGAN.
[2] https://sites.google.com/site/assistmentsdata/home/assistment-2009-2010-data.
[3] https://sites.google.com/site/assistmentsdata/home/2015-assistments-skill-builder-data.
[4] https://www.fi.muni.cz/adaptivelearning/?a=data.

- **DKVMN-E** is our supplement to DKVMN, which applies exercises as input instead of knowledge concepts.
- **SAKT** [9] is a representative method that purely uses self-attention mechanism for KT.
- **DKT+Forgetting** [12] is the first model that considers the forgetting behavior to DKT.
- **KTM** [16] adopts factorization machines to predict performance. Here, the implementation of KTM is the same as in [15].
- **AKT-R** [10] leverages a novel monotonic attention mechanism to make the prediction.
- **HawkesKT** [15] is the latest KT model, which focuses on fine-grained temporal cross-effects between interactions during learning.

It is worth noting that we do not list our supplement of DKT that applies exercises as input. The reason is that the direct use of exercise labels for one-hot encoding leads to out of memory seriously, even if it is a 128G CPU server.

Table 2. The performances of KSGAN with integration Function under different hyper-parameter λ.

Dataset	λ	ASSIST09		ASSIST12		slepemapy.cz.	
		AUC	ACC	AUC	ACC	AUC	ACC
KSGAN-C	0.1	0.7665	0.7261	0.7697	0.7526	0.7632	0.8101
	0.5	*0.7694*	*0.7311*	0.7705	0.7521	0.7644	0.8101
	1.0	0.7675	0.7309	0.7712	0.7539	**0.7667**	**0.8106**
KSGAN-M	0.1	0.7385	0.7090	0.7607	0.7469	0.7616	0.8089
	0.5	0.7369	0.7117	0.7614	0.7481	0.7638	0.8096
	1.0	0.7564	0.7246	0.7620	0.7498	0.7643	0.8101
KSGAN-CM	0.1	0.7690	0.7295	0.7714	0.7531	0.7623	0.8094
	0.5	0.7682	0.7299	*0.7732*	*0.7555*	0.7631	0.8098
	1.0	**0.7740**	**0.7355**	**0.7736**	**0.7557**	*0.7648*	*0.8103*
KSGAN-R	0.1	0.7594	0.7219	0.7621	0.7502	0.7636	0.8100
	0.5	0.7595	0.7225	0.7636	0.7510	0.7634	0.8099
	1.0	0.7606	0.7213	0.7653	0.7518	0.7639	0.8102

* The best results are bold, and the second best results are italic.

4.3 Implementation Details

The Area Under Curve (AUC) and Accuracy (ACC) are used as the metrics to report the performance. Moreover, the standard k-fold cross-validation (with $k = 5$) is used to evaluate all the models. In each experiment, Adam optimizer is adopted to minimize the loss value. The embedding dimension d, batch size, dropout rate, learning rate and maximum length N are set to 64, 32, 0.3, 0.005 and 100, respectively. Moreover, the candidate values for hyper-parameter λ are $\{1.0, 0.5, 0.1\}$. All the models are implemented using Python with Pytorch on a Linux server.

Table 3. Performance comparison of all KT methods.

Dataset		ASSIST09		ASSIST12		slepemapy.cz.	
		AUC	ACC	AUC	ACC	AUC	ACC
Baselines	DKT	0.7525	0.7247	0.7322	0.7371	0.7512	0.7820
	DKVMN	0.7326	0.7189	0.7057	0.7294	0.7371	0.7859
	DKVMN-E	0.6742	0.6946	0.6943	0.7255	0.7237	0.7847
	SAKT	0.6894	0.6864	0.6912	0.7216	0.6739	0.7711
	DKT+Forgetting	0.7573	0.7272	0.7462	0.7373	0.7574	0.7819
	KTM	0.7353	0.7178	0.7514	0.7412	0.7421	0.7772
	AKT-R	0.7519	0.7199	0.7649	*0.7523*	0.7547	*0.7827*
	HawkesKT	*0.7617*	*0.7305*	*0.7669*	0.7475	*0.7572*	0.7823
	KSGAN	**0.7740**	**0.7355**	**0.7736**	**0.7557**	**0.7648**	**0.8103**

* The best results are bold, and the second best results are italic.

4.4 Performance Analysis

Table 2 lists the performance of KSGAN with Integration Function under different hyper-parameter λ, wherein KSGAN-C, KSGAN-M, KSGAN-CM, and KSGAN-R represent KSGAN with Integration Function *Concatenation, Multiplication, Concatenation and Multiplication*, and *Rasch model*, respectively. Furthermore, Table 3 shows the performance of all compared models and KSGAN-CM. We find several observations as follows:

First, different kinds of Integration Functions show remarkable performance gaps. Overall, the KSGAN-CM yields the best performance on all datasets. The KSGAN with *Rasch model* is flexible to integrate exercise and knowledge tracing information, compared to KSGAN-C and KSGAN-M perform better sometimes. Additionally, the overall performance becomes better as the value of the hyper-parameter λ increases, all the variants of KSGAN achieve optimal AUC and ACC value when the λ is 1.0.

Second, the exercise-level KT models can perform better than knowledge concept-level KT models. Note that the performance of DKVMN-E on ASSIST09 shows a tremendous performance gap compared to DKVMN, but the performance gap is slight on slepemapy.cz.. This phenomenon is because the attempted exercises are highly sparse on ASSIST09 compared to slepemapy.cz., as observed in Table 1. Hence, the exercise-level models KTM, AKT-R, and HawkesKT address this issue differently and achieve better performance than knowledge concept-level models on several datasets.

Third, our model outperforms the other state-of-the-art models on three datasets. It is worth mentioning that these exercise-level KT models not only introduce exercise information into models but also consider additional information, which proves the effectiveness of KSGAN in exploring richer advanced information between knowledge concepts and exercises.

Table 4. Ablation study on three datasets.

Dataset	ASSIST09		ASSIST12		slepemapy.cz.	
	AUC	ACC	AUC	ACC	AUC	ACC
KSGAN-NGR	0.7464	0.7238	0.7433	0.7420	0.7565	0.8074
KSGAN-NG	0.7548	0.7270	0.7478	0.7453	0.7601	0.8079
KSGAN-NR	0.7688	0.7302	0.7661	0.7523	0.7621	0.8086
KSGAN	**0.7740**	**0.7355**	**0.7736**	**0.7557**	**0.7648**	**0.8103**

* The best results are bold.

4.5 Ablation Study

To evaluate the effect of graph attention layer and representation optimization, we perform an ablation study where we remove these two modules from KSGAN, respectively. In this section, the *Concatenation and Multiplication* is used for these models containing graph attention layers, and the hyper-parameter is set to 1.0. As shown in Table 4, it can be found that the graph attention layer shows a more significant improvement in prediction. Although the effect of loading the representation optimization is not noticeable, it has a positive.

- **KSGAN-NGR**: The graph attention layer and representation optimization are not loaded.
- **KSGAN-NG**: The graph attention layer is not loaded.
- **KSGAN-NR**: The representation optimization is not loaded.

5 Conclusion

This paper proposed a Knowledge Structure-aware Graph-Attention Network (KSGAN) to predict learners' performance at exercise level. KSGAN introduces a graph attention layer and representation optimization to deeply explore the richer advanced information between exercises and knowledge concepts. Compared to these exercise-level KT models, which consider additional information to improve prediction performance, our model is more effective because it only utilizes the knowledge structure between exercises and knowledge concepts. Experimental results on three real-world show that our model has outperformed other baselines in recent years.

Acknowledgements. The works described in this paper are supported by The National Natural Science Foundation of China under Grant Nos. 61772210 and U1911201; Guangdong Province Universities Pearl River Scholar Funded Scheme (2018); The Project of Science and Technology in Guangzhou in China under Grant No. 202007040006.

References

1. Corbett, A.T., Anderson, J.R.: Knowledge tracing: modeling the acquisition of procedural knowledge. User Model. User-Adap. Inter. **4**(4), 253–278 (1994)
2. Piech, C., et al.: Deep knowledge tracing. In: Advances in Neural Information Processing Systems, pp. 505–513 (2015)
3. Liu, Q., et al.: EKT: exercise-aware knowledge tracing for student performance prediction. IEEE Trans. Knowl. Data Eng. **33**(1), 100–115 (2021)
4. Pandey, S., Srivastava, J.: RKT: relation-aware self-attention for knowledge tracing. In: CIKM 2020: The 29th ACM International Conference on Information and Knowledge Management, pp. 1205–1214. ACM (2020)
5. Zhang, N., Li, L.: Knowledge tracing with exercise-enhanced key-value memory networks. In: Qiu, H., Zhang, C., Fei, Z., Qiu, M., Kung, S.-Y. (eds.) KSEM 2021. LNCS (LNAI), vol. 12815, pp. 566–577. Springer, Cham (2021). https://doi.org/10.1007/978-3-030-82136-4_46
6. Qiu, H., Zheng, Q., Msahli, M., Memmi, G., Qiu, M., Lu, J.: Topological graph convolutional network-based urban traffic flow and density prediction. IEEE Trans. Intell. Transp. Syst. **22**(7), 4560–4569 (2021)
7. Velickovic, P., Cucurull, G., Casanova, A., Romero, A., Liò, P., Bengio, Y.: Graph attention networks. In: 6th International Conference on Learning Representations, ICLR. OpenReview.net (2018)
8. Zhang, J., Shi, X., King, I., Yeung, D.: Dynamic key-value memory networks for knowledge tracing. In: Proceedings of the 26th International Conference on World Wide Web, WWW, pp. 765–774. ACM (2017)
9. Pandey, S., Karypis, G.: A self attentive model for knowledge tracing. In: Proceedings of the 12th International Conference on Educational Data Mining, EDM, pp. 384–389. International Educational Data Mining Society (IEDMS) (2019)
10. Ghosh, A., Heffernan, N.T., Lan, A.S.: Context-aware attentive knowledge tracing. In: The 26th ACM SIGKDD Conference on Knowledge Discovery and Data Mining, pp. 2330–2339. ACM (2020)
11. Nakagawa, H., Iwasawa, Y., Matsuo, Y.: Graph-based knowledge tracing: modeling student proficiency using graph neural network. In: 2019 IEEE/WIC/ACM International Conference on Web Intelligence, WI, pp. 156–163. ACM (2019)
12. Nagatani, K., Zhang, Q., Sato, M., Chen, Y., Chen, F., Ohkuma, T.: Augmenting knowledge tracing by considering forgetting behavior. In: The World Wide Web Conference, WWW, pp. 3101–3107. ACM (2019)
13. Shin, D., Shim, Y., Yu, H., Lee, S., Kim, B., Choi, Y.: SAINT+: integrating temporal features for ednet correctness prediction. In: LAK 2021: 11th International Learning Analytics and Knowledge Conference, pp. 490–496. ACM (2021)
14. Chen, P., Lu, Y., Zheng, V.W., Pian, Y.: Prerequisite-driven deep knowledge tracing. In: IEEE International Conference on Data Mining, ICDM, pp. 39–48. IEEE Computer Society (2018)

15. Wang, C., et al.: Temporal cross-effects in knowledge tracing. In: WSDM 2021, The Fourteenth ACM International Conference on Web Search and Data Mining, pp. 517–525. ACM (2021)

16. Vie, J., Kashima, H.: Knowledge tracing machines: factorization machines for knowledge tracing. In: The Thirty-Third AAAI Conference on Artificial Intelligence, pp. 750–757. AAAI Press (2019)

MCSN: Multi-graph Collaborative Semantic Network for Chinese NER

Yingqi Zhang[1], Wenjing Gu[1], Wenjun Ma[1(✉)], and Yuncheng Jiang[1,2(✉)]

[1] School of Computer Science, South China Normal University,
Guangzhou 510631, China
{zhangyingqi,gwen,jiangyuncheng}@m.scnu.edu.cn, phoenixsam@sina.com
[2] School of Artificial Intelligence, South China Normal University,
Foshan 528225, China

Abstract. Named Entity Recognition (NER) is not only one of the most important directions in Natural Language Processing (NLP), but also plays an essential pre-processing role in many downstream NLP tasks. In recent years, most of the existing methods solve Chinese NER tasks by leveraging word lexicon, which have been empirically proven to be effective. However, these methods that depend on lexical knowledge too much tend to be confused by lexicon words, which leads to recognizing false entities. In addition, the lexicon is just a method to augment performance for the NER models, but cannot provide the dependency information of every Chinese word in a sentence, which causes relatively poor results in complex text. In order to solve these issues, this paper proposes a Multi-graph Collaborative Semantic Network (MCSN) fusing the dependency information of Chinese words. We build the dependency relationships of Chinese words by leveraging Graph Attention Network. With the dependency relationships of Chinese words, MCSN not only overcomes the shortages of lexicon, but also better captures the semantic information of Chinese words. Experimental results on some Chinese benchmarking datasets show that our methods are not only effective, but also outperform the state-of-the-art (SOTA) results. Especially in the Weibo-NM dataset, our methods can outperform it more than 9.34% in F1 score, in contrast with the SOTA models.

Keywords: Chinese NER · Dependency information · Graph attention network

1 Introduction

NER is one of the most important directions of NLP, which is designed for identifying and classifying unstructured texts into predefined semantic categories such as person names, organizations, etc. [9,11]. Moreover, NER plays an essential role in a variety of NLP applications such as information extraction (IE) [2], text understanding [25], information retrieval [17], knowledge graph [1,23], recommendation system [22] etc.

© The Author(s), under exclusive license to Springer Nature Switzerland AG 2022
G. Memmi et al. (Eds.): KSEM 2022, LNAI 13368, pp. 322–334, 2022.
https://doi.org/10.1007/978-3-031-10983-6_25

In contrast with an English sentence, there is no space between characters in a Chinese sentence as word delimiters. Therefore, it is common for Chinese NER to first perform word segmentation by using an existing Chinese Word Segmentation (CWS) system and then apply a sequence labeling model based on word-level to segmented sentence [6, 21]. However, it is difficult for the CWS system to correctly segment query sentences, which will result in error propagation. In order to solve this problem, there are some methods resorting to performing Chinese NER directly at the character-level, which has been empirically proven to be effective [13]. However, such methods cannot exploit lexical knowledge. With this consideration, Zhang et al. [24] proposed the Lattice-LSTM model to exploit explicit word and word sequence information. Besides, Li et al. [10] presented a Flat-Lattice Transformer, which converts the lattice structure into a flat structure consisting of spans. These methods can increase the performance of NER models by leveraging lexical knowledge, but tend to neglect the dependency relationships of Chinese words, which leads to recognizing false entities.

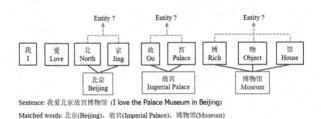

Sentence: 我爱北京故宫博物馆 (I love the Palace Museum in Beijing)

Matched words: 北京(Beijing)，故宫(Imperial Palace)，博物馆(Museum)

Fig. 1. A sentence just leveraging lexical knowledge

As shown in Fig. 1, for the sentence "我爱北京故宫博物馆" (I love the Palace Museum in Beijing), the matched word "北京" (Beijing) can better increase the relation between character "北" (North) and "京" (Jing), so the model is likely to recognize these two characters as an entirety, as well as other matched words. As a result, the model will recognize the word "北京" (Beijing), "故宫" (Imperial Palace) and "博物馆" (Museum) as an entity, respectively. But in fact, there is only one entity in this sentence, which is the word "北京故宫博物馆" (the Palace Museum in Beijing). To the best of our knowledge, the existing NER models cannot recognize the word "北京故宫博物馆" (the Palace Museum in Beijing) as an entity, due to lack of this word in the lexicon. In addition, it is impossible for the lexicon to contain all lexical matched words you want.

In order to solve this issue, this paper presents a MCSN model fusing dependency information of Chinese words. As shown in Fig. 2, we can use the dependency information of the word "北京" (Beijing). Obviously, the word "北京" (Beijing) in this sentence is a component that acts as attributive, as well as the word "故宫" (Imperial Palace). Because the word "博物馆" (Museum) is modified by both the words "北京" (Beijing) and "故宫" (Imperial Palace), we can build relationships among them by using their dependency information. With the relationships among these words, the word "北京故宫博物馆" (the

Palace Museum in Beijing) is seen as an entirety. Finally, the word "北京故宫博物馆" (the Palace Museum in Beijing) will be recognized as an entity.

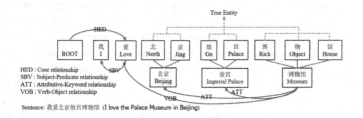

Fig. 2. A sentence fusing the dependency relationship of Chinese words

In order to achieve our methods, we construct three word-character interactive graphs. Specifically, The first graph is the Relation graph, and its function is to build the dependency relationships among Chinese words. The second graph is the Containing graph, which is designed for capturing contextual information in a sentence. The third graph is the Boundary graph, which is designed for confirming the boundaries of named entities, in order to solve the confusion of entity boundaries. Since different graphs have different functions, they will cooperate with each other via a fusion layer.

In summary, our main contributions are as follows:

- We propose a multi-graph collaborative semantic network for Chinese NER tasks.
- To the best of our knowledge, we are the first neural approach to NER that models the dependency information of Chinese words with multi-graph structure.
- Experimental results show that our methods are not only effective, but also outperform the SOTA models.

2   Related Work

There are two main types of enhanced performances in Chinese NER.

Lexical Knowledge. In recent years, many studies focus on character-based model by leveraging lexical knowledge. A representative method is the Lattice-LSTM model proposed by Zhang et al. [24], which not only avoids error propagation, but also models characters and potential words simultaneously. Moreover, Transformer-based methods have been used with lexical enhancement. Flat-Lattice Transformer proposed by Li et al. [10] can convert the lattice structure into a flat structure consisting of spans. This method has an excellent parallelization ability. Based on Flat-Lattice Transformer, Wu et al. [20] presents a novel Multi-metadata Embedding to improve the performance of the NER model by considering structural information about Chinese characters.

Glyph-Structural Methods. Compared with traditional neural network methods, graph neural networks can consider the relations among characters better, which has been proven by many excellent methods [5,16]. A lexicon-based graph network is proposed by Gui et al. [5]. This method treats the named entities as a node classification task, which can avoid error propagation and leverage lexical knowledge. In addition, Ding et al. [3] proposed a neural multi-digraph model for Chinese NER with Gazetteers.

Although the enhanced methods of those two main types can obtain great experimental results in Chinese NER datasets, they neglect one of the most important points in Chinese sentences, the dependency information among Chinese words. Due to the shortness of the lexicon and the lack of dependency information among Chinese words, these models may not only recognize false entities, but also cause relatively poor results in complex Chinese text. In this work, we propose a MCSN model fusing the dependency information of Chinese words. With the dependency relationships of Chinese words, MCSN not only overcomes the shortages of the lexicon, but also better captures the semantic information of Chinese words. Experimental results show that our methods are effective.

3   Methodology

In this section, we first introduce the construction of three word-character graphs to integrate lexical knowledge and the dependency information of Chinese words into sentences, and then introduce the structure of our training model.

3.1   The Construction of Graphs

In order to achieve our methods, we construct three word-character interactive graphs. The vertices of three interactive graphs are different, and the edges of each graph are different. For this, we introduce an adjacency matrix to represent the edges of each graph. The values in the adjacency matrix indicate whether there are relations between vertices or not in a graph.

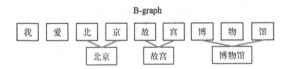

Fig. 3. The word-character Boundary graph

Boundary Graph. For the word-character Boundary graph (B-graph), the vertices of the B-graph consist of characters and lexical matched words of the corresponding character in a sentence. Take the sentence in Fig. 1 as an example. The sentence can be represented as $s = \{我,爱,北,京,故,宫,博,物,馆\}$. In order to utilize potential words in the sentence, we match all lexical words of every character. All matched words can be represented as $l = \{北京,故宫,博物馆\}$. Thus, the vertices of the B-graph is denoted as $V = \{我,\ldots,故宫,\ldots\}$. As shown in Fig. 3, if a lexical matched word l_i contains many characters, we need to leverage its contained first character or last character c. The (l_i, c)-entry of the B-graph corresponding adjacency matrix A^B is assigned a value of 1.

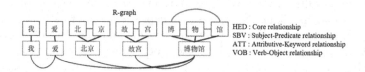

Fig. 4. The word-character Relation graph

Relation Graph. Taking the same sentence as an example, the vertex set of the word-character Relation graph (R-graph) consists of characters and words separated by the dependency parsing tool[1]. The sentence can be represented as $s = \{我,爱,\ldots,宫,博,物,馆\}$. The words separated by the dependency parsing tool, can be represented as $w = \{我,爱,北京,故宫,博物馆\}$. The dependency information of these words is as $f = \{SBV, HED, ATT, ATT, VOB\}$, which can be replace as the set $index = \{2, 0, 5, 5, 2\}$ (the value in set $index$ represents that the current node has a connection with the value-th node). With this R-graph, we build not only connections among characters, but also the dependency relationships among separated words in a sentence. As shown in Fig. 4, if a separated word w_n contains character set $C = \{c_1, c_2, \ldots, c_p\}, c_i, c_j \in C$, we will assign the (w_n, c_i)-entry of the R-graph corresponding adjacency matrix A^R a value of 1, as well as the (c_i, c_j)-entry. Moreover, if a separated word w_n has a relation with another separated word w_m, the (w_n, w_m)-entry of the R-graph corresponding adjacency matrix A^R is assigned a value of 1.

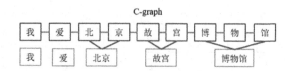

Fig. 5. The word-character Containing graph

Containing Graph. The vertices of the Containing graph (C-graph) consist of characters and words separated by the dependency parsing tool, as well as

---

[1] https://github.com/baidu/DDParser.

the R-graph. With this graph, the contextual information in the sentence can be captured by our model. As shown in Fig. 5, if a separated word w_n contains more than one character, we need to leverage its contained first character or last character i. Therefore, the (w_n, i)-entry of the C-graph corresponding adjacency matrix A^C is assigned a value of 1. Moreover, in the original sentence, if a character i has a predecessor or successor j, we will assign "$A^C_{ij} = 1$".

3.2 The Whole Architecture of Our Model

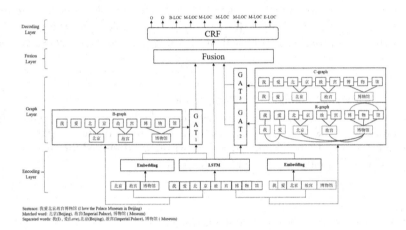

Fig. 6. The architecture of our model

The whole architecture of our model is shown in Fig. 6. For a sentence, we use the lexicon to obtain all matched words, and use the dependency parsing tool to obtain separated words. Then, those words are converted into dense vectors. Moreover, we first utilize a bidirectional LSTM model to capture contextual information of the input sequence, and then merge it with matched words and separated words, respectively. Furthermore, we fuse the merged results with three word-character interactive graphs in the graph layer, respectively. In order to fully use the merits of different graphs, a fusion layer is used for fusing these graphs. In the end, the results of the final predictions are obtained through the Conditional Random Field (CRF).

Encoding
For a Chinese NER model, the input of the training model based on characters is seen as $s = \{c_1, c_2, \cdots, c_n\}$, where c_i is the i-th character in a sentence. Each character c_i can be represented by looking up the embedding vector:

$$\mathbf{x}^c_i = e^c(c_i), \tag{1}$$

where e^c denotes the character embedding vector table.

Due to features of Long-Short Term Memory (LSTM) [7], LSTM can better capture contextual information of Chinese sentences, which has been empirically proven to be useful. In this paper, a bidirectional LSTM is applied to $\mathbf{x}^c = \{\mathbf{x}_1^c, \mathbf{x}_2^c, \cdots, \mathbf{x}_n^c\}$ to obtain the left-to-right and right-to-left LSTM hidden states. As shown in Eq. (2), the hidden vector representations of input sentence are denoted as $\mathbf{H} = \{\mathbf{h}_1, \mathbf{h}_2, \cdots, \mathbf{h_n}\}$.

$$\mathbf{h}_i = \overrightarrow{LSTM}\left(\mathbf{x}_i^c, \overrightarrow{\mathbf{h}}_{i-1}\right) \oplus \overleftarrow{LSTM}\left(\mathbf{x}_i^c, \overleftarrow{\mathbf{h}}_{i+1}\right). \tag{2}$$

Lexical knowledge can augment the character representation to enhance performance of the NER model. All lexical words matched by each character in the sentence are denoted as $l = \{l_1, l_2, \cdots, l_m\}$. By looking up the pre-trained embedding lookup table, each lexical word l_i is represented as a dense vector.

$$\mathbf{x}_i^l = e^w\left(l_i\right), \tag{3}$$

where e^w is a lexical embedding looking table.

In order to use the dependency relationships of Chinese words, we can obtain the separated words $w = \{w_1, w_2, \cdots, w_k\}$, by using dependency parsing tool. By looking up word embedding from a pre-train word embedding matrix, each separated word w_i can be represented as a dense vector.

$$\mathbf{x}_i^w = e^w\left(w_i\right), \tag{4}$$

where e^w is a lexical embedding looking table.

Graph Attention Networks over These Graphs

To give a graph architecture, meaningful outputs can be produced by graph neural network, or node representation can be learned through graph neural network [15]. Compared with other architectures of graph networks, we believe that Graph Attention Network (GAT) [18] is the most suitable for Chinese NER tasks, because GAT can allow for assigning different importances to different nodes with a neighborhood. Therefore, three word-character interactive graphs are modeled by GAT. Specifically, in a M-layer GAT, the input representation of j-th layer consists of a set of node features, $\mathbf{NF}^j = \{\mathbf{f}_1, \mathbf{f}_2, \ldots, \mathbf{f}_N\}$. In addition, an adjacency matrix $\mathbf{A}$ is needed, $\mathbf{f}_i \in \mathbb{R}^F, \mathbf{A} \in \mathbb{R}^{N \times N}$, where F denotes the dimension of features at j-th layer and N is the number of nodes. The output representation of j-th layer is a new set of node features differing with others $\mathbf{NF}^{(j+1)} = \{\mathbf{f}_1', \mathbf{f}_2', \ldots, \mathbf{f}_N'\}$. Every GAT operation with K different and independent attention heads is shown in Eqs. (5) and (6).

$$\mathbf{f}_i' = \mathop{\Big\|}_{k=1}^{K} \sigma\left(\sum_{j \in \mathcal{N}_i} \alpha_{ij}^k \mathbf{W}^k \mathbf{f}_j\right), \tag{5}$$

$$\alpha_{ij}^k = \frac{\exp\left(\text{LeakyReLU}\left(\mathbf{a}^T\left[\mathbf{W}^k\mathbf{f_i}\|\mathbf{W}^K\mathbf{f_j}\right]\right)\right)}{\Sigma_{k \in \mathcal{N}_i} \exp\left(\text{LeakyReLU}\left(\mathbf{a}^T\left[\mathbf{W}^k\mathbf{f_i}\|\mathbf{W}^K\mathbf{f_k}\right]\right)\right)}, \tag{6}$$

where concatenation operation is denoted as $\|$. The nonlinear activation function is denoted as σ. The adjacent nodes of node i in a graph are denoted as $\mathcal{N}_i$. The attention coefficients are denoted as α_{ij}^k, $\mathbf{W}^k \in \mathbb{R}^{F' \times F}$. The single-layer feed-forward neural network is denoted as $\mathbf{a} \in \mathbb{R}^{2F'}$. Note that, KF' is as the dimension of the output $\mathbf{f}_i'$. In the end, we will keep the averaging in the last layer, and F' is the dimension of the final output features we need.

$$\mathbf{f}_i^{final} = \sigma \left(\frac{1}{K} \sum_{k=1}^{K} \sum_{j \in \mathcal{N}_i} \alpha_{ij}^k \mathbf{W}^k \mathbf{f}_j \right). \tag{7}$$

Specifically, three independent graph attention networks are built for modeling three different word-character interactive graphs. Due to the different vertices of these three graphs, we denote these three independent graph attention networks as GAT_1, GAT_2, and GAT_3, respectively. The B-graph can capture the boundary information of the entity by using lexical knowledge. Therefore, the vertex set of B-graph can be denoted as $X_B = \{\mathbf{h}_1, \mathbf{h}_2, \cdots, \mathbf{h}_n, \mathbf{x}_1^l, \mathbf{x}_2^l, \cdots, \mathbf{x}_m^l\}$. The output node features of GAT_1 model is denoted as $\mathbf{G}_1$.

$$\mathbf{G}_1 = GAT_1 \left(X_B, A^B \right), \tag{8}$$

where $\mathbf{G}_1 \in \mathbb{R}^{F' \times (n+m)}$, n is the number of characters in the sentence, and m is the number of the lexical words matched by characters in the sentence. For the R-graph and the C-graph, these two graphs are shared the same vertex set $X = \{\mathbf{h}_1, \mathbf{h}_2, \cdots, \mathbf{h}_n, \mathbf{x}_1^w, \mathbf{x}_2^w, \cdots, \mathbf{x}_k^w\}$. The output node features of GAT_2 and GAT_3 model are denoted as $\mathbf{G}_2$ and $\mathbf{G}_3$, respectively.

$$\mathbf{G}_2 = GAT_2 \left(X, A^R \right), \tag{9}$$

$$\mathbf{G}_3 = GAT_3 \left(X, A^C \right), \tag{10}$$

where $\mathbf{G}_y \in \mathbb{R}^{F' \times (n+k)}$, $y \in \{2, 3\}$, n is the number of characters in the sentence, and k is the number of the words separated by dependency parsing tool. For the output node feature $\mathbf{G}_i, i \in \{1, 2, 3\}$, we keep the first n columns of these matrices, since only character representations are used to decode labels.

$$\mathbf{Q}_i = \mathbf{G}_i[:, 0 : n], i \in \{1, 2, 3\}. \tag{11}$$

Fusion
In order to use the merits of these interactive graphs, a fusion layer is adapted to fuse three graphs. Moreover, the contextual information of the input sentence is beneficial to Chinese NER. The input of the fusion layer is the contextual representation $\mathbf{H}$ and the output of the graph layer $\mathbf{Q}_i, i \in \{1, 2, 3\}$. The fusion equation is introduced below:

$$\mathbf{R} = \mathbf{W}_1\mathbf{H} + \mathbf{W}_2\mathbf{Q}_1 + \mathbf{W}_3\mathbf{Q}_2 + \mathbf{W}_4\mathbf{Q}_3, \tag{12}$$

where $\mathbf{W}_y, y \in \{1, 2, 3, 4\}$, is a trainable matrice. In the end, a collaborative matrix $\mathbf{R}$ can be obtained from a fusion layer. The matrix $\mathbf{R}$ integrate different functions of these different graphs.

Decoding

A standard CRF [8] layer is adopted to capture the dependencies between successive labels. For any input sentence $s = \{c_1, c_2, \cdots, c_n\}$, we obtain the input representation of CRF layer $\mathbf{R} = \{\mathbf{r}_1, \mathbf{r}_2, \cdots, \mathbf{r}_n\}$ from the fusion layer. Given the predicted tag sequence $y = \{y_1, y_2, \cdots, y_n\}$, the probability of the tag sequence y can be computed by:

$$p(y \mid s) = \frac{\exp\left(\sum_i \left(\mathbf{W}_{CRF}^{y_i}\mathbf{r}_i + \mathbf{b}_{CRF}^{(y_{i-1}, y_i)}\right)\right)}{\sum_{y'} \exp\left(\sum_i \left(\mathbf{W}_{CRF}^{y'_i}\mathbf{r}_i + \mathbf{b}_{CRF}^{(y'_{i-1}, y'_i)}\right)\right)}, \tag{13}$$

where y' denotes an arbitrary label sequence, $\mathbf{W}_{CRF}^{y_i}$ and $\mathbf{b}_{CRF}^{(y_{i-1}, y_i)}$ are trainable parameters. The first-order Viterbi algorithm [19] is used to find the highest scored label sequence over a character-based input representation. Given a manually labeled training data $\{(s_i, y_i)\}|_{i=1}^N$, the optimized model is obtained by using sentence-level log-likelihood loss with L_2 regularization.

$$L = \sum_{i=1}^N \log\left(P\left(y_i \mid s_i\right)\right) + \frac{\lambda}{2}\|\Theta\|^2. \tag{14}$$

As shown in Eq. 14, the L_2 regularization parameter is represented as λ, and the training parameters set is denoted as Θ.

4   Experiment

In this section, we show experimental processes, including tested datasets, evaluation metrics (P, R, F1) and so on. Specifically, our datasets include Weibo NER [13], OntoNotes [14] and E-commerce [3].

4.1   Overall Performance

Weibo and E-commerce. Chinese NER datasets on informal text are more challenging, due to the shortness and noisiness of the informal text. Compared with others, there are many informal texts in Weibo and E-commerce datasets, which may cause poor performance of the models. Moreover, the connections among entities are not close together. The R-graph can build closer relationships among characters by using the dependency information of Chinese words. Those close relationships are beneficial to the recognization of entities. The experimental results show that our methods are useful, as shown in Table 1. Compared with the MECT model [20], our model can outperform it by 9.34%, 1.82% and 3.33% in F1 score on Weibo-NM, Weibo-ALL and E-commerce, respectively.

Table 1. Main results on Weibo and E-commerce.

Models	Weibo-NE	Weibo-NM	Weibo-ALL	E-commerce
Lattice-LSTM [24]	53.04	62.25	58.79	–
CAN-NER [26]	55.38	62.98	59.31	–
LR-CNN [4]	57.14	66.67	59.92	–
LGN [5]	55.34	64.98	60.21	–
SoftLexicon (LSTM) [12]	59.08	62.22	61.42	73.59
+bichar [12]	58.12	64.20	59.81	73.88
MECT [20]	**61.91**	62.51	63.30	72.27
Ours	59.56	**71.85**	**65.12**	**75.60**

Table 2. Main results on OntoNotes.

Models	P	R	F1
Lattice-LSTM [24]	76.35	71.56	73.88
CAN-NER [26]	75.05	72.29	73.64
LR-CNN [4]	76.40	72.60	74.45
LGN [5]	76.13	73.68	74.89
SoftLexicon (LSTM) [12]	77.28	74.07	75.64
+bichar	77.13	75.22	76.16
MECT [20]	77.57	**76.27**	76.92
Ours	**79.89**	74.42	**77.06**

OntoNotes. There is a problem with the quality and consistency of the annotation in OntoNotes due to language ambiguity, which can lead to confusion in entity boundaries. The B-graph is capable of solving this problem. The results of the OntoNotes dataset indicate that our methods are effective. Detailed information about the main results can be known in Table 2. The MECT is proposed by Wu et al. [20], which is the SOTA model on OntoNotes dataset. Compared with the SOTA model, our methods gain 2.32%, 0.14% in Precision score and F1 score, respectively.

4.2 Effectiveness

The ablation experiments show the effectiveness of three interactive graphs.

Settings. The details of the ablation studies are as follows: 1) LSTM: we just use the LSTM model for training. 2) LSTM + B: we keep the LSTM and the B-graph for training. 3) LSTM + R + C: without the B-graph, etc.

Results. The results of the ablation study are shown in Table 3. We know that removing any graph can cause poor performance of the model in different

Table 3. Ablation study

Models	Weibo-NE	Weibo-NM	Weibo-ALL	Ontonotes
LSTM	46.51	54.98	52.14	61.89
LSTM + B	54.36	65.85	60.94	73.34
LSTM + R	55.77	66.56	61.78	74.86
LSTM + C	54.59	64.71	59.69	72.54
LSTM + B + R	57.89	70.01	63.36	76.10
LSTM + B + C	57.52	69.85	62.43	75.61
LSTM + R + C	56.97	67.38	62.16	75.96
Complete model	**59.56**	**71.85**	**65.12**	**77.06**

datasets. Specifically, the models with the R-graph can obtain better performances than others, which shows that the dependency information of Chinese words is beneficial to NER. However, the C-graph performs poorly without cooperating with other graphs. We guess that the contextual information of the sentence captured by "C-graph" is not enough to recognize the entities in informal text. In conclusion, the statistics of ablation experiments show that each graph is indispensable, but the best performance can be obtained by them together.

5   Conclusion

In this paper, we propose a Multi-graph Collaborative Semantic Network fusing the dependency information of Chinese words. The core of our model is three word-character interactive graphs. Specifically, The first graph is the Relation graph, and its function is to build the dependency relationships among Chinese words. The second graph is Containing graph, which is designed for capturing contextual information in a sentence. The third graph is the Boundary graph, which is designed for confirming the boundaries of named entities. With those three graphs, our model not only overcomes the shortages of lexicon, but also better captures the semantic information of Chinese words. Experimental results show that our methods are not only effective, but also outperform the SOTA results.

Acknowledgements. The works described in this paper are supported by The National Natural Science Foundation of China under Grant Nos. 61772210 and U1911201; Guangdong Province Universities Pearl River Scholar Funded Scheme (2018); The Project of Science and Technology in Guangzhou in China under Grant Nos.202007040006; Key Projects of the National Social Science Foundation of China under Grant Nos. 19ZDA041.

References

1. Chen, H., Yin, C., Fan, X., Qiao, L., Rong, W., Xiong, Z.: Learning path recommendation for MOOC platforms based on a knowledge graph. In: KSEM, pp. 600–611 (2021)
2. Cheng, D., Song, H., He, X., Xu, B.: Joint entity and relation extraction for long text. In: KSEM, pp. 152–162 (2021)
3. Ding, R., Xie, P., Zhang, X., Lu, W., Li, L., Si, L.: A neural multi-digraph model for Chinese NER with gazetteers. In: ACL, pp. 1462–1467 (2019)
4. Gui, T., Ma, R., Zhang, Q., Zhao, L., Jiang, Y.G., Huang, X.: CNN-based Chinese NER with lexicon rethinking. In: IJCAI, pp. 4982–4988 (2019)
5. Gui, T., et al.: A lexicon-based graph neural network for Chinese NER. In: EMNLP, pp. 1039–1049 (2019)
6. He, H., Sun, X.: F-score driven max margin neural network for named entity recognition in Chinese social media. In: EACL, pp. 713–718 (2017)
7. Hochreiter, S., Schmidhuber, J.: Long short-term memory. Neural Comput. **9**(8), 1735–1780 (1997)
8. Lafferty, J.D., McCallum, A., Pereira, F.C.N.: Conditional random fields: Probabilistic models for segmenting and labeling sequence data. In: Proceedings of the Eighteenth International Conference on Machine Learning, pp. 282–289 (2001)
9. Li, Q., Huang, Z., Dou, Y., Zhang, Z.: A framework of data augmentation while active learning for Chinese named entity recognition. In: KSEM, pp. 88–100 (2021)
10. Li, X., Yan, H., Qiu, X., Huang, X.: FLAT: Chinese NER using flat-lattice transformer. In: ACL, pp. 6836–6842 (2020)
11. Liu, P., Guo, Y., Wang, F., Li, G.: Chinese named entity recognition: the state of the art. Neurocomputing **473**, 37–53 (2022)
12. Ma, R., Peng, M., Zhang, Q., Wei, Z., Huang, X.: Simplify the usage of lexicon in Chinese NER. In: ACL, pp. 5951–5960 (2020)
13. Peng, N., Dredze, M.: Named entity recognition for Chinese social media with jointly trained embeddings. In: Proceedings of the EMNLP, pp. 548–554 (2015)
14. Pradhan, S., Ramshaw, L., Marcus, M., Palmer, M., Weischedel, R., Xue, N.: Conll-2011 shared task: modeling unrestricted coreference in ontonotes. In: Computational Natural Language Learning, pp. 1–27 (2011)
15. Qiu, H., Zheng, Q., Msahli, M., Memmi, G., Qiu, M., Lu, J.: Topological graph convolutional network-based urban traffic flow and density prediction. IEEE Trans. Intell. Transp. Syst. **22**(7), 4560–4569 (2021)
16. Sui, D., Chen, Y., Liu, K., Zhao, J., Liu, S.: Leverage lexical knowledge for Chinese named entity recognition via collaborative graph network. In: EMNLP-IJCNLP, pp. 3830–3840 (2019)
17. Tamine, L., Goeuriot, L.: Semantic information retrieval on medical texts: research challenges, survey, and open issues. ACM Comput. Surv. 146:1–146:38 (2022)
18. Velickovic, P., Cucurull, G., Casanova, A., Romero, A., Liò, P., Bengio, Y.: Graph attention networks. In: International Conference on Learning Representations (2018)
19. Viterbi, A.J.: Error bounds for convolutional codes and an asymptotically optimum decoding algorithm. IEEE Trans. Inf. Theory **13**(2), 260–269 (1967)
20. Wu, S., Song, X., Feng, Z.: MECT: Multi-metadata embedding based cross-transformer for Chinese named entity recognition. In: ACL-IJCNLP, pp. 1529–1539 (2021)

21. Yang, J., Teng, Z., Zhang, M., Zhang, Y.: Combining discrete and neural features for sequence labeling. In: International Conference on Intelligent Text Processing and Computational Linguistics, pp. 140–154 (2016)
22. Zhang, F., Li, R., Xu, K., Xu, H.: Similarity-based heterogeneous graph attention network for knowledge-enhanced recommendation. In: KSEM, pp. 488–499 (2021)
23. Zhang, Y., Gao, T., Lu, J., Cheng, Z., Xiao, G.: Adaptive entity alignment for cross-lingual knowledge graph. In: KSEM, pp. 474–487 (2021)
24. Zhang, Y., Yang, J.: Chinese NER using lattice LSTM. In: ACL, pp. 1554–1564 (2018)
25. Zhang, Z., Han, X., Liu, Z., Jiang, X., Sun, M., Liu, Q.: Ernie: enhanced language representation with informative entities. arXiv preprint arXiv:1905.07129 (2019)
26. Zhu, Y., Wang, G.: CAN-NER: convolutional attention network for Chinese named entity recognition. In: NAACL, pp. 3384–3393 (2019)

Text-Enhanced and Relational Context Based Hyperbolic Knowledge Graph Embedding

Xiang Ying[1,2,3], Minghao Li[1,2,3], Jian Yu[1,2,3], Mankun Zhao[1,2,3(✉)],
Tianyi Xu[1,2,3], Mei Yu[1,2,3], Hongwei Liu[4], and Xuewei Li[1,2,3]

[1] College of Intelligence and Computing, Tianjin University, Tainjin, China
{xiang.ying,lmh_tc,yujian,zmk,tianyi.xu,yumei,lixuewei,rgyu}@tju.edu.cn
[2] Tianjin Key Laboratory of Advanced Networking (TANKLab),
Tianjin University, Tainjin, China
[3] Tianjin Key Laboratory of Cognitive Computing and Application,
Tianjin University, Tainjin, China
[4] Foreign Language, Literature and Culture Studies Center,
Tianjin Foreign Studies University, Tainjin, China
liuhongwei@tjfsu.edu.cn

Abstract. Knowledge Graphs (KGs) are ubiquitous structures for information storage and increasingly becoming popular for a variety of downstream task, and KGs are often incomplete and knowledge graph embedding learn low-dimensional representations of entities and relations, which can be used for knowledge graph completion task. However, there still exists some problems. The important role of relational context which includes neighbor relations, head and tail entities is often overlooked in many existing methods. Entity semantic information contained in textual description of entities is not well used. Thus, we propose Text Enhanced Relational Context Hyperbolic Graph Convolution Network (TRHGCN) for knowledge graph completion. TRHGCN model utilize the hyperbolic space, which can better excavate the hierarchical structure of knowledge graph, and makes full use of text description and relational context to represent entities and relations in knowledge graph. Link prediction experiments are carried out on FB15K-237, WN18RR, NELL-995 datasets. We also do ablation studies on relational context and text description of entities. The results demonstrate that TRHGCN significantly outperforms the latest excellent methods such as CompGCN and ConvE, and our model performs better on hierarchical relations.

Keywords: Knowledge graph completion · Hyperbolic space ·
Relational context · Text enhancement · Hierarchical relations

1 Introduction

Knowledge graphs (KGs) is a semantic network to store structured information of real world entities and facts. KGs are multi-relational graphs whose nodes

G. Memmi et al. (Eds.): KSEM 2022, LNAI 13368, pp. 335–345, 2022.
https://doi.org/10.1007/978-3-031-10983-6_26

represent entities and edges represent relations, and the edges are labeled with different relations. A KG usually consists of a collection of triplets. Each triplet (h, r, t) indicates that head entity h is related to tail entity t through relation r. E.g., $(BeiJing, capitalof, China)$. A range of important applications, including search, question answering, recommendation systems, and machine reading comprehension all critically rely on existing KGs such as FreeBase [1], Word-Net [2], NELL [3], etc. Real-world KGs are usually incomplete, which motivates the research in knowledge graph completion (KGC), predicting missing links in knowledge graph, including search $(h, r, ?)$ or $(?, r, t)$.

KGC models usually predict missing links in KGs via embedding entities and relations into vector spaces. Therefore, a large number of state-of-the-art KGC models have been proposed, such as TransE [4], ComplEx [5], TuckER [6], BTDE [7], ConvE [8], ConvKB [9]. At present, hyperbolic graph convolution networks has been proved to be a better model for hierarchical data, such as HGCN [10], HGNN [11], LGCN [12]. However, all these models does not consider relational context and entity semantic information for knowledge graph completion.

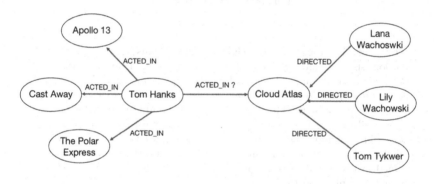

Fig. 1. An example of relational context.

Relations do not exist independently, they only make sense if they depend on the head and tail entity of the triplet [13]. The neighbor relations also has semantic relevance [14] to the current relation. As shown in Fig. 1, Tom Hanks has neighbor relation {ACTED_IN} with {Apollo 13, Cast Away, The Polar Express}, Cloud Atlas has neighbor relation {DIRECTED} with {Lana Wachoswki, Lily Wachoswki, Tom Tykwer}. From the neighbor relations we can infer the internal meaning of the entity, Tom Hanks may be an actor and Cloud Atlas may be a movie. The most likely relations between those two entities is {ACTED_IN}. Therefore, we define the relational context with the head and tail entity of triplet and their neighbor relations to represent current relation.

Entity description contains abundant entity information, which can be used as an auxiliary of the structured information with high confidence in the knowledge graph to help model build more accurate knowledge representation. As shown in Fig. 2, Barack Obama's entity description contains rich information, such as nationality, occupation, family. This can be a good supplement to the existing structured information in the knowledge graph, providing more in-depth detailed description, and even mining new knowledge that may be missing in the knowledge graph.

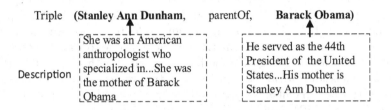

Fig. 2. An example of entity description in triplet.

In particular, our model can be summarized as follows. (i) When generating relation embedding in hyperbolic space, the context information of the relation is taken into account. Relational context information not only integrates the head entity information and tail entity information of the triplet, but also considers the neighbor relations. (ii) Text description information of entities is considered as auxiliary information to generate entity embedding using graph convolution network in hyperbolic space. The entity structure information extracted from TransE and entity semantic information in text description are integrated to obtain the entity embedding.

2   Related Work

2.1   Traditional KGC Models

TransE is one of the most widely used KGC models, which treats a relation as a translation from a head entity to a tail entity with translational constraint of $e_s + e_r \approx e_o$. Bi-linear models based models, which assume the score of a triple can be factorized into several tensors. In RESCAL [15], each entity was represented as a vector, tensor product is used to capture similarities between entities, and each relation is represented as a matrix to capture interactions of entities, utilizing the score function $\phi(e_s, r, e_o) = e_s^\top \mathbf{M}_r e_o$ to compute the scores of knowledge triples. ConvE [8] is a model based on Convolutional Neural Networks, which utilizes embedded two-dimensional convolution and multi-layer nonlinear features. In recent years, the research on GNNs [16] has developed rapidly, and has been further applied in the field of knowledge graph embedding. There are a large number of related studies that combine GCNs [17] and knowledge graph completion task. R-GCN [18] proposed the relation using specific parameter matrix to model the relation of knowledge graph, but the weight of each neighbor node in GCN is the same, and did not consider specific embedded vector relation, and when the relations are too many, model training are very slow, and requires a larger memory space.

2.2 Hyperbolic Embedding

HGCN [10] combines hyperbolic space with graph convolution network, by adding curvature as parameter, and using hyperbolic space, which can better model hierarchical data. HGCN achieves better results in node classification and link prediction tasks than traditional GCN. HGNN [11] also combines hyperbolic space with graph neural networks to transform operations in Euclidean space to hyperbolic space. LGCN [12] use Lorentzian model to do operations in hyperbolic space, such as linear transformation and nonlinear activation, and design an elegant neighborhood aggregation method. Compared with the existing HGCN [10], LGCN has lower distortion in learning tree representation. HypersphereE [19] also introduce an embedding method for knowledge graph completion based on hypersphere. MuRP [20] embedded multi-relational graph data into hyperbolic space model. Through hyperbolic calculus in hyperbolic space, such as Mobius multiplication and Mobius addition, MuRP can model hierarchical data better compared with methods in Euclidean space, and the model's expression in low-dimensional space is significantly better than others in Euclidean space.

2.3 Text Enhanced Model

In order to enhance the representation ability of knowledge graph, text enhanced representation model attempts to use text such as entity description and multiple knowledge bases to represent knowledge graph. DKRL [21] extends the translatation-based embedding approach from a specific triplet approach to a "text-enhanced" model. More importantly, DKRL adopts CNN structure to represent entity description, which improves the semantic representation of words. In this paper, we not only consider the strength of text-enhanced model and hyperbolic space but also use relational context to model relations.

3 Method

The TRHGCN model is divided into two parts: relation feature generator and entity feature generator. Our method use Lorentz hyperbolic model, which has lower distortion when learning the representation of tree-likeness graphs compared with existing hyperbolic GCNs.

3.1 Relation Feature Generator

The relation feature generator considers the influence of the relational context composed of the neighbor relations, head and tail entity. All the calculation process of the model is carried out in hyperbolic space, which can better model the hierarchical data. The detail of relation feature generator is shown in Fig. 3. The relation feature generator makes full use of the translation characteristics of TransE to obtains the relation embedding through the subtraction operation between the head and tail entities, and considers the neighborhood relations to perceive the position information of the triplet in which the relation is located.

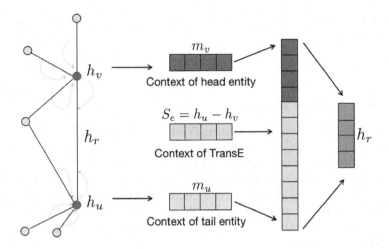

Fig. 3. Simple illustration of relation feature generator, which use TransE model to generate s_e^ℓ, and aggregate neighbor relations of head and tail entity as message m_v^ℓ and m_u^ℓ.

By sampling the neighbor relation of the head and tail entities, the embedded relation after sampling is mapped to Euclidean space by *log* operation, as shown in Eq. (1), the aggregation relation vectors m_u^ℓ and m_v^ℓ are obtained by summation operation in Euclidean space, which are used as the component of the context information of the relation.

$$m_{u,v}^\ell = \sum_{r \in N(u,v)} \log_o^{K_{\ell-1}} \left(h_r^{\ell-1,H} \right) \tag{1}$$

We can acquire relational context s_e^ℓ through tail entity embedding subtract head entity embedding in Euclidean space using translation feature of TransE, as show in Eq. (2), to generate the relational structural embedding s_e^ℓ.

$$s_e^\ell = \log_o^{K_\ell} \left(h_u^{\ell,H} \right) - \log_o^{K_\ell} \left(h_v^{\ell,H} \right) \tag{2}$$

Relation feature generator use full connection operation to combine m_v^ℓ, m_u^ℓ and s_e^{ell}, as shown in Eq. (3). The combined embedding vector $X_r^{\ell,H}$ is obtained, which not only considers the structure information of the relation in the triplet but also the location information of the current relation.

$$X_r^{\ell,H} = \exp_o^K \left(m_v^\ell \| m_u^\ell \| s_e^\ell \right), v, u \in \mathcal{N}(e) \tag{3}$$

The linear transformation process of relation feature generator is also completed in hyperbolic space. As shown in Eq. (4), the relational context output by the full connection layer is vetorized as $X_r^{\ell,H}$, then multiply the weighted matrix W and use nonlinear activation function $\sigma^{\otimes^{K_{\ell-1},K_\ell}}$ in hyperbolic space ,the relational vector is output finally as $h_r^{\ell,H}$. The $1/K_{\ell-1}$ and $1/K_\ell$ respectively represent the curvature of layer $\ell - 1$ and layer ℓ. $\otimes$ is mobius multiplication, and $\oplus$ is mobius addition.

$$h_r^{\ell,H} = \sigma^{\otimes^{K_{\ell-1},K_\ell}} \left(X_r^{\ell,H} \otimes^{K_{\ell-1}} W_r \oplus^{K_{\ell-1}} b^\ell \right) \tag{4}$$

3.2   Entity Feature Generator

As we see in Eq. (5), We use pre-trained TransE to obtain entity structural vector represented as e_s. Then we use BERT [22] to extract the textual description vector as e_i. Next, we use hadamard product to combine e_i and e_s to obtain entity interaction vector h_e which contains the entity textual information and the structural information of the triplet. Since some entity structure information may be lost during the training process, it is necessary to reconsider the entity structural information after obtaining the interactive vector. λ is the parameter to be learned.

$$h_e = \lambda \left(e_i \circ e_s \right) + (1 - \lambda)e_s \tag{5}$$

Entity feature generator adopts the combination idea in CompGCN [23] and obtains entity feature information based on hyperbolic graph convolution network. In this paper, entity embedding and relation embedding are used to obtain combined vector by circular correlation operation, then graph convolution operation is carried out in hyperbolic space, and weighted aggregation of neighborhood information is carried out by attention mechanism, finally generating entity feature information.

The scoring function of the training process of TRHGCN model adopts the scoring function of ConvE model to determine if each triple is the correct triple. The score function of ConvE is shown as Eq. (6), which $\overline{h}$ and $\overline{r}$ are vector of entities and relations. $\overline{h}, \overline{r} \in \mathbb{R}^{d_1 \times d_2}$ $h \in \mathbb{R}^{d'}$, $r \in \mathbb{R}^{d'}$, $h, r \in \mathbb{R}^{d'}$ then $d' = d_1 d_2$, ω represent a set of filter. $*$ represent convolution operation. $\mathrm{vec}(\cdot)$ is vectorized function, and Q is weighted matrix.

$$f(h, r, t) = \mathrm{ReLU}(\mathrm{vec}(\mathrm{ReLU}([\overline{h}; \overline{r}] * \omega))Q)t \tag{6}$$

4   Experiment

4.1   Datasets

This paper mainly conduct experiments on TRHGCN on three public datasets: WN18RR [8], FB15K-237 [8] and NELL-995[24]. The dataset used in our experiment is as Table 1 shows.

(1) WN18RR: WN18RR is a subset of WN18. The dataset removes inverse relations in WN18 dataset, but retains symmetric relations, asymmetric relations, where 18 means 18 kinds of relations and there are a lot of hierarchical relations in this dataset.

(2) FB15K-237: The FB15K-237 dataset is a subset extracted from the FreeBase dataset. Since inverse relation in FB15k would cause data leakage of test set, in order to avoid data leakage of test set, FB15K-237 are proposed, which removed the inverse relations from FB15k dataset.

(3) NELL-995: NELL-995 is a subset of NELL dataset. In this paper, four sub-datasets after the segmentation of NELL-995 dataset are adopted, and the proportion of hierarchical relations in the four sub-datasets are 100%, 75%, 50% and 25% respectively. We name these datasets NELL-995-h100, NELL-995-h75, NELL-995-h50 and Nell-995-h25, containing 43 hierarchical relations and 0, 14, 43, 129 non-hierarchical relations.

Table 1. Statistics of all datasets used in experiments.

	FB15K-237	WN18RR	NELL-995
Entity	14,541	40,943	63,917
Relation	237	11	198
Training	272,115	86,835	137,465
Validation	17,535	3,034	5,000
Test	20,466	3,134	5,000

4.2 Evaluation Protocol

In order to evaluate different models, for each test triple (e_i, r, e_j), we replace its head entity e_i with every entity $e_i' \in \mathcal{E}$ to calculate the scores of test triple (e_i, r, e_j) and every corrupted triple (e_i', r, e_j), and then compute the rank of test triple among these corrupted triples. Similarly, the head entity e_j of the test triple will be replaced as well. We evaluate our models using the evaluation metrics across the link prediction experiment: mean reciprocal rank (MRR) and Hits@ $k, k \in \{1, 3, 10\}$. Mean reciprocal rank is the average of the inverse of a mean rank assigned to the true triple over all evaluation triples. Hits@ k measures the percentage of the true triple appears in the top k to rank evaluation triples.

4.3 Experiment Results

Link Prediction Experiment. Link prediction results for all WN18RR and FB15k-237 are listed in Table 2. It can be seen that TRHGCN has achieved competitive results compared to other existing baselines. Hit@1 and Hit@3 are better than all of other methods in the experiments of two data sets, which indicates that adding relational context and entity description information can improve the performance of knowledge graph completion. There are more hierarchical relations in WN18RR than in FB15K-237, and our model uses hyperbolic space to do calculation, which can better represent the hierarchical relations. Experimental results in WN18RR has better performance than in FB15k-237.

Table 2. Results on WN18RR and FB15k-237. The best results are in bold.

	WN18RR				FB15k-237			
	MRR	Hits@10	Hits@3	Hits@1	MRR	Hits@10	Hits@3	Hits@1
DisMult [25]	.430	.490	.440	.390	.241	.419	.263	.155
ComplEx [5]	.440	.510	.460	.410	.247	.428	.275	.158
R-GCN [18]	–	–	–	–	.248	.417	.262	.151
ConvE [8]	.430	.520	.440	.400	.325	.501	.356	.237
HAKE [26]	.497	.582	.516	.452	.346	**.542**	.381	.250
HyperKG [27]	.41	.50	–	–	.28	.45	–	–
ATTH [28]	.486	.573	.499	.443	.348	.540	.384	.252
MURP [20]	.481	.566	.495	.440	.335	.518	.367	.243
CompGCN [23]	.479	.546	.494	.443	**.355**	.535	.390	.264
TRHGCN	**.512**	**.584**	**.516**	**.455**	.354	.536	**.402**	**.266**

Embedding Dimension and Hierarchical Relations. Table 3 shows link prediction results in NELL-995-h{100, 75, 50, 25} datasets for MuRP, CompGCN and TRHGCN at $d = 40$ and $d = 200$. It can be seen that TRHGCN performs better than MURP and CompGCN in all datasets. It is more obvious that our model can gain excellent performance than other model in lower dimension $d = 40$. As hierarchical relations increase gradually in NELL-995 dataset, the result of link prediction experiment also has improved. This shows that the model is effective in low dimensional space and can better model hierarchical relations.

Table 3. Results on NELL-995-h{100, 75, 50, 25} for $d = 40$ and $d = 200$.

Dataset	Model	$d = 40$				$d = 200$			
		MRR	Hits@10	Hits@3	Hits@1	MRR	Hits@10	Hits@3	Hits@1
NELL-995-h100	MuRP	.344	.511	.383	.261	.360	.529	.401	.274
	CompGCN	.362	.533	.398	.278	.372	.541	.414	.289
	TRHGCN	**.383**	**.550**	**.416**	**.293**	**.388**	**.556**	**.440**	**.312**
NELL-995-h75	MuRP	.365	.536	.405	.280	.359	.524	.401	.275
	CompGCN	.370	.542	.411	.284	.365	.536	.405	.280
	TRHGCN	**.379**	**.550**	**.423**	**.292**	**.363**	**.546**	**.412**	**.304**
NELL-995-h50	MuRP	.356	.519	.399	.271	.371	.539	.415	.284
	CompGCN	.362	.524	.403	.274	.375	**.551**	**.425**	**.290**
	TRHGCN	**.366**	**.530**	**.418**	**.281**	**.377**	.549	.423	.283
NELL-995-h25	MuRP	.343	.494	.379	.266	.359	.507	.397	.282
	CompGCN	.344	.511	.383	.261	375	**.538**	**.425**	**.308**
	TRHGCN	**.362**	**.524**	**.395**	**.275**	**.382**	.535	.425	.305

Ablation Study. We also conduct ablation study as shown in Table 4. The entity and relation vectors generated by the pre-trained TransE to do the ablation study about text description of entities. When the text description of the entity is removed, the result are not as good as before. We randomly generate relational embedding to do ablation study about relational context. When relational context is removed, the value of MRR decrease. The experimental result shows that text description and relational context both play important roles in our model.

Table 4. The ablation study on TRHGCN, -T represent removes textual descriptions of entities, -R represent removes relational context of relations.

	WN18RR			FB15k-237		
	MRR	Hits@10	Hits@1	MRR	Hits@10	Hits@1
TRHGCN	.512	.584	.455	.354	.536	.266
TRHGCN(-T)	.503	.573	.446	.348	.525	.257
TRHGCN(-R)	.507	.578	.448	.349	.530	.262
TRHGCN(-R & -T)	.481	.558	.432	.338	.512	.250

5 Conclusion and Future Work

In this paper, we introduced Text-Enhanced and Relational Context based Hyperbolic Knowledge Graph Embedding. Text description of entity is used as supplementary information for semantic representation of entities. Relational context are used to represent the relation embedding. We use hyperbolic space to model the hierarchical data in knowledge graphs. The experimental results show that our method can gain competitive result in link prediction experiments. In future work, we will consider the path information of the knowledge graph and try to carry out feature interaction between entity semantic information and structural information in more diversified ways.

Acknowledgements. This work is jointly supported by National Natural Science Foundation of China (61877043) and National Natural Science of China (61877044).

References

1. Bollacker, K.D., Evans, C., Paritosh, P., Sturge, T., Taylor, J.: Freebase: a collaboratively created graph database for structuring human knowledge. In: SIGMOD Conference, pp. 1247–1250 (2008)
2. Miller, G.A.: Wordnet: a lexical database for English. Commun. ACM **38**(11), 39–41 (1995)
3. Carlson, A., Betteridge, J., Kisiel, B., Settles, B., E.R.H. Jr., Mitchell, T.M.: Toward an architecture for never-ending language learning. In: AAAI (2010)
4. Bordes, A., Usunier, N., García-Durán, A., Weston, J., Yakhnenko, O.: Translating embeddings for modeling multi-relational data. In: NIPS, pp. 2787–2795 (2013)

5. Trouillon, T., Welbl, J., Riedel, S., Gaussier, É., Bouchard, G.: Complex embeddings for simple link prediction. In: ICML, pp. 2071–2080 (2016)
6. Balazevic, I., Allen, C., Hospedales, T.M.: Tucker: tensor factorization for knowledge graph completion. In: EMNLP/IJCNLP (1), pp. 5184–5193 (2019)
7. Luo, T., et al.: BTDE: block term decomposition embedding for link prediction in knowledge graph. In: ECAI, ser. Frontiers in Artificial Intelligence and Applications, vol. 325, pp. 817–824 (2020)
8. Dettmers, T., Minervini, P., Stenetorp, P., Riedel, S.: Convolutional 2d knowledge graph embeddings. In: AAAI, pp. 1811–1818 (2018)
9. Nguyen, D.Q., Nguyen, T.D., Nguyen, D.Q., Phung, D.Q.: A novel embedding model for knowledge base completion based on convolutional neural network. In: NAACL-HLT (2), pp. 327–333 (2018)
10. Chami, I., Ying, Z., Ré, C., Leskovec, J.: Hyperbolic graph convolutional neural networks. In: NeurIPS, pp. 4869–4880 (2019)
11. Liu, Q., Nickel, M., Kiela, D.: Hyperbolic graph neural networks. In: NeurIPS, pp. 8228–8239 (2019)
12. Zhang, Y., Wang, X., Shi, C., Liu, N., Song, G.: Lorentzian graph convolutional networks. Proc. Web Conf. **2021**, 1249–1261 (2021)
13. Msahli, M., Qiu, H., Zheng, Q., Memmi, G., Lu, J.: Topological graph convolutional network-based urban traffic flow and density prediction. IEEE Trans. Intell. Transp. Syst. **PP**(99) (2020)
14. Gao, T., Zhang, Y., Li, M., Lu, J., Cheng, Z., Xiao, G.: Representation learning of knowledge graph with semantic vectors. In: Qiu, H., Zhang, C., Fei, Z., Qiu, M., Kung, S.-Y. (eds.) KSEM 2021. LNCS (LNAI), vol. 12816, pp. 16–29. Springer, Cham (2021). https://doi.org/10.1007/978-3-030-82147-0_2
15. Nickel, M., Tresp, V., Kriegel, H.: A three-way model for collective learning on multi-relational data. In: ICML, pp. 809–816 (2011)
16. Zhou, J., et al.: Graph neural networks: a review of methods and applications. AI Open **1**, 57–81 (2020)
17. Kipf, T.N., Welling, M.: Semi-supervised classification with graph convolutional networks. In: ICLR (2017)
18. Schlichtkrull, M., Kipf, T.N., Bloem, P., van den Berg, R., Titov, I., Welling, M.: Modeling relational data with graph convolutional networks. In: Gangemi, A., et al. (eds.) ESWC 2018. LNCS, vol. 10843, pp. 593–607. Springer, Cham (2018). https://doi.org/10.1007/978-3-319-93417-4_38
19. Dong, Y., Guo, X., Xiang, J., Liu, K., Tang, Z.: HyspherE: an embedding method for knowledge graph completion based on hypersphere. In: Qiu, H., Zhang, C., Fei, Z., Qiu, M., Kung, S.-Y. (eds.) KSEM 2021. LNCS (LNAI), vol. 12815, pp. 517–528. Springer, Cham (2021). https://doi.org/10.1007/978-3-030-82136-4_42
20. Balazevic, I., Allen, C., Hospedales, T.M.: Multi-relational poincaré graph embeddings. In: NeurIPS, pp. 4465–4475 (2019)
21. Zuo, Y., Fang, Q., Qian, S., Zhang, X., Xu, C.: Representation learning of knowledge graphs with entity attributes and multimedia descriptions. In: Fourth IEEE International Conference on Multimedia Big Data, BigMM 2018, Xi'an, China, September 13–16, 2018, pp. 1–5 (2018)
22. Devlin, J., Chang, M., Lee, K., Toutanova, K.: BERT: pre-training of deep bidirectional transformers for language understanding. In: NAACL-HLT, pp. 4171–4186 (2019)
23. Vashishth, S., Sanyal, S., Nitin, V., Talukdar, P.P.: Composition-based multi-relational graph convolutional networks. In: ICLR (2020)

24. Xiong, W., Hoang, T., Wang, W.Y.: Deeppath: a reinforcement learning method for knowledge graph reasoning. In: EMNLP, pp. 564–573 (2017)
25. Yang, B., Yih, W., He, X., Gao, J., Deng, L.: Embedding entities and relations for learning and inference in knowledge bases. In: ICLR (Poster) (2015)
26. Zhang, Z., Cai, J., Zhang, Y., Wang, J.: Learning hierarchy-aware knowledge graph embeddings for link prediction. In: AAAI, pp. 3065–3072 (2020)
27. Kolyvakis, P., Kalousis, A., Kiritsis, D.: Hyperbolic knowledge graph embeddings for knowledge base completion. In: Harth, A., et al. (eds.) ESWC 2020. LNCS, vol. 12123, pp. 199–214. Springer, Cham (2020). https://doi.org/10.1007/978-3-030-49461-2_12
28. Chami, I., Wolf, A., Juan, D., Sala, F., Ravi, S., Ré, C.: Low-dimensional hyperbolic knowledge graph embeddings. In: ACL, pp. 6901–6914 (2020)

Cross-Sentence Temporal Relation Extraction with Relative Sentence Time

Pengyun Xie[1], Xinning Zhu[2(✉)], Chunhong Zhang[2], Zheng Hu[1], and Guanghua Yang[3]

[1] State Key Laboratory of Networking and Switching Technology, Beijing University of Posts and Telecommunications, Beijing, China
{xiepengyun,huzheng}@bupt.edu.cn
[2] School of Information and Communication Engineering, Beijing University of Posts and Telecommunications, Beijing, China
{zhuxn,zhangch}@bupt.edu.cn
[3] Jinan University, Zhuhai, China
ghyang@jnu.edu.cn

Abstract. Event temporal relation is capable to detect event evolution and plays an important role in natural language processing. Many recent studies which employ pre-trained language models have shown prominent performance improvement. However, due to more complex context, these approaches usually perform poorly when two events are not within the same sentence.

Thus in this paper, we propose a cross-sentence temporal relation extraction model which incorporates the prediction of temporal relations between sentences to enhance the performance of temporal event relation extraction. A multi-task learning framework is adopted by integrating the temporal relation classifier with an auxiliary task to predict the temporal order of the sentences. In addition, to deal with the problem of class-imbalanced data, we propose a sub-sampling method by decreasing the number of Vague relations. Compared to the baseline model, extensive experiments show that our model is capable to enhance the performance of cross-sentence temporal relation extraction while achieving state-of-the-art results on TimeBank-Dense, MATRES, and TCR dataset.

Keywords: Temporal relation extraction · Cross-sentence · Sentence temporal order · Relative time prediction · Multi-task

1 Introduction

Temporal relation extraction(TempRel) is a natural language understanding task. In general, this task requires to understand contextual semantics to extract temporal relation between events in a given text. Accurately understanding event order is beneficial for the development of downstream applications such as question answering [1], time line generation [2].

© The Author(s), under exclusive license to Springer Nature Switzerland AG 2022
G. Memmi et al. (Eds.): KSEM 2022, LNAI 13368, pp. 346–357, 2022.
https://doi.org/10.1007/978-3-031-10983-6_27

Fig. 1. Gold temporal relations in the cross sentence from a document excerpt. The yellow and blue boxes are two sentences respectively, which is separated by periods("."). Green arrow represents *After* relation and purple arrow represents *Before*

With the maturity of event extraction, more researchers have begun to pay attention to temporal relation extraction between events [2,3,8]. Compared to entity relation extraction, temporal relation extraction faces more challenges, such as low correlation between event type and relation type, more complex context and large span between events. As far as we know, the prior research in the temporal relation domain focused more on the setting where gold events are provided [3], and fed model with sentences extracted from a document. These models extract temporal relations without considering these relations are between events within the same sentence or in two consecutive sentences, thus leading to performance degradation in the latter case. Cross-sentence temporal relation extraction is more general in the document-level temporal relation extraction. For example, 76% of labeled temporal relations in TimeBank-Dense(TB-Dense) dataset [4] are not within the same sentence. Moreover, when evaluating the performance of some existing temporal relation extraction models [5] on TB-Dense dataset, almost 70% of the incorrect predicted temporal relations come from cross-sentence relation extraction.

Figure 1 shows the relations between events from one or two consecutive sentences. The nodes **trying, eliminate, restore, reported, killed clashes** are given events, and different color of edges specify different types of temporal relations. Edges between nodes of the same color represent the within-sentence temporal relations, while edges between nodes of different colors represent cross-sentence temporal relations. We observe that the topic described in the first sentence happens after the topic described in the second sentence. And all events labeled in the first sentence have the same relation with the events labeled in the second sentence. The consistency of the sentence order and event temporal relation is general. According to our statistics, 66% of the sentence pairs in the TB-Dense dataset and 71% of the sentence pairs in the MATRES dataset [6] follow this rule. Therefore, it is beneficial to make full use of this rule to improve the performance of temporal relation extraction. In this work, we propose a model that incorporates a the sentence temporal ordering task to enhance the ability to extract temporal relations across sentences. The traditional sentence ordering prediction(SOP) [7] task is to determine whether the order of sentence description is correct since the input sentence pairs may be incoherent. Different from the traditional sentence ordering prediction task, the input sentence pairs in our proposed model are coherent and have semantic logical order, but the temporal order of each sentence topic is unknown. In addition, even if the events in the two sentences are labeled incorrectly, sentence temporal ordering will not be affected. Hence, the method we proposed reduces the dependency on gold event annotations.

If we know the specific time that sentence describes, we can easily know the order of the sentence topic in the cross-sentence situations. However, the explicit time rarely appears in a sentence. Recently, Leeuwenberg [2] and Wen [8] propose to predict the relative event time and compare the relative timestamps of events to extract temporal relation. Inspired by this work, we use the similar method to predict relative sentence time for each sentence. In this way, we obtain the sentence order by comparing relative sentence time.

Besides, temporal relation extraction needs to struggle with the sparse event distribution in document and class-imbalanced data. Recently released temporal relation datasets, such as TB-Dense and MATRES datasets, still suffer from this issue. MATRES is relatively small in its size (15K TempRels). In the TB-Dense dataset, there are 3760 events and 5211 event pairs to predict temporal relation relations, but only 50% of all relations are *No-Vague* temporal relations, while the percentage of *Equal, Includes* and *Is_Included* are all less than 12%. To address this issue, we propose a *Vague* relation subsampling method to reduce excessive *Vague* relations.

Results of experiments show that we improve cross-sentence relation extraction by 1.3%-4.2% in $F1$ and obtain state-of-the-art performance across three common datasets TB-Dense, MATRES, TCR with 0.5%-1.3% improvement in $F1$, showing the effectiveness of our model.

In summary, our main contributions are presented as follows:

- We propose a sentence pair temporal ordering task to model the temporal ordering consistency of sentence pairs and event pairs and use relative sentence time to show the sentence temporal order of two consecutive sentences. What's more, a multi-task learning framework is employed to integrate the sentence pair temporal ordering task with a temporal relation classifier to improve the performance of cross-sentence temporal relation extraction. We evaluate the results for within- and cross-sentence relation extractions separately.
- We propose a *Vague* relation subsampling method to deal with the class-imbalanced data on the small datasets.

The paper is organized as follows: in Sect. 2, we describe the related work of TempRel. In Sect. 3, we will discuss our model for temporal relation extraction. The results and analysis of our experiments are shown in Sect. 4. Finally, we provide a conclusion in Sect. 5.

2   Related Work

In the temporal relation(TempRel) domain, various datasets are released and many methods are proposed. Early in the 2013 TempEval3 workshop, conventional machine learning models are used for extracting event TempRels, such as SVM, Max-entropy and logistic regression, and they all require expensive hand-crafted features. With the success of BERT [9], fine-tuning a pre-trained language model (LM) has become the de facto base model for temporal relation extraction between events. Some researchers leverage LSTM [10] or Graph Convolutional Networks (GCN) [11] to encode sequence, feeding the sentences or event pairs representations into a multi-layer perceptron for temporal relation classification. Recent approaches focus on modeling the dependency between relations using methods such as probabilistic soft logic (PSL) regularization [5] or Integer Linear Programming (ILP) [10]. In addition, Leeuwenberg [2] first proposes to predict relative event time and compare timestamps to get relation. However, this model can't handle the uncertain temporal boundary such as *Vague*. In order to solve this problem, Wen [8] incorporates the relative event time as additional features into training.

All the above works don't distinguish relations in within or cross sentences,, and temporal relation extraction models for in- and cross-domain are rarely studied. Lin and Miller [12] use BERT-finetuned model for sentence-agnostic temporal relation instances and evaluate the model for in- and cross-domain on the THYME corpus. Compared to the previous work, our model is distinguished by enhancing the cross-sentence temporal relation extraction, which treats within-sentence issue as a special case.

3 Approach

In this study, we are aiming at extracting temporal relations that occur within or cross sentences by inputting multiple sentences. Document D is divided into k sub-sentences, denoted as a sentence set $S = \{s_1, \cdots, s_k\}$. According to the position of the two events that labeled temporal relation within or across sentences, the input sequence $C = \{c_1, \cdots, c_n\}$ is denoted as $C = \{s_i, s_{i+1}\}$ for cross-sentence or $C = \{s_i\}$ for within-sentence, where $s_i \in S$ and c is a token representing a word and n is the total number of tokens. Given the input sequence C together with a set of l marked events $E = \{e_1, \cdots, e_l\}$, where $l \leq n$, we denote respectively the source and target events by e_s and e_t and these events make up the event pairs (e_s, e_t), where $s \geq 1$ and $t \leq n$. In general, we predict the temporal relation $y \in \mathcal{Y}$ between event pairs from a given sequence which contains relations within or across sentences. $\mathcal{Y}$ represents the set of relation classes.

The overall architecture of our model is shown in Fig. 2. The architecture consists of two components including a Temporal Relation Classifier and a Sentence Relative Timestamp Predictor. The Temporal Relation Classifier utilizes event pairs to classify temporal relations. For the sentence temporal ordering task, our model predicts the relative sentence time to facilitate the cross-sentence temporal relation extraction(Sect. 3.2). In order to solve the problem of class-imbalanced data, we propose a subsampling algorithm (Sect. 3.4).

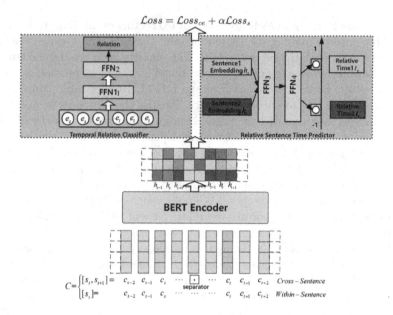

Fig. 2. Overview of our proposed model.

3.1   Temporal Relation Classifier

Our temporal relation classifier encodes the input sequence C by applying the pretrained language model BERT.

$$H = Bert(C) = \{h_1, h_2, \cdots, h_n\} \tag{1}$$

We denote contextualized representation of the sequence vector as H and each token $c_j \in C$ has a hidden representation vector h_j, which contains the syntactic and semantic features. Token c_s and c_t represent event e_s and e_t, respectively. Considering that the relation extracted from the sequence C is determined by two given event mentions e_s and e_t together, we use the contextualized representation of the event pair $h_{s,t}$ to predict temporal relation via concatenating the hidden representation vector h_s and h_t.

$$h_{s,t} = [h_s \oplus h_t] \tag{2}$$

where $\oplus$ is a concatenation operation. By feeding the event pair embedding $h_{s,t}$ to a two-layer feed-forward neural network(FNN) with a tanh activation function, we can predict the relation $\widehat{y}$ with the softmax function to convert the representation into a probability:

$$a_{s,t} = FFN_2(tanh(FFN_1(h_{s,t}))) \tag{3}$$

$$P(y|e_s, e_t) = softmax(W_f \cdot a_{s,t} + b_f) \tag{4}$$

where $FFN(x) = W \cdot x + b$, W and b are the weights and bias in the FFN layer

$$\widehat{y_i} = \underset{y_i \in \mathcal{Y}}{\arg\max} \, P(y_i | e_s, e_t) \tag{5}$$

we use cross-entropy objective for temporal relation classification.

$$\mathcal{L}_{ce} = -logP(y = \widehat{y} | e_s, e_t) \tag{6}$$

3.2 Sentence Relative Timestamp Predictor

The synergistic case between sentence pairs and event pairs has been shown in Fig. 1. To model the connection of two consecutive sentences, we use an auxiliary task to extract the temporal order of sentences. Inspired by Wen [8] and Leeuwenberg [2], we predict the relative sentence time for two consecutive sentences and anchor sentence temporal order by comparing the relative timestamp of each sentence. For two consecutive sentences, we use period ("*.*") to separate the input sequence $\mathcal{C}$, which corresponding the token c_m. The input sequence C can be denoted as:

$$\mathcal{C} = \{s_i, s_{i+1}\} = \{\{c_1, \cdots, c_m\}, \{c_{m+1}, \cdots, c_n\}\} \tag{7}$$

When dealing with within-sentence relation extraction, we treat it as a special case and set $m = 0$. We predict relative sentence time by mapping the representation of sentence s_i to a relative time $t_i \in (-1, 1)$. We obtain sentence embedding h_{s_i} and $h_{s_{i+1}}$ by averaging the embeddings for each token in sentence s_i and s_{i+1}. By feeding the sentence embedding to a two-layer feed-forward neural network(FFN), we get the relative timestamp t_i and t_{i+1}..

$$t_i = tanh(FFN_4(tanh(FFN_3(h_{s_i})))) \tag{8}$$

$$t_{i+1} = tanh(FFN_4(tanh(FFN_3(h_{s_{i+1}})))) \tag{9}$$

We use temporal order of sentences to assist temporal relation extraction. The temporal order of the two sentences is determined by the order of the events contained in them. To be specific, if the topic of the first sentence s_i is *Before* the second sentence s_{i+1}, their predicted time should be $t_i < t_{i+1}$. We use a margin-based optimization method to constrain relative sentence time. For example, if s_i is *Before* s_{i+1}, the optimization will maximize the distance between t_i and t_{i+1}. If s_i is *Equal* to s_{i+1}, it instead minimizes the distance. The same principle applies to other relations. The loss of sentence temporal ordering task is as follows:

$$\begin{aligned}
\mathcal{L}_S = \, & Rel[r_{(e_s, e_t)} = \text{BEFORE}]max(0, 1 - (t_{i+1} - t_i)) \\
& + Rel[r_{(e_s, e_t)} = \text{AFTER}]max(0, 1 - (t_i - t_{i+1})) \\
& + Rel[r_{(e_s, e_t)} = \text{INCLUDES}]max(0, 1 - (t_{i+1} - t_i)) \\
& + Rel[r_{(e_s, e_t)} = \text{IS\_INCLUDED}]max(0, 1 - (t_i - t_{i+1})) \\
& + Rel[r_{(e_s, e_t)} = \text{EQUAL}]|t_i - t_{i+1}|
\end{aligned} \tag{10}$$

where $Rel[r_{(e_s, e_t)} = \text{LABEL}] \in \{0, 1\}$, which indicates that relation label of (e_s, e_t) is LABEL.

3.3 Loss Function

We adopt a multi-task learning framework to connect two tasks, which are based on the same pretrained language model and sharing parameters. During training, we sum up the loss function (6) and (10) as the total loss, where α is a hyperparameter as the weight.

$$\mathcal{L} = \mathcal{L}_{ce} + \alpha \mathcal{L}_S \tag{11}$$

3.4 Subsampling Algorithm

Given l marked events in a document, it can combine $l \cdot (l-1)/2$ event pairs. However, when there are too many or even up to 10 events in a sentence, the samples of different relation classes will be seriously out of balance. This is because only a small number of event pairs have *No-Vague* temporal relations. When training a model by using a small dataset, such as TB-Dense, this problem is more serious. We propose a subsampling algorithm to reduce the impact of *Vague* relation, as described in Algorithm 1. If the proportion of *Vague* relation in the sequence $\mathcal{C}$ is greater than the threshold λ, we use parameter γ to control its proportion. We denote the proportion of *Vague* relations in the input sequence as $\mathcal{P}$:

$$\mathcal{P} = \frac{N_V}{N_{all}} \tag{12}$$

where N_V is the size of *Vague* relations set $R(Vague) = \{v_1, \cdots, v_j, \cdots, v_{N_V}\}$ and v_j is a *Vague* relation in the sequence $\mathcal{C}$. N_{All} is the size of all relations in the input sequence $\mathcal{C}$. If the proportion $\mathcal{P}$ is greater than the threshold λ $(0<\lambda<1)$, we tune the hyperparameters γ $(0<\gamma< 1)$ to control the proportion of the vague relation as follows:

$$R(Vague) = \begin{cases} Random(R(Vague), \gamma) & \mathcal{P} \geq \lambda \\ R(Vague) & \mathcal{P} < \lambda \end{cases} \tag{13}$$

where the function of $Random(\cdot, \cdot)$ is to randomly select γ proportion of *Vague* relation from set $R(Vague)$.

4 Experimental Results

4.1 Dataset

We train and test our model on the TB-Dense and MATRES dataset. Due to the limited size of Temporal and Causal Reasoning (TCR) dataset, we use it just as a test set to evaluate the performance of the model trained on MATRES dataset. TB-Dense has six relation classes and consists of 36 documents. MATRES and TCR dataset both have four relation classes. MATRES dataset consists of 281 documents and TCR is much smaller, consisting of just 25 documents and 2.6K relations. We show the number of relation classes in Table 1. On the MATRES dataset, we follow the official split that use TimeBank (183 docunments) and AQUAINT for training and Platinum for testing [6], and we randomly select 21 documents in training data as the validation set.

Table 1. The statistics of relations in Timebank-Dense, MATRES and TCR

Relation-type	TimeBank-dense			MATRES		TCR
	Trian	Dev	Test	Train	Test	Test
BEFORE	649	141	326	6425	427	1780
AFTER	565	136	233	4481	271	862
EQUAL	44	11	18	418	30	4
VAGUE	1800	226	571	1416	109	0
INCLUDES	168	12	47	–	–	–
IS_INCLUDED	203	14	47	–	–	–
Total	3429	540	1242	12740	837	2646

4.2 Experimental Settings

We use Precision, Recall, F1-score to evaluate our model performance. To be consistent with the baselines, we use standard Micro-average F1 scores [5] for TB-Dense dataset and F1 scores [8] where considering *Vague* as "no relation" for MATRES dataset. There are many pre-trained language models that we can utilize, such as BERT, RoBerta, RoBerta-large. In order to compare with other works, we use BERT as our pre-trained language model for TB-Dense dataset and RoBERTa-large for MATRES and TCR dataset. We use grid search for the learning rate from $\{1 \times 10^{-5}, 2 \times 10^{-5}, 4 \times 10^{-5}, 8 \times 10^{-5}\}$ and finally select 1×10^{-5} on the MATRES dataset and 2×10^{-5} on the TB-Dense dataset. Our best model is implemented in PyTorch framework and optimized using AdamW optimizer, which is completed on single NVIDIA TITAN RTX 2080 GPU. α in total loss function is set to 0.5 on the TB-Dense dataset and 1 on the MATRES dataset. The hyperparameters for vague relation subsampling γ and λ are both set to 0.8.

4.3 Overall Performance

Compared Baselines. We compare the proposed Relative Sentence Time model with the following baselines:

- **SP-ILP** [13] is a deep structured learning framework consisting of a RNN and a structured support vector machine(SSVM).
- **BiLSTM+MAP** [10] is a joint event and temporal relation extraction model with shared representations learning and structured prediction.
- **LSTM+TEMPROB+ILP** [14] is a neural system that applies word embeddings, temporal common sense knowledge, global inference via integer linear programming (ILP).
- **Joint Constrained Learning** [15] is a joint constrained learning model to solve the lack of jointly labeled data.
- **EventPlus** [16] is a temporal event understanding pipeline system that produces event understanding annotations including temporal relations.

- **CTRL-PG** [5] is a novel model with probabilistic soft logic and global inference to tackle the problem at the document level.
- **HGUR(RoBERTa) + knowledge** [17] is a model that embeds events into hyperbolic spaces for temporal relation extraction.
- **Event Relative time Comparison** [8] is a joint model for event relative prediction and event temporal relation classification.

Table 2. The results of experiments. The results of previous work are either directly taken from the cited papers or produced by the original source code. "-" represents this data is not shown or the dataset is not used in the paper.

Model	TB-Dense	MATRES			TCR
	F1_score	P	R	F1_score	F1_score
SP-ILP [13]	63.2	–	–	81.7	80.9
BiLSTM+MAP [10]	64.5	–	–	75.5	–
LSTM+TEMPROB+ILP [14]	–	71.3	82.1	76.3	–
Joint Constrained Learning [15]	–	73.4	85.0	78.8	–
EventPlus [16]	64.5	–	–	75.5	–
CTRL-PG [5]	65.2	–	–	–	–
HGRU(RoBERTa)+Knowledge [17]	–	79.2	81.7	80.5	83.5
Event Relative Time [8]	-	78.4	85.2	81.7	–
Our Model	**66.5**	**80.1**	**84.4**	**82.2**	**84.1**

Results. We show the experimental results in Table 2. Our model achieves state-of-the-art performance on all three datasets, showing that our method is successfully handling the relations within and across sentences. It outperforms the best baseline model by 0.5%–1.3% in $F1$.

4.4   Ablation Study

In order to study the impact of different components of our model, we conduct ablation study, as shown in Table 3. We evaluate the combination of relative time prediction and event embedding learning model using a multi-task framework(Multi-Task in Table 3). We see that multi-task module lift the performance by 0.4% on the TB-Dense dataset and 2.2% on the MATRES dataset in $F1$. Based on the multi-task module, our subsampling algorithm improves the performance by 1.3% on the TB-Dense dataset in $F1$. It's because only 11% of relations in the MATRES dataset are *Vague* relations but 89% of the other samples. Therefore, class-imbalanced data exists in temporal relation extraction. In comparison, 53% of relations in the TB-Dense dataset are *Vague* which is more than other relations, and 5% of relations are *Includes* or *Is_included*. During training, 27% of the input sequences in TB-Dense exceeded the threshold λ. In MATRES, it is only 5%.

Table 3. Ablation study

Model	TB-Dense			MATRES		
	P	R	F1_score	P	R	F1_score
Temporal relation classifier	64.8	64.8	64.8	75.0	85.7	80.0
Multi-Task	65.2	65.2	**65.2**	80.1	84.4	**82.2**
Multi-Task+Subsampling	66.5	66.5	**66.5**	77.8	85.9	81.7

4.5 Within- And Cross-Sentence Results Analysis

Table 4 exhibits the performance of our model for within- and cross-sentence temporal relation extraction. Compared to Relative Event Time Comparison model[1], the cross-sentence temporal extraction performance increased by 4.2% and 1.3% in $F1$ on the TB-Dense and MATRES datasets respectively. For within-sentence relation extraction, the performance decrease 0.6% in $F1$ on the TB-Dense and increase 0.5% in $F1$ on the MATRES dataset. The results show that our model effectively improve the ability of cross-sentence temporal relation extraction while guaranteeing the extraction of the within-sentence relation extraction.

Table 4. Within- and cross-sentence results

Dataset	Category	Model	P	R	F1_score
TimeBank-dense	Within-sentence	Event time Comparison	65.6	65.6	65.6
		Our model	65.0	65.0	65.0
	Cross sentence	Event time comparison	62.8	62.8	62.8
		Our model	**67.0**	**67.0**	**67.0**
MATRES	Within-sentence	Event time comparison	77.5	83.6	80.4
		Our model	78.3	83.6	80.9
	Cross-sentence	Event time comparison	82.2	84.8	83.5
		Our model	**83.7**	**86.0**	**84.8**

4.6 Case Study

Table 5 shows the results of a case study with the predicted relative sentence time and temporal relation extraction between events. In the first case, by comparing relative sentence time, the topic of Sentence1 is *After* the topic of Sentence2. We observe that the event pairs keep the same relation with the sentence pairs, and Sentence Relative Timestamp predictor module corrects the temporal relation between e_1 and e_5 which is predicted to be an incorrect *Vague* relation .

---

[1] The result of TimeBank Dense is reproduced using the same method by ourselves and the cited paper didn't experiment on this dataset

Table 5. Case study and the model predictions

1	Sentence1: Family friend and historian Dr Huw Lewis-Jones (**e1:paid**) tribute to a " gentle soul and fine climber " who (**e2:shunned**) the limelight. Sentence2: Mr Lowe also (**e3:took**) part in the trans-Antarctic expedition of 1957-58 , which (**e4:made**) the first successful overland (**e5:cross**) of Antarctica via the South Pole.
	$t_{s1} = -0.2307, \quad t_{s2} = -0.6905, \quad Sentence\ Temporal\ order = After$
	$r_{(e1,e3)} = After, \quad r_{(e1,e4)} = After, \quad r_{(e1,e5)} \neq Vague \rightarrow After$ $r_{(e2,e3)} = After, \quad r_{(e2,e4)} = After, \quad r_{(e2,e5)} \neq Vague \rightarrow After$
2	Sentence1:An Israeli raid on the ship (**e1:left**) nine passengers dead , all of them Turkish or of Turkish descent. Sentence2:" In light of the Israeli investigation into the incident , which (**e2:pointed**) out several operational errors , Prime Minister Netanyahu (**e3:apologized**) to the Turkish people for any errors that could have led to loss of life and (**e4:agreed**) to complete the agreement on compensation , " the statement (**e5:said**).
	$t_{s1} = -0.1391, \quad t_{s2} = 0.2152, \quad Sentence\ Temporal\ order = Before$
	$r_{(e1,e2)} = Before, \quad r_{(e1,e3)} = Before$ $r_{(e1,e5)} = Before, \quad r_{(e1,e4)} \neq Vague \rightarrow Before$

5 Conclusion

In this paper, we proposed to enhance cross-sentence temporal relation extraction. Our approach highlights the importance of sentence temporal order and we utilize the relative sentence time to model the temporal relation in the cross-sentence. Experiment results show our model not only outperforms SOTA methods on benchmarks, but also improves cross-sentence temporal relation extraction performance. In the future, we plan to focus on temporal relation in the within-sentence.

Acknowledgements. This work was supported by the Guangdong Province Science and Technology Project 2021A0505080015.

References

1. Ning, Q., Wu, H., Han, R., Peng, N., Gardner, M., Roth, D.: Torque: a reading comprehension dataset of temporal ordering questions. In: Proceedings of the 2020 Conference on Empirical Methods in Natural Language Processing, pp. 1158–1172 (2020)
2. Leeuwenberg, A., Moens, M.F.: Temporal information extraction by predicting relative time-lines. In: Proceedings of the 2018 Conference on Empirical Methods in Natural Language Processing, pp. 1237–1246 (2018)
3. Ning, Q., Feng, Z., Roth, D.: A structured learning approach to temporal relation extraction. In: Proceedings of the 2017 Conference on Empirical Methods in Natural Language Processing, pp. 1027–1037. Association for Computational Linguistics (2017)

4. Cassidy, T., McDowell, B., Chambers, N., Bethard, S.: An annotation framework for dense event ordering. In: Proceedings of the 52nd Annual Meeting of the Association for Computational Linguistics, pp. 501–506 (2014)
5. Zhou, Y., et al.: Clinical temporal relation extraction with probabilistic soft logic regularization and global inference. In: Proceedings of the AAAI Conference on Artificial Intelligence (2021)
6. Ning, Q., Wu, H., Roth, D.: A multi-axis annotation scheme for event temporal relations. In: Proceedings of the 56th Annual Meeting of the Association for Computational Linguistics, vol. 1: Long Papers, pp. 1318–1328 (2018)
7. Lan, Z., Chen, M., Goodman, S., Gimpel, K., Sharma, P., Soricut, R.: Albert: a lite bert for self-supervised learning of language representations (2019)
8. Wen, H., Ji, H.: Utilizing relative event time to enhance event-event temporal relation extraction. In: Proceedings of the 2021 Conference on Empirical Methods in Natural Language Processing, pp. 10431–10437 (2021)
9. Devlin, J., Chang, M.W., Lee, K., Toutanova, K.: Bert: pre-training of deep bidirectional transformers for language understanding. arXiv preprint arXiv:1810.04805 (2018)
10. Han, R., Ning, Q., Peng, N.: Joint event and temporal relation extraction with shared representations and structured prediction. In: Proceedings of the 2019 Conference on Empirical Methods in Natural Language Processing and the 9th International Joint Conference on Natural Language Processing, pp. 434–444 (2019)
11. Mathur, P., Jain, R., Dernoncourt, F., Morariu, V., Tran, Q.H., Manocha, D.: Timers: Document-level temporal relation extraction. In: Proceedings of the 59th Annual Meeting of the Association for Computational Linguistics and the 11th International Joint Conference on Natural Language Processing, vol. 2: Short Papers, pp. 524–533 (2021)
12. Lin, C., Miller, T., Dligach, D., Bethard, S., Savova, G.: A bert-based universal model for both within-and cross-sentence clinical temporal relation extraction. In: Proceedings of the 2nd Clinical Natural Language Processing Workshop, pp. 65–71 (2019)
13. Han, R., Hsu, I.H., Yang, M., Galstyan, A., Weischedel, R., Peng, N.: Deep structured neural network for event temporal relation extraction. In: Proceedings of the 23rd Conference on Computational Natural Language Learning, pp. 666–106 (2019)
14. Ning, Q., Subramanian, S., Roth, D.: An improved neural baseline for temporal relation extraction. In: Proceedings of the 2019 Conference on Empirical Methods in Natural Language Processing and the 9th International Joint Conference on Natural Language Processing, pp. 6203–6209 (2019)
15. Wang, H., Chen, M., Zhang, H., Roth, D.: Joint constrained learning for event-event relation extraction. In: Proceedings of the 2020 Conference on Empirical Methods in Natural Language Processing, pp. 696–706 (2020)
16. Ma, M.D., et al.: Eventplus: A temporal event understanding pipeline. In: Proceedings of the 2021 Conference of the North American Chapter of the Association for Computational Linguistics: Human Language Technologies: Demonstrations, pp. 56–65 (2021)
17. Tan, X., Pergola, G., He, Y.: Extracting event temporal relations via hyperbolic geometry. In: Proceedings of the 2021 Conference on Empirical Methods in Natural Language Processing, pp. 8065–8077 (2021)

Discourse Component Recognition via Graph Neural Network in Chinese Student Argumentative Essays

Sijie Wang, Ziwen Zhang, Yong Dou, Jun Luo, and Zhen Huang[✉]

National Key Laboratory of Parallel and Distributed Processing,
National University of Defense Technology, Changsha, China
{wangsijie,ziwen,yongdou,junluo,huangzhen}@nudt.edu.cn

Abstract. Identifying and classifying original discourse components is a prerequisite task for constructing the knowledge graph structure. Previous work suffers from the following problems. (i) Existing methods only rely on the discourse components themselves to extract the features of the text, and do not fully take into account the potential help of the context information of the discourse to consummate its own features. (ii) Most of the current methods usually combine multiple tasks for joint inference, with complementary effects among them, lacking methods focusing on the single-target task of discourse component recognition. To address these issues, we propose a graph neural network-based discourse component recognition model (**DCRGNN**), which enhances the interaction of sentence-level discourse component features through graph structure. Our experimental results show that **DCRGNN** achieves a relative improvement of up to 6% on Macro-F1 for specific discourse component types compared to the previous state-of-the-art methods on the Chinese dataset, and exceeds the baseline model in the single-target task on the English dataset.

Keywords: Discourse component recognition · Single-target task · Graph neural network

1 Introduction

Discourse component recognition (DCR) has been extensively studied for its potential assistance in many tasks such as argument knowledge graph construction, discourse parsing, and automatic essay scoring [17]. Nowadays, the scale of texts in electronic form is gradually increasing, so it is an indispensable task to analyze the discourse components in the text. Manual processing is time-consuming and technically demanding [10], so it is necessary to "automate" the processing of discourse texts.

Discourse component recognition is a sub-task of argument mining, which is mainly used to determine the categories of discourse elements and construct the internal structure of the essay. There are still problems with the existing

G. Memmi et al. (Eds.): KSEM 2022, LNAI 13368, pp. 358–373, 2022.
https://doi.org/10.1007/978-3-031-10983-6_28

discourse component recognition. (1) There is a strong confusion of discourse components. Even though the textual expressions are similar, there are still inconsistencies among different discourse component types. (2) The problem of data imbalance is serious. The gap between some discourse components with a small amount of data and those with a large amount of data even reaches 10 to 20 times. Among the six types of discourse components in the Chinese dataset, the proportion of Elaboration reaches more than 40%. In the three discourse components of the English dataset, Premise accounts for more than 50%. Although existing deep learning-based methods [2,19] achieve good performance, they only consider feature information of individual sentences to identify discourse components, ignoring that the meaning expressed by each sentence should not depend only on the sentence itself, but also contextual information of the context. Moreover, most of the existing methods train multiple tasks jointly, and the performance of multiple tasks is complementary to each other. There are few approaches that focus exclusively on the single-target task of discourse component recognition.

Towards these issues, we propose a framework for discourse component recognition combined with graph neural networks, called **DCRGNN**. We construct the graph neural network on sentence-level features to enhance the acquisition of contextual features by discourse components. At the same time, we adopt a composition method similar to sliding window to further optimize the graph structure.

Our experiments show that our framework outperforms the state-of-the-art in all six discourse components of Macro-F1 scores for Chinese student argumentative essays, and also outperforms the baseline model in the single-target task for English student argumentative essays. Our key contributions of this paper are as follows:

- We propose a graph neural network-based discourse component recognition model, named **DCRGNN**, which can effectively enhance the acquisition of contextual feature information by discourse components.
- We compare the effects of different types of graph neural networks and composition methods on the recognition of discourse components, and demonstrate the effectiveness of our constructed graph structure.
- Extensive experiments on two student argumentative essay datasets in Chinese and English show that the proposed **DCRGNN** achieves effective improvements over existing methods.

2   Related Work

Discourse component recognition can be considered as a sub-task of argument component type classification in the field of argument mining (AM), which mainly determines which discourse elements with argumentation nature belong to by modeling articles. Argument mining aims to automatically identify and extract argumentative structures from legal or argumentative texts, and is a challenging task in natural language processing [21]. Relevant methods can be roughly divided into the following categories.

ILP-based Method is typically aimed at joint modeling of multiple tasks. Persing [13] performed joint inference on the output of discourse component recognition and argument relation classification using ILP, which solves the error propagation problem of the pipelined approach. Stab [19] constructed a joint model for the two sub-tasks in order to ensure the consistency of global results, and optimizes the results of the two classifiers by ILP using its own constructed scoring formula. Afantenos [1] proposed a new ILP decoder and verified the importance of this decoder.

Feature-based Method typically combine multiple levels of structural features from different sources. Levy [11] mitigated the problem of data sparseness based on knowledge features such as topic word lists and lexical databases. Rinott [15] obtained complex features for classification by external classifiers such as subjectivity scores and named entity recognition. Stab [18] and Song [16] employed feature information such as location information, indicator features, and lexical features to assist in discourse component recognition.

Neural network-based Method occupy an essential place in the evolution of discourse component recognition tasks. Eger [5] defined the AM problem as dependence analysis problem, sequence labeling problem and multi-task problem, respectively, and proposed neural sequence tagging model combining with the neural network. But it requires a lot of text processing work in advance. Potash [14] applied pointer network with an attention mechanism to the discourse analysis task, handling both argument relation extraction and discourse component recognition tasks simultaneously. But they did not capture the connections between discourse components well. Daxenberger [4] modeled articles using CNN, LSTM, and BiLSTM respectively to identify claim data from multiple domains. However, they do not make full use of external features and contextual information in the text. Bao [2] proposed a neural transition-based argument mining model, which gradually builds argument graphs by generating a series of actions and can handle both tree-structured and non-tree-structured data. Despite the good performance, their method is not applicable to single-task targets and requires advanced labeling of the span range of each discourse component, which is not practical for practical use.

Therefore, we combine the feature-based approach, focus on the single-target task of discourse component recognition, and use graph-structured data [20] to alleviate the problem of insufficient contextual feature interaction.

3   Preliminary Problem Definition

Given an argumentative essay, the sentences in the essay are separated by delimiters, and the words in each sentence are also separated by commas. The task is to assign discourse component categories $\{q_1, \ldots, q_n\}$ to each sentence in the essay $E = \{s_1, \ldots, s_n\}$, where s_i is the i-th sentence in essay E, $1 \leq i \leq n$. q_i is the category of the corresponding sentence, $q_i \in \mathcal{Q}$, $\mathcal{Q}$ is a pre-defined set of discourse component types. There are seven types of Chinese dataset and four types of English dataset.

4   DCRGNN Framework

In this section, we will formally illustrate our framework **DCRGNN** in detail. **DCRGNN** consists of five parts: (1) Sentence Embedding Layer; (2) GNN Layer; (3) Position Information Encoding Layer; (4) Discourse-level Feature Extraction Layer; (5) Prediction Layer.

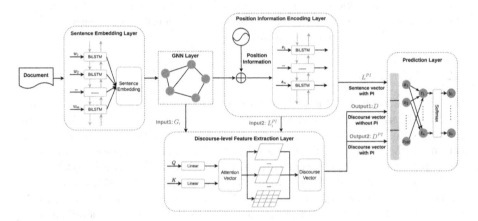

Fig. 1. The overall framework of DCRGNN. Sentence Embedding Layer and Position Information Encoding Layer perform word-level and sentence-level feature interactions, respectively. GNN Layer constructs graph structures based on sentence nodes. Discourse-level Feature Extraction Layer obtains discourse-level features through self-attention and adaptive pooling, and Prediction Layer performs the prediction of discourse components.

Sentence Embedding Layer encodes each word vector from the initial input text to obtain the initial sentence features and captures the connections between texts through Bi-LSTM. GNN layer further enhances the feature interaction between sentences and obtains richer contextual information. Additional position information is added to each sentence in the Position Information Encoding Layer to assist in classification. Discourse-level Feature Extraction Layer obtains feature vectors at the discourse level of each sentence and adds more complete characteristic information. Multiple feature vectors are combined to perform discourse component recognition at the Prediction layer. The architecture of **DCRGNN** is shown in Fig. 1.

4.1 Sentence Embedding Layer

We employs pre-trained word vectors from Tencent AI Lab[1] to convert each word into a corresponding representation vector. The input sentence sequence in each input essay is $S = \{w_1, w_2, \ldots, w_m\}$, w_i represents the i-th word in the sentence, and m represents the standard sentence length. In order to unify the length of all sentences in the essay and facilitate simultaneous training, the sentences exceeding the standard length are truncated to the standard length, while the remaining content is discarded. On the contrary, the sentences that are less than the standard length are filled with blank word information ([0]). The initialized feature vectors are fed into bidirectional LSTM (BiLSTM) to capture deep feature interactions. Ultimately, in order to obtain the initial features of the sentence, the sum of all feature vectors in each sentence is averaged, and the *tanh* function is put to use activating it.

4.2 GNN Layer

In this work, we utilize the feature information of sentences to construct graph neural networks to transform DCR into a node classification task. We employ SAGEConv [7], a network architecture that focuses on inductive node classification, as the framework for this section to obtain larger expressive capability and capture more adequate contextual feature information between nodes. Compared with the traditional GCN algorithm, whenever a new and unseen node is added, in order to obtain its characteristic information, it needs to be added to the graph and retrained with all nodes, which leads to a poor generalization of the model and high computational overhead. SAGEConv, on the other hand, is faster and more efficient as it only transfers feature information to neighboring nodes based on the selected node.

Graph Construction and Initialization
The whole essay is converted into an undirected partially connected graph, as shown in the Fig. 2, where each node represents a sentence.

The construction method is similar to the sliding window, with each node as the center, the w adjacent sentence nodes are selected forward and backward respectively to connect, thus forming a partially connected graph. In the writing habits of Chinese argumentative essays for senior high school students, the distance of sentences that produce meaningful associations with a sentence usually does not exceed three, because the longest meaning-penetrating sentence in Chinese writing, namely parallelism sentence, is usually only three sentences. Therefore, the range of w values is set to $\{1, 2, 3\}$ in this paper after experiments.

Originally, we tried the composition of the fully connected graph, hoping that each sentence node could aggregate more other sentence features, but the performance suffered. Because no matter how the feature matrix of the node is initialized, after multiple feature interactions, the features of all nodes in

---

[1] https://ai.tencent.com/ailab/nlp/en/embedding.html.

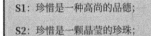

Essay

S1: 珍惜是一种高尚的品德;

S2: 珍惜是一颗晶莹的珍珠;

S3: 珍惜是使生命得到延伸的前提。

S4: 学会珍惜时间, 才不会让时间把我们消磨, 而是被我们所利用;

S5: 学会珍惜自己所拥有的, 才不会让平庸的情趣把我们迷恋, 而是被我们所排斥;

......

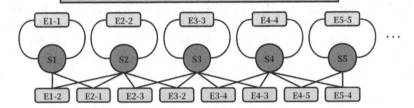

Fig. 2. Illustration of graph construction. Take $w = 1$ as an example. Each node is connected with w adjacent nodes. The blue box indicates the self-loop, and the green box indicates the directed connected edge. In the edge $Ep - q$, p denotes the starting node number and q denotes the ending node number. (Color figure online)

the same connected component will tend to be consistent, that is, the over-smoothing [8] problem will lead to the excessive similarity of feature matrices of sentences of different categories. Therefore, a partially connected graph is adopted in this paper, which can not only solve the over-smoothing problem, but also reduce the number of edges in the graph, thus greatly improving the training speed of the model.

Formally, we leverage an undirected partially connected graph $G = (V, E)$ to model an essay, V is a collection of all nodes, each node $v_i \in V$ represents a sentence, and the state of the node represents the initial feature corresponding to the sentence. E is the set of all edges, and the similarity of the features between the nodes at both ends of each edge is used as the weight of the edge. The weights of the edges are calculated using the cosine similarity or Euclidean distance. Assuming that the eigenvectors of nodes v_i and v_j at both ends of an edge are $[x_1, \ldots, x_{2d}]$ and $[y_1, \ldots, y_{2d}]$, respectively, the formula is as follows:

$$Similarity_1 = \frac{\sum_{t=1}^{2d}(x_t \times y_t)}{\sqrt{\sum_{t=1}^{2d}(x_t)^2} \times \sqrt{\sum_{t=1}^{2d}(y_t)^2}} \tag{1}$$

$$Dist(v_i, v_j) = \sqrt{\sum_{t=1}^{2d}(x_t - y_t)^2}$$

$$Similarity_2 = \frac{1}{(1 + Dist(v_i, v_j))} \tag{2}$$

wherein, $similarity_1$ in Eq. (1) is the cosine similarity, $dist$ in Eq. (2) is the Euclidean distance, and $similarity_2$ is the similarity based on Euclidean distance.

Node Aggregation and Update

Node Aggregation. For node v_i, the relevant information of the node is aggregated using the neighbor nodes connected to it. At the same time, the weight of the edge is used as the attention vector to obtain the different influences of different neighbor nodes on the current node. The aggregation formula of the node v_i at layer l (l starts from 1) can be expressed as follows:

$$h_{N(i)}^{(l)} = \text{Aggregate}\left(\left\{e_{ji} \cdot h_j^{(l-1)}, \forall j \in N(i)\right\}\right) \tag{3}$$

where l represents the number of layers of the network, that is, the number of hops that the current node can aggregate adjacent nodes, e_{ji} is the weight of the connecting edge between nodes j and i, $N(i)$ represents the set of neighbor nodes in the current layer of node v_i, and $h_{N(i)}^{(l)}$ denotes the feature representations of all neighbor nodes of node v_i in layer l. Aggregate denotes aggregate function, and this paper adopts the LSTM aggregator and the Max-Pooling aggregator respectively.

Node Update. For a general graph structure, the hidden states of nodes are usually updated based on recursive methods. At each iteration, the current node aggregates information from its local neighbors, and as the process iterates, the node acquires information from further afield.

For node v_i, each node in the graph is updated using the information of nodes in the previous layer, and the formula is as follows:

$$h_i^{(l)} = \sigma\left(W \cdot \text{Concat}\left(h_i^{(l-1)}, h_{N(i)}^{(l)}\right)\right)$$

$$h_i^{(l)} = \text{Norm}\left(h_i^{(l)}\right) = \frac{h_i^{(l)}}{\left\|h_i^{(l)}\right\|_2}, \forall i \in |V| \tag{4}$$

$h_i^{(l)}$ represents the feature vector of node v_i at the l-th layer, norm is normalization, $\|.\|_2$ denotes L2-norm, $|V|$ represents the number of nodes in the current graph.

4.3   Position Information Encoding Layer

Position information (PI) of the sentence is very essential for DCR in Chinese argumentative essays. For example, *Introduction* usually appears at the beginning of the essay, *Conclusion* is mostly at the end of the paragraph, and *Elaboration* mainly follows *Main Idea*.

We add global relative position information, paragraph relative position information and local relative position information for each sentence separately. Suppose there are E sentences and P paragraphs in the whole essay, the current paragraph has E_p sentences, the current sentence is the a-th sentence in the essay, the paragraph where the current sentence is located is the b-th paragraph in the essay, and the current sentence is the c-th sentence in the current paragraph, then the position information is as follows:

$$Pos_i^{global} = \frac{a}{E}$$

$$Pos_i^{para} = \frac{b}{P} \tag{5}$$

$$Pos_i^{local} = \frac{c}{E_p}$$

$$POS(i) = W_g \times Pos_i^{global} + W_p \times Pos_i^{para} + W_l \times Pos_i^{local} \tag{6}$$

W_g, W_p and W_l are the trainable parameters corresponding to the three position information respectively, and $POS(i)$ is the final sentence position vector. The sentence representation incorporating with PI is then re-modeled by a layer of BiLSTM, and the feature vector L_i of the i-th sentence with PI added is obtained as:

$$\boldsymbol{L}_i^{PI} = \tanh\left(\text{BiLSTM}\left(POS(i) + G_i\right)\right) \tag{7}$$

where G_i is the sentence node feature output from the GNN layer.

4.4   Discourse-level Feature Extraction Layer

The discourse feature extraction module accepts sentence feature vectors with and without PI added, respectively, and performs the same processing on both feature vectors. This module consists of two parts, which will be introduced separately.

Self-Attention

Attention mechanism begins as a process that mimics biological observation behavior, combining its own internal experience with external observation to increase the level of refinement of observation. The essence of attention can be described as a mapping function that maps a query to a sequence of key-value pairs, and it is widely used in multiple tasks in the field of natural language processing, especially machine translation [6]. The self-attention mechanism, on the other hand, removes the dependence on external information and can effectively capture the intrinsic correlation of data.

In this paper, the information of sentence features at different locations is modeled jointly to capture the internal structure between sentences in an essay. Only the vectors $\mathbf{Q}, \mathbf{K} \in n \times \mathbb{R}^{d_k}$ are defined, d_k is the dimension size. In order to increase the gap between features, we discard the traditional normalization function $softmax$, and adopt the $tanh$ activation function. The formula to obtain the self-attention weight vector is as follows:

$$\boldsymbol{w_s} = \text{Attn}(\mathbf{Q}, \mathbf{K}) = \tanh\left(\frac{\mathbf{Q}\mathbf{K}^{\mathrm{T}}}{\sqrt{d_k}}\right) \tag{8}$$

Adaptive Pooling

Adaptive pooling, also known as spatial pyramid pooling [9], can transform vector features of any input size into the same dimension, facilitating the processing of essays with different numbers of sentences in the same batch together. We perform multiple adaptive pooling in parallel to extract vectors of output dimensions 1, 2, 4, and 8, respectively. The obtained output features with different scales are spliced into a discourse feature vector of dimension 15, so as to more comprehensively reflect the feature representation of each sentence in the essay. Finally, the outputs corresponding to the input features with and without PI added are marked as $\boldsymbol{D}^{PI}$ and $\boldsymbol{D}$.

4.5   Prediction Layer

The prediction formula for discourse components is as follows:

$$\boldsymbol{Y} = \text{softmax}\left(\text{MLP}\left(\left[\boldsymbol{L}^{PI}; \boldsymbol{D}^{PI}; \boldsymbol{D}\right]\right)\right) \tag{9}$$

where $\boldsymbol{L}^{PI}$, $\boldsymbol{D}^{PI}$ and $\boldsymbol{D}$ are concatenated and spliced together.

Meanwhile, for training purposes, we minimize the cross-entropy loss as follows:

$$Loss(q, y) = -\sum_{i=1}^{n} (q_i * \log y_i) \tag{10}$$

where the true label is $q_i \in \boldsymbol{Q}$ and the predicted result is $y_i \in \boldsymbol{Y}$.

5   Experimental Setup

5.1   Evaluation Metrics and Dataset

In order to conduct an overall evaluation of the model, accuracy (Acc) and Macro-F1 are used as evaluation metrics in the experiments in this paper. Since the Chinese dataset for DCR is very limited, we only validate our model on the high school student argumentative essay dataset [16]. But we can be sure that our model will still be effective when more datasets in Chinese form are available in the future.

The specific discourse components can be divided into the following categories: **Introduction** describes the background environment in which the argument takes place. **Main Idea** is the author's own view expressed in response to certain events. **Thesis** is the area of discussion in which the author expresses his opinion. **Elaboration** is a further refinement of the author's description of his point of view. **Evidence** is used to provide examples to support the core ideas or topics. **Conclusion** is a summary of the essay and an overall statement of personal opinion. **N/A** is a discourse component unrelated to the above argumentative component. The dataset contains 1230 Chinese argumentative essays, and the statistical data are shown in Table 1.

Table 1. Detailed statistics of Chinese dataset.

#sentence								
Data	Type							
	Intro.	Main.	Thesis	Elabor.	Eviden.	Conclu.	N/A	Sum
Train	2.8k	4.44k	0.88k	12.4k	5.97k	3.08k	0.17k	29.8k
Test	0.3k	0.58k	0.15k	1.1k	0.68k	0.33k	0.02k	3.2k
Total	3.1k	5.02k	1.03k	13.5k	6.65k	3.41k	0.19k	33k
Proportion(%)	9.53	15.22	3.13	41.02	20.16	10.36	0.57	/

We also select the English student essay dataset [19] for testing, which contains three types of discourse components. **Main Claim** is the core argument of an argumentative essay, expressing the author's view on the topic. **Claim** is a specific argument that expresses support or opposition to the Main Claim. **Premise**, on the other hand, primarily provides justification for the Claim. **N/A** is the component that does not belong to any of these three. We utilize the PE dataset that researchers have already processed [16], containing a total of 322 essays, and the specific data are shown in Table 2.

Table 2. Detailed statistics of English dataset.

#sentence				
Data	Type			
	Main Claim	Claim	Premise	N/A	Sum
Train	0.6k	1.2k	3k	1k	5.8k
Test	0.15k	0.3k	0.8k	0.23k	1.5k
Total	0.75k	1.5k	3.8k	1.23k	7.3k
Proportion(%)	10.26	20.57	52.35	16.82	/

5.2   Implementation Details

In our experiments, we leverage the stochastic gradient descent (SGD) algorithm to optimize all training parameters, the standard length of the sentence is set to 40, the learning rate is initialized to 0.2, the dimension of word embedding is 200, the hidden layer dimension of the BiLSTM is 256, and the Dropout rate is 0.1. All models are implemented with Pytorch. For the Chinese dataset we utilize 10% of the training set as the validation set to select the model with the best performance, while for the English dataset we use 20%.

5.3   Baselines

To verify the performance of the model, we compared **DCRGNN** with the following baseline, which are listed as follows:

- **Double-BiLSTM**: We employ two BiLSTM to encode words and sentences in turn, and then directly use them for recognition.
- **Bert-Original**: We fine-tune on the most basic Bert model to directly train a sentence-level classifier.
- **Bert-DCR**: We leverage the 12-layer Bert model for fine-tuning, the subsequent model structure is the same as the model in this paper, but with the GNN layer removed.
- **DiSA** [16]: DiSA utilizes sentence position encoding and inter-sentence self-attention to enhance sentence representation and obtain more adequate sentence features.

6   Results and Analysis

6.1   Results on Chinese Dataset

Table 3 shows the performance of the baseline models and **DCRGNN** on the Chinese dataset. For each group of experiments, where the best results are highlighted in bold, and we calculate the average value according to the results of five random seeds. According to this table: (a) It can be observed from the results that **DCRGNN** is superior to all baseline models regardless of whether it is evaluated by Acc or Macro-F1, and the model with Max-Pooling aggregator outperforms the model with LSTM aggregator. The relative improvements (%) over the best baselines are nearly 1% for Acc and Macro-F1, respectively. (b) Among the Bert-based baseline models, Bert-Original has the worst performance, even lower than Double-BiLSTM, indicating that the effect of relying solely on pre-trained models is insufficient, and it is necessary to fully model word and sentence information to obtain more adequate contextual features. (c) The value of DiSA is the result given in the paper, and DiSA* is the average value after we conducted several experiments locally. The value of Acc is basically the same as that of the paper, but the value of Macro-F1 is lower than the result in the paper.

Table 3. Performance comparison on Chinese dataset.

Method	Acc.	Macro-F1
Double-BiLSTM	0.595	0.542
Bert-Original	0.572	0.510
Bert-DCR	0.647	0.638
DiSA	0.681	0.657
DiSA*(ours)	0.680	0.650
DCRGNN w. lstm agg.	**0.690**	0.661
DCRGNN w. pool agg.	**0.690**	**0.667**

Figure 3 shows the detailed Macro-F1 scores for each discourse component. Compared to the other two baseline models, **DCRGNN** maintains the best effect in the recognition of each discourse component. Bert-DCR is superior to DiSA in Main Idea, Thesis and Evidence. Conversely, DiSA performs better at Introduction, Elaboration and Conclusion. **DCRGNN**, on the other hand, improves in all six discourse components, especially in Main Idea, Thesis and Evidence compared with the existing best available model, with maximum improvements of 6%, 6% and 5.5%, respectively.

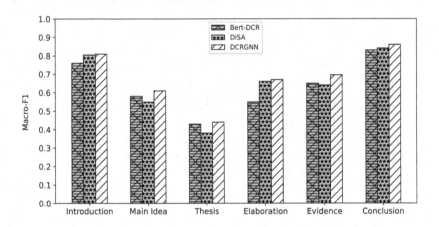

Fig. 3. Macro-F1 scores for the recognition of each discourse components.

6.2 Results on English Dataset

Table 4 reports the results of the four discourse components. **DCRGNN** achieves the best performance on both Acc and Macro-F1, while removing the GNN layer leads to a decrease in recognition.

Table 4. Performance comparison of four discourse components on English dataset.

Method	4-classes	
	Acc.	Macro-F1
Double-BiLSTM	0.681	0.502
DiSA	0.772	0.699
DCRGNN w/o. gnn	0.772	0.700
DCRGNN	**0.777**	**0.707**

Table 5 shows the recognition results of the three discourse components, with the N/A category data removed. As can be seen from the table, compared with other models, the performance of **DCRGNN** is poor. We employ additional manual features [16] to assist in DCR and replace BiLSTM with BiGRU, which improves the performance and is better than the effect of the single-target task. However, the performance of Span-LSTM and Bert-Trans, which combine two subtasks of discourse type classification and discourse relationship prediction, is significantly higher than the single-target task effect, indicating that the joint task helps to improve the overall performance.

Table 5. Performance comparison of three discourse components on English dataset.

Method	3-classes	
	Acc.	Macro-F1
DiSA	0.806	0.742
DCRGNN	0.811	0.750
DCRGNN w. extra Feature	0.843	0.811
St-SVM-full [12]	–	0.776
Single-Best [19]	–	0.773
ILP-Joint [19]	**0.850**	0.826
Span-LSTM [3]	–	0.873
Bert-Trans [2]	–	**0.884**

6.3   Ablation Study

In this subsection, we study the influence of different variations of **DCRGNN** on DCR. We present the results on the Chinese dataset in Table 6.

We observe that removing the GNN layer leads to a significant decrease in recognition performance, while switching the composition method to a fully connected graph also results in a certain extent of performance decrease. This indicates that the GNN layer based on partially connected graph composition method can well capture the interaction between sentences, enhance the representation of sentences, and effectively assist the recognition of discourse elements.

It can also be found that when using the Graph Attention Network (GAT), the performance is inferior to that of SAGEConv, regardless of using either of the two different composition methods. This shows that SAGEConv has a better performance in DCR.

Table 6. Ablation study on Chinese dataset.

Method	Acc.	Macro-F1
DCRGNN w/o. gnn	0.680	0.652
DCRGNN w. full	0.689	0.661
DCRGNN	**0.690**	**0.667**
DCRGNN w. gat	0.686	0.659
DCGGNN w. gat+full	0.685	0.659

6.4 Performance Variance Analysis

It can be clearly found that there are significant performance differences between the **DCRGNN** model on Chinese and English datasets, with performance fluctuations of more than 10% points in both the accuracy Acc and Macro-F1. For this reason, we conduct an in-depth error analysis.

Among the six main components of the Chinese dataset, the three components of main idea, thesis, and evidence have considerable confusion with the elaboration category, which is the main reason for the low performance of the Chinese dataset, especially the thesis category, which also generates confusion with the introduction, leading to a serious decline in performance, with less than 50% of Macro-F1. Thus, the overall performance on the Chinese dataset is less than 70%.

The three main components of the English dataset, on the other hand, are recognized to a more even degree and are therefore able to perform better overall.

7 Conclusion

In this paper, we mainly focus on the discourse component recognition task, and we proposed a GNN-based model named **DCRGNN**. **DCRGNN** enhances the interaction of contextual information between sentences, and the composition method of partially connected graph adopted further improves the performance of discourse component recognition while reducing training time. Extensive experimental results reveal that our model achieves the best results on the Chinese dataset, and validates the effectiveness of the model on the English dataset. In future work, we plan to incorporate bag-of-words (BoW) vectors to increase the features of the input and construct the graph in a more scientific way to further improve performance.

Acknowledgements. This work is supported by the National Key R&D Program of China under Grants (No. 2018YFB0204300).

References

1. Afantenos, S., Peldszus, A., Stede, M.: Comparing decoding mechanisms for parsing argumentative structures. Argument Comput. **9**(3), 177–192 (2018)
2. Bao, J., Fan, C., Wu, J., Dang, Y., Du, J., Xu, R.: A neural transition-based model for argumentation mining. In: Proceedings of the 59th Annual Meeting of the Association for Computational Linguistics and the 11th International Joint Conference on Natural Language Processing (Volume 1: Long Papers), pp. 6354–6364 (2021)
3. Chakrabarty, T., Hidey, C., Muresan, S., McKeown, K., Hwang, A.: Ampersand: Argument mining for persuasive online discussions (2020)
4. Daxenberger, J., Eger, S., Habernal, I., Stab, C., Gurevych, I.: What is the essence of a claim? cross-domain claim identification, pp. 2055–2066 (2017)
5. Eger, S., Daxenberger, J., Gurevych, I.: Neural end-to-end learning for computational argumentation mining, pp. 11–22 (2017)
6. Gehring, J., Auli, M., Grangier, D., Dauphin, Y.N.: A convolutional encoder model for neural machine translation. arXiv preprint arXiv:1611.02344 (2016)
7. Hamilton, W., Ying, Z., Leskovec, J.: Inductive representation learning on large graphs. In: Advances in Neural Information Processing Systems, vol. 30 (2017)
8. Hasanzadeh, A., et al.: Bayesian graph neural networks with adaptive connection sampling. In: International Conference on Machine Learning, pp. 4094–4104. PMLR (2020)
9. He, K., Zhang, X., Ren, S., Sun, J.: Spatial pyramid pooling in deep convolutional networks for visual recognition. IEEE Trans. Pattern Anal. Mach. Intell. **37**(9), 1904–1916 (2015)
10. Lawrence, J., Reed, C.: Argument mining: a survey. Comput. Linguist. **45**(4), 765–818 (2020)
11. Levy, R., Bilu, Y., Hershcovich, D., Aharoni, E., Slonim, N.: Context dependent claim detection. In: Proceedings of COLING 2014, the 25th International Conference on Computational Linguistics: Technical Papers, pp. 1489–1500 (2014)
12. Niculae, V., Park, J., Cardie, C.: Argument mining with structured SVMs and RNNs (2017)
13. Persing, I., Ng, V.: End-to-end argumentation mining in student essays. In: Proceedings of the 2016 Conference of the North American Chapter of the Association for Computational Linguistics: Human Language Technologies, pp. 1384–1394 (2016)
14. Potash, P., Romanov, A., Rumshisky, A.: Here's my point: Joint pointer architecture for argument mining, pp. 1364–1373 (2017)
15. Rinott, R., Dankin, L., Alzate, C., Khapra, M.M., Aharoni, E., Slonim, N.: Show me your evidence-an automatic method for context dependent evidence detection. In: Proceedings of the 2015 Conference on empirical methods in natural language processing, pp. 440–450 (2015)

16. Song, W., Song, Z., Fu, R., Liu, L., Cheng, M., Liu, T.: Discourse self-attention for discourse element identification in argumentative student essays. In: Proceedings of the 2020 Conference on Empirical Methods in Natural Language Processing (EMNLP), pp. 2820–2830 (2020)

17. Song, Y., Heilman, M., Klebanov, B.B., Deane, P.: Applying argumentation schemes for essay scoring. In: Proceedings of the First Workshop on Argumentation Mining, pp. 69–78 (2014)

18. Stab, C., Gurevych, I.: Identifying argumentative discourse structures in persuasive essays. In: Proceedings of the 2014 Conference on Empirical Methods in Natural Language Processing (EMNLP), pp. 46–56 (2014)

19. Stab, C., Gurevych, I.: Parsing argumentation structures in persuasive essays. Comput. Linguist. **43**(3), 619–659 (2017)

20. Sun, D., Huang, Z., Li, D., Ye, X., Wang, Y.: Improved partitioning graph embedding framework for small cluster. In: Qiu, H., Zhang, C., Fei, Z., Qiu, M., Kung, S.-Y. (eds.) KSEM 2021. LNCS (LNAI), vol. 12815, pp. 203–215. Springer, Cham (2021). https://doi.org/10.1007/978-3-030-82136-4_17

21. Wang, H., Huang, Z., Dou, Y., Hong, Y.: Argumentation mining on essays at multi scales. In: Proceedings of the 28th International Conference on Computational Linguistics, pp. 5480–5493 (2020)

A Rating Prediction Model Based on Knowledge Modeling

Maoyu Zhang[✉] and Haiming Li

College of Computer Science and Technology, Shanghai University of Electric Power,
Shanghai 201306, China
zmaoyu1995@163.com

Abstract. Traditional recommendation algorithms are prone to the problem of data sparsity and do not take full use of the semantic information about users and items. In order to alleviate these problems, a rating prediction model based on knowledge modelling (RPMKG) is proposed. The user knowledge model and the item knowledge model are built from user knowledge and item knowledge respectively. A knowledge model graph is constructed by linking the user knowledge model and the item knowledge model with rating relationships while maintaining the original knowledge links between the items. And an efficient algorithm is proposed to embed all knowledge into a unified vector space for knowledge representation learning. Then the rating prediction is performed directly based on the knowledge representation of the knowledge model. The experiments show that the knowledge model graph and learning algorithms proposed in this paper are effective in the field of recommendation systems.

Keywords: Knowledge model graph · Knowledge modelling · Knowledge embedding · Knowledge representation · Recommendation systems

1 Introduction

Technological advances and information technology services have brought a lot of convenience to our lives. But the unprecedented development of Internet technology has also brought about an exponential increase in the amount of information available. It is very difficult for people to find interested information, and recommendation systems appear to solve this problem [1]. The recommendation system is to filter out redundant data from overloaded data and make personalized recommendations. Traditional recommendation mainly includes collaborative filtering-based recommendation [3], content-based recommendation [6] and hybrid recommendation [5].

Collaborative filtering algorithm is the most widely used and most successful recommendation technology in recommendation systems by now [2]. The item-based collaborative filtering algorithm which was proposed in the literature [17]

G. Memmi et al. (Eds.): KSEM 2022, LNAI 13368, pp. 374–385, 2022.
https://doi.org/10.1007/978-3-031-10983-6_29

is a fairly classical algorithm. Potential connections between items are mined through historical user-item interactions and similar items are found. In the literature [9], the authors propose a combined model to improve prediction accuracy by exploiting the advantages of neighbourhood and latent factor approaches. Literature [8] proposes a neural network modelling approach for formal collaborative filtering. We focus on implicit feedback, which indirectly reflects users' preferences through behaviours such as watching videos, purchasing products and clicking on items. The collaborative filtering algorithm researches the user's historical behavior preference data, and then builds a model. The advantage of this method is that it does not require complex feature extraction and modeling of items like content-based recommendation algorithms [7]. The disadvantage is that it relies too much on the interaction information between the user and the item and does not take into account the characteristics of the user or the item itself. The recommendation performance of these algorithms can easily degrade when the information about the user's interaction with the item becomes sparse.

Extracting characteristics of users and items to aid recommendations has become a very important research. Researchers have found that deep learning algorithms can be used not only for prediction e.g. literature [16], but also to assist in feature extraction e.g. literature [13,23,24]. However, in recent years, there has been an increasing amount of research into knowledge graph-assisted recommendation systems. Inspired by the success of knowledge graphs applied to various tasks, researchers have also tried to use knowledge graphs to improve the performance of recommendation systems [19]. And semantic knowledge is the characteristics of the user and item. KGCN [20] takes samples from the neighbors of the entity as its receptive field, and then combines the neighborhood information with the bias to compute the representation of the entity. The receptive field can be extended to multiple hops away to simulate higher-order proximity information and capture the user's potential long-range interest. Studies have shown that calculating similarity from the semantic dimension has become one of the feasible ideas to improve the recommendation effect. Research has shown that calculating similarity from the semantic dimension becomes one of the feasible ideas to improve the effectiveness of recommendations. An algorithm (TransE-CF) is proposed in [14], they used a knowledge graph representation learning method to embed existing semantic data into a low-dimensional vector space. This method improves the semantic effect of collaborative filtering recommendation by calculating the semantic similarity between items and integrating them into collaborative filtering recommendation.

Few researchers have been able to use knowledge representation directly for interest prediction. So we make a bold conjecture to unify user knowledge, item knowledge and rating behaviour into the same graph. The entity-to-entity relationship in traditional knowledge graphs inspired us that could we create a relationship between user knowledge and item knowledge based on the history of user-item interactions? We know that knowledge graphs are generally built on specified domains and that it is difficult to unite knowledge from different domains without special connections. The connection between the user domain and the item domain generally relies only on the history of user-item interactions. Thus the sparsity of the knowledge connections between domains when the two domains are unified together depends on the sparsity of the user-item interaction data. This shows that the main challenge in realising our idea is to establish an effective linkage of knowledge between domains.

Based on the above motivation, this paper proposes a knowledge model graph. It first models users and items based on its own semantic knowledge and then links the user knowledge model and the item knowledge model by the corresponding user ratings of the items. The graph of the knowledge models of users and items is constructed while still maintaining the knowledge links between items. We embed the interlinked knowledge models into the same low-dimensional space, and to ensure an effective interface between the user knowledge model and the item knowledge model. We establish an equivalent embedding relationship between the two knowledge models based on user ratings, which can be directly used for rating prediction in recommendation systems after optimised representation learning. This method integrates knowledge embedding with rating prediction, reducing energy loss compared to traditional fusion methods and thus further enhancing the effectiveness of recommendations.

Some existing algorithms such as KGCN and TransE-CF is that only the knowledge of the items is considered without considering the user's own feature information. And they both perform knowledge for embedding learning in isolation from user rating information. Compared to the algorithms this paper introduces the users themselves and their rating habits as knowledge. Furthermore, a direct relationship of knowledge embedding is established between user knowledge, item knowledge and rating knowledge. This method will learn the connections between knowledge effectively and make more accurate prediction of ratings. An application of this is movie recommendations, where a user's rating of a movie is heavily influenced by factors such as the actor, director and genre of the movie. We can use the algorithm in this paper to learn the connection between users, ratings and the factors of movie. With the above algorithm, we can predict a rating of a user to an unrated movie based on the user and factors of the movie. This algorithm is also applicable in similar areas, such as music recommendations and book recommendations.

The rest of this paper is organized as follows. We introduce the related works in Sect. 2. Details of the model and the algorithm are given in Sect. 3. Sections 4 describes the experiment and the corresponding analysis. We conclude the research in Sect. 5.

2   Related Work

The Knowledge Graph is a knowledge base that was first conceived by Google to improve the search quality of search engines. A knowledge graph is a heterogeneous network of directed information. It contains node "entities" and directed edge "relations", and thus contains a great deal of background information about the items in the recommendation system, as well as the relationships between the items [26]. It can also be integrated with the user-item network consisting of user behaviour data [21,25], thus extending the hidden associations that exist between users and products, and complementing user-item interaction data.

Knowledge embedding techniques have been very successful in recent years e.g. TransE [4], TransH [22] and TransR [11]. And in the literature [10], researchers project the data into a different feature space by an extractor. Knowledge embedding allows for effective representation learning of knowledge. In contrast, representation learning of knowledge is a vector space mapping for entities and relations in the knowledge graph, and the resulting vectors can effectively represent the semantic links between entities and relations [27], which also helps in knowledge embedding in different scenarios.

The TransE algorithm is a classical algorithm that has the advantage of being easy to compute and understand. The model intuitively treats the relations in a triple (h indicates head entity, r indicates relations and t indicates tail entity) as translations from the head entity to the tail entity by continuously adjusting h, r and t so that $(h + r)$ is as equal to t as possible, i.e. $h + r \approx t$. If the above relationship is not satisfied, we consider this to be an erroneous triplet. And the aim of the training is to make the correct triad distances smaller and smaller and the incorrect triad distances larger and larger.

3   Rating Prediction Based on Knowledge Modeling

This section focuses on the construction of knowledge models, methods for learning knowledge representations and how to make score predictions.

3.1   Knowledge Model Graph

We take movie recommendations as an example. There are two domains of knowledge involved in movie recommendations, one in the movie domain and one in the user domain. Within the realm of movie are included the directors, actors, release dates and genres of the films. We use this knowledge information about the film to construct a film knowledge model.

Whereas information about the average user is prone to personal privacy, the amount of information in the user's domain is relatively small, making it more difficult to access the user's connections in terms of information. Therefore the only user information we can use includes only the user's unique identifier and the user's rating habits. We believe that every user has different criteria to follow when rating a film. For example, some users are more demanding and rarely give movies high ratings. Some users are relatively easy to satisfy and are used to giving high ratings. So there may be the case that the same rating may not be the same level of preference for different users. We therefore propose to tailor each user's own set of rating habits and to be different from anyone else's. Thus the user's knowledge model contains only the user's rating habits.

We link the user knowledge model and the item knowledge model together through a rating relationship to form a pair of model, as shown in Fig. 1.

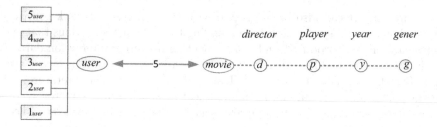

Fig. 1. A pair of model with the user knowledge model on the left, the rating in the middle and the movie knowledge model on the right

We form a pair of user-movie knowledge model (U, M) by linking the two knowledge models through user ratings of movies, with U denoting the user knowledge model and M denoting the movie knowledge model. The left half of the diagram shows the user knowledge model, the middle part shows the user rating of the movie, and the right half shows the movie knowledge model. The user knowledge model U has user identifiers $user$, and $1_{user}, 2_{user}, 3_{user}, 4_{user}$ and 5_{user} are the rating habits of $user$, corresponding to ratings 1, 2, 3, 4 and 5 respectively. The 5 on the middle line indicates the $user$'s rating of the film, which is equivalent to 5_{user} according to the $user$'s rating habits. In the movie knowledge model M, $movie$ denotes the movie identifiers, d denotes the movie director, p denotes the movie's player, y denotes the movie's release date, and g denotes the movie's genre.

Films can have the same director or actors etc. between them, so there are rich knowledge links between film knowledge models. We connect pairs of models through this linkage between films to build a knowledge model graph. This is shown in Fig. 2.

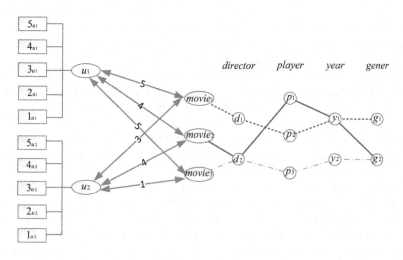

Fig. 2. Knowledge model graph.

As can be seen from the figure, we maintain the semantic connections between movies while unifying user and movie knowledge together. The benefit of the knowledge model graph constructed in this way is that the semantic relationships between films and users and ratings are learnt while still taking into account the knowledge links between films.

3.2 Knowledge Model Represent Learning

Unifying the knowledge models of users and films into the same graph, while maintaining links to existing film knowledge. This approach allows us to view different knowledge information in a unified way. We will perform optimal learning of knowledge representation on this knowledge model graph to obtain accurate knowledge representation of users, movies and ratings. Thus providing better recommendations to users. The idea of unifying user knowledge and item knowledge into the same graph and translating the act of rating into a knowledge link between the user and the film is a relatively novel one. But it is still possible to represent it for learning through knowledge embedding. We are inspired by the way knowledge is embedded in the TransE algorithm. Firstly, we embed the knowledge model into a uniform low-dimensional vector space. We fuse the film knowledge model into a whole by a method of vector summation. An approximate equivalence is then established between user knowledge model, film knowledge model and rating, i.e. $user + movie \approx rating$. We disperse the user's evaluation to the composition knowledge of the film. A user rating of a movie is equivalent to a user rating of data such as the director and actors of the movie. Our aim is to make the gap between the two sides of the approximate equals sign smaller and smaller, which we call the correct gap value. Conversely, the gap grows wider when the rating is wrong, which we call the incorrect gap value. The correct gap value formula is shown in Eq. (1).

$$gap(U, M) = ||u_{tag} + (m_{tag} + \sum_{f \in F} f) - u_r||_2^2 \tag{1}$$

where U represents the user knowledge model, $u_{tag} \in U$ denotes the embedding vector of users, $u_r \in U$ denotes the embedding vector of correct ratings. M represents the movie knowledge model, $m_{tag} \in M$ denotes the embedding vector of movie titles, and $F \subset M$ denotes the embedding set of movie attributes. The incorrect gap value formula is shown in Eq. (2).

$$gap'(U, M) = \sum_{u_r' \in R'_{(U)}} ||u_{tag} + (m_{tag} + \sum_{f \in F} f) - u_r'||_2^2 \tag{2}$$

where u_r' denotes the user's incorrect rating of the movie and $R'_{(U)}$ denotes the set of user's incorrect ratings of the movie.

Our overall desire is to have smaller and smaller correct gap values and larger and larger error gap values, calculated as shown in Eq. (3).

$$Loss = \sum_{(U,M)\in G} [gap(u,m) - gap'(u,m) + \zeta]_{+} \qquad (3)$$

Where G denotes the set of all model pairs in the training set, $[x]_{+}$ denotes the positive part of x, and ζ denotes the margin hyperparameter. In the loss function $Loss$, we subtract the wrong gap value from the correct gap value, which facilitates training the correct gap value to be naturally lower than the wrong gap value. With such a representation learning approach, we are able to effectively learn the knowledge representation of users' rating habits, thus improving the accuracy of rating prediction.

Our model can be learned by stochastic gradient descent (SGD), and the learning algorithm for the model is shown in Algorithm 1.

Algorithm 1. Knowledge Embedding Learning Algorithms

---
input: Input training set G
output: Embeddings of all knowledge subjects
1: Initialize all knowledge embedding values
2: **for** $i = 0 \rightarrow n$ **do** //n is the number of training sessions
3:     $S_{batch} \longleftarrow sample(G, b)$//$b$ is the batch size
4:     update embeddings according to $\nabla Loss$
5: **end for**
6: **return** All embeddings values

From the algorithm above we can see that the time complexity of this algorithm is $O(n)$. n is the number of training sessions defined by the experimenter, and we choose a number of training sessions that is generally no less than 100,000. As the amount of experiment data increases we also increase the value of n accordingly.

3.3   Rating Prediction

After learning the optimisation model we can obtain the embedding values of those knowledge. Assuming that the target user corresponds to the knowledge model U and the unrated movie corresponds to the knowledge model M, we need to calculate the rating gap value between the two knowledge models. As we expect the correct rating to correspond to the smallest gap value during training, we need to calculate the smallest rating gap value, the calculation is shown in Eq. (4). R represents the set of all habitual ratings of the user. The rating corresponding to the smallest rating gap value is the predicted rating of the movie by the target user.

$$P(U, M) = min\left(\left\| u_{tag} + (m_{tag} + \sum_{f\in F} f) - u_r \right\|_2^2 \middle| u_r \in R \right) \qquad (4)$$

4   Experiment Results

4.1   Experiment Environment and Data Set

The experiment hardware environment is Intel(R) Core (TM) i7-10750 with 32 GB of memory; software environment is Python 3.6; the operating system is Ubuntu18.04.

We selected the ML-Lastest-Small dataset, which is a set of movie ratings provided by MovieLens users from the end of the last century to the beginning of this century. The movie details were crawled from the IMDB website and the incomplete information data were removed, leaving 90637 ratings for 9013 movies from 593 users. We extracted the data into the knowledge model mapping. The total number of model pairs is 90637, total number of knowledge entities is 18667 and total number of user rating habits is 2965.

4.2   Evaluation Metrics and Experimental Steps

In this paper, MAE (Mean Absolute Error) and RMSE (Root Mean Square Error) are used to evaluate the recommended performance of the algorithm, which are calculated as shown in Eqs. (5) and (6) respectively.

$$MAE = \frac{\sum_{t=1}^{n} |\widehat{y}_t - y_t|}{n} \tag{5}$$

$$RMSE = \sqrt{\frac{\sum_{t=1}^{n} (\widehat{y}_t - y_t)^2}{n}} \tag{6}$$

where $\widehat{y}_t$ indicates the predicted rating y_t indicates the actual rating.

In order to accurately test the performance of the algorithm, the experiment data were randomly divided into 80% of the data as the training set and 20% as the test set, and a total of five experiments were conducted, with the average of the test results taken as the final result. The experiment steps are as follows: (1) Constructing a user and movie knowledge model. (2) Constructing a user-movie knowledge model graph. (3) Dividing the data set. (4) Knowledge embedding algorithm training. (5) Performing rating prediction on the test set. (6) Repeating steps (3), (4) and (5) in turn.

4.3   Results and Analysis

We take the following better performing methods for comparison:

-NSM-CF: An improved heuristic similarity measure model. The new similarity model combines the local context for common ratings of each pair users and global preference of each user ratings [12]. The new similarity model in this method overcomes the shortcomings of the traditional model. The improved similarity metric takes into account the proportion of common ratings between two users.

-NSMBC-CF: A similarity measure for neighborhood based CF, which uses all ratings made by a pair of users. Proposed measure finds importance of each pair of rated items by exploiting Bhattacharyya similarity [15]. Bhattacharyya distance is popular in the field of signal and image processing. The authors introduced it to recommendation systems to obtain correlations between items and obtained good recommendations.

-RKGE: A unified recurrent knowledge graph embedding framework. RKGE automatically mines all eligible paths between entity pairs from KG and then encodes them through a batch of recurrent networks, with each path modelled by a recurrent network. Recurrent networks in the batch share common parameters to avoid over-fitting. It then uses pooling operations to distinguish the importance of different paths to characterise user preferences for items. Finally, the recommendation layer is seamlessly integrated with the network, allowing RKGE to deliver training in an end-to-end manner [18].

The experimental results are shown in Fig. 3 below.

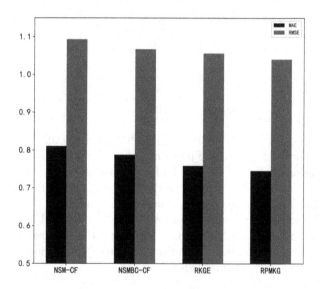

Fig. 3. experimental comparison results.

As can be seen from the figure, the algorithm proposed in this paper outperforms these comparative methods in terms of both MAE and RMSE values. The collaborative filtering algorithm above and the traditional collaborative filtering algorithms still rely heavily on historical user-item interaction data to mine similar items or users. These algorithms all lack the use of just information about the user or item itself. RKGE, like most recommendation algorithm models that fuse knowledge graphs, makes indirect use of knowledge information about items to assist with recommendations. The algorithm in this paper makes better use of the semantic knowledge of users and items than traditional collaborative filtering algorithms. The advantage of the algorithm over most fused knowledge graphs is that it unifies user knowledge, item knowledge and rating data into the same graph. The algorithm is also able to perform direct rating prediction through knowledge embedding.

5   Conclusion and Future Work

In this paper we proposed to model the knowledge of users and items. The rating is then used to link the knowledge models and this will be used to construct a knowledge model graph. The unification of user knowledge and film knowledge is achieved and the corresponding knowledge embedding learning algorithm was also proposed. The algorithm learns the relationship between user knowledge, item knowledge and ratings by embedding two interconnected knowledge model models into a unified low-dimensional space. The algorithm has the advantages of being easy to understand, containing fewer parameters and being easy to train. Through experiments, the proposed model and algorithm are proven to be effective in the field of recommendation systems.

Prior to this the construction of knowledge graphs was often restricted to within a domain. The model and algorithm were proposed in this paper, on the other hand, provide an idea for building knowledge graphs on hybrid domains. The key to this construction of hybrid domain knowledge graphs is how to establish the effectiveness of the knowledge articulation between domains. This may become a direction for future research.

References

1. Adomavicius, G., Zhang, J.: Stability of recommendation algorithms. ACM Trans. Inf. Syst. (TOIS) **30**(4), 1–31 (2012)
2. Aggarwal, C.C.: An Introduction to Recommender Systems. In: Recommender Systems, pp. 1–28. Springer, Cham (2016). https://doi.org/10.1007/978-3-319-29659-3_1
3. Bhagavatula, C., Feldman, S., Power, R., Ammar, W.: Content-based citation recommendation. arXiv preprint arXiv:1802.08301 (2018)
4. Bordes, A., Usunier, N., Garcia-Duran, A., Weston, J., Yakhnenko, O.: Translating embeddings for modeling multi-relational data. In: Advances in Neural Information Processing Systems, vol. 26 (2013)
5. Burke, R.: Hybrid recommender systems: survey and experiments. User Model. User-Adap. Inter. **12**(4), 331–370 (2002)
6. Chen, R., Hua, Q., Chang, Y.S., Wang, B., Zhang, L., Kong, X.: A survey of collaborative filtering-based recommender systems: From traditional methods to hybrid methods based on social networks. IEEE Access **6**, 64301–64320 (2018)
7. Guo, Q., et al.: A survey on knowledge graph-based recommender systems. IEEE Trans. Knowl. Data Eng. (2020)

8. He, X., Liao, L., Zhang, H., Nie, L., Hu, X., Chua, T.S.: Neural collaborative filtering. In: Proceedings of the 26th International Conference on World Wide Web, pp. 173–182 (2017)

9. Koren, Y.: Factorization meets the neighborhood: a multifaceted collaborative filtering model. In: Proceedings of the 14th ACM SIGKDD International Conference on Knowledge Discovery and Data Mining, pp. 426–434 (2008)

10. Li, Y., Song, Y., Jia, L., Gao, S., Li, Q., Qiu, M.: Intelligent fault diagnosis by fusing domain adversarial training and maximum mean discrepancy via ensemble learning. IEEE Trans. Industr. Inf. **17**(4), 2833–2841 (2020)

11. Lin, Y., Liu, Z., Sun, M., Liu, Y., Zhu, X.: Learning entity and relation embeddings for knowledge graph completion. In: Twenty-Ninth AAAI Conference on Artificial Intelligence (2015)

12. Liu, H., Hu, Z., Mian, A., Tian, H., Zhu, X.: A new user similarity model to improve the accuracy of collaborative filtering. Knowl.-Based Syst. **56**, 156–166 (2014)

13. Luo, Y., Wang, X., Cao, W.: A novel dataset-specific feature extractor for zero-shot learning. Neurocomputing **391**, 74–82 (2020)

14. Mu, R., Zeng, X.: Collaborative filtering recommendation algorithm based on knowledge graph. Mathematical Problems in Engineering 2018 (2018)

15. Patra, B.K., Launonen, R., Ollikainen, V., Nandi, S.: A new similarity measure using Bhattacharyya coefficient for collaborative filtering in sparse data. Knowl.-Based Syst. **82**, 163–177 (2015)

16. Qiu, H., Zheng, Q., Msahli, M., Memmi, G., Qiu, M., Lu, J.: Topological graph convolutional network-based urban traffic flow and density prediction. IEEE Trans. Intell. Transp. Syst. **22**(7), 4560–4569 (2020)

17. Sarwar, B., Karypis, G., Konstan, J., Riedl, J.: Item-based collaborative filtering recommendation algorithms. In: Proceedings of the 10th international conference on World Wide Web, pp. 285–295 (2001)

18. Sun, Z., Yang, J., Zhang, J., Bozzon, A., Huang, L.K., Xu, C.: Recurrent knowledge graph embedding for effective recommendation. In: Proceedings of the 12th ACM Conference on Recommender Systems, pp. 297–305 (2018)

19. Wang, H., et al.: Ripplenet: propagating user preferences on the knowledge graph for recommender systems. In: Proceedings of the 27th ACM International Conference on Information and Knowledge Management, pp. 417–426 (2018)

20. Wang, H., Zhao, M., Xie, X., Li, W., Guo, M.: Knowledge graph convolutional networks for recommender systems. corr abs/1904.12575 (2019). arXiv preprint arXiv:1904.12575 (2019)

21. Wang, X., He, X., Cao, Y., Liu, M., Chua, T.S.: KGAT: knowledge graph attention network for recommendation. In: Proceedings of the 25th ACM SIGKDD International Conference on Knowledge Discovery & Data Mining, pp. 950–958 (2019)

22. Wang, Z., Zhang, J., Feng, J., Chen, Z.: Knowledge graph embedding by translating on hyperplanes. In: Proceedings of the AAAI Conference on Artificial Intelligence, vol. 28 (2014)

23. Xie, Z., Cao, W., Ming, Z.: A further study on biologically inspired feature enhancement in zero-shot learning. Int. J. Mach. Learn. Cybern. **12**(1), 257–269 (2020). https://doi.org/10.1007/s13042-020-01170-y

24. Xie, Z., Cao, W., Wang, X., Ming, Z., Zhang, J., Zhang, J.: A biologically inspired feature enhancement framework for zero-shot learning. In: 2020 7th IEEE International Conference on Cyber Security and Cloud Computing (CSCloud)/2020 6th IEEE International Conference on Edge Computing and Scalable Cloud (EdgeCom), pp. 120–125. IEEE (2020)

25. Yu, X., et al.: Personalized entity recommendation: a heterogeneous information network approach. In: Proceedings of the 7th ACM International Conference on Web Search and Data Mining, pp. 283–292 (2014)
26. Zhang, F., Yuan, N.J., Lian, D., Xie, X., Ma, W.Y.: Collaborative knowledge base embedding for recommender systems. In: Proceedings of the 22nd ACM SIGKDD International Conference on Knowledge Discovery and Data Mining, pp. 353–362 (2016)
27. Zheng, L., Noroozi, V., Yu, P.S.: Joint deep modeling of users and items using reviews for recommendation. In: Proceedings of the Tenth ACM International Conference on Web Search and Data Mining, pp. 425–434 (2017)

Attending to SPARQL Logs
for Knowledge Representation Learning

Liu Yang[1], Bingyuan Xie[1], Jun Long[1], Wenti Huang[2], Shuyi Liu[3],
and Tingxuan Chen[1(✉)]

[1] School of Computer Science and Engineering, Central South University,
Changsha, China
{yangliu,xiebingyuan,jlong,chentingxuan}@csu.edu.cn
[2] Network Resources Management and Trust Evaluation Key Laboratory
of Hunan Province, Central South University, Changsha, China
[3] School of Electrical and Computer Technology, Xiamen University Malaysia,
Sepang, Darul Ehsan, Malaysia
cst1909144@xmu.edu.my

Abstract. Knowledge Representation Learning (KRL) maps entities
and relations to a continuous low-dimensional vector space, alleviating
data sparsity of Knowledge Graphs (KGs) and improving computing efficiency. However, most prior KRL models represented by TransE embed
all triple facts equally, without distinguishing latent semantic information of relations. In this paper, (1) we propose a novel correlation-aware
Knowledge Representation Learning framework, which integrates semantic features of relations while embedding; (2) we capture the semantics
by mining time-sequence and frequency characteristics of relations from
historical SPARQL logs; (3) we design a weighted encoder to distinguish correlation of each triple according to relational semantics, and
introduce the triple correlation into translation-based models to enhance
entity representations. Experimental results on Wikidata datasets show
that our proposed model significantly outperformed the state-of-the-art
translation-based models on both knowledge graph completion tasks and
triple classification tasks.

Keywords: Knowledge representation learning · Semantic
correlation · Knowledge graph · SPARQL

1 Introduction

Knowledge Graphs (KGs) such as Freebase and Wikipedia get widespread attention recently, which provide well-structured relational information among entities
and effectively organize the real-world facts. Further, KGs promote the development of knowledge-driven tasks like information retrieval and question answering. In KGs, knowledge can be expressed by triple facts in the form of (*head
entity, relation, tail entity*) or (*subject, predicate, object*) under Resource Description Framework (RDF) [1], which is also described as (h, r, t) or (s, p, o). For

ⓒ The Author(s), under exclusive license to Springer Nature Switzerland AG 2022
G. Memmi et al. (Eds.): KSEM 2022, LNAI 13368, pp. 386–399, 2022.
https://doi.org/10.1007/978-3-031-10983-6_30

example, (*Hugh, acted_in, Nirvana in Fire*) represents the fact that "*Hugh acted in the work Nirvana in Fire*". Such forms represent structured data in KGs effectively, but their symbolic nature also makes KGs hard to manipulate.

To solve the sparsity and computational inefficiency caused by the symbolic representation of KGs, Knowledge Representation Learning (KRL) methods present a powerful effect since they map entities and relations into a continuous low-dimensional vector space. Among these methods, translation-based models that view relations as translations from a head entity to a tail entity receive a lot of research. Although they are both simple and effective, they are still facing the challenges posed by the following limitations. Relations in KGs have different semantic features, characterizing various aspects of entity identities [2]. In other words, the importance of various relations differs greatly in embedding an entity. However, most KRL models ignore semantic features of relations and equally consider all neighboring relations for the embedding of central entities [3]. Only a few types of research consider relational semantics when embedding. Nathani et al. [4] assign different weight mass (attention) to entities in a neighborhood and propagate attention via layers in an iterative fashion. RGHAT [3] designs a novel hierarchical attention mechanism to compute different weights for different neighboring relations and entities. Nevertheless, they just utilize structural information of graphs to measure semantic features of relations and ignore semantic impacts of user preferences on relations [5].

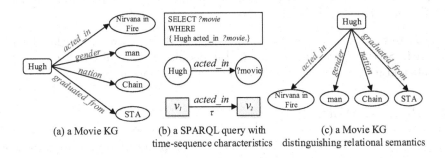

(a) a Movie KG   (b) a SPARQL query with   (c) a Movie KG
                    time-sequence characteristics   distinguishing relational semantics

Fig. 1. The example of movie KG and SPARQL query.

In this paper, we attempt to analyze SPARQL logs, which are kinds of structured representations of natural language questions executed on KGs, and to capture relational semantics by using the mined user preferences [6]. As the example illustrated in Fig. 1, in a movie KG, the central entity "Hugh" contains four neighboring relations (viz., *gender*, *nation*, *graduated_from*, and *acted_in*). Among them, "*acted_in*" can better recognize the identity of an actor than the other three relations, and users always prefer to search what movies the actor "*acted_in*". User preferences reflect the importance of the relation "*acted_in*" in real scenes. Hence, we focus on the triples connected by "*acted_in*" when embedding the entity "Hugh".

To this end, we propose a novel correlation-aware Knowledge Representation Learning framework, merging the semantic features of relations based on translation-based models. To integrate relational semantics and learn better knowledge representations, we introduce a new concept of triple correlation for each triple fact. Triple correlation describes the degree of semantic association between entities, which can be measured by the importance (semantic weight) of relations between entities. Specifically, we collect co-occurrence statistics of relation substructures to evaluate relational semantics and triple correlations from historical SPARQL logs grouped by query time. Then we utilize triple correlations as supervision to impose constraints on embedding, augmenting the accuracy of entity representation. Our contributions are summarized below:

- We develop a predicate-mine method with time-sequence, which measures relational semantics by analyzing time-sequence and frequency characteristics of SPARQL logs.
- We propose a Correlation-aware KRL model (C-KRL) following the translation-based framework, with a weighted encoder to set triple correlation for each triple connected by different relations according to semantics. C-KRL learns entity representations with triple correlation and keeps the distances between entities connected by the important relation closer in embedded spaces.
- We perform extensive experiments on Wikidata datasets, showing that C-KRL achieves a promising performance on knowledge graph completion tasks as well as triple classification tasks.

The rest of this paper is organized as follows: Sect. 2 introduces related work on KRL. Section 3 presents our method in detail. Section 4 discusses our experiments and results. Finally, we conclude the future work in Sect. 5.

2 Related Work

Inspired by word embeddings [7] which can well capture semantic information of words, researchers start to study distributed representations of knowledge graphs (aka, Knowledge Representation Learning) to solve sparsity and computational efficiency brought by structuring. KRL aims to express semantic information of entities and relations as low-dimensional real-valued vectors through machine learning. It can calculate complex semantic correlations between entities and relations, and well support downstream applications such as knowledge acquisition and link prediction. Among them, translation-based models are the most popular for their simplicity and effectiveness.

TransE [8] uses relation vector r as translation distance from head entity vector h to tail entity vector t, i.e., $h + r \approx t$, which is inspired by word embedding model of Word2Vec [9]. TransE works well for 1-n relationship with few parameters and low complexity, but the over-simplified translation assumptions [10] restrict performance: 1) it fails to model complex relationships (e.g., 1-n, n-1, n-n), and 2) it only focuses on local information of RDF triples and ignores reasoning logic between global structures as well as relations in KGs. TransH [11] adds relation-specific hyperplanes and represents entities distinctively under different relations to model complex relationships. TransR [12] embeds entities and relations in different entity spaces and multiple relation spaces to handle complex relations. PTransE [13] integrates relation paths in KGs, and breaks the limitations of other models to learn each triplet in isolation.

In addition, some methods integrate additional information that cannot be obtained from the original training data to improve the accuracy of knowledge embedding. DKRL [14] integrates entity descriptions to distinguish entity representation. TKRL [15] models the matrix of project entity by integrating rich hierarchical information of entities. CKRL [16] use confidence to learn knowledge representation while identifying possible noise in KGs, and breaks the unreasonable assumption that "all existing triples are correct" in KRL [17].

However, traditional KRL models mentioned above process each triple independently and fail to encapsulate the semantically rich latent relations in the vicinity of a given entity in a KG. They ignore that entities play different roles depending on different relations connected with other entities to a large extent. HINGE [18] considers that key-value pairs (k, v) on a hyper-relational fact should not be treated identically as base triplet (h, r, t), and hence captures the correlation between each triplet and its associated key-value pairs. LGGCN [19] captures semantic connection between facts and highlights the importance of key entities and relations when embedding.

In this paper, we introduce SPARQL historical data to analyze semantic information, and improve the basic translation model to verify whether user preferences contain relational semantics.

3   Methodology

In this section, we introduce our correlation-aware KRL framework in detail. We give the following definitions. A KG is a pair $\mathcal{K} = (\mathcal{E}, \mathcal{R}, \mathcal{F})$, where $\mathcal{E}$ denotes the set of entities, $\mathcal{R}$ indicates the set of relations, and $\mathcal{F}$ denotes the set of facts. A fact is a triple (h, r, t) or (s, p, o), where h (s) denotes head entity (subject), t (o) denotes tail entity (object), and r (p) is the relationship (project) between h and t. A SPARQL query (or simply called query) is a pair $Q = (\mathcal{V}, \mathcal{L})$, where $\mathcal{V}$ denotes the set of vertices, and $\mathcal{L}$ denotes the set of edges. Considering time-sequence of queries, we use $\mathbb{Q} = \{Q_{\tau_1}, Q_{\tau_2}, \ldots, Q_{\tau_k}\}$ to represent SPARQL logs, where $\mathcal{T} = \{\tau_1, \tau_2 \ldots \tau_k\}$ denotes time-windows. In other words, Q_{τ_k} represents the set of SPARQL queries occurred at τ_k.

In order to integrate semantic features of relations while embedding, we learn triple correlations, by capturing time-sequence and frequency characteristics of relations from historical SPARQL logs. Then, we introduce the triple correlation into translation-based models to improve the accuracy of entity embedding. Figure 2 depicts the framework of correlation-aware Knowledge Representation Learning. It mainly contains three steps: 1) Constructing semantic matrix $M_{n \times 1}$ of relations, by extracting time-sequence and frequency characteristics of predicates from historical SPARQL logs; 2) Scoring the correlation w of each triplet,

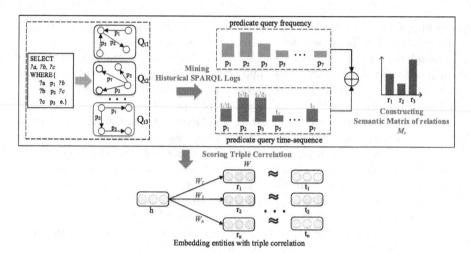

Fig. 2. Framework of correlation-aware knowledge representation learning model.

by designing a triple correlation function with M as input; 3) Embedding entities by introducing triple correlation w.

3.1   Semantic Matrix of Relations

SPARQL is a standard query language for Knowledge Graph developed by W3C [20]. In a SPARQL query, the query variables are primarily belong to the subjects or objects of triples and rarely appear in the predicates. Simultaneously, a statistical analysis [21] shows that 20% of the frequent predicate patterns cover 90% of historical queries, among the 8,151,238 actual SPARQL historical queries facing the knowledge graph of DBpedia. We believe that frequent predicate patterns reflect user preferences, which affect semantic features of relations. Therefore, we mine frequent predicate patterns to measure relational semantics, with a weighted encoder to assign correlation of each triple.

Given a set of historical SPARQL query $\mathcal{Q} = \{Q_1, Q_2, \ldots, Q_w\}$, we pattern each SPARQL query statement Q_j (subjects and objects in a query sentence are variables, and only predicates keep as constants, i.e., $v_1 \xrightarrow{p} v_2$), and mine a set of possible predicate patterns $\mathcal{P} = \{P_1, P_2, \ldots, P_n\}$. Then, we use formula (1) to calculate the frequency of each predicate pattern P_i in $\mathcal{Q}$.

$$Conf\left(P_i\right) = Conf\left(P_i | Q\right) = \frac{\sum_{j=1}^{w} count\left(Q_j, P_i\right)}{|Q|} \tag{1}$$

Among them, $count\left(Q_j, P_i\right)$ counts whether predicate pattern P_i exists in query statement Q_j. If exists, it will be assigned with 1; Otherwise, it will be assigned with 0. To distinguish frequency of predicate patterns, we set a threshold δ. If $Conf\left(P_i\right) \geq \delta$, we consider P_i as a frequent predicate pattern FP; Otherwise, P_i is an infrequent predicate pattern $\neg FP$.

As we all know, a query has time-sequence characteristics. The closer historical queries are related to the current time, the greater semantic impacts on the relations. Therefore, we specially consider the changing characteristics of SPARQL queries over time, and propose a predicate pattern with time-sequence characteristics. Firstly, we divide time into k periods. Given timestamp $T = \{\tau_1, \tau_2 \ldots \tau_k\}$, the historical SPARQL query set is $\mathbb{Q} = \{Q_{\tau_1}, Q_{\tau_2}, \ldots, Q_{\tau_k}\}$, and Q_{τ_k} represents the set of SPARQL query statements in τ_k period. Then, predicate patterns are represented as $v_1 \xrightarrow{p/\tau_k} v_2$. Querying entity variables v_1 or v_2 connected by the predicate p in the specific time frame τ_k.

Aiming at the predicate pattern with temporal features, we introduce a time trust factor λ_{τ_i}, and its value is related to time sequence. We set the corresponding trust factor value λ_{τ_i} for each time frame τ_i, and the sum of trust factors in all time frames is 1. As defined in formula (2):

$$\sum_{i=1}^{k} \lambda_{\tau_i} = \lambda_{\tau_1} + \lambda_{\tau_2} + \ldots + \lambda_{\tau_k} = 1 \tag{2}$$

$$\lambda_{\tau_1} < \lambda_{\tau_2} < \cdots < \lambda_{\tau_k} \tag{3}$$

In particular, as the time frame τ_i is closer to the current time, both the value λ_{τ_i} and trust degree are higher.

According to frequency statistics of predicate patterns, we calculate predicate semantics through weighted collaborative representations. The calculational model of predicate semantics shows as formula (4):

$$M(P_i) = \begin{cases} \sum_{j=1}^{k} \lambda_{\tau_j} \bullet Conf_{\tau_j}(P_i), & P_i \in FP \\ \beta \bullet Conf(P_i), & P_i \in \neg FP \end{cases} \tag{4}$$

where λ_{τ_j} is time trust factor, $Conf_{\tau_i}(P_i)$ calculates the frequency of predicate pattern P_i in Q_{τ_j}, and β is a hyper-parameter to balance the total frequency of infrequent predicate patterns $\neg FP$.

For infrequent predicate patterns $\neg FP$, we do not consider its dynamic changes. Contrarily, for frequent predicate patterns FP, we introduce the trust factor to capture dynamic changes of relational semantics. The higher score of $M(P_i)$, the more critical predicate pattern P_i and the higher semantic correlation of the triples connected by P_i.

3.2 Triple Correlation Function

Through analyzing time-sequence and frequent characteristics of historical SPARQL queries, we utilize the function $M(P_i)$ to construct a relational semantic matrix $M(r_i)$, which distinguishes the importance of each relation (obtained the different semantic features of relations). In KGs, for each head entity h, there is a relation r directly connected to it. We define $N(h) = \{r_1, r_2 \ldots r_m\}$ as the direct relation field of head entity h. Note that different relations express different semantics, thence the triples (h, r_i, t_{r_i}) which composed of head entity h

and different relations r_i contain different degrees of correlation. According to relational semantic matrix $M(r_i)$, we calculate the triple correlation by equation (5):

$$w(h, r_i, t_{r_i}) = \frac{M(r_i)}{\sum\limits_{j=1}^{m} M(r_j)} \tag{5}$$

According to the above calculation, a triple correlation composed of head entity h and different relations r_i should satisfy:

$$\sum_{i=1}^{m} w(h, r_i, t_{r_i}) = w(h, r_1, t_{r_1}) + w(h, r_2, t_{r_2}) + ... + w(h, r_m, t_{r_m}) = 1 \tag{6}$$

In this paper, we believe that relational semantics are positively correlated with the characteristics of frequency and time in SPARQL queries, thus we calculate triple correlation based on the importance of relations.

3.3   Correlation-Aware KRL Model

To merge relational semantics implied in a historical SPARQL query, we learn better knowledge representation with triple correlations taken into consideration, and pay more attention to those triples with high correlation. Following the assumption of $h + r \approx t$, we propose our correlation-aware KRL model (wTransE) and design an energy function as follows:

$$E(T) = \sum_{(h,r,t) \in T} E(h, r, t) * w(h, r, t) \tag{7}$$

The energy function consists of two parts: 1) $E(h, r, t) = \|\mathbf{h} + \mathbf{r} - \mathbf{t}\|$, derived from TransE, is the dissimilarity score under translation assumption. A low score implies an accurate embedding of entities and relations. 2) We introduce triple correlation based on TransE. A high score indicates the importance of relational semantics. We hope to concentrate more on the triples with high correlation when embedding.

As shown in Fig. 3, we observe that the distance between head entity and corresponding tail entity is randomly allocated in the vector space of traditional knowledge representation learning, which resulte in the lack of similarity between entities in the same class. We believe that head entity is closer to the tail entity corresponding to the core relation in vector space, and the semantics between two head entities pointed to the same tail entity by the core relation is more similar (d2<d1). Therefore, our model captures semantic features of different relations and introduces a triple correlation based on the assumption of translation. Triple correlation affects the similarity distance between entities, making entity embedding more accurate.

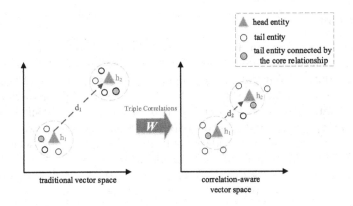

Fig. 3. Simple schematic diagram of wTransE.

During the training process, we define a score function with negative sampling as the training objective. This paired score function aims to make the score of positive triples lower than the score of the negative triples. Its optimized objective function is as the formula (8):

$$L = \sum_{(h,r,t)\in \mathcal{T}} \sum_{(h',r,t')\in \mathcal{T}'} max\left([\mathbb{E}],0\right) \cdot w\left(h,r,t\right) \tag{8}$$

$$\mathbb{E} = \gamma + E\left(h,r,t\right) - E\left(h',r,t'\right) \tag{9}$$

where γ is a hyper-parameter. $\mathcal{T}$ represents a set of positive triples, and $\mathcal{T}'$ represents a set of negative triples; $E\left(h,r,t\right) = d\left(h+r,t\right)$ represents the distance score of positive triples, and $E\left(h',r,t'\right) = d\left(h'+r,t'\right)$ represents the distance score of negative triples. Note that we add a triple correlation to distinguish semantic importance of different relations compared with the original translation model. For paired training, we extract negative triples from training set according to the rules defined by formula (10):

$$\mathcal{T}' = \{\{h',r,t\}|h' \in \mathcal{E}\} \cup \{\{h,r,t'\}|t' \in \mathcal{E}\} \tag{10}$$

For each positive triple $\mathcal{T} = (h,\ r,\ t)$, different entities will be extracted from the entity set $\mathcal{E}$ to replace head entity h or tail entity t in the process to form a negative triple. Through gradient descent training, we need to find the minimum value of L and continuously update vector value of entities to make it optimal.

4   Experiments

In this section, to test the effects of the knowledge representation learning model fused with historical SPARQL query information, we conducted experiments including knowledge graph completion tasks and triple classification tasks. The experimental results show that user preferences can distinguish the semantic degrees of different relations, and contribute to better knowledge representations.

4.1 Datasets

We use Wikidata datasets as knowledge graph datasets in our experiments, which contains facts about the director, actors, and genre of movies. We observed that the original data of Wikidata is large and very sparse and 53% of the entities only have one triple, making it difficult to evaluate the link prediction model. Therefore, Natalia et al. [22] filtered Wikidata datasets to retain a subset of entities that appear in at least two triples. We have followed two versions of Wikidata datasets, namely Wikidata-300K and Wikidata-1000k, which contain 300K and 1M triples respectively. We divide these triples into a training set, a validation set, and a test set. Table 1 shows the statistics of Wikidata datasets. We retrain the comparison model and our model on this new dataset.

Table 1. Details of the used datasets.

Datasets	#Rel	#Ent	#Train	#Valid	#Test
Wikidata-300k	294	36001	240000	23310	23373
Wikidata-1000k	394	104500	950000	18912	18984

As for datasets of historical SPARQL query, we use the anonymous SPARQL query logs provided by Wikipedia website [23]. The website offers a total of historical query logs, including six periods where each period counts 28-day SPARQL queries. Malyshev et al. [24] analyzed the number of valid queries (Valid) among total queries (Total), and the number of robot queries (Robotic) and organic queries (Organic) among valid queries. The statistics of SPARQL query logs are shown in Table 2.

Table 2. Details of SPARQL Query Logs.

No.	Start-End	#Total	#Valid	#Robotic	#Organic
1	2017.06.12–2017.07.09	79,082,916	59,555,701	59,364,020	191,681
2	2017.07.10–2017.08.06	82,110,141	70,397,955	70,199,977	197,978
3	2017.08.07–2017.09.03	90,733,013	78,393,731	78,142,971	250,760
4	2018.01.01–2018.01.28	106,074,877	92,100,077	91,504,428	595,649
5	2018.01.29–2018.02.25	109,617,007	96,407,008	95,526,402	880,606
6	2018.02.26–2018.03.25	100,133,104	84,861,808	83,998,328	863,480

The organic queries in SPARQL query logs are dominated by queries from users that require real-time information, so they can better reflect user needs. Therefore, this paper mainly analyzes and mines the organic queries.

4.2 Link Prediction

Task Definition. Link prediction is a classic task of knowledge graphs completion. Given a triple (h, r, t), we need to predict the missing item. Given $(?, r, t)$, it predicts head entity h, and given $(h, r, ?)$, it predicts tail entity t, and given $(h, ?, t)$, it predicts the relation r. The first two belong to entity prediction, and the latter is relation prediction. Nowadays the link prediction task has been used to estimate the effect of most existing Knowledge Representation Learning.

Evaluation Index. Referring to the experimental method developed in Bordes, we use evaluation indicators in the link prediction task: Mean Rank and Hits@N. For each test triple (h, r, t), we first remove head entity h, relation r, or tail entity t to obtain an incomplete triple. For example, we take the removal of tail entity (similar to the operation of head entity and relations) and get $(h, r, ?)$. Then we replace tail entity t with any entity e, and form a new triple (h, r, e). We calculate the score $f(h, r, e)$ of the new triplet and sort the score sequences in ascending order. The lower the score, the greater the probability of establishing the triple, and vice versa. Based on this ascending list, we use two evaluation indicators, i.e., Mean Rank and Hits@N.

Obviously, a fine knowledge representation learning model indicates lower Mean Rank and higher Hits@10 in the link prediction task. In fact, an artificially constructed negative triplet may be a fact triplet that exists in knowledge graph. If it exists, it will affect the evaluation results of the above evaluation methods and knowledge representation learning models. Therefore, we filter out these triples before ranking candidate entities, and then use link prediction to evaluate. We call the original evaluation method as "Raw" method, and the evaluation method that is filtered later as "Filter" method. For the negative sample sampling method, we use two different random sampling methods of uniform sampling and bernoulli sampling. Besides, uniform sampling method replaces head and tail entities with a uniform probability, named this method "unif"; and bernoulli sampling method utlizes different probabilities to replace head and tail entities, named "bern".

Parameter Settings. During the training process, mini-batch samples on each dataset take a value of 100, and L2 norm is used to measure the distance. Learning rate λ is the set in the range $\{0.1, 0.01, 0.001\}$; boundary distance value γ is the set in the range $\{1,2,4\}$, and the dimension d of the relation (entity) is the set in the range $\{20, 50, 100\}$. The number of iteration epochs during training is the set in the range $\{200, 500, 1000\}$. According to the minimum Mean Rank of the learning model, we find the most suitable parameters. For the Wikidata-300k dataset, we use the following parameters: learning rate $\lambda = 0.001$, boundary distance $\gamma = 1$, vector dimension $d = 100$, and the number of iterations $epoch = 200$. For Wikidata-1000k dataset, we use the following parameters: learning rate $\lambda = 0.1$, boundary distance $\gamma = 1$, vector dimension $d = 200$, and the number of iterations $epoch = 200$. To ensure fairness, we use the same parameter settings on the comparison models.

Result Analysis. For Wikidata-300k dataset, the results of the link prediction tasks are shown in Table 3. We add the triple correlation functions we proposed to TransE and TransR respectively to form wTransE and wTransR. Note that we re-test the four models on the new datasets and find out that our models are better than traditional embedding models. This indicates that different relations do have different semantic features, and user preferences have a clear impact on relational semantics. Our correlation-aware Knowledge Representation Learning framework distinguishes relational semantics and sets triple correlation for each triplet, thus it can achieve better knowledge embedding and improve the performances of link prediction. Because of the complexity and abundance of the entity set in datasets, we find that Mean Rank value changes significantly under different sampling methods. At the same time, the optimization effect on TransR compared to TransE is not apparent under the same sampling method.

Table 3. Comparison results of link prediction on Wikidata-300k.

Datasets	Wikidata-300k			
Metric	Mean rank		Hits@10(%)	
	Raw	Filter	Raw	Filter
TransE(unif)	3266.37	2783.27	30.46	31.82
TransE(bern)	1968.51	1150.31	30.28	33.04
wTransE(unif)	2758.14	2273.14	**32.04**	33.74
wTransE(bern)	1873.06	1041.25	30.91	**34.08**
TransR(unif)	3219.14	2730.95	29.62	30.85
TransR(bern)	1940.63	1102.59	29.11	32.26
wTransR(unif)	2684.32	2203.17	**32.83**	33.51
wTransR(bern)	1827.09	1004.71	31.42	**34.63**

For Wikidata-1000k dataset, the results of link prediction are shown in Table 4. We only increase the triple correlation function wTransE based on TransE, and find out that wTransE exhibits a more advantageous entity prediction than TransE. In addition, as the amount of data increases, the value of Mean Rank also increases accordingly. The growth in a dataset has brought about an increase in relation sets, which is twice of Wikidata-300k. We find out that the results of Hits@10 on Wikidata-1000k datasets are higher than those on Wikidata-300k datasets. This improvements fully implicate that relations contain different semantic information, and wTransE learning on a dataset with more relations can get a more pronounced improvement on the performances of link prediction.

Table 4. Comparison results of link prediction on Wikidata-1000k.

Datasets	Wikidata-1000k			
Metric	Mean rank		Hits@10(%)	
	Raw	Filter	Raw	Filter
TransE	4810.21	3680.23	29.91	33.11
wTransE	3605.60	2307.62	**33.33**	**37.67**

4.3   Triple Classification

Task Definition. Triple classification is to judge whether a given triple is correct or wrong, which is a binary classification task. A triple (h, r, t) is correct if the specified score function is below the threshold σ_r, and vice versa. σ_r is determined by the threshold when the verification set obtains the maximum classification accuracy.

Evaluation Index. Triple classification task uses accuracy rate as evaluation index. The higher the value of ACC, the better performances on triples classification tasks.

Parameter Settings. We only conduct experiments on Wikidata-300k dataset with the following parameters: learning rate $\lambda = 0.001$, boundary distance $\gamma = 1$, vector dimension $d = 100$, and the number of iterations $epoch = 200$. In order to ensure fairness, we use the same parameter settings on the comparison models.

Result Analysis. For Wikidata-300k dataset, the results of triple classification are shown in Table 5. Similarly, we add the triple correlation functions to TransE and TransR respectively to form wTransE and wTransR, both of which are improved comparing to the original methods. We weight relational semantics through triple correlation, so that entities with similar semantics in KG can be more closely represented in embedding space, which may help to improve the performances of triple classification.

Table 5. The Classification Results of Wikidata-300k triples (%).

Method	Wikidata-300k
TransE	63.2
wTransE	**64.8**
TransR	68.5
wTransR	**70.2**

5   Conclusion

In order to distinguish latent semantic features of relations, we proposed a novel correlation-aware Knowledge Representation Learning Framework, which fuses relational semantics through the triple correlation. Specifically, inspired by recommendation systems, we mined user preferences from historical SPARQL logs to capture relational semantics and introduced a triple correlation to distinguish the importance of triples linked by different relations. We hoped that entities with higher triple correlations are closer in embedding space. Therefore, we took the triple correlation as the regular term constraint when embedding, which obtained the representation of entities and relations with rich semantic features. Finally, we verified the effectiveness of our model through link prediction tasks and triple classification tasks.

Acknowledgements. This work is being supported by the National Natural Science Foundation of China under the Grant No. 62172451, and supported by Scientific and Technological Innovation 2030-Major Project of New Generation Artificial Intelligence under the Grant No. 2020AAA010961, by Open Research Projects of Zhejiang Lab under the Grant No. 2022KG0AB01, and in part by the Natural Science Foundation of Hunan under the Grant No. 2020JJ4754 and No. 2020JJ5775.

References

1. Ji, S., Pan, S., Cambria, E., Marttinen, P., Philip, S.Y.: A survey on knowledge graphs: representation, acquisition, and applications. IEEE Trans. Neural Networks Learn. Syst. **33**, 494–514 (2021)
2. Zhang, Q., Sun, Z., Hu, W., Chen, M., Guo, L., Qu, Y.: Multi-view knowledge graph embedding for entity alignment. arXiv preprint arXiv:1906.02390 (2019)
3. Zhang, Z., Zhuang, F., Zhu, H., Shi, Z., Xiong, H., He, Q.: Relational graph neural network with hierarchical attention for knowledge graph completion. In: Proceedings of the AAAI Conference on Artificial Intelligence, vol. 34, no. 05, pp. 9612–9619 (2020)
4. Nathani, D., Chauhan, J., Sharma, C., Kaul, M.: Learning attention-based embeddings for relation prediction in knowledge graphs. arXiv preprint arXiv:1906.01195 (2019)
5. Cao, Y., Wang, X., He, X., Hu, Z., Chua, T.-S.: Unifying knowledge graph learning and recommendation: towards a better understanding of user preferences. In: The World Wide Web Conference, pp. 151–161 (2019)
6. He, G., Li, J., Zhao, W.X., Liu, P., Wen, J.-R.: Mining implicit entity preference from user-item interaction data for knowledge graph completion via adversarial learning. In: Proceedings of The Web Conference 2020, pp. 740–751 (2020)
7. Mikolov, T., Sutskever, I., Chen, K., Corrado, G.S., Dean, J.: Distributed representations of words and phrases and their compositionality. In: Advances in Neural Information Processing Systems, pp. 3111–3119 (2013)
8. Bordes, A., Usunier, N., Garcia-Duran, A., Weston, J., Yakhnenko, O.: Translating embeddings for modeling multi-relational data. In: Advances in Neural Information Processing Systems, vol. 26 (2013)

9. Mikolov, T., Chen, K., Corrado, G., Dean, J.: Efficient estimation of word representations in vector space. arXiv preprint arXiv:1301.3781 (2013)
10. Chen, X., Jia, S., Xiang, Y.: A review: knowledge reasoning over knowledge graph. Expert Syst. Appl. **141**, 112948 (2020)
11. Wang, Z., Zhang, J., Feng, J., Chen, Z.: Knowledge graph embedding by translating on hyperplanes. In: Proceedings of the AAAI Conference on Artificial Intelligence, vol. 28, no. 1 (2014)
12. Lin, Y., Liu, Z., Sun, M., Liu, Y., Zhu, X.: Learning entity and relation embeddings for knowledge graph completion. In: Twenty-Ninth AAAI Conference on Artificial Intelligence (2015)
13. Lin, Y., Liu, Z., Luan, H., Sun, M., Rao, S., Liu, S.: Modeling relation paths for representation learning of knowledge bases. arXiv preprint arXiv:1506.00379 (2015)
14. Xie, R., Liu, Z., Jia, J., Luan, H., Sun, M.: Representation learning of knowledge graphs with entity descriptions. In: Proceedings of the AAAI Conference on Artificial Intelligence, vol. 30, no. 1 (2016)
15. Xie, R., Liu, Z., Sun, M., et al.: Representation learning of knowledge graphs with hierarchical types. In: IJCAI, pp. 2965–2971 (2016)
16. Xie, R., Liu, Z., Lin, F., Lin, L.: Does William Shakespeare really write hamlet? knowledge representation learning with confidence. In: Proceedings of the AAAI Conference on Artificial Intelligence, vol. 32, no. 1 (2018)
17. Chen, X., Chen, M., Shi, W., Sun, Y., Zaniolo, C.: Embedding uncertain knowledge graphs. In: Proceedings of the AAAI Conference on Artificial Intelligence, vol. 33, no. 01, pp. 3363–3370 (2019)
18. Rosso, P., Yang, D., Cudré-Mauroux, P.: Beyond triplets: hyper-relational knowledge graph embedding for link prediction. In: Proceedings of the Web Conference, pp. 1885–1896 (2020)
19. Huang, W., Mao, Y., Yang, L., Yang, Z., Long, J.: Local-to-global GCN with knowledge-aware representation for distantly supervised relation extraction. Knowl.-Based Syst. **234**, 107565 (2021)
20. Wang, X., Zou, L., Wang, C., Peng, P., Feng, Z.: Research on knowledge graph data management: a survey. J. Software **30**(7), 2140 (2019)
21. Peng, P., Zou, L., Guan, R.: Accelerating partial evaluation in distributed SPARQL query evaluation. In: 2019 IEEE 35th International Conference on Data Engineering (ICDE), pp. 112–123. IEEE (2019)
22. Ostapuk, N., Yang, J., Cudré-Mauroux, P.: Activelink: deep active learning for link prediction in knowledge graphs. In: The World Wide Web Conference, pp. 1398–1408 (2019)
23. Spitz, A., Dixit, V., Richter, L., Gertz, M., Geiß, J.: State of the union: a data consumer's perspective on wikidata and its properties for the classification and resolution of entities. In: Proceedings of the International AAAI Conference on Web and Social Media, vol. 10, no. 1 (2016)
24. Malyshev, S., Krötzsch, M., González, L., Gonsior, J., Bielefeldt, A.: Getting the most out of wikidata: semantic technology usage in Wikipedia's knowledge graph. In: Vrandečić, D., et al. (eds.) ISWC 2018. LNCS, vol. 11137, pp. 376–394. Springer, Cham (2018). https://doi.org/10.1007/978-3-030-00668-6_23

DBGARE: Across-Within Dual Bipartite Graph Attention for Enhancing Distantly Supervised Relation Extraction

Hejian Gu, Hang Yu$^{(\boxtimes)}$ ⓘ, and Xiangfeng Luo

Shanghai University, BaoShan, Shangai 200444, China
{ghj1819,yuhang,luoxf}@shu.edu.cn

Abstract. Recently, a kind of method based on single bipartite graph combined with single attention mechanism was proposed to solve the challenges of noisy labels and long-tailed distributions in distantly supervised relation extraction, which achieved competitive results. However, we argue that single bipartite graph will lose interactive information within each bipartite graph partition and single attention will cause attention bias. In order to improve the robustness of this method for noisy labels and long-tailed distributions, we propose a novel framework DBGARE, whereby graphs across and within each bipartite graph partition are constructed to enrich unbalanced relations dependency, based on which, a novel technique dual attention mechanism is devised to avoid attention bias and promote information dissemination from data-riches to data-poors. Multiple experiments on various widely-used real-world datasets show the state-of-the-art effectiveness of our framework in both challenges above. Furthermore, almost previous benchmark datasets are in English, we provide CIPDS∗, a new Chinese dataset collected from Chinese Corpus in Chinese search engine, to expand distantly supervised relation extraction research field.

Keywords: Distantly supervised relation extraction · Noisy labels · Long-tailed distributions · Dual attention · Bipartite graph

1 Introduction

Relation extraction (RE) attempts to extract relation knowledge between two entities under the semantic environment of unstructured text. The supervised methods have made a great success but been limited for the annotated training data, which cost a lot. To address this difficulty, [10] developed Distant Supervision (DS) to generate new training data automatically. Unfortunately, DS for relation extraction still suffers from two main challenges.

The first challenge is the noisy label, which is caused by the heuristic alignment that if two entities have a relationship in a known knowledge base, then

---

Supported by Shanghai Yangfan Program (22YF1413600).

G. Memmi et al. (Eds.): KSEM 2022, LNAI 13368, pp. 400–412, 2022.
https://doi.org/10.1007/978-3-031-10983-6_31

Table 1. Unbalanced distributions for the real-world dataset NYT-10 [14]. #Top-N, (N = 1,2,3,...) represents the relation type whose instances number ranked N.

Relations	#Top-1	#Top-2	#Top-3	...
Instances ratio	79.3%	10.0%	1.5%	...

all sentences that contain these two entities will express that relationship. But it can fail and result in the wrong label problem. The second challenge is the training data long-tailed distribution. The real-world datasets of distantly supervised relation extraction always have an unbalanced distribution with a long tail, which means a small proportion of relations may occupy the most of data, and it is difficult for model training. As shown in Table 1, take widely-used real-world dataset NYT-10 for example, the sum of the top 3 relations instances ratios is over 90%.

For alleviating the above two challenges, so as to achieve significant improvements in distantly supervised relation extraction, Liang et al. [8] introduced a constraint graph to model the dependency between relations for boosting the representation learning of long-tailed relations, and designed a constraint-aware attention to improve the noise immunity. However, the constraint graph is a bipartite digraph [8], which just processed as a single graph will lose the interactive information within each partition and dealing with the problem of noisy labels with single attention mechanism will cause attention bias. In addition, current datasets for distantly supervised relation extraction are almost in English. However, relation extraction tasks in NLP are also significant for other languages, such as Chinese. To achieve this, we investigate the Chinese Inter Person Distant Supervision (CIPDS*), a new dataset in Chinese for distantly supervised relation extraction.

In this paper, we propose a novel dual bipartite graph attention relation extraction framework (DBGARE) for distantly supervised relation extraction (see Fig. 1). As single bipartite graph loses the interactive information within the two partitions, we construct graphs across and within each partition to enrich unbalanced relations dependency. Then, we propose dual attention mechanism to pay attention to constructed graphs to avoid attention bias and promote information dissemination from data-riches to data-poors. The extensive experimental results show that our model achieves significant and consistent improvements. Moreover, we provide a novel dataset CIPDS* in Chinese to expand distantly supervised relation extraction research field. The contributions of this paper can be summarized as follows.

- We introduce a novel framework DBGARE. Different from focusing on the single bipartite graph, we construct the graphs both across and within the two partitions. While single attention can cause attention bias, we develop a novel technique dual bipartite graph attention mechanism.
- To our best knowledge, almost previous benchmark datasets for distantly supervised relation extraction are not in Chinese. So we also provide CIPDS*,

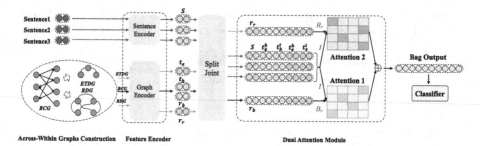

Fig. 1. The overview of DBGARE framework structure. Across-Within Graphs Construction is the construction of graphs across and within each bipartite graph partition. Feature Encoder is utilized to derive the representations for sentences and nodes of graphs. The split joint module simply aims to concatenate the split representations. In the dual attention module, two selective attentions are applied to pay attention to features from the constructed graphs and transform the sentences representations into two bag representations. Finally, bag representations from dual attention are aggregated into final bag representation, based on which the classifier predicts the entity-pair relation.

a new distantly supervised relation extraction dataset in Chinese to expand the research field.
- Our framework achieves significant and consistent improvements in addressing both the long-tailed distributions and the noisy labels, as multiple experiments shows.

2   Related Work

Traditional Feature-Based Methods: To address the problem of noisy labels, many traditional feature-based models [4,14,15] developed with the relaxed distant supervision assumption for multi-instance learning. These methods have shown their effectiveness for relation extraction. However, their performance relies strongly on the quality of designed features.

Neural Network-Based Methods: In the past few years, deep learning with neural networks [1,7,12,13] has reduced the dependence of models on manually designed features. [21] employed CNN based model for relation extraction, [20] proposed a Piecewise Convolutional Neural Network (PCNN) model, which used deep neural work to avoid feature engineering. With effectiveness of attention mechanisms, [9,19] have been proposed and achieved pretty good performance. Nevertheless, only driven by the noisy training data, these methods will hurt the robustness of the model.

Constraint Graph-Based Methods: Besides the information from sentences, the types of entities showed great potential for relation extraction [11, 18,23]. [8] explored a framework of constraint graph with single attention to handle the challenges noisy label and long-tailed distributions simultaneously, which achieved great improvement as compared to methods [4,10] on noisy label

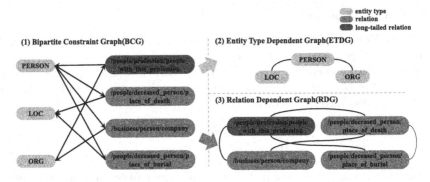

Fig. 2. Across-Within Graphs Construction. The graphs across and within each bipartite graph partition include: (1) The bipartite constraint graph (BCG) with relations partition and entity types partition. (2) The entity type-dependent graph (ETDG) consists of the entity types nodes from BCG with the connections sharing the same relations. (3) The relation-dependent graph (RDG) employs the relation nodes of BCG with the connections sharing the same entity types.

or methods on long-tailed distributions [3,9]. However, processing bipartite constraint graph as a single graph will lose the interactive information within the two partitions of it, and single attention mechanism can cause attention bias.

3   Framework

3.1   Across-Within Graphs Construction

The graphs across and within each bipartite graph partition include BCG, ETDG and RDG, which are showed in Fig. 2.

The bipartite constraint graph (BCG), which is defined as a triple $\mathcal{G} = \{\mathcal{T}, \mathcal{R}, \mathcal{C}\}$, consists of three main parts: $\mathcal{T}, \mathcal{R}, \mathcal{C}$, indicate the sets of entity types, relations and constraints, respectively. A constraint $(h_t, r, t_t) \in \mathcal{C}$ indicates that there are connections from entity type $h_t \in \mathcal{T}$ to relation $r \in \mathcal{R}$, and from relation $r \in \mathcal{R}$ to entity type $t_t \in \mathcal{T}$. As shown in Fig. 2, h_t can be 'PERSON' and r can be '/business/person/company', then h_t is 'ORG'.

However, there is no connection within each partition of the bipartite constraint graph (BCG), which will lose the interactive information within $\mathcal{T}$ and $\mathcal{R}$. As Fig. 2 shows, for sharing the same relations, we construct one partitioned graph named entity type-dependent graph (ETDG) to model the direct dependency information of partition $\mathcal{T}$. By sharing the same entity types, we also obtain the relation dependent graph (RDG).

3.2 Feature Encoder

Sentence Encoder. Given a sentence x consisting of m words $\{w_1, w_2, ..., w_m\}$, every word w_i is represented by a d_w−dimensional vector v_i, which is encoded by a pre-trained embedding matrix $V \in \mathbb{R}^{d_w \times |\mathcal{V}|}$, $\mathcal{V}$ is a fixed-sized vocabulary.

Firstly, the position-ware embeddings and entity-ware embeddings for the word w_i are obtained by concatenating:

$$x_i^p = [v_i; p_i^h; p_i^t] \in \mathbb{R}^{d_w + 2d_p},$$
$$x_i^e = [v_i; v^h; v^t] \in \mathbb{R}^{3d_w}. \tag{1}$$

For the sentence with words, the position-ware embeddings and the entity-ware embeddings represent as X^p and X^e, respectively.

Secondly, we employ linear layer and non-linear functions to map the position-ware and entity-ware embeddings into the same feature space:

$$\hat{X}^p = tanh(W_1 X^p + b_1),$$
$$\hat{X}^e = sigmoid(\lambda \cdot (W_2 X^e + b_2)), \tag{2}$$

where $tanh(x) = \frac{e^{2x}-1}{e^{2x}+1}$ and $sigmoid(x) = \frac{1}{1+e^{-x}}$ are activation functions, W_1 and W_2 are weight matrices, b_1 and b_2 are bias vectors, and λ is a hyper-parameter.

Thirdly, the features from $\hat{X}^p$ and $\hat{X}^e$ are aggregated to generate the final sentence embedding features:

$$X = \hat{X}^e \odot \hat{X}^e + (1 - \hat{X}^e) \odot \hat{X}^p, \tag{3}$$

where $\odot$ denotes element-wise product.

Finally, PCNN [20] is employed to capture the high-dimensional representation of the sentence $S \in \mathbb{R}^{3d^c}$, where d^c is the convolutional output dimension before piece-wise pooling.

Graph Encoder. Given a raw graph $\mathcal{G} = (\mathcal{N}, \mathcal{E})$, where $\mathcal{N}$ is the nodes set and $\mathcal{E}$ is the edges set. the adjacency matrix $\hat{A} \in \mathbb{R}^{n \times n}$ ($n = |\mathcal{N}|$) is defined as following:

$$\hat{A} = \begin{cases} 1 & if \ (n_i, n_j) \in \mathcal{E} \ or \ n_i = n_j, \\ 0 & otherwise. \end{cases} \tag{4}$$

Each node $n_i \in \mathcal{N}$ is randomly initialized as a d_v−dimensional embedding $v_i^{(0)}$. After initialization, the graph is transformed into an embedding matrix $V^{(0)} = \{v_i^{(0)}, ..., v_n^{(0)}\}$, with an adjacency matrix $\hat{A}$. With the initial layer nodes embeddings matrix $V^{(0)}$ and $\hat{A}$ as inputs, the computation of GCN for node n_i at the k_{th} layer can be defined as:

$$V_i^{(k)} = \rho \left(\sum_n^{j=1} \hat{A}_{ij} W^{(k)} v_j^{(k-1)} + b^k \right), \tag{5}$$

where $\mathbf{W}^{(k)}$ is weight martix , $\mathbf{b}^k$ is the bias vector and $\rho(\cdot)$ is performed as activation function (e.g. $RELU(x) = max(0, x)$). Because of BCG containing entities-type nodes and relation nodes, we can devide the second layer GCN output $\mathbf{V}^{(2)} \in \mathbb{R}^{n \times d_g}$ into relation representations $\mathbf{R}_b \in \mathbb{R}^{n_r \times d_g}$ and type representations $\mathbf{T}_b \in \mathbb{R}^{n_t \times d_g}$. ETDG is transformed as $\mathbf{T}_e \in \mathbb{R}^{n_t \times d_g}$ and RDG is encoded as $\mathbf{R}_r \in \mathbb{R}^{n_r \times d_g}$, where d_g is output feature dimension.

3.3   Dual Attention Module

For each sentence x_i contained entity pair with entities types(h, t), the sentence representation is S_i , the entities types in BCG can be obtained from $\mathbf{T}_b$ as (t_b^h, t_b^t), and the entities types in ETCG can also be obtained as (t_e^h, t_e^t). Then the instance representation is constructed by joining as follows:

$$I_i = \left[S_i; t_b^h; t_b^t; t_e^h; t_e^t \right] \in \mathbb{R}^{3d_c + 4d_g}. \tag{6}$$

Assume that the entity pair has the relation r. We take the average over the entity pairs for relation r. Entities representations of relation r are denoted as $t_{rb}^h, t_{rb}^t, t_{re}^h$ and t_{re}^t, and the representation of r in BCG is denoted as $\mathbf{r}_b$. BCG representations is constructed by joining as:

$$B_r = \left[\mathbf{r}_b; t_{rb}^h; t_{rb}^t; t_{re}^h; t_{re}^t \right] \in \mathbb{R}^{3d_c + 4d_g}. \tag{7}$$

We select the relation r representation from RDG as $\mathbf{r}_r$, similarly, we construct the representations of two partitioned graphs as follows:

$$R_r = \left[\mathbf{r}_r; t_{rb}^h; t_{rb}^t; t_{re}^h; t_{re}^t \right] \in \mathbb{R}^{3d_c + 4d_g}. \tag{8}$$

Attention 1. Given a bag of representations of instances I with relation r, the first attention is applied over each instance to the representations of BCG B_r. The attention weight α_{bi} for i_{th} instance can be calculated as:

$$
\begin{aligned}
e_{bi} &= I_i B_r, \\
\alpha_{bi} &= \frac{\exp(e_{bi})}{\sum_{j=1}^n \exp(e_{bj})}.
\end{aligned}
\tag{9}
$$

The bag representation for the first attention is derived as the weighted sum of all instances representations:

$$\mathbf{z}_{br} = \sum_{i=1}^n \alpha_{bi} I_i. \tag{10}$$

Attention 2. The second attention is adopted over each instance to the representations of RDG. Similarly, the bag representation for the second attention can be calculated as:

$$
\begin{aligned}
e_{ri} &= I_i R_r, \\
\alpha_{ri} &= \frac{\exp(e_{ri})}{\sum_{j=1}^n \exp(e_{rj})}, \\
\mathbf{z}_{rr} &= \sum_{i=1}^n \alpha_{ri} I_i.
\end{aligned}
\tag{11}
$$

Table 2. Hyper-parameters settings.

Components	Parameters	Values
Sentence encoder	Filter number	230
	Window size	3
	Word dimension	50
	Position dimension	3
	Lamda (λ)	5
Graph encoder	Initial dimension	700
	Layer 1 dimension	950
	Layer 2 dimension	690
Optimization	Batch size	256
	Learning rate	0.5
	Dropout rate	0.5

Finally, we integrate bag representations from dual attention output with adding to obtain the final bag representation, which fed into a softmax classifier to calculate the probability distribution over relation set as:

$$P(r|\mathcal{B};\mathcal{G}s;\theta) = softmax(\mathbf{W}\mathbf{z}_r + \mathbf{b}), \qquad (12)$$

where θ denotes the model parameters, $\mathbf{W}$ is the weight of the classifier, $\mathbf{z}_r = \mathbf{z}_{rr} + \mathbf{z}_{br}$ and $\mathbf{b}$ is the bias vector.

3.4 Optimization

We define the objective function by adopting cross-entropy at the bag level as:

$$\mathcal{J}(\theta) = -\frac{1}{N}\sum_{i=1}^{N}\log P(r_i|\mathcal{B}_i;\mathcal{G}s;\theta), \qquad (13)$$

Note that different from single graph input and single attention mechanism, $\mathcal{G}s$ represent multiple constructed graphs, and θ includes dual attention parameters.

4   Experiments

We set the parameters based on recommendations of [8]. In Table 2, we show all hyper-parameters which are used in our experiments.

4.1 Datasets

We evaluate our framework on three datasets, The overall statistics are shown in Table 3.

Table 3. Statistics of datasets used in our experiments.

Datasets	Splits	#Sentences	#Entity-pairs	#Instances	#Bags
NYT-10	Train	368099	279915	570088	293162
(#2010, English)	Test	61707	96678	172448	96678
GIDS	Train	11297	7570	11297	6502
(#2018, English)	Test	5663	3247	5663	3247
CIPDS*	Train	287351	37948	287400	37948
(#New, **Chinese**)	Test	38417	5416	41770	5416

CIPDS*: In this paper, we provide CIPDS*, a new dataset in Chinese for distantly supervised relation extraction. We align facts of Chinese KBs about inter-personal relationships with the Chinese corpus in Chinese search engine. Then we construct 34 relationships, including the special one "NA". In particular, to make an automatic evaluation more reliable and test if the models indeed obtain the true relation under the text environment, the train set structures by the heuristic alignment, but the test set is human-annotated. Similar to NYT-10, it has challenges of long-tailed distributions and noisy labels.

4.2 Evaluation Metrics

Similar to previous work [10], we evaluate our framework in the held-out evaluation. We report Hit@K (the count of how many instances prediction results are ranked in the top-n positions) widely used for long-tailed evaluation, while precision/recall curves and Precision@N (precisions at different recalls) for denoising evaluation.

4.3 Experimental Results for Long-Tailed Distributions

We employed various state-of-the-art models to be our baselines. The models without constraint graph include: PCNN+ATT, PCNN+HATT, PCNN+KATT, PCNN+HRS, PA-TRP, CoRA. While CGRE, BGRE-simple-add(ours), BGRE-simple-cat(ours), DBGARE(ours) belong to the constraint graph-based models. In the constraint graph-based models, BGRE-simple-add(ours), BGRE-simple-cat(ours) and DBGARE(ours) are proposed by us with graphs constructed across and within each bipartite graph partition. BGRE-simple-add(ours), BGRE-simple-cat(ours) and DBGARE(ours) are proposed to merge information from the constructed graph by simple adding, simple concatenating and dual attention, respectively. As dataset GIDS has no long-tailed distributions challenge, in this subsection, we do experiments on datasets NYT-10 and CIPDS*.

Table 4. (%) Accuracy of Hits@K on relations with training instances fewer than 100/200. Note that the K of Hit for CIPDS* is stricter because the count of relation types of CIPDS* is low, requiring stricter Hit@K.

Datasets	Training instances Hit@K(Macro)	<100			<200		
		10	15	20	10	15	20
NYT-10	PCNN+ATT [9]	<5.0	7.4	40.7	17.2	24.2	51.5
	PCNN+HATT [3]	29.6	51.9	61.1	41.4	60.6	68.2
	PCNN+KATT [22]	35.3	62.4	65.1	43.2	61.3	69.2
	PCNN+HRS [17]	36.8	64.0	68.8	44.8	62.0	71.5
	PA-TRP [2]	63.9	70.3	72.2	66.7	72.3	73.8
	CoRA [6]	59.7	63.9	73.6	65.4	69.0	77.4
	CGRE [8]	72.2	77.8	85.2	77.3	81.8	87.9
	BGRE-simple-add(ours)	77.8	85.2	85.2	81.8	87.9	87.9
	BGRE-simple-cat(ours)	77.8	**88.9**	**88.9**	81.8	**90.9**	**90.9**
	DBGARE(ours)	**83.3**	**88.9**	**88.9**	**86.4**	**90.9**	**90.9**
Datasets	Training instances Hit@K(Macro)	<100			<200		
		2	4	8	2	4	8
CIPDS*	PCNN+ATT [9]	<1.0	12.5	16.7	<2.0	9.4	25.0
	CGRE [8]	58.3	70.8	83.3	59.4	75.0	87.5
	BGRE-simple-add(ours)	66.1	87.5	91.7	71.9	87.5	93.8
	BGRE-simple-cat(ours)	**83.3**	**95.8**	99.1	78.1	90.6	93.8
	DBGARE(ours)	**83.3**	**95.8**	**99.2**	**84.4**	**96.9**	**99.9**

As shown in Table 4, we report accuracy of Hits@K on relations with training instances fewer than 100/200. As we can observe: (1) In datasets NYT-10 and CIPDS*, all Hit@K of the models in the rows below and including the CGRE (constraint graph-based models) are higher than the models in the rows above the CGRE (without constraint graph), which means the constraint graph-based frameworks bring better performance as compared to models without constraint graph, consistently. (2) In datasets NYT-10 and CIPDS*, all Hit@K of BGRE-simple-add(ours), BGRE-simple-cat(ours) and DBGARE(ours) are higher than CGRE, it indicates that the models with the interactive information within the two partitions get better performance than the single bipartite constraint graph framework. (3) In datasets NYT-10 and CIPDS*, all Hits@K of the model with the dual attention mechanism DBGARE(ours) are not lower, especially markedly improves in the Hit@10 of NYT-10 and the Hit@8 of CIPDS* as compared to BGRE-simple-add(ours) and BGRE-simple-cat(ours) in dataset NYT-10 and CIPDS*, it suggests that the dual attention mechanism behaves better than the common ways.

4.4   Experimental Results for Noisy Labels

According to the previous work [8,9], we select the following three groups of competitive models as baselines: (1) Traditional feature-based models including: Mintz, MultiR and MIMLRE. (2) Neural network-based models containing: PCNN, PCNN+ATT, BGWA, RESIDE, HATT and BATT. (3) Constraint graph-based framework: CGRE. As datasets NYT-10, GIDS and CIPDS∗ all have noisy labels challenge, in this subsection, we use all three datasets. Compared with NYT-10, the experimental results of the missing models in CIDS and CIPDS∗ are too low, so more sensible results are selected for presentation.

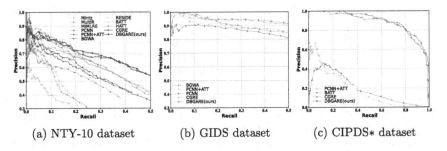

(a) NTY-10 dataset   (b) GIDS dataset   (c) CIPDS∗ dataset

Fig. 3. Precision-recall curves for different methods. DBGARE achieves higher precision over the most range recall compared to all the baselines on three datasets.

Figure 3 shows the precision/recall curves for different methods. We can observe that: (1) In dataset NYT-10, when the recall is greater than 0.1, the performance of traditional feature-based methods(Mintz, MultiR and MIMLRE) drops out quickly while neural network-based and constraint graph-based methods have reasonable precision. It demonstrates that human-designed features have limits to capture the semantic meaning of the sentences. (2) In datasets NYT-10, GIDS and CIPDS∗, the neural network-based models without constraint graphs also drop out quickly when the recall is greater than 0.2, compared to the constraint graph-based frameworks(CGRE and DBGARE(ours)). (3) In datasets NYT-10, GIDS and CIPDS∗, our framework DBGARE(ours) outperforms all other three groups of competitive models(traditional feature-based models, neural network-based models and constraint graph-based framework).

4.5   Evaluation of Attention Mechanism

To investigate the effect of different attention mechanisms, we select five the state-of-the-art models with attention mechanism to compare. Following the previous study[8], we employ Precision@N(N is the recall value), top-N, $N \in$ [100, 200, 300] and average of the all top-N for evaluations. We randomly select one/two/all sentences from each sentences bag with more than two sentences in the testing dataset to construct three new testing datasets: One/Two/All, and report the result values: P@100, P@200, P@300 and average of all.

Table 5 shows the denoising evaluation matric P@N. The framework DBGARE(ours) outperforms other methods at almost evolutional metrics on all datasets. We believe the reason is that single attention can only pay attention to single graph, which cases attention bias. In this contrast, the dual attention mechanism can pay attention to multiple graphs to avoid attention bias.

Table 5. (%) P@N values for relation extraction on the entity pairs with different number of instances.

Datasets	Test mode P@N	One				Two				All			
		100	200	300	Avg.	100	200	300	Avg.	100	200	300	Avg.
NYT-10	PCNN+ATT [9]	73.3	69.2	60.8	67.8	77.2	71.6	66.1	71.6	76.2	73.1	67.4	77.2
	RESIDE [16]	80.0	75.5	69.3	74.9	83.0	73.5	70.6	75.7	84.0	78.5	75.6	79.4
	PCNN+HATT [3]	84.0	76.0	69.7	76.6	85.0	76.0	72.7	77.9	88.0	79.5	75.3	80.9
	PCNN+BATT [19]	86.8	77.6	73.9	79.4	91.2	79.2	75.4	81.9	91.8	84.0	78.7	84.8
	CGRE [8]	**93.0**	84.5	77.7	85.1	91.0	85.5	81.7	85.9	**93.0**	88.0	86.0	89.0
	DBGARE(ours)	**93.0**	**87.5**	**82.0**	**87.5**	92.0	**88.0**	**84.3**	**88.1**	92.0	**88.5**	**86.7**	**89.1**
CIPDS*	PCNN+ATT [9]	28.0	23.5	20.0	23.8	31.0	24.5	19.3	24.9	43.0	36.0	29.7	36.2
	PCNN+BATT [19]	39.0	26.5	20.0	28.5	38.0	35.0	29.3	34.1	45.0	40.5	34.7	40.1
	CGRE [8]	**96.0**	74.0	**54.3**	**74.8**	94.0	**90.0**	70.3	84.8	97.0	93.0	84.0	91.3
	DBGARE(ours)	95.0	**75.5**	53.7	74.7	**98.0**	88.5	**71.7**	**86.1**	**99.0**	**94.5**	**83.7**	**92.4**

5 Conclusion and Future Works

In order to enhance the existing competitive method for solving noisy labels and long-tailed distributions of distantly supervised relation extraction, in this paper, we proposed a novel framework DBGARE. In DBGARE, we constructed graphs across and within each bipartite graph partition to enrich unbalanced relations dependency. In addition, we devised a novel technique dual attention mechanism to pay attention to multiple graphs for avoiding attention bias and promoting information dissemination from data-riches to data-poors. Multiple experimental results have shown the state-of-the-art effectiveness of our framework in both challenges. Furthermore, CIPDS*, a new distantly supervised relation extraction dataset in Chinese was proposed in this paper. In the future, we will use information about the directions of relations, which is significant for the model to understand the orientation semantics.

References

1. Bengio, Y.: Learning deep architectures for AI. Now Publishers Inc (2009)
2. Cao, Y., Kuang, J., Gao, M., Zhou, A., Wen, Y., Chua, T.S.: Learning relation prototype from unlabeled texts for long-tail relation extraction. IEEE Trans. Knowl. Data Eng. 1 (2021). https://doi.org/10.1109/TKDE.2021.3096200

3. Han, X., Yu, P., Liu, Z., Sun, M., Li, P.: Hierarchical relation extraction with coarse-to-fine grained attention. In: Proceedings of the 2018 Conference on Empirical Methods in Natural Language Processing, pp. 2236–2245 (2018)

4. Hoffmann, R., Zhang, C., Ling, X., Zettlemoyer, L., Weld, D.S.: Knowledge-based weak supervision for information extraction of overlapping relations. In: Proceedings of the 49th Annual Meeting of the Association for Computational Linguistics: Human Language Technologies, pp. 541–550 (2011)

5. Jat, S., Khandelwal, S., Talukdar, P.: Improving distantly supervised relation extraction using word and entity based attention. arXiv preprint arXiv:1804.06987 (2018)

6. Li, Y., Shen, T., Long, G., Jiang, J., Zhou, T., Zhang, C.: Improving long-tail relation extraction with collaborating relation-augmented attention. arXiv preprint arXiv:2010.03773 (2020)

7. Li, Y., Song, Y., Jia, L., Gao, S., Li, Q., Qiu, M.: Intelligent fault diagnosis by fusing domain adversarial training and maximum mean discrepancy via ensemble learning. IEEE Trans. Industr. Inf. **17**(60), 2833–2841 (2021). https://doi.org/10.1109/TII.2020.3008010

8. Liang, T., Liu, Y., Liu, X., Sharma, G., Guo, M.: Distantly-supervised long-tailed relation extraction using constraint graphs. arXiv preprint arXiv:2105.11225 (2021)

9. Lin, Y., Shen, S., Liu, Z., Luan, H., Sun, M.: Neural relation extraction with selective attention over instances. In: Proceedings of the 54th Annual Meeting of the Association for Computational Linguistics (vol. 1: Long Papers), pp. 2124–2133 (2016)

10. Mintz, M., Bills, S., Snow, R., Jurafsky, D.: Distant supervision for relation extraction without labeled data. In: Proceedings of the Joint Conference of the 47th Annual Meeting of the ACL and the 4th International Joint Conference on Natural Language Processing of the AFNLP, pp. 1003–1011 (2009)

11. Peng, H., et al.: Learning from context or names? An empirical study on neural relation extraction. arXiv preprint arXiv:2010.01923 (2020)

12. Peng, S., Zhang, Y., Yu, Y., Zuo, H., Zhang, K.: Named entity recognition based on reinforcement learning and adversarial training. In: Qiu, H., Zhang, C., Fei, Z., Qiu, M., Kung, S.-Y. (eds.) KSEM 2021. LNCS (LNAI), vol. 12815, pp. 191–202. Springer, Cham (2021). https://doi.org/10.1007/978-3-030-82136-4_16

13. Qiu, H., Zheng, Q., Msahli, M., Memmi, G., Qiu, M., Lu, J.: Topological graph convolutional network-based urban traffic flow and density prediction. IEEE Trans. Intell. Transp. Syst. **22**(7), 4560–4569 (2021). https://doi.org/10.1109/TITS.2020.3032882

14. Riedel, S., Yao, L., McCallum, A.: Modeling relations and their mentions without labeled text. In: Balcázar, J.L., Bonchi, F., Gionis, A., Sebag, M. (eds.) ECML PKDD 2010. LNCS (LNAI), vol. 6323, pp. 148–163. Springer, Heidelberg (2010). https://doi.org/10.1007/978-3-642-15939-8_10

15. Surdeanu, M., Tibshirani, J., Nallapati, R., Manning, C.D.: Multi-instance multi-label learning for relation extraction. In: Proceedings of the 2012 Joint Conference on Empirical Methods in Natural Language Processing and Computational Natural Language Learning, pp. 455–465 (2012)

16. Vashishth, S., Joshi, R., Prayaga, S.S., Bhattacharyya, C., Talukdar, P.: Reside: improving distantly-supervised neural relation extraction using side information. arXiv preprint arXiv:1812.04361 (2018)

17. Wang, J.: RH-Net: improving neural relation extraction via reinforcement learning and hierarchical relational searching. arXiv preprint arXiv:2010.14255 (2020)

18. Yao, Jinxin, Zhang, Min, Wang, Biyang, Xu, Xianda: A hybrid model with pre-trained entity-aware transformer for relation extraction. In: Li, Gang, Shen, Heng Tao, Yuan, Ye., Wang, Xiaoyang, Liu, Huawen, Zhao, Xiang (eds.) KSEM 2020. LNCS (LNAI), vol. 12274, pp. 148–160. Springer, Cham (2020). https://doi.org/10.1007/978-3-030-55130-8_13

19. Ye, Z.X., Ling, Z.H.: Distant supervision relation extraction with intra-bag and inter-bag attentions. arXiv preprint arXiv:1904.00143 (2019)

20. Zeng, D., Liu, K., Chen, Y., Zhao, J.: Distant supervision for relation extraction via piecewise convolutional neural networks. In: Proceedings of the 2015 Conference on Empirical Methods in Natural Language Processing, pp. 1753–1762 (2015)

21. Zeng, D., Liu, K., Lai, S., Zhou, G., Zhao, J.: Relation classification via convolutional deep neural network. In: Proceedings of COLING 2014, the 25th International Conference on Computational Linguistics: Technical Papers, pp. 2335–2344 (2014)

22. Zhang, N., et al.: Long-tail relation extraction via knowledge graph embeddings and graph convolution networks. arXiv preprint arXiv:1903.01306 (2019)

23. Zhong, Z., Chen, D.: A frustratingly easy approach for entity and relation extraction. arXiv preprint arXiv:2010.12812 (2020)

Concept Commons Enhanced Knowledge Graph Representation

Yashen Wang[1,2(✉)], Xiaoye Ouyang[1], Xiaoling Zhu[1], and Huanhuan Zhang[1]

[1] National Engineering Laboratory for Risk Perception and Prevention (RPP), China Academy of Electronics and Information Technology of CETC, Beijing 100041, China
yswang@bit.edu.cn, zhuxiaoling1@cetc.com.cn
[2] Information Science Academy of CETC, Beijing 100041, China

Abstract. Knowledge graphs (KGs) are regarded as important resources for a variety of artificial intelligence (AI) and auxiliary decision tasks but suffer from incompleteness. To address this challenge, a number of knowledge graph representation (KGR) and knowledge graph completion (KGC) methods have been developed using graph embeddings manners. Most existing methods focus on the structured information of native triples in encyclopaedia KG and maximize the likelihood of them. However, they neglect *semantic commons* contained in lexical KG. Recent researches aims at investigating the general framework for enhancing KGR or KGC methods with semantic signals (e.g., entity types, entity descriptions etc.,). However, their work almost modeled the semantic resources by an *implicit* way, leading their results lacked *interpretability*. To overcome this drawback, we propose a novel Concept Commons enhanced Knowledge Graph Representation model (named as **C^{2}KGR**), that integrates the structured information in encyclopaedia KG and the entity's concepts in lexical KG, via both implicit manner and *explicit* manner. Experimental results demonstrate the efficiency and interpretability of the proposed model on the real-world datasets.

Keywords: Knowledge graph representation · Concept commons · Knowledge graph completion · Representation learning · Interpretability

1 Introduction

Knowledge graphs (KGs) such as Freebase, YAGO, and Wikipedia are among the most widely used resources in the Natural Language Processing (NLP) applications [4,9,18,21,25,29]. Typically, a knowledge graph consists of a set of triples (h, r, t) where h, r, t stand for head entity, relation and tail entity respectively. KGs are widely used for many practical tasks, however, their completeness are *not* guaranteed. Although large-scale KGs have contained billions of triples [1,7,13], the extracted knowledge is still a small part of the real-world knowledge and probably contains errors and contradictions. For example, 71% of people in Freebase have no known place of birth, and 75% have no known nationality. For triple (h, r, t) embedded in given knowledge graph, Knowledge Graph Representation (KGR) models could learn the latent representations of the entities (head entity h and tail entity t) and relations (r), and

G. Memmi et al. (Eds.): KSEM 2022, LNAI 13368, pp. 413–424, 2022.
https://doi.org/10.1007/978-3-031-10983-6_32

have shown the best performance on the Knowledge Graph Completion (KGC) task [8,9,20]. However, most of the current KGR models such as TransE [2] and its variants TransH [22], TransR [8] relied heavily on KG's structure information, while ignoring the semantic information embedded in the given KGs.

Although these models have significantly improved the embedding representations and increased the prediction accuracy, there is still room for improvement by exploiting semantic information in the representation of entities. Generally speaking, *semantic information* includes entity concepts, types, descriptions, lexical categories and other textual information. Recent researches aims at investigating the genetic framework for enhancing KGR or KGC methods with semantic signals (e.g., entity type [9,11], entity description [25,27] and other semantic information). However, their work almost modeled the semantic resources by a implicit way, leading that the their results lacked *interpretability* [11]. Take entity type as example, it define categories of entities that are valid to enhance the representation of entities. In many type-embodied models such as TKRL [28] and TransT [9], the explicit types are necessary while some KGs (i.e., Word-Net) *lack* them, which limits the versatility of these models. [11] learns the latent entity type embedding of each entity by regarding each relation as a translation operation between the entity types of two entities with a relation-aware projection mechanism. However, this work only *implicitly* utilizes entity's extra semantics (e.g., entity type emphasized in this attempt), while does not *explicitly* incorporates with extra semantics, leading that the its results *lack* interpretability. To solve with these problems, TransC [20] leveraged entity's concept signals, which represents the domains or categories of entities in lexical KG Probase. In fact, all entities appearing in the head (or tail) with the same (specific) relation have some common concepts. For example, in the triple (David_Beckham, place_of_birth, London), David Beckham is a person, while in (David_Beckham, player_of, Manchester_United), David Beckham is a player or athlete (shown in Fig. 1).

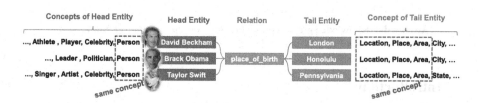

Fig. 1. An example showing that the entities in the head or tail of a relation share some common concepts from the lexical KG Probase [20].

In this work, we propose **C**oncept **C**ommons enhanced **K**nowledge **G**raph **R**epresentation model (named as **C²KGR**). The proposed work improves previous framework by the following two ways: (i) We try to leverage semantic constraints from lexical signals (i.e., concept emphasized here) for boosting the efficiency of knowledge graph embedding; (ii) We try to model the concept signals via not only a implicit manner but also a explicit manner. In the proposed model, we first embed the entities and relations into complex space via the *native* triple representations. Additionally, the *conceptual* triple representations is developed to learn concept-based embeddings. Especially, two kinds of concept-based semantic similarity constraints, are introduced into the proposed model, by leveraging concept commons explicitly and implicitly, inspired by [11] and [20]. Particularly, (i) the conceptual representations of head (or tail) entities involved in the triples with the same relation, are closer to each other; and (ii) all of the entities located in the head position (or tail position) with the same relation may have some common entity concepts.

2 Methodology

Our method is inspired by previous work [11]. This work proposed a general and generic framework, which aims at plugging *any* extra semantic signals (entity type used in this work) information into *any* knowledge graph embeddings models. Unfortunately, although entity type is shown as a beneficial semantic signal in previous works, this work introduces entity type only by a totally *implicit* manner, lacking of interpretability and explainability [10]. Instead, we improve this framework by the following two ways: (i) We try to leverage semantic constraints from lexical signals (i.e., concept emphasized here) for boosting the efficiency of knowledge graph embedding; (ii) We try to model the concept signals via not only a implicit manner but also a *explicit* manner. Hence, the proposed model is denoted as **C**oncept **C**ommons enhanced **K**nowledge **G**raph **R**epresentation model, i.e., **C²KGR**. Figure 2 sketches the architecture of the proposed model.

2.1 Native Triple Representations

To distinguish, we regard the structural (or topological) triples/entities/relations provided by the given KG are *native* triples/entities/relations. Nowadays, by combining symbolic reasoning methods or Bayesian models, deep representation learning techniques on knowledge graphs attempt to handle complex reasoning with relational path and symbolic logic and capture the uncertainty with probabilistic inference. For the native entities and relations, we project them into the high-dimension semantic space. Various Knowledge Graph Representation (KGR) models have been extensively developed for KG inference in recent years, and have achieved competitive performance in many KG-oriented tasks [3][17], have shown their ability to capture relational facts and model different scenarios with heterogenous information [6,21]. TransE [2] uses the structure information of triples ($\mathbf{h} + \mathbf{r} \approx \mathbf{t}$) to embed knowledge graphs into a continuous vector space, which is a very important component in knowledge representations. Many other translation-based methods are introduced, including TransH [22], TransD [5], TransR [8], TrasG [26] and RotatE [15]. Especially, following classic RotatE [15], for a specific triple (h, r, t), relation r is regarded as the *rotation operation* from the head entity h to the tail entity t. Note that, any current knowledge graph embedding methods could be adopted here, apart from RotatE [15]. We indicates Δ as the set of native triples embedded in current knowledge graph and we firstly update Δ by combing current knowledge graph with Probase: For each triple $(h, r, t) \in \Delta$, we distill the corresponding concepts of head entity h and tail entity t from Probase based

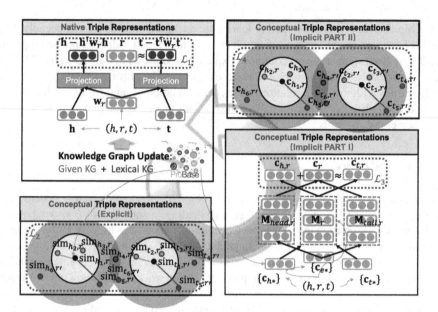

Fig. 2. The architecture of the proposed Concept Commons enhanced Knowledge Graph Representation model (C²KGR).

on instance conceptualization algorithm [4,19,24], as well as the relations[1] defined in Probase among these concepts and h (as well as t), and then we add aforementioned concepts (as newly-defined entity type) and relations into the current knowledge graph. With efforts above, we finish to leverage lexical semantic signals form Probase for enhancing the given knowledge graph. the energy function $\mathcal{E}_1(h, r, t)$ is defined as follows:

$$\mathcal{E}_1(h,r,t) = \| (\mathbf{h} - \mathbf{h}^\top \mathbf{w}_r \mathbf{h}) \circ \mathbf{r} - (\mathbf{t} - \mathbf{t}^\top \mathbf{w}_r \mathbf{t}) \| \tag{1}$$

Wherein, $\mathbf{h} \in \mathbb{R}^k$, $\mathbf{t} \in \mathbb{R}^k$ and $\mathbf{r} \in \mathbb{R}^k$ indicate the vector representation of head entity h, tail entity t and relation r, respectively. $\mathbf{w}_r \in \mathbb{R}^k$ denotes the normal vector of the hyper-plane involved in the relation r. With efforts above, we not only train vector representations for the native entities and relations embedded in the original knowledge graph, but also obtain the vector representations for associated concepts, which will be utilized in the following Sect. 2.5.

The corresponding loss function $\mathcal{L}_1$, could be defined as follows:

$$\mathcal{L}_1 = \log \phi[\eta_1 + \mathcal{E}_1(h,r,t) - \mathcal{E}_1(h_-, r, t_-)] \tag{2}$$

Wherein, notation η_1 denotes the fixed margins in $\mathcal{L}_1$. Function $\phi(\cdot)$ denotes the sigmoid function. (h_-, r, t_-) represents the negative instance of (h, r, t) by randomly replacing head entity h or tail entity t,

---

[1] Probase naturally provides two kinds of relation types: (i) occurrence co-occurrence frequencies among entities (or concepts); (ii) IsA probabilities ("belong" relation) between entity and concept.

2.2   Conceptual Triple Representations

Efficient representation learning and reasoning can be one of the paths towards the emulation of high-level cognition and human-level intelligence. Unfortunately, all the approaches above purely depend on the triples directly observed in KGs. On the other words, they relied heavily on KG's structural (also named as topological) information (Sect. 2.2), while *ignoring* the semantic information embedded in the given KGs. Recently, more and more methods investigate to improve the knowledge representation by exploiting additional information. E.g., the path information, entity type information (as well as entity description information) and logic rules etc., have been proved to be beneficial for various knowledge graph representation and inference task. [16,28]

This paper attempt at introducing concept semantic information Sect. 2.3 into knowledge graph representation task. That is, apart from naive triple representations generated in last section, the proposed model also want to generate the corresponding conceptual triple representation for each triple $(h, r, t) \in \Delta$. Especially, two kinds of concept-based semantic similarity constraints, are introduced into the proposed model, by leveraging concept commons explicitly Sect. 2.4 and implicitly Sect. 2.5. With efforts above, the conceptual triple representations could be constrained by the similarity between the entity's concepts, via explicit manner and implicit manner.

2.3   Motivation of Concept

The reason why concept is chosen is that: Compared with entity type [9,11], entity description [25,27] and other semantic information, concepts are simpler and more specific because concepts of an entity are unordered and contain less noise [4,14,18,23]. Moreover, Probase provide huge number of high-quality and robust concepts without builds.

2.4   Explicit Conceptual Triple Representations

The Similarity constraints strategy in [11] only *implicitly* utilizes entity's extra semantics, while does not *explicitly* incorporates with extra semantics, leading that the its results *lack* interpretability. Hence, to improve the model's interpretability, apart from [11], we introduce conceptual similarity constraint, inspired by [20]. As discussed in [20], all of the entities located in the head position (or tail position) with the *same* relation may have some *common* entity concepts, as shown in Fig. 1. In this example, all the head entities have "Person" concept and all the tail entities have concepts of "Location", "Place" and "Area". Therefore, we could see that, "Person" is the head concept of relation "palce_of_birth", and "Location", "Place" and "Area" are the tail concepts of this relation. Based on aforementioned correlation, this paper introduces a concept-based semantic similarity, which utilizes *entity concepts* to construct *relation concepts*, and then evaluate the conceptual similarity between entity and relation based on the aforementioned entity/relation concepts. Apparently, each relation (such as "palce_of_birth" in Fig. 1) relates two components, and thus each relation r has two concept sets: (i) head concept set C_r^{head}, consisting of concepts of the entities occurring in the head position; and (ii) tail concept set C_r^{tail}, consisting of concepts of the entities occurring in the tail position. From the lexical KG Probase [24], we could distill entities appearing in the head position of relation r to form the head entity set, denoted as E_r^{head}. Similarly, the tail entity set, denoted as E_r^{tail}, could be constructed in the same way. Moreover, given entity e, we denote its concept set as C_e, consisting the corresponding concepts deriving from Probase by leveraging single instance conceptualization algorithm [4,19,24]. With efforts above, given relation r, the corresponding C_r^{head} and C_r^{tail} could be defined as follows:

$$C_r^{head} = \bigcap_{e \in E_r^{head}} C_e \tag{3}$$

$$C_r^{tail} = \bigcap_{e \in E_r^{tail}} C_e \tag{4}$$

With efforts above, the semantic similarity between the relation r and its head entity h, to measure the distinction of entity semantics with the concept information, is defined as:

$$\text{sim}_{head}(r, h) = \frac{|C_r^{head} \bigcup C_h|}{|C_r^{head}|} \tag{5}$$

Similarly, the semantic similarity between the relation r and its tail entity t is defined as:

$$\text{sim}_{tail}(r, t) = \frac{|C_r^{tail} \bigcup C_t|}{|C_r^{tail}|} \tag{6}$$

Considering any two native triples $(h_1, r_1, t_1) \in \Delta$ and $(h_2, r_2, t_2) \in \Delta$ in given knowledge graph, we could design energy function for evaluating concept-driven semantic similarity as follows:

$$\mathcal{E}_2((h_1, r_1, t_1), (h_2, r_2, t_2))$$
$$= \frac{1}{2}(|\text{sim}_{head}(r_1, h_1) - \text{sim}_{head}(r_2, h_2)| \tag{7}$$
$$+ |\text{sim}_{tail}(r_1, t_1) - \text{sim}_{tail}(r_2, t_2)|)$$

Apparently, the value of $\mathcal{E}_2((h_1, r_1, t_1), (h_2, r_2, t_2))$, tends to be smaller if r_1 and r_2 are the same (or similar) relation. Therefore, for a specific triple $(h, r, t) \in \Delta$, the corresponding loss function $\mathcal{L}_2$, could be defined as follows:

$$\mathcal{L}_2 = \sum_{(h_+, r, t_+) \in \Delta_r} \sum_{(h_+, r', t_+) \in \Delta_{r'}}$$
$$\max[0, \eta_2 + \mathcal{E}_2((h, r, t), (h_+, r, t_+)) \tag{8}$$
$$- \mathcal{E}_2((h, r, t), (h_+, r', t_+))]$$

Wherein, notation η_2 denotes the margin parameter in $\mathcal{L}_2$. Function $\max[0, x]$ is the function to select the larger value between 0 and x. For each native triple $(h, r, t) \in \Delta$, (h_+, r, t_+) is a positive instance in the set Δ_r, which contains triples respect to relation r. (h_+, r', t_+) is positive instance in the set $\Delta_{r'}$, which is respect to relation r' and $r \neq r'$.

2.5 Implicit Conceptual Triple Representations

The conceptual representation for entity e respect to relation r is denoted as $\mathbf{c}_{e,r} \in \mathbb{R}^k$. Similarly, $\mathbf{c}_r \in \mathbb{R}^k$ denotes the conceptual representation of the relation r. Hence, First of all, based on translation-based embeeding manner, given (h, r, t), let us suppose that $\mathbf{c}_{h,r} + \mathbf{c}_r \approx \mathbf{c}_{t,r}$. Hence, we formulate the following energy function:

$$
\begin{aligned}
\mathbf{c}_{h,r} &= \mathbf{M}_r \cdot (\mathbf{c}_{h_1} + \mathbf{c}_{h_2} + \cdots + \mathbf{c}_{h_{|C_h|}}) \\
\mathbf{c}_{t,r} &= \mathbf{M}_r \cdot (\mathbf{c}_{t_1} + \mathbf{c}_{t_2} + \cdots + \mathbf{c}_{t_{|C_t|}}) \\
\mathbf{c}_r &= \mathbf{M}_{head,r} \cdot [\mathbf{c}_{e_1} + \mathbf{c}_{e_2} + \cdots + \mathbf{c}_{e_{|C_r^{head}|}}] \\
&+ \mathbf{M}_{tail,r} \cdot [\mathbf{c}_{e_1} + \mathbf{c}_{e_2} + \cdots + \mathbf{c}_{e_{|C_r^{tail}|}}]
\end{aligned}
\tag{9}
$$

$$
\mathcal{E}_3(h, r, t) = \parallel \mathbf{c}_{h,r} + \mathbf{c}_r - \mathbf{c}_{t,r} \parallel_l
$$

Wherein, $\mathbf{c}_{h_*}$ indicates the concept representation respect to concept h_* contained in the concept set C_h of entity h, which is initialized by RotatE (details in Sect. 2.2). Similarly, $\mathbf{c}_{e_*}$ indicates the concept representation according to concept e_* contained in the head (or tail) concept set C_r^{head} (or C_r^{tail}) respect to relation r. $\mathbf{c}_{h,r} \in \mathbb{R}^k$ and $\mathbf{c}_{t,r} \in \mathbb{R}^k$ are the conceptual representations of head entity h and tail entity t, associated with relation r, respectively. $\mathbf{M}_r \in \mathbb{R}^{k \times k}$ indicates the projection matrix to be trained, respect to relation r. Beside, $\mathbf{M}_{head,r} \in \mathbb{R}^{k \times k}$ and $\mathbf{M}_{tail,r} \in \mathbb{R}^{k \times k}$, indicate other trainable projection matrix respect the head and tail position of specific relation r, respectively.

The corresponding loss function $\mathcal{L}_3$, could be defined as follows:

$$
\mathcal{L}_3 = \sum_{(h_+, r, t_+) \in \Delta_r} \sum_{(h_-, r, t_-) \in \Delta_r'} \max[0, \eta_3 + \mathcal{E}_3(h_+, r, t_+) - \mathcal{E}_3(h_-, r, t_-)]
\tag{10}
$$

Wherein, notation η_3 denotes the margin in $\mathcal{L}_3$. $(h_-, r, t_-) \in \Delta_r'$ represents the negative instance of (h, r, t) by randomly replacing head entity h or tail entity t, and Δ_r' is the set of negative triples according to the given triple (h, r, t).

On the other hand, [11] learns the latent entity type embedding of each entity by regarding each relation as a translation operation between the entity types of two entities with a relation-aware projection mechanism. Following the similarity constraint strategy proposed by this work, our work also hypothesizes that: the conceptual representations of head (or tail) entities involved in the triples with the same relation, are closer to each other. Note that, this hypothesis is consistent with the explicit constraint proposed in Sect. 2.4. In other words, given triple (h_1, r, t_1) and triple (h_2, r, t_2) with the same relation r, we suppose that:

$$
\begin{aligned}
\mathbf{c}_{h_1,r} &\approx \mathbf{c}_{h_2,r} \\
\mathbf{c}_{t_1,r} &\approx \mathbf{c}_{t_2,r}
\end{aligned}
\tag{11}
$$

Given two triples (h_1, r_1, t_1) and (h_2, r_2, t_2), Thus, the energy function for evaluating the similarity from their conceptual perspective, is defined as follows:

$$
\begin{aligned}
&\mathcal{E}_4((h_1, r_1, t_1), (h_2, r_2, t_2)) \\
&= \frac{1}{2}(\parallel \mathbf{c}_{h_1,r_1} - \mathbf{c}_{h_2,r_2} \parallel_l + \parallel \mathbf{c}_{t_1,r_1} - \mathbf{c}_{t_2,r_2} \parallel_l)
\end{aligned}
\tag{12}
$$

Therefore, for a specific triple $(h, r, t) \in \Delta$, the corresponding loss function $\mathcal{L}_4$, could be defined as follows:

$$
\begin{aligned}
\mathcal{L}_4 = \sum_{(h_+, r, t_+) \in \Delta_r} \sum_{(h_+, r', t_+) \in \Delta_{r'}} \\
\max[0, \eta_4 + \mathcal{E}_4((h, r, t), (h_+, r, t_+)) \\
- \mathcal{E}_4((h, r, t), (h_+, r', t_+))]
\end{aligned}
\tag{13}
$$

Wherein, notation η_4 denotes the fixed margins in $\mathcal{L}_4$. Δ indicates the set of native triples embedded in current knowledge graph. For each native triple $(h, r, t) \in \Delta$, (h_+, r, t_+) is a positive instance in the set Δ_r, which containing triples respect to relation r. (h_+, r', t_+) is positive instance in the set $\Delta_{r'}$, which is respect to relation r' and $r \neq r'$.

2.6   Model Training

As sketched in Fig. 2, our optimization procedure has coupled all the four loss function defined above. Thus, the objective function of the proposed model, is defined as follows:

$$
\begin{aligned}
\mathcal{L} = \sum_{(h, r, t) \in \Delta} \{ \sum_{(h_-, r, t_-) \in \Delta'} [\alpha_1 \mathcal{L}_1 + \alpha_3 \mathcal{L}_4] \\
+ \alpha_2 \mathcal{L}_2 + \alpha_4 \mathcal{L}_4 \}
\end{aligned}
\tag{14}
$$

Wherein, parameter set $\{\alpha_1, \alpha_2, \alpha_3, \alpha_4\}$ denote the weights of $\mathcal{L}_1$, $\mathcal{L}_2$, $\mathcal{L}_3$ and $\mathcal{L}_4$ for trade-off. Δ indicates all the triples in the observable train set, while Δ' indicates the set of negative instance (h_-, r, t_-) generated by randomly replacing the entities in Δ.

3   Experiments

We evaluate our proposed concept commons enhanced knowledge graph representation model (named as $\mathbf{C^2KGR}$) on several experiments. We evaluate our model on standard Link Prediction task, Entity Prediction task and Triple Classification task with benchmark static datasets.

3.1   Datasets and Baselines

To evaluate entity prediction task, link prediction task and triple classification task, we conduct experiments on the **WN18** (WordNet) and **FB15k** (Freebase) introduced by [2] and use the same training/validation/test split as in [2]. The information of the two aforementioned datasets is reported in Table 1. Wherein, $\#E$ and $\#R$ denote the number of entities and relation types respectively. $\#Train$, $\#Valid$ and $\#Test$ are the numbers of triple in the training, validation and test sets respectively. As discussed above, concept signals of entities in FB15K and WN18 is generated by instance conceptualization algorithm [4, 19] based on Probase [12, 24]. As the datasets and their splitting manners, as well as the "unif." sampling strategy, are the same, we directly reuse the results of several baselines from the previous literature [8,22,28]. Under the "unif." sampling strategy [22], the optimal configurations are listed as follows: the batch size is set as 1024, learning rate $\epsilon = 0.001$, vector dimension $k = 100$, the fixed margins are set as $\eta_1 = 10$, $\eta_2 = 0.05$, $\eta_3 = 6$ and $\eta_4 = 3$ on WN18 dataset; $\epsilon = 0.00025$, $k = 300$, the fixed margins are set as $\eta_1 = 22$, $\eta_2 = 0.025$, $\eta_3 = 7$ and $\eta_4 = 5$ on FB15K dataset. We train the model until convergence. The baselines include five semantics-based models: **TKRL** [28] and **TransT** [9] utilize entity types; **DKRL** [27] and **SSP** [25] take advantage of entity descriptions; Apart from modeling semantic signals *implicitly*, **TransC** [20] try to utilize concept information *explicitly*.

Table 1. Statistics of FB15k and WN18 used in experiments.

Dataset	#E	#R	#Train	#Valid	#Test
WN18	40,943	18	141,442	5,000	5,000
FB15k	14,951	1,345	483,142	50,000	59,071

3.2 Evaluations on Entity Prediction Task

Table 2. Evaluation results of entity prediction on FB15k.

	Mean rank		HITS10(%)	
	Raw	Filter	Raw	Filter
TransE	238	143	46.4	62.1
TransH	212	87	45.7	64.4
TransR	199	77	47.2	67.2
DKRL	181	91	49.6	67.4
TKRL	202	87	50.3	73.4
SSP	**163**	82	57.2	73.4
TransT	199	**46**	53.3	73.4
TransC	175	44	58.4	86.7
C²KGR	166	**42**	**61.3**	**89.3**

Table 3. Evaluation results of entity prediction on WN18.

	Mean Rank		HITS10(%)	
	Raw	Filter	Raw	Filter
TransE	263	251	75.4	89.2
TransH	401	338	73.0	82.3
TransR	238	225	79.8	92.0
DKRL	202	198	77.4	92.4
TKRL	180	167	80.6	94.1
SSP	168	156	81.2	93.2
TransT	137	130	92.7	97.4
TransC	136	125	94.5	96.9
C²KGR	**131**	**121**	**97.3**	**97.8**

Entity prediction task aims at predicting the missing entity when given an entity and a relation, i.e., we infer tail entity t when given $(h, r, ?)$, or infer head entity h when given $(?, r, t)$. FB15K and WN18 are the benchmark dataset for this task. We adopt the same protocol used in previous studies. The overall entity prediction results on FB15K and WN18 are reported in Table 2 and Table 3. From the result, we observe that: **C²KGR** significantly outperforms all baselines on FB15k with "Filter" setting, which demonstrates that the proposed framework reasonably utilizes the concept commons and can capture the different semantics of every entity more accurately than linear transformations of single entity vector. Especially, These results shows that, (i) The conceptual representations learned from KGs are available to predict entities more accurately by restricting the entities with conceptual representations and concept-based semantic similarity constraints; (ii) As shown in TransC and our work, both implicit and explicit modeling are necessary for enhancing the expressive ability of commons.

3.3 Evaluations on Relation Prediction Task

Table 4. Evaluation results of relation prediction on FB15K.

	Mean Rank		HITS1(%)	
	Raw	Filter	Raw	Filter
TransE	2.91	2.53	69.5	90.2
TransH	8.25	7.91	60.3	72.5
TransR	2.49	2.09	70.2	91.6
DKRL	2.41	2.03	69.8	90.8
TKRL	2.47	2.07	68.3	90.6
SSP	1.87	1.47	70.9	90.9
TransT	1.59	**1.19**	72.0	94.1
TransC	1.37	1.38	73.6	95.2
C^2KGR	**1.33**	1.31	**74.3**	**97.1**

Table 5. Evaluation results of triple classification on FB15K.

	Accuracy(%)
TransE	85.7
TransH	87.7
TransR	86.4
DKRL	87.1
TKRL	88.5
SSP	90.1
TransT	91.0
TransC	93.4
C^2KGR	**95.3**

Relation prediction task attempts at predicting the missing relation type when given two entities, i.e., we predict r given $(h, ?, t)$. FB15K is the benchmark dataset for this task. The overall entity prediction results on FB15K and WN18 are reported in Table 4. From the result, we observe that: C^2**KGR** significantly outperforms all baselines in the most cases. Compared with **TransT**, which utilized type information, C^2**KGR** improves Mean Rank by 16.42% and HITS@1 by 3.24% in "Raw" setting. Similar to entity prediction task, the proposed C^2**KGR** still outperforms **TransC** which also introduces concept commons. However, our model achieve *explicit* ($\mathcal{E}_2$ in Eq. (7)) and *implicit* ($\mathcal{E}_3$ in Eq. (9) and $\mathcal{E}_4$ in Eq. (12)) concept modeling simultaneously, while **TransC** only model concept commons explicitly.

3.4 Evaluations on Triple Classification Task

Triple classification task aims at predicting whether a given triple is correct or incorrect. In other words, the comparative models are asked to predict the correctness of (h, r, t).

FB15K is the benchmark dataset of this task. Experimental results on FB15K dataset are shown in Table 5. Ours outperforms all baselines significantly, releasing that the conceptual representations learned by our model are more effective for inference than totally leveraging the *explicit* concepts (e.g., **TransC**). Moreover, compared with the best result, **TransT** and **SSP**, C^2KGR improves the accuracy by 4.69% and 5.74%.

4   Conclusions

This paper proposes a novel C^2KGR framework to learn concept commons representations for enriching knowledge graph representation task and knowledge graph completion task. Especially, the proposed model introduces two kinds of semantic representations for triple facts embedded in the given knowledge graph: (i) native triple representation, and (ii) conceptual triple representation. Meanwhile, we also constrain the conceptual representations by two kinds of the concept-based semantic similarities, by leveraging concept commons explicitly and implicitly. Our experiments on real-world datasets for several tasks, illustrate the superiority of the proposed model.

Acknowledgements. We thank anonymous reviewers for valuable comments. This work is funded by: (i) the National Natural Science Foundation of China (No. U19B2026, No. 62106243).

References

1. Bollacker, K., Evans, C., Paritosh, P., Sturge, T., Taylor, J.: Freebase: a collaboratively created graph database for structuring human knowledge. In: SIGMOD 2008, pp. 1247–1250 (2008)
2. Bordes, A., Usunier, N., Garcia-Duran, A., Weston, J., Yakhnenko, O.: Translating embeddings for modeling multi-relational data. In: NIPS 2013, pp. 2787–2795 (2013)
3. Guo, L., Wang, W., Sun, Z., Liu, C., Hu, W.: Decentralized knowledge graph representation learning. ArXiv abs/2010.08114 (2020)
4. Huang, H., Wang, Y., Feng, C., Liu, Z., Zhou, Q.: Leveraging conceptualization for short-text embedding. IEEE Trans. Knowl. Data Eng. **30**(7), 1282–1295 (2018)
5. Ji, G., He, S., Xu, L., Liu, K., Zhao, J.: Knowledge graph embedding via dynamic mapping matrix. In: ACL (2015)
6. Ji, S., Pan, S., Cambria, E., Marttinen, P., Yu, P.S.: A survey on knowledge graphs: representation, acquisition and applications. IEEE Trans. Neural Netw. Learn. Syst. **33**, 494–514 (2021)
7. Liang, Y., Xu, F., Zhang, S.-H., Lai, Y.-K., Mu, T.: Knowledge graph construction with structure and parameter learning for indoor scene design. Comput. Visual Media **4**(2), 123–137 (2018). https://doi.org/10.1007/s41095-018-0110-3
8. Lin, Y., Liu, Z., Sun, M., Liu, Y., Zhu, X.: Learning entity and relation embeddings for knowledge graph completion. In: AAAI 2015, pp. 2181–2187 (2015)
9. Ma, S., Ding, J., Jia, W., Wang, K., Guo, M.: Transt: type-based multiple embedding representations for knowledge graph completion. In: Joint European Conference on Machine Learning and Knowledge Discovery in Databases, pp. 717–733 (2017)
10. Marcinkevics, R., Vogt, J.E.: Interpretability and explainability: a machine learning zoo mini-tour. ArXiv abs/2012.01805 (2020)

11. Niu, G., Li, B., Zhang, Y., Pu, S., Li, J.: Autoeter: automated entity type representation for knowledge graph embedding. ArXiv abs/2009.12030 (2020)
12. Park, J.W., Hwang, S.W., Wang, H.: Fine-grained semantic conceptualization of framenet. In: AAAI, pp. 2638–2644 (2016)
13. Quan, W., Mao, Z., Wang, B., Li, G.: Knowledge graph embedding: a survey of approaches and applications. IEEE Trans. Knowl. Data Eng. **29**(12), 2724–2743 (2017)
14. Song, Y., Wang, H., Wang, Z., Li, H., Chen, W.: Short text conceptualization using a probabilistic knowledgebase. In: Proceedings of the Twenty-Second international joint conference on Artificial Intelligence, vol. Three, pp. 2330–2336 (2011)
15. Sun, Z., Deng, Z., Nie, J.Y., Tang, J.: Rotate: knowledge graph embedding by relational rotation in complex space. ArXiv abs/1902.10197 (2019)
16. Trouillon, T., Welbl, J., Riedel, S., Éric Gaussier, Bouchard, G.: Complex embeddings for simple link prediction. In: ICML (2016)
17. Wang, Q.S., Mao, Z., Wang, B., Guo, L.: Knowledge graph embedding: a survey of approaches and applications. IEEE Trans. Knowl. Data Eng. **29**, 2724–2743 (2017)
18. Wang, Y., Huang, H., Feng, C.: Query expansion based on a feedback concept model for microblog retrieval. In: International Conference on World Wide Web, pp. 559–568 (2017)
19. Wang, Y., Huang, H., Feng, C., Zhou, Q., Gu, J., Gao, X.: Cse: conceptual sentence embeddings based on attention model. In: 54th Annual Meeting of the Association for Computational Linguistics, pp. 505–515 (2016)
20. Wang, Y., Liu, Y., Zhang, H., Xie, H.: Leveraging lexical semantic information for learning concept-based multiple embedding representations for knowledge graph completion. In: APWeb/WAIM (2019)
21. Wang, Y., Zhang, H., Li, Y., Xie, H.: Simplified representation learning model based on parameter-sharing for knowledge graph completion. In: CCIR (2019)
22. Wang, Z., Zhang, J., Feng, J., Chen, Z.: Knowledge graph embedding by translating on hyperplanes. In: AAAI 2014, pp. 1112–1119 (2014)
23. Wang, Z., Zhao, K., Wang, H., Meng, X., Wen, J.R.: Query understanding through knowledge-based conceptualization. In: International Conference on Artificial Intelligence, pp. 3264–3270 (2015)
24. Wu, W., Li, H., Wang, H., Zhu, K.Q.: Probase: a probabilistic taxonomy for text understanding. In: SIGMOD Conference (2012)
25. Xiao, H., Huang, M., Meng, L., Zhu, X.: SSP: semantic space projection for knowledge graph embedding with text descriptions. In: AAAI (2017)
26. Xiao, H., Huang, M., Zhu, X.: Transg: a generative model for knowledge graph embedding. In: Meeting of the Association for Computational Linguistics, pp. 2316–2325 (2016)
27. Xie, R., Liu, Z., Jia, J.J., Luan, H., Sun, M.: Representation learning of knowledge graphs with entity descriptions. In: AAAI (2016)
28. Xie, R., Liu, Z., Sun, M.: Representation learning of knowledge graphs with hierarchical types. In: International Joint Conference on Artificial Intelligence, pp. 2965–2971 (2016)
29. Yi, T., Luu, A.T., Hui, S.C.: Non-parametric estimation of multiple embeddings for link prediction on dynamic knowledge graphs. In: Thirty First Conference on Artificial Intelligence (2017)

Relation Prediction Based on Source-Entity Behavior Preference Modeling via Heterogeneous Graph Pooling

Yashen Wang[1,2(✉)], Xiaoling Zhu[1], and Huanhuan Zhang[1]

[1] National Engineering Laboratory for Risk Perception and Prevention (RPP),
China Academy of Electronics and Information Technology of CETC, Beijing 100041, China
yswang@bit.edu.cn, zhuxiaoling1@cetc.com.cn
[2] Information Science Academy of CETC, Beijing 100041, China

Abstract. Recent years have witnessed great advance of representation learning (RL) based models for the knowledge graph relation prediction task. Most existing approaches represent graph nodes as vectors in a low-dimensional embedding space, ignoring the entity behavior preference and the beneficial semantic interactions in the real-world graphs. To address this challenge, this paper proposes a novel relation prediction model based on source-entity behavior preference modeling, which represents each source-entity as a heterogeneous graph released from their structure and semantic perspectives to better capture the behavior relatedness. Especially, a heterogeneous graph pooling method is leveraged for learning source-entity behavior embedding representation from this personalized heterogeneous graph. In our comprehensive experiments, we evaluate our model on real-world graphs, and the results demonstrate that the proposed model significantly outperforms existing state-of-the-art methods on benchmark datasets for the relation prediction and knowledge graph completion task.

Keywords: Knowledge graph representation · Knowledge graph completion · Relation prediction · Representation learning · Graph pooling

1 Introduction

Knowledge Graph (KG) is viewed as a visualization application to reveal the multiple relationships between the structure of scientific knowledge [8,36], wherein, the facts exist as triple (e_s, r, e_t), with e_s and e_t representing source-entity and target-entity, and r indicating a relation between entities. For example, in triple (David_Beckham, place_of_birth, London), there exists relation "place_of_birth" between source-entity "David_Beckham" and target-entity "London", which means that David Beckham was born in London.

Nowadays, many large-scale KGs, such as YAGO, Freebase, DBpedia and Probase etc., provide efficient knowledge basis for wide variety of tools, such as semantic search, recommender system, question answering, dialogue generation [8,23]. However, existing knowledge graphs still exist a huge amounts of missing triples and are far away from

G. Memmi et al. (Eds.): KSEM 2022, LNAI 13368, pp. 425–436, 2022.
https://doi.org/10.1007/978-3-031-10983-6_33

being *complete*. Therefore, the Knowledge Graph Completion (KGC) task, e.g., relation prediction, emerges as the times require. Relation prediction task could be defined as follows: given a KG, automatically predicting the *missing* link-formed relation between entities based on the current and known knowledge, and evaluating the credibility of triples *not* exist in the current KG [24]. Formally, we define the relation prediction task as follows: the relation prediction task takes a partial triple $(e_s, r, ?)$ as input (i.e., source-target e_s and relation r are known), and produces a ranked list of candidate target-entities $\hat{e}_t$ as output. It is a big challenging task because not only need to predict whether the relationship exists between two entities, but also need to predict which kind of relationship it is [8]. Knowledge Graph Embedding (KGE) methods [2, 19, 23], e.g., TransE [4] and a series of derivative models of its, such as TransH [27], TransR [12], TransD [9], TransG [32], RESCAL [15], SE [5], DKRL [33], etc., which transform high-dimensional and complex graph contents into low-dimensional vectors (or matrices, tensors) representations, to efficiently calculate the semantic relations among entities and relations via vectors, which is regarded as a common approach to accomplish relation prediction.

As a crucial step for representing entities in embedding based model, we must model source-entity's behavior preference from the perspectives of not only *structure* (e.g., who interact with it, etc.,) but also *semantics* (e.g., which semantic category it belongs to, etc.,). Precise source-entity behavior preference modeling is very important for accurate relation prediction. Existing methods for source-entity behavior preference modeling mainly model source-entity' topological structure information via neural network or attentive models. In fact, source-entity behavior modeling may have multiple kinds of relatedness: The entities belonging to the same *concept* have some relations in attracting new links, similar to the observation in [29], because concepts of entities are important indications of entity's semantic category, and precious research has demonstrated that entities in the head (or tail) position of a triple usually belong to the same or similar semantic category [22]. In other words, the similar semantic category indicates the similar entity behavior. For example, given (David_Beckham, place_of_birth, London), (Brack_Obama, place_of_birth, Honolulu) and (Taylor_Swift, place_of_birth, ?), in the first two triples, target-entities ("London" and "Honolulu") belong to concept "Location", "Place", "Area", etc., hence the candidate target-entity prefers to be derived from the similar concepts, for the same relation "place_of_birth". These can release some covert however useful vestiges for modeling the linking behaviors for more effective source-entity behavior modeling. However, in existing relation prediction methods that mainly represent source-entity only with their neighbor entities, the rich relatedness among user behaviors is unfortunately *ignored*.

To overcome this challenge, this paper proposes a novel relation prediction model based on source-entity behavior preference modeling, which represents each source-entity as a personalized heterogeneous graph revealed from their both structure perspective and semantic perspective (concept semantics emphasized here). The heterogeneous graph *nodes* contains the entities in source-category (i.e., entities in the same concept category with the given source-entity), the entities in target-category and the corresponding concepts. The *edges* are created between a existing relations among entities in source-category and target-category, and their concepts (derived from lexical knowledge graph Probase by instance conceptualization algorithm [7,23]), as well as co-occurrence relatedness among these concepts (derived from Probase directly). For efficiently learning entity behavior embeddings from the personalized heterogeneous graph, we leverage a heterogeneous graph pooling method recently investigated and demonstrated by [29] in news recommendation task, to iteratively condense the heterogeneous graph. Especially, for taking full use of interactions among different kinds of nodes, we introduce three kinds of pooling graph neural networks for different kinds of nodes (entity in source-category, entity in target-category and concept, respectively) to summarize type-specific graph information from the entire heterogeneous graph, and aggregates the same kinds of nodes based on their personalized features and the entire graph structure. Experiments show that the proposed model could not only effectively enhance the performance of entity behavior modeling, but also clearly distinguish the semantics, and perform well in knowledge graph embedding task.

2 Methodology

We describe our model for source-entity behavior modeling in relation prediction. In the proposed model, each source-entity is represented as a *heterogeneous graph*, which is built from their behaviors (i.e., the interactions with other entities in current KG and their corresponding concepts distilled from Prboase), shown as Fig. 1. To learn source-entity behavior embedding for relation prediction task from the aforementioned heterogeneous graph, we try to adapt a heterogeneous graph pooling method which is proved to be effective in domain of recommendation [29], for iteratively condensing this heterogeneous graph. Figure 2 overviews the overall architecture of the proposed method.

2.1 Heterogeneous Graph Construction

Firstly, we introduce the heterogeneous graph in our model for source-entity behavior modeling. An example of heterogeneous graph respect to source-entity "Taylor_Swift", is shown in Fig. 1, and in the given incomplete triple (Taylor_Swift, place_of_birth,?), the target-entity is our goal in relation prediction task. It contains three kinds of nodes, including: (i) entities in source-category (blue circles), (ii) entities in target-category (green circles), and (iii) concepts (orange circles). Especially:

(i) Entities in source-category: indicates entities which belong to the same concept category with the given source-entity and meanwhile once appear in the source-entity position of given relation. E.g., entities "David_Beckham" and "Brack_Obama" share the same concept "Preson" with source-entity "Taylor_Swift".

(ii) Entities in target-category: indicates entities which belong to the concept categories which appear in the target-entity position of given relation (in other words, it should once appear in the source-entity position of given relation), or is the target-entity of entity in source-category with the given relation. E.g., entities "London" and "Honolulu" belong to the concepts "Location", "Place", "Area" etc., which appear in the target-entity position of given relation "place_of_birth".

(iii) Concepts: indicate the concepts of aforementioned entities, which are derived from Probase by instance conceptualization algorithm. E.g., apart from the shared concepts "Person", entity "David_Beckham" belongs to concept "Athlete", and entity "Brack_Obama" belongs to concept "Politician".

Hence, given a source-entity e_s, we denote two kinds of entity set, interacted with e_s: (i) The set of entities belongs to source-category, $\mathcal{E}_s = \{e_i | i \in [1, \cdots, m_s]\}$; and (ii) The set of entities belongs to target-category, $\mathcal{E}_t = \{e_j | j \in [1, \cdots, m_t]\}$.

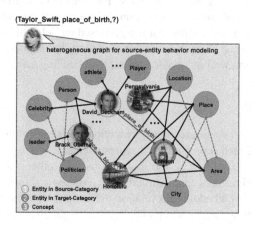

Fig. 1. An example of heterogeneous graph for source-entity behavior modeling.

In addition, entity's probabilistic *concepts* are very useful vestiges for modeling entity's semantic and behavior preference. The entities with the *same* concept may also have some relations in source-entity behavior modeling [22]. Because entities in the head (or tail) position of a triple usually belong to the same or similar semantic category. In other words, the similar semantic category indicates the similar entity behavior. Thus, we incorporate concept information [26,31], by leveraging instance acceptable conceptualization algorithm [21,23], into the heterogeneous graph by regarding each concept c_k as a node. Especially, Following [23], let C_Δ represent the complete set of concepts, and it is clear that the aforementioned $c_k \in C_\Delta$ indicate the concept defined in the lexical knowledge graph Probase [16,30].

Then, we connect each entity node e ($e \in \mathcal{E}_s$ or $e \in \mathcal{E}_t$) with its associated concept nodes (shown as black lines in Fig. 1), and connect entities with their corresponding interactions in the given knowledge graph (shown as purple lines). Co-occurrence relations among concepts are shown in orange dotted lines in Fig. 1. With efforts above, we finalize the heterogeneous graph $\mathcal{G}^0$.

2.2   Representation Initializations

We introduce how to learn initial node representations (respect to the node feature **E**), edge representations (respect to the edge feature **R**) and relatedness representations (respect to the relatedness matrix $\mathbf{A}$), in the heterogeneous graph mentioned above. For a heterogeneous graph with T types of nodes[1], we respectively denote its initial *node features*, *edge features* and *relatedness matrix* as $\mathbf{E}^0$, $\mathbf{R}^0$ and $\mathbf{A}^0$.

Node Representation Initialization: For nodes about entities in source-category ($e \in \mathcal{E}_s$) and entities in target-category ($e \in \mathcal{E}_t$), TransE [4] is used on the given knowledge graph, on which we would like to predict the missing relations, for learning entity embedding. For concept nodes, TransE is also leveraged on lexical knowledge graph Probase [31]. Note that, aforementioned entity node embeddings and concept node embeddings are all fine-tuned during model training.

Edge and Relatedness Representation Initialization: TrasnE is utilized for initialing the relations among entities and concepts for initializing edge representations. Probase naturally provides (i) occurrence frequencies among entities (or concepts), for the weights of edges between entities (or concepts) in our heterogeneous graph; (ii) IsA probabilities between entity and concept, for the weights of edges between concept and entity in our heterogeneous graph. For initial adjacent value between two entities (as well as between entities and concepts), we assign the frequency of them co-occurring in the same triples in the given knowledge graph.

2.3 Heterogeneous Graph Pooling

With efforts above, each source-entity e_s is represented as a specific heterogeneous graph $\mathcal{G}^0$, next question we faced with is: How to learn a source-entity behavior preference embedding θ_{e_s} from it for relation prediction task. To solve this problem, we investigate to adapt a recently proposed heterogeneous graph pooling method [29] into our relation prediction task.

In heterogeneous graphs studied in this work, different types of nodes obtain different types of features and topology, and describe the given source-entity e_s from different perspectives. Hence, we introduce and adapt a novel heterogeneous graph pooling method [29] for relation prediction task, which has been demonstrated able to consider the various characteristics of different types of nodes in news recommendation task. We applies conventional GAT [18] layers [20,35] to process the heterogeneous graph based on the input $\mathbf{E}^0$, $\mathbf{R}^0$, and $\mathbf{A}^0$. We denote the number of i-th type nodes in l-th layer, as m_i^l. Hence, $m^l = \sum_{i=1}^{T} m_i^l$ is defined as the sum of the number m_i^l of i-th kind of node, wherein $i \in [1, \cdots, T]$. The outputs from the l-th GNN layer, is denoted as: $\mathbf{E}^l \in \mathbb{R}^{m^l \times d}$, $\mathbf{R}^l \in \mathbb{R}^{m^l \times d}$ and $\mathbf{A}^l \in \mathbb{R}^{m^l \times m^l}$, respectively.

Specifically, for distinguishing the different characteristics and manners of different types of nodes in our specific heterogeneous graph, the graph relatedness matrix $\mathbf{A}^l$ is divided into $T \times T$ sub-matrices, according to node types. We denote the relatedness sub-matrix in the i-th row and the j-th column as $\mathbf{A}^l_{i,j \in \{1,\cdots,T\}} \in \mathbb{R}^{m_i^l \times m_j^l}$; Similarly, we also divide the entity feature $\mathbf{E}^l$ into T sub-matrices, according to node types: we

---

[1] $T = 3$ for $\mathcal{G}^0$ in our scene as shown in different colors in Fig. 1. However, due to the scalability of the proposed architecture, when more node types are introduced into the heterogeneous graph, our architecture is still at work.

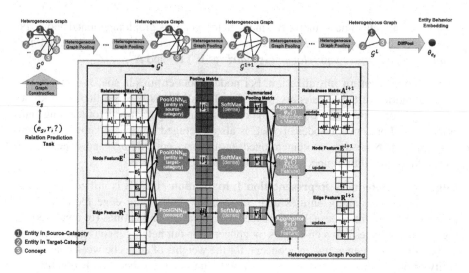

Fig. 2. The illustration of the proposed relation prediction model based on source-entity behavior preference modeling.

denote the i-th entity feature sub-matrix as $\mathbf{E}^l_{i\in\{1,\cdots,T\}} \in \mathbb{R}^{m^l_i \times d}$; Meanwhile, edge feature $\mathbf{R}^l$ is divided in the same way.

Motivated by [34], we apply T kinds of pooling graph neural networks, according T types of nodes, to *independently* learn a pooling matrix $\mathbf{U}^l_i \in \mathbb{R}^{m^l \times m^{l+1}_i}$ for each node type. Especially, for i-th kind of node, its pooling matrix can be formed as follows:

$$\mathbf{U}^l_{i\in[1,\cdots,T]} = \texttt{PoolGNN}_{\Theta^l_i}(\mathbf{E}^l_i, \mathbf{R}^l_i, \mathbf{A}^l_{i,\cdot}, \mathbf{A}^l_{\cdot,i}) \tag{1}$$

Then, we condense the pooling matrix $\mathbf{U}^l_i$ into a summarized pooling matrix, denoted $\mathbf{V}^l_i \in \mathbb{R}^{m^l_i \times m^{l+1}_i}$ as follows:

$$\mathbf{V}^l_{i\in[1,\cdots,T]} = \texttt{SoftMax}_i(\mathbf{W}^l_i\mathbf{U}^l_i + \mathbf{b}^l_i) \tag{2}$$

Wherein, $\mathbf{W}^l_i$ and $\mathbf{b}^l_i$ are the trainable parameter sets. With efforts above, for updating the representations mentioned above, we leverage threes kinds of aggregator (i.e., a node feature aggregator $\phi_E(\cdot)$, a edge feature aggregator $\phi_R(\cdot)$ and a relatedness matrix aggregator $\phi_A(\cdot)$) to compute the new node feature $\mathbf{E}^{l+1}$, edge feature $\mathbf{R}^{l+1}$ and relatedness matrix $\mathbf{A}^{l+1}$ in the next layer, details is described as follows:

(i) $\phi_A(\cdot)$: **Update of relatedness matrix A. Input.** the previous relatedness matrix $\mathbf{A}^l$ and the T summarized pooling matrices $\{\mathbf{V}^l_1, \cdots, \mathbf{V}^l_T\}$; **Output.** the new adjacent sub-matrix (of the $(l+1)$-th layer) in the i-th row and the j-th column as $\mathbf{A}^{l+1}_{i,j} \in \mathbb{R}^{m^{l+1}_i \times m^{l+1}_j}$, which is defined as follows:

$$\mathbf{A}^{l+1}_{i,j\in[1,\cdots,T]} = \mathbf{V}^{l\top}_i \mathbf{A}^l \mathbf{V}^l_j \tag{3}$$

(ii) $\phi_E(\cdot)$ **and** $\phi_R(\cdot)$: **Update of node and edge representations: Input**. the node feature $\mathbf{E}^l$ as well as $\mathbf{R}^l$, and the T summarized pooling matrices $\{\mathbf{V}_1^l, \cdots, \mathbf{V}_T^l\}$; **Output**. the new feature sub-matrix (of the $(l+1)$-th layer) of the i-th kind of nodes as $\mathbf{E}_i^{l+1}$ and $\mathbf{R}_i^{l+1}$, which is defined as:

$$\mathbf{E}_{i\in[1,\cdots,T]}^{l+1} = \mathbf{V}_i^{l\top}\mathbf{E}^l \tag{4}$$

$$\mathbf{R}_{i\in[1,\cdots,T]}^{l+1} = \mathbf{V}_i^{l\top}\mathbf{R}^l \tag{5}$$

Intuitively, we apply our heterogeneous graph pooling method to each GAT layer, and use multiple stacks of them, as shown in Fig. 2 (from left side to right side). After applying heterogeneous graph pooling iteratively for L rounds, the original heterogeneous graph $(\mathcal{G}^0)$ will be condensed into a small densely connected graph with T nodes (shown as $\mathcal{G}^L$ in Fig. 2), then we apply a DiffPool [34] layer to convert this graph $\mathcal{G}^L$ into a single node that summarizes the information of the entire graph. Accordingly, the embedding of this node, is output as the source-entity behavior embedding θ_{e_s} for relation prediction task.

2.4 Optimization

Given relation r and source-entity e_s, we predict the linked target entity $\hat{e}_t$ for model training, based on their relevance to the source-entity behavior preference embedding θ_{e_s} learned by our model (Sect. 2.3). The behavior preference score y^+ of the candidate target-entity $\hat{e}_t$ respect to given source-entity e_s under relation r, could be intuitively computed by the inner product between their embeddings, i.e., $y^+ = \mathtt{sigmoid}(\theta_{e_s}^\top \theta_{\hat{e}_t})$. Wherein, $\theta_{\hat{e}_t}$ is computed for the candidate target-entity $\hat{e}_t$, in the same way as θ_{e_s}. We denote Δ as the positive training set. Given relation r and source-entity e_s, for each target-entity $e_{t,?}$ (i.e., positive instance distilled from Δ), we *randomly* select several non-linked entities that are displayed in the same impression, as negative samples, to build training samples, denoted as Δ^-. The loss function for our relation prediction method is formed as follows:

$$\mathcal{L} = \sum_{i=1}^{|\Delta|}\sum_{j=1}^{|\Delta_i^-|}\max\{0, \gamma - y_i^+ + y_j^-\} \tag{6}$$

3 Experiment

3.1 Datasets and Baselines

To evaluate the proposed relation prediction model, we conduct experiments on the dataset WN18 (WordNet) and dataset FB15k (Freebase) introduced by [4,22,27], and use the same training\validation\test split settings as in previous work.

The baselines include **TransE** [4], **TransH** [27], **TransR** [12], **TransD** [9], **TransG** [32], **ComplEx** [17], **HolE** [14], **PTransE** [11], **SME** [3], **TransH** [27], **RESCAL**

[15], **SE** [5], **DKRL** [33], **TransT** [13], which are regarded as state-of-the-art baseline models recently proposed and verified. These models mentioned above usually learn continuous, low-dimensional vector representations (i.e., embeddings) for entities and relations by minimizing a margin-based pairwise ranking loss [11]. For evaluation, two widely-used measurements are considered as evaluation metrics in our experiments: (i) Mean Rank (MR), which indicates the mean rank of original triples in the corresponding probability ranks; and (ii) HITS@N, which indicates the proportion of original triples whose rank is not larger than N ($N = 10$ is utilized here). Note that, lower mean rank or higher HITS@10 means better performance.

3.2 Experimental Settings

The optimal-parameter configurations are described as follows: For dataset WN18, (i) the learning rate is 2e−5 (among 6e−5, 5e−5, 4e−5, 3e−5, and 2e−5), (ii) the vector dimension k is 300 (among 100, 150, 200, 300, 400 and 500), (iii) the size of set of entities belongs to source-category $\mathcal{E}_s$, m_s is 40 (among 20, 40, 60, 80, and 100), (iv) the size of set of entities belongs to target-category $\mathcal{E}_t$, m_t is 40 (among 20, 40, 60, 80, and 100). For dataset FB18K, (i) the learning rate is 3e−5 (among 6e−5, 5e−5, 4e−5, 3e−5, and 2e−5), (ii) the vector dimension k is 200 (among 100, 150, 200, 300, 400 and 500), (iii) the size of set of entities belongs to source-category $\mathcal{E}_s$, m_s is 60 (among 20, 40, 60, 80, and 100), (iv) the size of set of entities belongs to target-category $\mathcal{E}_t$, m_t is 40 (among 20, 40, 60, 80, and 100). We train the model until convergence. For the proposed model, we use basic GAT [18] to implement the graph neural networks, and ADAM [10] as the optimizer, similar to [29]. The hyperparameters 1are tuned on the validation set. Each experiment is repeated 5 times. All models are optimized simultaneously using Stochastic Gradient Descent (SGD) [6]. As the datasets are the same, we directly reuse the experimental settings of several baselines from the previous literature [1,22,25].

3.3 Experimental Results and Analysis

We adopt the same protocol used in previous studies [23]. The dataset WN18 and dataset FB15k are the benchmark datasets for this task following [22]. Table 1 reports the overall relation prediction results, as well as the average value of results on all the experimental datasets (as notated as "AVG."). The superscript † and ‡ respectively denote statistically significant improvements over **HolE** and **TransG**($p < 0.05$). The experimental and contrastive results, we observe that, in many instances, our heterogeneous graph pooling based relation prediction model (denoted as **Ours**) outperforms previous knowledge graph embedding (KGE) based models for relation prediction task. Especially: (i) **Ours** achieves the best results on metric HIT@10, and could also generate competitive results on metric MR; (ii) On dataset FB15K, compared with **TransG** [32], **ComplEx** [17], and **HolE** [14], the proposed **Ours** improves the HIT@10 by 2.95%, 8.13% and 21.75%, respectively; (iii) On dataset FB15K, compared with **TransG** [32] and **ComplEx** [17], the our **Ours** improves the HIT@10 by 33.25% and 3.56%, respectively. This result verifies that the proposed heterogeneous graph pooling mechanism and enhance with extra concept semantic (from lexical knowledge graph, e.g., Probase) are beneficial for relation prediction for knowledge graph completion

Table 1. Evaluation results of relation prediction task.

Models	WN18		FB15K		AVG.	
	MR	HIT@10	MR	HIT@10	MR	HIT@10
TransE [4]	243	86.5	121	45.7	182.4	66.1
TransH [27]	294	84.1	84	62.5	189.2	73.3
TransR [12]	212	88.9	76	63.5	144.0	76.2
TransD [9]	206	89.4	88	75.0	147.0	82.2
TransG [32]	335	$91.9^{\dagger}$	$49^{\dagger}$	$85.6^{\dagger}$	191.6	$88.7^{\dagger}$
ComplEx [17]	212	91.9	76	81.5	144.0	86.7
HolE [14]	**205**	89.7	65	71.7	**134.8**	80.7
PTransE [11]	220	82.8	52	81.1	136.3	82.0
SME [3]	517	71.9	149	39.6	333.2	55.7
RESCAL [15]	562	87.7	663	42.8	612.1	65.2
SE [5]	566	76.7	157	38.6	361.8	57.7
DKRL [33]	217	86.4	110	55.9	163.4	71.1
TransT [13]	235	90.2	82	75.4	158.5	82.8
Ours	$210^{\ddagger}$	$\mathbf{92.6}^{\dagger\ddagger}$	69	$\mathbf{88.1}^{\dagger\ddagger}$	$139.5^{\ddagger}$	$\mathbf{90.4}^{\dagger\ddagger}$

task. Note that, our approach outperforms the baseline methods on dataset FB15K, which is more sparse and complex, and hence this phenomenon demonstrates the efficiency and robustness of our heterogeneous graph pooling based relation prediction mechanism. This is because the we model entity behavior preference, from perspectives of not only structure but also semantics. Moreover, our approach models source-entity behavior embeddings via heterogeneous graph pooling and a hierarchical strategy (details in Sect. 2.3), which contributes greatly to capturing the high-order information on the specific heterogeneous graph (details in Sect. 2.1). The newest contributions in KGE-based work focus primarily on the changes in how the multiple/separate embedding hyper-planes are constructed. The proposed single hyper-plane **Ours** significantly outperforms these multiple/separate hyper-plane models: on average, the relative HIT@10 improvements over **TransH** [27] and **TransR** are 22.47% and 18.03%, respectively; and the relative MR improvements over **TransH** [27] and **TransR** are 25.56% and 4.95%, respectively.

Table 2. Evaluation on ablation study.

Models	WN18		FB15K	
	MR	HIT@10	MR	HIT@10
Ours	210	92.6	69	88.1
w/o source	227	90.7	75	86.3
w/o target	223	88.9	73	84.6
w/o concept	221	88.0	72	83.7

Ablation study respect to different kinds of nodes in the graph, i.e., entities in source-category, entities in target-category, and concepts, as shown in Table 2. Besides, as discussed in previous work such as [23,28], there exist different choices to construct the concept set C (details described in Sect. 2.1). To compare the effects of the different options for concept set C, following the feasible experimental settings in [23], we list the performances of our heterogeneous graph pooling based relation prediction model with option 2 (i.e., **Ours**) and with option 1 (denoted as **Ours+**), in Table 3.

Table 3. Different experimental effects respect to different options for concept set C.

Models	WN18		FB15K	
	MR	HIT@10	MR	HIT@10
TransG [32]	335	$91.9^{\dagger}$	$49^{\dagger}$	$85.6^{\dagger}$
HolE [14]	**205**	89.7	65	71.7
Ours	$210^{\ddagger}$	$\mathbf{92.6}^{\dagger\ddagger+}$	69^{+}	$88.1^{\dagger\ddagger}$
Ours+	**208**	91.5	74	**89.2**

4   Conclusion

This paper proposes a novel relation prediction method based on source-entity behavior modeling for knowledge graph completion task. By representing each source-entity as a heterogeneous graph built from their interactions among other entities and their corresponding concepts, it can capture the rich and beneficial relatedness between entity behaviors to enhance source-entity behavior modeling. We also introduce a heterogeneous graph pooling method to learn source-entity behavior embedding representation from the heterogeneous graph. Extensive experiments show that our proposed model could significantly outperforms several existing state-of-the-art methods on experimental datasets for the relation prediction task.

Acknowledgements. We thank anonymous reviewers for valuable comments. This work is funded by: (i) the National Natural Science Foundation of China (No. 62106243, U19B2026).

References

1. An, B., Chen, B., Han, X., Sun, L.: Accurate text-enhanced knowledge graph representation learning. In: NAACL-HLT (2018)
2. Arora, S.: A survey on graph neural networks for knowledge graph completion. arXiv: abs/2007.12374 (2020)
3. Bordes, A., Glorot, X., Weston, J., Bengio, Y.: Joint learning of words and meaning representations for open-text semantic parsing. In: AISTATS (2012)
4. Bordes, A., Usunier, N., Garcia-Duran, A., Weston, J., Yakhnenko, O.: Translating embeddings for modeling multi-relational data. In: NIPS 2013, pp. 2787–2795 (2013)

5. Bordes, A., Weston, J., Collobert, R., Bengio, Y.: Learning structured embeddings of knowledge bases. In: AAAI 2011, pp. 301–306 (2011)
6. Bottou, L.: Large-scale machine learning with stochastic gradient descent. In: COMPSTAT (2010)
7. Huang, H., Wang, Y., Feng, C., Liu, Z., Zhou, Q.: Leveraging conceptualization for short-text embedding. IEEE Trans. Knowl. Data Eng. **30**(7), 1282–1295 (2018)
8. Huxue, R., Huang, J., Wang, J., Li, Y.: Learning gaussian hierarchy embedding for relation prediction in knowledge graph. J. Phys. Conf. Ser. **1748**, 032039 (2021)
9. Ji, G., He, S., Xu, L., Liu, K., Zhao, J.: Knowledge graph embedding via dynamic mapping matrix. In: ACL (2015)
10. Kingma, D.P., Ba, J.: Adam: a method for stochastic optimization. CoRR abs/1412.6980 (2015)
11. Lin, Y., Liu, Z., Luan, H.B., Sun, M., Rao, S., Liu, S.: Modeling relation paths for representation learning of knowledge bases. In: EMNLP (2015)
12. Lin, Y., Liu, Z., Sun, M., Liu, Y., Zhu, X.: Learning entity and relation embeddings for knowledge graph completion. In: AAAI 2015, pp. 2181–2187 (2015)
13. Ma, S., Ding, J., Jia, W., Wang, K., Guo, M.: TransT: type-based multiple embedding representations for knowledge graph completion. In: Joint European Conference on Machine Learning and Knowledge Discovery in Databases, pp. 717–733 (2017)
14. Nickel, M., Rosasco, L., Poggio, T.: Holographic embeddings of knowledge graphs. In: Thirtieth AAAI Conference on Artificial Intelligence, pp. 1955–1961 (2016)
15. Nickel, M., Tresp, V., Kriegel, H.P.: A three-way model for collective learning on multi-relational data. In: International Conference on International Conference on Machine Learning, pp. 809–816 (2011)
16. Song, Y., Wang, S., Wang, H.: Open domain short text conceptualization: a generative + descriptive modeling approach. In: International Conference on Artificial Intelligence, pp. 3820–3826 (2015)
17. Trouillon, T., Welbl, J., Riedel, S., Éric Gaussier, Bouchard, G.: Complex embeddings for simple link prediction (2016)
18. Velickovic, P., Cucurull, G., Casanova, A., Romero, A., Lio', P., Bengio, Y.: Graph attention networks. arXiv:abs/1710.10903 (2018)
19. Wang, Q., Mao, Z., Wang, B., Guo, L.: Knowledge graph embedding: a survey of approaches and applications. IEEE Trans. Knowl. Data Eng. **29**, 2724–2743 (2017)
20. Wang, X., He, X., Cao, Y., Liu, M., Chua, T.S.: KGAT: knowledge graph attention network for recommendation. In: Proceedings of the 25th ACM SIGKDD International Conference on Knowledge Discovery & Data Mining (2019)
21. Wang, Y., yan Huang, H., Feng, C.: Query expansion with local conceptual word embeddings in microblog retrieval. IEEE Trans. Knowl. Data Eng. **33**, 1737–1749 (2021)
22. Wang, Y., Liu, Y., Zhang, H., Xie, H.: Leveraging lexical semantic information for learning concept-based multiple embedding representations for knowledge graph completion. In: APWeb/WAIM (2019)
23. Wang, Y., Zhang, H.: HARP: a novel hierarchical attention model for relation prediction. ACM Trans. Knowl. Discov. Data **15**, 17:1–17:22 (2021)
24. Wang, Y., Zhang, H.: Introducing graph neural networks for few-shot relation prediction in knowledge graph completion task. In: KSEM (2021)
25. Wang, Y., Zhang, H., Li, Y., Xie, H.: Simplified representation learning model based on parameter-sharing for knowledge graph completion. In: CCIR (2019)
26. Wang, Y., Zhang, H., Liu, Z., Zhou, Q.: Hierarchical concept-driven language model. ACM Trans. Knowl. Disc. Data (TKDD) **15**, 1–22 (2021)
27. Wang, Z., Zhang, J., Feng, J., Chen, Z.: Knowledge graph embedding by translating on hyperplanes. In: AAAI 2014, pp. 1112–1119 (2014)

28. Wang, Z., Zhao, K., Wang, H., Meng, X., Wen, J.R.: Query understanding through knowledge-based conceptualization. In: International Conference on Artificial Intelligence, pp. 3264–3270 (2015)
29. Wu, C., Wu, F., Huang, Y., Xie, X.: User-as-graph: User modeling with heterogeneous graph pooling for news recommendation. In: IJCAI (2021)
30. Wu, W., Li, H., Wang, H., Zhu, K.Q.: Probase: a probabilistic taxonomy for text understanding. In: Proceedings of the 2012 ACM SIGMOD International Conference on Management of Data, pp. 481–492 (2012)
31. Wu, W., Li, H., Wang, H., Zhu, K.Q.: Probase: a probabilistic taxonomy for text understanding. In: ACM SIGMOD International Conference on Management of Data, pp. 481–492 (2012)
32. Xiao, H., Huang, M., Zhu, X.: TransG : a generative model for knowledge graph embedding. In: Meeting of the Association for Computational Linguistics, pp. 2316–2325 (2016)
33. Xie, R., Liu, Z., Jia, J.J., Luan, H., Sun, M.: Representation learning of knowledge graphs with entity descriptions. In: AAAI (2016)
34. Ying, R., You, J., Morris, C., Ren, X., Hamilton, W.L., Leskovec, J.: Hierarchical graph representation learning with differentiable pooling. arXiv:abs/1806.08804 (2018)
35. Zhao, L., et al.: T-GCN: a temporal graph convolutional network for traffic prediction. IEEE Trans. Intell. Transp. Syst. **21**, 3848–3858 (2020)
36. Zhao, Y., et al.: Time-aware path reasoning on knowledge graph for recommendation. ACM Trans. Inf. Syst. (TOIS) (2022). https://doi.org/10.1145/3531267

KEAN: Knowledge-Enhanced and Attention Network for News Recommendation

Yuting Wang[1] [ID], Qian Gao[1]([⊠]) [ID], and Jun Fan[2]

[1] Qilu University of Technology (Shandong Academy of Sciences), Shandong, China
10431200638@stu.qlu.edu.cn, gq@qlu.edu.cn
[2] Business-Intelligence of Oriental Nations Corporation Ltd., Beijing, China
fanjun1@bonc.com.cn

Abstract. An important goal of online news system is to provide accurate personalized recommendation for users from mass news. One of the main problems in news recommendation is to obtain accurate news representation. Generally speaking, news is full of intellectual entities and common sense. However, existing news recommendation tends to ignore external knowledge and fail to fully detect potential knowledge links between news. In addition, news recommendation also faces the problem of user interest diversity. To solve the above problems, this paper proposes a knowledge enhancement and attention network based bnews recommendation model (KEAN) to enhance news title representation and user interest. The proposed model is mainly processed from two perspectives. First, for news titles, the entity embedding is enriched by aggregating information from its neighborhood in the knowledge graph, so as to obtain richer contextual embedding. Secondly, in order to meet the different interests in users, attention network is used to dynamically aggregate the information which is related to the current candidate news in user history. KEAN model can get rich feature representation by dealing with the correlation between entities and users' interests. The experimental results show that the proposed model performs better than the other compared models with F1 and AUC being increased by 0.8%–1.2%, 0.6%–1.8% in Bing News and MIND dataset.

Keywords: Recommendation system · Knowledge graph · Graph neural network · Attention network · News recommendation

1 Introduction

With the rapid development of the Internet, users prefer to read real-time news increasingly, such as news about COVID-19 and Winter Olympics. In the case of news, the title usually contains multiple entities which play an important role [1]. These entities are not independent, which can be linked to other entities through relationships. And they are organized in a graphical form. Therefore, knowledge graph (KG) is usually used to represent semantic association [2] between item entities in news recommendation scenarios. By exploring KG, the recommendation model can not only capture the underlying relationships between entities, but also take advantage of the semantic

© The Author(s), under exclusive license to Springer Nature Switzerland AG 2022
G. Memmi et al. (Eds.): KSEM 2022, LNAI 13368, pp. 437–449, 2022.
https://doi.org/10.1007/978-3-031-10983-6_34

relationships between entities to explain the underlying interests of users. For example, user clicks on a title as "The real time big data report of Novel Coronavirus Pneumonia in China" of the news (see Fig. 1), which contains two knowledge entities: "China" and "Novel Coronavirus Pneumonia". In fact, users may also be interested in stories with "COVID-19" in the title, or even in the causes and symptoms of "Novel Coronavirus pneumonia". So it is necessary to use KG to find some potential relationships.

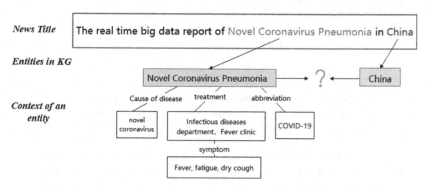

Fig. 1. News titles with multiple entities and contextual information in KG

Liu et al. [3] used external information of knowledge graph to model news titles in news recommendation. Wang et al. [4] proposed an end-to-end recommendation model (KGNN-LS). The trainable function is used to highlight the valuable relationship in KG. If KG is only used as auxiliary information in the process of news recommendation, it is difficult to find potential knowledge connections in news. In order to better understand the content of news, it is necessary to consider the relationship paths between multiple entities to achieve effective news modeling. Wang et al. [5] proposed deep knowledge-aware network (DKN), a deep recommendation model integrating knowledge graph information [5]. Although this method considers information at different levels, it still fails to take into account the complexity of entity representation.

In addition to knowledge graph, knowledge graph representation has also been widely studied in recent years. The purpose of knowledge graph representation is to learn a low-dimensional vector for each entity and relationship in the knowledge graph while maintaining the original graph structure. Hoffart et al. [7] proposed a knowledge graph convolution network for recommendation systems, which extended the non-spectral convolution network [8, 9] method to the knowledge graph through selective aggregation of neighborhood node features. Graph convolution network (KGCN) uses local graph convolution for classification tasks. Knowledge graph attention network (KGAT) which is proposed by Wang et al. [10] uses self-attention network to disseminate information, uses multi-attention mechanism to increase model capacity, and mines related neighbors in knowledge graph to enrich feature representation of items. KGAT has been used in the POI recommendation area [25] to capture the deep meaning between semantics, with significant improvements. However, at present, most of the news-based recommendation systems only learn news at the semantic level, ignoring the knowledge information contained in the news itself. And there are few related researches on the combination of news recommendation model and knowledge graph.

Although the above methods enhance the knowledge of news representation, they do not consider the impact of user interest diversity on news recommendation. In terms of user interest expression, Zhu et al. [11] proposed a model that utilizes multiple attention networks to dynamically extract user interest expression. Using attention mechanisms to highlight the user's current expression of interest. In addition, An Mingxiao et al. [12] used gated recurrent neural network to obtain users' long-term and short-term interest representation. But they do not consider the feature of the news and the interests of the users comprehensively, and only consider one-sided issues.

In view of the above problems, this paper proposes a network combining knowledge enhancement and deep attention neural network (KEAN) for news recommendation. First, KEAN uses knowledge graph and graph attention network to capture entity and context information in news titles, and TransE [13] is used to train the corresponding knowledge graph. Inspired by KGAT, this paper selects neighbor entities around the target entity to refine the representation of the entity. As well as enriching entity representation, context information is enriched. Thirdly, KEAN introduces an attention-based neural network (ANN) [11] component to model the current interests of users, and uses the attention mechanism to capture the different influences of users' clicking on news on candidate news, so as to model the current interests of users. Finally, the user's historical sequence features and current interests are combined to represent the user's features.

The main contributions of this paper are as follows:

- This paper adopts knowledge graph and graph attention network to conduct relevance retrieve for text features in news titles and obtain additional relevant entities and context representations to enhance text feature representation and obtain rich news features.
- In this paper, multiple attention networks are used to dynamically gather user interest representation based on user history behavior, so as to enhance the effect of user interest extraction and obtain user feature representation.
- Experiments on Bing News and Mind datasets show that the performance index is improved by 0.6%–1.8%, which proves that the performance of our proposed model in news recommendation is significantly better than that of the most advanced methods.

2   The KEAN Framework

2.1   Problem Formulation

In this paper, the key recommendation problem is to use a given user's click history to predict whether a user will click on a candidate story he hasn't seen before. Assume that the click history on the news of a user i is $\{t_1^i, t_2^i, \ldots, t_{N_i}^i\}$, including $t_j^i (j = 1, \ldots, N_i)$ which is the title of the news j clicked by the user i, N_i is the total number of stories clicked by the user i. For each title, it is a series of words, $t = [w_1, w_2, \ldots]$, where each word may be associated with an entity e in the knowledge graph. Based on a given user's click history and the connections between the words in a news title and the entities in the knowledge graph, we predict whether a user will click on a candidate story he hasn't seen before.

2.2 Model Framework

In this section, we describe the KEAN's framework from a bottom-up perspective in details (see Fig. 2). The input of KEAN is a candidate news and a historical news that the user ever clicked on. The output is the probability that the user clicks on the candidate news title. (1) When capturing news features, we consider using the idea of KGAT to enrich the physical representation of news. (2) This paper uses multiple attention networks to automatically match each clicked news with candidate news, and aggregates users' current interests with different weights. (3) The probability of users clicking on candidate news is obtained by multi-layer perceptron (MLP) with the input of candidate news features and user's dynamic interest features.

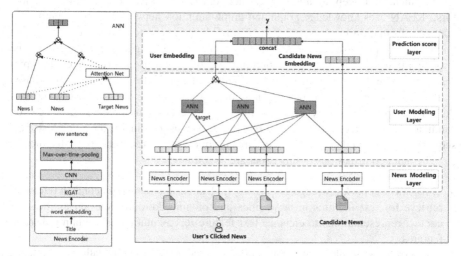

Fig. 2. Overall framework. The model is divided into three parts: news feature modeling layer, user interest modeling layer and prediction click score layer.

2.3 Knowledge Graph Construction

In order to utilize the information of the knowledge graph in the model, this paper first constructs a knowledge graph that is highly relevant to the task.

Firstly, the entities are identified from news titles, and the set E_{news} of news entities is obtained after processing all news titles. The original knowledge graph is large in scale and contains a large number of contents unrelated to the entities in the set E_{news}. In order to reduce the computational cost, a subgraph is extracted from the original knowledge graph according to the set E_{news}, i.e., for all relationships, the word frequency threshold is set to 10 times. When the word frequency of two entities appears more than 10 times, the relationship between two entities is constructed, and the nodes and corresponding edges that do not belong to the set E_{news} and are not on the path connecting any $e_i \in E_{news}$ are eliminated from the subgraph.

Then, knowledge representation learning methods, such as TransE, TransH [14], TransR [15], TransD [16], etc., are used to map the entities and relations in the knowledge mapping subgraph to a low-dimensional vector space to obtain the feature vectors of the entities and relations for subsequent models.

2.4 Construct News Features

This paper considers that an entity can be represented not only by its own embedding, but also by its neighbor parts. That is, each entity that appears in the news is retrieved for relevance. The weight of related edges is calculated within the appropriate number of steps, that is, the importance degree of the relationship, the reachable path between news entities is found. And the entities with high importance degree are selected for embedding.

We assume that entities in news articles can be linked to corresponding entities in knowledge graphs. Knowledge graph is represented as the set of entity-relations-entity.

Triples: $\mathcal{G} = \{(h, r, t) \mid h, t \in \mathcal{E}, r \in \mathcal{R}\}$, where $\mathcal{E}$ and $\mathcal{R}$ represents the set of entities and relations respectively, and (h, r, t) represents the existence of relations r from h to t. This paper uses TransE to learn the embedding vector $e \in \mathbb{R}^d$ for each entity and relationship. Let $\mathcal{N}_h$ represents the set of header entities h in the triplet. We apply KGAT [10] to get entity representations, as shown in the formula:

$$e_{\mathcal{N}_h} = ReLU(W_0(e_h \oplus \sum\nolimits_{(h,r,t) \in \mathcal{N}_h} \pi(h, r, t)e_t)) \tag{1}$$

Where $\oplus$ represents vector connection, and e_h and e_t are entity vectors learned from TransE. $\pi(h, r, t)$ is the attention weight to control how much information neighbor nodes need to propagate to the current entity, which can be calculated by double-layer fully connected neural network, as shown in the formula:

$$\pi_0(h, r, t) = W_2 ReLU(W_1(e_h \oplus e_r \oplus e_t) + b_1) + b_2 \tag{2}$$

$$\pi(h, r, t) = \frac{\exp(\pi_0(h, r, t))}{\sum_{\left(h, r', t'\right) \in \mathcal{N}_h} \exp(\pi_0(h, r', t'))} \tag{3}$$

Softmax function is used to normalize the coefficients. The trainable parameters are $\{W_0, W_1, W_2, b_1, b_2\}$. We can use the idea of graph neural networks to train models with higher-order information propagation in which neighborhood aggregation is stacked for multiple iterations.

By enriching the entity representation, the relevant context information [24] of the entity is enriched. Context embedding [5] is calculated as the average of its context entities, as shown in the formula:

$$context(e) = \{e_{\mathcal{N}_h} \mid (e, r, e_{\mathcal{N}_h}) \in \mathcal{G} \text{ or}(e_{\mathcal{N}_h}, r, e) \in \mathcal{G}\} \tag{4}$$

$$\bar{e} = \frac{1}{|context\ (e)|} \sum\nolimits_{e_i \in context(e)} e_{\mathcal{N}_h} \tag{5}$$

In view of the entity vector and word vector belong to different vector space, this paper uses the mapping function [5] to map the entity vector to the vector space with the same text features. The entity feature matrix is obtained. Considering that the adjacent entities of a node in the knowledge graph are usually closely connected semantically, the average node vector of adjacent entities is taken as the context node of the entity. At the same time, the same mapping function is used to map it to the same vector space as the text feature, which is extracted from the entity context feature matrix. Finally, text feature matrix, the three-channels input are constructed by entity feature matrix and entity context feature matrix t, and the news feature vector $e(t)$ are extracted through KCNN model, as shown in the formula:

$$e(t) = [\tilde{c}^{h_1} \tilde{c}^{h_2} \cdots \tilde{c}^{h_m}] \tag{6}$$

where $\tilde{c}^{h_i}$ is the output of the i convolution kernel, and m is the number of convolution kernels.

2.5 Construct User Interest Feature

Given the history of clicking news for user i is $\{t_1^i, t_2^i, \ldots, t_{N_i}^i\}$, corresponding news features are expressed as $e(t_1^i), e(t_2^i), \ldots, e(t_{N_i}^i)$. Because a user has multiple topics of interest, each news title that a user browses has a different degree of influence in predicting whether a user will click on a news title. Therefore, for the user representation i of the current candidate news t_j, we introduce ANN [11] to calculate the user's current interest representation, as shown in the formula:

$$e\left(t_k^i\right) = \tanh\left(W_w e\left(t_m^i\right) + b_w\right) \tag{7}$$

$$e(t_j) = \tanh(W_t e(t_j) + b_t) \tag{8}$$

$$s_j = softmax\left(\mathcal{H}\left(e\left(t_k^i\right), e(t_j)\right)\right) = \frac{\exp\left(\mathcal{H}\left(e\left(t_k^i\right), e(t_j)\right)\right)}{\sum_{k=1}^{N_i} \exp\left(\mathcal{H}\left(e\left(t_k^i\right), e(t_j)\right)\right)} \tag{9}$$

Where, s_j is used to measure the weight of the influence of historical click news $e(t_m^i)$ on candidate news $e(t_j)$. $m = 1, \ldots, N_i$, $W_w, W_t \in R^{d \times d}$, $b_w, b_t, v, e(t_m^i) \in R^d$, d is embedding dimension. The attention network $\mathcal{H}$ receives the embeddings of two news titles as input and output influence weights. Therefore, the dynamic interest feature $e(i)$ of user i can be calculated, as shown in the formula:

$$e(i) = \sum_{k=1}^{N_i} s_j e(t_k^i) \tag{10}$$

2.6 Predictive Click Probability

When predicting whether user i will click on candidate news title t_j, the model proposed in this paper takes user's dynamic interest feature and candidate news features into account. Another attention network $\mathcal{G}$ is used to predict the probability of user clicking on candidate news, and the formula is as follows:

$$p_{i,t_j} = \mathcal{G}(e(i), e(t_j)) \tag{11}$$

3 Experimental Setup and Result Analysis

3.1 Public Datasets

- **Bing News:** Each log contains information such as a user ID, news title, news link, number of clicks (0 means no clicks, 1 means clicks) and a timestamp. Through the Satori knowledge graph database information of Microsoft, the words in the news title are matched and disambiguated with the entities in the knowledge base, and the entities reachable with the entities are simultaneously obtained.

Table 1. Basic statistics of the news dataset and the extracted knowledge graph.

# users	141487	# entities	336350
# news	535145	# triples	4668
# logs	1025192	# relations	7145776
# words per title	7.9	# Contextual entities per entity	42.5
# entities per title	3.7		

# indicates the number of relation types.

- **MIND:** Each record contains user ID, news title, news link and click times. Microsoft Satori is used in this paper to obtain the corresponding knowledge graph content.

3.2 Parameter Settings

We choose TransE to deal with knowledge graphs and learn entity embedding, and use nonlinear transformation functions in KCNN. The dimension of both word embedding and entity embedding is set to 100. For each window of size 1, 2, 3, 4, set the number of filters to 64. We use Adam [17] to train KEAN by optimizing log losses. To compare KEAN with baseline, values of F1 and AUC were used as evaluation indicators.

3.3 Baselines

- **TextCNN** [18]: The text feature is extracted from the word vector of the news title as the vector representation of the news. The user feature is represented by the mean of the feature vector of the news that the user has browsed. A multi-layer perceptron is used to predict the probability of the user browsing the news based on the user feature and the candidate news feature.
- **KPCNN** [19]: Based on TextCNN, the vector of the entity corresponding to the word is introduced, which is spliced behind the word vector as the comprehensive vector of the word.
- **DMF** [20]: A depth matrix decomposition model for recommendation systems uses multiple nonlinear layers to process the original rating vectors of users and goods. We ignore news embedding and use implicit feedback as input to DMF.
- **DKN** [5]: TextCNN is used to learn the comprehensive features of news from the text features and entity features of news, and the user features are dynamically constructed by attention network structure.
- **DAN** [11]: Based on DKN, the attention network is improved to extract the user's current interest representation.
- **DKEN** [21]: This is an end-to-end knowledge enhancement model for item information sharing between user-item implicit interaction matrix and knowledge graph relationship matrix.
- **Wide&Deep** [22]: A general recommendation model consisting of a linear Wide channel and a nonlinear Deep channel.
- **LibFM** [23]: A classical CTR prediction model based on feature decomposition.

3.4 Baseline Model Comparison

In this experiment, we compared our KEAN to several baseline models and ran comparisons on a dataset. Table 2 and Fig. 3 shows the comparison results for the various models. Where Wide&Deep* and LibFM* represent the versions of Wide&Deep and LibFM after removing the input of entity vector respectively. From the comparison results we can see:

1) The performance of all models is better than that of DMF model based on CF. Because the attributes of news itself are very sensitive to time, the method based on CF is not effective in recommending news.
2) In addition to DMF model, LibFM performed the worst in all experiments. On the one hand, LibFM model has a relatively simple structure, which limits its expression ability. On the other hand, LibFM requires manual construction of news features and user features from word vectors, so it is difficult for manual construction of the most suitable features for the model.
3) Except LibFM, other models are all deep network models, among which Wide&Deep is a general recommendation model. When applied to the news recommendation problem described in this paper, news features also need to be constructed manually from word vectors as model input, so the effect is relatively poor. Both Wide&Deep and LibFM have improved their performance by introducing solid vectors as additional inputs.

Table 2. Comparison of experimental results between KEAN and baseline model

Models	Bing news		MIND	
	F_1 (%)	AUC (%)	F_1 (%)	AUC (%)
TextCNN	65.2	62.3	65.4	64.3
KPCNN	66.1	63.6	66.1	64.8
DMF	60.6	58.6	63.5	60.4
DKN	67.8	65.0	67.2	66.0
DAN	66.5	64.3	66.8	65.7
DKEN	68. 1	64.8	67.6	66.5
Wide&Deep	64.8	61.8	65.0	63.2
Wide&Deep*	63.7	60.7	64.2	61.5
LibFM	62.2	59.7	62.3	60.5
LibFM*	61.1	58.9	62.0	59.7
KEAN	**68.9**	**65.6**	**68.8**	**68.3**
Improve	↑ **0.8**	↑ **0.6**	↑ **1.2**	↑ **1.8**

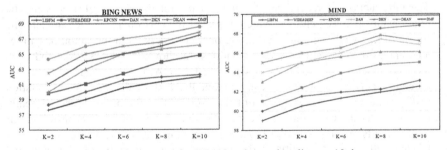

Fig. 3. AUC scores for KEAN and some baselines at 10 days

4) Except LibFM, other models are all deep network models, among which Wide&Deep is a general recommendation model. When applied to the news recommendation problem described in this paper, news features also need to be constructed manually from word vectors as model input, so the effect is relatively poor. Both Wide&Deep and LibFM have improved their performance by introducing solid vectors as additional inputs.

5) TextCNN, KPCNN, DKN, DAN and KEAN are all based on CNN to extract news features from the original word vector. Among them, TextCNN only considers the word vector of the news title text, and KPCNN splines the vector of the corresponding entity of the word behind each word vector as the comprehensive vector of the word on the basis of TextCNN. Compared with TextCNN, KPCNN has a little improvement. On the basis of TextCNN, DKN fuses word vector and entity vector in the form of multi-channel, and maps entity vector. Compared with KPCNN, this method

is more reasonable. In addition, attention network is introduced to better construct user features, so DKN has a greater improvement compared with KPCNN. On the basis of DKN, the proposed KEAN model introduces graph attention network to extract entities, enhances entity representation and context information representation, and further improves the information of entity vector. On the basis of DKN, multiple ANN attention networks are introduced to dynamically gather user interest representation and enhance the effect of user interest extraction. This is a further improvement over DKN.

6) This paper also compared with the latest model DKEN, these two models are used drawing attention network entities to get the neighbours, but at the same time of introducing KGAT, we use multiple attention network to carry on the dynamic and aggregation, so as to enrich the representation of user interest features. From the comparison results, our model is 1.8% higher than the accurate value of DKEN.

3.5 Model Ablation Experiment

In order to further illustrate the effects of various mechanisms in KEAN, this paper conducted comparative experiments on various variants of KEAN, and the results are shown in Table 3. Among them, KEAN without * (KGAT, Attention, etc.) represents that * is excluded from the KEAN model.

1) The introduction of KGAT can supplement the relationships and deep semantic relationships between entities, which improves the performance of the model. The fusion of knowledge graph information only considers the information of entities and ignores the connections between entities. As shown in Table 3, using KGAT in the model yields a gain of 1.3% on F1 and 2.1% on AUC of the dataset.

2) Attention network can dynamically obtain the historical sequence information and current interest representation of the user, so that the performance is greatly improved. As shown in Table 3, the introduction of attentional mechanism into our model results in 2.1% gain on F1 and 1.9% gain on AUC of the dataset.

3) Models with additional entities and context are more competitive than models that only consider news titles. This shows that entity and context information can provide indispensable and effective news feature information. As shown in Table 3, both entity vector and entity context vector can bring some improvement, and when these two vectors are used as inputs, they can play complementary roles and bring more improvement.

4) The introduction of nonlinear mapping function can effectively reduce the compatibility between entity vector and word vector, and the model performance is significantly improved after the introduction of mapping function, indicating that the heterogeneity between entity and entity type space can be alleviated by self-learning transformation function.

3.6 Impact of Embedding Dimension

This section focuses on the impact of entity embedding with different dimensions on the performance. In this experiment, all parameters except the measured parameters are set

Table 3. Comparative experimental results of KEAN direct variant

Model	F_1 (%)	AUC (%)
KEAN without KGAT	67.6	63.5
KEAN with KG	67.8	64.2
KEAN with KGAT	**68.9**	**65.6**
KEAN without Attention	66.8	63.7
KEAN with Attention	**68.9**	**65.6**
KEAN without context embedding	66.5	64.5
KEAN without entity embedding	66.3	64.3
KEAN with context and entity	**68.9**	**65.6**
KEAN without mapping	63.9	63.9
KEAN with linear mapping	65.6	64.7
KEAN with no-linear mapping	**68.9**	**65.6**

to the optimal configuration. We choose the dimensions d and k from all combinations of the set {20, 50, 100, 150, 200}, it gives plausible results (see Fig. 4).

1) This model has the best performance when $d = k = 100$ is set. Experiments show that this dimension can best express the semantic information of entity space and entity type space.

2) Given the entity embedding dimension d, the performance of the model will first increase with the increase of the number, and then decrease with the increase of the number after reaching the critical value. The experimental results fully show that too large or too small dimension will affect the performance of the model. This is because too low a dimension does not have enough ability to capture the necessary information and attributes, and too large a dimension introduces unnecessary noise and reduces generalization ability.

3.7 Impact of the Size for Each Hop

We have investigated for the selection of user neighbor node hops. There is a correlation between the performance of the model and the selection of the number of node hops (see Fig. 5).

1) The performance of the model improves while increasing the number of hops. However, increasing the number of hops in a single step does not lead to an increase in performance all the time. We find that the performance decreases when the number of hops reaches a critical points.

2) For large datasets like MIND, the best performance is achieved when it is 2. For small datasets like Bing News, other performance is achieved when it is 3. Experiments show that sparse data may require more space, but dense data requires only less space.

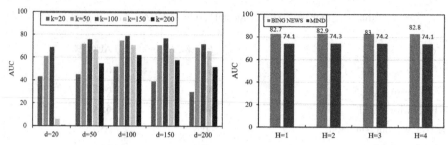

Fig. 4. AUC of embedding dimension   **Fig. 5.** AUC of hop counts

4   Conclusion and Future Work

Due to the existing news recommendation systems cannot accurately capture the deep semantic relations between entities, nor can they capture user's interest and preference well, KEAN model was put forward in this paper. For the embedding of entity vector and context information, considering the influence of entity's neighborhood value, we chose to use graph attention network to capture the one-hop neighborhood of entities, and removed irrelevant entities according to the number of occurrences between entities. At the same time, we used multiple attention networks to dynamically construct the user's interest feature based on the user's history of clicking on the title of news and the title of candidate news. Experimental results showed that the KEAN model is better than other news recommendation models. In the future work, we will further explore deep mining of user interest.

References

1. Okura, S., Tagami, Y., Ono, S., Tajima, A.: Embedding-based news recommendation for millions of users, pp. 1933–1942. ACM (2017)
2. Bansal, T., Das, M., Bhattacharyya, C.: Content driven user profiling for comment-worthy recommendations of news and blog articles, pp. 195–202. ACM (2015)
3. Liu, D., et al.: KRED: knowledge-aware document representation for news recommendations, pp. 200–209. ACM (2020)
4. Wang, H., Zhang, F., Zhang, M., Li, W., Wang, Z.: Knowledge-aware graph neural networks with label smoothness regularization for recommender systems, pp. 968–977. ACM (2019)
5. Wang, H., Zhang, F., Xie, X., Guo, M.: DKN: deep knowledge-aware network for news recommendation. In: 2018 World Wide Web Conference, pp. 1835–1844 (2018)
6. Kim, Y.: Convolutional neural networks for sentence classification. In: EMNLP (2014)
7. Niepert, M., Ahmed, M., Kutzkov, K.: Learning convolutional neural networks for graphs. In: The International Conference on Machine Learning, pp. 2014–2023 (2016)
8. Duvenaud, D.K., et al.: Convolutional networks on graphs for learning molecular fingerprints. In: Neural Information Processing Systems, pp. 2224–2232 (2015)
9. Hamilton, W., Ying, Z., Leskovec, J.: Inductive representation learning on large graphs. In: Neural Information Processing Systems, pp. 1024–1034 (2017)
10. Wang, X., He, X., Cao, Y., Chua, T.-S.: KGAT: knowledge graph attention network for recommendation, pp. 950–958. ACM (2019)

11. Zhu, Q., Zhou, X., Song, Z., et al.: DAN: deep attention neural network for news recommendation. In: AAAI (2019)
12. Mingxiao, An., et al.: Neural news recommendation with long- and short-term user representations. In: The Annual Meeting of the Association for Computational Linguistics (2019)
13. Bordes, A., Usunier, N., Garcia-Duran, A., Weston, J., Yakhnenko, O.: Translating embeddings for modeling multi-relational data. In: Advances in Neural Information Processing Systems, pp. 2787–2795 (2013)
14. Wang, Z., Zhang, J., Feng, J., Chen, Z.: Knowledge graph embedding by translating on hyperplanes. In: AAAI, pp. 1112–1119 (2014)
15. Ji, G., He, S., Xu, L., Liu, K., Zhao, J.: Knowledge graph embedding via dynamic mapping matrix. In: ACL, pp. 687–696 (2015)
16. Lin, Y., Liu, Z., Sun, M., Liu, Y., Zhu, X.: Learning entity and relation embeddings for knowledge graph completion. In: AAAI (2015)
17. Kingma, D., Ba, J.: Adam: a method for stochastic optimization (2014)
18. Kim, Y.: Convolutional neural networks for sentence classification. In: Empirical Methods in Natural Language Processing, pp. 1746–1751 (2014)
19. Wang, J, Wang, Z, Zhang, D, et al.: Combining knowledge with deep convolutional neural networks for short text classification. In: AAAI (2017)
20. Xue, H.J., Dai, X., Zhang, J., et al.: Deep matrix factorization models for recommender systems. In: AAAI (2017)
21. Guo, X., Lin, W., Li, Y.: DKEN: deep knowledge-enhanced network for recommender systems. Inform. Sci. **540**, 263–277 (2020)
22. Cheng, H.T., Koc, L., Harmsen, J., et al.: Wide & Deep Learning for Recommender Systems, pp. 7–10. ACM (2016)
23. Steffen, R.: Factorization Machines with libFM. ACM (2012)
24. Ma, P., Gao, Q., Fan, J.: Context aware feature interaction based recommendation system. In: IRC, pp. 485–489 (2020)
25. Zhang, C., Li, T., Gou, Y., Yang, M.: KEAN: knowledge embedded and attention-based network for POI recommendation. In: ICAICE (2020)

Labeled Knowledge-Based Decision Making with Assumption-Based Argumentation

Chuanqing Wang[1,2(✉)] 🄳, Yangyang Li[1], Chaoqun Fei[1], and Xikun Huang[1,2]

[1] Academy of Mathematics and Systems Science Key Lab of MADIS, Chinese Academy of Sciences, Beijing 100190, China
{tranking,yyli,cqfei,huangxikun}@amss.ac.cn
[2] University of Chinese Academy of Sciences, Beijing 100049, China

Abstract. Assumption-based Argumentation (ABA) has received a lot of attention and research attribute to its computability and interpretability. However, it is difficult for users to use ABA to represent the practical problems, especially for the data of problems involving natural language text/processing. Furthermore, since most arguments are derived by rules and some commonsense arguments are implied, massive rules need to be generated during representing practical problems by ABA, which reduces execution efficiency. Since the technologies of knowledge extraction from text and knowledge reasoning of knowledge graph are getting more and more efficient, it is possible to solve the above problems by using knowledge graph with ABA. In this paper, we propose a labeled RDF triple representation to enhance the semantics of triple and concise the process of triples extraction, and an abstract labeled knowledge-based decision making framework based on labeled triples for decision making. In order to apply the framework to the specific scene, we first give a detailed description of the definition and usage of labels in medical argumentation. Then we define an active decision framework for detecting the available decisions, and an optimal decision framework for computing the "best" decisions. Both of them build on argumentation-based computational mechanisms. Finally, we compute and explain the selected decisions by experimenting with the real argumentation record and demonstrate the applicability and rationality of our approach.

Keywords: Assumption-based argumentation · Labeled triple · Knowledge reasoning · Active decision · Optimal decision · Decision making

1 Introduction

Argumentation idea widely exists in human lives. For example, conflicting opinions always arise in the daily conversations where we defend our opinions and attack others' opinions by using argumentation ideas. Finally, some opinions will be selected as the final decisions when the conversation ends. Attributing to the powerful ability of reasoning and explanation, combining the realistic application requirements, argumentation-based decision making has attracted extensive research [1, 2]. The assumption-based argumentation [3, 4] which has a simple form to represent the arguments and can be easily used to

© The Author(s), under exclusive license to Springer Nature Switzerland AG 2022
G. Memmi et al. (Eds.): KSEM 2022, LNAI 13368, pp. 450–465, 2022.
https://doi.org/10.1007/978-3-031-10983-6_35

reason on its *rules* with *assumptions* and the *contraries* of assumptions, is one of the most popular research. Furthermore, the deduction trees of ABA can be used to represent the argument processes which show the relations among *arguments, rules, assumptions,* and *contraries.* Although ABA has many excellent features, it is difficult to split sentences into useful assumptions and generate rules from sentences in the realistic situations, such as in dialogue and medical argumentation. Besides, since commonsense knowledge is usually implied in arguments, massive rules need to be generated to explicitly declare the commonsense knowledge during representing practical problems by ABA. Therefore, structured data with formal specifications and extra reasoning technologies can facilitate the application of ABA in practical situations. Fortunately, the knowledge graph (KG) as a structured representation of knowledge may be a possible solution to these problems.

Knowledge graph was proposed by Google in 2012 [6], and it has been one of the hottest research in artificial intelligence. RDF [17] triples, which are structured and semantic knowledge representations, are usually used to describe the knowledge in KG. They have a simple and easy understanding format: (*subject, relation, object*) which means *subject* and *object* have a relationship *relation* or *subject* has the attribute *relation* with the attribute value *object*. Knowledge reasoning is one of the powerful features of KG. In recent years, with the improvement of reasoning technology [8], the application domains of KG are more and more extensive, such as commodity recommendation [18], smart medical [19, 22]. Therefore, it is possible to facilitate the knowledge representations of argument sentences by the technology of knowledge extraction, and simplify the generated rules by using the knowledge reasoning of KG.

To better combine the ABA framework and knowledge graph, we propose a labeled RDF triple representation and an abstract labeled knowledge-based decision making framework (LKDM). The labeled triples can enhance the semantics of knowledge representation. In addition, it can help users to extract the main knowledge of argumentation sentences more easily; the LKDM framework is based on labeled triples and used for decision making, and can simplify the generated rules by means of knowledge reasoning of KG. In practice, it is possible for an argumentation situation to generate multiple decisions that some of which are unavailable due to some background limitations. As in the medical argumentation situation argued for a patient, who is in an emergent state that needs multiple domain experts to solve it, most experts will make a decision (or suggestion) for the state based on their background knowledge. The final decision maker first needs to identify available decisions from these decisions. In fact, when an emergency happens, it will be a practical problem that some experts are very possible do not know the patient's situation in advance, which results in the decisions proposed by them may not satisfy the limitations with respect to the patient. For instance, the patient does not accept a surgery. In this case, it is necessary for the final decision maker to identify the available decisions quickly in an appropriate way. Therefore, we propose two specific sub-frameworks under the LKDM framework. One is active decision framework (ADF) for detecting the available decisions, and the other is optimal decision framework (ODF) for computing the "best" decisions from available decisions according to two decision criteria, including decisions that meet strongly dominant and weakly dominant. Both ADF and ODF use argumentation-based computational mechanisms to solve the problems. Finally, we conducted an experiment on the realistic medical argumentation record and did a brief time complexity analysis in terms of rules generation. The experimental results show that the labeled triples can be easily generated according to labels; the generated rules can be simplified; the selected decisions are rationality and can be explained by arguments or graphical deduction trees. The main contributions of this paper are summarized as follows and the processes of LKDM are shown in Fig. 1:

1. Introducing the labels into RDF triples to enhance the semantics of triples and facilitate knowledge extraction of argumentation sentences, and giving a detailed description on how to use the labels in the medical argumentation field.
2. Proposing an abstract LKDM framework to represent the argumentation abstractly, and two specific sub-frameworks, including ADF for detecting the active decisions and ODF for computing the optimal decisions with different measures. Both sub-frameworks are based on the argumentation-based computational mechanisms.
3. An experiment was carried out on the practical argumentation record to demonstrate the applicability and rationality of labeled triples and LKDM framework.

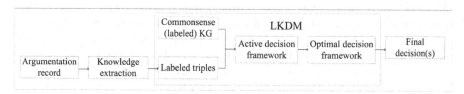

Fig. 1. The processes of LKDM framework

The rest of this paper is organized as follows. Section 2 discusses the related work. Section 3 simply describes the background knowledge of ABA. Section 4 describes the labeled RDF triples. Section 5 presents the framework of labeled knowledge-based decision making. Section 6 presents the experimental processes and results, and a briefly time complexity analysis. Finally, Sect. 7 concludes the paper.

2 Related Work

Different methods have been proposed to make decisions for argumentation. Amgoud and Prade [1] introduced abstract argumentation (AA) [7] into a decision making model to select and explain the "winning" decision by using a pair-wise comparison. Matt et al. [11] proposed an ABA-based decision making framework with one notion of dominant decision. Black and Atkinson [12] proposed a multi-agent dialogue model for the action making of agent. Fan and Toni [13] proposed a formal model with ABA for argumentation-based dialogues between agents, and gave a proof of a formal connection between these dialogues and argumentation semantics. Subsequently, they presented a multi-agent decision framework based on ABA in [14], and in the framework, two agents can argue towards "good" decisions by using the goals and attributes in a distributed manner. Fan et al. [9, 10] proposed a family of extended decision frameworks using

ABA, which studied decision making with preference over goals and sets of goals, and made explicit connections between "good" decisions and "acceptable" arguments. Zeng at el. [15] presented an argumentation-based approach to decision making with different kinds of preferences by using ABA. Wakaki [16] presented an ABA framework equipped with preferences to increase the kinds of preferences for decision making, and enhance the expressive power of ABA by P extensions. Notice that the above methods typically face two dilemmas. One is that users need to analyze the relationship between sentences in AA and ABA painstakingly, and the other is that users are hard to split sentences into main words so that it is difficult to obtain the assumptions and rules in ABA.

3   A Retrospective to ABA

An ABA framework is a tuple $\langle \mathcal{L}, \mathcal{R}, \mathcal{A}, \mathcal{C} \rangle$, where

- $\langle \mathcal{L}, \mathcal{R} \rangle$ is a deductive system, with $\mathcal{L}$ the *language* and $\mathcal{R}$ a set of *rules* of the form $s_0 \leftarrow s_1, ..., s_m (m \geq 0)$;
- $\mathcal{A} \subseteq \mathcal{L}$ is a (non-empty) set of *assumptions*;
- $\mathcal{C}$ is a total mapping from $\mathcal{A}$ into $2^{\mathcal{L}}$, where $\mathcal{C}(\alpha)$ is the *contrary* of $\alpha \in \mathcal{A}$.

Given a rule $s_0 \leftarrow s_1, ..., s_m$, we denote the head of the rule is s_0 and the body is $\{s_1, ..., s_m\}$. For an ABA framework, we always assume $\mathcal{L}$ contains all sentences appearing in $\mathcal{R}, \mathcal{A}$ and $\mathcal{C}$. As described by Dung et al. in [4], in this paper, we limit the ABA frameworks to flat, namely assumptions do not occur in the head of rules.

In ABA, arguments and assumptions are the primary objects around rules, and attacks are used to represent the relation between sets of assumptions. Simply, we just given the informal descriptions of arguments and attacks, as follows:

- *an argument for (the claim)* $c \in \mathcal{L}$ *supported by* $A \in \mathcal{A}$ (denoted as $A \vdash c$) is a finite tree with nodes labelled by sentences in $\mathcal{L}$ or by τ[1], and the root is labelled by c. Leaves are either τ or assumptions in A, and non-leaf s has many sub-nodes (leaves or non-leaves) that are the elements of body of a rule whose head is s.
- *an argument* $A_1 \vdash c_1$ *attacks an argument* $A_2 \vdash c_2$ if and only if (*iff* for short) c_1 is a contrary of one of the assumptions α in A_2, denoting as $c_1 = \mathcal{C}(\alpha)$ for $\alpha \in A_2$.

Attacks between sets of assumptions in ABA are different from the way of attacks between arguments. Concretely, a set of assumptions A attacks a set of assumptions B iff an argument supported by $A_1 \subseteq A$ attacks an argument supported by $B_1 \subseteq B$.

Some standard argumentation semantics have been introduced and discussed in AA [5, 6] and ABA [1, 4, 8]. Generally, the semantics of admissible is the most basic and important. In this paper, we focus on the semantics of admissible: a set of assumptions A_1 is admissible iff it is conflict-free (i.e. it does not attack itself) and it attacks all $A \subseteq \mathcal{A}$ that attack it; an argument $S_1 \vdash c$ belongs to an admissible extension supported by $S \subseteq \mathcal{A}$ iff $S_1 \subseteq S$ and S is admissible.

---

[1] As described in [4], $\tau \notin \mathcal{L}$ stands for "true" and is used to represent the empty body of rules.

4 Labeled RDF Triples

Although RDF triples can be used easily to represent knowledge, it is difficult for RDF triples to describe the sentence that has rich semantics. Generally, in the specific domain, people familiar with some words and word groups that are used frequently in this domain, and labeling these words with appropriate labels can not only preserve its rich semantic information but also represent the knowledge concisely. In this section, we will introduce labels into the knowledge representation of medical argumentation.

We introduce two kinds of labels into domain knowledge graph. One is used to mark the triple, and the other is used to mark the relation in the triple. Both two kinds of labels can be combined to increase richer semantics for triple. Specifically, we limit the work to the field of argumentation, where each argument generates/supports its decision by claiming some actions or attributes. Decision maker makes the final decision according to the attributes each decision has and the premise conditions each decision satisfies. The following parts give a formal description of labels.

Definition 1: In the field of argumentation, let the set of labels $L = \{a, b, c, d, f\}$, where a, b and c are *relation labels* used to mark the relation in the triple, d and f are *triple labels* used to mark the triple. The detailed description as follows:

- Label a (represents the word "action"): is used to claim a relation is an action. For example, the labeled triple (*patient, a: inject, anesthetic*) represents the relation "*inject*" is an action. The label a is usually used to claim a decision (or an argument) with the label d (see below).
- Label b ("benefit"): is used to claim the *benefit attribute* of a decision, and means the benefit will be gained when adopting this decision. For example, (*radiotherapy, b: cure_rate, 97%*) represents that the cure rate of radiotherapy is 97%, and the *object* 97% is the benefit value of *cure_rate*.
- Label c ("constraint"): is used to claim the *constraint attribute* of a decision. A decision can be selected only if the premise conditions of it satisfy all constraint attributes. For example, the labeled triple (*operation, c: age, le_75*) represents the constraint condition for operation is that the patient's age must be less than or equal to 75 years old.
- Label d ("decision"): is used to claim a decision generated by a triple. The relation labels a and b will be used when using the label d. The action label a acts on the *object* of triple to form a decision. For example, the labeled triple d: (*patient, a: take_out, larynx*) represents the decision "take out the patient's larynx" is generated, and we denote the decision as *take_out@larynx* (here uses the symbol "@" to represent this decision is a generated decision by *relation* and *object*). The *subject* of triple will be a decision when using label d to mark the triple and using benefit attribute b to mark the *relation*. For example, the labeled triple d: (*radiotherapy, b: cure_rate, 97%*) represents the cure rate of the decision *radiotherapy* is 97%.
- Label f ("fact"): is used to claim an indisputable objective fact. For example, the labeled triple f: (*patient, c: age, 75*) represents the patient's age is 75 years old.

5 LKDM Framework

In this section, we will give a detailed description of LKDM from three aspects which are the definition of LKDM, the active decision framework for detecting the available decisions, and the optimal decision framework for computing the optimal decision respectively.

5.1 Definition of LKDM

Definition 2: A LKDM framework is a tuple $\langle \mathcal{LT}, \mathcal{CKG}, \mathcal{L}, \mathcal{BF}, \mathcal{CF}, \mathcal{CR} \rangle$ where

- $\mathcal{LT}$, is a set of labeled triples, and is extracted from argumentation sentences;
- $\mathcal{CKG}$ is a domain-specific commonsense knowledge graph;
- $\mathcal{L}$ is a set of labels;
- $\mathcal{BF}$ is an ordered set of benefit functions. Each function in $\mathcal{BF}$ is used to measure benefit maximization with respect to a benefit attribute;
- $\mathcal{CF}$ is an ordered set of constraint functions. Each function in $\mathcal{CF}$ is used to measure whether the value of a constraint attribute is satisfied with respect to the constraint attribute;
- $\mathcal{CR}$ is used to represent the relationship among multiple constraint attributes.

In Sect. 4, we had given a detailed description of $\mathcal{LT}$ and $\mathcal{L}$. Here we give more information to $\mathcal{CKG}, \mathcal{BF}, \mathcal{CF}$ and $\mathcal{CR}$, as follows:

- $\mathcal{CKG}$. In LKDM framework, the domain-specific commonsense KG consists of labeled triples, and every relation in $\mathcal{CKG}$ has only one type of label. For example, if the relation "cure rate" belongs to $\mathcal{CKG}$ and is labeled by b, then its label remains unchanged in any LKDM frameworks used the $\mathcal{CKG}$. However, if a labeled triple is created according to some argument sentences, and its relation does not appear in the selected $\mathcal{CKG}$ (s), then users can use label a or b or c to mark the relation. Furthermore, the labels of relations in triples can be omitted if these relations have defined in a $\mathcal{CKG}$.
- $\mathcal{BF}$. Different functions need to be used to measure the quality of benefit attributes by their values. For example, for the benefit attribute "cure rate", the larger the value corresponding to it, the better it is. On the contrary, for the attribute "pain level", the smaller the value, the better. The functions in $\mathcal{BF}$ act on the values of benefit attributes, and we call these functions benefit functions. When the value of benefit attribute is equal to the result of the *benefit function* corresponded to the benefit attribute, we call the value satisfies this benefit function or the value *satisfies* this benefit attribute. For example, if the benefit attribute is *cure_rate*, and the benefit function is max which is used to obtain the maximum value of a set. Meanwhile, there are some labeled triples d: (*take_out@larynx, b: cure_rate,* 99%), d: (*radiotherapy, b: cure_rate,* 97%) and d: (*hemi_laryngectomy, b: cure_rate,* 97%), then $max(\{99\%, 97\%, 97\%\})$ is 99%, which means the value 99% is satisfies the benefit function *max* (we also say *take_out@larynx* satisfies *cure_rate*). Some basic benefit functions include *max, min, equal* and *has*.

- $\mathcal{CF}$. Similar to the $\mathcal{BF}$, the constraint functions are needed to measure whether the value of each constraint attribute satisfies the limitation on the constraint attribute. If one decision fails to satisfy constraint on a necessary constraint attribute, then it will be an *inactive decision* (describes in the next paragraph). For example, if a decision has the constraint attribute age with constraint function *less than or equal to 75 years old* (denoted as le_75 or formulated as $f(x) = x \leq 75$), and there is a labeled triple f: (*patient, c: age*, 75), then this decision can be selected for the *patient*. We call the value *satisfies* the constraint function (with respect to a constraint attribute), or the value *satisfies* the constraint attribute.
- $\mathcal{CR}$. When a decision was proposed, decision maker should determine whether the premise conditions of the decision are satisfied for a specific *subject* (e.g.: the *subject* is a patient in medical argumentation decision). We call the decisions that satisfy the premise conditions *active decisions*, otherwise *inactive decisions*. According to the practical experience, there are two relations among premise conditions. One is relation *and* that represents both premise conditions connected by it need to be satisfied, the other is relation *or* that represents at least one of the premise conditions connected by it need to be satisfied. For example, a decision which has the constraint attributes *age* and *status*. If the $\mathcal{CR}$ is *age* or *status*, then either *age* or *status* is satisfied the premise conditions of the decision are satisfied; if the $\mathcal{CR}$ is age and status, then only age and status are satisfied the premise conditions of the decision are satisfied. Simply, we call *constraint relation*.

5.2 Active Decision Framework

ADF is used to detect the active decisions, which is useful for the situation with many original decisions to reduce the time of decision making.

Definition 3: An ADF framework is a tuple $\langle \mathcal{LT}, \mathcal{CKG}, \mathcal{L}, \mathcal{CF}, \mathcal{CR} \rangle$, where elements of the tuple are same as LKDM framework. Let the number of decisions generated by $\mathcal{LT}$ be n, and the number of constraint attributes be r, then the ABA framework corresponding to $\langle \mathcal{LT}, \mathcal{CKG}, \mathcal{L}, \mathcal{CF}, \mathcal{CR} \rangle$ is $aba_{adf} = \langle \mathcal{L}, \mathcal{R}, \mathcal{A}, \mathcal{C} \rangle$, where

- $\mathcal{A}$ is such that: for all $i = 1, 2, ..., n, j = 1, 2, ..., r$:

  a. $s_i @ p_j$: for all the labeled triples with form d: $(s_i, a : p_j, o_{ij})$. For example, *take_out@larynx* can be obtained from the labeled triple d: (*patient, a: take_out, larynx*). Since the relation labels can be omitted, the form d: $(s_i, a : p_j, o_{ij})$ is a completion form. Same below.
  b. s_i: for all the labeled triples with form d: $(s_i, b : p_j, o_{ij})$. For example, *radiotherapy* can be obtained from the labeled triple d: (*radiotherapy, b: cure_rate*, 97%).
  c. Let S be the assumption set which is obtained by above a and b, we take into account the constraint relation $\mathcal{CR}$, and use specific examples to describe how to obtain the assumptions:

    (1) For the relation *or*: for example, *age or status*, which represents either constraint attribute *age* or *status* is satisfied the relation *or* is satisfied. Simply,

we consider the case where the decision has only two constraint attributes *age* and *status*. We construct two new decisions s_{i1} and s_{i2} with respect to the decisions_i, so that s_{i1} has the constraint attribute *age* and the attribute value of *age* of s_i (means that creates a labeled triple $(s_{i1}, c: age, age\_value)$), and s_{i2} has *status* and the attribute value. Hence, there are arguments $\{s_{i1}\} \vdash s_{i1}$ and $\{s_{i2}\} \vdash s_{i2}$ hold, and we can determine s_i is an active decision by proving s_{i1} or s_{i2} is an active decision. Therefore, removing s_i from S and adds s_{i1} and s_{i2} to S.

(2) For the relation *and*: according to the introduction of rules of ABA, no assumptions need to be produced.

d. $Nts_i p_j Sa$: the contrary of $ts_i p_j Sa$.

- C is such that: for all $i = 1, 2, ..., n, j = 1,2,...,r$, t such that $f : (t, c : p_j, o_j)$ exists in $\mathcal{LT}$ or $\mathcal{CKG}$, and s_i is a decision:

a. $C(s_i) = \{Nts_i p_1 Sa, Nts_i p_2 Sa, ..., Nts_i p_r Sa\}$, which means s_i does not satisfy the constraint attributes $p_1, p_2, ..., p_r$ with respect to t.
b. $C(Nts_i p_j Sa) = \{ts_i p_j Sa\}$.

- $\mathcal{R}$ is such that: for all $i = 1, 2, ..., n, j = 1, 2, ..., r$ and $s_i \in S$. The underscore "_" appears in the following triples means any non-empty entity, and the string "Sa" is used to distinguish the rule heads which satisfy some conditions:

a. If triple $(s_i, c : p_j, \_)$ exists or can be acquired by reasoning in $\mathcal{LT}$ with $\mathcal{CKG}$, which means that the decision s_i has the constraint attribute p_j, then generates the rule: $s_i p_j \leftarrow$;
b. We denote the j-th element of $\mathcal{CF}$ as g_j. If triple $f : (t, c : p_j, o_j)$ exists and the result of $g_j(o_j)$ is "true", which means that the actual value o_j of p_j satisfies g_j with respect to t, then generates the rule: $tg_j o_j Sa \leftarrow$;
c. If triple $(s_i, c : p_j, \_)$ not exists and cannot be acquired by reasoning in $\mathcal{LT}$ with $\mathcal{CKG}$, then generates the rule:

$$ts_i p_j Sa \leftarrow, \text{ for all t such that } f : \Big(t, c : p_j, o_j\Big) \text{exists in or } \mathcal{CFG};$$

d. $ts_i p_j Sa \leftarrow s_i p_j, tg_j o_j Sa$.

The rule head $ts_i p_j Sa$ in d of R means that if the decision s_i has the constraint attribute p_j (so can acquire a labeled triple (s_i, p_j, o_{ij})), and there is also a fact whose subject is t and object satisfies j-th element g_j of CF, then s_i can satisfy the constraint condition with respect to p_j according to the realistic case for the t. Hence, t can select s as its decision while limiting the constraint attribute to p_j. The rule in c of $\mathcal{R}$ means that the decision s_i has no constraint attribute p_j, so p_j does not limit s_i. In other words, s_i is satisfied w.r.t constraint attribute p_j.

We can use ABA framework to solve the problem of detecting the active decisions. In order to prove the correctness of correspondence described in Definition 3, the following theorem gives a formal proof.

Theorem 1: Given adf $= \langle \mathcal{LT}, \mathcal{CKG}, \mathcal{L}, \mathcal{CF}, \mathcal{CR} \rangle$, let $aba_{adf} = \langle \mathcal{L}, \mathcal{R}, \mathcal{A}, \mathcal{C} \rangle$ be the ABA framework corresponding to adf, then the decision s generated by $\mathcal{LT}$ for subject t is an active decision iff argument $\{s\} \vdash s$ is admissible in aba_{adf}.

Proof: We first prove if the decision s in adf is an active decision for t, then $\{s\} \vdash s$ is admissible in aba_{adf}. Let there are r constraint attributes $p_1, p_2, ..., p_r$. Simplicity, let s have the constraint attributes $p_1, p_2, ..., p_k (0 \leq k \leq r)$. Since s is an active decision for t, then there are labeled triples $(s, c : p_u, \_)$ and labeled triples $f : (t, c : p_u, o_u)$ for all $0 \leq u \leq k$, such that o_u satisfies the u-th constraint function g_u of CF (means the result of $g_u(o_u)$ is "true"). Hence the rules $sp_u \leftarrow$ and $tg_u o_u Sa \leftarrow$ hold. According to the rule $ts_i p_j Sa \leftarrow s_i p_j, tg_j o_j Sa$, we can obtain $tsp_u Sa$. Since s has no constraint attributes $p_{k+1}, p_{k+2}, ..., p_r$, the rule $tsp_v Sa \leftarrow$ holds $(k < v \leq r)$. Therefore, we can obtain $\{\} \vdash tsp_j Sa$ for all j $(0 \leq j \leq r)$ and $\{\} \vdash tsp_j Sa$ cannot be attacked. We know that only $\{Ntsp_j Sa\}$ can attack $\{s\}$ according to the Definition 1 and the ways of attack in ABA. Since $\{Ntsp_j Sa\} \vdash Ntsp_j Sa$ is attacked by $\{\} \vdash tSp_j Sa$ for all j, and $\{s\}$ not attacks itself (i.e. $\{s\}$ is conflict-free), $\{s\} \vdash s$ is admissible.

Then we prove that if $\{s\} \vdash s$ is admissible in aba_{adf}, then s is an active decision in adf with respect to some t. We have $C(s) = \{Ntsp_1 Sa, Ntsp_2 Sa, ..., Ntsp_r Sa\}$, which $Ntsp_j Sa$ is assumption for all j. Let $\{Ntsp_j Sa\} \vdash Ntsp_j Sa$ be attackers of $\{s\} \vdash s$. Since $\{s\} \vdash s$ is admissible, it defends all of its attacks. Hence, $\{Ntsp_j Sa\} \vdash Ntsp_j Sa$ is attacked for all j. Since $C(Ntsp_j Sa) = \{tsp_j Sa\}$, $\{\} \vdash tsp_j Sa$ must exist for all j. According to the rules of aba_{adf}, there are two rules with head $tsp_j Sa$ are $ts_i p_j Sa \leftarrow s_i p_j, tg_j o_j Sa$ and $ts_i p_j Sa \leftarrow$ respectively, which represent that either s has no constraint attribute p_j or s has p_j such that $(s, c : p_j, o_{ij})$ and $f : (t, c : p_j, o_j)$ exist (or can be acquired by reasoning) and o_j satisfies the j-th constraint function g_j of CF with respect to t. Therefore, s is an active decision. $\square$

5.3 Optimal Decision Framework

In the previous section, we described and proved how to use ABA framework to detect the active decisions. In this section, we will show two kinds of optimal decision frameworks which are strongly dominant ODF and weakly dominant ODF respectively. Both of them are used to compute and explain the optimal decision with ABA. Firstly, we give the definitions of strongly dominant and weakly dominant with respect to labeled knowledge decision.

Definition 4: A strongly dominant of the labeled knowledge decision is such that given the labeled knowledge base LK with n decisions and m benefit attributes, the decision s is a strongly dominant decision iff s has all the benefit attributes in LK, and for every benefit attribute p there is a labeled triple (or can be acquired by reasoning in LK) d: (s, b: p, o) in LK such that the object o is the best value for p.

Definition 5: A weakly dominant of the labeled knowledge decision is such that given the labeled knowledge base LK with n decisions and m benefit attributes, the decision s is a weakly dominant decision iff:

1. s has some benefit attributes in LK, and some of its benefit attributes (denoted as BP) have the best attribute values;
2. There is no other weakly dominant decision (let be s') in LK, such that for each bp in BP there is a labeled (or can be acquired by reasoning in LK) d: $(s', b: bp, o')$ that the *object* o' is the best value for bp, and there is a benefit attribute p' not in bp such that s' satisfies p'.

Definition 6: A strongly dominant ODF framework odf_{sd} is a tuple $\langle \mathcal{LT}, \mathcal{CKG}, \mathcal{L}, \mathcal{BF} \rangle$, where elements of the tuple are same as LKDM framework. Let the number of decisions generated by $\mathcal{LT}$ be n and the number of benefit attributes be m, then the ABA framework corresponding to odf_{sd} is $aba_{odf\_sd} = \langle \mathcal{L}, \mathcal{R}, \mathcal{A}, \mathcal{C} \rangle$, where

- $\mathcal{A}$ is such that: for all $i = 1,2,...,n, j = 1,2,...,m$:

   a. All the decisions that are acquired in the following ways:

      (1) $s_i @ p_j$: for all the labeled triples with form d: $(s_i, a : p_j, o_{ij})$.
      (2) s_i: for all the labeled triples with form d: $(s_i, b : p_j, o_{ij})$.

   b. $Nh_j s_i p_j Sa$: for all s_i and p_j such that either s_i has benefit attribute p_j whose attribute value does not satisfy the j-th element h_j of $\mathcal{BF}$ or s_i has no benefit attribute p_j. In other words, $Nh_j s_i p_j Sa$ represents s_i does not satisfy p_j.

- $\mathcal{C}$ is such that: for all $i = 1,2,...,n, j = 1,2,...,m$, and s_i is a decision:

   a. $C(s_i) = \{Nh_1 s_i p_1 Sa, Nh_2 s_i p_2 Sa, ..., Nh_t s_i p_m Sa\}$, which means s_i does not satisfy the benefit function h_j with respect to p_j for all j.
   b. $C(Nh_j s_i p_j Sa) = \{h_j s_i p_j Sa\}$.

- $\mathcal{R}$ is such that: for all $i = 1,2,...,n, j = 1,2,...,m$, and s_i is a decision:

   - If triple $(s_i, b : p_j, o_{ij})$ exists or can be acquired by reasoning in $\mathcal{LT}$ with $\mathcal{CKG}$ (denoted the j-th element of $\mathcal{BF}$ as h_j), and the result of $h_j(o_{ij})$ is "true", which means that o_{ij} satisfies g_j. Then generates the rule: $h_j s_i p_j Sa \leftarrow$;

There is only one rule in $\mathcal{R}$, the reason for this situation can be contributed to the capacity of knowledge reasoning. That is to say, there might be a series of complicated knowledge reasoning behind the triple $(s_i, b : p_j, o_{ij})$.

As described in Sect. 5.2, we can also use an ABA framework to correspond a strongly dominant ODF, and the following theorem gives a formal declaration.

Theorem 2: Given $odf_{sd} = \langle LT, CKG, L, BF \rangle$, let $aba_{odf\_sd} = \langle L, R, A, C \rangle$ be the ABA framework corresponding to odf_{sd}, then the decision s generated by LT is a strongly dominant optimal decision iff $\{s\} \vdash s$ is admissible in aba_{odf_sd}.

Proof: The proof processes are similar to Theorem 1 and are omitted.

In practice, almost each decision either does not have all benefit attributes or cannot satisfy all the benefit attributes. Therefore, the weakly dominant ODF is the most realistic optimal decision framework.

Definition 7: A weakly dominant ODF framework odf_{wd} is a tuple $\langle LT, CKG, L, BF \rangle$ where elements of the tuple are same as LKDM framework. Let the number of decisions generated by LT be n and the number of benefit attributes be m, then the ABA framework corresponding to odf_{wd} is $aba_{odf\_wd} = \langle L, R, A, C \rangle$, where

- A is such that: for all $i = 1,2,...,n, j = 1,2,...,m$:

  a. All the decisions that are acquired in the following ways:

      (1) $s_i @ p_j$: for all the labeled triples with form d: $(s_i, a : p_j, o_{ij})$.
      (2) s_i: for all the labeled triples with form d: $(s_i, b : p_j, o_{ij})$.

  b. $Nh_j s_i p_j Sa$: for all s_i and p_j such that either s_i has benefit attribute p_j whose attribute value does not satisfy the j-th element h_j of BF or s_i has no benefit attribute p_j.
  c. $NRPs_k s_i$: for $k = 1,2,...n, k \neq i$.

- C is such that: for all $i = 1,2,...,n, j = 1,2,...,m$, and s_i is a decision:

  a. $C(s_i) = \{Ps_1 s_i, ..., Ps_{i-1} s_i, Ps_{i+1} s_i, ..., Ps_n s_i\}$;
  b. $C(Nh_j s_i p_j Sa) = \{h_j s_i p_j Sa\}$;
  c. $C(NRPs_k s_i) = \{RPs_k s_i\}$;

- R is such that: for all $i = 1,2,...,n, j = 1,2,...,m$, and s_i is a decision:

  a. If triple $(s_i, b : p_j, o_{ij})$ exists or can be acquired by reasoning in LT with CKG, (denote the j-th element of BF as h_j) and the result of $h_j(o_{ij})$ is "true", which means that o_{ij} satisfies g_j. Then generates the rule: $h_j s_i p_j Sa \leftarrow$;
  b. for all $k, i = 1,2,...,n, k \neq i, j = 1,2,...,m$:

      (1) $Ps_k s_i \leftarrow h_j s_k p_j Sa, Nh_j s_i p_j Sa, NRPs_k s_i$;
      (2) $RPs_k s_i \leftarrow Nh_j s_k p_j Sa, h_j s_i p_j Sa$;

The rule head $RPs_k s_i$ in b. (2) of R means that there is a benefit attribute p_j such that the decision s_k does not satisfy p_j but s_i satisfies (grammatically, the former symbol represents satisfaction while the latter does not. Hence, using the latter "R" to represent the reverse). The rule head $Ps_k s_i$ in b. (1) of R means that if s_i satisfies p_j for each p_j of s_i, then s_k satisfies p_j, and there is at least one benefit attribute p_j' can be satisfied by s_k but not by s_i.

As described in Sect. 5.2, we can also use an ABA framework to correspond a weakly dominant ODF, and the following theorem gives a formal declaration.

Theorem 3: Given $odf_{wd} = \langle \mathcal{LT}, \mathcal{CKG}, \mathcal{L}, \mathcal{BF} \rangle$, let $aba_{odf\_wd} = \langle \mathcal{L}, \mathcal{R}, \mathcal{A}, \mathcal{C} \rangle$ be the ABA framework corresponding to odf_{wd}, then the decision s generated by $\mathcal{LT}$ is a weakly dominant optimal decision iff $\{s\} \vdash s$ is admissible in aba_{odf_wd}.

Proof: We first prove that if the decision s in odf_{wd} is a weakly dominant optimal decision, then $\{s\} \vdash s$ is admissible in aba_{odf_wd}. Let there be m benefit attributes $p_1, p_2, ..., p_m$. Since s is a weakly dominant optimal decision, s has r benefit attributes that can be satisfied by itself, and there is no other decision s' such that s' satisfies not only these r benefit attributes but also at least one benefit attribute that is not in these r benefit attributes. Now we use proof by contradiction to prove current conclusion. Suppose $\{s\} \vdash s$ is not admissible, since $\{s\}$ does not attack itself and the contrary of s_t: $C(s_t) = \{Ps_1s_t, ..., Ps_{t-1}s_t, Ps_{t+1}s_t, ..., Ps_ns_t\}$, there is at least one Ps_is holds ($s_i \neq s$). Hence, the rule $Ps_is \leftarrow h_js_ip_jSa, Nh_jsp_jSa, NRPs_is$ holds, whose first two elements of body mean there is a benefit attribute p_j such that s_i satisfies p_j but s does not, and the last element of body means that there is no such decision s_i such that there is a benefit attribute p'_j that is satisfied by s but not by s_i, in other words, the last element of body represents that for each benefit attribute satisfied by s is also satisfied by s_i. Since the benefit attribute p'_j is satisfied by s_i but not by s, s is not a weakly dominant optimal decision according to Definition 5. Therefore, $\{s\} \vdash s$ is admissible.

Then we prove that if $\{s\} \vdash s$ is admissible in aba_{odf_wd}, then s is a weakly dominant optimal decision. Simplicity, Suppose the benefit attributes $p_1, p_2, ..., p_r (1 \leq r \leq m)$ are satisfied by s. We know that the contrary of s (suppose $s = s_t$) is $\{Ps_1s, ..., Ps_{t-1}s, Ps_{t+1}s, ..., Ps_ns\}$. We also use proof by contradiction to prove current conclusion. Suppose s is not a weakly dominant optimal decision, then: 1) There is at least one decision s_i such that all the benefit attribute $p_k (1 \leq k \leq r)$ satisfied by s is satisfied by s_i, in other words, there is no benefit attribute p' that satisfied by s but not by s_i, hence the rule $RPs_is \leftarrow Nh_ls_ip_lSa, h_lsp_lSa$ is not held for all $l (0 < l \leq m)$, then $NRPs_is$ holds. 2) There is at least one benefit attribute $p_j (r < j \leq m)$ that is satisfied by s_i but not by s, hence the item $h_js_ip_jSa$ and Nh_jsp_jSa hold. Therefore, the rule $Ps_is \leftarrow h_js_ip_jSa, Nh_jsp_jSa, NRPs_is$ holds, which means $\{s\} \vdash s$ is not admissible. Hence, s is a weakly dominant optimal decision. □

6 Experiment

We use the medical argumentation record to test our LKDM framework. Since there are few public medical argumentation records, we select the most commonly used record reported by Chang et al. [20] as our experimental data (see Fig. 2).

The final labeled triples ($\mathcal{LT}$) extracted from the record are as follows (we used the symbol "-" to separate two items. Concisely, in the following, we denote the decisions *take_out@larynx* as *tol*, *radiotherapy* as *rad*, *hemi-laryngectomy* as *hl*, and denote the benefit attributes *cure_rate* as *cr*, *voice_quality* as *vq*, *operation* as *opt*, *patient* as *pt*):

d:(*pt, a:take_out, larynx*);   *d*:(*tol, b:cr, 99%*);   *d*:(*tol, b:vq, 0*);
d:(*rad, b:cr, 97%*);   *d*:(*rad, b:vq, 97%*);   *d*:(*hl, b:cr, 97%*);
d:(*hl, b:vq, 50%*);   *f*:(*pt, c:age, 75*);   *f*:(*pt, c: status, good*);
(*opt, c:age, le_75*);   (*opt, c:status, good*);

The following are necessary labeled triples used in this example that are either acquired from the $\mathcal{CKG}$ or newly generated by debaters:

(*tol, b:is_a, opt*);   (*rad, b:is_a, opt*);   (*hl, b:is_a, opt*).

S1:   (A1) My opinion is to take out the patient's larynx. This is has the best cure rate of 99%.
S2:   (A2) I agree, taking out the patient's larynx would provide the best cure potential.
S3:   (A3) I also agree, taking out the patient's larynx would provide the best cure potential.
RT1: (A4) But if you take out the patient's larynx, the patient will have no voice.
RT1: (A5) However, if you use radiotherapy, there is a 97% cure rate from the radiotherapy and about 97% voice quality, which is very good. The 3% who fail radiotherapy can have their larynx removed and most of these will be cured too.
S2:   (A6) My opinion is also that the patient should have a hemi-laryngectomy. This will give a cure rate is as good as radiation therapy.
S3:   (A7) I agree, performing a hemi-laryngectomy would give a cure rate as good as radiotherapy.
RT1: (A8) Yes, I have performed many hemi-laryngectomies, and when I reviewed my case load, the cure rate was 97%, which is as good as that reported internationally for radiotherapy.
RT2: (A9) I agree, however, you fail to take into account the patient's age. Given the patient is over 75, operating on the patient is not advisable as the patient may not recover from an operation.
RT1: (A10) Yes, however, in this case, the patient's performance status is extremely good, the patient will most likely recover from an operation. (i.e. the general rule does not apply)
S2:   (A11) Reviewing our past case decisions, evidence suggest that the we have always performed a hemilaryngectomy, hence my preference is to do the same.
S3:   (A12) I agree, however, there is some new medical literature reporting that the voice quality after a hemilaryngectomy was only 50% acceptable and the reporting institution was the North American leaders in hemilaryngectomy, hence we should perform radiotherapy.

Fig. 2. Argumentation record [20]

The set of labels $\mathcal{L}$ is $\{a, b, c, d, f\}$; the set of benefit functions $\mathcal{BF}$ is $\{cr : max, vq : max\}$; the set of constraint functions $\mathcal{CF}$ is $\{age : X \leq 75, status : X = good\}$; the constraint relation $\mathcal{CR}$ is $\{ageorstatus\}$. In order to save space, we only give the specific correspondence between strongly dominant ODF and ABA, as follows:

$\mathcal{A}$ (assumptions): *tol, rad, hl, Nmax-rad-cr-Sa, Nmax-hl-cr-Sa, Nmax-tol-vq-Sa, Nmax-hl-vq-Sa.*

$\mathcal{C}$ (contraries): *C(hl)={Nmax-hl-cr-Sa, Nmax-hl-vq-Sa}*,

C(tol)={Nmax-tol-cr-Sa,   Nmax-tol-vq-Sa},   *C(Nmax-tol-cr-Sa)={max-tol-cr-Sa},*
C(rad)={Nmax-rad-cr-Sa, Nmax-rad-vq-Sa},   *C(Nmax-tol-vq-Sa)={max-tol-vq-Sa},*
C(Nmax-rad-cr-Sa)={max-rad-cr-Sa},   *C(Nmax-hl-cr-Sa)={max-hl-cr-Sa},*
C(Nmax-rad-vq-Sa)={max-rad-vq-Sa},   *C(Nmax-hl-vq-Sa)={max-hl -vq-Sa}.*

$\mathcal{R}$ (rules): *max-tol-cr-Sa←; max-hl-vq-Sa← .*

We use CaSAPI [21] to compute the admissible decisions. The result shows that there is no admissible decision in this example. That is to say, there is no strongly dominant optimal decision. However, if we apply this example to the weakly dominant ODF, the decisions tol and rad are weakly dominant optimal decisions, and the reason for selecting them can be explained by using the deduction trees (only displaying the main part of the trees) in Fig. 3. Furthermore, if we consider the number of benefit attributes that a weakly dominant optimal decision has, since rad has extra benefit attribute *vq*, *rad* will be better than *tol*, which is consist with the result in [23].

Finally, we simply compare our work with others. Because of lacking appropriate works and criteria, in this paper, we briefly analyze the superiority of our work by comparing with Fan's in [10] which is classical. In order to enable two methods to compare, we just roughly estimate the time complexity of rules generation according to the same data (or information or knowledge).

We consider computing the strongly dominant decisions, and we assume the data has m active decisions and n goals and t (benefit) attributes. For Fan's method, each attribute of a decision generates a rule; each attribute of a goal generates a rule; a rule is generated by any attribute with any decision with any goal. Therefore, the time complexity of Fan's method is $O(mnt)$. For our method, a rule is generated only if the triple $(s_i, b : p_j, o_{ij})$ exists or can be acquired by reasoning, and o_{ij} satisfies j-th element of constraint function. Therefore, the maximal time complexity of ours is $O(mn)$. The above analysis represents that our method is better than Fan's in terms of rules generation.

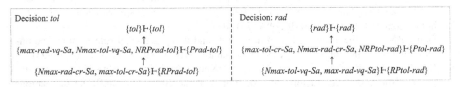

Fig. 3. The deduction trees of weakly dominant optimal decisions *tol* and *rad*.

7 Conclusion

In this paper, we proposed a systemic model for decision making with ABA. It consists of a method for labeling the label to RDF triple and an abstract labeled knowledge-based decision making (LKDM) framework for decision making. On the one hand, the labels can enhance the semantic information of triple and facilitate the work of main knowledge extraction from argumentation sentences. In addition, we gave a detailed description of the meaning and usage of the labels in medical argumentation field. On the other hand, the LKDM framework can simplify the rules generated during using ABA to represent real-world situations by means of the reasoning ability of KG. In order to apply the LKDM framework to the practical situation, we defined two specific sub-frameworks with argumentation-based computational mechanisms, which are active decision framework for detecting the active decisions and optimal decision framework for computing the "best" decision. Both of them are given the formal definitions as well as the theorems which are used to prove their correctness. Moreover, we studied two measures with respect to the "best" decision of optimal decision framework. One is the strongly dominant optimal decision framework, and the other is the weakly dominant optimal decision framework. Finally, we used the real case of medical argumentation to demonstrate the applicability and rationality of our model, and did a brief time complexity analysis in terms of rules generation for our model. In the future, there is still many deep works to do, such as constructing a complete domain labeled knowledge base, designing more measures for optimal decision framework, adding the preference to the model.

Acknowledgements. This work has been supported by National Key Research and Development Program of China under grant 2016YFB1000902, NSFC Project 61621003, 61872352, 62006125.

References

1. Amgoud, L., Prade, H.: Using arguments for making and explaining decisions. Artif. Intell. **173**(3–4), 413–436 (2009)
2. Fox, J., Krause, P., Elvang-Gøransson, M.: Argumentation as a general framework for uncertain reasoning. In: Uncertainty in Artificial Intelligence, pp. 428–434. Morgan Kaufmann (1993)
3. Cyras, K., Schulz, C., Toni, F., et al.: Assumption-based argumentation: disputes, explanations, preferences (2017)
4. Dung, P.M., Kowalski, R.A., Toni, F.: Assumption-based argumentation. In: Simari, G., Rahwan, I. (eds.) Argumentation in Artificial Intelligence, pp. 199–218. Springer, Boston (2009). https://doi.org/10.1007/978-0-387-98197-0_10
5. Dung, P.M.: On the acceptability of arguments and its fundamental role in nonmonotonic reasoning, logic programming and n-person games. Artif. Intell. **77**(2), 321–357 (1995)
6. Dong, X., Gabrilovich, E., Heitz, G., et al.: Knowledge vault: a web-scale approach to probabilistic knowledge fusion. In: Proceedings of the 20th ACM SIGKDD International Conference on Knowledge Discovery and Data Mining, pp. 601–610 (2014)
7. Baroni, P., Toni, F., Verheij, B.: On the acceptability of arguments and its fundamental role in nonmonotonic reasoning, logic programming and n-person games: 25 years later. Argument Comput. **11**(1–2), 1–14 (2020)
8. Chen, X., Jia, S., Xiang, Y.: A review: knowledge reasoning over knowledge graph. Expert Syst. Appl. **141**, 112948 (2020)
9. Fan, X., Craven, R., Singer, R., Toni, F., Williams, M.: Assumption-based argumentation for decision-making with preferences: a medical case study. In: Leite, J., Son, T Cao, Torroni, P., van der Torre, L., Woltran, S. (eds.) CLIMA 2013. LNCS (LNAI), vol. 8143, pp. 374–390. Springer, Heidelberg (2013). https://doi.org/10.1007/978-3-642-40624-9_23
10. Fan, X., Toni, F.: Decision making with assumption-based argumentation. In: Black, E., Modgil, S., Oren, N. (eds.) TAFA 2013. LNCS (LNAI), vol. 8306, pp. 127–142. Springer, Heidelberg (2014). https://doi.org/10.1007/978-3-642-54373-9_9
11. Matt, P.-A., Toni, F., Vaccari, J.R.: Dominant decisions by argumentation agents. In: McBurney, P., Rahwan, I., Parsons, S., Maudet, N. (eds.) ArgMAS 2009. LNCS (LNAI), vol. 6057, pp. 42–59. Springer, Heidelberg (2010). https://doi.org/10.1007/978-3-642-12805-9_3
12. Black, E., Atkinson, K.: Choosing persuasive arguments for action. In: AAMAS 2011, The 10th International Conference on Autonomous Agents and Multiagent Systems-Volume 3. International Foundation for Autonomous Agents and Multiagent Systems, pp. 905–912 (2011)

13. Fan, X., Toni, F.: Assumption-based argumentation dialogues. In: Twenty-Second International Joint Conference on Artificial Intelligence (2011)
14. Fan, X., Toni, F., Mocanu, A., et al.: Dialogical two-agent decision making with assumption-based argumentation. In: Proceedings of the 2014 International Conference on Autonomous Agents and Multi-agent Systems, pp. 533–540 (2014)
15. Zeng, Z., Fan, X., Miao, C., et al.: Context-based and explainable decision making with argumentation. In: AAMAS, pp. 1114–1122 (2018)
16. Wakaki, T.: Assumption-based argumentation equipped with preferences and its application to decision making, practical reasoning, and epistemic reasoning. Comput. Intell. **33**(4), 706–736 (2017)
17. Pan, J.Z.: Resource description framework. In: Staab, S., Studer, R. (eds.) Handbook on Ontologies, pp. 71–90. Springer, Heidelberg (2009). https://doi.org/10.1007/978-3-540-926 73-3_3
18. Sun, Z., Yang, J., Zhang, J., et al.: Recurrent knowledge graph embedding for effective recommendation. In: Proceedings of the 12th ACM Conference on Recommender Systems, pp. 297–305 (2018)
19. Ernst, P., Meng, C., Siu, A., et al.: Knowlife: a knowledge graph for health and life sciences. In: 2014 IEEE 30th International Conference on Data Engineering. IEEE, pp. 1254–1257 (2014)
20. Chang, C.F., Miller, A., Ghose, A.: Mixed-initiative argumentation: group decision support in medicine. In: Kostkova, P. (ed.) eHealth 2009. LNICSSITE, vol. 27, pp. 43–50. Springer, Heidelberg (2010). https://doi.org/10.1007/978-3-642-11745-9_8
21. Gartner, D., Toni, F.: CaSAPI: a system for credulous and sceptical argumentation. Proc. ArgNMR 80–95 (2007)
22. Hu, F., Lakdawala, S., Hao, Q., et al.: Low-power, intelligent sensor hardware interface for medical data preprocessing. IEEE Trans. Inf Technol. Biomed. **13**(4), 656–663 (2009)
23. Al Qassas, M., Fogli, D., Giacomin, M., et al.: Analysis of clinical discussions based on argumentation schemes. Procedia Comput. Sci. **64**, 282–289 (2015)

MGR: Metric Learning with Graph Neural Networks for Multi-behavior Recommendation

Yuan Yuan⬛, Yan Tang$^{(\boxtimes)}$⬛, Luomin Du⬛, and Yingpei Chen⬛

College of Computer and Information Science, Southwest University,
Chongqing, China
{y947136085,duluomin5686,chenyingpei}@email.swu.edu.cn, ytang@swu.edu.cn

Abstract. Traditional recommendation methods often suffer from the problems of sparsity and cold start. Therefore, researchers usually leverage Knowledge Graph as a kind of side information to alleviate these issues and improve the accuracy of recommendation results. However, most existing studies focus on modeling the single behavior of user-item interactions, ignoring the active effects of the multi-type behavior information in the recommendation performance. In view of this, we propose Metric Learning with Graph Neural Networks for Multi-behavior Recommendation (MGR), a novel sequential recommendation framework that considers both temporal dynamics and semantic information. Specifically, the temporal encoding strategy is used to model dynamic user preferences. In addition, the Graph Neural Network is utilized to capture the information from high-order nodes so as to mine the semantic description in multi-behavior interactions. Finally, symmetric metric learning helps to sort the item list to accomplish the Top-K recommendation task. Extensive experiments in three real-world datasets demonstrate that MGR outperforms the state-of-the-art recommendation methods.

Keywords: Recommender system · Knowledge graph · Graph neural networks · Temporal information · Metric learning

1 Introduction

Recommender systems, as an essential branch of data mining, have been successfully applied in various fields such as healthcare [8], e-commerce [13], social media [14] and so on. Traditional recommendation algorithms such as collaborative filtering [3] relies heavily on the historical behavior of users, which often suffers from the data sparsity and cold start problems. Therefore, researchers propose to leverage Knowledge Graph (KG) as a kind of side information to enrich the semantic description of users and items in the recommender systems. However, most of the existing studies focus on modeling the single interaction of users, but the actual recommendation scenario usually contains multi-type user behaviors [1]. As shown in Fig. 1, in the online e-commerce platforms, users

© The Author(s), under exclusive license to Springer Nature Switzerland AG 2022
G. Memmi et al. (Eds.): KSEM 2022, LNAI 13368, pp. 466–477, 2022.
https://doi.org/10.1007/978-3-031-10983-6_36

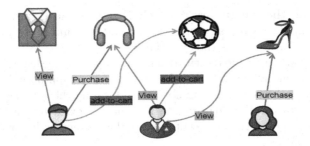

Fig. 1. An illustration of multiple types of user behavior.

have a variety of behaviors, such as page view, add-to-cart, and purchase, which are crucial for capturing the fine-grained user preferences. In addition, previous studies [6, 10, 11] only extract the static relevance between users and items, ignoring the dynamic changes of user preference implied in the historical interaction sequence. With the gradual diversification and complexity of recommendation scenarios, the above methods are inadequate.

Motivated by the above observations, we propose MGR, an end-to-end framework for knowledge graph enhanced multi-behavior sequential recommendation. Specifically, the temporal encoding strategy [4] is used to convert the time information into trainable vectors so as to incorporate the behavior dynamics into our model. In order to obtain fine-grained user preferences, Graph Neural Network (GNN) is used to sufficiently extract the information from high-order nodes.

The main contributions of this paper can be highlighted as follows:

1. We propose an end-to-end framework, which creatively considers the semantic relevance and temporal dynamics of items.
2. We design a multi-behavior mutual dependency encoder scheme to capture the dependencies between different behavior types through the multi-head attention mechanism and discriminate the different contribution in predicting stage.
3. Extensive experiments are conducted on three benchmark datasets to demonstrate that MGR significantly outperforms the state-of-the-art baselines, and the knowledge graph is further helpful to enhance the interpretability of the recommendation model.

2 Related Work

2.1 Graph Neural Network

Recently, the algorithms based on Graph Neural Network (GNN) have achieved remarkable results in recommendation [5, 10, 11]. GNN-based methods utilize the connectivity of the graph to extract structural information, so as to enrich the representation of users and items. These methods are mainly divided into the following steps:

(1) Sample the Neighbors of Each Node in the Graph: In order to reduce the computational cost, usually only a certain number of neighbor nodes are sampled for each node as the candidates.

(2) Information Aggregation: The propagation mechanism is used to capture the information from high-order nodes, and the appropriate aggregation function is selected to extract the information from neighbor nodes.

(3) Information Updating: The information extracted in the previous step is used to update the representation of the current node for downstream recommendation tasks.

2.2 Metric Learning

Metric learning aims to learn distance functions to measure the similarity between the samples so that similar samples have a small distance and dissimilar samples are far away from each other.

Euclidean distance has been widely used in various fields, and the calculation formula is as follows:

$$d(u, v) = \|\boldsymbol{\alpha}_u - \boldsymbol{\beta}_v\|_2^2 \tag{1}$$

Previous studies [2,9] often use the user-center metric to narrow the distance between the user and positive samples and push away negative samples. For example, u_1 and u_2 have common preferences, given a triple (u_1, v_1, v_2^-), where v_1 represents the positive sample, and v_2^- represents the negative one. According to the triple loss function proposed by CML [2], the distance between the user and negative sample should be larger than that between the user and positive sample, which is formula as follows:

$$d(u_1, v_1) + m \le d(u_1, v_2^-) \tag{2}$$

Metric learning avoids the limitation of using inner product as the prediction function and enhances the mining ability of recommendation algorithm.

3   Model

The framework of MGR is illustrated in Fig. 2, which consists of four parts: (1) Temporal Information Encoding Module, (2) Multi-Behavior Mutual Dependency Encoder, (3) Information Fusion Module and (4) Symmetic Metric Learning.

3.1   Problem Formulation

Table 1 summarizes the key notations used in this paper, which define our proposal and review the literature.

   Input : Given the G_u, G_v, and the historical interaction sequence S_U^T.

   Output : The probability $y_{i,j}^k$ of interaction between user u_i and item v_j under the target behavior type k.

Table 1. Notations

Notation	Description
U	The set of users
I	The set of items
R	The set of relations
K	The number of behavior types
L	The number of layers in GNN
u_i	The embedding for user i
v_j	The embedding for item j
G_u	User-item interaction knowledge graph
G_v	Item-item relation knowledge graph
$t_{i,j}^k$	u_i interacted with v_j under the behavior type of k
S_U^T	The historical interaction sequence before target time T

3.2 Temporal Information Encoding Module

In the recommendation scenario, temporal evolution is essential for modeling user preferences. Inspired by previous research [4], the temporal information encoding strategy generates the vectors containing time information. Specifically, we convert the temporal information, which is hard to train, into the low dimensional vectors, and the formula is as follows:

$$T_{i,j}^{k,(2l)} = \sin \frac{\tau\left(t_{i,j}^k\right)}{10000^{\frac{2l}{d}}} \tag{3}$$

$$T_{i,j}^{k,(2l+1)} = \cos \frac{\tau\left(t_{i,j}^k\right)}{10000^{\frac{2l+1}{d}}} \tag{4}$$

where superscript $(2l)$ and $(2l + 1)$ represent odd and even positions in the temporal embedding vector, respectively. In order to enhance the tunable ability of temporal encoding, Multi-layer Perceptron (MLP) is further applied to obtain $\overline{T}_{i,j}^k \in \mathbb{R}^d$. Finally, temporal information is integrated into the embeddings:

$$u_i = e_i \oplus \overline{T}_{i,j}^k \tag{5}$$

$$v_j = e_j \oplus \overline{T}_{i,j}^k \tag{6}$$

where e_i and e_j are the initial embeddings of user and item, respectively.

We leverage the connectivity of the graph structure to transfer the temporal information between the current node and the target one, with the following graph attention mechanism:

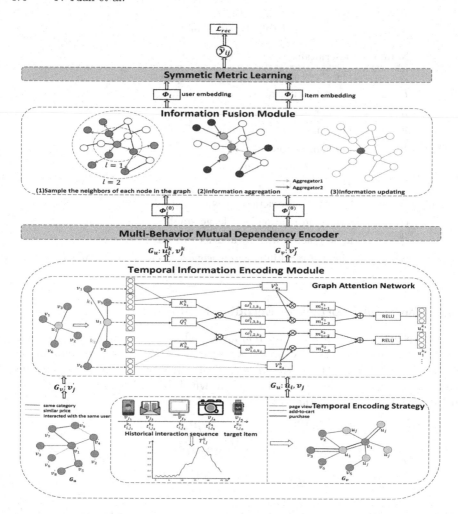

Fig. 2. Framework of MGR.

(1) Message Propagation Mechanism

$$m_{i \leftarrow j}^{k} = \overset{H}{\underset{h=1}{||}} \omega_{i,j,k}^{h} \cdot V_k^h v_j \tag{7}$$

$$m_{j \leftarrow i}^{k} = \overset{H}{\underset{h=1}{||}} \omega_{j,i,k}^{h} \cdot V_k^h u_i \tag{8}$$

where $m_{i \leftarrow j}^{k}$ denotes the information transmission process from the item j to the user i. Similarly, $m_{j \leftarrow i}^{k}$ represents the information transmission between the user i and the item j. In addition, $\omega_{i,j,k}^{h}$ represents the propagation weight and

Q_k^h, K_k^h, V_k^h represent the transformation matrixes:

$$Q_k^h = \sum_{m=1}^{M} \alpha_m^k \overline{Q}_m^h \tag{9}$$

$$K_k^h = \sum_{m=1}^{M} \beta_m^k \overline{K}_m^h \tag{10}$$

$$V_k^h = \sum_{m=1}^{M} \gamma_m^k \overline{V}_m^h \tag{11}$$

(2) Information Aggregation

Accumulate the information from $m_{i \leftarrow j}^k$ and $m_{j \leftarrow i}^k$ to update the representation of the current node. The calculation process is as follows:

$$u_i^k = f \left(\sum_{v_j \in N_i} m_{i \leftarrow j}^k \right) \tag{12}$$

$$v_j^k = f \left(\sum_{u_i \in N_j} m_{j \leftarrow i}^k \right) \tag{13}$$

where N_i and N_j denote the neighbors of user i and item j respectively, and $f(\cdot)$ represents the activation function RELU.

Similarly, for graph G_v, the heterogeneous information from items is aggregated and calculated to obtain the item embedding v_j^r:

$$v_j^r = f \left(\sum_{v_{j'} \in N_j} m_{j \leftarrow j'}^r \right) \tag{14}$$

where N_j denotes the neighbors of item j.

3.3   Multi-behavior Mutual Dependency Encoder

In the multi-behavior recommendation scenario, different types of behavior interacted in a complex way, but most previous studies [1,5] only used a relatively independent and local manner to model multi-type interaction. In this paper, we leverage a multi-behavior encoding scheme [13] to capture the dependencies between distinct behaviors with the multi-head attention mechanism.

The representations of user and item are formally defined as follows:

$$\tilde{u}_i^k = \text{MH-Att}\left(u_i^k\right) = \sum_{k'=1}^{K} \psi_{k,k'}^{i,h} \cdot \overline{V}^h \cdot u_i^{k'} \tag{15}$$

$$\tilde{v}_j^k = \text{MH-Att}\left(v_j^k\right) = \sum_{k'=1}^{K} \psi_{k,k'}^{j,h} \cdot \overline{V}^h \cdot v_j^{k'} \tag{16}$$

$$\tilde{v}_j^r = \text{MH-Att}\left(v_j^r\right) = \sum_{r'=1}^{R} \psi_{r,r'}^{j,h} \cdot \overline{V}^h \cdot v_j^{r'} \tag{17}$$

where the relational intensity ψ is calculated as follows:

$$\psi_{k,k'}^{i,h} = \frac{\exp\left(\overline{\psi_{k,k'}^{i,h}}\right)}{\sum_{k'=1}^{K} exp(\overline{\psi_{k,k'}^{i,h}})} \tag{18}$$

$$\overline{\psi_{k,k'}^{i,h}} = \frac{\left(\overline{Q}^h \cdot u_i^k\right)^\top \left(\overline{K}^h \cdot u_i^{k'}\right)}{\sqrt{d/H}} \tag{19}$$

where $\overline{Q}^h, \overline{K}^h, \overline{V}^h$ represent the projection matrixes in the h-th subspace.

Through the above pairwise manner, obtain the relational intensity between different behaviors. Next, in order to promote the cooperation between different behaviors, the gated fusion mechanism is used to calculate the user embedding $\Phi_i^{(0)}$ and item embedding $\Phi_j^{(0)}$:

$$\Phi_i^{(0)} = \sum_{k=1}^{K} \eta_i^k \tilde{u}_i^k \tag{20}$$

$$\Phi_j^{(0)} = \sum_{k=1}^{K} \eta_j^k \tilde{v}_j^k \oplus \sum_{r=1}^{R} \xi_j^r \tilde{v}_j^r \tag{21}$$

In the above formulas, $\eta_i^k, \eta_j^k, \xi_j^r$ represent the importance score of the behavior, which is trained by MLP.

3.4   Information Fusion Module

In the actual recommendation scenario, users have different interaction behaviors with the item, which reflect the users' preferences for the item. In this regard, GNN is used to introduce behavior information into the recommendation module, according to the message propagate mechanism, the $(l+1)$-th layer is calculated as follows:

$$\Phi_i^{(l+1)} = \sum_{j \in N_u(i)} \text{Propagate}\left(\Phi_j^{(l)}\right) \tag{22}$$

$$\Phi_j^{(l+1)} = \sum_{i \in N_u(j); j' \in N_v(j)} \text{Propagate}\left(\Phi_i^{(l)}, \Phi_{j'}^{(l)}\right) \tag{23}$$

In the above formulas, Propagate $(\cdot)$ is the information propagation function. The final embeddings of users and items are calculated as follows:

$$\Phi_i = \Phi_i^{(1)} \oplus \Phi_i^{(2)} \oplus \cdots \oplus \Phi_i^{(L)} \tag{24}$$

$$\Phi_j = \Phi_j^{(1)} \oplus \Phi_j^{(2)} \oplus \cdots \oplus \Phi_j^{(L)} \tag{25}$$

3.5   Symmetric Metric Learning

Although the existing metric learning recommendation methods are very effective, when the distance between positive and negative samples is too close, it is easy to mislead other users in the prediction process. Therefore, Li et al. [7] propose a symmetric metric learning algorithm SML. In addition to calculating the user-center metric, SML [7] also symmetrically introduces the positive item-center metric, which maintains a closer distance between the positive sample and the user and pushes the negative sample away from the positive sample.

Firstly, from a geometric perspective, the user-center metric is to take user u_1 as the center of the sphere and $r_u + m_u$ as the radius of the sphere. Similarly, from the perspective of the item: v_j and v_j^- respectively represent the positive and negative samples of the same user, it can be inferred that v_j and v_j^- are not similar, which means that the distance between them should be large enough, so the distance function is defined as:

$$d\left(\Phi_i, \Phi_j\right) + n_j \leq d\left(\Phi_j, \Phi_j^-\right) \tag{26}$$

where n denotes the margin in item-center metric.

Considering that different users have different preferences, the margin m should be personalized for each user. Similarly, due to the symmetrical measurement, the margin n should also be changed with different items. In view of this, the loss function with adaptive margin strategy is proposed as follows:

$$\mathcal{L}_{AM} = -\left(\frac{1}{|U|}\sum_u m_u + \frac{1}{|I|}\sum_v n_v\right) \tag{27}$$

We use Euclidean distance $d\left(\Phi_i, \Phi_j\right)$ as the prediction function $\hat{y}_{ij}$ of the recommendation task, and the loss function of the recommendation task is defined as follows:

$$\mathcal{L}_{rec} = \sum_{(u_i,v_j)\epsilon G_u} \sum_{\left(u_i,v_j^-\right)\notin G_u} \left(\left[d\left(\Phi_i, \Phi_j\right) - d\left(\Phi_i, \Phi_j^-\right) + m_u\right]_+\right.$$
$$\left. + \lambda\left[d\left(\Phi_i, \Phi_j\right) - d\left(\Phi_j, \Phi_j^-\right) + n_v\right]_-\right) + \gamma\mathcal{L}_{AM} \tag{28}$$

4   Experiments

To demonstrate the effectiveness of MGR, we conduct experiments on three publicly accessible datasets and report the comparison results.

Table 2. Dataset statistics

Dataset	#User	#Item	#Interaction	Behavior type
MovieLens-10M	67,788	8,704	9,922,036	Dislike, Neural, Like
Yelp	19,800	22,734	1,400,002	Tip, Dislike, Neural, Like
Retail	147,894	99,037	7,658,926	Page View, Cart, Purchase

4.1 Datasets

Experiments are performed on three real-world datasets, namely MovieLens-10M[1], Yelp[2] and Retail[3]. We transform the explicit feedback into implicit feedback following the previous data processing method [13]. Table 2 shows the statistics of the experimental datasets.

4.2 Evaluation Metrics

To evaluate the quality of Top-K recommendation methods, we use industry standard Hit Ratio (HR) and Normalized Discounted Cumulative Gain (NDCG) as the evaluation standard. HR@K is a commonly used indicator to measure the accuracy of recommendation, while NDCG@K pay more attention to the position in the ranking list.

4.3 Baselines

We compare MGR with following baselines, including traditional recommendation (BiasMF [6]), GNN-based recommendation (NGCF [11], KGAT [10]), and multi-behavioral recommendation (MATN [12], MBGCN [5], KHGT [13]).

(1) BiasMF [6]: This is a traditional recommendation model, which enhances the matrix factorization paradigm by combining user and item biases with corresponding implicit feedback.
(2) NGCF [11]: This is a classic model that extends GNN to collaborative filtering. It obtains the structural information in the user-item graph through the propagation mechanism, thereby effectively making up for the data sparse.
(3) KGAT [10]: This model explicitly captures the structural information in the KG, and adaptively learns the information from neighbor nodes through the propagation layer to obtain the fine-grained representation of the current node.
(4) MATN [12]: This model designs a multi-behavior-dependent encoder, introduces different types of user interaction into the recommendation module, and uses the attention mechanism to strengthen the semantics of specific behaviors and enhance the accuracy of user preference expression.

---

[1] https://grouplens.org/datasets/movielens/10m/.
[2] https://www.yelp.com/dataset/download.
[3] https://github.com/akaxlh/KHGT/tree/master/Datasets/retail.

Table 3. Recommendation performance in three datasets

Model	MovieLens-10M		Yelp		Retail	
	HR@10	NDCG@10	HR@10	NDCG@10	HR@10	NDCG@10
BiasMF	0.7831	0.5012	0.7631	0.4921	0.2731	0.1642
NGCF	0.8014	0.5108	0.8103	0.5084	0.3143	0.1947
KGAT	0.8203	0.5217	0.8426	0.5507	0.3844	0.2206
MATN	0.8498	0.5732	0.8493	0.5396	0.3617	0.2144
MBGCN	0.8379	0.5641	0.8074	0.5088	0.3706	0.2312
KHGT	0.8657	0.5986	0.8917	0.6073	0.4712	0.2843
MGR	**0.8762**	**0.6104**	**0.9023**	**0.6185**	**0.4801**	**0.2905**

(5) MBGCN [5]: This model uses graph convolution networks to obtain the implicit semantic information in historical interaction sequence. It can distinguish the different effects of behaviors on the target item and improve the recommendation performance.
(6) KHGT [13]: This model integrates the dynamics of multi-type interactions through temporal encoding strategy and uses GNN to capture high-order neighbor information of users and items. Finally predicts output through the inner product.

4.4 Results

The results of MGR and other baselines in Top-K recommendation are presented in Table 3, from which we have the following observations:

1. MGR achieves the best performance on three datasets, indicating that our method can effectively utilize graph-structured data to improve recommendation quality.
2. Compared with the traditional algorithm BiasFM [6], the recommendation based on KGs (NGCF [11], KGAT [10] and MGR) can easily obtain more accurate recommendation results with the help of a large amount of side information.
3. Algorithms with multi-behavior data (MATN [12], MBGCN [5], KHGT [13] and MGR), their recommendation performances are all the better than other baselines, which demonstrates that user's multi-behavior data has a positive impact on the recommendation task.
4. Although KHGT [13] outperforms other baselines, it limits the data mining ability due to violation of triangular inequality in the prediction stage.

4.5 Ablation Study

In this section, we compare some model variants of MGR and analyze their efforts.

- MGR-Ti: This model removes the temporal encoding strategy and only considers the influence of multiple behavior types on the recommendation task.
- MGR-MB: This model removes multi-behavior module and only uses GNN to extract the representations of user and item.
- MGR-ML: This model removes symmetric metric learning and utilizes the inner product to predict recommendation results.

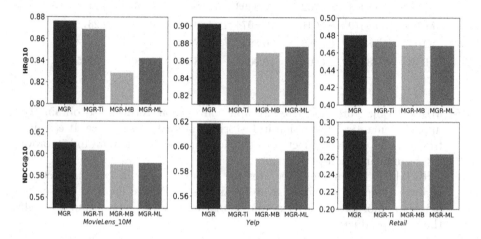

Fig. 3. Ablation study of MGR.

The experimental results are shown in Fig. 3, from which we have the following observations:

1. The positive effect of temporal information in assisting recommendation task.
2. The multi-type behavior information helps capture user preferences more accurately.
3. Symmetric metric learning with adaptive margin can obtain more fine-grained user representation than inner product, which helps to improve recommendation accuracy.

5   Conclusion

In this paper, we   propose a multi-behavioral recommendation model based on GNN and metric learning. Specifically, temporal encoding strategy is leveraged to model user dynamic preferences. Then GNN is leveraged to capture the fine-grained semantic information from the high-order nodes. Finally, we use the symmetric metric learning to predict recommendation results. Extensive experiments demonstrate our model can effectively improve the recommendation quality. For future work, we intend to use the path information from the KGs, which will help to enhance the interpretability of recommendation algorithms.

References

1. Gao, C., et al.: Learning to recommend with multiple cascading behaviors. IEEE Trans. Knowl. Data Eng. **33**(6), 2588–2601 (2019)
2. Hsieh, C.K., Yang, L., Cui, Y., Lin, T.Y., Belongie, S., Estrin, D.: Collaborative metric learning. In: Proceedings of the 26th International Conference on World Wide Web, pp. 193–201 (2017)
3. Hu, Y., Koren, Y., Volinsky, C.: Collaborative filtering for implicit feedback datasets. In: 2008 Eighth IEEE International Conference on Data Mining, pp. 263–272. IEEE (2008)
4. Hu, Z., Dong, Y., Wang, K., Sun, Y.: Heterogeneous graph transformer. In: Proceedings of the Web Conference 2020, pp. 2704–2710 (2020)
5. Jin, B., Gao, C., He, X., Jin, D., Li, Y.: Multi-behavior recommendation with graph convolutional networks. In: Proceedings of the 43rd International ACM SIGIR Conference on Research and Development in Information Retrieval, pp. 659–668 (2020)
6. Koren, Y., Bell, R., Volinsky, C.: Matrix factorization techniques for recommender systems. Computer **42**(8), 30–37 (2009)
7. Li, M., et al.: Symmetric metric learning with adaptive margin for recommendation. In: Proceedings of the AAAI Conference on Artificial Intelligence, vol. 34, pp. 4634–4641 (2020)
8. Sharma, D., Singh Aujla, G., Bajaj, R.: Deep neuro-fuzzy approach for risk and severity prediction using recommendation systems in connected health care. Trans. Emerg. Telecommun. Technol. **32**(7), e4159 (2021)
9. Tay, Y., Tuan, L.A., Hui, S.C.: Latent relational metric learning via memory-based attention for collaborative ranking. In: Proceedings of the 2018 World Wide Web Conference, pp. 729–739 (2018)
10. Wang, X., He, X., Cao, Y., Liu, M., Chua, T.S.: KGAT: knowledge graph attention network for recommendation. In: Proceedings of the 25th ACM SIGKDD International Conference on Knowledge Discovery & Data Mining, pp. 950–958 (2019)
11. Wang, X., He, X., Wang, M., Feng, F., Chua, T.S.: Neural graph collaborative filtering. In: Proceedings of the 42nd International ACM SIGIR Conference on Research and Development in Information Retrieval, pp. 165–174 (2019)
12. Xia, L., Huang, C., Xu, Y., Dai, P., Zhang, B., Bo, L.: Multiplex behavioral relation learning for recommendation via memory augmented transformer network. In: Proceedings of the 43rd International ACM SIGIR Conference on Research and Development in Information Retrieval, pp. 2397–2406 (2020)
13. Xia, L., et al.: Knowledge-enhanced hierarchical graph transformer network for multi-behavior recommendation. In: Proceedings of the AAAI Conference on Artificial Intelligence, vol. 35, pp. 4486–4493 (2021)
14. Zheng, H., Wu, K., Park, J.H., Zhu, W., Luo, J.: Personalized fashion recommendation from personal social media data: an item-to-set metric learning approach. In: 2021 IEEE International Conference on Big Data (Big Data), pp. 5014–5023. IEEE (2021)

Recomposition of Process Choreographies Using a Graph-Based Model Repository

Piotr Wiśniewski[1], Krzysztof Kluza[1(✉)], Anna Suchenia[2], Leszek Szała[3], and Antoni Ligęza[1]

[1] AGH University of Science and Technology,
al. A. Mickiewicza 30, 30-059 Krakow, Poland
{wpiotr,kluza,ligeza}@agh.edu.pl
[2] Cracow University of Technology, ul. Warszawska 24, 31-155 Kraków, Poland
asuchenia@pk.edu.pl
[3] Department of Mathematics, Faculty of Chemical Engineering, University of
Chemistry and Technology, Prague, Technicka 5, 166 28 Prague 6, Czech Republic
leszek.szala@vscht.cz

Abstract. Modeling process choreographies is a key activity to illustrate collaboration between different organizations. In this paper, we propose a method to automatically generate BPMN Choreography Diagrams based on existing models. A process choreography can be decomposed into a number of reusable parts. Such parts are then stored in a web-based repository, which uses the BPMN Ontology to describe structural properties of each component. New diagrams are generated by composing a graph based on the general connectivity rules and requirements provided by the user. Our results show that composing new models in such a way may serve as decision support to domain experts and reduce the risk of designing a flawed diagram.

1 Introduction

In our previous paper [1], we proposed a process recomposition method to build a process model from a set of reusable components (from diagram decomposition [2]). However, our method did not cover interactions between participants.

In this paper, we applied our concept to recompose process choreographies, which usually define collaboration between process participants. We introduce a novel way to automate choreography modeling based on the reuse of the existing components. Such a solution might be used for redesigning or creating new models based on the general requirements and criteria provided by the user.

The paper is organized as follows. Section 2 provides an overview of process choreography modeling. Section 3 includes an analysis of existing works related to the generation of process choreographies. The algorithm of model decomposition is presented in Sect. 4. Section 5 presents a novel method to generate choreography diagrams based on reusable components. Finally, conclusions and plans for future work are described in Sect. 6.

G. Memmi et al. (Eds.): KSEM 2022, LNAI 13368, pp. 478–488, 2022.
https://doi.org/10.1007/978-3-031-10983-6_37

2   Process Choreography Modeling

The concept of process choreography originated from web service coordination [3]. However, it is a broader term that covers the aspects of business-to-business collaboration between partners. A choreography model shows how information is exchanged between processes taking place in different organizations.

BPMN (Business Process Model and Notation) is a widely used standard for business process modeling. Choreography diagrams were introduced as a part of BPMN in 2011 along with its current version (2.0) [4]. However, first attempts to model process choreographies with BPMN were made four years before [5].

Although BPMN Choreography diagrams include the same groups of elements as process diagrams, their subsets are different. The following elements are considered essential from the purpose of choreography modeling:

1. Flow Objects, including:
    - activities – Choreography Tasks and Sub-Choreographies,
    - events – a limited set of start, intermediate and end events shared with BPMN process diagrams,
    - gateways – exclusive (XOR), inclusive (OR), parallel (AND), and event-based.
2. Connecting objects, including sequence flows and message flows (only if pools are used to represent participants).
3. Swimlanes, only in the form of pools to represent message flow between participants of a Choreography Task.
4. Artifacts, including annotations and groups.

Figure 1 presents an example BPMN choreography diagram with a simple exclusive gateway structure.

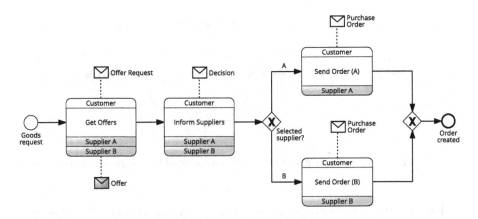

Fig. 1. Choreography diagram of purchase order creation. Based on [6].

2.1   Graph-Based Representations for Choreography Diagrams

Process models are commonly represented by directed graphs [7,8]. Since choreography diagrams base on the same concept of activities, events, and gateways as other BPMN models, it is possible to adapt the graph representation for this type of workflow. In our approach, we use the concept of business process graph previously presented in [2]. Similarly to the business process graph, a choreography graph is a connected, directed graph $G_C = (V_O, E_F)$, where:

- V_O is a non-empty set of vertices that represents all flow objects (activities, events, and gateways) in a diagram, together with their annotations;
- E_F is a non-empty set of edges that represents all connecting objects (sequence flows).

As choreography diagrams do not use the concept of lanes, the list of properties for a vertex is limited compared to a process model and include: object ID, object type (task, start event, AND split etc.), and object name/description. In addition, vertices that represent activities have four additional properties: initiator, recipient, message, and return message (optional).

Exactly as in the case of process graphs, all vertices in a choreography graph are connected by a directed edge $e \in E_F$, which is a pair of its endpoints. Edges that follow an alternative gateway (OR/XOR) contain also the information about the condition that needs to be fulfilled for the flow to continue along that sequence flow.

Figure 2 shows a graph-based representation of the choreography diagram from Fig. 1. To clarify the representation, vertices were colored according to the corresponding flow object type. Properties of the first choreography task were summarized in Table 1.

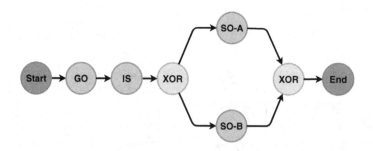

Fig. 2. Example choreography diagram represented by a directed graph.

The last step of creating a choreography graph is building its adjacency matrix D of size $n \times n$, where n is the number of flow objects in the diagram. Such a matrix defines flow connections between objects in the diagram, which is useful during the decomposition phase.

Table 1. Properties of the vertex representing the first task – Get Offers.

Property	Value
Object ID	GO
Object type	Choreography task
Object name	Get offers
Initiator	Customer
Recipient	Supplier A, Supplier B
Message	Offer request
Return message	Offer

2.2   BPMN Ontology

An ontology for BPMN 2.0 diagrams was proposed by Rospocher et al. in 2014 [9]. It provides a formalization of BPMN components in OWL 2 DL language, including classes and object properties for choreography diagrams. Representation of a process model in an ontology can lead to multiple benefits such as collecting process knowledge, as well as model querying and validation [10]. The purpose of using the BPMN ontology for the component repository is the possibility to add semantic annotations to the sub-diagrams created as a result of model decomposition. Provided that such annotations are both generate automatically based on the existing models and prepared by the repository users, it would be easier to retrieve elements while creating new models.

Assuming that CD corresponds to the entire choreography, example ABox statements [11] for the choreography diagram presented in Fig. 1 are as follows:

```
choreogrpahy(CD)
choreographyTask(Get Offers)
has_flowElement(CD, Get Offers)
has_Participant(Get Offers, Customer)
has_Participant(Get Offers, Supplier A)
has_initiatingParticipantRef(Get Offers, Customer)
has_messageFlow(Get Offers, Offer Request)
```

3   Related Works

Although choreography models are part of the BPMN 2.0 standard since its introduction in 2011, there exist several underspecification issues of the language, such as the possibility to specify the message recipient (in case of multiple participants) or to specify relations between different collaborators [12]. It might be one of the reasons why BPMN choreography diagrams are much less frequently considered than collaboration models.

Nevertheless, there exist several papers related to the automated support of choreography modeling. Nguyen et al. [13] proposed a framework in which choreography diagrams are represented as Symbolic Transition Graphs. These structures are then used to check the realizability of a process choreography and create behavioral skeletons for its participants. Requirement analysis for the automation of choreography model treatment was conducted by Cortes-Cornax et al. [14]. The authors provided a multi-factor evaluation of the BPMN capabilities for modeling service interactions.

Automated support for choreography modeling can also be achieved by detecting synchronization points in the multi-instance process model, where choreography is required [15]. Next, diagrams are enhanced in a database-aided online tool. Such an approach may lead to the automatic generation of choreography models which is mentioned by the authors in their plans for future work.

4   Decomposition of Choreography Diagrams

The first step in the recomposition approach consists in extracting sub-diagrams from existing models and storing them in a model repository. The input choreography diagram is transformed into a graph representation and then divided into k-element subgraphs. The parameter k that determines the number of flow objects can be adjusted based on the business case.

In [2], we discussed solving possibilities for $k = 2$ (bi-gram decomposition) and $k = 3$ (tri-gram decomposition). A general problem for $2 <= k < n$ is solvable as a Constraint Satisfaction Problem of finding all subgraphs of a given graph. However, such problems are exponential [16]. Therefore, we based our research on three-element sub-diagrams. In this case, the resulting tri-grams are found, by taking for every flow object v in the diagram: v with its two direct predecessors, v with one predecessor and one successor or v with two direct successors. Based on this assumption, it is possible to estimate the cardinality of the set S_3, i.e., the number of tri-grams in a choreography model. It is expressed by Formula 1, which is based on the BPMN formal model presented in [17].

$$|S_3| = |\mathbb{T}| + \sum_{g \in \mathbb{G}} \binom{\sigma_I(g)}{2} + \sum_{m \in \mathbb{M}} \binom{\sigma_O(m)}{2} + |\mathbb{I}^*|, \tag{1}$$

where:

- $\mathbb{T}$ is the set of choreography tasks in the diagram,
- $\mathbb{G}$ is the set of split gateways in the diagram,
- $\mathbb{M}$ is the set of merge gateways in the diagram,
- $\mathbb{I}^*$ is the set of SESE (Single Entry Single Exit) intermediate events,
- $\sigma_I : \mathbb{O} \longrightarrow \mathbb{N}_0$ determines the number of sequence flows incoming to a flow object and $\mathbb{N}_0$ stands for non-negative integers,
- $\sigma_O : \mathbb{O} \longrightarrow \mathbb{N}_0$ determines the number of sequence outgoing from a flow object.

It can be seen that, in the choreography graph presented in Fig. 2, ten different tri-grams can be identified: one per each task and three per each gateway. Figure 3 shows four sub-diagrams created from an example choreography model.

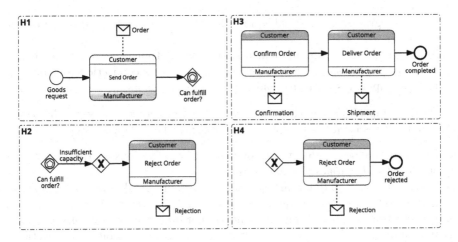

Fig. 3. Component models created as a result of choreography diagram decomposition.

As the next step, sub-diagrams are filtered based on the assumption that each component should contain a choreography activity or an event. After filtering, semantic annotations are added to each of the created sub-diagrams, using the BPMN ontology presented in Sect. 2.2. Finally, annotated components can be saved to a repository in the form of a database containing the subgraph structure, flow object properties, and automatically generated semantic annotations.

5   Generating New Models from Reusable Components

In the proposed approach, the recomposition of choreography diagrams is formulated as a problem of composing a graph that satisfies the predefined conditions. It is assumed that the final choreography model should have only one start event, but it can have multiple end events. Therefore, the user is responsible for specifying one of the available initial events, the initiating collaborator, as well as a set of potential end events. It is also possible to indicate a set of existing activities and sub-diagrams that must be included in the resulting model.

5.1   Algorithm

In order to compose a correct choreography diagram, it is necessary to define when a pair of sub-diagrams are connectable. Based on the BPMN standard and empirical analysis, the following set of connectivity requirements was specified for two tri-grams s_1 and s_2:

- sub-diagrams s_1 and s_2 contain different sets of elements,
- s_1 has at least one output and s_2 has at least one input,
- if s_1 ends with a gateway and s_2 starts with a gateway, the gateway types must match (e.g. XOR split – XOR merge),

- the choreography is enforceable, i.e., the initiator of the first activity in s_2 is present in s_1,
- if s_1 and s_2 have common elements, then the output of s_1 must match the input of s_2 or s_1 and s_2 must have only one possible connection (one output and one input, respectively) and two common elements.

The recomposition algorithm generates a set of choreography graphs based on sub-diagrams from the repository. It consists of the following steps:

1. Provided that $l_S = |S_3|$ is the number of sub-diagrams in the repository, create a $l_s \times l_S$ adjacency matrix A_0.
2. If two different sub-diagrams s_i and s_j ($i, j \in \{1, ..., l_S\}$) are connectable so that s_j follows s_i, then assign $A_0(i, j) = 1$ and $A_0(j, i) = -1$.
3. Remove from matrix A_0 all components that do not have any connection.
4. If a sub-diagram has only one input and the number of incoming connections in matrix A_0 exceeds 1, or this sub-diagram has only one output and the number of outgoing connections in matrix A_0 exceeds 1, then create matrices $A_1, A_2, ..., A_x$ for every possible input/output configuration.
5. From the created matrices, remove all sub-diagrams that do not have any incoming connections except the initial component.
6. From the created matrices, remove all sub-diagrams that do not contain any end event and do not have any outgoing connections.
7. For each of the created matrices, check if there exists a path from the initial sub-diagram to any of the components that have an end event. If so, add the matrix to the final set of models C_R.
8. Provided that the set C_R is non-empty, the recomposition was successful.

The final step of the recomposition process is the removal of doubled flow objects that occurred after connecting overlapping sub-diagrams and removal of gateways that have only one input and one output. If multiple solutions exist, the user can select one of several models that have been recomposed and choose one that fits best to the business case.

5.2 Illustrative Example

The proposed recomposition algorithm was implemented in Python language with a preliminary repository in the form of a CSV file. The example presented in this section shows the recomposition process based on four sub-diagrams (H1–H4) shown in Fig. 3.

Let us assume the following requirements for the generated diagram: the choreography should start with a goods request which is initiated by the customer. As a result of the process, a purchase order can be completed or rejected.

Taking into account the provided requirements and a repository consisting of four component models, the algorithm from Sect. 5.1 was executed. The initial adjacency matrix A_0 is shown in Formula 2. Its indices correspond to the order of the example sub-diagrams.

$$A_0 = \begin{bmatrix} 0 & 1 & 1 & 1 \\ -1 & 0 & 1 & 0 \\ 1 & -1 & 0 & 0 \\ -1 & 0 & 0 & 0 \end{bmatrix} \tag{2}$$

After removing non-admissible connections and unnecessary flow objects (steps 4–6), we obtain two matrices: A_1 (Formula 3) and A_2 (Formula 4). Although component H2 was removed from matrix A_1, the corresponding row and column were kept to clarify the example.

$$A_1 = \begin{bmatrix} 0 & 0 & 1 & 1 \\ 0 & 0 & 0 & 0 \\ -1 & 0 & 0 & 0 \\ -1 & 0 & 0 & 0 \end{bmatrix} \tag{3}$$

$$A_2 = \begin{bmatrix} 0 & 1 & 0 & 1 \\ -1 & 0 & 1 & 0 \\ 0 & -1 & 0 & 0 \\ -1 & 0 & 0 & 0 \end{bmatrix} \tag{4}$$

It is clear that the initial sub-diagram must be H1, as it is the only one that contains a start event. Likewise, the choreography should end with component H3 or H4. In the graph represented by matrix A_1, there are two admissible paths induced by two sub-diagrams: (H1, H3) and (H1, H4). In matrix A_2, one can also identify two paths: (H1, H2, H3) and (H1, H4). Since paths can be determined in both cases, the final set contains two choreography models:

$$C_R = \{A_1, A_2\}. \tag{5}$$

Figure 4 shows a BPMN choreography diagram created based on matrix A_1. The final adjustment to be done by the algorithm is to remove the XOR split gateway, which was initially part of the sub-diagram H4. Since it has only one input, it is unnecessary in the resulting model. The last step of the model adjustment is adding labels on the sequence flows outgoing from the event-based gateway with the condition "Can fulfill order?". This can be done manually by the user or based on the analysis of other sub diagrams, e.g., from the component H3, one can determine that the order is rejected if the manufacture does not have sufficient capacity to produce the requested goods.

The diagram created based on matrix A_2 is syntactically correct after removing unnecessary gateways (see Fig. 5). However, it makes no sense from the business perspective, as a rejected order cannot be later confirmed by the manufacturer. This example shows that the solutions provided by the algorithm should be considered preliminary and must be revised by business users before selecting the final model.

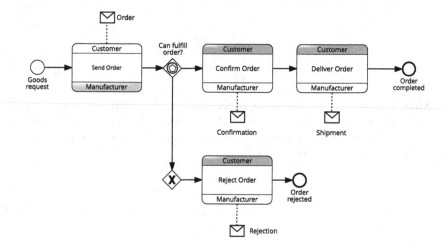

Fig. 4. Recomposed choreography diagram before final adjustments.

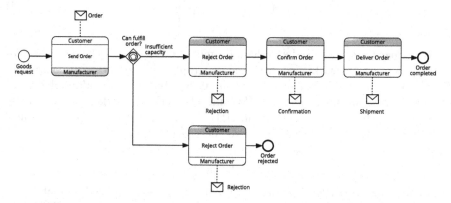

Fig. 5. Second choreography diagram after final adjustments.

6   Concluding Remarks

In this paper, we presented a method to generate BPMN choreography diagrams based on a repository of component models extracted from the existing choreography models. Our approach can be seen as a support for choreography modeling that automates activities performed by different process collaborators.

The algorithm generates a set of admissible solutions from which users can select a diagram that corresponds best to their requirements. A model created in such a way can be a firm basis for the final choreography diagram and thus, it can reduce the time spent on collaboration between different organizations.

As future work, we plan to extend the recomposition approach by ranking the generated solutions using constraint optimization, as well as collecting user requirements based on natural language descriptions.

References

1. Wiśniewski, P., Kluza, K., Jemioło, P., Ligęza, A., Suchenia, A.: Business process recomposition as a way to redesign workflows effectively. In: 2021 16th Conference on Computer Science and Intelligence Systems (FedCSIS). IEEE, pp. 471–474 (2021)
2. Wiśniewski, P.: Decomposition of business process models into reusable subdiagrams. In: ITM Web of Conferences, vol. 15, EDP Sciences, p. 01002 (2017)
3. Barros, A., Hettel, T., Flender, C.: Process choreography modeling. In: Handbook on Business Process Management 1. Springer, pp. 257–277 (2010). https://doi.org/10.1007/978-3-642-00416-2_12
4. Chinosi, M., Trombetta, A.: BPMN: an introduction to the standard. Comput. Stand. Interf. **34**(1), 124–134 (2012)
5. Decker, G., Barros, A.: Interaction modeling using BPMN. In: International Conference on Business Process Management. Springer, pp. 208–219 (2007)
6. Weske, M.: Business Process Management: Concepts, Languages, Architectures 2nd Edition. Springer (2012). https://doi.org/10.1007/978-3-642-32885-5_5
7. Semantic Methods for Execution-level Business Process Modeling. LNBIP, vol. 40. Springer, Heidelberg (2009). https://doi.org/10.1007/978-3-642-05085-5
8. Parody, L., Gómez-López, M., Varela-Vaca, A., Gasca, R.: Business process configuration according to data dependency specification. Appl. Sci. **8**(10), 2008 (2018)
9. Rospocher, M., Ghidini, C., Serafini, L.: An ontology for the business process modelling notation. In: Garbacz, P., Kutz, O. (eds.) Formal Ontology in Information Systems - Proceedings of the Eighth International Conference, FOIS2014, 22–25 September 2014, Rio de Janeiro, Brazil, vol. 267. IOS Press, pp. 133–146 (2014)
10. Thomas, O., Fellmann, M.: Semantic EPC: enhancing process modeling using ontology languages. In: Proceedings of the Workshop on Semantic Business Process and Product Lifecycle Management SBPM 2007, Held in Conjunction with the 3rd European Semantic Web Conference (ESWC 2007), Innsbruck, Austria, 7 June 2007, CEUR WS (2007)
11. Roy, S., Dayan, G.S., Holla, V.D.: Modeling industrial business processes for querying and retrieving using OWL + SWRL. In: OTM Confederated International Conferences On the Move to Meaningful Internet Systems. Springer, pp. 516–536 (2018). https://doi.org/10.1007/978-3-030-02671-4_31
12. Adamo, G., Borgo, S., Di Francescomarino, C., Ghidini, C., Rospocher, M.: BPMN 2.0 choreography language: interface or business contract? In: JOWO - Proceedings of the Joint Ontology Workshops 2017, CEUR-WS (2017)
13. Nguyen, H.N., Poizat, P., Zaïdi, F.: Automatic skeleton generation for data-aware service choreographies. In: IEEE 24th International Symposium on Software Reliability Engineering (ISSRE). IEEE, pp. 320–329 (2013)
14. Cortes-Cornax, M., Dupuy-Chessa, S., Rieu, D., Mandran, N.: Evaluating the appropriateness of the BPMN 2.0 standard for modeling service choreographies: using an extended quality framework. Softw. Syst. Model. **15**(1), 219–255 (2014). https://doi.org/10.1007/s10270-014-0398-0
15. Gómez-López, M.T., Pérez-Álvarez, J.M., Varela-Vaca, A.J., Gasca, R.M.: Guiding the creation of choreographed processes with multiple instances based on data models. In: International Conference on Business Process Management. Springer, pp. 239–251 (2016). https://doi.org/10.1007/978-3-319-58457-7_18

16. Riicker, G., Riicker, C.: Automatic enumeration of all connected subgraphs. MATCH-Commun. Math. Comput. Chem **41**, 145–149 (2000)
17. Ligęza, A.: BPMN - a logical model and property analysis. Decis. Making Manuf. Serv. **5**(1–2), 57–67 (2011)

Combining Knowledge Graphs with Semantic Similarity Metrics for Sentiment Analysis

Piotr Swędrak, Weronika T. Adrian[(✉)], and Krzysztof Kluza

AGH University of Science and Technology, al. Mickiewicza 30,
30-059 Krakow, Poland
{wta,kluza}@agh.edu.pl

Abstract. The paper proposes a new semantic similarity method with an asymmetry coefficient. The motivation behind this idea is that in some cases it is justified to break the symmetry while comparing certain entities. Such semantic similarity in some cases might be desirable from the psychological point of view. It allows us to enrich embedding methods with knowledge graphs by adding additional information about the specificity of a concept. For the evaluation of the proposed solution, the method has been used as a component for determining a sentiment of reviews. The values of the asymmetry coefficient for the selected set of chosen pairs of words were computed and compared. We present the results of series of experiments comparing the accuracy of different methods in the context of sentiment analysis in various configurations.

Keywords: Semantic similarity · Embedding methods · Knowledge graphs

1 Introduction

Concept of semantic similarity is crucial in many applications because of the increased interest in fields related to Natural Language Processing and recommendation systems. Recently, much attention has been brought to the structural representation of knowledge with use of knowledge graphs [3,10] that gather knowledge from various sources and can be of different structures and granularity. The abundance of entities that a user might be potentially interested in results in willingness to restricting this vast amount of possibilities only to those that are the best choices because of their similarity to the ones that are liked or interesting for a user.

The natural outcome of ubiquity of using semantic similarity is the a great deal of different metrics that aim to achieve the best evaluation of similarity. We can distinguish two main types of scoring semantic similarity between words: corpus-based and knowledge-based methods [6]. Corpus-based methods assess

G. Memmi et al. (Eds.): KSEM 2022, LNAI 13368, pp. 489–501, 2022.
https://doi.org/10.1007/978-3-031-10983-6_38

the similarity based on the information derived from big corpora. The knowledge-based ones use information in the form of the structured knowledge. One of the most widely used structured resource about language is a lexical database WordNet.

The goal of the presented research is to combine embedding methods and knowledge graphs to improve and enrich models for chosen problems by miti-gating shortcomings of one approach by advantages of the other. Therefore, we introduce and implement a new method with an asymmetry coefficient[1], and apply it to the sentiment analysis problem.

The paper is structured as follows. In the next section, we present some preliminaries concerning metrics and semantic similarities. Section 3 presents the description of our method. In Sect. 4, we present the comparison of the results of method application for sentiment analysis. Section 5 provides the discussion of our results. The final section summarizes the paper.

2   Preliminaries

The function f is a metric if it satisfies the following conditions for every pair of points (x, y):

– identity of indiscernibles

$$f(x, y) = 0 \iff x = y$$

– symmetry

$$f(x, y) = f(y, x)$$

– the triangle inequality

$$f(x, y) \leq f(x, z) + f(z, y)$$

Intuitively, words are similar to each other if the distance between them is small. Although the above definition requires the metric to be symmetric, Amos Tversky in [11] argues that similarity does not have to be a symmetric relation. He proposes that the similarity scale S for object A and B can be written using a non-negative scale f:

$$S(a, b) = \theta f(A \cap B) - \alpha f(A - B) - \beta f(B - A)$$

for $\theta, \alpha, \beta \geq 0$ where $A \cap B$ is a set of features shared by both A and B, $A - B$ is a set of features of A that are not present in B and $B - A$ is a set of features of B that are not present in A. In such a model, the symmetry of similarity is not necessary:

$$S(a, b) = S(b, a) \iff$$

---

[1] The repository with the implementation of our experiments is publicly available on: https://github.com/pswedrak/Embedding-Knowledge-Graphs.

$$\theta f(A \cap B) - \alpha f(A - B) - \beta f(B - A) = \theta f(B \cap A) - \alpha f(B - A) - \beta f(A - B)$$

$$S(a, b) = S(b, a) \iff -\alpha f(A - B) - \beta f(B - A) = -\alpha f(B - A) - \beta f(A - B)$$

$$S(a, b) = S(b, a) \iff (-\alpha + \beta) f(A - B) = (-\alpha + \beta) f(B - A)$$

$$S(a, b) = S(b, a) \iff (\alpha = \beta) \vee (A = B)$$

Let us define two types of similarity tasks:

- non-directional ($\alpha = \beta$), this indicates how much objects a and b are similar
- directional ($\alpha \neq \beta$), this indicates how much the object a is similar to b

In general, in case of the directional similarity the relation does not have to be symmetric.

3   Description of the Proposed Method

Our proposed method takes into consideration the degree of specificity of given concepts. In order to be able to differentiate levels of specificity we build a tree of concepts using the knowledge graph called WordNet. This step is inspired by the paper [1] but instead of using this graph to directly compute semantic similarity, we use it to examine the depth of a concept in the graph. For our further considerations, it is necessary to introduce the following concepts:

- hypernym – a word whose meaning includes the meaning of a more specific word, so "pet" is the hypernym of "dog",
- hyponym – a word whose meaning is included in the meaning of another more general word, so "dog" is the hyponym of "pet",
- meronym – a term used to denote a thing that it is a part of, so the "eye" is the meronym of "face",
- holonym – a term that denotes a whole whose part is denoted by another term, so the "face" is the holonym of "eye".

In the following subsections, we describe the method in details.

3.1   Creating the Concept Graph

We start by inserting a root node which is the most generic concept in the taxonomy. For every concept $c \in s(w_1) \cup s(w_2)$ where w_1 and w_2 are input words and s denotes all senses of a word we recursively add hypernyms on the path from c to the root. We use WordNet to find senses and hypernyms of words. Then, for every concept $c \in s(w_1) \cup s(w_2)$ where w_1 we create $hyp(c)$ which is the set of all direct hyponyms of c. Then, we insert to the graph every concept $h \in hyp$. Subsequently, we perform the same actions for meronyms and holonyms.

3.2   Computing the Asymmetry Coefficient

Let us now introduce the α (asymmetry) coefficient in order to implement the asymmetry in similarity.

$$asim(a, b) = sim(a, b) + \alpha$$

$$asim - \text{asymmetric similarity}$$

$$sim - \text{similarity}$$

$$\alpha = \frac{dist_a - dist_b}{dist_{lch}}$$

$dist_a$ – The average distance from the root to the concepts of a

$dist_b$ – The average distance from the root to the concepts of b

$dist_{lch}$ – The distance from the root to the lowest common hypernym of a and b

3.3   Explanation with an Example

Let us observe a visualization of the concept graph constructed for the pair of words: *psychology* and *discipline* in Fig. 1.

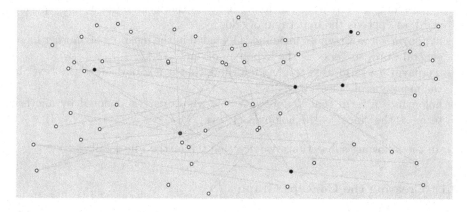

Fig. 1. Visualization of a graph created for words *psychology* and *discipline*

For the visibility purposes the labels of nodes were hidden, but they are visible when the user hovers the mouse pointer over the node. The red node is the only sense of the *psychology* in the knowledge base, the black nodes are senses of *discipline*.

Let us now calculate the asymmetry coefficient:

– $dist_a = 8$ - The average distance from the root to the concepts of *psychology*

- $dist_b = 4$ - The average distance from the root to the concepts of *discipline*
- $dist_{lch} = 3$ - The distance from the root to the lowest common hypernym that is *cognition*

$$\alpha = \frac{dist_a - dist_b}{dist_{lch}} = \frac{8 - 4}{3} \approx 1.33$$

The asymmetry coefficient is bigger that 0 which means that *psychology* is supposed to be more specific entity that *discipline* which is consistent with the common intuition.

3.4   Observations over Selected Pairs of Words

The asymmetry coefficient has been computed for the selected set of pairs of words derived from the WordSim-353 and SimLex-999 datasets.

```
tiger cat -0.2222222222222222 6.474888920783997
media radio -0.8 5.733585953712463
money cash -0.16666666666666666 8.412792086601257
magician wizard 0.0 5.971980094909668
food fruit -1.5 6.110004782676697
bird cock -0.2 3.681226074695587
money dollar 0.16666666666666666 7.003531455993652
tiger animal -0.25 4.9998050928115845
tiger organism 0 1.7651548981666565
psychology science 1.0 8.005320429801941
psychology discipline 1.3333333333333333 4.589941203594208
cup object 1.5 1.745162457227707
hospital infrastructure 1.0 2.3060832917690277
phone equipment -0.2 3.192112147808075
liquid water 0.3333333333333333 6.573084592819214
seafood food 0.5 6.669999957084656
lobster food 1.5 5.389065742492676
man governor -0.6 2.8041106462478638
aluminum metal 0.3333333333333333 5.0359392166137695
book text -0.3333333333333333 4.94172602891922
alcohol brandy -0.4 2.9130783677101135
book bible -0.3333333333333333 6.757094860076904
winter season 0.25 6.21617317199707
alcohol gin -0.4 3.902214765548706
father parent 0.0 6.519390940666199
parent adult 0.25 4.9013859033584595
metal aluminum -0.3333333333333333 5.0359392166137695
lens camera -0.2857142857142857 6.777362823486328
meal dinner -0.25 8.077412843704224
wall brick -0.5 5.993028283119202
```

```
noise rattle -0.25 4.0961554646492
beer beverage 0 5.651609301567078
man uncle -0.75 5.1382410526275635
bird turkey 0.0 3.6010897159576416
sandwich lunc 0 1.7489011585712433
```

We performed experiments in order to compare different method of determining the sentiment of a text. We examined the accuracy of different methods and their combination in order to find out if it is possible to achieve better results by combining machine learning and knowledge graphs approaches. In the primary experiments, we differentiate two kinds of sentiment – positive and negative. In additional experiments, we introduce the neutral label as well.

4   Comparison of Results for Sentiment Analysis

In order to compute the embedded vectors we used the subset of Yelp Open Dataset. It consists of information about businesses, reviews and users for personal, educational and academic purposes[2]. The whole dataset includes more than 8 million reviews and 200 thousand pictures for approximately 160 thousand businesses in 8 metropolitan areas in the United States.

The dataset has a form of JSON files. The most interesting one in terms of these experiments, the review.json file, contains a collection of reviews as a text data containing:

- review id (22 characters)
- user id (22 characters) that maps to the user data in user.json
- business id (22 characters) that map to the business data in business.json
- number of stars (from 1 to 5)
- date (in format YYYY-MM-DD)
- the review
- number of received "useful votes"
- number of received "funny votes"
- number of received "cool votes"

What is crucial for these experiments is that every review is associated with the number of stars that assesses the quality of the business. This number is in range 1–5, where 1 is the most negative opinion and 5 is the most positive one. We assume that reviews with 1 or 2 stars are negative while the reviews with 4 or 5 stars are positive.

Due to the heavy computational requirements the 2000 reviews were chosen in order to perform experiments. The reviews were split into two datasets: the training one and the test one. The training dataset contains 1500 reviews, the test dataset contains 500 reviews.

---

[2] See: https://www.yelp.com/dataset.

4.1   Simon Vector

In the process of computing the Similarity-based sentiment projection (SIMON) vector, we receive a two-dimensional matrix (see Fig. 2). On the y-axis we can find lexicon words derived from the dataset that have been used to score the sentiment. On x-axis there are all tokens from the document. Such matrix is computed for every document in the dataset. The vector for the document is obtained by applying the pooling function column-wise (see Fig. 3 and 4).

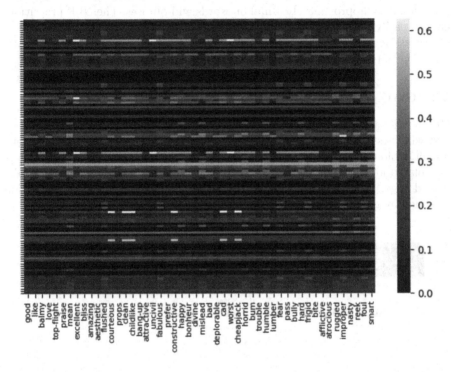

Fig. 2. Example of the SIMON matrix

Fig. 3. The SIMON vector obtained by applying the max function

4.2 Word2Vec

Word2Vec is one of the popular techniques that is employed for the improvement of the outcomes of the model is exploiting the pre-trained embedded vectors that were obtained by being trained with the use of the computational power that is unavailable for the ordinary user. It allows to take much more data into account which usually results in achieving better accuracy.

The popular pre-trained word vectors are published by Google. The model [2] was trained on the subset of Google News dataset (100 billion words). It contains embeddings of approximately 3 million words and phrases. The NLP practitioners can easily obtain those vectors with the use of the gensim downloader. It is also possible to train the model on your own corpus using the gensim library, analogously to the Doc2Vec model.

4.3 GloVe

GloVe (Global Vectors) method [7] aims to mitigate the drawbacks of local context windows models, e.g. Word2Vec. They perform well on many tasks but they do not exploit the global statistics of a corpus since the models are trained only on isolated local contexts. Similarly to Wor2Vec, we used the pre-trained GloVe embeddings [8], as it is possible to train the model using the implementation provided by the Stanford University.

Fig. 4. The SIMON vector obtained by applying the mean function

4.4 Doc2Vec

Doc2Vec [5] (Paragraph Vector) is an algorithm that is conceptually similar to Word2Vec but instead of learning embedded representations of words we focus on longer fragments of texts such as sentences or whole documents. For Doc2Vec embeddings, we used the gensim [9] library. The Doc2Vec model in this library requires a few parameters (for other parameters we use the default values):

- documents – the list (or an iterable) of the documents from the dataset
- vector size – the dimensions of the embedded vector (100)
- window – the biggest allowed distance between the context and predicted word (3)
- minimal count – the model takes into consideration words that occur in the dataset at least that many times (1)

4.5   Classification with a Feed-Forward Neural Network and LSTM

For classification, the neural network model has been used. It has been implemented in the keras library (see the summary in Fig. 5). In every experiment the model was trained during 100 epochs.

The model exploits the binary cross-entropy loss as there are just two classes in the problem: positive and negative. It is defined as [4]:

$$J = -\frac{1}{M} \sum_{m=1}^{M} [y_m log(h_\theta(x_m)) + (1 - y_m)log(1 - h_\theta(x_m)]$$

where M − the number of training examples , y_m − the correct label,

x_m − the training example (input) , h_θ − the neural network model.

4.6   Results

Every model was trained 10 times and the accuracy in Table 1 is the mean of achieved results.

```
Model: "sequential"
```

Layer (type)	Output Shape	Param #
dense (Dense)	(None, 100)	10100
dense_1 (Dense)	(None, 50)	5050
dense_2 (Dense)	(None, 2)	102

```
Total params: 15,252
Trainable params: 15,252
Non-trainable params: 0
```

Fig. 5. Summary of the classification model.

Moreover, the LSTM models were trained for 16 epochs as they are more computationally demanding and training them requires more time than training ordinary feed-forward neural networks but it does not affect the LSTM model negatively as values of the loss function decrease very fast in initial epochs. The summary of the LSTM model is presented in Fig. 6.

```
Model: "sequential"
_____
Layer (type)                 Output Shape              Param #
=================================================================
embedding (Embedding)        (None, 100, 128)          12800

spatial_dropout1d (SpatialDr (None, 100, 128)          0

lstm (LSTM)                  (None, 196)               254800

dense (Dense)                (None, 2)                 394
=================================================================
Total params: 267,994
Trainable params: 267,994
Non-trainable params: 0
```

Fig. 6. Summary of the LSTM model

4.7 Introducing the Asymmetry Coefficient

In this experiment we included the asymmetry coefficient while computing the semantic similarity for SIMON vectors (Table 2).

Table 1. The mean accuracy on the training and test data for the models

Method	Accuracy on the training data	Accuracy on the test data
(pre-trained) Word2Vec	100%	88.73%
(pre-trained) GloVe	100%	87.72%
Word2Vec	75.31%	75.44%
GloVe	100%	86.67%
Doc2Vec	75.31%	75.45%
SIMON	75.50%	73.24%
(pre-trained) Word2Vec + SIMON	98.97%	89.91%
(pre-trained) GloVe + SIMON	99.39%	87.68%
Word2Vec + SIMON	75.64%	73.46%
GloVe + SIMON	75.31%	75.44%
Doc2Vec + SIMON	76.08%	73.73%
LSTM	100%	87.77%
LSTM for SIMON	74.78%	75.44%

Table 2. The mean accuracy on the training and test data for the SIMON models

Method	Accuracy on the training data	Accuracy on the test data
SIMON	75.50%	73.24%
SIMON with the asymmetry coefficient	75.39%	**75.31%**

4.8   Introducing the Neutral Class

In this experiment (Table 3), we attempt to introduce the third class of reviews – the neutral one. In the YELP dataset we may associate these reviews with reviews that achieved 3 stars from the user. For computing SIMON vectors we use words that have zero scores of positive and negative features according to the SentiWordNet.

5   Discussion

The first conclusion is that the pre-trained vectors allow to achieve much better results in comparison to the word vectors that were trained on the subset of our dataset. This is because the word vectors that can be found on the Internet were trained on huge datasets using resources that are not available for a single user. What is interesting, the difference in accuracy varies in case of Word2Vec and GloVe. Pre-trained Word2Vec is better by above 13% points than non-pre-trained vectors while pre-trained GloVe is better by approximately only one percentage point.

Table 3. The mean accuracy on the training and test data for the models

Method	Accuracy on the training data	Accuracy on the test data
(pre-trained) Word2Vec	100%	77.52%
(pre-trained) GloVe	99.99%	76.62%
Word2Vec	67.93%	67.6 %
GloVe	100%	75.54%
Doc2Vec	67.91%	67.6%
SIMON	68.05%	65.36%
(pre-trained) Word2Vec + SIMON	93.7%	79.52%
(pre-trained) GloVe + SIMON	95.33%	77.1%
Word2Vec + SIMON	68.01%	66.04%
GloVe + SIMON	67.93%	67.6%
Doc2Vec + SIMON	68.6%	65.86%

The SIMON method of creating word vectors seems to be the least effective which is quite intuitive because we use far less data when compared to machine learning models. Even though the knowledge base that is used to compute semantic similarity for SIMON is big, we use only a small part of it while computing a similarity score for a single pair. Even though the SIMON method itself cannot be used to build a very accurate model, it contributes to the small improvement of pre-trained Word2Vec and GloVe models. We achieve the best results when we build a model concatenating pre-trained Word2Vec and SIMON vectors. This might be a result of adding some new data from WordNet to the word vectors.

One experiment involved classification with the use of Long short-term memory (LSTM) model. We can notice an improvement when we use this architecture because even though we train it on our dataset we achieve accuracy that is comparable with the results obtained with the use of pre-trained vectors. This method is definitely worthy of attention when planning further experiments.

The important experiment was connected with introducing the asymmetry coefficient for the SIMON method. The SIMON technique uses the semantic similarity computation so if it is changed we can affect the accuracy of this method. The experiment shows that we can increase the accuracy on the test data by 2% points when we introduce the asymmetry coefficient. The possible explanation for this is that we include more data from the WordNet knowledge base because the semantic similarity metric uses different parts of knowledge contained in WordNet than the method that we use to compute the asymmetry coefficient.

The final experiments aimed to include the neutral class representing reviews that were not scored neither very positively nor negatively. One can notice a decrease in accuracy when we take into consideration the neutral class. The reduction of accuracy approximately amounts to 10% points. This is connected with the problem that purely neutral reviews are very rare. The strength of opinion and degree of positivity or negativity of the review may vary but they are usually closer to the positive or negative label than the neutral one.

6   Conclusions

In this paper, we introduced a new semantic similarity method. The key contribution is introducing the asymmetry coefficient in order to break the symmetry while computing the semantic similarity as in some cases it is desirable from the psychological point of view. It allows us to enrich embedding methods with knowledge graphs by adding additional information about the specificity of a concept. We presented the results of series of experiments comparing the accuracy of different methods in the context of sentiment analysis in various configurations.

The future work might involve developing different ways of computing the asymmetry coefficient in semantic similarity methods. For the time being, we support the different level of specificity as a basis for the asymmetry but there are other possibilities that can be explored. For example it could be an interesting idea to take into consideration the popularity or prominence of concepts.

References

1. Alvarez, M.A., Lim, S.: A graph modeling of semantic similarity between words. In: International Conference on Semantic Computing (ICSC 2007), pp. 355–362. IEEE (2007)
2. Google: Pre-trained word2vec embeddings. https://code.google.com/archive/p/word2vec/
3. Gutierrez, C., Sequeda, J.F.: Knowledge graphs. Commun. ACM **64**(3), 96–104 (2021)
4. Ho, Y., Wookey, S.: The real-world-weight cross-entropy loss function: modeling the costs of mislabeling. IEEE Access **8**, 4806–4813 (2019)
5. Le, Q., Mikolov, T.: Distributed representations of sentences and documents. In: International Conference on Machine Learning, pp. 1188–1196 (2014)
6. Mihalcea, R., Corley, C., Strapparava, C., et al.: Corpus-based and knowledge-based measures of text semantic similarity. In: AAAI 2006: Proceedings of the 21st National Conference on Artificial Intelligence, vol. 1, pp. 775–780 (2006)
7. Pennington, J., Socher, R., Manning, C.D.: Glove: global vectors for word representation. In: Proceedings of the 2014 Conference on Empirical Methods in Natural Language Processing (EMNLP), pp. 1532–1543 (2014)
8. Pennington, J., Socher, R., Manning, C.D.: Glove: global vectors for word representation. https://nlp.stanford.edu/projects/glove/
9. Řehůřek, R., Sojka, P.: Software framework for topic modelling with large corpora. In: Proceedings of the LREC 2010 Workshop on New Challenges for NLP Frameworks, pp. 45–50. ELRA, Valletta, Malta (2010)
10. Slimani, T.: Description and evaluation of semantic similarity measures approaches. arXiv preprint arXiv:1310.8059 (2013)
11. Tversky, A.: Features of similarity. Psychol. Rev. **84**(4), 327 (1977)

Enhanced Simple Question Answering with Contrastive Learning

Xin Wang[1] , Lan Yang[2], Honglian He[1]([⊠]), Yu Fang[1], Huayi Zhan[2],
and Ji Zhang[3]

[1] Southwest Petroleum University, Chengdu, China
{xinwang,fangyu}@swpu.edu.cn, 202121000475@stu.swpu.edu.cn
[2] Sichuan Changhong Electric Co. Ltd, Mianyang, China
{lan.yang,huayi.zhan}@changhong.com
[3] University of Southern Queensland, Toowoomba, Australia
Ji.Zhang@usq.edu.cn

Abstract. Answer natural language questions on knowledge bases
(KBQA) has attracted wide attention. Several techniques have been
developed for answering *simple questions*. These techniques mostly rely
on deep networks to perform classification for relation prediction. Nowadays, contrastive learning has shown its powers in improving performances of classification, while most prior techniques do not gain benefit
from this. In light of these, we propose a novel approach to answering simple questions on knowledge bases. Our approach has two key
features. (1) It leverages pre-trained transformers to gain better performance on entity linking. (2) It employs a contrastive learning based
model for relation prediction. We experimentally verify the performance
of our approach, and show that our approach achieves an accuracy of
83.54%, which beats existing state-of-the-art techniques, on a typical
benchmark dataset; we also conduct a deep analysis to show advantages
of our technique, especially its sub-modules.

Keywords: Knowledge base · Question answering · Contrastive
learning · Transfer learning · Pre-trained model

1 Introduction

In our society today, there is an unprecedented proliferation of knowledge bases
(KBs), *e.g.,* Freebase [4], YAGO [34], DBPedia [21], etc. Due to massive coverage
of knowledge, these knowledge bases have been come to an important semantic
database for supporting open domain question answering (QA).

Knowledge in KBs is typically organized in a structured manner, *e.g.,* RDF,
hence searches on KBs, that are performed via query languages, are not friendly
for end-users, since people not only need to master a query language but also
familiar with the structure and relations of the underlying knowledge base. In
practice, a KBQA system should automatically translate a natural language

© The Author(s), under exclusive license to Springer Nature Switzerland AG 2022
G. Memmi et al. (Eds.): KSEM 2022, LNAI 13368, pp. 502–515, 2022.
https://doi.org/10.1007/978-3-031-10983-6_39

question (or a fragment thereof) posed by users into a structured query (e.g. SPARQL), and find answers by querying a knowledge base. This calls for effective techniques to search KBs for natural language questions. While the scale of the data and the difficulty for question understanding leads to KBQA problem a challenging task.

Most existing KBQA systems are neural-network (NN) based, whose performance highly relies on the quantity and quality of the training data. While it is often difficult to obtain such training data, due to high labor cost. To answer simple questions, a key challenge is the relation prediction, *i.e.*, find the correct predicate (*a.k.a.* relation) from a knowledge base based on the given subject. This task mostly resolved via classification models. However, existing models rarely incorporate contrastive learning, which shows superior performance for classification. In addition, fine-tuned pre-trained models have shown effectiveness in improving performances of downstream tasks [13,20,23,26].

Motivated by these, we propose an approach to answering simple questions on KBs. Our approach leverages pre-trained models for entity linking and constrastive learning for relation prediction and gain superior performance on one typical benchmark dataset `SimpleQuestions` [6]. This shows that our approach yields a promising technique for QA systems.

Contributions. The contributions of the paper are listed as follows.

- We introduce a comprehensive technique for entity linking. The technique consists of two components, one for span detection and the other one for entity linking. For span detection, a model that integrates a pre-trained transformer is developed. The entity linking is performed via a *level-wise* searching strategy.
- We introduce an approach for relation prediction. The approach relies on two networks and works in pipeline. The first network, which leverages pre-trained transformer, implements a classification model to identify candidate relation. Based on the candidate relation, a contrastive learning-based model is developed for relation prediction.
- We perform a thorough evaluation of our proposed approach, compared with typical state-of-the-art methods. We show that our approach beats most existing techniques in sub-tasks and outperforms the state-of-the-art methods in question answering. This shows the power of our approach that is boosted by contrastive learning and transfer learning.

Organization. The remainder of the paper is organized as follows. We review related works in Sect. 2 and introduce preliminary information in Sect. 3. In Sect. 4, we illustrate details of our approach. Experimental studies in Sect. 5 demonstrate the overall performance of our approach. Section 6 concludes the paper.

2   Related Work

We categorize prior works *w.r.t.* KBQA into three types: Semantic Parsing (SP-based) [2,3,8,15,32,35,38], Information Retrieval (IR-based) [5–7,37] and Neural Network-based (NN-based) [11,14,16,18,23–25,29,30,33,39,40,42]. We also revisit contrastive learning due to its importance.

SP-Based. Semantic Parser usually translates a natural language question into a logical form like CCG (combinatory categorial grammar) [8,32], "λ-DCS" [3], SQL [35] and other formal queries [15], which can be executed to retrieval the answer. The main challenge of the semantic parsing is how to match a natural language phrase to predicates in the logical form. [2] adopts a learning-to-rank methodology to match an input question with a SPARQL query according to the predefined patterns. [38] uses a staged search method to generate a query graph and search the knowledge base in an early stage to reduce candidate list. By applying an advanced entity linking system and a deep convolutional neural network model that matches question and query graph, [38] achieves a new state-of-the-art result on a typical dataset. However, these methods still relied on lexical triggers or manually defined features.

IR-Based. This type of technique first generates candidate entities from the KB according to the topic entity of a given question. Then scoring or ranking methods are introduced to select answers by calculating the information extracted from both question and candidate answers. [37] first represents questions and answers by the dependency parser and Freebase structure respectively and then calculates the association between question features and answer features. They also introduce CluewebMapping which is used to calculate how likely one relation maps to the original question. Some other works [5–7] learn the distributed embedding of the question and answer by mapping them to the low dimensional space and then calculate the correlation score. The candidate answer with a higher score is more likely to be the right answer.

NN-Based. The procedure of NN-based methods can be split into two successive sub-processes: candidate generation and answer filtering. Moreover, pretrained models are also involved.

Candidate Generation. Many works first identify the topic entity and initialize a candidate list with entities (along with their relations) around the topic entity in a knowledge base (KB). They then use a substring of the question, which we call mention, to match entities in the KB. The substring can be generated by *e.g.,* sequence labeling techniques (*e.g.,* CRF [30,39], and chunk). The main challenge of this task is that there may exist excessive entities with the same name. Then Extra information associated with entities is introduced to narrow down the candidate list [24].

Answer Filtering. The key issue is the representation of the question and answer pair as well as the calculation of their similarity score. [14] used multi-column CNN to represent questions from three aspects, *i.e.,* the path, context, and type of an answer. Inspired by [14], some attention-based neural networks were introduced to represent words in a question by using different attention of each aspect of the candidate answer [30]. Since questions can be answered according to the topic entity and relation path, some works convert the answer selection process

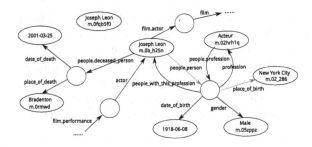

Fig. 1. A subgraph centered at "Joseph Leon" in Freebase

into a relation matching task. For example, [40] introduced BiLSTM to represent question and candidate relations. Some other works try to match the question with candidate facts, *e.g.*, [16] introduces CNNs to learn the representation of the question and candidate tuples; [39] uses two different levels of CNNs to represent the distribution of subject-mention pair and predicate-question pattern pair. Analogous to [39], GRU [24] and LSTM [18] are used to encode the question-entity and question-predicate pair. [29] applied a global-local attentive relation detection model to consider local semantic information on interaction cases between questions and relations sequences. [42] utilized an attention neural network fused with structural features to rank candidate facts jointly.

Transformer Networks. Transformer networks, *e.g.*, BERT [13], have been proposed and shown advantages in improving performances of downstream tasks. To show how well BERT performs for KBQA, [23] introduces BERT-based models for entity span detection and relation prediction. [25] uses a BERT-based model with relation-aware attention to preserve the original interaction information between a question and its candidate facts. [33] employs BERT to embed a question along with its context information, and uses the embedding for the answer prediction. [11] proposed a general model with relation reasoning capability to score the predicates through an attention mechanism. Observe that [23] trains a single model to cope with two subtasks in a single pass; [33] just follows an end-to-end manner without considering subtasks. On the contrary, our approach handles KBQA problem by solving inherent subtasks separately, which eases the understanding and tuning of the models and achieves even better performances. We are not aware any prior work in this direction.

Contrastive Learning. Contrastive learning is a kind of self-supervised learning. Its core idea is to shorten the distance between positive samples and anchor samples in the vector representation space, and widen the distance between negative samples and anchor samples. Contrastive learning was first applied in computer vision(CV), *e.g.*, [10,17,19]. The idea was then borrowed by people from field of natural language processing (NLP). They leverage contrastive learning into language model pre-training, e.g. BERT-CT [9] and IS-BERT [41]. There exists a few works in KBQA. Jinfeng Rao et al. [31] developed a model for answer selection. The model applied a pairwise ranking method, based on

Noise-Contrastive Estimation (NCE) for model training. To further improve the ranking performance for QA pairs, Deng et al. [12] introduced a ranking technique by leveraging generation-augmented contrastive data. The ERICA [28] framework proposed by Qin et al. boosts contrastive learning to improve the performance of pre-trained models. Inspired by [12,28,31], we incorporate contrastive learning as well as fine-tuned pre-trained models to rank entity-relation pairs and obtain optimal answers to ensure KBQA performance.

3   Preliminaries

In this section, we introduce preliminary information.

Knowledge Base. Let $\mathcal{E}$ denote a set of entities (*e.g.*, Joseph Leon), and $\mathcal{P}$ denote a set of predicates (*e.g.*, people.person.place_of_birth). Then the knowledge base consists of a collection of subject-predicate-object triples (e_1, p, e_2), where $e_1, e_2 \in \mathcal{E}$ are the entities that refer to subject and object, respectively, and $p \in \mathcal{P}$ is a predicate. A knowledge base can also be represented as a graph G, *i.e.*, each entity can be viewed as a node, and two related entities are connected by a directed edge labeled with the predicate. Then, we can denote a knowledge base as a knowledge graph and use the terms interchangeably.

In this work, we use Freebase [4] as our knowledge base, since it is a large-scale knowledge base consisting of numerous general facts. In Freebase, each fact represents a relationship between two entities. For example, the fact ⟨Joseph Leon, people.person.place_of_birth, New York City⟩ tells us that a person named as "Joseph Leon" was born in "New York City", where the predicate has the same semantic as the relation "born in". Figure 1 shows a fraction of Freebase centered at "Joseph Leon". Nodes are the entities with a unique identifier (id), and directed edges indicate the relation between two entities, labeled by a predicate.

Questions. The benchmark of simple QA task, *i.e.*, SimpleQuestions[6] is used as our question set. Though being easier to handle than questions with multiple relations, answering single-relation questions is still far from being solved. The difficulty lies in the mapping from a question to a particular predicate as well as an entity in a KB (see example above).

Problem Formulation. The task of simple QA over KB can be put more formally as follows. Let G be a background knowledge graph represented as a set of triples (e_i, p, e_j). Given a natural language question represented as a sequence of words $Q = \{w_1, \cdots, w_T\}$, the task of simple QA is to find the right triple (s, p, o) from G such that o is the intended answer for Q.

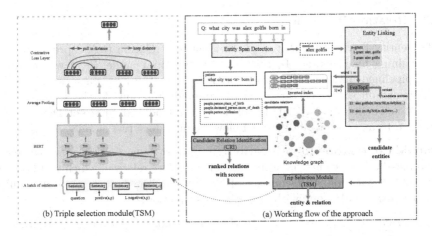

Fig. 2. Overall architecture

4 An Approach

In this section, we introduce our approach. The overall architecture of our approach, shown in Fig. 2, consists of two main modules, *i.e.*, entity linking module and relation prediction module. Below, we illustrate each of them with details.

4.1 Entity Linking

The task works in two stages, *i.e.*, entity span detection and entity linking.

Entity Span Detection. Before entity linking, an entity span (entity mention or mention m_e for short) needs to be detected for a question Q. To this end, we develop a model SDM, which achieves high performance by combining BERT [13] with BiLSTM and CRF. The network follows a standard training procedure of most deep networks for the span detection task.

Entity Linking. Given a mention m_e, the task of entity linking is to identify the best entity from a KB, that can semantically "match" m_e. While the ambiguity brings a big challenge for the task. Hence, we develop an entity linking module (ELM) for the task. The core part of module ELM is the algorithm EntityLink, which works as follows. Given an entity mention m_e, EntityLink generates a set $\mathcal{S}$ of sub-strings of m_e by following n-gram model. It next iteratively identifies candidate entities by using $\mathcal{S}$, an inverted index and the procedure EvaTopE. Note that the inverted index maintains the $\langle$key, value$\rangle$ pairs, where the key s_k refers to the name (resp. alias) of an entity, and the value is a set of entities including s_k as a part of its name (resp. alias). The procedure EvaTopE simply identifies entities whose name (resp. alias) is similar to a string in $\mathcal{S}$.

4.2   Relation Prediction

After entity linking, one still needs to identify a relation (*a.k.a.* predicate) for determining final answer. To this end, we develop a model RPM which works in a pipelined manner for relation prediction. In the first stage, a sub-model CRI is introduced to generate a set of candidate relation. At the second stage, a contrastive learning based model TSM is introduced to select the optimal relation, from a set of candidates. Below we introduce two models, one by one.

Candidate Relation Identification. In contrast to most techniques that select relations directly, we first identify a set of candidate relation, which will be used for further selection. CRI consists of a BERT as the base layer and a fully-connected-network along with a special loss function.

Task-Oriented Input. According to the specific task (relation prediction), CRI customizes the input (training data) as follows. It masks the entity mention in a question sentence with a special symbol, *e.g.,* <e>, and generates an input pattern that combines the masked question sentence along with a candidate relation. For example, given the question "what city was joseph leon born in", it is firstly masked as "what city was <e> born in" by replacing the entity mention joseph leon with <e>, and then associated with a candidate relation, *e.g.,* "people.person.place_of_birth", thereby forming an input pattern $Pat_Q = \langle$what city was <e> born in, people.person.place_of_birth$\rangle$.

Sampling Strategy. For model training, we introduce a sampling strategy to generate the training data, *i.e.,* patterns. Specifically, for a question Q and a mention m_e appeared in Q, we extract a set of relations, where each of them forms a triple of G with a candidate entity in C_s (a set that includes candidate entities of m_e and is produced by EntityLink). We then pick L_1 relations as *negative samples* and produce a new set of patterns Pat_Q for Q. This process is performed for each question and the patterns generated are used for model training. The rationale behind the strategy is that the newly selected *negative samples* are more close to the correct relation, thus learning from these samples may bring the model even higher resolving power.

Loss Function. Loss functions often have an impact on model performance and training procedure. In addition, training data used by CRI exhibit an imbalance in positive/negative and easy/hard samples, which may also influence model performance. Taking this into consideration, we applied an α-balanced variant of the focal loss [22] as the loss function to resolve the unbalanced distribution of positive/negative as well as easy/hard samples. The function is defined as follows:

$$FL = \begin{cases} -\alpha(1-p)^\gamma \, log(p), & if \; y = 1, \\ -(1-\alpha)p^\gamma \, log(1-p), & if \; y = 0. \end{cases} \tag{1}$$

Here, $y \in \{1, 0\}$ specifies the ground-truth class and $p \in [0, 1]$ is the model's estimated probability for the class with label $y = 1$. The parameter α is introduced to adjust the imbalance between positive/negative samples. While the parameter γ is used for smoothly adjusting the rate at which easy examples are down-weighted.

Triple Selection Model. Given a set of candidate relation, we develop a triplet selection model (TSM) to choose the best relation. The module adopts the idea of contrastive learning to select the best (s, p). As shown in Fig. 2(b), TSM consists of a BERT as the base layer, an average pooling and an infoNCE loss layer. Below, we show key features of the model.

Model Input. According to the specific task (triple selection), TSM customizes the input (training data) along the same line as CRI. For each question in the training data, it is associated with a positive sample (s, p) and L_2 pairs as negative samples. The entities and relationship in the positive and negative samples are the data inferred earlier. Ultimately, TSM selects the most similar (s, p) pairs for the question.

InfoNCE Loss. The infoNCE loss is used as the contrastive loss layer. The purpose for incorporating infoNCE is to draw the question Q closer to the positive sample, and keep distances from the negative samples. The function is defined as follows:

$$Loss^{infoNCE} = -log\frac{exp(Sim(Q, (s, p)^+)/\tau)}{\sum_{i=0}^{L} exp(Sim(Q, (s, p))/\tau)} \tag{2}$$

Here, $Sim(Q, (s, p))$ represents the dot product of Q and (s, p) pairs. $(s, p)^+$ is the positive sample (s,p) pair. L represents the number of negative samples. We set the hyper-parameter τ of infoNCE to 0.05.

5   Experimental Studies

5.1   Settings

Implementation and Dataset. We start from implementation and dataset used.

Model Implementation. Our models are built on the small uncased pre-trained BERT model. They were implemented in Keras v2.2.5 with CUDA 9.0 running on an NVIDIA Tesla P100 GPU. For Levenshtein Distance, we used the process function in the "fuzzywuzzy" python package.

Knowledge Base. We used FB2M, which is a subset of Freebase and contains $2, 150, 604$ entities, $6, 701$ predicates, and $14, 180, 937$ atomic facts, as the underlying knowledge base.

Questions. We used SimpleQuestions [6] for the KBQA task. The question set contains $108, 442$ question/answer pairs, where all the answers were manually annotated using facts of FB2M. We split the question set into three parts, *i.e.*, training, validation and testing, which account for $75, 910$, $10, 845$ and $21, 687$, respectively. We removed 431 questions from the test set, since either these questions contain unseen entities in FB2M or mentions (subjects) of these questions have

Table 1. Performance comparisons

Approaches	Tasks (%)		
	ELM ($R@k$)	RPM ($R@k$)	System (Acc)
Bordes et al. 2015 [6]	-	-	63.9
Lukovnikov et al. 2017 [24]	91.8	-	71.2
Mohammed et al. 2018 [27]	93.1	82.8	74.9
Yin et al. 2016 [39]	91.6	-	76.4
Lukovnikov et al. 2019 [23]	95.2	83.5	77.3
Qu et al. 2018 [30]	95.8	73.7	77.9
Yu et al. 2016 [40]	-	-	78.7
Vishal et al. 2018 [16]	-	-	80.0
Hao et al. 2018 [18]	-	-	80.2
Wang et al. 2018 [36]	-	-	81.5
Luo et al. 2020 [25]	**97.1**	-	80.9
Qiu et al. 2021 [29]	-	-	81.3
Cheng et al.2020 [11]	-	-	82.3
Zhang et al. 2021 [42]	-	-	82.9
Ours	96.4	**95.91**	**83.54**

very different surface format with corresponding GT subjects, which brings a big challenge for entity linking (see [1] for the list of removed questions). Then, the test set contains $21,256$ questions, in total.

Evaluation Metrics. We define the following metric to measure the accuracy of the predicted results.

$$\mathsf{Acc} = \frac{\sum_{i=1}^{N} h(\hat{w}, w)}{N}. \tag{3}$$

Here, N indicates the size of the question set; $\hat{w}$ and w refers to the predicted results and ground truth (abbr. GT) results of a question Q, respectively; function $h(\cdot)$ takes $\hat{w}$ and w as input, and evaluates whether $\hat{w}$ and w are equivalent not, i.e., $h(\hat{w}, w) = 1$ if $\hat{w} = w$, and $h(\hat{w}, w) = 0$, otherwise.

Performance of the System. Following the measurement proposed by [6], the predicted answer (object) is correct *if* the subject, the relationship (predicate) and the object are predicted correctly, simultaneously. Thus, $\hat{w}$ and w are two triples $(\hat{s}, \hat{p}, \hat{o})$ and (s, p, o), and $h(\hat{w}, w) = 1$ if $\hat{s} = s$, $\hat{p} = p$ and $\hat{o} = o$.

Performance of Sub-modules. (1) We evaluate recall (denoted as $R@k$) of ELM and RPM with top-k strategy, *i.e.*, whether the correct answer appears in the k top-ranked results that are predicted. For entity linking, the predicted answer $\hat{w}$ refers to an entity (as subject) $\hat{s}$, and $h(\hat{w}, w) = 1$ if $\hat{s}$ is the same as the GT subject s. For relation prediction, the predicted answer $\hat{w}$ is a pair $(\hat{s}, \hat{p})$ such that $h(\hat{w}, w) = 1$ if $\hat{s} = s$ and $\hat{p} = p$, *i.e.*, the predicted relation $\hat{p}$ equals to the

GT predicate, and moreover the subject $\hat{s}$ associated on $\hat{p}$ is also the same as the GT entity s. This metric turns to accuracy, when $k = 1$. (2) We also evaluate the accuracy, denoted as Acc_{RPM}, of the sub-module RPM by varying L, i.e., the amount of negative samples used for model training.

Baseline Methods. We used a list of models [6,11,16,18,23–25,27,29,30,36, 39,40,42] as baseline methods, for performance comparison.

5.2   Results and Analysis

System Assessment. We perform a comprehensive experimental studies to show performances of our approach.

Overall Accuracy. As shown in Table 1, the overall accuracy of our approach reaches 83.54%, which ranks the top among all baseline methods. This shows the superior performance of our approach. Though [11,42] report similar overall accuracy as ours, they do not show their capability for dealing with sub-tasks, i.e., entity linking and relation prediction. This brings trouble to the interpretation and evaluation of underlying networks. In addition, [36] uses a relation filter to filter invalid relations. This filter strategy essentially simulates the searching mechanism, by using a lookup table. In the table, a set of candidate relations are stored, where the GT relation is in place. While, this can not guaranteed happen in practice.

Performances of Sub-modules. We also evaluate performances of our sub-modules ELM and RPM, by comparing their recalls to the baseline methods. As different methods used different k to show its influence on $R@k$. To ease comparison, we choose the largest $R@k$ for each method, and report the results in Table 1. As is shown, only [23–25,27,30,39] reported performances of their entity linking sub-modules, and [23,27,30] exhibits recalls of their relation prediction sub-module. Our sub-modules beat all of these approaches on both of the tasks.

Influences by Parameters. We show how parameters influence performances of the system and its key components ELM and RPM.

Varying k. We show the influence on ELM with varied k. Using different k, we evaluated $R@k$ of ELM and report our findings in Table 2. As is shown, with the increase of k, the recall grows as well and reaches 96.4% when k is set as an arbitrarily large integer. This performance is superior to [24] for a large k and comparable to the results of [27], that was tested on the validation set.

Fixing $\alpha = 0.9$, $\gamma = 3$, we varied k from 1 to U (unlimited) to see the influence of k on RPM. The results shown in Table 2 tell us that $R@k$ grows from 88.84% to 95.69% with the increase of k, that is consistent as the results on ELM.

Varying γ & α. We first show the influence of γ on RPM. Fixing $k = 1$, $\alpha = 0.6$, we varied γ from 2 to 4 and got $R@1 = 88.84\%$, 88.76% and 88.7%, respectively. This shows that varying γ does not have substantial impact on the performance of RPM. We also show the influence of α. Fixing $k = 1$, $\gamma = 2$, we varied α from

Table 2. Influence on components by varying k. $R@U$ indicates that k is set as Unlimited, thus there is no constraint on the size of candidate set.

$R@k$	$R@1$	$R@5$	$R@10$	$R@100$	$R@400$	$R@U$
ELM	66.6	82.1	85.8	91.8	94.9	96.4

$R@k$	$R@1$	$R@2$	$R@3$	$R@U$
RPM	89.20	94.62	95.29	95.91

Table 3. Influence on the accuracy of the system and RPM by varying L.

L_1	1	3	5	10
Acc$_{RPM}$	85.93	**89.2**	88.75	88.98
L_2	1	2	3	
Acc	83.14	82.23	**83.54**	

0.2 to 0.9 in 0.1 increment, and find that $R@1$ is very steady, around 88% with small changes. A similar trend also appears when γ is set at 3 and 4. The results tell us that RPM is insensitive to the change of α and γ.

Varying L_1 and L_2. We show the influence of L_1 and L_2 on Acc and Acc$_{RPM}$. Fixing k=1, we set L_1 as 1, 3, 5 and 10, and train CRI model. As shown in Table 3, when L=3, CRI model achieves the best performances. The reason is that a balance between positive and negative samples needs to be elaborately chosen. On one hand, the model needs negative samples to learn knowledge for classification, especially for distinguishing true negatives; on the other hand, too many negative samples will lead to more misclassifications for some true negatives. Fixing L_1=3, we employed CRI model to infer the training data, which is later used to train TSM. Letting L_2 as 1, 2 and 3, we train TSM and find that when L_2=3, the model gets the best accuracy of 83.54%.

6   Conclusion

In this paper, we proposed a comprehensive approach that leverages pre-trained transformers (BERT) and contrastive learning for answering simple questions on knowledge bases. Extensive experiments on a typical benchmark dataset show that our approach outperforms most of existing methods. This verifies that contrastive learning along with pre-trained transforms can boost performances for *e.g.,* simple KBQA. In the future, we would like to explore techniques for answering even more complex questions, *e.g.,* WebQuestions, in the meanwhile, we will also investigate the impact from contrastive learning and transfer learning.

Acknowledgement. This work is supported by Sichuan Scientific Innovation Fund (No. 2022JDRC0009) and the National Key Research and Development Program of China (No. 2017YFA0700800).

References

1. Removed Questions. https://github.com/Mycatinjuly/SimpleQuestion_QA
2. Bast, H., Haussmann, E.: More accurate question answering on freebase. In: Proceedings of the 24th ACM International on Conference on Information and Knowledge Management, pp. 1431–1440 (2015)
3. Berant, J., Chou, A., Frostig, R., Liang, P.: Semantic parsing on freebase from question-answer pairs. In: Proceedings of the 2013 Conference on Empirical Methods in Natural Language Processing, pp. 1533–1544. ACL (2013)
4. Bollacker, K.D., Evans, C., Paritosh, P., Sturge, T., Taylor, J.: Freebase: a collaboratively created graph database for structuring human knowledge. In: Proceedings of the ACM SIGMOD International Conference on Management of Data, pp. 1247–1250 (2008)
5. Bordes, A., Chopra, S., Weston, J.: Question answering with subgraph embeddings. In: Proceedings of the 2014 Conference on Empirical Methods in Natural Language Processing, pp. 615–620 (2014)
6. Bordes, A., Usunier, N., Chopra, S., Weston, J.: Large-scale simple question answering with memory networks. CoRR abs/1506.02075 (2015)
7. Bordes, A., Weston, J., Usunier, N.: Open question answering with weakly supervised embedding models. In: Calders, T., Esposito, F., Hüllermeier, E., Meo, R. (eds.) ECML PKDD 2014. LNCS (LNAI), vol. 8724, pp. 165–180. Springer, Heidelberg (2014). https://doi.org/10.1007/978-3-662-44848-9_11
8. Cai, Q., Yates, A.: Large-scale semantic parsing via schema matching and lexicon extension. In: Proceedings of the 51st Annual Meeting of the Association for Computational Linguistics (Volume 1: Long Papers), pp. 423–433 (2013)
9. Carlsson, F., Gyllensten, A.C., Gogoulou, E., Hellqvist, E.Y., Sahlgren, M.: Semantic re-tuning with contrastive tension. In: International Conference on Learning Representations (2020)
10. Chen, T., Kornblith, S., Norouzi, M., Hinton, G.: A simple framework for contrastive learning of visual representations. In: International Conference on Machine Learning, pp. 1597–1607. PMLR (2020)
11. Cheng, L., Chen, Z., Ren, J.: Enhancing question answering over knowledge base using dynamical relation reasoning. In: 2020 International Joint Conference on Neural Networks (IJCNN), pp. 1–8. IEEE (2020)
12. Deng, Y., Zhang, W., Lam, W.: Learning to rank question answer pairs with bilateral contrastive data augmentation. In: Proceedings of the Seventh Workshop on Noisy User-generated Text, pp. 175–181 (2021)
13. Devlin, J., Chang, M., Lee, K., Toutanova, K.: BERT: pre-training of deep bidirectional transformers for language understanding. In: Proceedings of the 2019 Conference of the North American Chapter of the Association for Computational Linguistics: Human Language Technologies, pp. 4171–4186 (2019)
14. Dong, L., Wei, F., Zhou, M., Xu, K.: Question answering over freebase with multicolumn convolutional neural networks. In: Proceedings of the 53rd Annual Meeting of the Association for Computational Linguistics and the 7th International Joint Conference on Natural Language Processing, pp. 260–269 (2015)
15. Fader, A., Zettlemoyer, L.S., Etzioni, O.: Paraphrase-driven learning for open question answering. In: Proceedings of the 51st Annual Meeting of the Association for Computational Linguistics, pp. 1608–1618 (2013)

16. Gupta, V., Chinnakotla, M., Shrivastava, M.: Retrieve and re-rank: a simple and effective IR approach to simple question answering over knowledge graphs. In: Proceedings of the First Workshop on Fact Extraction and VERification), pp. 22–27, November 2018

17. Hadsell, R., Chopra, S., LeCun, Y.: Dimensionality reduction by learning an invariant mapping. In: 2006 IEEE Computer Society Conference on Computer Vision and Pattern Recognition (CVPR 2006), vol. 2, pp. 1735–1742. IEEE (2006)

18. Hao, Y., Liu, H., He, S., Liu, K., Zhao, J.: Pattern-revising enhanced simple question answering over knowledge bases. In: Proceedings of the 27th International Conference on Computational Linguistics, pp. 3272–3282 (2018)

19. He, K., Fan, H., Wu, Y., Xie, S., Girshick, R.: Momentum contrast for unsupervised visual representation learning. In: Proceedings of the IEEE/CVF Conference on Computer Vision and Pattern Recognition, pp. 9729–9738 (2020)

20. Howard, J., Ruder, S.: Universal language model fine-tuning for text classification. In: Proceedings of the 56th Annual Meeting of the Association for Computational Linguistics, pp. 328–339 (2018)

21. Lehmann, J., et al.: DBpedia - a large-scale, multilingual knowledge base extracted from Wikipedia. Semant. Web 6(2), 167–195 (2015)

22. Lin, T., Goyal, P., Girshick, R.B., He, K., Dollár, P.: Focal loss for dense object detection. In: IEEE International Conference on Computer Vision, pp. 2999–3007 (2017)

23. Lukovnikov, D., Fischer, A., Lehmann, J.: Pretrained transformers for simple question answering over knowledge graphs. In: Ghidini, C., et al. (eds.) ISWC 2019. LNCS, vol. 11778, pp. 470–486. Springer, Cham (2019). https://doi.org/10.1007/978-3-030-30793-6_27

24. Lukovnikov, D., Fischer, A., Lehmann, J., Auer, S.: Neural network-based question answering over knowledge graphs on word and character level. In: Barrett, R., Cummings, R., Agichtein, E., Gabrilovich, E. (eds.) Proceedings of the 26th International Conference on World Wide Web, pp. 1211–1220. ACM (2017)

25. Luo, D., Su, J., Yu, S.: A Bert-based approach with relation-aware attention for knowledge base question answering. In: 2020 International Joint Conference on Neural Networks (IJCNN), pp. 1–8. IEEE (2020)

26. Maheshwari, G., Trivedi, P., Lukovnikov, D., Chakraborty, N., Fischer, A., Lehmann, J.: Learning to rank query graphs for complex question answering over knowledge graphs. In: Ghidini, C., et al. (eds.) ISWC 2019. LNCS, vol. 11778, pp. 487–504. Springer, Cham (2019). https://doi.org/10.1007/978-3-030-30793-6_28

27. Mohammed, S., Shi, P., Lin, J.: Strong baselines for simple question answering over knowledge graphs with and without neural networks. In: Walker, M.A., Ji, H., Stent, A. (eds.) Proceedings of the 2018 Conference of the North American Chapter of the Association for Computational Linguistics: Human Language Technologies, pp. 291–296. Association for Computational Linguistics (2018)

28. Qin, Y., et al.: ERICA: improving entity and relation understanding for pre-trained language models via contrastive learning. In: Proceedings of the 59th Annual Meeting of the Association for Computational Linguistics, pp. 3350–3363 (2021)

29. Qiu, C., Zhou, G., Cai, Z., Søgaard, A.: A global-local attentive relation detection model for knowledge-based question answering. IEEE Trans. Artif. Intell. 2(2), 200–212 (2021)

30. Qu, Y., Liu, J., Kang, L., Shi, Q., Ye, D.: Question answering over freebase via attentive RNN with similarity matrix based CNN. CoRR abs/1804.03317 (2018)

31. Rao, J., He, H., Lin, J.: Noise-contrastive estimation for answer selection with deep neural networks. In: Proceedings of the 25th ACM International on Conference on Information and Knowledge Management, pp. 1913–1916 (2016)

32. Reddy, S., Lapata, M., Steedman, M.: Large-scale semantic parsing without question-answer pairs. Trans. Assoc. Comput. Linguist. **2**, 377–392 (2014)

33. Sharath, J.S., Rekabdar, B.: Question answering over knowledge base using language model embeddings. In: 2020 International Joint Conference on Neural Networks, pp. 1–8. IEEE (2020)

34. Suchanek, F.M., Kasneci, G., Weikum, G.: Yago: a core of semantic knowledge. In: Proceedings of the 16th International Conference on World Wide Web, pp. 697–706 (2007)

35. Sun, Y., et al.: Semantic parsing with syntax- and table-aware SQL generation. In: Proceedings of the 56th Annual Meeting of the Association for Computational Linguistics, pp. 361–372 (2018)

36. Wang, Y., Zhang, R., Xu, C., Mao, Y.: The APVA-TURBO approach to question answering in knowledge base. In: Proceedings of the 27th International Conference on Computational Linguistics, pp. 1998–2009 (2018)

37. Yao, X., Durme, B.V.: Information extraction over structured data: question answering with freebase. In: Proceedings of the 52nd Annual Meeting of the Association for Computational Linguistics, pp. 956–966 (2014)

38. Yih, W., Chang, M., He, X., Gao, J.: Semantic parsing via staged query graph generation: question answering with knowledge base. In: Proceedings of the Annual Meeting of the Association for Computational Linguistics, pp. 1321–1331 (2015)

39. Yin, W., Yu, M., Xiang, B., Zhou, B., Schütze, H.: Simple question answering by attentive convolutional neural network. In: COLING 2016, 26th International Conference on Computational Linguistics, Proceedings of the Conference: Technical Papers, pp. 1746–1756 (2016)

40. Yu, M., Yin, W., Hasan, K.S., dos Santos, C.N., Xiang, B., Zhou, B.: Improved neural relation detection for knowledge base question answering. In: Proceedings of the 55th Annual Meeting of the Association for Computational Linguistics, pp. 571–581 (2017)

41. Zhang, Y., He, R., Liu, Z., Lim, K.H., Bing, L.: An unsupervised sentence embedding method by mutual information maximization. In: Proceedings of the Conference on Empirical Methods in Natural Language Processing, pp. 1601–1610 (2020)

42. Zhang, Y., Jin, L., Zhang, Z., Li, X., Liu, Q., Wang, H.: SF-ANN: leveraging structural features with an attention neural network for candidate fact ranking. Appl. Intell. 1–16 (2021)

ConCas: Cascade Popularity Prediction Based on Topic-Aware Graph Contrastive Learning

Chen Ling[1], Xianren Zhang[2], Jiaxing Shang[1(✉)], Dajiang Liu[1], Yong Li[1], Wu Xie[3], and Baohua Qiang[3]

[1] College of Computer Science, Chongiqng University, Chongqing, China
lingchen20638@163.com, {shangjx,liudj,yongli}@cqu.edu.cn
[2] CQU-UC Joint Co-op Institute, Chongqing University, Chongqing, China
zhangxr2000@foxmail.com
[3] Guangxi Key Laboratory of Trusted Software,
Guilin University of Electronic Technology, Guilin, China
xiesixchannels@126.com, qiangbh@guet.edu.cn

Abstract. Cascade popularity prediction on social networks has attracted much attention from scholars over the past few years. Many existing methods take cascade size during the observation period as a key feature. However, when making early predictions where the observation period is short, the difference in cascade size between popular and unpopular contents becomes insignificant. Therefore, this paper proposes a topic-aware graph pre-training model based on the self-supervised learning termed **ConCas**, which fully utilizes graph structural and content topic information for accurate cascade popularity prediction. Specifically, graph contrastive learning is used on cascade graphs to identify the key structural characteristics that discriminate the popular and unpopular cascades. To further improve the model performance, the underlying social network is used to obtain embeddings as node features. Besides, Latent Dirichlet Allocation (LDA) topic modeling is performed on the message content to generate topic tags, which are further embedded in the cascade graph as node features. Finally, the embeddings of the learned cascade graph are fed to downstream learning models for popularity prediction. Experimental results on the Weibo dataset show that ConCas achieves higher prediction accuracy than the state-of-the-art baselines.

Keywords: Popularity prediction · Graph neural networks · Contrastive learning · LDA topic modeling

1 Introduction

Recently, with the prosperity of online social networking platforms, the research on information popularity prediction [15] has received extensive attention from

G. Memmi et al. (Eds.): KSEM 2022, LNAI 13368, pp. 516–528, 2022.
https://doi.org/10.1007/978-3-031-10983-6_40

both academia and industry. It finds application in a lot of important scenarios such as rumor detection, social advertising, etc. Recently, due to the superiority of deep learning models, deep learning-based popularity prediction methods has gained more attention [8]. Most existing methods either explicitly or implicitly regard cascade size during the observation period as a key feature. However, when we need to make early predictions where the observation period is short, the difference in cascade size between popular and unpopular contents becomes insignificant. Therefore, how to take full advantage of other available data such as graph structural and content topic information to improve prediction performance, is a key issue worth investigating. Unfortunately, most existing methods still lack sufficient consideration of such information.

To address the above issue and inspired by the latest progress in self-supervised learning, this paper proposes a topic-aware graph pre-training model termed **ConCas**, which fully utilizes graph structural and content topic information for accurate cascade popularity prediction. Specifically, to capture the cascade graph information, we utilize the graph contrastive learning model [11] to identify the key structural characteristics that discriminate popular and unpopular cascades. Moreover, unlike existing methods which treat each cascade graph independently, we aggregate popular and unpopular cascades into the corresponding large cascade graphs for contrastive learning, so that the interactions among different cascades can be captured. To learn more structural information, we feed the underlying user social network into Node2vec [5] to generate node embeddings as user features. Considering the importance of content information, we further adopt LDA topic modeling and TF-IDF algorithm to extract the latent topics and generate topic tags. Experiments on a Weibo dataset validated the effectiveness of the ConCas model over the state-of-the-art baselines.

In short, the main contributions of our work are as follows:

- For the early cascade popularity prediction problem where the observation period is short and the cascade size is no longer a predictive feature, we propose a self-supervised graph contrastive learning-based approach for more accurate popularity prediction. To the best of our knowledge, it is the first effort to apply graph contrastive learning to cascade popularity prediction.
- To improve the prediction accuracy of the model, we apply Node2vec on the underlying social network to get node embeddings, and adopt LDA topic modeling and TF-IDF algorithm to extract topic tags from message content.
- We conduct extensive experiments on a real Weibo dataset. The results show that ConCas achieves higher prediction accuracy than the baselines. Besides, considering the underlying social relation and content topic information can both benefit the prediction performance.

2 Related Work

We briefly review the related works from two aspects, i.e., information diffusion prediction and self-supervised learning on the graph.

Information Diffusion Prediction. In recent years, deep neural networks have shown powerful capabilities in modeling information diffusion as sequential data and usually yield significantly better prediction performance. Li et al. [8] proposed the first popularity prediction deep learning model DeepCas, which converts the information cascade graph into a set of node sequences based on the random walk algorithm, and automatically learns the representation of the cascade graph. Cao et al. [1] propose a novel method CoupledGNN, which uses two coupled graph neural networks to capture the interplay between node activation states and the spread of influence. Chen et al. [4] proposed a semi-supervised method CasCN under an end-to-end deep learning framework, which predicts information popularity by learning latent representations of structural and temporal features. Yang et al. [13] proposed a reinforcement learning-based multi-scale diffusion prediction model, and incorporate the macroscopic diffusion size information into the RNN-based microscopic diffusion model. Zhou et al. [16] proposed VaCas which learns node-level and graph-level embeddings via variational auto-encoders and Bi-GRU, and predicts the size of cascades by MLP.

Graph Self-Supervised Learning. For network-related tasks, the internal graph structure often contains richer information. Therefore, graph self-supervised learning has become a promising approach to learn predictive feature representations. GPT-GNN [7] initializes the framework of GNN through generative pre-training, and introduces a self-supervised attribute graph generation task. Recently, Qiu et al. [11] proposed GCC model, which makes the first attempt to take contrastive learning as a pre-training method to enable graph neural networks to learn internal and transferable structural representations. As far as we know, the graph contrastive learning model has not yet been applied on the popularity prediction task.

3   The Proposed Method

3.1   Problem Formulation

Definition 1 (Cascade Graph). *For message m posted by user u_0, based on the repost data observed within a time window T, a directed cascade graph $G_m^T(V_m^T, E_m^T)$ can be constructed, where V_m^T consists of users who have involved in the message diffusion process and each directed edge $e(v_i, v_j) \in E_m^T$ indicates that user v_j reposted the message from v_i.*

Considering the interactions among different cascades, we aggregate multiple cascade graphs to construct the following aggregated cascade graph:

Definition 2 (Aggregated Cascade Graph). *Given a set of M cascade graphs $\{G_m^T(V_m^T, E_m^T)|m = 1, \cdots, M\}$, an aggregated cascade graph $G^T(V^T, E^T)$ is constructed where $V^T = \bigcup_{m=1}^{M} V_m^T$ and $E^T = \bigcup_{m=1}^{M} E_m^T$.*

Based on the above definitions, we give the definition of cascade popularity prediction problem as follows:

Definition 3 (Cascade Popularity Prediction Problem). *Given the social network, the contents and cascade graphs for a set of messages within observation time T, the cascade popularity prediction problem aims to learn a function that predicts whether a piece of message will become popular in the future.*

The popularity label of a message is determined by its final cascade size (number of reposts) in the dataset.

Definition 4 (r-ego Network [11]). *For an aggregated cascade graph $G^T(V^T, E^T)$ and a node $v \in V^T$, the r-neighbors of v are defined as $N_r(v) = \{u | d(v, u) \leq r\}$, where $d(v, u)$ is the shortest path distance between v and u. The r-ego network of v, i.e., G_v, is a subgraph induced by $N_r(v)$.*

Definition 5 (Generalized Positional Embedding [11]). *Given a subgraph with adjacency matrix A and degree matrix D, the normalized graph Laplaciade-composen matrix is eigen-decomposed, i.e., $I - D^{-1/2}AD^{1/2} = U\Lambda U^T$. Then, the top feature vectors in U are defined as generalized positional embedding for the subgraph.*

3.2 ConCas Model

The core idea of ConCas is to pre-train a GNN model to capture the key cascade graph patterns that discriminate popular and unpopular messages through self-supervised contrastive learning. The overall framework is shown in Fig. 1, which consists of five main components to be introduced in the following.

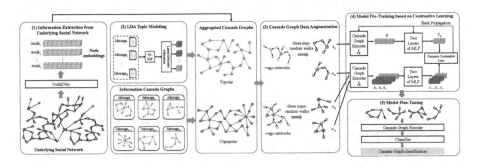

Fig. 1. The framework of ConCas model

Information Extraction from Underlying Social Network. The underlying social network gives an overview of the structural patterns and diffusion channels among users, which is beneficial to popularity prediction. To learn relevant information from the underlying social network, the graph embedding method is utilized. In our method, we mainly aim to preserve both homogeneity and structural similarity among users from the learned embeddings. To this end, we use Node2vec [5], as the graph embedding method.

LDA Topic Modeling Contents and topics may also affect the popularity of a message. In order to extract the topic features, then use the TF-IDF method to extract keywords. The key step of TF-IDF is to calculate the importance score of a word with respect to a message. After calculating the importance scores, for each message, we select the top 50% important words as the keywords, based on which we further apply the LDA topic model to extract the topic features. Through the TF-IDF step, the less informative words will be filtered out, which is beneficial to the LDA topic modeling in terms of both effectiveness and efficiency.

The LDA model can learn the topic distribution over each document (i.e., message) and the word distribution over each topic. For each message, given the learned topic distribution, we select the topic tag with the highest probability as the topic feature. Then for each user who participated in the message, the topic feature will be added into the node feature vector.

Node Feature. The complete node feature vector in cascade graph includes node embedding learned from the underlying social network and the topic tag. Besides, in order to avoid possible noise, we follow the procedure of GCC [11], and add the generalized position embedding, the one-hot encoding of vertex degree, and the binary indicator of ego vertex to the node feature vector. The final feature vectors are then normalized by their L2-Norm [6].

Data Augmentation for Information Cascade Graph. For self-supervised learning on the aggregated cascade graph, in order to improve the model discriminability, a random data augmentation strategy is used. Specifically, graph instance pairs randomly sampled from the same r-ego network are treated as positive instance pairs, while those sampled from different r-ego networks are treated as negative instance pairs. To sample a graph instance from the aggregated cascade graph, we use the following three-step random walk-based method [11].

Random Walk with Restart: We start a random walk on cascade graph from the ego vertex v. The walker iteratively traverses its neighborhood with the probability proportional to the edge weight. In addition, at each step, with a none-zero probability the walker returns back to the starting vertex v.

Subgraph Induction: The random walk with restart collects a subset of vertices surrounding v, denoted by S_v. The sub-graph induced by S_v is then regarded as an augmented graph instance of the r-ego network.

Anonymization: We anonymize the sampled graph by renumbering its vertices to $\{1, 2, \cdots, |\hat{S}_v|\}$ in arbitrary order. The anonymization step ensures that the model will focus on the structural information.

Model Pre-training Based on Contrastive Learning. Graph contrastive learning learns graph-level representations by comparing positive and negative graph samples. For the popularity prediction problem investigated in this paper, we mainly aim to learn the structural and content information from the information cascade graph, so as to distinguish between popular and unpopular messages. For any graph instance x, the purpose of graph contrastive learning is to learn the encoder f, which maps a graph to a low-dimensional feature vector such that f satisfies:

$$sim(f(x), f(x^+)) \gg sim(f(x), f(x^-)) \tag{1}$$

where x^+ is a positive subgraph sampled from the same r-ego network of x, x^- is a negative subgraph sampled from a different r-ego network, $sim(\cdot)$ is a similarity measure, which is defined as the dot product in this paper. To achieve the above goal, the learning model has to maximize the similarity between positive sample pairs while minimize the similarity between negative sample pairs in a given mini-batch. Specifically, given an encoded query vector q and a dictionary containing $K + 1$ encoded key vectors $\{k_0, k_1, \cdots, k_K\}$, which consists of one positive key (denoted as k_+) and K negative keys, the graph contrastive learning model aims to minimize the following InfoNCE [10] loss:

$$L = -\log \frac{\exp(sim(q, k_+)/\tau)}{\sum_{i=0}^{K} \exp(sim(q, k_i)/\tau)} \tag{2}$$

where τ is the temperature hyper-parameter and $sim(\cdot)$ is the aforementioned similarity function. Here, $q = f_q(x_q)$ is a query representation, $k_+ = f_k(x_{k_+})$ is a representation of positive (similar) key, $k_i = f_k(x_{k_i})$ $(k_i \neq k_+)$ is a representation of negative key. It is worth noting that we follow the design of GCC [11] and use two separate graph neural network encoders (f_q and f_k) whose parameters are not shared.

Contrastive Learning Strategies. Since a large number of negative samples are needed for learning, it is required to maintain the K-size dictionary and encoders while the value of K is extremely large. The most commonly used designs at this stage are end-to-end (E2E), momentum comparison (MoCo) [6], and SimCLR [2]. Recently, MoCo v2 [3] was proposed to replace the projection head in MoCo with a 2-layer MLP head, which was only used in the pre-training stage. Experiments showed that MoCo v2 leads to better classification performance. Compared with SimCLR's 4k∼8k batch size that requires TPU support, MoCo v2 can run on a typical 8-GPU machine and achieve better results than SimCLR. Therefore, in this paper, we will use MoCo v2 to maintain the dictionary, which uses a two-layer MLP projection head to obtain a new embedding representation, i.e., $z_q = MLP(q)$ and $z_k = MLP(k)$. Then the loss calculated through Eq. (2) is propagated back through the query encoder to update the parameters of f_q. Finally, the updated parameters of f_q will be used to update the parameters of f_k through a momentum coefficient.

Graph Neural Network Encoder. The graph neural network encoder maps the input graph sample to a low-dimensional vector space. The goal of the pre-training step is to train the graph neural network encoder which captures the structural and content information from the popular and unpopular information cascade graphs, so as to support the downstream popularity prediction task. To this end, we take InfoNCE [10] as the learning objective and use the afore-mentioned data augmentation strategy to obtain similar and dissimilar sample pairs. These pairs are input into the encoder to obtain vector representations. Here, we choose GIN[12] as the graph neural network encoder since it can gener-ate graph-level embeddings and exhibit good performance in graph classification tasks. GIN updates node representations as:

$$h_v^{(l)} = MLP^{(l)}((1 + \epsilon^{(l)}) \cdot h_v^{(l-1)} + \sum_{u \in N(v)} h_u^{(l-1)})) \tag{3}$$

The final graph representation is obtained by concatenating across all itera-tions/layers of the GIN:

$$h_G = CONCAT(sum(\{h_v^{(l)} | v \in G\}) | l = 0, 1, \cdots, L) \tag{4}$$

3.3   Model Fine-Tuning

After pre-training, we get the f_q and f_k encoder parameters, and the trained query encoder f_q will be used to perform downstream graph classification tasks for further fine-tuning. We consider two fine-tuning modes, freeze mode and full training mode. Specifically, the frozen mode will fix the f_q encoder parameters, and only train the downstream classifier parameters. The full training mode will directly connect the downstream classifier to the graph encoder for end-to-end training, i.e., parameters of f_q and the downstream classifier will be updated simultaneously. The full training mode is more time-consuming than the freeze mode and requires more GPU resources. However, in terms of prediction accu-racy, the full training mode performs much better.

4   Evaluation

4.1   Dataset

Our experiments are mainly based on the Weibo dataset provided by the Dat-aCastle competition platform[1]. We conducted a data preprocessing procedure by filtering out the following data: (1) users who have never been reposted from by others; (2) source messages with empty content. The popularity label of a message is determined by its 3-day cascade size (i.e., number of reposts). Specif-ically, if the cascade size within the future three days is greater than 300, then it is a popular message. If the cascade size is less than 30, then it is an unpopular

---

[1] https://challenge.datacastle.cn/v3/cmptDetail.html?id=166.

message. The observation period parameter T is set to one hour, i.e., we use 1-hour data to predict the future 3-day popularity. In order to eliminate the impact of cascade size during the observation period, we only select messages whose 1-hour cascade sizes range from 10 to 30 as the training set. Table 1 shows the statistics of the processed dataset. Here we use the ten-fold cross-validation method for hyper-parameter tuning.

4.2 Baseline and Evaluation Metric

Baseline. We consider four state-of-the-art baselines, i.e., Node2vec [5], Graph2vec [9], DGCNN [14], and DeepCas [8], for comparison. These methods can be divided into two groups according to their fine-tuning strategies. Specifically, baselines with freezing fine-tuning strategy include Node2vec and Graph2vec, and the remaining DGCNN and DeepCas baselines utilize a full training strategy.

Table 1. Statistics of the Weibo dataset

Datasets		# cascades	# nodes	# edges	Avg. # nodes
Weibo (total)	Popular (300+)	250	4,845	4.892	19.38
	Unpopular ($\leq$30)	1,000	13,907	11.929	13.91
Weibo (pre-training)	Popular (300+)	200	3,740	3,655	18.70
	Unpopular ($\leq$30)	800	11,101	9,559	13.88
Weibo (testing)	Popular (300+)	50	1,105	1,237	22.10
	Unpopular ($\leq$30)	200	2,806	2,370	14.03

We also compare the performance of each method under four different node feature groups: **(1) CG (nan):** no node feature will be used, **(2) CG (text):** content topic feature will be used, **(3) CG (social):** features learned from underlying social network will be used, and **(4) CG (text & social):** both text and social features will be used.

Evaluation Metric. We choose F1 score to measure the accuracy of the above baselines and our proposed ConCas model.

4.3 Settings

Pre-training Settings. We follow the settings of GCC [11], train 75,000 steps and use the Adam optimizer with the following parameters: $\beta_1 = 0.9, \beta_2 = 0.999, \varepsilon = 1 \times 10^{-8}$. For MoCo, the initial learning rate is 0.005, the weight decay is 1×10^{-4}, the learning rate warms up during the first 7500 iterations, and then linearly decays during the following steps. For MoCo v2, we use the cosine learning rate schedule, the initial learning rate is set to 0.005, and the decay period is set to 10. Gradient norm clipping is applied to the range $[-1, 1]$. For MoCo and MoCo v2, we use a batch size of 32, a dictionary size of 1024 and a momentum m of 0.999, epoch set to 300, and temperature $\tau = 0.2$. For E2E, we use mini-batch size of 1,024, a dictionary size of 1,023, and the other settings are the same as MoCo. Among them, the MLP projection head of MoCo v2 is a two-layer fully connected layer. Note that we are not using the "extra blur augmentation" of MoCo v2 here. We use GIN as the encoder, with a total of 5 layers, each layer has 64 hidden units.

Fine-Tuning Settings. For the freezing mode, we choose SVM as the classifier. For full training mode, we use the Adam optimizer with a learning rate of 0.005.

4.4 Result

LDA Topic Modeling. We compare the LDA algorithm using only the bag-of-words model and the LDA algorithm using TF-IDF. The results of perplexity and model coherence scores with respect to the number of topics are shown in the Fig. 2 (a) and (b) respectively.

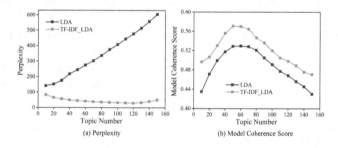

Fig. 2. Perplexity and model coherence score of LDA and TF-IDF_LDA

The perplexity and coherence scores are used to determine the optimal number of topics for the LDA model. A lower perplexity value usually indicates better generalization performance, and a high coherence score usually indicates better model performance. From the results in Fig. 2, it can be seen that TF-IDF based LDA model performs significantly better. Based on the results, we set the number of topics to 50. We use the generated topic tags as node features and embed them in the information cascade graph.

Table 2. F1-Score results of different methods under different feature groups

Datasets	CG (nan)	CG (text)	CG (social)	CG (social & text)
Number of graphs	250			
Number of classes	2			
Number of nodes	3911			
Avg. number of nodes	15.64			
Node2vec (freeze)	50.27	49.50	55.30	55.53
Graph2vec (freeze)	72.50	72.79	83.27	84.06
ConCas (freeze, E2E)	71.29	69.36	78.41	80.03
ConCas (freeze, MoCo)	72.96	**76.07**	83.18	83.14
ConCas (freeze, MoCo v2)	**74.69**	74.27	**84.78**	**84.83**
DGCNN (full)	68.73	70.66	72.07	71.95
DeepCas (full)	76.37	**81.70**	84.79	85.50
ConCas (full, E2E)	74.43	71.99	80.09	81.50
ConCas (full, MoCo)	76.74	76.16	83.85	84.16
ConCas (full, MoCo v2)	**79.78**	80.58	**87.21**	**86.84**

Popularity Prediction. Table 2 shows the results of F1-score for different methods under different feature groups. It can be seen that the node embedding-based method Node2vec exhibit the worst performance. This indicates that simply averaging the node embeddings as the graph representation cannot capture sufficient graph structural information. By comparing different fine-tuning strategies, it is observed that full training-based methods generally perform better. For the freezing fine-tuning strategy, ConCas (freeze, MoCo v2) performs the best under the CG (nan), CG (social) and CG (social & text) feature groups. In terms of end-to-end full training strategy, ConCas (full, MoCo v2) exhibits the best performance under the CG (nan), CG (social), and CG (social & text) feature groups. Although the best performance under CG (text) feature group is provided by DeepCas, the difference between DeepCas and ConCas (full, MoCo v2) is insignificant. By comparing the results under different feature groups, we see that in most cases, both social and text features are beneficial to the classification performance. Specifically, the embedding learned from the underlying social network plays a vital role in popularity prediction. In sum, the results in Table 2 validate the effectiveness of our method.

To show that the performance differences between the baselines and our method are statistically significant, we compare ConCas with two best performed baselines, i.e., Graph2vec and DeepCas. Figure 3 shows the F1-Score results under different feature groups, where the data point shows the average value of 10 experiments, the lower and upper bonds correspond to the minimum and maximum values. The results show that ConCas (full, MoCo v2) performs better than the other methods and the differences are statistically significant.

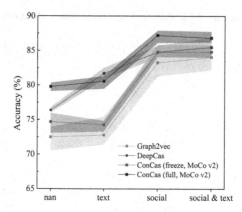

Fig. 3. Significance of performance difference between ConCas and two best performed baselines

Since our ConCas model takes MoCo and MoCo v2 as the contrastive learning strategy, we further investigate the impact of different parameters on their performance. Figure 4 shows the change of accuracy (F1-Score) for MoCo and MoCo v2 with respect to the change of different parameters. It can be seen from Fig. 4(a) that when the dictionary size increases, the model performance also increases and peaks at $K = 1024$. However, the increasing trend becomes insignificant as the dictionary size becomes very large. Therefore, choosing $K = 1024$ would be an economic choice. Figure 4 (b) shows that when $m = 0.999$, the result is optimal. But when m increases to 0.9999, the accuracy value drops. Therefore, we choose $m = 0.999$ in our method. From Fig. 4(c) it is observed that the increase

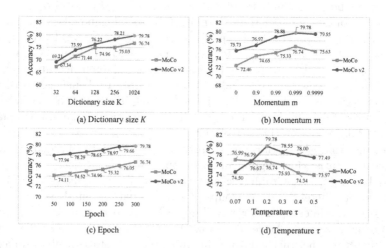

Fig. 4. Parameter sensitivity results for ConCas with MoCo and MoCo v2 contrastive learning strategies

of epoch is also helpful for the model performance. However, when the epoch size is higher than 250, the gain in accuracy becomes insignificant. Figure 4(d) shows that MoCo and MoCo v2 have different sensitivities to temperature, and they reach the optimal state at $\tau = 0.07$ and $\tau = 0.2$, respectively.

5 Conclusion

In this paper, we investigated the early popularity prediction problem and proposed a graph contrastive learning-based method named ConCas which takes fully advantage of both graph structural and message content information. Experimental results on a real Weibo dataset validated the effectiveness of the proposed approach as compared to the state-of-the-art methods. In the future, we will consider more available data, such as the videos/images associated with the message, and other user information to further improve the model accuracy.

Acknowledgements. This work was supported in part by: National Natural Science Foundation of China (Nos. 61966008, U2033213), Sichuan and Chongqing Joint Key R&D Project (No. 2021YFQ0058).

References

1. Cao, Q., Shen, H., Gao, J., Wei, B., Cheng, X.: Popularity prediction on social platforms with coupled graph neural networks. In: Proceedings of the 13th International Conference on Web Search and Data Mining, pp. 70–78 (2020)
2. Chen, T., Kornblith, S., Norouzi, M., Hinton, G.: A simple framework for contrastive learning of visual representations. In: International Conference on Machine Learning, pp. 1597–1607. PMLR (2020)
3. Chen, X., Fan, H., Girshick, R., He, K.: Improved baselines with momentum contrastive learning. arXiv preprint arXiv:2003.04297 (2020)
4. Chen, X., Zhou, F., Zhang, K., Trajcevski, G., Zhong, T., Zhang, F.: Information diffusion prediction via recurrent cascades convolution. In: 2019 IEEE 35th International Conference on Data Engineering (ICDE), pp. 770–781. IEEE (2019)
5. Grover, A., Leskovec, J.: node2vec: Scalable feature learning for networks. In: Proceedings of the 22nd ACM SIGKDD International Conference on Knowledge Discovery and Data Mining, pp. 855–864 (2016)
6. He, K., Fan, H., Wu, Y., Xie, S., Girshick, R.: Momentum contrast for unsupervised visual representation learning. In: Proceedings of the IEEE/CVF Conference on Computer Vision and Pattern Recognition, pp. 9729–9738 (2020)
7. Hu, Z., Dong, Y., Wang, K., Chang, K.W., Sun, Y.: GPT-GNN: generative pre-training of graph neural networks. In: Proceedings of the 26th ACM SIGKDD International Conference on Knowledge Discovery and Data Mining, pp. 1857–1867 (2020)
8. Li, C., Ma, J., Guo, X., Mei, Q.: DeepCAS: an end-to-end predictor of information cascades. In: Proceedings of the 26th International Conference on World Wide Web, pp. 577–586 (2017)
9. Narayanan, A., Chandramohan, M., Venkatesan, R., Chen, L., Liu, Y., Jaiswal, S.: graph2vec: Learning distributed representations of graphs. arXiv preprint arXiv:1707.05005 (2017)

10. Van den Oord, A., Li, Y., Vinyals, O.: Representation learning with contrastive predictive coding. arXiv preprint arXiv:1807.03748 (2018)
11. Qiu, J., et al.: GCC: graph contrastive coding for graph neural network pre-training. In: Proceedings of the 26th ACM SIGKDD International Conference on Knowledge Discovery and Data Mining, pp. 1150–1160 (2020)
12. Xu, K., Hu, W., Leskovec, J., Jegelka, S.: How powerful are graph neural networks? arXiv preprint arXiv:1810.00826 (2018)
13. Yang, C., Tang, J., Sun, M., Cui, G., Liu, Z.: Multi-scale information diffusion prediction with reinforced recurrent networks. In: IJCAI, pp. 4033–4039 (2019)
14. Zhang, M., Cui, Z., Neumann, M., Chen, Y.: An end-to-end deep learning architecture for graph classification. In: Thirty-second AAAI Conference on Artificial Intelligence (2018)
15. Zhou, F., Xu, X., Trajcevski, G., Zhang, K.: A survey of information cascade analysis: models, predictions, and recent advances. ACM Comput. Surv. (CSUR) 54(2), 1–36 (2021)
16. Zhou, F., Xu, X., Zhang, K., Trajcevski, G., Zhong, T.: Variational information diffusion for probabilistic cascades prediction. In: IEEE INFOCOM 2020-IEEE Conference on Computer Communications, pp. 1618–1627. IEEE (2020)

GADN: GCN-Based Attentive Decay Network for Course Recommendation

Wen Chen, Wenjun Ma$^{(\boxtimes)}$, Yuncheng Jiang$^{(\boxtimes)}$, and Xiaomao Fan

School of Computer Science, South China Normal University, Guangzhou, China
ethan@m.scnu.edu.cn, {mawenjun,ycjiang}@scnu.edu.cn

Abstract. Course recommendation in online platforms aims to address the information explosion problem and make personalized recommendations for users. Most of the recent recommendation models mainly strive to model inherent user preference while ignoring the users' learning process and overlooking the relations among courses (e.g., The prerequisite course for Deep Learning is Linear Algebra). This paper proposes an innovative model named GCN-based Attentive Decay Network for Course Recommendation (GADN). Specifically, (1) we utilize the GCN-based Knowledge Extraction Layer to explicitly model the relationships on Collaborative Sequence Graph (CSG), which incorporates user-item interactions and course sequence information; (2) we incorporate the Knowledge Evolution Layer with a monotonic attention decay mechanism to model users' learning process. At the Knowledge Evolution Layer, we calculate attention weights using exponential decay and an absolute distance measure, in addition to the similarity between courses; (3) our method has a specific explanation through visualizing attention weight. Systematically, we conduct a series of experiments to demonstrate the effectiveness of our model on several prevalent metrics compared to the other prevailing baseline methods.

Keywords: Course recommendation · Sequence recommendation · Graph neural network · Attention mechanism · Explainable recommendation

1 Introduction

Nowadays, as Internet technologies become prevalent, online platforms such as Coursera, edX, and Udacity are accessible to most users. The surging number of online courses has put forward a more demanding need for more accurate and targeted recommendations for users.

Unlike other recommendation tasks, course recommendation is confronted with three vital challenges as it is highly related to learning input and the learning process. (1) According to the Input Hypothesis [11] in educational field, the input addressed to a learner should be "i+1", in which "i" refers to the current stage of knowledge, and "i+1" means the next stage of learning. In other words, the knowledge that learners are exposed to should be just far enough

G. Memmi et al. (Eds.): KSEM 2022, LNAI 13368, pp. 529–541, 2022.
https://doi.org/10.1007/978-3-031-10983-6_41

beyond their current competence that they can understand most of it but still be challenged to make progress. In light of the fact that most courses require some prerequisite knowledge, users are apt to enroll in the courses of which they have mastered the prior knowledge to guarantee the comprehensible input. For instance, the course "Machine Learning" will be more of a candidate course if a user is in possession of pre-knowledge of "Linear Algebra" and "Probability Theory". Hence, we argue that course recommendations should consider the information of courses' prior knowledge. (2) An intuitive fact is often overlooked that most users' enrolled courses demonstrate an onward trend of difficulty level during their learning process, indicating that enrolled courses in the distant past are not as informative as recently enrolled courses when we recommend courses to them. (3) An explainable recommendation can guide students to conduct a targeted review and consolidation, enhancing users' enthusiasm for the recommended courses and subsequent learning.

Traditional methods [3,12], deep learning methods [6,7,16,19] and specific methods [1,3,4,8,13,20,21] for course recommendation have all ignored the above three challenges in real-world course recommendation scenarios.

Therefore, we proposed a novel explainable model GADN based on the CSG and users' learning process. Specifically, (1) We constructed CSG which contained users' interactions and the sequence information of courses. For each user and corresponding historical enrolled courses, we obtained their embedding through the Embedding Layer and then fed them to the GCN-based Knowledge Extraction layer to explicitly model their high-order connectivity; (2) We incorporated the Knowledge Evolution Layer with monotonic attention decay mechanism to model users' learning process. At the Knowledge Evolution Layer, we calculated attention weights using exponential decay and an absolute distance measure, in addition to the similarity between courses; (3) Our method can provide explanation through visualizing attention weight, enabling users to select specific courses to review and consolidate before moving on.

The key contributions can be summarized as follows: (1) Inspired by the Input Hypothesis, we placed an emphasis on the information of courses' prior knowledge in the field of course recommendation. (2) We proposed a novel GCN-based method of course recommendation, dependent on monotonic attention decay mechanism. (3) The effectiveness of the proposed model was confirmed by serial experiments with real-world data collected from XuetangX.

2   Related Work

Course Recommendation. Traditional methods typically utilize Collaborative Filtering (CF) [12] or Matrix Factorization (MF) [10] to model users' preferences based on their interactions. For instance, MF transforms users and items into a generic vector space and estimates a user's preference on an item by the inner product between their vectors. Prevalent and effective as these methods are, they are criticised for data sparsity and the inability to model such side information as user/item attributes.

Recently, deep learning has revolutionized recommendation systems dramatically. One line of deep learning methods such as NeuFM [7] seek to improve the recommendation performance by incorporating auxiliary information with user ID and item ID, then estimating user preferences via Multi-Layer Perceptions (MLP) and Factorization machines (FM). Another line leverages multiple recommendation techniques to overcome the limitation of using only one method. For instance, (1) CKE [19] integrates Knowledge Graph(KG) and CF for joint training to take auxiliary information into full consideration; (2) LightGCN [6] utilizes the most crucial components of Graph Convolution Network(GCN) - neighborhood aggregation - for recommendation to exploit high-order collaborative signals; (3) KGAT [16] incorporates KG and the Graph Neural Network framework to achieve high-order relation modeling in an explicit and end-to-end manner. (4) Zhao et al. [21] propose a knowledge-aware recommendation which applies rich side information including Keyword Knowledge Graph and Course Knowledge Graph. But none of these took advantage of users' historical enrolled courses to capture their preferences.

Users' historical enrolled courses serves as a promising solution to model users' preferences. HRL [20] proposes a hierarchical reinforcement learning algorithm to revise the user profiles and tune the course recommendation model on the revised profiles. As two industrial methods, DIN [22] and BST [2] employs Deep Interest Network and Transformer [15] to model user behavior sequences.

In this paper, we use the monotonic attention decay mechanism to model learning processing for each enrolled courses in users' behavior sequences.

Graph Neural Network in Recommendation. Graphs play a crucial role in modern machine learning[17]. Recently, graph neural networks [4,6,16,17] have become recurrent topics in Recommendation and both have broad applicability. However, these methods do not pay attention to the sequence information of the course. In this paper, we propose the GCN-based Knowledge Extraction Layer to explicitly model the relationships between courses.

3   Problem Formulation

In this section, we first introduce the Collaborative Sequence Graph (CSG) which encodes user-item bipartite graph and course sequence graph into a unified graph, and then formalize the problem of course recommendation.

Collaborative Sequence Graph(CSG): In the course recommendation scenario, we generally have a historical record of user-course interactions. Therefore, we represent interaction data as a user-item bipartite graph $\mathcal{G}_1$, which is defined as $\{(u, Interact, i) \mid u \in \mathcal{U}, i \in \mathcal{I}\}$, where $\mathcal{U}$ and $\mathcal{I}$ denote user and course sets respectively. The enrolled courses typically require some reserve of prior knowledge. We can find the prerequisite knowledge of each course on the XuetangX platform. We organize that sequence information between courses as a course sequence graph. $\mathcal{G}_2$, which is presented as $\{(i_n, r_{nm}, i_m) \mid i_n, i_m \in \mathcal{I}, r \in \mathcal{R})\}$. Note that $\mathcal{R}$ contains two kinds of relations: prerequisite and successor. Then The bipartite graph can be seamlessly integrated with $\mathcal{G}_2$ as a unified graph (CSG) $\mathcal{G} = \{(h, r, t) \mid h, t \in \mathcal{E}', r \in \mathcal{R}'\}$, where $\mathcal{E} = \mathcal{U} \cup \mathcal{I}$ and $\mathcal{R}' = \mathcal{R} \cup \{Interact\}$.

Course Recommendation: Given a target user with corresponding interaction data, we strive to calculate the user's preference score for a series of candidate courses and recommend a top N list of courses. More formally, for a user u, we denote his enrolled courses sequence as $\{i_1^u, i_2^u, ..., i_n^u \mid i_t^u \in \mathcal{I}\}$, where i_k^u is the $k-th$ enrolled course by the user u. Each user u and each course i has a corresponding entity e in the CSG $\mathcal{G}$. The goal is to learn a predict function f that predicts the user u preference score $\tilde{y}_{ui}$ about the course i.

4   Proposed Method

In this section, we introduce the details of the GADN model, which contains two main aspects: (1) the GCN-based Knowledge Extraction Layer which is an end-to-end fusion that exploits the higher-order relationships of CSG to enrich users' and courses' representations, and (2) the Knowledge Evolution Layer including a monotonic attention decay mechanism that generates a modified representation of each course for better modeling users' learning process. The framework of our model is illustrated in Fig. 1.

The input is a user, corresponding enrolled courses, and target course. We obtain their embedding through the Embedding Layer, then feed them into the Knowledge Extraction Layer and the Knowledge Evolution Layer successively, and finally obtain the user's enrollment probability of the target course through the Prediction Network.

4.1   Embedding Layer

As in the mainstream recommendation model, we describe each user u and item i as a corresponding embedding vector $\mathbf{e}_u \in \mathbb{R}^d$ and $\mathbf{e}_i \in \mathbb{R}^d$, where d denotes the embedding size. This can be seen as building a parameter matrix as an embedding look-up table:

$$\mathbf{E} = [\ \underbrace{\mathbf{e}_{u_1}, \cdots, \mathbf{e}_{u_N}}_{\text{users embeddings}}, \underbrace{\mathbf{e}_{i_1}, \cdots, \mathbf{e}_{i_M}}_{\text{item embeddings}}\ ]. \tag{1}$$

where N represents the number of users, M the number of courses.

Typically, this embedding table serves as an initial state for user and item embeddings, which need to be optimized end-to-end before completing the recommendation task. In many classical recommendation methods, these ID embeddings are directly fed into the prediction layer to predict the user's preference score. In contrast, in our GADN framework, we refine these embeddings by propagating them over the CSG. This leads to more efficient embeddings for recommendation, as the embedding refinement step explicitly injects collaborative signals and sequence information of the course into the embeddings.

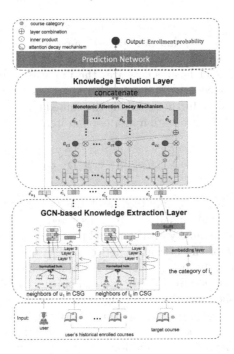

Fig. 1. An illustration of our proposed model GADN.

4.2   GCN-based Knowledge Extraction Layer

Inspired by the GCN-based recommendation method [6], we design a light information propagation structure, which can better capture collaborative filtering signals and course sequence information in the CSG. This does not result in any additional tunable parameter or burden of high-quality recommendations. Such information propagation can be abstracted as:

$$\mathbf{e}_i^{(k+1)} = \text{AGG}\left(\mathbf{e}_i^{(k)}, \left\{\mathbf{e}_u^{(k)} \cup \mathbf{e}_{i'}^{(k)} : u, i' \in \mathcal{N}_i\right\}\right) \tag{2}$$

The AGG is an aggregation function that considers the k-th layer's representation of the target user (or item) and its neighbor nodes. In the k-th Knowledge Extraction Layer, we adopt the simple weighted sum aggregator. The knowledge extraction operation in our model is defined as:

$$
\begin{aligned}
\mathbf{e}_u^{(k+1)} &= \sum_{i \in \mathcal{N}_u} \frac{1}{\sqrt{|\mathcal{N}_u|}\sqrt{|\mathcal{N}_i|}} \mathbf{e}_i^{(k)} \\
\mathbf{e}_i^{(k+1)} &= \sum_{u \in \mathcal{N}_i} \frac{1}{\sqrt{|\mathcal{N}_i|}\sqrt{|\mathcal{N}_u|}} \mathbf{e}_u^{(k)} + \sum_{i' \in \mathcal{N}_i} \frac{1}{\sqrt{|\mathcal{N}_i|}\sqrt{|\mathcal{N}_{i'}|}} \mathbf{e}_u^{(k)}
\end{aligned}
\tag{3}
$$

Given a target user(or a course), we only aggregate the neighbors' node connected in the CSG and do not integrate the target node because the following layer combination operation essentially captures the target node's information. However, it is worth noting that our special course aggregation operation differs from the existing operation. As defined in Eq. 3, for each target course, the embedding in the higher layer aggregates the upper-level user embedding and the prerequisite and successor courses for the target course. After the aggregation operation at K layers, we further combine the embeddings obtained at each layer to compose the final representation of a user(an item):

$$\mathbf{e}_u = \sum_{k=0}^{K} \alpha_k \mathbf{e}_u^{(k)}; \quad \mathbf{e}_i = \sum_{k=0}^{K} \alpha_k \mathbf{e}_i^{(k)} \tag{4}$$

where $\alpha_k \geq 0$ indicates the importance of the k-th layer embedding in constituting the final embedding. It can be considered as a hyper-parameter that needs to be adjusted manually or as a model parameter for automatic optimization (e.g.the output of the attention network [22]). Our experiments discover that setting α_k uniformly to $1/(k+1)$ has generally achieved good performance. Therefore, we do not design a dedicated component to optimize α_k to avoid unnecessarily complicating the knowledge extraction layer and to reduce the overall burdensome of the recommendation algorithm.

There are two main reasons we utilize the knowledge extraction layer: (1) the high-order connectivity information and the sequence information of the courses in CSG can significantly improve the performance of the recommendation algorithm; (2) the activation function and linear transformation layer are dispensed with in the AGG, consequently obtaining a more comprehensive embedding without increasing the number of tunable parameters.

4.3   Attention-Based Knowledge Evolution Layer

The Monotonic Attention Decay Mechanism. Inspired by the outstanding achievements of Transformer [15] in the field of natural language processing and sequence modeling, we adopt a monotonic decaying version of the scaled dot-product attention mechanism to model users' historical enrolled courses. First, we briefly summarize the original attention mechanism. Each course has a key, query, and value embedding layer in this framework, which maps the input to the output queries, keys, and values of dimensions D_q, D_k, and D_v respectively. Let $\mathbf{q}_t \in \mathbb{R}^{D_k \times 1}$ represent the query corresponding to the course that the user enrolls in at time step t, and we use the Softmax function to calculate the scaled point product attention value as:

$$\alpha_{t,\tau} = \text{Softmax}\left(\frac{\mathbf{q}_t^\top \mathbf{k}_\tau}{\sqrt{D_k}}\right) = \frac{\exp\left(\frac{\mathbf{q}_t^\top \mathbf{k}_\tau}{\sqrt{D_k}}\right)}{\sum_{\tau'} \exp\left(\frac{\mathbf{q}_t^\top \mathbf{k}_\tau}{\sqrt{D_k}}\right)} \in [0,1] \tag{5}$$

The output of the scaled dot-product attention mechanism is then given by $\sum_\tau \alpha_{t,\tau} \mathbf{v}_\tau \in \mathbb{R}^{D_v \times 1}$. $\mathbf{q}_\tau \in \mathbb{R}^{D_q \times 1}$, $\mathbf{k}_\tau \in \mathbb{R}^{D_k \times 1}$ and $\mathbf{v}_\tau \in \mathbb{R}^{D_v \times 1}$ denote the query, key and value for the enrolled course at time step τ, respectively.

However, this basic scaled dot-product attention mechanism will be inadequate for course recommendation. Considering most users' enrolled courses display an onward trend of difficulty level, users' enrolled courses in the distant past are not as informative as recent enrolled courses when we recommend their courses, that is, when users enroll in a new course, past knowledge in unrelated courses and that from too long ago should be relatively irrelevant. Specifically, we add a multiplicative exponential decay term to the attention coefficient as:

$$\alpha_{t,\tau} = \frac{\exp\left(s_{t,\tau}\right)}{\sum_{\tau'} \exp\left(s_{t,\tau'}\right)} \tag{6}$$

with

$$s_{t,\tau} = \frac{\exp(-\theta \cdot d(t,\tau)) \cdot q_t^\top k_\tau}{\sqrt{D_k}} \tag{7}$$

where $\theta > 0$ is a tunable decay rate parameter and $d(t,\tau)$ is relative distance measure between t-th and τ-th user enrolled courses. It is straightforward that the distance between two time steps is defined as their absolute value difference:

$$d(t,\tau) = |t - \tau| \tag{8}$$

In summary, the current course attention coefficient on a past course depends not only on the similarity between courses but also on the relative distance.

Transformer's Sub-layers. As the Transformer [15], we also use several sub-layers, including one for layer normalization [18], one for dropout [14], a fully-connected feedforward network, and a residual connection layer in Knowledge Evolution Layer.

4.4   Prediction Network

After concatenating the embedding of the user and the output of the Knowledge Evolution Layer, we use three fully-connected layers to predict the preference score, which is a prevailing practice in the Recommendation tasks.

To predict whether a user will enroll in the target course, we model it as a binary classification problem and use the sigmoid function as the output unit after Prediction Network. To train the model, we use the cross-entropy loss:

$$\mathcal{L} = -\frac{1}{N} \sum_{(x,y) \in \mathcal{D}} (y \log p(x) + (1 - y) \log(1 - p(x))) \tag{9}$$

where $\mathcal{D}$ represent all the samples, and $y \in \{0, 1\}$ is the label representing whether the user has enrolled in a course or not, $p(x)$ is the output of the Prediction Network after the sigmoid unit, representing the predicted enrollment probability of sample x.

5   Experiments

5.1   Dataset Description

We collect the users' activity data of the real-world XuetangX platform[1] from August 1, 2015, to August 1, 2017. Those who enrolled in at least five courses are selected users, and only the latest 100 enrolled courses are kept in the dataset for those who have enrolled in more than 100 courses. We combine over 6000 courses with repetition into 2583 courses. Since the original data[2] do not contain the prerequisite knowledge of the course, we crawl this information on the course detailed pages. Then we form it into the course sequence graph.

The resulting dataset is comprised of 58907 users, 2583 courses of 23 distinct categories, 586442 records of user-course interactions and 2404 course prerequisites. The distributions of the dataset are shown in the Fig. 2.

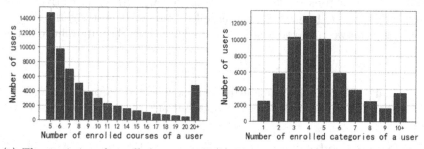

(a) The statistics of enrolled courses of users

(b) The statistics of enrolled categories of users

Fig. 2. Data statistics

5.2   Setting

Data Processing. After de-duplicating user activities, we take the last course enrolled by 20% of users in the dataset as the test set and the rest as the training set. Each sample in the training or the test set is a sequence of historical enrolled courses paired with a target course. During the training process, we build up 4 negative samples for each positive samples by replacing the target course with each of 4 randomly candidate courses. We consider each enrolled course in the test set as the target course and the corresponding courses of the same user in the training set as the historical courses during the test process. Each positive sample in the test set is paired with 99 randomly sampled negative courses.

Hyper-Parameters. Our model is implemented with Python 3.8 and Pytorch 1.5+, and the Adam [9] is chosen as the optimizer. Besides, we give the detail of the model parameters in Table 1.

---

[1] http://www.xuetangx.com.

[2] The original dataset is available at http://moocdata.cn/data/user-activity.

Table 1. Configuration of GADN.

Embedding size	100	Batch size	1024
Sequence length	20	Dropout	0.2
Epochs	20	Knowledge Extraction	$1 \sim 3$
Knowledge Evolution Layer	1	FFN hidden size	512
Prediction Network	$1024 * 512 * 256$	Learning rate	0.01

Evaluation Metrics. We evaluate all the methods in terms of the widely used metrics [5], including Hit Ratio (HR@K), Normalized Discounted Cumulative Gain (NDCG@K), and mean reciprocal rank (MRR). We set K to 5 and 10, and report the average metrics for all users in the test set.

5.3 Performance Comparison with Other Methods.

The methods in comparison include:

- **MLP** [7]: It adopts a multi-layer perception to predict the probability of recommending a course to the user.
- **NeuMF** [7]: It combines the traditional matrix factorization and multi-layer perceptron, which can extract low-dimensional and high-dimensional features simultaneously and can exert a good recommendation effect.
- **CKE** [19]: It is a KG-based representative regularization-based method, which exploits semantic embedding to enhance matrix factorization.
- **LightGCN** [6]: It learns user and item embeddings by linearly propagating them on the user-item interaction graph, and then calculates the final prediction score.
- **KGAT** [16]: It integrates the knowledge graph and interaction graph into a unified graph space and uses the knowledge-aware attention to distinguish the importance of neighbor embedding.
- **HRL** [20]: It utilizes the hierarchical reinforcement model to modify the user's profile, which is in aid of prediction score.
- **DIN** [22]: It uses attention to capture users' interest in the historical behavior. The users' embedding changes with candidate products, which effectively improves the performance of model.
- **BST** [2]: It introduces the Transformer layer to model the user's historical behavior sequence, so as to capture users' dynamic interest.

The Table 2 shows the comparison with the above methods. Due to the lack of relevant Keyword Knowledge Graph and Course Knowledge Graph, we do not compare with the model proposed by Zhao et al. [21].

Table 2. Performance comparison.

Models	HR@5	HR@10	NDCG@5	NDCG@10	MRR
MLP	0.4427	0.6480	0.3059	0.3624	0.3026
NeuMF	0.4944	0.6534	0.3518	0.4033	0.3429
CKE	0.4472	0.6055	0.3126	0.3623	0.3050
LightGCN	0.4834	0.6434	0.3457	0.3973	0.3385
KGAT	0.4871	0.6533	0.3477	0.4013	0.3403
HRL	0.4854	0.6567	0.3430	0.3984	0.3367
DIN	0.5331	0.6923	0.3795	0.4310	0.3654
BST	0.5376	0.6990	0.3853	0.4374	0.3718
GADN-1	**0.5630**	**0.7156**	**0.4081**	**0.4576**	**0.3920**

It can be noticed that our method is superior than other methods in various evaluation metrics:

- Our proposed method GADN-1 outperforms the comparison baseline in all cases. The value of 1 refers to the number of knowledge extraction layers.
- MLP and NeuMF cannot effectively extract users' potential interests from users' historical behavior, negatively affecting their performance.
- Regarding the methods based on GCN or the Knowledge Graph, we organize user-courses interaction and CSG into a knowledge graph for KGAT and CKE. It turns out that performance of the graph-based methods discussed above is ineffective owing to the same deficiency as MLP and NeuMF.
- The sequence-based methods excel in all the methods in comparison in that they overcome the problem of users' preference deviation. But the performance of HRL is criticised that the interactions of users in the dataset are relatively short, and it will be more challenging to capture users' interests after screening. As two industrial methods, DIN and BST are also under attack for not capturing side information (e.g. the sequence information between courses) or modelling users' learning process.

5.4   Ablation and Visualization

Ablation Study. To prove the two critical innovations of the method, the GCN-based knowledge extraction layer and monotonic attention decay mechanism, we conduct several additional ablation experiments and compare the results. Firstly, we utilize Knowledge Evolution layer with the basic scaled dot-product attention as a basemodel. Following, we use the monotonic attention decay mechanism instead of the basic attention. Finally, to investigate with how many knowledge extraction layers can achieve the best performance, we add the knowledge extraction layer and search the layer numbers in the range of {1,2,3}. Table 3 summarizes the experimental results, where the value of each number

Table 3. Results from ablation experiments.

Model	Knowledge extraction	Monotonic attention decay	HR@5	HR@10	NDCG@5	NDCG@10	MRR
Basemodel	✗	✗	0.5376	0.6990	0.3853	0.4374	0.3718
Basemodel-D	✗	✓	0.5469	0.7058	0.3941	0.4456	0.3799
GADN-1	1	✓	**0.5630**	**0.7156**	**0.4081**	**0.4576**	**0.3920**
GADN-2	2	✓	0.5621	0.7150	0.4059	0.4554	0.3893
GADN-3	3	✓	0.5573	0.7098	0.4024	0.4516	0.3860

in Knowledge Extraction column refers to the number of knowledge extraction layers in the model.

We can observe that the basemodel is overtaken by basemodel-D which possesses a monotonic attention decay that can better model users' learning process. Then we add the knowledge extraction layer to capture side information and collaborative filtering signals, which improve the model's performance with no increase of tunable parameters. Most notably, when the number of knowledge extraction layers is 1, the model performance outstrips any other model. A possible explanation is that the typical problem of Graph Convolutional Network - over smoothing leads to the descent of the model's performance while the number of knowledge extraction layers is increasing.

Visualization. Figure 3 visualizes the attention weights in the Knowledge Evolution Layer for a single user for twelve consecutive steps. The first eleven time steps are the historical enrolled courses which follow a hierarchy of ascending difficulty level, and the last one "Advanced Database System" refers to the recommended course. It's shown that "Database System (Part 1)" and "Operating System" attribute the most attention weights to course recommendation, while English-related courses attribute the least. And the attention weights of the courses in the distant past are not as informative as those in the immediate past. Similarity and recency are key factors that control the attention weights.

These observations suggest that our monotonic attention decay mechanism can provide user feedback by linking a user's target course to their enrolled courses in the past and this information may enable users to select specific courses to review and consolidate before moving on.

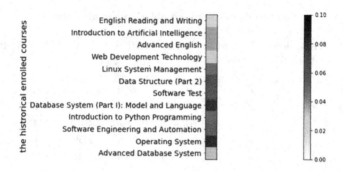

Fig. 3. Attention weights for the enrolled courses of a user

6   Conclusion and Future Work

In this paper, we proposed a new GCN-based method of course recommendation, dependent on monotonic attention decay mechanism. Our method improved the existing course recommendation methods by constructing the embedding of users and courses through the Knowledge Extraction Layer, using modified attention to model the users' learning process on the appropriate time scale. The experimental results in a benchmark real-world dataset showed that our method outweighed the majority of prominent recommendation methods and had certain explanation through visualizing attention weight.

The way of future work includes adding relevant texts of the courses to further improve the explanation and extending the monotonic attention decay module to other algorithms to prove its effectiveness.

Acknowledge. The works described in this paper are supported by Key Projects of the National Social Science Foundation of China (No. 19ZDA041), the National Natural Science Foundation of China under Grant Nos. 61772210 and U1911201; Guangdong Province Universities Pearl River Scholar Funded Scheme (2018); The Project of Science and Technology in Guangzhou in China under Grant No. 202007040006.

References

1. Bulathwela, S., Perez-Ortiz, M., Yilmaz, E., Shawe-Taylor, J.: TrueLearn: a family of Bayesian algorithms to match lifelong learners to open educational resources. In: AAAI, pp. 565–573 (2020)
2. Chen, Q., Zhao, H., Li, W., Huang, P., Ou, W.: Behavior sequence Transformer for E-commerce recommendation in Alibaba. In: Proceedings of the 1st International Workshop on Deep Learning Practice for High-Dimensional Sparse Data with KDD, pp. 1–4 (2019)
3. Elbadrawy, A., Karypis, G.: Domain-aware grade prediction and top-N course recommendation. In: Proceedings of the 10th ACM Conference on Recommender Systems, pp. 183–190 (2016)
4. Gong, J., et al.: Attentional graph convolutional networks for knowledge concept recommendation in MOOCs in a heterogeneous view. In: SIGIR, pp. 79–88 (2020)

5. Gunawardana, A., Shani, G.: Evaluating recommender systems. In: Ricci, F., Rokach, L., Shapira, B. (eds.) Recommender Systems Handbook, pp. 265–308. Springer, New York (2015). https://doi.org/10.1007/978-1-0716-2197-4_15

6. He, X., Deng, K., Wang, X., Li, Y., Zhang, Y., Wang, M.: LightGCN: Simplifying and powering graph convolution network for recommendation. In: SIGIR. p. 639–648 (2020)

7. He, X., Liao, L., Zhang, H., Nie, L., Hu, X., Chua, T.S.: Neural collaborative filtering. In: WWW, pp. 173–182 (2017)

8. Jiang, W., Pardos, Z.A., Wei, Q.: Goal-based course recommendation. In: Learning Analytics and Knowledge (LAK), pp. 36–45 (2019)

9. Kingma, D.P., Ba, J.: Adam: a method for stochastic optimization. In: ICLR, pp. 1–15 (2015)

10. Koren, Y., Bell, R., Volinsky, C.: Matrix factorization techniques for recommender systems. Computer, 30–37 (2009)

11. Krashen, S.D.: The input hypothesis: issues and implications. Language, 171–173 (1985)

12. Sarwar, B., Karypis, G., Konstan, J., Riedl, J.: Item-based collaborative filtering recommendation algorithms. World Wide Web J. 285–295 (2001)

13. Sheng, D., Yuan, J., Xie, Q., Luo, P.: MOOCRec: an attention meta-path based model for top-K recommendation in MOOC. In: KSEM, pp. 280–288 (2020)

14. Srivastava, N., Hinton, G., Krizhevsky, A., Sutskever, I., Salakhutdinov, R.: Dropout: a simple way to prevent neural networks from overfitting. JMLR, 1929–1958 (2014)

15. Vaswani, A., et al.: Attention is all you need. In: NIPS (2017)

16. Wang, X., He, X., Cao, Y., Liu, M., Chua, T.S.: KGAT: knowledge graph attention network for recommendation. In: DMKD, pp. 950–958 (2019)

17. Wu, Z., Pan, S., Chen, F., Long, G., Zhang, C., Philip, S.Y.: A comprehensive survey on graph neural networks. TNNLS, 4–24 (2020)

18. Xu, J., Sun, X., Zhang, Z., Zhao, G., Lin, J.: Understanding and improving layer normalization. In: NIPS (2019)

19. Zhang, F., Yuan, N.J., Lian, D., Xie, X., Ma, W.Y.: Collaborative knowledge base embedding for recommender systems. In: DMKD, pp. 353–362 (2016)

20. Zhang, J., Hao, B., Chen, B., Li, C., Chen, H., Sun, J.: Hierarchical reinforcement learning for course recommendation in MOOCs. In: AAAI, pp. 435–442 (2019)

21. Zhao, Y., Ma, W., Jiang, Y., Zhan, J.: A MOOCs recommender system based on user's knowledge background. In: KSEM, pp. 140–153 (2021)

22. Zhou, G., et al.: Deep interest evolution network for click-through rate prediction. In: AAAI, pp. 5941–5948 (2019)

Discrimination of News Political Bias Based on Heterogeneous Graph Neural Network

Yanze Ren[1(✉)], Yan Liu[1(✉)], Guangsheng Zhang[2], Lian Liu[2], and Peng Lv[1]

[1] Henan Key Laboratory of Cyberspace Situation Awareness, Zhengzhou, China
ryz0721@163.com, ms.liuyan@foxmail.com
[2] Investigation Technology Center PLCMC, Beijing 100000, China

Abstract. The polarization of western political ideology is becoming more and more serious, and it is difficult for news articles to keep objective justice. Their contents are often biased towards a particular political party to guide the trend of public opinion. Therefore, judging the political inclination of news texts is of great significance to national election prediction and public opinion control. The existing modeling methods based on news content mostly rely on the semantic information of news. The combination of various element features and structural information in the news is insufficient. This paper proposes a political bias discrimination method of news based on a heterogeneous neural network, with multiple information related to prejudice in the news as the nodes of a heterogeneous network. By enriching the representation of nodes through a heterogeneous graph neural network and using the fused node features to distinguish the political news bias. The experimental results show that our model can achieve 84.30% accuracy and 83.34% Macro F1 value in news political bias classification. Compared with the baseline model Bert +CNN with the best experimental results, the accuracy and Macro F1 are improved by 1.92% and 0.4%, respectively.

Keywords: News political bias discrimination · Heterogeneous neural network · Entity recognition · LDA

1 Introduction

The discrimination of political bias has essential research significance. Over the past decade, we have witnessed the intensification of civil discourse and the increasing polarization of political ideology. As the Associated Press said, "Americans are more divided than ever before, and they are deadlocked in social issues, race, gender, and economy". A political position has become the dominant factor in daily activities, and we live in an era of the echo chamber and the proliferation of erroneous information about parties. These unprecedented situations require researchers to strengthen the recognition of political views.

Nowadays, news released by news media is widely spread on social networks, and people's political views are influenced by political news. However, it is difficult to detect bias in the news because the content in the news is richer, and the expression of political inclination is reflected in many details. Moreover, the expression is more obscure

G. Memmi et al. (Eds.): KSEM 2022, LNAI 13368, pp. 542–555, 2022.
https://doi.org/10.1007/978-3-031-10983-6_42

than the short text. The two political news items shown in Fig. 1 respectively describe the left-leaning and right-leaning political attitudes of the United States towards the "Russian-Ukrainian military conflict." Right-leaning news shows more disappointment with Biden's introduction of relevant policies; Left-leaning news supports Biden's promulgation of applicable laws. In the above examples, some media help their political parties by publishing news covering tendentious views, guiding the masses' judgement of the "Russia-Ukraine Incident", changing the masses' political views and paving the way for the next election. Therefore, it is critical important to choose the traditional news without political bias to ensure the objectiveness of audience towards current news.

Several Senate Republicans continue to drill the Biden administration after denying Poland's proposal to send fighter jets to Ukraine. In a joint press conference Thursday, Senate Minority Leader Mitch McConnell (R-Ky.) expressed his frustration at the lack of urgency from Joe Biden's White House. "This administration has been a step behind every, every step of the way, if you will," stated the Kentucky lawmaker. "Never quite doing things soon enough.

In spite of its immense danger, the campaign for a "no-fly zone" in Ukraine seems to be gaining momentum, with twenty-seven foreign policy luminaries signing a letter earlier this week calling on the Joe Biden administration to set up a "limited" one over the country, to protect the humanitarian corridors recently agreed to in Russia-Ukraine talks. The letter has already been widely cited in the press, giving the disastrous idea more legitimacy.

Fig. 1. Different political tendencies of news

In order to determine the political orientation of the news, current research mainly focuses on content analysis and analysis based on various external information. The work based on content often relies on the semantic information of news texts. Ahmed et al. [1] and Bhatia et al. [2] modeled the ideological perspective at the thematic level respectively to infer the political bias of news. Iyyer et al. [3] and Chen et al. [4] all applied recursive neural network (RNN) to identify political bias at the sentence level. Li et al. [5] injected entity information into the text model to identify the differences between news narratives from different perspectives. The discrimination of news political tendency based on external information is gradually diversified. Baly et al. [6] comprehensively judged the political bias of news by combining the multi-source information of news, that is, who wrote it, described it on social media, and who read it. Chen et al. [7] proposed a method to predict political bias based on an opinion knowledge graph. Li et al. [8] captured how news spread in social networks and used graph convolutional networks to judge news orientation. The above modeling method based on news content is not comprehensive enough to consider elements. It does not make use of the information such as subject, entities and sentences at the same time for modeling and does not consider the structural relations of the information.

Therefore, this paper puts forward a news political tendency discrimination model based on a heterogeneous graph neural network, which can comprehensively judge the political bias of news by combining the essential elements of information and the structural relationship between them. Specifically, the political orientation of news is not purely emotional analysis but highly related to the theme and entity. Thus the discrimination of news orientation needs to emphasize the critical role of the research object. Firstly, this paper uses named entity recognition technology and the LDA topic model [9]. The entity and topic information in the news is extracted, and the graph network model is established by associating it with sentences. Secondly, the node representations are obtained by a heterogeneous graph convolution algorithm. Finally, all node representations output by the heterogeneous networks is fused to judge the political tendency of news. On the whole, this paper has made the following contributions:

- In this paper, we propose a novel end-to-end graph neural model. As far as we know, this is the first time that the heterogeneous network of modeling news content has been used to judge the political tendency of news.
- In this paper, a heterogeneous network containing news entities, topics, and sentences is designed, and a fusion method is intended for the nodes of the heterogeneous network output. The fused features are used to distinguish the political orientation of news. The ablation experiment results show that our method is effective in the selection of feature nodes and node fusion strategy.
- We conduct extensive experiments to evaluate our method and competitive baselines. As a result, our method out-performs all state-of-the-art approaches. It is proved that the heterogeneous network model can represent political news features more effectively.

2 Related Work

2.1 Discrimination of Political News Inclination

The analysis of ideology in news is currently in the development stage. People are increasingly interested in detecting political bias from large text corpora automatically. Sinno et al. [10] proposed a multidimensional framework to measure ideology's time, distance and other aspects. Li et al. [11] proposed a pretraining model, making it easier to detect news bias by utilizing information from rich social backgrounds and language. Guo et al. [12] conducted a case study on the influence of ideological topic bias on the pretraining model of natural language processing. Feng et al. [13] constructed an American political knowledge map containing 10,703 triples to strengthen the representation of the political bias of the news. Feng et al. [14] also proposed the entity detection of political stance and the judgment of political ideology of social entities.

Generally speaking, among the current news political orientation analysis tasks, the mainstream research mostly base on the emotion classification of the pretraining model, with the introduction of external information to enhance the pretraining model of the entity and other information representation. The work also goes deeper into time-related measurements and the propensity analysis of entities in the news. In this paper, we intend to combine the feature representation method of the above related research, and focus on the news content to distinguish its political orientation.

2.2 Heterogeneous Graph Neural Network

In recent years, Graph Neural Networks (GNN) has become a research hotspot in deep learning, which can only be used to deal with homogeneous graphs. However, the types of nodes and edges between nodes of various graphs are different in reality. To solve this problem, the heterogeneous networks have been created, which can aggregate data of different attributes together. HAN [15] used semantic-level attention and node-level attention to learn the importance of meta-path and node neighbor at the same time and obtained the final node representation through corresponding aggregation operations. HetGNN [16] used LSTM to aggregate the node neighbors under a special relationship and update the node representation. Its neighbors are selected through random walk restart. Yang Hu [17] created the HGAT model to classify short texts, extract entities and topics from texts to construct heterogeneous networks, and capture their rich relationships to solve semantic sparsity of short texts. Linmei Hu [18] created the CompareNet model to extract information from news to construct a heterogeneous network and compare it with Wikipedia knowledge to detect fake news.

The modeling of homogeneous information networks will inevitably lead to the loss of a large amount of information. Modeling data into heterogeneous networks can enrich the expression of information, thus mining more meaningful information. This paper focuses on combining the above heterogeneous network modeling methods and using heterogeneous graph representation learning to solve the feature representation of news.

3 Methods

3.1 Problem Definition

Sentences in the news are split according to symbols to get multiple sentences of a document. News entity is about people, places, institutions, things, locations, and other entity types. The topic of news is obtained from the news corpus by LDA model.

News political bias can also be defined as the following form: aiming at the sentence $S = \{s_1, s_2, \cdots, s_m\}$ in every political news d, where m indicates the number of sentences in the news, and s_n is for one of the sentences. The NLTK(Natural Language Toolkit) named entity recognition technology is used to obtain the entities in the news. The entities in the sentence are identified as $E = \{e_1, e_2, \cdots, e_n\}$, and n indicates the number of entities in the sentence. Get the topic $T = \{t_1, t_2, \cdots, t_K\}$ in the news corpus, where K is the total number of topics set, and associate each sentence with P most relevant topics. The expression of political inclination can generally be distinguished by parties, political institutions, etc., and the division of people's political factions gradually shows a concentrated distribution according to regions. At the same time, the emotions presented on different topics also show different political positions. The goal is to judge the political inclination y of given news by combining the above information. According to our task, we define the political inclination as left-leaning, neutral, and right-leaning, $y \in \{0, 1, 2\}$.

3.2   Overall Framework of the Model

As shown in Fig. 2, this section focuses on the overall process of news political bias discrimination. (1) Extract entity and topic information from news and build a heterogeneous network with sentences. (2) Using the heterogeneous graph convolution algorithm of double attention, the vector representation of all nodes is obtained. (3) Fusion of node information. (4) Discrimination of political news bias.

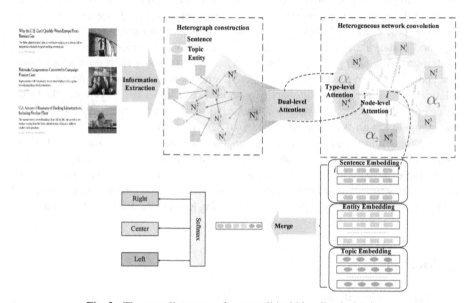

Fig. 2.   The overall process of news political bias discrimination

3.3   Heterogeneous Network Construction

News heterogeneous network includes three types of nodes and three types of edges:

The first type is sentence node, which uses LSTM to encode a sentence $s = \{\omega_1, \omega_2, \cdots, \omega_m\}$, ω_m represents every word in the sentence, and the feature vector of the sentence is $x_s \in R^M$. The second type is the topic node. The initial vector representation of topic $t \in T$ is encoded by one-hot, and its feature vector representation is $x_t \in R^K$. The third type is the entity node. For the encoding of entities, we use randomly initializing word vectors. For words appearing in the corpus, a fixed dictionary size is adopted, dimensions are defined, and word vectors are randomly initialized to obtain $x_e \in R^N$, N is the dimension of word vectors. This representation method will not make the entity acquire any external knowledge.

The three types of edges are sentence to sentence bidirectional connection, subject to sentence bidirectional connection, sentence to entity unidirectional connection. Note that a one-way connection between a sentence and an entity is different from a two-way connection between a sentence and a topic because the topic is the global information of the sentence; in contrast, the entity exists in different positions in the sentence. A one-way connection between sentences and entities is established to not disturb the meaning of different parts of a sentence by the entity information of different places.

These nodes and edges form a text network graph $G = (v, \varepsilon)$, where v represents the set of nodes $v = \{S \cup T \cup E\}$, ε represents the edges between nodes, $\varepsilon = \{(S \leftrightarrow S) \cup (S \leftrightarrow T) \cup (S \rightarrow E)\}$.

3.4 Heterogeneous Network Convolution Algorithm

We use the heterogeneous graph neural network to deal with the heterogeneous graph constructed by the above pairs. Consider the differences between various types of information; for example, given a particular node, different types of neighboring nodes may have different influences on it and different adjacent nodes of the same type may also have different importance. This paper uses a heterogeneous network convolution algorithm with double attention.[19]. They are projected into an implicit public space by their respective transformation matrices.

The calculation method is that the matrix $H^{(l+1)}$ representation of heterogeneous convolution $l+1$ layer is updated by aggregating different neighboring nodes H_τ^l. The initial node vector matrix is $H^{(0)} = X$, the rows of X are all nodes, and the columns are the characteristics of all nodes. The specific formula is:

$$H^{(l+1)} = \sigma(\sum_{\tau \in T} \mathcal{B}_\tau \cdot H_\tau^{(l)} \cdot W_\tau^{(l+1)}) \tag{1}$$

In the formula, $\sigma(\cdot)$ denotes the activation function, and the nodes τ have different transfer matrices $W_\tau^{(l)}$. The transfer matrix $W_\tau^{(l)}$ considers different feature spaces and projects into the same feature space. $\mathcal{B}_\tau \in R^{|v| \times |v_\tau|}$ is the attention transfer matrix, whose rows represent all the nodes and columns represent their neighboring nodes with type τ. Its element $\mathcal{B}_\tau$ in the v throw and the v' column is computed as follows:

$$\beta_{vv'} = Softmax_{v'}\left(\sigma\left(v^T \cdot \alpha_\tau[h_v, h_{v'}]\right)\right) \tag{2}$$

where v is the attention vector, α_τ is the attention weight of different types of nodes. h_v and $h_{v'}$ respectively represent the current node vector and the vector of its neighboring node v'. Softmax function is used to normalize the adjacent nodes of node v.

In the aggregation of information, the calculation method of attention weight α_τ of different types of nodes is as follows:

$$\alpha_\tau = Softmax_\tau\left(\sigma\left(\mu_\tau^T \cdot [h_v, h_\tau]\right)\right) \tag{3}$$

Among them, the Softmax function is used for normalization across all types, μ_τ is the attention weight under τ type, h_v is the embedded representation of the current node, and h_τ is the sum of the weights of all neighboring nodes $h_{v'}$ under the τ type. The above $\sigma(\cdot)$ is the activation function, specifically using Leaky Relu.

We can get node vector representation with rich semantic and structural information through an L-layer heterogeneous graph convolution network.

3.5 Learning Optimization

For all node eigenvectors output by heterogeneous networks, we adopt the strategy of fusing node representations to judge political tendencies comprehensively. Firstly, for all sentence node representations output by heterogeneous networks, we get the vector of sentence classes by averaging, and the entities and topics are also calculated by attention. We believe that the political orientation of news is highly correlated with the subject entity and sentence, and the judgment of political orientation solely relying on a specific type of node output by a heterogeneous network will lead to insufficient information aggregation and affect the judgment effect. In this paper, three kinds of nodes are spliced to get H_d as the final representation of news and then introduced into the softmax layer to detect the political tendency:

$$Z = \text{softmax}(W_0 H_d + b_0) \tag{4}$$

where W_0 is the parameter matrix, and b_0 is the intercept of linear change. In the training process of the model, the cross-entropy loss function is used:

$$L = -\sum_D \sum_{i=1}^{Y} y_i \log(\tilde{y}_i) + \lambda \sum_{w \in q} w^2 \tag{5}$$

where Y is the number of predicted labels, y is the annotation of news articles, q are all learnable parameters in our proposed model, and λ is a hyperparameter.

We use biased labels on the whole news article during the training process. Although this labeling method is not perfect, the narratives about some aspects in the articles may be inconsistent with the overall political views. However, this is a reasonable approximation because it is difficult to obtain a label for something in the news, but it can present a particular political concept as a whole. In the test, we used the attention mechanism to aggregate nodes of the same type, enhance some words with political ideas, and re-spliced node information to represent the whole news, which combined the political views of each interest in the news.

4 Experiment

4.1 Experimental Setup

4.1.1 Datasets and Evaluation Methods

Our experiment is completed on the ALLsides news data set. ALLsides website will push news articles from all aspects of the political spectrum for every popular event. The website will hide the source of the articles and give the final value according to readers' evaluation of the political tendency of the articles. Baly et al. [20] used the large-scale news data set created by the website to publish 37,554 news articles from 73 news media obtained on the website, covering more than 100 topics. This dataset represents real political scenes. Table 1 shows the statistical results of the data set. Data set division: 1300 data sets are used as test sets in the experiment, which is close to the data set division ratio of Ramy Baly et al. [23].

Table 1. The statistical results of the ALLsides data set

	Political inclination	News quantity	Proportion of
ALLsides	Left tilt (0)	13005	34.6%
	Neutral (1)	10815	28.8%
	Right (2)	13734	36.6%

Evaluation method: The political tendency is judged as three classification results, and the Accuracy and Macro F1 values are used as the evaluation indexes of the experimental effect.

4.1.2 Baseline Model

We compare the model of this experiment with several baseline methods with better text information processing effects, including the following methods.

SkipThought [21]: Each document is regarded as a long sentence, and the skip-gram model in word2vec is used for reference. The previous sentence and the next sentence of this sentence are predicted by one sentence, and unsupervised sentence representation is generated.

HAN [22]: Use word-level and sentence-level bidirectional LSTM to construct vector representation for each sentence and document. At the lexical and sentence levels, self-attention is used to aggregate hidden states.

FastText [23]: The input is several words and their n-gram features to represent a single document. The words and n-gram vectors of the whole document are superimposed and averaged to get the document vector, and then the document vector is used for classification.

TextCNN [24]: The convolution neural network CNN is applied to text classification. Several convolution kernels of different sizes extract the critical information in sentences so that the local relevance can be better captured.

Bert [25]: The goal of the BERT model is to use the large-scale unlabeled corpus to train and obtain the representation of the text with rich semantic information. The pre-training process is carried out using the word MASK and the prediction of the following sentence on the large corpus. The finetune process of the Bert model is suitable for all kinds of text tasks.

ERNIE [26]: It aims to learn the language representation enhanced by a knowledge masking strategy. Unlike Bert, the masking strategy includes entity masking and phrase masking, which implicitly learns information about knowledge and long semantic dependency to guide word embedding learning.

4.1.3 Model Parameter Setting

In this paper, the Pytorch deep learning framework is used as the development environment for the experiment, the NVIDIA GV100 graphics card is used for the deep learning server, and NLTK is used for entity extraction in the news. The ALLsides dataset comes

Table 2. Parameter setting

Hyperparameter	Value
Number of topics	100
Each sentence is associated with P topics	3
Heterogeneous network layer L	1
Hide dimension	300
Node embedding dimension	32
Maximum sentence length	50
Batch size	32
Learning rate	1×10^{-5}
Dropout	0.3
Epochs	20
Optimizer	Adam

from more than 100 topics, and the number of LDA topics is set to 100. Other related parameters are set in Table 2.

4.2 Experimental Results

4.2.1 The Influence of Topic Number on Experimental Results

In constructing a heterogeneous network, we compare different numbers of topic associated with each sentence, and obtain the results shown in Fig. 3. The results show that the classification accuracy and Macro F1 both show a trend of first increasing and then decreasing with the number of topics, and the best is reached at 3. The model's classification accuracy for political tendencies is 84.30%, and the Macro F1 value is 83.34%. This may be since sentences are related to topics with low probability, which leads to increased noise and does not play a role in distinguishing content differences by topic information. Therefore, the follow-up work of this experiment will set the P-value to 3.

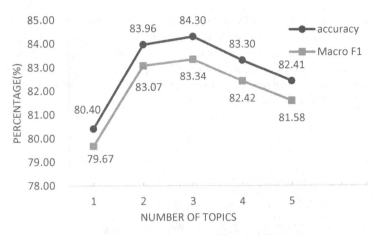

Fig. 3. Experimental results under different number of topics

4.2.2 Influence of Heterogeneous Networks with Different Node Types on Experimental Results

In the process of constructing a heterogeneous network of news texts, to prove the effectiveness of selecting topic and entity nodes in judging political tendency, we separately constructed sentence, and topic network (ST), sentence and entity network (SE) and sentence, topic and entity network (STE). As can be seen from Fig. 4 that the heterogeneous network constructed by selecting two types of nodes has a lower discrimination effect on political inclination than selecting three types of nodes. It is proved that extracting entity topic information at the same time will be more suitable for the task of judging political inclination.

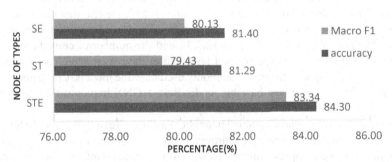

Fig. 4. Experimental results of heterogeneous networks with different types of nodes

4.2.3 Influence of Node Category Fusion on Experimental Results

After initially passing through heterogeneous networks, the nodes fused the information of other nodes, and the same type of nodes was merged by the method of average pooling. We conducted the following experiment to judge whether a specific type of node can be directly classified for political bias, using a specific type of nodes output from heterogeneous networks to directly judge political bias. And the results shown in Fig. 5 are obtained by fusing the three types of nodes. The results show that in evaluating the political inclination of news, using a specific type of node to judge will weaken the information of other attributes, thus fusing all kinds of nodes again will enhance the expression of political inclination of news.

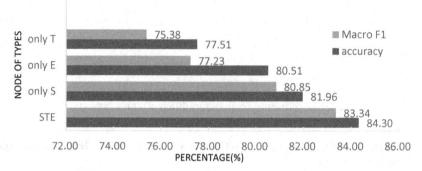

Fig. 5. Influence of graph node fusion on experimental results

4.2.4 The Comparison of the Experimental Results of the Baseline Model

To prove the effectiveness of our model, we compared the optimal model obtained from the above experiment with the baseline model. SkipThought and HAN used the results in the article [5]. FastText and TextCNN model parameters are set to batch size = 128, pad size = 512, learning rate is set to 1e–4, and hidden layer dimension is 256. For Bert and ERNIE, batch size is set to 32, pad size = 512, the learning rate is set to 5e–5, and hidden layer dimension is 768. Bert + CNN adds a convolution layer to Bert's output. The convolution kernel size is (2,3,4), and the number of convolution kernels is 256. Table 3 shows the experimental results after the experiment. The results show that our model is superior to seven commonly used baseline models. Compared with the experimental results, the best baseline model Bert + CNN improves the accuracy and Macro F1 by 1.92% and 0.4%, respectively.

Generally, models such as SkipThought, FastText, TextCNN, and HAN get the feature representation of sentences through modeling, but the expression of political inclination is more complex. Simply relying on the semantic information of sentences will lead to indistinguishable differences in political bias, and the experimental results are poor. The effect of Bert, ERNIE, and Bert +CNN is greatly improved because they use the method of generating dynamic word vectors, Adjusting the vector representation of words according to the semantic information of the context, to learn subtle political bias in the news. Our method highlights the importance of topics and entities in the news based on sentence semantic information representation, and modeling heterogeneous networks can enhance the interaction between information. The experimental results show that this modeling method is very effective for political bias discrimination. At

Table 3. Baseline comparison results

Model	Accuracy	Macro F1
SkipThounght	68.67	–
FastText	65.00	65.71
TextCNN	69.22	70.12
HAN	74.9	–
Bert	78.46	78.88
ERNIE	81.08	81.28
Bert+CNN	82.38	82.94
Ours	**84.30**	**83.34**

the same time, this method may apply to more fields of text classification research. The heterogeneous network model may apply to more scenarios like recommendation systems and social networks.

5 Conclusion

In this paper, we propose a news political tendentiousness discrimination model based on a heterogeneous graph neural network, which can extract essential elements from a piece of news to build a heterogeneous network and enrich the representation of news documents through the heterogeneous network model. For each piece of news, extract its theme and entity, and establish a heterogeneous document graph with the sentences. It can make the information containing political elements conveyed in sentences and obtain a news political bias classifier to learn the news representation with rich features. The model has achieved the best classification effect on the ALLsides data set, which proves the effectiveness of our method.

In future work, we will continue to work on three aspects. First, we will choose more effective entities, classify the types of entities, and inject the external knowledge information of entities into the model to further improve the discrimination effect of political news bias. Second, we consider extracting more element information from news content to establish heterogeneous networks. Third, we consider combining social networks or domain knowledge graph to judge the political bias of news.

Acknowledgments. This work is supported by the Science and Technology Department of Henan Province in China. The project name is the research on false information detection and dissemination suppression technology for social media. (No. 222102210081). And it's also supported by the National Natural Science Foundation of China (No. U1804263, U1736214, 62172435, 62002386) and the Zhongyuan Science and Technology Innovation Leading Talent Project (No. 214200510019).

References

1. Ahmed, A., Xing, E.P.: Staying informed: supervised and semi-supervised multi-view topical analysis of ideological perspective. In: Proceedings of the 2010 Conference on Empirical Methods in Natural Language Processing, pp. 1140–1150 (2010)
2. Bhatia, S.P.D.: Topic-specific sentiment analysis can help identify political ideology, 79–84 (2019). https://doi.org/10.18653/v1/w18-6212
3. Iyyer, M., Enns, P., Boyd-Graber, J., Resnik, P.: Political ideology detection using recursive neural networks. In: Proceedings of the 52nd Annual Meeting of the Association for Computational Linguistics (volume 1: Long Papers), vol. 1, pp. 1113–1122 (2014). https://doi.org/10.3115/v1/p14-1105
4. Chen, W.-F., Al Khatib, K., Wachsmuth, H., Stein, B.: Analyzing political bias and unfairness in news articles at different levels of granularity, 149–154 (2020). https://doi.org/10.18653/v1/2020.nlpcss-1.16
5. Li, C., Goldwasser, D.: MEAN: multi-head entity aware attention network for political perspective detection in news media. In: Proceedings of the Fourth Workshop on NLP for Internet Freedom: Censorship, Disinformation, and Propaganda, pp. 66–75 (2021). https://doi.org/10.18653/v1/2021.nlp4if-1.10
6. Baly, R., et al.: What was written vs. who read it: news media profiling using text analysis and social media context, pp. 3364–3374 (2020). https://doi.org/10.18653/v1/2020.acl-main.308
7. Chen, W., Zhang, X., Wang, T., Yang, B., Li, Y.: Opinion-aware knowledge graph for political ideology detection. In: IJCAI, vol. 17, pp. 3647–3653 (2017). https://doi.org/10.24963/ijcai.2017/510
8. Li, C., Goldwasser, D.: Encoding social information with graph convolutional networks for political perspective detection in news media. In: Proceedings of the 57th Annual Meeting of the Association for Computational Linguistics, pp. 2594–2604. Association for Computational Linguistics, Stroudsburg, PA, USA (2019). https://doi.org/10.18653/v1/P19-1247
9. Campbell, J.C., Hindle, A., Stroulia, E.: Latent dirichlet allocation: extracting topics from software engineering data. Art Sci. Anal. Softw. Data. **3**, 139–159 (2015). https://doi.org/10.1016/B978-0-12-411519-4.00006-9
10. Sinno, B., Oviedo, B., Atwell, K., Alikhani, M., Li, J.J.: Political ideology and polarization of policy positions: a multi-dimensional approach (2021)
11. Li, C., Goldwasser, D.: Using social and linguistic information to adapt pretrained representations for political perspective identification. In: Findings of the Association for Computational Linguistics: ACL-IJCNLP 2021, pp. 4569–4579 (2021). https://doi.org/10.18653/v1/2021.findings-acl.401
12. Guo, M., Hwa, R., Lin, Y.-R., Chung, W.-T.: Inflating topic relevance with ideology: a case study of political ideology bias in social topic detection models, 4873–4885 (2021). https://doi.org/10.18653/v1/2020.coling-main.428
13. Feng, S., Luo, M., Chen, Z., Li, Q., Chang, X., Zheng, Q.: Knowledge graph augmented political perspective detection in news media (2021)
14. Feng, S., Luo, M., Chen, Z., Yu, P., Chang, X., Zheng, Q.: Encoding heterogeneous social and political context for entity stance prediction (2021)
15. Wang, X., Ji, H., Cui, P., Yu, P., Shi, C., Wang, B., Ye, Y.: Heterogeneous graph attention network. In: Web Conference 2019 - Proceedings World Wide Web Conference WWW 2019, pp. 2022–2032 (2019) https://doi.org/10.1145/3308558.3313562
16. Zhang, C., Song, D., Huang, C., Swami, A., Chawla, N.V.: Heterogeneous graph neural network. In: Proceedings of the 25th ACM SIGKDD International Conference on Knowledge Discovery \& Data Mining, pp. 793–803 (2019). https://doi.org/10.1145/3292500.3330961

17. Hu, L., Yang, T., Shi, C., Ji, H., Li, X.: Heterogeneous graph attention networks for semi-supervised short text classification. In: Proceedings of the 2019 Conference on Empirical Methods in Natural Language Processing and the 9th International Joint Conference on Natural Language Processing (EMNLP-IJCNLP), pp. 4821–4830 (2020). https://doi.org/10.18653/v1/d19-1488

18. Hu, L., et al.: Compare to the knowledge: graph neural fake news detection with external knowledge. In: Proceedings of the 59th Annual Meeting of the Association for Computational Linguistics and the 11th International Joint Conference on Natural Language Processing (volume 1: Long Papers), pp. 754–763 (2021). https://doi.org/10.18653/v1/2021.acl-long.62

19. Yang, T., Hu, L., Shi, C., Ji, H., Li, X., Nie, L.: HGAT: Heterogeneous graph attention networks for semi-supervised short text classification. ACM Trans. Inf. Syst. 39 (2021). https://doi.org/10.1145/3450352

20. Baly, R., Da San Martino, G., Glass, J., Nakov, P.: We can detect your bias: predicting the political ideology of news articles. In: Proceedings of the 2020 Conference on Empirical Methods in Natural Language Processing (EMNLP), pp. 4982–4991. Association for Computational Linguistics, Stroudsburg, PA, USA (2020). https://doi.org/10.18653/v1/2020.emnlp-main.404

21. Kiros, R., et al.: Skip-thought vectors. Adv. Neural Inf. Process. Syst. 3294–3302 (2015)

22. Seo, P.H., Lin, Z., Cohen, S., Shen, X., Han, B.: Hierarchical Attention Networks. ArXiv. 1480–1489 (2016)

23. Joulin, A., Grave, E., Bojanowski, P., Mikolov, T.: Bag of tricks for efficient text classification. In: 15th Conference European Chapter Association Computer Linguistics EACL 2017 - Proceedings Conference, vol. 2, pp. 427–431 (2017). https://doi.org/10.18653/v1/e17-2068

24. Vieira, J.P.A., Moura, R.S.: An analysis of convolutional neural networks for sentence classification. In: 2017 43rd Latin American Computer Conference CLEI 2017. 2017-January, pp. 1–5 (2017). https://doi.org/10.1109/CLEI.2017.8226381

25. Devlin, J., Chang, M.W., Lee, K., Toutanova, K.: BERT: Pre-training of deep bidirectional transformers for language understanding. In: NAACL HLT 2019 - 2019 Conference North American Chapter Association Computer Linguists Human Language Technology - Proceedings Conference, vol. 1, pp. 4171–4186 (2019)

26. Sun, Y., et al.: ERNIE: enhanced representation through Knowledge Integration (2019)

Graph-Based Neural Collaborative Filtering Model for Drug-Disease Associations Prediction

Xiaotian Xiong[1], Qianshi Yuan[2], Maoan Zhou[1], and Xiaomei Wei[1(✉)]

[1] College of Informatics, Huazhong Agricultural University, Wuhan, China
{xxt,zma}@webmail.hzau.edu.cn, may@mail.hzau.edu.cn
[2] School of Artificial Intelligence, Hebei University of Technology, Tianjin, China
185510@stu.hebut.edu.cn

Abstract. Traditional drug discovery process has made a major contribution to pharmacotherapy, but also confer big challenges: it is time-consuming, expensive, and laborious. In recent years, the computational drug repositioning methods are used to address such challenges and bring up new opportunities. The drug-disease association prediction is a crucial task towards computational drug repositioning. In this paper, we propose a new computational method termed CFDDA which employs graph-based neural collaborative filtering to effectively predict the potential indications of existing drugs. 10-fold cross validation on benchmark dataset shows that the proposed model achieves a promising performance in predicting drug-disease association compared with other state-of-the-art methods. The obtained AUPR of 0.539 absolutely outperforms the baselines and the AUC of 0.9103 is comparative to the best model. Moreover, the predicted drug indications are validated by published literature to confirm the effectiveness of our method in practical application.

Keywords: Embeddings · Drug repositioning · Collaborative filtering · GCN

1 Introduction

Traditional drug development is a time-consuming, expensive and high-risk process. According to reports, the total development time of a new drug is at least 10–15 years, with an average cost of \$2.6 billion [1]. In view of the difficulties and challenges of traditional drug development, it is worth the effort to identify new therapeutic uses for existing drugs. This kind of drug development methods is known as drug repositioning. Computational drug repositioning helps rapidly identify new indications for market drugs using computation-based methods, such as network inference, machine learning and deep learning.

To date, the computational methods used to predict the undetected drug-disease association can be classified into three categories: network-based propagation, machine learning-based methods and deep learning-based methods. Network-based propagation

---

X. Xiong and Q. Yuan---These authors contributed equally to this work.

G. Memmi et al. (Eds.): KSEM 2022, LNAI 13368, pp. 556–567, 2022.
https://doi.org/10.1007/978-3-031-10983-6_43

methods generally spread information iteratively to neighboring nodes through edges in the network [2]. Traditional machine learning techniques have been widely used to build biological entity association prediction model [3]. However, feature engineering in machine learning is a laborious and time-consuming task which requires a decent amount of domain knowledge. Instead, deep learning is thriving owing to its capacity of learning distributed feature representation automatically through multi-level nonlinear transformation, and is widely used to complete complex downstream tasks. For instance, an increasing number of deep learning-based recommendation algorithms are used to predict potential drug-disease association [4]. The extensively used techniques in CF recommendation include matrix factorization (MF), neural collaborative filtering (NCF) and graph neural network (GNN), etc. [5–7]. Recently, neural graph collaborative filtering (NGCF) model has attracted more and more attention [7, 8]. Inspired by such studies, graph neural collaborative filtering (GNCF) has been used in biological entity prediction tasks such as drug-disease associations prediction and polypharmacy side effects prediction [9, 10].

Inspired by the succeed of CF methods in recommendations, this paper focuses on collaborative filtering models for drug-disease associations (DDA) extraction, especially on NGCF model. Here we propose a new end-to-end framework, termed CFDDA, using collaborative filtering methods for DDA prediction. First, we conduct a comparative study on various collaborative filtering algorithms and investigate their advantages in our task. Next, we combine the advantages of several typical CF models to explore diverse perspectives of node representation for purpose of enhanced prediction performance. Further, considering the cold start problem which is most common in CF recommendation system, we add the auxiliary information from drug/disease similarity measures to our framework. Finally, CFDDA is applied to predict the potential drug-disease associations accurately and effectively. The overall schematic framework of CFDDA is shown in Fig. 1.

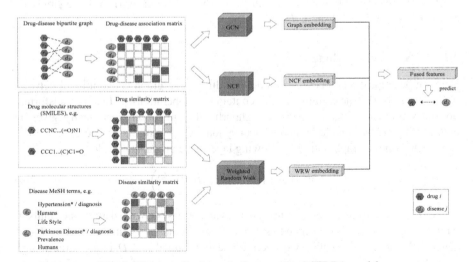

Fig. 1. The overall schematic framework of CFDDA model

2 Materials and Methods

2.1 Dataset

Known Drug-Disease Associations

Two published datasets, i.e. PREDICT [11] and CDataset [12], were employed in our experiment to validate the proposed model. There are 1933 known drug-disease associations involving 593 drugs and 313 diseases in the PREDICT, and 2532 known drug-disease associations including 663 drugs and 409 diseases in the CDataset. For each dataset, drugs were derived from DrugBank [13], while diseases were acquired from Online Mendelian Inheritance in Man database (OMIM) [14]. The known associations can be viewed as a bipartite network between drugs and diseases. For convenience, the bipartite network is presented as a binary matrix $Y \in R^{m \times n}$, where m and n denote the dimension of the matrix same as the number of drugs and diseases. The entry y_{ij} in the matrix is set as 1 if drug r_i has a known association with disease d_j, or $y_{ij} = 0$ conversely. It is worth to mention that verified interactions between drugs and diseases are very sparse, and the percentage of unverified associations is above 98%.

Similarity Matrices

The molecular structure of drugs is denoted by the notation of Simplified Molecular Input Line Entry Specification (SMILES) [15]. Base on the SMILES, PubChem fingerprint descriptors are calculated via the Chemical Development Kit (CDK) [16]. Then, pairwise drug similarity based on their feature profiles, i.e. fingerprint, is measured by the Tanimoto score. The calculated drug similarities are denoted by a $m \times m$ matrix s_r, where the entry $s_r(i, j)$ is the similarity between drug r_i and drug r_j. The similarities between diseases are obtained from MimMiner [17], which used text mining approach to compute similarity between two diseases from the OMIM database. The disease similarities are represented by a $n \times n$ matrix s_d, where the entry $s_d(i, j)$ is the similarity between disease d_i and disease d_j.

2.2 GCN-Based CF Module

Here we descript the procedure of node encoding using graph convolutional network (GCN) framework. The common GCNs contain three operations: 1) feature transformation, 2) non-linear activation, and 3) neighborhood aggregation. Specifically, given an undirected graph with nodes X and adjacency matrix A, a multi-layer neural network is constructed on the graph with the following layer-wise propagation rule:

$$H^{(l+1)} = f\left(\tilde{D}^{-\frac{1}{2}}\tilde{A}\tilde{D}^{-\frac{1}{2}}H^{(l)}W^{(l)}\right) \tag{1}$$

where $H^{(l+1)}$ is the eigenvector matrix of drugs and diseases obtained after l step embedding propagation. $H^{(0)}$ is assigned as X that can be randomly initialized. $\tilde{A} = I + A$ denotes the adjacency matrix with self-connection added and D is a degree matrix such that $D_{ii} = \sum_i \tilde{A}_{ij}$, thus entry d_{ii} denotes the number of non-zero elements of the i-th row vector in the adjacency matrix A. The Laplacian matrix is defined as

$\tilde{L} = \tilde{D}^{-\frac{1}{2}}\tilde{A}\tilde{D}^{-\frac{1}{2}}$, $\tilde{D} = I + D$, and I denotes the identity matrix. $W^{(l)}$ is a layer-specific trainable transformation matrix.

In our experiment, we find that the three-operations in GCN not always are necessary to strengthen a model. So we build two types of GCN models with different components, which are termed as GCN1 and GCN2 respectively. GCN1 combines all the three operations of feature transformation, nonlinear activation and neighborhood aggregation but GCN2 only contains neighborhood aggregation.

GCN1 Formulation

Given the drug-disease interaction matrix R, we get the adjacent matrix A and its degree matrix D, shown in formula (2). The Laplacian matrix L is calculated as follows:

$$A = \begin{bmatrix} 0 & R \\ R^T & 0 \end{bmatrix}, L = D^{-\frac{1}{2}}AD^{-\frac{1}{2}} \tag{2}$$

According to the propagation rules, the network embeddings of nodes are calculated as follows:

$$H^{(l)} = LeakyReLU\left(\tilde{L}H^{(l-1)}W_1^{(l)} + LH^{(l-1)} \odot H^{(l-1)}W_2^{(l)}\right) \tag{3}$$

where $H^{(l)}$ is the node embeddings obtained by l iterations of information propagation; $\tilde{L} = L + I$, and $\odot$ denotes the element-wise product. *LeakyReLU* is the activation function. The other symbols' definition is similar to formula (1). Finally, we concatenate the outputs of all convolutional layers to obtain the embedding of drug r_i as formula (4):

$$e_{r_i}^{GCN} = h_{r_i}^{(0)}|| \ldots ||h_{r_i}^{(l)} \tag{4}$$

where $h_{r_i}^{(l)}$ and $h_{d_j}^{(l)}$ denote the l-th layer embeddings of drug r_i and disease d_j respectively; || means concatenation. Similar as $e_{r_i}^{GCN}$, we can obtain $e_{d_i}^{GCN}$ as the GCN embedding of disease d_i. Then the interaction feature of drug-disease pair (r_i, d_j) are calculated by a elements-wise product $\odot$ in formula (5):

$$e_{ij}^{GCN} = e_{r_i}^{GCN} \odot e_{d_j}^{GCN} \tag{5}$$

GCN2 Formulation

Compared to GCN1, GCN2 only use the convolutional operation as formula (6):

$$H^{(l)} = LH^{(l-1)} \tag{6}$$

Considering that different convolutional layer has different contribution to the final node embeddings. Instead of equally concatenating the embeddings from different layers as formula (4) did, we apply a weighted sum method to aggregate the embeddings as follows:

$$e_{r_i}^{GCN} = \alpha_0 h_{r_i}^{(0)} + \alpha_1 h_{r_i}^{(1)} + \alpha_2 h_{r_i}^{(2)} + \ldots + \alpha_l h_{r_i}^{(l)} \tag{7}$$

where α_i is a trainable weight for the l-th layer embedding $h^{(l)}$. Similar as $e_{r_i}^{GCN}$, we can obtain $e_{d_i}^{GCN}$ as the GCN embedding of disease d_i. Then the two node embeddings are integrated by a elements-wise product $\odot$:

$$e_{ij}^{GCN} = e_{r_i}^{GCN} \odot e_{d_j}^{GCN} \tag{8}$$

2.3 Neural CF Module

The Neural CF module is borrowed from NCF framework which was originally proposed for recommendation [6]. It consists of two parts: MF layer and multiple linear perceptron (MLP) layers.

MF Layer

We use $e_{r_i}^{MF}$ and $e_{d_j}^{MF}$ to respectively denote the embeddings of drug r_i and disease d_j that are learned from the input of their one-hot vector pair. MF layer leverages a linear operation $\odot$ to get the interaction characteristics of the pair (r_i, d_j):

$$e_{ij}^{MF} = e_{r_i}^{MF} \odot e_{d_j}^{MF} \tag{9}$$

MLP Layers

First, we learn the node representations $e_{r_i}^{MLP}$ and $e_{d_j}^{MLP}$ from embedding layer for drug r_i and disease d_j. Then they are concatenated to get the simple interaction feature $e^{MLP(0)}$. Next, an l-layers MLP uses the non-linear function $ReLU$ to explore the deep interaction features:

$$e_{ij}^{MLP(0)} = e_{r_i}^{MLP} \oplus e_{d_j}^{MLP} \tag{10}$$

$$e_{ij}^{MLP(l)} = ReLU(e_{ij}^{MLP(l-1)} W^l + b^{(l)}) \tag{11}$$

where $\oplus$ is the concatenation operation; $W^{(l)}$ and $b^{(l)}$ are the trainable weight and bias value of the l-th MLP layer respectively.

2.4 Learning Similarity Features by Weighted Random Walk

We view the similarity as a weighted network, then the weighted random walk algorithm (WRW) derived from Deepwalk [18] is employed to learn comprehensive features of drugs and diseases. First, given a start node in the network, the random walk algorithm is used to extract node sequence on the walk path, and then the SkipGram [19] model is applied to learn node embeddings. In this way, we obtain drug embedding $e_{r_i}^{WRW}$ and disease $e_{d_j}^{WRW}$ respectively. Finally, we take $e_{r_i}^{WRW}$ and $e_{d_j}^{WRW}$ as the input to learn further feature representation by MLP. The procedure is similar to formula (11), so we don't repeat it. The outputs of MLP are interacted by a elements-wise product:

$$e_{ij}^{WRW} = e_{r_i}^{WRW(l)} \odot e_{d_j}^{WRW(l)} \tag{12}$$

2.5 CFDDA Model

Model Formulation

We model the drug-disease relationships prediction process as a binary classification problem. The output of the model is a probability $\hat{y}_{ij}$, which is used to predict whether there is a potential treatment relationship between sample pair:

$$\hat{y}_{ij} = \sigma\left(h\left(e_{ij}^{MF} \oplus e_{ij}^{MLP} \oplus e_{ij}^{GCN} \oplus e_{ij}^{WRW}\right) + b\right) \tag{13}$$

where e_{ij}^{MF}, e_{ij}^{MLP}, e_{ij}^{GCN} and e_{ij}^{WRW} have been mentioned above; σ, h and b denote the activation function, weight and bias value of the output layer respectively. Here, we choose sigmoid as the activation function and update the h value through back propagation in the training stage.

Loss Function and Training Process

The loss between the predicted value and the target value is defined as binary cross-entropy loss:

$$L(\theta) = -\sum_{(i,j)} y_{i,j} log\hat{y}_{i,j} + \left(1 - y_{i,j}\right) log\left(1 - \hat{y}_{i,j}\right) + \lambda\|\theta\| \tag{14}$$

where $y_{i,j}$ denotes whether there is an observed association between the drug r_i and the disease d_j (0 or 1), $\hat{y}_{i,j}$ denotes the predicted drug-disease association score, (i, j) denotes a training sample. θ denotes the model parameters, λ denotes the regularization parameter. $L(\theta)$ is the loss function to be minimized, and we use Adam optimizer to minimize the loss function.

Parameter Settings

The training epochs is 80. The learning rate is 0.001. The batch training size is 64. The number of negative samples is 5. The embedding size of MF part is 16. The embedding size of the MLP part is 64, and the dimension of the subsequent hidden layer is [64, 32, 16]. The embedding size of GCN part is 16, and the number of convolution layers is 3. The embedding size of WRW part is 16. Researchers can adjust regularization coefficient by themselves.

3 Results and Discussion

3.1 Evaluation Metrics

We conducted a 10-fold cross-validation using golden standard datasets PREDICT and CDataset to evaluate the performance of CFDDA. In the 10-fold cross-validation, all known drug-disease associations in the dataset are randomly divided into 10 subsets. Each subset in turn serves as the test set, and the other 9 subsets serve as the training set. The cross-validation process is repeated 10 times and the averaged result is taken as the final performance report. In each fold, CFDDA model is trained on the training set, and then used to predict the associations in the test set. According to the prediction scores, the area under curve (AUC) and the area under precision-recall curve (AUPR) are selected as metrics to evaluate the prediction model. Since recent studies have shown that AUPR can provide more informative assessments than AUC on highly unbalanced datasets [20], we attach more importance to AUPR in the following experiments. Besides, we also use the metric of hit ratio (HR)@n that is usually adopted in recommendation system to measure the accuracy of top-n recommendations in the ranking list.

3.2 Performance Comparison of Various CF Models

Each CF model has its distinct advantage in feature representation so as to have different recommendation performance. Here we conducted experiments to explore the properties of several typical CF models, such as MF, NCF, GCN. It is worth mentioning that we developed two different GCN-based models: GCN1 and GCN2. The parameters involved in these CF methods are set through grid search, and the default values will refer to the original papers that proposed these methods. Table 1 shows the AUC, AUPR and HR@10 obtained by four prediction methods on PREDICT.

Table 1. Performance of CF models on PREDICT

	AUC	AUPR	HR@10
MF	0.8771	0.4221	0.6612
NCF	0.8856	0.4994	0.6648
GCN1	0.8989	**0.5234**	**0.6912**
GCN2	**0.9005**	0.3926	0.6813

As the result shown in Table 1, two GCN models achieve better performance than MF and NCF in all metrics, except the AUPR of GCN2. Moreover, GCN1 outperforms GCN2 with the AUPR of 0.5234 and HR@10 of 0.6912 respectively. Specifically, the AUPR of GCN1 is 13% higher than GCN2 method.

MF is a linear model that only uses simple and fixed inner product to estimate complex drug-disease associations in low-dimensional potential space. NCF framework integrates MF and MLP methods. Since MLP uses nonlinear function to learn deep interaction features of drugs and diseases, it greatly enhances NCF performance. However, MF and NCF cannot encode topological information. Comparatively, GCN-base methods perform information propagation on the bipartite graph from drug-disease associations to model the high-order connectivity of the graph structure. Specifically, GCN2 only retains neighborhood aggregation to reduce the model complexity and speeds up the training progress. Accordingly, it achieves a slightly lower performance than GCN1.

3.3 Performance of Integrated CF Models

In light of the results of CF model comparison, we focus on the GCN model as the main framework. To include the ability of various CF model in capturing features of drugs and disease, we try several combinations and compare their contribution to prediction model. The results are reported in Table 2.

Table 2. Performance of integrated CF model on PREDICT

	AUC	AUPR	HR@10
GCN1	0.8989	0.5234	0.6912
GCN2	0.9005	0.3926	0.6813
GCN1 + NCF	0.8905	0.5225	0.6792
GCN2 + NCF	**0.9047**	**0.5360**	**0.7289**

From the results, we can see that the addition of NCF to GCN1 almost has no positive effect on the prediction performance. In contrast, the combination of NCF and GCN2 make a significant improvement on AUC, AUPR, and HR@10 which reach to 0.9047, 0.536 and 0.7289 respectively. In particular, the AUPR is 14.3% higher than simple GNC2. Since GCN2 and NCF pay attention to distinct aspect information of drug-disease associations, their combination helps to obtain comprehensive feature representation.

We analyze that GCN1's complex network structure is enough to model high-order connectivity from bipartite graphs, so adding NCF will not significantly improve performance. Here, we add auxiliary information of drugs and disease from knowledge database to alleviate the cold start problem in CF model. The experiment results demonstrate that the auxiliary information has positive contribution to CFADD as expected, shown in Table 3. Finally, considering the best performance we take NCF + GCN2 + SIM as our standard model, referred to as CFDDA.

Table 3. Ablation experimental results on PREDICT

	AUC	AUPR
GCN2 + NCF	0.9047	0.5360
GCN2 + NCF + SIM(CFDDA)	**0.9103**	**0.5390**

3.4 Comparisons with the State-of-the-Arts Models

In this section, we compare CFDDA with four recent methods: NIMCGCN [21], LAGCN [9], DisDrugPred [22], MBiRW [12]. We adopt the published results or open source code in the following experiments. The comparison between baselines and CFDDA is shown in Table 4.

Table 4. Comparison to baselines in the 10-fold cross validation on PREDICT

	AUC	AUPR
NIMCGCN	0.8352	0.1216
LAGCN	0.7617	0.1566
DisDrugPred	0.8900	0.0700
MBiRW	**0.9110**	0.1290
CFDDA	0.9103	**0.5390**

As the results shown in Table 4, we can see that CFDDA has the absolute advantage over all baseline methods with respect to the value of AUPR which reach to 0.539. It is crucial to the model with sparse data. As we above-mentioned, for highly unbalanced datasets, AUPR can provide a more significant evaluation than AUC. AUPR comprehensively considers both real positive rate and false positive rate, so the biased dataset has little effect on it. From Table 5 we can see that AUC of CFDDA is 0.9103 which is a bit lower than the best model MBiRW. The reason may be that our model uses fewer prior auxiliary information by comparison to MBiRW.

3.5 Evaluation on Extra Dataset

In order to make the prediction more convincing, we repeated the above experiment on another dataset. The comparison results are shown in Table 5.

Table 5. Comparison to baselines in the 10-fold cross validation on CDataset

	AUC	AUPR
NIMCGCN	0.8654	0.1352
LAGCN	0.7890	0.1698
DisDrugPred	0.9080	0.0670
MBiRW	**0.9320**	0.1990
CFDDA	0.9216	**0.5917**

Clearly, we can see that CFDDA has the absolute advantage over all baseline methods with respect to value of AUPR which reaches to 0.5917. It shows that the performance of CFDDA on different datasets is certainly stable.

3.6 Prediction of Novel Drug-Disease Associations

To further validate the prediction ability of CFDDA, we investigate the prediction results of the model and cite the evidence for the discoveries. The prediction scores at top 10 are considered, shown in Table 6. We find that eight out of ten predicted associations to be proved in published literature. After retrieval in PubMed, we find that Trihexyphenidyl has been proved to be one of the most useful drugs to treat Parkinson's disease [23]. In addition, some publications confirmed that Tiagabine is a novel antiepileptic drug that was designed to block gamma-aminobutyric acid uptake by presynaptic neurons and glial cells [24].

Table 6. Top 10 drug-disease associations predicted by CFDDA

Drug	Disease	Evidence
Pilocarpine	Hypertension	[25]
Methyclothiazide	Enteropathy, familial	NA
Melphalan	Mismatch repair cancer syndrome	[26]
Clofarabine	Mismatch repair cancer syndrome	[27]
Biperiden	Parkinson disease, late-onset	[28]
Orphenadrine	Dystonia	[29]
Trihexyphenidyl	Parkinson disease, late-onset	[23]
Isoleucine	Spastic paraplegia	NA
Bromocriptine	Parkinson disease, late-onset	[30]
Tiagabine	Seizures	[24]

4   Conclusion

In this paper, we formalized the DDA prediction problem into a CF recommendation task aiming to computational drug repositioning. For the purpose of ranking the association probabilities of drug-disease pairs, we investigated several typical collaborative filtering recommendation methods, such as Matrix Factorization (MF), Neural Collaborative Filtering (NCF), Graph Convolutional Network (GCN). The comparison experiment shows that these CF methods provide unique contribution to the overview prediction performance. Understandably, MFs' linearity limits the ability of feature representation. Both NCF and GNN-based CF leverage the neural network framework to encode the features of drugs and diseases, but GNN-based models focus more on topological neighbors. Correspondingly, we combined the two CF framework aiming to derive comprehensive feature representation. In addition, the addition of auxiliary information contributes to the improvement of system performance through relieving the cold start problem. The final experimental results show that CFDDA has considerable competitiveness compared with other state-of-the-art methods. Moreover, the predicted recommendation list of drug indications is verified by publicly available literatures.

Acknowledgments. This work is supported by the Fundamental Research Funds for the Central Universities (No: 2662020XXPY08).

References

1. Chan, H.C.S., Shan, H., et al.: Advancing drug discovery via artificial intelligence. Trends Pharmacol Sci. **40**(8), 592–604 (2019)
2. Cowen, L., Ideker, T., et al.: Network propagation: a universal amplifier of genetic associations. Nat. Rev. Genet. **18**(9), 551–562 (2017)
3. Wei, X., Zhang, Y., et al.: Predicting drug–disease associations by network embedding and biomedical data integration. Data Technol. Appl. **53**(2), 217–229 (2019)
4. Yuan, Q., Wei, X., et al.: A hybrid neural collaborative filtering model for drug reposition-ing. In: 2020 IEEE International Conference on Bioinformatics and Biomedicine (BIBM), pp. 515–518 (2020)
5. He, X., Zhang, H., et al.: Fast matrix factorization for online recommendation with implicit feedback. In: Proceedings of the 39th International ACM SIGIR Conference on Research and Development in Information Retrieval, pp. 549–558 (2016)
6. He, X., Liao, L., et al.: Neural collaborative filtering. In: Proceedings of the 26th International Conference on World Wide Web, pp. 173–182 (2017)
7. Wang, X., He, X., et al.: Neural graph collaborative filtering. In: Proceedings of the 42nd Inter-national ACM SIGIR Conference on Research and Development in Information Retrieval, pp. 165–174 (2019)
8. He, X., Deng, K., et al.: LightGCN: simplifying and powering graph convolution network for recommendation. In: Proceedings of the 43rd International ACM SIGIR Conference on Research and Development in Information Retrieval, pp. 639–648, (2020)
9. Yu, Z., Huang, F., et al.: Predicting drug-disease associations through layer attention graph convolutional network. Brief Bioinform. **22**(4) (2021)
10. Zitnik, M., Agrawal, M., et al.: Modeling polypharmacy side effects with graph convolutional networks. Bioinformatics **34**(13), i457–i466 (2018)
11. Gottlieb, A., Stein, G.Y., et al.: PREDICT: a method for inferring novel drug indications with application to personalized medicine. Mol. Syst. Biol. **7**, 496 (2011)
12. Luo, H., Wang, J., et al.: Drug repositioning based on comprehensive similarity measures and bi-random walk algorithm. Bioinformatics **32**(17), 2664–2671 (2016)
13. Law, V., Knox, C., et al.: DrugBank 4.0: shedding new light on drug metabolism. Nucleic Acids Res. **42**, Database issue, D1091–7 (2014)
14. Hamosh, A., Scott, A.F., et al.: Online Mendelian Inheritance in Man (OMIM), a knowledge-base of human genes and genetic disorders. Nucleic Acids Res. **33**, Database issue, D514–7 (2005)
15. Weininger, D.: SMILES, a chemical language and information system. 1. introduction to methodology and encoding rules. J. Chem. Inf. Comput. Sci. **28**(1), 31–36 (1988)
16. Steinbeck, C., Hoppe, C., et al.: Recent developments of the chemistry development kit (CDK) - an open-source java library for chemo- and bioinformatics. Curr. Pharm. Des. **12**(17), 2111–2120 (2006)
17. van Driel, M.A., Bruggeman, J., et al.: A text-mining analysis of the human phenome. Eur. J. Hum. Genet. **14**(5), 535–542 (2006)
18. Perozzi, B., Al-Rfou, R., et al.: DeepWalk: online learning of social representations. In: Proceedings of the 20th ACM SIGKDD International Conference on Knowledge Discovery and Data Mining, pp. 701–710: Association for Computing Machinery, New York, New York, USA (2014)
19. Mikolov, T., Sutskever, I., et al.: Distributed representations of words and phrases and their compositionality. In: Advances in Neural Information Processing Systems, vol. 26, pp. 3111–3119, Lake Tahoe, NV(US) (2013)

20. Saito, T., Rehmsmeier, M.: The precision-recall plot is more informative than the ROC plot when evaluating binary classifiers on imbalanced datasets. PLoS ONE **10**(3), e0118432 (2015)
21. Li, J., Zhang, S., et al.: Neural inductive matrix completion with graph convolutional networks for miRNA-disease association prediction. Bioinformatics **36**(8), 2538–2546 (2020)
22. Xuan, P., Cao, Y., et al.: Drug repositioning through integration of prior knowledge and projections of drugs and diseases. Bioinformatics **35**(20), 4108–4119 (2019)
23. Schwab, R.S., Doshay, L.J.: Slow-release trihexyphenidyl in Parkinson's disease. JAMA **180**(2), 159–161 (1962)
24. Shinnar, S.: Tiagabine. In: Seminars in Pediatric Neurology, vol. 4, no. 1, pp. 24–33 (1997)
25. van Charldorp, K.J., de Jonge, A., et al.: Subclassification of muscarinic receptors in the heart, urinary bladder and sympathetic ganglia in the pithed rat. Naunyn Schmiedebergs Arch. Pharmacol. **331**(4), 301–306 (1985)
26. Gajek, A., Poczta, A., et al.: Chemical modification of melphalan as a key to improving treatment of haematological malignancies. Sci. Rep. **10**(1), 4479 (2020)
27. Faderl, S., Gandhi, V., et al.: The role of clofarabine in hematologic and solid malignancies—development of a next-generation nucleoside analog. Cancer **103**(10), 1985–1995 (2005)
28. Kostelnik, A., Cegan, A., et al.: Anti-parkinson drug biperiden inhibits enzyme acetylcholinesterase. Biomed. Res. Int. **2017**, 2532764 (2017)
29. Jacob, A.: A case of torsion dystonia treated with orphenadrine. Scott. Med. J. **7**(3), 139–140 (1962)
30. DA agonists - Ergot derivaties: Bromocriptine. Mov. Disord. **17**, S4, S53–S67 (2002)

ECCKG: An Eventuality-Centric Commonsense Knowledge Graph

Ya Wang[1,2], Cungen Cao[1], Zhiwen Chen[1,2], and Shi Wang[1(✉)]

[1] Key Laboratory of Intelligent Information Processing, Institute of Computing Technology,
Chinese Academy of Sciences, Beijing 100190, China
{wangya,cgcao,chenzhiwen20s,wangshi}@ict.ac.cn
[2] University of Chinese Academy of Sciences, Beijing, China

Abstract. Eventuality-centric knowledge graphs are essential resources for many downstream applications. However, current knowledge graphs mainly focus on knowledge about entities while ignoring the real-world eventualities (including events and states). To fill this gap, we propose to build ECCKG, a high-quality eventuality-centric commonsense knowledge graph. We argue that rule-based methods are of great value for knowledge graph construction, but must be used in conjunction with other techniques such as crowdsourcing. We thus create ECCKG by combining rule-based reasoning with crowdsourcing. We first acquire seed ECCKG by manually filtering out the incorrect and duplicate eventuality-related commonsense assertions in ConceptNet 5.5. Then we enrich the seed ECCKG with a set of logical rules iteratively. Finally, we generate new commonsense assertions by instantiating the existing eventualities. The resulting ECCKG contains more than 1.3 million eventuality-centric commonsense knowledge tuples which is about 15 times larger than ConceptNet 5.5. A manual evaluation shows that ECCKG outperforms other eventuality-centric commonsense knowledge graphs in terms of both quality and quantity. We also demonstrate the usefulness of ECCKG by the extrinsic use case of commonsense knowledge acquisition. ECCKG is available at https://zenodo.org/record/6084081.

Keywords: Eventuality-centric knowledge graph · Knowledge graph completion · Commonsense knowledge acquisition

1 Introduction

Eventuality-centric knowledge graphs are crucial for a variety of applications such as natural language processing [1], question answering [2] and event prediction [3]. However, existing large-scale knowledge graphs including YAGO [4], DBpedia [5] and Wikidata [6] focus mostly on entity-centric information and are insufficient in terms of their coverage with respect to eventualities. In this paper, both events (e.g. buy hamburger) and states (e.g. hungry) are eventualities following the commonly adopted terminology proposed by Mourelatos [7]. To the best of our knowledge, currently there are no dedicated commonsense knowledge graphs collecting eventuality-centric information. For example, ConceptNet [8] is limited to entity-centric commonsense knowledge and does not

© The Author(s), under exclusive license to Springer Nature Switzerland AG 2022
G. Memmi et al. (Eds.): KSEM 2022, LNAI 13368, pp. 568–584, 2022.
https://doi.org/10.1007/978-3-031-10983-6_44

provide much commonsense knowledge about eventualities. Another notable example is ATOMIC [9], which ignores many other types of commonsense knowledge with an emphasis on commonsense causal knowledge for daily events.

To address the limitations of prior works, we propose a framework to construct an eventuality-centric commonsense knowledge graph (ECCKG) with high accuracy. We make use of the fact that significant efforts have already been made to create existing commonsense knowledge graphs. Thus, we exploit the information of ConceptNet [10] rather than starting our project from scratch. Our framework is a three-step pipeline composed of seed knowledge graph acquisition, seed knowledge graph completion and new eventuality generation.

Seed ECCKG Acquisition. ConceptNet is the most prominent and widely used project on commonsense knowledge acquisition [11]. It has been proven a useful resource for various AI downstream tasks [12–14]. Therefore, we select ConceptNet as our source of seed ECCKG. ConceptNet is a commonsense knowledge graph (CSKG) which contains general commonsense facts for a small number of human-defined relations (e.g. IsA, Causes and CapableOf) about the world. Since the information is collected relying mostly on human crowdsourcing, the accuracy of commonsense knowledge in Concept-Net is fairly high. Nevertheless, data errors are in the nature of knowledge graphs and thus ConceptNet still has been found to be noisy [15], e.g. the nonsensical commonsense tuples < buy hamburger, causes, bad conscience> and <buy hamburger, causes, world hunger>. There also exists duplicate assertions in ConceptNet, such as "eating hamburger" and "eating hambuger" as results of "buying hamburger". The goal of this paper is to build a high-quality eventuality-centric commonsense knowledge graph. To this end, we remove the incorrect and duplicate commonsense knowledge tuples that involve eventualities in ConceptNet to get a seed ECCKG with high accuracy. Moreover, the data quality of seed ECCKG is crucial for enriching it using a rule-based approach in the second step as it determines the ultimate performance of the rules. Since the number of eventuality-related commonsense tuples in ConceptNet is limited, we decide to clean relevant tuples in ConceptNet with human efforts to guarantee the quality of seed ECCKG.

Seed ECCKG Completion. Despite its success in AI tasks, ConceptNet is often criticized for the small scale which restricts its usage in many real-world applications. Many methods have been developed to increase the scale of knowledge graphs by discovering missing relations [16]. The task of inferring missing relations between existing nodes is known as knowledge graph completion. As a valuable type of means for knowledge graph completion, rule-based methods have been studied by many researchers [17–20]. Implicit relations can be derived by applying inference rules on existing knowledge to make a knowledge graph more complete. The rules can also be used to detect incorrect knowledge to improve the quality of the knowledge graph. Moreover, rules provide us with interpretable reasoning for predicting implicit relations. Compared to traditional knowledge graphs that usually contain thousands of types of relations between entities, there are very few kinds of relations between eventualities in an eventuality-centric knowledge graph. For instance, ConceptNet only has 7 relations between eventualities. Limited relation types result in finite rules. Therefore, for eventuality-centric commonsense knowledge graph construction, it is much easier to manually collect rules than to automatically learn these rules. In this paper, we aim to exploit the seed ECCKG to infer implicit relations between events without adding much wrong information. For this purpose, we manually obtain the 18 Horn rules of length 1 or length 2 contained in ECCKG. These rules reason over the seed ECCKG to correctly generate missing relations. They are of the form "**Causes(x, z)** ∧ **IsA(y, x)** → **Causes(y, z)**" or "**HasPrerequisite(x, y)** → **Before(y, x)**". These are Horn rules on binary predicates [21]. These commonsense rules capture the eventuality-independent relational semantics of the seed ECCKG. One of the key advantages of these rules is their inductive ability to generalize to new eventualities. With the power of these inference rules, we can add correct missing information to the seed ECCKG iteratively. During each iteration, the newly discovered triples from the previous iteration are used as facts to trigger relevant rules.

New Eventuality Generation *is a* relations are important semantic relations and are presented in almost every knowledge graph. Human annotation could provide a high-quality CSKG, yet its high cost often results in relatively low coverage of concepts. For instance, ConceptNet merely contains 4,757 events. Consequently, there exist very few *isa* relations between eventualities in ConceptNet. For this reason, we propose to generate new eventualities by instantiating existing eventualities to automatically produce new *isa* relations between eventualities. In ECCKG, an eventuality is a verb (adjective) or a combination of a verb (adjective) with nouns. We instantiate an eventuality by replacing the verb (adjective) and nouns with their proper hyponyms exploiting WN18 [22], a subset of WordNet [23]. In WordNet, one word is a hyponym of another if it is a subtype or instance of the second word. For example, "apple" is a hyponym of "fruit" and "jog" is a hyponym of "run". In this manner, we can generate novel eventualities (e.g. "eating apple" and "jog") by instantiating the verb (adjective) or nouns in an existing eventuality. The task of generating new eventualities is the process of producing new *isa* relations.

In the context of artificial intelligence, commonsense knowledge is the set of background information that a person is intended to know or assume. Commonsense knowledge is instrumental in many AI applications [24–26]. Commonsense knowledge including knowledge about everyday concepts and typical human behavior is usually not expressed explicitly but resides in the mind of humans. Consequently, commonsense knowledge acquisition remains long-standing challenges in general artificial intelligence. Many efforts have been devoted to collecting commonsense knowledge. However, there have been very few works on commonsense knowledge acquisition using CSKGs. In this paper, we propose to exploit eventuality-centric commonsense knowledge graph for commonsense knowledge acquisition to evaluate the usefulness of ECCKG. Due to the space limitations, we take commonsense knowledge acquisition of human desires as an example. Commonsense knowledge about human desires is an important part of human commonsense knowledge. For example, a person wants to be healthy and rich. It is worth mentioning that, although Desires relations in ConceptNet involve such commonsense knowledge, the coverage is very limited. We aim to complement existing commonsense knowledge about human desires in ConceptNet by providing more information with the help of ECCKG.

In summary, we make three main contributions in this paper. First, we construct ECCKG, a high-quality eventuality-centric commonsense knowledge graph with more than 15 times as many commonsense knowledge tuples as ConceptNet. Second, we are the first to propose a rule-based method for eventuality-centric commonsense knowledge graph completion. Third, we make the first attempt to acquire commonsense knowledge from an eventuality-centric commonsense knowledge graph.

2 Related Work

2.1 Eventuality-Centric Knowledge Graph

Recently, constructing eventuality-centric knowledge graphs have gained much attention [1] presented an eventuality-centric document representation model based on sentence-level event mentions. In this work, Event graphs are extracted by combining machine learning and rule-based models. These event graphs consist of event mentions and the temporal relations between them. However, knowledge contained in [1] is not commonsense knowledge [3] proposed an event logic graph (ELG). ELG is a directed cyclic graph, whose nodes are events, and edges stand for the temporal, causal, conditional or hypernym-hyponym relations between events. Events and relations between these events are acquired from large-scale unstructured text. For the task of script event prediction, [27] constructed a narrative event evolutionary graph (NEEG) based on the narrative event chains extracted from news corpus. This event graph is also a directed cyclic graph in which nodes are narrative events and edges are relations connecting two events (mainly temporal relations and causal relations). But both ELG and NEEG do not cover other commonsense relations in ECCKG [2] developed ASER, a large-scale eventuality knowledge graph extracted from unstructured textual data. ASER is a knowledge graph about eventualities and their relations. These eventualities are extracted using syntactic patterns based on dependency grammar. ASER contains 15 relation types. Different from ECCKG, most of the relations are discourse relations rather than commonsense relations [28] crowdsourced GLUCOSE, a large-scale dataset of implicit commonsense causal knowledge about everyday situations. Each GLUCOSE entry includes a specific causal statement and an inference rule generalized from this statement. GLUCOSE captures ten dimensions of causal explanation related to a sentence. These dimensions can be mapped to causal, part-whole and conditional relations in ECCKG, respectively. However, many commonsense relations in ECCKG are absent in GLUCOSE [29] built a hierarchical causality network to discover high-level abstract causality rules. The causality network is generalized from a specific one, with abstract events denoted by frequently co-occurring word pairs. Causal relations in this network are extracted from news headlines exploiting four common causal connectives [30] presented EventKG, a multilingual eventuality-centric temporal knowledge graph. In EventKG, relations are extracted from several large-scale knowledge graphs and semi-structured sources. Both [29] and [30] are ignorant regarding other relation types in ECCKG and statements included in them are not commonsense knowledge [31] constructed an activity knowledge graph with activities extracted from narrative text. In the knowledge graph, activities are linked by four types of relations (parent, previous, next and similarity). These relations are inferred using logical rules [9] introduced ATOMIC, a knowledge graph that involves social commonsense knowledge about events. ATOMIC focuses on inferential *if-then* knowledge that covers causal and conditional relations. ATOMIC is collected completely through crowdsourcing. Similar to other eventuality-centric knowledge graph, ATOMIC neglects other commonsense relations in ECCKG except causal and conditional relations.

These eventuality-centric knowledge graphs are automatically constructed using extraction techniques [1, 3, 27, 2, 29, 30, 31] or crowdsourced completely through human computation [9, 28]. Unfortunately, a hand-crafted knowledge graph typically suffers from limited coverage and automatic approaches often introduce noisy information to the knowledge graph. Compared to prior works, we combine human crowdsourcing and automatic rule-based methods to construct ECCKG.

2.2   Rule-Based Knowledge Graph Completion

Since incompleteness is in the nature of any significant knowledge graph, many attempts have been made to add new information to a knowledge graph. Rule-based methods are prominent solutions in this line of research [32] used distant supervision to mine rules based on the relationships between the subject entities of a listing (e.g. table and list) and the listing context. These rules can be applied to extend a knowledge graph like DBpedia and YAGO with novel entities and assertions [18] proposed an anytime bottom-up technique for learning logical rules from large knowledge graphs. Experimental results show that these rules are useful for the task of knowledge graph completion [33] proposed DRUM, a model to learn first-order logical rules from knowledge graphs for inductive and interpretable knowledge graph completion. DRUM makes a connection between learning confidence for each rule and low-rank tensor approximation. Meanwhile, it uses bidirectional RNNs to share useful information across the tasks of learning rules for different relations [34] presented RuDiK, a system for discovering declarative rules from knowledge graphs. RuDiK aims to discover positive rules that express relations between entities and negative rules which identify contradictions in a knowledge graph. The positive rules can be used to enrich the knowledge graphs with new facts and negative rules are beneficial to improve the quality of the knowledge graphs [35] proposed an algorithm for extracting rules from knowledge graphs by combining embedding techniques with a new sampling method. This algorithm uses embedding models to prune the rule search space and introduces a new sampling method to restrict the range of entities to be considered. For knowledge graph completion, it outperforms a state-of-the-art system in terms of efficiency and accuracy.

However, all these rules are automatically mined from the knowledge graphs using frequency-based approaches. As a result, these approaches depend on the quality of the knowledge graphs and prone to errors and incompleteness. Furthermore, the mined rules are applied primarily to traditional entity-centric knowledge graphs rather than eventuality-centric knowledge graphs. In contrast, the rules in our work are correct hand-collected commonsense rules which always hold. Since ECCKG involve a limited number of relation types, it does not require much human efforts to create these rules. Thus, we can effectively extend the seed ECCKG with limited human intervention.

3   Construction of ECCKG

We start by defining the task of constructing ECCKG. Given a subset of ConceptNet **C** which contains **m** validated eventuality-centric commonsense tuples, a rule set **R** which consists of **n** Horn rules and a list **E** which includes **k** eventualities that are new to **C**. Our objective is to produce a new high-quality commonsense knowledge graph $\mathbf{C}^+$ (with m^+ pieces of eventuality-centric commonsense knowledge) with the help of **R** and **E** such that $m << m^+$. The proposed framework is shown in Fig. 1.

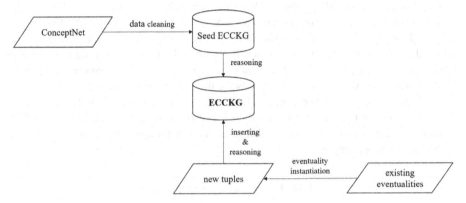

Fig. 1. The overall framework.

3.1 Acquisition of Seed ECCKG from ConceptNet

ConceptNet is a CSKG whose nodes are concepts and edges are relations between concepts. A concept consists of a single word or multi-word phrase, and all its 34 relations are human-defined. In ConceptNet, commonsense knowledge is represented in the form of tuple (triple) <head concept, relation, tail concept>, e.g. <buy hamburger, Causes, eat hamburger>. ConceptNet is built relying mostly on human efforts and thus is known for its high quality. In addition, ConceptNet is the largest publicly available CSKG. We aim to acquire a high-quality seed ECCKG to facilitate the rule-based knowledge graph completion in next section. As a result, we choose ConceptNet as our knowledge source to obtain the seed ECCKG. Specifically, we adopt the English subset of Conceptnet 5.5 as the source of seed ECCKG and only eight relations which connects eventualities are selected as presented in Table 1. It is worth noting that we introduce a new relation type, i.e. temporal relation in ECCKG compared to ConceptNet.

Despite its indisputable value, ConceptNet is noisy due to the constructing process. For example, ConceptNet partly contains unverified crowdsourced assertions and many commonsense statements are true only under some circumstances. To acquire a cleaner subgraph from ConceptNet as a seed ECCKG, we take the following steps:

- remove incorrect tuples, e.g. <buy hamburger, causes, bad conscience>.
- discard context-dependent triples, e.g. <buy hamburger, causes, have heart attack>.
- correct misspellings, e.g. "eat hambuger" to "eat hamburger".
- delete duplicate tuples, e.g. <buy hamburger, causes, eating hamburger> and <buy hamburger, causes, eating hambuger> after correction.

ConceptNet puts its emphasis mostly on entity-centric facts and does not deliver much information about relations between eventualities. Therefore, it's feasible to obtain a seed ECCKG by manually checking a small number of eventuality-centric triples included in the original ConceptNet. For this task, we recruit 20 college students. Each student is equally given a number of knowledge tuples. There is often a strong agreement among humans about judging the validity of commonsense knowledge. Therefore, we assign the students different tuples. They are asked to verify every tuple with above steps. It takes them ten days to complete this task. A total of 37659 triples in ConceptNet are retained as the seed ECCKG as detailed in Table 1. It is worth pointing out that the English subset of ConceptNet 5.5 does not involve *ObstructedBy* relations. Motivated by the observation that if the preconditions for the occurrence of an eventuality are not true, this eventuality will be prevented. Therefore, we collect triples about *ObstructedBy* relation by making the prerequisite in triples about *HasPrerequisite* relation untrue. For instance, we can obtain <eat apple, ObstructedBy, not get apple based on <eat apple, HasPrerequisite, get apple>.

Table 1. Statistics of ConceptNet.

Relation	Example	Initial size	Retained size
Causes	<get job, Causes, earn money>	16800	11084
HasSubevent	<eat, HasSubevent, chew>	25236	2304
HasPrerequisite	<hear music, HasPrerequisite, not deaf>	22709	5678
ObstructedBy	<lose weight, ObstructedBy, eat cake>	5676	5676
Before	<bake cake, Before, eat cake>	0	0
CausesDesire	<be hungry, CausesDesire, eat>	4687	2830
IsA	<jog, IsA, run>	2681	1327
OppositeTo	<sad, OppositeTo, happy>	11669	8760

3.2 Completion of Seed ECCKG with Logical Rules

We obtain the seed ECCKG in the section above. However, there is a huge gap between the small scale of seed ECCKG and the broad demands of downstream applications, motivating us to acquire more larger eventuality-centric commonsense knowledge, a task referred to as knowledge graph completion or link prediction. Recent approaches in commonsense knowledge graph completion tasks have mostly centered on embedding techniques that involve learning and operating on the latent representations of entities and relations [36, 37, 38]. Unfortunately, these embedding-based methods do not explicitly capture the compositional logical rules underlying a knowledge graph and are limited to the transductive setting where the full set of entities must be known during the training stage. These embedding-based models are highly dependent on training on a set of static entities and have low performance when new triples are presented. To overcome these limitations, we propose a rule-based approach to enriching the seed ECCKG.

In this paper, we restrict each rule to be a first-order Horn rule of length 1 or length 2, where the conclusion contains only a single atom and the premise is a single atom or a conjunction of two atoms, because longer rules can be very costly in terms of correct human identifications. The atom is acquired by converting commonsense triples <head event, relation, tail event> in the seed ECCKG into the logical formula "relation(head event, tail event)". To the best of our knowledge, our work is the first attempt to exploit logical rules in eventuality-centric knowledge graph completion. These rules are commonsense rules. In other words, these rules are commonsense knowledge about the relationships between two different types of relations. The approach of acquiring this kind of commonsense knowledge, or discovering these rules, works as follows: given a relation R_1 between eventuality x and eventuality y and a relation R_2 between eventuality y and eventuality z, the rule creators check whether there exists a relation R_3 between eventuality x and eventuality z; or given a relation R_1 between eventuality x and eventuality y, the rule curators decide whether another relation R_2 holds between them. R_1, R_2 and R_3 are one of the eight relations covered by the seed ECCKG. For example, we assume that R_1 is *Before* and R_2 is also *Before*, we only need to investigate whether R_1, R_2 and R_3 is *Causes, HasSubevent, HasPrerequisite, ObstructedBy, Before, CausesDesire, IsA* or *OppositeTo*. We obtain a complete set of 18 commonsense rules as illustrated below after a total of 576 (8 * 8 * 8 + 8 * 8) checks. Therefore, it is trivial to discover all these rules for humans using this approach but rather difficult to automatically learn them from the seed ECCKG. These rules reason over the existing knowledge tuples in the seed ECCKG to correctly predict new relations. Only 4 of them are illustrated below due to the limited space. The full list of rules is publicly available at https://zenodo.org/record/6084081.

1. **Causes(x, z) ∧ IsA(y, x) → Causes(y, z):**
   Causes(buy, have less money) ∧ IsA(buy hamburger, buy) → Causes(buy hamburger, have less money)
2. **HasSubevent(x, y) ∧ Before(x, z) → Before(y, z):**
   HasSubevent(eat apple, swallow) ∧ Before(eat apple, digest apple) → Before(swallow, digest apple)
3. **Before(x, y) ∧ Before(y, z) → Before(x, z):**
   Before(buy apple, eat apple) ∧ Before(eat apple, digest apple) → Before(buy apple, digest apple)
4. **HasPrerequisite(x, y) → Before(y, x):**
   HasPrerequisite (eat hamburger, make hamburger) → Before(make hamburger, eat hamburger)

We manually acquire these logical rules for two reasons. First, there usually exists many types of relations between entities in traditional large-scale knowledge graph. As a result, a knowledge graph can have rules in the thousands and it is infeasible to rely on human crowdsourcing for rule discovery in such a huge number. Contrary to this, an eventuality-centric commonsense knowledge graph includes a small number of relation types, making it possible to enumerate all rules with little manual efforts. Second, most rule-based approaches learn probabilistic logical rules with a statistical measure. This measure is derived from the facts in the knowledge graph and assumes these facts are correct. In practice, this dependence often leads to incorrect confidence value of a rule. In contrast, although it requires manual effort to discover and validate, our rules are hard rules which always hold with no exception. Consequently, most of the new relations (knowledge tuples) generated by these rules are true which enables us to enrich the seed ECCKG with high-quality commonsense knowledge.

These logical rules capture the eventuality-independent relational semantics of an eventuality-centric commonsense knowledge graph and provide us with interpretable reasoning for relation predictions which is not the case for embedding-based methods. In addition to providing interpretability, one of the key advantages of these logical rules is their inductive ability to generalize to new events which can be useful for reasoning over large-scale dynamic CSKG. The inherent inductive ability of these logical rules is complementary to the current state-of-the-art knowledge graph completion approaches. Many large-scale knowledge graphs have been created using automatic or semi-automatic methods. But these methods do not guarantee that the resulting knowledge graphs are free from errors. Our logical rules can also serve to discover logical inconsistencies and identify erroneous triples.

We apply the rules to knowledge tuples in the seed ECCKG to iteratively infer new relations. These newly inferred relations can be used as the atoms of premises for the next iteration. For example, if the new relation is HasPrerequisite(eat hamburger, make hamburger), then we can take this relation as the premise of rule 4 to infer Before(make hamburger, eat hamburger) in the next iteration. Table 2 presents the overall results before and after using rules after four iterations. 5K new random instances are selected from each relation for human evaluation. We can observe that these rules extend the seed ECCKG by more than 34 times at a high level of accuracy.

Table 2. Effect of inference rules.

Relation	Before inference	After inference	Accuracy
Causes	11,084	748,016	83.1%
HasSubevent	2,304	5,424	85.1%
HasPrerequisite	5,678	30,224	88.5%
ObstructedBy	5,676	443,595	84.5%
Before	0	52,065	83.4%
CausesDesire	2,830	3,141	87.7%
IsA	1,327	1,904	93.1%
OppositeTo	8,760	13,492	92.5%
Total	**37659**	**1,297,861**	**87.2%**

3.3 Generation of New Eventualities Using *isa* Relations

Though we have collected a considerable number of commonsense tuples after the rule-based knowledge graph completion, the coverage of events is rather low. For this reason, we further expand the knowledge graph by adding novel events to it.

WordNet is one of the most popular and widely used lexical resources. In WordNet, semantically equivalent concepts are grouped into synsets. The synsets are linked by a small set of relations, including hypernyms (isa), hyponyms (reverse of isa), meronym (part–whole), etc. A hyponym of one word is more concrete and covers a narrower range of semantic concepts than the word itself. For example, "apple" is called a hyponym of "fruit" and "dark red" is a hyponym of "red". *isa* relations are transitive. If A is a hypernym of B while B is a hypernym of C, then A is also a hypernym of C. In ECCKG, an eventuality is represented by a verb/adjective (predicate) or a combination of a verb/adjective with nouns (arguments). This allows us to leverage the taxonomic hierarchy of WordNet to generate new eventualities by replacing the predicates or arguments with their hyponyms. For example, if the eventuality is "eat fruit", then we can produce the new instantiated eventuality "eat apple" by substituting "fruit" with "apple". New *isa* relations are also produced when new eventualities are created. To do so, we first decompose an eventuality into two dimensions: predicate and argument. We use the Stanford POS Tagger to part-of-speech tag an eventuality to extract its predicate and arguments information. In the tagging output, verb (v)/adjective (a) denotes the predicate and nouns (n) are the arguments. A word may have different meanings and thus can be mapped to different synsets in WordNet. Therefore, disambiguating the semantic of predicate and arguments is crucial for constructing a high-quality ECCKG. For this task, we adopt the disambiguation techniques in Knowlywood [31] to map the predicate or arguments to their proper senses in WordNet. In particular, we instantiate an eventuality with WN18, a subset of WordNet which only contains synsets with at least fifteen connections to other synsets. It is worth mentioning that, we do not generate new eventualities using the hypernyms in WordNet. This is because hypernyms are not required in the logical rules and thus contribute little to the knowledge graph completion. To avoid more errors, we restrict our attention to hyponyms.

Table 3. Effect of event instantiation.

Relation	Before instantiation	After instantiation	Accuracy
Causes	748,016	748,352	98.1%
HasSubevent	5,424	5,563	96.7%
HasPrerequisite	30,224	30,514	98.5%
ObstructedBy	443,595	44,3836	97.5%
Before	52,065	52,532	97.4%
CausesDesire	3,141	3,147	100%
IsA	1,904	58,972	95.5%
OppositeTo	13,492	13,492	–
Total	**1,297,861**	**1,356,408**	**97.7%**

We generate a total of 237,386 new *isa* relations by generating 50,561 new eventualities. Then we apply the logical rules in Sect. 3.2 to these relations to infer more commonsense tuples. The statistics of new tuples are reported in Table 3. Most of the errors stem from semantic parsing.

Finally, we obtain the ECCKG which consists of 60,531 eventuality nodes and more than 1.3 million directed edges. A subgraph of ECCKG is shown in Fig. 2.

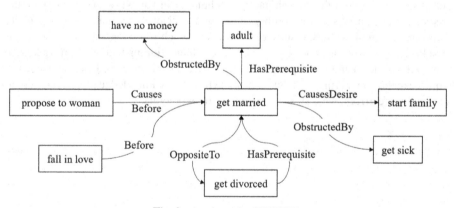

Fig. 2. A subgraph of ECCKG.

4 Intrinsic Evaluation

We compare our ECCKG to three relevant prominent CSKGs, i.e. ATOMIC-20, ConceptNet and TransOMCS. Since ATOMIC-20 is built on ATOMIC, we only consider the extended version. We evaluate the quality of each CSKG in terms of accuracy and coverage. We first map relations involving eventualities in these CSKGs to the relations in ECCKG. ECCKG covers more eventuality-centric relation types than the other CSKGs. It means ECCKG can cover more diverse types of commonsense knowledge about eventualities.

4.1 Accuracy Evaluation

In order to assess the accuracy of the commonsense knowledge contained in these CSKGs, we randomly select 8K instances for each relation. We rely on the same annotators that acquire seed ECCKG in Sect. 3.1 for this evaluation task. Annotators are presented with commonsense instances in the form of <head event, relation, tail event>. For each instance, the students are asked if it makes sense to them. If so, they should label it with "True". Otherwise, they should label it with "False". Most commonsense knowledge do not hold as absolute universal truths but rather be a reflection of overall tendencies. Therefore, the annotators are also given a choice to label a tuple with "Unclear" if they are not sure about the validity. For each tuple, we invite three students to label it and if at least two of them label it as "True", we consider it valid. The annotation results are reported in Table 4. From the result we can see that ECCKG outperforms other CSKGs in terms of accuracy.

Table 4. Knowledge graph accuracy.

Knowledge graph	Total	True	False	Unclear
ECCKG	1,356,408	87.4%	11.5%	1.1%
ConceptNet	89,458	57.5%	38.5%	4.0%
ATOMIC	1,246,582	80.3%	17.3%	2.4%
TransOMCS	394,561	43.8%	51.4%	4.8%

4.2 Coverage Evaluation

We also make a pairwise comparison between the four CSKGs to assess their coverage with respect to the commonsense knowledge they contain. For concepts mapping, we preprocess the events of each triple in a similar way to ATOMIC-20 [39]. We use two metrics to evaluate the coverage of a CSKG: Coverage precision and Coverage recall. Coverage precision evaluates the proportion of triples in the source CSKG that are correct is found in the target CSKG. Coverage recall reflects the proportion of triples in the target CSKG that are correct is contained in the source CSKG. Table 5 and Table 6 illustrate the results. We can observe from the results that ECCKG has the widest coverage.

Table 5. Coverage precision (%).

Source	Target			
	TransOMCS	ConceptNet	ATOMIC	ECCKG
TransOMCS	–	0.4	0.3	0.6
ConceptNet	5.5	–	45.6	100.0
ATOMIC	1.4	9.3	–	17.5
ECCKG	7.9	38.5	55.3	–

Table 6. Coverage recall (%).

Source	Target			
	TransOMCS	ConceptNet	ATOMIC	ECCKG
TransOMCS	–	7.6	1.3	9.2
ConceptNet	0.3	–	8.9	39.6
ATOMIC	0.4	47.8	–	76.9
ECCKG	0.7	100.0	19.1	–

5 Extrinsic Evaluation

In this section, we assess the performance of ECCKG on commonsense knowledge acquisition. Our focus is particularly on commonsense knowledge about human goals due to space limitation.

Emotions are associated with desires. Usually, emotions result from what is happening to our desires. Events that satisfy the desires of an individual yield positive emotions, and events that harm his or her desires lead to negative emotions [40]. Most of the commonsense tuples in ECCKG are commonsense knowledge relating to human activities. Therefore, causal tuples with emotional state as tail eventuality in ECCKG are a useful resource for obtaining commonsense knowledge about human desires. For instance, <get good grade, Causes, happy> and <get divorced, Causes, sadness>. The head events are considered as commonsense knowledge about human desires in these causal tuples.

We first need to discover information about emotion in the tail events of causal tuples. One emotion can be expressed in various ways in English. For example, the emotional response to "get good grade" can be "happiness", "feel happy", "feelings of joy" in ConceptNet. We argue that the way emotions are expressed does not affect the acquisition of commonsense knowledge about human goals. It is the emotion itself that has an influence on the acquisition of commonsense knowledge. Moreover, an exhaustive list of these ways usually requires extensive manual effort. We note that, if we translate these events into Chinese using Google Translate Tool, we obtain the results containing three emotion-related adjectives (i.e. happy, joyful and delighted). All these adjectives denote positive emotions. There is a limited number of Chinese adjectives that typically encode positive (e.g. 高兴|happy and 骄傲|proud) and negative emotions (e.g. 愤怒|angry and 失望|disappointed). When these adjectives appear in the tail eventuality of a causal triple, they are effective emotional information that helps us collect commonsense knowledge about human goals. Therefore, we manually collect these Chinese daily emotion adjectives and semantically organize them into a taxonomy. In total, we acquire 115 emotion-related adjectives exploiting the book *"Usage Dictionary of Chinese Adjectives"* [41].

For each causal commonsense tuple in ECCKG, we translate its tail eventuality using the popular Google Translate Tool. Then we check whether the resulting eventuality contains Chinese emotion adjectives or not. If the eventuality contains positive emotion adjectives, the corresponding head eventuality is the desire humans want to satisfy. If it includes negative emotion adjectives, the head eventuality is the desire humans want to avoid. Moreover, desires of humans are usually the desires of their families (i.e. parents, spouses and children), close friends and lovers. Thus, we can automatically acquire the desires of a mother or father, a husband or wife, and a son or daughter of a person when we are equipped with his or her desires. A total of 92,095 human desires are acquired from ECCKG with a high accuracy of 94.6%. We do not extract much commonsense knowledge about human desires from ECCKG, which is unsurprising as ECCKG has only few causal tuples with an emotion-related eventuality as tail eventuality. But the accuracy is high enough to prove the applicability of ECCKG to certain commonsense knowledge acquisition. Some human desires are illustrated in Table 7.

Table 7. Commonsense knowledge about human desires.

Humans	Desires	Not desires
Self	destroy enemy/find lost item/get good grade	be insulted/arrive late/get divorced
Parents	children to destroy enemy/children to find lost item/children to get good grade	children to be insulted/children to arrive late/children to get divorced
Children	parents to destroy enemy/parents to find lost item/parents to get good grade	parents to be insulted/parents to arrive late/parents to get divorced
Spouse	spouse to destroy enemy/spouse to find lost item/spouse to get good grade	spouse to be insulted/spouse to arrive late/spouse to get divorced

6 Conclusion

We presented ECCKG, a large-scale and high-quality commonsense knowledge graph about eventualities. ECCKG is a commonsense repository of textual descriptions that encode the social aspects of human everyday experiences. It is constructed with the aim of being complementary to current CSKGs. ECCKG introduces 8 eventuality-centric relations concerning situations surrounding a given eventuality of interest. Intrinsic evaluation showed the superior coverage, size and quality of ECCKG. Furthermore, an extrinsic evaluation for human desires acquisition showed that ECCKG is useful for extracting some kinds of commonsense knowledge.

References

1. Glavaš, G., Šnajder, J.: Event graphs for information retrieval and multi-document summarization. Expert Syst. Appl. **41**(15), 6904–6916 (2014)
2. Zhang, H., Liu, X., Pan, H., et al.: ASER: a large-scale eventuality knowledge graph. In: Proceedings of The Web Conference 2020, pp. 201–211 (2020)
3. Ding, X., Li, Z., Liu, T., et al.: ELG: an event logic graph. arXiv preprint arXiv:1907.08015 (2019)
4. Suchanek, F.M., Kasneci, G., Weikum, G.: Yago: a core of semantic knowledge. In: Proceedings of the 16th International Conference on World Wide Web, pp. 697–706 (2007)
5. Auer, S., Bizer, C., Kobilarov, G., et al.: Dbpedia: A Nucleus for a Web of Open Data the Semantic Web, pp. 722–735. Springer, Berlin, Heidelberg (2007)
6. Vrandečić, D., Krötzsch, M.: Wikidata: a free collaborative knowledge base. Commun. ACM **57**(10), 78–85 (2014)
7. Mourelatos, A.: Events, processes, and states. Linguist. Philos. **2**(3), 415-434 (1978)
8. Speer, R., Chin, J., Havasi, C.: Conceptnet 5.5: an open multilingual graph of general knowledge. In: Thirty-first AAAI Conference on Artificial Intelligence (2017)
9. Sap, M., Le Bras, R., Allaway, E., et al.: Atomic: An atlas of machine commonsense for if-then reasoning. In: Proceedings of the AAAI Conference on Artificial Intelligence, vol. 33, no. 01, pp. 3027–3035 (2019)
10. Liu, H., Singh, P.: ConceptNet—a practical commonsense reasoning tool-kit. BT Technol. J. **22**(4), 211–226 (2004)
11. Nguyen, T.P., Razniewski, S., Weikum, G.: Advanced semantics for commonsense knowledge extraction. In: Proceedings of the Web Conference 2021, pp. 2636–2647 (2021)
12. Mihaylov, T., Frank, A.: Knowledgeable reader: enhancing cloze-style reading comprehension with external commonsense knowledge. In: Proceedings of the 56th Annual Meeting of the Association for Computational Linguistic, pp. 821–832 (2018)
13. Vijayaraghavan, P., Roy, D.: Modeling human motives and emotions from personal narratives using external knowledge and entity tracking. In: Proceedings of the Web Conference 2021, pp. 529–540 (2021)
14. Bauer, L., Wang, Y., Bansal, M.: Commonsense for generative multi-hop question answering tasks. In: Proceedings of the 2018 Conference on Empirical Methods in Natural Language Processing, pp. 4220-4230 (2018)
15. Zhou, Y., Schockaert, S., Shah, J.: Predicting ConceptNet path quality using crowdsourced assessments of naturalness. In: The World Wide Web Conference, pp. 2460–2471 (2019)
16. Meilicke, C., Fink, M., Wang, Y., Ruffinelli, D., Gemulla, R., Stuckenschmidt, H.: Fine-grained evaluation of rule- and embedding-based systems for knowledge graph completion. In: Vrandečić, D., Bontcheva, K., Suárez-Figueroa, M.C., Presutti, V., Celino, I., Sabou, M., Kaffee, L.-A., Simperl, E. (eds.) ISWC 2018. LNCS, vol. 11136, pp. 3–20. Springer, Cham (2018). https://doi.org/10.1007/978-3-030-00671-6_1
17. Teru, K., Denis, E., Hamilton, W.: Inductive relation prediction by subgraph reasoning. In: International Conference on Machine Learning. PMLR, pp. 9448–9457 (2020)
18. Meilicke, C., Chekol, M.W., Fink, M., et al.: Reinforced anytime bottom-up rule learning for knowledge graph completion. arXiv preprint arXiv:2004.04412 (2020)

19. Wang, Q., Wang, B., Guo, L.: Knowledge base completion using embeddings and rules. In: Twenty-fourth International Joint Conference on Artificial Intelligence. (2015)
20. Yang, F., Yang, Z., Cohen, W.W.: Differentiable learning of logical rules for knowledge base reasoning. In: Proceedings of the 31st International Conference on Neural Information Processing Systems, pp. 2316–2325 (2017)
21. Galárraga, L.A., Teflioudi, C., Hose, K., et al.: AMIE: association rule mining under incomplete evidence in ontological knowledge bases. In: Proceedings of the 22nd International Conference on World Wide Web, pp. 413–422 (2013)
22. Bordes, A., Glorot, X., Weston, J., et al.: A semantic matching energy function for learning with multi-relational data. Mach. Learn. **94**(2), 233–259 (2014)
23. Miller, G.A.: WordNet: An Electronic Lexical Database. MIT Press (1998)
24. Murugesan, K., Atzeni, M., Kapanipathi, P., et al.: Text-based RL agents with commonsense knowledge: new challenges, environments and baselines. In: Thirty Fifth AAAI Conference on Artificial Intelligence (2021)
25. Chen, H., Huang, Y., Takamura, H., et al.: Commonsense knowledge aware concept selection for diverse and informative visual storytelling. In: Proceedings of the AAAI Conference on Artificial Intelligence, vol. 35, no. 2, pp. 999–1008 (2021)
26. Wu, S., Li, Y., Zhang, D., et al.: Diverse and informative dialogue generation with context-specific commonsense knowledge awareness. In: Proceedings of the 58th Annual Meeting of the Association for Computational Linguistics, pp. 5811–5820 (2020)
27. Li, Z., Ding, X., Liu, T.: Constructing narrative event evolutionary graph for script event prediction. In: Proceedings of the 27th International Joint Conference on Artificial Intelligence, pp. 4201–4207 (2018)
28. Mostafazadeh, N., Kalyanpur, A., Moon, L., et al.: GLUCOSE: generalized and contextualized story explanations. In: Proceedings of the 2020 Conference on Empirical Methods in Natural Language Processing (EMNLP), pp. 4569-4586 (2020)
29. Zhao, S., Wang, Q., Massung, S., et al.: Constructing and embedding abstract event causality networks from text snippets. In: Proceedings of the Tenth ACM International Conference on Web Search and Data Mining, pp. 335–344 (2017)
30. Gottschalk, S., Demidova, E.: Eventkg: a multilingual eventuality-centric temporal knowledge graph. In: European Semantic Web Conference, pp. 272-287. Springer, Cham (2018)
31. Tandon, N., De Melo, G., De, A., et al.: Knowlywood: mining activity knowledge from hollywood narratives. In: Proceedings of the 24th ACM International on Conference on Information and Knowledge Management, pp. 223–232 (2015)
32. Heist, N., Paulheim, H.: Information extraction from co-occurring similar entities. In: Proceedings of the Web Conference 2021, pp. 3999–4009 (2021)
33. Sadeghian, A., Armandpour, M., Ding, P., et al.: DRUM: end-to-end differentiable rule mining on knowledge graphs. Adv. Neural. Inf. Process. Syst. **32**, 15347–15357 (2019)
34. Ortona, S., Meduri, V.V., Papotti, P.: Robust discovery of positive and Negative rules in knowledge bases. In: 2018 IEEE 34th International Conference on Data Engineering (ICDE), pp. 1168–1179. IEEE (2018)
35. Omran, P.G., Wang, K., Wang, Z.: Scalable rule learning via learning representation. In: IJCAI, pp. 2149–2155 (2018)
36. Rossi, A., Barbosa, D., Firmani, D., et al.: Knowledge graph embedding for link prediction: a comparative analysis. ACM Trans. Knowl. Discov. Data (TKDD) **15**(2), 1–49 (2021)
37. Rosso, P., Yang, D., Cudré-Mauroux, P.: Beyond triplets: hyper-relational knowledge graph embedding for link prediction. In: Proceedings of The Web Conference 2020, pp. 1885–1896 (2020)
38. Wang, Z., Yang, J., Ye, X.: Knowledge graph alignment with entity-pair embedding. In: Proceedings of the 2020 Conference on Empirical Methods in Natural Language Processing (EMNLP), pp. 1672–1680 (2020)

39. Hwang, J.D., Bhagavatula, C., Le Bras, R., et al.: (Comet-) Atomic 2020: on symbolic and neural commonsense knowledge graphs. In: Proceedings of the AAAI Conference on Artificial Intelligence, vol. 35, no. 7, pp. 6384–6392 (2021)
40. Zurbriggen, E.L., Sturman, T.S.: Linking motives and emotions: a test of Mcclelland's hypotheses. Pers. Soc. Psychol. Bull. **28**(4), 521–535 (2002)
41. Usage Dictionary of Chinese Adjectives. Commercial Press (2003)

CKGAC: A Commonsense Knowledge Graph About Attributes of Concepts

Ya Wang[1,2], Cungen Cao[1], Zhiwen Chen[1,2], and Shi Wang[1(✉)]

[1] Key Laboratory of Intelligent Information Processing, Institute of Computing Technology, Chinese Academy of Sciences, Beijing 100190, China
{wangya,cgcao,chenzhiwen20s,wangshi}@ict.ac.cn
[2] University of Chinese Academy of Sciences, Beijing, China

Abstract. This paper presents a method for building a large commonsense knowledge graph about attributes of concepts, called CKGAC. CKGAC contains triples that connect concepts (nouns) with attribute values (adjectives) via corresponding attributes like *color*, *taste* and *age*. We first manually construct a seed commonsense knowledge graph for CKGAC based on a limited set of Chinese adjectives. Then we add new triples to this seed commonsense knowledge graph by extracting < concept, adjective> pairs from unstructured Web documents. We further extend the commonsense knowledge graph using *isa* relations between concepts. Finally, we obtain CKGAC which consists of 4,490,768 high-quality commonsense triples covering 187 concept attributes. Experimental results show the effectiveness of our approach in terms of both precision and coverage through human evaluation. In order to prove the utility of CKGAC, we demonstrate an application of it to commonsense knowledge acquisition. CKGAC is available at https://zenodo.org/record/6084143.

Keywords: Concept attribute · Commonsense knowledge graph · Commonsense knowledge acquisition

1 Introduction

Information about attributes of concepts tells us from what viewpoints concepts are usually understood or described. However, in order to truly understand a concept, knowing that a concept can be described by a certain set of attributes is not enough. We also have to know the values of attributes when we want to know about a concept that have these attributes. For example, the attributes of an apple will be *color* (red) and *taste* (sweet). Therefore, commonsense knowledge about concept attributes and their possible values is of great practical importance for a variety of downstream applications such as product search [1, 2], question answering [3, 4] and information retrieval [5, 6]. Unfortunately, state-of-the-art commonsense knowledge graphs [7, 8] focus on generic *hasProperty* relation and neglect fine-grained relations like *hasColor* and *hasTaste*.

To overcome the limitations of existing commonsense knowledge graphs, we propose an approach to constructing a commonsense knowledge graph about attributes of concepts (CKGAC). CKGAC provides commonsense knowledge in the form of <concept,

G. Memmi et al. (Eds.): KSEM 2022, LNAI 13368, pp. 585–601, 2022.
https://doi.org/10.1007/978-3-031-10983-6_45

attribute, adjective> triple where concept is a noun or noun phrase. The commonsense knowledge included in these triples is: 1) concept has attribute; 2) adjective can modify concept; and 3) adjective describe the attribute of concept. The second type of commonsense knowledge is linguistic commonsense knowledge. Our construction method consists of three stages: (1) acquisition of an initial seed of triples based on a set of frequently used Chinese adjectives; (2) extraction of new triples from Web texts using two linguistic patterns; and (3) completion of knowledge graph after stage 1 and stage 2 by replacing the existing concepts with their sub-concepts. It is worth stating that we focus on the Chinese language.

Construction of Seed CKGAC. The relationship between a concept, a particular attribute and an adjective is rarely explicitly observed in natural language text. Consequently, automatic acquisition of an initial seed of triples with high precision is challenging because of sparseness and bias in corpora. The quality of the seed knowledge graph severely impacts the whole performance of our approach. This is because the errors in the seed knowledge graph will produce a snowball effect and propagate in stage 2 and stage 3. Thus, achieving high precision of the seed CKGAC is our most important objective. The main function of an adjective is the modification of concepts by describing some attributes of them [9]. For example, "sad" is used to describe the feelings of a person or an animal and "expensive" provides possible value for the attribute *price*. Although the attributes are implicitly conveyed by adjectives, they can be easily inferred by humans. Moreover, the number of commonly used Chinese adjectives is limited. Motivated by these observations, we propose to acquire the seed CKGAC based on Chinese adjectives by tapping human intelligence. This stage results in 3,020 triples covering a large-scale set of 187 attributes, e.g. <person, emotion, sad> and <product, price, expensive>. These triples will be used as gold standard to guide the extraction of triples in stage 2 and completion of knowledge graph in stage 3.

Extraction of New Triples from Web Texts. After stage 1, we obtain a concise and clean set of commonsense tuples that covers only abstract concepts such as people and product. Although commonsense knowledge about concept attributes can be manually collected like WordNet [10] or GerCo [11], problems are cost and coverage. Therefore, we need to increase the coverage of the seed CKGAC by automatically discovering new concepts and assigning appropriate attributes and adjectives to these concepts. The Web is the biggest repository of information available which covers almost any possible domain. There has been an extensive body of Web-based work on the acquisition of information about concept attributes [12, 13]. In this paper, we follow this trend and extract attribute knowledge from Chinese web text. Using linguistic patterns to extract knowledge about concept attributes from unstructured text has been demonstrated to be an effective approach [14, 15]. We specifically employ two syntactic patterns, **adjective-noun** and **noun-adverb-adjective** where adverb is adverb of degree (i.e. "很", "非常", "十分" and "特别" in Chinese), to extract <noun, adjective> pairs. For instance, <mom, sad> and <jewelry, expensive>. The two patterns are relatively restrictive. We tried several variations of them, but came to the conclusion that the two patterns offer the best tradeoff between precision and recall for our application. Our design of the extraction and filtering mechanisms prioritizes precision over recall since the removal of probable errors in this stage will prevent a snowball effect that leads incorrect triples to proliferate in stage 3. We also attempted to leverage two linguistic patterns involving attribute to extract <attribute, adjective> pairs, i.e. **adjective-attribute** and **attribute-adverb-adjective**. However, we discarded them for yielding very low recall. We collect a set of <noun, adjective> pairs after extraction. In order to generate candidate triples, we need to add attributes to these pairs. Firstly, we check whether the noun in a pair is an attribute. If the noun is not an attribute, we then investigate whether the adjective in the same pair describe only one attribute based on the seed CKGAC. The details of candidate triples generation will be given in Sect. 4.2. Due to the nature of automatic part-of-speech tagging, the generated candidate triples are quite noisy. Therefore, we introduce some filtering rules to remove the incorrect or ambiguous triples.

Completion of knowledge graph using *isa* relations *isa* relation is a relationship between a sub-concept and a concept (e.g. a girl is a person). This type of relationship is a backbone of almost every traditional knowledge graph such as WordNet [10]. The sub-concepts of a concept inherit the attributes this concept has. In addition, these sub-concepts can be associated with the adjectives that modify this concept. Therefore, we can further enrich the commonsense knowledge graph acquired after stage 1 and stage 2 with the sub-concepts of the existing concepts in it. For example, we can produce a new triple <girl, appearance, beautiful> by replacing the concept in the existing triple <person, appearance, beautiful> with its sub-concept (i.e. girl). For this purpose, we utilize English WordNet as the source of sub-concepts. WordNet is a commonsense knowledge graph that manually organizes nouns and adjectives into lexical classes according to *isa* relations. For instance, "girl" and "person" are connected by an indirect edge. Here, "girl" is considered as a hyponym of "person" and "person" is a hypernym of "girl". Human construction could provide high-quality commonsense knowledge which serves well our most important goal, namely high accuracy. Furthermore, WordNet has good coverage of common concepts. We argue that WordNet is a suitable resource for extending the existing commonsense knowledge graph. Unlike most existing work, we focus on non-English language in our current research, namely Chinese. As a result, we need to translate the target concepts and their sub-concepts in WordNet into Chinese.

The main contributions of this work are threefold. (1) We construct a high-quality and large-scale commonsense knowledge graph about concept attributes. To the best of our knowledge, this is the first Chinese resource involving attributes of concepts; (2) We establish a gold standard of adjective-noun collocations for Chinese that supports collocation research; (3) We collect a set of attributes that can be used as dimensions of commonsense knowledge acquisition.

The rest of the paper is organized as follows. We start by introducing previous work in Sect. 2. In Sect. 3, we describe the approach to constructing CKGAC. We conduct an experiment to evaluate the quality of CKGAC and make a comparison with an existing commonsense knowledge graph in Sect. 4. Section 5 provides an application of CKGAC to demonstrate its utility. We make a conclusion about our work in Sect. 6.

2 Related Work

2.1 Commonsense Knowledge Graph Construction

Many efforts have been made to construct commonsense knowledge graph. WordNet [10] categorizes semantically equivalent concepts into synsets. In WordNet, nouns and adjectives are connected by the sparse *attribute* relation. For example, <age, *attribute*, mature> and <color, *attribute*, colorful>. In fact, these nouns are attributes themselves. WordNet completely lacks the commonsense information about the concepts that have these attributes. ConceptNet [7] is the most prominent and extensively used commonsense knowledge graphs. Commonsense statements in ConceptNet are acquired using crowdsourcing efforts of Web users. ConceptNet does not provide much commonsense knowledge about concept attributes except for generic *hasProperty* relation. SenticNet [16] is a commonsense knowledge graph for opinion mining and sentiment analysis. SenticNet provides commonsense information about the polarity and affective values of commonsense concepts. Atomic [17] puts its emphasis on the inferential commonsense knowledge, i.e. causal and conditional relations between events. GLUCOSE [18] is a large-scale commonsense knowledge graph with its focus on causal, part-whole and conditional relations between events. Both Atomic and GLUCOSE are event-centric commonsense knowledge graphs. Consequently, SenticNet, Atomic and GLUCOSE are fairly ignorant regarding commonsense knowledge about concept attributes. The closest related work is the WebChild [19] knowledge graph with triples of nouns, attributes and adjectives. However, WebChild convers only 19 fine-grained relations such as *hasShape*, *hasColor* and *hasWeight*, etc.

2.2 Attribute Selection

Another close body of work is the research on attribute selection. The task of attribute selection is to predict the hidden attribute expressed by an adjective in composition with a noun. There has been much prior research on attribute selection [20] used CBOW word embeddings to represent adjective and noun meaning and learned a compositionality function to compute an adjective-noun phrase representation to capture the compositional attribute meaning [21] presented a distributional framework to model hidden attributes in the compositional semantics of adjective-noun phrase [8] formulated attribute selection task in a vector space model that represents adjectives and nouns as vectors in a semantic space defined over possible attributes. An attribute model that captures semantic information encoded in adjectives and nouns using Latent Dirichlet Allocation [22] presented a study on attribute selection for German. Previous work on attribute selection focus primarily on English or German data. In contrast, this paper presents the first work on attribute selection in Chinese adjective-noun phrases. Furthermore, these studies have in common that they perform attribute selection for a small number of adjective-noun phrases compared to our work.

3 Construction of CKGAC

CKGAC is a Chinese commonsense knowledge graph containing triples of the form <concept, attribute, adjective>. The overall framework of CKGAC construction is shown in Fig. 1. We will introduce each part of the framework separately in the following sub-sections.

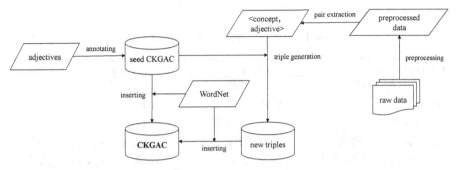

Fig. 1. Overall framework of CKGAC construction.

3.1 Construction of Seed CKGAC

A Chinese adjective is one that ascribes a value of an attribute to a noun (concept). The semantic representation is ATTRIBUTE (concept) = adjective. That is to say, for a given adjective, there exists a concept and an ATTRIBUTE such that ATTRIBUTE (concept) = adjective. For example, TASTE (apple) = sweet. Therefore, we can exploit an adjective to acquire commonsense knowledge about the concepts and attributes that are relevant to this adjective, i.e. <concept, attribute, adjective> triples. For a language, most of its native speakers are equipped with this kind of commonsense knowledge or background knowledge. Additionally, the number of frequently used Chinese adjectives is limited. Thus, it is feasible to manually construct the seed CKGAC to guarantee its accuracy. For these reasons, we select three advanced students of computational linguistics with a solid background in Chinese lexical semantics to accomplish this task.

The task of building the seed CKGAC is defined as follows: given an adjective, firstly determine the concepts used to form <concept, adjective> pairs, and then annotate each pair with the appropriate attribute, i.e. determine the attribute conveyed by a pair. It is worth noting that the pairs must match the linguistic patterns introduced above. Take "sweet (甜)" as an example, we can obtain pairs such as <voice, sweet> and <apple, sweet> whereas <pen, sweet> or <chair, sweet> does not make much sense. An abstract concept can include many sub-concepts or instances, for example, there are millions of different kinds of **food** in the world. Manually enumerating all the food is a work that requires a great deal of time and effort, which we will do in an automatic way in the next section. The job of the students is to contribute the most abstract concepts that are correct and could cover all their correct sub-concepts or instances of them. From the two pairs, we can infer the corresponding attributes, i.e. *tone* and *taste*. In total, we collect 3,020 triples that constitute the seed CKGAC based on 1,632 selected Chinese adjectives in the book "*A Dictionary of Common Adjectives Taxonomy*" [23]. There are about 4100 Chinese adjectives (including many adjectives that people usually don't use in daily conversations) in this book. These adjectives are classified into 41 categories according to their meanings. This dictionary is composed of four parts: adjectives, phonetic notations, definitions and example sentences. Some triples in the seed CKGAC are shown in Table 1.

Table 1. Example triples of the seed CKGAC.

Concept	Attribute	Adjective
physical object (物体)	taste (味道)	sweet (甜)
person (人)	feeling (情绪)	sad (悲伤)
animal (动物)	feeling (情绪)	sad (悲伤)
physical space (物理空间)	area (面积)	bright and spacious (敞亮)
physical space (物理空间)	light (光线)	bright and spacious (敞亮)
food (食物)	taste (味道)	delicious (可口)
food (食物)	hardness (硬度)	delicious (可口)
food (食物)	temperature (温度)	delicious (可口)
product (商品)	price (价格)	expensive (昂贵)
product (商品)	price (价格)	cheap (便宜)
physical object (物体)	taste (味道)	sweet (甜)
person (人)	feeling (情绪)	sad (悲伤)

The seed CKGAC covers 187 attributes and 88 abstract concepts. The full list of attributes is publicly available at https://zenodo.org/record/6084143. It will serve as the empirical basis for extracting new triples in Sect. 4.2 and enriching the knowledge graph with the sub-concepts in Sect. 4.3. This small-scale but high-quality commonsense knowledge graph can be used not only for the problem studied in this paper, but also in computational linguistics [24]. It is worth mentioning that, the seed CKGAC also includes a dataset of adjective-noun collocations. Adjective-noun collocations for non-Chinese language have been extensively studied [11, 21, 24]. Either manually creating or automatically extracting this type of collocations is a challenging task that requires clear definitions of adjectives and nouns. As a result, there exist only a few resources that can serve as gold standards in adjective-noun collocations research. This dataset will be a reliable and valuable resource for the studies of adjective-noun collocations and attribute knowledge for Chinese.

In the process of building the seed CKGAC, we find that attributes are themselves concepts (i.e. attribute concept) and have their own attributes. For example, *brightness* (亮度) is the attribute of *light* (光线). We call the attribute of an attribute *part-attribute*. If a concept C1 has an attribute A1 which is composed of some part-attributes such as A2 and A3, then A2 and A3 are also the attributes of C1. Another discovery is that an attribute may be an instance of another attribute. For instance, *altitude* (海拔) is an instance of *height* (高度). We call the more specific attribute *sub-attribute*. If a concept C1 has an attribute A1 that is a sub-attribute of attribute A2, then A2 is also the attribute of C1. In this paper, all attribute concepts in the triples that serve as concepts are treated as general concepts rather than attributes unless otherwise specified.

3.2   Extraction of New Triples from Web Texts

The extraction process involves three steps: 1) extracting <*noun, adjective*> pairs; 2) generating candidate triples; and 3) filtering out noisy triples.

Extracting <concept, adjective> Pairs. It has been proved that using the Web as a corpus greatly reduces the problem of data sparseness. Web documents provide a great deal of information about <noun, adjective> (<concept, adjective>) pairs. Therefore, we take advantage of the significant amounts of textual content available in Web documents to extract <noun, adjective> pairs. Our Web document corpus is collected by extracting news articles from famous Chinese websites such as Tencent and Baidu. The total size of the corpus is over 1.6 GB. Pattern-based approaches have been widely used to extract knowledge from unstructured text [25, 26]. <noun, adjective> pairs could also be automatically extracted from corpora by searching for syntactic patterns.

We use the following text patterns to extract <concept, adjective> pairs: "adj * (形容词 的*)" and "* adv adj (* 程度副词 形容词)", where *adj* is a given adjective introduced above, *advs* are different forms of " 很(very)", " 非常(extremely)", " 特别(particularly)" and " 十分(completely)", and the wildcard denotes an unspecified noun. Examples are "sweet soup (甜 的 汤)" and "the soup is very sweet (汤 很 甜)". We find that when using the Web, the two simple text patterns are sufficient to extract large numbers of <noun, adjective> pairs with a good degree of precision and recall.

We only use simple text patterns to identify nominal concepts, whereas parsers are used in most work of this kind. In this paper, the part-of-speech tagging of text corpora is performed using the ICTCLAS tagger [27] which is a free Chinese Lexical Analysis System. We remove the sentences in which a given adjective is not contained. Only the sentences including at least one of the 1,632 adjectives are retained. Next, we match the remaining sentences with the patterns. For the first pattern, we select the nearest words tagged as /n, /nr, /ns, /nt and /nz after a given adjective as the target concept we want to obtain. Consider the tagged sentence " 最/d 贫穷/a 的/u 国家/n 付出/v 了/u 最/d 昂贵/a 的/u 代价/n", we select " 国家(country)" to generate the < 国家 贫穷 > (<country, poor>) pair. And for the second pattern, we take the nearest words tagged as /n, /nr, /ns, /nt and /nz before a given adjective as the valid concept for this adjective. For example, " 意图(purpose)" is regarded as the correct concept in the sentence " 可见/c 其/r 去/v 头条/n 化/k 的/u 意图/n 已经/d 十分/d 明显/a/a". One thing worth mentioning is that when both patterns are matched by a sentence, e.g. " 成为/v 我国/n 十分/d 珍贵/a 的/u 历史/n 珍宝/n/n", the first pattern has priority over the second one. The result of the extraction is a large set of <concept, adjective> pairs as shown in Table 2.

Generating Candidate Triples. We are ultimately interested in <concept, attribute, adjective> triples that define the compositional semantics of <concept, adjective> pairs. For this purpose, we need to assign an attribute to a <concept, adjective> pair to produce

Table 2. Example <concept, adjective> pairs.

Concept	Adjective	Validity
colleague (同事)	happy (高兴)	true
mouth (嘴巴)	dry (干)	true
shape (外形)	peculiar (独特)	true
lawyer (律师)	excellent (优秀)	true
heart (心脏)	strong (强大)	true
mind (思维)	clear (清晰)	true
house (房子)	cheap (便宜)	true
house (房子)	early (早)	false

a triple. As previously mentioned, the seed CKGAC as a gold standard of <concept, adjective> pairs and <concept, attribute, adjective> triples can help to generate triples. We will describe the generation method in detail in the next paragraph. We consider the triples generated in this step as candidate triples since the error-prone nature of the extracted <noun, adjective> pairs.

We begin by checking whether the noun in an <noun, adjective> pair is an attribute.the noun is an attribute, it is regarded as an attribute rather than a concept. We then convert this <noun, adjective> pair to a <attribute, adjective> pair and examine whether the <attribute, adjective> pair is included in at least one of the triples in the seed CKGAC. If not, the <attribute, adjective> pair is considered as invalid. If the <attribute, adjective> pair is contained in at least one of the triples in the seed CKGAC, we cannot generate new triples. If the noun in an <noun, adjective> pair is not an attribute, we further investigate whether the adjective in this pair has only one sense. An adjective having single sense describes only one attribute in the seed CKGAC. We add the at-tribute conveyed by an adjective with one meaning to the <noun, adjective> pair to generate a new <noun, attribute, adjective> candidate triple. Otherwise, if the adjective has more than one senses, in other words, if the adjective expresses more than one at-tributes in the seed CKGAC, we match the noun with the concepts this adjective mod-ifies in the triples of the seed CKGAC. If the noun is not an existing concept or a sub-concept of at least one of the existing concepts, the <noun, adjective> pair will be con-sidered as an incorrect pair. If the noun is a sub-concept of at least one of the existing concepts, we add the corresponding attribute the adjective describes to the <noun, adjective> pair to generate a novel candidate triple. And if the noun is an existing concept, the <noun, adjective> pair is not useful for candidate triple generation. The algorithm Fig. 2 describes the process of candidate triples generation.

Observe that candidate triples generation requires identifying the sub-concepts of a concept. We leverage WordNet which contains a large number of isa relationships be-tween concepts for this task. We will use a Chinese subset of WordNet since we have chosen Chinese as our language of research.

Filtering Out Noisy Triples. Automatically part-of-speech tagging could produce noisy results. Moreover, Chinese is a language whose expressions are complex and di-verse. Consequently, the candidate triples created after step 2 are quite noisy. There-fore, we need to filter out the incorrect triples to improve the quality of the resulting com-monsense knowledge graph in this stage. We completely remove a triple whose concept containing any of the following: letters, numbers, punctuation marks or Chinese char-acter "一"; Chinese family name at the beginning of the concept; Chinese character "性" at the end of the concept; Chinese character "阿"; Chinese concept "实体"; and one-character concept that does not appear in WordNet.

```
1: // E: seed attribute set; T: seed concept set
2: // A: seed <attribute, adjective> pairs; W: sub-concepts in WordNet
3: for <noun, adjective>
4:    if noun∈ E
5:        Convert <noun, adjective> to <attribute, adjective>
6:        if <attribute, adjective> ∉ A
7:            remove <attribute, adjective>
8:    if noun ∉ E
9:        Regard <noun, adjective> as <concept, adjective>
10:       if adjective occurs more than once in A
11:           if noun ∈ W
12:               generate candidate triple
13:           if noun ∉ T and noun ∉ W
14:               remove <noun, adjective>
15: end for
16: return candidate triple
```

Fig. 2. Algorithm of generating candidate triples.

The output of stage 2 is a knowledge graph composed of 188,074 triples (including seed triples) as illustrated in Fig. 3. From the subgraph, we can draw the following conclusions: 1) some adjectives are likely to express different attributes depending on the nouns they modify; 2) concepts have many different attributes; 3) the attributes of a concept are inherited by its sub-concepts; 4) the adjectives modify a concept can also describe its sub-concepts; 5) some adjectives can describe different attributes of a concept; and 6) for some attributes, different adjectives could denote values of them. Studying the concepts, attributes and adjectives involved in a language based on these conclusions are not easy even for humans. We argue that it is non-trivial to construct a commonsense knowledge graph like CKGAC for any language.

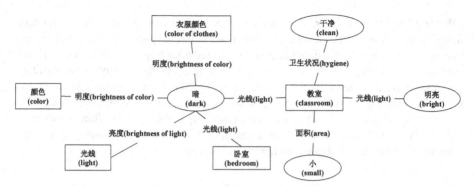

Fig. 3. A subgraph of CKGAC. Concepts and adjectives are indicated with rectangles and circles respectively.

3.3 Completion of Knowledge Graph Using *Isa* Relations

isa is an important commonsense relation between a concept and its sub-concepts. In this relation, the concept is called a hypernym and its sub-concept is a corresponding hyponym, e.g. an apple is a kind of fruit and cats are animals. As stated above, the sub-concepts of a concept share not only the attributes of this concept but also the adjectives modify it. For example, apples and bananas have the same attribute taste which is an attribute of fruits. In addition, we can describe the taste of apples and bananas with the same adjective delicious, i.e. delicious apples and delicious bananas. Inspired by these findings, we propose to further extend the commonsense knowledge graph to include the sub-concepts acquired from WordNet. Specifically, we replace the concept in an existing triple with its sub-concepts to generate new triples.

We take two main steps for the task of commonsense knowledge graph completion. In the first step, we search for the existing concepts already translated into English and their sub-concepts in WN18 [28]. WN18 is a subset of WordNet 3.0 in which most of the triples involve *isa* relations. Note that *isa* is a transitive relation. If concept C1 is a hypernym of concept C2 while concept C2 is a hypernym of concept C3 then concept C1 is also a hypernym of concept C3. That is to say, C1 is considered a hypernym of C2 regardless of how much higher in the hierarchy it is with respect to C2. Next, we translate the sub-concepts in these matching triples (i.e. triples containing existing concepts) into corresponding Chinese concepts, e.g. "apple" into "苹果". We manually translate these concepts for two reasons. First, the number of these sub-concepts is limited. Second, nouns are often highly ambiguous and may have many different meanings. For example, chair is a piece of furniture (i.e. 椅子in Chinese) in <chair, isa, furniture> but a person (i.e. 主席in Chinese) in <chair, isa, person>. Thus, we decide to rely on human translators for the translation task to acquire disambiguated triples. In the second step, we create novel triples by replacing the concept contained in an existing triple with its sub-concepts. For example, we can acquire <apple, taste, delicious> based on <fruit, taste, delicious>. The results of this stage are depicted in Fig. 4.

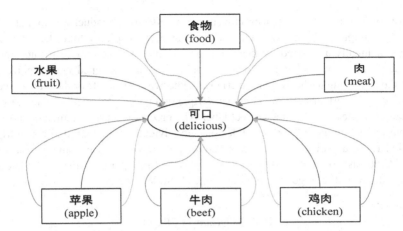

Fig. 4. A subgraph of CKGAC. The attribute *hardness, taste* and *temperature* are indicated with red, blue and green directed edges. (Color figure online)

There exists few *isa* relations between adjectives, e.g. angry (生气) and furious (愤怒). We do not take this type of *isa* relation into account since they contribute little to the knowledge graph completion. For the *isa* relations between attributes, they also play a minor role in enriching the knowledge graph because of their limited coverage.

The resulting CKGAC contains 4,490,768 triples and involves 15,356 concepts. The statistics of CKGAC are summarized in Table 3.

Table 3. CKGAC statistics.

Commonsense tuples	Coverage (tuples/arguments)	Arguments
<concept, attribute>	←769, 793/1,632→	Adjective
<concept, adjective>	←3,456,140/187→	Attribute
<concept, attribute, adjective>	←4,490,768/15,356→	Concept

4 Experiment

4.1 Quality of CKGAC

A triple is considered as correct based on three criteria: (1) the concept has the attribute; (2) the adjective can modify the concept; and (3) the attribute is correctly selected based on the combination of the concept and the adjective. Consequently, we evaluate the quality of CKGAC by assessing the precision of <noun, attribute> pairs, <noun, adjective> pairs and <noun, attribute, adjective> triples.

We ask the three students constructing the seed CKGAC to conduct the evaluation. We randomly sampled 5 triples for each adjective (i.e. 8,160 triples in total) from CKGAC that are manually annotated by them. For each triple, we decompose it into <noun, attribute> and <noun, adjective> pairs. A triple or a pair is assigned a label "correct" if it is valid according to the evaluation criteria; Otherwise, the triple or the pair is labeled as "incorrect". Furthermore, we consider a triple or a pair as "correct" if at least two of the human judges agree on the correct label. The precision scores are then obtained by computing the number of correct triples or pairs divided by the total number of triples or pairs. The evaluation results are reported in Table 4. We can see from the results that CKGAC consists of commonsense knowledge with high quality. Almost all the errors are introduced in the stage of extracting triples from Web texts.

Table 4. Quality of CKGAC.

Commonsense Tuples	True	False	Precision
<concept, attribute>	1289	112	0.92
<concept, adjective>	6165	126	0.98
<concept, attribute, adjective>	7276	899	0,89

4.2 Comparison with WebChild

There is no direct competitor that provides commonsense triples covering all the attributes in CKGAC. WebChild is the closest available resource. WebChild is a commonsense knowledge graph which contains triples of concepts, attributes and adjectives that are automatically acquired from book n-grams. The goal of WebChild is similar to CKGAC to associate a concept with all applicable adjectives through its attributes. However, WebChild covers only 19 attributes in CKGAC as presented in Table 5. WebChild lack triples about many other attributes included in CKGAC such as price and location that play an important role in various AI applications. We compare CKGAC against WebChild with respect to individual performance per sharing attribute.

Table 5 clearly conveys that CKGAC achieves a better precision per attribute than WebChild except for emotion. However, WebChild outperforms CKGAC in terms of coverage of most attributes. This is not surprising, because CKGAC is mainly constructed from a much smaller text (1.6G) corpus compared to a huge N-gram corpus (1T) used in WebChild. The slightly lower coverage led by such a small corpus also reflects the effectiveness of our method. We argue that the coverage limitation of CKGAC could be easily addressed by exploiting a bigger corpus.

Table 5. Comparison with WebChild.

WebChild (Precision / Coverage)	attribute (WebChild / CKGAC)	CKGAC (Precision / Coverage)
0.80 / 90,288	ability / 能力	0.84 / 9,610
0.95 / 365,201	appearance / 外观	0.97 / 127,236
0.70 / 95,838	beauty / 容貌	0.73 / 39,946
0.70 / 494,380	color / 颜色	0.84 / 96,027
0.90 / 79,630	emotion / 情感	0.90 / 34,646
0.91 / 141,453	feeling / 情绪	0.92 / **247,129**
0.70 / 90,021	length / 长度	0.95 / 13,510
0.80 / 146,148	motion / 行为	0.81 / **171,492**
0.82 / 25,347	smell / 气味	0.85 / 22,183
0.82 / 793,484	quality / 质量	0.85 / 13,062
0.70 / 5,727	sensitivity / 知觉	0.83 / **78,921**
0.80 / 359,789	shape / 形状	0.94 / 77,655
0.82 / 910,901	size / 体积	0.89 / 34,666
0.71 / 130,952	sound / 声音	0.75 / 13,459
0.88 / 563,022	state / 状态	0.90 / 8,740
0.82 / 165,412	strength / 力量	0.83 / 85,163
0.70 / 19,892	taste / 味道	0.76 / **41,166**
0.80 / 27,399	temperature / 温度	0.83 / **57,534**
0.70 / 144,587	weight / 重量	0.74 / 36,011

5 Application: Commonsense Knowledge Acquisition

Commonsense knowledge is usually not explicitly mentioned but resides in the mind of humans. Acquiring commonsense knowledge is known as an extremely difficult task [29, 30]. Attributes in this paper can serve as dimensions of collecting commonsense knowledge. These dimensions provide a basis for commonsense knowledge acquisition as they illustrate the facets of commonsense knowledge. For example, drinking pure water can quench your thirst (function) and apples are opaque (opacity). Consequently, we can effectively crowdsource commonsense knowledge along these dimensions. To confirm this assumption, we select two random events (i.e. that boy is eating an apple and that boy is running on the playground) to collect the preconditions that enable them to occur, e.g. you need to have an apple before you eat it.

For this goal, we ask two college students to provide preconditions expressed in natural language for the events. The students first try to exhaust all possible preconditions associated with each event. Then they are offered the attributes of the concepts in an event as clues to contribute preconditions. The students are asked to complete the tasks with and without the attributes in half an hour for a fair comparison. Given an event, we only suggest the attributes that the concepts in this event have as clues for the students to provide preconditions since only these relevant attributes are useful. For example, the attribute gender cannot help to acquire preconditions for the two events. The results are reported in Table 6 before and after offering attributes. The students equipped with the attributes provide more than two times as much commonsense knowledge as when they are not given the attributes.

Understanding the circumstances in which an event is possible or impossible to happen is a key aspect of human intelligence [30]. Accordingly, we have expected it will be trivial for humans to contribute commonsense knowledge about preconditions. Quite the contrary, the results indicate that it is difficult to come up with preconditions even for humans who possess them. The results prove the effectiveness of attributes as dimensions of commonsense knowledge acquisition.

Table 6. Results with and without attributes.

Event	Before	After
That boy is eating an apple	1) The boy has an apple	8) The boy has the strength to swallow the apple. (*strength*)
	2) The boy is alive	9) The boy has the strength to bite the apple. (*strength*)
	3) The boy can open his mouth	10) The apple is near the boy. (*position*)
	4) The apple is soft enough	11) The boy is old enough to eat an apple. (*age*)
	5) The boy knows how to eat an apple	12) The apple is not too hot to eat. (*temperature*)
	6) The boy has the ability to swallow the apple	13) The boy can stand the taste of the apple. (*taste*)
	7) The boy has the ability to bite the apple	14)......
	1) The boy is alive	9) The playground is safe enough. (*safety*)
	2) The boy has legs	10) The surface of the playground is not too hot. (*temperature*)
	3) The boy is awake	11) The playground is bright enough. (*light*)
	4) The boy can run	12) The playground is long enough. (*length*)
That boy is running on the playground	5) The playground is big enough	13) The playground is wide enough. (*width*)
	6) The playground is strong enough	14) The area of the playground is larger than that of the boy. (*area*)

(*continued*)

Table 6. (*continued*)

Event	Before	After
	7) The boy has enough strength to run	15) The boy can stand. (*ability*)
	8) The boy is not a baby	16)......

6 Conclusion

We constructed a commonsense knowledge graph about attributes of concepts for Chinese by combining human efforts and information extraction techniques, called CKGAC. Current CKGAC is composed of 4,490,768 <concept, attribute, adjective> triples covering 1,632 adjectives, 187 attributes and 15,356 concepts. CKGAC also provides 3,456,140 <concept, adjective> pairs which is a valuable resource for collocation research. Experiment results showed the high quality and wide coverage of CKGAC. In addition, we proved the utility of CKGAC by applying it to commonsense knowledge acquisition. In particular, we focused on acquiring commonsense knowledge about the preconditions that make it possible for an event to happen.

References

1. Wang, Q., Yang, L., Kanagal, B., et al.: Learning to extract attribute value from product via question answering: a multi-task approach. In: Proceedings of the 26th ACM SIGKDD International Conference on Knowledge Discovery & Data Mining, pp. 47–55 (2020)
2. Lin, R., He, X., Feng, J., et al.: PAM: Understanding Product Images in Cross Product Category Attribute Extraction. arXiv preprint arXiv:2106.04630 (2021)d
3. Romero, J., Razniewski, S., Pal, K., et al.: Commonsense properties from query logs and question answering forums. In: Proceedings of the 28th ACM International Conference on Information and Knowledge Management, pp. 1411–1420 (2019)
4. Nguyen, T.P., Razniewski, S., Weikum, G.: Advanced semantics for commonsense knowledge extraction. In: Proceedings of the Web Conference 2021, pp. 2636–2647 (2021)
5. Halevy, A., Noy, N., Sarawagi, S., et al.: Discovering structure in the universe of attribute names. In: Proceedings of the 25th International Conference on World Wide Web, pp. 939–949 (2016)
6. Bhutani, N., Qian, K., Li, Y., et al.: Exploiting structure in representation of named entities using active learning. In: Proceedings of the 27th International Conference on Computational Linguistics, pp. 687–699 (2018)
7. Speer, R., Chin, J., Havasi, C.: Conceptnet 5.5: An open multilingual graph of general knowledge. In: Thirty-first AAAI Conference on Artificial Intelligence (2017)
8. Hartung, M., Frank, A.: Exploring supervised lda models for assigning attributes to adjective-noun phrases. In: Proceedings of the 2011 Conference on Empirical Methods in Natural Language Processing, pp. 540–551 (2011)
9. Bakhshandeh, O., Allen, J.: From adjective glosses to attribute concepts: Learning different aspects that an adjective can describe. In: Proceedings of the 11th International Conference on Computational Semantics, pp. 23–33 (2015)
10. Fellbaum, C., Miller, G.: WordNet: An Electronic Lexical Database. MIT Press (1998)

11. Strakatova, Y., Falk, N., Fuhrmann, I., et al.: All that glitters is not gold: a gold standard of adjective-noun collocations for German. In: Proceedings of the 12th Language Resources and Evaluation Conference, pp. 4368–4378 (2020)

12. Tokunaga, K., Kazama, J., Torisawa, K.: Automatic discovery of attribute words from web documents. In: Dale, R., Wong, K.-F., Su, J., Kwong, O.Y. (eds.) IJCNLP 2005. LNCS (LNAI), vol. 3651, pp. 106–118. Springer, Heidelberg (2005). https://doi.org/10.1007/11562214_10

13. Lee, T., Wang, Z., Wang, H., et al.: Attribute extraction and scoring: a probabilistic approach. In: 2013 IEEE 29th International Conference on Data Engineering (ICDE), pp. 194–205. IEEE (2013)

14. Pasca, M.: Weakly-supervised acquisition of open-domain classes and class attributes from web documents and query logs. In: Proceedings of the 46th Annual Meeting of the Association for Computational Linguistics, pp. 19–27 200 (2008)

15. Bing, L., Lam, W., Wong, T.L.: Wikipedia entity expansion and attribute extraction from the web using semi-supervised learning. In: Proceedings of the Sixth ACM International Conference on Web Search and Data Mining, pp. 567–576 (2013)

16. Cambria, E., Li, Y., Xing, F.Z., et al.: SenticNet 6: Ensemble application of symbolic and sub-symbolic AI for sentiment analysis. In: Proceedings of the 29th ACM International Conference on Information & Knowledge Management, pp. 105–114 (2020)

17. Sap, M., Le Bras, R., Allaway, E., et al.: Atomic: an atlas of machine commonsense for if-then reasoning. In: Proceedings of the AAAI Conference on Artificial Intelligence, vol. 33, no. 01, pp. 3027–3035 (2019)

18. Mostafazadeh, N., Kalyanpur, A., Moon, L., et al.: GLUCOSE: generalized and contextualized story explanations. In: Proceedings of the 2020 Conference on Empirical Methods in Natural Language Processing (EMNLP), pp. 4569-4586 (2020)

19. Tandon, N., De Melo, G., Suchanek, F., et al.: Webchild: harvesting and organizing common-sense knowledge from the web. In: Proceedings of the 7th ACM International Conference on Web Search and Data Mining, pp. 523–532 (2014)

20. Hartung, M., Kaupmann, F., Jebbara, S., et al.: Learning compositionality functions on word embeddings for modelling attribute meaning in adjective-noun phrases. In: Proceedings of the 15th Conference of the European Chapter of the Association for Computational Linguistics: vol. 1, Long Papers, pp. 54–64 (2017)

21. Hartung, M., Frank, A.: A structured vector space model for hidden attribute meaning in adjective-noun phrases. In: Proceedings of the 23rd International Conference on Computational Linguistics (Coling 2010), pp. 430–438 (2010)

22. Falk, N., Strakatova, Y., Huber, E., et al.: Automatic classification of attributes in German adjective-noun phrases. In: Proceedings of the 14th International Conference on Computational Semantics (IWCS), pp. 239–249 (2021)

23. Fu, Y.F.: A Dictionary of Common Adjectives Taxonomy. Shanghai University Press (2007)

24. Anke, L.E., Schockaert, S., Wanner, L.: Collocation classification with unsupervised relation vectors. In: Proceedings of the 57th Annual Meeting of the Association for Computational Linguistics, pp. 5765–5772 (2019)

25. Zhang, H., Liu, X., Pan, H., et al.: ASER: a large-scale eventuality knowledge graph. In: Proceedings of the Web Conference 2020, pp. 201–211 (2020)

26. Gottschalk, S., Demidova, E.: EventKG–the hub of event knowledge on the web–and biographical timeline generation. Semant. Web 10(6), 1039–1070 (2019)

27. Zhang, H.P., Yu, H.K., Xiong, D., et al.: HHMM-based Chinese lexical analyzer ICTCLAS. In: Proceedings of the second SIGHAN workshop on Chinese language processing, pp. 184–187 (2003)

28. Bordes, A., Glorot, X., Weston, J., et al.: A semantic matching energy function for learning with multi-relational data. Mach. Learn. 94(2), 233–259 (2014)

29. Fang, T., Zhang, H., Wang, W., et al.: DISCOS: bridging the gap between discourse knowledge and commonsense knowledge. In: Proceedings of the Web Conference 2021, pp. 2648–2659 (2021)
30. Chemero, A.: An outline of a theory of affordances. Ecol. Psychol. **15**(2), 181–195 (2003)

Attentive Capsule Graph Neural Networks for Session-Based Recommendation

Yingpei Chen and Yan Tang[(✉)]

School of Computer and Information Science, Southwest University,
Chongqing, China
chenyingpei1@email.swu.edu.cn, ytang@swu.edu.cn

Abstract. Considering recommendation scenarios in that user profiles are anonymous, the session-based recommendation is proposed to predict the items users are interested in from short sessions. However, most existing methods for session-based recommendation are insufficient to obtain diverse user interests. Meanwhile, they are susceptible to the negative impact of the cold start. To solve these problems, we propose a novel attentive capsule graph neural network for session-based recommendation (ACGNN) to mine more profound user preferences and minimize the impact of the cold start on the recommendation. In ACGNN, we model historical session sequences as graph-structured data and leverage graph neural networks to learn low-level item embedding to represent each session, which can capture complex transitions of items. Various low-level item embeddings are then aggregated into high-level item embeddings by an attentive capsule network, which significantly improves the expressiveness of the model. It can also enrich the features of cold-start users and items, which were difficult to be revealed by previous methods. Our experiments on two real-world datasets consistently show the superior performance of ACGNN over state-of-the-art methods.

Keywords: Session-based recommendation · Graph neural network · Capsule network

1 Introduction

In many online platforms, user behavior data is frequently anonymous. In order to predict the interested items of users, the session-based recommendation is used to mine user preferences.

Session-based recommendation [12] is a recommendation task that is only based on anonymous user behavior and uses implicit user feedback to predict interested items of users, such as purchases and clicks. A session defines a set of interactive behavior sequences generated by a user in a given period, which can be divided according to a custom time interval. In particular, users in the session-based recommendation are anonymous, and user behavior is limited. Therefore,

© The Author(s), under exclusive license to Springer Nature Switzerland AG 2022
G. Memmi et al. (Eds.): KSEM 2022, LNAI 13368, pp. 602–613, 2022.
https://doi.org/10.1007/978-3-031-10983-6_46

when there is insufficient user-item interaction data, session-based recommendation performs better than the traditional recommendation.

Recently, due to the impact of deep learning, Hidasi et al. [2] applied recurrent neural networks (RNNs) with gated recurrent units (GRUs) for a session-based recommendation. On this basis, Tan et al. [14] further proposed an improved method by data augmentation to improve the robustness of training by pre-training to sufficiently consider the transitions of user behavior over time. Li et al. [4] proposed NARM, a new method, adding an attention mechanism to RNN, which can simultaneously capture the users' continuous behavior and interest. Liu et al. [7] proposed STAMP, a method similar to NARM, by employing simple multilayer perceptron (MLP) networks and attention mechanisms. It can also sufficiently consider the users' global preferences and current preferences. SR-GNN, proposed by Wu et al. [16], combines graph neural networks (GNNs) with RNN for the first time and applies it to a session-based recommendation. By modeling session sequences into graph-structured data and attention mechanisms, complex transitions of the items in sessions are captured. Recently, Yu et al. [17] proposed TAGNN based on SR-GNN, using an attentive module to reveal the relevance of historical actions given a particular target item, further improving session representations.

Although the methods above achieve significant results, becoming state-of-the-art, they still have some limitations:

- They highly depend on the relevance between the last item in the session and the user's interest in the current session, which is not conducive to capturing diverse user interests.
- They are susceptible to the negative impact of the cold start.

To overcome the limitations above, we propose an attentive capsule graph neural network for session-based recommendation (ACGNN) method. At first, historical session sequences are modeled as session graphs. After that, the features of each session graph are captured through GNN, generate the user preference embedding vector for each session, and represent it as item embedding. Then, adopt a novel dynamic routing capsule network with attention mechanisms to obtain multiple user preferences and aggregate low-level item embeddings into higher-level user preference vectors. Each is called high-level item embedding, which further represents each session. As high-level item embeddings enrich the features for cold-start users and items, the novel module helps predict the next-click item more accurately. Our experiments on real datasets show the superiority of ACGNN over state-of-the-art methods and can reduce the impact of the cold start on the recommendation scenarios.

2 Related Work

This section reviews the related work on session-based recommendation, including deep-learning-based methods and graphs-based neural network methods. Besides, the capsule network is mentioned in the end.

2.1   Deep-Learning-Based Methods

Hidasi et al. [2] proposed a recurrent neural network (RNN) approach for the first time. In the same year, they proposed a parallel RNN approach [3], which not only considers the basic information of clicked items but also uses some other features to improve the recommendation result. On this basis, Tan et al. [14] improved the performance of the model above by data augmentation, pre-training, and taking temporal shifts in user behavior into account. Li et al. [4] proposed NARM, similar to the Transformer [15], which is commonly used in natural language processing. It has an encoder-decoder neural network structure and uses an RNN approach with an attention mechanism to capture users' sequential behavior features. Liu et al. [7] proposed STAMP, using simple multilayer perceptron (MLP) networks and attention mechanisms to achieve users' global preference and current preference.

2.2   Graph-Based Neural Network Methods

The classical neural network CNN and RNN are deployed on graph-structured data in increasing research. Gated graph neural networks (GGNNs), a variant of the graph neural network (GNN) proposed by Li et al. [5], are also widely used. It applies gated recurrent units (GRUs) and relies on the backpropagation through time (BPTT) algorithm to calculate the gradient.

In session-based recommendation, SR-GNN proposed by Wu et al. [16] combines GGNNs, RNN, and attention network. It models session sequences into graph-structured data and captures complex transitions of the items in sessions. After that, Yu et al. [17] proposed TAGNN on this basis, which employs a new attentive module to reveal the relevance of historical actions given a particular target item, further improving session representations. These graph-based neural network methods have shown a promising direction for the session-based recommendation. However, these methods cannot effectively capture profound dependencies and have poor ability against the cold start.

2.3   Capsule Network

Hinton et al. [10] proposed a capsule network to replace the traditional convolutional neural network (CNN). Unlike CNN, it uses vectors to represent features, which can enrich feature representations. The appearing capsule network solves two shortcomings of CNN, the low ability to recognize rotated objects and the poor spatial recognition between objects.

Last few years, it has been widely used in other recommendation scenarios [6,8,13], most achieve good results compared with previous methods. Inspired by them, the capsule network is considered to cope with the cold start for the session-based recommendation.

3   Proposed Method

This section focuses on the proposed ACGNN method in detail. The framework of the proposed ACGNN method is illustrated in Fig. 1.

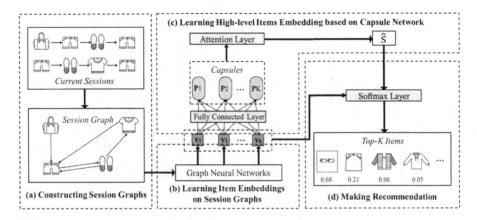

Fig. 1. Overview of the proposed ACGNN method. (a) We model all session graphs based on historical session sequences. (b) Each session graph proceeds one by one, and the resulting item embeddings can be generated through a gated graph neural network. (c) A dynamic routing capsule network with an attention mechanism is used to obtain multiple preferences of users, and low-level item embeddings are aggregated into a higher-level user preference vector for each session. (d) We predict the probability of the user's next-click item in session.

3.1 Notations

The target of session-based recommendation is to predict a user's next-click item solely based on the user's historical session sequences without the long-term preference profile. Here are the notations of this problem as follows.

Let $V = \{v_1, v_2, \ldots, v_m\}$ represent all items clicked by a user in session. At the same time, $s = [v_{s,1}, v_{s,2}, \ldots, v_{s,n}]$ sorted by timestamp is used to represent an anonymous session sequence. Let $v_{s,n+1}$ represent the user's next-click item. Finally, a probabilistic ranking list of all candidate items is generated, and the item with top-k probability will be the candidate item for the recommendation.

3.2 Constructing Session Graphs

Referring to [16,17], we model each session sequence s into a directed session graph $G = (V, E, A_s)$, where V is the point set, E is the edge set, and A_s is the adjacency matrix. In other words, each node $v_{s,i} \in V$ in G represents an item, and each edge $(v_{s,i-1}, v_{s,i}) \in E$ represents that the user clicks item $v_{s,i-1}$ and item $v_{s,i}$ one by one. We define the out-degree matrix A_{out} and the in-degree matrix A_{in} to represent the weighted connection of the outgoing edge and the incoming edge, respectively. Since A_{out} is the same size as A_{in}, we concatenate A_{out} and A_{in} horizontally into an adjacency matrix A_s to represent the complex transitions of items in each session. For clarity, the s subscript for mentioned item embeddings below is omitted.

3.3 Learning Item Embeddings on Session Graphs

Then, we map each node $v_{s,i} \in V$ to a unified embedding vector space, and let a d-dimensional vector $v_i \in \mathbb{R}^d$ represent each learned item v_i. Besides, we use item embeddings to represent each session s. Next, we present how to learn item embeddings via graph neural network. Using a graph neural network (GNN) can learn complex node connections and capture the features of session graphs. Hence, it is especially well-suited for session-based recommendation. In order to reduce the negative impact of vanishing gradient on recommendation accuracy, we employ gated graph neural networks (GGNNs) [5], a variant of GNN, to learn item embeddings. Formally, for the node $v_{s,i}$ of graph G, the update functions are shown as follows:

$$\mathbf{a}_{s,i}^t = \mathbf{A}_{s,i:}^t \left[\mathbf{v}_1^{t-1}, \ldots, \mathbf{v}_n^{t-1} \right]^{\mathrm{T}} \mathbf{H} + \mathbf{b} \tag{1}$$

$$\mathbf{z}_{s,i}^t = \sigma \left(\mathbf{W}_z \mathbf{a}_{s,i}^t + \mathbf{U}_z \mathbf{v}_i^{t-1} \right) \tag{2}$$

$$\mathbf{r}_{s,i}^t = \sigma \left(\mathbf{W}_r \mathbf{a}_{s,i}^t + \mathbf{U}_r \mathbf{v}_i^{t-1} \right) \tag{3}$$

$$\widetilde{\mathbf{v}}_i^t = \tanh \left(\mathbf{W}_o \mathbf{a}_{s,i}^t + \mathbf{U}_o \left(\mathbf{r}_{s,i}^t \odot \mathbf{v}_i^{t-1} \right) \right) \tag{4}$$

$$\mathbf{v}_i^t = \left(1 - \mathbf{z}_{s,i}^t \right) \odot \mathbf{v}_i^{t-1} + \mathbf{z}_{s,i}^t \odot \widetilde{\mathbf{v}}_i^t \tag{5}$$

where $\mathbf{A}_{s,i:}^t \in \mathbb{R}^{1 \times 2n}$ represents the two columns of adjacency matrix $\mathbf{A}_s$ corresponding to node $\mathbf{v}_{s,i}$ and determines how nodes in the graph communicate with each other, $\left[\mathbf{v}_1^{t-1}, \ldots, \mathbf{v}_n^{t-1} \right]$ represents all item vectors in session s, $\mathbf{H} \in \mathbb{R}^{d \times 2d}$ is the weight matrix, $\mathbf{b} \in \mathbb{R}^d$ is the bias vector, the result in Eq. (1) $\mathbf{a}_{s,i}^t$ is the input corresponding to the i-th clicked item in session s at time t. $\sigma(\cdot)$ in Eq. (2), Eq. (3), Eq. (4) represents the sigmoid function, $\mathbf{W}_z, \mathbf{W}_r, \mathbf{W}_o, \mathbf{U}_z, \mathbf{U}_r, \mathbf{U}_o$ are parameters that can be learned. $\mathbf{z}_{s,i}^t$ and $\mathbf{r}_{s,i}^t$ denote the reset and update gates in gated recurrent units (GRUs), respectively, $\odot$ denotes element-wise multiplication. $\widetilde{\mathbf{v}}_i^t$ is a candidate state generated based on the reset gate, the current state, and the previous state, while the final output $\mathbf{v}_i^t$ is the final state constructed based on the candidate state.

The GGNNs model transfers information through adjacent nodes, in which the update and reset gates of GRUs respectively control the information that needs to be discarded and retained. After updating all nodes in session graphs until convergence, we can obtain all latent item embeddings on session graphs.

3.4 Learning High-Level Item Embedding Based on Capsule Network

The latest research only uses attention networks to integrate user preferences in session, which can neither be conducive to capturing diverse user interests nor reduce the impact of the cold start on the recommendation. It is not very objective if highly dependent on the relevance between the last item in the session and the user's interest in the current session. Inspired by [6,8,13], we employ a novel dynamic routing capsule network with an attention mechanism for these problems. It helps obtain multiple user preferences and aggregate low-level item embeddings into high-level user preference vectors, called high-level item embeddings, which further represent each session. There are richer features for cold-start users and items in high-level item embeddings, which are insufficient in low-level item embeddings. Thus, aggregating high-level item embeddings is so significant that it helps predict the next-click item more accurately.

We use multi-layer preference capsules to complete information aggregation. Considering that not all preference capsules contribute equally to the process of aggregation, thus an attention mechanism is further added to emphasize the capsules with significant contributions, which can represent diverse user preferences.

The final state $\mathbf{v}_i^t$ output by GGNNs is used to form low-level embedding representations of user preferences $E_i = \{\mathbf{e}_j, j \in \mathbf{v}_i^t\}$. Then, the preference capsule vectors are iteratively calculated through dynamic routing. In each iteration, we take the embedding vector $\mathbf{e}_j \in \mathbb{R}^d$ of the final state j after linear transformation and the vector $\mathbf{p}_k \in \mathbb{R}^d$ of preference capsule k, calculate the routing logit value l_{jk} by the following formula:

$$l_{jk} = \mathbf{p}_k^{\mathrm{T}} \mathbf{S} \mathbf{e}_j \tag{6}$$

where $\mathbf{S} \in \mathbb{R}^{d \times d}$ is the bilinear mapping matrix parameter shared between $\mathbf{e}_j$ and $\mathbf{p}_k$.

By performing the "routing softmax" on logits, the sum of the coupling coefficient between the final state j and all preference capsules is 1. The calculated coupling coefficient d_{jk} is as follows:

$$d_{jk} = softmax\,(l_{jk}) \tag{7}$$

After getting the coupling coefficient d_{jk} , we can calculate the candidate vector $\mathbf{z}_k$ of the preference capsule k by multiplying by the weighted sum of all final states, which is as follows:

$$\mathbf{z}_k = \sum_j d_{jk} \mathbf{S} \mathbf{e}_j \tag{8}$$

Especially, we obtain the embedding representation $\mathbf{p}_k$ of the preference capsule k through the nonlinear "squash" function, as shown below:

$$\mathbf{p}_k = squash\,(\mathbf{z}_k) = \frac{\mathbf{z}_k}{\|\mathbf{z}_k\|} \frac{\|\mathbf{z}_k\|^2}{1 + \|\mathbf{z}_k\|^2} \tag{9}$$

The number of preference capsules is equivalent to the number of different user preferences captured from user sessions by GGNNs, which received positive feedback from users. Suppose we have K preference capsules, meaning that K different user preferences are extracted from the historical items on which users gave positive feedback. We add an attention layer to emphasize the capsules with significant contributions and calculate the attention score $\hat{s}_k$ through a multilayer perceptron (MLP), as follows:

$$\hat{s}_k = softmax\left(\mathbf{h}_a^{\mathrm{T}} ReLU\left(\mathbf{W}_a\mathbf{p}_k + \mathbf{b}_a\right)\right) \tag{10}$$

where $\mathbf{h}_a \in \mathbb{R}^{d \times d_a}$, $\mathbf{W}_a \in \mathbb{R}^{d \times d_a}$, $\mathbf{b}_a \in \mathbb{R}^{d \times d_a}$ are the parameters of the attention layer.

After that, with the attentive weights assigned to the preference capsules, the high-level user preference score $\hat{s}$ is obtained in the form of a weighted sum, as shown below:

$$\hat{\mathbf{s}} = \sum_{k=1}^{K} \hat{s}_k\mathbf{p}_k \tag{11}$$

3.5   Making Recommendation

Let $\hat{\mathbf{y}}_i$ denote the probability of the user's next click on the item $\mathbf{v}_i$ in session, as shown in Eq. (12) below. We take the top-k probability items in $\hat{\mathbf{y}}_i$ as the recommended results.

$$\hat{\mathbf{y}}_i = softmax\left(\hat{\mathbf{s}}^{\mathrm{T}}\mathbf{v}_i\right) \tag{12}$$

Besides, we define the loss function of each session graph as the cross-entropy of the predicted value and the ground truth. It can be written as follows:

$$L\left(\mathbf{y}, \hat{\mathbf{y}}\right) = -\sum_{i=1}^{m} \mathbf{y}_i \log \hat{\mathbf{y}}_i \tag{13}$$

where $\mathbf{y}$ is a one-hot encoding vector, which denotes the ground truth of the next-clicked item.

At last, we use the Back Propagation Through Time (BPTT) paradigm to train the proposed ACGNN model.

4   Experiments

In this section, we demonstrate the effectiveness of ACGNN by comparing it with baselines and making a detailed analysis. Besides, we design an experiment to confirm the performance of ACGNN for cold start.

4.1   Experimental Setup

Datasets. We choose two representative public datasets in our experiments, i.e., Diginetica and Yoochoose. We follow the same data preprocessing method as baselines to make it fair. Due to the Yoochoose dataset being quite large, following [4,7], we divide the Yoochoose training sequence by time and use the recent 1/64 part of the training sequence. The statistics of datasets are shown in Table 1:

Table 1. Statistics of the datasets.

Statistics	Diginetica dataset	Yoochoose1/64 dataset
Total clicks	982961	557248
Training sessions	719470	369859
Test sessions	60858	55898
Total items	43097	16766
Average session length	5.12	6.16

Baselines. We compare the proposed ACGNN method with the following representative baselines. Following previous methods [4,7,16,17], we adopt the commonly used HR@20 (Hit Rate)[1] and MRR@20 (Mean Reciprocal Rank) as evaluation metrics. Baselines are listed as follows:

- POP and S-POP. POP always recommends the most top-k popular items in the training set. In contrast, S-POP recommends them in the current session.
- Item-KNN [1]. A traditional method of recommendation based on the cosine similarity between session vectors.
- BPR-MF [11]. A Bayesian personalized ranking method using stochastic gradient descent proposed by Rendle et al.
- FPMC [9]. A session-based recommendation method based on Markov chain.
- GRU4REC [3]. The first session-based recommendation method based on deep learning uses a recurrent neural network to model session sequences.
- NARM [4]. A deep learning method that mines sequential behavior features of users through RNN and attention mechanism.
- STAMP [7]. A short-term attention memory priority model can effectively capture the user's global and current preference.
- SR-GNN [16]. A session-based recommendation method based on a graph neural network (GNN) can capture the user's global and current preferences.
- TAGNN [17]. A session-based recommendation method based on GNN and the target attention unit is introduced.

Parameter Settings. In our experiments, the number of preference capsules is set to 5, the batch size is set to 100, the dimension of the attention layer is set to 200, and the L2 penalty is set to 10^{-5}. Besides, we select a random 10% subset of the training set as the validation set and select other hyper-parameters on it. All parameters are initialized using a Gaussian distribution with a mean value of 0 and a standard deviation of 0.1. After that, the mini-batch Adam optimizer with the initial learning rate of 0.001 is adopted, which will decay at a rate of 0.05 every three epochs.

---

[1] Note that [4,7,16,17] used different metric names for HR@20 (e.g., Precision@20 and Recall@20). However, they used the same formula to obtain this measurement (i.e., the proportion of cases when the desired item is among the top-20 items in all cases).

4.2 Model Comparison

To verify the overall performance of ACGNN, we compare it with existing representative baseline methods. The overall performance in terms of HR@20 and MRR@20 is shown in Table 2, where the best results are highlighted in bold.

Table 2. Comparison results on two datasets.

Method	Diginetica		Yoochoose1/64	
	HR@20	MRR@20	HR@20	MRR@20
POP	0.88	0.19	6.71	1.65
S-POP	21.06	13.67	30.44	18.35
Item-KNN	35.75	11.57	51.60	21.81
BPR-MF	5.22	1.96	31.31	12.08
FPMC	26.53	6.95	45.62	15.01
GRU4REC	29.40	8.31	60.64	22.89
NARM	49.70	16.17	68.32	28.63
STAMP	45.64	14.32	68.74	29.67
SR-GNN	50.77	17.62	70.57	30.94
TAGNN	51.29	18.01	70.97	31.01
ACGNN	**51.83**	**18.37**	**71.46**	**31.12**

ACGNN aggregates the separated session sequences into graph-structured data, which can sufficiently consider higher-level user preferences. As shown in Table 2, ACGNN reaches the optimal HR@20 and MRR@20 on the Diginetica dataset and the Yoochoose1/64 dataset, which shows the superiority and effectiveness of ACGNN. We analyze the reasons from the following aspects.

Firstly, it can be found from Table 2, the performance of traditional methods is generally low. POP, S-POP, Item-KNN, and BPR-MF are early traditional recommendation methods, while FPMC is recommended based on the Markov chain. None of them work on advanced deep neural networks, so their performance is worse than that of ACGNN.

Secondly, the performance of the latest deep-learning-based methods is significantly better than that of the traditional methods because of the more vital ability to capture complex user behaviors. For example, GRU4REC and NARM are sequence models based on recurrent neural networks (RNNs), which can consider the one-way transitions between consecutive items. STAMP takes a different approach, employing simple multilayer perceptron (MLP) networks and an attention mechanism to obtain and integrate the user's global and current preferences.

Thirdly, it is easy to find that after introducing a graph neural network (GNN), the performance of methods can be significantly improved. The reason is that modeling session sequences into graph-structured data can sufficiently consider the complex transitions among the items in sessions, rather than only considering the one-way transitions between consecutive items. For example, SR-GNN models session sequences into graph-structured data through GNN. Thus it can capture more implicit connections between clicked items. TAGNN further considers user preferences with target-aware attention improving recommendation accuracy. However, the performance of these methods is still lower than that of ACGNN. ACGNN extends the graph structure in SR-GNN and TAGNN and sufficiently activates user preferences through the latest capsule network structure to effectively improve the performance of the session model. In summary, Table 2 sufficiently illustrates the superiority and effectiveness of ACGNN.

4.3   Ablation Studies

This section performed some ablation studies to show the effectiveness of the proposed modules. We compare the session embedding strategy with the other three approaches, including low-level item embedding only (GGNN), high-level item embedding without attention mechanism (ACGNN-F), and high-level item embedding with average pooling (ACGNN-AVG). The results of four different session embedding strategies are shown in Table 3.

Table 3. The performance of different session embedding strategies.

Strategy	Diginetica		Yoochoose1/64	
	HR@20	MRR@20	HR@20	MRR@20
GGNN	49.83	16.51	69.89	30.46
ACGNN-F	51.70	18.16	71.37	31.08
ACGNN-AVG	50.12	16.79	70.43	30.82
ACGNN	**51.83**	**18.37**	**71.46**	**31.12**

It can be observed that the proposed session embedding strategy ACGNN is consistently better than other session embedding strategies, which validates the effectiveness of the proposed modules. Furthermore, GGNN performs worse because it only generates low-level item embeddings, which is insufficient to capture diverse user interests. ACGNN and its variants outperform GGNN, indicating the effectiveness of aggregating high-level item embeddings. Besides, ACGNN performs better than ACGNN-F and ACGNN-AVG on both datasets, which indicates that there may be some noises in the session. Attention mechanisms can help capture significant features of users and items from session data to aggregate high-level item embeddings.

4.4   Impact of Cold Start

To verify that ACGNN can reduce the negative impact of cold start on recommendation, we compare and analyze the performance of TAGNN and our proposed ACGNN at the beginning of the session.

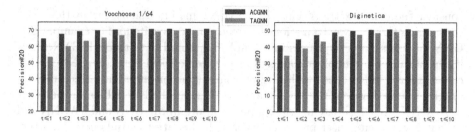

Fig. 2. Performance comparisons of the proposed method and TAGNN.

Figure 2 records the average value of HR@20 in each session's first ten time steps when TAGNN and ACGNN respectively make predictions on the Yoochoose1/64 dataset and Diginetica dataset. It is apparent that the HR@20 of ACGNN is higher than that of TAGNN in all the time steps at the beginning of the session, whether on the Yoochoose1/64 dataset or the Diginetica dataset, which sufficiently demonstrates the superiority of ACGNN. Besides, within the first three time steps after the start of the session ($t \leqslant 1, t \leqslant 2, t \leqslant 3$), the HR@20 of TAGNN is significantly lower than that in other time steps, which is the main feature of cold start. It is susceptible to a cold start when making personalized recommendations because anonymous users in the session-based recommendation are similar to the new users without historical actions.

In contrast, in the first several time steps after the start of the session, the HR@20 of ACGNN is not significantly lower than that in other time steps. It reveals that the cold start has little impact on the recommendation accuracy of ACGNN. The capsule network can better represent actual user preferences through high-level user preferences because it can enrich the features for cold-start users and items available. In summary, it shows that ACGNN can effectively reduce the negative impact of cold start on the recommendation accuracy of the session-based recommendation.

5   Conclusion

This paper presents an attentive capsule graph neural network for the session-based recommendation (ACGNN) method. We model historical session sequences as graph-structured data and use graph neural networks learning item embeddings to represent each session, which can capture rich transitions of items. A variety of low-level item embeddings are then aggregated into high-level item embeddings by capsule network, enriching the features for cold-start users and items that are difficult to reveal by previous methods. Our experiments on real datasets confirm the superiority over state-of-the-art methods and can reduce the impact of the cold start on the recommendation. Some potential future work includes: (1) considering more metadata to improve performance further; (2) trying to combine prior knowledge with an attention mechanism.

References

1. Davidson, J., et al.: The youtube video recommendation system. In: Proceedings of the Fourth ACM Conference on Recommender Systems, pp. 293–296 (2010)
2. Hidasi, B., Karatzoglou, A., Baltrunas, L., Tikk, D.: Session-based recommendations with recurrent neural networks. arXiv preprint arXiv:1511.06939 (2015)
3. Hidasi, B., Quadrana, M., Karatzoglou, A., Tikk, D.: Parallel recurrent neural network architectures for feature-rich session-based recommendations. In: Proceedings of the 10th ACM Conference on Recommender Systems, pp. 241–248 (2016)
4. Li, J., Ren, P., Chen, Z., Ren, Z., Lian, T., Ma, J.: Neural attentive session-based recommendation. In: Proceedings of the 2017 ACM on Conference on Information and Knowledge Management, pp. 1419–1428 (2017)
5. Li, Y., Tarlow, D., Brockschmidt, M., Zemel, R.: Gated graph sequence neural networks. arXiv preprint arXiv:1511.05493 (2015)
6. Liu, P., Yu, W.: Capsrec: a capsule graph neural network model for social recommendation. In: 2021 IEEE 33rd International Conference on Tools with Artificial Intelligence (ICTAI), pp. 359–363. IEEE (2021)
7. Liu, Q., Zeng, Y., Mokhosi, R., Zhang, H.: Stamp: short-term attention/memory priority model for session-based recommendation. In: Proceedings of the 24th ACM SIGKDD International Conference on Knowledge Discovery & Data Mining, pp. 1831–1839 (2018)
8. Patil, S., Banerjee, D., Sural, S.: A graph theoretic approach for multi-objective budget constrained capsule wardrobe recommendation. ACM Trans. Inf. Syst. (TOIS) **40**(1), 1–33 (2021)
9. Rendle, S., Freudenthaler, C., Gantner, Z., Schmidt-Thieme, L.: BPR: bayesian personalized ranking from implicit feedback. arXiv preprint arXiv:1205.2618 (2012)
10. Sabour, S., Frosst, N., Hinton, G.E.: Dynamic routing between capsules. Adv. Neural Inf. Process. Syst. **30**, 1–11 (2017)
11. Sarwar, B., Karypis, G., Konstan, J., Riedl, J.: Item-based collaborative filtering recommendation algorithms. In: Proceedings of the 10th International Conference on World Wide Web, pp. 285–295 (2001)
12. Schafer, J.B., Konstan, J., Riedl, J.: Recommender systems in e-commerce. In: Proceedings of the 1st ACM Conference on Electronic Commerce, pp. 158–166 (1999)
13. Song, Z., Yuan, J., Wang, X., Ji, W.: Capturing multi-granularity interests with capsule attentive network for sequential recommendation. In: Zhang, W., Zou, L., Maamar, Z., Chen, L. (eds.) WISE 2021. LNCS, vol. 13081, pp. 147–161. Springer, Cham (2021). https://doi.org/10.1007/978-3-030-91560-5_11
14. Tan, Y.K., Xu, X., Liu, Y.: Improved recurrent neural networks for session-based recommendations. In: Proceedings of the 1st Workshop on Deep Learning for Recommender Systems, pp. 17–22 (2016)
15. Vaswani, A., et al.: Attention is all you need. In: Advances in Neural Information Processing Systems, pp. 5998–6008 (2017)
16. Wu, S., Tang, Y., Zhu, Y., Wang, L., Xie, X., Tan, T.: Session-based recommendation with graph neural networks. In: Proceedings of the AAAI Conference on Artificial Intelligence, vol. 33, pp. 346–353 (2019)
17. Yu, F., Zhu, Y., Liu, Q., Wu, S., Wang, L., Tan, T.: Tagnn: target attentive graph neural networks for session-based recommendation. In: Proceedings of the 43rd International ACM SIGIR Conference on Research and Development in Information Retrieval, pp. 1921–1924 (2020)

Integrating Quaternion Graph Convolutional Networks with Tucker Decomposition for Link Prediction on Knowledge Graphs

Thanh Le[1,2]([✉]) [ID], Chi Tran[1,2] [ID], Loc Tran[1,2] [ID], and Bac Le[1,2] [ID]

[1] Faculty of Information Technology, University of Science,
Ho Chi Minh City, Vietnam
{lnthanh,lhbac}@fit.hcmus.edu.vn, {tdchi18,txloc18}@clc.fitus.edu.vn
[2] Vietnam National University, Ho Chi Minh City, Vietnam

Abstract. A knowledge graph is a knowledge base that provides a structured representation of real-world entities, i.e., objects, events, or concepts. Interactions between these entities are illustrated through relationships. However, we can not integrate all human knowledge into graphs. Besides, the real world is dynamic and ever-evolving, so they typically suffer from incompleteness. The task of link prediction is to solve this challenge by inferring missing associations between entities based on existing ones. In this paper, we introduce a new model named QTuckER, which utilizes a pointwise mutual information (PMI) word-word matrix as an adjacency matrix for Graph Convolutional Networks via quaternion multiplication. Specifically, an adjacent matrix is created based on the co-occurrence probability of entities and relations divided by the probabilities of them appearing individually. Then, Quaternion Graph Convolutional Networks are given as an encoder module to update entity and relation vector representations from a row-normalized PMI matrix. Finally, the TuckER model is used as a decoder module to calculate the score for each triple in the graph. Experimental results show that QTuckER obtains better results than previous translation-based and tensor decomposition-based models on two standard benchmark datasets.

Keywords: Knowledge graph embedding · Link prediction · Graph convolutional networks · Quaternion multiplication · Tensor factorization

1 Introduction

Knowledge graphs (KGs) are represented in terms of entities and relations denoted as (h, r, t) (where h and t are head and tail entities, and r is a relation) that contain large amounts of information about the real world. Nowadays, it plays an essential role in different applications such as recommendation systems, question answering, and information retrieval.

G. Memmi et al. (Eds.): KSEM 2022, LNAI 13368, pp. 614–626, 2022.
https://doi.org/10.1007/978-3-031-10983-6_47

However, most KGs are still incomplete [17], requiring us to create algorithms that can infer the missing links in the graph based on the existing ones. Therefore, many different methods have been proposed to solve this problem by embedding entities and relations of KGs into a low-dimensional embedding space. Then a scoring function is given to evaluate each triple so that actual triples will have higher scores than invalid ones.

Despite achieving good results, current geometry-based and tensor factorization-based methods have almost reached their limitations. Recent approaches are gradually using Graph Neural Networks (GNNs) to improve performance for embedding models where GNNs are used as an encoder to update entity and relation vector representations. Then, these vectors are passed to a decoder that takes advantage of the scoring function in ComplEx [15], DistMult [18], and ConvE [5] models to compute the score for each triple. We observe that entities and relations in triples can form similar characteristics. For instance, *Washington* co-occurs with *USA* when given a triple (*Washington, isCaptialOf, USA*). From this observation, entities and relations in KGs can be considered as words in a sentence so that we could build a word-word co-occurrence matrix representing their co-occurrence probabilities.

In this paper, we proposed an embedding model named QTuckER, which is a GNN-based model to solve link prediction through quaternion multiplication. Given a knowledge graph, a skip-gram vocabulary is first built by counting the co-occurrence of each pair (word, context), where the word and the context are entities and relations. Then, it is used to create a word-word count sparse matrix to fit into memory. Next, PMI's formula [4] is applied to this matrix to calculate data values for (entity, entity) and (entity/relation, relation/entity) pairs, leading to a sparse adjacency matrix. The quaternion multiplication [6] is incorporated into Graph Convolutional Networks (GCNs) for the encoder module to use this adjacency matrix. Finally, QTuckER takes advantage of the scoring function from TuckER [1] to calculate the score for each triple.

In summary, our main contribution to this paper is as follows:

- We introduce QTuckER, a GNN-based model for link prediction on KGs that achieve better results than GNN-based and tensor factorization-based methods across two standard benchmark datasets.
- Showing how efficient quaternion multiplication can be when combined with GNNs architectures as an encoder module for decomposition-based models, such as the TuckER model.

The rest of this paper consists of five sections. In Sect. 2, we briefly mention the typical models based on the translation, tensor factorization, and graph neural networks. The background knowledge that led to our improved idea are shown in Sect. 3. In Sect. 4, we illustrate the architecture of QTuckER. Section 5 shows our experimental results with other methods on FB15k-237 and WN18RR. The conclusion and the future directions are discussed in Sect. 6.

2   Related Work

2.1   Translation-based Methods

In 2013, Border et al. introduced a model named TransE [2], which could be considered the first translation-based model for link prediction in KGs. Given a triplet (h, r, t), the main idea of TransE is that if this triplet holds, then the sum of vector $\mathbf{h}$ and vector $\mathbf{r}$ is as close to vector $\mathbf{t}$ as possible, i.e. $\mathbf{h} + \mathbf{r} \approx \mathbf{t}$. Although TransE is quite simple and has an impressive performance, it has two problems: i) TransE uses Euclidean distance for the scoring function, which limits the flexibility of the model; ii) TransE has difficulty dealing with complex relational patterns such as 1-N, N-1, N-N relations.

Based on the idea of TransE, later improved models of Trans series such as TransH [16], TransR [8], and TransD [7] are introduced to overcome these weaknesses of TransE.

2.2   Tensor Factorization-Based Methods

In 2011, Nickel presented RESCAL [10], which could capture the latent semantics by defining a scoring function that uses the bilinear product between head and tail entity vectors with a full rank relation matrix. Although RESCAL is an expressive model and has the ability to perform collective learning through latent components, a large number of parameters ($O(d^2)$ parameters per relation) makes this model easy to overfitting.

To reduce the runtime of RESCAL, Yang et al. came up with DistMult [18], which is a special case of RESCAL. In this architecture, the relational asymmetric matrix used in RESCAL is replaced by a diagonal square matrix. By this way, the number of parameters per relation becomes $O(d)$. However, this model only focuses on learning symmetric relations and can not model asymmetric relations.

To create an efficient model and capture anti-symmetric relations, Trouillon introduced ComplEx [15], which changes embeddings from real space to a complex space because the composition of complex embeddings allows the model to handle many types of relations, such as symmetric and antisymmetric.

2.3   GNN-Based Methods

Introduced by Schlichtkrull et al. in 2018, R-GCN [11] propagates information from the target entity to its neighbors by using two graph convolutional layers to update the target entity's embedding, then using these embeddings for the decoder DistMult. Although R-GCN introduces new regularization methods, including block-diagonal and basis decomposition, semantic information in relation embeddings is ignored in the encoder phase. Thus, the embeddings of both entity and relation are not enriched. Moreover, the decoder can not handle asymmetric relations. SACN [12] leverages the integration between Weighted GCNs architecture and ConvTransE [12] to create a noval combination architecture between GNNs and Convolutional Neural Networks (CNNs) for improving the performance of link prediction tasks and handle better different types of relation. However, the relation embeddings are still skipped in the encoder phase.

3 Background

3.1 Problem Formulation

Let $\mathcal{E}$ denote the set of all entities, and $\mathcal{R}$ the set of all relations. A knowledge graph is a collection of triples (h, r, t), where $h, t \in \mathcal{E}$ is the head, and tail entities and $r \in \mathcal{R}$ is the relation between them. If (h, r, t) holds, then head entity (h) is related to tail entity (t) via relation (r). Our target is to embed entities and relations into a low-dimensional space while preserving their semantic meaning. These embeddings are used to predict a head entity $(?, r, t)$ or a tail entity $(h, r, ?)$. Commonly, a scoring function $s = \phi(h, r, t)$ is defined to compute the score for each triple. A non-linearity function such as logistic sigmoid is applied to convert the score to a probability prediction $p = \sigma(s) \in [0, 1]$ of the triple being true.

3.2 Quaternion

A quaternion $Q \in \mathbb{H}$ [6] extends the complex number to the hypercomplex number system and is applied in three-dimensional space. It consists of one real part and three imaginary parts, defined as $Q = a + b\mathbf{i} + c\mathbf{j} + d\mathbf{k}$, where a, b, c and $d \in \mathbb{R}$ are real numbers and $\mathbf{i}, \mathbf{j}$ and $\mathbf{k}$ are imaginary units that satisfy $\mathbf{i}^2 = \mathbf{j}^2 = \mathbf{i}^2 = \mathbf{ijk} = -1$. In addition, quaternion multiplication is not commutative, i.e. $q \otimes p \neq p \otimes q$, but it is associative, i.e. $(p \times q) \times r = p \times (q \times r)$ and $(p + q) \times r = p \times r + q \times r$ (where p, q and r are three quaternions). Some operations for the Quaternion algebra $\mathbb{H}$ are described as follows:

Conjugate: The conjugate of a quaternion Q is defined as $Q^* = \text{conj}(a + b\mathbf{i} + c\mathbf{j} + d\mathbf{k}) = a - b\mathbf{i} - c\mathbf{j} - d\mathbf{k}$

Norm: The norm of a quaternion Q is defined as $||Q|| = \sqrt{a^2 + b^2 + c^2 + d^2}$. To normalize a quaternion, we simply divide it by its magnitude $||Q||$: $Q^\triangleleft = \frac{Q}{||Q||}$

Addition: The addition of two quaternion $Q = a_1 + b_1\mathbf{i} + c_1\mathbf{j} + d_1\mathbf{k}$ and $P = a_2 + b_2\mathbf{i} + c_2\mathbf{j} + d_2\mathbf{k}$ is given by: $Q + P = (a_1 + a_2) + (b_1 + b_2)\mathbf{i} + (c_1 + c_2)\mathbf{j} + (d_1 + d_2)\mathbf{k}$

Inner Product: The inner product $\cdot$ between two quaternions Q and P is computed by taking the inner product of each corresponding component in each quaternion and summing up the four inner products $Q \cdot P = <a_1, a_2> + <b_1, b_2> + <c_1, c_2> + <d_1, d_2>$

Hamilton Product: The Hamilton product between two quaternion Q and P is defined as $Q \otimes P = (a_1a_2 - b_1b_2 - c_1c_2 - d_1d_2) + (a_1b_2 + b_1a_2 + c_1d_2 - d_1c_2)\mathbf{i} + (a_1c_2 - b_1d_2 + c_1a_2 + d_1b_2)\mathbf{j} + (a_1d_2 + b_1c_2 - c_1b_2 + d_1a_2)\mathbf{k}$

Inverse: The inverse of a quaternion Q is defined as $Q^{-1} = \frac{Q^*}{\|Q\|^2}$

3.3   Tucker Decomposition

Tucker decomposes a tensor into a set of matrices and a small core tensor. Given a 3rd-order tensor $\mathcal{X} \in \mathbb{R}^{I \times J \times K}$, tucker decomposition can be defined as $\mathcal{X} = \mathcal{Z} \times_1 \mathbf{A} \times_2 \mathbf{B} \times_3 \mathbf{C}$ (where $\mathcal{Z} \in \mathbb{R}^{P \times Q \times R}$ is the core tensor, x_n is the n-mode product, and $\mathbf{A} \in \mathbb{R}^{I \times P}$, $\mathbf{B} \in \mathbb{R}^{J \times Q}$, $\mathbf{C} \in \mathbb{R}^{K \times R}$ are three matrices).

4   Methodology

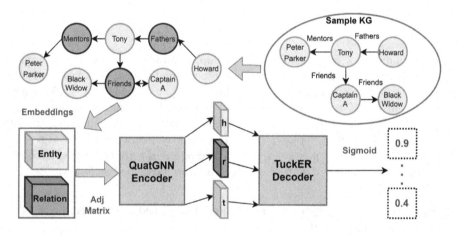

Fig. 1. The architecture of our proposed model QTuckER

The illustration of QTucER is shown in Fig. 1. To create an adjacency matrix for the encoder module, we consider entities and relations in KGs as words in a sentence, and these words can form triples with a co-occurrence. Specifically, a skip-gram vocabulary is computed by iterating over each triple. At each iteration, skip-grams are formed by using the back_window and front_window words of the focus word. For example, we have a triple (*Elon Musk, ceoOf, Tesla*). Assuming back_window = front_window = 2, skip-grams can be procedure such as (*Elon Musk, ceoOf*), (*Elon Musk, Tesla*), (*ceoOf, Elon Musk*), (*ceoOf, Tesla*), (*Tesla, Elon Musk*) and (*Tesla, ceoOf*). After that, with pairs that occur more than twice, the total number of occurrences of them is stored. In the next step, a word-word count matrix is created from these pairs. In turn, PMI's formula is applied to this matrix to form a PMI matrix used as data values for the adjacency matrix. Specifically, PMI for a pair $(word_1, word_2)$ is defined as follows:

$$\text{PMI}(word_1, word_2) = \log \frac{\text{p}(word_1, word_2)}{\text{p}(word_1) * \text{p}(word_2)} \tag{1}$$

where $\text{p}(word_1, word_2) = \frac{C_{i,j}}{\sum_{i=1}^{N}\sum_{j=1}^{N} W_{i,j}}$, $\text{p}(word_1) = \frac{\sum_{j=1}^{N} C_{i,j}}{\sum_{i=1}^{N}\sum_{j=1}^{N} W_{i,j}}$, $\text{p}(word_2)$ $= \frac{\sum_{i=1}^{N} C_{i,j}}{\sum_{i=1}^{N}\sum_{j=1}^{N} W_{i,j}}$, $C_{i,j}$ is the number of co-occurrence of $word_1$ and $word_2$ in the skip-gram vocabulary, $\sum_{j=1}^{N} C_{i,j}$ is the sum of columns in the word-word count matrix with $word_1$ index, $\sum_{i=1}^{N} C_{i,j}$ is the sum of rows in the word-word count matrix with $word_2$ index and $W_{i,j}$ is the sum of all elements in the word-word count matrix.

However, we have two cases for the pair $(word_1, word_2)$. In the first case, if $(word_1, word_2)$ is (entity, entity), we take $\text{PMI}(word_1, word_2)$ as co-occurrence values. In the other case, if $(word_1, word_2)$ is (entity/relation, relation/entity), we take $\text{p}(word_1, word_2)$. After that, a new sparse matrix is constructed based on these co-occurrence values. Next, an adjacency matrix is formed by adding a self-loop, i.e. adding the sparse matrix with an identity matrix. Since the adjacency matrix is still a sparse matrix, the rows need to be normalized. Finally, it is converted to a torch sparse tensor by using coordinate format (COO) before coming to the encoder module.

4.1 Encoder

Most GNNs focus on embedding nodes into Euclidean space. However, Euclidean space limits the model performance to hierarchical data types. To solve this problem, embedding models have recently turned to the Hyperbolic space because its tree-like structure allows good handling of hierarchical relationships. HGCN [3] has succeeded in extending GCNs to Hyperbolic space to learn node representations for hierarchical scale-free graphs. Besides these two spaces, hypercomplex space also demonstrates efficiency through the QuatE model [19]. Because of the potential of this space, Nguyen et al. incorporated GCNs into hypercomplex space to create QGNN [9]. In this paper, QGNN is used as our main encoder module. The aggregation function of QGNN is defined as follows:

$$\mathbf{H}^{(l+1)} = \sigma(\tilde{\mathbf{D}}^{-\frac{1}{2}}\tilde{\mathbf{A}}\tilde{\mathbf{D}}^{-\frac{1}{2}}\mathbf{W}^{(l)} \otimes \mathbf{H}^{(l)}) \tag{2}$$

where $\tilde{\mathbf{D}}$ is the diagonal node degree matrix, $\mathbf{W}^{(l)}$ is the quaternion weight matrix, $\mathbf{H}^{(l)}$ is the quaternion vector in the lth layer, $\sigma(.)$ is a nonlinear activation function such as ReLU or tanh, $\otimes$ is the quaternion multiplication, wherein $\tilde{\mathbf{A}} = \mathbf{A} + \mathbf{I}$ where $\mathbf{A}$ is the adjacency matrix and $\mathbf{I}$ is the identity matrix.

The quaternion multiplication between quaternion vector $\mathbf{H}^{(l)} \in \mathbb{H}^n$ and the quaternion weight matrix $\mathbf{H}^{(l)} \in \mathbb{H}^{m \times n}$ is represented as:

$$\mathbf{H}^{(l)} = \mathbf{H}_1^{(l)} + \mathbf{H}_2^{(l)}\mathbf{i} + \mathbf{H}_3^{(l)}\mathbf{j} + \mathbf{H}_4^{(l)}\mathbf{k} \tag{3}$$

$$\mathbf{W}^{(l)} = \mathbf{W}_1^{(l)} + \mathbf{W}_2^{(l)}\mathbf{i} + \mathbf{W}_3^{(l)}\mathbf{j} + \mathbf{W}_4^{(l)}\mathbf{k} \tag{4}$$

where $\mathbf{H}_1^{(l)}, \mathbf{H}_2^{(l)}, \mathbf{H}_3^{(l)}, \mathbf{H}_4^{(l)} \in \mathbb{R}^n$ and $\mathbf{W}_1^{(l)}, \mathbf{W}_2^{(l)}, \mathbf{W}_3^{(l)}, \mathbf{W}_4^{(l)} \in \mathbb{R}^{m \times n}$

The Hamilton product $\otimes$ between $\mathbf{W}^{(l)}$ and $\mathbf{H}^{(l)}$ are computed as follows:

$$
\begin{aligned}
\mathbf{W}^{(l)} \otimes \mathbf{H}^{(l)} = &(\mathbf{W}_1^{(l)}\mathbf{H}_1^{(l)} - \mathbf{W}_2^{(l)}\mathbf{H}_2^{(l)} - \mathbf{W}_3^{(l)}\mathbf{H}_3^{(l)} - \mathbf{W}_4^{(l)}\mathbf{H}_4^{(l)}) \\
+&(\mathbf{W}_1^{(l)}\mathbf{H}_2^{(l)} + \mathbf{W}_2^{(l)}\mathbf{H}_1^{(l)} + \mathbf{W}_3^{(l)}\mathbf{H}_4^{(l)} - \mathbf{W}_4^{(l)}\mathbf{H}_3^{(l)})\mathbf{i} \\
+&(\mathbf{W}_1^{(l)}\mathbf{H}_3^{(l)} - \mathbf{W}_2^{(l)}\mathbf{H}_4^{(l)} + \mathbf{W}_3^{(l)}\mathbf{H}_1^{(l)} + \mathbf{W}_4^{(l)}\mathbf{H}_2^{(l)})\mathbf{j} \\
+&(\mathbf{W}_1^{(l)}\mathbf{H}_4^{(l)} + \mathbf{W}_2^{(l)}\mathbf{H}_3^{(l)} - \mathbf{W}_3^{(l)}\mathbf{H}_2^{(l)} + \mathbf{W}_4^{(l)}\mathbf{H}_1^{(l)})\mathbf{k}
\end{aligned}
\tag{5}
$$

When performing the Hamilton product between $\mathbf{W}^{(l)}$ and $\mathbf{H}^{(l)}$, any error related to the sign causes different outputs and hence, can lead to worse performance. Therefore, the computation of the Hamilton product in hypercomplex space needs to be more careful than in Euclidean space.

4.2   Decoder

After obtaining quaternion vector representations of entities and relations from the QGCN layer, they are passed to the TuckER model as a decoder module. The scoring function of the decoder is defined as follows:

$$\phi(\mathrm{h,r,t}) = \mathcal{W} \times_1 \mathbf{e}_h \times_2 \mathbf{w}_r \times_3 \mathbf{e}_t \tag{6}$$

where $\mathbf{e}_h, \mathbf{e}_t \in \mathbb{R}^{d_e}$ are embeddings for head and tail entities and $\mathbf{e}_h \in \mathbb{R}^{d_r}$ is the embedding for relation entity, d_e and d_r are the embedding dimensions of the entity and relation vectors, $\mathcal{W} \in \mathbb{R}^{d_e \times d_r \times d_e}$ is the core tensor.

The logistic sigmoid is applied to each score $\phi(\mathrm{h, r, t})$ to get the predicted probability $\mathrm{p} \in [0, 1]$ of a triple being true. Since the number of parameters of $\mathcal{W}$ does not depend on the number of entities or relations, the number of parameters of the decoder increases linearly with the dimensionality of entity and relation embeddings. As a result, it can be scalable to large KGs. Following Balazevic [1], some learned knowledge is stored in the core tensor instead of embeddings, enabling parameter-sharing among entities and relations through multi-task learning. Hence, it makes the decoder module highly beneficial for datasets with a large number of relations, such as FB15k-237. Furthermore, to enhance the quality of the decoder, we apply a nonlinear activation function f such as ReLU or tanh to the scoring function. Equation 6 is now re-written as follows:

$$\phi(\mathrm{h,r,t}) = \mathbf{e}_t^T \cdot f(\mathcal{W} \times_1 \mathbf{e}_h \times_2 \mathbf{w}_r) \tag{7}$$

4.3   Training

QTuckER is trained by minimizing a binary cross-entropy loss (BCE) as follows:

$$\mathcal{L}(y, p) = -\sum_{i=1}^{N}(y^{(i)} log(p^{(i)}) + (1 - y^{(i)}) log(1 - p^{(i)})) \tag{8}$$

where $y^{(i)}$ is the binary label with $y^{(i)} = 1$ if (h, r, t) $\in$ G and $y^{(i)} = 0$ if (h, r, t) $\in$ G', G and G' are collection of valid and invalid triples, $p^{(i)} = $ sigmoid(ϕ(h, r, t)) $\in [0, 1]$ is the predicted probabilities and N is the number of training samples.

To speed up training and improve the performance for embedding models, the 1-N scoring strategy [5] is used. Specifically, instead of using 1-1 scoring where all triples (h, r, t) are trained one at a time, a pair (h, r) with all tail entities t $\in \mathcal{E}$ is used to calculate the score. Furthermore, to enhance data quantity for training, we also use the standard data augmentation technique [1] by adding reciprocal relations (t, r^{-1}, h) for every triple (h, r, t) in KGs.

5 Experiments

5.1 Datasets and Evaluation Metrics

To evaluate the performance of our model and avoid test leakage problem, we utilized two standard benchmark datasets, including FB15k-237 [14] and WN18RR [5]. Table 1 summarizes the detailed statistics of these datasets.

Similar to previous works, we use two ranking-based metrics, Hits@k (k $\in$ {1, 3, 10}) and Mean Reciprocal Rank (MRR) to evaluate our model. The filtered setting [2] is also applied as standard evaluation method.

Table 1. Dataset summary

Dataset	Entities	Relations	Train	Valid	Test
FB15k-237	14,541	237	272,115	17,535	20,466
WN18RR	40,943	11	86,835	3,034	3,134

5.2 Settings and Hyperparameters

QTuckER is implemented based on Pytorch version 1.10.1+cu111, Intel Xeon processor and NVIDIA Tesla A100-PCIE-40 GB. Hyperparameters includes the number of epochs, learning rate, embedding dim, hidden dim, input dropout rate, hidden dropout rate at layer 1 and 2, which are found by conducting the grid-search as follows: FB15k-237: {6000, 0.0005, 200, 200, 0.3, 0.2, 0.4}; and WN18RR: {10000, 0.003, 500, 500, 0.1, 0.2, 0.7}.

5.3 Results and Analysis

In this section, our work is compared with the pioneer of the translation-based model, TransE, and other geometric models, RotatE and QuatE. Furthermore, QTuckER is also evaluated with standard bilinear models, including DistMult, ComplEx, TuckER, and CNN&GNN-based models such as ConvE, R-GCN, and SACN. Table 2 shows the experimental results on FB15k-237 and WN18RR.

Table 2. Link prediction results of QTuckER and other baseline models on FB15k-237 and WN18RR.

Model	FB15k-237				WN18RR			
	MRR	Hits@1	Hits@3	Hits@10	MRR	Hits@1	Hits@3	Hits@10
TransE [2]	0.294	–	–	0.465	0.226	–	–	0.501
DistMult [16]	0.241	0.155	0.263	0.419	0.430	0.390	0.440	0.490
ComplEx [15]	0.247	0.158	0.275	0.428	0.440	0.410	0.460	0.510
TuckER [1]	<u>0.358</u>	<u>0.266</u>	<u>0.394</u>	0.544	0.470	<u>0.443</u>	0.482	0.526
RotatE [13]	0.338	0.241	0.375	0.533	0.476	0.428	0.492	0.571
QuatE [19]	0.348	0.248	0.382	**0.550**	<u>0.488</u>	0.438	**0.508**	**0.582**
R-GCN [11]	0.248	0.153	0.258	0.417	0.402	0.345	0.437	0.494
SACN [12]	0.350	0.260	0.390	0.540	0.470	0.430	0.480	0.540
ConvE [5]	0.325	0.237	0.356	0.501	0.430	0.400	0.440	0.520
QTuckER (Our)	**0.365**	**0.270**	**0.405**	<u>0.549</u>	**0.489**	**0.444**	<u>0.503</u>	<u>0.566</u>
% Improvement	**2.0%**	**1.5%**	**2.8%**	**0.9%**	**4.0%**	**0.2%**	**4.4%**	**7.6%**

On FB15k-237, our model achieved the best performance except for Hits@10, at 54.9%. In comparison with the baseline model TuckER, QTuckER outperforms TuckER on all of the metrics, and the percentage improvement ranges from 0.9% to 2.8%. The result confirms the efficiency of quaternion embeddings and the effect of graph features in the encoder phase. Compared with TransE, DistMult and ComplEx, QTuckER outperforms in all four metrics. The improvement of QTuckER indicates the ability of our model to enhance the decomposition phase by the quality embeddings from the encoder.

In group models using CNNs and GNNs, 10% improves compared with R-GCN, about 1%–1.5% on SACN on Hits@k, and more than 3% on metrics of the ConvE model. This result validates our approach to leveraging the robust property of decomposition in the TuckER model compared with the convolutional operator in ConvTransE of the SACN and ConvE models.

On WN18RR, QTuckER has the best Hits@1 and MRR results, with 48.9% and 44.4%, while acquiring the second position in Hits@3 and Hits@10, respectively. Our work indicated a substantial improvement of 26.3% on MRR and 6.5% on Hits@10 in TransE model in the geometric direction. However, the figure for Hits@10 is 0.5% lower than RotatE and 1.6% lower on QuatE. The lower outcomes demonstrate the weak power when modeling the hierarchical structure of WN18RR. Moreover, it could be explained by the advantages of the natural characteristic of rotation operation in RotatE and the ability to handle the hierarchical structure in the scoring function QuatE.

Whereas compared with the DistMult, ComplEx, and TuckER model, our approach outperforms in all metrics. In conclusion, our proposed framework performs efficiently on WN18RR, particularly in combining the graph features represented as quaternion embeddings to enhance the power of modeling the hierarchical structure of the TuckER model.

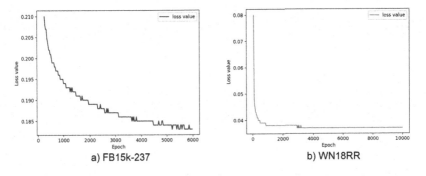

Fig. 2. The loss coverage research of QTuckER on the datasets.

We also analyze the coverage process of the loss function and Hits@10 on FB15k-237 and WN18RR in Fig. 2. Overall, the coverage process of WN18RR is more stable than FB15k-237, and the loss value of WN18RR is consistently lower than that of the remaining dataset during the learning phase. Although the process is stable on WN18RR, the improvement percentage on this dataset is less significant than the statistic for FB15k-237. This phenomenon could be explained by the limitation of the scoring function on WN18RR when modeling the hierarchical structure.

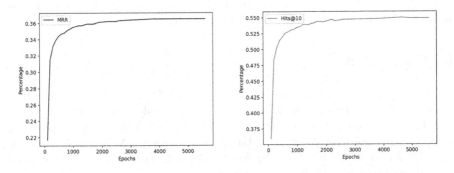

Fig. 3. The metric convergence process of QTuckER on FB15k-237.

Figure 3 illustrates the converge process on FB15k-237. Overall, the figures for both metrics indicate a stable and quick process. Specifically, MRR has witnessed remarkable growth from 21.7% to 35.5% at epoch 1000th, while Hits@10 has experienced the same trend but more significantly, from 36% to 53.5%. In the remaining process, MRR continued to follow its trend but less substantially, reaching the global maximum at 3800th epoch with an improvement of 1.1%. Meanwhile, the statistic for Hits@10 hit the highest point at 55.0% at 4600th epoch. Although it takes at least 5000 epochs on FB15k-237, the training time of each epoch is low and about thirty seconds per epoch.

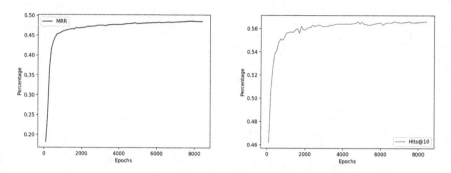

Fig. 4. The metric convergence process of QTuckER on WN18RR

In Fig. 4, the convergence process experienced the same tendency in FB15k-237 on MRR, but it takes longer and is unstable on the Hits@10 metric. Specifically, in the first 1000 epochs, MRR increased by about 27.9%, while Hits@10 is only about 9.4%. Furthermore, in the remaining phase, the coverage process of MRR is prolonged and tends to reach a maximum in the last epochs. Meanwhile, it is unstable and fluctuates between 56.2% and 56.6% on Hits@10.

In summary, the convergence progress of our model indicates that it is fast and tends to converge very slowly in the last epochs, so we suggest using at least 6000 epochs on the FB15k-237 and 10000 epochs on WN18RR so that the result is not too different from the actual result. In addition, the model training time is swift, so it is possible to apply the model to large KGs.

6   Conclusion

In this paper, we proposed an embedding model for link prediction on KGs named QTuckER by constructing a pointwise mutual information word-word matrix for the co-occurrence of entities and relations. This matrix is then fed to an encoder module, Quaternion Graph Convolutional Network. Finally, the decoder module which is a factorization-based model such as TuckER is utilized to compute the score for triples. Experiment results show that QTuckER achieves better results than neural network-based, decomposition-based and translation-based models on two standard benchmark datasets, WN18RR, and FB15k-237.

In future work, we might utilize other state-of-the-art factorization-based models for the encoder module, or replace the decoder module with a better Graph Neural Network architecture such as Graph Attention Network so that the results can be obtained better.

Acknowledgement. This research is funded by the University of Science, VNU-HCM, Vietnam under grant number CNTT 2022-2 and Advanced Program in Computer Science.

References

1. Balažević, I., Allen, C., Hospedales, T.: Tucker: Tensor factorization for knowledge graph completion. ArXiv Preprint ArXiv:1901.09590. (2019)
2. Bordes, A., Usunier, N., Garcia-Duran, A., Weston, J., Yakhnenko, O.: Translating embeddings for modeling multi-relational data. Adv. Neural Inf. Process. Syst. **26**, 1–9 (2013)
3. Chami, I., Ying, Z., Ré, C., Leskovec, J.: Hyperbolic graph convolutional neural networks. Adv. Neural Inf. Process. Syst. **32**, 1–12 (2019)
4. Church, K., Hanks, P.: Word association norms, mutual information, and lexicography. Comput. Linguist. **16**, 22–29 (1990)
5. Dettmers, T., Minervini, P., Stenetorp, P., Riedel, S.: Convolutional 2D knowledge graph embeddings. In: Proceedings of the AAAI Conference on Artificial Intelligence, vol. 32 (2018)
6. Hamilton, W.: Xi, on quaternions; or on a new system of imaginaries in algebra. Lond. Edinburgh Dublin Phil. Mag. J. Sci. **33**, 58–60 (1848)
7. Ji, G., He, S., Xu, L., Liu, K., Zhao, J.: Knowledge graph embedding via dynamic mapping matrix. In: Proceedings of the 53rd Annual Meeting of the Association for Computational Linguistics and the 7th International Joint Conference on Natural Language Processing, vol. 1: Long Papers, pp. 687–696 (2015)
8. Lin, Y., Liu, Z., Sun, M., Liu, Y., Zhu, X.: Learning entity and relation embeddings for knowledge graph completion. In: Twenty-Ninth AAAI Conference on Artificial Intelligence (2015)
9. Nguyen, T., Phung, D., et al.: Quaternion graph neural networks. In: Asian Conference on Machine Learning, pp. 236–251 (2021)
10. Nickel, M., Tresp, V., Kriegel, H.: A three-way model for collective learning on multi-relational data. In: ICML (2011)
11. Schlichtkrull, M., Kipf, T., Bloem, P., Berg, R., Titov, I., Welling, M.: Modeling relational data with graph convolutional networks. In: European Semantic Web Conference, pp. 593–607 (2018)
12. Shang, C., Tang, Y., Huang, J., Bi, J., He, X., Zhou, B.: End-to-end structure-aware convolutional networks for knowledge base completion. In: Proceedings of the AAAI Conference on Artificial Intelligence, vol. 33, pp. 3060–3067 (2019)
13. Sun, Z., Deng, Z., Nie, J., Tang, J.: Rotate: knowledge graph embedding by relational rotation in complex space. ArXiv Preprint ArXiv:1902.10197 (2019)
14. Toutanova, K., Chen, D., Pantel, P., Poon, H., Choudhury, P., Gamon, M.: Representing text for joint embedding of text and knowledge bases. In: Proceedings of the 2015 Conference on Empirical Methods in Natural Language Processing, pp. 1499–1509 (2015)
15. Trouillon, T., Welbl, J., Riedel, S., Gaussier, É., Bouchard, G.: Complex embeddings for simple link prediction. In: International Conference on Machine Learning, pp. 2071–2080 (2016)
16. Wang, Z., Zhang, J., Feng, J., Chen, Z.: Knowledge graph embedding by translating on hyperplanes. In: Proceedings of the AAAI Conference on Artificial Intelligence, vol. 28 (2014)
17. West, R., Gabrilovich, E., Murphy, K., Sun, S., Gupta, R., Lin, D.: Knowledge base completion via search-based question answering. In: Proceedings of the 23rd International Conference on World Wide Web, pp. 515–526 (2014)

18. Yang, B., Yih, W., He, X., Gao, J., Deng, L.: Embedding entities and relations for learning and inference in knowledge bases. ArXiv Preprint ArXiv:1412.6575 (2014)
19. Zhang, S., Tay, Y., Yao, L., Liu, Q.: Quaternion knowledge graph embeddings. Adv. Neural Inf. Process. Syst. **32**, 1–11 (2019)

Implementing Large-Scale ABox Materialization Using Subgraph Reasoning

Xixi Zhu, Bin Lin, Zhaoyun Ding, Li Yao, and Cheng Zhu[✉]

Science and Technology on Information Systems and Engineering Laboratory,
National University of Defense Technology, Changsha 410073, China
{zhuxixi14,liubin11,zyding,zhucheng}@nudt.edu.cn, liyao6522@sina.com.cn

Abstract. The ontology knowledge base can be divided into two parts: TBox and ABox, where the former models schema-level knowledge within the domain, and the latter is a statement of assertions or facts about a set of instances. ABox materialization is the process of discovering implicit assertions in ABox by reasoning based on existing knowledge, which is important in knowledge base applications. Ontology reasoning is a common method for ABox materialization. However, it is considered to be a computationally intensive operation and does not scale well for large-scale ABox. To solve this problem, this paper proposes an approximate reasoning hypothesis: materialization on the overall ABox is approximately equivalent to the collection of subgraph reasoning on ABox. Based on this hypothesis, a subgraph reasoning method for large-scale ABox materialization is proposed. Subgraph reasoning first divides ABox into instance-centered multi-hops subgraphs, then performs ontology reasoning on each subgraph, and finally takes the collection of all subgraph reasoning results as the result of ABox materialization. We conduct experiments on multiple open-source ontologies, and analyze the rationality of the approximate reasoning hypothesis. The experimental results show that subgraph reasoning can effectively improve the reasoning efficiency and achieve superior scalability for large-scale ABox materialization reasoning.

Keywords: ABox materialization · Subgraph reasoning · Large-scale ABox · OWL DL · SWRL

1 Introduction

Ontology is an important form of explicit modeling of human knowledge through symbols, and it is the core of the Semantic Web framework [1–3]. The ontology knowledge base can usually be divided into two parts: TBox and ABox [4]. The former is the schema-level knowledge of the knowledge base, which is used to describe the relationship between the recognized concepts and attributes in

© The Author(s), under exclusive license to Springer Nature Switzerland AG 2022
G. Memmi et al. (Eds.): KSEM 2022, LNAI 13368, pp. 627–643, 2022.
https://doi.org/10.1007/978-3-031-10983-6_48

the domain, and the latter is a collection of instance assertions or fact statements. The effective application of ontology knowledge base is relied on reasoning. ABox materialization [5] refers to the process of ontology reasoning to reason more implicated assertions in ABox, which can discover implicit class labels of instances and implicit relationships between instances. ABox materialization is widely used in event knowledge management [6], network security intelligence management [7], gene-disease analysis [8] and other fields. Recently, with the explosive growth of data and the improvement of knowledge extraction technology, ontology knowledge bases containing large-scale ABox are increasingly common, which brings new challenges to the reasoning task of ABox materialization [9–11].

Ontology reasoning is a computationally intensive operation, and its reasoning efficiency is limited by the complexity of TBox [9]. OWL (Web Ontology Language) and its extension OWL2 are the mainstream ontology modeling languages recommended by W3C [4,12], and its logical basis is Description Logic (DL) [13]. Ontology reasoning is generally considered as a computationally intensive operation, and its inference complexity in OWL DL is at least EXPTIME-complete [9]. In order to obtain efficient reasoning support, W3C introduces a series of tractable description logic languages, such as OWL EL, Horn DL, DL-lite, corresponding to three sub-languages of OWL: OWL2 EL, OWL2 RL, and OWL2 QL [14]. In these sublanguages, the time complexity of the standard reasoning problem is PTIME complete. However, real-world knowledge is not limited to these sub-languages, and often requires complex expressive capabilities and OWL DL-oriented reasoner to reason.

The SWRL (Semantic Web Rule Language) rule language is commonly used in ontology modeling, which can combine Horn-like rules with the OWL knowledge base to provide an advanced abstract syntax for ontology modeling and extend the semantics and syntax of OWL [15]. SWRL rules include antecedent and consequent: the former is also called the rule body, and the latter is called the rule head. The rule body defines the preconditions of the rule, and the rule head gives the implied conclusion, which means that the preconditions specified in the antecedent are holded, the conclusion in the consequent must also be holded. SWRL rules can effectively describe the composite relationship between instances in ABox, which is a considerable factor in ABox materialization, but it also further increases reasoning costs.

The scale of ABox also influences the reasoning task of ABox materialization. Tableau [16] or Hypertableau [17] is the classical algorithms of ontology reasoning, and both of them are memory algorithms. The reasoning of Tableau is to construct a model to detect the consistency of the ontology, and reduce other reasoning tasks as consistency testing. For the ontology knowledge base containing a large-scale ABox, the calculation process needs to construct a huge abstract model. Thus, either the reasoning fails due to memory overflow, or the reasoning efficiency is decreased due to a large amount of frequent internal and external memory data exchanges. Therefore, ontology reasoning does not have good scalability for large-scale ABox reasoning tasks.

In order to realize the reasoning task of large-scale ABox materialization, this paper proposes the approximate reasoning hypothesis that the materialization on the overall ABox is approximately equivalent to the union of the subgraph reasoning on the ABox. Based on this hypothesis, a subgraph-based reasoning method is proposed. The subgraph reasoning method firstly divides the ABox into instance-centered multi-hops subgraphs, then performs ontology reasoning on each subgraph, and finally merges the results of all subgraph reasoning as the result of ABox materialization. Subgraph reasoning can effectively improve the scalability of ontology reasoning for large-scale ABox. The main contributions of this paper are as follows:

(1) We propose approximate reasoning hypothesis and a subgraph reasoning method for large-scale ABox materialization based on the hypothesis. The reasoning task of large-scale ABox materialization is realized by subgraph reasoning, which can approximate the reasoning results on the overall ABox.
(2) We conduct experiments to analyze the similarity between ABox subgraph reasoning and overall ABox reasoning on multiple open-source ontologies constructed by OWL DL and OWL DL+SWRL respectively, which verifies the rationality of the approximate reasoning hypothesis.
(3) We perform experiments on multiple knowledge bases containing ABox of different scales. The results show that the reasoning efficiency of large-scale ABox can be effectively improved by subgraph reasoning, which indicates that subgraph reasoning achieves superior scalability. Meanwhile, the experiments also find that subgraph reasoning can handle the condition where cannot be reasoned directly on the whole ABox.

This paper is organized as follows. In Sect. 2, we introduce the relevant preliminary knowledge, and describe the research points of this paper; Sect. 3 analyzes experimental results, and Sect. 4 is the conclusion of this paper.

2   Preliminaries

This paper considers the reasoning task of large-scale ABox materialization, and therefore assumes the TBox to be completely correct, while disregarding the data properties in the assertion set. The basis of OWL DL is description logic. Common description logic is mainly obtained by adding or deleting different constructors on $\mathcal{ALC}$ [13]. These constructors become the main evidence for distinguishing different specific description logics[1]. For example, $\mathcal{ALCN}$ is obtained by adding the number restrictions in $\mathcal{ALC}$, and $\mathcal{ALCF}$ is obtained by adding the functionality constraint. In the practical application of Semantic Web, it not only needs to describe concepts, but also to enhance the expression ability of relationships. For example, $\mathcal{ALC}$ with a transitive relationship trans(R) is also called $\mathcal{S}$. If adding role hierarchy axioms or the role inverse axiom to $\mathcal{S}$, we obtain the $\mathcal{SH}$ language and the $\mathcal{SI}$ language, respectively. OWL DL is corresponding to $\mathcal{SHOIN}$, which is the description logic language with strong expressive ability.

   In order to describe the problem of this paper, some concepts need to be explained.

---

[1] http://www.cs.man.ac.uk/~ezolin/dl/.

Definition 1. *The class assertion $C(e)$ indicates that e is an instance of class C; The role assertion $r(s, o)$ indicates that there is a role r between instance s and instance o. In this paper, the set composed of class assertions and role assertions is called the assertion set, denoted as ABox.*

Although class assertions are unary relations and role assertions are binary relations, both can be expressed intactly using RDF graph [24]. To be specific, $C(e)$ is represented as $(e, rdf : type, C)$ and $r(s, o)$ is represented as (s, r, o), where $rdf : type$ is a reserved word in RDF, representing the *Class* of the instance.

Definition 2. *Given an OWL DL knowledge base $KB = (TBox, ABox)$, the knowledge base obtained by ontology reasoning is called an extended knowledge base, denoted as $KB_{ext} = (TBox, ABox_{ext})$. In this paper, the process of acquiring the extended knowledge base KB_{ext} from the knowledge base KB is called ABox materialization, and the process of ontology reasoning is represented as $KB_{ext} = Reasoner(KB)$.*

The computation complexity of ontology reasoning in OWL DL is at least EXPTIME-complete, making it not scalable for ontology knowledge bases containing large-scale ABox. Therefore, this paper proposes a method based on subgraph reasoning.

Definition 3. *Suppose e is an instance in the ontology knowledge base* **KB**, *then in the RDF graph composed of all assertions of ABox, the subgraph composed of entities and relation assertions within k hops centered on e is called the subgraph of e, denoted as $\mathbf{g}_e^k$.*

According to Definition 3, it can be seen that the 1-hop subgraph of e is represented as:

$$\mathbf{g}_e^1 = \{r(e, a_i^1) | r(e, a_i^1) \in ABox\} \cup \{r(a_i^1, e) | r(a_i^1, e) \in ABox\} \cup \{C(e) | C(e) \in ABox\}$$

2-hop subgraph can is represented as:

$$\mathbf{g}_e^2 = \mathbf{g}_e^1 \cup \{r(a_i^1, a_i^2) | r(a_i^1, a_i^2) \in ABox\} \cup \{r(a_i^2, a_i^1) | r(a_i^2, a_i^1) \in ABox\}$$
$$\cup \{C(a_i^1) | C(a_i^1) \in ABox\}$$

And so on, k-hop is reprensented as:

$$\mathbf{g}_e^k = \mathbf{g}_e^{k-1} \cup \{r(a_i^{k-1}, a_i^k) | r(a_i^{k-1}, a_i^k) \in ABox\} \cup \{r(a_i^k, a_i^{k-1}) | r(a_i^k, a_i^{k-1}) \in ABox\}$$
$$\cup \{C(a_i^{k-1}) | C(a_i^{k-1}) \in ABox\}$$

The k-hops subgraph is an important concept in this paper, so its explanation is shown in Example 1.

Example 1 (Example of a k-hops subgraph for an instance e). The RDF graph
of the example ABox is given in Fig. 1, where C_i ($i = 1, 2, 3, ..., n$, n is the number
of classes defined in the TBox) represents the *Class* defined in the TBox, and
the line legend represents different *Role*, and a_1–a_8 represent instances in ABox.

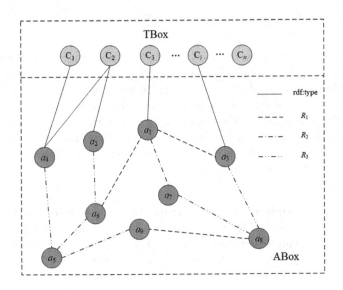

Fig. 1. RDF graph of example ABox.

Taking instance a_1 as an example, the assertion sets (triples) contained in
the 1-hop subgraph, the 2-hop subgraph and the 3-hop subgraph are represented
respectively:

$$\mathbf{g}_{a_1}^1 = \{(a_1, rdf:type, C_3), (a_1, R_1, a_3), (a_1, R_1, a_6), (a_1, R_2, a_7)\}$$

$$\mathbf{g}_{a_1}^2 = \mathbf{g}_{a_1}^1 \cup \{(a_6, R_3, a_2), (a_6, R_2, a_5), (a_3, R_3, a_8), (a_7, R_3, a_8), (a_3, rdf:type, C_i)\}$$

$$\mathbf{g}_{a_1}^3 = \mathbf{g}_{a_1}^2 \cup \{(a_5, R_3, a_4), (a_5, R_2, a_9), (a_8, R_1, a_9)\}$$

According to Definition 3, if all instances in ABox are traversed, a large-scale
ABox can be represented as:

$$ABox = \mathbf{g}_{e_1}^k \cup \mathbf{g}_{e_2}^k \cup \ldots \cup \mathbf{g}_{e_i}^k \cup \ldots \cup \mathbf{g}_{e_N}^k \tag{1}$$

where e_i represents the entity number in the ABox, $i = 1, 2, \ldots N$, N represents
the number of instances in the ABox, and k represents the hops of the subgraph.
Example 1 shows that, with the increases of hops, the obtained subgraph is
closer to the complete ABox. Then, how to make the subgraph reasoning closer
to reasoning on the overall ABox, the value of k is critical.

Definition 4. *In ABox, if the reasoning of an implicit assertion requires multiple assertions as the precondition, then the inference process to obtain the implicit assertion is called chain reasoning. In chain reasoning, the number of role assertions in the precondition is represented as n and the length of the reasoning chain is represented as l, where $l = n - 1$. The maximum length of the reasoning chain in the knowledge base is represented as l_{max}: if $n = 2$ or there is no chain reasoning, then $l_{max} = 1$.*

According to Definition 4, in OWL DL, the reasoning about the transitive attributes $Trans(R)$ is a kind of chain reasoning, and the complex class construction may also be a kind of chain reasoning. In addition, reasoning about SWRL rules is also a kind of chain reasoning, as described in Example 2. $l = n - 1$ is to ensure the consistency of the reasoning chain length l and the subgraph hops k. As shown in Example 2, although the precondition of the chain reasoning represented by SWRL contains two role assertions, the 1-hop subgraph of x_2 can divide x_1 and x_3 into the same RDF graph.

Example 2 (Chain reasoning example).

i. Chain reasoning resulting from transitive roles in knowledge bases. Suppose *ancestorOf* is a role with transitive attributes in the knowledge base, which can be represented to be $Trans(ancestorOf)$. The semantics of $ancestorOf(x, y)$ are: x is the ancestor of y, then for the instances $a_1 \ a_n$ in ABox, if:

$$ancestorOf(a_1, a_2), ancestorOf(a_2, a_3), \ldots, ancestorOf(a_{n-1}, a_n)$$

Then it can be inferred that: $ancestorOf(a_1, a_n)$ also holds. It is found that the process of implicitly asserting $ancestorOf(a_1, a_n)$ is a kind of chain reasoning, and the length of reasoning chain is $l = n - 1$.

ii. Chain reasoning arising from complex concept constructions in knowledge bases. Suppose *Class:Person, Student, Course, University* are in the knowledge base, *roles: takeCourse(x, y), studyIn(x, y)* and *hasAdvisor(x, w)* indicate that x takes course y, x studies in school z and the advisor of x is w. If the following axioms exist in the knowledge base:

Student EquivalentTo (Person and *(takeCourse* some *Course)* and *(studyIn* some *University)* and *(hasAdvisor* some *Person))*

Then, for an instance e of the *Person*, the reasoning process of judging whether he/she is a *Student* is a chain reasoning, and the length of the reasoning chain is $l = 2$.

iii. Chain reasoning composed of SWRL rules in a knowledge base. Suppose the SWRL rule in the knowledge base is:

$hasParent(?x_1, ?x_2) \wedge hasBrother(?x_2, ?x_3) \Rightarrow hasUncle(?x_1, ?x_3)$

For instances $a_1 \ a_3$ in ABox, if $hasParent(a_1, a_2)$ and $hasBrother(a_2, a_3)$ hold, $hasUncle(a_1, a_3)$ can be inferred. The process of obtaining the implicit assertion $hasUncle(a_1, a_3)$ is chain reasoning, and the length of the reasoning chain is $l = 1$.

It can be found from Example 2 that if we want to obtain the implicit assertion of chain reasoning, it is necessary to ensure that all instances involved in the chain reasoning are in the same RDF graph, which means that when the hops k of the subgraph is bigger than or equal to the maximum inference chain length l_{max}, the implicit assertion of the chain inference can be completely discovered in the subgraph inference. The paradox is that with the increases of the hops, the efficiency of subgraph reasoning becomes lower. In real reasoning problems, there may be only a small proportion of assertions related to the maximum chain reasoning, so it can be appropriate to choose k according to the actual situation.

It is necessary to define a criterion to evaluate the similarity of results between subgraph reasoning and overall ABox reasoning. Similarity is measured with a broad recall, namely:

$$Semilarity = \frac{len(\{a \wedge a \in ABox^{k}_{\mathbf{g}\_ext}\})}{len(ABox_{ext})} \tag{2}$$

In the formula, a represents a class assertion or a role assertion, and $len(*)$ represents the length of $*$, and $ABox^{k}_{\mathbf{g}\_ext}$ represents the collection of k-hop subgraph reasoning.

Based on the above analysis, the approximate reasoning hypothesis can be expressed as hypothesis 1.

Hypothesis 1. For a given similarity threshold α, when the hops k of the subgraph is bigger than, equal to or slightly smaller than the maximum reasoning chain length l_{max}, the similarity between the results of the subgraph reasoning and the overall ABox reasoning is recorded as *Similarity*. If there is *Similarity* $\geq \alpha$, then the union of subgraph reasoning is considered to be approximately equivalent to the result of overall ABox reasoning, which is the approximate reasoning hypothesis in this paper.

In Hypothesis 1, the similarity threshold α represents the expected value of subgraph reasoning approximation for the overall ABox reasoning in applications. When Hypothesis 1 holds, the following formula can be obtained:

$$ABox_{ext} \approx ABox^{k}_{\mathbf{g}\_ext} = \mathbf{g}^{k}_{e1\_ext} \cup \mathbf{g}^{k}_{e2\_ext} \cup \dots \mathbf{g}^{k}_{ei\_ext} \dots \cup \mathbf{g}^{k}_{eN\_ext} \tag{3}$$

where $\mathbf{g}^{k}_{ei\_ext}$ represents the reasoning extension on the subgraph $\mathbf{g}^{k}_{ei}$.

The reason for using approximate equivalence is that there may be information loss in subgraph reasoning compared to overall ABox reasoning, so that the reasoning results cannot be completely same, mainly in two aspects: One is that the subgraph may not contain the information expressed in the TBox. For example, in chain reasoning, if the two instances in the conclusion are not on the same subgraph, the implicit assertion of the chain reasoning cannot be found; The second is the loss of information that may be caused by iterative reasoning. In the process of ontology reasoning, the discovered conclusions can be used as the premise of other implicit assertions, so more assertions can be inferred. However, there is no assertion updating transfer between different subgraphs in the subgraph reasoning, which causes information loss partly. The information loss in both aspects can be compensated by increasing the hops of the subgraph.

The method of subgraph reasoning can effectively enhance the scalability of ontology reasoning for large-scale ABox. The main reasons are as follows:

(1) Suppose the scale of the overall ABox is N_A, and the average scale of the k-hop subgraphs of instances in the ABox is N_g, then $N_g \ll N_A$. Suppose the computation complexity on the overall ABox is $O(2^{p(N_A)})$, the computation complexity of the subgraph inference is represented as $O(N \times 2^{p(N_g)})$, where $p(*)$ is the polynomial function of $*$, and N is the number of instances in ABox. It can be seen that the subgraph reasoning can convert the reasoning problem on a large-scale ABox into a linear superposition of small-scale subgraph reasoning, which effectively improves the reasoning efficiency.

(2) The subgraph reasoning method can further improve efficiency through parallel reasoning. The subgraph reasoning method divides the overall ABox into instance-centric k-hop subgraphs, and then infers all subgraphs with the full TBox where the inference of each subgraph is independent, so parallelism can be used to speed up the subgraph reasoning.

The reasoning efficiency is evaluated by reasoning time t, which is the average of 3 experiments and the unit is seconds, namely:

$$t_{ext} = \frac{Time_1(ABox_{ext}) + Time_2(ABox_{ext}) + Time_3(ABox_{ext})}{3} \quad (4)$$

$$t_{\mathbf{g\_ext}}^k = \frac{Time_1(ABox_{\mathbf{g\_ext}}^k) + Time_2(ABox_{\mathbf{g\_ext}}^k) + Time_3(ABox_{\mathbf{g\_ext}}^k)}{3} \quad (5)$$

where t_{ext} represents the average time of inference under the overall ABox, $t_{\mathbf{g\_ext}}^k$ represents the average time of k-hop subgraph inference, and $Time_i$ represents the time consumed by the $i-th$ acquisition of the corresponding extended assertion set.

3 Experiment and Analysis

This section mainly consists of three parts: firstly, we introduce the open-source ontology and ABox data used in the experiment; Then we analyze the rationality of the approximate reasoning hypothesis through the similarity of the subgraph reasoning and the overall ABox reasoning; Finally, the scalability of subgraph reasoning for large-scale ABox materialization reasoning tasks is verified by comparing the time consumption of subgraph reasoning and overall ABox reasoning.

3.1 Ontology and Data

The experiments in this paper are carried out on four open-source knowledge bases, namely the univ-bench.owl[2] ontology released by the Oxford University

---

[2] http://krr-nas.cs.ox.ac.uk/ontologies/lib/LUBM/.

ontology database [18], referred as Lubm; the family.swrl[3] ontology released by the Stanford University ontology database [19], referred as Family ; sem_r.swrl[4] from the ontology library of the University of Toronto, referred as Sem [20]; the last one is the time-qualitative-only[5] ontology [21] released by Batsakis et al., referred as Time.

The statistics of the four open-source knowledge bases are shown in Table 1. In the table, # *Axios* represents the number of axioms contained in the TBox, and # *SWRL* represents the number of rules defined in the knowledge base, and # *Classes* and # *Roles* respectively represent the number of concepts and relations defined in the ontology, and *isABox* refers to whether there is an existing ABox set in the knowledge base, and *Complexity* corresponds to the description logic language of the knowledge base. Both subgraph reasoning and overall ABox reasoning use the ontology reasoner Pellet, which is a relatively mature and widely used ontology reasoner [22].

Table 1. The statistical information of knowledge base

Ontology	# Axioms	# SWRL	# Classes	# Roles	isABox	Complexity
Lubm	243	0	43	25	Yes	ALEHI+
Family	153	12	18	16	No	ALCHOIQ
Sem	355	19	19	35	No	SRIQ
Time	82	10	2	17	No	SRIF

Table 2. Scale of knowledge base for approximate reasoning hypothesis analysis and its extended knowledge base

Ontology	Label	Scale of ABox			Reasoning (OWL DL) Scale of ABox$_{ext}$			Reasoning (OWL DL+SWRL) Scale of ABox$_{ext}$		
		# CA	# RA	# A	# CA	# RA	# A	# CA	# RA	#A
Lubm	# L1	18128	49336	67464	21853	16082	37935	–	–	–
Family	# F1	196	991	1187	1445	2344	3789	1497	4910	6407
Sem	# S1	195	416	611	340	8274	8614	341	10777	11118
Time	# T1	211	1015	1226	0	10710	10710	0	11412	11412

From Table 1, it can be found that except for Lubm, the rest of the knowledge bases do not contain ABox, so this paper uses the method of literature [23] to synthesize a logically consistent set of assertions. For the verification experiment of approximate reasoning hypothesis, this paper synthesized small-scale ABox on

---

[3] http://protege.cim3.net/file/pub/ontologies/family.swrl.owl/family.swrl.owl.
[4] http://stl.mie.utoronto.ca/ontologies/simple_event_model/sem_r.swrl.
[5] https://github.com/sbatsakis/TemporalRepresentations.

Family, Sem and Time respectively as the experimental data. At the same time, in order to analyze the impact of chain reasoning on approximate reasoning assumptions, two groups of comparing experiments are conducted. The first group is to delete the SWRL rules in the knowledge base, and only reason on the knowledge base constructed based on OWL DL; The second group is to keep SWRL rules and reason on the knowledge base constructed based on OWL DL+SWRL.

Table 3. The scale of knowledge base for scalability analysis

Ontology	Label	Scale of ABox		
		# CA	# RA	# A
Family	# F1	196	991	1187
	# F2	331	1796	2127
	# F3	1722	9298	11020
	# F4	3618	19295	22913
Time	# T1	211	1015	1226
	# T2	525	2529	3054
	# T3	914	4019	4933
	# T4	5003	22752	27755

Then, the similarity between the subgraph reasoning and the overall ABox reasoning is analyzed in two groups of experiments. In the experiment, we set the similarity threshold $\alpha=99\%$. In fact, this is a relatively high similarity expectation. The scales of ABox and its corresponding extended assertion set in the four knowledge bases are shown in Table 2. In the table, $ABox_{ext}$ represents the extended assertion set on the overall ABox, $\# CA$ represents the number of class assertions in the assertion set, $\# RA$ represents the number of role assertions number, $\# A$ indicates the number of all assertions, and '-' indicates that there is no assertions.

For the scalability analysis experiment, this paper selects the Family and Time ontology, and synthesizes ABox knowledge bases of different scales to analyze and compare the scalability of the subgraph reasoning and the overall ABox reasoning. The reason for choosing Family and Time is that they have strong expression ability and contain SWRL rules, which are closer to the ontology knowledge base in real applications. The scales of the knowledge bases are shown in Table 3.

3.2   Approximate Reasoning Hypothesis Verification

This section firstly analyzes the similarity of the subgraph reasoning to the overall ABox reasoning on OWL DL, in which the SWRL rules in # F1, # S1, and

T1 are removed. For # L1 and # F1, their maximum length of chain reasoning is $l_{max} = 1$. In order to verify the rationality of the subgraph inference hypothesis, we set the hops of subgraph $k = \{1, 2\}$. In # S1 and # T1, there are transitive roles, and $l_{max} = 3$ for both of them, so let $k = \{1, 2, 3, 4\}$. The reasoning results are shown in Table 4. In the table, $ABox^k_{g\_ext}$ represents the extended assertion set obtained by subgraph reasoning, and *Similarity* represents the defined similarity criterion in Sect. 2, which is used to measure the similarity between subgraph reasoning and overall ABox reasoning.

It can be seen from Table 4 that for # L1 and # F1, when $k = 1$, their *Similarity* reaches 100%, indicating that $ABox^1_{g\_ext}$ and $ABox_{ext}$ are the same

Table 4. Reasoning on OWL DL (without SWRL)

Label	l_{max}	k	Scale of ABox$^k_{g\_ext}$			Similarity
			# CA	# RA	#A	
# L1	1	1	21853	16082	37935	100%
		2	21853	16082	37935	100%
# F1	1	1	1445	2344	3789	100%
		2	1445	2344	3789	100%
# S1	3	1	329	586	915	10.62%
		2	336	1926	2262	26.26%
		3	340	8274	8614	100%
		4	340	8274	8614	100%
# T1	3	1	0	1898	1898	17.72%
		2	0	9368	9368	87.47%

Table 5. Reasoning on OWL DL + SWRL

Label	l_{max}	k	Scale of ABox$^k_{g\_ext}$			Similarity
			# CA	# RA	#A	
# F1	2	1	1462	3703	5165	79.26%
		2	1503	5041	6544	98.77%
		3	1518	5189	6707	99.64%
# S1	6	1	329	649	978	8.63%
		2	336	2173	2509	22.41%
		3	341	10795	11136	99.99%
		4	341	10795	11136	99.99%
# T1	3	1	0	1940	1940	17.0%
		2	0	9690	9690	84.91%
		3	0	11372	11372	99.65%
		4	0	11412	11412	100%

in this situation, which illustrates that subgraph reasoning can achieve a good approximation to the overall ABox reasoning. For # S1, when $k = 1$, the *Similarity* is only 10.62%. The value of *Similarity* increases with k. When $k = 2$, the *Similarity* is 26.26%. However, when $k = l_{max} = 3$, the value of *Similarity* quickly reaches 100%. At this time, the k-hop subgraph contains all the instances involved in the chain reasoning, thus perfectly approximating the overall ABox inference. For # T1, it shows similar results to #S1, but the difference is that when $k = l_{max} = 3$, the value of *Similarity* is 99.98% (comparing to 100% achieved in #S1). Although the subgraph contains all instances in chain reasoning, this suggests that the loss of information caused by iterative reasoning affects the *Similarity* at this time. When continuing to increase $k = 4$, the *Similarity* reaches 100%, which means that by increasing the hops of the subgraph, the loss caused by iterative reasoning is compensated.

Through the above analysis, it can be found that for the ontology knowledge base represented by OWL DL, when the hops of subgraph is equal to the maximum length of the reasoning chain, the subgraph reasoning can nicely approximate the result of the overall ABox reasoning. Even if the value of *Similarity* cannot reach 100% in some cases, it exceeds 99.9%, which is bigger than the similarity threshold α set in the experiment. The experimental results indicate that the approximate reasoning hypothesis is holded on the knowledge base constructed by OWL DL.

Next, we analyze the reasoning results of subgraph reasoning on OWL DL + SWRL knowledge base, as shown in Table 5. Since # L1 does not contain SWRL rules, the experiment is only carried out on the remaining three knowledge bases. It can be found from the table that with the introduction of SWRL rules, the maximum length of the reasoning chain of knowledge base increases. At this time, we set $k = \{1, 2, 3\}$ for # F1, $k = \{1, 2, 3, 4\}$ for # S1 and # T1. There are two reasons why $k = l_{max}$ is not obtained: First, in practical applications, the proportion of implicit assertions discovered by the largest reasoning chain may be very small, and can be discarded if not necessary; The second is that increasing the hops of subgraph will bring large computation costs, which should be avoided in large-scale ABox materialization.

Comparing Table 4 and Table 5 horizontally, it can be found that after the introduction of SWRL rules, more implicit assertions are inferred. With the increase of the maximum length of reasoning chain, the k value with better approximation can be obtained in OWL DL, but becomes worse in the knowledge base of OWL DL + SWRL. Such as for # F1, when $k = 1$ in Table 4, the *Similarity* is 100%, while it is only 79.26% in Table 5. This shows that with the introduction of SWRL rules and the increases of the length of the maximum reasoning chain in the knowledge base, the hops of subgraph needs to be increased accordingly.

Table 4 and Table 5 also show the same characteristics. Obviously, with the increases of the hops of subgraph, the value of *Similarity* increases, and the maximum value on the three data all exceeds 99%, which is bigger than the similarity threshold α set by the experiment. It is shown that for the knowledge base constructed by OWL DL + SWRL, subgraph reasoning can also perfectly approximate the reasoning results of the overall ABox. For # S1, although its k value is less than l_{max}, it still achieves good results. In practical applications, if the length of the maximum reasoning chain is too large and the result is not necessary, it can be appropriately discarded, and takes a smaller k in exchange for the improvement of reasoning efficiency.

In a word, whenever the ontology knowledge base is represented by OWL DL or OWL DL + SWRL, the subgraph reasoning can effectively approximate the reasoning results of the overall ABox, which shows that the approximate reasoning hypothesis proposed in this paper is reasonable and it is feasible to try the reasoning task for large-scale ABox materialization through subgraph reasoning.

3.3   Scalability Analysis

In the case that the subgraph reasoning can effectively approximate the overall ABox reasoning, the scalability of the subgraph reasoning is analyzed and compared. On datasets of different scales, subgraph reasoning and overall ABox reasoning are performed respectively to compare the time consumption. The results are shown in Table 6. For # F1 to # F4, we set $k = 2$ and for # T1 to # T4, we set $k = 3$. In the table, $t^k_{g\_ext}$ and t_{ext} represent the time consumption by subgraph reasoning and overall ABox reasoning, respectively. The time consumption is only referred to the reasoning time and does not includes the result serialization time. '-' indicates that the reasoning cannot be done due to memory overflow or the reasoning result is not obtained for more than 10 h. In addition, for subgraph reasoning, a single thread (not parallel), 2-thread parallel, and 4-thread parallel comparison are performed respectively.

Table 6. Reasoning time consumption analysis comparison table

Ontology	Label	Consumption of time(s)			
		$t^k_{g\_ext}$ single-thread	$t^k_{g\_ext}$ 2-thread parallel	$t^k_{g\_ext}$ 4-thread parallel	t_{ext}
Family	# F1	26	14	8	174
	# F2	43	23	12	387
	# F3	215	120	84	18451
	# F4	447	251	163	-
Time	# T1	190	98	97	57
	# T2	368	193	151	-
	# T3	518	279	205	-
	# T4	3150	1666	-	-

As can be seen from Table 6, from # F1 to # F4, $t^k_{\mathbf{g}\text{-}ext}$ is smaller than t_{ext} in all experiments, which indicates that the time consumption by subgraph reasoning is less than the overall ABox reasoning. In addition, as the scale of the knowledge base increases, the time advantage of subgraph reasoning becomes more obvious. For example, for # F1, the time consumption achieved by single-thread subgraph reasoning is 26 s, and the time consumption of overall ABox reasoning is 174 s. To be more specific, the time consumption of overall ABox reasoning is about 7 times that of the single-thread subgraph reasoning, while for # F4, the times is about 85. It means that subgraph reasoning method achieves higher reasoning efficiency.

It can also be found from Table 6 that for # T1, $t^k_{\mathbf{g}\text{-}ext}$ is slightly larger than t_{ext}, which shows that subgraph reasoning consumes a little more time. However, from # T2 to # T4, the ontology reasoner cannot perform inference on the overall ABox because of memory overflow or no results returned for more than 10 h. At this time, subgraph reasoning can still be performed and the reasoning result can be obtained effectively. It means that subgraph reasoning achieves better scalability for large-scale knowledge bases, and can perform effective reasoning when the overall ABox reasoning cannot be adapted. The results of # F4 also verifies this point of view.

In addition, as shown in Table 6, compared with single-thread reasoning, the efficiency of subgraph reasoning can be further improved through multi-thread parallel computing. For example, for # F1, the time consumption is 26 s for single-thread subgraph reasoning, 14 s for 2-thread parallel, and only 8 s for 4-thread parallel. However, it does not mean that the efficiency of reasoning is improved with the increases of parallel threads, and it is affected by computing

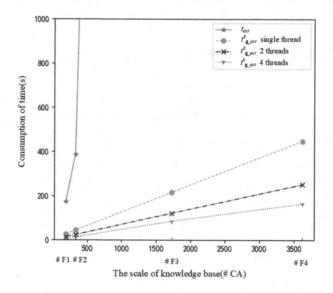

Fig. 2. Time-consumption comparison of different scale knowledge base.

resources. For example, for # F4, the time consumption of single-thread reasoning is about 2.74 times that of 4-thread parallel, and for #F1, it is 3.25 times, which is significantly decreased. This is because when the scale of the knowledge base is large, too many parallel threads will occupy a large amount of computing resources, resulting in a decrease in reasoning efficiency. Obviously, for # T4, due to memory overflow, 4-thread parallel reasoning cannot obtain inference results.

In order to further analyze the reasoning efficiency of subgraph reasoning and the overall ABox reasoning, the curve of its reasoning time consumption changing with the scale of the knowledge base is shown in Fig 2. It can be found that with the increase of the scale of the knowledge base, the time consumption of reasoning on the overall ABox increases exponentially, showing an approximately vertical growth curve in the figure. While for subgraph reasoning, the time consumption is almost a straight line with the growth of the knowledge base, presenting a linear growth. This verifies the previous analysis on reasoning efficiency. The subgraph reasoning can convert the inference problem on a large-scale ABox into a linear superposition of small-scale subgraph reasoning, which effectively improves the reasoning efficiency.

From the above experiments, it can be seen that subgraph reasoning has higher reasoning efficiency and better scalability than the overall ABox reasoning. It can convert the reasoning problem on a large-scale ABox into a linear superposition of small-scale subgraph reasoning, and its reasoning efficiency can be further improved with parallel computing. At the same time, for large-scale ABox, when the direct reasoning cannot be performed, subgraph reasoning can still effectively obtain reasoning results.

4   Conclusion

To solve the problem that ontology reasoning cannot be applied to large-scale ABox materialization reasoning, this paper proposes an approximate reasoning hypothesis that approximates the overall ABox reasoning result through the collection of subgraph reasoning. Based on this hypothesis, a subgraph reasoning method for large-scale ABox materialization is proposed. The subgraph reasoning firstly divides the ABox into instance-centered k-hop subgraphs, and then takes the collection of subgraph inference results as the result of the overall ABox reasoning. Through experiments, this paper verifies the rationality of the approximate reasoning hypothesis, and analyzes the scalability of subgraph reasoning to large-scale ABox. The experimental results on multiple open-source ontologies show that subgraph reasoning can effectively approximate the reasoning results of the overall ABox in the knowledge base of OWL DL or OWL DL+SWRL. Compared with the overall ABox reasoning, the subgraph reasoning achieves higher reasoning efficiency and can be adapted to situations where the overall ABox reasoning cannot be directly performed. The subgraph reasoning provides a feasible idea for solving the reasoning task for large-scale ABox materialization in applications.

References

1. Guarino, N., Oberle, D., Staab, S.: What is an ontology? In: Staab, S., Studer, R. (eds.) Handbook on Ontologies. IHIS, pp. 1–17. Springer, Heidelberg (2009). https://doi.org/10.1007/978-3-540-92673-3_0
2. Ian, H.: Historical ontology. In: In the Scope of Logic, Methodology, and Philosophy of Science, pp. 583–600. Springer, Dordrecht (2002). https://doi.org/10.1007/978-94-017-0475-5_13
3. Berners-Lee, T., Hendler, J., Lassila, O.: The semantic web. Sci. Am. **284**(5), 34–43 (2001). https://doi.org/10.1038/35074206
4. Horrocks, I.: OWL: a description logic based ontology language. In: van Beek, P. (ed.) CP 2005. LNCS, vol. 3709, pp. 5–8. Springer, Heidelberg (2005). https://doi.org/10.1007/11564751_2
5. Glimm, B., Kazakov, Y., Liebig, T., Tran, T.-K., Vialard, V.: Abstraction refinement for ontology materialization. In: Mika, P., et al. (eds.) ISWC 2014. LNCS, vol. 8797, pp. 180–195. Springer, Cham (2014). https://doi.org/10.1007/978-3-319-11915-1_12
6. Gottschalk, S., Demidova, E.: EventKG: a multilingual event-centric temporal knowledge graph. In: Gangemi, A., et al. (eds.) ESWC 2018. LNCS, vol. 10843, pp. 272–287. Springer, Cham (2018). https://doi.org/10.1007/978-3-319-93417-4_18
7. Jia, Y., Qi, Y., Shang, H., Jiang, R., Li, A.: A practical approach to constructing a knowledge graph for cybersecurity. Engineering **4**(01), 117–133 (2018). https://doi.org/10.1016/j.eng.2018.01.004
8. Alshahrani, M., Khan, M.A., Maddouri, O., et al.: Neuro-symbolic representation learning on biological knowledge graphs. Bioinformatics **33**(17), 2723–2730 (2017). https://doi.org/10.1093/bioinformatics/btx275
9. Pan, J.Z., Ren, Y., Zhao, Y.: Tractable approximate deduction for OWL. Artif. Intell. **235**, 95–155 (2016). https://doi.org/10.1016/j.artint.2015.10.004
10. Narayanan, S., Catalyurek, U., Kurc, T., et al.: Parallel materialization of large ABoxes. In: Proceedings of the 2009 ACM Symposium on Applied Computing, pp. 1257–1261 (2009). https://doi.org/10.1145/1529282.1529564
11. Rabbi, F., MacCaull, W., Faruqui, R.U.: A scalable ontology reasoner via incremental materialization. In: Proceedings of the 26th IEEE International Symposium on Computer-Based Medical Systems, pp. 221–226. IEEE (2013). https://doi.org/10.1109/CBMS.2013.6627792
12. Grau, B.C., Horrocks, I., Motik, B., et al.: OWL 2: the next step for OWL. J. Web Semant. **6**(4), 309–322 (2008). https://doi.org/10.1016/j.websem.2008.05.001
13. Baader, F., Calvanese, D., McGuinness, D., Patel-Schneider, P., Nardi, D. (eds.): The Description Logic Handbook: Theory, Implementation and Applications. Cambridge University Press, Cambridge (2003)
14. Krötzsch, M.: OWL 2 profiles: an introduction to lightweight ontology languages. In: Eiter, T., Krennwallner, T. (eds.) Reasoning Web 2012. LNCS, vol. 7487, pp. 112–183. Springer, Heidelberg (2012). https://doi.org/10.1007/978-3-642-33158-9_4
15. Mehla, S., Jain, S.: Rule languages for the semantic web. In: Abraham, A., Dutta, P., Mandal, J.K., Bhattacharya, A., Dutta, S. (eds.) Emerging Technologies in Data Mining and Information Security. AISC, vol. 755, pp. 825–834. Springer, Singapore (2019). https://doi.org/10.1007/978-981-13-1951-8_73
16. Schmidt-Schauß, M., Smolka, G.: Attributive concept descriptions with complements. Artif. Intell. **48**(1), 1–26 (1991). https://doi.org/10.1016/0004-3702(91)90078-X

17. Baumgartner, P.: Hyper tableau—the next generation. In: de Swart, H. (ed.) TABLEAUX 1998. LNCS (LNAI), vol. 1397, pp. 60–76. Springer, Heidelberg (1998). https://doi.org/10.1007/3-540-69778-0_14
18. Guo, Y., Pan, Z., Heflin, J.: LUBM: a benchmark for OWL knowledge base systems. J. Web Semant. **3**(2–3), 158–182 (2005). https://doi.org/10.1016/j.websem.2005.06.005
19. Golbreich, C.: Combining rule and ontology reasoners for the semantic web. In: Antoniou, G., Boley, H. (eds.) RuleML 2004. LNCS, vol. 3323, pp. 6–22. Springer, Heidelberg (2004). https://doi.org/10.1007/978-3-540-30504-0_2
20. Katsumi, M., Grüninger, M.: Using PSL to extend and evaluate event ontologies. In: Bassiliades, N., Gottlob, G., Sadri, F., Paschke, A., Roman, D. (eds.) RuleML 2015. LNCS, vol. 9202, pp. 225–240. Springer, Cham (2015). https://doi.org/10.1007/978-3-319-21542-6_15
21. Batsakis, S., Tachmazidis, I., Antoniou, G.: Representing time and space for the semantic web. Int. J. Artif. Intell. Tools **26**(03), 1750015.1-1750015.30 (2017). https://doi.org/10.1142/S0218213017600156
22. Sirin, E., Parsia, B., Grau, B.C., et al.: Pellet: a practical owl-dl reasoner. J. Web Semant. **5**(2), 51–53 (2007). https://doi.org/10.1016/j.websem.2007.03.004
23. Bin, L., Hang, C., Min, L., et al.: A graph data synthesis method, device, computer device and storage medium. Patent for Invention (2021)
24. Lassila, O., Swick, R.R.: Resource description framework (RDF) model and syntax specification (1998)

BPMN4SBP for Multi-dimensional Modeling of Sensitive Business Processes

Mariam Ben Hassen[(✉)], Mohamed Turki, and Faïez Gargouri

MIRACL Laboratory - B.P. 242, University of Sfax, ISIMS, 3021 Sfax, Tunisia
{mariem.benhassen,mohamed.turki,faiez.gargouri}@isims.usf.tn

Abstract. This research article proposes a conceptual solution for the Sensitive Business Processes (SBPs). It aims at systematically developing a valid and rigorous BPMN extension, called "BPMN4SBP", supporting the multi-dimensional modeling of SBPs (i.e., the knowledge, functional, organizational, behavioral, informational and intentional dimensions). The objective of the new extension is to explicitly integrate all the relevant issues and aspects relevant at the coupling/intersection of the busine ss process modeling (BPM) domain and the knowledge management (KM) domain for improving the identification and management of crucial knowledge which are mobilized and created by these processes. Based on a Core Ontology of SBP, need for extension is identified and the valid BPMN4SBP extension is designed by the construction of a conceptional domain model and the corresponding BPMN extension model. This extended BPMN4SBP meta-model is derived by applying model transformation rules and by adapting, also, the UML profile mechanism to BPMN.

Keywords: Business process modeling · Knowledge management · Sensitive business process · Core domain ontologies · BPMN 2.0.2 extension · DSR methodology

1 Introduction

Nowadays, modern organizations have become aware of the necessity to identify and model their sensitive business processes (SBPs) in order to improve the management of their individual and collective knowledge. An SBP is a particular type of business process centered on knowledge, information and data. It includes a large number of critical activities (individual and/or collective), mobilizing crucial knowledge, on which it is necessary to capitalize. It contains knowledge-intensive activities that value the acquisition, storage, dissemination, sharing, conversion and creation of individual and collective knowledge (tacit and explicit). Thus, it mobilizes a wide variety of knowledge sources recording a very large mass of heterogeneous knowledge. Its execution involves the collaboration and interaction of many participants (who can be internal and/or external to the organization) and heavily depends on the tacit and strategic knowledge of experts with heterogeneous levels of expertise and skills. This type of process can be semi-structured, structured or unstructured, possessing a high degree of complexity, flexibility

G. Memmi et al. (Eds.): KSEM 2022, LNAI 13368, pp. 644–657, 2022.
https://doi.org/10.1007/978-3-031-10983-6_49

and dynamism. Besides, its contribution to reach strategic objectives of the organization and its realization duration are very important [1–3]. Due to its characteristics, modeling and organizing the knowledge involved in SBP is relatively critical. Therefore, it is important that an appropriate BPM language provides an explicit representation of relevant SBP dimensions, viz. the functional dimension, the organizational dimension, the behavioral dimension, the informational dimension, the intentional dimension and the knowledge dimension [2, 3]. In this context, the SBPs can be graphically represented, using the well-known standard for BPM, the Business Process Model and Notation (BPMN 2.0.2) [4], in order to localize and identify the knowledge that is mobilized and created by different activities of these processes. BPMN 2.0 was selected as the most suitable BPM notations for SBP representation, because it offers a good variety of characteristics and functionalities to support SBP modeling (e.g., ontological completeness, strong expressiveness, (process flow aspects), understandability, ease of interpretation, level of adoption in professional practice, availability of tools, well-defined meta model, flexibility, extensibility, etc.) better than other BPM languages [2]. However, despite its expressive representational capabilities, BPMN 2.0.2 diagrams are still incomplete to explicitly and adequately support and specify the core dimensions and concepts of SBP. So, to overcoming the shortcomings of BPMN, some of its concepts must be adapted and extended to be convenient for a rich and expressive representation of SBPs, integrating all or at least most of the relevant issues at the intersection of KM and BPM (e.g., the dynamic, interaction and knowledge aspects).

To the best of our knowledge, there is no rigorous scientific work on the extension of BPMN 2.0 for KM. Thus, we proposed EM-BPMN4SBP, a rigorous scientific method for the design and development of the BPMN4SBP extension for the identification and management of crucial knowledge. We support our work with the design-oriented branch of management infor-mation science, the Design Science Research Methodology (DSRM) [5–7] as it aims to de-velop new artifacts (e.g., a domain-oriented development method for valid BPMN exten-sions, instantiation of the method for implementing the BPMN4SBP extension, ontological conceptual patterns, meta-models and a new BPMN4SBP notation). The design of the various artefacts is mainly driven by the adaptation and the extension of adequate techniques and methods from the field of method engineering and BPMN extensions development [4, 8–10] in order to ensure relevance and rigor [5, 6]. The objective of our "EM-BPMN4SBP" extension method is to develop rigorous, complete and expressive graphical representation models of SBPs that explicitly and adequately integrate all the issues and aspects relevant to the coupling/integration of the BPM and KM domains (*i.e.,* the knowledge, functional, organizational, behavioral, informational and intentional dimensions) for improving the management of crucial knowledge (*i.e.,* the identification, the sharing, the valorization and the exploitation of the knowledge that are necessary for the realization of SBP). This makes it possible to optimize the SBP modeling operation and reduces the cost of the capitalization operations of the crucial knowledge on which it is necessary to capitalize.

2 Scientific Problem and Motivation

2.1 Limitations of BPMN 2.0.2 in the Context of SBP Modeling

BPMN 2.0.2 [4] is considered the most widespread standard for BP modeling and the most suitable for SBP specification since it takes into account the different requirements of SBP modeling better than other BPM languages [2]. However, the generic concepts of this notation are insufficient to specify and cover perfectly and completely some relevant characteristics of SBP [2, 3, 10–13]:

- BPMN is not suitable for modeling the knowledge dimension, *i.e.,* the types of knowledge that are mobilized, generated and/or modified by each type of SBP activity (*e.g.,* the individual/collective aspect, the tacit/explicit aspect, the factual/procedural aspect of the knowledge) as well as the different sources of knowledge;
- BPMN is not suitable for modeling the different possibilities of knowledge conversion, *i.e.,* the dynamics of sharing, transferring and creating knowledge (and information sources of knowledge) within SBP activities;
- Limited representation capacity to explicitly distinguish individual actions from collective actions carried out collectively by individuals (forming a collective);
- Limited capacity to represent knowledge-intensive actions/activities;
- Limited ability to explicitly represent the roles of the different agentive entities that carry out the different types of SBP actions and that communicate, exchange and share knowledge (*e.g.,* collective tacit knowledge);
- Limited capacity to represent collaboration and (inter) human interactions aspects (between several agents);
- Limited ability to explicitly and separately represent the data (and their sources) and the information (and their sources) that are needed to carry out SBP/BP activities (and that are shared among different participants);
- Limited ability to explicitly and separately represent data flows, information flows, and knowledge flows between sources and among activities;
- Limited capacity to explicitly represent the different resources allowing to carry out the different SBP actions (*i.e.,* material resources, immaterial resources and human resources);
- Limited ability to perfectly and completely support the dynamic aspects of SBP modeling, i.e., the representation of highly flexible complex BPs that can be unstructured or semi-structured;
- Abandonment of the intentional aspect of SBP/BP modeling (e.g., the modeling of objectives and intentions). In contrast, in order to overcome the various shortcomings identified, the BPMN 2.0.2 specification provides an extension mechanism [4] to integrate and explicitly represent new SBP concepts and dimensions (not supported by the BPMN meta-model and notation) in order to improve the localization, identification, transfer, sharing, generation, valorization and exploitation of different knowledge types.

2.2   BPMN Extensibility in General

Adding new concepts and dimensions to an existing meta-model affects both the abstract syntax and the concrete syntax. It is therefore necessary to examine the extensibility of BPMN.

BPMN 2.0.2 Extension Mechanism and its Shortcomings. In the perspectives of extending the use cases of the BPMN 2.0.2 specification and enriching, in particular, the modeling of SBPs, the OMG [4] provides a built-in extension mechanism (based on the Meta Object Facility) that enables the definition and integration of additional domain-specific concepts and attributes and ensures the validity of the core BPMN elements. This extension mechanism is composed of the following generic extension elements: An Extension Definition specifies a named group of new attributes (and associations) which can be used by standard BPMN elements. It is not inevitably a new element, since it can also be intended as a single additional attribute of a BPMN element. An Extension Definition consists of several Extension Attribute Definitions which define particular attributes of new or original BPMN elements. Values of these Extension Attribute Definitions can be defined by the Extension Attribute Value class. Therefore, primitive types from the MOF can be used [15]. The element Extension binds and imports the entire Extension Definition and its attributes to a BPMN model definition. By doing so, all extension elements are accessible for existing BPMN elements [4]. Although the extension mechanism of BPMN provides relevant classes and relations for the extension of the meta-model, there are still some obscurities and syntactic inaccuracies of the extension mechanism which nevertheless cause confusions and uncertainties regarding its implementation [9]. For example, it does not define type structures for new attributes. Thus, it is not clear whether a BPMN extension generates a new meta-model version or constitutes a profile in the sense of UML profiles. Furthermore, the BPMN specification does not provide any methodological guidelines for the (standard) extension elements, for the simple and straightforward development of the envisaged extensions as well as to generate graphical notations for these elements. So, the comprehensibility, quality and exchangeability of the developed models are considerably hampered [13, 14].

3   Objectives of Our Approach

Anyway, most BPMN extensions considered in the literature are not rigorously designed. There seems to be a (semantic) gap between the definition of domain-specific requirements of the extension, their conceptualization and their implementation as a valid extended BPMN meta-model. This last aspect is successfully addressed by STROPPI ET AL. [8] and few extensions exploit its proclaimed transformation approach (e.g., [9–21]). However, the first phases of preparation and design of BPMN extensions are not always perfectly guided. Concretely, we note the absence of an in-depth analysis of the new domain-specific requirements (which must be satisfied by the extended BPMN notation) as well as a specification of a precise, common and consensual conceptualization of this extension domain (with rigorous and formal definitions of domain concepts) which is the basis of all subsequent transformation steps and which promotes better communication with domain experts. In addition, the step "Element Equivalence Check" ([9, 15]) is not explained in depth. In particular, the correspondence between domain concepts and BPMN meta-model concepts is not based on clear and rigorous semantic definitions of the concepts involved in the extension domain. However, a thorough and precise discussion on the semantic adequacy of the domain concepts with standard elements of BPMN is necessary to ensure and justify the real need for a BPMN extension and to determine which elements to adapt or reuse. We argue that further analysis and ex-planation of the conceptual modeling phase of an extension in the BPMN extension development process is needed for several reasons: (i) better description and understanding of domain knowledge through explanation of its requirements and concepts, (ii) validation of the choice of BPMN as the most adequate BPM language for the objective considered (which adequately satisfies these requirements), (iii) rigorous design and logical explanation of domain-specific extension elements through a detailed semantic comparison with standard BPMN elements, (iv) Methodical guidance for the whole extension process: from domain concepts (semi-formal, informal) to BPMN and BPEL concepts (formal, semi-formal), (v) Improvement of the understandability and reusability level.

In the perspective of fulfilling the previously stated shortcomings, improving the design and development process of valid BPMN extensions and thus enriching the BPMN 2.0.2 specification to perfectly support the new SBP modeling requirements, we propose in this article, to make two new contributions (conceptual and methodological) to the BPMN extensions development domain as well as to the DSR (Design Science Research) domain [5–7]:

1. Proposition of a generic, holistic and coherent method to support the implementation of valid, rigorous, well-defined and understandable BPMN 2.0 meta-model and notation extensions, which we call EM-BPMN + X (Methodology for the development of BPMN Plus Extensions). This new approach extends and consolidates the BPMN extension method of STROPPI et AL. [8] as well as the research work of [9, 14–16] (which are based on the work of STROPPI et AL.). Its objective consists in optimizing, on the one hand, the extension preparation phase, i.e., the domain analysis of the extension and the design of the CDME model, and, on the other hand, the extension meta-model definition phase (BPMN + X) (its abstract syntax and concrete syntax) in order to develop a valid, complete and accurate domain/context-specific extension of BPMN 2.0.2. The domain analysis considers the analysis of extension domain requirements, the design of core ontology and domain ontological conceptual patterns, as well as a better consideration of the mapping of extension concepts semantics with standard BPMN concepts.

2. Development of the new BPMN4SBP extension by applying the generic method "EM-BPMN + X" for the graphical specification of SBPs for the identification and management of crucial knowledge. The objective of BPMNSBP is twofold: (i) to represent and manage the BP/SBP of the KM domain (i.e., to improve the identification, sharing, enhancement and exploitation of knowledge) and (ii) to extend and enrich the BPMN 2.0.2 specification with new functionalities and new modeling requirements for SBPs (e.g., modeling the knowledge-intensity perspective of

organizational actions/activities, modeling collaborative interactions, modeling the different types/natures of knowledge, modeling highly dynamic flexible processes, etc. (Cf. Sect. 4). The aim is to extend and improve, on the one hand, the modeling of relevant aspects of SBP relating to the functional, organizational, informational and intentional dimensions, and on the other hand, to explicitly integrate the new knowledge dimension into the BPMN models. In other words, the new BPMN4SBP notation should perfectly support the modeling of the relevant SBP characteristics, i.e., the modeling of complex, flexible, highly dynamic, collaborative/interactive and information-intensive and crucial knowledge-intensive processes.

In the following, we first present the consolidated method that we propose to develop domain-specific BPMN extensions. Secondly, we detail its application to enrich the multi-dimensional modeling of SBPs.

Figure 1 outlines the consolidated method that we propose for the design and development of valid BPMN extensions (EM-BPMN + X) and its application for SBP modeling. With respect to the limited space of this paper, the EM-BPMN + X method cannot be presented.

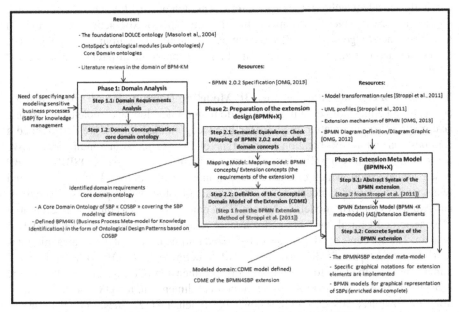

Fig. 1. EM-BPMN + X and its application for SBP

4 The EM-BPMN4SBP Method: An Extension of BPMN 2.0.2 for the Multi-dimensional Specification of SBP

In this section, we apply the methodological principles of the extension (BPMN + X) for the graphical specification of SBPs. Our BPMN Extension Methodology for SBP

Specification "EM-BPMN4SBP" extends the BPMN 2.0.2 meta-model and notation to perfectly support the modeling and visualization of specific requirements relating to the different SBP modeling dimensions (the functional, organizational, behavioral, informational, intentional and knowledge dimensions).

4.1 Phase 1: Analysis and Conceptualization of the SBP Modeling Domain

Step 1.1: Requirements Analysis for SBP Modeling (and for the BPMN4SBP Extension). An SBP involves many subjective and complex concepts. Taking into account, on the one hand, the recurrent elements in the analysis of the requirements of BPM-KM languages [2], and on the other hand, the new characteristics of SBP [2, 3], we have defined 14 specific requirements for SBP modeling that are related to the different dimensions of SBP (R1−R14): the functional dimension (R1−R4), the organizational dimension (R5), the knowledge dimension (R6−R8), the informational dimension (R9−R11), the behavioral dimension (R12, R13) and the intentional dimension (R14). These requirements address issues relevant to the intersection/coupling of BPM and KM (see [2, 3] for a detailed description). For example, the objective of BPMN4SBP is to extend and improve the modeling of the **organizational dimension** by considering and integrating explicitly and adequately: (i) the explicit representation of the different types of agentive entities that are capable of carrying out the different types of SBP actions and who hold and share knowledge (e.g., a collective, an expert, an informal group, an organization, an internal actor or an external actor), (ii) the modeling of the different roles of agents **[R5]**.

Step 1.2: Conceptualization of the SBP Modeling Domain. In order to deepen the concepts and dimensions defining the SBP domain for developing complete and expressive graphical representation models (for knowledge management), we first defined a rigorous conceptual specification for this type of BP, organized in a multi-perspective formal ontology, the Core Ontology of Sensitive Business Processes (COSBP). COSBP is semantically rich, which extends the top foundational ontology DOLCE[1] [23] and reuses and specializes concepts of «core» domain ontologies[2]. It specifies, formalizes, and explicates the SBP modeling domain. This ontology offers a consensual referential of generic and central concepts and semantic relationships relevant to the BPM-KM domain. The concepts of COSBP are categorized into six classes of ontological modules (OMs) relating to the six dimensions of SBP modeling, viz. the OM for the functional dimension [11], the OM for the organizational dimension (Cf. Fig. 2), the OM for the behavioral dimension, the OM for the intentional dimension, the OM for the informational dimension and the OM for the knowledge dimension [12]. These OMs provide sets of basic concepts to analyze static and dynamic aspects of SBPs, including their knowledge intensive activities, collective actions, knowledge conversion actions, interaction, collaboration, information and knowledge sharing, and intentional aspects.

For example, to account for the organizational aspects of the SBP (Cf. Fig. 2), we reused generic concepts (and semantic relations) which are defined in the following

---

[1] http://www.loa-cnr.it/DOLCE.html.

[2] These ontological modules are accessible online: http://home.mis.u-picardie.fr/~site-ic/site/spip.php?article53.

ontological modules: Agentive Entity-OS, Organization-OS, Particpation-role-OS (see http://home.mis.u-picardie.fr/~site-ic/site/spip.php?article53).

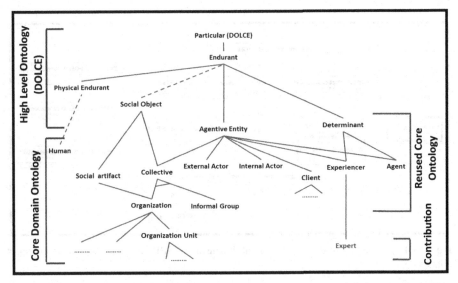

Fig. 2. Ontological module for the intentional dimension of SBP modeling. extension of the ontological module «Participant-role-OS».

This reference ontology will be used to define a generic meta-model for specifying SBPs, called "BPM4KI: Business Process Meta-model for Knowledge Identification" [1, 2][3]. The goal is to obtain an enriched consensus modeling covering all generic concepts, semantic relationships and properties needed for the exploitation of SBPs, known as core modeling [2]. The concepts of BPM4KI are categorized into six *Ontological Design Patterns (ODPs)* [50] representing the six aspects of SBP modeling. The design of these ODPs is based on the reuse of the different ontological modules of COSBP. For example, Fig. 3 represent the ODP relating to the organizational dimension of SBP modeling. The ODP-O includes all the concepts and semantic relations of SBP already defined in the ontological module of COSBP relating to this dimension (Cf. Fig. 2), in addition to the inter-aspect relationships (the different concepts are recognizable by their thicker borders). The new extended SBP concepts defined in COSBP are marked in blue.

4.2 Phase 2: Preparation of the BPMN4SBP Extension Design

The objective of this phase is to establish a semantic comparison between the new SBP domain concepts and the standard BPMN elements, in order to express the semantics of

---

[3] https://www.dropbox.com/s/9ipgzx8oertwg65/An%20extract%20of%20the%20BPM4KI%20meta-model%20for%20modeling%20SBPs.pdf?dl=0. The core concepts of BPM4KI are marked in grey. The new extended SBP concepts (relating to each dimension) defined in COSBP are marked in blue.

the extension elements and define the conceptual domain model of BPMN4SBP. This is allowing to vigorously and adequately define the (valid) BPMN4SBP meta-model by applying model transformation rules.

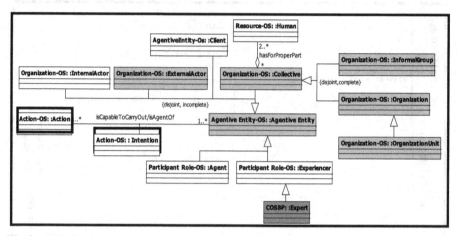

Fig. 3. ODP-O relating to the organizational dimension of SBP modeling (with its inter-aspect relationships)

Step 2.1. Semantic Equivalence Check: Correspondence Between BPM4KI Concepts and BPMN 2.0.2 Concepts. In accordance with the BPM4KI meta-model, each (ontological) concept of SBP is examined with regard to its semantic equivalence (mapping) to the standard element(s) of BPMN 2.0. 2, based, on the one hand, on the rigorous and formal definitions of SBP concepts offered by the COSBP ontology and, on the other hand, on detailed descriptions of the standard element defined in the BPMN 2.0.2 specification documentation [4]. At the end of this equivalence verification study, a classification as a «BPMN Concept» or as an «Extension Concept» is considered for each concept. With respect to the limited space of this paper, the conducted equivalence check cannot be presented.

Step 2.2. Definition of the Conceptual Domain Model of the Extension (CDME) of BPMN4SBP. Based on the equivalence check, we defined the CDME model of the BPMN4SBP extension comprising basic BPMN elements as well as extension elements, properties, and their semantic relationships with BPMN classes (using a set of two colors). Fig. 4 illustrates an excerpt of class diagrams related to the CDME model created. This model is the result of the integration of the ODP-O of BPM4KI on certain classes of the BPMN 2.0.2 meta-model. Two types of stereotypes are specified for the different classes of the CDME model. We distinguish the stereotyped classes «Extension Concepts» indicating the standard elements of BPMN (e.g., *Process, Participant, Resource Role, Human Performer*, etc.). These extended classes are marked in gray for better visual differentiation. While stereotyped classes like «Extension Concepts» specify new extension elements (e.g., `Agentive Entity`, `Organization,Collective`, `Expert`, `External Actor`, etc.).

4.3 Phase 3: The BPMN4SBP Meta-model: Abstract Syntax and Concrete Syntax

The extended BPMN4SBP meta-model is derived and designed from the CDME model designed in the previous step that adequately integrates the new key concepts of SBP relating to the different modeling dimensions. Due to the increased number of extension elements and the large extent of the resulting extended BPMN meta-model, we present in Fig. 5 an excerpt illustrating the BPMN4SBP meta-model (in accordance with CDME (Fig. 4)). The semantics and abstract syntax of the BPMN4SBP extension are based on the BPMN 2.0.2 extension mechanism specification [4] and the adaptation of the profile mechanism [9, 23].

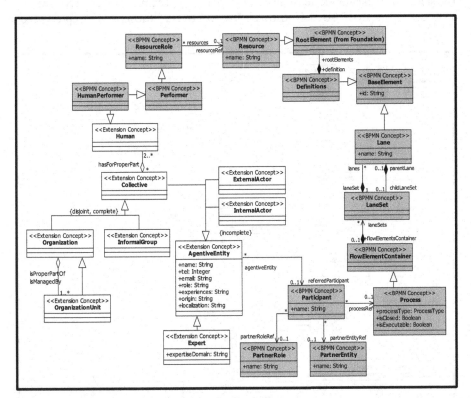

Fig. 4. The CDME model of the BPMN4SBP extension (an extract - CDME of the extension of the organizational dimension of SBP)

Moreover, for the design of the BPMN4SBP meta-model, our approach consists in adopting and applying the fifteen model transformation rules defined in [8] allowing the passage of the CDME model from our extension to a valid BPMN4SBP extension profile, by analyzing the different properties and the different generalization relationships of the CDME classes (Cf. Fig. 4). The application of each rule is presented in detail in [8]. These different rules cover all possible configurations of CDME (e.g., application of additional properties to BPMN meta-classes, definition of new concepts, definition of new meta-class specifications) allowing to create and represent in a rigorous way the BPMN4SBP elements from the *Extension Concepts* defined in the underlying CDME model, by strictly applying the extension mechanism of the BPMN 2.0.2 specification and by adapting the BPMN + X profile mechanism (Cf. Fig. 5). As a UML profile, the BPMN4SBP meta-model consists of several stereotypes: *BPMN Element, Extension Element, Extension Definition, Extension Relationship* and *Extension Enum* [8] (Cf. Fig. 4). The stereotyped classes « BPMNElement» represent the standard elements defined in the BPMN 2.0.2 metamodel (marked in gray). The stereotyped classes « ExtensionDefinition» (e.g.,AgentiveEntity,Human,Collective,Organization) group the attributes and elements that can be associated with the predefined elements of BPMN. The stereotyped classes «ExtensionElement» (e.g., TacitKnowledge, IndividualKnowledge,CollectiveKnowledge,ExternalKnowledge) represent new

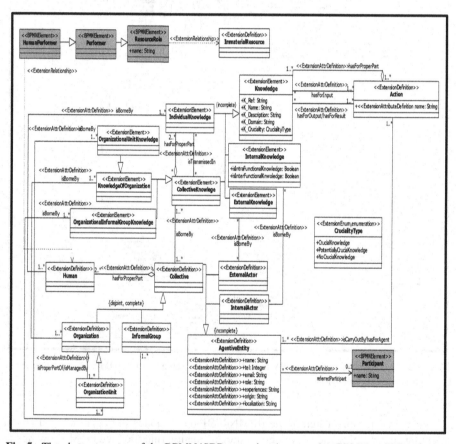

Fig. 5. The abstract syntax of the BPMN4SBP extension (an extract – BPMN + SBP organizational dimension)

types of SBP specific elements that are created independently from any BPMN element. In addition, stereotypical dependencies « ExtensionRelationship» document the BPMN element to be extended by an ExtensionDefinition.

Besides the abstract syntax of the BPMN extension, it is important to provide a standardized definition of the graphical notations (according to BPMN specification guidelines) in order to facilitate the exchangeability of the models and the integration of the proposed extension into BPMN tools. Thus, this step consists of (systematically) defining the concrete syntax of the new elements of the BPMN + X extension based on the OMG Diagram Graphics (DG) package of the Diagram Definition (DD) standard specification [24] (which should be instantiated to BPMN DG. In Fig. 6, an extract of the concrete syntax with the extension of graphical notation is presented. Furthermore, the new BPMN4SBP extension is deployed in practice on real cases in order to evaluate and approve its usefulness and added values and to subsequently improve it. A case study was conducted in a real practical scenario in the healthcare domain in the context of the Association of Protection of the Motor-disabled people of Sfax-Tunisia. We are interested, particularly, in the early care of the disabled children with cerebral palsy. With respect to the limited space of this paper, the practical applicability of the BPMN4SBP extension is not demonstrated by realized SBP graphical representation models in this paper. The research work of [2] presented a detailed description of this case study as well as SBP model examples using the BPMN4SBP Modeler Tool.

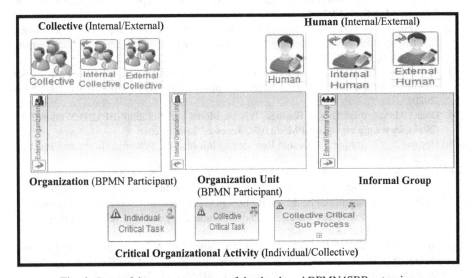

Fig. 6. Parts of the concrete syntax of the developed BPMN4SBP extension.

5 Conclusion and Perspectives

The contributions in this research article provide solutions to the problem of developing valid (domain-specific) BPMN extensions. In particular, these contributions propose a conceptual solution for the specification of SBPs using the extended BPMN notation (BPMN4SBP). Our work is the first approach that systematically adapts the BPMN standard to SBP modeling in the KM domain, which explicitly addresses the integration and representation of the knowledge dimension and all other aspects relevant at the coupling/intersection of BPM-KM in the BPMN 2.0.2 meta-model and notation. The evolved extension allows to enrich and improve, on the one hand, the functional, organizational, behavioral and informational dimensions of the BPMN 2.0.2 specification, and on the other hand, to integrate the new aspects relating to the knowledge dimension as well as the intentional dimension of SBP. BPMN4SBP was designed in accordance with the DSR paradigm based on a set SBP modeling requirements identified and previous versions ([1, 10–14] in order to ensure domain adequacy (the semantics) and the design of a valid and consistent BPMN4SBP meta-model (the syntax). In brief, the BPMN4SBP extension provides a solid foundation for both semi-formal modeling of SBPs and for deriving executable workflow models in BPEL due to its conformance to the BPMN specification. Thus, this extension can be applied by domain experts or even customized/adapted by model engineers.

References

1. Ben Hassen, M., Turki, M., Gargouri, F.: Comparative analysis of contemporary modeling languages based on BPM4KI meta-model for sensitive business processes representation. Int. J. Enterpr. Inf. Syst. **14**(3), 41–78 (2018)
2. Ben Hassen, M., Turki, M., Gargouri, F.: A Multicriteria evaluation approach for selecting a sensitive business process modeling language for knowledge management. J. Data Semant. (JODS), **8**(3), 157–202 (2019)
3. Ben Hassen, M., Turki, M. and Gargouri, F.: Analyse conceptuelle des processus métier sensibles. 38ème édition de la manifestation scientifique INFORSID, Dijon, France, pp. 53–68 (2020)
4. Object Management Group. Business Process Model and Notation (BPMN) Version 2.0.2 (2013) www.omg.org/spec/BPMN/2.0.2/. Accessed 22 Nov 2018
5. Hevner, A., Chatterjee, S.: Design Research in Information Systems: Theory and Practice, p. 320. Springer, New York (2010)
6. Peffers, K., Tuunanen, T., Rothenberger, M.A., Chatterjee, S.: A design science research methodology for information systems research. J. Manag. Inf. Syst. **24**, 45–77 (2008)
7. Peffers, K., Tuunanen, and Niehaves, B.: Design science research genres: introduction to the special issue on exemplars and criteria and applicable design science research. Europ. J. Inf. Syst. **27**(2), 129 (2018)
8. Stroppi, L.J.R., Chiotti, O., Villarreal, P.D.: Extending BPMN 2.0: method and tool support. In: Dijkman, R., Hofstetter, J., Koehler, J. (eds.) BPMN 2011. LNBIP, vol. 95, pp. 59–73. Springer, Heidelberg (2011). https://doi.org/10.1007/978-3-642-25160-3_5
9. Braun, R., Schlieter, H., Burwitz, M., Esswein, W.: Extending a business process modeling language for domain-specific adaptation in healthcare. In: Thomas. O., Osnabrück, S., (Hrsg.): Proceedings der 12. Internationalen Tagung Wirtschaftsinformatik (WI 2015), pp. 468–481 (2015)
10. Ben Hassen, M., Turki, M., Gargouri, F.: Modeling dynamic aspects of sensitive business processes for knowledge localization. In Proceedings of the 21st International Conference on Knowledge Based and Intelligent Information and Engineering Systems (KES2017), Marseille, France. Procedia Computer Science, vol. 112, pp. 731–740. Elsevier (2017)

11. Ben Hassen, M., Turki, M., Gargouri, F.: Extending sensitive business process modeling with functional dimension for knowledge identification. In: Proceedings of the 14th International Conference on e-Business (ICE-B 2017), Madrid, Spain. In: Proceedings of the 14th International Joint Conference on e-Business and Telecommunications (ICETE 2017), vol. 2, pp. 38–51 (2017)

12. Ben Hassen, M., Turki, M., Gargouri, F.: Using core ontologies for extending sensitive business process modeling with the knowledge perspective. In: Proceedings of the Fifth European Conference on the Engineering of Computer-Based Systems (ECBS'2017), Larnaca, Cyprus, p. 2. ACM (2017)

13. Ben Hassen, M., Turki, M., Gargouri, F.: BPMN4KM: design and implementation of a BPMN extension for modeling the knowledge perspective of sensitive business processes. J. Procedia Comput. Sci. **121**, 1119–1134 (2017)

14. Braun, R., Schlieter, H.: Requirements-based development of BPMN extensions: the case of clinical pathways. In: IEEE 1st International Workshop on the Interrelations between Requirements Engineering and Business Process Management, pp. 39–44 (2014)

15. Braun, R., Schlieter, H., Burwitz, M., Esswein, W.: BPMN4CP: design and implementation of a BPMN extension for clinical pathways. In: IEEE International Conference on Bioinformatics and Biomedicine, pp. 9–16 (2014)

16. Braun, R., Esswein, W.: Towards multi-perspective modeling with BPMN. In: Aveiro, D., Pergl, R., Valenta, M. (eds.) EEWC 2015. LNBIP, vol. 211, pp. 67–81. Springer, Cham (2015). https://doi.org/10.1007/978-3-319-19297-0_5

17. Chergui, M., Benslimane, S.M.: Towards a BPMN security extension for the visualization of cyber security requirements. Int. J. Technol. Diffus. (IJTD) **11**(2), 1–17 (2020)

18. Zarour, K., Benmerzoug, D., Guermouche, N., Drira, K.: A BPMN extension for business process outsourcing to the cloud. In: Rocha, Á., Adeli, H., Reis, L., Costanzo, S. (eds.) New Knowledge in Information Systems and Technologies. WorldCIST'19 2019. Advances in Intelligent Systems and Computing, vol. 930, pp. 833-843. Springer, Cham (2019).https://doi.org/10.1007/978-3-030-16181-1_78

19. Abouzid, I., Saidi, R.: Proposal of BPMN extensions for modelling manufacturing processes. In: Proceedings of the 5th International Conference on Optimization and Applications, pp. 1–6 (2019)

20. Intrigila, B., Della Penna, G., D'Ambrogio, A.: A lightweight BPMN extension for business process-oriented requirements engineering. Computers **10**, 171 (2021)

21. Masolo, C., et al.: The WonderWeb Library of Foundational Ontologies and the DOLCE ontology. WonderWeb Deliverable D18, Final Report (version 1.0, 31–12–2003) (2003)

22. Object Management Group. Meta Object Facility (MOF), Version 2.4.2. (2014). http://www.omg.org/spec/MOF/

23. Object Management Group. Diagram Definition (DD), Version 1.0. (2012). http://www.omg.org/spec/DD/1.0/PDF/

Attention-based Learning for Multiple Relation Patterns in Knowledge Graph Embedding

Tengwei Song[ID] and Jie Luo[✉][ID]

State Key Laboratory of Software Development Environment,
School of Computer Science and Engineering, Beihang University, Beijing, China
{songtengwei,luojie}@buaa.edu.cn

Abstract. Relations in knowledge graphs often exhibit multiple relation patterns. Various knowledge graph embedding methods have been proposed to modelling properties in relation patterns. However, relations with a certain relation pattern actually only account for a small proportion in the knowledge graph. Relations with no explicit relation patterns also show complicated properties which is rarely studied. To this end, we argue that a property of a relation should either be *global* or be *partial*, and propose an **A**ttention-based **L**earning framework for **M**ulti-relation **P**atterns (ALMP) for expressing complex properties of relations. ALMP adopts a set of affine transformations to express corresponding global relation properties. Furthermore, ALMP utilizes a module of attention mechanism to integrate the representations. Experimental results show that ALMP outperforms baseline models on the link prediction task.

Keywords: Knowledge graph · Representation learning · Attention

1 Introduction

In recent years, knowledge graphs (KG), a data structure depicting the correlation of real word entities, has enhanced reasoning capability and interpretability of deep learning methods by combining knowledge and intelligence. Therefore, learning the representation of knowledge graphs in vector space for downstream deep learning systems becomes a task that attracts much attention.

The most important feature that distinguishes knowledge graphs from general graphs is that relations between entities have specific properties, which are regarded as *relation pattern* in some KG embedding methods (e.g. symmetry, transitivity, etc.). Furthermore, for capturing these properties, existing methods try to model the relation as a certain mapping approach between the head and tail entities. For example, RotatE [16] defines each relation as a rotation from the head entity to the tail entity to modeling and inferring relation patterns like symmetry/asymmetry, inversion, and composition. Such modeling principle is

G. Memmi et al. (Eds.): KSEM 2022, LNAI 13368, pp. 658–670, 2022.
https://doi.org/10.1007/978-3-031-10983-6_50

consistent with the idea of *relational inductive biases*, which enables relational reasoning by imposing constraints on the relations as well as the interactions among entities.

The relation with a certain relation pattern actually refers to that all instances related to the relation satisfy the rule form of the relation pattern. Here we use *global relation property* to refer to such pattern of relations. On the other hand, in most KGs, the amount of relations with no explicit relation patterns is far larger than relations with a certain pattern. According to the schema of YAGO3 [11] , there are 91.9% of relations with undefined relation patterns[1]. In fact, these relations may also follow some relation patterns on some observed facts but violate the patterns on other/unobserved facts. It means that, for a relation with no relation property, it may also shows several relation patterns simultaneously on its different instances. We use *partial relation property* to refer to such properties that hold over some subsets of entities but not all. Therefore, a pertinent question for KG embedding methods is: can we learn an integrated representation which combines various multiple relation properties so that it could better express the complicated interactions between entities?

To this end, we propose a novel framework based on KG embedding with affine transformations, namely the **A**ttention-based **L**earning for **M**ultiple relation **P**atterns (ALMP). ALMP is inspired by various relational inductive biases imposed by the KG embedding models according to different relation patterns. We systematically combine the geometric transformations with the properties of relation patterns from the perspective of relational inductive biases. Then, we learn integrated KG representation utilizing attention mechanism to incorporate features of various relation properties. Finally, we show experimental results on the link prediction task over public benchmarks, where ALMP showed better performance comparing to the baseline methods with single relational inductive biases.

2 Related Work

We categorize KG embedding models into the following different types according to the approaches they choose to utilize relational inductive biases.

Translation as Relational Inductive Bias. KG embedding models of this type implicitly models the relation as a vector addition from a head entity to a tail entity. The well-known series of models in KG embedding area are the translation-based models represented by TransE [5]. TransE proposed a distance-based scoring function, which assumes the added embedding of subject entity h and relation r should be close to the embedding of object entity t. To solve the 1-To-N problem in TransE, variants of translational architectures have been developed. TransH [22] projects entities and relations into a relation-specific hyperplanes, which enables different projections of an entity in different relations. TransR [23] introduces relation-specific spaces, which builds entity and relation embeddings in different spaces separately. A recent model BoxE [1],

---

[1] https://github.com/yago-naga/yago3/tree/master/schema.

embeds entities as points, and relations as a set of boxes, for yielding a model that could express multiple relation patterns.

Linear Mapping as Relational Inductive Biases. KG embedding models of this type modeling the relations as linear mappings from head entities to tail. Dist-Mult [2] model the relation as a bilinear diagonal matrix between head and tail entities for multiple relational representation learning. To expand Euclidean space, ComplEx [17] firstly introduces complex vector space which can capture both symmetric and asymmetric relations. Similarly, RotatE [16] models in complex space and can capture additional inversion and composition patterns by introducing rotational Hadamard product. Extending the embedding from complex space to quaternary space, QuatE [24] use a quaternion inner product and gains more expressive semantic learning capability. Tucker [3] utilize Tucker decomposition of the binary tensor representation of triples. Recently, PairRE [7] proposed a method to model each relation with paired vectors to project the corresponding head and tail entities for better handle multiple relation patterns. To remedy the drawback that previous models cannot model the transitive relation pattern, Rot-Pro [14] imposes projection on both source and target entities for expressing transitivity, and utilize a rotation operation as RotatE to underpin other relation patterns.

Attention Mechanism as Relational Inductive Biases. KBGAT [13] is an attention-based embedding model that captures both entity and relation features of neighborhoods of any given entities. The latest model GAATs [21] integrates an attenuated attention mechanism to assign different weight in different relation path and acquire the information from the neighborhoods so that entities and relations can be learned in any neighbors. Beyond the scope of graph neural network, ATTH [6] recently proposes a low-dimensional hyperbolic knowledge graph embedding method to capture tree-like structures and hence modeling hierarchy data. It further conducts attention-based transformations of reflection and rotation for multiple relation patterns, which is similar to our proposal. The main difference between ATTH and our method is that ATTH focused on the hyperbolic embedding for hierarchical data, while we emphasize on integrating multiple transformations for modeling complex interactions among different relation patterns.

3   Multiple Relation Property Problem

Relation patterns play important role in KG completion because missing/unobserved facts can be inferred based on these patterns. Existing methods dedicate a lot to model such patterns. A general methods is regarding relations as translation or linear transformations from head entity to tail entity. We list the five common relation patterns mentioned on previous work in Table 1, and the corresponding transformations form that could model these patterns.

However, Battaglia et al. have pointed out that, ideally, inductive biases both improve the search for solutions as well as finding solutions that generalize in

Table 1. Rule form of relation patterns and the attributes of their corresponding mapping matrix, where LT form represents linear transformation form [25] and TT represents translation transformation.

Relation pattern	Rule form	LT form	TT form
Symmetry	$r(x,y) \Rightarrow r(y,x)$	$\mathbf{M}_r\mathbf{M}_r = \mathbf{I}$	$\mathbf{r} + \mathbf{r} = 0$
Asymmetry	$r(x,y) \Rightarrow \neg r(y,x)$	$\mathbf{M}_r\mathbf{M}_r \neq \mathbf{I}$	$\mathbf{r} + \mathbf{r} \neq 0$
Inversion	$r_2(x,y) \Rightarrow r_1(y,x)$	$\mathbf{M}_{r_1}\mathbf{M}_{r_2} = \mathbf{I}$	$\mathbf{r}_1 + \mathbf{r}_2 = 0$
Composition	$r_2(x,y) \wedge r_3(y,z) \Rightarrow r_1(x,z)$	$\mathbf{M}_{r_2}\mathbf{M}_{r_3} = \mathbf{M}_{r_1}$	$\mathbf{r}_1 + \mathbf{r}_2 = \mathbf{r}_3$
Transitivity	$r(x,y) \wedge r(y,z) \Rightarrow r(x,z)$	$\mathbf{M}_r^n = \mathbf{M}_r$	$n\mathbf{r} = \mathbf{r}$

a desirable way, however, when the introduced inductive biases are too strong, it tends to lead to sub-optimal performance [4]. Similarly, as mentioned above, most relations in KGs do not exhibit a global pattern, and hence these KG embedding methods may tend to over fit for a certain relation pattern since the model forces all relations to follow a certain transformation.

Therefore, we seek to explore the multiple relation property problem. We observed that the multiple relation property problem can be divided into two circumstances:

(1) Multiple *global relation properties* (i.e. relation patterns) can exhibit in a relation simultaneously. For example, relation *isLocatedIn* in YAGO3-10 describes the relations of geographical locations. Obviously, it shows global transitive as well as asymmetric property among all its instances.

(2) Relations with no explicit relation pattern may also show one/multiple *partial relation properties* over some subsets of entities. For example, relation *isConnectedTo* in YAGO3 describes the connectivity between different airports. It exhibits partial symmetry or transitivity pattern on certain subsets airports.

Current models with so-called fully expressiveness mainly focus on modeling single relation pattern. For example, in Rot-Pro [14], the solution space of modeling transitivity is that when the relational rotation phase is $2n\pi$ while that of modeling symmetric is that when the relational rotation phase is $n\pi$. Therefore, it theoretically could not modeling relations with both transitivity and asymmetric pattern like *isLocatedIn*.

Therefore, we introduce a generic framework ALMP to integrate the multiple representations of various relation properties.

4   Attention-based Learning for Multiple Relation Patterns

4.1   Parameterization

We parameterize the the embedding of entity and relation in 2D vector space and denote them by $\mathbf{e}$ and $\mathbf{e}_r$ respectively. The embedding dimension is an even

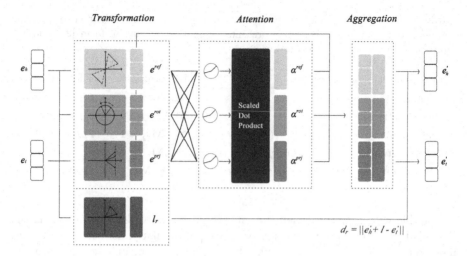

Fig. 1. The structure of the ALMP framework. The transformation module obtains the entity embedding via three linear transformation as well as the translation. Then the attention module learns the attention weight assigned to each element of each transformed embedding. Finally, the aggregation module obtains the final embedding by integrating the attention with the corresponding embeddings.

number d, then the set of parameters $\Theta := \{\Theta_e, \Theta_r\}$.

$$\Theta_e := \begin{bmatrix} \mathbf{e}_i^x \\ \mathbf{e}_j^y \end{bmatrix}, (i \in \{1, ..., \frac{d}{2}\}, j = i + \frac{d}{2}), \tag{1}$$

where e_i^x and e_j^y are the corresponding components on each dimension of the x and y axis.

The relation parameterization is composed of the following components:

$$\Theta_r := \begin{cases} \Theta_{r,i}^{\text{ref}} = diag\left(T_{r,i}^{\text{ref}}(\theta_{r_1})\right), \\ \Theta_{r,i}^{\text{rot}} = diag\left(T_{r,i}^{\text{rot}}(\theta_{r_2})\right), \\ \Theta_{r,i}^{\text{prj}} = diag\left(T_{r,i}^{\text{prj}}(\theta_{r_3}, a_r, b_r)\right), \\ \Theta_{r,i}^l = l_{r,i}, (i \in \{1, ..., \frac{d}{2}\}) \end{cases} \tag{2}$$

where $\Theta_{r,i}^{\text{ref}}, \Theta_{r,i}^{\text{rot}}$, and $\Theta_{r,i}^{\text{prj}}$ are the geometric-specific parameters on each dimension i, and $T_{r,i}^{\text{ref}}(\theta_{r_1}), T_{r,i}^{\text{rot}}(\theta_{r_2})$, and $T_{r,i}^{\text{prj}}(\theta_{r_3}, a_r, b_r)$ are the 2D matrix form of each geometric transformation. We will illustrate the geometric details in the next section. Meanwhile, in the rest of paper, we will omit the dimensional index i in vectors for simplicity.

4.2   Core Modules

The general structure of the ALMP framework is illustrated in Fig. 1, which contains the following core modules.

Transformation Module. We uniformly taking relations as four representative affine transformations, which are translation, reflection, rotation, for capturing various partial properties in relations. The reason for taking relations as affine transformations is that they could naturally express geometric operations and fit the different partial properties of relations. The four transformations and their corresponding properties that they could capture are illustrated in the following items:

– **Reflection**: An informal description of reflection in KG embedding is that: the head entity will return to itself after transforming twice. Therefore, it could naturally represent *symmetric* relation pattern geometrically[2]. According to the linear algebra theorem [20], the corresponding 2D matrix form of reflection in Eq. 2 is as follows:

$$T_r^{\text{ref}}(\theta_{r_1}) = \begin{bmatrix} \cos\theta_{r_1} & \sin\theta_{r_1} \\ -\sin\theta_{r_1} & \cos\theta_{r_1} \end{bmatrix} \tag{3}$$

– **Rotation**: Regarding relations as rotations from head entities to tail entities could naturally model *inverse, asymmetry* and *composition* patterns since the relation with such patterns involve the matching with other relations. RotatE [16] utilize the relational rotation in complex space, which is analogous with 2D euclidean space. The matrix form of rotation in Eq. 2 is:

$$T_r^{\text{rot}}(\theta_{r_2}) = \begin{bmatrix} \cos\theta_{r_2} & -\sin\theta_{r_2} \\ \sin\theta_{r_2} & \cos\theta_{r_2} \end{bmatrix} \tag{4}$$

– **Projection**: Projection in vector space is equivalent to the idempotent transformation, which could express the *transitivity* relation pattern. However, conducting projection on a vector will cause the loss of dimensional information. Therefore, models such as Rot-Pro [14] expressed projection in the form of similarity of idempotent transformation. According to Rot-Pro, the matrix form of projection in Eq. 2 is defined as:

$$T_r^{\text{prj}}(\theta_{r_3}, a_r, b_r) = S_r^{-1}(\theta_{r_3}) \begin{bmatrix} a_r & 0 \\ 0 & b_r \end{bmatrix} S_r(\theta_{r_3}), \tag{5}$$

where $S_r(\theta_{r_3})$ is an invertible matrix with parameter θ_{r_3}, and $a_r, b_r \in \{0, 1\}$.
– **Translation**: The corresponding geometric operation of translation in vector space is the addition of vector (l_r in Eq. 2). Translation could model relation patterns such as *asymmetry, inversion,* and *composition*.

The initial embeddings of the head and tail entity h, t are denoted by $\mathbf{e}_h, \mathbf{e}_t$, which are obtained via a shallow encoder[3]. Then $\mathbf{e}_h$ and $\mathbf{e}_t$ are simultaneously

---

[2] Note that relational rotation can model symmetric pattern only when the relational rotation phase is $n\pi$, ($n = 0, 1, 2, \ldots$). While reflection is more general and straightforward for modeling symmetric pattern.

[3] A shallow encoder in KG embedding can be viewed as a lookup function that finds the hidden representation corresponding to an entity or a relation given its index [9].

transformed by three types of linear transformations, which represents reflection, rotation, and projection respectively.

Theoretically, each transformation is prone to learn independently the corresponding relation patterns which fit itself. We use the form:

$$\mathbf{e}_h^{\text{ref}} = T_r^{\text{ref}}(\mathbf{e}_h), \mathbf{e}_h^{\text{rot}} = T_r^{\text{rot}}(\mathbf{e}_h), \mathbf{e}_h^{\text{prj}} = T_r^{\text{prj}}(\mathbf{e}_h) \tag{6}$$

$$\mathbf{e}_t^{\text{ref}} = \mathbf{e}_t, \mathbf{e}_t^{\text{rot}} = \mathbf{e}_t, \mathbf{e}_t^{\text{prj}} = T_r^{\text{prj}}(\mathbf{e}_t) \tag{7}$$

to denote the transformed embeddings of $\mathbf{e}_h$ and $\mathbf{e}_t$ after reflection, rotation and projection. Note that due to the principle of transitivity modeling, the projection operation should be conducted simultaneously on both head and tail entities.

Attention Module. For integrating the expressiveness of the three embeddings aforementioned, it is natural to utilize attention mechanism to focus on specific transformation that fits the relation pattern [6]. Here we employ an element-wise attention, which learns the attention weights on each dimension, since we assume that each dimension of a well-learned representation is a disentangled factor and should be assigned with different attention weight from different relation patterns. The attention weight can be obtained based on the following equation.

$$[\alpha^{\text{ref}}; \alpha^{\text{rot}}; \alpha^{\text{prj}}] = \sigma(\mathbf{W}_r \cdot [\mathbf{e}^{\text{ref}}; \mathbf{e}^{\text{rot}}; \mathbf{e}^{\text{prj}}]), \tag{8}$$

where $\mathbf{W}_r \in \mathbb{R}^d$ is a trainable vector; $[\cdot; \cdot]$ denotes the concatenation operation; The vector α^{ref}, α^{rot}, and $\alpha^{\text{prj}} \in \mathbb{R}^d$, and each α_i^ν scores how much the i-th component of the embedding is related to the corresponding transformation ($\nu \in \{\text{ref}, \text{rot}, \text{prj}\}$); and σ refers to an non-linear activation function such as softmax.

Aggregation Module. Based on various linear transformation and the attention mechanism, we have obtained the three transformed embeddings along with their corresponding element-wise attention weights. To integrate them together, multiple aggregating methods could be considered as long as it is permutation invariant (e.g. summation or average over $\{\text{ref}, \text{rot}, \text{prj}\}$). The general form of the aggregation can be defined as follows:

$$\mathbf{e}' = agg(\alpha^\nu \odot \mathbf{e}^\nu), \tag{9}$$

where $\nu \in \{\text{ref}, \text{rot}, \text{prj}\}$ and $\odot$ denotes the Hadamard product.

4.3   Scoring Function

For each triple (h, r, t), the distance function of the ALMP model is defined as the following form:

$$d_r(\mathbf{e}_h, \mathbf{e}_t) = \|agg(\alpha^\nu \odot \mathbf{e}_h^\nu) + l_r - agg(\alpha^\nu \odot \mathbf{e}_t^\nu)\|, \tag{10}$$

where l_r is a vector in $\mathbb{R}^d$ to integrate translation transformation for relation r. The final scoring function is defined as:

$$f_r(\mathbf{e}_h, \mathbf{e}_t) = -d_r(\mathbf{e}_h, \mathbf{e}_t) + b_h + b_t, \tag{11}$$

where b_h and b_t are the head and tail entity biases that act as margins in the scoring function [6].

5   Experiment

5.1   Datasets

We evaluate our method on three well-known benchmarks, which are FB15k-237 [19], WN18RR [18], and YAGO3-10 [11].

FB15k-237 [19] is a modified version of FB15k extracted from Freebase [8], which excludes inverse relations to resolve a flaw with FB15k [18]. The main relation patterns in FB15k-237 are asymmetry and composition.

WN18RR [18] is a subset of WN18 [5] from WordNet [12], which retains most of the symmetric, asymmetric and compositional relations while removing the inversion relations.

YAGO3-10 is a subset of YAGO [15], a dataset which integrates vocabulary definitions of WordNet with classification system of Wikipedia.

5.2   Experimental Settings

Training Details. During optimization procedure, we additionally adopted the following techniques for obtaining better performance. First, when preprocessing datasets, we follow the data augmentation protocol in [10] by using reciprocal relations. Second, we utilized nuclear p-Norm regularization method proposed by [10]. The reported result is the average result after three runnings.

Evaluation Protocol. We evaluate the ALMP and baseline models on two widely used evaluation metrics: mean reciprocal rank (MRR), and top-k Hit Ratio (Hit@k). For each valid triples (h, r, t) in the test set, we replace either h or t with every other entities in the dataset to create corrupted triples in the link prediction task. Following previous work [5,13,18], all the models are evaluated in a *filtered* setting, i.e., corrupt triples that appear in training, validation, or test sets are removed during ranking. The valid triple and filtered corrupted triples are ranked in ascending order based on their prediction scores. Higher MRR or Hit@k indicate better performance.

Model Setting. We simply denote the model with the classic ALMP framework as the ALMP model. The attention module of ALMP adopts an element-wise scaled dot-product attention, which is similar to [6]. The aggregation module of ALMP adopts a simple Hadamard product and a summation over all dimensions.

Table 2. Link prediction results on FB15k-237, WN18RR and YAGO3-10. Results of models with [†] are taken from [16]. The result of ATTE is reproduced by us with suggested hyper-parameters. Other results are taken from the original paper of corresponding model.

	FB15k-237				WN18RR				YAGO3-10			
	MRR	Hit@1	Hit@3	Hit@10	MRR	Hit@1	Hit@3	Hit@10	MRR	Hit@1	Hit@3	Hit@10
TransE [†]	.294	–	–	.465	.226	–	–	.501	–	–	–	–
ComplEx [†]	.247	.158	.275	.428	.44	.41	.46	.51	.36	.26	.40	.55
RotatE [†]	.338	.241	.375	.533	.476	.428	.492	.571	.495	.402	.550	.670
Rot-Pro	.344	.246	.383	.540	.457	.397	.482	.577	.542	.443	.596	.699
ATTE	.351	.255	.386	.543	.489	.443	.504	.577	.525	.440	.574	.680
BoxE	.337	.238	.347	.538	.451	.400	.472	.541	.560	.484	.608	.691
TuckER	.358	.266	.394	.544	.470	.443	.482	.526	–	–	–	–
PairRE	.351	.256	.387	.544	–	–	–	–	–	–	–	–
DLMP	.348	.253	.384	.543	.498	.451	.516	.589	.539	.451	.604	.696
ALMP⁻	.347	.250	.386	.542	.454	.399	.473	.577	.515	.439	.558	.656
ALMP*	.353	.257	.390	.548	.494	.448	.511	.585	.542	.462	.586	.688
ALMP	.355	.260	.319	.548	.488	.439	.506	.586	.566	.489	.612	.702

Baselines. We compared ALMP with a number of representative baselines, which are TransE, ComplEx, RotatE, Rot-Pro [14], ATTE, BoxE [1], TuckER [3], and PairRE [7]. ATTE is the variant of ATTH [6] on euclidean space, which integrated two geometric operation: rotation and refection. We choose ATTE instead of ATTH to focus on the knowledge graph embedding models on euclidean space.

ALMP Variants. We further build a set of ALMP variants by modifying a specific module in ALMP for the ablation study afterwards. The illustration of ALMP variants is as follows.

- **DLMP** (Disentangled Learning for Multi-relation Patterns) is a variant whose entity embeddings under reflection, rotation, and projection are disentangled from each other.
- **ALMP*** utilizes non-element-wise attention instead of the element-wise attention mechanism in ALMP.
- **ALMP⁻** is another variant of ALMP with no additional step of translation transformation.

Hyper-parameter Settings. We train ALMP and its variants using a grid search of hyper-parameters: embedding dimensions in $\{400, 500, 600\}$; learning rate in $\{1e^{-5}, 1e^{-4}, 5e^{-4}\}$; batch size in $\{512, 1024, 2048\}$; number of negative sampling in $\{0, 50, 100, 200\}$.

5.3 Main Results

The experimental results on three datasets are reported in Table 2. We can see that ALMP with its variants outperforms most the baseline models across all common evaluation metrics, which empirically show the effectiveness of integrating affine transformations with attention to model complex interactions among relational patterns.

Furthermore, the performance gains over Rot-Pro could confirm the stronger expressiveness of integrated relational inductive bias than single bias. In other words, although relation patterns can be theoretically modeled separately by Rot-Pro, integrating them can indeed gain better performance, which coincides with our suppose of partial and global relation patterns. Meanwhile, the performance gain over AttE illustrates that integrating more forms of transformations gains better performance on expressiveness.

5.4   Ablation Study on ALMP Variants

According to the results of three variants of ALMP, we could draw some experimental conclusions of ALMP according to their difference.

First, we could find that the performance of ALMP$^-$ is lower than other variants, which demonstrates that the effectiveness of using translation transformation as relational inductive biases. Second, DLMP outperforms other variants on WN18RR and have a reasonable performance on the other two datasets, which shows disentangled learning is also an effective approach for integrating various relation patterns for certain knowledge graphs. Furthermore, the link prediction result on ALMP* is similar to that on ALMP, where ALMP* shows more robust result across the three datasets, while ALMP show better results on both FB15k-237 and YAGO3-10.

In summary, the variants of ALMP show overall strong capability for knowledge graph completion. Also, for different knowledge graphs, it is feasible to fine tune the result with a specific variant.

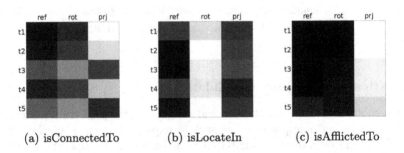

(a) isConnectedTo   (b) isLocateIn   (c) isAfflictedTo

Fig. 2. The attention visualization result of ALMP. Figure (a), (b), (c) represent the results of five triples randomly selected on the test set with different relations. Darker block represents lower attention value distributed to each transformation.

5.5   Case Study

For case study, we evaluate the MRR result for specific relations on WN18RR and YAGO3-10.

The relations we select basically contains the common global or partial relation patterns mentioned above. We compare the case study result with Rot-Pro, which is proved that could model the five relation patterns separately. The result is summarized in Table 3. The relations are selected manually with multiple relation properties. The case study result reflects that ALMP shows superior link prediction capability in modelling multiple relation patterns compared with KG embedding methods that model the relational properties separately.

Table 3. Comparison of MRR on Rot-Pro and ALMP for typical relations on WN18RR and YAGO3-10.

Relation	Rot-Pro	ALMP
isConnectedTo	0.405	**0.423**
isLocatedIn	0.297	**0.335**
isAffiliatedTo	0.664	**0.725**
playsFor	0.630	**0.667**
hypernym	0.150	**0.199**
derivationally_related_form	**0.958**	0.956
instance_hypernym	0.325	**0.389**
also_see	**0.627**	0.618
member_meronym	0.256	**0.266**
synset_domain_topic_of	0.347	**0.411**
has_part	0.197	**0.198**
member_of_domain_usage	0.308	**0.382**
member_of_domain_region	0.251	**0.402**

5.6   Attention Distribution Validation

Having confirmed that ALMP could indeed gain better prediction performance on relations of multiple patterns, we seek to explore that for a specific relation, how the attention value is distributed to each geometric operation. In other words, we would figure out that, for two specific entities with a partial relational property annotated by humans, does the learned attention distributions accurately reflect it? To this end, we select five triples for three relations in YAGO3-10 respectively and draw the attention visualization graph in Fig. 2.

We could find that there is obvious difference of attention distribution. For relation *isConnectedTo*, the attention distributed to three geometric operation is almost equal. It is may caused by that *isConnectedTo* is a relation with partial pattern of both symmetry, which can be learnt by both reflection and rotation, and transitivity, which can be modeled by projection. For relation *isLocatedIn*, the model tends to focus more attention on the rotation transformation. The possible reason might be that *isLocatedIn* is a relation with both global transitivity and asymmetry patterns, and asymmetry pattern could not be modeled by projection or reflection. As for relation *isAfflictedTo*, it is a relation with partial transitivity, hence the model prone to pay attention to the projection transformation.

6 Conclusion

In this paper, we proposed ALMP, a generic framework for knowledge graph embedding. ALMP could help handle the problem of the multiple relational properties by utilizing attention mechanism to integrating common affine transformation methods. On common KG embedding benchmarks, ALMP and its variants show effectiveness on link prediction task. According to the attention analysis and case study, ALMP is capable of capturing multiple relational properties.

Acknowledgement. This work was supported by the National Key R&D Program of China (Grant No. 2021ZD0112901).

References

1. Abboud, R., İsmail İ.C., Lukasiewicz, T., Salvatori, T.: BoxE: a box embedding model for knowledge base completion (2020)
2. Yang, B., Yih, W. T., He, X., Gao, J., Deng, L.: Embedding entities and relations for learning and inference in knowledge bases. In: ICLR, pp. 1–13 (2015)
3. Balazevic, I., Allen, C., Hospedales, T.: Tucker: tensor factorization for knowledge graph completion. Proceedings of the 2019 Conference on Empirical Methods in Natural Language Processing and the 9th International Joint Conference on Natural Language Processing (EMNLP-IJCNLP) (2019). https://doi.org/10.18653/v1/d19-1522
4. Battaglia, P.W., et al.: Relational inductive biases, deep learning, and graph networks. CoRR (2018)
5. Bordes, A., Usunier, N., Garcia-Duran, A., Weston, J., Yakhnenko, O.: Translating embeddings for modeling multi-relational data. Adv. Neural Inf. Process. Syst. **26**, 2787–2795 (2013)
6. Chami, I., Wolf, A., Juan, D.C., Sala, F., Ravi, S., Ré, C.: Low-dimensional hyperbolic knowledge graph embeddings. In: Proceedings of the 58th Annual Meeting of the Association for Computational Linguistics, pp. 6901–6914. Association for Computational Linguistics (Jul 2020)
7. Chao, L., He, J., Wang, T., Chu, W.: PairRE: knowledge graph embeddings via paired relation vectors. In: Proceedings of the 59th Annual Meeting of the Association for Computational Linguistics and the 11th International Joint Conference on Natural Language Processing, vol. 1: Long Papers, pp. 4360–4369. Association for Computational Linguistics, Online (2021). https://aclanthology.org/2021.acl-long.336

8. Bollacker, K., Evans, C., Paritosh, P., Sturge, T., Taylor, J.: Freebase: a collaboratively created graph database for structuring human knowledge. In: SIGMOD, pp. 1247–1250 (2008)

9. Kazemi, S.M., et al.: Representation learning for dynamic graphs: a survey (2020)

10. Lacroix, T., Usunier, N., Obozinski, G.: Canonical tensor decomposition for knowledge base completion (2018)

11. Mahdisoltani, F., Biega, J., Suchanek, F.: Yago3: a knowledge base from multilingual wikipedias. In: Proceedings of CIDR 2015 (2015)

12. Miller, G.A.: Wordnet: a lexical database for English. Commun. ACM **38**(11), 39–41 (1995)

13. Nathani, D., Chauhan, J., Sharma, C., Kaul, M.: Learning attention-based embeddings for relation prediction in knowledge graphs. In: Proceedings of the 57th Annual Meeting of the Association for Computational Linguistics, pp. 4710–4723 (2019)

14. Song, T., Luo, J., Huang, L.: Rot-pro: modeling transitivity by projection in knowledge graph embedding. In: Proceedings of the Thirty-Fifth Annual Conference on Advances in Neural Information Processing Systems (NeurIPS) (2021)

15. Suchanek, F.M., Kasneci, G., Weikum, G.: Yago: a core of semantic knowledge. In: Proceedings of the 16th International Conference on World Wide Web, pp. 697–706 (2007)

16. Sun, Z., Deng, Z.H., Nie, J.Y., Tang, J.: Rotate: knowledge graph embedding by relational rotation in complex space. In: International Conference on Learning Representations (2019)

17. Trouillon, T., Welbl, J., Riedel, S., Gaussier, E., Bouchard, G.: Complex embeddings for simple link prediction. In: Proceedings of 33rd International Conference on Machine Learning, pp. 2071–2080 (2016)

18. Dettmers, T., Minervini, P., Stenetorp, P., Riedel, S.: Convolutional 2D knowledge graph embeddings. In: Proceedings of the 32nd AAAI Conference on Artificial Intelligence (2018)

19. Toutanova, K., Chen, D.: Observed versus latent features for knowledge base and text inference. In: Proceedings of the 3rd Workshop on Continuous Vector Space Models and their Compositionality, pp. 57–66 (2015)

20. Valenza, R.: Linear algebra: an introduction to abstract mathematics. In: Undergraduate Texts in Mathematics. Springer, New York (2012). https://doi.org/10.1007/978-1-4612-0901-0

21. Wang, R., Li, B., Hu, S., Du, W., Zhang, M.: Knowledge graph embedding via graph attenuated attention networks. IEEE Access **8**, 5212–5224 (2020)

22. Wang, Z., Zhang, J., Feng, J., Chen, Z.: Knowledge graph embedding by translating on hyperplanes. In: AAAI Conference on Artificial Intelligence (2014)

23. Lin, Y., Liu, Z., Sun, M., Liu, Y., Zhu, X.: Learning entity and relation embeddings for knowledge graph completion. In: Proceedings of the 29th AAAI Conference on Artificial Intelligence, pp. 2181–2187 (2015)

24. Zhang, S., Tay, Y., Yao, L., Liu, Q.: Quaternion knowledge graph embedding. In: Advances in Neural Information Processing Systems, pp. 2731–2741 (2019)

25. Zhang, W., et al.: Iteratively learning embeddings and rules for knowledge graph reasoning (2019)

Recognition of Mechanical Parts Based on Improved YOLOv4-Tiny Algorithm

Baoshuai Du, Tong Fang, Lulu Gao, Guang Yang, and Jingbo Zhao[✉]

School of Information and Control Engineering, Qingdao University of Technology, Qingdao, Shandong, China
zhaoyancheng2021@163.com

Abstract. In order to improve the recognition, detection and grasping of mechanical parts by mechanical arm of factory automatic assembly line and solve the problems of large detection error and low accuracy in traditional mechanical parts feature extraction algorithm, common mechanical parts were taken as the research target and combined lightweight network in deep learning algorithm as the base model for optimization. CSP-Darknet53 was used to extract the feature. An improved MA-RFB module was added in front of the prediction end, and multi-branch convolution and empty convolution were introduced to strengthen the receptive field. In addition, the neck network was improved, PANet was selected to replace FPN, and attention module CBAM was added to form RC-PANet for multiscale detection of parts targets. AP reaches 96.47% in the self-made part dataset, and detection speed is 0.00138s per sample. Without losing too much speed, compared with the original YOLOv4-Tiny network, AP improved by 2.80%, and the improved algorithm achieved a balance in speed and precision, which reflected the theoretical and application value of the research.

Keywords: Lightweight network · Parts testing · Receptive field module

1 Introduction

As a modern technology to replace manual labor with machinery, automatic assembly was widely used in major enterprises and factories to improve production efficiency and reduce labor costs. As a key link in assembly, object detection of parts has important research significance to improve its detection accuracy and speed. Most of the traditional part detection algorithms were based on machine learning, which is to extract the features of assembled mechanical parts manually and used the machine learning algorithm to identify the target parts. However, the feature extraction process has strong artificiality and unpredictability.

Commonly used detection areas are traffic [1], aviation, fault [2], pedestrian and so on. In recent years, deep learning was widely popular, the application of this technology in target recognition greatly increased the accuracy and speed of detection. The target detection algorithm based on deep learning is divided into one stage and two stage detection algorithm [3], the two-stage algorithm traversed the input image using selective

G. Memmi et al. (Eds.): KSEM 2022, LNAI 13368, pp. 671–682, 2022.
https://doi.org/10.1007/978-3-031-10983-6_51

search, extracted candidate regions that may contain target objects, and sent the features into the convolutional neural networks for feature extraction. Finally, the features were sent into SVM or iterative classification algorithm for target classification, representative algorithms include SPP-Net, Fast R-CNN, Faster R-CNN and so on. The one-stage detection algorithm abandoned the process of candidate region extraction, and only carried out feature extraction once, and directly treated the detection target information for classification and regression. The two-stage detection algorithm had higher detection accuracy due to the multiple candidate regions extracted and sufficient feature extraction, while the one-stage detection algorithm omitted candidate region recommendation and had lower detection accuracy than the two-stage detection algorithm, but the detection speed was greatly improved and the real-time performance was better, representative algorithms included SSD [4] and YOLO. In the existing studies, Huang jiacai [5] pruned YOLOv3 and reduced a detection scale, improved the detection speed of parts to nearly two times under the condition of ensuring the detection accuracy and small loss. Yu Yongwei et al. [6] integrated the CFE module into the YOLOv3 trunk feature network Darknet-53 and used the improved k-means algorithm to improve the detection accuracy of parts by more than 10%.

Due to the poor identification accuracy and speed of traditional parts detection algorithm, it can not meet the requirements of accuracy and real-time in parts assembly process. In this paper, by integrating the advantages and disadvantages of various network models in deep learning detection algorithm, one-stage detection algorithm YOLOv4-Tiny was selected as the infrastructure. This algorithm was the lightweight version of target detection network YOLOv4, which has good real-time performance. In order to improve the accuracy of YOLOv4-Tiny, PANet was used to replace FPN in the neck network, and depthwise separable convolution and receptive field module RFB were introduced to optimize the network. By reducing the number of parameters and enhancing the receptive field, the accuracy and speed of part identification reached a good level.

2   Yolov4-Tiny Algorithm Model

Yolov4-tiny is a lightweight version of the one-stage detection algorithm YOLOv4, which was proposed by Alexey Bochkovskiy in 2020. Based on YOLOv3, a series of techniques were used to improve the algorithm, and the detection accuracy and speed were much better than YOLOv3. The network structure of YOLOv4-Tiny was mainly composed of feature extraction network, neck pyramid network and prediction network, as shown in Fig. 1.

The feature extraction network of YOLOv4-Tiny uses CSPDarknet53-Tiny, which was composed of several convolutional modules and CSPBlocks. CSPBlock adopted CSPnet structure, which disintegrated the stack of residual blocks in YOLOv3 into two parts, and the main part still used the stack of residual blocks. The other part used a large residual edge directly and connected at the end after simple processing to fuse with the main part. Residual structure can greatly alleviate problems such as gradient disappearance and gradient explosion caused by the network being too deep [7]. The main feature extraction network had eliminated the spatial pyramid SPP and changed the

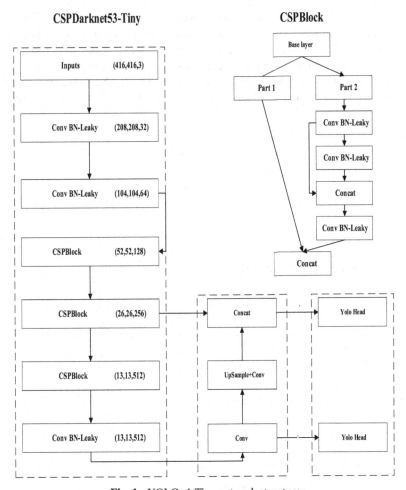

Fig. 1. YOLOv4-Tiny network structure

activation function from Mish used in YOLOv4 to LeakyRelu. The neck structure had replaced FPN structure with PANet and the output terminals have been changed from 3 detection terminals to 2 detection terminals. By simplifying the overall structure of the network, the parameters of YOLOv4-Tiny were reduced to only one tenth of those of YOLOv4. Although the detection accuracy was reduced, the detection speed was up to 10 times of YOLOv4.

3   Improvement Measures

3.1   Enhancement of Receptive Field Based on RFB Module

In order to increase the receptive field of the network and improve the detection accuracy of the lightweight network, the RFB module was added behind the FPN of the neck network and in front of the prediction end. This structure was a multi-branch convolution module composed of ordinary convolution layer and dilated convolution layer. Feature maps were input to dilated convolution layers with different expansion rates through convolution kernels of different sizes. Feature layers of different scales were fused through concating splicing operation, and the final feature vectors were obtained after 1×1 convolution. The RFB module drew on the Inception[6] and ResNet residual architecture, the dalited convolution and residual connection can effectively enhance the receptive

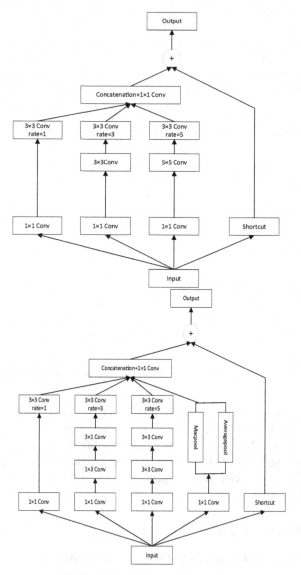

Fig. 2. RFB and improved MA-RFB

field and integrate feature maps of multiple scales to obtain more comprehensive feature information while keeping the scale features unchanged.

This section has been improved based on the RFB module. Firstly, the 3×3 convolution layer was replaced with 1×3 and 3×1 convolution, and the 5×5 convolution was replaced with two 3×3 convolution, and a branch combined by average pooling and maximum pooling was added to further reduce the number of parameters and retain more feature information of the target while increasing the receptive field. The original RFB structure and the improved MA-RFB structure are shown in Fig. 2.

3.2 Improvement Based on Attention Module CBAM

As the layers of neural network deepen, the complexity of network increased gradually, which not only brought gradient disappearance and gradient explosion, but also made the information storage of network became large. In the state of limited computing resources, it was difficult to process the image information at each position. The application of attention module effectively solved this problem. At present, the more classical attention modules mainly included SENet [7] and CBAM [8]. The main difference between CBAM and SENet lied in that CBAM has an additional information of spatial attention, while SENet solved the problem of different importance of feature map channels extracted by neural network in the process of convolutional layer and pooling layer, and focused on

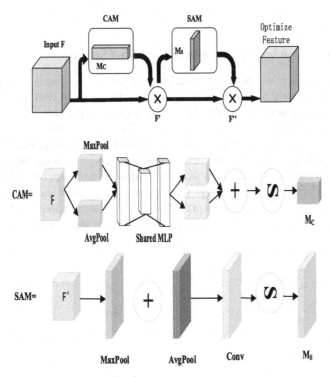

Fig. 3. CBAM structure

the feature information of different channels. CBAM added spatial channel information while focusing on channel information, and distributes computing resources reasonably by weighted fusion of the two information. The structure of CBAM is shown in Fig. 3, mainly composed of CAM and SAM modules.

CBAM is a general lightweight attention module, which can be added in any position of the commonly used convolutional neural networks to effectively improve the detection performance of the network through the dual improvement of channel and spatial attention module. In this paper, CBAM is combined with FPN of neck network, and the improved structure is shown in Fig. 4.

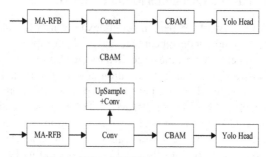

Fig. 4. CBAM-FPN network structure

3.3 Feature Fusion Improvement Based on PANet Structure

In order to simplify the network structure and reduce the number of parameters, YOLOv4-Tiny algorithm changes the PANet structure in YOLOv4 neck network to FPN [9] feature pyramid. Although the detection speed of the network was improved, the accuracy of the network was greatly reduced. Therefore, this paper reused the PANet [10] network structure and added a bottom-up channel on the basis of FPN feature pyramid, which solved the problem that the original network only combines the semantic information of the deep feature map with the shallow feature map, but did not combine the location information of the shallow feature map with the deep feature map. The neck network structure of PANet that integrated the receptive field module of MA-RFB and the attention module of CBAM was named RC-PANet, as shown in Fig. 5.

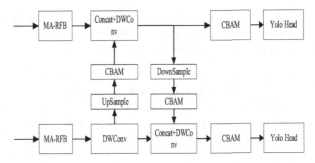

Fig. 5. RC-PANet network structure

4 Experimental

4.1 Dataset

At present, there are few open datasets about mechanical parts and most of them are the detection of a single part. This paper focuses on multi-object detection. Therefore, a mechanical parts dataset is self-made by taking photos of specific parts and obtaining them through the network. This dataset mainly includes five categories: nut, bolt, bearing, gear and washer. Some datas are shown in Fig. 6.

Fig. 6. Parts image dataset

In order to reduce network overfitting caused by too small dataset, data enhancement was used to expand the dataset, mainly including rotation, horizontal mirror, adding noise, cutmix [11], etc. The expanded dataset was composed of 5000 images, which were divided into training set and test set in the ratio of 9:1. LabelImg annotation tool was used to annotate the images in the dataset. A total of 12,532 parts were labeled with

5000 pictures, and the total number of 5 types of parts is shown in Table 1. The number of parts of each type is evenly distributed, which meets the requirements of training sample set in convolutional neural networks.

Table 1. Mark quantity of various parts

Category	Nut	Bearing	Washer	Bolt	Gear
Number	2518	2428	2440	2474	2672

4.2 Evaluation Indicators

In order to verify the improved algorithm structure, TTP of each image was used as an index to evaluate the model speed, Precision and Recall were calculated, and P-R curves of accuracy and recall were established. Then the Mean Average Precision is calculated as the index to evaluate the model accuracy[12], and its calculation formula is shown as follows.

$$R_{Recall} = \frac{T_{TP}}{T_{TP} + F_{FN}} \tag{1}$$

$$P_{Precision} = \frac{T_{TP}}{T_{TP} + F_{FP}} \tag{2}$$

$$mAP = \frac{1}{C} \sum_{c \in C} AP(c) \tag{3}$$

Where: TP indicates that samples belonging to positive class are divided into positive class; FN represents that the model is incorrectly classified and the samples that should belong to the positive category are classified into the negative category; FP means that the samples whose model classification error should belong to negative category are divided into positive category.

4.3 Ablation Experiment with Improved Algorithm

According to the improved strategies in this paper, the accuracy and speed effects of each improved point are tested to form the improved RCP-YOLOv4-Tiny network in this paper. The algorithm with addition of MA-RFB module was denoted as B, the algorithm with addition of CBAM attention module was denoted as C, and the algorithm with PANet structure was denoted as D. After adjusting parameters, the algorithm was denoted as algorithm E, and the comparison experiment was conducted with the original YOLOv4-Tiny network. Meanwhile, the ablation experiment was completed based on the experimental results above. The experimental results are shown in Table 2.

Compared with the original network YOLOv4-Tiny, the AP of the improved algorithm increases by 2.80%, and the detection speed of single image only increases by

Table 2. Impact of each module on performance

	MA-RFB	CBAM	PANet	AP/%	TTP/s
A				93.67	0.0093
B	√			94.82	0.0119
C		√		94.94	0.0105
D			√	94.35	0.0094
E	√	√	√	96.47	0.0138

0.0045s. Each module has a certain improvement effect on the network. According to the analysis in Table 5, the detection accuracy of the network after the combination of the three improvement points is slightly lower than 0.3% of the sum of the detection accuracy of the three improvement points, because the number of network parameters after the combination is much higher than the sum of the parameters added by the three alone, but the dataset is too small and the feature quantity extracted from the network is limited. Therefore, the next improvement point of this paper is to expand the dataset and eliminate the influence of multiple improvement points against each other, but the improved network still effectively solves the problems of error detection and missing detection and improves the detection accuracy. The comparison figures of the test results in the experimental part are shown in Fig. 7 and 8.

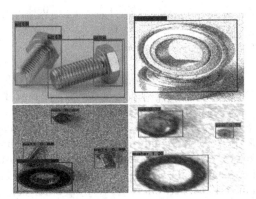

Fig. 7. YOLOv4-Tiny

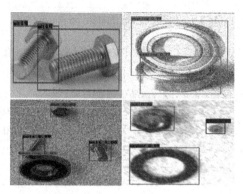

Fig. 8. RCP-YOLOv4-Tiny

The improved algorithm in this paper is compared with the mainstream algorithm in the first stage, and the experimental results are shown in Table 3.

Table 3. Each algorithm detects performance

Algorithm	AP/%	TTP/s
YOLOv3	97.17	0.0373
YOLOv3-Tiny	90.02	0.0082
YOLOv4	98.84	0.0431
YOLOv4-Tiny	93.67	0.0093
RCP-YOLOv4-Tiny	96.47	0.0138

Compared with YOLOv4, the proposed algorithm is 3.12 times faster than YOLOv4 in detection accuracy, which is suitable for embedded equipment with limited resources. Compared with the lightweight network YOLOv3-Tiny, the detection accuracy is improved by 5.58%. Because the number of parameters of the improved network is much higher than that of YOLOv3-Tiny itself, the speed is increased. Compared with YOLOv3 with similar accuracy, the speed is about 3 times higher. In this paper, the use of lightweight with the original network is not very big difference on precision, shows that under the condition of the same dataset has an impact on the detection performance, network structure in the dataset is less, less testing category, environment more easily and less number of network under the condition of easy training, this article put forward on the comprehensive performance of network better, In the detection accuracy and speed is located in a balanced position, suitable for real-time high-precision parts detection.

5 Conclusion

In order to improve the mechanical parts precision and speed of detection algorithm, the network model can be deployed on the equipment of limited resources, this article is based on the neck of the network structure optimization to improve the algorithm, by increasing the RFB multi-branch convolution pyramid structure, attention mechanism CBAM module, PANet features to improve the lightweight network accuracy was not high. Compared with the original YOLOv4-Tiny network, the AP of the improved network model increased by 2.80%, and the detection time of each image increased by 0.0045 s, but it was still faster than the current mainstream network detection speed. The target detection algorithm of mechanical parts proposed in this paper could meet the requirements of real-time in the process of automatic assembly and achieve high detection accuracy. The subsequent work will further study the balance between detection accuracy and speed, adopt the current method of double prediction head and depth separable convolution to improve detection accuracy and optimize detection speed, so as to achieve better performance of network model accuracy and speed.

Acknowledgment. This work is supported in part by the National Natural Science Foundation of China under Grant 51475251, the Natural Science Foundation of Shandong Province under Grant ZR2013FM014 and in part by the Qingdao Municipality Livelihood Plan Pro-ject under Grant 22–3-7-xdny-18-nsh.

References

1. Qiu, H., Zheng, Q., Msahli, M., et al.: Topological graph convolutional network-based urban traffic flow and density prediction. IEEE Trans. Intell. Transp. Syst. **22**(07), 4560–4569 (2020)
2. Li, Y., Song, Y., Jia, L., et al.: Intelligent fault diagnosis by fusing domain adversarial training and maximum mean discrepancy via ensemble learning. IEEE Trans. Ind. Inform. **17**(04), 2833–2841 (2021)
3. Zhao, J.Q., Du, B.S.: Development of small target detection technology based on deep learning. Electrooptics Optics Control, 1–10 (2022)
4. Liu, W., Anguelov, D., Erhan, D., Szegedy, C., Reed, S., Fu, C.-Y., Berg, A.C.: SSD: Single shot multibox detector. In: Leibe, B., Matas, J., Sebe, N., Welling, M. (eds.) ECCV 2016. LNCS, vol. 9905, pp. 21–37. Springer, Cham (2016). https://doi.org/10.1007/978-3-319-464 48-0_2
5. Huang, J.C., Zhou, J., Ding, L., et al.: Fast detection method of part target based on improved YOLOv3 algorithm. J. Nanjing Inst. Tech. **18**(03), 6–11 (2020)
6. Yu, Y.W., Peng, X., Du, L.Q., et al.: Real-time detection of parts by assembly robot based on deep learning framework. Acta Armamentarii **41**(10), 2122–2130 (2020)
7. Zhong, B.H., Wang, L., Zhong, S.S.: Selective assembly for coordinator parts by rngru based on comprehensive grey relational order model. China Mech. Eng. **32**(03), 314–320+356 (2021)
8. Szegedy, C., Liu, W., Jia, Y., et al.: Going deeper with convolutions. In: Proceedings of IEEE Conference on Computer Vision and Pattern Recognition, pp. 1-9. IEEE Press, USA (2015)
9. Yang, Z.Y, Wang, J.J, Jin, L.: Human fall detection method based on SE-CNN. Comput. Eng. 1–10 (2022)
10. Cai, G.Y., Chu, Y.Y.: Visual sentiment analysis based on multi-level features fusion of dual attention. Comput. Eng. **47**(09), 227–234 (2021)
11. Lin, T.Y., Dollár, P., Girshick, R., et al.: Feature pyramid networks for object detection. In: Proceedings of the IEEE Conference on Computer Vision and Pattern Recognition, pp. 2117–2125. IEEE, New York (2017)

12. Liu, S., Qi, L., Qin, H., et al.: Path aggregation network for instance segmentation. In: IEEE Conference on Computer Vision and Pattern Recognition, pp. 8759–8768. IEEE, Piscataway (2018)

13. Yun, S., Han, D., Oh, S.J., et al.: Cutmix: regularization strategy to train strong classifiers with localizable features. In: Proceedings of the IEEE/CVF International Conference on Computer Vision. IEEE, New York, 6023–6032 (2019)

14. Wang, X.P, Wang, X.Q, Lin, Hao.: Review on improvement of typical object detection algorithms in deep learning. Comput. Eng. Appl. **58**(06), 42–57(2022)

Asymmetric Neighboring Context Modeling for Knowledge Graph Embedding

Yuanhao Hu[1], Yuanxin Ouyang[2(✉)], Jun Bai[2], Chuanrui Wang[1], Wenge Rong[2], and Zhang Xiong[2]

[1] Sino-French Engineer School, Beihang University, Beijing, China
{huyuanhao,buaa_wcr}@buaa.edu.cn
[2] School of Computer Science and Engineering, Beihang University, Beijing, China
{oyyx,bai_jun,w.rong,xiongz}@buaa.edu.cn

Abstract. Knowledge graph embedding (KGE) is to learn how to represent the low dimensional vectors for entities and relations based on the observed triples. When dealing with surrounding information, recent models either ignore the interactions between triples within the knowledge graph or use too many parameters to take the surrounding information into the model. Besides, the asymmetric information in the surrounding triples deserves further investigation. In this paper, we propose an Asymmetric Context Aware Representation for Knowledge Graph Embedding method (AcarE). Specifically, we first use an asymmetric context encoder to introduce the surrounding triples information to the head and relation entity. Afterwards we use an encoding system based on convolutional neural network (CNN) to encode the context-aware head and context-aware relation. Experimental results on both WN18RR and FB15K-237 datasets demonstrate the AcarE's promising potential.

Keywords: Knowledge graph embedding · Asymmetric neighboring information · Attention mechanism

1 Introduction

Recently, the knowledge graphs (KG) have been attached much attention in the community and also successfully applied in various natural language processing applications [7]. Typically, a KG stores factual knowledge in the form of structural triples, i.e., (h, r, t), which means there is a kind of relation (r) from head entity (h) to tail entity (t). The goal of knowledge graph embedding (KGE) is to project massive interconnected triples into a low-dimensional space and preserve the initial semantic information at the same time.

Earlier KGE models tend to ignore the interactions among different triples [2]. Though this kind of mechanism is easy in implementation, the topology of knowledge graph, which may contain vital information, is neglected. Therefore some KGE models introduce the neighboring information into the calculation

© The Author(s), under exclusive license to Springer Nature Switzerland AG 2022
G. Memmi et al. (Eds.): KSEM 2022, LNAI 13368, pp. 683–695, 2022.
https://doi.org/10.1007/978-3-031-10983-6_52

of knowledge graph embedding [4,24]. Introducing extra information can significantly improve the KGE's performance, while it is also becoming a challenging task to make a proper trade-off between the model complexity (the number of parameters) and the model expressiveness (the performance in capturing semantic information). Furthermore, during utilizing neighboring information, most models do not consider the asymmetric relation within triples. In fact, one entity can be one triple's head entity and also other triple's tail entity. Such asymmetric information is important for triples [11], thereby inspiring an interesting question: is such asymmetric information can be further utilized in KGE task?

Inspired by the above discussion, in this paper we propose a lightweight framework, Asymmetric Context Aware Representation for Knowledge Graph Embedding model (AcarE), for the KGE task. This method can achieve highly competitive results without the sacrifice in the model complexity. The contribution of this work is three-folders: 1) we proposed a neighboring information encoding mechanism while preserving the asymmetric information; 2) we developed an efficient neighboring information aggregating strategy to keep model parameters as small as possible; 3) we conducted comprehensive experiments to evaluate the performance of the proposed method. Experimental results have shown this proposed framework's promising potential.

2   Related Work

Most existing KGE models can be classified into three categories, i.e., translation-based models, tensor factorization-based models and neural network-based models. A representative translation-based model is TransE [2]. TransR [10] and TransH [23] extend TransE by projecting entities or relations into different vector space. These models introduced the idea of translation invariance into the knowledge graph embedding field.

Some models are based on tensor factorization. For example, RESCAL [13] applies a tensor to express the inherent structure of a KG and uses the rank-d factorization to obtain its latent semantics. Comparing to RESCAL, DistMult [26] uses bi-linear transformations to reduce the number of parameters. However, DistMult can only handle symmetric relations. Inspired by Euler's identity, RotatE [17] introduces the rotational Hadamard product, and it treats the relation as a rotation between the head and tail entity in complex space.

Recently neural network based approach gains much attention. ConvE [5] and ConvKB [12] employ convolutional network for this task. AcrE [14] employs atrous convolutional network to increase the interactions between head and relation embedding. ReInceptionE [24] takes in the surrounding information to increase the interactions of different triples, but adds many extra parameters.

3   Methodology

3.1   Problem Definition

A knowledge graph G can be denoted as $G = (E, R)$, where E contains $|E|$ different entities, R contains $|R|$ different relations. The knowledge graph is formed by a number of triples, i.e., $G = \{(h_i, r_i, t_i)|(h_i, r_i, t_i) \in E \times R \times E\}$.

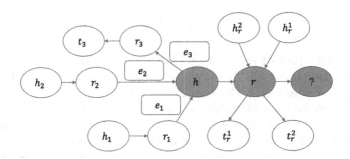

Fig. 1. The neighboring information of the head entity and relation

As shown in Fig. 1, the KGE task is to predict tail entity (?), given the head entity (h) and relation (r). The proposed framework consists of three modules: 1) Asymmetric context encoder, which is used to encode the surrounding triples of head entity (h), e.g., (h_2, r_2, h) and (h, r_3, t_3), to embedding-dimensional vectors e_2 and e_3. 2) Attention-based aggregating mechanism, which aims to aggregate the context information using a gated linear layer and attention mechanism. The context-aware head entity representation $h_{context}$ and relation representation $r_{context}$ are calculated in this step. 3) Convolutional query encoder is used to transform the query ($h_{context}, r_{context}, ?$) into an embedding-dimensional vector t'. Finally, we compute the score for the given triple (h, r, t) as the dot product of the query embedding t' and the tail entity embedding.

3.2   Asymmetric Context Encoder

As shown in Fig. 1, given a triple ($h, r, ?$) for which we need to predict the tail entity, the asymmetric context encoder is used to encode the neighboring triples of the head entity (h). The head entity h can be head entity or tail entity in the surrounding triples, e.g., tail entity of (h_1, r_1, h) and head entity of (h, r_3, t_3). The surrounding triples of h are defined as $N(h) = \{(h_i, r_i)|(h_i, r_i, h) \in G\} \cup \{(t_i, r'_i)|(h, r_i, t_i) \in G\}$, where r'_i is a new relation we create different from r_i to keep the asymmetric information. r'_i is the reversed version of the relation r_i, e.g. the relation *PartOf* is the reversed version of the relation *Contain*.

Figure 2 shows the whole architecture of asymmetric context encoder, which consists of two structures, i.e., 1) asymmetric LSTM [8] encoder (on the left), and 2) gated linear encoder (on the right).

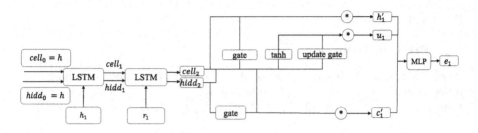

Fig. 2. Asymmetric head surrounding information encoder

The asymmetric LSTM encoder is used to capture the asymmetric or serial information. $cell_i$ and $hidd_i$ are the cell and hidden state of the LSTM structure. h denotes the center head entity embedding (h in Fig. 1), h_i and r_i are the head and relation embedding of the triples surrounding h. Here we use h_1 and r_1 in Fig. 1 as an example. The embedding of the center head entity h is used as the initial hidden state and cell state of the LSTM model. This is to let the encoder be aware of the center query head entity embedding to be aggregated in advance. As such in the learning process, it can better encode the surrounding triples $(h_i, r_i) \in N(h)$. The asymmetric LSTM encoder conserves the asymmetric information of surrounding triples whether h is a head entity or tail entity in the surrounding triples, i.e. the form of surrounding triples can be (h_i, r_i, h) or (h, r_i, t_i). The information always flows in the right direction within the triple, from h_i to r_i or from t_i to r_i' depending on the position of the center head entity in the surrounding triple. The output of the asymmetric LSTM encoder is the cell state $cell_2$ and hidden state $hidd_2$ of the second LSTM cell.

Afterwards we use a gated linear encoder to encode the output of the asymmetric LSTM encoder. We first concatenate the cell state $cell_2$ and hidden state $hidd_2$. Then we calculate the information to conserve in $cell_2$ and $hidd_2$ as c' and h'. $W_{c_{gate}} \in R^{d \times 2d}$ and $b_{c_{gate}} \in R^d$ are trainable transformation matrix and bias to calculate the forget gate for $cell_2$, d is the KGE dimension. $W_{h_{gate}} \in R^{d \times 2d}$ and $b_{h_{gate}} \in R^d$ have the same role and calculate forget gate for $hidd_2$. x_{update} is the candidate update vector and x_{update_gate} is the update gate vector. The update vector u is the element-wise multiplication of x_{update} and x_{update_gate}. These three vectors c', h' and u are then concatenated and transformed into the embedding dimension through linear transformation matrix $W_{concat_1} \in R^{d \times 3d}$ and bias $b_{concat_1} \in R^d$. The encoded information of the surrounding triples can be noted as $N(h) = \{e_1, e_2, e_3, ..., e_n\}$, calculated as follows:

$$cell_2, hidd_2 = LSTM(h, h_1, r_1) \tag{1}$$

$$c_1' = sigmoid(W_{c_{gate}} \cdot [cell_2; hidd_2] + b_{c_{gate}}) \circ cell_2 \tag{2}$$

$$h_1' = sigmoid(W_{h_{gate}} \cdot [cell_2; hidd_2] + b_{h_{gate}}) \circ hidd_2 \tag{3}$$

$$x_{update} = tanh(W_{update} \cdot [cell_2; hidd_2] + b_{update}) \tag{4}$$

$$x_{update\_gate} = sigmoid(W_{update\_gate} \cdot [cell_2; hidd_2] + b_{update\_gate}) \tag{5}$$

$$u_1 = x_{update} \circ x_{update\_gate} \tag{6}$$

$$e_1 = relu(W_{concat_1} \cdot [c_1'; h_1'; u_1] + b_{concat_1}) \tag{7}$$

3.3 Attention-based Aggregating Mechanism

After encoding the surrounding triple information, we adopt the attention mechanism to assist the framework in aggregating the surrounding information with the center query information, as shown in Fig. 3.

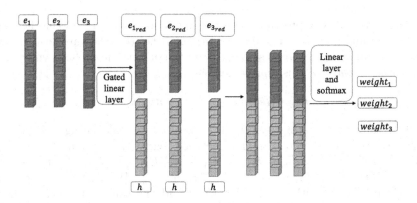

Fig. 3. Aggregate surrounding encode into head embedding

To balance the importance of the surrounding information and the center query information, the dimension of surrounding encode $e_i \in N(\mathbf{h})$ is first reduced based on the gated linear structure. After concatenating with the center embedding, the weight of the surrounding triples is calculated as below.

$$e_{i_{gate}} = sigmoid(W_{e_{gate}} \cdot e_i + b_{e_{gate}}) \tag{8}$$

$$e_{i_{update}} = tanh(W_{e_{update}} \cdot e_i + b_{e_{update}}) \tag{9}$$

$$e_{i_{red}} = e_{i_{gate}} \circ e_{i_{update}} \tag{10}$$

$$weight_i = softmax(leaky\_relu(W_{concat_2} \cdot [e_{i_{red}}, h] + b_{concat_2})) \tag{11}$$

$$context_h = weight^{\mathsf{T}} \cdot N(\mathbf{h}) \tag{12}$$

$e_{i_{red}} \in R^{d'}$ is the surrounding encode after reducing dimension and $d' < d$. $W_{concat_2} \in R^{1 \times (d+d)'}$ and $b_{concat_2} \in R$ are linear parameters to fuse the reduced surrounding encode and center information. $weight$ is the weight of the surrounding triples. Calculated with attention mechanism, $context_h$ is the context information of head h. The aggregating process for calculating the head context is noted as $context_h = attention\_aggregate(h, N(\mathbf{h}))$. It should be noted that although the softmax activation function ensures that the sum of the weights for context triples is 1, in practice we add a few zero vectors to the surrounding triples encode set $N(\mathbf{h})$. Therefore, the attention model can assign relatively large weights to the zero vectors in $N(\mathbf{h})$. The sum of the effective weights could be less than 1. This helps the model to adjust the importance of surrounding information during training, and avoids adding too much invalid noise under the condition that the number of surrounding triples is too large. Next, $context_h$ is concatenated with the head entity embedding. $W_{imp_h} \in R^{d \times 2d}$ and $b_{imp_h} \in R^d$ are trainable linear transformation matrix and bias to calculate the significance gate noted as imp_gate_h.

$$imp\_gate_h = sigmoid(W_{imp_h} \cdot [context_h; h] + b_{imp_h}) \qquad (13)$$

The final context representation is the Hadamard product between the significance gate and $context_h$. The representation of the context-aware head entity is sum of the final context representation and the original query head embedding. The context-aware head is represented as $h_{context}$.

$$h_{context} = imp\_gate_h \circ context_h + h \qquad (14)$$

The same aggregating system is also used in calculating the context-aware relation representation. The relation entity r is connected to head entities $N_h(r) = \{h_r^i | (h_r^i, r, t_r^i) \in G, h_r^i \in E, t_r^i \in E\}$ and tail entities $N_t(r) = \{t_r^i | (h_r^i, r, t_r^i) \in G, h_r^i \in E, t_r^i \in E\}$. We aggregate separately the relation entity with the head entities and the tail entities, $context_{r_h} = attention\_aggregate(r, N_h(\mathbf{r}))$, $context_{r_t} = attention\_aggregate(r, N_t(\mathbf{r}))$. Finally, the head-context representation $context_{r_h}$ and the tail-context representation $context_{r_t}$ will be fused.

$$context_r = relu(W_{fusion} \cdot [context_{r_h}; context_{r_t}] + b_{fusion}) \qquad (15)$$

$$imp\_gate_r = sigmoid(W_{imp_r} \cdot [context_r; r] + b_{imp_r}) \qquad (16)$$

$$r_{context} = imp\_gate_r \circ context_r + r \qquad (17)$$

$context_r$ is context information of the relation r, imp_gate_r is the significance gate for $context_r$. $W_{fusion} \in R^{d \times 2d}$, $b_{fusion} \in R^d$ are all trainable linear parameters for fusing $context_{r_h}$ and $context_{r_t}$. W_{imp_r} and b_{imp_r} are used to calculate the significance gate. The context-aware relation is represented as $r_{context}$. $h_{context}$ and $r_{context}$ calculated above are the inputs to the query encoder.

3.4   Query Encoder

Query encoder is used to transform the input query $q = (h_{context}, r_{context}, ?)$ into vector t' and calculate the score function using t' and tail entity embedding. As shown in Fig. 4, given a query $q = (h_{context}, r_{context}, ?)$, we first reshape the context-aware head and context-aware relation representation to 2D matrices denoted as $h'_{context}$ and $r'_{context}$. Afterwards, the 2D embeddings are viewed as two channels of the input for the query encoder. Thus, compared to ConvE [5], the convolution operations can increase the interactions between the head

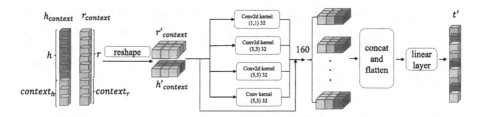

Fig. 4. Query encoder

Table 1. Dataset statistics

Dataset	Entity	Relation	Train	Validation	Test
WN18RR	40943	11	86835	3034	3134
FB15K-237	14541	237	272115	17535	20466

and relation embeddings. Several convolution operations are applied in parallel. Specifically, we use 4 convolutions of 1×1, 3×3, 5×5 and 5×5 to capture the direct interactions. This process can be formulated as:

$$A_i = [h'_{context}||r'_{context}] * W_{size \times size} \tag{18}$$

where $||$ denotes the concatenation operation, $*$ denotes the convolution operation and $W_{size \times size}$ is the parameter of convolution filters. For A_1 and A_2, $size$ is 1 and 3, for A_3 and A_4, $size$ is 5. Finally, the output interaction features with different scales are concatenated.

Although convolution layers extract useful interactions between $h_{context}$ and $r_{context}$, we lose some original information in this process. Besides, there is an inherent vanishing gradient issue in the deep networks. As such we use the residual learning method to include the original information $h_{context}$ and $r_{context}$. We first expand $[h'_{context}||r'_{context}]$ to A_0 according to the number of filters used in the convolution layer. A_0 has the same dimension as A_1, A_2, A_3 and A_4. Finally, the concatenated result A is flattened and projected into the embedding space through the transformation matrix W and the bias b.

$$A = A_0 \oplus A_1 \oplus A_2 \oplus A_3 \oplus A_4. \tag{19}$$

$$t' = relu(W \cdot Flatten(A) + b) \tag{20}$$

4 Experimental Study

4.1 Experiment Configuration

Dataset. The experimental study is conducted on two datasets, i.e., WN18RR [5] and FB15K-237 [18]. They are respectively subsets of WN18 and FB15k, which contain a large number of inverse relations, thereby making it possible for the triples in the test set be obtained simply by inverting triples in the training set. Therefore, both WN18RR and FB15k-237 are generated by removing the inverse relations [2]. The statistics of these two datasets are shown in Table 1. FB15K-237 contains almost 20 times more relations than WN18RR.

Evaluation Metric. We use link prediction, one of the most frequently used benchmark evaluation tasks for KGE methods, to evaluate our model. Link prediction is to predict the missing h or t for a correct triple (h, r, t). Rather than requiring one best answer, this task emphasizes more on ranking a set of candidate entities from the KG. Hits@k and MRR are often used for the evaluation.

Table 2. Hyper-parameters used in experiments

Hyper-parameters	FB15K-237	WN18RR
Entity embedding dimension(d)	200	200
Relation embedding dimension(d)	200	200
Reduced dimension during aggregation(d')	60	60
Number of triples surrounding head entity	200	200
Number of surrounding entities of relation	50	50
Number of false triples generated	1000	1000
Number of kernels for convolution	32	32
hidden_size of LSTM	200	200
num_layers of LSTM	1	1
learning_rate	0.001	0.002
batch_size	128	256
Epoch number	200	200

Model Training. To optimize the parameters , we follow ConvE [5] and apply sigmoid function to the scores. The loss function is depicted in Eq. 21, where $y_i = 1$ if $(h, r, t_i) \in G$, otherwise $y_i = 0$. $p(t_i|h, r)$ is the probability that (h, r, t_i) actually holds, i.e. $t'_i = query\_encoder(h_{context}, r_{context})$ and $p(t_i|h, r) = sigmoid(t'_i \cdot t_i)$. The model is trained with Adam optimization and the hyperparameters are listed in Table 2.

$$L = -\frac{1}{N} \sum_{i=1}^{N} [y_i \log p(t_i|h, r) + (1 - y_i) \log (1 - p(t_i|h, r))] \tag{21}$$

4.2   Results and Discussion

We compare our results with various benchmark methods, and the experimental results are summarized in Table 3. It is noted that our framework's performance on WN18RR is not the best. It is because: 1) WN18RR contains fewer triples and the knowledge graph structure is simpler. 2) due to the relatively small training set, the mechanism of introducing surrounding information may not be fully trained. 3) compared with FB15K-237 which contains 237 relations, WN18RR knowledge graph contains only 11 relations. Since the structure of the knowledge graph is relatively simple, the improvement effect of introducing context information is limited as expected.

Table 3. Overall results on FB15K-237 and WN18RR

Models	FB15K-237				WN18RR			
	MRR	H@1	H@3	H@10	MRR	H@1	H@3	H@10
TransE [2]	0.279	–	–	44.1	0.243	–	–	53.2
ConvE [5]	0.312	22.5	34.1	49.7	0.43	40.0	44.0	52.0
ConvKB [12]	0.243	15.5	37.1	42.1	0.249	35.7	41.7	52.4
RotatE [17]	0.338	24.1	37.5	53.3	0.476	42.8	49.2	57.1
D4-STE [25]	0.320	23.0	35.3	50.2	0.480	45.2	49.1	53.6
DistMult [26]	0.241	15.5	26.3	41.9	0.430	39.0	44.0	49.0
SACN [16]	0.35	26.0	39.0	54.0	0.470	43.0	48.0	54.0
R-GCN+ [15]	0.249	15.1	26.4	41.7	–	–	–	–
ConvR [9]	0.350	26.1	38.5	52.8	0.475	44.3	48.9	53.7
VR-GCN [27]	0.248	15.9	27.2	43.2	–	–	–	–
RSNs [6]	0.280	20.2	–	45.3	–	–	–	–
CompGCN [21]	0.355	26.4	39.0	53.5	0.479	44.3	49.4	54.6
InteractE [20]	0.354	26.3	–	53.5	0.463	43.0	–	52.8
AcrE [14]	0.358	26.6	39.3	54.5	0.459	42.2	47.3	53.2
HAKE [29]	0.346	25.0	38.1	54.2	**0.497**	**45.2**	**51.6**	**58.2**
QuatE [28]	0.311	22.1	34.2	49.5	0.481	43.6	50.0	56.4
PairRE [3]	0.351	25.6	38.7	54.4	–	–	–	–
ComplEx [19]	0.343	25.0	37.7	53.2	0.479	44.1	49.5	55.2
ReInceptionE [24]	0.349	–	–	52.8	0.483	–	–	58.2
HypER [1]	0.341	25.2	37.6	52.0	0.465	43.6	47.7	52.2
AcarE	**0.363**	**27.0**	**40.0**	**54.6**	0.466	42.4	48.1	55.0

As to the performance on FB15K-237, our proposed model achieves large performance gains. The reason is mainly: 1) instead of concatenating the head and relation embeddings from left to right, our model takes the two inputs as two channels. Therefore the convolution based encoder can learn more interactions between the context-aware head and the context-aware relation. 2) we introduce surrounding information to both head entity and relation, the context-aware representation can gather relevant local neighbors to help encode the given query and the asymmetric context encoder conserves the asymmetric information within the triple. 3) when aggregating surrounding information with the center query information, we use the gated linear model and add special zero vectors to the surrounding information encode. Thus, we can balance the importance of the neighboring information and the center information.

4.3 Ablation and Parameter Efficiency

Table 4 shows the ablation experiments of our framework on the larger FB15k-237 dataset. There is an evident difference between the performance with or without the asymmetric LSTM encoder. Besides, although the performance improves if we take in the relation context or the head context, the model taking in both relation context and head context has the best performance.

With regard to the model complexity, as shown in Table 5, although our model fully introduces the context information, the asymmetric context encoder is lightweight and the attention-based aggregating mechanism is mainly based on gated linear structure, the number of parameters used is still relatively small. Our model has the closest number of parameters to ConvE [5], but it is far superior compared to ConvE [5] in all evaluation metrics. This indicates that our lightweight model could be used in large knowledge graphs.

Table 4. Experimental results of ablation experiments on FB15K-237

	MRR	H@1	H@3	H@10
AcarE	**0.363**	**27.0**	**40.0**	**54.6**
w/o relation and head context	0.356	26.3	39.0	54.2
w/o relation context	0.357	26.4	39.5	54.3
w/o head context	0.357	26.4	39.2	54.3
w/o asymmetric LSTM encoder	0.360	26.6	39.7	54.3

Table 5. Parameter efficiency on FB15K-237

Models	Number of parameters (Millions)
ConvE [5]	4.96
RotatE [17]	29.32
SACN [16]	9.63
InteractE [20]	10.70
CompGCN [21]	9.45
HAKE [29]	29.79
CoKE [22]	10.19
AcarE	6.70

5   Conclusion and Future Work

In this paper, we proposed an advanced context-aware framework for knowledge graph embedding, which first employed two different encoder mechanisms to encode respectively the surrounding information and the center query information. The convolution based query encoder increased the interactions between the context-aware head and relation representations. The asymmetric context encoder conserved the asymmetric information in the context triples. Furthermore, the head and relation context information were fused with the center query information based on the gated linear structure, which assured the importance of context information compared to center information, while keeping parameter efficient. Empirical studies demonstrated that our proposed framework achieved competitive performance on two widely used benchmark datasets WN18RR and FB15k-237, with satisfied balance of model complexity and overall performance.

Concerning the future work, we plan to take the asymmetric information of triples into the query encoder. Furthermore, it deserves further investigation to design more flexible attention structure in the process of aggregating context information and center query information.

Acknowledgements. This work was partially supported by the National Key Research and Development Program of China (No. 2018YFB2101502) and the Natural Science Foundation of China (No. 61977002).

References

1. Balažević, I., Allen, C., Hospedales, T.M.: Hypernetwork knowledge graph embeddings. In: Proceedings of 2019 International Conference on Artificial Neural Networks, pp. 553–565 (2019)
2. Bordes, A., Usunier, N., García-Durán, A., Weston, J., Yakhnenko, O.: Translating embeddings for modeling multi-relational data. In: Proceedings of the 26th International Conference on Neural Information Processing Systems, pp. 2787–2795 (2013)
3. Chao, L., He, J., Wang, T., Chu, W.: PairRE: knowledge graph embeddings via paired relation vectors. In: Proceedings of the 59th Annual Meeting of the Association for Computational Linguistics, pp. 4360–4369 (2021)
4. Chen, S., Liu, X., Gao, J., Jiao, J., Zhang, R., Ji, Y.: HittER: hierarchical transformers for knowledge graph embeddings. In: Proceedings of the 2021 Conference on Empirical Methods in Natural Language Processing, pp. 10395–10407 (2021)
5. Dettmers, T., Minervini, P., Stenetorp, P., Riedel, S.: Convolutional 2D knowledge graph embeddings. In: Proceedings of the 32nd AAAI Conference on Artificial Intelligence, pp. 1811–1818 (2018)
6. Guo, L., Sun, Z., Hu, W.: Learning to exploit long-term relational dependencies in knowledge graphs. In: Proceedings of the 36th International Conference on Machine Learning, pp. 2505–2514 (2019)
7. Hao, Y., et al.: An end-to-end model for question answering over knowledge base with cross-attention combining global knowledge. In: Proceedings of the 55th Annual Meeting of the Association for Computational Linguistics, pp. 221–231 (2017)

8. Hochreiter, S., Schmidhuber, J.: Long short-term memory. Neural Comput. **9**(8), 1735–1780 (1997)
9. Jiang, X., Wang, Q., Wang, B.: Adaptive convolution for multi-relational learning. In: Proceedings of the 2019 Conference of the North American Chapter of the Association for Computational Linguistics, pp. 978–987 (2019)
10. Lin, Y., Liu, Z., Sun, M., Liu, Y., Zhu, X.: Learning entity and relation embeddings for knowledge graph completion. In: Proceedings of the 29th AAAI Conference on Artificial Intelligence, pp. 2181–2187 (2015)
11. Liu, Y., Wang, P., Li, Y., Shao, Y., Xu, Z.: AprilE: attention with pseudo residual connection for knowledge graph embedding. In: Proceedings of the 28th International Conference on Computational Linguistics, pp. 508–518 (2020)
12. Nguyen, D.Q., Nguyen, T.D., Nguyen, D.Q., Phung, D.Q.: A novel embedding model for knowledge base completion based on convolutional neural network. In: Proceedings of the 2018 Conference of the North American Chapter of the Association for Computational Linguistics, pp. 327–333 (2018)
13. Nickel, M., Tresp, V., Kriegel, H.: A three-way model for collective learning on multi-relational data. In: Proceedings of the 28th International Conference on Machine Learning, pp. 809–816 (2011)
14. Ren, F., et al.: Knowledge graph embedding with atrous convolution and residual learning. In: Proceedings of the 28th International Conference on Computational Linguistics, pp. 1532–1543 (2020)
15. Schlichtkrull, M.S., Kipf, T.N., Bloem, P., van den Berg, R., Titov, I., Welling, M.: Modeling relational data with graph convolutional networks. In: Proceedings of 15th International Conference on Semantic Web, pp. 593–607 (2018)
16. Shang, C., Tang, Y., Huang, J., Bi, J., He, X., Zhou, B.: End-to-end structure-aware convolutional networks for knowledge base completion. In: Proceedings of the 33rd AAAI Conference on Artificial Intelligence, pp. 3060–3067 (2019)
17. Sun, Z., Deng, Z., Nie, J., Tang, J.: RotatE: knowledge graph embedding by relational rotation in complex space. In: Proceedings of the 7th International Conference on Learning Representations (2019)
18. Toutanova, K., Chen, D., Pantel, P., Poon, H., Choudhury, P., Gamon, M.: Representing text for joint embedding of text and knowledge bases. In: Proceedings of the 2015 Conference on Empirical Methods in Natural Language Processing, pp. 1499–1509 (2015)
19. Trouillon, T., Welbl, J., Riedel, S., Gaussier, É., Bouchard, G.: Complex embeddings for simple link prediction. In: Proceedings of the 33nd International Conference on Machine Learning, pp. 2071–2080 (2016)
20. Vashishth, S., Sanyal, S., Nitin, V., Agrawal, N., Talukdar, P.P.: InteractE: improving convolution-based knowledge graph embeddings by increasing feature interactions. In: Proceedings of the 34th AAAI Conference on Artificial Intelligence, pp. 3009–3016 (2020)
21. Vashishth, S., Sanyal, S., Nitin, V., Talukdar, P.P.: Composition-based multi-relational graph convolutional networks. In: Proceedings of the 8th International Conference on Learning Representations (2020)
22. Wang, Q., et al.: CoKE: contextualized knowledge graph embedding. CoRR abs/1911.02168 (2019)
23. Wang, Z., Zhang, J., Feng, J., Chen, Z.: Knowledge graph embedding by translating on hyperplanes. In: Proceedings of the 28th AAAI Conference on Artificial Intelligence, pp. 1112–1119 (2014)

24. Xie, Z., Zhou, G., Liu, J., Huang, J.X.: ReInceptionE: relation-aware inception network with joint local-global structural information for knowledge graph embedding. In: Proceedings of the 58th Annual Meeting of the Association for Computational Linguistics, pp. 5929–5939 (2020)
25. Xu, C., Li, R.: Relation embedding with Dihedral group in knowledge graph. In: Proceedings of the 57th Conference of the Association for Computational Linguistics, pp. 263–272 (2019)
26. Yang, B., Yih, W., He, X., Gao, J., Deng, L.: Embedding entities and relations for learning and inference in knowledge bases. In: Proceedings of the 3rd International Conference on Learning Representations (2015)
27. Ye, R., Li, X., Fang, Y., Zang, H., Wang, M.: A vectorized relational graph convolutional network for multi-relational network alignment. In: Proceedings of the 28th International Joint Conference on Artificial Intelligence, pp. 4135–4141 (2019)
28. Zhang, S., Tay, Y., Yao, L., Liu, Q.: Quaternion knowledge graph embeddings. In: Proceedings of 2019 Annual Conference on Neural Information Processing Systems, pp. 2731–2741 (2019)
29. Zhang, Z., Cai, J., Zhang, Y., Wang, J.: Learning hierarchy-aware knowledge graph embeddings for link prediction. In: Proceedings of the 34th AAAI Conference on Artificial Intelligence, pp. 3065–3072 (2020)

IMDb30: A Multi-relational Knowledge Graph Dataset of IMDb Movies

Wenying Feng[1,2], Daren Zha[1], Lei Wang[1], and Xiaobo Guo[1,2(✉)]

[1] Institute of Information Engineering, Chinese Academy of Sciences, Beijing, China
{fengwenying,zhadaren,wanglei,guoxiaobo}@iie.ac.cn
[2] School of Cyber Security, University of Chinese Academy of Sciences, Beijing, China

Abstract. Most knowledge graph embedding (KGE) models are trained and evaluated through common benchmark datasets such as WN18 and FB15k. However, these datasets belong to the general filed and have been utilized as link prediction benchmarks for many years. In addition, some of them suffer from test leakage, thus cannot evaluate KGE models effectively. To provide a new link prediction benchmark of field-specific knowledge graph without test leakage, we proposed a new dataset called **IMDb30**, which incorporate knowledge of IMDb (Internet Movie Database) movies. We construct IMDb30 based on the public relational data released on IMDb website. The complete IMDb30 contains more than 6 million triplets, and a subset of IMDb30 is also constructed to conduct experiments. IMDb30 subset contains 115080 triplets formed by 31343 entities and 30 relations. We conduct link prediction experiments for 3 convolutional neural network models of KGE on the subset and the results show that IMDb30 can effectively train and evaluate KGE models. The complete dataset and the construction process are made publicly available.

Keywords: Knowledge graph · KG construction · Knowledge graph completion · Link prediction

1 Introduction

Knowledge Graph (KG) is graph-structured knowledge base, first proposed by Google. Some famous KGs, such as WordNet, Freebase and YAGO, have been widely used in various AI applications such as expert system, semantic search, and Q&A. Knowledge Graph Embedding (KGE) is the main method for KG representation. It embeds entities and relations of KG into low dimensional continuous vector space, thus makes the knowledge can be calculated and reasoned. KGE is applied directly to link prediction for Knowledge Graph Completion (KGC). Many KG datasets are used to evaluate KGE models on link prediction, such as WN18, FB15k, WN18RR and FB15k-237. WN18 and FB15k are first proposed in TransE [3] for training and evaluating the link prediction capability

G. Memmi et al. (Eds.): KSEM 2022, LNAI 13368, pp. 696–708, 2022.
https://doi.org/10.1007/978-3-031-10983-6_53

of TransE. WN18RR and FB15k are the subsets of WN18 and FB15k, respectively. They are proposed to fix the test leakage of original datasets by removing the reversal triplets in test set compared to them in training set.

Even though there are many datasets for KG link prediction, these datasets still suffer from several problems that restrict them from evaluating KGE models comprehensively and fairly. **Firstly**, WordNet datasets (WN18 and WN18RR) and Freebase datasets (FB15k and FB15k-237) have been used for a long time, and some excellent models have achieved very high percentage of link prediction accuracy[1], so there is not so much utilization potentiality of these datasets, therefore a new challenging dataset needs to be proposed. **Secondly**, some datasets (WN18 and FB15k) suffer from test leakage. For example, the test set frequently contains triplets such as $(s, \text{hyponym}, o)$ while the training set contains its reverse $(o, \text{hypernym}, s)$ [5]. This will lead to false high accuracy of link prediction. **Thirdly**, these link prediction datasets are basically in general field which contain general knowledge. There is few field-specific KG datasets for link prediction such as movie KG. Existing movie datasets [6,15] are not constructed specially for link prediction and are in small scale, thus cannot evaluate KGE model performance fairly and fully in specific field.

Focusing on these problems, we propose a movie KG dataset **IMDb30**. We build this dataset based on the public IMDb list dataset following three steps: requesting, filtering, and partitioning. We first construct the subset which contains 115080 triplets composed by 31343 entities and 30 relations, and then incrementally build the whole dataset. Our proposed IMDb30 is a movie relational KG dataset, its head entities are movies and the tail entities are persons or production companies. The test set are parted from the whole original triplet set, thus there is no test leakage. We train and evaluate three convolution KGE models (Conv1D, Conv2D, and Conv3D) on IMDb30 subset. The model performance results are the same as them on traditional datasets, but the prediction accuracy are not as high as on them. This indicates our proposed benchmark IMDb30 can evaluate KGE models correctly and has a stricter requirement for the embedding capability of KGE models. We also visualize the embedding vectors of entities and relations in IMDb30 subset trained by Conv3D. The visualization results show that convolution model can capture entity semantics.

In summary, Our contributions are as follows:

Contribution I: We propose and construct a movie KG dataset IMDb30, which contains more than 6 million triplets. To the best of our knowledge, IMDb30 is the largest movie KG dataset for link prediction, covering the information of most IMDb movies.

Contribution II: Based on the subset of IMDb30 obtained so far, we train and evaluate three convolutional KGE models, and the comparison results are the same as on traditional KG datasets.

---

[1] https://paperswithcode.com/sota/link-prediction-on-wn18
https://paperswithcode.com/sota/link-prediction-on-fb15k
https://paperswithcode.com/sota/link-prediction-on-wn18rr
https://paperswithcode.com/sota/link-prediction-on-fb15k-237.

Contribution III: We visualize the embedded vectors of the entities and relations in IMDb30 trained by Conv3D. The embedded entity scatters show clustering, denoting the embedded vectors have learned entity semantics.

The rest of the paper is structured as follows. We provide a summary of related work of link prediction datasets and convolutional KGE models in Sect. 2. Then we introduce the construction process of IMDb30 in Sect. 3. Experiment results across 3 convolution models are reported and analysed in Sect. 4, followed by conclusion and future work in Sect. 5.

2   Related Work

In this section we introduce the commonly used link prediction datasets and the 3 convolutional KGE models we train on our proposed IMDb30 dataset.

2.1   Link Prediction Datasets

Several link prediction datasets are constructed based on open knowledge graph WordNet and Freebase. WN18 and FB15k are used as link prediction datasets in TransE [3]. **WN18** is a subset of WordNet [11], containing lexical relational data of synsets. WordNet is designed to produce an intuitively usable dictionary and thesaurus, and support automatic text analysis. Its entities (termed synsets) correspond to word senses, and relations define lexical relations between them [3]. WN18 considers the data version used in SME [2], in which the example triplet is like (*_score_NN_2, _has_part, _musical_notation_NN_1*). **FB15k** is a subset of Freebase [1], describing general facts about movies, actors, awards, sports, and sports teams. Freebase is a huge knowledge base of general facts. Antoine et al. select the subset of entities that are present in Wikilinks database and also have at least 100 mentions in Freebase (for both entity and relation). Then they remove relations which just reverse the head and tail to generate the dataset FB15k [3]. WN18 and FB15k are used to train and evaluate many KGE models such as TransE [3], TransH [17], TransR [10], ConvE [5], R-GCN [14], ConvR [8], et al. Even these two datasets are commonly used, Toutanova and Chen [16] note that WN18 and FB15k suffer from test leakage through inverse relations: a large number of test triplets can be obtained by simply inverting triplets in the training set. Thus they introduce **FB15k-237**, a subset of FB15k where inverse relations are removed. In addition, Dettmers et al. introduce **WN18RR** to fix the same flaw of WN18.

In addition to the general field datasets described above, there are field-specific KG datasets. Han and Wang [6] extract knowledge from movie data crawled from Baidu Encyclopedeia. They also use a movie scoring dataset called Movie-Lens constructed from 3900 movies for recommendation algorithm evaluation. Shuai and Zhang [15] construct a Chinese movie KG for Q&A. However these field-specific datasets are in small scale and are not specially designed for link prediction. So there is no large scale movie KG for link prediction, and the

KG datasets of general field lack the capability of evaluating the model performance in specific field.

Focus on this problem, we propose and construct a large scale movie KG dataset IMDb30. This dataset contains information of most movies in IMDb website[2]. IMDb[3] is an online database of information related to films, television series, and streaming content online, including cast, production crew, plot summaries, critical reviews, et al. As of December 2021, the database contains 8,744,296 titles (including some 600 thousand films), and the total number of data items is 428,149,001[4].

2.2 Convolutional KGE Models

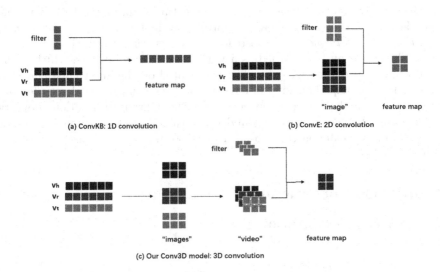

(a) ConvKB: 1D convolution

(b) ConvE: 2D convolution

(c) Our Conv3D model: 3D convolution

Fig. 1. 3 convolutional models for KGE

Since most KGs suffer from information loss, various KGE models are proposed to conduct link prediction for KGC. KGE models can be classified into three major categories: translation-based model (e.g. TransE [3]), bilinear model (e.g. DistMult [18]), and neural network model (e.g. ConvE [5], ConvKB [12]). In neural network models, convolution (including regular convolution and graph convolution) is a commonly used operation for capturing the interactions between entities and relations. Graph convolutional network (GCN) is also used in traffic flow and density prediction [13]. In addition, generating adversarial network (GAN) is used both in KGE [4] and intelligent fault diagnosis [9].

---

[2] https://www.imdb.com/.

[3] https://en.wikipedia.org/wiki/IMDb.

[4] https://www.imdb.com/pressroom/stats/.

Futhermore, the development of hardware has also contributed to the improvement of detection and prediction [7].

We train and evaluate three convolutional KGE models on the IMDb30 subset, as shown in Fig. 1. Among them, ConvKB use 1D convolution and ConvE use 2D convolution, respectively. Based on ConvKB and ConvE, we extend the convolution form to 3D and propose Conv3D. For convenience of illustration, we denote three models as Conv1D, Conv2D, and Conv3D, respectively. Figure 1(a) shows 1D convolution used in Conv1D. Conv1D stacks the embeddings of h, r, t into a matrix as the input of convolution. The filter in 1D convolution is a vector, which is repeatedly operated over every row of the input matrix, and produces a feature map. Figure 1(b) shows 2D convolution used in Conv2D. Conv2D first reshapes the embeddings of h and r into *images* (matrices) and concatenates them into a big *image* as the input of 2D convolution. Here the filter is also a matrix, operated on the *image* to generate a feature map. Figure 1(c) shows the core idea of our Conv3D. Following Conv2D, we first reshape the embeddings of h, r, and t into *images*. Then instead of concatenation, we stack them into a cube. This cube can be regarded as a video with 3 image frames, which is the input of 3D convolution. A cube filter is operated on the input cube and generates a feature map. This kind of convolution form can capture deeper feature interaction than shallow convolution form without losing translation property of knowledge triplet. By training and evaluating these three model Conv1D, Conv2D, and Conv3D on the subset of IMDb30, we verify the usability of our proposed dataset.

3   IMDb30 Construction

3.1   Properties of IMDb30

Table 1. Statistics of Common Datasets and our IMDb30

Dataset	$|\mathcal{E}|$	$|\mathcal{R}|$	Train	Valid	Test
WN18	40943	18	141442	5000	5000
WN18RR	40943	11	86835	3034	3134
FB15k	14951	1345	483142	50000	59071
FB15k-237	14541	237	272115	17535	20466
IMDb30 subset	**31343**	**30**	**91909**	**11585**	**11586**

Dataset Scale. Since it will take much more time (about 600 h) to build the whole dataset, thus we first construct the subset to verify the feasibility of the construction scheme and the evaluation capability of this dataset. The basic statistic information of IMDb30 subset is shown in the last line of Table 1.

IMDb30 subset contains 31343 entities and 30 relations, constructing 115080 triplet samples. The whole samples are divided into training set, validation set, and test set, following a proportion of 8:1:1 (91909 for training, 11585 for validation, and 11586 for test). The entity and relation number of IMDb30 is more balanced than the four common datasets. And the appropriate division proportion of triplet samples can effectively train and evaluate model performance.

The subset triplets are collected from 10000 IMDb movies. Building them takes about 8 h and they occupy 3.41 MB of hardware space. The subset of is 1/60 of the complete dateset, because there are about 600 thousand movies in IMDb. We have already finished constructing the complete dataset and make it publicly available in GitHub[5], along with the construction code. Data scale and construction time comparison of the subset and complete dataset is listed in Table 2. So far as we know, IMDb30 based on IMDb is the largest movie KG for link prediction.

Table 2. Comparison of IMDb30 subset and complete IMDb30

Dataset scale	Subset	Complete dataset
Movie number	10000	593631
Entity number	31343	About 1.8 million
Relation number	30	30
Triplet number	115080	About 6 million
Occupied space	3.41 M	About 350 M
Construction time	8 h	About 25 d

Table 3. 30 Relations in IMDb30

cast	art_directors	location_management
directors	set_decorators	music_department
writers	costume_designers	stunts
producers	make_up_department	camera_department
composers	production_managers	casting_department
cinematographers	assistant_directors	costume_departmen
editors	art_department	script_department
editorial_department	sound_department	transportation_department
casting_directors	special_effects	production_companies
production_designers	visual_effects	distributors

---

[5] https://github.com/fengwenying/IMDb30.

Entities and Relations. There are two kinds of elements in IMDb30: entity and relation. The logical relationships of IMDb30 entities form a large graph, which is stored as triplets. The nodes of the graph are entities, and the edges of the graph are the relations between entities. For example, in triplet (*tt0111161*, *directors*, *nm0001104*), *tt0111161* is the ID of the movie entity *The Shawshank Redemption*, and *nm0001104* is the ID of the director person *Frank Darabont*. This triplet denotes that there is a relation of *directors* between entity *The Shawshank Redemption* and entity *Frank Darabont*. There are three types of entities: movie, person, and company. The head entities of all triplets are movies, and the tail entities are persons or companies. Every entity is denoted as a string of 7 digits, with prefix *tt* for movie entities, *nm* for person entities, and *co* for company entities. The string is also the unique identification of IMDb webpage for the entity. Table 3 list the 30 relations, denoted by words or phrases connected with underline.

3.2 Construction Process

The process for constructing IMDb30 contains 3 stages: requesting, filtering, and partitioning.

Requesting. We use open-source toolkit Cinemagoer[6] (previously known as IMDbPY) to request movie information with a specified ID. Cinemagoer is a Python package for retrieving and managing entities such as movies and characters in IMDb movie database. It can be regarded as an encapsulated crawler, getting and returning assigned movie information in the form of dictionary.

Filtering. Cinemagoer return all information according to specified movie ID, we select the information related to attribute fields in Table 3 for triplet construction. Since there are many entities for some attribute fields (for example, one movie may have dozens of actors), the low-frequency entities ranked behind may cause long-tail phenomenon. This feature makes the KG difficult to be embedded and represented. Therefore we restrict the entity number of each attribute field for each movie to k (k=5). In addition, illegal representation occasionally exists in the returned information (for example, the tail entity type is not person or company), thus we need to filter out illegal information. The filtered information is assembled into triplets, which are added into triplet set of IMDb30.

Partitioning. We build the dataset in blocks for debug convenience and avoiding data storage. The triplets of every 10000 movies are collected as one block, and the subset contains 10 blocks. We splice the blocks into complete triplet set and shuffle. Then we divide the triplet set into training set, validation set, and test set following specified proportion.

---

[6] https://imdbpy.readthedocs.io/en/latest/index.html.

In the process of IMDb30 construction, we mainly solve the following two problems:

1. How to specify movie IDs?

There are about 600 thousand movies on IMDb website, each movie is identified by an string ID with prefix *tt* followed by 7 digits. However, some IDs have no corresponding movie entity, and we are unable to determine the one-to-one correspondence between each movie and the ID. It will lead to serious waste of requesting resources and increase the requesting load if we make traversal search and request for all the candidate IDs of the permutation and combination of 7 digits. If we carry out incremental crawling according to the recommended movies of seed movies, we cannot guarantee to traverse all the movie entities in IMDb, and this may cause type offset. To solve this problem, we use IMDb official public dataset[7] to assign movie IDs. This official public dataset contains the information of almost all of the IMDb movies, documentaries, TV series et al. We make information request with the dataset samples whose type is *movie*, thus can obtain the information of assigned attribute field accurately and save request resources.

2. Which attribute fields are specified as relations?

Since the head and tail of the triplet in IMDb30 are entities, the relation between head entity and tail entity is their corresponding relationship.

The constructed triplet is relational triplet in the form of (head entity, relation, tail entity), rather than attribute triplet in the form of (entity, attribute, value). Whereas in IMDb website, most of the movie information is attribute information, like *release date, movie genre*. Their value is abstract date or type, rather than real entity, thus cannot be utilized to construct relational triplet. Only the attribute fields that the attribute value is real entity like person or company can be selected to construct relational triplets. To solve this problem, we select 30 attribute fields whose value are entities, listed in Table 3. These 30 relations can be classified into two categories: *production_companies* and *distributors* belong to *movie-company* relation, the other relations in Table 3 belong to *movie-person* relation. In this way, we can make sure that the tail entity of IMDb30 triplet are real entity in physical world with independent IMDb webpage rather than abstract particular year or movie type.

4 Experiments

We conduct experiments to explore whether the proposed KG dataset is practical. Specifically, we consider two tasks: performance evaluation of convolutional models, and visualization of embedded entities and relations.

---

[7] https://www.imdb.com/interfaces/.

4.1   Performance Evaluation of Convolutional Models

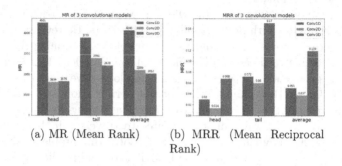

(a) MR (Mean Rank)   (b) MRR (Mean Reciprocal Rank)

Fig. 2. MR and MRR of link prediction on IMDb30 subset

We use IMDb30 subset to train and test three convolutional models: Conv1D, Conv2D, and Conv3D. We use link prediction task to evaluate model performance. The purpose of link prediction is to deduce whether there is some relationship between two entities, i.e., inferring missing h given $(?, r, t)$, or inferring missing t given $(h, r, ?)$. The results are obtained by calculating and ranking the scores on test set using score function $f(\cdot)$. We use two series of metrics to quantitatively indicate the results of link prediction: MR/MRR and Hits@n. Mean Rank (MR) calculates the average value of all ranked numbers of predicted entity in test set. Mean Reciprocal Rank (MRR) is a transformation form of MR, which is the mean of reciprocals of the ranked numbers. Hits@n counts the quantity ratio of right entities in test set that are ranked in top n. We take n=1, 3, 10 in implementation. Lower MR, higher MRR, or higher Hits@n indicates better link prediction performance. Following TransE, for valid triplet (h, r, t), we replace h or t with each entity in $\mathcal{E}$ except for the ground truth entity to generate a set of corrupted triplets. We take *filter* setting protocol, i.e., not taking the mis-generated valid triplets into account while counting the rank number of the ground truth entity. We set the same hyper-parameters while training the three models for comparing model performance fairly.

The comparison results of three models on 5 link prediction metrics (MR, MRR, Hits@1, Hits@3, Hits@10) are showed in Fig. 2 and Fig. 3. From the 5 metrics as a whole, the comparison results of three models are basically consistent. On our IMDb30 subset, the performance of Conv3D (green) is better than that of Conv1D (blue) and Conv2D (orange), which is consistent with the comparison results on other KG dataset such as WN18 and WN18RR. From each bar chart separately, the prediction accuracy of each model for tail entity (person, company) is higher than that for head entity (movie). The reason for this phenomenon is that the samples in training set are all forward triplets. The triplets are 1-N, which means one movie entity may correspond to multiple persons or companies. In this situation, when the model are predicting tail entity,

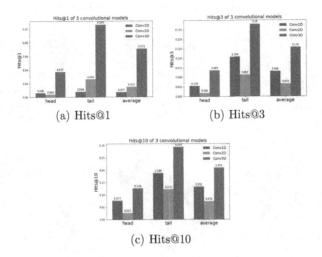

(a) Hits@1   (b) Hits@3

(c) Hits@10

Fig. 3. Hits@n of link prediction on IMDb30 subset

the number of candidate entities are more than 1, so the prediction accuracy is improved. On the contrary, there is only one ground-truth candidate entity when predicting head entity, resulting in low prediction accuracy.

This part of experiments demonstrate that our IMDb30 subset can evaluate and compare KGE model performance effectively and fairly. Despite this, the metric results of these three models are much worse than those on WordNet and Freebase datasets. This indicates that IMDb30 is more complicated than common datasets in graph structure. IMDb30 is more difficult to be embedded and predicted, thus raises higher requirement for the embedding capability of KGE model.

4.2 Visualization of Embedded Entities and Relations

To explore the distribution of entities and relations of IMDb30 in semantic space, we visualize the embedded vectors trained by Conv3D with toolkit tSNE[8]. Figure 4 showed the variation trend of two-dimensional distribution of entity embedding vectors along with the training epochs. The embedded entities before training show irregular loose sand distribution. With the increase of the epoch number, the whole distribution gradually presents large and small clustering. The scattered points at the edge move closer to the center, and outliers decrease. Finally, three large classes containing several small clusters are formed. This phenomenon indicates that the embedded vectors capture certain semantics for entities after training, and form clusters according to the semantics. However, the relation embedding vectors do not show clustering or special evolution trend. This is because relation is an abstract existence, and has no apparent relationship with each other. So we do not put the visualization figure here.

---

[8] http://lvdmaaten.github.io/tsne/.

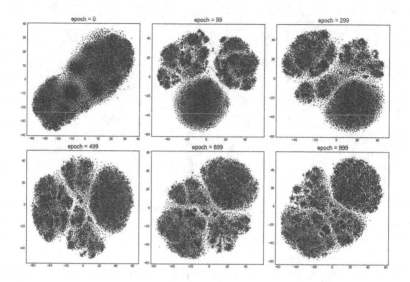

Fig. 4. Visualization of IMDb30 entities

5 Conclusion

In this paper, we proposed IMDb30, a movie knowledge graph dataset, containing 30 relations and more than 6 million triplets. We built this dataset based on IMDb public relational dataset through three steps: requesting, filtering, and partitioning. We conducted link prediction experiments with three convolutional KGE models on IMDb30 subset. The results show that our proposed dataset can train and evaluate KGE model and make a fair comparison. The visualization experiment for embedded entities shows that the embedding vectors trained by KGE model can capture entity semantics. Since the triplet number of the whole IMDb30 is so large that KGE model needs a lot of training time, and there are some low-frequency entities resulting in unbalanced graph structure, we plan to futher filter the triplets, and perform accurate statistics of entity number and triplet number. In addition, We will also conduct detailed analysis for the graph structure and provide a public Python package on Github in the future. We hope IMDb30 can facilitate KG researchers with model test benchmark of specific field, so as to evaluate KGE model in different scenarios.

Acknowledgements. The author would like to thank IMDb.com, Inc., the subsidiary of Amazon for releasing the IMDb movie datasets in text format, which help us construct our knowledge graph dataset. In addition, we would like to thank the reviewers for their valuable comments and suggestions that help improving the quality of this paper.

References

1. Bollacker, K., Evans, C., Paritosh, P., Sturge, T., Taylor, J.: Freebase: a collaboratively created graph database for structuring human knowledge. In: Proceedings of the 2008 ACM SIGMOD International Conference on Management of Data, pp. 1247–1250 (2008)
2. Bordes, A., Glorot, X., Weston, J., Bengio, Y.: A semantic matching energy function for learning with multi-relational data. Mach. Learn. **94**(2), 233–259 (2013). https://doi.org/10.1007/s10994-013-5363-6
3. Bordes, A., Usunier, N., Garcia-Duran, A., Weston, J., Yakhnenko, O.: Translating embeddings for modeling multi-relational data. Adv. Neural Inf. Process. Syst. **26**, 1–9 (2013)
4. Cai, L., Wang, W.Y.: Kbgan: adversarial learning for knowledge graph embeddings. arXiv preprint arXiv:1711.04071 (2017)
5. Dettmers, T., Minervini, P., Stenetorp, P., Riedel, S.: Convolutional 2D knowledge graph embeddings. In: Thirty-Second AAAI Conference on Artificial Intelligence (2018)
6. Han, W., Wang, Q.: Movie recommendation algorithm based on knowledge graph. In: 2019 2nd International Conference on Safety Produce Informatization (IICSPI), pp. 409–412. IEEE (2019)
7. Hu, F., Lakdawala, S., Hao, Q., Qiu, M.: Low-power, intelligent sensor hardware interface for medical data preprocessing. IEEE Trans. Inf. Technol. Biomed. **13**(4), 656–663 (2009)
8. Jiang, X., Wang, Q., Wang, B.: Adaptive convolution for multi-relational learning. In: Proceedings of the 2019 Conference of the North American Chapter of the Association for Computational Linguistics: Human Language Technologies, vol. 1 (Long and Short Papers), pp. 978–987 (2019)
9. Li, Y., Song, Y., Jia, L., Gao, S., Li, Q., Qiu, M.: Intelligent fault diagnosis by fusing domain adversarial training and maximum mean discrepancy via ensemble learning. IEEE Trans. Ind. Inf. **17**(4), 2833–2841 (2020)
10. Lin, Y., Liu, Z., Sun, M., Liu, Y., Zhu, X.: Learning entity and relation embeddings for knowledge graph completion. In: Twenty-Ninth AAAI Conference on Artificial Intelligence (2015)
11. Miller, G.A.: Wordnet: a lexical database for English. Commun. ACM **38**(11), 39–41 (1995)
12. Nguyen, D.Q., Nguyen, T.D., Nguyen, D.Q., Phung, D.: A novel embedding model for knowledge base completion based on convolutional neural network. arXiv preprint arXiv:1712.02121 (2017)
13. Qiu, H., Zheng, Q., Msahli, M., Memmi, G., Qiu, M., Lu, J.: Topological graph convolutional network-based urban traffic flow and density prediction. IEEE Trans. Intell. Transp. Syst. **22**(7), 4560–4569 (2020)
14. Schlichtkrull, M., et al.: Modeling relational data with graph convolutional networks. In: Gangemi, A., et al. (eds.) ESWC 2018. LNCS, vol. 10843, pp. 593–607. Springer, Cham (2018). https://doi.org/10.1007/978-3-319-93417-4_38
15. Shuai, Q., Zhang, C.: Question answering system based on knowledge graph of film culture. In: 2020 International Conference on Culture-oriented Science & Technology (ICCST), pp. 150–153. IEEE (2020)
16. Toutanova, K., Chen, D.: Observed versus latent features for knowledge base and text inference. In: Proceedings of the 3rd Workshop on Continuous Vector Space Models and their Compositionality, pp. 57–66 (2015)

17. Wang, Z., Zhang, J., Feng, J., Chen, Z.: Knowledge graph embedding by translating on hyperplanes. In: Proceedings of the AAAI Conference on Artificial Intelligence, vol. 28 (2014)
18. Yang, B., Yih, W.T., He, X., Gao, J., Deng, L.: Embedding entities and relations for learning and inference in knowledge bases. arXiv preprint arXiv:1412.6575 (2014)

KnowReQA: A Knowledge-aware Retrieval Question Answering System

Chuanrui Wang[1], Jun Bai[2], Xiaofeng Zhang[1], Cen Yan[2], Yuanxin Ouyang[2(✉)],
Wenge Rong[2], and Zhang Xiong[1]

[1] Sino-French Engineer School, Beihang University, Beijing, China
{buaa_wcr,xiaofeng_z,xiongz}@buaa.edu.cn
[2] School of Computer Science and Engineering, Beihang University, Beijing, China
{bai_jun,cenyan,oyyx,w.rong}@buaa.edu.cn

Abstract. Retrieval question answering (ReQA) is an essential mechanism to automatically satisfy the users' information needs and overcome the problem of information overload. As a promising solution to achieve fast retrieval from large-scale candidate answers, dual-encoder framework has been widely studied to improve its representation quality for text in the recent years. Inspired by that humans usually answer the question using their background knowledge, in this work, we explore the way to incorporate knowledge entities into the retrieval model to build high-quality text representations and propose novel knowledge-aware text encoding and knowledge-aware text matching modules to facilitate the fusion between text and knowledge. The promising experimental results on various benchmarks prove the potential of the proposed approach.

Keywords: Retrieval question answering · Dual-encoder · Knowledge aware retrieval · Natural language processing

1 Introduction

Question Answering (QA) system is an essential application, which could automatically return suitable answers to the questions posed by users [1]. With the rapid accumulation of question-answer pairs, retrieval question answering (ReQA) has become a promising mechanism for QA system, which propose to directly retrieve the most relevant candidate answer from large-scale database in an end-to-end fashion [2]. Traditional ReQA approaches rely merely on the correlation between questions and answers at the level of the text surface instead of the deep semantic meaning, e.g., BM25 [15]. Recently, with the development of data-driven models, neural retrievers have significantly improved the performance of QA and drawn increasing attention from both academia and industries.

The mainstream neural retrievers consist of interaction-based retrievers and representation-based retrievers. Interaction-based retriever, e.g., BERT$_{QA}$ model [4] extracts rich interaction between questions and answers by conducting stacked transformer layers on concatenated QA pairs. Though effective on accuracy, the

© The Author(s), under exclusive license to Springer Nature Switzerland AG 2022
G. Memmi et al. (Eds.): KSEM 2022, LNAI 13368, pp. 709–721, 2022.
https://doi.org/10.1007/978-3-031-10983-6_54

interaction-based retriever has low computational efficiency due to the extensive needs for early interaction. The representation-based retriever is built on the dual-encoder framework. It first extracts the sentence-level representations of questions and answers separately by encoders. Then a matching operation (e.g., dot-product or cosine similarity) is conducted between the sentence-level representations to produce the matching score. In this way, the sentence-level representations of candidate answers could be obtained and stored in advance which saves a lot of time in practical. Therefore, a representation-based retriever is more suitable for a retrieval question answering system.

Since the matching operation in dual-encoder is simple, the qualities of the sentence-level representations decide the final retrieval accuracy. Recently Variational Autoencoders (VAEs) [17,22] and Knowledge Distillation (KD) [19] techniques have been explored to enhance such qualities. Intuitively, the knowledge related to the texts is another source worth utilizing, e.g., the entities related to certain concepts which provide essential clues for text understanding. Various works have been proposed to incorporate the entity information into text encoding. For example, Zhang et al. [23] employed a masked entity prediction task to tell the knowledge entity information to the model. It has been proven effective in extractive question answering [20] and generative dialogue systems [24].

Nevertheless, such approaches do not explicitly distinguish text tokens and knowledge entities where the entity information would be disturbed by noise within the text tokens. Unlikely the above method, Yamada et al. [21] proposed a pre-trained language model encoding text tokens and knowledge entities using an entity-aware self-attention mechanism to explicitly capture the difference as well as the interaction between them, which could effectively help the model to understand the types of tokens and show brilliant empirical results on knowledge-intensive tasks such as relation classification and entity typing. Inspired by this remarkable work, we employ the entity-aware self-attention mechanism in the encoder to achieve Knowledge-aware Text Encoding (KTE) for both question and candidate answer. To make use of the entity information in the q-a matching process, we also propose a Knowledge-aware Text Matching (KTM) module to build knowledge-aware sentence-level representations by considering both text tokens and entity tokens, which further improves the accuracy of retrieval.

Therefore, in this paper we propose a Knowledge-aware Retrieval Question Answering (KnowReQA) system, in which the Wikipedia as background knowledge base is first utilized to represent the knowledge entities related to questions and candidate answers. Then entity-aware self-attention mechanism is employed to explicitly capture the interaction between knowledge entities and text tokens for the knowledge-aware text encoding. Finally, the token representations from both text and entities are utilized to form sentence-level representations for the knowledge-aware text matching. The experiments on widely used ReQA datasets, i.e., ReQA SQuAD and ReQA NQ have shown our proposal's potential.

2   Related Work

Early answer retrieval systems are usually implemented by TF-IDF [13] and BM25 [15], which benefit from simple lexical overlap. Though lightweight and efficient, they fail to retrieve some answers which are not related semantically but logically. To address this issue, neural dual-encoder model [16] is proposed, which employs two encoders to compute the sentence-level representations of questions and answers independently and estimates the relevance between them by cosine or dot-product similarity. By leveraging the advanced pre-trained language models [11], the dual-encoder obtains high efficiency and promising performance.

A critical problem of dual-encoder is that the computation of matching score is conducted without any token-level interaction between question and answer, which impairs the retrieval accuracy. Several methods are proposed to overcome this challenge. On one hand, some works implement more complex matching functions on the token-level representations (e.g. Poly-Encoder [8] and ColBert [10]) which are more like a combination of the interaction-based model and the representation-based model. However, these works lose the fast retrieval ability of typical dual-encoder. On the other hand, some advanced methods focus on improving the quality of sentence-level representations. They propose to train the dual-encoder with auxiliary generative task, e.g., Yu et al. [22] proposed the Cross-VAEs model with question-to-answer and answer-to-question reconstruction tasks which can better capture the aligned semantics between questions and answers. Additionally, some researchers [18] adopt the teacher-student framework to make an interaction-based model as additional guidance for dual-encoder during training, which can provide a smooth matching distribution of question-answer pairs. Considering it is difficult for dual-encoder to model the whole complex geometry of interaction-based model in high dimensional space through element-wise alignment directly, recently Wang et al. [19] further proposed the geometry alignment mechanism to align the geometry of sentence-level representations from dual-encoder with that from an interaction-based model.

3   Methodology

3.1   Problem Definition and Overview

Given a question q and a set $S_a = (a_1, a_2, ..., a_K)$ of K candidate answers, the objective of a typical retrieval question answering task is to find the best-matched answer from all candidate answers for the posed question q. In this work, we propose a knowledge-aware retrieval question answering model, in which the knowledge entity sets E_q and E_a related respectively to questions and candidate answers need to be exploited.

The proposed KnowReQA model consists of knowledge-aware text encoding and knowledge-aware text matching. The former is used to extract the interaction between text and knowledge entities. The latter further compute the matching score by considering both text tokens and entity tokens, which results in knowledge-aware text matching.

3.2   Knowledge Entity Extraction

We need to firstly obtain the knowledge entities related to questions and candidate answers. Considering Wikipedia as the knowledge source, we employ the entity linking tool, i.e., TagMe [5], to extract commonsense knowledge entities from questions and candidate answers and to map them to entities in Wikipedia. As shown in Fig. 1, given a text, TagMe returns a list of entity candidates with corresponding confidence scores. The entities with scores higher than a confidence threshold are considered to be text-related entities.

[Question text]: where is the **charging bull** located in **NYC**?
[Linked entity]: Charging Bull, New York City.

[Answer text]: **Charging Bull** , which is sometimes referred to as the **Wall Street Bull** or the **Bowling Green Bull** , is a **bronze sculpture** that stands in **Bowling Green** in the **Financial District** in **Manhattan**, **New York City**.
[Linked entities]: Charging Bull, Bull, Bronze sculpture, Bowling Green, Kentucky, Financial District, Manhattan, New York City]

Fig. 1. A pair of question and answer with their related entities, the boldfaced tokens are entities extracted, which are then linked to standard entities in Wikipedia.

In order to introduce knowledge information into retrieval question answering task, we use the TagMe tool [5] to extract commonsense knowledge entities in question and answer sentences and map them to specific entities in Wikipedia one-to-one.

3.3   Knowledge-Aware Text Encoding

During the text encoding stage, the model should be explicitly aware of the text-related knowledge entities and interactively encode the text and entities. Given the text (question or answer candidate) $T = (t_1, t_2, ..., t_m)$ and the text-related entities $E = (e_1, e_2, ..., e_n)$, where t_i is the i_{th} token and e_i is the i_{th} entity; m and n are the length of text and the number of entities, the **Knowledge-Aware Text Encoding (KTE)** module explicitly distinguish the tokens from text and entities and employ entity-aware self-attention mechanism to model the relation between text and entities. Finally, the token representations of text and entities with rich text-entity interaction are obtained.

As shown in Fig. 2, to explicitly distinguish the tokens from text and entities, we use different embedding layers to obtain the embeddings of text tokens and entity tokens. Then we concatenate the corresponding token embeddings of text and entities as the initial token representations:

$$H^0 = [\text{TextEmbedding}(T), \text{EntityEmbedding}(E)] = [h_1^0, h_2^0, ..., h_p^0] \quad (1)$$

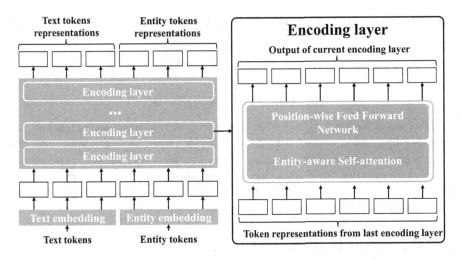

Fig. 2. The knowledge-aware text encoding module, where the text as well as the text-related entities are input to encoder with entity-aware self-attention mechanism to extract the interaction between text and entities.

where $p = m + n$; $H^0 \in \mathbb{R}^{p \times D}$ is the matrix of initial encoding representation; h_i^0 is the i_{th} vector of initial representation; D is the dimension of hidden space.

The typical encoding is conducted by stacking various encoding layers on the initial token representations, where the widely used transformer-based encoding layer is built upon the Self-Attention (SA) mechanism and position-wise Feed-Forward Network (FFN). The self-attention mechanism can be formulated as Eq. 2, where H is the representation of tokens, and $W^Q, W^K, W^V \in \mathbb{R}^{D \times D}$ are the trainable parameters.

$$\text{SA}(H) = \text{Softmax}(\frac{HW^Q(HW^K)^T}{\sqrt{d}})HW^V = M_{\text{SA}} HW^V \qquad (2)$$

However, the original self-attention mechanism does not consider the difference between the text tokens and entity tokens when computing the attention scores, thus being not well suitable to capture their interaction. In order to differently treat text tokens and entity tokens, we employ the entity-aware self-attention mechanism [21] that uses different query transformation parameters W_{EASA}^Q for different types of token pairs.

$$W_{\text{EASA}}^Q = \begin{cases} W_{t2t} & \text{if } h_i \text{ and } h_j \text{ are from text tokens} \\ W_{t2e} & \text{if } h_i \text{ is from text token and } h_j \text{ is from entity token} \\ W_{e2t} & \text{if } h_i \text{ is from entity token and } h_j \text{ is from text token} \\ W_{e2e} & \text{if } h_i \text{ and } h_j \text{ are from entity token} \end{cases} \qquad (3)$$

For the l_{th} encoding layer, the input representation is the corresponding token representations $H^{l-1} = [h_1^{l-1}, h_2^{l-1}, ..., h_p^{l-1}]$ output from the last encoding layer.

The Entity-Aware Self-Attention (EASA) mechanism can be thus formulated by Eqs. 4 and 5.

$$M_{\text{EASA}_{i,j}} = \text{Softmax}\left(\frac{h_i W_{\text{EASA}}^Q (h_j W^K)^T}{\sqrt{d}}\right) \tag{4}$$

$$\text{EASA}(H^{l-1}) = M_{\text{EASA}} H^{l-1} W^V \tag{5}$$

After encoding by L transformer layers with entity-aware self-attention, the corresponding token representations $H^L = (h_1^L, h_2^L, ..., h_p^L)$ are split into the token representations of text H_t^L and that of entities H_e^L. Finally, through the encoding process described above we could obtain the text token representations of question and answer candidate (H_t^q and H_t^a), as well as their entity token representations (H_e^q and H_e^a).

3.4   Knowledge-Aware Text Matching

At the matching stage, typically the sentence-level representations of question and answer candidate are extracted from the outputs of encoder and the cosine similarity between them is computed as matching score. To further incorporate the knowledge of entities in the matching time, we propose **Knowledge-aware Text Matching (KTM)** module which fully considers the different importances of text tokens and entity tokens by conducting attention mechanism among the token representations from both text and entities. Specifically, linear layers are employed to compute the attention scores among the concatenated token representations of text and entities where the attention scores are then used to perform weighted summation of token representations to produce the sentence-level representation:

$$A = \text{softmax}(W_A^1(\text{Tanh}(W_A^2(H_t \oplus H_e)^T))) \tag{6}$$

$$y = A(H_t \oplus H_e) \tag{7}$$

where $\oplus$ denote concatenation; $W_A^1 \in \mathbb{R}^{1 \times \frac{1}{2}D}$ and $W_A^2 \in \mathbb{R}^{\frac{1}{2}D \times D}$ are parameters of linear layers; $A \in \mathbb{R}^{1 \times (m+n)}$ is the attention scores over all token representations; $y \in \mathbb{R}^{1 \times D}$ is the sentence-level representation. As shown in Fig. 3, we could obtain the knowledge-aware sentence-level representations of question and answer candidate in this way, i.e., y_q and y_a, then the knowledge-aware text matching could be achieved by computing cosine similarity between them:

$$\text{KTM}(y_q, y_a) = \frac{y_q \cdot y_a}{||y_q|| \times ||y_a||} \tag{8}$$

in which $\cdot$ represents the dot-product operation and $||y||$ denotes the $L2$ norm.

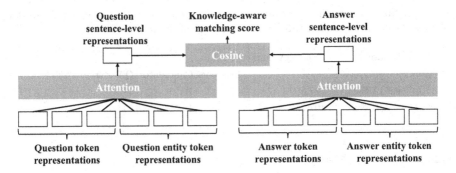

Fig. 3. The knowledge-aware text matching module first attentively extracts sentence-level representations for question and answer, then cosine similarity between the sentence-level representations is calculated for the knowledge-aware matching score.

3.5 Model Training

To train KnowReQA model, we employ the widely used in-batch negative sampling strategy which build negative question-answer pairs from the batch of data. And the corresponding loss function for a data batch could be defined as:

$$\mathcal{L} = -\frac{1}{N} \sum_{i=1}^{N} \log \frac{\mathrm{KTM}(y_q^i, y_a^i)/\tau}{\sum_{j=1}^{N} \mathrm{KTM}(y_q^i, y_a^j)/\tau} \tag{9}$$

where N is number of sample within a data batch; τ is the temperature factor to adjust the numerical range of the scores [3].

4 Experimental Study

4.1 Datasets

The widely used ReQA benchmarks are built from the SQuAD and NQ datasets where the data samples consist of question, document and span-level answer within the document [2]. To make these datasets suitable to large-scale retrieval question answering system, the sentence containing the span-level answer is taken as the true answer, other sentences in the document are also used as false candidate answers. Then the processed versions of SQuAD and NQ datasets are ReQA SQuAD and ReQA NQ datasets.

We show the statistics of ReQA SQuAD and ReQA NQ in Table 1. The degree of token overlap between the question and the correct answer is considered to compare the difficulties of these datasets. As shown as Table 1, ReQA SQuAD dataset has a overlap rate of 43.03% (that is, 43.03% of the tokens in the question also appear in the correct answer), while the ReQA NQ dataset has only 23.50% [6]. This means that the answer retrieval on the ReQA NQ should depend less on text surface matching, and it is more necessary to correctly understand the semantics of question and answer sentences.

Table 1. Statistics of the retrieval question answering datasets, where QA overlap denotes the token repetition rate of the question and matched answer.

Dataset	Train QA pairs	Test		
		Questions	Candidates	QA overlap (%)
ReQA SQuAD	87,599	10,539	10,246	43.03
ReQA NQ	107,252	4,177	19,551	23.50

4.2 Evaluation Metrics

Following previous works [2,19], we adopt Mean Reciprocal Rank (MRR) and Recall@K as evaluation metrics. Their definitions are as Eqs. 10 and 11.

$$MRR = \frac{1}{N_q} \sum_{i}^{N_q} \frac{1}{\mathrm{rank}_i} \tag{10}$$

$$R@K = \frac{1}{N_q} \sum_{i}^{N_q} \frac{|\mathrm{top}_K(P_i) \cap G_i|}{|G_i|} \tag{11}$$

where N_q is the number of questions; rank_i is the highest rank of true answers to the i_{th} question; P_i is the list of all candidate answers sorted in reserve by the matching scores; $\mathrm{top}_K(P_i)$ is the operation to extract the top-K candidate answers from P_i; G_i is the set of true answer to the i_{th} question.

4.3 Compared Methods

We compare the proposed KnowReQA model with following methods:

- **BM25** [15] The traditional model employing the correlation at the level of surface, specifically it considers the different importance of each question token as well as the relevance between the question tokens and answer text.
- **Dual-VAEs** [17] It introduces VAE into dual-encoder based on GRU, where auxiliary reconstruction tasks for both question and answer are proposed to improve the qualities of the sentence-level representations.
- **Cross-VAEs** [22] Similar to Dual-VAEs, it reconstruct answer using question and vice versa which could help capture the QA interaction.
- **Dual-BERTs** [14] The dual-encoder model using BERT as encoder, where attentive pooling is conducted to form the sentence-level representations.
- **ENDX-BERTs** [19] It utilizes knowledge distillation technique to enhance Dual-BERTs by the knowledge from interaction-based model.
- **Know Dual-BERTs** A baseline method that employs knowledge information. It is also built on Dual-BERTs, while two special tokens, i.e., [bok] and [eok] referring to "begin of knowledge" and "end of knowledge", are added before and after each knowledge entity, which has been proven useful [9].

4.4   Implementation Details

For the implementation of KnowReQA, we initialize the encoder with entity-aware self-attention mechanism using the pre-trained weights from [21], where the hidden dimensions D, number of encoding layers L are 768 and 12. To train KnowReQA, we set batch size and number of epochs to 12 and 30, which are the same settings used in [19]. AdamW [12] is employed as optimizer with learning rate of 1e-5 and a linear warmup [7] of 3 epochs is used.

Table 2. Results on ReQA SQuAD and ReQA NQ datasets, the scores of compared methods are reported from [19] where '-' denotes the score is not reported.

Method	ReQA SQuAD			ReQA NQ		
	MRR	R@1	R@5	MRR	R@1	R@5
BM25	52.96	45.81	61.31	12.54	8.77	16.48
Dual-VAEs	61.48	55.01	68.49	–	–	–
Cross-VAEs	62.29	55.60	70.05	–	–	–
Dual-BERTs	71.06	61.24	83.09	52.02	36.22	72.66
ENDX-BERTs	73.43	63.94	85.18	57.76	43.32	76.15
Know Dual-BERTs	71.65	61.95	83.70	62.28	49.77	78.05
KnowReQA	**74.11**	**64.58**	**85.76**	**62.87**	**50.54**	**85.76**

4.5   Main Results

The results on ReQA SQuAD and ReQA NQ are listed in Table 2. BM25 is based on bag-of-words retrieval function, it show comparable results on ReQA SQuAD due to the high overlap rate between question and answer, while its performance turns down significantly on ReQA NQ since the questions share few co-occurrence tokens with answers. The other models are all neural dual-encoder models and significantly outperform BM25 due to their strong ability to extract deep semantic meaning, where Dual-BERTs and ENDX-BERTs (BERT-based models) significantly outperform Dual-VAEs and Cross-VAEs (GRU-based models) which show the effectiveness of pre-trained language model. For the models enhanced by knowledge information, Know Dual-BERTs effectively improves the Dual-BERTs espically on ReQA NQ, which is because that ReQA NQ is harder than ReQA SQuAD and the knowledge entities are useful information when less lexical overlap between question and answer exist. However, Know Dual-BERTs only implicitly implements knowledge and could not effectively distinguish the knowledge from text, while our KnowReQA explicitly encode the knowledge information and utilize it during matching stage.

The proposed KnowReQA model surpasses all compared methods with regard to all three metrics on both ReQA SQuAD and ReQA NQ. Compared to the current state-of-the-art model ENDX-BERTs, our KnowReQA outperforms it on MRR, R@1, R@5 by 0.93%, 1.00% and 0.68% on ReQA SQuAD and by 8.85%, 16.67% and 12.62% on ReQA NQ, which shows that our proposed KnowReQA can successfully make use of knowledge and achieve new state-of-the-art result on benchmarks of retrieval question answering.

Table 3. Comparative experimental results about the effect of entity quantity. The first column reports the confidence threshold used to extract entities, the second and third columns count the average number of extracted entities among questions or answers. The fourth column shows the MRR metric to illustrate the final performance on ReQA SQuAD.

Threshold setting	#KE in Q	#KE in A	MRR
1	0	0	76.00
0.4	0.352	1.221	76.23
0.25	0.988	3.377	76.43
0.1	2.321	6.821	78.08

4.6   Effect of Entity Quantity

To better understand the effectiveness brought by knowledge entities and examine whether KnowReQA model successfully makes use of the entity information, we set different confidence thresholds when extracting the knowledge entities from questions and answers using TagMe, consequently different numbers of entities are obtained. We train KnowReQA four times on ReQA SQuAD by setting the confidence threshold to 1, 0.4, 0.25 and 0.1, respectively. In order to speed up the training, the experiment settings were modified to batch size 24 in 5 epochs. Since we increase the batch size which results in more negative question-answer pairs, the corresponding results are better than the results in Table 2.

As shown in Table 3, the number of knowledge entities increases as the confidence threshold decreases, and the MRR score increases as the number of knowledge entities grows, which shows that more knowledge entities provide more useful information and improve the retrieval performance.

Table 4. Ablation experiment on ReQA SQuAD.

Method	MRR	R@1	R@5
KnowReQA	78.08	70.01	88.21
w/o KTM	77.86	69.67	88.10
w/o KTM&KTE	76.26	67.98	86.70

4.7 Ablation Study on Knowledge-Aware Model Structure

We further perform the ablation study on ReQA SQuAD dataset. Two ablation tests are conducted by removing the knowledge-aware text matching where only text token representations are used to form the sentence-level representation (w/o KTM), and further removing the knowledge-aware text encoding where no entities are input to the encoder (w/o KTM&KTE).

The results are shown in Table 4, which show that each component in our proposed model has its benefits. The result of model without the knowledge-aware text matching drops about 0.48% on Recall@1, and that of the model without knowledge-aware text matching and knowledge-aware text encoding has another performance loss of 1.60% absolutely concerning MRR.

5 Conclusion and Future Work

In this paper, we presented a KnowReQA system in order to solve the problem of insufficient understanding of sentence. The proposed model can seize knowledge entities from text and improve the retrieval accuracy throughout knowledge-aware text encoding and knowledge-aware text matching. Experiments on multiple datasets demonstrate our superior performance. As part of future work, we also focus on applying the model on closed-domain such as biomedical field and make use of rich domain-specific knowledge.

Acknowledgements. This work was partially supported by the National Key Research and Development Program of China (No. 2018YFB2101502) and the Natural Science Foundation of China (No. 61977002).

References

1. Abbasiantaeb, Z., Momtazi, S.: Text-based question answering from information retrieval and deep neural network perspectives: a survey. WIREs Data Min. Knowl. Disc. **11**(6), e1412 (2021)
2. Ahmad, A., Constant, N., Yang, Y., Cer, D.: ReQA: an evaluation for end-to-end answer retrieval models. In: Proceedings of the 2nd Workshop on Machine Reading for Question Answering, pp. 137–146 (2019)
3. Chen, T., Kornblith, S., Norouzi, M., Hinton, G.E.: A simple framework for contrastive learning of visual representations. In: Proceedings of the 37th International Conference on Machine Learning, pp. 1597–1607 (2020)
4. Devlin, J., Chang, M., Lee, K., Toutanova, K.: BERT: pre-training of deep bidirectional transformers for language understanding. In: Proceedings of the 2019 Conference of the North American Chapter of the Association for Computational Linguistics: Human Language Technologies, pp. 4171–4186 (2019)
5. Ferragina, P., Scaiella, U.: Fast and accurate annotation of short texts with wikipedia pages. IEEE Softw. **29**(1), 70–75 (2011)
6. Guo, M., Yang, Y., Cer, D., Shen, Q., Constant, N.: MultiReQA: A cross-domain evaluation for retrieval question answering models. CoRR arXiv:abs/2005.02507 (2020)

7. He, K., Zhang, X., Ren, S., Sun, J.: Deep residual learning for image recognition. In: Proceedings of the 2016 IEEE Conference on Computer Vision and Pattern Recognition, pp. 770–778 (2016)

8. Humeau, S., Shuster, K., Lachaux, M., Weston, J.: Poly-encoders: architectures and pre-training strategies for fast and accurate multi-sentence scoring. In: Proceedings of the 8th International Conference on Learning Representations (2020)

9. Jeong, M., et al.: Transferability of natural language inference to biomedical question answering. In: Working Notes of CLEF 2020 - Conference and Labs of the Evaluation Forum, Thessaloniki, Greece, 22–25 September 2020, vol. 2696 (2020)

10. Khattab, O., Zaharia, M.: Colbert: efficient and effective passage search via contextualized late interaction over BERT. In: Proceedings of the 43rd International ACM SIGIR Conference on Research and Development in Information Retrieval, pp. 39–48 (2020)

11. Lin, D., Wang, J., Li, W.: Target-guided knowledge-aware recommendation dialogue system: an empirical investigation. In: Proceedings of the 3rd Edition of Knowledge-aware and Conversational Recommender Systems and the 5th Edition of Recommendation in Complex Environment (2021)

12. Loshchilov, I., Hutter, F.: Decoupled weight decay regularization. In: Proceedings of the 7th International Conference on Learning Representations (2019)

13. Lowe, R., Pow, N., Serban, I., Pineau, J.: The ubuntu dialogue corpus: a large dataset for research in unstructured multi-turn dialogue systems. In: Proceedings of the 16th Annual Meeting of the Special Interest Group on Discourse and Dialogue, pp. 285–294 (2015)

14. Reimers, N., Gurevych, I.: Sentence-bert: sentence embeddings using siamese bert-networks. In: Proceedings of the 2019 Conference on Empirical Methods in Natural Language Processing, pp. 3980–3990 (2019)

15. Robertson, S.E., Zaragoza, H.: The probabilistic relevance framework: BM25 and beyond. Found. Trends Inf. Retrieval $3(4)$, 333–389 (2009)

16. Seo, M.J., Lee, J., Kwiatkowski, T., Parikh, A.P., Farhadi, A., Hajishirzi, H.: Real-time open-domain question answering with dense-sparse phrase index. In: Proceedings of the 57th Conference of the Association for Computational Linguistics, pp. 4430–4441 (2019)

17. Shen, D., Zhang, Y., Henao, R., Su, Q., Carin, L.: Deconvolutional latent-variable model for text sequence matching. In: Proceedings of the 32nd AAAI Conference on Artificial Intelligence, pp. 5438–5445 (2018)

18. Tahami, A.V., Ghajar, K., Shakery, A.: Distilling knowledge for fast retrieval-based chat-bots. In: Proceedings of the 43rd International ACM SIGIR Conference on Research and Development in Information Retrieval, pp. 2081–2084 (2020)

19. Wang, Y., et al.: Enhancing dual-encoders with question and answer cross-embeddings for answer retrieval. In: Findings of the Association for Computational Linguistics: EMNLP 2021, pp. 2306–2315 (2021)

20. Xu, G., Rong, W., Wang, Y., Ouyang, Y., Xiong, Z.: External features enriched model for biomedical question answering. BMC Bioinf. $22(1)$, 272 (2021)

21. Yamada, I., Asai, A., Shindo, H., Takeda, H., Matsumoto, Y.: LUKE: deep contextualized entity representations with entity-aware self-attention. In: Proceedings of the 2020 Conference on Empirical Methods in Natural Language Processing, pp. 6442–6454 (2020)

22. Yu, W., Wu, L., Zeng, Q., Tao, S., Deng, Y., Jiang, M.: Crossing variational autoencoders for answer retrieval. In: Proceedings of the 58th Annual Meeting of the Association for Computational Linguistics, pp. 5635–5641 (2020)

23. Zhang, Z., Han, X., Liu, Z., Jiang, X., Sun, M., Liu, Q.: ERNIE: enhanced language representation with informative entities. In: Proceedings of the 57th Conference of the Association for Computational Linguistic,. pp. 1441–1451 (2019)
24. Zhou, H., Young, T., Huang, M., Zhao, H., Xu, J., Zhu, X.: Commonsense knowledge aware conversation generation with graph attention. In: Proceedings of the 27th International Joint Conference on Artificial Intelligence, pp. 4623–4629 (2018)

Dynamic Embedding Graph Attention Networks for Temporal Knowledge Graph Completion

Jingqi Wang$^{(\boxtimes)}$ (ID), Cui Zhu, and Wenjun Zhu

College of Computer Science, Faculty of Information Technology,
Beijing University of Technology, Beijing, China
{wangjq1,cuizhu,zhuwenjun}@emails.bjut.edu.cn

Abstract. Most link prediction algorithms are designed for static knowledge graphs (KGs). Notably, KGs usually evolve with time. Currently, researchers pay more attention to temporal knowledge graph completion (TKGC). However, existing methods are insufficient to utilize the complex structure between entities and their neighbor nodes, and modeling of entities is not comprehensive enough. Therefore, we propose DEGAT (Dynamic Embedding Graph Attention Networks), an attention-based TKGC method. Specifically, we use a generalized graph attention network as an encoder to aggregate the features of neighbor nodes and relations. Thus, the model can learn the features of entities from their neighbors without complicated matrix operations. In decoder, we introduce a diachronic embedding function for entities. We build a novel model DE-ConvKB for TKGC by equipping static models with a dynamic entity embedding function that provides the features of entities at any point time. The results show significant improvements over the state-of-the-art methods on three public datasets.

Keywords: Link prediction · Graph attention networks · Temporal

1 Introduction

KGs consist of entities, relations, and semantic descriptions. Entities can be objects in the real world, relations represent associations between entities, and semantic descriptions include types and attributes. KGs have a wide range of applications such as recommendation systems [14] and semantic search [15].

However, existing large-scale KGs are often incomplete due to the insufficiency of techniques [2]. Therefore, the link prediction task is generated, which aims to complete the KG. Knowledge is time-oriented when representing genuine relations. The TKG is a tuple (subject, predicate, object, timestamp) formed by adding timestamps to the triplet. The TKGC task can be expressed as a query predicting missing entities in the form of (subject, predicate, ?, timestamp).

KBGAT [9] applies the graph attention mechanism, effectively aggregating neighbor nodes and assigning different weights. However, it is not particularly

© The Author(s), under exclusive license to Springer Nature Switzerland AG 2022
G. Memmi et al. (Eds.): KSEM 2022, LNAI 13368, pp. 722–734, 2022.
https://doi.org/10.1007/978-3-031-10983-6_55

efficient for the problem of link prediction under temporal constraints. DE-SimplE [7] provides a diachronic entity embedding function. The model defines an entity embedding function that takes an entity and a timestamp as inputs. It offers a hidden representation for the entity so that the model can obtain entity features at any given time. However, the diachronic embedding function only extends some static bilinear models. We consider applying the time-embedding function to a neural network model to learn entity vectors with temporal information while aggregating multi-hop neighbor nodes.

To sum up, we propose the DEGAT model. Our architecture is an end-to-end model. The encoder exploits a modified graph attention mechanism to enhance the link prediction ability of the decoder DE-ConvKB. Specifically, the encoder specifies different weights to different nodes in a neighborhood without relying on knowing the graph structure upfront. It can also holistically capture multi-hop and semantically similar relations in the neighborhood of any given entity. The decoder uses the diachronic embedding function to control the closure of states at different time points. Furthermore, we add a diachronic embedding function to ConvKB [10] to learn the entity embeddings from multiple angles. Our contributions are summarized as follows:

1. We propose a graph attention model that can deal with the temporal information.
2. We design a new decoder model DE-ConvKB.
3. We assign different weights for dynamic and static features, then use the weighted average method to obtain the final embedding vector of the entity.
4. We show the effectiveness of our model on subsets of GDELT and ICEWS datasets.

The remainder of the paper is structured as follows: Sect. 2 discusses the related work. Section 3 discusses the background and introduces our model. Section 4 presents the experimental setup and results. Section 5 concludes the paper.

2   Related Work

Static Link Prediction Methods. Traditional representation learning algorithms for static KGs are roughly divided into three categories: methods based on translational distance models, matrix decomposition methods, and neural network methods. TransE [1] models entities and relations by regarding as relation vector as a translational operation of head and tail entity vectors. It cannot deal with complex relational types. DistMult [16] treats the relational dependent matrix as a diagonal matrix composed of real numbers. ComplEx [12] improves DistMult by complex-valued embedding to model asymmetric relations. ConvE [4] uses embedded two-dimensional convolution to model interactions between entities and relations. MINERVA [3] solves the task of answering questions with known relations when there is only one entity. R-GCN [11] uses relation-specific weight matrices, which are defined as a linear combination of a set of basis matrices. KBGAT [9] invests a generalized attention-based graph embedding for link prediction. However, these models cannot deal effectively with the temporal information among facts.

Temporal Link Prediction Methods. Temporal methods can be roughly divided into two categories: timestamp separately encoding methods and sequence learning-based methods. The former is to model the timestamp as a vector, matrix, or plane and then directly use it for KGC. The latter fuses temporal information into the representation vector of an entity or relation, then uses the existing representation learning model to estimate the triplet with the temporal information. RE-NET [6] combines an RGCN-based [11] snapshot graph and an RNN-based [17] event encoder to model the sequence of facts. CyGNet [18] leverages the copy mechanism to characterize and infer temporal knowledge. DE-SimplE [5] can learn the different states of entities at different time by using diachronic embedding. It combines with SimplE [7] as a scoring function to focus more on changing entities. CluSTeR [8] applies clue searching and temporal reasoning to predict future facts in two-stage and extends two models, RGCRN [8] and EvolveRGCN [8]. In summary, these models underutilized graph structure features, which may lose other valuable historical facts. Inspired by the graph attention mechanism, we propose the DEGAT model based on entity joint embedding to complete the TKG.

3   Methodology

Firstly, we denote the KG as $G = (E, R)$, where E and R are the set of entities and relations. A triplet is represented as (e_i, r_k, e_j) where e_i denotes a head entity, e_j denotes a tail entity, and r_k denotes a relation linking e_i and e_j.

3.1   Graph Attention Networks

The input feature of the entity-set is $\mathbf{z} = \{z_1, z_2, \ldots, z_N\}$, the output features of entities are $\mathbf{z}' = \{z'_1, z'_2, \ldots, z'_N\}$, where N is number of entities. z_i and z'_i are input and output embedding of the entity e_i [13]. The attention value of the edge (e_i, e_j) can be formalized as:

$$r_{ij} = f(Wz_i, Wz_j) \qquad (1)$$

where W is a parametric linear transformation matrix mapping the input features to high-dimensional output feature space. f represents an attention function, r_{ij} indicates the edge between node e_i and node e_j. Then, we compute the relative attention through *softmax function* over all the values in the neighborhood as:

$$\alpha_{ij} = softmax_j(r_{ij}) \qquad (2)$$

where α_{ij} is the relative attention coefficient, which is used to update the initial feature vector of the central node. The output of a layer shows as:

$$z_i' = \sigma \left(\sum_{j \in N_i} \alpha_{ij} W z_j \right) \tag{3}$$

In order to stabilize the training process, GAT uses *multi-head attention*.

$$z_i' = \|_{k=1}^{K} \sigma \left(\sum_{j \in \mathcal{N}_i} \alpha_{ij}^k W^k z_j \right) \tag{4}$$

where $\|$ represents a concatenate operation, σ represents a nonlinear activation function, α_{ij}^k is the weight obtained by the k-th attention mechanism, W^k is a linear mapping matrix of the k-th attention mechanism. K is the number of attention. We can also use the averaging method to get the final node representation as follows:

$$z_i' = \sigma \left(\frac{1}{K} \sum_{k=1}^{K} \sum_{j \in N_i} \alpha_{ij}^k W^k z_j \right) \tag{5}$$

3.2 Encoder

Learning Graph Attention. For triplets $t_{ij}^k = (e_i, r_k, e_j)$, vectors h_i, r_k and h_j represent the initial vector of head entities, relations and tail entities. We concatenate the entity embedding with the relation vector to obtain t_{ijk}, which is the initial representation of the triplet.

$$t_{ijk} = W_1 [h_i \| h_j \| r_k] \tag{6}$$

where W_1 is the linear transformation matrix. In order to find the attention value of the triplet, we process the embedding vector by the LeakyRelu non-linearity.

$$m_{ijk} = LeakyReLU (t_{ijk}) \tag{7}$$

Then we use softmax function to calculate the relative attention value α_{ijk} of the triplet t_{ij}^k.

$$\alpha_{ijk} = softmax_{jk} (m_{ijk}) = \frac{\exp (m_{ijk})}{\sum_{n \in \mathcal{N}_i} \sum_{r \in \mathcal{R}_{in}} \exp (m_{inr})} \tag{8}$$

where $\mathcal{N}_i$ represents the neighborhood of entity e_i, $\mathcal{R}_{ij}$ represents the set of relations connecting entities e_i and e_j. Then we can get the new embedding of the entity e_i, which is the sum of each triplet representation weighted by their attention values.

$$h_i' = \sigma \left(\sum_{j \in \mathcal{N}_i} \sum_{k \in \mathcal{R}_{ij}} \alpha_{ijk} t_{ijk} \right) \tag{9}$$

Our encoder model is as show in Fig. 1. We get the embedding vectors of entities as shown in the yellow and green circles. Then the embedding vectors of entities and relations enter the first GAT layer. At the same time, we update the relation vectors. Next, we concatenate the entity and relation vectors and feed them into the second GAT layer. At last, we calculate the loss function of the triplet.

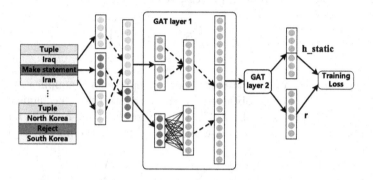

Fig. 1. This figure is the encoder of our model. Yellow circles represents initial entity embedding vectors and green circles represents initial relation embedding vectors. (Color figure online)

At the first attention layer, we employ a multi-head attention mechanism similar to GAT, where q represents the number of attention heads, then concatenated them, resulting in the following representation:

$$h_i' = \|_{q=1}^{Q} \sigma \left(\sum_{j \in \mathcal{N}_i} \alpha_{ijk}^q c_{ijk}^q \right) \tag{10}$$

We define the initial relation embedding matrix $G^0 \in R^{N_r \times D_r}$, N_r is the total number of relations, D_r represents the dimension of the initial relation embedding vectors. $G \in R^{N_r \times D_r'}$ is the output matrix embedding of the relation. In this step, we use linear transformation matrix W_r to update the relation vector, where $W_r \in R^{D_r \times D_r'}$.

$$G = G^0 W_r \tag{11}$$

It is not efficient if we use the concatenate operation again at the second attention layer. So we apply the averaging operation to get the final embedding vector of the entity.

$$h_i' = \sigma \left(\frac{1}{Q} \sum_{q=1}^{Q} \sum_{j \in N_i} \alpha_{ijk}^q c_{ijk}^q \right) \tag{12}$$

We use the margin-based ranking loss to train our model to get the embedding vectors for entities and relations, the idea is that the functional relation induced by the edges corresponds to a translation of the embeddings. When (h, r, t) holds, t should be a nearest neighbor of $h + r$ $(h + r \approx t)$, the loss function is as:

$$L = \sum_{(h,r,t) \in S} \sum_{(h',r,t' \in S')} [\beta + d(h + r, t) - d(h' + r, t')]_+ \tag{13}$$

where β is a hyper-parameter, $[x]_+$ denotes the positive part of x. S is a set of positive samples, and S' is a set of negative samples combine.

3.3 Decoder

Joint Embedding of Entities. We need to learn different entity features for the triplets at different time to adapt to the changing factual relations. To this end, we find a way to perceive the dynamic features of entities and learn the changing features of entities over time. Therefore, we employ the diachronic embedding to divide the representation of entity into temporal part and static part. The former change with the evolution of the event, while the latter retain the fixed attributes of the entity.

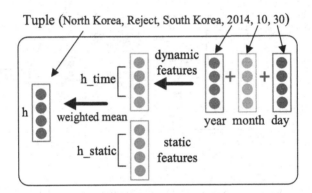

Fig. 2. The joint embedding process of entities. We use a tuple in the ICEWS dataset to illustrate the computational process of entity joint embedding. (Color figure online)

The diachronic embedding function of entities uses the concatenation operation for static features and dynamic features before. The disadvantage of the method is that the ability to extract features is insufficient, and it is not easy to show the effect of dynamic embedding on entity vectors. Here we use the method of weighted mean to obtain the partial entity vectors.

As shown in Fig. 2, the input triplet has a specific timestamp, which is the format of year, month, and day. The blue circles represent dynamic features and the grey circles represent static features. Part of the gray circles represents the entity features calculated by encoder. The diachronic embedding function obtains the dynamic features shown in blue circles. The function is as follows:

$$e^i_{(h,\tau)} = \begin{cases} \alpha^i_h \sigma \left(w^i_h \tau + b^i_h \right), & 1 \leq i \leq \varphi u \\ \alpha^i_h & \varphi u < i \leq u \end{cases} \tag{14}$$

where $e^i_{(h,\tau)}$ is the ith component of $e_{(h,\tau)}$. $e_{(h,\tau)}$ is the embedding of the head entity h under the time τ. τ is the timestamp expressed in the form of year, month, or day. $\alpha^i_h \in R^u$, $w^i_h \in R^{\varphi u}$, $b^i_h \in R^{\varphi u}$ are learnable parameters. u is the embedding dimension of the entity. φ is a hyper-parameter of the model, which is the proportion of temporal feature. We use the first φu elements of $e_{(h,\tau)}$ to capture the dynamic features of the entity, and $(1 - \varphi)u$ presents the static features of the entity. h_time is the dynamic features derived from an entity and a timestamp through the diachronic embedding function. h_static represents the partial entity static features obtained by the graph attention mechanism.

DE-ConvKB. As show in Fig. 3, we improve a decoder model DE-ConvKB based on the temporal embedding function. $h_{i\_}static$ and $h_{i\_}time$ represent the static and dynamic features of h_i. $h_{j\_}static$ and $h_{j\_}time$ represent the static and dynamic features of h_j.

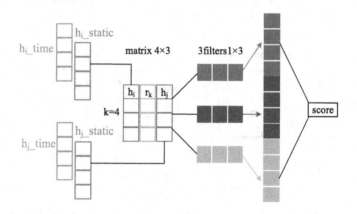

Fig. 3. The decoder DE-ConvKB of our model.

Each triplet has a hidden time vector, which is expressed as a 3-column matrix $A = [h_i, r_k, h_j] \in R^{k \times 3}$ where each column vector denotes a triplet element. We feed A to a convolution layer, then we process A with multiple filters to generate different feature maps. The feature maps are concatenated into a single feature vector standing for the input triplet. Finally, the score of the triplet t^k_{ij} is calculated by the dot product with the weight vector. The score function can be written formally as:

$$f\left(t^k_{ij}\right) = \left(\prod_{m=1}^{\Omega} ReLU\left([h_i, r_k, h_j] * \omega^m\right)\right).\mathbf{W} \tag{15}$$

where Ω is a hyper-parameter representing number of filters used, ω^m is the mth convolutional filter, and we use a linear transformation matrix $\mathbf{W} \in R^{\Omega k \times 1}$ to compute the final score of the triplet. $*$ is a convolution operator. For example, given the head entity and the relation, we select the one with the highest score from the set of tail entities as the result of the tail entity prediction. The model use the Adam optimizer and the soft margin loss as follows:

$$\mathcal{L} = \sum_{t_{ij}^k \in \{S \cup S'\}} \log\left(1 + \exp\left(l_{t_{ij}^k} \cdot f\left(t_{ij}^k\right)\right)\right) + \frac{\lambda}{2}\|\mathbf{W}\|_2^2 \qquad (16)$$

4   Experiments

4.1   Experimental Setup

Datasets. We evaluate DEGAT on three TKG datasets: ICEWS14, ICEWS05-15 and GDELT.ICEWS14 is a short-range dataset consisting of the events that occurred in 2014. ICEWS05-15 is a long-range dataset consisting of the events that occurred between 2005 to 2015. GDELT project is a global initiative that consists of real-time data from print, broadcast, and web news media worldwide. Notably, since GDELT has a larger data scale than the first two datasets, we select part of the whole sample instead. The selected sample statistics are also listed in Table 1. We take the same partition proportion for training/validation/test sets as DE [5]. The statistics of the three datasets are listed in Table 1.

Table 1. Dataset statistics.

Dataset	#Ents	#Rels	#Time Gap	Training	Validation	Test	Total
ICEWS14	7,128	230	365	72,826	8,941	8,963	90,730
ICEWS05-15	10,488	251	4,017	386,962	46,275	46,092	479,329
GDELT	500	20	366	2,735,685	341,961	341,961	3,419,607
GDELT-s	500	20	366	373,018	45,995	49,545	468,558

Evaluation Metrics. For every test tuple, we replace the missing entity with every candidate entity in the entity set to generate a set of corrupt tuples. Then we calculate a score for these tuples with TKG embedding models. To compare the model performance quantitatively, we take the widely used MR (Mean Rank), MRR (Mean Reciprocal Rank), and Hits@n (n = 1, 3, 10) as employed metrics.

Implementation. Following KBGAT [9], we take a two-step training procedure. We first train the encoder, generalized GAT [13] to encode the static graph information about the entities and relations. Then we train the decoder, diachronic ConvKB [10] to perform the TKGC task. We do not search for the optimal hyper-parameter setting but still get excellent performance. For encoder: the learning rate is 0.001, the batch size is the sample number of the training set, the negative ratio is 2, embedding size is 50, the dropout probability for GAT layer is 0.3, output embedding dimension is 100. For decoder: the learning rate is the same as encoder, the batch size is 128, the negative ratio is 40, the input dimension is the output embedding dimension of GAT, the output channels in convolution layer is 50, and there is no dropout in it. For neither encoder nor decoder, we do not use pre-trained embeddings. To combine the static features trained by GAT and the dynamic feature trained by ConvKB, we introduce a hyper-parameter γ to denote the proportion of the static features, and set γ to 0.68 as the default value.

4.2 Experimental Results

Table 2, 3, and 4 present the prediction results on the test sets of ICEWS14, ICEWS05-15, and GDELT, respectively. The best results are in bold, and the second best results are underlined. Hits@n results are in percentage. Retention of decimals is subject to the rounding principle. The reported models are classified into three parts: static models, temporal models, and the models that are most relevant to our model. The results of static and temporal models are from CluSTeR [8], and the missing items are marked as -.

Table 2. TKGC results on ICEWS14.

Model	MR	MRR	Hits@1	Hits@3	Hits@10
DistMult [2014]	–	0.249	17.3	–	40.2
ComplEx [2016]	–	0.319	22.2	–	50.7
RGCN [2018]	–	0.271	18.4	–	44.2
ConvE [2018]	–	0.309	21.7	–	50.1
RotatE [2018]	–	0.275	18.0	–	47.2
MINERVA [2018]	–	0.332	25.7	–	48.3
RGCRN [2021]	–	0.369	27.0	–	56.1
EvolveRGCN [2021]	–	0.371	27.0	–	57.0
CyGNet [2020]	–	0.365	27.4	–	54.4
RE-NET [2020]	–	0.389	29.3	–	57.5
CluSTeR [2021]	–	0.460	33.8	–	71.2
DE-TransE [2020]	–	0.326	12.4	46.7	68.6
DE-DistMult [2020]	–	0.501	39.2	56.9	70.8
DE-SimplE [2020]	–	0.526	41.8	59.2	72.5
KBGAT [2019]	133	0.539	42.2	61.0	76.1
DEGAT(ours)	168	0.633	53.8	69.8	79.7

As shown in the tables, our DEGAT consistently outperforms the baselines and achieves SOTA (state-of-the-art) results on three datasets, which convincingly verifies its effectiveness. Specifically, on ICEWS14, DEGAT achieves the

Table 3. TKGC results on ICEWS05-15.

Model	MR	MRR	Hits@1	Hits@3	Hits@10
DistMult [2014]	–	0.164	9.8	–	29.9
ComplEx [2016]	–	0.231	14.5	–	40.6
RGCN [2018]	–	0.273	19.1	–	43.6
ConvE [2018]	–	0.252	16.0	–	44.4
RotatE [2018]	–	0.199	10.9	–	38.7
MINERVA [2018]	–	0.307	25.8	–	39.9
RGCRN [2021]	–	0.394	28.7	–	60.4
EvolveRGCN [2021]	–	0.407	30.3	–	61.3
CyGNet [2020]	–	0.374	27.5	–	56.1
RE-NET [2020]	–	0.417	31.1	–	62.0
CluSTeR [2021]	—	0.446	34.9	–	63.0
DE-TransE [2020]	–	0.314	10.8	45.3	68.5
DE-DistMult [2020]	–	0.484	36.6	54.6	71.8
DE-SimplE [2020]	–	0.513	39.2	57.8	74.8
KBGAT [2019]	**136**	<u>0.655</u>	<u>56.8</u>	<u>70.5</u>	<u>82.0</u>
DEGAT(ours)	<u>241</u>	**0.777**	**72.4**	**81.4**	**87.1**

improvements of 0.301 in MRR, 28.1% in Hits@1, and 31.4% in Hits@10 over the best static baseline model MINERVA [3]. Compared with the best temporal baseline model CluSTeR [8], DEGAT achieves the improvements of 0.173 in MRR, 20.0% in Hits@1, and 8.5% in Hits@10. More obviously, the baseline models all perform poorly on GDELT. But our DEGAT still significantly achieves high prediction accuracy. We notice that our MR is slightly inferior to that of KBGAT. Due to tens of thousands of entities in ICEWS datasets, the MR differences within a few tens can be ignored. Besides, there are few abnormal test samples, and their MR cannot be lowered to the front.

4.3 Auxiliary Experiments

Ablation Study. DEGAT mainly benefits from two critical modules: GAT for aggregating graph information, DE for encoding temporal information. We carry out an ablation study on three datasets to explore how the two modules contribute to the results. The ablation experiment results are also listed in Table 2, 3, and 4.

Influence of Static Feature Proportion. Figure 4 shows the test MR of DEGAT on ICEWS14 as a function of γ, the static feature proportion.

Table 4. TKGC results on GDELT.

Model	MR	MRR	Hits@1	Hits@3	Hits@10
DistMult [2014]	–	0.156	9.3	–	28.0
ComplEx [2016]	–	0.123	8.0	–	20.6
RGCN [2018]	–	0.109	4.6	–	22.6
ConvE [2018]	–	0.173	10.4	–	31.3
RotatE [2018]	–	0.053	1.2	–	12.5
MINERVA [2018]	–	0.121	10.0	–	16.7
RGCRN [2021]	–	0.177	10.9	–	30.9
EvolveRGCN [2021]	–	0.174	11.0	–	29.9
CyGNet [2020]	–	0.180	10.9	–	31.6
RE-NET [2020]	–	0.190	11.6	–	33.5
CluSTeR [2021]	–	0.183	11.6	–	31.9
DE-TransE [2020]	–	0.126	0.0	18.1	35.0
DE-DistMult [2020]	–	0.213	13.0	22.8	37.6
DE-SimplE [2020]	–	0.230	14.1	24.8	40.3
KBGAT [2019]	46	<u>0.487</u>	<u>43.1</u>	<u>50.2</u>	<u>59.0</u>
DEGAT(ours)	**46**	**0.543**	**49.9**	**55.3**	**62.3**

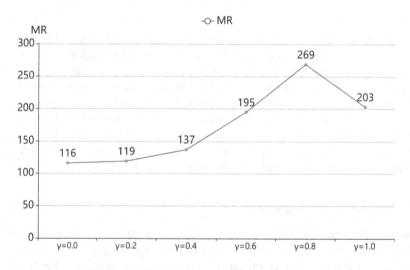

Fig. 4. Test MR of DEGAT on ICEWS14 as a function of γ.

According to the Fig. 4, along with the features becoming static (γ changes from 0.0 to 1.0), MR shows a significant boost. Since lower MR denotes better performance, this observation indicates the importance of integrating temporal information. As γ becomes larger, up to 1.0, MR decreases instead. This may be due to overfitting on the static feature and cannot learn enough temporal information, thus the model does not rely on temporal information for inference. However, in the actual application scenario of TKG, the utilization of temporal information is important. According to the experiments, the Hits@n will be reduce if γ to $0 \sim 0.4$. We suggest to set the static proportion γ to $0.5 \sim 0.7$. This setting will help for the model aggregating static graph structure meanwhile integrating temporal information.

5   Conclusion

We proposed DEGAT, a new TKGC model based on the graph attention mechanism. The static embedding vectors of entities that aggregate adjacent node and relation information are combined with the dynamic embedding vectors generated by the diachronic embedding function. We extended the static KG embedding method to TKG to enhance the knowledge representation ability of the model. Experiments on link prediction used three benchmark datasets to demonstrate the superiority of our model.

References

1. Bordes, A., Usunier, N., Garcia-Duran, A., Weston, J., Yakhnenko, O.: Translating embeddings for modeling multi-relational data. Adv. Neural Inf. Process. Syst. **26** (2013)
2. Cai, B., Xiang, Y., Gao, L., Zhang, H., Li, Y., Li, J.: Temporal knowledge graph completion: a survey. arXiv preprint arXiv:2201.08236 (2022)
3. Das, R., et al.: Go for a walk and arrive at the answer: reasoning over paths in knowledge bases using reinforcement learning. arXiv preprint arXiv:1711.05851 (2017)
4. Dettmers, T., Minervini, P., Stenetorp, P., Riedel, S.: Convolutional 2D knowledge graph embeddings. In: Proceedings of the AAAI Conference on Artificial Intelligence, vol. 32 (2018)
5. Goel, R., Kazemi, S.M., Brubaker, M., Poupart, P.: Diachronic embedding for temporal knowledge graph completion. In: Proceedings of the AAAI Conference on Artificial Intelligence, vol. 34, pp. 3988–3995 (2020)
6. Jin, W., Qu, M., Jin, X., Ren, X.: Recurrent event network: autoregressive structure inference over temporal knowledge graphs. arXiv preprint arXiv:1904.05530 (2019)
7. Kazemi, S.M., Poole, D.: Simple embedding for link prediction in knowledge graphs. Adv. Neural Inf. Process. Syst. **31** (2018)
8. Li, Z., et al.: Search from history and reason for future: Two-stage reasoning on temporal knowledge graphs. arXiv preprint arXiv:2106.00327 (2021)
9. Nathani, D., Chauhan, J., Sharma, C., Kaul, M.: Learning attention-based embeddings for relation prediction in knowledge graphs. arXiv preprint arXiv:1906.01195 (2019)
10. Nguyen, D.Q., Nguyen, T.D., Nguyen, D.Q., Phung, D.: A novel embedding model for knowledge base completion based on convolutional neural network. arXiv preprint arXiv:1712.02121 (2017)

11. Schlichtkrull, M., Kipf, T.N., Bloem, P., van den Berg, R., Titov, I., Welling, M.: Modeling relational data with graph convolutional networks. In: Gangemi, A., et al. (eds.) ESWC 2018. LNCS, vol. 10843, pp. 593–607. Springer, Cham (2018). https://doi.org/10.1007/978-3-319-93417-4_38
12. Trouillon, T., Welbl, J., Riedel, S., Gaussier, É., Bouchard, G.: Complex embeddings for simple link prediction. In: International Conference on Machine Learning, pp. 2071–2080. PMLR (2016)
13. Veličković, P., Cucurull, G., Casanova, A., Romero, A., Lio, P., Bengio, Y.: Graph attention networks. arXiv preprint arXiv:1710.10903 (2017)
14. Wang, X., Wang, D., Xu, C., He, X., Cao, Y., Chua, T.S.: Explainable reasoning over knowledge graphs for recommendation. In: Proceedings of the AAAI Conference on Artificial Intelligence, vol. 33, pp. 5329–5336 (2019)
15. Xiong, C., Power, R., Callan, J.: Explicit semantic ranking for academic search via knowledge graph embedding. In: Proceedings of the 26th International Conference on World Wide Web, pp. 1271–1279 (2017)
16. Yang, B., Yih, W.T., He, X., Gao, J., Deng, L.: Embedding entities and relations for learning and inference in knowledge bases. arXiv preprint arXiv:1412.6575 (2014)
17. Zaremba, W., Sutskever, I., Vinyals, O.: Recurrent neural network regularization. arXiv preprint arXiv:1409.2329 (2014)
18. Zhu, C., Chen, M., Fan, C., Cheng, G., Zhan, Y.: Learning from history: Modeling temporal knowledge graphs with sequential copy-generation networks. arXiv preprint arXiv:2012.08492 (2020)

Cross-CAM: Focused Visual Explanations for Deep Convolutional Networks via Training-Set Tracing

Yu Sun[1], Kailang Ma[1] , Xuanxin Liu[2], and Jian Cui[1(✉)]

[1] School of Cyber Science and Technology, Beihang University, Beijing 100191, China
{sunyv,makailang,cuijianw}@buaa.edu.cn
[2] College of Forestry, Beijing Forestry University, Beijing 100191, China
liuxuanxin@bjfu.edu.cn

Abstract. In recent years, the widely used deep learning technologies have always been controversial in terms of reliability and credibility. *Class Activation Map* (CAM) has been proposed to explain the deep learning models. Existing CAM-based algorithms highlight critical portions of the input image, but they don't go any farther in tracing the neural network's decision-basis. This work proposes Cross-CAM, a visual interpretation method which supports deep traceability for prediction-basis samples and focuses on similar regions of the category based on the input image and the prediction-basis samples. The Cross-CAM extracts deep discriminative feature vectors and screens out the prediction-basis samples from the training set. The similarity-weight and the grad-weight are then combined to form the cross-weight, which highlights similar regions and aids in classification decisions. On the ILSVRC-15 dataset, the proposed Cross-CAM is tested. The new weakly-supervised localization evaluation metric IoS (*Intersection over Self*) is proposed to effectively evaluate the focusing effect. Using Cross-CAM highlight regions, the top-1 location error for weakly-supervised localization achieves 44.95% on the ILSVRC-15 validation set, which is 16.25% lower than Grad-CAM. In comparison to Grad-CAM, Cross-CAM focuses on the key regions using the similarity between the test image and the prediction-basis samples, according to the visualisation results.

Keywords: Interpretability · CAM · Traceability · Prediction-decision sample

1 Introduction

In recent years, neural networks have made major breakthroughs in the fields of image classification [1, 2], object detection [3, 4], speaker recognition [5], and so on, thanks to the rapid development of hardware capability [6–8], and new algorithms [9–11]. However, due to the lack of transparency in the model structure and the training process users

Supported by the National Natural Science Foundation of China (32071775) and 2020 Industrial Internet Innovation and Development Project - Malicious Code Analysis Equipment Project of Security and Controlled System, No.: TC200H02X.
First Author and Second Author contribute equally to this work.

can neither understand the operation mechanism of the model nor judge the reliability of the results. So it is difficult for users to establish trust with the neural networks [12–14]. In addition, the black box problem of neural networks causes challenges for researchers to effectively trace or analyze the wrong results, leading to great risks in practical applications [15].

The interpretable neural network gives the decision basis of each prediction result [16]. At present, the interpretability methods of neural network are mainly divided into four kinds: visual interpretation methods, disturbance-based interpretation methods [17–19], knowledge-based interpretation methods [20] and causal interpretation methods [21, 22]. As visual interpretation methods are in line with human cognitive habits, the corresponding researches are the most in-depth. Visual interpretation methods mainly include methods based on back propagation and activation mapping. Back propagation based methods include Gradient [23], Guided Backpropagation [24], Integrated Gradient [25] and so on. Activation mapping based methods are mainly the series of *Class Activation Mapping* (CAM), including CAM [26], Grad-CAM [27], Score-CAM [28] and so on. The CAM-based methods have become one of the most commonly used neural network interpretation methods.

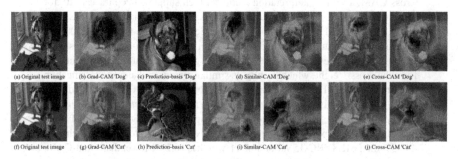

Fig. 1. Outputs from a number of visualizations of different methods (Grad-CAM, Similar-CAM and Cross-CAM) for the boxer (dog) class (top) and tiger cat class (bottom).

However, CAM only focused on a single image to find the region of interest (see Fig. 1 (b) and (g)) and the improvements of follow-up CAMs were limited. Actually when people judge the category for one image, they usually notice some key regions and compare them with images of already known categories. The above mode can also be used to explain the recognition process of the neural network. The classification ability of the neural network is obtained by learning the training images, thus the training images can be analogized to the images of known categories for people, and the training images most similar with one test image can be regarded as the basis for supporting classification, which are the prediction-basis samples of the test image. Combining the test image with prediction-basis samples of different categories, different similar regions are generated (see Fig. 1 (a)(c) and (f)(h)). The similar regions are also the key regions to explain the network, which correspond to different important key regions when considering different categories (see Fig. 1 (d) and (i)). In addition, the gradients of the target categories can be used to further focus on the regions related to the categories (see Fig. 1 (e) and (j)).

To summarize, the contributions of the paper are as follows:

(1) Cross-CAM, a visual interpretation method which supports the deep traceability for prediction-basis samples without requiring architectural changes is proposed. The most similar images are selected from thousands of training images automatically as the prediction-basis samples for interpretation.
(2) Cross-CAM further focuses on the similar regions based on the existing CAM method. The method identifies the discriminative regions integrating the test image and the corresponding prediction-basis samples. It highlights similar key regions that affect the classification decision while excluding irrelevant regions. In addition, CAM provides an intuitive explanation for the misjudgment of the model.
(3) The IoS (*Intersection over Self*) is proposed as a suitable weakly-supervised localization evaluation metric measuring the attention level of the CAM method to the key regions of images.

The rest of the paper is organised as follows: Sect. 2 briefly describes the two directions that the Cross-CAM method proposed in this paper draws on: CAM and ReID. Section 3 presents our approach in two sequential steps, prediction-based samples tracking and similar region visualization. Section 4 provides the visualization results and the comparison with the previous advanced Grad-CAM in weakly supervised performance, illustrating the advantages of Cross-CAM in interpretation fineness and robustness, and Sect. 5 concludes the paper.

2 Related Work

The proposed method draws on both the recent CAM methods and the ReID (*person re-identification*) methods while the former provide the visualization principle and the latter provide the feature comparison principle.

CAM was first proposed in 2016 and obtained the heat map reflecting the regions of interest by weighting the feature map. The *Global Average Pooling* (GAP) layer was used to build a generic localizable deep representation for object localization without using any bounding box annotations. The top-5 error achieved was remarkably close to that achieved by the fully supervised approach [29]. Based on CAM, Grad-CAM used the gradients of the target as the weights for feature maps to highlight the important regions, avoiding the dependence on the GAP layer, and the localization result was superior than CAM. The variants of Grad-CAM mainly optimized the ability to explain multiple object instances in a single image such as Grad-CAM+ + [30] and Smooth Grad-CAM+ + [31]. Although the above visualization methods have produced good visualization effects in weakly-supervised location, these methods lack the ability to further determine the core regions of the objects as almost all pixels of the objects are highlighted. In addition, the previous CAMs only explained what the neural network paid attention to, but not why.

The comparison between known and unknown data is the basic pattern of face recognition and *Person Re-identification* (ReID). Comparing with the generic object recognition referred as the close-set identification, face recognition task is required to identify new unseen classes without labels. In order to match a given probe image to the ones of the same person, the discriminative features for each image are extracted and the distances between the features are computed. The distances of the same person should be small while those of different persons be large [26, 32, 33]. ReID task also identifies the same person from multiple images, with the only difference being that the recognition regions extend from the face to the whole body [34–36].

Integrating the feature comparison method and the CAM visualization method, this work proposes Cross-CAM, which supports the deep traceability for prediction-basis samples and focuses on key regions according to the similarity between the original image and the prediction-basis samples. Through the combination of the two methods, not only the regions of interest are visualized, but also the reasons why the neural network pays attention to the regions are explained.

3   Approach

Cross-CAM consists of two step. The first step is tracing prediction-basis samples which supports the classification decision. The second step is visualization of the similar regions based on the classification target. In order to combine the similarity with the classification results, the visualization process includes similarity weight extraction and gradient weight fusion.

3.1   Prediction-Basis Samples Tracing

The similarity between images can be measured by the distances between the discriminative feature vectors. So choosing the suitable discriminative features is the key of prediction-basis samples tracing. The previous works have shown that the deeper features are usually more discriminative, which contain more semantic information and represent the main image region better [37]. So the inputs of the final fully-connected layer are used as the discriminative features. In the retrieval process, the Euclidean distance between the features is calculated as follows:

$$D = \sqrt{\sum_i^n \left(F_{train}^i - F_{test}^i\right)^2} \tag{1}$$

where F_{train} is the discriminative features of the training image, F_{test} is the discriminative feature of the test image and n is the dimension of the features vectors. The training images can be sorted according to the similarity degree to the test image. The most similar images are selected as the prediction-basis samples of the test image.

3.2   Similar Region Visualization

The prediction-basis samples of the test image reflect the similarity in the image level. As shown in Fig. 2, in order to locate the similar regions in the image, Cross-CAM weights the image feature maps using cross-weight w_{cross}. The cross-weight w_{cross} is composed of similarity-weight $w_{similarity}$ and grad-weight w_{grad}:

$$w_{cross} = w_{similarity} \cdot w_{grad} \tag{2}$$

Thus the similar regions can be located and correlated with the classification results at the same time.

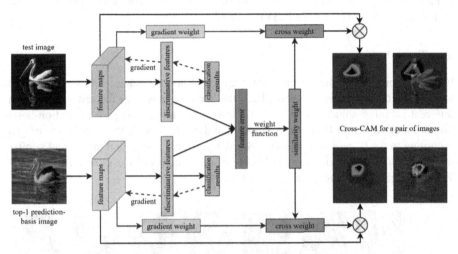

Fig. 2. The visualization process of Cross-CAM.

Similarity Weight Generation. The similarity-weight is negatively correlated with the discriminative feature error. The function of similarity-weight designed in the work is shown as follows:

$$w_{similarity} = \begin{cases} -ln(F_{error} + 10^{-6}) - 5, w_{similarity} > 0 \\ 0, w_{similarity} \leq 0 \end{cases} \tag{3}$$

$$F_{error} = |F_{ss} - F_{test}| \tag{4}$$

where F_{ss} is the discriminative feature of the prediction-basis sample, and F_{error} is the discriminative feature error. The logarithm operation is used to enlarge the small error and the nonnegative function avoids leading into negative values.

Gradient Weight Fusion. The gradient of the class score with respect to the feature maps is used to get the grad-weight w_{grad}. Because we are only interested in the features that are positively correlated with the class of interest, the grad-weight w_{grad} is designed as follows:

$$gradient = \sum_i \sum_j \frac{\partial Y^c}{\partial A_{ij}^k} \tag{5}$$

$$w_{grad} = \begin{cases} GAP(gradient), GAP(gradient) > 0 \\ 0, GAP(gradient) \leq 0 \end{cases} \tag{6}$$

where Y^c is the classification score for class c, A_{ij}^k is the feature maps for activation including K feature maps and with locations indexed by i, j. GAP is the global average pooling function.

4 Visualization Results and Evaluation

In this section, the interpretability and robustness of Cross-CAM are evaluated with the pretrained ResNet50 [1] on the ILSVRC-15 [2].

4.1 Traceability

Figure 3 shows the prediction-basis samples for some test images. As we can see, the top-1 of prediction-basis samples all are the same objects with the test images with different shooting angles. In Fig. 3 (b), the second similar image in prediction-basis samples looks different from the test image but they are actually the same beach wagon according to the license plate number. Similarly, the test image and the second similar image in Fig. 3 (e) are the front and back shooting angles of the same reflex camera. These examples show the traceability of Cross-CAM.

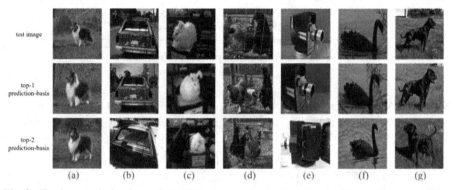

Fig. 3. Tracing result for Cross-CAM. The images in the first line are the test images in the ILSVRC-15 validation set while the images in the second and third lines are the prediction-basis samples Cross-CAM searched from the ILSVRC-15 training set.

4.2 Highlight Similar Key Regions

Visualization results for some correctly classified images are shown in Fig. 4. For contrast, Grad-CAM, Similar-CAM and Cross-CAM are visualized at the same time. Similar-CAM is the weakened version of Cross-CAM without fusing the grad-weight. As we can see, Grad-CAM highlights the total regions of the target object while Similar-CAM and Cross-CAM mainly focus on the key regions. Comparing Similar-CAM and Cross-CAM, the latter only follows the most important region in one object while the former may care more than one region such as the limpk (Fig. 4 (a))and the drake (Fig. 4. (b)). The key region that Cross-CAM highlights tallies with the cognition of human such as the flame in the stove (Fig. 4. (c)) and the keys and the finger shapes in the saxophone playing (Fig. 4. (d)).

(a) limpkin   (b) drake

(c) stove   (d) sax

Fig. 4. Visualization results of highlighting similar key regions.

4.3 Weakly-Supervised Localization

Cross-CAM is generic and can be used in weakly supervised localization, localizing objects in images using only whole image class labels. The localization capability of Cross-CAM is evaluated in the context of image classification. The ImageNet localization challenge requires to provide classification labels and bounding boxes at the same time. Given an image, the class prediction is obtained from the pretrained off-the-shelf ResNet50 network and then the Cross-CAM map is generated and binarized with a threshold of 15% of the max intensity like Grad-CAM. Then all the contours are extracted in the binary map and the bounding boxes are generated as the circumscribed rectangle of the contours.

The bounding boxes of some test images generated by CAM, Similar-CAM and Cross-CAM are shown in Fig. 5, and it is obvious that Similar-CAM and Cross-CAM have advantages in locating the key image regions than CAM. In ILSVRC-15, the location result is regarded as incorrect when the IoU (Intersection over Union) of the annotation box and the predicted box is less than 0.5. However, for some images with large annotation boxes, the metric of IoU with 0.5 threshold do not reflect the attention of the methods, as Cross-CAM only focuses on some key regions of the objects rather than the whole objects.

In order to effectively evaluate the attention of CAM to the key regions of the objects, the evaluation metric called IoS (Intersection over Self) is used to replace IoU. IoS is

Fig. 5. Comparison of the location results between Grad-CAM, Similar-CAM and Cross-CAM.

defined as the ratio of the area of the intersection of the annotation box and the predicted box to the area of predicted box. In the actual prediction, some predicted boxes within the scope of annotation boxes are too small to reflect the features of objects. Therefore, the IoS is defined as 0 if the area of the predicted box divided by the area of the annotation box is less than 0.1. The IoS is formulated as follows:

$$IoS = \begin{cases} \frac{P \cap A}{P}, & \frac{P}{A} \geq 0.1 \\ 0, & \frac{P}{A} < 0.1 \end{cases} \tag{7}$$

Following IoS, the top-1 localization errors on the validation set are shown in Table 1. Similar-CAM and Cross-CAM are significantly better than Grad-CAM and the location error is decreased by 10.59% and 16.25%, respectively. The results showed that Similar-CAM and Cross-CAM have obvious advantages in locating the key regions of the objects.

Table 1. Localization error % on ILSVRC-15 validation set (lower is better) for ResNet50.

Model	Localization error with IoS %
Grad-CAM	61.20
Similar-CAM	50.61
Cross-CAM	44.95

4.4 Discussion

On one hand, Cross-CAM uses highlight key regions to indicate the judgment basis of the model. On the other hand, Cross-CAM applies visual explanations for the causes of misjudgment through the traceable prediction-basis samples. As shown in Fig. 6, if there are more than one object in the image, the reason of misjudgment is usually recognizing the wrong target object in the image meanwhile the correct object appears in the top-5 classification results. According to the highlight regions of Similar-CAM, the network shows the ability to correctly locate the labelled category through prediction-basis samples. The analysis reflects the recognition ability of the model, which is helpful for users to establish trust in the model and improve the usability of the model.

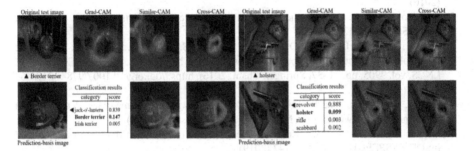

(a) Border terrier is misclassified as jack-o'-lantern   (b) Holster is misclassified as revolver

(c) Sussex spaniels is misclassified as clumber   (d) Sports car is misclassified as castle

Fig. 6. The intuitive explanation for the misjudgment of the model.

5   Conclusion

We presented a novel improvement to the CAM-based visual interpretation method called Cross-CAM. The proposed method supports the deep traceability for prediction-basis samples and further focuses the key regions that support classification decisions based on traceability results. Cross-CAM successfully searched for the same object photographed from different angles in the training set, according to the visualisation results on the ILSVRC-15 validation set. With the help of the prediction-basis samples, Cross-CAM further focused the key regions of the target object compared with Grad-CAM. To effectively evaluate the focusing effect, the method was evaluated using the new weakly-supervised localization evaluation metric IoS on the ILSVRC-15 validation set and achieved 44.95% for top-1 localization error rate. In the future, the proposed method would be generalized to more data types such as encrypted traffic, medical imaging and so on. And the trace process would be strengthened using metric learning methods to optimize the focusing effect of CAM methods.

744   Y. Sun et al.

References

1. He, K., Zhang, X., Ren, S., Sun, J.: Deep residual learning for image recognition. In: Proceedings of the IEEE Conference on Computer Vision and Pattern Recognition, pp. 770–778 (2016)
2. Russakovsky, O., et al.: Imagenet large scale visual recognition challenge. Int. J. Comput. Vis. **115**(3), 211–252 (2015)
3. Liu, W., Anguelov, D., Erhan, D., Szegedy, C., Reed, S., Fu, C.-Y., Berg, A.C.: Ssd: Single shot multibox detector. In: Leibe, B., Matas, J., Sebe, N., Welling, M. (eds.) ECCV 2016. LNCS, vol. 9905, pp. 21–37. Springer, Cham (2016). https://doi.org/10.1007/978-3-319-464 48-0_2
4. Ren, S., He, K., Girshick, R., Sun, J.: Faster r-cnn: Towards real-time object detection with region proposal networks. Adv. Neural Inf. Process. Syst. **28** (2015)
5. Bhattacharya, G., Alam, M.J., Kenny, P.: Deep speaker recognition: Modular or monolithic? In: INTERSPEECH, pp. 1143–1147 (2019)
6. Qiu, M., Xue, C., Shao, Z., Sha, E.:Energy minimization with soft real-time and DVS for uniprocessor and multiprocessor embedded systems. In: IEEE DATE Conference, pp. 1–6 (2007)
7. Qiu, M., Liu, J., Li, J., et al.: A novel energy-aware fault tolerance mechanism for wireless sensor networks. In: IEEE/ACM International Conference on GCC (2011)
8. Qiu, M., Li, H., Sha, E.: Heterogeneous real-time embedded software optimization considering hardware platform. In: Proceedings of the 2009 ACM symposium on Applied Computing, pp. 1637–1641 (2009)
9. Wu, G., Zhang, H., et al.: A decentralized approach for mining event correlations in distributed system monitoring. JPDC **73**(3), 330–340 (2013)
10. Niu, J., Gao, Y., et al.: Selecting proper wireless network interfaces for user experience enhancement with guaranteed probability. JPDC **72**(12), 1565–1575 (2012)
11. Liu, M., Zhang, S., et al.: H infinite state estimation for discrete-time chaotic systems based on a unified model. IEEE Trans. Syst. Man Cybern. **42**(4), 1053–1063 (2012)
12. Li, Y., Song, Y., Jia, L., et al.: Intelligent fault diagnosis by fusing domain adversarial training and maximum mean discrepancy via ensemble learning. IEEE Trans. Ind. Inform. **17**(4), 2833–2841 (2020)
13. Shao, Z., Xue, C., Zhuge, Q., et al.: Security protection and checking for embedded system integration against buffer overflow attacks via hardware/software. IEEE Trans. Comput. **55**(4), 443–453 (2006)
14. Qiu, H., Qiu, M., Liu, M., Memmi, G.: Secure health data sharing for medical cyber-physical systems for the healthcare 4.0. IEEE J. Biomed. Health Inform. **24**(9), 2499–2505 (2020)
15. Qiu, H., Zheng, Q., et al.: Topological graph convolutional network-based urban traffic flow and density prediction. IEEE Trans. ITS (2020)
16. Hua, Y., Zhang, D., Ge, S.: Research progress in the interpretability of deep learning models. J. Cyber Secur. **5**(3), 1–12 (2020)
17. Cui, X., Wang, D., Wang, Z.J.: Chip: Channel-wise disentangled interpretation of deep convolutional neural networks. IEEE Trans. Neural Netw. Learn. Syst. **31**(10), 4143–4156 (2019)
18. Fong, R.C., Vedaldi, A.: Interpretable explanations of black boxes by meaningful perturbation. In: Proceedings of the IEEE International Conference on Computer Vision, pp. 3429–3437 (2017)
19. Ribeiro, M.T., Singh, S., Guestrin, C.: Why should i trust you? explaining the predictions of any classifier. In: Proceedings of the 22nd ACM SIGKDD International Conference on Knowledge Discovery and Data Mining, pp. 1135–1144 (2016)

20. Kong, X., Tang, X., Wang, Z.: A survey of explainable artificial intelligence decision Xitong Gongcheng Lilun yu Shijian. Syst. Eng. Theory Pract. **41**(2), 524–536 (2021)
21. Parafita, A., Vitria, J.: Explaining visual models by causal attribution. In: 2019 IEEE/CVF International Conference on Computer Vision Workshop (ICCVW), pp. 4167–4175. IEEE (2019)
22. Zhao, Q., Hastie, T.: Causal interpretations of black-box models. J. Bus. Econ. Stat. **39**(1), 272–281 (2021)
23. Simonyan, K., Vedaldi, A., Zisserman, A.: Deep inside convolutional networks: Visualising image classification models and saliency maps. arXiv preprint arXiv:1312.6034 (2013)
24. Springenberg, J.T., Dosovitskiy, A., Brox, T., Riedmiller, M.: Striving for simplicity: The all convolutional net. arXiv preprint arXiv:1412.6806 (2014)
25. Sundararajan, M., Taly, A., Yan, Q.: Axiomatic attribution for deep networks. In: International Conference on Machine Learning, pp. 3319–3328. PMLR (2017)
26. Wen, Y., Zhang, K., Li, Z., Qiao, Y.: A discriminative feature learning approach for deep face recognition. In: Leibe, B., Matas, J., Sebe, N., Welling, M. (eds.) ECCV 2016. LNCS, vol. 9911, pp. 499–515. Springer, Cham (2016). https://doi.org/10.1007/978-3-319-46478-7_31
27. Selvaraju, R.R., Cogswell, M., Das, A., Vedantam, R., Parikh, D., Batra, D.: Grad-cam: visual explanations from deep networks via gradient-based localization. In: Proceedings of the IEEE International Conference on Computer Vision, pp. 618–626 (2017)
28. Wang, H., et al.: Score-cam: score-weighted visual explanations for convolutional neural networks. In: Proceedings of the IEEE/CVF Conference on Computer Vision and Pattern Recognition Workshops, pp. 24–25 (2020)
29. Zhou, B., Khosla, A., Lapedriza, A., Oliva, A., Torralba, A.: Learning deep features for discriminative localization. In: Proceedings of the IEEE Conference on Computer Vision and Pattern Recognition, pp. 2921–2929 (2016)
30. Chattopadhay, A., Sarkar, A., Howlader, P., Balasubramanian, V.N.: Grad-cam++: Generalized gradient-based visual explanations for deep convolutional networks. In: 2018 IEEE Winter Conference on Applications of Computer Vision (WACV), pp. 839–847. IEEE (2018)
31. Omeiza, D., Speakman, S., Cintas, C., Weldermariam, K.: Smooth gradcam++: An enhanced inference level visualization technique for deep convolutional neural network models. arXiv preprint arXiv:1908.01224 (2019)
32. Schroff, F., Kalenichenko, D., Philbin, J.: Facenet: a unified embedding for face recognition and clustering. In: Proceedings of the IEEE Conference on Computer Vision and Pattern Recognition, pp. 815–823 (2015)
33. Wu, B., Wu, H.: Angular discriminative deep feature learning for face verification. In: ICASSP 2020–2020 IEEE International Conference on Acoustics, Speech and Signal Processing (ICASSP), pp. 2133–2137. IEEE (2020)
34. Chen, T., et al.: Abd-net: Attentive but diverse person re-identification. In: Proceedings of the IEEE/CVF International Conference on Computer Vision, pp. 8351– 8361 (2019)
35. Dai, Z., Chen, M., Gu, X., Zhu, S., Tan, P.: Batch dropblock network for person re-identification and beyond. In: Proceedings of the IEEE/CVF International Conference on Computer Vision, pp. 3691–3701 (2019)
36. Zheng, Z., Yang, X., Yu, Z., Zheng, L., Yang, Y., Kautz, J.: Joint discriminative and generative learning for person re-identification. In: Proceedings of the IEEE/CVF Conference on Computer Vision and Pattern Recognition, pp. 2138–2147 (2019)
37. Zeiler, M.D., Fergus, R.: Visualizing and understanding convolutional networks. In: Fleet, D., Pajdla, T., Schiele, B., Tuytelaars, T. (eds) Computer Vision – ECCV 2014. ECCV 2014. LNCS, vol. 8689, pp. 818–833. Springer, Cham (2014). https://doi.org/10.1007/978-3-319-10590-1_53

Author Index

Printed in the United States
by Baker & Taylor Publisher Services